4299

Strategic Management

Columbus St.

Community College

Business Management

INTRODUCTION TO INFORMATION SYSTEMS

INTRODUCTION TO INFORMATION SYSTEMS

Sixteenth Edition

GEORGE M. MARAKAS
KU School of Business
University of Kansas

JAMES A. O'BRIEN
College of Business Administration
Northern Arizona University

McGraw-Hill
Irwin

McGraw-Hill
Irwin

INTRODUCTION TO INFORMATION SYSTEMS

Published by McGraw-Hill/Irwin, a business unit of The McGraw-Hill Companies, Inc., 1221 Avenue of the Americas, New York, NY, 10020.

Some ancillaries, including electronic and print components, may not be available to customers outside the United States.

This book is printed on acid-free paper.

1 2 3 4 5 6 7 8 9 0 DOW/DOW 1 0 9 8 7 6 5 4 3 2

ISBN 978-0-07-337688-2 (student edition)
MHID 0-07-337688-4 (student edition)
ISBN 978-0-07-750643-X (instructor edition)
MHID 0-07-750643-X (instructor edition)

Vice president and editor-in-chief: *Brent Gordon*
Editorial director: *Paul Ducham*
Executive director of development: *Ann Torbert*
Senior development editor: *Trina Hauger*
Editorial coordinator: *Jonathan Thornton*
Vice president and director of marketing: *Robin Zwettler*
Marketing director: *Amee Mosley*
Marketing manager: *Donielle Xu*
Vice president of editing, design, and production: *Sesha Bolisetty*
Lead project manager: *Harvey Yep*
Senior buyer: *Carol Bielski*
Senior designer: *Mary Kazak Sander*
Senior photo research coordinator: *Keri Johnson*
Photo researcher: *Jennifer Blankenship*
Media project manager: *Suresh Babu, Hurix Systems Pvt. Ltd.*
Cover design: *Pam Verros*
Cover image: *© 2011 Masterfile Corporation*
Interior design: *Gino Cieslik*
Typeface: *10/12 Janson*
Compositor: *Aptara®, Inc.*
Printer: *R. R. Donnelly*

Library of Congress Cataloging-in-Publication Data

Marakas, George M.
    Introduction to information systems / George Marakas, James O'Brien.—16th ed.
        p. cm.
    In previous ed. James O'Brien is named as first author.
    Includes bibliographical references and index.
    ISBN-13: 978-0-07-337688-2 (student edition : alk. paper)
    ISBN-10: 0-07-337688-4 (student edition : alk. paper)
    ISBN-13: 978-0-07-750643-8 (instructor edition : alk. paper)
    ISBN-10: 0-07-750643-X (instructor edition : alk. paper)
    1. Business—Data processing.   2. Management—Data processing.   3. Management information systems.   4. Electronic commerce.   I. O'Brien, James A., 1936-   II. O'Brien, James A., 1936-
    Introduction to informaton systems.   III. Title.
HR5548.2.O23 2013
658.4'038—dc23
                                                                                2011042215

www.mhhe.com

dedication

**Dedicated to our families, friends, and students.
You make everything possible.**

The world of information systems presents new and exciting challenges each and every day. Creating a textbook to capture this world is a formidable task, to be sure. This, the 16th edition of *Introduction to Information Systems*, represents a major upgrade in both content and style. We are excited about all of the changes and take pride in delivering this new edition to you. Moreover, we thank all of you for your loyalty to the book and the input you provided that was instrumental in its development and constant revision. Your continued support fills us with joy and a sense of both accomplishment and contribution.

We are very excited about the new Real World Challenge and Solution boxes. We believe this new element will bring to life the importance of each topic area and how they truly relate to a better understanding of the field.

We are pleased and excited to welcome back Miguel Aguirre-Urreta as a major contributor to the cases and text content. His work and effort on the Real World Challenges, Real World Cases, and green box content will be apparent as we bring you new content in every chapter of the book. Please join us in welcoming Miguel back to this new edition.

On behalf of Jim, Miguel, and myself, please accept our sincere appreciation for your support and loyalty. As always, we hope you enjoy and benefit from this book.

Dr. George M. Marakas

George M. Marakas is a professor of Information Systems at the School of Business at the University of Kansas. His teaching expertise includes Systems Analysis and Design, Technology-Assisted Decision Making, Electronic Commerce, Management of IS Resources, Behavioral IS Research Methods, and Data Visualization and Decision Support. In addition, George is an active researcher in the area of Systems Analysis Methods, Data Mining and Visualization, Creativity Enhancement, Conceptual Data Modeling, and Computer Self-Efficacy.

George received his PhD in Information Systems from Florida International University in Miami and his MBA from Colorado State University. Prior to his position at the University of Kansas, he was a member of the faculties at the University of Maryland, Indiana University, and Helsinki School of Economics. Preceding his academic career, he enjoyed a highly successful career in the banking and real estate industries. His corporate experience includes senior management positions with Continental Illinois National Bank and the Federal Deposit Insurance Corporation. In addition, George served as president and CEO of CMC Group Inc., a major RTC management contractor in Miami, Florida, for three years. Throughout his academic career, George has distinguished himself both through his research and in the classroom. He has received numerous national teaching awards, and his research has appeared in the top journals in his field. In addition to this text, he is the author of four textbooks in the field of information systems: *Management Information Systems; Decision Support Systems for the 21st Century; Systems Analysis and Design: An Active Approach;* and *Data Warehousing, Mining, and Visualization: Core Concepts.*

Beyond his academic endeavors, George is also an active consultant and has served as an advisor to a number of organizations, including the Central Intelligence Agency, Brown & Williamson, the Department of the Treasury, the Department of Defense, Xavier University, Citibank Asia-Pacific, Nokia Corporation, Professional Records Storage Inc., Heineken International, and United Information Systems. His consulting activities are concentrated primarily on e-commerce strategy, the design and deployment of global IT strategy, workflow reengineering, e-business strategy, and ERP and CASE tool integration.

George is also an active member of a number of professional IS organizations and an avid golfer, a motorcyclist, a second-degree black belt in tae kwon do, a PADI master scuba diver trainer and IDC staff instructor, and a member of Pi Kappa Alpha fraternity.

James A. O'Brien was an adjunct professor of Computer Information Systems in the College of Business Administration at Northern Arizona University. He completed his undergraduate studies at the University of Hawaii and Gonzaga University and earned an MS and PhD in Business Administration from the University of Oregon. He was professor and coordinator of the CIS area at Northern Arizona University; professor of Finance and Management Information Systems and chairman of the Department of Management at Eastern Washington University; and a visiting professor at the University of Alberta, the University of Hawaii, and Central Washington University.

Dr. O'Brien's business experience included working in the Marketing Management Program of the IBM Corporation, as well as serving as a financial analyst for the General Electric Company. He was a graduate of General Electric's Financial Management Program. He also served as an information systems consultant to several banks and computer services firms.

Jim's research interests were in developing and testing basic conceptual frameworks used in information systems development and management. He wrote eight books, including several that have been published in multiple editions and translated into Chinese, Dutch, French, Japanese, and Spanish. He also contributed to the field of information systems through the publication of many articles in business and academic journals, as well as through his participation in academic and industry associations in the field of information systems.

brief contents

contents

ix

module II
Information Technologies

chapter 3

chapter 4

chapter 6

Telecommunications and Networks 230

THE NETWORKED ENTERPRISE 231

TELECOMMUNICATIONS
NETWORK ALTERNATIVES 248

module III
e-Business Applications

module IV
Development Processes

chapter 11

chapter 12

module V
Management Challenges

chapter 13

A Business and Managerial Perspective

The Sixteenth Edition is designed for business students who are or who will soon become business professionals in today's fast-changing business world. The goal of this text is to help business students learn how to use and manage information technologies to revitalize business processes, improve business decision making, and gain competitive advantage. Thus, it places a major emphasis on up-to-date coverage of the essential role of Internet technologies in providing a platform for business, commerce, and collaboration processes among all business stakeholders in today's networked enterprises and global markets. This is the business and managerial perspective that this text brings to the study of information systems. Of course, as in all Marakas and O'Brien texts, this edition:

- Loads the text with **Real World Challenges and Solutions, Real World** Cases, in-depth examples **(Green Boxes),** and questions that help develop critical thinking skills (**Real World Activities, Case Study Questions, Discussion Questions,** and **Analysis Exercises**).

- Provides opportunities to learn about real people and companies in the business world with **Real World Challenges** and **Real World Solutions.**

- Organizes the text around a simple **Five-Area Information Systems Framework** that emphasizes the IS knowledge a business professional needs to know.

- Places a **major emphasis on the strategic role of information technology** in providing business professionals with tools and resources for managing business operations, supporting decision making, enabling enterprise collaboration, and gaining competitive advantage.

One note for clarification—the new look and feel to this sixteenth edition has changed the previous blue boxes to green. Although we now call them by their new name, their intention remains the same—to help develop a more focused, and in-depth understanding of the topic area under study.

Modular Structure of the Text

The text is organized into modules that reflect the five major areas of the framework for information systems knowledge. Each chapter is then organized into two or more distinct sections to provide the best possible conceptual organization of the text and each chapter. This organization increases instructor flexibility in assigning course material because it structures the text into modular levels (i.e., modules, chapters, and sections) while reducing the number of chapters that need to be covered.

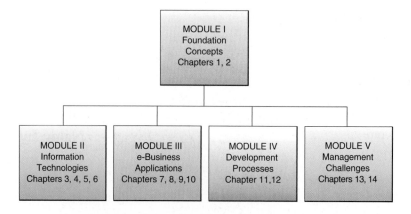

an information systems framework

Foundation Concepts
Fundamental business information systems concepts, including trends, components, and roles of information systems (Chapter 1) and competitive advantage concepts and applications (Chapter 2). Selective coverage of relevant behavioral, managerial, and technical concepts.

Development Processes
Developing and implementing business/IT strategies and systems using several strategic planning and application development approaches (Chapters 11 and 12).

Management Challenges
The challenges of business/IT technologies and strategies, including security and ethical challenges and global IT management (Chapters 13 and 14).

e-Business Applications
How businesses use the Internet and other information technologies to support their business processes, e-business and e-commerce initiatives, and business decision making (Chapters 7, 8, 9, and 10).

Information Technologies
Includes major concepts, developments, and managerial issues involved in computer hardware, software, telecommunications networks, data resource management technologies, and other technologies (Chapters 3, 4, 5, and 6).

INFORMATION SYSTEMS

DEVELOPMENT PROCESSES · FOUNDATION CONCEPTS · e-BUSINESS APPLICATIONS · INFORMATION TECHNOLOGIES · MANAGEMENT CHALLENGES

real world approach

Real World Challenges, Solutions, and Cases

Each chapter provides a **Real World Challenge**, a **Real World Solution,** and two **Real World Cases:** all in-depth examples that illustrate how prominent businesses and organizations have attempted to implement the theoretical concepts students have just learned.

Each chapter will begin with a Real World Challenge–an actual business problem taken from current events that is focused on the topic area associated with the chapter. The Real World Challenge is intended to serve as a basis for discussion and point of reference that relates the material being presented to an actual business situation. At the end of each chapter, the Real World Solution is presented to demonstrate how the problem was solved by applying many, or all, of the concepts presented throughout the chapter. In this way, we can bring to life the importance of understanding each of the topic areas that combine to reflect the current state of affairs in the field of information systems.

A full list of cases is available inside the front cover.

real world
CASE 1

AstraZeneca, UnitedHealth, and Others: IT-Asset Management– Do You Know What You've Got?

Global pharmaceuticals giant AstraZeneca needed some strong medicine of its own to fix a burgeoning IT-asset-management problem brought about by multiple acquisitions and their nonstandard gear, a high-tech workforce spread across 255 facilities in 147 countries, and in total more than 67,000 employees using more than 90,000 hardware and software assets ranging from notebooks up to SAP and Oracle enterprise applications and databases.

With software vendors becoming more aggressive on audits as sales of new products are generally weak, and with greater internal collaboration requiring a more consistent set of tools to simplify processes and maintenance, the $31 billion pharmaceuticals company realized a few years ago that Microsoft's Systems Management Server was simply overmatched for the job of managing the global enterprise's complex base of IT assets.

So Microsoft recommended the asset-management products offered by a French company called PS'Soft, which is a subsidiary of BDNA Corp., a top provider of IT infrastructure inventory and analysis solutions. And in the years that AstraZeneca has been steadily getting its IT assets under control, PS'Soft has distinguished itself like few other IT vendors, according to AstraZeneca Global IT Asset leader Bernard Warrington.

"In all my years, our engagement with PS'Soft was one of the first and only times we had an IT vendor show such willingness to work as a true partner and really try to solve our problems with us," Warrington says. Referring to PS'Soft's Julian Moreau, Warrington described the uniquely open collaboration that allowed him and his team to understand the problem, design the solution, and then execute that plan.

"Julian and I worked extremely closely together, and from there our partnership cascaded down to the other members of the team," Warrington says. "But I need to be very clear about that: In the beginning, the knowledge and expertise were clearly with them—they were teaching and we were learning."

The problem, Warrington says, is that in the increasingly strategic world of IT-asset management, "the tool set itself meets only 30 percent of the overall need: On top of that, you need to build the processes, understand the costs, come up with standards, develop interfaces with

other major vendors, and much more—we simply didn't have all the skills necessary to cover that total life cycle. But PS'Soft did have those skills, both in-house and through their contacts."

In addition, says Warrington, PS'Soft and BDNA had the global experience necessary to help AstraZeneca get its arms around its global sprawl of IT gear, which was essential for two reasons: First, so that the company could begin to gain greater leverage in purchasing negotiations, and second, so it could be able to fairly, but aggressively, hold its own during audits by software vendors.

"In so many countries where we operate, the tradition has been that budgets are managed locally, making it impossible to see the global aggregate in detail," Warrington says. "We simply did not have the ability to get a global view. The old tools we used gave us something of a snapshot, but didn't let us have enough insight to be able to manage the situation. At the same time, the IT vendors are getting very aggressive with audits, and without offering a specific number I can tell you that millions and millions of dollars are at stake—and before our engagement with PS'Soft, no matter how hard we tried with the old tool set, we were just not able to achieve those potential cost savings from vendors."

Over time, Warrington says, AstraZeneca gained that necessary level of control and knowledge: "Now Astra-Zeneca is in a position to enter negotiations from a position of strength, confidence, and knowledge." And that achievement has given the company a new perspective on the realm of IT-asset management, Warrington said: "Too many companies just look on IT- asset management as nothing more than bean counting, versus looking deeper and understanding the ROI and ROA that can be achieved.

"But we learned firsthand that there is a huge opportunity to get control over what you have, to satisfy even the most rigorous audit, and to negotiate better contracts. And that's a lot more than bean counting," says Warrington.

IT organizations in diversified companies—particularly those grown through acquisition—wage a seemingly endless battle against unnecessary IT diversity and related costs. Conceived, planned, and executed in 18 months, UnitedHealth Group's (UHG) Hercules program proves

128

real-life lessons

Use Your Brain

Traditional case study questions promote and provide opportunity for critical thinking and classroom discussion.

Use Your Hands

The Real World Activities section offers possibilities for hands-on exploration and learning.

the complexity can be conquered, while protecting or improving IT's service levels. By creating a standard desktop configuration and consistent management processes, Hercules reduced total cost of ownership to $76 per month per desktop, from more than $240.

In 2004, with the CEO's support, Alistair Jacques, then SVP of UHG-IT, launched Hercules, focusing it on standardizing and streamlining the processes behind desktop management: procurement, configuration, installation, life cycle and asset management. In addition to this focus on process, two techniques stand out as key to the program's success. Working with finance, IT developed a chargeback model that imposes a premium on nonstandardized desktop configurations: $170 per month versus $45 per month for a standard configuration. This value price encourages business managers to choose the more efficient infrastructure. UHG also reduced costly on-site support by reorganizing it: A central IT team manages high-level support activities, completing 95 percent remotely, while select, on-site end users (often non-IT administrative staff trained by IT) provide basic support to colleagues.

UHG-IT treated desktop management as a business process challenge rather than a technology issue. This approach freed them to employ tactics like non-IT staff for desktop support and value pricing. To date, UHG has converted 75,000 out of 90,000 devices to the new standards, delivering $42 million in annual savings. Effectively, UHG can now manage nearly four times the number of end users with the same number of IT personnel as in 2004. All while actually improving—not diminishing—service levels: IT now deploys 99.4 percent of releases, updates and patches in three hours, instead of 65 percent in three weeks.

Indeed, companies that blow off asset management do so at their own peril. At the same time, 99 percent of companies that her organization comes across don't have a proper asset management process in place, according to Elisabeth Vanderveldt, vice president of business development at Montreal-based IT services and consulting firm Conamex International Software Corp. That's a staggering number, considering the value that life-cycle management can bring to an organization. And it's indicative of the widespread lack of respect for this important aspect of IT operations.

The ideal time to start considering an asset management program is before the business and its IT infrastructure is even up and running, but the common scenario is that corporations look to asset management after they've encountered a problem running the infrastructure.

The mentality around asset management is evolving, however. Companies used to consider only reliability, availability, and overall equipment effectiveness in that equation. But now there is recognition of factors like continuing pressures on cost, and green technology. "It really requires a mature organization to understand what's going to be needed to assess and execute a life-cycle management strategy," says Don Barry, associate partner in global business services in the supply chain operations and asset management solutions group at IBM.

Why is a life-cycle management program important? For one thing, it puts IT in much better control of its assets, and this can have a number of benefits.

"IT can make really intelligent decisions around what they should get rid of, and they might even find they have more money in the budget and they can start taking a look at newer technology and see if they can bring it in-house. Without that big picture, they just end up spending more and more money than had they been proactive," says Vanderveldt.

Life-cycle management also has value as a risk management tool and it aids in the disaster recovery process as well, she adds. "It's also beneficial for those moments that are just completely out of your control, like mergers, acquisitions and uncontrolled corporate growth, either organic or inorganic," says Darin Stahl, an analyst at London, Ontario-based Info-Tech Research Group. "IT leaders without this tool set are now charged with pulling all this information together on short notice. That could be diminished considerably in terms of turnaround time and effort for IT guys if they have a holistic asset management program in place."

SOURCE: Adapted from Bob Evans, "Global CIO Quick Takes: AstraZeneca Saves Millions with BDNA," *InformationWeek*, February 22, 2010; Rick Swanborg, "Desktop Management: How UnitedHealth Used Standardization to Cut Costs," *CIO.com*, April 28, 2009; and Kathleen Lau, "Asset Management: Do You Know What You've Got?" *CIO Canada*, August 13, 2008.

▼ CASE STUDY QUESTIONS

1. What are the companies mentioned in the case trying to control, or manage, through these projects? What is the problem? And how did they get there?
2. What are the business benefits of implementing strong IT-asset management programs? In what ways have the companies discussed in the case benefited? Provide several examples.
3. One of the companies in the case, UnitedHealth Group, tackled the issue by imposing standardization and charging those stepping outside standard models. How should they balance the need to standardize with being able to provide business units with the technologies best suited to their specific needs? Justify your answer.

▼ REAL WORLD ACTIVITIES

1. An important metric in this area considered by companies is the Total Cost of Ownership (TCO) of their IT assets. Go online and research TCO and how it is related to IT-asset management. How are companies using TCO to manage their IT investments? Prepare a presentation to share your research with the rest of your class.
2. What does Don Barry of IBM mean by "life-cycle" in the context of this case? How would this life-cycle management work when it comes to IT assets? Break into small groups with your classmates and create a working definition of life-cycle management and how it works as you understand it from the case.

strategy, ethics . . .

Competitive Advantage

Chapter 2 focuses on the use of IT as a way to surpass your competitors' performance.

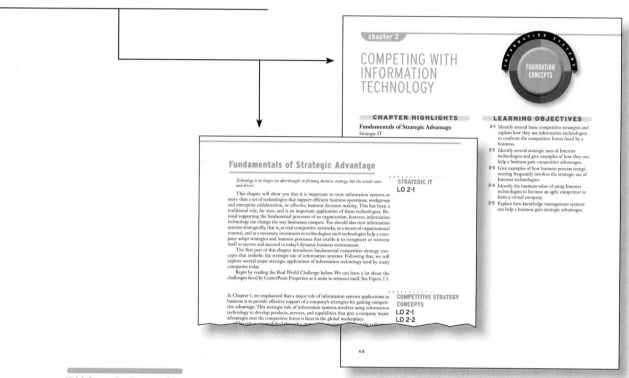

Ethics & Security

Chapter 13 discusses the issues surrounding these topics and the challenges IT faces.

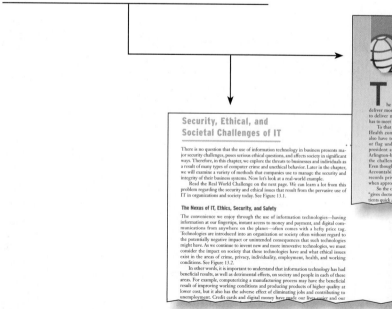

. . . and beyond

Managing Global IT

Whether they are in Berlin or Bombay, Kuala Lumpur or Kansas, San Francisco or Seoul, companies around the globe are developing new models to operate competitively in a digital economy. These models are structured, yet agile; global, yet local; and they concentrate on maximizing the risk-adjusted return from both knowledge and technology assets.

International dimensions have become a vital part of managing a business enterprise in the inter-networked global economies and markets of today. Whether you become a manager in a large corporation or the owner of a small business, you will be affected by international business developments and deal in some way with people, products, or services whose origin is not your home country.

Figure 14.11 illustrates the major dimensions of the job of managing global information technology that we cover here. Notice that all global IT activities must be adjusted to take into account the cultural, political, and geoeconomic challenges that exist in the international business community. Developing appropriate business and IT strategies for the global marketplace should be the first step in **global information technology management**. Once that is done, end users and IS managers can move on to developing the portfolio of business applications needed to support business/IT strategies; the hardware, software, and Internet-based technology platforms to support those applications; the data resource management methods to provide necessary databases; and finally the systems development projects that will produce the global information systems required.

THE INTERNATIONAL DIMENSION

GLOBAL IT MANAGEMENT
LO 14-4

FIGURE 14.11
The major dimensions of global e-business technology management.

[Diagram: Global IT Management → Cultural, Political, and Geoeconomic Challenges → Business/IT Strategies | Business Application Portfolios | Internet-Based Technology Platforms | Data Resource Management | Systems Development]

We seem to have reached a point where virtually every chief information officer is a global chief information officer—a leader whose sphere of influence (and headaches) spans continents. The global chief information officer's most common challenge, according to CIO Executive Council members, is managing global virtual teams. In an ideal world, human-resources policies across the global IT team should be consistent, fair, and responsive. Titles and reporting structures (if not compensation) should be equalized.

The council's European members, representing Royal Dutch Shell, Galderma, Olympus, and others, commissioned a globalization playbook that collects and codifies best practices in this and other globalization challenges.

Global Teams: It's Still a Small World

FIGURE 14.1

A global company serving global customers requires a global IT infrastructure.
SOURCE: © Getty Images.

with large volumes of assets an
orative partner they need to rea
is a fundamental part of everyth
says Christopher Perretta, exe
chief information officer.

Nowhere is this clearer than
that the company has historica
and technology development: A
operating expense budget under
formation officer goes to new p
year. Over the years, the comp
known for its "green" IT effort
merous distinctions for these ef
rankings at places such as Comp
Newsweek. Starting in early 2
center was designed to minimi
and the company started to tra
tube monitors and into flat scre
use and environmental impact a

Go Global with IT
This text closes with Chapter 14, an in-depth look at IT across borders.

Expand Your Knowledge
Green boxes in each chapter provide brief, in-depth examples of how corporations apply IS concepts and theories.

Expand Your Horizons
Globe icons indicate examples with an international focus so that your knowledge makes you truly worldly.

Exploring Virtual Worlds as Collaboration Tools

For emergency responders working along Interstate 95, accidents aren't a game; they're a way of life (and death). So it seemed odd to a group of firefighters, cops, and medics when researchers from the University of Maryland suggested that they use a virtual world to collaborate on training for rollovers, multicar pileups, and life-threatening injuries.

The phrase *virtual world* is often associated with Second Life, the much-hyped 3-D environment hosted by Linden Lab that allows users to talk to friends, sell T-shirts, fly around on carpets, and even build amusement parks—in other words, to play. "It wasn't until we started to do elaborate demos that the first responders started to realize the true potential," says Michael Pack, director of research with the University of Maryland's Center for Advanced Transportation Technology, who has since begun rolling out a virtual world pilot project that could accommodate training for hundreds of emergency workers.

Industry analysts and developers of virtual worlds believe that by immersing users in an interactive environment that allows for social interactions, virtual worlds have the potential to succeed where other collaborative technologies, like teleconferencing, have failed. Phone-based

Amazon.com has just launched an application on Facebook that enables members of the social network to buy gifts for each other based on wish lists registered with the online retailer. *Amazon Giver* also provides Facebook members with the option of viewing suggested items for friends based on interests listed on their profile pages. A second Facebook application, *Amazon Grapevine*, provides a news feed of friends' activity on Amazon, such as when they update their wish lists, write reviews, or tag products. Both applications share information only with Facebook members who have opted in to the service.

"By combining Amazon's vast selection of products with Facebook's millions of users, we are able to make activities like gift-giving more efficient and rewarding for Facebook users," says Eva Manolis, vice president of Amazon.

By adding the *Amazon Giver* application to their profile, Facebook members get the option of clicking directly to a secure Amazon checkout page. If the recipient has a wish list, then Amazon can ship the item without the buyer entering a shipping address, which would already be on file. In order for people to view a wish list, it would have to be set as "public." With *Amazon Grapevine*, people have the option to choose what type of activity they would be willing to share with friends through the news feed. Activity updates are entirely opt-in.

Amazon.com has also introduced a new way for online merchants to leverage Amazon's infrastructure to ship their physical products. "The *Amazon Fulfillment Web Service* (Amazon FWS), allows merchants to sign in to A

Amazon.com: Partnering and Leveraging Infrastructure

Borders Group Inc. is an international book and music retailer based in Ann Arbor, Michigan. Before filing for bankruptcy protection in 2011 and later going out of business, the company operated close to 1,000 stores in the United States under the Borders and Waldenbooks brands. Computerworld columnist Frank Hayes believes there are a number of IT lessons to be learned from this debacle:

First, you cannot run a company without IT-savvy management. When founded by brothers Tom and Louis Borders, the company had what was then a state-of-the-art punch card system that allowed them to track and adjust inventory in a near real-time basis. It was reportedly one of the main reasons Kmart bought Borders in 1992: to use the system to run its Waldenbooks chain. The brothers, however, cashed out and all managers who came after them never had a strong grasp of IT. Sometimes even the best technology does not scale well; the system worked fine for a few stores, but not for hundreds.

Companies need to keep getting better all of the time. In 2000, according to Forrester, Borders overtook Amazon.com as the best online bookseller. Amazon kept improving, while Borders turned its attention elsewhere. Borders also missed the chance to emulate, borrow, or steal the best ideas that were introduced in the Web site of its main competitor, Amazon. At some point, Borders fell too far behind.

Right now most analysts decry the deal that, in 2001, gave Amazon.com control of the Borders online operations. Then, however, Gartner called it "a step in the right direction for both companies," which would allow Borders a

IT Lessons from the Demise of Borders

what's new?

The Sixteenth Edition includes significant changes to the Fifthteenth Edition's content that update and improve its coverage, many of them suggested by an extensive faculty review process. Highlights of key changes for this edition include the following:

- Real World Cases provide current, relevant, and in-depth examples of IS theory applications. A combination of *Case Study Questions* and *Real World Activities* allows you to engage students on a variety of levels.

- More new Real World Cases: More than two-thirds of the cases are new to the Sixteenth Edition. These up-to-date cases provide students with in-depth business examples of the successes and challenges that companies are experiencing in implementing the information technology concepts covered in each chapter.

- Real World Challenges and Solutions provide students with an applied perspective for each of the topic areas and concepts presented in the text.

- Chapter 1: *Foundations of Information Systems in Business* provides an expanded discussion of IS careers and the job market outlook.

- Chapter 2: *Competing with Information Technology* has added coverage on core competency.

- Chapter 3: *Computer Hardware* provides a streamlined coverage of input/output technologies and added coverage of solid-state drives and Microsoft ReadyBoost.

- Chapter 4: *Computer Software* includes updated coverage of cloud computing and software as a service.

- Chapter 5: *Data Resource Management* includes an updated discussion of database fundamentals.

- Chapter 6: *Telecommunications and Networks* provides an added discussion of thin and thick client/server approach and updated discussions of telecommunication fundamentals.

- Chapter 7: *e-Business Systems* includes an updated discussion on digital billboards.

- Chapter 8: *Enterprise Business Systems* provides updated discussions of new Internet search engines.

- Chapter 9: *e-Commerce Systems* provides an added discussion of autoresponder event notification and an updated discussion of new Internet search engines.

- Chapter 10: *Supporting Decision Making* includes an expanded discussion of decision structure and updated discussions of knowledge management systems, executive information systems, artificial intelligence, and virtual reality.

- Chapter 11: *Business/IT Strategies for Development* has expanded coverage of scenario planning and implementation challenges.

- Chapter 12: *Implementing Business/IT Solutions* has increased coverage of system thinking and implementation challenges.

- Chapter 13: *Security and Ethical Challenges* includes an updated discussion on denial of service attacks, new coverage of cyber warfare, and expanded discussions of business and technology ethics, computer crime, and coverage of recent court decisios related to email privacy.

- Chapter 14: *Enterprise and Global Management of Information Technology* provides expanded coverage of global IT governance.

student support

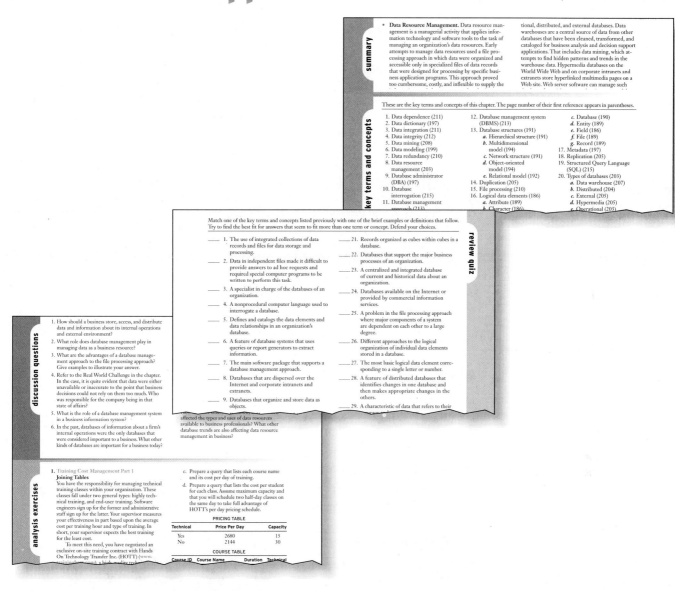

Each chapter contains *complete pedagogical support* in the form of:

- **Summary.** Revisiting key chapter concepts in a bullet-point summary.

- **Key Terms and Concepts.** Using page numbers to reference where terms are discussed in the text.

- **Review Quiz.** Providing a self-assessment for your students. Great for review before an important exam.

- **Discussion Questions.** Whether assigned as homework or used for in-class discussion, these complex questions will help your students develop critical thinking skills.

- **Analysis Exercises.** Each innovative scenario presents a business problem and asks students to use and test their IS knowledge through analytical, Web-based, spreadsheet, and/or database skills.

- **Closing Case Studies.** Reinforcing important concepts with prominent examples from businesses and organizations. Discussion questions follow each case study.

instructor support

Online Learning Center

Available to adopting faculty, the Online Learning Center provides one convenient place to access the Instructor's Manual, PowerPoint slides, and videos.

INSTRUCTOR'S MANUAL (IM) To help ease your teaching burden, each chapter is supported by solutions to Real World Case questions, Discussion Questions, and Analysis Exercises.

TEST BANK Choose from more than 1,3000 true/false, multiple-choice, and fill-in-the-blank questions of varying levels of difficulty. Complete answers are provided for all test questions. By using the **EZ Test Computerized Test Bank,** instructors can design, save, and generate custom tests. EZ Test also enables instructors to edit, add, or delete questions from the test bank; analyze test results; and organize a database of tests and student results.

POWERPOINT SLIDES A set of visually stimulating PowerPoint slides accompanies each chapter, providing a lecture outline and key figures and tables from the text. Slides can be edited to fit the needs of your course.

VIDEOS Videos will be downloadable from the instructor side of the OLC.

MBA MIS Cases

Developed by Richard Perle of Loyola Marymount University, these 14 cases allow you to add MBA-level analysis to your course. See your McGraw-Hill/Irwin sales representative for more information.

Online Course Formats

Content for the Sixteenth Edition is available in WebCT, Blackboard, and PageOut formats to accommodate virtually any online delivery platform.

Online Learning Center

Visit www.mhhe.com/marakas for additional instructor and student resources.

acknowledgments

The Sixteenth Edition represents an ongoing effort to improve and adapt this text to meet the needs of students and instructors. For this revision, we received the guidance of more than 80 reviewers over the course of several months of review work. We thank all of them for their insight and advice.

Hans-Joachim Adler, *University of Texas at Dallas*

Shoshana Altschuller, *Iona College*

Beni Asllani, *University of Tennessee—Chattanooga*

Mary Astone, *Troy University*

Michel Benaroch, *Syracuse University*

James P. Borden, *Villanova University*

Kevin Brennan, *University of Rochester*

Richard L. Brozovic, *McMurry University*

Mari W. Buche, *Michigan Technological University*

Jane Carey, *Arizona State University*

Arthur E. Carter, *Radford University*

Steve Casarow, *Clearwater Christian College*

Carl J. Case, *St. Bonaventure University*

Mary Ann Cassidy, *Westchester Community College*

David Chao, *San Francisco State University*

Edward J. Cherian, *George Washington University*

Robert Chi, *California State University—Long Beach*

Dale Chisamore, *University of Texas at Dallas*

Michael Cummings, *Georgia Institute of Technology*

Andy Curran, *University of Cincinnati—Clermont*

Joanna DeFranco-Tommarello, *New Jersey Institute of Technology*

Carolyn Dileo, *Westchester Community College*

Robin L. Dillon-Merrill, *Georgetown University*

Kevin Lee Elder, *Ohio University*

Kurt Engemann, *Iona College*

Roger Finnegan, *Metropolitan State University*

Gary Fisher, *Angelo State University*

Thomas Franza, *Dowling College*

Carl Friedman, *University of the District of Columbia*

Zbigniew J Gackowski, *California State University—Stanislaus*

Maria R. Garcia, *Franklin Pierce University*

Leo Gemoets, *University of Texas at El Paso*

Richard T. Grenci, *John Carroll University*

Bernard Han, *Western Michigan University—Kalamazoo*

Joseph T. Harder, *Indiana State University*

David Harris, *University of New Mexico—Albuquerque*

Nik Hassan, *University of Minnesota—Duluth*

James He, *Fairfield University*

Jun He, *University of Pittsburgh*

Mary Hollingsworth, *George Perimeter College*

Fred Hughes, *Faulkner University*

Lynn Isvik, *Upper Iowa University*

A. T. "Tom" Jarmoszko, *Central Connecticut State University*

Jeanne Johnson, *Culver-Stockton University*

Surinder Kahai, *Binghamton University*

Arnold Kamis, *Suffolk University*

(David) Wei Kang, *University of California—Irvine*

Rex Karsten, *University of Northern Iowa*

Ranjan B. Kini, *Indiana University Northwest*

Ronald Kizior, *Loyola University—Chicago*

Rebecca Berens Koop, *University of Dayton*

Linda Lau, *Longwood University*

Al Lederer, *University of Kentucky*

Anita Lee-Post, *University of Kentucky*

John D. "Skip" Lees, *California State University—Chico*

David Lewis, *University of Massachusetts—Lowell*

Dahui Li, *University of Minnesota—Duluth*

Shin-jeng Lin, *Le Moyne College*

Rob Lipton, *Penn State University*

Celia Romm Livermore, *Wayne State University*

Mohamed Lotfy, *Regis University*

John Lundin, *San Jose State University*

Sharad K. Maheshwari, *Hampton University*

Yogish Malhotra, *Syracuse University*

Victor Mbarika, *Louisiana State University*

Denise McManus, *University of Alabama—Tuscaloosa*

William A. McMillan, *Madonna University*

Patricia McQuaid, *California State Polytechnic University—San Luis Obispo*

Luvai Motiwalla, *University of Massachusetts—Lowell*

David Nickels, *University of North Alabama*

Janet T. Nilsen, *Metropolitan State University*

Peter Otto, *Dowling College*

Shailendra C. Palvia, *Long Island University*

Panagiotis Petratos, *California State University—Stanislaus*

William Pritchard, *Wayne State University*

Mahesh S. Raisinghani, *University of Dallas*

Frederick Rodammer, *Michigan State University*

Paula Ruby, *Arkansas State University*

Mark B. Schmidt, *Mississippi State University*

Roy Schmidt, *Bradley University*

Ganesan Shankar, *Boston University*

Betsy Page Sigman, *Georgetown University*

K. David Smith, *Cameron University*

Marion Smith, *Texas Southern University*

Bill Sodeman, *Hawaii Pacific University*

Toni M. Somers, *Wayne State University*

Richard W. Srch, *DeVry University*

Godwin Udo, *University of Texas at El Paso*

Gregory W. Ulferts, *University of Detroit Mercy*

David A. Vance, *Mississippi State University*

Sameer Verma, *San Francisco State University*

Padmal Vitharana, *Syracuse University*

Anita Whitehill, *Foothill College*

G. W. Willis, *Baylor University*

Wita Wojtkowski, *Boise State University*

Marie Wright, *Western Connecticut State University*

Robert Wurm, *Nassau Community College*

Yue "Jeff" Zhang, *California State University—Northridge*

Robert Zwick, *Baruch College (CUNY)*

Our thanks also go to Lawrence Andrew of Western Illinois University for his contribution to the analysis exercises and to Richard Perle of Loyola Marymount University for his MBA cases that so many instructors use in conjunction with this text.

Much credit should go to several individuals who played significant roles in this project. Thus, special thanks go to the editorial and production team at McGraw-Hill/Irwin: Paul Ducham, editorial director; Trina Hauger, senior developmental editor; Donielle Xu, marketing manager; Harvey Yep, senior project manager; Keri Johnson, photo coordinator; and Mary Sander, designer. Their ideas and hard work were invaluable contributions to the successful completion of the project. The contributions of many authors, publishers, and firms in the computer industry that contributed case material, ideas, illustrations, and photographs used in this text are also thankfully acknowledged.

Acknowledging the Real World of Business

The unique contribution of the hundreds of business firms and other computer-using organizations that are the subjects of the Real World Cases, exercises, and examples in this text is gratefully acknowledged. The real-life situations faced by these firms and organizations provide readers of this text with valuable demonstrations of the benefits and limitations of using the Internet and other information technologies to enable electronic business and commerce, as well as enterprise communications and collaboration in support of the business processes, managerial decision making, and strategic advantage of the modern business enterprise.

George M. Marakas
James A. O'Brien
Miguel Aguirre-Urreta

Assurance of Learning Ready

Many educational institutions today are focused on the notion of assurance of learning, an important element of some accreditation standards. *Introduction to* Information Systems is designed specifically to support your assurance of learning initiatives with a simple, yet powerful, solution.

Each test bank question for *Introduction to Information Systems* maps to a specific chapter's learning outcome/objective listed in the text. You can use our test bank software, *EZ Test*, to query about learning outcomes/objectives that directly relate to the learning objectives for your course. You can then use the reporting features of *EZ Test* to aggregate student results in similar fashion, making the collection and presentation of assurance of learning data simple and easy.

AACSB Statement

McGraw-Hill Companies is a proud corporate member of AACSB International. Recognizing the importance and value of AACSB accreditation, the authors of *Introduction to Information Systems* 16e have sought to recognize the curricula guidelines detailed in AACSB standards for business accreditation by connecting selected questions in *Introduction to Information Systems* or its test bank with the general knowledge and skill guidelines found in the AACSB standards. It is important to note that the statements contained in *Introduction to Information Systems* 16e are provided only as a guide for the users of this text.

The statements contained in *Introduction to Information Systems* 16e are provided only a guide for the users of this text. The AACSB leaves content coverage and assessment clearly within the realm and control of individual schools, the mission of the school, and the faculty. The AACSB charges schools with the obligation of doing assessments against their own content and learning goals. Although *Introduction to* Information Systems 16e and its teaching package make no claim of any specific AACSB qualification or evaluation, we have, within *Introduction to Information Systems* 16e, labeled selected questions according to the six general knowledge and skills areas. The labels or tags within *Introduction to Information Systems* 16e are as indicated. There are, of course, many more within the test bank, the text, and the teaching package, which might be used as a "standard" for your course. However, the labeled questions are suggested for your consideration.

list of real world challenges and cases

Chapter 1: Foundations of Information Systems in Business

- Modernizing Legacy Systems at Crescent Healthcare Inc.
- eCourier, Cablecom, and Bryan Cave: Delivering Value through Business Intelligence
- *The New York Times* and Boston Scientific: Two Different Ways of Innovating with Information Technology

Chapter 2: Competing with Information Technology

- CenterPoint Properties—Creating a New Company for a New Business
- How to Win Friends and Influence Business People: Quantify IT Risks and Value
- For Companies Both Big and Small: Running a Business on Smartphones

Chapter 3: Computer Hardware

- Budway Enterprises Inc.—Looking for a Low-Cost, High-Return Alternative to Paper
- AstraZeneca, UnitedHealth, and Others: IT-Asset Management—Do You Know What You've Got?
- IT in Health Care: Voice Recognition Tools Make Rounds at Hospitals

Chapter 4: Computer Software

- Japan Post Network—from Government Entity to Private Company
- GE, H.B. Fuller Co., and Others: Successful Implementations of Software as a Service
- U.S. Department of Defense: Enlisting Open-Source Applications

Chapter 5: Data Resource Management

- U.S. Xpress—Lots of Data, Not Enough Quality
- Beyond Street Smarts: Data-Driven Crime Fighting
- Duke University Health System, Beth Israel Deaconess Medical Center, and Others: Medical IT Is Getting Personal

Chapter 6: Telecommunications and Networks

- Adena Health System and Cherokee Health Systems—The Challenges of Medicine in the Rural United States
- DLA Piper, MetLife, PepsiCo, and Others: Telepresence Is Finally Coming of Age
- Brain Saving Technologies Inc. and the T-Health Institute: Medicine through Videoconferencing

Chapter 7: e-Business Systems

- Qualcomm—Silos, Silos, Everywhere
- Toyota Europe, Campbell Soup Company, Sony Pictures, and W.W. Grainger: Making the Case for Enterprise Architects
- Nationwide Insurance: Unified Financial Reporting and "One Version of the Truth"

Chapter 8: Business Across the Enterprise

- Jelly Belly Candy Company—Getting Your Arms Around Sales
- Kennametal, Haworth, Dana Holding, and Others: ERPs Get a Second Lease on Life
- Cisco Systems, Black & Decker, and O'Reilly Auto Parts: Adapting Supply Chains to Tough Times

Chapter 9: e-Commerce Systems

- Ticketmaster—New Clients, New Outlets, New Needs
- Sony, 1-800-Flowers, Starbucks, and Others: Social Networks, Mobile Phones, and the Future of Shopping
- LinkedIn, Umbria, Mattel, and Others: Driving the "Buzz" on the Web

Chapter 10: Supporting Decision Making

- Deutsche Post DHL—The Challenges of Creating and Managing a Global Brand
- Valero Energy, Elkay Manufacturing, J&J, and Overstock.com: The Move Toward Fact-Based Decision Making
- Kimberly-Clark Corp.: Shopping for Virtual Products in Virtual Stores

Chapter 11: Business/IT Strategies for Development

- Sloan Valve Company—ERP, Business Processes, and the Need to Change
- IT Leaders: IT/Business Alignment Takes on a Whole New Meaning
- Centene, Flowserve, and Shaw Industries: Relationships, Collaboration, and Project Success

Chapter 12: Implementing Business/IT Solutions

- Starwood Hotels and Resorts—Success and Growth Bring on IT Challenges
- Microsoft, SiCortex, and Others: How Virtualization Helps Software Developers
- JetBlue Airways, WestJet Airlines, and Others: The Difficult Path to Software Upgrades

Chapter 13: Security and Ethical Challenges

- Harland Clarke—Reinventing the Company, Reinventing Security
- Texas Health Resources and Intel: Ethics, IT, and Compliance
- Wyoming Medical Center, Los Angeles County, and Raymond James: End-Point Security Gets Complicated

Chapter 14: Enterprise and Global Management of Information Technology

- State Street Corporation—The Need to Reshape IT Infrastructure
- Reinventing IT at BP
- Cadbury, Forrester Research, A.T. Kearney, and Others: IT Leaders Face New Challenges in a Globalized World

INTRODUCTION TO INFORMATION SYSTEMS

FOUNDATION CONCEPTS

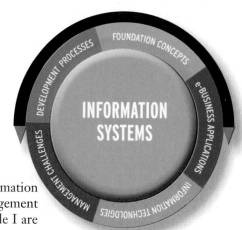

Why study information systems? Why do businesses need information technology? What do you need to understand about both the use and management of information technologies in business? The introductory chapters of Module I are designed to answer these fundamental questions about the role of information systems in business.

- **Chapter 1: Foundations of Information Systems in Business** presents an overview of the five basic areas of information systems knowledge needed by business professionals, including the conceptual system components and major types of information systems. In addition, trends in information systems and an overview of the managerial challenges associated with information systems are presented.

- **Chapter 2: Competing with Information Technology** introduces fundamental concepts of competitive advantage through information technology and illustrates major strategic applications of information systems.

Completing these chapters will prepare you to move on to study chapters on information technologies (Module II), e-business applications (Module III), systems development processes (Module IV), and the management challenges of information systems (Module V).

chapter 1

FOUNDATIONS OF INFORMATION SYSTEMS IN BUSINESS

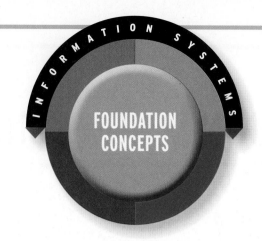

CHAPTER HIGHLIGHTS

Foundation Concepts: Information Systems in Business

The Real World of Information Systems

REAL WORLD CHALLENGE: Modernizing Legacy Systems at Crescent Healthcare Inc.

The Fundamental Roles of IS in Business

Trends in Information Systems

The Role of e-Business in Business

Types of Information Systems

Managerial Challenges of Information Technology

Foundation Concepts: The Components of Information Systems

System Concepts: The Foundation for Business Processes

Components of Information Systems

Information System Resources

Information System Activities

Recognizing Information Systems

REAL WORLD SOLUTION: Crescent Healthcare Inc.: From Green Screens to Online Access

REAL WORLD CASE: eCourier, Cablecom, and Bryan Cave: Delivering Value through Business Intelligence

REAL WORLD CASE: The New York Times and Boston Scientific: Two Different Ways of Innovating with Information Technology

LEARNING OBJECTIVES

1-1 Understand the concept of a system and how it relates to information systems.

1-2 Explain why knowledge of information systems is important for business professionals, and identify five areas of information systems knowledge that they need.

1-3 Give examples to illustrate how the business applications of information systems can support a firm's business processes, managerial decision making, and strategies for competitive advantage.

1-4 Provide examples of several major types of information systems from your experiences with business organizations in the real world.

1-5 Identify several challenges that a business manager might face in managing the successful and ethical development and use of information technology in a business.

1-6 Provide examples of the components of real world information systems. Illustrate that in an information system, people use hardware, software, data, and networks as resources to perform input, processing, output, storage, and control activities that transform data resources into information products.

1-7 Demonstrate familiarity with the myriad of career opportunities in information systems.

Foundation Concepts:
Information Systems in Business

The question of why we need to study information systems and information technology has evolved into a moot issue. We now live in a world where the majority—if not all—of those who will read this text have always had desktop computers, laptops, mobile phones, video games, and the Internet in their daily lives. They literally know of no other world. Information systems have become so integrated into the daily business activities of accounting, finance, operations management, marketing, human resource management, or any other major business function that we cannot imagine any other way to perform them. Information systems and technologies are vital components of successful businesses and organizations—some would say they are business imperatives.

The sentences above make the strongest and most logical argument for why you are reading this text. Information systems constitute an essential field of study in business administration and management, which is why most business majors include a course in information systems. You very likely intend to be a manager, entrepreneur, or some form of business professional and, as such, it is just as important to have a basic understanding of information systems as it is to understand your chosen area of career focus. We may live in a world where we can't remember when we didn't have computing technologies at our fingertips, but we have only begun to scratch the surface of our understanding of what we can do with them. It is the reason you are taking this course. You need to understand the computing technologies and use them to your advantage, because you simply can't live without them.

Information systems and technologies, including Internet-based information systems, are playing vital and expanding roles in business. Information technology can help all kinds of businesses improve the efficiency and effectiveness of their business processes, managerial decision making, and workgroup collaboration, which strengthens their competitive positions in rapidly changing marketplaces. This benefit occurs irrespective of whether the information technology is used to support product development teams, customer support processes, e-commerce transactions, or any other business activity. Information technologies and systems are, quite simply, an essential ingredient for business success in today's dynamic global environment.

THE REAL WORLD OF INFORMATION SYSTEMS
LO 1-1

Let's take a moment to bring the real world into our discussion of the importance of information systems (IS) and information technology (IT). See Figure 1.1, and read the Real World Challenge. Using information systems and technologies to solve a problem like this will be our focus for this chapter.

If we are to understand information systems and their functions, we first need to be clear about the concept of a *system*. We use the word all the time, often without really understanding exactly what it is we are talking about. In its simplest form, a system is a *set of interrelated components, with a clearly defined boundary, working together to achieve a common set of objectives.* Using this definition, it becomes easy to see that virtually everything you can think of is a system, and one system can be made up of other systems or be part of a bigger system. We will expand on this idea later in the next section, but for now, this definition gives us a good foundation for understanding the focus of this textbook: information systems.

Modernizing Legacy Systems at Crescent Healthcare Inc.

Changing jobs is always a challenge. Changing industries while changing jobs is an even bigger challenge. When Brett Michalak left his job as CIO of Tickets.com in May 2010 to take over the top IT position at Crescent Healthcare Inc., he found something he was very likely not expecting: green screen applications and a lot of homegrown software that had hardly been touched since the company was founded about 20 years earlier. Now that's a challenge. The entertainment business and the health care industry are very different environments when it comes to culture, success drivers, and day-to-day operations. As it turns out, they are also very different industries when it comes to IT.

Crescent Healthcare was founded in 1992 as an alternate-site provider of intravenous immune globulin therapy services, and expanded into nursing and comprehensive care services for patients with chronic and acute illnesses by 1995. The acquisition of Apria Healthcare, with operations in California, in 1998 and the injection of private capital in 2004 led Crescent Healthcare to become a leader in infusion services and therapy with more than 500 employees and a large network of partners, including health plans, hospitals, nurses, and physician groups. Today, Crescent Healthcare operates nine clinical centers across the United States.

Crescent Healthcare is a pharmacy, but not the kind of pharmacy you may be used to. Instead of dispensing antibiotics, aspirin, and cold medication to walk-ins at retail stores, the company is one of between 700 to 1,000 providers who specialize in infusion therapy. This is a field of patient care that involves the administration of medication using intravenous or subcutaneous routes. Common applications of infusion therapy include chemotherapy, antibiotics, pain management medication, and others. Most commonly, these therapies are conducted at home or at an outpatient center, which allows patients to live a more normal lifestyle and does not require them to come to a hospital or facility and be admitted for the procedures to take place.

Both the medications and their administration are complicated and expensive. Providers must also manage the logistics for the entire ecosystem involved in the delivery of these treatments. This includes arranging for visit times with nurses, the particular treatments to be received, any medications that are necessary, and any equipment used to deliver the medications. And any one of these can change up to the minute the nurse leaves the company to visit the patient at home. After that very moment, however, the company loses touch with the nurse, and data only get back into the system after the nurse comes back from her visit. That introduces a fair amount of delay in the entire process. These are, on the other hand, Crescent Healthcare's core business processes—those that make or break the company. And IT is a major force in making sure those work just fine, all the time.

"What we are trying to do is give all our customers—hospitals, physicians, payers, and patients—the most up-to-date clinical information on the status of their patients and our service to them," says Michalak.

The company has a long way to go before they get there, however. When Michalak started working at Crescent, he was faced with an aged IT infrastructure that had essentially been in place since the company was founded. No major updates or upgrades, no new applications. No color in the screens. The core, central application—the one that supported all those ever-important business processes—was a homegrown pharmacy management system. It was character-based and accessible only from dumb terminals. That means no mouse, no point-and-click, only green letters on a black background.

The challenge Michalak faced was more extensive than improving usability and reliability of the existing technology. The system does work well—kind of. That is, as long

FIGURE 1.1

Legacy applications and infrastructure can constrain the ability to compete in the 21st century.

SOURCE: © Fotosearch.

as you do not need to extract data from the system and use them for planning future capacity expansions, run alternative scenarios of what the future might hold, or do any kind of market analysis or business intelligence. If you can do without any of these applications—and without anything else for which you might need data—then the current system works just fine. Crescent Healthcare could not get any of these applications to work with the current system, and so the company did without them. At some point, however, management decided that things had to change.

"Most of the real business applications were homegrown and a lot of them have to be replaced," says Michalak. "The idea is to do a wholesale legacy replacement—create from scratch a pharmacy management system that is essentially soup to nuts, that touches all aspects of the functional business departments," he says.

The core business process of the company—the arrangement and delivery of infusion therapy services—is very slow. The goal is to cut down latency throughout the process every-

where possible, except in direct, hands-on patient care. The big question now is how to get there—and without affecting the most important aspect of Crescent Healthcare's business. "In health care, the quality of patient care is paramount, so that is one of the immovable priorities," says Michalak.

To summarize, Crescent Healthcare is a leader in a growing segment—infusion therapies—of a growing industry: health care. Their core business process is very complicated and drawn out, out of touch with the systems at times, and with a central outcome—quality of patient care—that accepts no compromises. All of this is supported by an IT infrastructure that has remained essentially unchanged for the last 20 years, and is starting to constrain what the company can do. The new CIO is charged with revamping these homegrown applications while keeping the lights on.

SOURCE: Kevin Fogarty, "From Green Screen Apps to the Cloud: One CIO's Challenge," *CIO.com*, January 27, 2011, and Crescent Healthcare, Inc. *www.crescenthealthcare.com*, accessed May 2, 2011.

▼ QUESTIONS TO CONSIDER

1. Why does Crescent Healthcare need to replace its current technologies? The company has very likely invested huge sums in its core applications over time, they do seem to work as expected, and people know how to use them, even if they have some quirks. Is it worth starting all over again?

2. What are some of the alternatives that Michalak has for achieving these objectives? That is, in which ways

could the revamping of existing applications be accomplished? What are the advantages and disadvantages of each?

3. Beyond replacing the current systems with more modern ones, what other functionality would you add to Crescent's IT infrastructure? In what ways would you make the new systems different from the current ones?

What Is an Information System?

We begin with a simple definition that we can expand upon later in the chapter. An *information system* (IS) can be any organized combination of people, hardware, software, communications networks, data resources, and policies and procedures that stores, retrieves, transforms, and disseminates information in an organization. People rely on modern information systems to communicate with one another using a variety of physical devices (*hardware*), information processing instructions and procedures (*software*), communications channels (*networks*), and stored data (*data resources*). Although today's information systems are typically associated with computers, we have been using information systems since the dawn of civilization. Even today we make regular use of information systems that have nothing to do with a computer. Consider some of the following examples of information systems:

- **Smoke signals for communication** were used as early as recorded history and can account for the human discovery of fire. The pattern of smoke transmitted valuable information to others who were too far to see or hear the sender.

- **Card catalogs in a library** are designed to store data about the books in an organized manner that allows readers to locate a particular book by its title, author name, subject, or a variety of other approaches.

- **Your book bag, day planner, notebooks, and file folders** are all part of an information system designed to help you organize the inputs provided to you via handouts, lectures, presentations, and discussions. They also help you process these inputs into useful outputs: homework and good exam grades.

- **The cash register at your favorite fast-food restaurant** is part of a large information system that tracks the products sold, the time of a sale, inventory levels, and the amount of money in the cash drawer; it also contributes to the analysis of product sales in any combination of locations anywhere in the world.

- **A paper-based accounting ledger** as used before the advent of computer-based accounting systems is an iconic example of an information system. Businesses used this type of system for centuries to record the daily transactions and to keep a record of the balances in their various business and customer accounts.

Figure 1.2 illustrates a useful conceptual framework that organizes the knowledge presented in this text and outlines areas of knowledge you need about information systems. It emphasizes that you should concentrate your efforts in the following five areas of IS knowledge:

- **Foundation Concepts.** Fundamental behavioral, technical, business, and managerial concepts about the components and roles of information systems. Examples include basic information system concepts derived from general systems theory or

✳FIGURE 1.2

A framework that outlines the major areas of information systems knowledge needed by business professionals.

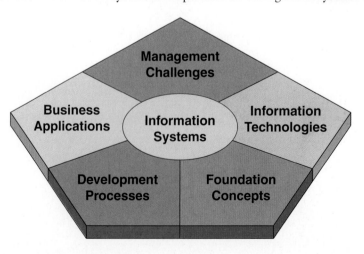

competitive strategy concepts used to develop business applications of information technology for competitive advantage. Chapters 1 and 2 and other chapters of the text support this area of IS knowledge.

- **Information Technologies.** Major concepts, developments, and management issues in information technology—that is, hardware, software, networks, data management, and many Internet-based technologies. Chapters 3 and 4 provide an overview of computer hardware and software technologies, and Chapters 5 and 6 cover key data resource management and telecommunications network technologies for business.

- **Business Applications.** The major uses of information systems for the operations, management, and competitive advantage of a business. Chapters 7 and 8 cover applications of information technology in functional areas of business such as marketing, manufacturing, and accounting. Chapter 9 focuses on e-commerce applications that most companies use to buy and sell products on the Internet, and Chapter 10 covers the use of information systems and technologies to support decision making in business.

- **Development Processes.** How business professionals and information specialists plan, develop, and implement information systems to meet business opportunities. Several developmental methodologies are explored in Chapters 11 and 12, including the systems development life cycle and prototyping approaches to business application development.

- **Management Challenges.** The challenges of effectively and ethically managing information technology at the end-user, enterprise, and global levels of a business. Thus, Chapter 13 focuses on security challenges and security management issues in the use of information technology, while Chapter 14 covers some of the key methods business managers can use to manage the information systems function in a company with global business operations.

Although a seemingly endless number of software applications exist, there are three fundamental reasons for all business applications of information technology. They are found in the three vital roles that information systems can perform for a business enterprise:

- Support of business processes and operations.
- Support of decision making by employees and managers.
- Support of strategies for competitive advantage.

Figure 1.3 illustrates how these fundamental roles interact in a typical organization. At any given moment, information systems designed to support business processes and operations may also be providing data to, or accepting data from, systems

THE FUNDAMENTAL ROLES OF IS IN BUSINESS
LO 1-2
LO 1-3

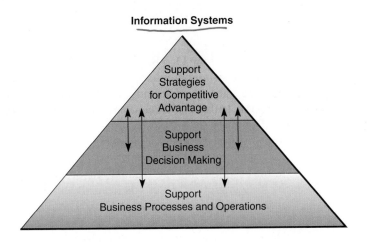

Information Systems

Support Strategies for Competitive Advantage

Support Business Decision Making

Support Business Processes and Operations

FIGURE 1.3

The three fundamental roles of the business applications of information systems. Information systems provide an organization with support for business processes and operations, decision making, and competitive advantage.

focused on business decision making or achieving competitive advantage. The same is true for the other two fundamental roles of IS. Today's organizations are constantly striving to achieve integration of their systems to allow information to flow freely through them, which adds even greater flexibility and business support than any of the individual system roles could provide.

Let's look at a typical retail store as a good example of how these *roles of IS in business* can be implemented.

The Fundamental Roles of IS in Business

Support of Business Processes and Operations. As a consumer, you regularly encounter information systems that support the business processes and operations at the many retail stores where you shop. For example, most retail stores now use *computer-based information systems* to help their employees record customer purchases, keep track of inventory, pay employees, buy new merchandise, and evaluate sales trends. Store operations would grind to a halt without the support of such information systems.

Support of Business Decision Making. Information systems also help store managers and other business professionals make better decisions. For example, decisions about what lines of merchandise need to be added or discontinued and what kind of investments they require are typically made after an analysis provided by computer-based information systems. This function not only supports the decision making of store managers, buyers, and others, but also helps them look for ways to gain an advantage over other retailers in the competition for customers.

Support of Strategies for Competitive Advantage. Gaining a strategic advantage over competitors requires the innovative application of information technologies. For example, store management might make a decision to install touch-screen kiosks in all stores, with links to the e-commerce Web site for online shopping. This offering might attract new customers and build customer loyalty because of the ease of shopping and buying merchandise provided by such information systems. Thus, strategic information systems can help provide products and services that give a business a comparative advantage over its competitors.

Welch's: Balancing Truckloads with Business Intelligence

Given dramatic fluctuations in gas prices, it's no surprise that companies want to find ways to rein in transportation costs. One company finding success in that endeavor is Welch's, a well-known purveyor of food and packaged consumer goods. The company is tapping the power of business intelligence for better insight into its supply-chain operations, which in turn can help keep transportation expenses lower. Welch's, the $654 million manufacturer known for its jams, jellies, and juices, recently installed an on-demand BI application from Oco.

One way Welch's is leveraging the Oco BI application is to ensure that truckloads delivered by its carriers go out full.

The idea is that customers are already paying for the full truck when it delivers goods, even if it's only halfway or three-quarters loaded. With the BI system, Welch's can tell if a buyer's shipment is coming up short of full capacity and help them figure out what else they can order to max it out, thus saving on future shipping costs.

"Welch's can go to the customer and say, 'You're only ordering this much. Why not round out the load with other things you need? It will be a lot cheaper for you,'" says Bill Copacino, president and CEO of Oco. "If you're able to put

4,000 more pounds on the 36,000-pound shipment, you're getting a 10 percent discount on transportation costs," he adds.

"We're essentially capturing every element—from the customer orders we receive, to bills of lading on every shipment we make, as well as every data element on every freight bill we pay," says Bill Coyne, director of purchasing and logistics for Welch's. "We dump them all into one data warehouse [maintained by Oco], and we can mix-and-match and slice-and-dice any way we want." Coyne says that Welch's tries to ship its products out of its distribution center five days a week. "But we found ourselves just totally overwhelmed on Fridays," he says. "We would complain, 'How come there are so many orders on Friday?'"

Now, the new system helps Welch's balance its daily deliveries so that it uses about the same number of trucks, rather than hiring seven trucks on a Monday, five on a Tuesday, eight on a Wednesday, and so forth.

The company reaps transportation savings by using a stable number of trucks daily—"as capacity is not jumping all over the place," Copacino says.

"We are gaining greater visibility into cost-savings opportunities, which is especially important in light of rising fuel and transportation costs," says Coyne. Welch's spends more than $50 million each year on transportation expenses, and the Oco BI application and reporting features have become critical in a very short period of time. "We literally can't go any amount of time without knowing this stuff," Coyne says.

SOURCE: Ted Samson, "Welch's Leverages BI to Reduce Transport Costs," *InfoWorld*, October 16, 2008; and Thomas Wailgum, "Business Intelligence and On-Demand: The Perfect Marriage?" *CIO Magazine*, March 27, 2008.

TRENDS IN INFORMATION SYSTEMS
LO 1-3

The business applications of information systems have expanded significantly over the years. Figure 1.4 summarizes these changes.

Until the 1960s, the role of most information systems was simple: transaction processing, record keeping, accounting, and other *electronic data processing* (EDP) applications. Then another role was added, namely, the processing of all these data into useful, informative reports. Thus, the concept of *management information systems* (MIS) was born. This new role focused on developing business applications that provided managerial end users with predefined management reports that would give managers the information they needed for decision-making purposes.

By the 1970s, it was evident that the standard "off-the-shelf" information products produced by management information systems were not adequately meeting the decision-making needs of management, so the concept of *decision support systems* (DSS) was born. The new role for information systems was to provide managers with ad hoc, interactive support of their decision-making processes. This support would be tailored to the unique decisions and decision-making styles of managers as they confronted specific types of problems in the real world.

In the 1980s, several new roles for information systems appeared. First, the rapid development of microcomputer processing power, application software packages, and telecommunications networks gave birth to the phenomenon of *end-user computing*. End users could now use their own computing resources to support their job requirements instead of waiting for the indirect support of centralized corporate information services departments.

Second, it became evident that most top corporate executives did not directly use (read "have time to use") either the voluminous reports from management information systems or the complex analytical modeling capabilities of decision support systems, so the concept of *executive information systems* (EIS) developed. These "executive summary" information systems were created to give top executives an easy way to get

FIGURE 1.4

The expanding roles of the business applications of information systems. Note how the roles of computer-based information systems have expanded over time. Also, note the impact of these changes on the end users and managers of an organization.

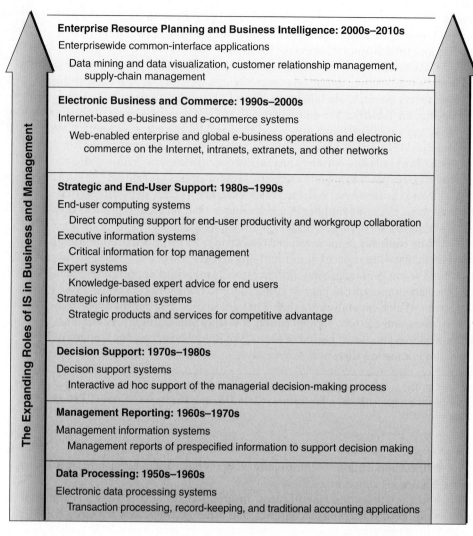

The Expanding Roles of IS in Business and Management

Enterprise Resource Planning and Business Intelligence: 2000s–2010s

Enterprisewide common-interface applications

Data mining and data visualization, customer relationship management, supply-chain management

Electronic Business and Commerce: 1990s–2000s

Internet-based e-business and e-commerce systems

Web-enabled enterprise and global e-business operations and electronic commerce on the Internet, intranets, extranets, and other networks

Strategic and End-User Support: 1980s–1990s

End-user computing systems

Direct computing support for end-user productivity and workgroup collaboration

Executive information systems

Critical information for top management

Expert systems

Knowledge-based expert advice for end users

Strategic information systems

Strategic products and services for competitive advantage

Decision Support: 1970s–1980s

Decison support systems

Interactive ad hoc support of the managerial decision-making process

Management Reporting: 1960s–1970s

Management information systems

Management reports of prespecified information to support decision making

Data Processing: 1950s–1960s

Electronic data processing systems

Transaction processing, record-keeping, and traditional accounting applications

the critical information they wanted, when they wanted it, and tailored to the formats they preferred.

Third, breakthroughs occurred in the development and application of artificial intelligence (AI) techniques to business information systems. Today's systems include intelligent software agents that can be programmed and deployed inside a system to act on behalf of their owner, system functions that can adapt themselves on the basis of the immediate needs of the user, virtual reality applications, advanced robotics, natural language processing, and a variety of applications for which artificial intelligence can replace the need for human intervention, thus freeing up knowledge workers for more complex tasks. *Expert systems* (ES) and other *knowledge-based systems* also forged a new role for information systems. Today, expert systems can serve as consultants to users by providing expert advice in limited subject areas. One look at Watson playing *Jeopardy* against the two best players in the world shows the power of machine learning to rapidly bring us new knowledge.

An important new role for information systems appeared in the 1980s and continued through the 1990s: the concept of a strategic role for information systems, sometimes called *strategic information systems* (SIS). In this concept, information technology becomes an integral component of business processes, products, and services that help a company gain a competitive advantage in the global marketplace.

The mid- to late 1990s saw the revolutionary emergence of *enterprise resource planning* (ERP) systems. This organization-specific form of a strategic information system integrates all facets of a firm, including its planning, manufacturing, sales, resource management, customer relations, inventory control, order tracking, financial management, human resources, and marketing—virtually every business function. The primary advantage of these ERP systems lies in their common interface for all computer-based organizational functions and their tight integration and data sharing, necessary for flexible strategic decision making. We explore ERP and its associated functions in greater detail in Chapter 8.

We are also entering an era where a fundamental role for IS is *business intelligence* (BI). BI refers to all applications and technologies in the organization that are focused on the gathering and analysis of data and information that can be used to drive strategic business decisions. Through the use of BI technologies and processes, organizations can gain valuable insight into the key elements and factors—both internal and external—that affect their business and competitiveness in the marketplace. BI relies on sophisticated metrics and analytics to "see into the data" and find relationships and opportunities that can be turned into profits. We'll look closer at BI in Chapter 10.

Finally, the rapid growth of the Internet, intranets, extranets, and other interconnected global networks in the 1990s dramatically changed the capabilities of information systems in business at the beginning of the 21st century. Further, a fundamental shift in the role of information systems occurred. Internet-based and Web-enabled enterprises and global e-business and e-commerce systems are becoming commonplace in the operations and management of today's business enterprises. Information systems is now solidly entrenched as a strategic resource in the modern organization.

A closer look at Figure 1.4 suggests that though we have expanded our abilities with regard to using information systems for conducting business, today's information systems are still doing the same basic things that they began doing more than 50 years ago. We still need to process transactions, keep records, provide management with useful and informative reports, and support the foundational accounting systems and processes of the organization. What has changed, however, is that we now enjoy a much higher level of integration of system functions across applications, greater connectivity across both similar and dissimilar system components, and the ability to reallocate critical computing tasks such as data storage, processing, and presentation to take maximum advantage of business and strategic opportunities. Because of these increased capabilities, the systems of tomorrow will be focused on increasing both the speed and reach of our systems to provide us with greater decision-making accuracy, speed, and insight.

THE ROLE OF e-BUSINESS IN BUSINESS

The Internet and related technologies and applications have changed the ways businesses operate and people work, as well as how information systems support business processes, decision making, and competitive advantage. Thus, many businesses today are using Internet technologies to Web-enable their business processes and create innovative *e-business applications.* See Figure 1.5.

In this text, we define *e-business* as the use of Internet technologies to work and empower business processes, e-commerce, and enterprise collaboration within a company and with its customers, suppliers, and other business stakeholders. In essence, e-business can be more generally considered an *online exchange of value.* Any online exchange of information, money, resources, services, or any combination thereof falls under the e-business umbrella. The Internet and Internet-like networks—those inside the enterprise *(intranet)* and between an enterprise and its trading partners *(extranet)*—have become the primary information technology infrastructure that supports the e-business applications of many companies. These companies rely on e-business applications to (1) reengineer internal business processes, (2) implement e-commerce systems with their customers and suppliers, and (3) promote enterprise collaboration among business teams and workgroups.

Enterprise collaboration systems involve the use of software tools to support communication, coordination, and collaboration among the members of networked teams and workgroups. A business may use intranets, the Internet, extranets, and other

FIGURE 1.5

Businesses today depend on the Internet, intranets, and extranets to implement and manage innovative e-business applications.

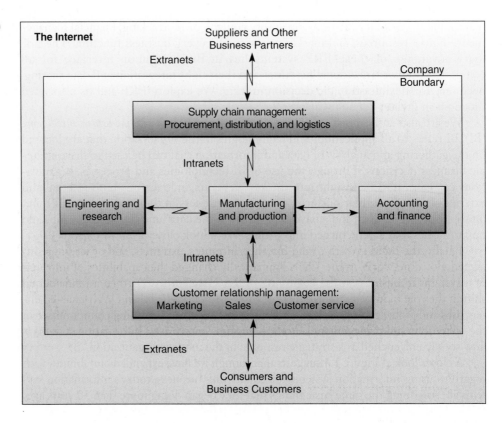

networks to implement such systems. For example, employees and external consultants may form a *virtual team* that uses a corporate intranet and the Internet for e-mail, videoconferencing, e-discussion groups, and Web pages of work-in-progress information to collaborate on business projects.

E-commerce is the buying, selling, marketing, and servicing of products, services, and information over a variety of computer networks. Many businesses now use the Internet, intranets, extranets, and other networks to support every step of the commercial process, including everything from advertising, sales, and customer support on the World Wide Web to Internet security and payment mechanisms that ensure completion of delivery and payment processes. For example, e-commerce systems include Internet Web sites for online sales, extranet access to inventory databases by large customers, and the use of corporate intranets by sales reps to access customer records for customer relationship management.

TYPES OF INFORMATION SYSTEMS
LO 1-4

Information systems are a "one-size-fits-all" concept. IS can be developed to perform a wide variety of related tasks or just a single task; for example, several *types of information systems* can be classified either as operations or management information systems. Figure 1.6 illustrates this conceptual classification of information systems applications. Information systems are categorized this way to spotlight the major role each plays in the operations and management of a business. Note, however, that there are many subcategories of information systems, and each plays an essential role in either the operation of the business or the execution of its chosen strategy. Let's look briefly at some examples of such information systems categories.

Operations Support Systems

Information systems have always been needed to process data generated by, and used in, business operations. Such *operations support systems* produce a variety of information products for internal and external use; however, they do not emphasize the specific

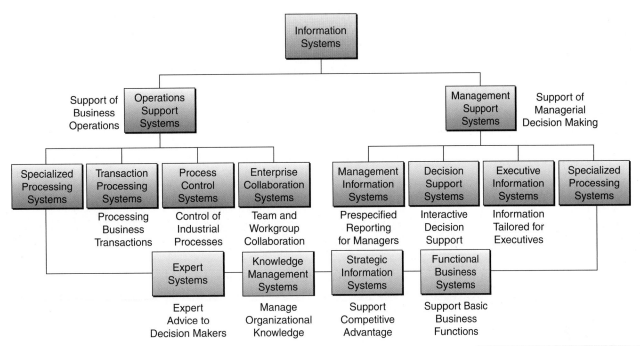

FIGURE 1.6

Operations and management classifications of information systems. Note how this conceptual overview emphasizes the main purposes of information systems that support business operations and managerial decision making.

information products that can best be used by managers. Further processing by management information systems is usually required. The role of a business firm's operations support systems is to process business transactions, control industrial processes, support enterprise communications and collaborations, and update corporate databases efficiently. See Figure 1.7.

Transaction processing systems are important examples of operations support systems that record and process the data resulting from business transactions. They process transactions in two basic ways. In *batch processing*, transactions data are accumulated over a period of time and processed periodically. In *real-time* (or *online*) processing, data are processed immediately after a transaction occurs. For example, point-of-sale (POS) systems at many retail stores use electronic cash register terminals to capture and transmit sales data electronically over telecommunications links to regional computer centers for immediate (real-time) or nightly (batch) processing. Figure 1.8 is an example of software that automates accounting transaction processing.

Process control systems monitor and control physical processes. For example, a petroleum refinery uses electronic sensors linked to computers to monitor chemical processes continually and make instant (real-time) adjustments that control the refinery process. *Enterprise collaboration systems* enhance team and workgroup communications and productivity and include applications that are sometimes called *office automation*

FIGURE 1.7

A summary of operations support systems with examples.

Operations Support Systems
• **Transaction processing systems.** Process data resulting from business transactions, update operational databases, and produce business documents. Examples: sales and inventory processing and accounting systems.
• **Process control systems.** Monitor and control industrial processes. Examples: petroleum refining, power generation, and steel production systems.
• **Enterprise collaboration systems.** Support team, workgroup, and enterprise communications and collaborations. Examples: e-mail, chat, and videoconferencing groupware systems.

FIGURE 1.8

QuickBooks is a popular accounting package that automates small office or home office (SOHO) accounting transaction processing while providing business owners with management reports.

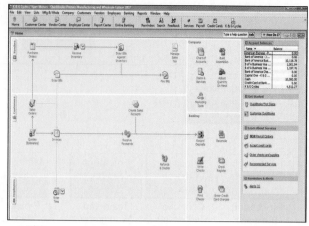

SOURCE: Courtesy of Quickbooks.

systems. For example, knowledge workers in a project team may use e-mail to send and receive e-messages or use videoconferencing to hold electronic meetings to coordinate their activities.

Management Support Systems

When information system applications focus on providing information and support for effective decision making by managers, they are called ***management support systems.*** Providing information and support for decision making by all types of managers and business professionals is a complex task. Conceptually, several major types of information systems support a variety of decision-making responsibilities: (1) management information systems, (2) decision support systems, and (3) executive information systems. See Figure 1.9.

Management information systems (MIS) provide information in the form of reports and displays to managers and many business professionals. They are the most common form of information system in an organization. For example, sales managers may use their networked computers and Web browsers to receive instantaneous displays about the sales results of their products and access their corporate intranet for daily sales analysis reports that evaluate sales made by each salesperson. *Decision support systems* (DSS) give direct computer support to managers during the decision-making process. These types of systems fall under the business intelligence or business analytics umbrella and will be discussed in detail in Chapter 10. For example, an advertising manager may use a DSS to perform a what-if analysis as part of the decision to determine how to spend advertising dollars. A production manager may use a DSS to decide how much product to manufacture, based on the expected sales associated with a future promotion and the location and availability of the raw materials necessary to

FIGURE 1.9

A summary of management support systems with examples.

Management Support Systems
• **Management information systems.** Provide information in the form of prespecified reports and displays to support business decision making. Examples: sales analysis, production performance, and cost trend reporting systems.
• **Decision support systems.** Provide interactive ad hoc support for the decision-making processes of managers and other business professionals. Examples: product pricing, profitability forecasting, and risk analysis systems.
• **Executive information systems.** Provide critical information from MIS, DSS, BI, and other sources tailored to the information needs of executives. Examples: systems for easy access to analyses of business performance, actions of competitors, and economic developments to support strategic planning.

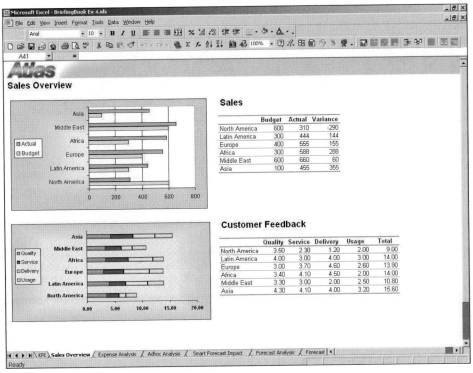

FIGURE 1.10

Management information systems provide information to business professionals in a variety of easy-to-use formats.

SOURCE: Courtesy of Infor.

manufacture the product. *Executive information systems* (EIS) provide critical information from a wide variety of internal and external sources in easy-to-use displays to executives and managers. Think of an EIS as a "30,000-foot-high view of the organization." For example, top executives may use touch-screen terminals for an instant view of text and graphics displays that highlight key areas of organizational and competitive performance. Figure 1.10 is an example of an MIS report display.

Other Classifications of Information Systems

Several other categories of information systems can support either operations or management applications. For example, *expert systems* can provide expert advice for operational chores like equipment diagnostics or managerial decisions such as loan portfolio management. IBM's famous supercomputer, Watson, is an example of an expert system that can translate text input and use a complex search algorithm to find answers to questions. *Knowledge management systems* are knowledge-based information systems that support the creation, organization, and dissemination of business knowledge to employees and managers throughout a company. Information systems that focus on operational and managerial applications in support of basic business functions such as accounting or marketing are known as **functional business systems.** Finally, *strategic information systems* apply information technology to a firm's products, services, or business processes to help it gain a strategic advantage over its competitors. See Figure 1.11.

It is also important to realize that business applications of information systems in the real world are typically integrated combinations of the several types of information systems just mentioned. That is because conceptual classifications of information systems are designed to emphasize the many different roles of information systems. In practice, these roles are combined into integrated or **cross-functional informational systems** that provide a variety of functions. Thus, most information systems are designed both to produce information and to support decision making for various levels of management and business functions, as well as perform record-keeping and transaction-processing chores. Whenever you analyze an information system, you

FIGURE 1.11

A summary of other categories of information systems with examples.

Other Categories of Information Systems
• **Expert systems.** Knowledge-based systems that provide expert advice and act as expert consultants to users. Examples: credit application advisor, process monitor, and diagnostic maintenance systems.
• **Knowledge management systems.** Knowledge-based systems that support the creation, organization, and dissemination of business knowledge within the enterprise. Examples: intranet access to best business practices, sales proposal strategies, and customer problem resolution systems.
• **Strategic information systems.** Support operations or management processes that provide a firm with strategic products, services, and capabilities for competitive advantage. Examples: online stock trading, shipment tracking, and e-commerce Web systems.
• **Functional business systems.** Support a variety of operational and managerial applications of the basic business functions of a company. Examples: information systems that support applications in accounting, finance, marketing, operations management, and human resource management.

probably see that it provides information for a variety of managerial levels and business functions. The enterprise resource planning systems discussed in Chapter 8 are examples of information systems that combine virtually all of the processes of an organization into a single system that spans all organizational boundaries. It's like one big information system that runs the whole organization. We will discuss that more later.

MANAGERIAL CHALLENGES OF INFORMATION TECHNOLOGY
LO 1-5
LO 1-7

Figure 1.12 illustrates the scope of the challenges and opportunities facing business managers and professionals in effectively managing information systems and technologies. Success in today's dynamic business environment depends heavily on maximizing the use of Internet-based technologies and Web-enabled information systems to meet the competitive requirements of customers, suppliers, and other business partners in a global marketplace. Figure 1.12 also emphasizes that information systems and their associated technologies must be managed to support the business strategies, business processes, and organizational structures and culture of a business enterprise. That is because information systems are designed, operated, and used by people in a variety of organizational settings and business environments. The goal of many companies today is to maximize their customer and business value by using information technology to help their employees implement cooperative business processes with customers, suppliers, and others.

FIGURE 1.12

Examples of the challenges and opportunities that business managers face in managing information systems and technologies to meet business goals.

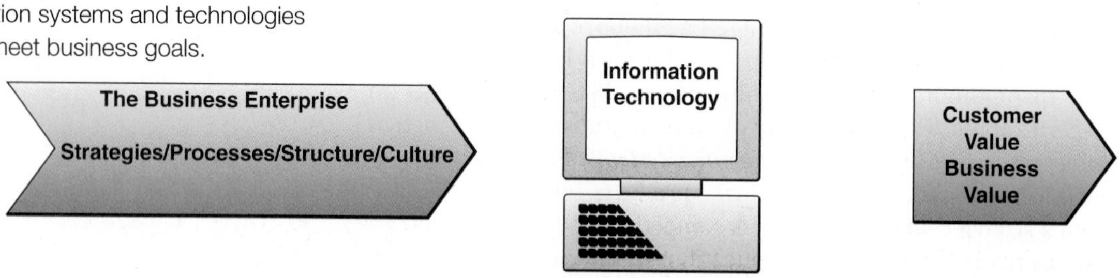

The Business Enterprise
Strategies/Processes/Structure/Culture

Information Technology

Customer Value Business Value

Business / IT Challenges
- Speed and flexibility requirements of product development, manufacturing, and delivery cycles.
- Reengineering and cross-functional integration of business processes using Internet technologies.
- Integration of e-business and e-commerce into the organization's strategies, processes, structure, and culture.

Business / IT Developments
- Use of the Internet, intranets, extranets, and the Web as the primary IT infrastructure.
- Diffusion of Web technology to internetwork employees, customers, and suppliers.
- Global networked computing, collaboration, and decision support systems.

Business / IT Goals
- Give customers what they want, when and how they want it, at the lowest cost.
- Coordination of manufacturing and business processes with suppliers and customers.
- Marketing channel partnerships with suppliers and distributors.

Success and Failure with IT

By now you should be able to see that the success of an information system should not be measured only by its *efficiency* in terms of minimizing costs, time, and the use of information resources. Success should also be measured by the *effectiveness* of the information technology in supporting an organization's business strategies, enabling its business processes, enhancing its organizational structures and culture, and increasing the customer and business value of the enterprise.

It is important to realize, however, that information technology and information systems can be mismanaged and misapplied in such a way that IS performance problems create both technological and business failures. Let's look at an example of what happens after these failures occur, as well as what can be done to avoid these situations.

Your department—information technology—has just played a starring role in blowing a multimillion-dollar enterprise software project. The intense glare from the CEO, CFO, and other business leaders is squarely focused on the CIO, vice president of applications, project managers, and business analysts charged with making sure that this didn't happen. Of course, IT is never 100 percent at fault for any massive project—whether an ERP or CRM implementation, mainframe migration, or networking upgrade. The business side usually plays its part.

But the unfortunate and unfair fact is that because these initiatives are considered "technology projects," the business will almost always look in IT's direction when there's blame to be tossed around. "That's just a fact of life in IT," says Chris Curran, who's both a consulting partner at Diamond Management & Techonology Consultants and its Chief Technology Offer.

No sane executive would dismiss the strategic importance of IT today. And most don't: An IT Governance Institute study, consisting of more than 250 interviews with executives of both large and small companies in a variety of industry sectors, found that half of the respondents said that IT is "very important to the enterprise," and three-quarters stated that they align IT and business strategies.

When it came to IT project accountability, "executive management" was identified as the group held accountable for IT governance in 71 percent of the enterprises. That's all well and good, but when it comes to walking the walk with technology projects, non-IT executives appear to fall back on familiar rhetoric. In a similar 2009 survey of more than 500 IT professionals by ISACA, a nonprofit trade group focusing on corporate governance, almost half of respondents said "the CIO is responsible for ensuring that stakeholder returns on IT-related investments are optimized," notes the survey report.

Curran takes those results a step further. "Business investments need to have business accountability," Curran says. "But when a project goes south, especially high-profile ERP implementations, IT gets blamed—but it's not an IT project."

Curran's advice for such massive undertakings, which CIOs and analysts talk up but many don't follow, is practical: Think bite-sized project chunks and set proper expectations. He also advises his clients and their IT shops to embrace change and transparency—even if it hurts at first. "The corporate culture—the status quo—tends to be: 'Everything's good. We don't talk about problems until they are near unrecoverable, because we know people don't like bad news,'" Curran says.

But there are always going to be problems. That, also, is "just a fact of life in IT."

Responsibility and Accountability for Project Success (and Failure)

SOURCE: Thomas Wailgum, "After a Massive Tech Project Failure: What IT Can Expect," CIO.com, August 5, 2009.

FIGURE 1.13

Developing information systems solutions to business problems can be implemented and managed as a multistep process or cycle.

Developing IS Solutions

Developing successful information system solutions to business problems is a major challenge for business managers and professionals today. As a business professional, you will be responsible either for proposing, assisting with development, or developing new or improved uses of information technologies for your company. As a business manager, you will frequently manage the development efforts of information systems specialists and other business end users.

Most computer-based information systems are conceived, designed, and implemented using some form of systematic development process. Figure 1.13 shows that several major activities must be accomplished and managed in a complete IS development cycle. In this development process, end users and information specialists *design* information system applications on the basis of an *analysis* of the business requirements of an organization. Examples of other activities include *investigating* the economic or technical feasibility of a proposed application, acquiring and learning how to use any software necessary to *implement* the new system, and making improvements to *maintain* the business value of a system.

We discuss the details of the information systems development process in Chapters 11 and 12. We will explore many of the business and managerial challenges that arise in developing and implementing new uses of information technology in Chapters 13 and 14. Now let's look at one way in which the upgrading of legacy applications can be approached. This example emphasizes the importance of carefully considering all possible alternatives when thinking about deploying new technology.

Modernize (Don't Replace!) Your Legacy Applications

Over time, all companies find themselves facing outdated legacy systems—those technologies that were developed long ago and that, while still working today, are lacking in one or more major aspects. The interface may look strange (monochromatic green letters over a black background!), business needs may have changed, and there are new functions that the system can no longer perform. Documentation is often missing or outdated, and the original developers are long gone. Current IT staff are not entirely sure how the old system works. Where to go from here?

Many companies would undertake a massive system development effort at this point. They would obtain requirements for a new set of applications, which would be designed and either coded or acquired, then tested and implemented. And then would come training, data conversion, implementation rollouts, and the like. And the initial release would likely not work as well as the "old" system it is replacing, although things would get better as time (and money) goes into it. This is not, however, the only way.

There are tools (which used to be called "screen scrappers") by vendors such as IBM, Attachmate, and Rocket Seagull Software that put a web-browser front-end between the old green screens of yore and the users of today. These tools capture the data directly from the legacy system and present it to users in an appealing graphical interface developed with current technologies and standards, while minimizing the amount of tinkering necessary in the background. In fact, the point of contact with the legacy system can be completely revamped without modifying it in any significant way. Taking this route automatically allows employees and users to access the system from any device that supports a browser, while giving the IT staff time to gradually transition out of the legacy system, but only for those modules that need changing.

This solution is not always the best one—sometimes, it does make sense to replace the old system with a new one, just as replacing an old car is more cost effective than buying the old car a new transmission. Other times, however, companies are faced with systems that are ugly, but otherwise work fine. The system might be mission-critical, and thus the replacement process must be approached with extreme care. Or the necessary resources (budget, time) may not be there at this time. In those scenarios, on the other hand, extending the life of those systems with new and updated interfaces may be the way to go.

SOURCE: Mike Kinrys, "Avoid Costly System Replacements by Modernizing Old Applications," *CMA Management*, July 2008.

Challenges and Ethics of IT

As a prospective manager, business professional, or knowledge worker, you will very likely be challenged by the ethical responsibilities generated by the use of information technology. For example, what uses of information technology might be considered improper, irresponsible, or harmful to other people or to society? What is the proper business use of the Internet and an organization's IT resources? What does it take to be a *responsible end user* of information technology? How can you protect yourself from computer crime and other risks of information technology? These are some of the questions that outline the ethical dimensions of information systems that we will discuss and illustrate with real world cases throughout this text and in detail in Chapter 13. Figure 1.14 outlines some of the ethical risks that may arise in the use of several major applications of information technology. The following example illustrates some of the security challenges associated with conducting business over the Internet.

FIGURE 1.14

Examples of some of the ethical challenges that must be faced by business managers who implement major applications of information technology.

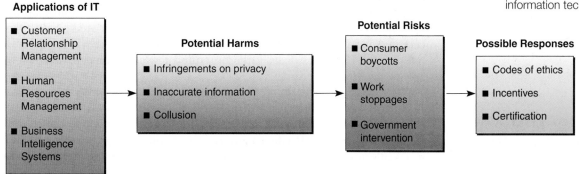

Hannaford Bros.: The Importance of Securing Customer Data

Hannaford Bros. may have started as a fruit and vegetable stand in 1883, but it has expanded from its Maine roots to become an upscale grocer with more than 160 stores throughout Maine, Massachusetts, New Hampshire, upstate New York, and Vermont. In March 2008, the supermarket chain disclosed a data security breach; Hannaford said in a notice to customers posted on its Web site that unknown intruders had accessed its systems and stolen about 4.2 million credit and debit card numbers between December 7 and March 10. The breach affected all of Hannaford's 165 supermarkets in New England and New York, as well as 106 stores operated under the Sweetbay name in Florida and 23 independently owned markets that sell Hannaford products.

In a likely precursor of what was yet to come, two class-action lawsuits were filed against the company within the week. The filers argued that inadequate data security at Hannaford had resulted in the compromise of the personal financial data of consumers, thereby exposing them to the risk of fraud. They also claimed the grocer also appeared not to have disclosed the breach to the public quickly enough after discovering it.

Even though the Hannaford breach is relatively small compared with some other corporate security problems, it is likely to result in renewed calls for stricter regulations to be imposed on companies that fail to protect consumer data. In addition to facing the likelihood of consumer lawsuits, retailers who suffer breaches have to deal with banks and credit unions, which are getting increasingly anxious about having to shell out tens of thousands of dollars to pay for the cost of notifying their customers and reissuing credit and debit cards.

Retailers, on the other hand, have argued that the commissions they pay to card companies on each transaction are supposed to cover fraud-related costs, making any additional payments a double penalty. They also have said that the only reason they store payment card data is because of requirements imposed on them by the major credit card companies.

While the ultimate impact of these and other security breaches may be hard to quantify, it represents one of the most important challenges resulting from the ubiquitous use of electronic transaction processing and telecommunication networks in the modern networked enterprise, and one that is likely to keep growing every day. The security of customer and other sensitive data also represents one of the primary concerns of IT professionals.

SOURCE: Jaikumar Vijayan, "Hannaford Hit by Class-Action Lawsuits in Wake of Data-Breach Disclosure," *Computerworld*, March 20, 2008.

Challenges of IT and IS Careers

Both information technology and the myriad of information systems it supports have created interesting, challenging, and lucrative career opportunities for millions of men and women all over the globe. At this point in your life you may still be uncertain about the career path you wish to follow, so learning more about information technology may help you decide if you want to pursue an IT/IS-related career. One thing is certain: You will either work in an IT/IS-related career or you will regularly work with one or more IS professionals. Either way, the knowledge you gain here will be invaluable throughout your career.

In recent years, economic downturns have affected all job sectors, including IT. Further, rising labor costs in North America, Canada, and Europe have resulted in a large-scale movement to outsource basic software programming functions to India, the Middle East, and Asia-Pacific countries. Despite this move, employment opportunities in the information systems field are strong, with more new and exciting jobs emerging each day as organizations continue to expand their use of information technology. In addition, these new jobs pose constant human resource management challenges to all organizations because shortages of qualified information systems personnel frequently occur. Dynamic developments in business and information technologies cause constantly changing job requirements in information systems, which will ensure that the long-term job outlook in IT remains both positive and exciting.

Along with the myth that there are no jobs for IS professionals (we will dispel this one below!), another common myth is that IS professionals are computer geeks who live in a cubicle. Once again, nothing could be further from the truth! Today's IS professional must be highly skilled in communication, able to deal with people, and, most of all, articulate in the fundamentals of business and strategy. The marketplace is demanding a *business technologist* with a big "B" and a big "T." The world of the IS professional is filled with constant challenge, variety, social interaction, and cutting-edge decision making. No desks and cubicles here. If action is what you are after, then you have found it here.

One major recruiter of IS professionals is the IT industry itself. Thousands of companies develop, manufacture, market, and service computer hardware, software, data, and network products and services. The industry can also provide e-business and e-commerce applications and services, end-user training, or business systems consulting. The biggest need for qualified people, however, comes from the millions of businesses, government agencies, and other organizations that use information technology. They need many types of IS professionals, such as systems analysts, software developers, and network managers to help them plan, develop, implement, and manage today's Internet-based and Web-enabled business/IT applications.

The accounting industry is a major recruiter of IS professionals. Legislation, entitled the Sarbanes-Oxley Act of 2002, required major changes with regard to auditing practices by public accounting firms and internal control processes within publicly held organizations of all sizes and industries. Many of these changes directly affect the IT/IS practices of all parties involved. To facilitate the execution of the covenants of Sarbanes-Oxley, the accounting industry is actively recruiting graduates from accounting programs that have a significant emphasis on IS education. In addition, they are spending equal energy to recruit IS/IT professionals to work within the accounting industry. In either case, the result is a significant increase in demand for graduates with an IS/IT background or emphasis. Figure 1.15 lists just a few of the many career roles available to the modern IT professional.

According to recent reports by the U.S. Department of Labor, computer systems analysts, database administrators, and other managerial-level IS positions are expected to be among the fastest-growing occupations through 2015. Employment of IS professionals is expected to grow more than 36 percent (much higher than average) for all occupations as organizations continue to adopt and integrate increasingly sophisticated technologies. Job increases will be driven by very rapid growth in computer system design and related services, which is projected to be one of the fastest-growing

FIGURE 1.15

Careers in IS are as diverse and exciting as the technologies used in them; IS professionals have career opportunities in every business environment and activity throughout the world.

Systems Analyst	System Consultant	Business Applications Consultant
Chief Information Officer	Computer Operator	Computer Serviceperson
Network Administrator	Data Dictionary Specialist	Network Manager
Database Administrator	Database Analyst	Documentation Specialist
IS Auditor	End-User Computer Manager	Equipment Manufacturer Representative
PC Sales Representative	Programmer	Program Librarian
Project Manager	Records Manager	Hardware Sales Representative
Scheduling and Control Person	Security Officer	Office Automation Specialist
Senior Project Leader	Service Sales Representative	Software Sales Representative
Technical Analyst	Software Quality Evaluator	Technical Writer
Telecommunications Specialist	Training & Standards Manager	User Interface Specialist

industries in the U.S. economy. In addition, many job openings will arise annually from the need to replace workers who move into managerial positions or other occupations or who leave the labor force. Most important to you, IS/IT graduates generally receive some of the highest starting salaries compared with other college graduates.

Despite the recent economic downturn among information technology firms, IS professionals still enjoy favorable job prospects. The demand for networking to facilitate sharing information, expanding client/server environments, and the need for specialists to use their knowledge and skills in a problem-solving capacity will be major factors in the rising demand for computer systems analysts, database administrators, and other IS professionals. Moreover, falling prices of computer hardware and software should continue to induce more businesses to expand their computerized operations and integrate new technologies. To maintain a competitive edge and operate more efficiently, firms will keep demanding the services of professionals who are knowledgeable about the latest technologies and can apply them to meet the needs of businesses.

Perhaps the time has come to put a sharper edge on this message: The field of information systems is growing at an increasingly rapid pace, and there is little risk of being unemployed upon graduation! I believe that the concern over a lack of IT/IS-related jobs was fueled by the news media and is now, quite simply, unfounded. Headlines proclaimed the death of IS and the lack of jobs in the United States due to massive outsourcing and offshoring. The jobs that were being sent overseas were real ones, to be sure. They were, however, not the jobs that you or your fellow students were ever going to train for during your stay in college—unless, of course, you aspire to being a faceless voice in a call center. These jobs are service-related jobs that, while vital to the big picture, are not the management level, creative business technologist positions that colleges and universities typically train their students to obtain. The real problem facing the IS field today is the lack of graduates! Students are choosing other professions because they fear low pay and unemployment, whereas recruiters are simultaneously begging for more graduates to feed their voracious appetites for more IS professionals. If you choose to avoid a career in information systems, it should not be because you think there are no jobs, that it does not have to do with people, or that it is no fun. Over the course of this book, we will dispel, with strong evidence, all of these rumors and myths. Let's start with some facts related to the first one.

The Bureau of Labor Statistics has some compelling evidence in favor of a career in information systems:

> *Prospects for qualified computer and information systems managers should be excellent. Workers with specialized technical knowledge and strong communications and business skills, as well as those with an MBA with a concentration in information systems, will have the best prospects. Job openings will be the result of employment growth and the need to replace workers who transfer to other occupations or leave the labor force. Fast-paced occupational growth and the limited supply of technical workers will lead to a wealth of opportunities for qualified individuals. While technical workers remain relatively scarce in the United States, the demand for them continues to rise. This situation was exacerbated by the economic downturn in the early 2000s, when many technical professionals lost their jobs. Since then, many workers have chosen to avoid this work since it is perceived to have poor prospects. (Bureau of Labor Statistics Occupational Outlook Handbook, 2010–2011)*

Increasingly, more sophisticated and complex technology is being implemented across all organizations, which will continue to fuel the demand for these IT/IS occupations. The demand for systems analysts continues to grow to help firms maximize their efficiency with available technology. Expansion of e-commerce—doing business on the Internet—and the continuing need to build and maintain databases that store critical information about customers, inventory, and projects are fueling demand for database administrators familiar with the latest technology. Finally, the increasing importance placed on "cybersecurity"—the protection of electronic information—will result in a need for workers skilled in information security. Let's take a look at the emerging role of business analysts as liaisons between IT specialists and their business customers.

The Critical Role of Business Analysts

For two decades, the CIO has been viewed as the ultimate broker between the business and technology functions. But while that may be an accurate perception in the executive boardroom, down in the trenches, business analysts (BA) have been the ones tasked with developing business cases for IT application development, in the process smoothing relations among competing parties and moving projects along.

The 21st century business analyst is a liaison, bridge, and diplomat who balances the oftentimes incongruous supply of IT resources and demands of the business. A recent Forrester Research report found that those business analysts who were most successful were the ones who could "communicate, facilitate and analyze." The business analyst is a hot commodity right now due to business reliance on technology, according to Jim McAssey, a principal at The W Group, a consulting firm. "The global delivery capabilities of technology today make the challenges of successfully bridging the gap between business and IT even harder," he says.

"Companies typically don't invest in an IT project without a solid business case," says Jeff Miller, senior vice president of Aetea, an IT staffing and consulting firm.

A good business analyst is able to create a solution to a particular business problem and act as a bridge to the technologists who can make it happen. "Without the BA role, CIOs are at significant risk that their projects will not solve the business problem for which they were intended," says Miller.

The ideal candidate will have 5 to 10 or more years of experience (preferably in a specific industry), a technical undergraduate degree, and an MBA.

Strong risk-assessment, negotiation, and problem-resolution skills are key, and hands-on experience is critical. Business analysts must be process-driven and able to see a project through conflict and change, from start to finish. "The BA also must have the ability to learn new processes," says Miller. "A good BA learns business concepts and can quickly relate them to the specific needs of the project."

In the end, the more business technology analysts that are working in the business, the better off the CIO and IT function will be—whether the business technology analysts are reporting into IT or the business side. That's because those IT-savvy analysts, who will have a more in-depth understanding of and more expertise in technologies, will "ultimately help the business make better decisions when it comes to its interactions with IT," contend the Forrester analysts. And "CIOs have new allies in the business." Salaries range from $45,000 (entry level) to $100,000 (senior business analyst) per year.

SOURCE: Thomas Wailgum, "Why Business Analysts Are So Important for IT and CIOs," *CIO Magazine*, April 16, 2008; and Katherine Walsh, "Hot Jobs: Business Analyst," *CIO Magazine*, June 19, 2007.

The IS Function

The successful management of information systems and technologies presents major challenges to business managers and professionals. Thus, the information systems function represents:

- A major functional area of business equally as important to business success as the functions of accounting, finance, operations management, marketing, and human resource management.

- An important contributor to operational efficiency, employee productivity and morale, and customer service and satisfaction.

- A recognized source of value to the firm.
- A major source of information and support needed to promote effective decision making by managers and business professionals.
- A vital ingredient in developing competitive products and services that give an organization a strategic advantage in the global marketplace.
- A dynamic, rewarding, and challenging career opportunity for millions of men and women.
- A key component of the resources, infrastructure, and capabilities of today's networked business enterprises.
- A strategic resource.

Foundation Concepts:
The Components of Information Systems

System concepts underlie all business processes, as well as our understanding of information systems and technologies. This is why we need to understand how generic system concepts apply to business firms and the components and activities of information systems. A grasp of system concepts will help you better understand many other concepts in the technology, applications, development, and management of information systems that we cover in this text. For example, system concepts help us understand:

● ● ● ● ● ● ● ● ● ● ● ● ● ●
**SYSTEM CONCEPTS:
THE FOUNDATION FOR
BUSINESS PROCESSES**
LO 1-6

- **Technology.** Computer networks are systems of information processing components that use a variety of hardware, software, data management, and telecommunications network technologies.

- **Applications.** E-business and e-commerce applications involve interconnected business information systems.

- **Development.** Developing ways to use information technology in business includes designing the basic components of information systems.

- **Management.** Managing information technology emphasizes the quality, strategic business value, and security of an organization's information systems.

What Is a System?

We have used the term *system* more than 100 times already and will use it thousands more times before we are done. It therefore seems reasonable that we focus our attention on exactly what a **system** is. As we discussed at the beginning of the chapter, a system is defined as *a set of interrelated components, with a clearly defined boundary, working together to achieve a common set of objectives by accepting inputs and producing outputs in an organized transformation process*. Many examples of systems can be found in the physical and biological sciences, in modern technology, and in human society. Thus, we can talk of the physical system of the sun and its planets, the biological system of the human body, the technological system of an oil refinery, and the socioeconomic system of a business organization. See Figure 1.16.

Systems have three basic functions:

- **Input** involves capturing and assembling elements that enter the system to be processed. For example, raw materials, energy, data, and human effort must be secured and organized for processing.

- **Processing** involves transformation processes that convert input into output. Examples are manufacturing processes, the human breathing process, or mathematical calculations.

- **Output** involves transferring elements that have been produced by a transformation process to their ultimate destination. For example, finished products, human services, and management information must be transmitted to their human users.

SOME EXAMPLES. A transport system is made up of many interrelated components including the chassis, drivetrain, body, user interface, and environment. Each of these components is assembled in a manner to allow for either a specific application or a variety of contexts and uses. The transport system boundary is such that it can easily be identified and differentiated from other

FIGURE 1.16

An example of a system: Interrelated components, in the form of pipes, meters, and valves, work together to supply energy to a large building.

SOURCE: © Brian Kennedy/Flickr/Getty Images.

similar systems. It accepts inputs from its operator and produces acceleration, deceleration, or directional outputs as a result of an organized transformation process. This is just a fancy way of describing a car, truck, bicycle, jet aircraft, or a space shuttle. They are all just systems.

A manufacturing system accepts raw materials as input and produces finished goods as output. An information system accepts resources (data) as input and processes them into products (information) as output. A business organization is a system in which human and economic resources are transformed by various business processes into goods and services. Systems are everywhere. Even we are systems!

Feedback and Control

The system concept becomes even more useful by including two additional elements: *feedback* and *control*. A system with feedback and control functions is sometimes called a *cybernetic* system, that is, a system that is both self-monitoring and self-regulating. Again, it sounds kind of like the way we function.

- *Feedback* is data about the performance of a system. For example, data about sales performance are feedback to a sales manager. Data about the speed, altitude, attitude, and direction of an aircraft are feedback to the aircraft's pilot or autopilot.

- *Control* involves monitoring and evaluating feedback to determine whether a system is moving toward the achievement of its goal. The control function then makes the necessary adjustments to a system's input and processing components to ensure that it produces proper output. For example, a sales manager exercises control when reassigning salespersons to new sales territories after evaluating feedback about their sales performance. An airline pilot, or the aircraft's autopilot, makes minute adjustments after evaluating the feedback from the instruments to ensure that the plane is exactly where the pilot wants it to be.

EXAMPLE. Figure 1.17 illustrates a familiar example of a self-monitoring, self-regulating, thermostat-controlled heating system found in many homes; it automatically monitors and regulates itself to maintain a desired temperature. Another example is the human body, which can be regarded as a cybernetic system that automatically monitors and adjusts many of its functions, such as temperature, heartbeat, and breathing. A business also has many control activities. For example, computers may monitor and control manufacturing processes, accounting procedures help control financial systems, data entry displays provide control of data entry activities, and sales quotas and sales bonuses attempt to control sales performance.

Other System Characteristics

Figure 1.18 uses a business organization to illustrate the fundamental components of a system, as well as several other system characteristics. Note that a system does not exist in a vacuum; rather, it exists and functions in an *environment* containing other systems. If a system is one of the components of a larger system, it is referred to as a *subsystem*, and the larger system is its environment.

Several systems may share the same environment. Some of these systems may be connected to one another by means of a shared boundary, called the *interface*.

FIGURE 1.17

A common cybernetic system is a home temperature control system. The thermostat accepts the desired room temperature as input and sends voltage to open the gas valve, which fires the furnace. The resulting hot air goes into the room, and the thermometer in the thermostat provides feedback to shut the system down when the desired temperature is reached.

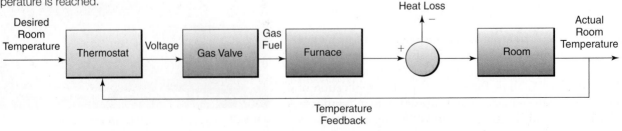

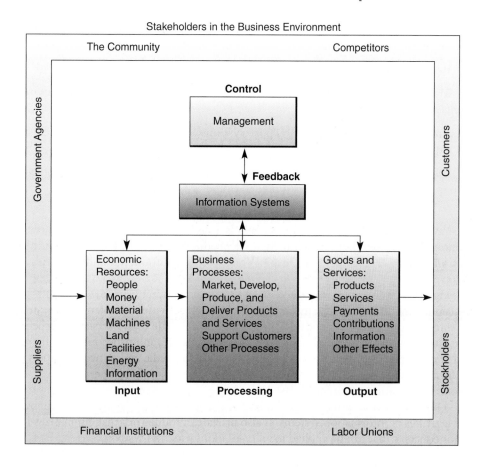

Stakeholders in the Business Environment

FIGURE 1.18
A business is an example of an organizational system in which economic resources (input) are transformed by various business processes (processing) into goods and services (output). Information systems provide information (feedback) about the operations of the system to management for the direction and maintenance of the system (control) as it exchanges inputs and outputs with its environment.

Figure 1.18 also illustrates the concept of an *open system*, that is, a system that interacts with other systems in its environment. In this diagram, the system exchanges inputs and outputs with its environment. Thus, we could say that it is connected to its environment by input and output interfaces. Finally, a system that has the ability to change itself or its environment to survive is called an *adaptive system*.

SOME MORE EXAMPLES. Organizations such as businesses and government agencies are good examples of the systems in society, which is their environment. Society contains a multitude of such systems, including individuals and their social, political, and economic institutions. Organizations themselves consist of many subsystems, such as departments, divisions, process teams, and other workgroups. Organizations are examples of open systems because they interface and interact with other systems in their environment. Finally, organizations are examples of adaptive systems because they can modify themselves to meet the demands of a changing environment.

If we apply our understanding of general system concepts to information systems, it should be easy to see the parallels. Information systems are made up of interrelated components:

* People, hardware, software, peripherals, and networks.

   They have clearly defined boundaries:

* Functions, modules, type of application, department, or end-user group.

   All the interrelated components work together to achieve a common goal by accepting inputs and producing outputs in an organized transformation process:

* Using raw materials, hiring new people, manufacturing products for sale, and disseminating information to others.

Information systems make extensive use of feedback and control to improve their effectiveness:

- Error messages, dialog boxes, passwords, and user rights management.

Many information systems are designed to change in relation to their environments and are adaptive:

- Intelligent software agents, expert systems, and highly specialized decision support systems.

Information systems are systems just like any other system. Their value to the modern organization, however, is unlike any other system ever created.

COMPONENTS OF INFORMATION SYSTEMS

LO 1-1
LO 1-6

We have noted that an information system is a system that accepts data resources as input and processes them into information products as output. How does an information system accomplish this task? What system components and activities are involved?

Figure 1.19 illustrates an *information system model* that expresses a fundamental conceptual framework for the major components and activities of information systems. An information system depends on the resources of people (end users and IS specialists), hardware (machines and media), software (programs and procedures), data (data and knowledge bases), and networks (communications media and network support) to perform input, processing, output, storage, and control activities that transform data resources into information products.

This information system model highlights the relationships among the components and activities of information systems. It also provides a framework that emphasizes four major concepts that can be applied to all types of information systems:

- People, hardware, software, data, and networks are the basic resources of information systems.

FIGURE 1.19

The components of an information system. All information systems use people, hardware, software, data, and network resources to perform input, processing, output, storage, and control activities that transform data resources into information products.

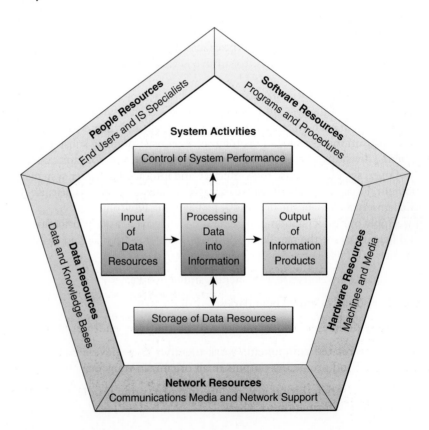

- People resources include end users and IS specialists, hardware resources consist of machines and media, software resources include both programs and procedures, data resources include data and knowledge bases, and network resources include communications media and networks.

- Data resources are transformed by information processing activities into a variety of information products for end users.

- Information processing consists of the system activities of input, processing, output, storage, and control.

Our basic IS model shows that an information system consists of five major resources: *people*, *hardware*, *software*, *data*, and *networks*. Let's briefly discuss several basic concepts and examples of the roles these resources play as the fundamental components of information systems. You should be able to recognize these five components at work in any type of information system you encounter in the real world. Figure 1.20 outlines several examples of typical information system resources and products.

INFORMATION SYSTEM RESOURCES

People Resources

People are the essential ingredient for the successful operation of all information systems. These *people resources* include end users and IS specialists.

- *End users* (also called users or clients) are people who use an information system or the information it produces. They can be customers, salespersons, engineers, clerks, accountants, or managers and are found at all levels of an organization. In fact, most of us are information system end users. Most end users in business are referred to as *knowledge workers,* that is, people who spend most of their time communicating and collaborating in teams and workgroups and creating, using, and distributing information.

- *IS specialists* are people who develop and operate information systems. They include systems analysts, software developers, system operators, and other managerial, technical, and clerical IS personnel. Briefly, systems analysts design information systems based on the information requirements of end users, software developers create computer programs based on the specifications of systems analysts, and system operators help monitor and operate large computer systems and networks.

Information System Resources and Products
People Resources
Specialists—systems analysts, software developers, systems operators.
End Users—anyone else who uses information systems.
Hardware Resources
Machines—computers, video monitors, magnetic disk drives, printers, optical scanners.
Media—floppy disks, magnetic tape, optical disks, plastic cards, paper forms, removable storage media.
Software Resources
Programs—operating system programs, spreadsheet programs, word processing programs, payroll programs.
Procedures—data entry procedures, error correction procedures, paycheck distribution procedures.
Data Resources
Product descriptions, customer records, employee files, inventory databases.
Network Resources
Communications media, communications processors, network access, control software.
Information Products
Management reports and business documents using text and graphics displays, audio responses, and paper forms.

FIGURE 1.20

Examples of information system resources and products.

Hardware Resources

The concept of *hardware resources* includes all physical devices and materials used in information processing. Specifically, it includes not only *machines,* such as computers and other equipment, but also all data *media,* that is, tangible objects on which data are recorded, from sheets of paper to magnetic or optical disks. Examples of hardware in computer-based information systems are:

- **Computer systems,** which consist of central processing units containing microprocessors and a variety of interconnected peripheral devices such as printers, scanners, monitors, and so on. Examples are handheld, laptop, tablet, or desktop microcomputer systems, midrange computer systems, and large mainframe computer systems.

- **Computer peripherals,** which are devices such as a keyboard, electronic mouse, trackball, or stylus for the input of data and commands, a video screen or printer for the output of information, and magnetic or optical disk drives for the storage of data resources.

Upgrade Your Legacy Systems in Three Steps

Replacing existing hardware and software with new technologies is both difficult and painful. Even when everybody involved (IT staff, users, other stakeholders) agree that is the best way to move forward, it is still painful. Specifying and implementing a replacement system is fraught with difficulties and requires some tough decisions. Robert C. Seacord of Carnegie Mellon University's Software Engineering Institute outlines a three-step process for moving forward:

Analyze the Current System in Place. The focus should be on what the existing application is doing, rather than on the technology on which it has been implemented, which users are sometimes fast to pinpoint as the culprit. Sometimes, however, the current system may no longer fulfill user needs. Or, the business is growing too rapidly and the technology does not scale well. Or, the system is no longer supported or understood. "We were facing a system running on a DOS- and Fox-based platform that no one knew much about, and the only guy who did understand it was about to retire," says Gerry Doan of Santa Cruz County, California, who supports a 500-person department. Other times, systems become outdated due to changes in hardware, as companies facing the move to 64-bit operating systems are starting to discover (16-bit applications will no longer run on those). The key issue in this step is to understand why it is that the current system should be replaced, as those reasons will have a major influence on what the new system should do and look like.

Understand the Requirements for the New System. All system changes, even seemingly simple performance upgrades, require an understanding of what users actually do with them. One key indicator that an application is no longer satisfying the needs of the user community is the existence of "off-system" workarounds in the form of spreadsheets and databases that users have developed to cope with the shortcomings of the current technology. These are often a rich source of ideas for what the new system should do. Standardizing on a small set of key technologies may also simplify the life of everyone involved, both users and IT staff. "Our management's intention is to mainstream as much technology as possible so everyone in IT will be using the same skill set," says Santa Cruz County's Doan. It's a lot easier to maintain and upgrade systems when they are all the same.

Make the Business Case for the New Project. Cost-benefit analyses of upgrading legacy technologies are not always as straightforward as they seem.

Some costs are easy to measure; for example, the cost of hardware and packaged software upgrades. Others, like the cost of the migration itself, are hard to estimate. And if understanding costs is tough, benefits may feel like mostly guesswork, since so many of them are really hard to quantify. Sometimes a single issue may be important enough to make the project be worth undertaking. When Santa Cruz County upgraded, "we lost the requirement to support a handful of nonstandard machines, that included some Windows 95 equipment, and a computer running an older Linux version," says Doan. That was a big relief to the busy department. And then there are the unexpected benefits. After users get familiar with the new technology, they can start doing things nobody had originally envisioned. Santa Cruz "users had to be taught new ways to get to their data," says Doan, "but the payoff was new things they could do that they couldn't do before."

SOURCE: John Dickinson, "Upgrading Your Legacy Systems," *InformationWeek*, August 28, 2007.

Software Resources

The concept of *software resources* includes all sets of information processing instructions. This generic concept of software includes not only the sets of operating instructions called *programs,* which direct and control computer hardware, but also the sets of information processing instructions called *procedures* that people need.

It is important to understand that even information systems that do not use computers have a software resource component. This claim is true even for the information systems of ancient times or the manual and machine-supported information systems still used in the world today. They all require software resources in the form of information processing instructions and procedures to properly capture, process, and disseminate information to their users.

The following are examples of software resources:

- **System software,** such as an operating system program, which controls and supports the operations of a computer system. Microsoft Windows and Unix are two examples of popular computer operating systems.

- **Application software,** which are programs that direct processing for a particular use of computers by end users. Examples are sales analysis, payroll, and word processing programs.

- **Procedures,** which are operating instructions for the people who will use an information system. Examples are instructions for filling out a paper form or using a software package.

Data Resources

Data are more than the raw material of information systems. The concept of *data resources* has been broadened by managers and information systems professionals. They realize that data constitute valuable organizational resources. Thus, you should view data just as you would any organizational resource that must be managed effectively to benefit all stakeholders in an organization.

The concept of data as an organizational resource has resulted in a variety of changes in the modern organization. Data that previously were captured as a result of a common transaction are now stored, processed, and analyzed using sophisticated software applications that can reveal complex relationships among sales, customers, competitors, and markets. In today's wired world, the data to create a simple list of an organization's customers are protected with the same energy as the cash in a bank vault. Data are the lifeblood of today's organizations, and the effective and efficient management of data is considered an integral part of organizational strategy. Data can be thought of as an asset of the organization just like vehicles, building, inventory, and money.

Data can take many forms, including traditional alphanumeric data, composed of numbers, letters, and other characters that describe business transactions and other events and entities; text data, consisting of sentences and paragraphs used in written communications; image data, such as graphic shapes and figures or photographic and video images; and audio data, including the human voice and other sounds.

The data resources of information systems are typically organized, stored, and accessed by a variety of data resource management technologies into:

- Databases that hold processed and organized data.
- Knowledge bases that hold knowledge in a variety of forms, such as facts, rules, and case examples about successful business practices.

For example, data about sales transactions may be accumulated, processed, and stored in a Web-enabled sales database that can be accessed for sales analysis reports by managers and marketing professionals. Knowledge bases are used by knowledge management systems and expert systems to share knowledge or give expert advice on specific subjects. We explore these concepts further in subsequent chapters.

DATA VERSUS INFORMATION. The word ***data*** is the plural of *datum*, although *data* commonly represents both singular and plural forms. Data are raw facts or observations, typically about physical phenomena or business transactions. For example, a spacecraft launch or the sale of a hamburger each generate a lot of data describing those events. More specifically, data are objective measurements of the *attributes* (the characteristics) of *entities* (e.g., people, places, things, and events).

EXAMPLE. Business transactions, such as buying a car or an airline ticket, can produce a lot of data. Just think of the hundreds of facts needed to describe the characteristics of the car you want and its financing, or the intricate details for even the simplest airline reservation.

People often use the terms *data* and *information* interchangeably. However, it is better to view data as raw material resources that are processed into finished information products. Then we can define ***information*** as data that have been converted into a meaningful and useful context for specific end users. Thus, data are usually subjected to a value-added process (*data processing* or *information processing*) during which (1) their form is aggregated, manipulated, and organized; (2) their content is analyzed and evaluated; and (3) they are placed in a proper context for a human user. A good metaphor is to think of *data* as the raw materials necessary to create and explosion and *information* as the explosion.

The issue of context is really at the heart of understanding the difference between information and data. Data can be thought of as context independent: A list of numbers or names, by itself, does not provide any understanding of the context in which it was recorded. In fact, the same list could be recorded in a variety of contexts. In contrast, for data to become information, both the context of the data and the perspective of the person accessing the data become essential. The same data may be considered valuable information to one person and completely irrelevant to the next. Just think of data as potentially valuable to all and information as valuable relative to its user.

EXAMPLE. Names, quantities, and dollar amounts recorded on sales forms represent data about sales transactions. However, a sales manager may not regard these as information. Only after such facts are properly organized and manipulated can meaningful sales information be furnished and specify, for example, the amount of sales by product type, sales territory, or salesperson.

Network Resources

Telecommunications technologies and networks like the Internet, intranets, and extranets are essential to the successful e-business and e-commerce operations of all types of organizations and their computer-based information systems. Telecommunications networks consist of computers, communications processors, and other devices interconnected by communications media and controlled by communications software. The concept of *network resources* emphasizes that communications technologies and networks are fundamental resource components of all information systems. Network resources include:

- **Communications media.** Examples include twisted-pair wire, coaxial and fiber-optic cables, and microwave, cellular, and satellite wireless technologies.

- **Network infrastructure.** This generic category emphasizes that many hardware, software, and data technologies are needed to support the operation and use of a communications network. Examples include communications processors, such as modems and inter-network processors, and communications control software, such as network operating systems and Internet browser packages.

Regardless of the type of information system, the same basic *information system activities* occur. Let's take a closer look now at each of the basic *data or information processing* activities. You should be able to recognize input, processing, output, storage, and control activities taking place in any information system you are studying. Figure 1.21 lists business examples that illustrate each of these information system activities.

INFORMATION SYSTEM ACTIVITIES
LO 1-6

Input of Data Resources

Data about business transactions and other events must be captured and prepared for processing by the *input* activity. Input typically takes the form of *data entry* activities such as recording and editing. End users usually enter data directly into a computer system or record data about transactions on some type of physical medium such as a paper form. This entry includes a variety of editing activities to ensure that they have recorded the data correctly. Once entered, data may be transferred onto a machine-readable medium, such as a magnetic disk, until needed for processing.

For example, data about sales transactions may be recorded on source documents such as paper order forms. (A *source document* is the original, formal record of a transaction.) Alternatively, salespersons might capture sales data using computer keyboards or optical scanning devices; they are visually prompted to enter data correctly by video displays. This method provides them with a more convenient and efficient *user interface*, that is, methods of end-user input and output with a computer system. Methods such as optical scanning and displays of menus, prompts, and fill-in-the-blank formats make it easier for end users to enter data correctly into an information system.

Processing of Data into Information

Data are typically subjected to *processing* activities, such as calculating, comparing, sorting, classifying, and summarizing. These activities organize, analyze, and manipulate

Information System Activities
• **Input.** Optical scanning of bar-coded tags on merchandise.
• **Processing.** Calculating employee pay, taxes, and other payroll deductions.
• **Output.** Producing reports and displays about sales performance.
• **Storage.** Maintaining records on customers, employees, and products.
• **Control.** Generating audible signals to indicate proper entry of sales data.

FIGURE 1.21

Business examples of the basic activities of information systems.

data, thus converting them into information for end users. The quality of any data stored in an information system must also be maintained by a continual process of correcting and updating activities.

EXAMPLE. Data received about a purchase can be (1) *added* to a running total of sales results, (2) *compared* to a standard to determine eligibility for a sales discount, (3) *sorted* in numerical order based on product identification numbers, (4) *classified* into product categories (e.g., food and nonfood items), (5) *summarized* to provide a sales manager with information about various product categories, and finally (6) used to *update* sales records.

Output of Information Products

Information in various forms is transmitted to end users and made available to them in the *output* activity. The goal of information systems is the production of appropriate *information products* for end users. Common information products include messages, reports, forms, and graphic images, which may be provided by video displays, audio responses, paper products, and multimedia. We routinely use the information provided by these products as we work in organizations and live in society. For example, a sales manager may view a video display to check on the performance of a salesperson, accept a computer-produced voice message by telephone, and receive a printout of monthly sales results.

Storage of Data Resources

Storage is a basic system component of information systems. Storage is the information system activity in which data are retained in an organized manner for later use. For example, just as written text material gets organized into words, sentences, paragraphs, and documents, stored data are commonly organized into a variety of data elements and databases. This organization facilitates their later use in processing or retrieval as output when needed by users of a system. Such data elements and databases are discussed further in Chapter 5, Data Resource Management.

Control of System Performance

An important information system activity is the *control* of system performance. An information system should produce feedback about its input, processing, output, and storage activities. This feedback must be monitored and evaluated to determine whether the system is meeting established performance standards. Then appropriate system activities must be adjusted so that proper information products are produced for end users.

For example, a manager may discover that subtotals of sales amounts in a sales report do not add up to total sales. This conflict might mean that data entry or processing procedures need to be corrected. Then changes would have to be made to ensure that all sales transactions would be properly captured and processed by a sales information system.

RECOGNIZING INFORMATION SYSTEMS

As a business professional, you should be able to recognize the fundamental components of information systems you encounter in the real world. This demand means that you should be able to identify:

- The people, hardware, software, data, and network resources they use.
- The types of information products they produce.
- The way they perform input, processing, output, storage, and control activities.

This kind of understanding will help you be a better user, developer, and manager of information systems. As we have pointed out in this chapter, this is important to your future success as a manager, entrepreneur, business professional, or modern business technologist.

Let's see how things turned out . . .

$35,000.^{00}$
$4,500.^{00}$

Crescent Healthcare Inc.: From Green Screens to Online Access

When we last saw Brett Michalak and Crescent Healthcare Inc., they were involved in the planning for a new solution to replace their existing homegrown pharmacy management software, which supported their core business processes. The current IT infrastructure in place was about 20 years old and had not been the focus of any major upgrades or improvements since. In addition to less-than-user-friendly graphical interfaces (or lack thereof, as their applications were character-based), getting data out of this system and into others to support more advanced planning and analysis was not feasible, and the company had decided that a comprehensive revamping of their application base was in order. This section discusses in more detail the approach taken by the company to tackle this project.

"The original intent was to do all the development with a cloud-based solution to get the cost and efficiency benefits available there and a path to other initiatives," says Michalak. As a first step, Crescent catalogued all of their legacy systems and then analyzed each to identify the specific business processes, or portions of them, that each legacy application supported. This apparently simple process of listing applications and how they were used brought about its own share of unanswered questions. Over time, many companies continue to support applications well after their business need has ceased to exist. This is particularly prevalent when nobody is really sure what would happen if a particular application were unplugged, as there is no clear architecture relating applications to each other.

After the list was scrubbed, the next step was to identify ways in which existing functionality could be replicated using Force.com services, their chosen alternative for cloud computing services [Force.com is one of the major cloud platforms for building and running applications—this particular platform provides customers with programmable logic, user interface, and workflow tools that can be used to design and run applications that are also remotely hosted and accessible through a Web site, thus greatly reducing the need for customers to support their own IT infrastructure]. Whereas some portion of the existing business processes of Crescent could be migrated to the cloud environment, others proved more troublesome in this regard. "The initial approach was to do a full Force.com development, but as we moved through that we had to make some adjustments based on specific requirements that didn't quite fit the cloud plan," says Michalak.

Trade-offs with regard to required functionality are a staple of migrations from custom legacy systems to commercial software applications, but they are especially notable when moving to a cloud environment. In those cases, the important thing is for companies to take a step back and ask themselves where they want to be in the future, rather than worry about the technology that will be implemented right now. And at the end of the day, functionality—that is, getting this done—will usually beat technology issues, particularly for mission-critical applications. One of the trade-offs Crescent had to make involved their central application, which was devoted to pharmacy management.

Instead of attempting to migrate that into the cloud, they replaced their green-screen pharmacy management software with specialized software from Definitive Homecare Solutions: something called CPR+. This application is especially designed for specialty pharmacies like Crescent Healthcare, which work rather differently from their retail counterpart. The application provides patient assessments that are customizable by therapy, medication, or disease state, as well as tracking and logistics tools designed to manage treatment progress, patient appointments, lab tracking, and scheduling. As a rather specialized type of service, even within health care, CPR+ supports the unique reimbursement processes related to the provision of infusion therapy.

By acquiring commercial software instead of attempting to develop its own set of applications, Crescent Healthcare was able to leverage the expertise of one of the few specialized software vendors in this segment of the industry. It also provides the company with a platform for future growth and expansion into related areas, should the business need ever arise. In addition to the core functionality described above, CPR+ also provides additional modules that can be added on to the base implementation. One of those, which provides access to patient information through a Web portal, is also being implemented by Crescent. Before rolling out the application to their employees, however, Michalak and the IT staff are conducting extensive testing to reduce the possibility of any major issues arising during implementation—that is, as much as one can when working with large system implementations.

Applications, however, are not any good without data. Crescent also had to gather, clean, and recycle their data to make it compatible with systems other than the home-grown software being phased out. That involved the deployment of a data warehouse where the data could be loaded and worked upon to make them ready for the transition to the new application environment. Having that data warehouse in place also got them thinking about the future deployment of business intelligence and analytics tools. Health care organizations are notorious for generating large amounts of data, which can possibly be leveraged to better serve their customers with new products and services, or improve the provision of existing ones. The ultimate goal, however, is to make all this data and functionality available to those who need it most: the caregivers in the field, those who have direct contact with the patient and who are, as far as the patients are concerned, the visible face of Crescent Healthcare.

"We'll be giving nurses, people in the field a user friendly interface we can use to get the most current information into their hands and that of patients to improve the logistics, improve the care, and get information back from the field as quickly as possible, " says Michalak.

The next stage of the process will focus on mobile connectivity. One of the major challenges the company is facing right now is the time between the last point of contact with the nurse or caregiver before she leaves to visit her patients and the next contact when the nurse returns from the field and updates the system with information about all visits that happened in between. When those routes are long or caregivers do not return to the office until the next day, there can be some lengthy delays in updating the data in the system. Eventually, the system will be able to allow nurses to log in remotely, either through browsers or apps in a smart phone.

Beyond gains in operational efficiency, the company sees all these developments as a source of competitive advantage. In a growing industry with 700 to 1,000 competitors, Crescent Healthcare is one of the larger providers of infusion services. And they need all the help they can get in staying ahead of everybody else. "I absolutely do see this as a competitive advantage in attracting clients and caregivers and payers; being able to keep everyone up-to-date in real time is light years ahead of where we were," Michalak says.

SOURCE: Kevin Fogarty, "From Green Screen Apps to the Cloud: One CIO's Challenge", *CIO.com*, January 27, 2011, and Definitive Homecare Solutions, *cprplus.com*, accessed May 2, 2011.

▼ QUESTIONS TO CONSIDER

1. Brett Michalak sees the efforts undertaken by Crescent Healthcare as providing the company with a competitive advantage over others in its industry. Why do you think he is making this statement? Can you provide three examples of how these technologies may provide them with a competitive advantage?

2. Based on your experience with the health care industry, what other projects do you see a company like Crescent Healthcare undertaking in the future? Does their new infrastructure position them well for those future initiatives? Why or why not?

- **IS Framework for Business Professionals.** The IS knowledge that a business manager or professional needs to know is illustrated in Figure 1.2 and covered in this chapter and text. This knowledge includes (1) foundation concepts: fundamental behavioral, technical, business, and managerial concepts like system components and functions, or competitive strategies; (2) information technologies: concepts, developments, or management issues regarding hardware, software, data management, networks, and other technologies; (3) business applications: major uses of IT for business processes, operations, decision making, and strategic/competitive advantage; (4) development processes: how end users and IS specialists develop and implement business/IT solutions to problems and opportunities arising in business; and (5) management challenges: how to manage the IS function and IT resources effectively and ethically to achieve top performance and business value in support of the business strategies of the enterprise.

- **Business Roles of Information Systems.** Information systems perform three vital roles in business firms. Business applications of IS support an organization's business processes and operations, business decision making, and strategic competitive advantage. Major application categories of information systems include operations support systems, such as transaction processing systems, process control systems, and enterprise collaboration systems; and management support systems, such as management information systems, decision support systems, and executive information systems. Other major categories are expert systems, knowledge management systems, strategic information systems, and functional business systems. However, in the real world, most application categories are combined into cross-functional information systems that provide information and support for decision making and also performing operational information processing activities. Refer to Figures 1.7, 1.9, and 1.11 for summaries of the major application categories of information systems.

- **System Concepts.** A system is a group of interrelated components, with a clearly defined boundary, working toward the attainment of a common goal by accepting inputs and producing outputs in an organized transformation process. Feedback is data about the performance of a system. Control is the component that monitors and evaluates feedback and makes any necessary adjustments to the input and processing components to ensure that proper output is produced.

- **Information System Model.** An information system uses the resources of people, hardware, software, data, and networks to perform input, processing, output, storage, and control activities that convert data resources into information products. Data are first collected and converted to a form that is suitable for processing (input). Then the data are manipulated and converted into information (processing), stored for future use (storage), or communicated to their ultimate user (output) according to correct processing procedures (control).

- **IS Resources and Products.** Hardware resources include machines and media used in information processing. Software resources include computerized instructions (programs) and instructions for people (procedures). People resources include information systems specialists and users. Data resources include alphanumeric, text, image, video, audio, and other forms of data. Network resources include communications media and network support. Information products produced by an information system can take a variety of forms, including paper reports, visual displays, multimedia documents, e-messages, graphic images, and audio responses.

These are the key terms and concepts of this chapter. The page number of their first reference appears in parentheses.

1. Computer-based information system (8)
2. Control (26)
3. Data (32)
4. Data or information processing (33)
5. Data resources (31)
6. Developing successful information system solutions (18)
7. E-business (11)
8. E-business applications (11)
9. E-commerce (12)
10. Enterprise collaboration systems (11)
11. Extranet (11)
12. Feedback (26)
13. Hardware resources (30)
    a. Machines (30)
    b. Media (30)
14. Information (32)
    a. Information products (34)
15. Information system (6)
16. Information system activities (33)
    a. Input (33)
    b. Processing (33)
    c. Output (34)
    d. Storage (34)
    e. Control (34)
17. Information system model (28)
18. Intranet (11)

19. Knowledge workers (29)
20. Management information systems (14)
21. Network resources (33)
22. People resources (29)
    a. IS specialists (29)
    b. End users (29)
23. Roles of IS in business (8)
    a. Support of business processes and operations (8)
    b. Support of business decision making (8)
    c. Support of strategies for competitive advantage (8)
24. Software resources (31)
    a. Programs (31)
    b. Procedures (31)
25. System (25)
26. Types of information systems (12)
    a. Cross-functional informational systems (15)
    b. Management support systems (14)
    c. Operations support systems (12)
    d. Functional business systems (15)
    e. Transaction processing systems (13)
    f. Process control systems (13)
    g. Enterprise collaboration systems (13)

Match one of the previous key terms and concepts with one of the following brief examples or definitions. Look for the best fit for answers that seem to fit more than one key term or concept. Defend your choices.

_____ 1. People who spend most of their workday creating, using, and distributing information.

_____ 2. Information systems support an organization's business processes, operations, decision making, and strategies for competitive advantage.

_____ 3. Using IT to reengineer business processes to support e-business operations.

_____ 4. Using Web-based decision support systems to support sales managers.

_____ 5. Using information technology for e-commerce to gain a strategic advantage over competitors.

_____ 6. A system that uses people, hardware, software, and network resources to collect, transform, and disseminate information within an organization.

_____ 7. An information system that uses computers and their hardware and software.

_____ 8. Anyone who uses an information system or the information it produces.

_____ 9. Applications using the Internet, corporate intranets, and interorganizational extranets for e-business operations, e-commerce, and enterprise collaboration.

_____ 10. The buying, selling, marketing, and servicing of products over the Internet and other networks.

_____ 11. Groupware tools to support collaboration among networked teams.

_____ 12. A group of interrelated components with a clearly defined boundary working together toward the attainment of a common goal.

_____ 13. Data about a system's performance.

_____ 14. Making adjustments to a system's components so that it operates properly.

_____ 15. Facts or observations.

_____ 16. Data that have been placed into a meaningful context for an end user.

_____ 17. Converting data into information is a type of this kind of activity.

_____ 18. An information system uses people, hardware, software, network, and data resources to perform input, processing, output, storage, and control activities that transform data resources into information products.

_____ 19. Machines and media.

_____ 20. Computers, disk drives, video monitors, and printers are examples.

_____ 21. Magnetic disks, optical disks, and paper forms are examples.

_____ 22. Programs and procedures.

_____ 23. A set of instructions for a computer.

_____ 24. A set of instructions for people.

_____ 25. End users and information systems professionals.

_____ 26. Using the keyboard of a computer to enter data.

_____ 27. Computing loan payments.

_____ 28. Printing a letter you wrote using a computer.

_____ 29. Saving a copy of the letter on a magnetic disk.

_____ 30. Having a sales receipt as proof of a purchase.

_____ 31. Information systems can be classified into operations, management, and other categories.

_____ 32. Includes transaction processing, process control, and end-user collaboration systems.

review quiz

_____ 33. Includes management information, decision support, and executive information systems.

_____ 34. Information systems that perform transaction processing and provide information to managers across the boundaries of functional business areas.

_____ 35. Internet-like networks and Web sites inside a company.

_____ 36. Interorganizational Internet-like networks among trading partners.

_____ 37. Using the Internet, intranets, and extranets to empower internal business operations, e-commerce, and enterprise collaboration.

_____ 38. Information systems that focus on operational and managerial applications in support of basic business functions such as accounting or marketing.

_____ 39. Data should be viewed the same way as any organizational resource that must be managed effectively to benefit all stakeholders in an organization.

_____ 40. A major challenge for business managers and professionals today in solving business problems.

_____ 41. Examples include messages, reports, forms, and graphic images, which may be provided by video displays, audio responses, paper products, and multimedia.

_____ 42. These include communications media and network infrastructure.

_____ 43. People who develop and operate information systems.

_____ 44. The execution of a set of activities in order to convert data into information.

_____ 45. Those systems implemented in order to direct physical conversion processes, such as oil refinement.

_____ 46. The second stage of information systems evolution, focused on providing managerial users with information relevant to decision making in the form of predefined reports.

_____ 47. A type of operation support systems geared toward the recording and processing of data captured as a result of business transactions.

_____ 48. A type of operation support systems that enhance team and workgroup communication and productivity.

1. How can information technology support a company's business processes and decision making and give it a competitive advantage? Give examples to illustrate your answer.

2. How does the use of the Internet, intranets, and extranets by companies today support their business processes and activities?

3. One major issue in the Real World Challenge outlined in the chapter was the lack of upgrades and new applications undertaken ever since the company was founded and the original IT infrastructure put in place. How does a company ever get to the place where Crescent is in the opening to this chapter? What do you think prevented them from taking action earlier?

4. Why do big companies still fail in their use of information technology? What should they be doing differently?

5. How can a manager demonstrate that he or she is a responsible end user of information systems? Give several examples.

6. Refer to the Real World Solution in the chapter. Has Crescent Healthcare applied the "three steps for the upgrading of legacy systems" outlined in the chapter? Which of those have been done in more or less detail? Can you fill in the blanks for any that you see lacking?

7. What are some of the toughest management challenges in developing IT solutions to solve business problems and meet new business opportunities?

8. Why are there so many conceptual classifications of information systems? Why are they typically integrated in the information systems found in the real world?

9. In what major ways have information systems in business changed during the last 40 years? What is one major change you think will happen in the next 10 years? Refer to Figure 1.4 to help you answer.

10. Refer to the Real World Case on eCourier, Cablecom, and Bryan Cave in the chapter. Jay Bregman, CTO and cofounder of eCourier, notes that the company hopes their innovative use of technology will become a differentiator in their competitive market. More generally, to what extent do specific technologies help companies gain an edge over their competitors? How easy or difficult would it be to imitate such advantages?

Complete the following exercises as individual or group projects that apply chapter concepts to real-world business situations.

1. Understanding the Information System

The Library as an Information System

A library makes an excellent information systems model. It serves as a very large information storage facility with text, audio, and video data archives. Look up the definitions for each term listed below and briefly explain a library's equivalents.

   a. Input

   b. Processing

   c. Output

   d. Storage

   e. Control

   f. Feedback

The Library of Congress, occupying three buildings in Washington, D.C., is the largest library in the world.

   a. Use a Web browser and a search engine to locate the home URL (Web address) of the Library of Congress and access that page. What is the URL (home page) of the Library of Congress?

   b. Examine the Collection Highlights; how many types of data can be accessed directly from that page? Locate and select one collection of interest to you and write a one-page synopsis of that collection. Be sure to include the URL (Web address) of that collection.

2. Careers in IT

Are You Ready?

If you are looking for a job in information technology, it helps to know what's hot. Read the CIO article "IT Graduates Not 'Well-Trained, Ready-to-Go'" (http://bit.ly/h9GAw7), and answer the questions below.

   a. What four skills from higher-education institutions are in demand?

   b. For each skill above, list the associated course numbers and names offered by your college or university. Use **_bold italics_** to denote courses required for all business majors; use **bold** to denote courses required for all information technology majors.

   c. Are the required courses sufficient to give you the competitive edge you need (given your major)? Explain.

   d. List three required general education or "core curriculum" courses you believe provide you with the least value in the job market. Justify your answers.

3. Skydive Chicago: Efficiency and Feedback

Digital Data

Skydive Chicago (www.SkydiveChicago.com) is one of the premier skydiving resorts in the United States, serving skydivers ranging in skills from first-time jumpers to internationally competitive freefly teams.

Each student in Skydive Chicago's training program makes a series of progressive training jumps under the direct supervision of a U.S. Parachute Association–rated jumpmaster. The training program gears each jump in the series toward teaching one or two new skills. Jumpmasters videotape their students' jumps. Students use the feedback these videos provide to identify mistakes. They often copy their videos onto a personal computer or DVD for future reference.

Jumpmasters may also copy well-executed student skydives to the facility's video library. All students are given access to the drop zone's training room and are encouraged to watch video clips in preparation for their next training jump. This saves jumpmasters, who are paid per jump, considerable time. Jumpmasters also use these videos to evaluate their training method's effectiveness.

   a. How can this information system benefit the skydiving student?

   b. How can this information system benefit Skydive Chicago?

   c. Draw the information systems model (Figure 1.19, the information system model). Fill in your diagram with people, hardware, software, and other information from this exercise.

4. Are Textbooks History?

Trends in Information Systems

The wealth of free information available via the Internet continues to grow at incredible rates. Search engines such as Google make it easier to locate useful information. This textbook often explores the Internet's impact on various industries, and the textbook industry is no exception. Is it possible that free Internet content might one day replace textbooks?

   a. Go to www.google.com and use the search box to look up "End-user." Were any of Google's first five search results useful with respect to this course?

   b. Go to www.wikipedia.com and use the search box to look up "Knowledge worker." Compare Wikipedia's article to the information provided within this textbook. Which source did you find easiest to use? What advantages did Wikipedia provide? What advantages did this textbook provide?

c. Go to http://www.wikiversity.org and use the search box to look up "Information system." How does this description of Information Systems differ from the text description? Which one provides enough information for you to understand what an information system is without providing too much information (information overload)?

d. Between Google, Wikipedia, Wikiversity, and this textbook, which source provides the most useful information about "Information Systems"? Why?

e. Go to http://www.gcflearnfree.org and http://www.free-ed.net, and look at the course offerings. If you choose to pursue a future in information systems and information technology, what constraints (limits) do these Web sites pose in terms of teaching you to be an educated professional in this field? What differences do you see between the two "schools"?

5. **Careers in IS**
Disaster Recovery
"How important are your data to you?" "What would happen if . . . ?" While business managers focus on solving business problems and determining what their information systems should do, disaster recovery consultants ask what would happen if things go wrong.

With careful advanced planning, disaster recovery specialists help their clients prevent calamity. While this topic covers a wide variety of software issues, installation configuration issues, and security threats, examining common end-user mistakes may also prove enlightening. Common end-user mistakes include:

a. Failure to save work in progress frequently.

b. Failure to make a backup copy.

c. Storing original and backup copies in the same location.

For each of the common end-user mistakes listed above, answer the following questions.

a. How might this mistake result in data loss?

b. What procedures could you follow to minimize this risk?

eCourier, Cablecom, and Bryan Cave: Delivering Value through Business Intelligence

Visitors to the eCourier Web site are greeted with the words "*How happy are you? Take the eCourier happy test today!*" Those words and the playful purple Web site represent the company's customer satisfaction focus. And a key for the company in achieving that happiness is through its focus on operational business intelligence.

Business intelligence is moving out of the ivory tower of specialized analysts and is being brought to the front lines. In the case of eCourier, whose couriers carry 2,000 packages around London each day, operational business intelligence allows the company to keep real-time tabs on customer satisfaction. "This is a crucial differentiator in London's competitive same-day courier market, where clients are far more likely to take their business elsewhere than they are to report a problem to their current courier," says the company's Chief Technology Officer and cofounder Jay Bregman. Online directory London Online shows about 350 listings for courier services.

Before implementing operational business intelligence, eCourier sought to define IT as a crucial differentiator. Cofounders Tom Allason, eCourier's CEO, and Bregman ditched the idea of phone dispatchers and instead gave their couriers GPS-enabled handhelds, so couriers can be tracked and orders can be communicated electronically. They also focused on making online booking easy and rewarding; and much was invested in user-friendly applications: Customers can track online exactly where their courier is, eliminating the package delivery guesswork.

Today, 95 percent of deliveries are booked online, meaning that eCourier needs a much smaller staff for monitoring, tracking and placing orders, which in turn makes the company more scalable. Bregman says this is notable in a market where many courier companies use telephone dispatchers and guesswork about package whereabouts. Although innovative, booking and tracking automation did not complete the customer happiness puzzle. Without leading-edge business intelligence, account managers could miss the same issues that plagued other courier services: late deliveries, surly couriers, or even an unnoticed ramp-up in deliveries. "We're only one delivery away from someone deciding to use a different delivery firm," says Bregman.

So eCourier started using software from a company called SeeWhy to try to generate customer data more quickly. "What's unique about SeeWhy," says Bregman, "is its ability to report what's happening with customers instantly." When a new booking enters eCourier's database, the information is duplicated and saved into a repository within SeeWhy. The software then interprets the data by comparing it with previous information and trends, and if it notices an anomaly, it takes action. If a customer typically places an eCourier order every Thursday morning between 9:30 and 10 and there's been no contact during that time, eCourier's CRM team will receive an alert shortly after 10 that includes the client's history and the number of bookings it typically places in a day.

Bregman says there's a fair amount of tuning to get the metrics right. For example, the company had to tweak the system to recognize expected shifts in activity, so it doesn't send a slew of alerts once the after-Christmas drop in business occurs. Getting that perfect balance of when to send alerts and how best to optimize the system is an ongoing process, he says.

The SeeWhy software is designed to establish a "normal" client booking pattern from the first use, which is deepened with each subsequent booking. A sharp drop-off in bookings, an increase in bookings, or a change in dormant account activity generates an alert that is sent to that client's account manager, who then uses the opportunity to problem-solve, or in the case of increased activity, upsell—for example, to overnight or international services. These capabilities have provided a big payoff, says Bregman. He also believes the system saves his company the expense of having to hire people to monitor for "who's happy and who's not—we're able to do a lot more on our customer team with a lot less." There are other approaches to judging customer dissatisfaction, however. Cablecom, a Swiss telecom company, used SPSS's statistical software to mine customer data, primarily from trouble tickets—such as the average duration of a ticket, or how many tickets had been opened for a customer over a specific time period—to build a model that could flag when a customer was at a high risk of leaving. But the model proved to be only about 70 percent accurate, says Federico Cesconi, director of customer insight and retention.

So Cesconi used SPSS's Dimensions survey research software to create an online customer survey, and from that he was able to determine that customer dissatisfaction usually begins around the ninth month of service, with the bulk of the customer losses occurring between months 12 and 14. Cesconi then created another survey that he now offers to customers in the seventh month of service, and that includes an area where they can type in specific complaints and problems. "Cablecom calls customers within 24 hours of completing the survey," Cesconi says. "The two approaches together provide the best view of customers ready to bolt, and the best chance at retaining them."

In 2002, global law firm Bryan Cave faced the million-dollar question: How do you make the most money with your resources while simultaneously delivering the highest customer value? The problem was pressing. Clients of the firm, which now has 800 lawyers in 15 offices worldwide, were demanding alternatives to the traditional hourly fee structure. They wanted new models, such as fixed pricing and pricing that was adjusted during a project.

But making money from these new billing strategies required the complicated balance of staffing and pricing. Projects weighted too heavily with a law partner's time would be expensive (for the law firm) and not optimized for profit. Devoting too little of a partner's time would leave clients feeling undervalued. Optimizing profit and perceived value had to be achieved by spreading partners' time throughout a number of cases and balancing the remaining resources needed for a case with the less-expensive fees of associates and paralegals. "Clients are most likely to stay with you if you deliver just the right mix," says Bryan Cave CIO John Alber.

The law firm's traditional method of analyzing collected fees and profit used a spreadsheet that was complicated and took too long. "Spreadsheets provide a level of detail that can be valuable for analysts," says Alber, "but the information in a spreadsheet can be confusing and difficult to work with." Alber says he decided it was better to build an easy-to-understand interface using business intelligence tools. Although the company will not release specific figures, Alber says that since the company implemented its first BI tool in 2004, both profitability and hours leveraged (the hours worked by equity partners and all other fee earners at the firm) have increased substantially.

The tools also allow lawyers to track budgets in real time so they can quickly make adjustments. The BI tools even provide a diversity dashboard, which tracks the hourly mix of women and minorities working on the firm's cases, a feature the company will license to Redwood Analytics for sale to other law firms. The firm developed this diversity tool to bring transparency to the diversity reporting process required by many clients. In other words, the tools provide Bryan Cave with a method of customizing its fees and helping clients better understand what they get for their money.

As an illustration, Alber points to the customized pricing one lawyer gave to his real estate client. Developers think in terms of square feet, says Alber, and this client couldn't understand why legal fees for a 400,000-square-foot building might be the same as legal fees for a 4,000-square-foot building, even though it required the same amount of the lawyer's time. So the lawyer used the pricing and staffing modeling tools and historical analysis tools to determine whether it made sense for the law firm to charge clients based on the size of their projects. He found that while there was risk of underpricing large buildings, the deal volume in small buildings offset that risk for the law firm. The result made per-square-foot pricing possible.

"It may be possible that someone with enough will-power or manpower could do that using traditional analysis," says Alber, "but this lawyer had the information right at his fingertips." Business intelligence enables "us to be in touch with clients and shift things around in response to what customers are asking," says Alber. Adopting new and improved project management, pricing, and customer service capabilities required planning, appropriate pacing, and user buy-in.

"In today's environment, you can't do value innovation without being in touch with the economics of your business, without really understanding where you make money and where you don't, and that's what business intelligence tools do," says Alber. "Our goal," he says, "is to build the best long-term relationships in the world."

SOURCE: Diann Daniel, "Delivering Customer Happiness through Operational Business Intelligence," *CIO Magazine*, December 6, 2007; Diann Daniel, "How a Global Law Firm Used Business Intelligence to Fix Customer Billing Woes," *CIO Magazine*, January 8, 2008; and Mary Weier, "Dear Customer: Please Don't Leave," *InformationWeek*, June 18, 2007.

▼ CASE STUDY QUESTIONS

1. How do information technologies contribute to the business success of the companies depicted in the case? Provide an example from each company explaining how the technology implemented led to improved performance.

2. In the case of law firm Bryan Cave discussed above, the use of BI technology to improve the availability, access, and presentation of existing information allowed them to provide tailored and innovative services to their clients. What other professions could benefit

from a similar use of these technologies, and how? Develop two different possibilities.

3. Cablecom developed a prediction model to better identify those customers at risk of switching to another company in the near future. In addition to those noted in the case, what other actions could be taken if that information were available? Give some examples. Would you consider letting some customers leave anyway? Why?

▼ **REAL WORLD ACTIVITIES**

1. Use the Internet to research the latest offerings in BI technologies and their uses by companies. What differences can you find with those reviewed in the case? Prepare a report to summarize your findings and highlight new and innovative uses of these technologies.

2. Why do some companies in a given industry, like eCourier above, adopt and deploy innovative technologies while others in the same line of business do not? Break into small groups with your classmates to discuss what characteristics of companies could influence their decision to innovate with the use of information technologies.

CASE 2

The New York Times and Boston Scientific: Two Different Ways of Innovating with Information Technology

Almost everybody has a theory about how to save the U.S. newspaper industry. The only consensus, it seems, is that it needs to change fundamentally or it could all but disappear. At *The New York Times*, tough times have elevated IT-enabled innovation to the top of the agenda.

A research and development group, created in 2006, operates as a shared service across nearly two dozen newspapers, a radio station, and more than 50 Web sites. "Our role is to accelerate our entry onto new platforms by identifying opportunities, conceptualizing, and prototyping ideas," explains Michael Zimbalist, the company's vice president of R&D.

Zimbalist's staff of 12 includes experts in rapid prototyping, specialists in areas like mobile or cloud computing, and data miners who probe Web site data for insight into what visitors do. They work within a common framework based on idea generation, development, and diffusion throughout the business. Recent projects included prototypes for new display ad concepts, as well as BlackBerry applications for Boston.com and the expert site About.com. The team's work is intended to supplement and support innovation taking place within the business units. For example, the team is prototyping E-Ink, an emerging display technology that some business units can't spare the resources to investigate.

At NYTimes.com, CTO of Digital Operations Marc Frons's design and product development group worked with Zimbalist's team and Adobe developers on the Times Reader 2.0 application—the next generation, on-screen reading system it developed on the Adobe AIR platform. Frons further encourages forward thinking among his 120-person team with twice-annual innovation contests. Winners receive cash, recognition, and the resources to turn their ideas into reality. Typical projects are measured against criteria like revenue potential or journalistic value, but R&D projects aren't. "Since we build software, there's no huge capital investment up front," Frons says, "which allows us to experiment. The emphasis is on rapid development."

Times Widgets, a widget-making platform, was a contest winner, as was the recently launched Times Wire, a near real-time customizable interface for online content. "We're trying to solve specific problems and think about where the business is going," Frons says. Frons is focused on enhancing revenue, cutting costs, and increasing efficiency through process improvements and automation.

The New York Times has launched a cool interactive map that shows the most popular Netflix rentals across 12 U.S. metropolitan areas: New York, San Francisco/Bay Area, Boston, Chicago, Washington, Los Angeles, Seattle, Minneapolis, Denver, Atlanta, Dallas, and Miami. If you're a Netflix junkie and a closet Twilight fan (and you live in a major U.S. city), your rental habits are now on display. To create the map, *The New York Times* partnered with Netflix. The map is a graphical database of the top 100 most-rented Netflix films of 2009 laid on top of maps. With it, you can graphically explore top 2009 Netflix movies based on three criteria: films that were hated/loved by critics, an alphabetical list, and most rented. For example, select most rented and when you mouse-over a ZIP code, a window pops up that shows you what the top Netflix rentals are for that specific region.

Some trends are not surprising: the most Netflixed movie of 2009 was *The Curious Case of Benjamin Button*, though *Slumdog Millionaire* and *Twilight* were both in the top ten. Milk, the story of San Francisco activist Harvey Milk, was popular in San Francisco and other city centers, but not so much in the suburbs of southern cities (such as Dallas and Atlanta). *Mad Men*, the 1960s-set drama about advertising execs, was hot in parts of Manhattan and Brooklyn, but not in any other major cities (it barely got mention in Denver and Dallas, and not at all in Miami).

The map does show some interesting trends: Big blockbusters were not as popular in city centers (*Wanted* and *Transformers: Revenge of the Fallen*, barely made a splash in the city centers of Manhattan and San Francisco), although this could be due to the fact that a lot of people see blockbusters in movie theaters. *Last Chance Harvey*, a romantic comedy starring Dustin Hoffman and Emma Thompson, was enjoyed in wealthier suburbs (such as Scarsdale), but not in city centers (such as Manhattan). Tyler Perry's movies (*Tyler Perry's Madea Goes to Jail* and *Tyler Perry's The Family That Preys*) were popular in predominantly black neighborhoods.

Much of what has come down the innovation pike thus far at *The New York Times* can be classified as process or product innovation. Typically, a healthy and growing company should be content with focusing 90 to 95 percent of its innovation dollars on such core business innovation and 5 percent or 10 percent on new business models, says Mark Johnson, chairman of strategic innovation consultancy Innosight. However, he adds, "The newspaper industry is in so much trouble that business model innovation is more important than ever."

Now is a good—and bad—time for fostering such innovation. "You've got the leadership's attention you need," says Johnson. "But it's harder in the sense that there's an urgency to fix the financials, and being patient in the way you need to be for a new business model to unfold is a very difficult thing to do."

While *The New York Times* is focused on experimenting with a number of different initiatives, Boston Scientific faces a much different challenge: how to foster innovation without risking the disclosure and leakage of very valuable intellectual property. And the company has turned to technology to help find the right mix of access and security.

Boston Scientific wants to tear down barriers that prevent product developers from accessing the research that went into its successful medical devices so that they can create new products faster. But making data too easily accessible could open the way to theft of information potentially worth millions or billions of dollars. It's a classic corporate data privacy problem. "The more info you give knowledge workers, the more effective they can be in creating a lot of value for the company," says Boris Evelson, a principal analyst at Forrester. "This creates disclosure risks—that someone's going to walk away with the data and give it to a competitor."

This tension compels the $8 billion company to seek out software that allows the broader engineering community to share knowledge while managing access to product development data, says Jude Currier, cardiovascular knowledge management and innovation practices lead at Boston Scientific. "Active security is the way to address this problem," Currier says. That is, regularly monitor who's accessing what and adjust permissions as business conditions change.

Keeping the pipeline of new stents, pacemakers, and catheters fresh is especially important because heart-related items account for 80 percent of Boston Scientific's sales. Over the past few years, engineers have been focused on quality system improvements, Currier says. Boston Scientific had inherited regulatory problems from acquisitions it made during that time. Now that those situations have been addressed, the company is ready to reinvigorate internal innovation.

Boston Scientific is piloting Invention Machine's Goldfire software, which, Currier says, provides the right mix of openness and security for data. Before, Boston Scientific's product developers worked in silos with limited access to research by colleagues on different product lines. Information was so locked down that even if scientists found something useful from a past project, they often didn't have access to it. "We're changing that," Currier says.

Goldfire makes an automated workflow out of such tasks as analyzing markets and milking a company's intellectual property. It combines internal company data with information from public sources—such as federal government databases. Researchers can use the software to find connections among different sources—for instance, by highlighting similar ideas. Engineers can use such analysis to get ideas for new products and begin to study their feasibility. The goal is to have any engineer access any other's research. "The people in the trenches can't wait for that day to arrive," he says.

Although the goal is more openness, not all data stays open forever. For example, as a project gets closer to the patent application stage, access to the data about it is clipped to fewer people, Currier says.

He adds that since installing Goldfire, patent applications are up compared to similar engineering groups that do not use the Goldfire tool. "We have had to educate people that we aren't throwing security out the window but making valuable knowledge available to the organization," he says.

SOURCE: Stephanie Overby, "Rapid Prototyping Provides Innovation that Fits at *The New York Times*," *CIO.com*, June 24, 2009; Sarah Jacobson, "Netflix Map Shows What's Hot in Your Neighborhood," *PCWorld.com*, January 11, 2010; and Kim S. Nash, "Innovation: How Boston Scientific Shares Data Securely to Foster Product Development," *CIO.com*, November 23, 2009.

▼ **CASE STUDY QUESTIONS**

1. As stated in the case, *The New York Times* chose to deploy their innovation support group as a shared service across business units. What do you think this means? What are the advantages of choosing this approach? Are there any disadvantages?

2. Boston Scientific faced the challenge of balancing openness and sharing with security and the need for restricting access to information. How did the use of technology allow the company to achieve both objectives at the same time? What kind of cultural changes were required for this to be possible? Are these more important than the technology-related issues? Develop a few examples to justify your answer.

3. The video rental map developed by *The New York Times* and Netflix graphically displays movie popularity across neighborhoods from major U.S. cities. How would Netflix use this information to improve its business? Could other companies also take advantage of these data? How? Provide some examples.

▼ REAL WORLD ACTIVITIES

1. The newspaper industry has been facing serious challenges to its viability ever since the Internet made news available online. In addition to those initiatives described in the case, how are *The New York Times* and other leading newspapers coping with these challenges? What do you think the industry will look like five or ten years from now? Go online to research these issues and prepare a report to share your findings.

2. Go online and search the Internet for other examples of companies using technology to help them innovate and develop new products or services. Break into small groups with your classmates to share your findings and discuss any trends or patterns you see in current uses of technology in this regard.

chapter 2

COMPETING WITH INFORMATION TECHNOLOGY

INFORMATION SYSTEMS

FOUNDATION CONCEPTS

CHAPTER HIGHLIGHTS

Fundamentals of Strategic Advantage

Strategic IT

Competitive Strategy Concepts

REAL WORLD CHALLENGE: CenterPoint Properties—Creating a New Company for a New Business

Strategic Uses of Information Technology

Building a Customer-Focused Business

The Value Chain and Strategic IS

Using Information Technology for Strategic Advantage

Strategic Uses of IT

Reengineering Business Processes

Becoming an Agile Company

Creating a Virtual Company

Building a Knowledge-Creating Company

Knowledge Management Systems

REAL WORLD SOLUTION: CenterPoint Properties—Reinventing a Company with the Help of IT

REAL WORLD CASE: How to Win Friends and Influence Business People: Quantify IT Risks and Value

REAL WORLD CASE: For Companies Both Big and Small: Running a Business on Smartphones

LEARNING OBJECTIVES

2-1 Identify several basic competitive strategies and explain how they use information technologies to confront the competitive forces faced by a business.

2-2 Identify several strategic uses of Internet technologies and give examples of how they can help a business gain competitive advantages.

2-3 Give examples of how business process reengineering frequently involves the strategic use of Internet technologies.

2-4 Identify the business value of using Internet technologies to become an agile competitor or form a virtual company.

2-5 Explain how knowledge management systems can help a business gain strategic advantages.

Fundamentals of Strategic Advantage

Technology is no longer an afterthought in forming business strategy, but the actual cause and driver.

This chapter will show you that it is important to view information systems as more than a set of technologies that support efficient business operations, workgroup and enterprise collaboration, or effective business decision making. This has been a traditional role, for sure, and is an important application of these technologies. Beyond supporting the fundamental processes of an organization, however, information technology can change the way businesses compete. You should also view information systems strategically, that is, as vital competitive networks, as a means of organizational renewal, and as a necessary investment in technologies; such technologies help a company adopt strategies and business processes that enable it to reengineer or reinvent itself to survive and succeed in today's dynamic business environment.

The first part of this chapter introduces fundamental competitive strategy concepts that underlie the strategic use of information systems. Following that, we will explore several major strategic applications of information technology used by many companies today.

Begin by reading the Real World Challenge below. We can learn a lot about the challenges faced by CenterPoint Properties as it seeks to reinvent itself. See Figure 2.1.

In Chapter 1, we emphasized that a major role of information systems applications in business is to provide effective support of a company's strategies for gaining competitive advantage. This strategic role of information systems involves using information technology to develop products, services, and capabilities that give a company major advantages over the competitive forces it faces in the global marketplace.

This role is accomplished through a *strategic information architecture*: the collection of **strategic information systems** that supports or shapes the competitive position and strategies of a business enterprise. So a strategic information system can be any kind of information system (e.g., TPS, MIS, and DSS) that leverages information technology to help an organization gain a competitive advantage, reduce a competitive disadvantage, or meet other strategic enterprise objectives.

Figure 2.2 illustrates the various competitive forces a business might encounter, as well as the competitive strategies that can be adopted to counteract such forces. It is important to note that the figure suggests that any of the major strategies may be deemed useful against any of the common competitive forces. Although it is rare and unlikely that a single firm would use all strategies simultaneously, each has value in certain circumstances. For now, it is only important that you become familiar with the available strategic approaches. Let us look at several basic concepts that define the role of competitive strategy as it applies to information systems.

Competitive Forces and Strategies

How should a business professional think about competitive strategies? How can a business use information systems to apply competitive strategies? Figure 2.2 illustrates an important conceptual framework for understanding forces of competition and the various competitive strategies employed to balance them.

A company can survive and succeed in the long run only if it successfully develops strategies to confront five **competitive forces** that shape the structure of competition in its industry. In Michael Porter's classic model of competition, any business that

STRATEGIC IT
LO 2-1

COMPETITIVE STRATEGY CONCEPTS
LO 2-1
LO 2-2

CenterPoint Properties— Creating a New Company for a New Business

CenterPoint Properties, headquartered in Oak Brook, Illinois, is a leading real estate company focused on the development, ownership, and management of industrial real estate and infrastructure assets in the logistics and transportation arena, such as rail depots, roads, and port facilities. The company started its operations in 1984 as Capital and Regional Properties Corporation, a subsidiary of Capital and Regional plc, which was traded on the London Stock Exchange. In 1993 the company successfully completed its initial public offering in the United States, structured as a publicly traded REIT (Real Estate Investment Trust, a security that sells like a stock on the major exchanges but is limited in focus to investing in real estate properties, either directly or through mortgage-backed securities) after acquiring and consolidating the operations of FCLS Investor Group, an industrial development company based in Chicago.

Since then and more than halfway through the first decade of the 21st century, CenterPoint Properties became the largest real estate company in the Chicago region. An undisputed successful performer, the company consistently increased shareholder value and outperformed every related market index. At the same time, however, management started to realize that their current business model, which had brought them to this point, was not going to last forever. Every successful business model has a life cycle, in which competitors start to understand what makes a successful company successful, and slowly begin to catch up with market leaders. Under those conditions, innovation is key. Management realized that if CenterPoint wanted to continue to grow and remain one step ahead of the competition, it would need to evolve. And that would not be easy—real estate companies are hardly known for their introduction of innovative products and services. In fact, CenterPoint realized that it would need to transform itself into an entirely different player—a developer and provider of logistic solutions.

In hindsight, it all started when CenterPoint became involved in the development of some of the largest intermodal transportation facilities in the United States. An intermodal facility is one where an interface occurs between two or more different modes of transportation. For passenger traffic, a terminal where riders transfer from train service to a bus would be an example of an intermodal facility. When freight and cargo are of interest, these may involve the loading and unloading of cargo from trucks to railroads, or port facilities where container ships are unloaded and the containers are then transferred by a different means of transportation to their final destination.

After years of experience managing those facilities and the significant real estate developments associated with them, management came to realize that they had been providing supply chain solutions to their customers under the guise of real estate management. As the logistics industry became more and more competitive and globalized, management saw an opportunity to transform the company into a provider of business solutions to their clients. "We saw the opportunity to become a leader in developing intermodal, port, and transportation-related real estate solutions, but we knew the window of opportunity wouldn't be open forever," says Scott Zimmerman, Chief Information Officer for CenterPoint.

For that to happen, however, CenterPoint found it would have to reinvent itself as a different organization. An entirely new financial and capital structure would be needed, as public markets with their focus on short-term measures of profitability were not ideally suited to the kind of large-scale, long-term, and capital-intensive projects the

FIGURE 2.1

CenterPoint Properties faces some tough decisions as it seeks to transform itself into a world-class provider of real estate solutions—and IT is at the center of those solutions.

SOURCE: © Phil Boorman/agefotostock.

company had in mind. This would in turn mandate a new and redesigned reporting structure, and extensive collaboration with stakeholders beyond the traditional boundaries of the existing corporation. One of the keys to success in this new endeavor would be the ability to grow the business exponentially without a commensurate growth in head count. In other words, CenterPoint needed a way to make their business very scalable—something for which IT is the perfect candidate. Doing so, however, would require a degree of integration between IT and the business that was unprecedented both at CenterPoint and within the real estate industry in general. But management knew there was no other way in which they could accomplish this major transformation without heavy involvement from IT.

"We needed an intuitive, scalable enterprise solution designed specifically to support our unique business processes, yet agile enough to adapt to our new lines of business; we needed an inviting and secure system that would not only process data, but also help turn it into real-time information, providing CenterPoint with a significant competitive advantage," says Zimmerman. Intuitive, scalable, and secure. Supportive and customized, but adaptive and agile at the same time. Real-time information and competitive advantage. A tall order for anything and anyone, but the company knew that the new IT infrastructure they needed was at the heart of the entire project.

Unfortunately, whatever it was that Zimmerman envisioned, it was clearly not available in commercial form. Most commercially available real estate software packages were designed for, well, real estate companies. Their functionality was geared toward the administration of few but large multitenant buildings, where the central processes dealt with contract management, maintenance, billing and collections, and the like. CenterPoint, on the other hand, needed a solution for managing a large number of properties, but each with fewer tenants and involving the full life cycle of the facility, from acquisition through disposition. Commercial real estate software was mostly limited only to the property management phase of that life cycle.

In addition, there was also some skepticism from within the ranks of management as to what IT CenterPoint would need to move forward with its transformation. Specifically, it was difficult to visualize what the final system would look like, not only aesthetically, but also regarding required functionality. The company also had a number of software products that had been working well for some time, and some felt that it would be both faster and less expensive to modify or retool the existing technologies to support the new business model than to implement a new system from scratch, particularly if no commercial software were readily available.

At this juncture, CenterPoint management needed to decide on the best way to move forward. Without a doubt, the company would emerge as a radically different organization, focused on a new business model, which would in turn require the development of new competencies if it wanted to be successful. It was also clear that IT would be at the core of the transformation. The best way to move forward, however, was not as evident.

SOURCE: "CenterPoint Properties," *Computerworld Honors Program Case Study*, www.centerpoint-prop.com, accessed May 9, 2011, and "Office Business Application at the Heart of Commercial Real-Estate Company's Success," *Microsoft Office System Customer Solution Case Study*.

▼ QUESTIONS TO CONSIDER

1. What do you think will be the major challenges CenterPoint will face as it embarks on its transformation from real estate manager into a provider of logistic solutions? What part of those challenges will be related to IT? What does your answer say about the importance of IT in organizations today?
2. What are some of the alternatives that CenterPoint has for procuring the new functionality required from their IT for the new business model? What are the advantages and disadvantages of each of those alternatives?
3. Is it a good idea to roll out a new, large IT implementation at the same time the company is embarking on a major transformation? On the other hand, is it possible to radically transform a company without major changes in IT?

FIGURE 2.2

Businesses can develop competitive strategies to counter the actions of the competitive forces they confront in the marketplace.

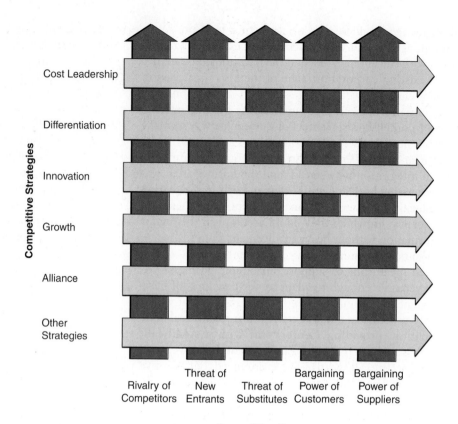

Competitive Forces

wants to survive and succeed must effectively develop and implement strategies to counter (1) *the rivalry of competitors within its industry,* (2) *the threat of new entrants into an industry and its markets,* (3) *the threat posed by substitute products that might capture market share,* (4) *the bargaining power of customers,* and (5) *the bargaining power of suppliers.*

Competition is a positive characteristic in business, and competitors share a natural, and normally healthy, rivalry. This rivalry encourages and sometimes requires a constant effort to gain competitive advantage in the marketplace. This ever-present competitive force requires a commitment of significant resources on the part of a firm.

Guarding against the threat of new entrants also requires the expenditure of significant organizational resources. Not only do firms need to compete with other firms in the marketplace, but they must also work to create significant barriers to the entry of new competition. This competitive force has always been difficult to manage, but it is even more so today. The Internet has created many ways to enter the marketplace quickly and with relatively low cost. In the Internet world, a firm's biggest potential competitor may be one that is not yet in the marketplace but could emerge almost overnight.

The threat of substitutes is another competitive force that confronts a business. The effect of this force is apparent almost daily in a wide variety of industries, often at its strongest during periods of rising costs or inflation. When airline prices get too high, people substitute car travel for their vacations. When the cost of steak gets too high, people eat more hamburger and fish. Most products or services have some sort of substitute available to the consumer.

Finally, a business must guard against the often opposing forces of customer and supplier bargaining powers. If customers' bargaining power gets too strong, they can drive prices to unmanageably low levels or just refuse to buy the product or service. If a key supplier's bargaining power gets too strong, it can force the price of goods and services to unmanageably high levels or just starve a business by controlling the flow of parts or raw materials essential to the manufacture of a product.

Figure 2.2 also illustrates that businesses can counter the threats of competitive forces that they face by implementing one or more of the five basic *competitive strategies.*

- **Cost Leadership Strategy.** Becoming a low-cost producer of products and services in the industry or finding ways to help suppliers or customers reduce their costs or increase the costs of competitors.
- **Differentiation Strategy.** Developing ways to differentiate a firm's products and services from those of its competitors or reduce the differentiation advantages of competitors. This strategy may allow a firm to focus its products or services to give it an advantage in particular segments or niches of a market.
- **Innovation Strategy.** Finding new ways of doing business. This strategy may involve developing unique products and services or entering unique markets or market niches. It may also involve making radical changes to the business processes for producing or distributing products and services that are so different from the way a business has been conducted that they alter the fundamental structure of an industry.
- **Growth Strategies.** Significantly expanding a company's capacity to produce goods and services, expanding into global markets, diversifying into new products and services, or integrating into related products and services.
- **Alliance Strategies.** Establishing new business linkages and alliances with customers, suppliers, competitors, consultants, and other companies. These linkages may include mergers, acquisitions, joint ventures, formation of virtual companies, or other marketing, manufacturing, or distribution agreements between a business and its trading partners.

One additional point regarding these strategies is that they are not mutually exclusive. An organization may make use of one, some, or all of the strategies in varying degrees to manage the forces of competition. Therefore, a given activity could fall into one or more of the categories of competitive strategy. For example, implementing a system that allows customers to track their orders or shipments online could be considered a form of differentiation if the other competitors in the marketplace do not offer this service. If they do offer the service, however, online order tracking would not serve to differentiate one organization from another.

If an organization offers its online package tracking system in a manner that allows its customers to access shipment information via not only a computer but a mobile phone as well, then such an action could fall into both the differentiation and innovation strategy categories. Think of it this way: Not everything innovative will serve to differentiate one organization from another. Likewise, not everything that serves to differentiate organizations is necessarily viewed as innovative. These types of observations are true for any combination of the competitive strategies, thus making them complementary to each other rather than mutually exclusive.

How can business managers use investments in information technology to support a firm's competitive strategies? Figure 2.3 answers this question with a summary of the many ways that information technology can help a business implement the five basic competitive strategies. Figure 2.4 provides examples of how specific companies have used strategic information systems to implement each of these five basic strategies for competitive advantage. Note the major use of Internet technologies for e-business and e-commerce applications. In the rest of this chapter, we discuss and provide examples of many strategic uses of information technology.

STRATEGIC USES OF INFORMATION TECHNOLOGY
LO 2-3

Other Strategic Initiatives

While Porter's Five Forces (as shown in Figure 2.2) are considered the basic foundation for understanding business strategy, there are many strategic initiatives available to a firm in addition to the five basic strategies of cost leadership, differentiation, innovation,

FIGURE 2.3

A summary of how information technology can be used to implement the five basic competitive strategies. Many companies are using Internet technologies as the foundation for such strategies.

Basic Strategies in the Business Use of Information Technology
Lower Costs
• Use IT to substantially reduce the cost of business processes.
• Use IT to lower the costs of customers or suppliers.
Differentiate
• Develop new IT features to differentiate products and services.
• Use IT features to reduce the differentiation advantages of competitors.
• Use IT features to focus products and services at selected market niches.
Innovate
• Create new products and services that include IT components.
• Develop unique new markets or market niches with the help of IT.
• Make radical changes to business processes with IT that dramatically cut costs; improve quality, efficiency, or customer service; or shorten time to market.
Promote Growth
• Use IT to manage regional and global business expansion.
• Use IT to diversify and integrate into other products and services.
Develop Alliances
• Use IT to create virtual organizations of business partners.
• Develop interenterprise information systems linked by the Internet and extranets that support strategic business relationships with customers, suppliers, subcontractors, and others.

growth, and alliance. Let's look at several key strategies that can also be implemented with information technology. They include locking in customers or suppliers, building switching costs, raising barriers to entry, and leveraging investment in information technology.

Investments in information technology can allow a business to *lock in customers and suppliers* (and therefore lock out competitors) by building valuable new relationships with them. These business relationships can become so valuable to customers or suppliers that they deter them from abandoning a company for its competitors or intimidate them into accepting less profitable business arrangements. Early attempts to use information systems technology in these relationships focused on significantly improving the quality of service to customers and suppliers in a firm's distribution,

FIGURE 2.4

Examples of how, over time, companies have used information technology to implement five competitive strategies for strategic advantage.

Strategy	Company	Strategic Use of Information Technology	Business Benefit
Cost Leadership	Dell Computer Priceline.com eBay.com	Online build to order Online seller bidding Online auctions	Lowest-cost producer Buyer-set pricing Auction-set prices
Differentiation	AVNET Marshall Moen Inc. Consolidated Freightways	Customer/supplier of e-commerce Online customer design Customer online shipment tracking	Increase in market share Increase in market share Increase in market share
Innovation	Charles Schwab & Co. Federal Express Amazon.com	Online discount stock trading Online package tracking and flight management Online full-service customer systems	Market leadership Market leadership Market leadership
Growth	Citicorp Walmart Toys 'R' Us Inc.	Global intranet Merchandise ordering by global satellite network POS inventory tracking	Increase in global market Market leadership Market leadership
Alliance	Walmart/Procter & Gamble Cisco Systems Staples Inc. and Partners	Automatic inventory replenishment by supplier Virtual manufacturing alliances Online one-stop shopping with partners	Reduced inventory cost/ increased sales Agile market leadership Increase in market share

Other Strategic Uses of Information Technology
• Develop interenterprise information systems whose convenience and efficiency create switching costs that lock in customers or suppliers.
• Make major investments in advanced IT applications that build barriers to entry against industry competitors or outsiders.
• Include IT components in products and services to make substitution of competing products or services more difficult.
• Leverage investment in IS people, hardware, software, databases, and networks from operational uses into strategic applications.

FIGURE 2.5

Additional ways that information technology can be used to implement competitive strategies.

marketing, sales, and service activities. More recent projects characterize a move toward more innovative uses of information technology.

A major emphasis in strategic information systems has been to find ways to **create switching costs** in the relationships between a firm and its customers or suppliers. In other words, investments in information systems technology can make customers or suppliers dependent on the continued use of innovative, mutually beneficial interenterprise information systems. They then become reluctant to pay the costs in time, money, effort, and inconvenience that it would take to switch to a company's competitors.

By making investments in information technology to improve its operations or promote innovation, a firm could also **raise barriers to entry** that would discourage or delay other companies from entering a market. Typically, these barriers increase the amount of investment or the complexity of the technology required to compete in an industry or a market segment. Such actions tend to discourage firms already in the industry and deter external firms from entering the industry.

Investing in information technology enables a firm to build strategic IT capabilities so that they can take advantage of opportunities when they arise. In many cases, this happens when a company invests in advanced computer-based information systems to improve the efficiency of its own business processes. Then, armed with this strategic technology platform, the firm can **leverage investment in IT** by developing new products and services that would not be possible without a strong IT capability. An important current example is the development of corporate intranets and extranets by many companies, which enables them to leverage their previous investments in Internet browsers, PCs, servers, and client/server networks. Figure 2.5 summarizes the additional strategic uses of IT we have just discussed.

Boeing: Saving Big by Cutting Imaging Costs

Hitting "Ctrl+P" can cost your business more than you think. It certainly did at aerospace giant Boeing. Imaging services—which includes production printing, office printing, faxing, scanning, and related supplies—used to cost the company nearly $150 million annually. The problem, says Earl Beauvais, Boeing's director of print, plot, and scan services, was that imaging wasn't centrally controlled, and the company used several vendors. Boeing also owned, operated, and maintained about 32,000 imaging devices. The lack of an enterprise-wide solution meant, among other things, that each department was responsible for purchasing its own toner, paper, and other supplies.

To increase efficiency and reduce cost, Beauvais and his team sought a managed services solution to handle everything from print cartridges to printer upkeep across Boeing's 195 domestic sites and 168 international sites. Beauvais spent 18 months researching and interviewing vendors, who had to show how they would manage the company's imaging technology needs while providing the greatest efficiency at the best price. He and his team chose a partnership comprising Dell (for maintenance and asset management) and Lexmark (for devices). They picked them in part because Dell had infrastructure in place at Boeing.

To prove the concept, a six-month pilot implementation launched at Boeing's St. Louis office in May 2007. The St. Louis system included 47 new Lexmark device categories, including printers, copy machines, and scanners. "We replaced the devices because we didn't want variability of age," says Beauvais.

The beauty of managed services is that Dell owns the devices and handles maintenance, a key goal for Beauvais.

Boeing saw ROI immediately because Dell's service contract cost less than its existing agreements. In the end, Boeing saved about 30 percent of its imaging maintenance and supplies costs, and 27 percent of its overall imaging costs annually at locations with the new system. The initiative began rolling out companywide at the end of 2007.

For Boeing, the benefits couldn't be clearer. Beauvais's staff can now focus more on other business needs, and the company's total imaging spending has been reduced to $110 million annually. Both will aid Boeing as it navigates a turbulent economy.

SOURCE: Jarina D'Auria, "Boeing Saves Big by Cutting Imaging Costs," *CIO.com*, March 25, 2009.

Competitive Advantage and Competitive Necessity

The constant struggle to achieve a measurable competitive advantage in an industry or marketplace occupies a significant portion of an organization's time and money. Creative and innovative marketing, research and development, and process reengineering, among many other activities, are used to gain that elusive and sometimes indescribable competitive advantage over rival firms.

The term *competitive advantage* is often used when referring to a firm that is leading an industry in some identifiable way such as sales, revenues, or new products. In fact, the definition of the term suggests a single condition under which competitive advantage can exist: When a firm sustains profits that exceed the average for its industry, the firm is said to possess competitive advantage over its rivals. In other words, competitive advantage is all about profits. Of course, sales, revenues, cost management, and new products all contribute in some way to profits, but unless the contribution results in sustained profits above the average for the industry, no measurable competitive advantage has been achieved. The real problem with a competitive advantage, however, is that it normally doesn't last very long and is generally not sustainable over the long term. Figure 2.6 illustrates this cycle. Once a firm figures out how to gain an advantage over its competitors (normally through some form of innovation), the competitors figure out how it was done through a process referred to as organizational learning. To combat the competitive advantage, they adopt the same, or some similar, innovation. Once this occurs, everyone in the industry is doing what everyone else is doing; what was once a competitive advantage is now a competitive necessity. Instead of creating an advantage, the strategy or action becomes necessary to compete and do business in the industry. When this happens, someone has to figure out a new way to gain a competitive edge, and the cycle starts all over again.

Every organization is looking for a way to gain competitive advantage, and many have successfully used strategic information systems to help them achieve it. The important point to remember is that no matter how it is achieved, competitive advantage doesn't last forever. Arie de Geus, head of strategic planning for Royal Dutch Shell, thinks there may be one way to sustain it: "The ability to learn faster than your competitors may be the only sustainable competitive advantage in the future." This suggests an important role for information systems if any competitive advantage is to be achieved.

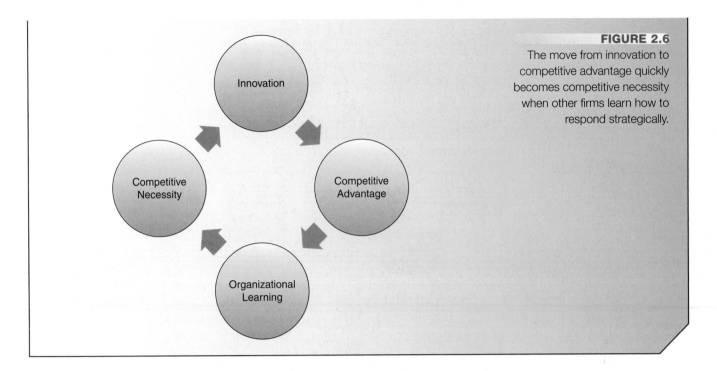

The driving force behind world economic growth has changed from manufacturing volume to improving customer value. As a result, the key success factor for many firms is maximizing customer value.

BUILDING A CUSTOMER-FOCUSED BUSINESS
LO 2-2

For many companies, the chief business value of becoming a customer-focused business lies in its ability to help them keep customers loyal, anticipate their future needs, respond to customer concerns, and provide top-quality customer service. This strategic focus on ***customer value*** recognizes that quality, rather than price, has become the primary determinant in a customer's perception of value. Companies that consistently offer the best value from the customer's perspective are those that keep track of their customers' individual preferences; keep up with market trends; supply products, services, and information anytime and anywhere; and provide customer services tailored to individual needs. Thus, Internet technologies have created a strategic opportunity for companies, large and small, to offer fast, responsive, high-quality products and services tailored to individual customer preferences.

Internet technologies can make customers the focal point of customer relationship management (CRM) and other e-business applications. In combination, CRM systems and Internet, intranet, and extranet Web sites create new channels for interactive communications within a company, as well as communication with customers, suppliers, business partners, and others in the external environment. Such communications enable continual interaction with customers by most business functions and encourage cross-functional collaboration with customers in product development, marketing, delivery, service, and technical support. We will discuss CRM systems in Chapter 8.

Typically, customers use the Internet to ask questions, lodge complaints, evaluate products, request support, and make and track their purchases. Using the Internet and corporate intranets, specialists in business functions throughout the enterprise can contribute to an effective response. This ability encourages the creation of cross-functional discussion groups and problem-solving teams dedicated to customer involvement, service, and support. Even the Internet and extranet links to suppliers and business partners can be used to enlist them in a way of doing business that ensures the prompt delivery of quality components and services to meet a company's commitments to its customers. This process is how a business demonstrates its focus on customer value.

FIGURE 2.7

How a customer-focused business builds customer value and loyalty using Internet technologies.

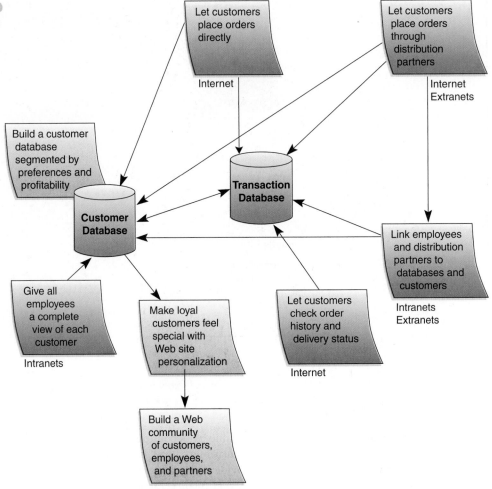

Figure 2.7 illustrates the interrelationships in a customer-focused business. Intranets, extranets, e-commerce Web sites, and Web-enabled internal business processes form the invisible IT platform that supports this e-business model. The platform enables the business to focus on targeting the kinds of customers it really wants and "owning" the customer's total business experience with the company. A successful business streamlines all business processes that affect its customers and develops CRM systems that provide its employees with a complete view of each customer, so they have the information they need to offer their customers top-quality personalized service. A customer-focused business helps its e-commerce customers help themselves while also helping them do their jobs. Finally, a successful business nurtures an online community of customers, employees, and business partners that builds great customer loyalty as it fosters cooperation to provide an outstanding customer experience. Let's review a real-world example.

Universal Orlando: IT Decisions Driven by Customer Data

Michelle McKenna is the CIO of Universal Orlando Resort, but she is also a mother of two and the planner of family vacations.

In fact, she thinks of herself first as a theme park customer, second as a senior leader at Universal, and finally as the company's CIO. "Recently we were brainstorming new events that would bring more Florida residents to our theme parks during off-peak tourist periods. Our in-house marketing group was pitching proposals, and I offered the idea of a Guitar Hero competition. Everyone loved it. But that idea didn't come from being a CIO—it came from being a mother of two," she says.

"Thinking like our customers and focusing on our company's markets are among the most important ways we can fulfill our responsibility to contribute to informed decision making," says McKenna. Moving forward, it's more critical than ever for CIOs to study market trends and find ways to maximize business opportunities.

Universal Orlando is one of many brands in the travel and entertainment industry competing for discretionary dollars spent by consumers on leisure time and vacations. Of course, the competition boils down to a market of one—the individual consumer. People often assume that because of the high volume of guests, the experience at Universal Orlando has to be geared for the masses. But digital technology now enables guests to customize their experience. For example, the new Hollywood Rip Ride RockIt Roller Coaster will allow guests to customize their ride experience by choosing the music that plays around them while on the roller coaster. When the ride ends, guests will be able to edit video footage of that experience into a music video to keep, share with friends, or post online.

Any CIO can take a few steps to get market savvy. Management gets weekly data about what happened in the park and what the spending trends are per guest. CIOs should get copied on any reports like that. They should study them and look for patterns. "Don't be afraid to ask questions about it; give yourself permission to be a smart (and inquisitive) businessperson. When I first joined the company and asked about market issues, people looked at me and thought, 'Why did she ask that? It doesn't have anything to do with technology.' Over time they realized that I needed to understand our data in order to do my job," says McKenna.

Knowledge of market data helps Universal Orlando drill down to understand what is really happening in business. For example, trends indicated that annual pass holders—Florida residents, primarily—spend less on food, merchandise, and other items than day-pass guests.

It turned out that some pass holders do spend on par with day guests, particularly when they attend special events, Mardi Gras, and Halloween Horror Nights. "This analysis showed that we needed to segment those annual pass holders more deeply in order to better understand them and market to them. So we are building a new data warehouse and business intelligence tools that will calculate spending by hour and by pass type. The initiative started in IT, and we can find many similar opportunities if we look at market details and ask questions," McKenna says.

SOURCE: Michelle McKenna, "Customer Data Should Drive IT Decisions," *CIO Magazine*, June 2, 2008.

THE VALUE CHAIN AND STRATEGIC IS
LO 2-1

Let's look at another important concept that can help you identify opportunities for strategic information systems. The *value chain* concept, developed by Michael Porter, is illustrated in Figure 2.8. It views a firm as a series, chain, or network of basic activities that add value to its products and services and thus add a margin of value to both the firm and its customers. In the value chain conceptual framework, some business activities are primary processes; others are support processes. *Primary processes* are those business activities that are directly related to the manufacture of products or the delivery of services to the customer. In contrast, *support processes* are those business activities that help support the day-to-day operation of the business and that indirectly contribute to the products or services of the organization. This framework can highlight where competitive strategies can best be applied in a business. So managers and business professionals should try to develop a variety of strategic uses of the Internet and other technologies for those basic processes that add the most value to a company's products or services and thus to the overall business value of the company.

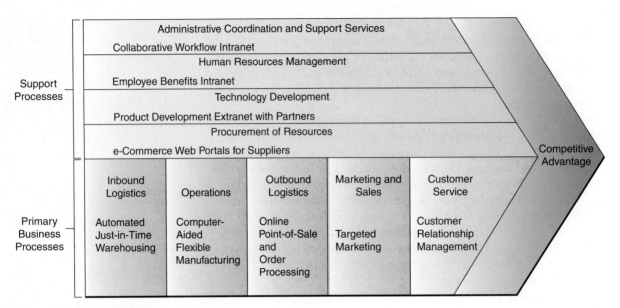

FIGURE 2.8

The value chain of a firm. Note the examples of the variety of strategic information systems that can be applied to a firm's basic business processes for competitive advantage.

Value Chain Examples

Figure 2.8 provides examples of how and where information technologies can be applied to basic business processes using the value chain framework. For example, the figure illustrates that collaborative workflow intranets can increase the communications and collaboration required to improve administrative coordination and support services dramatically. An employee benefits intranet can help the human resources management function provide employees with easy, self-service access to their benefits information. Extranets enable a company and its global business partners to use the Web to design products and processes jointly. Finally, e-commerce Web portals can dramatically improve procurement of resources by providing online marketplaces for a firm's suppliers.

The value chain model in Figure 2.8 also identifies examples of strategic applications of information systems technology to primary business processes. These include automated just-in-time warehousing systems to support inbound logistic processes that involve inventory storage, computer-aided flexible manufacturing systems, as well as online point-of-sale and order processing systems to improve the outbound logistics processes that handle customer orders. Information systems can also support marketing and sales processes by developing an interactive targeted marketing capability on the Internet and the Web. Finally, a coordinated and integrated customer relationship management system can dramatically improve customer service.

Thus, the value chain concept can help you identify where and how to apply the strategic capabilities of information technology. It shows how various types of information technologies might be applied to specific business processes to help a firm gain competitive advantages in the marketplace.

Using Information Technology for Strategic Advantage

Organizations may view and use information technology in many ways. For example, companies may choose to use information systems strategically, or they may be content to use IT to support efficient everyday operations. If a company emphasized strategic business uses of information technology, its management would view IT as a major competitive differentiator. They would then devise business strategies that use IT to develop products, services, and capabilities that give the company major advantages in the markets in which it competes. In this section, we provide many examples of such strategic business applications of information technology. See Figure 2.9.

One of the most important implementations of competitive strategies is **business process reengineering** (BPR), often simply called *reengineering*. Reengineering is a fundamental rethinking and radical redesign of business processes to achieve dramatic improvements in cost, quality, speed, and service. BPR combines a strategy of promoting business innovation with a strategy of making major improvements to business processes so that a company can become a much stronger and more successful competitor in the marketplace.

However, Figure 2.10 points out that although the potential payback of reengineering is high, so too is its risk of failure and level of disruption to the organizational environment. Making radical changes to business processes to dramatically improve efficiency and effectiveness is not an easy task. For example, many companies have used cross-functional enterprise resource planning (ERP) software to reengineer, automate, and integrate their manufacturing, distribution, finance, and human resource business processes. Although many companies have reported impressive gains with such ERP reengineering projects, many others either have experienced dramatic failures or did not achieve the improvements they sought.

Many companies have found that *organizational redesign* approaches are an important enabler of reengineering, along with the use of information technology. For

SOURCE: © The McGraw-Hill Companies Inc./John Flournoy.

FIGURE 2.9

Companies of all sizes can benefit from using smartphones to improve their business processes.

FIGURE 2.10

Some of the key ways that business process reengineering differs from business improvement.

	Business Improvement	Business Process Reengineering
Level of Change	Incremental	Radical
Process Change	Improved new version of process	Brand-new process
Starting Point	Existing processes	Clean slate
Frequency of Change	One-time or continuous	Periodic one-time change
Time Required	Short	Long
Typical Scope	Narrow, within functions	Broad, cross-functional
Horizon	Past and present	Future
Participation	Bottom-up	Top-down
Path to Execution	Cultural	Cultural, structural
Primary Enabler	Statistical control	Information technology
Risk	Moderate	High

SOURCE: Howard Smith and Peter Fingar, *Business Process Management: The Third Wave* (Tampa, FL: Meghan-Kiffer Press, 2003), p. 118.

example, one common approach is the use of self-directed cross-functional or multi-disciplinary *process teams*. Employees from several departments or specialties, including engineering, marketing, customer service, and manufacturing, may work as a team on the product development process. Another example is the use of *case managers*, who handle almost all tasks in a business process instead of splitting tasks among many different specialists.

The Role of Information Technology

Information technology plays a major role in reengineering most business processes. The speed, information-processing capabilities, and connectivity of computers and Internet technologies can substantially increase the efficiency of business processes, as well as communications and collaboration among the people responsible for their operation and management. For example, the order management process illustrated in Figure 2.11 is vital to the success of most companies. Many of them are reengineering this process with ERP software and Web-enabled e-business and e-commerce systems, as outlined in Figure 2.12.

FIGURE 2.11

The order management process consists of several business processes and crosses the boundaries of traditional business functions.

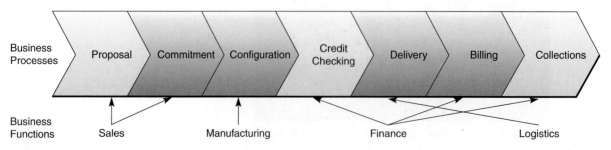

Reengineering Order Management
• Customer relationship management systems using corporate intranets and the Internet.
• Supplier-managed inventory systems using the Internet and extranets.
• Cross-functional ERP software for integrating manufacturing, distribution, finance, and human resource processes.
• Customer-accessible e-commerce Web sites for order entry, status checking, payment, and service.
• Customer, product, and order status databases accessed via intranets and extranets by employees and suppliers.

FIGURE 2.12

Examples of information technologies that support reengineering the order management processes.

To Build or to Buy—Is That Really the Question?

To build or to buy? Software, that is. This is one of the most enduring, persistent questions in the world of IT. Should a company license (i.e., buy) a commercial application that will do 75 percent of what is needed, or should it develop its own applications that will support the requirements as closely as possible? The traditional answer has been that one buys to standardize—that is, to automate necessary but not strategic business processes—and builds to compete—that is, to support those core processes that make your company different from its competitors.

But things may be more complicated than that. In some cases, homegrown systems may currently be handling menial, less-than-strategic tasks, but switching costs make it difficult to replace them with commercial software. In other cases, packaged software may do exactly what the company needs, even if those needs are strategic in nature. Then, why develop your own?

Many IT executives will evaluate commercial software before even considering building their own. Buying commercial software as often as possible frees up resources for those times when you really, really need to build your own software. When making those decisions, it is important to understand the entire life cycle of software applications and not only the development stage. Many applications will last at least seven or eight years, and due to ongoing maintenance and improvements, 70 percent of the costs will be incurred after the software has been officially implemented. It thus seems that buying or building may be much more complicated than previously thought.

Consider financial services giant Visa. Due to a major emphasis on security, reliability, and privacy concerns of its customers, Visa has an IT organization that is historically biased toward building in-house. This is also due to the sheer size of their global financial network—when you are that large, there is really nobody else you can turn to; all other provider organizations are small in comparison, and the benefits are just not there. However, even an IT organization that traditionally builds can turn to commercial software—even open-source software, of all things—when the economics make sense. Infrastructure and tools are just an example.

"They work, and there is no competitive advantage to build," says David Allen, a consultant who served as Visa's CTO for three years. "Those systems are built at a scale because you're leveraging the technology across many companies." Further, the the company has embraced the availability of mature and reliable open-source tools, particularly in areas such as development, databases, and programming languages. "The combination of low-cost tools and having the source code available can be like getting the best of both worlds [of buying and building]," Allen says. "We have gotten as good if not better in deploying new services on open source as on commercially available software like Windows."

> The best bet may be to put together all available data about business processes, assets and requirements, people, software, hardware, architecture, and compliance and present it with detailed alternatives—each with its advantages and disadvantages, benefits and consequences—to the business stakeholders, and let them make that decision. Inevitably, however, politics will raise its ugly head sooner or later.

SOURCE: Traylor, P. "To build or to buy IT applications?" *InfoWorld*, February 13, 2006.

BECOMING AN AGILE COMPANY
LO 2-4

We are changing from a competitive environment in which mass-market products and services were standardized, long-lived, information-poor, and exchanged in one-time transactions, to an environment in which companies compete globally with niche market products and services that are individualized, short-lived, information-rich, and exchanged on an ongoing basis with customers.

To be an **agile company,** a business must use four basic strategies. First, the business must ensure that customers perceive the products or services of an agile company as solutions to their individual problems. Thus, it can price products on the basis of their value as solutions, rather than their cost to produce. Second, an agile company cooperates with customers, suppliers, other companies, and even with its competitors. This cooperation allows a business to bring products to market as rapidly and cost-effectively as possible, no matter where resources are located or who owns them. Third, an agile company organizes so that it thrives on change and uncertainty. It uses flexible organizational structures keyed to the requirements of different and constantly changing customer opportunities. Fourth, an agile company leverages the impact of its people and the knowledge they possess. By nurturing an entrepreneurial spirit, an agile company provides powerful incentives for employee responsibility, adaptability, and innovation.

Figure 2.13 summarizes another useful way to think about agility in business. This framework emphasizes the roles that customers, business partners, and information technology can play in developing and maintaining the strategic agility of a company. Notice how information technology can enable a company to develop relationships

FIGURE 2.13

How information technology can help a company be an agile competitor, with the help of customers and business partners.

Type of Agility	Description	Role of IT	Example
Customer	Ability to co-opt customers in the exploitation of innovation opportunities • As sources of innovation ideas • As co-creators of innovation • As users in testing ideas or helping other users learn about the idea	Technologies for building and enhancing virtual customer communities for product design, feedback, and testing	eBay customers are its de facto product development team because they post an average of 10,000 messages each week to share tips, point out glitches, and lobby for changes
Partnering	Ability to leverage assets, knowledge, and competencies of suppliers, distributors, contract manufacturers, and logistics providers in the exploration and exploitation of innovation opportunities	Technologies facilitating interfirm collaboration, such as collaborative platforms and portals, supply chain systems	Yahoo! has accomplished a significant transformation of its service from a search engine into a portal by initiating numerous partnerships to provide content and other media-related services from its Web site
Operational	Ability to accomplish speed, accuracy, and cost economy in the exploitation of innovation opportunities	Technologies for modularization and integration of business processes	Ingram Micro, a global wholesaler, has deployed an integrated trading system allowing its customers and suppliers to connect directly to its procurement and ERP systems

SOURCE: V. Sambamurthy, Anandhi Bhaharadwaj, and Varun Grover, "Shaping Agility through Digital Options: Reconceptualizing the Role of Information Technology in Contemporary Firms," *MIS Quarterly*, June 2003, p. 246.

with its customers in virtual communities that help it be an agile innovator. As we will see repeatedly throughout this textbook, information technologies enable a company to partner with its suppliers, distributors, contract manufacturers, and others via collaborative portals and other Web-based supply chain systems that significantly improve its agility in exploiting innovative business opportunities.

In today's dynamic global business environment, forming a ***virtual company*** can be one of the most important strategic uses of information technology. A virtual company (also called a *virtual corporation* or *virtual organization*) is an organization that uses information technology to link people, organizations, assets, and ideas.

Figure 2.14 illustrates that virtual companies typically form virtual workgroups and alliances with business partners that are interlinked by the Internet, intranets, and extranets. Notice that this company has organized internally into clusters of process and cross-functional teams linked by intranets. It has also developed alliances and extranet links that form ***interenterprise information systems*** with suppliers, customers, subcontractors, and competitors. Thus, virtual companies create flexible and adaptable virtual workgroups and alliances keyed to exploit fast-changing business opportunities.

Virtual Company Strategies

Why do people form virtual companies? It is the best way to implement key business strategies and alliances that promise to ensure success in today's turbulent business climate. Several major reasons for virtual companies stand out and are summarized in Figure 2.15.

For example, a business may not have the time or resources to develop the necessary manufacturing and distribution infrastructure, personnel competencies, and information technologies to take full advantage of a new market opportunity in a timely manner. It can assemble the components it needs to provide a world-class solution for customers and capture the market opportunity only by quickly forming a virtual company through a strategic alliance of all-star partners. Today, of course, the Internet, intranets, extranets, and a variety of other Internet technologies are vital components in creating such successful solutions.

CREATING A VIRTUAL COMPANY LO 2-4

FIGURE 2.14

A virtual company uses the Internet, intranets, and extranets to form virtual workgroups and support alliances with business partners.

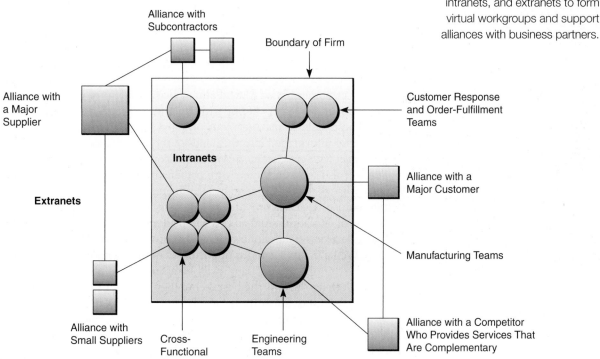

Alliance with Subcontractors

Boundary of Firm

Alliance with a Major Supplier

Customer Response and Order-Fulfillment Teams

Intranets

Alliance with a Major Customer

Extranets

Manufacturing Teams

Alliance with Small Suppliers

Cross-Functional Teams

Engineering Teams

Alliance with a Competitor Who Provides Services That Are Complementary

FIGURE 2.15

The basic business strategies of virtual companies.

Strategies of Virtual Companies
• Share infrastructure and risk with alliance partners.
• Link complementary core competencies.
• Reduce concept-to-cash time through sharing.
• Increase facilities and market coverage.
• Gain access to new markets and share market or customer loyalty.
• Migrate from selling products to selling solutions.

Sysco: Transforming a Company with the Help of IT

Sysco, headquartered in Houston, Texas, is a major distributor of food products to restaurants, schools, hospitals, and hotels and is also a provider of equipment and supplies to the hospitality and food service industries. Sysco employs approximately 45,000 with sales for the 2010 fiscal year surpassing $37 billion. It operates more than 180 locations in the United States, Canada, and Ireland, from which it serves more than 400,000 customers. The company is organized into a series of large operating companies with geographical responsibilities, and a smaller group of specialty food companies that cater to particular segments of the market.

Sysco has embarked on a new project to standardize and unify business processes across its operating companies and distribution centers. The overarching goals of the effort are to increase efficiency and improve sales and marketing, as well as provide increased transparency through improved data management. Not surprisingly, IT is an integral part of this transformation.

"This is more than an IT project—it is truly a business transformation," says Jim Hope, executive vice president. "Using the power of SAP as the foundation for our transformation, Sysco intends to improve productivity, retain and expand business with existing customers, and understand where market opportunities lie so we can do a better job attracting and pursuing new business."

The company chose SAP Business Suite and Business Objects business intelligence platforms as the centerpieces after a series of pilots and demonstrations convinced senior management this was the way to go. As everybody in IT knows, one of the most important keys to the success of this kind of large project is executive commitment. And so Sysco started by getting this first, and then figuring out the details later. "We're starting to pilot some of the customer-facing applications, and in particular, an improved ordering platform for our customers," said Mark Palmer, vice president of corporate communication. "So far, we're very happy with what we're seeing."

These "details" include a four-pronged approach focused on getting more and better information into the hands of their sales associates (Sysco's main point of contact with customers), a Web-based complete order management system that will also assist customers with personalized recommendations, a consolidated back office that will be shared by all affiliates, and standardized reporting across the company that will provide management with up-to-date information on all aspects of operations. And all this will be done with commercial software that will replace existing stand-alone systems that just could not deliver anymore.

"We have a tremendous opportunity to use technology to continue to sharpen our operations," says Twila Day, senior vice president and chief information officer. "SAP is the best technology provider to help us with our plans to integrate all of our software needs into a single platform, giving us the visibility required to efficiently manage our business end-to-end."

SOURCE: Schneider, I. "Sysco Taps SAP For BI, CRM," *InformationWeek*, May 6, 2010 and www.sysco.com, accessed May 9, 2011.

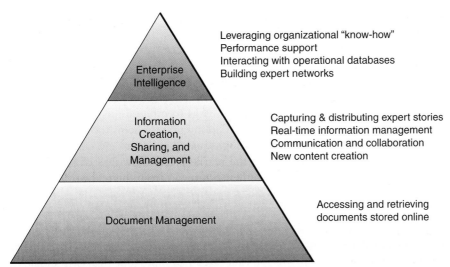

FIGURE 2.16
Knowledge management can be viewed as three levels of techniques, technologies, and systems that promote the collection, organization, access, sharing, and use of workplace and enterprise knowledge.

SOURCE: Marc Rosenberg, *e-Learning: Strategies for Delivering Knowledge in the Digital Age* (New York: McGraw-Hill, 2001), p. 70.

In an economy where the only certainty is uncertainty, the one sure source of lasting competitive advantage is knowledge. When markets shift, technologies proliferate, competitors multiply, and products become obsolete almost overnight, successful companies are those that consistently create new knowledge, disseminate it widely throughout the organization, and quickly embody it in new technologies and products. These activities define the "knowledge-creating" company, whose sole business is continuous innovation.

Many companies today can only realize lasting competitive advantage if they become knowledge-creating companies or learning organizations. That means consistently creating new business knowledge, disseminating it widely throughout the company, and quickly building the new knowledge into their products and services.

Knowledge-creating companies exploit two kinds of knowledge. One is *explicit knowledge*, which is the data, documents, and things written down or stored on computers. The other kind is *tacit knowledge,* or the "how-tos" of knowledge, which resides in workers. Tacit knowledge can often represent some of the most important information within an organization. Long-time employees of a company often "know" many things about how to manufacture a product, deliver the service, deal with a particular vendor, or operate an essential piece of equipment. This tacit knowledge is not recorded or codified anywhere because it has evolved in the employee's mind through years of experience. Furthermore, much of this tacit knowledge is never shared with anyone who might be in a position to record it in a more formal way because there is often little incentive to do so or simply, "Nobody ever asked."

As illustrated in Figure 2.16, successful knowledge management creates techniques, technologies, systems, and rewards for getting employees to share what they know and make better use of accumulated workplace and enterprise knowledge. In that way, employees of a company are leveraging knowledge as they do their jobs.

Making personal knowledge available to others is the central activity of the knowledge-creating company. It takes place continuously and at all levels of the organization.

Knowledge management has thus become one of the major strategic uses of information technology. Many companies are building ***knowledge management systems*** (KMS) to manage organizational learning and business know-how. The goal of such systems is to help knowledge workers create, organize, and make available important business knowledge, wherever and whenever it's needed in an organization. This information includes processes, procedures, patents, reference works, formulas, best practices, forecasts, and fixes. As you will see in Chapter 10, Internet and intranet Web

BUILDING A KNOWLEDGE-CREATING COMPANY
LO 2-5

KNOWLEDGE MANAGEMENT SYSTEMS

sites, groupware, data mining, knowledge bases, and online discussion groups are some of the key technologies that may be used by a KMS.

Knowledge management systems also facilitate organizational learning and knowledge creation. They are designed to provide rapid feedback to knowledge workers, encourage behavior changes by employees, and significantly improve business performance. As the organizational learning process continues and its knowledge base expands, the knowledge-creating company works to integrate its knowledge into its business processes, products, and services. This integration helps the company become a more innovative and agile provider of high-quality products and customer services, as well as a formidable competitor in the marketplace. Now let's close this chapter with an example of knowledge management strategies from the real world.

Goodwin Procter Makes a Strong Case for Knowledge Management

If anyone knows that time is money, it's an attorney. The 850 attorneys and their staff at Goodwin Procter LLP were spending too much time assembling documents and looking up information, which meant cases took more time than they should to proceed. The $611 million law firm's eight offices used seven different applications to manage more than 2 terabytes of data for Goodwin Procter's more than 60,000 cases—close to 10 million documents. CIO Peter Lane wanted to integrate the data. Using Microsoft SharePoint, his team created the Matter Page System as a hub through which attorneys could access business data and client information.

What's more, the firm has been able to use the platform to share its notes and work in progress. It's now easy for an attorney to find a colleague who can help with a similar case. Matter Pages took a year to implement, but it immediately changed how Goodwin Procter's attorneys work.

When a client called with a question, finding the answer used to mean launching more than one application and looking up the data in different systems. Attorneys needed contact information, documents, billing information, and more. The process sometimes took hours.

"Now, instead of having to launch the different systems from the desktop, or the Web interface, or the document management system, we were able to pull all of this information into a one-stop-shop view for the users in our company," says Andrew Kawa, Goodwin Procter's development manager, who leads its system development efforts.

The system increases efficiency for the attorneys because they can find previous matters that they or others have worked on and gain extra information much more quickly than before. They spend less time researching and more time moving a case forward. The initial success of Matter Pages has Lane investigating new SharePoint features, such as wikis and blogs. He expects to deploy these new capabilities widely over the next few months.

For example, each matter has a wiki that is used to track notes, or other unstructured data that relates to it. These notes are open for editing by all users. Blogs tend to be used for discussions that are not case-specific, although when a matter or set of matters apply to the topic of the blog, users can add links to related cases.

"One of the IT goals is to take advantage of the new technology as it becomes available," Lane adds. With that goal in mind, says Lane, the Matter Pages System won't ever truly be completed. Currently, Kawa is looking to integrate Goodwin Procter's patent and trademark information with data about their patent applications from the U.S. Patent and Trademark Office. The integration would allow attorneys to retrieve real-time information on their pending patents and actions they need to take. "I don't think we will ever declare the project done or say we don't have to put any more time or effort in," he says.

SOURCE: Jarina D'Auria, "Goodwin Procter Makes Strong Case for Knowledge Management," *CIO.com*, August 1, 2008.

CenterPoint Properties— Reinventing a Company with the Help of IT

CenterPoint Properties is a large real estate company making the transition into a world-class provider of intermodal transportation and logistics solutions. Such a radical transformation in its business model requires major changes in all aspects of the organization, from capital structure and ownership to the underlying technologies needed to run the new business. And that is where IT comes in. The challenge for CenterPoint is how to best deploy new applications and functionality for a business model that is largely unique and innovative, while at the same time keeping the day-to-day aspects of the real estate business chugging along.

Early on, CenterPoint Properties realized that commercial software was not going to cut it, at least not completely. Although there is no shortage of good software on the market, most vendors typically focus on the more streamlined or commoditized part of the business: back-end processes. While those are certainly important, the company started looking for a solution that would provide all the functionality required by the new business model. "To be successful, we were going to have to buy what we could, develop what was unique and strategic, and then integrate it into a single system," says Scott Zimmerman, Chief Information Officer at CenterPoint. Out of this vision, the CUB System (CenterPoint's Universal Business System) was born.

Everyday real estate functions—the ones that are neither unique nor strategic—were addressed by implementing a leading real estate ERP package called Yardi. This allowed CenterPoint to benefit from a stable and well-tested platform that was very reliable and cost-efficient for the essential transactions that all real estate companies have to deal with, such as sending rent statements, writing and processing checks, and so on. Because the underlying technology on which Yardi was built (the Microsoft.NET framework) was compatible with CenterPoint's infrastructure, developers were able to tap into the functionality of Yardi directly from other parts of CUB, thus allowing multiple applications to communicate with each other without human intervention. This was not as straightforward as it sounds; it was necessary to fly back and forth to Yardi's offices in California, and have a number of distance meetings between developer teams. Nevertheless, the benefits outweighed those costs.

Today, large real estate projects are a team effort. Members of those teams may include CenterPoint employees—in Chicago or elsewhere—plus participants from the client company. Sometimes consultants to either of the two parties are also part of the team, and all of the various team members are likely to be geographically dispersed. In short, enabling collaboration is a key success driver for these efforts. To address this, CenterPoint developed a custom CRM (Customer Relationship Management) system on top of Microsoft's SharePoint 2007 platform. While SharePoint 2007 takes care of the "plumbing" (hosting Web sites, security and access issues, and storing all data), CenterPoint focuses on creating the tools they need. These include a separate Web site and blog for each different project that team members can use to keep updated about new developments; the Web site and blog also function as a central repository of project information that everyone can access anywhere at any time. Instant Messaging and e-mail are integrated so that all members are kept up-to-date on any new development in the project in their preferred way. The system also handles routing and approval of documents to the proper parties, as well as managing a digital library of all documents in the project—which are thus also available anytime, anywhere.

The old saying that real estate is all about "location, location, location" also holds true for CenterPoint. In order to take advantage of the most recent breakthroughs on GIS (Geographic Information Systems) technology, CUB integrates GIS functionality with Microsoft's Virtual Earth Web service. Executives can then analyze existing or potential properties by using maps and aerial images that are overlaid with demographic, market, census and economic data. These data can be rearranged to create maps exposing different aspects of the site, which are all color-coded. Examples include vacancy and rent levels, new sales and construction, sale prices in the area, population growth, age and income, and any other relevant market trends.

All of these pieces—and others still under development—are tied together by a common interface based on a mix of ASP.NET, AJAX and JavaScript. Having a single, unified "look and feel" for the application has contributed to greatly reduced training costs, as well as improved employee productivity. Indeed, the underlying goal behind the custom interface was to minimize the amount of searching and clicking required before users could find what they were looking for. In CUB, 80 percent of the information is within one or fewer clicks of a mouse (fewer meaning that important data will be displayed in a pop-up window when a user hovers the pointer over an object). CUB also integrates RSS feeds so that users can get up-to-date information on important industry and market trends, and it implements enterprise search functionality in a single place: All data stores of the company can be searched with a single keyword search box at the top of the portal.

The key to this effort has been the ability (and willingness) to pick and choose the best technology for each job, and make them all work together. This best-of-breed approach provides CenterPoint with a unique set of applications well suited to their business needs; at the same time, the applications are highly modular and extensible for when those needs change—and they will change, that much is guaranteed. "CUB is less a story about implementing a single technology and more a case study of how to successfully integrate the best parts a given technology has to offer into a cohesive system using progressive design techniques and pragmatic analysis of problem domains to efficiently support a business strategy," says Zimmerman.

While all of this was going on, CenterPoint Properties went private. In March 2006, the California Public Employees' Retirement System (CalPers) agreed to purchase CenterPoint Properties. As the details of the deal were ironed out, one of the lead advisers to CalPers was not convinced: A relatively small Chicago firm with only a hundred employees would not be able to execute the vision that the executives had put in place—at least not in the time frame that was necessary for it to be successful. At that time, CenterPoint's CEO asked the CIO to give a demonstration of CUB. That was all it took.

"Had CenterPoint not had the foresight to invest early in this system to support and drive our new business model, we wouldn't have been able to go private and we'd be trading at $25 per share [half of CalPers' purchase price] like our competition instead of experiencing double-digit growth. It was the straw that broke the camel's back," says Mike Mullen, CEO.

CenterPoint has started to reap many of those benefits as CUB went online. The integrated nature of all data provided, as well as the efficient and automated processing of routine transactions in the background, has freed property managers to concentrate on the most value-added aspects of the business. Their productivity has markedly gone up, as well. Today, CenterPoint estimates its property managers are handling twice as much square footage as their counterparts in other real estate companies. Faster and more accurate decision making, coupled with increased deal volume per employee—both of which have been made possible by CUB—have had a major impact on business results. CenterPoint has increased the turnover rate for properties from five or six years to three, which doubled the transaction volume the company can handle from the properties in its portfolio. Since CUB was implemented, CenterPoint has increased its investment volume by 80 percent and grown at an annual rate of 15 to 20 percent without an increase in staff.

It is surprising how many companies have approached CenterPoint about purchasing or licensing CUB for their own internal use. Every time CenterPoint makes a sales pitch to a potential partner, they do a demonstration of CUB—pretty much like the one that convinced CalPers that CenterPoint was ready to make the vision a reality. Often this demonstration becomes the focus of attention, and follow-up calls ensue from other real estate executives. CenterPoint is now considering the possibility of licensing the software or, even further, acting as a service provider to other companies in the industry. None of these were on the radar when CUB was first proposed, but that is what happens when one company has a technology that is so far superior to anything else.

"While many things contributed to our success—the development of our new business plan, and our evolution into a private company—it was CUB that ultimately made our vision a reality," says Paul Fisher, CenterPoint's President. "Developing CUB was worth every penny."

SOURCE: "CenterPoint Properties," *Computerworld Honors Program Case Study*, www.centerpoint-prop.com, accessed May 9, 2011, and "Office Business Application at the Heart of Commercial Real-Estate Company's Success," *Microsoft Office System Customer Solution Case Study*.

▼ **QUESTIONS TO CONSIDER**

1. To build or to buy is one of the central questions when it comes to provisioning technologies. How did CenterPoint choose what to buy and what to develop internally? What lessons can be synthesized from its approach that can be applied to other companies in the future?

2. What is your opinion on whether CenterPoint should possibly license CUB or act as a service provider? Do you think this would dilute CenterPoint's competitive position? What are the advantages and disadvantages of moving forward with this idea?

- **Strategic Uses of Information Technology.** Information technologies can support many competitive strategies. They can help a business cut costs, differentiate and innovate in its products and services, promote growth, develop alliances, lock in customers and suppliers, create switching costs, raise barriers to entry, and leverage its investment in IT resources. Thus, information technology can help a business gain a competitive advantage in its relationships with customers, suppliers, competitors, new entrants, and producers of substitute products. Refer to Figures 2.3 and 2.5 for summaries of the uses of information technology for strategic advantage.

- **Building a Customer-Focused Business.** A key strategic use of Internet technologies is to build a company that develops its business value by making customer value its strategic focus. Customer-focused companies use Internet, intranet, and extranet e-commerce Web sites and services to keep track of their customers' preferences; to supply products, services, and information anytime or anywhere; and to provide services tailored to the individual needs of the customers.

- **Reengineering Business Processes.** Information technology is a key ingredient in reengineering business operations because it enables radical changes to business processes that dramatically improve their efficiency and effectiveness. Internet technologies can play a major role in supporting innovative changes in the design of work flows, job requirements, and organizational structures in a company.

- **Becoming an Agile Company.** A business can use information technology to help it become an agile company. Then it can prosper in rapidly changing markets with broad product ranges and short model lifetimes in which it must process orders in arbitrary lot sizes; it can also offer its customers customized products while it maintains high volumes of production. An agile company depends heavily on Internet technologies to help it respond to its customers with customized solutions, and to cooperate with its customers, suppliers, and other businesses to bring products to market as rapidly and cost effectively as possible.

- **Creating a Virtual Company.** Forming virtual companies has become an important competitive strategy in today's dynamic global markets. Internet and other information technologies play a key role in providing computing and telecommunications resources to support the communications, coordination, and information flows needed. Managers of a virtual company depend on IT to help them manage a network of people, knowledge, financial, and physical resources provided by many business partners to take advantage of rapidly changing market opportunities.

- **Building a Knowledge-Creating Company.** Lasting competitive advantage today can only come from the innovative use and management of organizational knowledge by knowledge-creating companies and learning organizations. Internet technologies are widely used in knowledge management systems to support the creation and dissemination of business knowledge and its integration into new products, services, and business processes.

These are the key terms and concepts of this chapter. The page number of their first reference appears in parentheses.

1. Agile company (64)
2. Business process reengineering (61)
3. Competitive forces (49)
4. Competitive strategies (53)
5. Create switching costs (55)
6. Customer value (57)
7. Interenterprise information systems (65)
8. Knowledge-creating company (67)
9. Knowledge management system (67)
10. Leverage investment in IT (55)
11. Lock in customers and suppliers (54)
12. Raise barriers to entry (55)
13. Strategic information systems (49)
14. Value chain (59)
15. Virtual company (65)

Match one of the key terms and concepts listed previously with one of the brief examples or definitions that follow. Try to find the best fit for answers that seem to fit more than one term or concept. Defend your choices.

_____ 1. A business must deal with customers, suppliers, competitors, new entrants, and substitutes.

_____ 2. Cost leadership, differentiation of products, and new product innovation are examples.

_____ 3. Using investments in technology to keep firms out of an industry.

_____ 4. Making it unattractive for a firm's customers or suppliers to switch to its competitors.

_____ 5. Strategies designed to increase the time, money, and effort needed for customers or suppliers to change to a firm's competitors.

_____ 6. Information systems that reengineer business processes or promote business innovation are examples.

_____ 7. This strategic focus recognizes that quality, rather than price, has become the primary determinant in customers choosing a product or service.

_____ 8. Highlights how strategic information systems can be applied to a firm's business processes and can support activities for competitive advantage.

_____ 9. A business finding strategic uses for the computing and telecommunications capabilities it has developed to run its operations.

_____ 10. Information technology helping a business make radical improvements in business processes.

_____ 11. A business can prosper in rapidly changing markets while offering its customers individualized solutions to their needs.

_____ 12. A network of business partners formed to take advantage of rapidly changing market opportunities.

_____ 13. Learning organizations that focus on creating, disseminating, and managing business knowledge.

_____ 14. Information systems that manage the creation and dissemination of organizational knowledge.

_____ 15. Using the Internet and extranets to link a company's information systems to those of its customers and suppliers.

1. Suppose you are a manager being asked to develop computer-based applications to gain a competitive advantage in an important market for your company. What reservations might you have about doing so? Why?

2. How could a business use information technology to increase switching costs and lock in its customers and suppliers? Use business examples to support your answers.

3. How could a business leverage its investment in information technology to build strategic IT capabilities that serve as a barrier to new entrants into its markets?

4. Review the Real World Challenge introduced in the chapter. In such a major transformative project where no one can really envision what the end product (or end company) will look like, how should organizations set out to create these technology-enabled solutions? What kind of approaches would work best? Worst?

5. What strategic role can information play in business process reengineering?

6. How can Internet technologies help a business form strategic alliances with its customers, suppliers, and others?

7. How could a business use Internet technologies to form a virtual company or become an agile competitor?

8. Consider the Real World Solution discussed in the chapter. Do you think CenterPoint Properties' success is the result of the new business model or the new technology deployed to support it (i.e., CUB)? Is it possible to distinguish one from the other? What are the implications for other companies as they seek to reinvent themselves in the future?

9. Information technology can't really give a company a strategic advantage because most competitive advantages don't last more than a few years and soon become strategic necessities that just raise the stakes of the game. Discuss.

10. MIS author and consultant Peter Keen says: "We have learned that it is not technology that creates a competitive edge, but the management process that exploits technology." What does he mean? Do you agree or disagree? Why?

1. **End-User Computing**
Skills Assessment

Not all programs are written by dedicated programmers. Many knowledge workers write their own software using familiar word processing, spreadsheet, presentation, and database tools. This textbook contains end-user computing exercises representing a real-world programming challenge. This first exercise will allow your course instructor to assess the class. Assess your skills in each of the following areas:

a. *Word processing:* Approximately how many words per minute can you type? Do you use styles to manage document formatting? Have you ever set up your own mail-merge template and data source? Have you created your own macros to handle repetitive tasks? Have you ever added branching or looping logic in your macro programs?

b. *Spreadsheets:* Do you know the order of operations your spreadsheet program uses (what does "=5*2^2-10" equal)? Do you know how to automatically sort data in a spreadsheet? Do you know how to create graphs and charts from spreadsheet data? Can you build pivot tables from spreadsheet data? Do you know the difference between a relative and a fixed cell reference? Do you know how to use functions in your spreadsheet equations? Do you know how to use the IF function? Have you created your own macros to handle repetitive tasks? Have you ever added branching or looping logic in your macro programs?

c. *Presentations:* Have you ever used presentation software to create presentation outlines? Have you added your own multimedia content to a presentation? Do you know how to add charts and graphs from spreadsheet software into your presentations so that they automatically update when the spreadsheet data change?

d. *Database:* Have you ever imported data into a database from a text file? Have you ever written queries to sort or filter data stored in a database table? Have you built reports to format your data for output? Have you built forms to aid in manual data entry? Have you built functions or programs to manipulate data stored in database tables?

e. *File Management:* Can you store or locate a specific file on a particular storage device? If you receive an attachment on an e-mail, can you store it on your hard drive in a location where you can find it again? Can you create a specific folder for a group of related files, then navigate to it when necessary, or direct someone else to that location?

f. *Internet:* Do you know how to navigate your way around the Internet? If someone gives you a specific URL, can you access that location? Do you know what a URL is? Can you modify your home page on your favorite Web browser? Do you know how to use an anti-virus program? Can you use the Status Bar to determine if a link is trying to spoof you to another site? E-mail is arguably the largest use of the Internet today. Can you send and receive e-mail, build a mailing list, and send and receive attachments?

2. **Marketing: Competitive Intelligence**
Strategic Marketing

Marketing professionals use information systems to gather and analyze information about their competitors. They use this information to assess their product's position relative to the competition and make strategic marketing decisions about their *product*, its *price*, its distribution (*place*), and how to best manage its *promotion*. Michael Bloomberg, founder of Bloomberg (www.bloomberg.com), and others have made their fortunes gathering and selling data about businesses. Marketing professionals find information about a business's industry, location, employees, products, technologies, revenues, and market share useful when planning marketing initiatives.

During your senior year you will find yourself in close competition for jobs. You can take the same intelligence-gathering approach used by professional marketers when planning how to sell your own skills. Use the following questions to help you prepare for your job search.

a. Product: Which business majors are presently in greatest demand by employers? Use entry-level salaries as the primary indicator for demand.

b. Product: Which colleges or universities in your region pose the greatest competitive threat to students with your major?

c. Price: What is the average salary for entry-level employees in your major and geographic region? Is salary your top concern? Why or why not?

d. Place: Which areas of the country are currently experiencing the greatest employment growth?

e. Promotion: What is your marketing plan? Describe how you plan to get your name and qualifications in front of prospective employers. How can the Internet help you get noticed?

3. Competing against Free

Wikipedia Faces Down Encyclopedia Britannica
The record and movie industries are not the only industries to find themselves affected by free access to their products. Encyclopedia Britannica faces challenges by a nonprofit competitor that provides its services without charge or advertising, Wikipedia.org. Wikipedia depends on volunteers to create and edit original content under the condition contributors provide their work without copyright.

Who would work for free? During its creation in the 19th century, the Oxford English Dictionary editors solicited word articles and references from the general public. In the 20th century, AOL.com found thousands of volunteers to monitor its chat rooms. Amazon.com coaxed more than 100,000 readers to post book reviews on its retail Web site. Outdoing them all in the 21st century, Wikipedia published its 1,000,000th English language article in March 2006. Wikipedia includes more than 2,000,000 articles in more than 200 languages, all created and edited by more than 4,800,000 million users.

Can Wikipedia compete on quality? Wikipedia provides its users with both editing and monitoring tools. This allows users to self-police. Wikipedia also uses voluntary administrators who block vandals, temporarily protect articles, and manage arbitration processes when disputes arise. A paper published by *Nature* in December 2005 evaluated 50 Wikipedia articles and found an average of four factual errors per Wikipedia article as compared with an average of three errors per article in the *Encyclopedia Britannica*. More significantly, Wikipedians (as the volunteers call themselves) corrected each error by January 2006. Alexa.com rated Wikipedia.com as the 17th most visited Web site on the Internet, while Britannica.com came in 2,858th place (Yahoo and Google ranked in first and second place).

Wikipedia has already built on its success. In addition to offering foreign language encyclopedias, it also provides a common media archive (commons.wikimedia.org), a multilingual dictionary (www.wiktionary.org), and a news service (www.wikinews.org).

One of the latest Wikipedia projects is Wikiversity, a Web site devoted to free learning, Web education, open educational resources, and collaborative learning communities (www.wikiversity.com).

a. How does the Wikimedia Foundation meet the criteria for an agile company?

b. How does the Wikimedia Foundation meet the criteria for a virtual company?

c. How does the Wikimedia Foundation meet the criteria for a knowledge-creating organization?

d. How would you recommend that Encyclopedia Britannica adapt to this new threat?

e. How does Wikiversity compare as an educational resource to traditional colleges and schools? How would a degree earned online from wikiversity.com be viewed compared with a degree earned in a traditional learning environment? What learning resources are at Wikiversity that you can use to further your education right now?

4. Knowledge Management

Knowing What You Know
Employees often receive a great deal of unstructured information in the form of e-mails. For example, employees may receive policies, announcements, and daily operational information via e-mail. However, e-mail systems typically make poor enterprisewide knowledge management systems. New employees don't have access to e-mails predating their start date. Employees typically aren't permitted to search others' e-mail files for needed information. Organizations lose productivity when employees spend time reviewing and organizing their e-mail files. Lastly, the same information might be saved across thousands of different e-mail files, thereby ballooning e-mail file storage space requirements.

Microsoft's Exchange server, IBM's Domino server, and Interwoven's WorkSite, along with a wide variety of open standard Web-based products aim to address an organization's need to share unstructured information. These products provide common repositories for various categories of information. For example, management may use a "Policy" folder in Microsoft Exchange to store all of its policy decisions. Likewise, sales representatives may use a "Competitive Intelligence" database in IBM's Domino server to store information obtained during the sales process about competing products, prices, or marketplace rumors. WorkSite users categorize and store all of their electronic documents in a large, searchable, secured, common repository. Organizations using these systems can secure them, manage them, and make them available to the appropriate personnel. Managers can also appoint a few specific employees requiring little technical experience to manage the content.

However, these systems cannot benefit an organization if its employees fail to contribute their knowledge, if they fail to use the system to retrieve information, or if the system just isn't available where and when needed. To help managers better understand how employees use these systems, knowledge management systems include usage statistics such as date/time, user name, reads, writes, and even specific document access information.

Research each of these products mentioned above and answer the following questions:

a. What steps might a manager take to encourage his or her employees to use the organization's knowledge management system?

b. Should managers set minimum quotas for system usage for each employee? Why or why not?

c. Aside from setting employee usage quotas, how might an organization benefit from knowledge management system usage statistics?

5. Crowd-Sourcing Ad Reviews

Do You Like This Ad?

Marketers dream of their ads going viral, but what works, what flops, and when is it time to change approaches? Facebook may be on the verge of turning advertising on its head with its automated user feedback system. Read CNNTech's article *How Facebook killed (most) spam* (http://bit.ly/fE5NMS), and then answer the questions below:

a. List each type of user-generated feedback Facebook automatically monitors.

b. How do the users benefit?

c. How do advertisers benefit?

d. How does Facebook benefit?

e. In your opinion, what obstacles will competitors have to overcome to compete with Facebook's approach to managing advertising?

How to Win Friends and Influence Business People: Quantify IT Risks and Value

CIO Tim Schaefer thinks words do matter.

He looked at the words IT used inside Northwestern Mutual Life, and felt they sent exactly the wrong message about IT's role in meeting business goals. So, over the last 18 months, these words are out: IT costs, internal customers, IT leaders, Alignment, IT systems, and "IT and the business." In are these: IT investments, external customers, business leaders, integration, service levels, IT assets, and "our business."

"We came to realize we ourselves were building the wall. We were distinguishing ourselves from the rest of the company," says Schaefer. "We were somehow different. We had all this special knowledge. So this whole concept of black box, and the gap in the relationship, we came to realize was of our own doing." As part of a broader change of IT strategy and culture, Schaefer has asked the top 150 leaders in IT to commit to being business leaders, not IT leaders.

Symbolic, semantics, and a whole lot of hoo-hah? Sure—if IT continued to behave exactly the same way it always has. At Northwestern Mutual, a life insurance and investment company with more than $155 billion in assets, IT has not. IT started by working very hard to put a real value on IT assets. Although the process is ongoing, Schaefer says the company now knows it has IT assets worth "somewhere north of $3 billion." It can talk about service levels in terms business units care about—that causing problems in the underwriting process costs $11,000 an hour in lost productivity, and problems that keep the field force from using their client management tools costs $25,000 an hour.

Schaefer's goal is to get IT systems to be viewed as a business asset, with a value every bit as real as the buildings and land the company owns. Getting there requires a portfolio approach to all of its IT assets. That's not a project portfolio approach many IT teams have, but an investment portfolio with the same type of processes the company uses to manage holdings in stocks, bonds, real estate, or private equity. Instead of considering whether to buy, hold, or sell assets, though, the IT asset portfolio assesses IT systems and applications through a framework called TIME: Tolerate, Invest, Migrate, or Eliminate.

Putting a value on an IT asset isn't easy. Northwestern Mutual's IT team does so by working hand-in-hand with the business units that rely on them. How many more employees would it take to process claims if the software system used for that didn't exist? What's the replacement cost? What's the cost per hour to the business if it goes down? Getting an asset value is only the first step, though. All these factors go into whether and how to invest more into that asset. "If we don't do the right things with these $3 billion worth of assets, we're not going to optimize the value," Schaefer says.

This asset-and-investment philosophy drives what IT projects the company puts money behind. Lots of companies have a technology strategy committee that helps guide IT spending, and Northwestern Mutual Life does too. "We're transitioning them into an investment management board," Schaefer says. Northwestern Mutual Life has a number of boards to guide its investment into financial asset classes on behalf of policyholders—boards that set broad strategy for where the best opportunities are for return in those categories. Discussions in the technology strategy committee are moving to that same thinking.

From that process, they've targeted specific high-return investment opportunities for technology. For example, technology that reduces barriers of time and space is on that list. Northwestern Mutual's network includes more than 7,000 financial representatives, and those in the Western U.S. states cover massive territory. Yet they're obligated to meet with clients regularly, to make sure they're recommending suitable investments. A video link that lets a Colorado-based representative do live meeting conversations with his three clients in Wyoming in a half-day instead of three days on the road offers a measurable value. There's another word that matters to Schaefer, which fits this financial discussion: partner. Of course, IT wants to be considered a partner with business units on projects, but it has a clear definition for that: IT shares the business risk and benefits, including financial, from IT investments. "We should feel as bad when they aren't meeting their objectives as they do," he says.

Conventional wisdom, decades worth of IT project failures, and less-than-desirable outcomes tell us that every tech-related investment—from a massive SAP ERP rollout to a small CRM deployment—comes with some amount of risk. In fact, according to Forrester Research VP and principal analyst Chip Gliedman, "of all investments within an organization, investment in IT is generally assumed to have the most risk associated with it. Yet, it is surprising that IT investment has traditionally received the least amount of attention when it comes to risk management."

Since 2003, when the software and equipment components of the U.S. GDP took their largest fall in 15 years, most CEOs have viewed technology as a cost, not an investment. Although budgets have expanded during the past few years, the growth rates have been modest, and most of the money has gone toward fortifying financial systems, while front-office systems have ranked the lowest. Companies, having neglected the customer far too long in their technology investments, are likely to start feeling the effect as frustrated customers go elsewhere. Customers' frustration will grow all the more when they deal with clunky corporate systems after years of enjoying tremendous innovation in the consumer technology they use.

The contrast is a direct result of treating technology as a cost. This viewpoint has preserved an older set of technologies that weren't built for the Internet. Many large enterprises are now realizing that without investment in new systems, no new wave of productivity improvement is possible. How to manage this new wave of investment, and keep costs under control, however, is still baffling to even the best of them.

The process of risk measurement has been "confounding decision makers within IT for some time," Gliedman asserts. As a result, companies rely on weak qualitative analysis that only loosely ties to enterprise-application project outcomes, he says. Gliedman breaks down IT risk factors into two categories: implementation and impact risks. Implementation-based risks relate to areas such as project size ("the larger the project, the higher the level of uncertainty about the outcome") and the technology and vendor (will they both deliver on the intended benefits?). Impact-based risks include cultural, training, and managerial factors that can all significantly affect any project's outcome and benefits.

"While the risk analysis cannot on its own point to the best course of action, it can provide the additional shading to management so that the eventual decision is an informed one," Gliedman notes. "Likewise, expectations can be set properly, avoiding overly rosy ROI projections that will lead to inevitable disappointment."

Most IT departments today could use help in the ongoing struggle to align IT with the business, and vice versa. Business executives are frustrated by application uptime challenges and their significant costs to the company's bottom line, although IT isn't fully aware of that. The business side is also not at all excited about long-term enterprise projects. As a consequence of both, business executives are feeling animosity toward IT.

Providing more risk transparency to the Mahogany Row on all IT projects could be a huge win for IT departments right now.

One more thing about the words IT uses. Schaefer and his leadership team made a deliberate choice not to rename the IT department to become the business technology department, even though that's their mindset. They worried that a name change might sound superficial to the business units. Instead, they focused on how they talk about IT every day. The message alone doesn't mean a thing if the IT team doesn't act differently, by valuing IT assets and then optimizing them. But the message does matter, because it very likely reflects how IT thinks about its role in the business and how business units perceive IT. And it's critical to changing the culture of the organization.

Schaefer has an advantage in getting the company to think and talk about IT as a financial asset. Assets, investments, and returns are the natural language at Northwestern Mutual, as a financial services company. But it is not a stretch for nonfinancial IT organizations to embrace this framework and to put hard values on IT assets.

"Listen to the words you use," Schaefer advises.

SOURCE: Chris Murphy, "Global CIO: What's IT Worth? Northwestern Mutual Life CIO Knows," *InformationWeek*, March 8, 2010; Thomas Wailgum, "How to Win CFO Friends and Influence Business People: Quantify IT Investment Risk," *CIO.com*, April 22, 2009; and Bob Suh, "Gearing Up for Recession: Technology as an Investment, not a Cost," *Computerworld*, March 14, 2008.

▼ CASE STUDY QUESTIONS

1. By changing the way his group talks about IT investments, CIO Tim Schaefer is trying to change the way the rest of the company sees IT. Why do you think this is necessary? What would be the prevailing mindset about IT in his company, such that he needs to do something about it? Provide some examples of how IT may be regarded in this organization.

2. Chip Gliedman of Forrester Research breaks down IT risks into implementation and impact considerations. Why do you think these are so difficult to manage? What makes IT investments different from investments in other areas of a company?

3. Do you agree with the notion that IT investments can be treated in the same manner as financial investments, and similarly quantified by putting a dollar value to them? Why or why not? Would your answer change depending on the type of IT investment under consideration?

▼ REAL WORLD ACTIVITIES

1. Do you agree with the approach and metrics employed by Northwestern Mutual to value their IT investments? Can you think of alternative ways, and how those might stack up against those discussed in the case? Break into small groups with your classmates to discuss the pros and cons of alternative approaches to valuing the impacts of IT in a company.

2. Go online and search for examples of IT projects that have been successful, and those that have failed. Make a list of the different factors that seem to influence the outcome of these implementations. Can you group them into the categories discussed in the case? Which seem to be the most important? Prepare a presentation to share your findings.

CASE 2

For Companies Both Big and Small: Running a Business on Smartphones

In early 2006, San-Antonio, Texas–based CPS Energy, the nation's largest municipally owned energy provider, was by all accounts riding the road to riches. The company had the highest bond ratings of any such utility provider. Its workforce and customer base in general expressed satisfaction. And most importantly, it was profitable. In other words, there were no external signs that the company was about to launch a technology program that would redefine the way it did business and reshape its workforce of roughly 4,000.

There weren't external signs, but for those in the know, including Christopher Barron, CPS Energy's vice president and chief information officer, it couldn't have been more clear that a change was imminent—and that the future of the company might depend on it. "We had a much larger workforce than a business our size maybe should have," Barron says.

Barron looked at other companies with large mobile workforces like its own, companies like UPS and FedEx, and saw a huge disparity in the way his business was operating. For instance, specific CPS workers had little or no access to IT systems and resources while away from the office or warehouse. They were often required to visit work sites or customer locations to diagnose issues or suggest fixes before reporting back to the appropriate departments or parties, which would then initiate the next step of the resolution process. That could mean dispatching additional workers, and the whole ordeal could take days.

"If we kept with the amount of manual labor that it took for us to accomplish that work, we would not be in the position to be competitive in the future," Barron says. From this realization, the company's Magellan Program was born.

Barron and his colleagues envisioned the Magellan Program as a way to better mobilize and connect its traditionally siloed workforce to the people and systems they needed to do their jobs. The goals of the program: Extend CPS's networking infrastructure, build its own secure Wi-Fi networks in offices and warehouses, and deploy smartphones and custom mobile applications to all CPS staffers who didn't currently have a laptop or other mobile device. For Barron, the first and most significant challenge in deploying smartphones to such a large user base was getting executive buy-in. "One of our biggest headaches has been, and continues to be, the perception that the technology brings little to the table other than e-mail, and it costs a lot," Barron says.

"For a CIO to try to eliminate all the resistance from a senior executive might take forever," Barron says. "So rather than try to get to the execs and mollify all their fears about cost, usage and safety, we've gone to specific groups, engineers, line workers, office workers, and because it's so cheap we've been able to give the devices out on 'experimental basis.' There's so much value in these handheld devices and two or three applications that they prove themselves," he says. "You just have to get them into the hands of the people that actually need to use them in order to demonstrate that."

Three innovative ways CPS staffers employ their smartphones are as digital cameras at work sites, as GPS tracking mechanisms, and as emergency notification receivers. In the past, CPS might have had to dispatch a small group of "generalist" workers to a service call to make sure the correct person was there. Today, a single worker can visit a site, take a photo of a damaged piece of equipment or infrastructure, and then send it back to headquarters or the office. Then an expert diagnoses the issue and sends along instructions to fix the problem or dispatches the appropriate worker—who's available immediately via voice, e-mail, and SMS text via smartphone.

"The Magellan Program, through the use of smartphones and other technology, has or will empower all employees, no matter what work they perform, to become part of the greater company's 'thought network'," Barron says. "Each person is now like a node in our network." The company is also seeing significant gains in supply chain efficiency related to Magellan and the smartphone deployment, he says. For instance, smartphones help speed up the purchase order process, because in the past a specific person or group of people needed to be onsite to approve orders. Now the approvers can be practically anywhere with cellular coverage. The company's supply chain buyers can also visit warehouses to work with the people who actually order parts, leading to faster order times, and more proactive supply chain management overall. In just one year, the time it takes to close purchasing and procurement deals decreased by more than 65 percent. Also, inventory levels were reduced by more than $8 million dollars since the Magellan Program began.

Additionally, both employee and customer satisfaction levels are up, Barron notes, due to the fact that staffers now have more access to corporate systems and information and feel closer to the business. Because CPS can now resolve more customer issues with fewer processes, they've reduced

79

the time it takes to complete most service calls, leading to happier customers. In fact, the company received the highest score in J.D. Power and Associates 2007 Gas Utility Residential Customer Satisfaction Survey.

The technology, however, is no longer the exclusive purview of large companies with significant IT budgets, at least not anymore. Lloyd's Construction in Eagan, Minnesota, might not seem as though it needs flashy phone software. The $9-million-a-year demolition and carting company has been run by the same family for the past 24 years. Lloyd's takes down commercial and residential buildings, then hauls them away. What could be more simple?

That is, if wrangling 100 employees, 30 trucks, and more than 400 dumpsters can be called simple. Coordinating those moving parts is crucial to growing the business—and to saving the sanity of Stephanie Lloyd, 41, who has run the company for the past four years. Until recently, Lloyd's used a hodge-podge of spreadsheets, paper ledgers, and accounting software on company PCs to keep track of its workers and equipment. To make matters worse, the company used radios to coordinate with its workers on the job, and the more cell phone towers that came online in Minnesota, the worse Lloyd's radio reception got. It was time, the Lloyds decided, to drag their company into the 21st-century world of smartphones.

Lloyd's considered a half-dozen mobile-productivity software suites before settling on eTrace, which happened to come from a company called GearWorks based just across town. Not only was GearWorks local, but its software worked on Sprint Nextel's i560 and i850 phones, which are aimed at the construction industry. Lloyd's had already started buying these push-to-talk phones to wean workers from their dying radios. Immediately, there were troubles with technophobic staff. Employees had to be guided up a steep learning curve in order to master even basic features on their new phones. For 18 months the two systems ran side by side: eTrace as it was phased in, and the old paper-and-pencil system as it was phased out. Accounting inconsistencies quickly crept in.

And eTrace gave rise to a delicate labor problem. The software featured integrated mapping and travel data that showed the real-time locations of all company assets. To their chagrin, the Lloyds discovered that those assets were spending too much time parked outside the same lunch spots—ones that were not on prescribed routes. Lloyd was sympathetic to workers' needs for breaks—"we've all worked demolition here," she says—but quickly clamped down on unauthorized ones.

GearWorks' CEO says the challenges Lloyd's faced are to be expected. "All these products operate under the ominous pendulum of challenge and opportunity," says Todd Krautkremer, 47. "But our software does a good job of letting the customer control that rate of change in the business."

Once the deployment dust had settled, the savings became clear. The company employs 12 drivers, 22 foremen, and seven office workers who use 41 phones running eTrace. The company buys an unlimited data package for each phone, which totals about $4,000 a month. Add other networking charges, and Lloyd's spends about $50,000 a year for a complete business, accounting, and communications solution. Before eTrace, the company paid an accountant 40 hours a week to do the books. Now that person comes in one day a week for six hours, saving roughly $1,000 a week.

Data entry and job logging by the dispatcher and foremen, Lloyd says, is roughly 1½ times faster than paper and radio. More efficient routing has cut fuel costs by about 30 percent. And employees have stopped making unauthorized stops. Lloyd estimates a net improvement in performance of 10 percent to 12 percent, or roughly $1 million for 2007—not a bad return on $50,000.

"It really does work," she says.

SOURCE: Jonathan Blum, "Running an Entire Business from Smart-phones," *FORTUNE Small Business*, March 12, 2008; and Al Sacco, "How Smartphones Help CPS Energy Innovate and Boost the Bottom Line," *CIO Magazine*, July 11, 2008.

▼ CASE STUDY QUESTIONS

1. In which ways do smartphones help these companies be more profitable? To what extent are improvements in performance coming from revenue increases or cost reductions? Provide several examples from the case.
2. The companies described in the case encountered a fair amount of resistance from employees when introducing smartphone technologies. Why do you think this happened? What could companies do to improve the reception of these initiatives? Develop two alternative propositions.
3. CPS Energy and Lloyd's Construction used smartphones to make existing processes more efficient. How could they have used the technology to create new products and services for their customers? Include at least one recommendation for each organization.

▼ REAL WORLD ACTIVITIES

1. In addition to the companies featured in the case, others like FedEx and UPS, which have large mobile workforces, heavily use mobile communication technologies. What other companies could benefit from these innovations? Go online and research uses of smartphones in industries different from the ones reviewed here. Prepare a report to share your findings.
2. Use the Internet to research the latest technological developments in smartphones, and imagine how those could be used by companies to deliver value to customers and shareholders.

INFORMATION TECHNOLOGIES

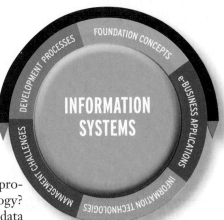

What challenges do information system technologies pose for business professionals? What basic knowledge should you possess about information technology? The four chapters of this module give you an overview of the hardware, software, data resource management, and telecommunications network technologies used in information systems and their implications for business managers and professionals.

- **Chapter 3: Computer Hardware** reviews history, trends, and developments in computer technologies and systems; basic computer hardware concepts; and the major types of technologies used in peripheral devices for computer input, output, and storage.

- **Chapter 4: Computer Software** reviews the basic features and trends in the major types of application software and system software used to support both enterprise and end-user computing.

- **Chapter 5: Data Resource Management** emphasizes management of the data resources of computer-using organizations. This chapter reviews key database management concepts and applications in business information systems.

- **Chapter 6: Telecommunications and Networks** presents an overview of the Internet and other telecommunication networks, business applications, and trends, and reviews technical telecommunications alternatives.

Chapter 3

COMPUTER HARDWARE

INFORMATION
TECHNOLOGIES

CHAPTER HIGHLIGHTS

Computer Systems: End User and Enterprise Computing

Introduction

A Brief History of Computer Hardware

REAL WORLD CHALLENGE: Budway Enterprises Inc.—Looking for a Low-Cost, High-Return Alternative to Paper

Types of Computer Systems

Microcomputer Systems

Midrange, Mainframe, and Supercomputer Systems

Technical Note: The Computer System Concept

Moore's Law: Where Do We Go from Here?

Computer Peripherals: Input, Output, and Storage Technologies

Peripherals

Input Technologies

Output Technologies

Storage Trade-Offs

Semiconductor Memory

Magnetic Disks

Magnetic Tape

Optical Disks

Radio Frequency Identification

Predictions for the Future

REAL WORLD SOLUTION: Budway Enterprises Inc.— Custom Technology with Standard Components

REAL WORLD CASE: AstraZeneca, UnitedHealth, and Others: IT-Asset Management—Do You Know What You've Got?

REAL WORLD CASE: IT in Health Care: Voice Recognition Tools Make Rounds at Hospitals

LEARNING OBJECTIVES

3-1 Understand the history and evolution of computer hardware.

3-2 Identify the major types and uses of micro-computer, midrange, and mainframe computer systems.

3-3 Outline the major technologies and uses of computer peripherals for input, output, and storage.

3-4 Identify and give examples of the components and functions of a computer system.

3-5 Identify the computer systems and peripherals you would acquire or recommend for a business of your choice, and explain the reasons for your selections.

Computer Systems: End User and Enterprise Computing

INTRODUCTION

All computers are systems of input, processing, output, storage, and control components. In this section, we discuss the history, trends, applications, and some basic concepts of the many types of computer systems in use today. In the next section, we will cover the changing technologies for input, output, and storage that are provided by the peripheral devices that are part of modern computer systems.

Read the Real World Challenge regarding Budway Enterprises Inc. We can learn a lot about the challenges faced by small business from this case. See Figure 3.1.

A BRIEF HISTORY OF COMPUTER HARDWARE
LO 3-1

Today we are witnessing rapid technological changes on a broad scale. However, many centuries elapsed before technology was sufficiently advanced to develop computers. Without computers, many technological achievements of the past would not have been possible. To fully appreciate their contribution, we must understand their history and evolution. Although a thorough discussion of computing history is beyond the scope of this text, a brief consideration of the development of the computer is possible. Let's look quickly into the development of computers.

At the dawn of the human concept of numbers, humans used their fingers and toes to perform basic mathematical activities. Then our ancestors realized that by using some objects to represent digits, they could perform computations beyond the limited scope of their own fingers and toes. Can't you just see in your mind a cave full of cavemen performing some group accounting function using their fingers, toes, sticks, and rocks? It creates a comical, yet accurate, picture.

Shells, chicken bones, or any number of objects could have been used, but the fact that the word *calculate* is derived from *calculus*, the Latin word for "small stone," suggests that pebbles or beads were arranged to form the familiar abacus, arguably the first human-made computing device. By manipulating the beads, it was possible with some skill and practice to make rapid calculations.

Blaise Pascal, a French mathematician, invented what is believed to be the first mechanical adding machine in 1642. The machine partially adopted the principles of the abacus but did away with the use of the hand to move the beads or counters. Instead, Pascal used wheels to move counters. The principle of Pascal's machine is still being used today, such as in the mechanical counters of tape recorders and odometers. In 1674, Gottfried Wilhelm von Leibniz improved Pascal's machine so that the machine could divide and multiply as easily as it could add and subtract.

When the age of industrialization spread throughout Europe, machines became fixtures in agricultural and production sites. An invention that made profound changes in the history of industrialization, as well as in the history of computing, was the mechanical loom, invented by a Frenchman named Joseph Jacquard. With the use of cards punched with holes, it was possible for the Jacquard loom to weave fabrics in a variety of patterns. Jacquard's loom was controlled by a program encoded into the punched cards. The operator created the program once and was able to duplicate it many times over with consistency and accuracy.

The idea of using punched cards to store a predetermined pattern to be woven by the loom clicked in the mind of Charles Babbage, an English mathematician who lived in the 19th century. He foresaw a machine that could perform all mathematical calculations, store values in its memory, and perform logical comparisons among values. He called it the *Analytical Engine*. Babbage's analytical engine, however, was never built. It lacked one thing: electronics. Herman Hollerith eventually

Budway Enterprises Inc.– Looking for a Low-Cost, High-Return Alternative to Paper

Budway Enterprises Inc. is a family-owned company originally founded in 1948 as a same-day pickup and delivery service in the downtown Los Angeles area. It is still a family business, and the current president is the grandson of the founder. Ever since the late 1940s, however, Budway's operations have changed dramatically. In 1990 the company expanded into the use of flatbed trailers to carry full loads of steel coil for USS/POSCO Industries, a steel mill located in northern California. The significant efficiencies and savings that accrued to both partners led Budway to build a large, state-of-the-art railroad transloading

facility in Fontana, California, where a large number of railroad cars can be received and unloaded simultaneously. With 120,000 square feet of warehouse and facilities and two 30-ton overhead cranes, Budway has transformed itself into the nation's largest provider of transloading services for the Burlington Northern Santa Fe (BNSF) Railway, handling more than 6,000 railroad cars per year.

These services include the handling, storage, and transportation of products largely for the steel industry. Each of these products has been created by the manufacturing mills to the unique specifications of their final customers; while seemingly identical, two coils of steel may differ in width, gauge, length, resistance to heat, and so forth. As a result, it is imperative that Budway uniquely identifies and tracks each unit or bundle of units from receipt until its later delivery to its final destination. This is an industry where mistakes happen often, and the incorrect items are delivered to the wrong destination because it is sometimes difficult to tell them apart. Budway, however, is becoming more than a warehouse and ship operation; rather, it is turning into the nation's largest provider of inventory management and distribution services for products moving into southern California by truck, rail, or container ship.

As these products move from one form of transportation to another, it is critical to be able to pinpoint their location accurately at all times. The individual value of each item is quite high, and lost or wrongly delivered items cost Budway dearly, not only in the form of claims or lost time, but in reputation as well. A customer that received the wrong product is a customer that is now not able to keep its own manufacturing lines going—a rather unhappy customer. As the business continued to grow, executives at Budway realized that traditional paper documentation was not going to be able to provide the kind of real-time information on product location that was necessary to take their business to the next level. A lot of things can happen to paper: It gets misplaced, lost, not filled out properly, or not filled out at all. A more secure, timely, and accessible solution was needed—one based on information technology.

Budway management decided to launch a project with the ultimate goal of providing their customers with peace of mind at all times about their products. The project was

FIGURE 3.1

Doing away with paper documents may hold the key to growth and new products and services for Budway Enterprises Inc.
SOURCE: Image Source/Getty Images.

aimed, however, at providing much more than timely access to delivery information and a reduction in the amount of clerical work required to process it—both of which are important. The goal was to go beyond automating their current business processes into faster and more efficient completion, and rather to provide access to new data and services that are just not possible in the world of paper. After much analysis and consultation with clients, four key goals were identified for the project.

First, the new system should eliminate all kinds of paper-based documentation currently being used in the business. Although management realized this would take some time for their clients to get used to—after all, paper was the most widely used medium in the industry—it believed that completely eliminating paper would provide many benefits in the long term, not the least of which were a significant reduction in the cost of producing, organizing, and storing all those documents. Second, the new process should be able to capture proof-of-delivery (POD) signatures electronically as products were delivered to their final recipients. Third, for all items that were under the custody of Budway, real-time tracking data of their location should be available, allowing them to pinpoint both the exact location and status of each item in the warehouse, loading docks, or trucks. Finally, it should be easy for customers to confirm delivery through the Internet, both internally and remotely.

Given the major role that technology was going to play in this project, management undertook a comprehensive search of some of the options then available in the market, and found the results somewhat discouraging. While many of the necessary pieces were out there, none seemed to be exactly what Budway was looking for. For example, the wireless hand-held devices that the large small-package freight companies (e.g., UPS, FedEx, DHL) used had the ability to capture electronic signatures, but none of the hardware vendors provided any software that would suit the different business environment in which Budway operates. They were also costly—about $3,500 each for small orders. For a small, family-owned business where all software was written internally by a member of management, large up-front capital outlays were just not possible. This extensive search, however, helped management identify the four key characteristics that any technology should have if it was to help move the project forward:

1. Capture proof-of-delivery (POD) signatures electronically and in real time; no loads should be released to the recipients without accepted delivery first.

2. GPS capabilities are a must. Accurate and real-time tracking of the location of each individual item or bundle over a large geographical area (i.e., southern California) cannot be accomplished otherwise.

3. Employees must be able to access and update work orders while deliveries are in progress and obtain reports on their status. These must be able to integrate with the in-house software that already exists in the company.

4. Any chosen solution must be cost-effective. This applies both to the initial investment and to ongoing service, maintenance, and modifications. As noted above, Budway does not have the same financial resources as some of the larger companies in the industry. Furthermore, any implementation expenses must be offset by savings because rates are competitive, and increasing them would not be feasible.

To summarize, Budway Enterprises Inc. is a growing, family-owned business that is the leader in the unloading, storage, and delivery of specialty metal products in southern California. In order to expand its competitive position in this industry, the company has decided to undertake a major renovation of its current business processes, today largely based on paper documents and forms that constrain the timeliness and availability of data throughout the company and with its customers. Although no out-of-the-box solution appears to exist, management has identified the key characteristics of the project that any solution must be able to satisfy. Financial aspects of the chosen solution are also a consideration, as it must imply a limited initial investment and not negatively affect the rates Budway charges.

SOURCE: "Low-Cost GPS Tracking and Digital PODs Using Smartphones," *Computerworld Honors Program Case Study,* http://www.cwhonors.org/viewCaseStudy2008.asp?NominationID=2056, accessed May 14, 2011, and "Productivity Picks Up for Budway by Use of Tracking and Resource Management Software," *Agilis Systems Case Study.*

▼ QUESTIONS TO CONSIDER

1. In this scenario, management was able to outline some specific characteristics that the resulting technology must have. Is this a good idea? On the one hand, it provides clear criteria against which proposals can be evaluated; on the other hand, it limits solutions to what management has thought of, which is likely derived from what exists today, not what might exist in the future. How do you balance these two aspects of the problem?

2. Beyond obvious efficiencies, is management taking a leap of faith when it assumes that going digital will open the door to new products and services, or is it a foregone conclusion? Can you provide some examples of what would be possible with digital PODs that would not be possible with paper-based ones?

3. What are some of the challenges Budway Enterprises faces as it seeks to modernize its business processes? Which are technical in nature, and which are business-related? How do the challenges you identified generalize to other companies?

adapted Jacquard's concept of the punched card to record census data in the late 1880s. Census data were translated into a series of holes in a punched card to represent the digits and the letters of the alphabet. The card was then passed through a machine with a series of electrical contacts that were either turned off or on, depending on the existence of holes in the punched cards. These different combinations of off/on situations were recorded by the machine and represented a way of tabulating the result of the census. Hollerith's machine was highly successful; it cut the time it took to tabulate the result of the census by two-thirds, and it made money for the company that manufactured it. In 1911, this company merged with its competitor to form International Business Machines. You probably know it better as IBM.

The ENIAC (Electronic Numerical Integrator and Computer) was the first electronic digital computer. It was completed in 1946 at the Moore School of Electrical Engineering of the University of Pennsylvania. With no moving parts, ENIAC was programmable and had the capability to store problem calculations using vacuum tubes (about 18,000).

A computer that uses vacuum tube technology is called a first-generation computer. The ENIAC could add in 0.2 of a millisecond, or about 5,000 computations per second. The principal drawback of ENIAC was its size and processing ability. It occupied more than 1,500 square feet of floor space and could process only one program or problem at a time. As an aside, the power requirements for ENIAC were so great that adjacent common-area lighting dimmed during the power-up and calculation cycles. Figure 3.2 shows the ENIAC complex.

In the 1950s, Remington Rand manufactured the UNIVAC I (Universal Automatic Calculator). It could calculate at the rate of 10,000 additions per second. In 1957, IBM developed the IBM 704, which could perform 100,000 calculations per second.

In the late 1950s, transistors were invented and quickly replaced the thousands of vacuum tubes used in electronic computers. A transistor-based computer could perform 200,000–250,000 calculations per second. The transistorized computer represents the second generation of computer. It was not until the mid-1960s that the third generation of computers came into being. These were characterized by solid-state technology and integrated circuitry, coupled with extreme miniaturization.

No history of electronic computing would be complete without acknowledging Jack Kilby. Kilby was a Nobel Prize laureate in physics in 2000 for his invention of the integrated circuit in 1958 while working at Texas Instruments (TI). He is also the inventor of the handheld calculator and thermal printer. Without his work that generated

FIGURE 3.2

ENIAC was the first digital computer. It is easy to see how far we have come in the evolution of computers.

SOURCE: Photo courtesy of United States Army.

a patent for a "Solid Circuit made of Germanium," our worlds, and most certainly our computers, would be much different and less productive than we enjoy today.

In 1971, the fourth generation of computers was characterized by further miniaturization of circuits, increased multiprogramming, and virtual storage memory. In the 1980s, the fifth generation of computers operated at speeds of 3–5 million calculations per second (for small-scale computers) and 10–15 million instructions per second (for large-scale computers).

The age of microcomputers began in 1975 when a company called MITS introduced the ALTAIR 8800. The computer was programmed by flicking switches on the front. It came as a kit and had to be soldered together. It had no software programs, but it was a personal computer available to the consumer for a few thousand dollars when most computer companies were charging tens of thousands of dollars. In 1977 both Commodore and Radio Shack announced that they were going to make personal computers. They did, and trotting along right beside them were Steve Jobs and Steve Wozniak, who invented their computer in a garage while in college. Mass production of the Apple began in 1979, and by the end of 1981, it was the fastest selling of all the personal computers. In August 1982 the IBM PC was born, and many would argue that the world changed forever as a result.

Following the introduction of the personal computer in the early 1980s, we used our knowledge of computer networks gained in the early days of computing and combined it with new and innovative technologies to create massive networks of people, computers, and data on which anyone can find almost anything: the Internet. Today we continue to see amazing advancements in computing technologies.

Okay, it's time to slow down a bit and begin our discussion of today's computer hardware.

Today's computer systems come in a variety of sizes, shapes, and computing capabilities. Rapid hardware and software developments and changing end-user needs continue to drive the emergence of new models of computers, from the smallest handheld personal digital assistant/cell phone combinations to the largest multiple-CPU mainframes for enterprises. See Figure 3.3.

TYPES OF COMPUTER SYSTEMS
LO 3-2

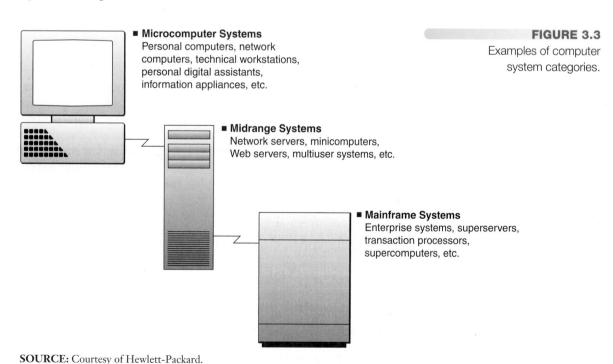

FIGURE 3.3
Examples of computer system categories.

■ **Microcomputer Systems**
Personal computers, network computers, technical workstations, personal digital assistants, information appliances, etc.

■ **Midrange Systems**
Network servers, minicomputers, Web servers, multiuser systems, etc.

■ **Mainframe Systems**
Enterprise systems, superservers, transaction processors, supercomputers, etc.

SOURCE: Courtesy of Hewlett-Packard.

Categories such as *mainframe, midrange,* and *microcomputer* systems are still used to help us express the relative processing power and number of end users that can be supported by different types of computers. These are not precise classifications, and they do overlap each other. Thus, other names are commonly given to highlight the major uses of particular types of computers. Examples include personal computers, network servers, network computers, and technical workstations. In most cases, you will work with either a desktop, laptop, or handheld personal computer in your daily life and business dealings.

In addition, experts continue to predict the merging or disappearance of several computer categories. They feel, for example, that many midrange and mainframe systems have been made obsolete by the power and versatility of networks composed of microcomputers and servers. Other industry experts have predicted that the emergence of network computers and *information appliances* for applications on the Internet and corporate intranets will replace many personal computers, especially in large organizations and in the home computer market. Still others suggest that the concept of *nanocomputers* (computing devices that are smaller than micro) will eventually pervade our entire understanding of personal computing. Only time will tell whether such predictions will equal the expectations of industry forecasters.

MICROCOMPUTER SYSTEMS

The entire center of gravity in computing has shifted. For millions of consumers and business users, the main function of desktop PCs is as a window to the Internet. Computers are now communications devices, and consumers want them to be as cheap as possible.

Microcomputers are the most important category of computer systems for both businesspeople and consumers. Although usually called a *personal computer,* or PC, a microcomputer is much more than a small computer for use by an individual as a communication device. The computing power of microcomputers now exceeds that of the mainframes of previous computer generations, at a fraction of their cost. Thus, they have become powerful networked *professional workstations* for business professionals.

Consider the computing power on the *Apollo 11* spacecraft. Most certainly, landing men on the moon and returning them safely to earth was an extraordinary feat. The computer that assisted them in everything from navigation to systems monitoring was equally extraordinary. *Apollo 11* had a 2.048 MHz CPU that was built by MIT. Today's standards can be measured in the 4 GHz in many home PCs (MHz is 1 million computing cycles per second and GHz is 1 billion computing cycles per second). Further, the *Apollo 11* computer weighed 70 pounds versus today's powerful laptops weighing in as little as 1 pound. This is progress, for sure.

Microcomputers come in a variety of sizes and shapes for a variety of purposes, as Figure 3.4 illustrates. For example, PCs are available as handheld, notebook, laptop, tablet, portable, desktop, and floor-standing models. Or, based on their use, they include home, personal, professional, workstation, and multiuser systems. Most microcomputers are *desktops* designed to fit on an office desk or laptops for those who want a small, portable PC. Figure 3.5 offers advice on some of the key features you should consider when acquiring a high-end professional workstation, multimedia PC, or beginner's system. This breakdown should give you some idea of the range of features available in today's microcomputers.

Some microcomputers are powerful **workstation computers** (technical workstations) that support applications with heavy mathematical computing and graphics display demands, such as computer-aided design (CAD) in engineering or investment and portfolio analysis in the securities industry. Other microcomputers are used as **network servers.** These are usually more powerful microcomputers that coordinate telecommunications and resource sharing in small local area networks (LANs) and in Internet and intranet Web sites.

a. A notebook microcomputer.
SOURCE: © 2011 Lenovo. All rights reserved.

b. The microcomputer as a professional workstation.
SOURCE: Corbis.

FIGURE 3.4

Examples of microcomputer systems:

c. The microcomputer as a technical workstation.
SOURCE: Courtesy of Hewlett-Packard.

Business Pro	Multimedia Heavy or Gamer	Newcomer
To track products, customers, and firm performance, more than just a fast machine is necessary:	Media pros and dedicated gamers will want at least a Mac G4 or a 2–3 GHz Intel dual-core chip, and	Save some money with a Celeron processor in the 2–3 GHz range while looking for
• 3–4 GHz dual-core processor • 4–8 GB RAM • 500 GB+ hard drive • Up to 32-inch flat-panel display • CD-RW/DVD+RW • Network interface card • Color laser printer	• 4–8 GB RAM • 1 TB+ hard drive • 27-inch or better flat-panel display • 32× or better DVD+RW • Video cards (as fast and as powerful as budget permits) • Sound cards • Laser printer (color or B&W)	• 2 GB RAM • 120–160 GB hard drive • 15- to 17-inch flat-panel or wide-screen • CD-RW/DVD • USB port • Inkjet printer

FIGURE 3.5

Examples of recommended features for the three types of PC users. Note: www.dell.com and www.gateway.com are good sources for the latest PC features available.

Corporate PC Criteria

What do you look for in a new PC system? A big, bright screen? Zippy new processor? Capacious hard drive? Acres of RAM? Sorry, none of these is a top concern for corporate PC buyers. Numerous studies have shown that the price of a new computer is only a small part of the total cost of ownership (TCO). Support, maintenance, and other intangibles contribute far more heavily to the sum. Let's take a look at four top criteria.

Solid Performance at a Reasonable Price. Corporate buyers know that their users probably aren't mapping the human genome or plotting trajectories to Saturn. They're doing word processing, order entry, sales contact management, and other essential business tasks. They need a solid, competent machine at a reasonable price, not the latest whizbang.

Many organizations are adopting a laptop, rather than desktop, strategy. Using this approach, the employee uses his or her laptop while in the office and out in the field. With the proliferation of wireless Internet access, this strategy allows employees to take the desktop with them wherever they may be—at their desk, in a conference room, at a meeting off-site, or in a hotel room in another country.

One outcome of this strategy is the development and acquisition of more powerful laptops with larger and higher-quality screens. This demand presents a challenge to laptop manufacturers to provide higher quality while continuing to make the laptop lightweight and portable.

Operating System Ready. A change in the operating system of a computer is the most disruptive upgrade an enterprise has to face. That's why many corporate buyers want their machines to be able to handle current operating systems and anticipate new ones. Although most organizations have adopted Windows XP or Vista, some enterprises still use operating systems of an earlier vintage. Ultimately, they must be able to make the transition to Windows 7 (the newest OS from Microsoft) and even to OS versions expected three to five years from now. Primarily, that demand means deciding what hard disk space and RAM will be sufficient.

Connectivity. Networked machines are a given in corporate life, and Internet-ready machines are becoming a given. Buyers need machines equipped with reliable wireless capabilities. With fewer cables to worry about, wireless networks, especially when combined with laptop PCs, contribute to the flexibility of the workplace and the simplicity of PC deployment. Many organizations are planning for Internet-based applications and need machines ready to make fast, reliable, and secure connections.

Security-Equipped. Most of the data that is processed by networked workstations in a modern corporate environment can be considered proprietary, if not mission-critical. A major criterion for corporate purchase is the degree to which the device can accept or conform to the myriad of security measures in use in that organization. Can it accept a USB dongle, smartcard reader, biometric access device, and so forth? We will cover this aspect in greater detail in Chapter 13.

Computer Terminals

Computer terminals, essentially any device that allows access to a computer, are undergoing a major conversion to networked computer devices. Also included are *network terminals,* which may be *Windows terminals* that depend on network servers for Windows software, processing power, and storage, or *Internet terminals,* which depend on Internet or intranet Web site servers for their operating systems and application software.

Intelligent terminals take many forms and can perform data entry and some information processing tasks independently. These tasks include the widespread use of transaction terminals in banks, retail stores, factories, and other work sites. Examples are automated teller machines (ATMs), factory production recorders, airport check-in kiosks, and retail point-of-sale (POS) terminals. These intelligent terminals use keypads, touch screens, bar code scanners, and other input methods to capture data and interact with end users during a transaction, while relying on servers or other computers in the network for further transaction processing.

Network Computers

Network computers (NCs) are a microcomputer category designed primarily for use with the Internet and corporate intranets by clerical workers, operational employees, and knowledge workers with specialized or limited computing applications. These NCs are low-cost, sealed microcomputers with no or minimal disk storage that are linked to the network. Users of NCs depend primarily on network servers for their operating system and Web browser, application software, and data access and storage.

One of the main attractions of network computers is their lower TCO (total cost of ownership), that is, the total of all costs associated with purchasing, installing, operating, and maintaining a computer. Purchase upgrades, maintenance, and support cost much less than for full-featured PCs. Other benefits to business include the ease of software distribution and licensing, computing platform standardization, reduced end-user support requirements, and improved manageability through centralized management and enterprisewide control of computer network resources.

Information Appliances

PCs aren't the only option: A host of smart gadgets and information appliances—from cellular phones and pagers to handheld PCs and Web-based game machines—promise Internet access and the ability to perform basic computational chores.

Handheld microcomputer devices known as personal digital assistants (PDAs) are some of the most popular devices in the ***information appliance*** category. Web-enabled PDAs use touch screens, pen-based handwriting recognition, or keypads so that mobile workers can send and receive e-mail, access the Web, and exchange information such as appointments, to-do lists, and sales contacts with their desktop PCs or Web servers.

Now a mainstay of PDA technology is the RIM BlackBerry, a small, pager-sized device that can perform all of the common PDA functions, plus act as a fully functional mobile telephone. What sets this device apart from other wireless PDA solutions is that it is always on and connected. A BlackBerry user doesn't need to retrieve e-mail; the e-mail finds the BlackBerry user. Because of this functionality, there is no need to dial in or initiate a connection. The BlackBerry doesn't even have a visible antenna. When a user wishes to send or reply to an e-mail, the small keyboard on the device allows text entry. Just like a mobile telephone, the BlackBerry is designed to remain on and continuously connected to the wireless network, allowing near real-time transfer of e-mail. Furthermore, because the BlackBerry uses the same network as most mobile telephone services, the unit can be used anywhere that a mobile phone can be used.

Two relatively new entrants to this field (although gaining favor in leaps and bounds) are the Apple iPhone and iPad (Figure 3.6). The iPhone essentially combines three products—a revolutionary mobile phone, a wide-screen iPod music and video player with touch controls, and a breakthrough Internet communications device with desktop-class e-mail, Web browsing, maps, and searching—into one small and lightweight handheld device. The iPhone also introduces an entirely new user interface based on a large, multitouch display and pioneering new software, letting users control

FIGURE 3.6

The Apple iPad—a revolutionary player in the information appliance and PDA marketplace.

SOURCE: © The McGraw-Hill Companies.

everything with just their fingers. The iPad, essentially a large iPhone without calling capabilities (although my guess is that calling on an iPad is just around the corner), is becoming the standard for tablet-type Internet appliances.

The iPhone and iPad have truly ushered in an era of software power and sophistication never before seen in a mobile device, completely redefining what people can do on a mobile phone. We can expect to see even more sophisticated mobile PDA-type devices in the future as Moore's law continues to prevail and the marketplace continues to demand more functionality (see the discussion on Moore's law later in this chapter for more details on this concept).

Information appliances may also take the form of video game consoles and other devices that connect to your home television set. These devices enable people to surf the World Wide Web, send and receive e-mail, and watch television programs or play video games, all at the same time. Other information appliances include wireless PDAs and Internet-enabled cellular and PCS phones, as well as wired, telephone-based home appliances that can send and receive e-mail and access the Web.

MIDRANGE, MAINFRAME, AND SUPERCOMPUTER SYSTEMS

Midrange systems are primarily high-end network servers and other types of servers that can handle the large-scale processing of many business applications. Although not as powerful as mainframe computers, they are less costly to buy, operate, and maintain than mainframe systems and thus meet the computing needs of many organizations. See Figure 3.7.

> *Burgeoning data warehouses and related applications such as data mining and online analytical processing are forcing IT shops into higher and higher levels of server configurations. Similarly, Internet-based applications, such as Web servers and electronic commerce, are forcing IT managers to push the envelope of processing speed and storage capacity and other [business] applications, fueling the growth of high-end servers.*

Midrange systems have become popular as powerful network servers (computers used to coordinate communications and manage resource sharing in network settings) to help manage large Internet Web sites, corporate intranets and extranets, and other

FIGURE 3.7
Midrange computer systems can handle large-scale processing without the high cost or space considerations of a large-scale mainframe.

SOURCE: China Foto Press/Getty Images.

networks. Internet functions and other applications are popular high-end server applications, as are integrated enterprisewide manufacturing, distribution, and financial applications. Other applications, like data warehouse management, data mining, and online analytical processing (which we will discuss in Chapters 5 and 10), are contributing to the demand for high-end server systems.

Mainframe systems are large, fast, and powerful computer systems. For example, mainframes can process thousands of million instructions per second (MIPS). Mainframes can also have large primary storage capacities. Their main memory capacity can range from hundreds of gigabytes to many terabytes of primary storage. Mainframes have slimmed down drastically in the last few years, dramatically reducing their air-conditioning needs, electrical power consumption, and floor space requirements—and thus their acquisition and operating costs. Most of these improvements are the result of a move from cumbersome water-cooled mainframes to a newer air-cooled technology for mainframe systems. Thus, mainframe computers continue to handle the information processing needs of major corporations and government agencies with high transaction processing volumes or complex computational problems. See Figure 3.8.

The term *supercomputer* describes a category of extremely powerful computer systems specifically designed for scientific, engineering, and business applications requiring extremely high speeds for massive numeric computations. The market for supercomputers includes government research agencies, large universities, and major corporations. They use supercomputers for applications such as global weather forecasting, military defense systems, computational cosmology and astronomy, microprocessor research and design, and large-scale data mining. Purchase prices for large supercomputers are in the $5 million to $50 million range.

The ASCI White supercomputer system, shown in Figure 3.9, consists of three IBM RS/6000 SP systems: White, Frost, and Ice. White, the largest of these systems, is a 512-node, 16-way SMP supercomputer with a peak performance of 12.3 teraflops. Frost is a 68-node, 16-way SMP system; and Ice is a 28-node, 16-way SMP system. Supercomputers like these continue to advance the state of the art for the entire computer industry.

FIGURE 3.8

Mainframe computer systems are the heavy lifters of corporate computing.

SOURCE: © Royalty Free/Corbis.

FIGURE 3.9

The ASCI White supercomputer system at Lawrence Livermore National Laboratory in Livermore, California.

SOURCE: Image courtesy of Silicon Graphics, Inc.

Supercomputers Aid Satellite Launches

Satellite launches are a noisy affair, especially for the satellite atop the rocket. Vibration and noise, unless compensated, could render it useless before it reaches orbit, so researchers spend a lot of time on complex computer simulations that help them insulate the delicate craft. Now those simulations are about to get much more accurate, thanks to a new supercomputer that recently began work in Japan.

The Fujitsu FX1 computer was inaugurated in 2009 by the Japan Aerospace Explorations Agency (JAXA). It has 3,008 nodes, each of which has a 4-core Sparc64 VII microprocessor. The machine has 94 terabytes of memory and a theoretical peak performance of 120 teraflops. Running standard benchmarks, it achieved a peak performance of 110.6 teraflops, which ranks it not only the most powerful machine in Japan but also the most efficient supercomputer in the world. Its peak performance represents 91.2 percent of its theoretical performance and outranks the previous record holder, a machine at the Leibniz Rechenzentrum in Munich. Ranked below the German computer is another JAXA machine. "Performance is about 15 times higher than the system we had before," said Kozo Fujii, director of JAXA's Engineering Digital Innovation Center.

Two rows of computer racks make up the main system, and a third row alongside is a second, less powerful FX1 machine. In an adjoining room sits an NEC SX-9 vector computer for running specialized tasks and the storage that augments the entire system. All together, a petabyte of disk storage space and 10 petabytes of tape storage are connected to the system (a petabyte is a million gigabytes). And between the lot, there are many big, industrial air conditioners to keep the room cool and extract the heat generated by this mass of hardware.

JAXA intends to put it to work on simulations such as the acoustic noise experienced by a satellite at launch, said Fujii. "There is a wide band of frequencies and usually the peak frequencies are located between 60 and 100 Hertz and we can capture at that level of frequencies. But hopefully with the new computer we can capture frequencies of 150 or 200 Hz that are difficult for the current computer."

SOURCE: Martyn Williams, "World's Most Efficient Supercomputer Gets to Work," *CIO Magazine*, April 2, 2009.

The Next Wave of Computing

Interconnecting microprocessors to create minisupercomputers is a reality, as discussed above. The next wave is looking at harnessing the virtually infinite amount of unused computing power that exists in the myriad of desktops and laptops within the boundaries of a modern organization.

Distributed or *grid computing* in general is a special type of parallel computing that relies on complete computers (with onboard CPU, storage, power supply, network interface, and so forth) connected to a network (private, public, or the Internet) by a conventional network interface. This is in contrast to the traditional notion of a supercomputer, which has many processors connected together in a single machine. The grid could be formed by harnessing the unused CPU power in all of the desktops and laptops in a single division of a company (or in the entire company, for that matter).

The primary advantage of distributed computing is that each node can be purchased as commodity hardware; when combined, it can produce similar computing resources to a multiprocessor supercomputer, but at a significantly lower cost. This is due to the economies of scale of producing desktops and laptops, compared with the lower efficiency of designing and constructing a small number of custom supercomputers.

One feature of distributed grids is that they can be formed from computing resources belonging to multiple individuals or organizations (known as multiple administrative domains). This can facilitate commercial transactions or make it easier to assemble volunteer computing networks.

A disadvantage of this feature is that the computers that are actually performing the calculations might not be entirely trustworthy. The designers of the system must thus introduce measures to prevent malfunctions or malicious participants from producing false, misleading, or erroneous results, and from using the system as a platform for a hacking attempt. This often involves assigning work randomly to different nodes (presumably with different owners) and checking that at least two different nodes report the same answer for a given work unit. Discrepancies would identify malfunctioning and malicious nodes.

Another challenge is that because of the lack of central control over the hardware, there is no way to guarantee that computers will not drop out of the network at random times. Some nodes (like laptops or dial-up Internet customers) may also be available for computation but not for network communications for unpredictable periods. These variations can be accommodated by assigning large work units (thus reducing the need for continuous network connectivity) and reassigning work units when a given node fails to report its results as expected.

Despite these challenges, grid computing is becoming a popular method of getting the most out of the computing resources of an organization. Check out the Internet for grid projects ending with "@home". These projects allow you to contribute some of your free and idle computing resources to grid projects ranging from looking at the human genome to searching for extra-terrestrial life.

TECHNICAL NOTE: THE COMPUTER SYSTEM CONCEPT
LO 3-3

As a business professional, you do not need detailed technical knowledge of computers. However, you do need to understand some basic concepts about computer systems, which should help you be an informed and productive user of computer system resources.

A computer is more than a high-powered collection of electronic devices performing a variety of information processing chores. A computer is a *system*, an interrelated combination of components that performs the basic system functions of input, processing, output, storage, and control, thus providing end users with a powerful information processing tool. Understanding the computer as a **computer system** is vital to the effective use and management of computers. You should be able to visualize any computer this way, from the smallest microcomputer device to the largest computer networks whose components are interconnected by telecommunications network links throughout a building complex or geographic area.

Figure 3.10 illustrates that a computer is a system of hardware devices organized according to the following system functions:

- **Input.** The input devices of a computer system include computer keyboards, touch screens, pens, electronic mice, and optical scanners. They convert data into

FIGURE 3.10

The computer system concept. A computer is a system of hardware components and functions.

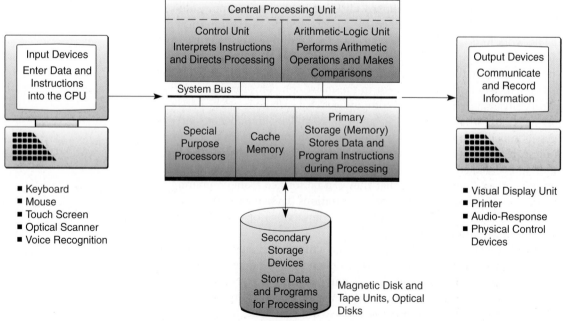

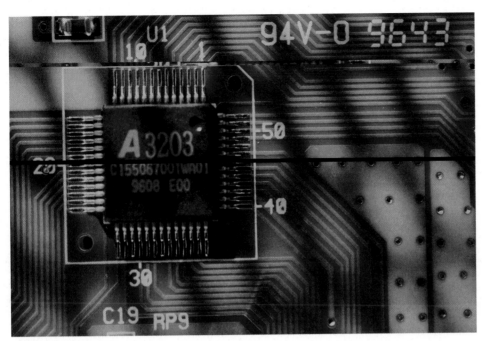

SOURCE: © Getty Images.

FIGURE 3.11

Mobile CPU chips, such as the one shown here, can reach speeds up to 3 Ghz to bring desktop-like power to a mobile setting.

electronic form for direct entry or through a telecommunications network into a computer system.

- **Processing.** The ***central processing unit*** (CPU) is the main processing component of a computer system. (In microcomputers, it is the main *microprocessor*. See Figure 3.11.) Conceptually, the circuitry of a CPU can be subdivided into two major subunits: the arithmetic-logic unit and the control unit. The electronic circuits (known as *registers*) of the *arithmetic-logic unit* perform the arithmetic and logic functions required to execute software instructions.

- **Output.** The output devices of a computer system include video display units, printers, and audio response units. They convert electronic information produced by the computer system into human-intelligible form for presentation to end users.

- **Storage.** The storage function of a computer system takes place in the storage circuits of the computer's ***primary storage unit,*** or *memory*, supported by ***secondary storage*** devices such as magnetic disk and optical disk drives. These devices store data and software instructions needed for processing. Computer processors may also include storage circuitry called *cache memory* for high-speed, temporary storage of instruction and data elements.

- **Control.** The control unit of a CPU is the control component of a computer system. Its registers and other circuits interpret software instructions and transmit directions that control the activities of the other components of the computer system.

We will explore the various hardware devices associated with each of these system functions later in this chapter.

Computer Processing Speeds

How fast are computer systems? Early computer ***processing speeds*** were measured in ***milliseconds*** (thousandths of a second) and ***microseconds*** (millionths of a second). Now computers operate in the ***nanosecond*** (billionth of a second) range, with ***picosecond*** (trillionth of a second) speed being attained by some computers. Such speeds seem almost incomprehensible. For example, an average person taking one step each nanosecond would circle the earth about 20 times in one second!

We have already mentioned the *teraflop* speeds of some supercomputers. However, most computers can now process program instructions at **million instructions per second (MIPS)** speeds. Another measure of processing speed is *megahertz* (MHz), or millions of **cycles per second,** and *gigahertz* (GHz), or billions of cycles per second. This rating is commonly called the *clock speed* of a microprocessor because it is used to rate microprocessors by the speed of their timing circuits or internal clock rather than by the number of specific instructions they can process in one second.

However, such ratings can be misleading indicators of the effective processing speed of microprocessors and their *throughput*, or ability to perform useful computation or data processing assignments during a given period. That's because processing speed depends on a variety of factors, including the size of circuitry paths, or *buses*, that interconnect microprocessor components; the capacity of instruction-processing *registers*; the use of high-speed cache memory; and the use of specialized microprocessors such as a math co-processor to do arithmetic calculations faster.

MOORE'S LAW: WHERE DO WE GO FROM HERE?

Can computers get any faster? Can we afford the computers of the future? Both of these questions can be answered by understanding **Moore's law.** Gordon Moore, cofounder of Intel Corporation, made his famous observation in 1965, just four years after the first integrated circuit was commercialized. The press called it "Moore's law," and the name has stuck. In its form, Moore observed an exponential growth (doubling every 18 to 24 months) in the number of transistors per integrated circuit and predicted that this trend would continue. Through a number of advances in technology, Moore's law, the doubling of transistors every couple of years, has been maintained and still holds true today. Figure 3.12 illustrates Moore's law as it relates to the evolution of computing power.

Despite our regular use of exponential growth when predicting the future, particularly the future of technology, humans are often not very good at realizing what exponential growth really looks like. To understand this issue better, let's take a moment to reflect on what Moore's law would mean to us if it applied beyond the number of transistors on a computer chip:

- According to Moore's law, the estimated number of transistors shipped in 2003 was 10^{18}. That's just about 100 times the estimated number of ants in the world.

- In 1978, a commercial flight between New York and Paris cost about $900 and took about seven hours. If Moore's law could be applied to commercial aviation, that same flight today would cost about a penny and would take less than one second.

FIGURE 3.12

Moore's law suggests that computer power will double every 18 to 24 months. So far, it has.

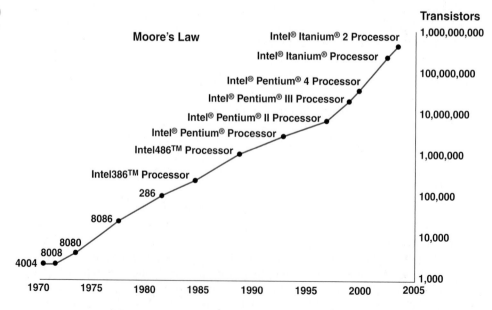

Over the years, Moore's law has been interpreted and reinterpreted such that it is commonly defined in a much broader sense than it was originally offered. Nonetheless, its application, and its relative accuracy, is useful in understanding where we have been and in predicting where we are going. For example, one common corollary of Moore's law is that the price of a given level of computing power will be cut in half about every 18 to 24 months. Moore didn't specifically predict this effect, but it has been shown to be rather consistently accurate as well. This trend is also true for the cost of storage (we will explore this further later in the chapter).

Although Moore's law was initially made in the form of an observation and prediction, the more widely it became accepted, the more it served as a goal for an entire industry. This caused both marketing and engineering departments of semiconductor manufacturers to focus enormous energy on the specified increase in processing power that it was presumed one or more of their competitors would soon actually attain. Expressed as "a doubling every 18 to 24 months," Moore's law suggests the phenomenal progress of technology in recent years. Expressed on a shorter timescale, however, Moore's law equates to an average performance improvement in the industry as a whole of more than 1 percent *per week*. For a manufacturer competing in the processor, storage, or memory markets, a new product that is expected to take three years to develop and is just two or three months late is 10–15 percent slower or larger than the directly competing products, thus rendering it harder to sell.

A sometimes misunderstood point is that exponentially improved hardware does not necessarily imply that the performance of the software is also exponentially improved. The productivity of software developers most assuredly does not increase exponentially with the improvement in hardware; by most measures, it has increased only slowly and fitfully over the decades. Software tends to get larger and more complicated over time, and Wirth's law (Niklaus Wirth, a Swiss computer scientist) even states humorously that "Software gets slower faster than hardware gets faster."

Recent computer industry studies predict that Moore's law will continue to hold for the next several chip generations (at least another decade). Depending on the doubling time used in the calculations, this progress could mean up to a 100-fold increase in transistor counts on a chip in the next 10 years. This rapid exponential improvement could put 100 GHz personal computers in every home and 20 GHz devices in every pocket. It seems reasonable to expect that sooner or later computers will meet or exceed any conceivable need for computation. Intel, however, suggests that it can sustain development in line with Moore's law for the next 20 years *without* any significant technological breakthroughs. Given the frequency of such breakthroughs in today's marketplace, it is conceivable that Moore's law can be sustained indefinitely. Regardless of what the end of Moore's law may look like, or when it may arrive, we are still moving along at a phenomenal rate of evolution, and the best may be yet to come.

Computer Peripherals: Input, Output, and Storage Technologies

The right peripherals can make all the difference in your computing experience. A top-quality monitor will be easier on your eyes—and may change the way you work. A scanner can edge you closer to that ever-elusive goal: the paperless office. Backup storage systems can offer bank-vault security against losing your work. CD and DVD drives have become essential for many applications. Thus, the right choice of peripherals can make a big difference. See Figure 3.13.

PERIPHERALS

Peripherals is the generic name given to all input, output, and secondary storage devices that are part of a computer system but are not part of the CPU. Peripherals depend on direct connections or telecommunications links to the central processing unit of a computer system. Thus, all peripherals are ***online*** devices; that is, they are separate from, but can be electronically connected to and controlled by, a CPU. (This is the opposite of ***off-line*** devices that are separate from and not under the control of the CPU.) The major types of peripherals and media that can be part of a computer system are discussed in this section. See Figure 3.14.

INPUT TECHNOLOGIES
LO 3-4
LO 3-5

Input technologies now provide a more natural user interface for computer users. You can enter data and commands directly and easily into a computer system through pointing devices like electronic mice and touch pads and with technologies like optical scanning, handwriting recognition, and voice recognition. These developments have made it unnecessary to record data on paper *source documents* (e.g., sales order forms) and then keyboard the data into a computer in an additional data-entry step. Further improvements in voice recognition and other technologies should enable an even more natural user interface in the future. Keyboards are still the most widely used devices for entering data and text into computer systems. However, ***pointing devices*** are a better alternative for issuing commands, making choices, and responding to prompts displayed on your video screen. They work with your operating system's ***graphical user interface*** (GUI), which presents you with icons, menus, windows, buttons, and bars for your selection. For example, pointing devices such as an electronic

FIGURE 3.13

Smart use of voice recognition technologies allows hospitals to improve the quality of care while keeping costs under control.

SOURCE: ERproductions Ltd./Getty Images.

FIGURE 3.14
Some advice about peripherals
for a business PC.

Peripherals Checklist

- **Monitors.** Bigger is better for computer screens. Consider a high-definition 19-inch or 21-inch flat screen CRT monitor, or LCD flat-panel display. That gives you much more room to display spreadsheets, Web pages, lines of text, open windows, and so on. An increasingly popular setup uses two monitors that allow multiple applications to be used simultaneously.

- **Printers.** Your choice is between laser printers and color inkjet printers. Lasers are better suited for high-volume business use. Moderately priced color inkjets provide high-quality images and are well suited for reproducing photographs; per-page costs are higher than for laser printers.

- **Scanners.** You'll have to decide between a compact, sheet-fed scanner and a flatbed model. Sheet-fed scanners will save desktop space, while bulkier flatbed models provide higher speed and resolution.

- **Hard Disk Drives.** Bigger is better; as with closet space, you can always use the extra capacity. So go for 80 gigabytes at the minimum to 160 gigabytes and more.

- **CD and DVD Drives.** CD and DVD drives are a necessity for software installation and multimedia applications. Common today is a built-in CD-RW/DVD drive that both reads and writes CDs and plays DVDs.

- **Backup Systems.** Essential. Don't compute without them. Removable magnetic disk drives and even CD-RW and DVD-RW drives are convenient and versatile for backing up your hard drive's contents.

mouse, trackball, and touch pads allow you to choose easily from menu selections and icon displays using point-and-click or point-and-drag methods. See Figure 3.15.

The electronic mouse is the most popular pointing device used to move the cursor on the screen, as well as issue commands and make icon and menu selections. By moving the mouse on a desktop or pad, you can move the cursor onto an icon displayed on the screen. Pressing buttons on the mouse initiates various activities represented by the icon selected.

The trackball, pointing stick, and touch pad are other pointing devices most often used in place of the mouse. A trackball is a stationary device related to the mouse. You turn a roller ball with only its top exposed outside its case to move the cursor on the screen. A pointing stick (also called a *trackpoint*) is a small button-like device, sometimes likened to the eraser head of a pencil. It is usually centered one row above the space bar of a keyboard. The cursor moves in the direction of the pressure you place on the stick. The touch pad is a small rectangular touch-sensitive surface usually placed below the keyboard. The cursor moves in the direction your finger moves on the pad. Trackballs, pointing sticks, and touch pads are easier to use than a mouse for portable computer users and are thus built into most notebook computer keyboards.

FIGURE 3.15
Many choices exist for pointing devices including the trackball, mouse, pointing stick, and touch screen.

SOURCE: (left to right) Courtesy of Logitech, Microsoft®, International Business Machines Corporation, and © Don Wright/AP Images.

Touch screens are devices that allow you to use a computer by touching the surface of its video display screen. Some touch screens emit a grid of infrared beams, sound waves, or a slight electric current that is broken when the screen is touched. The computer senses the point in the grid where the break occurs and responds with an appropriate action. For example, you can indicate your selection on a menu display just by touching the screen next to that menu item.

Gati Limited: Real-Time Delivery with Handheld Technology

Gati Limited is one of the leading distribution and supply chain solutions companies in India. Launched in 1989 as a small cargo management company, Gati has grown to employ more than 3,500 people. Reaching more than 90 percent of India, Gati operates a fleet of more than 4,000 trucks of various capacities—containers, refrigerated, freight, and so forth—and does it all, from flexible point-to-point services to complex logistics and supply chain management. Rapid growth, however, is not without its disadvantages. As the company reached farther and farther into the country, it sought to keep the same level of customer service for which it had always been known: If Gati said it would be delivered, then it would be. And on time.

At the center of the freight business lies the POD, or proof-of-delivery, document. This piece of paper, when signed by the recipient acknowledging the time and completeness of the delivery, provides evidence to all involved in the transaction that Gati fulfilled its part of the bargain. This document, however, needs to find its way back to the sender to be of any use. With hundreds of thousands of shipments somewhere in the country at any given time—the company covers 3.2 lakh, or 320,000, kilometers every day—the resources needed to get ship those documents around are substantial, and time-consuming.

For instance, it took Gati about three days to send the PODs back to the original shippers. In this day and age, that just does not cut it anymore. "We needed to provide customers with real-time delivery results and eliminate the risk of losing physical copies of PODs," says G.S. Ravi Kumar, CIO. Any solution would need to be relatively inexpensive and easy to implement across a workforce that was largely nontechnical.

Gati opted for inexpensive handheld devices with GPRS (General Packet Radio Service, a 2G/3G robust packet mobile data service that supports Internet Protocols) and image-capturing functionality. As deliveries are made, the driver captures an image of the signed POD document and other package information and transmits it to a central database. Many benefits accrued to Gati out of this simple design. For example, Gati no longer needs an army of data entry operators who would type details in the physical PODs to update the data stores of the company. Delivery information is now available almost in real time, and the costs of tracking and shipping physical PODs have largely disappeared. Although sometimes GPRS connectivity would be a challenge in rural areas, the company also developed a way to work around this issue: Custom software would capture the image and delivery information and then transmit it when it detected that connectivity had been established again. This way drivers could continue their routes without worrying about any of these issues.

"Today, we have eliminated the cost of couriering PODs, and updated delivery information is almost in real time," says G. S. Ravi Kumar. The entire project, which cost Rs 90 lakh (about 200,000 dollars) was rolled out to more than 240 locations and more than 900 users, processing over 20,000 transactions a day. The simplicity of the solution was largely responsible for Gati Limited achieving ROI in less than six months.

SOURCE: "Handhelds Helped Gati Deliver Real-Time Reports," CIO India Case Study, CIO.in, and www.gati.com, accessed May 15, 2011.

FIGURE 3.16

Many PDAs accept pen-based input.

SOURCE: © Comstock/PunchStock.

Pen-based computing technologies are still being used in many handheld computers and personal digital assistants. Despite the popularity of touch-screen technologies, many still prefer the use of a stylus rather than a fingertip. *Tablet* PCs and PDAs contain fast processors and software that recognizes and digitizes handwriting, handprinting, and hand drawing. They have a pressure-sensitive layer, similar to that of a touch screen, under their slate-like liquid crystal display (LCD) screen. Instead of writing on a paper form fastened to a clipboard or using a keyboard device, you can use a pen to make selections, send e-mail, and enter handwritten data directly into a computer. See Figure 3.16.

Speech Recognition Systems

Speech recognition is gaining popularity in the corporate world among nontypists, people with disabilities, and business travelers, and is most frequently used for dictation, screen navigation, and Web browsing.

Speech recognition may be the future of data entry and certainly promises to be the easiest method for word processing, application navigation, and conversational computing because speech is the easiest, most natural means of human communication. Speech input has now become technologically and economically feasible for a variety of applications. Early speech recognition products used *discrete speech recognition*, for which you had to pause between each spoken word. New *continuous speech recognition* software recognizes continuous, conversationally paced speech. See Figure 3.17.

Speech recognition systems digitize, analyze, and classify your speech and its sound patterns. The software compares your speech patterns to a database of sound patterns in its vocabulary and passes recognized words to your application software. Typically, speech recognition systems require training the computer to recognize your voice and its unique sound patterns to achieve a high degree of accuracy. Training such systems involves repeating a variety of words and phrases in a training session, as well as using the system extensively.

Continuous speech recognition software products like Dragon Naturally Speaking and ViaVoice by IBM have up to 300,000-word vocabularies. Training to 95 percent accuracy may take several hours. Longer use, faster processors, and more memory

Using speech recognition
technology for word processing.

SOURCE: © Tim Pannell/Corbis.

make 99 percent accuracy possible. In addition, Microsoft Office Suite 2007 has built-in speech recognition for dictation and voice commands of a variety of software processes.

Speech recognition devices in work situations allow operators to perform data entry without using their hands to key in data or instructions and to provide faster and more accurate input. For example, manufacturers use speech recognition systems for the inspection, inventory, and quality control of a variety of products; airlines and parcel delivery companies use them for voice-directed sorting of baggage and parcels. Speech recognition can also help you operate your computer's operating systems and software packages through voice input of data and commands. For example, such software can be voice-enabled so you can send e-mail and surf the World Wide Web.

Speaker-independent voice recognition systems, which allow a computer to understand a few words from a voice it has never heard before, are being built into products and used in a growing number of applications. Examples include *voice-messaging computers*, which use speech recognition and voice response software to guide an end user verbally through the steps of a task in many kinds of activities. Typically, they enable computers to respond to verbal and Touch-Tone input over the telephone. Examples of applications include computerized telephone call switching, telemarketing surveys, bank pay-by-phone bill-paying services, stock quotation services, university registration systems, and customer credit and account balance inquiries.

One of the newest examples of this technology is Ford SYNC. SYNC is a factory-installed, in-car communications and entertainment system jointly developed by Ford Motor Company and Microsoft. The system was offered on 12 different Ford, Lincoln, and Mercury vehicles in North America for the 2008 model year and is available on most current model year Ford offerings.

Ford SYNC allows a driver to bring almost any mobile phone or digital media player into a vehicle and operate it using voice commands, the vehicle's steering wheel, or manual radio controls. The system can even receive text messages and read them aloud using a digitized female voice named "Samantha." SYNC can interpret a hundred or so shorthand messages, such as LOL for "laughing out loud," and it will read swear words; it won't, however, decipher obscene acronyms. Speech recognition is now common in your car, home, and workplace.

Optical Scanning

Few people understand how much scanners can improve a computer system and make your work easier. Their function is to get documents into your computer with a minimum of time and hassle, transforming just about anything on paper—a letter, a logo, or a photograph—into the digital format that your PC can read. Scanners can be a big help in getting loads of paper off your desk and into your PC.

Optical scanning devices read text or graphics and convert them into digital input for your computer. Thus, optical scanning enables the direct entry of data from source documents into a computer system. For example, you can use a compact desktop scanner to scan pages of text and graphics into your computer for desktop publishing and Web publishing applications. You can scan documents of all kinds into your system and organize them into folders as part of a *document management* library system for easy reference or retrieval. See Figure 3.18.

Another optical scanning technology is called optical character recognition (OCR). The OCR scanners can read the characters and codes on merchandise tags, product labels, credit card receipts, utility bills, insurance premiums, airline tickets, and other documents. In addition, OCR scanners are used to automatically sort mail, score tests, and process a wide variety of forms in business and government.

Devices such as handheld optical scanning wands are frequently used to read *bar codes*, codes that use bars to represent characters. One common example is the Universal Product Code (UPC) bar coding that you see on just about every product sold. For example, the automated checkout scanners found in supermarkets read UPC bar coding. Supermarket scanners emit laser beams that are reflected off a code. The reflected image is converted to electronic impulses that are sent to the in-store computer, where they are matched with pricing information. Pricing information is returned to the terminal, visually displayed, and printed on a receipt for the customer. See Figure 3.19.

FIGURE 3.18

A modern document management system can serve as an optical scanner, copier, fax, and printer.

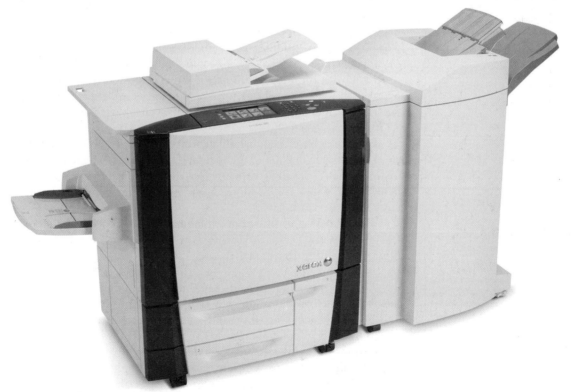

SOURCE: Courtesy of Xerox.

FIGURE 3.19

Using an optical scanning wand to read bar coding of inventory data.

SOURCE: © Jeff Smith/Getty Images.

Forget the ATM: Deposit Checks without Leaving Home

First, we didn't need to visit the bank teller anymore. Then we were able to stick our checks right into the ATM without an envelope. Now we won't have to leave the house to make deposits.

Based in Sacramento, California, Schools Financial Credit Union is one of the latest banks to allow customers to scan checks at home and deposit them over the Internet. Golden One Credit Union, also from California, had introduced scanner-based check deposits in July 2009. "Banking's not the way it was 5 or 10 years ago," said Nathan Schmidt, a vice president at Schools Financial. "With any type of technology, it becomes more convenient to self-service."

Even with the widespread use of direct deposit and online banking, people still write and receive millions of paper checks each year. And for the most part, when we have to deposit a paper check, we still need to go to an ATM to do it.

Businesses have been making deposits over the Internet far longer, ever since the passage in 2004 of the federal Check 21 Act, which made a digital image of a check legally acceptable for payment. Businesses quickly saw the benefits of the new law. Sending checks as digital images eliminated courier costs and paperwork.

The extension of the service to consumers has come much more slowly. Cary Whaley, a director at Washington, D.C.–based Independent Community Bankers of America, says financial institutions have been wary about potential fraud.

"For many banks, it remains a business application," Whaley says. "The next step is the consumer side, but a lot of community banks are a little wary. When you're getting into thousands of consumers, the challenge for banks and credit unions is not only monitoring risk, but monitoring for changes in transactions and transaction amounts."

But some bankers say consumers are increasingly demanding the same convenience given to their business counterparts, and it's just a matter of time before remote deposits become much more widespread.

When Schools Financial Credit Union decided to take the plunge, it included safeguards to prevent abuse. Customers must use their existing secure online banking log-in, and they can't transmit items more than twice a day.

Users have a time limit to scan and deposit the check online, and checks must meet specific requirements before they are deposited. Post-dated, damaged, or lightly printed checks, for instance, will not scan properly and cannot be deposited.

"So many people prefer to do self-service. They choose to go online—maybe they're parents with small kids, or they might not want to go to an ATM at 3 a.m.," says Golden One's chief executive officer, Teresa Halleck.

"People are already online," she says. "They're comfortable with electronic delivery and they're looking for more."

SOURCE: Darrell Smith, "Forget the ATM—Some Banks Allow Check Deposits via Scanner, iPhone," *The Sacramento Bee*, October 26, 2009.

Other Input Technologies

Magnetic stripe technology is a familiar form of data entry that helps computers read credit cards. The coating of the magnetic stripe on the back of such cards can hold about 200 bytes of information. Customer account numbers can be recorded on the magnetic stripe so that it can be read by bank ATMs, credit card authorization terminals, and many other types of magnetic stripe readers.

Smart cards that embed a microprocessor chip and several kilobytes of memory into debit, credit, and other cards are popular in Europe and becoming available in the United States. One example is in the Netherlands, where millions of smart debit cards have been issued by Dutch banks. Smart debit cards enable you to store a cash balance on the card and electronically transfer some of it to others to pay for small items and services. The balance on the card can be replenished in ATMs or other terminals. The smart debit cards used in the Netherlands feature a microprocessor and either 8 or 16 kilobytes of memory, plus the usual magnetic stripe. The smart cards are widely used to make payments in parking meters, vending machines, newsstands, pay telephones, and retail stores.

Digital cameras represent another fast-growing set of input technologies. Digital still cameras and digital video cameras (digital camcorders) enable you to shoot, store, and download still photos or full-motion video with audio into your PC. Then you can use image-editing software to edit and enhance the digitized images and include them in newsletters, reports, multimedia presentations, and Web pages. Today's typical mobile phone includes digital camera capabilities as well.

The computer systems of the banking industry can magnetically read checks and deposit slips using magnetic ink character recognition (MICR) technology. Computers can thus sort and post checks to the proper checking accounts. Such processing is possible because the identification numbers of the bank and the customer's account are preprinted on the bottom of the checks with an iron oxide–based ink. The first bank receiving a check after it has been written must encode the amount of the check in magnetic ink on the check's lower righthand corner. The MICR system uses 14 characters (the 10 decimal digits and 4 special symbols) of a standardized design. *Reader-sorter* equipment reads a check by first magnetizing the magnetic ink characters and then sensing the signal induced by each character as it passes a reading head. In this way, data are electronically captured by the bank's computer systems.

Computers provide information in a variety of forms. Video displays and printed documents have been, and still are, the most common forms of output from computer systems. Yet other natural and attractive output technologies, such as voice response systems and multimedia output, are increasingly found along with video displays in business applications.

OUTPUT TECHNOLOGIES
LO 3-3
LO 3-4

FIGURE 3.20

The flat-panel LCD video monitor is becoming the de facto standard for a desktop PC system.

SOURCE: Courtesy of Hewlett-Packard.

For example, you have probably experienced the voice and audio output generated by speech and audio microprocessors in a variety of consumer products. Voice messaging software enables PCs and servers in voice mail and messaging systems to interact with you through voice responses. Of course, multimedia output is common on the Web sites of the Internet and corporate intranets.

Video Output

Video displays are the most common type of computer output. Many desktop computers still rely on video monitors that use a *cathode ray tube* (CRT) technology similar to the picture tubes used in home television sets. Usually, the clarity of the video display depends on the type of video monitor you use and the graphics circuit board installed in your computer. These can provide a variety of graphics modes of increasing capability. A high-resolution, flicker-free monitor is especially important if you spend a lot of time viewing multimedia on CDs, or on the Web, or the complex graphical displays of many software packages.

The biggest use of liquid crystal displays (LCDs) has been to provide a visual display capability for portable microcomputers and PDAs. However, the use of "flat-panel" LCD video monitors for desktop PC systems has become common as their cost becomes more affordable. See Figure 3.20. These LCD displays need significantly less electric current and provide a thin, flat display. Advances in technology such as *active matrix* and *dual scan* capabilities have improved the color and clarity of LCD displays. In addition, high-clarity flat-panel televisions and monitors using *plasma* display technologies are becoming popular for large-screen (42- to 80-inch) viewing.

Printed Output

Printing information on paper is still the most common form of output after video displays. Thus, most personal computer systems rely on an inkjet or laser printer to produce permanent (hard-copy) output in high-quality printed form. Printed output is still a common form of business communication and is frequently required for legal documentation. Computers can produce printed reports and correspondence; documents such as sales invoices, payroll checks, and bank statements; and printed versions of graphic displays. See Figure 3.21.

FIGURE 3.21

Modern laser printers produce high-quality color output with high speed.

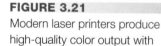

SOURCE: Courtesy of Xerox.

Inkjet printers, which spray ink onto a page, have become the most popular, low-cost printers for microcomputer systems. They are quiet, produce several pages per minute of high-quality output, and can print both black-and-white and high-quality color graphics. Laser printers use an electrostatic process similar to a photocopying machine to produce many pages per minute of high-quality black-and-white output. More expensive color laser printers and multifunction inkjet and laser models that print, fax, scan, and copy are other popular choices for business offices.

STORAGE TRADE-OFFS
LO 3-3
LO 3-4

Data and information must be stored until needed using a variety of storage methods. For example, many people and organizations still rely on paper documents stored in filing cabinets as a major form of storage media. However, you and other computer users are more likely to depend on the memory circuits and secondary storage devices of computer systems to meet your storage requirements. Progress in very-large-scale integration (VLSI), which packs millions of memory circuit elements on tiny semiconductor memory chips, is responsible for continuing increases in the main-memory capacity of computers. Secondary storage capacities are also escalating into the billions and trillions of characters, due to advances in magnetic and optical media.

There are many types of storage media and devices. Figure 3.22 illustrates the speed, capacity, and cost relationships of several alternative primary and secondary storage media. Note the cost/speed/capacity trade-offs as you move from semiconductor memories to magnetic disks to optical disks and to magnetic tape. High-speed storage media cost more per byte and provide lower capacities. Large-capacity storage media cost less per byte but are slower. These trade-offs are why we have different kinds of storage media.

However, all storage media, especially memory chips and magnetic disks, continue to increase in speed and capacity and decrease in cost. Developments like automated high-speed cartridge assemblies have given faster access times to magnetic tape, and the speed of optical disk drives continues to increase.

Note in Figure 3.22 that semiconductor memories are used mainly for primary storage, although they are sometimes used as high-speed secondary storage devices. Magnetic disk and tape and optical disk devices, in contrast, are used as secondary storage devices to enlarge the storage capacity of computer systems. Also, because most primary storage circuits use RAM (random-access memory) chips, which lose their contents when electrical power is interrupted, secondary storage devices provide a more permanent type of storage media.

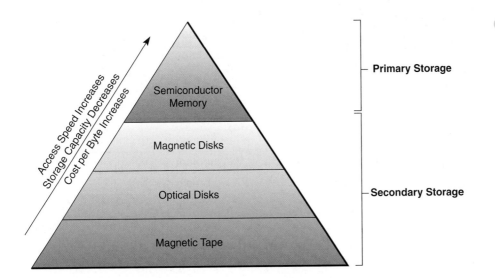

FIGURE 3.22

Storage media cost, speed, and capacity trade-offs. Note how cost increases with faster access speeds but decreases with the increased capacity of storage media.

Computer Storage Fundamentals

Data are processed and stored in a computer system through the presence or absence of electronic or magnetic signals in the computer's circuitry or in the media it uses. This character is called "two-state" or ***binary representation*** of data because the computer and the media can exhibit only two possible states or conditions, similar to a common light switch: "on" or "off." For example, transistors and other semiconductor circuits are in either a conducting or a nonconducting state. Media such as magnetic disks and tapes indicate these two states by having magnetized spots whose magnetic fields have one of two different directions, or polarities. This binary characteristic of computer circuitry and media is what makes the binary number system the basis for representing data in computers. Thus, for electronic circuits, the conducting ("on") state represents the number 1, whereas the nonconducting ("off") state represents the number 0. For magnetic media, the magnetic field of a magnetized spot in one direction represents a 1, while magnetism in the other direction represents a 0.

The smallest element of data is called a ***bit,*** short for *binary digit*, which can have a value of either 0 or 1. The capacity of memory chips is usually expressed in terms of bits. A ***byte*** is a basic grouping of bits that the computer operates as a single unit. Typically, it consists of eight bits and represents one character of data in most computer coding schemes. Thus, the capacity of a computer's memory and secondary storage devices is usually expressed in terms of bytes. Computer codes such as ASCII (American Standard Code for Information Interchange) use various arrangements of bits to form bytes that represent the numbers 0 through 9, the letters of the alphabet, and many other characters. See Figure 3.23.

Since childhood, we have learned to do our computations using the numbers 0 through 9, the digits of the decimal number system. Although it is fine for us to use 10 digits for our computations, computers do not have this luxury. Every computer processor is made of millions of tiny switches that can be turned off or on. Because these switches have only two states, it makes sense for a computer to perform its computations with a number system that has only two digits: the *binary number system*. These digits (0 and 1) correspond to the off/on positions of the switches in the computer processor. With only these two digits, a computer can perform all the arithmetic that we can with 10 digits. Figure 3.24 illustrates the basic concepts of the binary system.

FIGURE 3.23

Examples of the ASCII computer code that computers use to represent numbers and the letters of the alphabet.

Character	ASCII Code	Character	ASCII Code	Character	ASCII Code
0	00110000	A	01000001	N	01001110
1	00110001	B	01000010	O	01001111
2	00110010	C	01000011	P	01010000
3	00110011	D	01000100	Q	01010001
4	00110100	E	01000101	R	01010010
5	00110101	F	01000110	S	01010011
6	00110110	G	01000111	T	01010100
7	00110111	H	01001000	U	01010101
8	00111000	I	01001001	V	01010110
9	00111001	J	01001010	W	01010111
		K	01001011	X	01011000
		L	01001100	Y	01011001
		M	01001101	Z	01011010

2^7	2^6	2^5	2^4	2^3	2^2	2^1	2^0
128	64	32	16	8	4	2	1
0 or 1	0 or 1	0 or 1	0 or 1	0 or 1	0 or 1	0 or 1	0 or 1

To represent any decimal number using the binary system, each place is simply assigned a value of either 0 or 1. To convert binary to decimal, simply add up the value of each place.

Example:

2^7	2^6	2^5	2^4	2^3	2^2	2^1	2^0
1	0	0	1	1	0	0	1
128	0	0	16	8	0	0	1
128 +	0 +	0 +	16 +	8 +	0 +	0 +	1 = 153

10011001 = 153

FIGURE 3.24

Computers use the binary system to store and compute numbers.

The binary system is built on an understanding of exponentiation (raising a number to a power). In contrast to the more familiar decimal system, in which each place represents the number 10 raised to a power (ones, tens, hundreds, thousands, and so on), each place in the binary system represents the number 2 raised to successive powers (2^0, 2^1, 2^2, and so on). As shown in Figure 3.24, the binary system can be used to express any integer number by using only 0 and 1.

Storage capacities are frequently measured in *kilobytes* (KB), *megabytes* (MB), *gigabytes* (GB), or *terabytes* (TB). Although *kilo* means 1,000 in the metric system, the computer industry uses K to represent 1,024 (or 2^{10}) storage positions. For example, a capacity of 10 megabytes is really 10,485,760 storage positions, rather than 10 million positions. However, such differences are frequently disregarded to simplify descriptions of storage capacity. Thus, a megabyte is roughly 1 million bytes of storage, a gigabyte is roughly 1 billion bytes, and a terabyte represents about 1 trillion bytes, while a *petabyte* is more than 1 quadrillion bytes.

To put these storage capacities in perspective, consider the following: A terabyte is equivalent to about 20 million typed pages, and it has been estimated that the total size of all the books, photographs, video and sound recordings, and maps in the U.S. Library of Congress approximates 3 petabytes (3,000 terabytes).

Direct and Sequential Access

Primary storage media such as semiconductor memory chips are called *direct access* memory or random-access memory (RAM). Magnetic disk devices are frequently called direct access storage devices (DASDs). In contrast, media such as magnetic tape cartridges are known as *sequential access* devices.

The terms *direct access* and *random access* describe the same concept. They mean that an element of data or instructions (such as a byte or word) can be directly stored and retrieved by selecting and using any of the locations on the storage media. They also mean that each storage position (1) has a unique address and (2) can be individually accessed in about the same length of time without having to search through other storage positions. For example, each memory cell on a microelectronic semiconductor RAM chip can be individually sensed or changed in the same length of time. Also, any data record stored on a magnetic or optical disk can be accessed directly in about the same period. See Figure 3.25.

Sequential access storage media such as magnetic tape do not have unique storage addresses that can be directly addressed. Instead, data must be stored and retrieved using a sequential or serial process. Data are recorded one after another in a predetermined sequence (e.g., numeric order) on a storage medium. Locating an

Sequential Access Storage Device

Read/Write Head

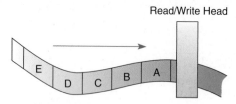

Direct Access Storage Device

Read/Write Head

FIGURE 3.25

Sequential versus direct access storage. Magnetic tape is a typical sequential access medium. Magnetic disks are typical direct access storage devices.

individual item of data requires searching the recorded data on the tape until the desired item is located.

SEMICONDUCTOR MEMORY

Memory is the coal man to the CPU's locomotive: For maximum PC performance, it must keep the processor constantly stoked with instructions. Faster CPUs call for larger and faster memories, both in the cache where data and instructions are stored temporarily and in the main memory.

The primary storage (main memory) of your computer consists of microelectronic *semiconductor memory* chips. It provides you with the working storage your computer needs to process your applications. Plug-in memory circuit boards containing 256 megabytes or more of memory chips can be added to your PC to increase its memory capacity. Specialized memory can help improve your computer's performance. Examples include external cache memory to help your microprocessor work faster or a video graphics accelerator card for faster and clearer video performance. Removable credit-card-size and smaller "flash memory" RAM devices like a jump drive or a memory stick can also provide gigabytes of erasable direct access storage for PCs, PDAs, or digital cameras.

Thus, there are two basic types of semiconductor memory: *random-access memory (RAM)* and *read-only memory (ROM)*.

- **RAM, random-access memory.** These memory chips are the most widely used primary storage medium. Each memory position can be both sensed (read) and changed (written), so it is also called read/write memory. This is a *volatile* memory.

- **ROM, read-only memory.** Nonvolatile random-access memory chips are used for permanent storage; ROM can be read but not erased or overwritten. Frequently used control instructions in the control unit and programs in primary storage (such as parts of the operating system) can be permanently burned into the storage cells during manufacture, sometimes called *firmware*. Variations include PROM (programmable read-only memory) and EPROM (erasable programmable read-only memory), which can be permanently or temporarily programmed after manufacture.

A now common, but still quite innovative, form of storage that uses semiconductor memory is the *flash drive* (sometimes referred to as a *JumpDrive*). Figure 3.26 shows a common flash memory drive.

Flash memory uses a small chip containing thousands of transistors that can be programmed to store data for virtually unlimited periods without power. The small drives can be easily transported in your pocket and are highly durable. Storage capacities currently range as high as 250 gigabytes, but newer flash technologies are making even higher storage capacities a reality. The advent of credit-card-like memory cards and ever-smaller storage technologies puts more data into the user's pocket every day.

FIGURE 3.26

A USB flash memory drive.

ReadyBoost

The higher storage volumes provided by flash drives require new technologies intended to take advantage of it. Microsoft's *ReadyBoost* is one such example. ReadyBoost is a disk cache component, first introduced with Microsoft's Windows Vista in 2006 and bundled with Windows 7 in 2009. It works by using the flash drive, SD card, or any kind of portable flash mass-storage system as a cache.

Using ReadyBoost-capable flash memory (NAND memory devices) for caching allows Windows 7 to service random disk reads with performance that is typically 80–100 times faster than random reads from traditional hard drives. This caching applies to all disk content, not just the page file or system DLLs. Flash devices typically are slower than a hard disk for sequential input/output so, to maximize performance, ReadyBoost includes logic that recognizes large, sequential read requests and makes sure the hard disk services these requests. When a compatible device is plugged in, the Windows AutoPlay dialog offers an additional option to use the flash drive to speed up the system; an additional "ReadyBoost" tab is added to the drive's properties dialog where the amount of space to be used can be configured. The system can use up to 256 GB of flash memory.

Solid-State Drive

Semiconductor memory has also allowed for the successful development of the *solid-state drive*. A solid-state drive (SSD) is a data storage device that uses semiconductor memory to store persistent data with the intention of providing access in the same manner as that of a hard disk drive. SSDs are distinguished from traditional hard disk drives (HDDs), which are electromechanical magnetic storage devices containing spinning disks and movable read/write heads. SSDs, in contrast, use microchips which retain data in nonvolatile memory chips and contain no moving parts. Compared to electromechanical HDDs, SSDs are typically less susceptible to physical shock, are silent, and have lower access times and latency. SSDs use the same connector interface as hard disk drives, thus making them easy to add to an existing computer.

As of 2010, most SSDs use NAND-based flash memory, which retains memory even without power. SSDs using volatile random-access memory (RAM) also exist for situations that require even faster access, they but do not necessarily need data persistence after power loss, or use external power or batteries to maintain the data after power is removed. A hybrid drive combines the features of an HDD and an SSD in one unit, containing a large HDD, with a smaller SSD cache to improve performance of frequently accessed files. These can offer near-SSD performance in most applications (such as system start-up and loading applications) at a lower price than an SSD. Regardless of the configuration, SSDs that have the operating system loaded display significant performance improvements over even the fastest of hard drives.

Work 7×24: Collaboration Technology for Small Companies

Technology is becoming more and more pervasive in all industries throughout the world. All companies that are either very large, large, or medium-sized are already greatly based on technology in one way or the other. On the consumer side of things, new products are introduced almost every day, from social media innovations to tablets to cloud-based music services. Many of these products are based on mobile platforms that come with cameras and GPS systems as defaults. But smaller companies have yet to fully embrace all of these developments.

"There are a lot that focus on consumers, but nothing for smaller enterprises and the like," says Jens Lundström, CEO of Two Story Software, the Swedish start-up behind Work 7×24, a service that allows small businesses with employees out on the field to collaborate and keep everybody updated without the need to fill out paperwork. To make things easier for smaller businesses with more limited resources and technical expertise, the service is hosted remotely and can be accessed from any device with a connection to the Internet.

"Usually handymen, including electricians, plumbers, and installers, have a mobile phone and a notepad, and that is their back office support. When they head out in the field they have work orders written on a note," says Lundström. The service is targeted to organizations where a large portion of their workforce does not work at an office all day, but is rather out in the field and, most often, out of touch with headquarters for hours at a time. The goal is to take advantage of already built-in features of mobile phones to give these smaller businesses a leg up against larger operations.

Work 7×24 allows managers to enter new work orders or update existing ones from the office and then notifies employees through an e-mail or text message, which contains a link that can be used to access the update and enter any necessary information. It can also be used to provide information on the customer or location the employee is about to visit. Any images or instructions that can be of help can also be included.

After the visit to the customer is over, employees can use the same service to upload information back to the office, which can then be shared with other employees in the future. For example, salespeople can include photographs of new equipment installed at a customer site so that repair technicians know what to expect when they go out in the field to service it. They can also include useful nearby locations, or geo-tagged directions when customers are located in remote and hard-to-access rural areas. Work 7×24 also includes support for quotes and invoicing on the spot, as well as reporting of any materials used and the number of hours worked.

And the best part? It is all paperless. "Our goal is to make it simpler for small companies to work together and document what they have done, and do it faster with less paperwork," says Lundström.

SOURCE: Mikael Ricknäs, "Camera Phones and GPS are for SMBs Too, Says Startup," *IDG News Service*, November 7, 2008, and www.twostorysoftware.com, accessed May 15, 2011.

MAGNETIC DISKS

Multigigabyte magnetic disk drives aren't extravagant, considering that full-motion video files, sound tracks, and photo-quality images can consume colossal amounts of disk space in a blink.

Magnetic disks are the most common form of secondary storage for your computer system. That's because they provide fast access and high storage capacities at a reasonable cost. Magnetic disk drives contain metal disks that are coated on both sides with an iron oxide recording material. Several disks are mounted together on a vertical shaft, which typically rotates the disks at speeds of 3,600 to 7,600 revolutions per minute (rpm). Electromagnetic read/write heads are positioned by access arms between the slightly separated disks to read and write data on concentric, circular tracks. Data are recorded on tracks in the form of tiny magnetized spots to form the binary digits of common computer codes. Thousands of bytes can be recorded on each track, and there are several hundred data tracks on each disk surface, thus providing you with billions of storage positions for your software and data. See Figure 3.27.

RAID Storage

RAID computer storage equipment—big, refrigerator-size boxes full of dozens of interlinked magnetic disk drives that can store the equivalent of 100 million tax returns—hardly gets the blood rushing. But it should. Just as speedy and reliable networking opened the floodgates to cyberspace and e-commerce, ever-more-turbocharged data storage is a key building block of the Internet.

SOURCE: © Royalty Free/Corbis.

FIGURE 3.27

Magnetic disk media: a hard magnetic disk drive and a 3½-inch floppy disk.

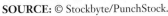

SOURCE: © Stockbyte/PunchStock.

Disk arrays of interconnected microcomputer hard disk drives have replaced large-capacity mainframe disk drives to provide virtually unlimited online storage. Known as ***RAID (redundant arrays of independent disks),*** they combine from 6 to more than 100 small hard disk drives and their control microprocessors into a single unit. These RAID units provide large capacities (as high as 1–2 terabytes or more) with high access speeds because data are accessed in parallel over multiple paths from many disks. Also, RAID units provide a *fault-tolerant* capacity, in that their redundant design offers multiple copies of data on several disks. If one disk fails, data can be recovered from backup copies automatically stored on other disks. Storage area networks (SANs) are high-speed *fiber channel* local area networks that can interconnect many RAID units and thus share their combined capacity through network servers with many users.

There are a variety of classifications of RAID, and newer implementations include not only hardware versions, but also software methods. The technical aspects of RAID are beyond the scope of this text and probably beyond the needs of the modern business technologist as well. It is sufficient to note that the storage mechanisms in the modern organization are probably using some type of RAID technology. If you are interested in drilling deeper into this technology and how it works, a wide variety of Internet resources are available.

MAGNETIC TAPE

Tape storage is moving beyond backup. Although disk subsystems provide the fastest response time for mission-critical data, the sheer amount of data that users need to access these days as part of huge enterprise applications, such as data warehouses, requires affordable (magnetic tape) storage.

Magnetic tape is still being used as a secondary storage medium in business applications. The read/write heads of magnetic tape drives record data in the form of magnetized spots on the iron oxide coating of the plastic tape. Magnetic tape devices include tape reels and cartridges in mainframes and midrange systems and small cassettes or cartridges for PCs. One growing business application of magnetic tape involves the use of high-speed 36-track magnetic tape cartridges in robotic automated drive assemblies that can directly access hundreds of cartridges. These devices provide lower-cost storage to supplement magnetic disks to meet massive data warehouse and other online business storage requirements. Other major applications for magnetic tape include long-term *archival* storage and backup storage for PCs and other systems.

OPTICAL DISKS

Optical disk technology has become a necessity. Most software companies now distribute their elephantine programs on CD-ROMs. Many corporations are now rolling their own CDs to distribute product and corporate information that once filled bookshelves.

Optical disks, a fast-growing type of storage media, use several major alternative technologies. See Figure 3.28. One version is called CD-ROM (compact disk–read-only memory). CD-ROM technology uses 12-centimeter (4.7-inch) compact disks (CDs) similar to those used in stereo music systems. Each disk can store more than 600 megabytes. That's the equivalent of more than 400 1.44-megabyte floppy disks or more than 300,000 double-spaced pages of text. A laser records data by burning permanent microscopic pits in a spiral track on a master disk from which compact disks can be mass produced. Then CD-ROM disk drives use a laser device to read the binary codes formed by those pits.

CD-R (compact disk–recordable) is another popular optical disk technology. CD-R drives or CD *burners* are commonly used to record data permanently on CDs. The major limitation of CD-ROM and CD-R disks is that recorded data cannot be erased. However, CD-RW (CD-rewritable) drives record and erase data by using a laser to heat a microscopic point on the disk's surface. In CD-RW versions using magneto-optical technology, a magnetic coil changes the spot's reflective properties from one direction to another, thus recording a binary 1 or 0. A laser device can then read the binary codes on the disk by sensing the direction of reflected light.

DVD technologies have dramatically increased optical disk capacities and capabilities. DVD (digital video disk or digital versatile disk) optical disks can hold from

FIGURE 3.28

Comparing the capabilities of optical disk drives.

Optical Disk Drive Capabilities
CD-ROM A CD-ROM drive provides a low-cost way to read data files and load software onto your computer, as well as play music CDs.
CD-RW A CD-RW drive allows you to easily create your own custom data CDs for data backup or data transfer purposes. It will also allow you to store and share video files, large data files, digital photos, and other large files with other people that have access to a CD-ROM drive. This drive will do anything your CD-ROM drive will do; it reads all of your existing CD-ROMs, audio CDs, and CDs that you have created with your CD burner.
CD-RW/DVD A CD-RW/DVD combination drive brings all of the advantages of CD-RW, CD-ROM, and DVD-ROM to a single drive. With a CD-RW/DVD combo drive, you can read DVD-ROM and CD-ROM disks, as well as create your own custom CDs.
DVD-ROM A DVD-ROM drive allows you to enjoy the crystal-clear color, picture, and sound clarity of DVD video on your PC. It will also prepare you for future software and large data files that will be released on DVD-ROM. A DVD-ROM drive can also read CD-ROM disks, effectively providing users with full optical read capability in one device.
DVD+RW/+R with CD-RW A DVD+RW/+R with CD-RW drive is a great all-in-one drive, allowing you to burn DVD+RW or DVD+R disks, burn CDs, and read DVDs and CDs. It enables you to create DVDs to back up and archive up to 4.7GB of data files (that's up to 7 times the capacity of a standard 650MB CD) and store up to to 2 hours of MPEG2 digital video.

SOURCE: "Learn More—Optical Drives," www.dell.com.

FIGURE 3.29

Optical disk storage includes CD
and DVD technologies.

SOURCE: Photodisc/Getty Images.

3.0 to 8.5 gigabytes of multimedia data on each side. The large capacities and high-quality images and sound of DVD technology are expected to replace CD technologies for data storage and promise to accelerate the use of DVD drives for multimedia products that can be used in both computers and home entertainment systems. Thus, DVD-ROM disks are increasingly replacing magnetic tape videocassettes for movies and other multimedia products, while DVD+RW disks are being used for backup and archival storage of large data and multimedia files. See Figure 3.29.

RADIO FREQUENCY IDENTIFICATION

One of the newest and most rapidly growing storage technologies is *radio frequency identification (RFID),* a system for tagging and identifying mobile objects such as store merchandise, postal packages, and sometimes even living organisms (like pets). Using a special device called an RFID reader, RFID allows objects to be labeled and tracked as they move from place to place.

The RFID technology works using small (sometimes smaller than a grain of sand) pieces of hardware called RFID chips. These chips feature an antenna to transmit and receive radio signals. Currently, there are two general types of RFID chips: *passive* and *active*. Passive RFID chips do not have a power source and must derive their power from the signal sent from the reader. Active RFID chips are self-powered and do not need to be close to the reader to transmit their signal. Any RFID chips may be attached to objects or, in the case of some passive RFID systems, injected into objects. A recent use for RFID chips is the identification of pets, such as dogs or cats. By having a tiny RFID chip injected just under their skin, they can be easily identified if they become lost. The RFID chip contains contact information about the owner of the pet. Taking this a step further, the Transportation Security Administration is considering using RFID tags embedded in airline boarding passes to keep track of passengers.

Whenever a reader within range sends appropriate signals to an object, the associated RFID chip responds with the requested information, such as an identification number or product date. The reader, in turn, displays the response data to an operator. Readers may also forward data to a networked central computer system. Such RFID systems generally support storing information on the chips as well as just reading data.

The RFID systems were created as an alternative to common bar codes. Relative to bar codes, RFID allows objects to be scanned from a greater distance, supports storing of data, and allows more information to be tracked per object.

Recently RFID has raised some privacy concerns as a result of the invisible nature of the system and its capability to transmit fairly sophisticated messages. As these types of issues are resolved, we can expect to see RFID technology used in just about every way imaginable.

RFID Privacy Issues

How would you like it if, for instance, one day you realized your underwear was reporting on your whereabouts?—California State Senator Debra Bowen, at a 2003 hearing on RFID privacy concerns.

The use of RFID technology has caused considerable controversy and even product boycotts by consumer privacy advocates who refer to RFID tags as *spychips*. The two main privacy concerns regarding RFID are:

- Because the owner of an item will not necessarily be aware of the presence of an RFID tag, and the tag can be read at a distance without the knowledge of the individual, it becomes possible to gather sensitive data about an individual without consent.

- If a customer pays for a tagged item by credit card or in conjunction with a loyalty card, then it would be possible to deduce the identity of the purchaser indirectly by reading the globally unique ID of that item (contained in the RFID tag).

Most concerns revolve around the fact that RFID tags affixed to products remain functional even after the products have been purchased and taken home; thus, they can be used for surveillance and other purposes unrelated to their supply chain inventory functions.

Read range, however, is a function of both the reader and the tag itself. Improvements in technology may increase read ranges for tags. Having readers very close to the tags makes short-range tags readable. Generally, the read range of a tag is limited to the distance from the reader over which the tag can draw enough energy from the reader field to power the tag. Tags may be read at longer ranges by increasing reader power. The limit on read distance then becomes the signal-to-noise ratio of the signal reflected from the tag back to the reader. Researchers at two security conferences have demonstrated that passive UHF RFID tags (not the HF-type used in U.S. passports), normally read at ranges of up to 30 feet, can be read at ranges of 50–69 feet using suitable equipment. Many other types of tag signals can be intercepted from 30–35 feet away under good conditions, and the reader signal can be detected from miles away if there are no obstructions.

The potential for privacy violations with RFID was demonstrated by its use in a pilot program by the Gillette Company, which conducted a "smart shelf" test at a Tesco in Cambridge, England. They automatically photographed shoppers taking RFID-tagged safety razors off the shelf to see if the technology could be used to deter shoplifting. This trial resulted in consumer boycott against Gillette and Tesco. In another incident, uncovered by the *Chicago Sun-Times*, shelves in a Wal-Mart in Broken Arrow, Oklahoma, were equipped with readers to track the Max Factor Lipfinity lipstick containers stacked on them. Webcam images of the shelves were viewed 750 miles away by Procter & Gamble researchers in Cincinnati, Ohio, who could tell when lipsticks were removed from the shelves and observe the shoppers in action.

The controversy surrounding the use of RFID technologies was furthered by the accidental exposure of a proposed Auto-ID consortium public relations campaign that was designed to "neutralize opposition" and get consumers to "resign themselves to the inevitability of it" while merely pretending to address their concerns. During the U.N. World Summit on the Information Society (WSIS) on November 16–18, 2005, Richard Stallman, founder of the free software movement, protested the use of RFID security cards. During the first meeting, it was agreed that future meetings would no longer use RFID cards; upon finding out this assurance was broken, he covered his card in tin foil and would uncover it only at the security stations. This protest caused the security personnel considerable concern. Some did not allow him to leave a conference room in which he had been the main speaker, and then prevented him from entering another conference room, where he was due to speak.

The Food and Drug Administration in the United States has approved the use of RFID chips in humans. Some business establishments have also started to "chip" customers, such as the Baja Beach Nightclub in Barcelona. This has provoked concerns into privacy of individuals, as they can potentially be tracked wherever they go by an identifier unique to them. There are concerns that this could lead to abuse by an authoritarian government or lead to removal of other freedoms.

In July 2006, Reuters reported that Newitz and Westhues, two hackers, showed at a conference in New York City that they could clone the RFID signal from a human-implanted RFID chip, which proved that the chip is not as secure as was previously believed.

All of these examples share a common thread, showing that whatever can be encoded can also be decoded. RFID presents the potential for enormous efficiencies and cost savings. It also presents significant challenges to privacy and security. Until these issues are worked through, much controversy will continue to surround RFID technologies.

Kimberly-Clark: Secrets to RFID Success

While you may not immediately recognize the name Kimberly-Clark, you have surely purchased one or more of its products: Scott, Huggies, Pull-Ups, Kleenex, and Kotex are some of its better-known brands. In fact, the company holds the number 1 or 2 spot in market share in more than 80 countries. At last count, more than 1.3 billion people use its products every day, which helps explain how sales for 2010 topped $19.7 billion. None of this would be possible without a razor-sharp global supply chain that coordinates manufacturing operations in 37 different countries, and distribution and sales in 150 countries overall—that is pretty much every country on the planet. Radio Frequency Identification (RFID) is the key to that effort.

Kimberly-Clark was one of the first large companies to get heavily involved with RFID, and it has been a strong believer in the technology. "Our goal is to evolve the capabilities of our supply chain to a demand-driven network. One of the keys to achieving that vision is to have a highly integrated suite of supply chain systems that provide end-to-end visibility and as close to real-time information as possible," says Mark Jamison, vice president of customer supply chain management at Kimberly-Clark.

How much "real-time" should real-time data be is an important issue. It is unlikely that most companies will need to know, on an hour-by-hour basis, what is going on with their products and customers; getting that information two or three times a day may be enough to understand the market. Yet being able to see how promotions are taking off, which products are moving more or less than expected, and how production volumes are coming along allows Kimberly-Clark to keep its products always on the shelf in the right quantity— so they're are not too many and not too few.

"Our strategy around RFID has been to focus on business processes and develop repeatable, scalable business processes that are enabled by the technology. The technology in and of itself is not going to bring value to the supply chain. The value to the supply chain comes from reengineering your business processes and enabling those new business processes to work with the technology," notes Jamison.

Consider, for example, product promotions and their delivery and execution. Kimberly-Clark managers found out that their promotional materials and displays arrive in the stores only 55 percent of the time to meet promotion or advertising dates. Only 55 percent of the time! The company redesigned the process to start tracking these materials using real-time data. They began to chart progress against plans, and they also involved their retail operation employees, who are the ones in daily contact with the stores and chains. Now, on a day-to-day basis, managers know which stores have not executed the promotions as necessary, and they can then send people to make those promotions happen immediately. Timely execution of promotions went up to 75 percent afterwards, resulting also in increased sales. And all of this was possible thanks to the timely data afforded by their RFID deployment.

"In the supply chain, potentially, we could bring RFIDs back into the manufacturing environment, and trace raw materials. We've found that the bigger payback in the short term for us has been reducing out-of-stocks on the shelf. But we believe there are a lot more opportunities with RFID," says Jamison.

SOURCE: Thomas Wailgum, "Kimberly-Clark's Secrets to RFID Success," *CIO Magazine*, July 30, 2007, and www.kimberly-clark.com, accessed May 11, 2011.

PREDICTIONS FOR THE FUTURE

If Moore's law prevails and technology advancement continues, we can expect to see our lives change in remarkable and unimaginable ways. Although we cannot really predict the future, it is interesting and fun to read the predictions of futurists— people whose job is to think about what the future might bring. Here's one man's perspective on what computing technology might do to change our lives in the decades to come.

Computers Will Enable People to Live Forever

In just 15 years, we'll begin to see the merger of human and computer intelligence that ultimately will enable people to live forever. At least that's the prediction of author and futurist Ray Kurzweil. Kurzweil suggests that nanobots will roam our bloodstreams, fixing diseased or aging organs, while computers will back up our human memories and rejuvenate our bodies by keeping us young in appearance and health.

The author of the book *The Singularity Is Near*, Kurzweil says that within a quarter of a century, nonbiological intelligence will match the range and subtlety of human intelligence. He predicts that it will then soar past human ability because of the continuing acceleration of information-based technologies, as well as the ability of machines to share their knowledge instantly.

Kurzweil predicts people and computers will intermix with nanobots, blood cell-sized robots, that will be integrated into everything from our clothing to our bodies and brains. People just need to live long enough—another 15–30 years—to live forever. Think of it as replacing everyone's "human body version 1.0" with nanotechnology that will repair or replace ailing or aging tissue, he says. Parts will become easily replaceable." A $1,000 worth of computation in the 2020s will be 1,000 times more powerful than the human brain," says Kurzweil, adding that in 25 years we'll have multiplied our computational power by a billion. "Fifteen years from now, it'll be a very different world. We'll have cured cancer and heart disease, or at least rendered them to manageable chronic conditions that aren't life threatening. We'll get to the point where we can stop the aging process and stave off death." Actually, we'll hit a point where human intelligence just can't keep up with, or even follow, the progress that computers will make, according to Kurzweil. He expects that nonbiological intelligence will have access to its own design plans and be able to improve itself rapidly. Computer, or nonbiological, intelligence created in the year 2045 will be one billion times more powerful than all human intelligence today.

"Supercomputing is behind the progress in all of these areas," says Kurzweil, adding that a prerequisite for nonbiological intelligence is to reverse-engineer biology and the human brain. That will give scientists a "toolkit of techniques" to apply when developing intelligent computers. In a written report, he said, "We won't experience 100 years of technological advance in the 21st century; we will witness on the order of 20,000 years of progress, or about 1,000 times greater than what was achieved in the 20th century."

According to Kurzweil, here's what we can expect in the not-so-distant future:

- Doctors will be doing a backup of our memories by the late 2030s.

- By the late 2020s, doctors will be sending intelligent bots, or nanobots, into our bloodstreams to keep us healthy, and into our brains to keep us young.

- In 15 years, human longevity will be greatly extended. By the 2020s, we'll be adding a year of longevity or more for every year that passes.

- In the same time frame, we'll routinely be in virtual reality environments. Instead of making a call on a cell phone, we will "meet" someone in a virtual world, take a walk on a virtual beach, and chat. Business meetings and conference calls will be held in calming or inspiring virtual locations.

- When you're walking down the street and see someone you've met before, background information about that person will pop up on your glasses or in the periphery of your vision.

- Instead of spending hours in front of a desktop machine, computers will be more ingrained in our environment. For instance, computer monitors could be replaced by projections onto our retinas or on a virtual screen hovering in the air.

- Scientists will be able to rejuvenate all of someone's body tissues and organs by transforming his or her skin cells into youthful versions of other cell types.

- Need a little boost? Kurzweil says scientists will be able to regrow our own cells, tissues, and even whole organs, and then introduce them into our bodies, all without surgery. As part of what he calls the "emerging field of rejuvenation medicine," new tissue and organs will be built out of cells that have been made younger.

- Got heart trouble? No problem, says Kurzweil. "We'll be able to create new heart cells from your skin cells and introduce them into your system through the bloodstream. Over time, your heart cells get replaced with these new cells, and the result is a rejuvenated, young heart with your own DNA."

- One trick we'll have to master is staying ahead of the game. Kurzweil warns that terrorists could obviously use this same technology against us. For example, they could build and spread a bioengineered biological virus that's highly powerful and stealthy.

According to Kurzweil, we're not that far away from solving a medical problem that has plagued scientists and doctors for quite some time now: the common cold. He notes that although nanotechnology could go into our bloodstreams and knock it out, before we even get to that stage, biotechnology should be able to cure the cold in just 10 years.

SOURCE: Sharon Gaudin, "Kurzweil: Computers Will Enable People to Live Forever," *InformationWeek*, November 21, 2006.

real world SOLUTION

Budway Enterprises Inc.–Custom Technology with Standard Components

Budway Enterprises, a family-owned business, is one of the leading providers of transloading, logistics solutions and supply chain services for the specialty metals industry in southern California. Operating out of a major facility in Fontana, the company has grown from a same-day delivery service for downtown Los Angeles into the largest rail-transloader for the Burlington Northern Santa Fe Railway. As the company continued to grow and sought to expand into more value-added services, management realized that its reliance on paper documents to run the business would only allow the company to get so far, and decided to launch an initiative to go all digital. Although the company has clearly identified the major business and technological objectives that any solution must be able to deliver, it has become apparent that no existing alternatives in the market are exactly what the company is looking for. In addition, given the limited resources of a family-owned enterprise, financial constraints must also be taken into account.

Budway executives looked at the handheld devices that the small package delivery companies, such as FedEx or UPS, use. Although these devices offered wireless access as well as data collection and scanning capabilities, none of the hardware vendors provided software that would connect these devices to the existing systems at Budway. They were also more expensive than a small company could afford. Budway also looked at GPS tracking solutions, which are transmitters that are installed on vehicles to provide real-time data about the locations visited and routes taken. Although much less expensive, these solutions did not provide digital Proof-of-Delivery (POD— the central document in the freight industry) or work order monitoring. It quickly became evident that the company would need to create its own solution by integrating parts of existing technologies.

In the end, Budway opted for a smartphone combined with other technologies and service providers to achieve the required functionality. As its hardware platform the company selected the Palm Treo Smartphone, which at the time was one of only two cell phones that had touch-screen capabilities that would allow the capture of signatures using a stylus pen. Given the wide availability of these phones and their relatively low cost compared to more specialized handheld devices, such as those used by FedEx or UPS, this was an attractive alternative. Budway chose Sprint as the

service provider, through its Sprint Business Mobility Framework offerings. Given the extensive coverage that Sprint offered within Budway's area of operations, this ensured that employees would always be within reach of the wireless service.

The Palm Treo Smartphone already had an integrated GPS device which, when used within Sprint's network, automatically provided location updates every 10 minutes. Testing determined that this time frame was more than adequate for the needs of Budway. Having found an adequate hardware and communications setup, the company now turned to the software needed to support their business processes. Although the phones themselves did not come with any work order management applications, Agilis Systems, a Sprint partner, offered work-flow software that could be customized and integrated with current software at Budway, which was an important consideration. Best of all, this hybrid solution came at a low cost to the company: Initial cost for each phone was $250 with a $ 75-per-month service charge, which included both Sprint service and the software packages developed by Agilis.

The resulting benefits are too long to list, but a few samples will give you an idea of the value that Budway has been able to deliver from this project. For example, clients can confirm receipt of products within minutes of delivery, helping their invoicing efforts. All parties involved have real-time access to tracking information about products being shipped, and clients can see what products are en route and when they will reach their destination. Having access to better and more updated information allowed Budway to offer new services, such as optimizing delivery schedules and redirecting drivers to take advantage of any opportunities, as well as being more proactive overall in managing any issues that may arise, sometimes even before drivers get to their destination.

Many clients have been very impressed by Budway's ability to deliver a rather sophisticated solution and help them improve their own business processes. One particular customer, Harbor Pipe & Steel Inc., has gone one step further. It now uses Budway almost exclusively for inbound materials coming into the ports of Los Angeles and Long Beach that need to be delivered to its facility in Riverside, California. Harbor Pipe & Steel uses the digital POD data and other online tools that Budway provides to track its products from the harbor to its facilities. "With the use of the Web site, I can see where my material is located at all times. This allows me to see if the material is in Budway's yard or on a truck heading our way with an estimated time of arrival," says Bob Line, Transportation Manager at Harbor Pipe & Steel. Making POD documents available electronically has been a major cost- and time-saver for this customer. "If there is any problem or question that arises on any coil, we can easily download the POD. This has taken a huge burden off of my shoulders since I have to reconcile all of the loads being picked up and shipped from the harbor," says Line.

Budway management has always been committed to using technology to gather as much data as possible and improving the way they run their business, so top management support was easy to come by. Prior to this project, all software had been developed by a member of management. The company had to hire a full-time programmer to work on the software integration between the components developed by Agilis Systems and internal Budway systems, but the benefits provided by the new technology, as well as its low initial cost of deployment, also made this decision a clear one. There were some issues along the way. For instance, Agilis had not fully developed the programming interface that Budway needed to communicate with the smartphones, and so the provider was building features as Budway was requesting them.

Although digital PODs are quite common, they had never been used in this particular industry before. As a result, some clients were initially skeptical about the new technology and insisted on signing an actual document in addition to the touch screen. Budway was happy to oblige, providing drivers with both options until customers became more comfortable with the new approach. However, once clients started to realize the many benefits associated with the technology, the need for actual paper documents quickly evaporated. These days, nobody wants to go back to "good old paper" anymore.

The most significant aspect of this project is that, taken individually, none of the technologies involved in the final solution was, by itself, terribly innovative. Taken together, however—and properly integrated—the resulting functionality was original enough that none of the other companies involved in the project had ever conceptualized it before getting involved with Budway. Using a cell phone as the only device also provided some unexpected benefits, as drivers only needed to use a single piece of hardware for all of their work. This helped simplify training and reduce barriers to adoption for the new technology. Although major carriers have the human and financial resources necessary to develop a custom solution, smaller companies like Budway are forced to think creatively about the best way to use standard, off-the-shelf technologies in ever more innovative ways. While large companies may have the scale necessary to justify proprietary developments, smaller businesses will not likely see a return on investment that justifies going to those lengths. Moreover, Budway management believes that the resulting solution is actually more powerful than any of the higher-end alternatives on the market at the time, and all for a fraction of the cost.

SOURCE: "Low-Cost GPS Tracking and Digital PODs Using Smartphones," *Computerworld Honors Program Case Study*, Budway Enterprises Inc., http://www.cwhonors.org/viewCaseStudy2008. asp?NominationID=2056, accessed May 14, 2011, and "Productivity Picks Up for Budway by Use of Tracking and Resource Management Software," *Agilis Systems Case Study*.

▼ QUESTIONS TO CONSIDER

1. Did Budway management take on an unnecessary risk by becoming the principal integrator of all of these components, instead of delegating the task to an outside partner, such as a consulting company? What are the advantages and disadvantages of each approach?

2. Now that the new systems are in place and working properly, what is the next step for Budway? Where do you think management could still improve their operations with the use of technology?

- **Computer Systems.** Major types of computer systems are summarized in Figure 3.3. Microcomputers are used as personal computers, network computers, personal digital assistants, technical workstations, and information appliances. Midrange systems are increasingly used as powerful network servers and for many multiuser business data processing and scientific applications. Mainframe computers are larger and more powerful than most midsize systems. They are usually faster, have more memory capacity, and can support more network users and peripheral devices. They are designed to handle the information processing needs of large organizations with high volumes of transaction processing or with complex computational problems.

Supercomputers are a special category of extremely powerful mainframe computer systems designed for massive computational assignments.

- **The Computer Systems Concept.** A computer is a system of information processing components that perform input, processing, output, storage, and control functions. Its hardware components include input and output devices, a central processing unit (CPU), and primary and secondary storage devices. The major functions and hardware in a computer system are summarized in Figure 3.10.

- **Peripheral Devices.** Refer to Figures 3.14 and 3.22 to review the capabilities of peripheral devices for input, output, and storage discussed in this chapter.

These are the key terms and concepts of this chapter. The page number of their first reference appears in parentheses.

1. Binary representation (110)
2. Central processing unit (97)
3. Computer system (96)
4. Computer terminal (90)
5. Cycles per second (98)
6. Direct access (111)
7. Graphical user interface (100)
8. Information appliance (91)
9. Magnetic disks (114)
   a. RAID (redundant array of independent disks) (115)
10. Magnetic stripe (107)
11. Magnetic tape (115)
12. Mainframe system (93)
13. Microcomputer (88)
14. Midrange system (92)
15. MIPS (million instructions per second) (98)
16. Moore's law (98)
17. Network computer (91)
18. Network server (88)
19. Network terminal (90)
20. Off-line (100)
21. Online (100)
22. Optical disks (116)
23. Optical scanning (105)
24. Peripherals (100)
25. Pointing devices (100)
26. Primary storage unit (97)
27. Processing speed (97)
    a. Millisecond (97)
    b. Microsecond (97)
    c. Nanosecond (97)
    d. Picosecond (97)
28. RFID (radio frequency identification) (117)
29. Secondary storage (97)
30. Semiconductor memory (112)
    a. RAM (random-access memory) (112)
    b. ROM (read-only memory) (112)
31. Sequential access (111)
32. Speech recognition (103)
33. Storage capacity (111)
    a. Bit (110)
    b. Byte (110)
    c. Kilobyte (111)
    d. Megabyte (111)
    e. Gigabyte (111)
    f. Terabyte (111)
    g. Petabyte (111)
34. Supercomputer (93)
35. Volatility (112)
36. Workstation computer (88)

Match one of the previous key terms and concepts with one of the following brief examples or definitions. Try to find the best fit for answers that seem to fit more than one term or concept. Defend your choices.

_____ 1. A computer is a combination of components that perform input, processing, output, storage, and control functions.

_____ 2. The main processing component of a computer system.

_____ 3. A measure of computer speed in terms of processor cycles.

_____ 4. Devices for consumers to access the Internet.

_____ 5. The memory of a computer.

_____ 6. Magnetic disks and tape and optical disks perform this function.

_____ 7. Input/output and secondary storage devices for a computer system.

_____ 8. Connected to and controlled by a CPU.

_____ 9. Separate from and not controlled by a CPU.

_____ 10. Results from the presence or absence or change in direction of electric current, magnetic fields, or light rays in computer circuits and media.

_____ 11. A common computer interface using a desktop metaphor and icons.

_____ 12. Can be a desktop/laptop or handheld computer.

_____ 13. A computer category between microcomputers and mainframes.

_____ 14. Low-cost microcomputers for use with the Internet and corporate intranets.

_____ 15. A redundant array of inexpensive hard drives.

_____ 16. A terminal that depends on network servers for its software and processing power.

_____ 17. A computer that manages network communications and resources.

_____ 18. The most powerful type of computer.

_____ 19. A magnetic tape technology for credit cards.

_____ 20. One-billionth of a second.

_____ 21. Roughly 1 billion characters of storage.

_____ 22. Includes electronic mice, trackballs, pointing sticks, and touch pads.

_____ 23. The largest of the three main types of computers.

_____ 24. Processor power measured in terms of number of instructions processed.

_____ 25. Prediction that computer power will double approximately every 18 to 24 months.

_____ 26. Promises to be the easiest, most natural way to communicate with computers.

_____ 27. Capturing data by processing light reflected from images.

_____ 28. The speed of a computer.

_____ 29. One one-thousandth of a second.

_____ 30. 1,024 bytes.

_____ 31. A device with a keyboard and a video display networked to a computer is a typical example.

_____ 32. The amount of data a storage device can hold.

_____ 33. A personal computer used as a technical workstation.

_____ 34. The smallest unit of data storage.

_____ 35. One trillion bytes.

_____ 36. You cannot erase the contents of these storage circuits.

_____ 37. The memory of most computers consists of these storage circuits.

_____ 38. The property that determines whether data are lost or retained when power fails.

_____ 39. Each position of storage can be accessed in approximately the same time.

_____ 40. Each position of storage can be accessed according to a predetermined order.

_____ 41. Microelectronic storage circuits on silicon chips.

_____ 42. Uses magnetic spots on metal or plastic disks.

_____ 43. Uses magnetic spots on plastic tape.

_____ 44. Uses a laser to read microscopic points on plastic disks.

_____ 45. A millionth of a second.

_____ 46. A trillionth of a second.

_____ 47. A grouping of eight bits that represents one alphabetic or special character.

_____ 48. A short-range wireless technology most commonly used to tag, track, and identify objects.

_____ 49. Around a million bytes; more precisely, 2 to the 20th power.

_____ 50. A unit of information or computer storage equal to one quadrillion bytes, or 1,024 terabytes.

discussion questions

1. What trends are occurring in the development and use of the major types of computer systems?

2. Will the convergence of PDAs, subnotebook PCs, and cell phones produce an information appliance that will make all of those categories obsolete? Why or why not?

3. Review the Real World Challenge introduced in the chapter. Since the proof-of-delivery (POD) documents are in essence the only binding evidence that products were delivered safe, sound, and on time, what are some of the issues that customers may raise when Budway proposes to do away with this document? What are some strategies Budway can use to assuage any concerns?

4. Do you think that information appliances like PDAs will replace personal computers (PCs) in business applications? Explain.

5. Are networks of PCs and servers making mainframe computers obsolete? Explain.

6. Consider the Real World Solution discussed in the chapter. How are the challenges encountered by a small company, such as Budway, different from those faced by larger enterprises? How was it possible for Budway to create a superior solution at a lower cost than some of the higher-end systems used by major companies in their industry?

7. What are several trends that are occurring in computer peripheral devices? How do these trends affect business uses of computers?

8. What are several important computer hardware developments that you expect to happen in the next 10 years? How will these affect the business use of computers?

9. What processor, memory, magnetic disk storage, and video display capabilities would you require for a personal computer that you would use for business purposes? Explain your choices.

10. What other peripheral devices and capabilities would you want to have for your business PC? Explain your choices.

analysis exercises

1. Hardware Costs
   Purchasing Computer Systems for Your Workgroup
   You have been asked to get pricing information for a potential purchase of PCs for the members of your workgroup. Go to the Internet to get prices for these units from Dell and Hewlett Packard. Look for a high-end office desktop model.

   The list below shows the specifications for the basic system you have been asked to price and potential upgrades to each feature. You will want to get a price for the basic system described below and a separate price for each of the upgrades shown.

Component	Basic Unit	Upgrade
CPU (gigahertz)	2.8	3.4
Hard Drive (gigabytes)	160	500
RAM (gigabytes)	1	2
Removable media	16× DVD-R/W	48× DVD-R/W
Monitor	17-inch flat screen	19-inch flat screen

   Select the standard software licenses; your IT department will install the necessary software for your workgroup. Take a two-year warranty and servicing coverage offered by each supplier. If a two-year warranty is not available, simply note any differences in the coverage with the closest match.

   a. Prepare a spreadsheet summarizing this pricing information and showing the cost, from each supplier, of the following options:
      a. units with the basic configuration,
      b. the incremental cost of each upgrade separately, and
      c. the cost of a fully upgraded unit. If you cannot find features that exactly match the requirements, then use the next higher standard for comparison and make a note of the difference.
   b. Prepare a set of PowerPoint slides summarizing your results. Include a discussion of the warranty and servicing contract options offered by each supplier.

2. Price and Performance Trends for Computer Hardware
   Hardware Analysis
   The table below details price and capacity figures for common components of personal computers. Typical prices for microprocessors, Random Access Memory (RAM), and hard disk storage prices are displayed. The performance of typical components has increased substantially over time, so the speed (for the microprocessor) or the capacity (for the storage devices) is also listed for comparison purposes. Although not all of the improvements in these components are reflected in these capacity measures, it is interesting to examine trends in these measurable characteristics.

   a. Create a spreadsheet based on the figures below and include a new row for each component showing the price per unit of capacity (cost per megahertz of speed for microprocessors and cost per megabyte of storage for RAM and hard disk devices).
   b. Create a set of graphs highlighting your results and illustrating trends in price per unit of performance (speed) or capacity.
   c. Write a short paper discussing the trends you found. How long do you expect these trends to continue? Why?
   d. Prepare a summary presentation outlining the points from your paper (above). Be sure to *link* your Excel chart into the PowerPoint presentation so it automatically updates when any data changes in the spreadsheet.

3. Can Computers Think Like People?
   The Turing Test
   The Turing Test is a hypothetical test to determine whether or not a computer system reached the level of "artificial intelligence." If the computer can fool a person into thinking it is another person, then it has artificial intelligence. Except in very narrow areas, no computer has passed the Turing Test.

   Free e-mail account providers such as Hotmail or Yahoo take advantage of this fact. They need to distinguish between new account registrations generated by a person and registrations generated by spammers' software. Why? Spammers burn through thousands of e-mail accounts in order to send

	1991	1993	1995	1997	1999	2001	2003	2005
Processor Speed MHz	25	33	100	125	350	1000	3,000	3,800
Cost	$180	$125	$275	$250	$300	$251	$395	$549
RAM Chip Mb per Chip	1	4	4	16	64	256	512	2,000
Cost	$55	$140	$120	$97	$125	$90	$59	$149
Hard Drive Gb per drive	.105	.250	.540	2.0	8.0	40.0	160.0	320
Cost	$480	$375	$220	$250	$220	$138	$114	$115

millions of e-mails. To help them, spammers need automated tools to generate these accounts. Hotmail fights this practice by requiring registrants to correctly enter an alphanumeric code hidden within an image. Spammers' programs have trouble correctly reading the code, but most humans do not. With this reverse Turing test, also called a "captcha," Hotmail can distinguish between a person and program and allow only humans to register. As a result, spammers must look elsewhere for free accounts.

a. Aside from those mentioned above, in what applications might businesses find it useful to distinguish between a human and a computer?

b. Describe a Turing test that a visually impaired person but not a computer might pass.

c. Search the Internet for the term "captcha" and describe its strengths and weaknesses.

4. Radio Frequency Identification

Input Device or Invasion of Privacy?

Punch cards, key boards, bar code scanners—the trend is clear. Input devices have continued to promote faster and more accurate data entry. Key to this is capturing data at its source, and no tool does this better than radio frequency identification systems (RFID). An RFID transmitter sends out a coded radio signal. An RFID tag changes and reflects this signal back to an antenna. The RFID system can read the reflection's unique patter and record it in a database. Depending on the system, this pattern may be associated with a product line, shipping pallet, or even a person. Although an RFID system's range is limited to a few dozen feet, this approach enables remarkable inventory tracking that doesn't rely on a human to keyboard or scan. Except for the presence of a 1-inch square (5-cm square) RFID tag, humans may have no idea an RFID system is in operation.

Indeed, that may be part of the problem. Consumers have expressed concern that RFID chips attached to products they purchase may be used to track them. Others fear the government may require embedded RFID chips as a form of personal identification and tracking. What started as a new and improved input device has devolved into a matter of public policy.

a. How would you feel if your university used RFID tags embedded in your student IDs to replace the magnetic "swipe" strip? On a campus, RFID tags might be used to control building access, manage computer access, or even automatically track class attendance.

b. Enter "RFID" into an Internet search engine and summarize the search results. Of the top twenty results, how many were positive, negative, or neutral?

c. Enter "RFID" and "privacy" into an Internet search engine, select a page expressing privacy concerns, and summarize them in a brief essay. Do you find these concerns compelling?

5. Gadgets

Getting to Know All about You

For two decades, user input devices typically comprised a keyboard and a mouse. This left computers virtually "blind" to the world. A whole new class of devices has now changed this. Read Wired.com's article *How Context-Aware Computing Will Make Gadgets Smarter* (http://bit.ly/av0V7w) and answer the following questions:

a. What additional context-sensitive inputs are computing devices now able to acquire automatically?

b. Briefly explain the difference between "hard-sensing" and "soft-sensing." Provide an example of each.

c. The more our computers know about us, the more useful they can become—and the more invasive. Hundreds of detective stories and spy novels feature futuristic tracking devices, yet here we are in the future and we're carrying them willingly, albeit perhaps unknowingly. Read MSNBC.com's article, *Government officials want answers to secret iPhone tracking* (http://bit.ly/fR3SVu), and answer the following questions.

d. Do you agree with researchers Allan and Warden that "there's no immediate harm that would seem to come from the availability of this data"? Give several examples of harm that might arise from having this information fall into the wrong hands.

e. Has Apple's response to this revelation been adequate? Why or why not?

AstraZeneca, UnitedHealth, and Others: IT-Asset Management— Do You Know What You've Got?

Global pharmaceuticals giant AstraZeneca needed some strong medicine of its own to fix a burgeoning IT-asset-management problem brought about by multiple acquisitions and their nonstandard gear, a high-tech workforce spread across 255 facilities in 147 countries, and in total more than 67,000 employees using more than 90,000 hardware and software assets ranging from notebooks up to SAP and Oracle enterprise applications and databases.

With software vendors becoming more aggressive on audits as sales of new products are generally weak, and with greater internal collaboration requiring a more consistent set of tools to simplify processes and maintenance, the $31 billion pharmaceuticals company realized a few years ago that Microsoft's Systems Management Server was simply overmatched for the job of managing the global enterprise's complex base of IT assets.

So Microsoft recommended the asset-management products offered by a French company called PS'Soft, which is a subsidiary of BDNA Corp., a top provider of IT infrastructure inventory and analysis solutions. And in the years that AstraZeneca has been steadily getting its IT assets under control, PS'Soft has distinguished itself like few other IT vendors, according to AstraZeneca Global IT Asset leader Bernard Warrington.

"In all my years, our engagement with PS'Soft was one of the first and only times we had an IT vendor show such willingness to work as a true partner and really try to solve our problems with us," Warrington says. Referring to PS'Soft's Julian Moreau, Warrington described the uniquely open collaboration that allowed him and his team to understand the problem, design the solution, and then execute that plan.

"Julian and I worked extremely closely together, and from there our partnership cascaded down to the other members of the team," Warrington says. "But I need to be very clear about that: In the beginning, the knowledge and expertise were clearly with them—they were teaching and we were learning."

The problem, Warrington says, is that in the increasingly strategic world of IT-asset management, "the tool set itself meets only 30 percent of the overall need: On top of that, you need to build the processes, understand the costs, come up with standards, develop interfaces with other major vendors, and much more—we simply didn't have all the skills necessary to cover that total life cycle. But PS'Soft did have those skills, both in-house and through their contacts."

In addition, says Warrington, PS'Soft and BDNA had the global experience necessary to help AstraZeneca get its arms around its global sprawl of IT gear, which was essential for two reasons: First, so that the company could begin to gain greater leverage in purchasing negotiations, and second, so it could be able to fairly, but aggressively, hold its own during audits by software vendors.

"In so many countries where we operate, the tradition has been that budgets are managed locally, making it impossible to see the global aggregate in detail," Warrington says. "We simply did not have the ability to get a global view. The old tools we used gave us something of a snapshot, but didn't let us have enough insight to be able to manage the situation. At the same time, the IT vendors are getting very aggressive with audits, and without offering a specific number I can tell you that millions and millions of dollars are at stake—and before our engagement with PS'Soft, no matter how hard we tried with the old tool set, we were just not able to achieve those potential cost savings from vendors."

Over time, Warrington says, AstraZeneca gained that necessary level of control and knowledge: "Now AstraZeneca is in a position to enter negotiations from a position of strength, confidence, and knowledge." And that achievement has given the company a new perspective on the realm of IT-asset management, Warrington said: "Too many companies just look on IT- asset management as nothing more than bean counting, versus looking deeper and understanding the ROI and ROA that can be achieved.

"But we learned firsthand that there is a huge opportunity to get control over what you have, to satisfy even the most rigorous audit, and to negotiate better contracts. And that's a lot more than bean counting," says Warrington.

IT organizations in diversified companies—particularly those grown through acquisition—wage a seemingly endless battle against unnecessary IT diversity and related costs. Conceived, planned, and executed in 18 months, UnitedHealth Group's (UHG) Hercules program proves the complexity can be conquered, while protecting or improving IT's service levels. By creating a standard desktop configuration and consistent management processes, Hercules reduced total cost of ownership to $76 per month per desktop, from more than $240.

In 2004, with the CEO's support, Alistair Jacques, then SVP of UHG-IT, launched Hercules, focusing it on standardizing and streamlining the processes behind desktop management: procurement, configuration, installation, life cycle and asset management. In addition to this focus on process, two techniques stand out as key to the program's success. Working with finance, IT developed a chargeback model that imposes a premium on nonstandardized desktop configurations: $170 per month versus $45 per month for a standard configuration. This value price encourages business managers to choose the more efficient infrastructure. UHG also reduced costly on-site support by reorganizing it: A central IT team manages high-level support activities, completing 95 percent remotely, while select, on-site end users (often non-IT administrative staff trained by IT) provide basic support to colleagues.

UHG-IT treated desktop management as a business process challenge rather than a technology issue. This approach freed them to employ tactics like non-IT staff for desktop support and value pricing. To date, UHG has converted 75,000 out of 90,000 devices to the new standards, delivering $42 million in annual savings. Effectively, UHG can now manage nearly four times the number of end users with the same number of IT personnel as in 2004. All while actually improving—not diminishing—service levels: IT now deploys 99.4 percent of releases, updates and patches in three hours, instead of 65 percent in three weeks.

Indeed, companies that blow off asset management do so at their own peril. At the same time, 99 percent of companies that her organization comes across don't have a proper asset management process in place, according to Elisabeth Vanderveldt, vice president of business development at Montreal-based IT services and consulting firm Conamex International Software Corp. That's a staggering number, considering the value that life-cycle management can bring to an organization. And it's indicative of the widespread lack of respect for this important aspect of IT operations.

The ideal time to start considering an asset management program is before the business and its IT infrastructure is even up and running, but the common scenario is that corporations look to asset management after they've encountered a problem running the infrastructure.

The mentality around asset management is evolving, however. Companies used to consider only reliability, availability, and overall equipment effectiveness in that equation. But now there is recognition of factors like continuing pressures on cost, and green technology. "It really requires a mature organization to understand what's going to be needed to assess and execute a life-cycle management strategy," says Don Barry, associate partner in global business services in the supply chain operations and asset management solutions group at IBM.

Why is a life-cycle management program important? For one thing, it puts IT in much better control of its assets, and this can have a number of benefits.

"IT can make really intelligent decisions around what they should get rid of, and they might even find they have more money in the budget and they can start taking a look at newer technology and see if they can bring it in-house. Without that big picture, they just end up spending more and more money than had they been proactive," says Vanderveldt.

Life-cycle management also has value as a risk management tool and it aids in the disaster recovery process as well, she adds. "It's also beneficial for those moments that are just completely out of your control, like mergers, acquisitions and uncontrolled corporate growth, either organic or inorganic," says Darin Stahl, an analyst at London, Ontario–based Info-Tech Research Group. "IT leaders without this tool set are now charged with pulling all this information together on short notice. That could be diminished considerably in terms of turnaround time and effort for IT guys if they have a holistic asset management program in place."

SOURCE: Bob Evans, "Global CIO Quick Takes: AstraZeneca Saves Millions with BDNA," *InformationWeek*, February 22, 2010; Rick Swanborg, "Desktop Management: How UnitedHealth Used Standardization to Cut Costs," *CIO.com*, April 28, 2009; and Kathleen Lau, "Asset Management: Do You Know What You've Got?" *CIO Canada*, August 13, 2008.

▼ CASE STUDY QUESTIONS

1. What are the companies mentioned in the case trying to control, or manage, through these projects? What is the problem? And how did they get there?

2. What are the business benefits of implementing strong IT-asset management programs? In what ways have the companies discussed in the case benefited? Provide several examples.

3. One of the companies in the case, UnitedHealth Group, tackled the issue by imposing standardization and charging those stepping outside standard models. How should they balance the need to standardize with being able to provide business units with the technologies best suited to their specific needs? Justify your answer.

REAL WORLD ACTIVITIES

1. An important metric in this area considered by companies is the Total Cost of Ownership (TCO) of their IT assets. Go online and research TCO and how it is related to IT-asset management. How are companies using TCO to manage their IT investments? Prepare a presentation to share your research with the rest of your class.

2. What does Don Barry of IBM mean by "life-cycle" in the context of this case? How would this life-cycle management work when it comes to IT assets? Break into small groups with your classmates and create a working definition of life-cycle management and how it works as you understand it from the case.

IT in Health Care: Voice Recognition Tools Make Rounds at Hospitals

The infamous doctor's scrawl may finally be on its way out.

Voice technology is the latest tool health care providers are adopting to cut back on time-consuming manual processes, freeing clinicians to spend more time with patients and reduce costs.

At Butler Memorial Hospital, voice-assisted technology has dramatically reduced the amount of time the Butler, Pa., hospital's team of intravenous (IV) nurses spends recording information in patients' charts and on other administrative tasks. And at the Cleveland Clinic's Fairview Hospital, doctors are using speech recognition to record notes in patients' e-medical records.

Butler recently completed a pilot project where three IV nurses used Vocollect's AccuNurse hands-free, voice-assisted technology along with Boston Software System's work-flow automation tools. The nurses were able to cut the time they spend on phone calls and manual processes, including patient record documentation, by at least 75 percent. Now Butler is rolling out the voice technology for its full IV team of four nurses and seven other clinicians to use for patient care throughout the facility.

The productivity boost from the voice-assisted tools also helps with the hospital's expansion plans, says Dr. Tom McGill, Butler vice present of quality and safety. Butler will soon add about 70 beds—growing from 235 beds now to more than 300—but it won't need to expand the IV nursing team because of the time savings from the voice-assisted technology, McGill says.

In the past, when a patient needed IV care, such as a change in the intravenous medication being administered, an IV nurse would be paged. The nurse would have to call the patient's nursing station or the doctor requesting the IV to obtain details. The nurse then would prioritize the request with all of the existing IV orders. Once IV care was completed, nurses would record what they did in the patient's e-medical record.

With the AccuNurse, which combines the use of speech recognition and synthesis for charting and communication, Butler's IV nurses wear lightweight headsets and small pocket-sized wireless devices that enable them to hear personalized care instructions and other information about patients' IV needs.

IV requests are entered into Butler's computer system, which sends them through the Vocollect system to the appropriate headset. IV nurses listen to details about new orders and use the system to prioritize IV orders.

When they finish caring for a patient, nurses record what they did in the patient's e-medical record using voice commands. "The nurses can document as they're walking to the next patient's room," says McGill. Once they finish with one patient, nurses say "next task" to obtain instructions for the next patient, McGill says.

The system has shown itself to be capable of understanding different accents, he said. Butler is evaluating expanding use of the voice-assisted technology to other clinical areas, including surgery. The technology could be used to help ensure that surgical staff complete patient safety checklists.

McGill wouldn't say how much Butler paid for the system, but he expects the ROI will be realized in 12 to 18 months. "It's very affordable," he notes. Meanwhile, Dr. Fred Jorgenson, a faculty physician at Cleveland Clinic's Fairview Hospital, is using Nuance's Dragon Medical speech recognition technology to speak patient notes into the hospital's Epic EMR (electronic medical records) system.

"I'm not a fast typist," Jorgenson says. "Many doctors over a certain age aren't. If I had to type all the time, I'd be dead." And, at 13 cents to 17 cents per line, dictation transcription services are expensive. "In primary care, patient notes can be 30 to 40 lines. That adds up," he says. Fairview is saving about $2,000 to $3,000 a month that might have otherwise been spent on transcription, Jorgenson said. It cost about $3,500 to get Dragon up and running.

With transcription services, the turnaround time is 24 to 36 hours before information is available in the EMR. Spoken notes are available immediately.

Jorgensen describes the accuracy of Dragon Medical's speech-to-text documentation as "very good," especially with medical terms and prescriptions. "It rarely gets medical words wrong," he says. "If you see a mistake, it's usually with 'he' or 'she,' and you can correct it when you see it."

Mount Carmel St. Ann's hospital in Columbus, Ohio, has been among the early wave of health care providers using electronic clinical systems bolstered with speech recognition capabilities. About seven years ago, emergency department doctors at Mount Carmel St. Ann's hospital began having access to Dragon's speech recognition software not long after an e-health record system from Allscripts was rolled out there.

When the e-health record was first rolled out—without the voice capabilities—Mount Carmel St. Ann's doctors didn't necessarily see the kind of productivity boost they had been hoping for, in large part because they found themselves spending a lot of time typing notes, notes Dr. Loren Leidheiser, chairman and director of emergency medicine at Mount Carmel St. Ann's emergency department. But as more of Mount Carmel St. Ann's ER doctors began incorporating the speech recognition capabilities into their work flow—whether speaking notes into a lapel microphone or into a computer in the patient room or hallway—the efficiency picked up tremendously, says Leidheiser.

Also, before using the Dragon software, the ER department spent about $500,000 annually in traditional dictation transcription costs for the care associated with the hospital's 60,000 to 70,000 patient visits yearly at the time. That was cut down "to zero," he says. The return on investment on the speech recognition, combined with the use of the e-health record system, was "within a year and a half," notes Leidheiser.

Leidheiser also makes use of time stuck in traffic to dictate notes that are later incorporated into patient records or turned into e-mails or letters. Using a Sony digital recorder, Leidheiser can dictate a letter or note while in his car, then later plug the recorder into his desktop computer, where his spoken words are converted to text.

Speech recognition technology is also helping U.S. military doctors keep more detailed patients notes while cutting the time they spend typing on their computers. By 2011, the U.S. Department of Defense expects to have implemented its integrated, interoperable electronic medical record system, AHLTA, at more than 500 military medical facilities and hospitals worldwide.

The system will be used for the care of more than 9 million active military personnel, retirees, and their dependents. Military doctors using the AHLTA system also have access to Dragon NaturallySpeaking Medical speech recognition technology from Nuance Communications' Dictaphone health care division, allowing doctors to speak "notes" into patient records, as an alternative to typing and dictation. Over the last year, the adoption of Dragon has doubled, with approximately 6,000 U.S. military doctors using the software at health care facilities of all military branches, including the Air Force, Army, Navy, and Marine Corps.

The use of Dragon Naturally Speaking voice recognition software with the AHLTA e-health record systems is freeing doctors from several hours of typing into the AHLTA their various patient notes each week, he said. Being able to speak notes into an e-health record at the patient's bedside—rather than staring at a computer screen typing—also helps improves doctors' bedside manner and allows them to narrate more comprehensive notes while the patients are there, or right after a visit. That cuts down on mistakes caused by memory lapses and boosts the level of details that are included in a patient record, says Dr. Robert Bell Walker, European Regional Medical Command AHLTA consultant and a family practice physician for the military.

The voice capability "saves a lot of time and adds to the thoroughness of notes from a medical and legal aspect," says Dr. Craig Rohan, a U.S. Air Force pediatrician at Peterson Air Force base in Colorado. The ability to speak notes directly into a patient's electronic chart is particularly helpful in complicated cases, where a patient's medical history is complex, he says. Text pops up on the computer screen immediately after words are spoken into the system, so doctors can check the accuracy, make changes, or add other details.

Also, because spoken words are immediately turned into text, the medical record has "a better flow" to document patient visits. Previously, "the notes that had been created by [entering] structured text into the AHLTA system looks more like a ransom note," says Walker, with information seemingly randomly pasted together.

Doctors can speak into a microphone on their lapels to capture notes in tablet PCs during patient visits, or speak into headsets attached to desktop or wall-mounted computers. The storage requirement of voice notes is "small," especially when compared with other records, such as medical images, says Walker. By adding spoken notes to medical records, e-mails, and letters, "it's easier to tell the story," remarks Leidheiser.

SOURCE: Marianne Kolbasuk McGee, "Voice Recognition Tools Make Rounds at Hospitals," *InformationWeek*, September 17, 2009; Marianne Kolbasuk McGee, "Doctors Use Speech Recognition Tools to Enhance Patient E-Health Records," *InformationWeek*, May 19, 2008; and Matt Hamblen, "Doctors' Notes Get Clearer with Speech Recognition Software," *Computerworld*, May 16, 2008.

▼ CASE STUDY QUESTIONS

1. What are some of the benefits afforded to organizations implementing voice recognition technologies in these settings? How can you quantify these benefits to assess the value of the investment? Provide several examples from the case.

2. There is no margin for error when working in a health care setting. How would you go about implementing these technologies in this high-risk environment? What precautions or approaches would you take to minimize risks? Develop some recommendations.

3. In what other areas of medicine would you expect technology to make inroads next? Where do you think it would be most beneficial, and how would it change the way doctors and nurses work today? Provide several examples.

▼ REAL WORLD ACTIVITIES

1. The case talks about electronic medical or health records systems. These are slowly becoming standard in many hospitals and clinics, both private and public. Go online and search for reports of these implementations. What are the main benefits derived from their adoption? What have been the major roadblocks preventing their acceptance? Prepare a report to share your findings.

2. The case above was presented from the perspective of practitioners and hospital administrators. How comfortable would you feel, as a patient, knowing that your health care providers are using these technologies? Would you have any concerns? Break into small groups with your classmates to discuss this issue.

chapter 4

COMPUTER SOFTWARE

INFORMATION SYSTEMS

INFORMATION TECHNOLOGIES

CHAPTER HIGHLIGHTS

Application Software: End-User Applications

Introduction to Software

REAL WORLD CHALLENGE: Japan Post Network—from Government Entity to Private Company

Business Application Software
Software Suites and Integrated Packages
Web Browsers and More
Electronic Mail, Instant Messaging, and Blogs
Word Processing and Desktop Publishing
Spreadsheets
Presentation Graphics
Personal Information Managers
Groupware
Software Alternatives

System Software: Computer System Management

System Software Overview
Operating Systems
Other System Management Programs
Programming Languages
Web and Internet Languages and Services
Programming Software

REAL WORLD SOLUTION: Japan Post Network—Savings and Competitive Advantage with Software as a Service and Cloud Computing

REAL WORLD CASE: GE, H.B. Fuller Co., and Others: Successful Implementations of Software as a Service

REAL WORLD CASE: U.S. Department of Defense: Enlisting Open-Source Applications

LEARNING OBJECTIVES

4-1 Describe several important trends occurring in computer software.

4-2 Give examples of several major types of application and system software.

4-3 Explain the purpose of several popular software packages for end-user productivity and collaborative computing.

4-4 Define and describe the functions of an operating system.

4-5 Describe the main uses of computer programming software, tools, and languages.

4-6 Describe the issues associated with open-source software.

Application Software:
End-User Applications

This chapter provides an overview of the major types of software you depend on as you work with computers and access computer networks. It discusses their characteristics and purposes and gives examples of their uses. Before we begin, let's look at an example of the changing world of software in business.

INTRODUCTION
TO SOFTWARE
LO 4-1
LO 4-2

Read the Real World Challenge discussing the problems that Japan Post Network faced as it transitioned from government entity to private company. We can learn a lot about how to develop new systems under severe time constraints from this case. See Figure 4.1.

What Is Software?

To fully appreciate the need for—and value of—the wide variety of software available, we should be sure we understand what software is. *Software* is the general term for a myriad of programs used to operate and manipulate computers and their peripheral devices or to perform a specific task using a computer as the vehicle. One common way of describing hardware and software is to say that software can be thought of as the variable part of a computer and hardware as the invariable part. Think of the hardware as your iPod, Blu-Ray player, or CD player and the software as the song, movie, or game you want to enjoy. As you can imagine, there are many types and categories of software. In this chapter, we'll try to unravel the basic categories of software and the common uses for it.

Types of Software

Let's begin our overview of software by looking at an organizational chart of the major types and functions of software. The two main categories available to computer users are *application* software and *system* software as shown in Figure 4.2. This method of organizing software is the method we will use for our detailed discussion in this chapter. Of course, this figure is a conceptual illustration. The types of software you will encounter depend primarily on the types of computers and networks you use and on the specific tasks you want to accomplish. Nonetheless, once you understand the basics, the rest will be easy.

Application Software for End Users

Figure 4.2 shows that **application software** includes a variety of programs that can be further subdivided into *general-purpose* and *application-specific* categories. **General-purpose application programs** are programs that perform common information processing jobs for end users. For example, word processing, spreadsheet, database management, and graphics programs are popular with users for home, education, business, scientific, and many other purposes. Because they significantly increase the productivity of end users, they are sometimes known as *productivity packages*. Other examples include Web browsers, e-mail, and groupware, which help support communication and collaboration among workgroups and teams. In today's environment, it is hard to imagine a computer user, regardless of job role or intention, who has not encountered a word processor, spreadsheet, or Web browser in some form or another. These applications are essential.

An additional common way of classifying software is based on how the software was developed. **Custom software** is the term used to identify software applications that

Japan Post Network– from Government Entity to Private Company

In a former life, Japan Post was a government-owned corporation offering postal and package delivery services, banking, and life insurance. With more than 400,000 employees and 24,700 postal offices throughout Japan, it was the largest employer in the country; one-third of all government employees worked for Japan Post. The company was born on April 2, 2003 to replace the existing Postal Services Agency, and it was taken private in October 2007 after a heated political contest decided the issue in favor of making the company a privately owned entity. At its height, Japan Post ran the largest postal savings system in the world, with approximately 224 trillion yen (about $2.1 trillion) in its savings accounts, and 126 trillion yen (about $1.2 trillion) in life insurance services. To put these numbers in context, they represented about 25 percent of all household assets in Japan at the time. Japan Post also held about 140 trillion yen, one-fifth of the Japanese national debt, in its bond accounts.

After being privatized, Japan Post became the Japan Post Group, which operates four separate businesses (Japan Post Service, Japan Post Network, Japan Post Bank, and Japan Post Insurance) under an umbrella corporation called Japan Post Holdings. Japan Post Network operates more than 24,000 post offices in Japan and provides

Japan Post Network needs to develop new systems to integrate operations with three other companies in a short time frame.

SOURCE: Image Source/Jupiterimages.

contracted sales agency service to the other three businesses in the group. It is also responsible for providing customer service and sales of products and services for the other companies. Now a private company, Japan Post Network needed to get its systems quickly integrated with those of the other companies and start competing in a new marketplace. For a company of this size, which was accustomed to being a government entity, the challenge was nothing short of formidable.

"We only had three months to develop and implement a system that would allow us to consolidate paper-based customer data and feedback taken from our branch offices to be used for systems development," says Akira Iwasaki, CIO. In particular, Japan Post Network identified two major business challenges that would need to be addressed if the new company was to be successful as a private entity— and all in the short deadline imposed by the privatization schedule. The first one was a compliance issue. As a separate company providing bank agency services, Japan Post Network was involved in the cross-selling of various products and services provided by the other sister entities in the holding group. In order to comply with various banking, financial instruments, exchange, and insurance business laws and regulations, Japan Post Network was required to obtain prior consent from customers "in writing or other appropriate methods." This was a new business requirement; when Japan Post Network was part of the government-owned Japan Post, this was not necessary, since the customer was dealing with a single company. Now, as a third-party agent, Japan Post Network had to ensure that customers knew with whom they were ultimately contracting.

The second challenge was also a result of the privatization process that split the giant Japan Post into four legally distinct companies. The new holding group had set a goal of improving customer service throughout all entities by better collecting and sharing information between post offices and branches. Before, Japan Post Network had relied on a system that used e-mail and paper-based documentation to gather and manage information about customer inquiries, complaints, or any other interactions at its offices. Now that the company was about to compete in the private sector, that process would no longer do. New technology was needed to achieve rapid and appropriate responses to customer demands, as well as more accurate gathering of interaction information, which was key to the development of new products and services.

With only a short period of time before the privatization was completed, speed in new systems creation and deployment was Japan Post Network's major concern. At the same time, given the large size of its operations and the coming transition from a government-owned and government-run entity into a private, competitive company looming ahead, quality of service was paramount. None of its soon-to-be customers had ever known anything but the "old" Japan Post. (At the time of privatization, Japan Post—counting its predecessor, the Postal Services Agency—was more than 130 years old and had always existed as a government-owned entity.) Outages and errors in its first day of business in the private world just could not happen. To make things even more complicated, Japan Post Network had a team of about 60 IT staff members in charge of systems development and planning for a company with nearly 120,000 employees, so IT attention was in short supply.

In order to achieve its goals while taking into account all of these constraints, Japan Post Network submitted a general competitive bidding process to select the new technologies it would deploy. (This is a process in which information about the conditions that the winning bidder must satisfy is made public, and competition among candidates is used to determine to whom the contract would be awarded.) The company compiled its list of requirements for each system and evaluated each vendor on how well they were able to satisfy those requirements. Any vendors selected would need to be able to deploy the new systems in a short period of time. How short? The public bid was announced in January 2007, and all systems should be operational nine months later.

Japan Post was broken up into four different operations as part of the Japanese government's long-term plan to introduce private ownership and competition in what were traditionally government monopolies. One of the new four companies, Japan Post Network, will operate the postal service branches and serve as an agent of the other three enterprises, selling various financial and insurance products, and would also be the main physical point of contact with customers. Now a commercial entity, Japan Post Network needed to transform its postal business from being operations oriented to generating increasing revenues. This translates into transforming post offices into a single point of contact with customers that is able to serve all of their banking, insurance, brokerage, and shipping needs. And all this must be accomplished with customer-facing systems that are efficient, easy to use, and reliable. Did we mention they only have nine months to do so?

SOURCE: Pete Swabey, "Japan Post," *InformationAge*, March 12, 2009, Charles Babcock, "How Cloud Computing Changes IT Organizations," *InformationWeek*, November 28, 2009, Koji Motoyoshi and Yefim Natis, "Case Study: Japan Post Improves Customer Service Effectiveness with Saas and APaaS," *Gartner Research*, July 15, 2008, "Japan Post Expands Salesforce Platform Deployment to 45,000 Users," *Salesforce.com Press Release*, September 5, 2008, IDC ExpertROI Spotlight, December 2009, and www.japanpost.com, accessed May 16, 2011.

▼ **QUESTIONS TO CONSIDER**

1. What will be the business model of the new Japan Post Network? How will it be different from what was done when all companies worked together as Japan Post? How will the new applications support, or enable, that business model?

2. What are some of the challenges that Japan Post Network and its employees and customers will face as the company seeks to roll out these new applications in such a short time frame? What are some strategies that could be used to address these challenges?

3. Why do you think Japan Post Network opted for a formal, public, competitive bidding process? What are the advantages and disadvantages of taking this approach? What were they looking to accomplish?

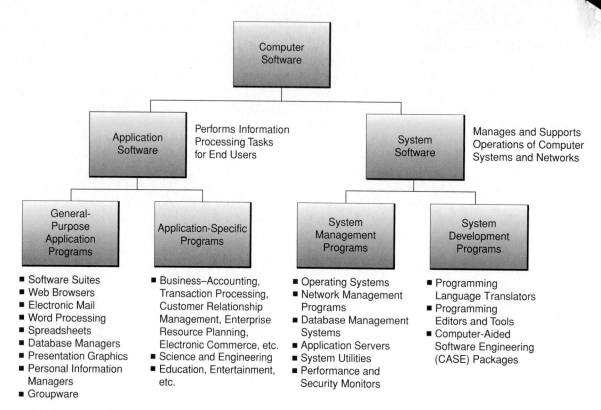

FIGURE 4.2

An organizational chart of computer software. Note the major types and examples of application and system software.

are developed within an organization for use by that organization. In other words, the organization that writes the program code is also the organization that uses the final software application. This means the custom application can be designed to do exactly what the organization wants or needs. It also means that the software will work only for that organization and only for its intended purpose. In contrast, **COTS software** (an acronym that stands for *commercial off-the-shelf*) is developed with the intention of selling the software in multiple copies (and usually for a profit). In this case, the organization that writes the software is not the intended target audience for its use. Examples of common COTS applications include Microsoft Office, Adobe Acrobat, or Intuit's Quickbooks.

Several characteristics are important when describing COTS software. First, as stated in our definition, COTS software products are sold in many copies with minimal changes beyond scheduled upgrade releases. Purchasers of COTS software generally have no control over the specification, schedule, evolution, or access to either the source code or the internal documentation. A COTS product is sold, leased, or licensed to the general public, but in virtually all cases, the vendor of the product retains the intellectual property rights to the software. Custom software, in contrast, is generally owned by the organization that developed it (or that paid to have it developed), and the specifications, functionality, and ownership of the final product are controlled or retained by the developing organization. We'll get into this in a little more depth later in the chapter.

The newest innovation in software development is called *open-source software*. In this approach, developers collaborate on the development of an application using programming standards that allow anyone to contribute to the software. Furthermore, as each developer completes his or her project, the code for the application becomes available and free to anyone else who wishes to use it. We will discuss this new approach to software development in greater detail later in this chapter.

Germany-based SAP AG is tackling business processes in a novel way with the newest version of its Business Suite, which embeds analytics acquired from Business Objects SA and introduces industry-specific "value scenarios." Version 7.0 of SAP Business Suite, a library of business processes, adds industry best practices through more than 30 modular value scenarios—such as Superior Customer Value and Product Lifecycle Management (PLM)—designed to cross traditional organizational boundaries.

These " predefined end-to-end business processes" are intended to be implemented in small steps by organizations as they need it, says Jim Hagemann Snabe, SAP executive board member. The value scenarios basically illustrate interrelationships between SAP product capabilities using graphical guides and business terms, not feature and function lists. The customer can also see the impact on the associated systems, and ultimately, the specific SAP modules that would need to be activated.

Ray Wang, vice president at Cambridge, Massachusetts–based Forrester Research Inc., says customers will find the value scenarios "compelling as they align with the key business drivers users face." But as with all best practices, Wang notes that "SAP will need to make it easy for customers to modify those scenarios, reduce the overall cost of owning SAP, and provide more frequent levels of innovation."

One customer, Colgate-Palmolive Co., has large implementations in CRM and PLM that would benefit from the new capabilities of version 7.0, says the company's senior vice president of IT and business services, Ed Toben. "Particularly when you look at PLM, which is newer, the processes and the enhancement-pack concept of turning on pieces should make us move faster," says Toben.

Another customer, pharmaceutical company Roche, requires the flexibility and ability to scale as the business changes in order to remain current, says chief information officer Jennifer Allerton. "IT investments . . . have got to make sense in their own right," she says. "And, the pharmaceuticals business is one where you invest for the long term and when you make investments about IT packages, you're not going to change your mind the next day about them."

IBM Corp., also a customer, is focused on a number of transformation programs, including the area of operational efficiency, says Jeannette Horan, vice president of enterprise business transformation with the office of the chief information officer at IBM. To that end, the company's strategy, says Horan, is to integrate the enterprise globally through common processes, using the Business Suite to "mix and match components of the business to go to market in new and interesting ways."

But while companies are taking a hard look at spending and reviewing projects, "that does not mean . . . that companies do not spend, they just spend very smartly and very wisely," says Léo Apotheker, co-CEO of SAP AG. There is a need, says Apotheker, "to provide better and faster insight, a higher level of efficiency, a need to introduce a whole new degree of flexibility in the way we do business."

SAP Business Suite7: Introducing Modular Scenarios Cutting across Organizational Functions

SOURCE: Kathleen Lau, "Industry 'Value Scenarios' in SAP Business Suite 7," *Computerworld Canada,* February 12, 2009.

The best thing about software is that it can literally be designed to do whatever you want. Thousands of *function-specific application software* packages are available to support needs of end users in business, education, and day-to-day activities. For example, business application software supports the reengineering and automation of business processes with strategic e-business applications like *customer relationship management, enterprise resource planning,* and *supply chain management.* Other examples are

BUSINESS APPLICATION SOFTWARE
LO 4-2

ORACLE E-BUSINESS SUITE

Advanced Planning	Business Intelligence	Contracts
e-Commerce	Enterprise Asset Management	Exchanges
Financials	Human Resources	Interaction Center
Manufacturing	Marketing	Order Fulfillment
Procurement	Product Development	Professional Services Automation
Projects	Sales	Service
Training	Treasury	

FIGURE 4.3

The business applications in Oracle's E-Business Suite software illustrate some of the many types of business application software being used today.

SOURCE: Oracle Corp., "Oracle Enterprise Performance Management and Business Intelligence," Oracle.com, 2011.

software packages that Web-enable online applications or apply to the internal activities of organizations like *human resource management, accounting,* and *finance.* Still other software empowers managers and business professionals with decision support tools like *data mining, enterprise information portals,* or *knowledge management systems.*

We will discuss these applications again in upcoming chapters and will go into more detail about these business software tools and applications. For example, data warehousing and data mining are discussed in Chapters 5 and 10; accounting, marketing, manufacturing, human resource management, and financial management applications are covered in Chapters 7 and 8. Customer relationship management, enterprise resource planning, and supply chain management are also covered in Chapter 8. Electronic commerce is the focus of Chapter 9, and decision support and data analysis applications are explored in Chapter 10. Figure 4.3 illustrates some of the many types of business application software that are available today. These particular applications are integrated in the Oracle E-Business Suite software product of Oracle Corp.

SOFTWARE SUITES AND INTEGRATED PACKAGES
LO 4-3

FIGURE 4.4

The basic program components of the top four software suites. Other programs may be included, depending on the suite edition selected.

From business application software, we move to the more general-purpose applications and uses of software. The best place to start our discussion is by looking at *software suites,* which are very likely the most widely used productivity software packages. Software suites bundle together a variety of general-purpose software applications. Examples of popular software suites include Microsoft Office, Lotus SmartSuite, Corel WordPerfect Office, Sun's StarOffice, and their open-source product, OpenOffice. Examining their components gives us an overview of the important software tools that you can use to increase your productivity.

Figure 4.4 compares the basic programs that make up the top four software suites. Notice that each one integrates software applications for word processing,

Programs	Microsoft Office	Lotus SmartSuite	Corel WordPerfect Office	Sun Open Office
Word Processor	Word	WordPro	WordPerfect	Writer
Spreadsheet	Excel	1-2-3	Quattro Pro	Calc
Presentation Graphics	PowerPoint	Freelance	Presentations	Impress
Database Manager	Access	Approach	Paradox	Base
Personal Information Manager	Outlook	Organizer	Corel Central	Schedule

spreadsheets, presentation graphics, database management, and personal information management. Microsoft, Lotus, Corel, and Sun bundle several other useful programs in each suite, depending on which version you select. Examples include programs for Internet access, e-mail, Web publishing, desktop publishing, voice recognition, financial management, and electronic encyclopedias.

The biggest advantage of a software suite is that it generally costs a lot less than the total cost of buying its individual packages separately. Another advantage is that all programs use a similar *graphical user interface* (GUI) of icons, tool and status bars, menus, and so on, which gives them the same look and feel and makes them easier to learn and use. Software suites also share common tools, such as spell checkers and help wizards, to increase their efficiency. Another big advantage of suites is that their programs are designed to work together seamlessly and import each other's files easily, no matter which program you are using at the time. These capabilities make them more efficient and easier to use than a hodgepodge of individual package versions from a variety of vendors.

Of course, putting so many programs and features together in one supersize package does have some disadvantages. Industry critics argue that most end users never use many software suite features. The suites take up a lot of disk space (often upward of 1+ gigabytes), depending on which version or functions you install. Because of their size, software suites are sometimes derisively called *bloatware* by their critics. The cost of suites can vary from as low as $100 for a competitive upgrade to more than $700 for a full version of some editions of the suites.

These drawbacks are one reason for the continued use of ***integrated packages*** like Microsoft Works, Lotus eSuite WorkPlace, and AppleWorks. Integrated packages combine some, but not all, of the functions of several programs—word processing, spreadsheets, presentation graphics, database management, and so on—into one software package.

Because integrated packages leave out many features and functions that are in individual packages and software suites, they are considered less powerful. Their limited functionality, however, requires a lot less disk space (often less than 10 megabytes), costs less than $100, and is frequently preinstalled on many low-end microcomputer systems. Integrated packages offer enough functions and features for many computer users while providing some of the advantages of software suites in a smaller package.

WEB BROWSERS AND MORE

Without a doubt, the most important and most widely used software application—even more than e-mail—is the ***Web browser.*** Once simple and limited, Web browsers are now incredibly powerful and feature-rich. Browsers such as Microsoft Explorer, Mozilla Firefox, Google Chrome, and Opera are software applications designed to support navigation through the point-and-click hyperlinked resources of the World Wide Web and the rest of the Internet, as well as corporate intranets and extranets. Once limited to surfing the Web, browsers are becoming the universal software platform from which end users launch information searches, e-mail, multimedia file transfers, discussion groups, and even productivity applications.

Figure 4.5 illustrates the use of the Microsoft Internet Explorer browser to access the Google search engine. Google.com is the largest search engine today with more than 1 billion searches per month. Other useful search engines include Yahoo, Ask Jeeves, Look Smart, Lycos, and Overture. Using search engines to find information has become an indispensable part of business and personal Internet, intranet, and extranet applications.

Industry experts predict that the Web browser will be the model for how most people use networked computers in the future. Even today, whether you want to watch

FIGURE 4.5

Using the Microsoft Internet Explorer browser to access a popular Web site.

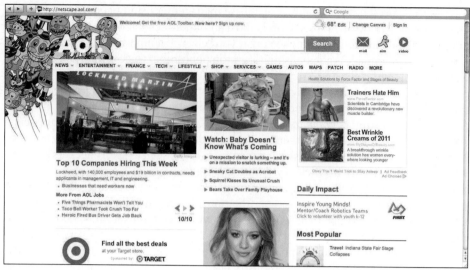

SOURCE: Content © 2011 AOL Inc. Used with permission.

a video, make a phone call, download some software, hold a videoconference, check your e-mail, or work on a spreadsheet of your team's business plan, you can use your browser to launch and host such applications. That's why browsers are sometimes called the *universal client*, that is, the software component installed on all of the networked computing and communications devices of the clients (users) throughout an enterprise. As an aside, this entire book was revised and edited in a browser-based authoring program called PowerXEditor (we will learn more about PowerXEditor later in this chapter).

ELECTRONIC MAIL, INSTANT MESSAGING, AND BLOGS

The first thing many people do at work (and the thing they do most often), all over the world, is check their electronic mail. *E-mail* has changed the way people work and communicate. Computer users depend on e-mail software to communicate with one another by sending and receiving electronic messages and file attachments via the Internet or their organizations' intranets or extranets. E-mail is stored on networked mail servers and can be read whenever you are ready by using either an e-mail application or just a browser. So, with only a few minutes of effort (and a few microseconds of transmission time), a message to one or many individuals can be composed, sent, and received.

As we mentioned previously, e-mail software is a mainstay component of top software suites and Web browsers. Free e-mail packages such as Google gmail, Microsoft Hotmail, and Yahoo! Mail are available to Internet users from online services and Internet service providers. Most e-mail software like Microsoft Outlook or Windows Live Mail can route messages to multiple end users based on predefined mailing lists and provide password security, automatic message forwarding, and remote user access. They also allow you to store messages in folders and make it easy to add documents and Web file attachments to e-mail messages. E-mail packages enable you to edit and send graphics and multimedia files, as well as text, and provide computer conferencing capabilities. In addition, your e-mail software may automatically filter and sort incoming messages (even news items from online services) and route them to appropriate user mailboxes and folders. Finally, many e-mail clients also include calendaring and contact management functions.

Instant messaging (IM) is an e-mail/computer-conferencing hybrid technology that has grown so rapidly that it has become a standard method of electronic messaging for millions of Internet users worldwide. By using instant messaging, groups of business professionals or friends and associates can send and receive electronic messages instantly and thus communicate and collaborate in real time in a near-conversational mode. Messages pop up instantly in an IM window on the computer screens of everyone in your business workgroup or friends on your IM "buddy list," as long as they are online, no matter what other tasks they are working on at that moment. Instant messaging software can be downloaded and IM services implemented by subscribing to many popular IM systems, including AOL's Instant Messenger and ICQ, MSN Messenger, Yahoo Messenger and Skype. See Figure 4.6.

A *blog* (shortened from the word Weblog or written as "Web log") is a Web site of personal or commercial origin that uses a dated log format updated, daily or very frequently, with new information about a particular subject or range of subjects. The information can be written by the site owner, gleaned from other Web sites or other sources, or contributed by users via e-mail.

A blog often has the quality of being a kind of online diary from a particular point of view. Generally, blogs are devoted to one or several subjects or themes, usually of topical interest. In general, blogs can be thought of as developing commentaries, individual or collective, on their particular themes. A blog may be any individual's recorded ideas (a sort of diary), a commercial information source open only to subscribers, or a complex collaboration open to anyone. Most of the latter are *moderated discussions*.

Because there are a number of variations on this idea and new variations can easily be invented, the meaning of this term is apt to gather additional connotations with time. As a formatting and content approach for a Web site, the blog seems popular because the viewer knows that something changes every day, there is a personal (rather than bland commercial) point of view, and, on some sites, there is an opportunity to collaborate with or respond to the Web site and its participants.

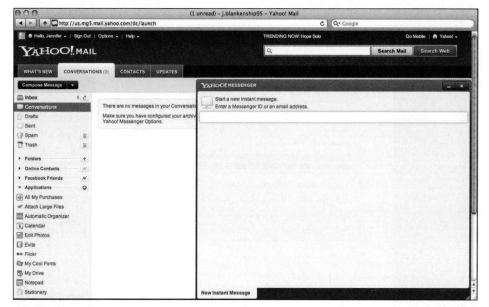

FIGURE 4.6

Using the e-mail features of the Yahoo! instant messaging system.

SOURCE: YAHOO! and the YAHOO! logo are trademarks of Yahoo! Inc. Reproduced with permission of Yahoo! Inc.

WORD PROCESSING AND DESKTOP PUBLISHING

Software for ***word processing*** has transformed the process of writing just about anything. Word processing packages computerize the creation, editing, revision, and printing of *documents* (e.g., letters, memos, reports) by electronically processing *text data* (words, phrases, sentences, and paragraphs). Top word processing packages like Microsoft Word, Lotus WordPro, Corel WordPerfect, and OpenOffice Writer can provide a wide variety of attractively printed documents with their desktop publishing capabilities. These packages can also convert documents to HTML format for publication as Web pages on corporate intranets or the World Wide Web.

Word processing packages also provide other helpful features. For example, a *spelling checker* capability can identify and correct spelling errors, and a *thesaurus* feature helps you find a better choice of words to express ideas. You can also identify and correct grammar and punctuation errors, as well as suggest possible improvements in your writing style, with grammar and style checker functions. In addition to converting documents to HTML format, you can use the top packages to design and create Web pages from scratch for an Internet or intranet Web site. See Figure 4.7.

End users and organizations can use ***desktop publishing (DTP)*** software to produce their own printed materials that look professionally published. That is, they can design and print their own newsletters, brochures, manuals, and books with several type styles, graphics, photos, and colors on each page. Word processing packages and desktop publishing packages like Adobe InDesign, Microsoft Publisher, and QuarkXPress are used for desktop publishing. Typically, text material and graphics can be generated by word processing and graphics packages and imported as text and graphics files. Optical scanners may be used to input text and graphics from printed material. You can also use files of *clip art*, which are predrawn graphic illustrations provided by the software package or available from other sources.

FIGURE 4.7

Using the Microsoft Word word processing package. Note the insertion of a table in the document.

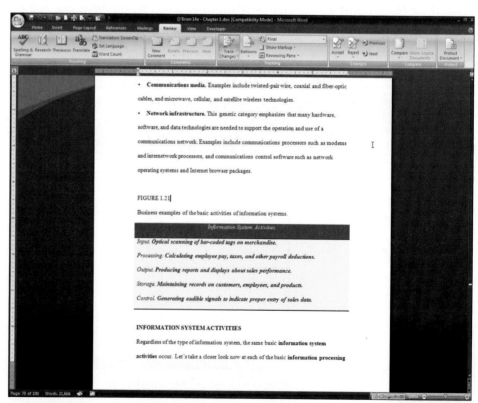

SOURCE: Courtesy of Microsoft®.

SPREADSHEETS

Spreadsheet packages like Microsoft Excel, OpenOffice Calc, and Corel QuattroPro are used by virtually every business for analysis, planning, and modeling. They help you develop an *electronic spreadsheet*, which is a worksheet of rows and columns that can be stored on your PC or on a network server, or converted to HTML format and stored as a Web page or Web sheet on the World Wide Web. Developing a spreadsheet involves designing its format and developing the relationships (formulas) that will be used in the worksheet. In response to your input, the computer performs necessary calculations according to the formulas you defined in the spreadsheet and displays the results immediately, whether on your workstation or Web site. Most packages also help you develop charts and graphic displays of spreadsheet results. See Figure 4.8.

For example, you could develop a spreadsheet to record and analyze past and present advertising performance for a business. You could also develop hyperlinks to a similar Web sheet on your marketing team's intranet Web site. Now you have a decision support tool to help you answer *what-if questions* you may have about advertising. For example, "What would happen to market share if advertising expenses were to increase by 10 percent?" To answer this question, you would simply change the advertising expense formula on the advertising performance worksheet you developed. The computer would recalculate the affected figures, producing new market share figures and graphics. You would then have better insight into the effect of advertising decisions on market share. Then you could share this insight with a note on the Web sheet on your team's intranet Web site.

Basically, a spreadsheet can be thought of as a giant electronic piece of paper. You can put your work, or parts of it, anywhere you like on the paper and refer to it in whatever way you want from other parts of the paper. You can even refer to work in one spreadsheet from another spreadsheet. Their versatility is almost endless. Microsoft's Excel boasts dimensions of 65,536 rows by 256 columns. The columns can be

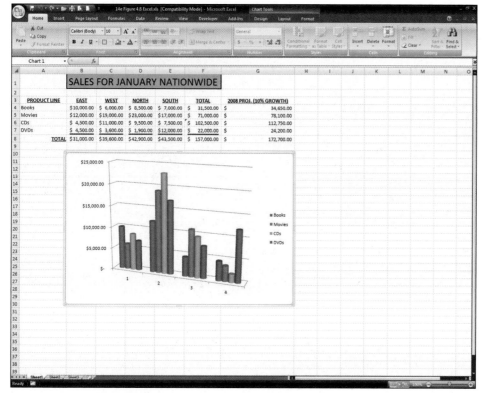

FIGURE 4.8

Using an electronic spreadsheet package, Microsoft Excel. Note the use of graphics.

SOURCE: Courtesy of Microsoft®.

sized to display up to 255 characters and each cell (the intersection of a column and row) can contain up to 32,767 characters. Assuming a typical cell size of 1/4″ high by 1″ wide, if an electronic spreadsheet were actually spread out as a piece of paper, it would be over 1,300 feet high by 21 feet wide!

PRESENTATION GRAPHICS

Presentation graphics software packages help you convert numeric data into graphics displays such as line charts, bar graphs, pie charts, and many other types of graphics. Most of the top packages also help you prepare multimedia presentations of graphics, photos, animation, and video clips, including publishing to the World Wide Web. Not only are graphics and multimedia displays easier to comprehend and communicate than numeric data, but multiple-color and multimedia displays can more easily emphasize key points, strategic differences, and important trends in the data. Presentation graphics have proved to be much more effective than tabular presentations of numeric data for reporting and communicating in advertising media, management reports, or other business presentations. See Figure 4.9.

Presentation graphics software packages like Microsoft PowerPoint, OpenOffice Impress, Lotus Freelance, or Corel Presentations give you many easy-to-use capabilities that encourage the use of graphics presentations. For example, most packages help you design and manage computer-generated and orchestrated *slide shows* containing many integrated graphics and multimedia displays. You can select from a variety of predesigned *templates* of business presentations, prepare and edit the outline and notes for a presentation, and manage the use of multimedia files of graphics, photos, sounds, and video clips. Of course, the top packages help you tailor your graphics and multimedia presentation for transfer in HTML format to Web sites on corporate intranets or the World Wide Web.

FIGURE 4.9

Using the slide preview feature of a presentation graphics package, Microsoft PowerPoint.

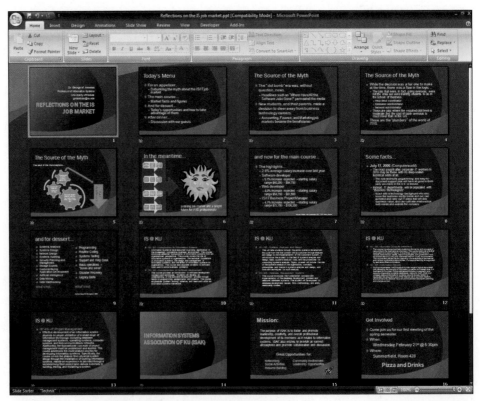

SOURCE: Courtesy of Microsoft®.

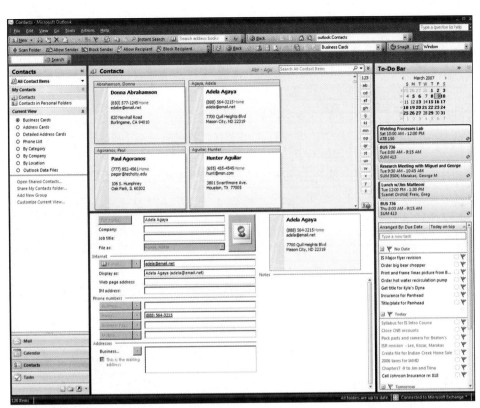

FIGURE 4.10

Using a personal information manager (PIM): Microsoft Outlook.

SOURCE: Courtesy of Microsoft®.

PERSONAL INFORMATION MANAGERS

The *personal information manager (PIM)* is a popular software package for end-user productivity and collaboration, as well as a popular application for personal digital assistant (PDA) handheld devices. Various PIMs such as Lotus Organizer and Microsoft Outlook help end users store, organize, and retrieve information about customers, clients, and prospects or schedule and manage appointments, meetings, and tasks. A PIM package will organize data you enter and retrieve information in a variety of forms, depending on the style and structure of the PIM and the information you want. For example, information can be retrieved as an electronic calendar or list of appointments, meetings, or other things to do; as the timetable for a project; or as a display of key facts and financial data about customers, clients, or sales prospects. Most PIMs now include the ability to access the World Wide Web and provide e-mail capability. Also, some PIMs use Internet and e-mail features to support team collaboration by sharing information such as contact lists, task lists, and schedules with other networked PIM users. See Figure 4.10.

GROUPWARE

Groupware is software that helps workgroups and teams collaborate to accomplish group assignments. Groupware is a category of general-purpose application software that combines a variety of software features and functions to facilitate collaboration. For example, groupware products like Lotus Notes, Novell GroupWise, and Microsoft Exchange support collaboration through e-mail, discussion groups and databases, scheduling, task management, data, audio and videoconferencing, and so on.

Groupware products rely on the Internet and corporate intranets and extranets to make collaboration possible on a global scale by *virtual teams* located anywhere in the world. For example, team members might use the Internet for global e-mail, project discussion forums, and joint Web page development. Or they might use corporate

Lotus Sametime enables work-groups and project teams to share spreadsheets and other work documents in an interactive online collaboration process.

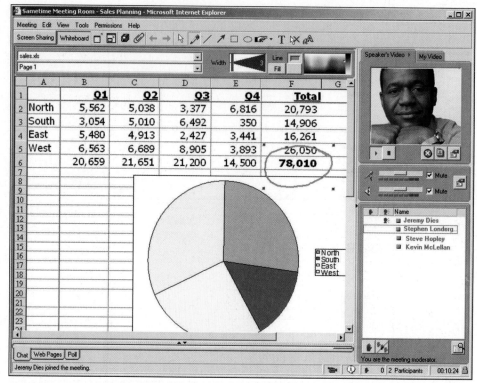

SOURCE: Courtesy of International Business Machines Corporation. Unauthorized use not permitted.

intranets to publish project news and progress reports and work jointly on documents stored on Web servers. See Figure 4.11.

Collaborative capabilities are also being added to other software to give it groupware-like features. For example, in the Microsoft Office software suite, Microsoft Word keeps track of who made revisions to each document, Excel tracks all changes made to a spreadsheet, and Outlook lets you keep track of tasks you delegate to other team members. Recently, the Microsoft Office suite has included functions that allow multiple people to work on and edit the same document at the same time. Using this feature, any changes made by one team member will become visible to all team members as they are being made.

Two recent additions to the collaborative software marketplace are Microsoft's Windows SharePoint Services and IBM's WebSphere. Both products allow teams to create sophisticated Web sites for information sharing and document collaboration quickly. Furthermore, businesses can use these products as a platform for application development to facilitate the efficient creation of Web-based business portals and transaction processing applications. Web sites built with collaborative development tools can integrate a wide variety of individual applications that can help increase both individual and team productivity.

SOFTWARE ALTERNATIVES
LO 4-1

Many businesses are finding alternatives to acquiring, installing, and maintaining business application software purchased from software vendors or developing and maintaining their own software in-house with their own software developer employees. For example, as we will discuss further in Chapter 14, many large companies are *outsourcing* the development and maintenance of software they need to *contract programming* firms and other software development companies, including the use of *offshore* software developers in foreign countries, and using the Internet to communicate, collaborate, and manage their software development projects.

FIGURE 4.12

Salesforce.com is a leading application service provider of Web-based sales management and customer relationship management services to both large and small businesses.

SOURCE: Courtesy of Salesforce.com.

Application Service Providers

A large and fast-growing number of companies are turning to *application service providers (ASPs),* instead of developing or purchasing the application software they need to run their businesses. Application service providers are companies that own, operate, and maintain application software and the computer system resources (servers, system software, networks, and IT personnel) required to offer the use of the application software for a fee as a service over the Internet. The ASP can bill their customers on a per-use basis or on a monthly or annual fee basis.

Businesses are using an ASP instead of owning and maintaining their own software for many reasons. One of the biggest advantages is the low cost of initial investment, and in many cases, the short time needed to get the Web-based application set up and running. The ASP's pay-as-you-go fee structure is usually significantly less expensive than the cost of developing or purchasing, as well as running and maintaining, application software. In addition, using an ASP eliminates or drastically reduces the need for much of the IT infrastructure (servers, system software, and IT personnel) that would be needed to acquire and support application software, including the continual challenges of distributing and managing companywide software patches and upgrades. Consequently, the use of ASPs by businesses and other organizations is expected to accelerate in the coming years. See Figure 4.12.

Santa Clara, California–based security vendor McAfee Inc. released a Software as a Service (SaaS) Web security tool for protecting a distributed workforce from Web threats, while rendering IT departments fewer upfront costs in light of current budgetary constraints.

Especially in tough economic times, a SaaS model of software delivery, like the McAfee Web Protection Service, saves cash-strapped organizations money because IT staff members don't have to spend valuable time managing on-site equipment, says Mark Campbell, senior product marketing manager with McAfee Inc. "They get the advantages of having a tool that is always on, always up-to-date, and with uptime guarantees," says Campbell. One challenge with on-premise tools, he continues, is that when vendors issue a feature update, a period of time can elapse before the enhancements are up and running in the environment, says Campbell. That problem goes away when the software is hosted centrally.

Features of the hosted security offering include reputation-based filtering, based on McAfee's reputation system TrustedSource, to block constantly morphing threats. There's flexible policy manager for setting policies for certain employee groups like access to certain social networking sites by contract employees versus executive management. Users have the ability to run reports and use dashboards to gain insight into an organization's Web usage. "Are

McAfee Inc.: Security under a Software-as-a-Service Model

employees spending all day on Facebook, and does this align with our appropriate usage of Web tools?" says Campbell. Other features include malware protection, remote office and user support, and transparent user authentication.

James Quin, senior research analyst with London, Ontario–based Info-Tech Research Group Ltd., can't yet say if McAfee's SaaS offering will be cheaper in the long run given monthly recurring costs for the service. That said, in this climate of eliminated capital budgets, Quin says "a solution like this offers them value there." Small organizations in particular, says Quin, will benefit from not having to retain as much security expertise.

Offering a SaaS option for malware technology that is "pretty commoditized" is certainly a move by McAfee to differentiate itself in a crowded space, says Quin. "And it puts them out front first because they're not going to be the last ones to offer this kind of service," he says.

Campbell thinks customers' perception of hosted security products has changed for the better, helped along by the successful adoption of hosted CRM tools like salesforce.com. "More and more IT departments are beginning to accept and really realize the benefits of it," says Campbell.

SOURCE: Kathleen Lau, "SaaS Web Security a Cheaper Option, McAfee Says," *CIO.com*, April 30, 2009.

Cloud Computing

One of the most recent advances in computing and software delivery is called *cloud computing*. Cloud computing is a style of computing in which software and, in some cases, virtualized hardware resources are provided as a service over the Internet. Users need not have knowledge of, expertise in, or control over the technology infrastructure "in the cloud" that supports them. The term cloud is used as a metaphor for the Internet, based on how the Internet is often depicted in computer network diagrams.

The concept incorporates technology trends that have the common theme of reliance on the Internet for satisfying the computing needs of the users. Examples of vendors providing cloud services include SAP Business ByDesign, MidlandHR's "iTrent as a Service," Salesforce.com, and Google Apps, which provide common business applications online that are accessed from a Web browser, while the software and data are stored on the servers.

Cloud computing is often confused with grid computing (recall the concept from Chapter 3 where the CPU power of multiple computers is harnessed to act like one big computer when necessary). Indeed, many cloud computing deployments depend on grids, but cloud computing can be seen as a natural next step from the grid model. The majority of cloud computing infrastructure consists of reliable services delivered through data centers and built on servers with different levels of virtualization technologies. The services are accessible anywhere that has access to networking infrastructure. The cloud appears as a single point of access for all the computing needs of consumers.

As many computer software users generally do not own the infrastructure around them, they can avoid capital expenditure and consume resources as a service, paying instead for what they use. If this sounds a lot like how you pay for your electricity or natural gas, it is because the same basic model has been adopted. Many cloud computing offerings have adopted the utility computing model, which is analogous to how traditional utilities like electricity are consumed, while others are billed on a subscription basis. Sharing "perishable and intangible" computing power among multiple users or enterprises can improve utilization rates, as servers are left idle less often because more people are accessing and using the computing resources. Through this approach, significant reductions in costs can be realized while increasing the overall speed of application development. An advantage to this approach is that a given user's or enterprise's computing capacity can be scaled upward almost instantly as needed without having to own an infrastructure that is engineered to be ready for short-term peak loads. Cloud computing has been enabled by large increases in available commercial bandwidth, which makes it possible to receive the same response times from centralized infrastructure at other sites.

The real benefit to the organization comes from the cost savings. Cloud computing users can avoid capital expenditure on hardware, software, and services, by simply paying a provider only for what they use. As stated above, consumption is billed on a utility basis (e.g., resources consumed, as in electricity) or subscription basis (e.g., time-based, as in a newspaper), with little or no up-front cost. Other benefits of this timesharing-style approach are low barriers to entry, shared infrastructure and costs, low management overhead, and immediate access to a broad range of applications. Users can generally terminate the contract at any time, and the services are often covered by service-level agreements with financial penalties in the event the agreed-upon service levels are not delivered. It is predicted that someday, everyone will compute "in the cloud."

Australian Maritime Safety Authority: Cloud Computing? Nothing New

The Australian Maritime Safety Authority (AMSA) is a self-funded government authority tasked with the provision of safety and administrative services to the Australian maritime industry. These include maritime safety, environmental protection, maritime and aviation search and rescue, and a host of clerical services such as ship registration, audit, and inspection. As part of the latter, AMSA operates the International Safety Management (ISM) program, which keeps track of audits to international ships according to agreed-upon industry standards and best practices. The IT behind this process records these audits and issues certificates of compliance that remain valid for a period of time. Information is stored centrally in Canberra and accessed and collected from 14 different ports. While certainly important, this is a low-volume system. The AMSA makes about two dozen of these inspections a month.

While the current application was based on Microsoft Excel, over time AMSA became interested in creating something with a Web presence, which would be easy to access from all locations and eventually by the public at large. Since most of its system development was done in-house at the time, AMSA started by looking there first, but did not see anything it liked. The traditional approach to system development would take about six months and cost between 200,000 and 300,000 Australian dollars (between about $210,000 and $315,000).

AMSA therefore started looking for alternatives. In a conference in 2008 it learned about salesforce.com, one of the leading providers of cloud-based Software as a Service (or SaaS). At this time, developing the ISM application using the Force.com cloud computing platform would not only be a first in Australian government, it would be the first-ever Force.com development in the country. The better part? Both cost and time required were an order of magnitude smaller than what AMSA had estimated it would cost to develop the application internally.

Salesforce.com consultants estimated it would take about six weeks of development time, which would cost 30,000 Australian dollars; this included development, training, and one year of licensing, with additional licensing and maintenance fees on an ongoing basis for about 8,000 Australian dollars a year. At these rates, the low estimate for the internal development alternative would cover development plus about 20-some years of licensing if going for the cloud-based alternative. While hard to pin down exactly, AMSA estimated ongoing maintenance costs for an internally developed application at about 20,000 Australian dollars a year.

While not everything went perfectly—an important requirement was completely overlooked in the alpha version, which required extensive rework later on—business users of the new ISM application were quite satisfied with the many improvements over the existing Excel-based technology. One thing to keep in mind, however, is what would happen if AMSA decided to terminate the relationship. Since the application runs only on the Force.com platform, there is little that could be recovered other than the data contained in it, which would be returned to AMSA within 24 hours of termination. AMSA management underscores that it is important to go into this type of arrangement knowing how one would get out, if ever needed.

SOURCE: Andrea Di Maio and Steve Bittinger, "Case Study: Australian Maritime Safety Authority Proves that Cloud is Nothing New," *Gartner Research*, November 22, 2010, and www.amsa.gov.au, accessed May 16, 2011.

Software Licensing

Regardless of whether a software application is purchased COTS or accessed via an ASP, the software must be licensed for use. Software licensing is a complex topic that involves considerations of the special characteristics of software in the context of the underlying intellectual property rights, including copyright, trademark, and trade secrets, as well as traditional contract law, including the Uniform Commercial Code (UCC).

Contrary to what many believe, an individual or company that buys a software application has not purchased rights of ownership. Rather, the individual or company has purchased a license to use the software under the terms of the software licensing agreement. Software is generally licensed to protect the vendor's intellectual property rights. The license often prohibits reverse engineering, modifying, disclosing, or transferring the software. In most cases, the license also gives the purchaser permission to sell or dispose of the rights provided by the license but not to duplicate or resell multiple copies of the software. In simple terms, when you purchase software, you do not *own* the software. Rather, you are allowed to *use* the software. The only way to own software is either to write it yourself or pay someone to write it for you.

The requirement for licensing does not disappear when use of the software is obtained through an ASP. In this case, the license to dispense use of the software is granted to the ASP by the various software vendors, and in return, the ASP agrees to pay the software vendor a royalty based on the number of user accounts to which the ASP resells the rights.

Software vendors are working hard to provide easy licensing and access to their products while simultaneously preventing software piracy, which serves only to raise the ultimate cost of the product and is, quite simply, illegal.

Later in this chapter we will learn about an entirely new approach to software licensing: open-source code. See Figure 4.13.

FIGURE 4.13

The U.S. Department of Defense is becoming both an adopter and a provider of open-source software.

SOURCE: Andrea Comas/Reuters/Landov.

System Software:
Computer System Management

System software consists of programs that manage and support a computer system and its information processing activities. For example, operating systems and network management programs serve as a vital *software interface* between computer networks and hardware and the application programs of end users. We can think of system software much like the central nervous system in the human body. It is responsible for making sure all of the parts are connected properly to the brain so the "system" (in this case, the human body) will respond properly to commands sent from the brain.

SYSTEM SOFTWARE OVERVIEW
LO 4-4
LO 4-6

Overview

We can group system software into two major categories (see Figure 4.14):

- **System Management Programs.** Programs that manage the hardware, software, network, and data resources of computer systems during the execution of the various information processing jobs of users. Examples of important system management programs are operating systems, network management programs, database management systems, and system utilities.

- **System Development Programs.** Programs that help users develop information system programs and procedures and prepare user programs for computer processing. Major software development programs are programming language translators and editors, and a variety of CASE (computer-aided software engineering) and other programming tools. We will take a closer look at CASE tools later in this chapter.

The most important system software package for any computer is its operating system. An *operating system* is an integrated system of programs that manages the operations of the CPU, controls the input/output and storage resources and activities of the

OPERATING SYSTEMS

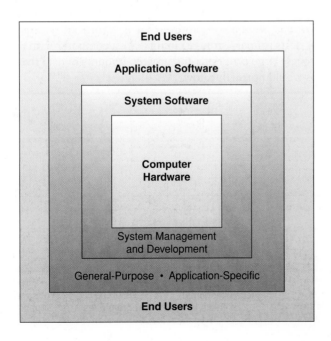

FIGURE 4.14
The system and application software interface between end users and computer hardware.

computer system, and provides various support services as the computer executes the application programs of users.

The primary purpose of an operating system is to maximize the productivity of a computer system by operating it in the most efficient manner. An operating system minimizes the amount of human intervention required during processing. It helps your application programs perform common operations such as accessing a network, entering data, saving and retrieving files, and printing or displaying output. If you have any hands-on experience with a computer, you know that the operating system must be loaded and activated before you can accomplish other tasks. This requirement emphasizes that operating systems are the most indispensable components of the software interface between users and the hardware of their computer systems. In today's world, the two most popular operating systems are Microsoft's Windows 7 and Apple's OS X.

Operating Systems Functions

An operating system performs five basic functions in the operation of a computer system: providing a user interface, resource management, task management, file management, and utilities and support services. See Figure 4.15.

THE USER INTERFACE. The *user interface* is the part of the operating system that allows you to communicate with it so you can load programs, access files, and accomplish other tasks. Three main types of user interfaces are the *command-driven, menu-driven,* and *graphical user interfaces.* The trend in user interfaces for operating systems and other software is moving away from the entry of brief end-user commands, or even the selection of choices from menus of options. Instead, most software provides an easy-to-use graphical user interface (GUI) that uses icons, bars, buttons, boxes, and other images. These GUIs rely on pointing devices like the electronic mouse or touch pad to make selections that help you get things done. Currently, the most common and widely recognized GUI is the Microsoft Windows desktop.

RESOURCE MANAGEMENT. An operating system uses a variety of resource management programs to manage the hardware and networking resources of a computer system, including its CPU, memory, secondary storage devices, telecommunications processors, and input/output peripherals. For example, memory management programs keep track of where data and programs are stored. They may also subdivide memory into a number of sections and swap parts of programs and data between memory and magnetic disks or other secondary storage devices. This process can provide a computer system with a *virtual memory* capability that is significantly larger than the real memory capacity of its primary storage circuits. So, a computer with a virtual memory capability can process large programs and greater amounts of data than the capacity of its memory chips would normally allow.

FIGURE 4.15

The basic functions of an operating system include a user interface, resource management, task management, file management, and utilities and other functions.

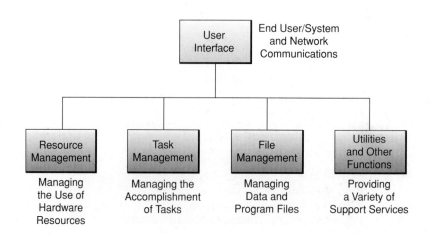

FILE MANAGEMENT. An operating system contains *file management* programs that control the creation, deletion, and access of files of data and programs. File management also involves keeping track of the physical location of files on magnetic disks and other secondary storage devices. So operating systems maintain directories of information about the location and characteristics of files stored on a computer system's secondary storage devices.

TASK MANAGEMENT. The *task management* programs of an operating system help accomplish the computing tasks of end users. The programs control which task gets access to the CPU and for how much time. The task management functions can allocate a specific slice of CPU time to a particular task and interrupt the CPU at any time to substitute a higher priority task. Several different approaches to task management may be taken, each with advantages in certain situations.

Multitasking (sometimes referred to as *multiprogramming* or timesharing) is a task management approach that allows for several computing tasks to be performed in a seemingly simultaneous fashion. In reality, multitasking assigns only one task at a time to the CPU, but it switches from one program to another so quickly that it gives the appearance of executing all of the programs at the same time. There are two basic types of multitasking: *preemptive* and *cooperative*. In preemptive multitasking, the task management functions parcel out CPU *time slices* to each program. In contrast, cooperative multitasking allows each program to control the CPU for as long as it needs it. If a program is not using the CPU, however, it can allow another program to use it temporarily. Most Windows and UNIX-based operating systems use the preemptive approach, whereas most Apple-style platforms use cooperative multitasking. Although the terms *multitasking* and *multiprocessing* are often used interchangeably, they are actually different concepts based on the number of CPUs being used. In multiprocessing, more than one CPU is being accessed, but in multitasking, only one CPU is in operation.

Most computers make use of some sort of multitasking. On modern microcomputers, multitasking is made possible by the development of powerful processors and their ability to address much larger memory capacities directly. This capability allows primary storage to be subdivided into several large partitions, each of which is used by a different software application.

In effect, a single computer can act as if it were several computers, or *virtual machines*, because each application program runs independently at the same time. The number of programs that can be run concurrently depends on the amount of memory that is available and the amount of processing each job demands. That's because a microprocessor (or CPU) can become overloaded with too many jobs and provide unacceptably slow response times. However, if memory and processing capacities are adequate, multitasking allows end users to switch easily from one application to another, share data files among applications, and process some applications in a *background* mode. Typically, background tasks include large printing jobs, extensive mathematical computations, or unattended telecommunications sessions.

Microsoft Windows

For many years, MS-DOS (Microsoft Disk Operating System) was the most widely used microcomputer operating system. It is a single-user, single-tasking operating system but was given a graphical user interface and limited multitasking capabilities by combining it with Microsoft Windows. Microsoft began replacing its DOS/Windows combination in 1995 with the Windows 95 operating system, featuring a graphical user interface, true multitasking, networking, multimedia, and many other capabilities. Microsoft introduced an enhanced Windows 98 version during 1998, and a Windows Me (Millennium Edition) consumer PC system in 2000.

Microsoft introduced its Windows NT (New Technology) operating system in 1995. Windows NT is a powerful, multitasking, multiuser operating system that was

FIGURE 4.16

Comparing the purposes of the four versions of the Microsoft Windows Server 2008 R2 operating system.

Microsoft Windows Server 2008 R2 Comparisons
• **Windows Server 2008, Standard Edition** For smaller server applications, including file and print sharing, Internet and intranet connectivity, and centralized desktop application deployment.
• **Windows Server 2008, Enterprise Edition** For larger business applications, XML Web services, enterprise collaboration, and enterprise network support.
• **Windows Server 2008, Datacenter Edition** For business-critical and mission-critical applications demanding the highest levels of scalability and availability.
• **Windows Server 2008, Web Edition** For Web serving and hosting, providing a platform for developing and deploying Web services and applications.

installed on many network servers to manage PCs with high-performance computing requirements. New Server and Workstation versions were introduced in 1997. Microsoft substantially enhanced its Windows NT products with the Windows 2000 operating system during the year 2000.

Late in 2001, Microsoft introduced Windows XP Home Edition and Professional versions, and thus formally merged its two Windows operating system lines for consumer and business users, uniting them around the Windows NT and Windows 2000 code base. With Windows XP, consumers and home users finally received an enhanced Windows operating system with the performance and stability features that business users had in Windows 2000 and continue to have in Windows XP Professional. Microsoft also introduced four new Windows Server 2003 versions in 2008, which are summarized and compared in Figure 4.16.

In 2006, Microsoft released their next operating system called Vista. Vista contains hundreds of new features; some of the most significant include an updated graphical user interface and visual style dubbed Windows Aero, improved search features, new multimedia creation tools such as Windows DVD Maker, and completely redesigned networking, audio, print, and display subsystems. Vista also aims to increase the level of communication between machines on a home network using peer-to-peer technology, making it easier to share files and digital media between computers and devices.

For developers, Vista introduced version 3.0 of the .NET Framework, which aims to make it significantly easier for developers to write high-quality applications than with the previous versions of Windows.

Microsoft's primary stated objective with Vista, however, was to improve the state of security in the Windows operating system. One of the most common criticisms of Windows XP and its predecessors has been their commonly exploited security vulnerabilities and overall susceptibility to malware, viruses, and buffer overflows. In light of these complaints, then-Microsoft chairman Bill Gates announced in early 2002 a companywide "Trustworthy Computing Initiative" to incorporate security work into every aspect of software development at the company. Microsoft claimed that it prioritized improving the security of Windows XP and Windows Server 2003 rather than finishing Windows Vista, significantly delaying its completion.

During 2008, a new server product, entitled (appropriately enough) Windows Server 2008, has emerged. Windows Server 2008 is built from the same code base as Windows Vista; therefore, it shares much of the same architecture and functionality. Because the code base is common, it automatically comes with most of the technical, security, management, and administrative features new to Windows Vista such as the rewritten networking processes (native IPv6, native wireless, speed, and security improvements); improved image-based installation, deployment, and recovery; improved diagnostics, monitoring, event logging, and reporting tools; new security features;

improved Windows Firewall with secure default configuration; .NET Framework 3.0 technologies; and the core kernel, memory, and file system improvements. Processors and memory devices are modeled as Plug and Play devices, to allow hot-plugging of these devices.

Windows Server 2008 is already in release 2 as several performance and security enhancements required a major upgrade.

In 2009, Microsoft released their newest operating system, Windows 7. Unlike its predecessor, Vista, which introduced a large number of new features, Windows 7 was intended to be a more focused and incremental upgrade with the goal of being fully compatible with applications and hardware with which Vista was already compatible. Windows 7 has been very well received and is rapidly replacing the installed base of Vista without receiving any of the complaints and struggles encountered by Vista adopters and users.

UNIX

Originally developed by AT&T, UNIX is now also offered by other vendors, including Solaris by Sun Microsystems and AIX by IBM. UNIX is a multitasking, multiuser, network-managing operating system whose portability allows it to run on mainframes, midrange computers, and microcomputers. UNIX is still a popular choice for Web and other network servers.

Linux

Linux is a low-cost, powerful, and reliable UNIX-like operating system that is rapidly gaining market share from UNIX and Windows servers as a high-performance operating system for network servers and Web servers in both small and large networks. Linux was developed as free or low-cost *shareware* or *open-source software* over the Internet in the 1990s by Linus Torvald of Finland and millions of programmers around the world. Linux is still being enhanced in this way but is sold with extra features and support services by software vendors such as Red Hat, Caldera, and SUSE Linux. PC versions, which support office software suites, Web browsers, and other application software, are also available.

Open-Source Software

The concept of *open-source software* (OSS) is growing far beyond the Linux operating system. The basic idea behind open source is very simple: When programmers can read, redistribute, and modify the source code for a piece of software, the software evolves. People improve it, people adapt it, people fix bugs. This development can happen at a speed that, if one is accustomed to the slow pace of conventional software development, seems astonishing. The open-source community of software developers has learned that this rapid evolutionary process produces better software than the traditional commercial (closed) model, in which only a very few programmers can see the source. The concept of open source, admittedly, runs counter to the highly commercial (and proprietary) world of traditional software development. Nonetheless, an increasingly large number of developers have embraced the open-source concept and come to realize that the proprietary approach to software development has hidden costs that can often outweigh its benefits.

Since 1998, the OSS movement has become a revolution in software development. This revolution, however, can actually trace its roots back more than 30 years. Typically, in the PC era, computer software had been sold only as a finished product, otherwise called a *precompiled binary*, which is installed on a user's computer by copying files to appropriate directories or folders. Moving to a new computer platform (Windows to Macintosh, for example) usually required the purchase of a new license. If the company went out of business or discontinued support of a product, users of that product had no recourse. Bug fixes were completely dependent on the organization that sold the software. In contrast, OSS is software that is licensed to guarantee free access to the programming behind the precompiled binary, otherwise called the *source code*. This access allows the user to install the software on a new platform without an additional purchase and to get support (or create a support consortium with other like-minded users) for a product whose creator no longer supports it. Those who are technically inclined can fix bugs themselves rather than waiting for someone else to do so. Generally, there is a central distribution mechanism that allows users to obtain the source code, as well as precompiled binaries in some cases. There are also mechanisms by which users may pay a fee to obtain the software, such as on a CD-ROM or DVD, which may also include some technical support. A variety of licenses are used to ensure that the source code will remain available, wherever the code is actually used.

To be clear, there are several things open source is not: It is not shareware, public-domain software, freeware, or software viewers and readers made freely available without access to source code. Shareware, whether or not the user registers it and pays the registration fee, typically allows no access to the underlying source code. Unlike freeware and public-domain software, OSS is copyrighted and distributed with license terms designed to ensure that the source code will always be available. Although a fee may be charged for the software's packaging, distribution, or support, the complete package needed to create files is included, not just a portion needed to view files created elsewhere.

The philosophy of open source is based on a variety of models that sometimes conflict; indeed, it often seems there are as many philosophies and models for developing and managing OSS as there are major products. In 1998, a small group of open-source enthusiasts decided it was time to formalize some things about open source. The newly formed group registered themselves on the Internet as www.open-source.org and began the process of defining exactly what is, and what is not, open-source software. As it stands today, open-source licensing is defined by the following characteristics:

- The license shall not restrict any party from selling or giving away the software as a component of an aggregate software distribution containing programs from several different sources.
- The program must include source code and must allow distribution in source code, as well as compiled form.
- The license must allow modifications and derived works and must allow them to be distributed under the same terms as the license of the original software.
- The license may restrict source code from being distributed in modified form only if the license allows the distribution of patch files with the source code for the purpose of modifying the program at build time.
- The license must not discriminate against any person or group of persons.
- The license must not restrict anyone from making use of the program in a specific field of endeavor.
- The rights attached to the program must apply to all to whom the program is redistributed without the need for execution of an additional license by those parties.
- The license must not be specific to a product.
- The license must not contaminate other software by placing restrictions on any software distributed along with the licensed software.

This radical approach to software development and distribution is not without its detractors—most notably Microsoft. Nonetheless, the open-source movement is flourishing and stands to continue to revolutionize the way we think about software development.

OpenOffice.org 3

A relative newcomer to the open-source arena is an entire office suite offered by Sun Microsystems called OpenOffice.org 3. This product, built under the open-source standards described above, is a complete integrated office suite that provides all the common applications including word processing, spreadsheet, presentation graphics, and database management. It can store and retrieve files in a wide variety of data formats, including all of the file formats associated with the other major office suite applications on the market.

Best of all, OpenOffice.org 3 can be downloaded and used *entirely free of any license fees*. OpenOffice.org 3 is released under the LGPL license. This means you may use it for any purpose: domestic, commercial, educational, or public administration. You may install it on as many computers as you like, and you may make copies and give them away to family, friends, students, employees—anyone you like.

Mac OS X

Actually based on a form of UNIX, the Mac OS X (pronounced MAC OS 10) is the latest operating system from Apple for the iMac and other Macintosh microcomputers. The Mac OS X version 10.6 Snow Leopard has an advanced graphical user interface and multitasking and multimedia capabilities, along with an integrated Web browser, e-mail, instant messaging, search engine, digital media player, and many other features.

Mac OS X was a radical departure from previous Macintosh operating systems; its underlying code base is completely different from previous versions. Its core, named Darwin, is an open-source, UNIX-like operating system. Apple layered over Darwin a number of proprietary components, including the Aqua interface and the Finder, to complete the GUI-based operating system that is Mac OS X.

Mac OS X also included a number of features intended to make the operating system more stable and reliable than Apple's previous operating systems. Preemptive multitasking and memory protection, for example, improved the ability of the operating system to run multiple applications simultaneously that don't interrupt or corrupt each other.

The most visible change was the Aqua theme. The use of soft edges, translucent colors, and pinstripes—similar to the hardware design of the first iMacs—brought more texture and color to the interface than OS 9's "Platinum" appearance had offered. Numerous users of the older versions of the operating system decried the new look as "cutesy" and lacking in professional polish. However, Aqua also has been called a bold and innovative step forward at a time when user interfaces were seen as "dull and boring." Despite the controversy, the look was instantly recognizable, and even before the first version of Mac OS X was released, third-party developers started producing skins (look-and-feel colors and styles for application interfaces) for customizable applications that mimicked the Aqua appearance.

Mac OS X also includes its own software development tools, most prominently an integrated development environment called Xcode. Xcode provides interfaces to compilers that support several programming languages including C, C++, Objective-C, and Java. For the Apple Intel Transition, it was modified so that developers could easily create an operating system to remain compatible with both the Intel-based and PowerPC-based Macintosh.

Application Virtualization

Consider all of the various types of software applications we discussed earlier in the chapter, along with the multiple operating systems we just discussed. What happens when a user who has a machine running Windows needs to run an application designed specifically for a machine running Mac OS X? The answer used to be "Borrow someone's Mac." Through the development of application virtualization, a much more useful and productive answer exists. *Application virtualization* is an umbrella term that describes software technologies that improve portability, manageability, and compatibility of applications by insulating them from the underlying operating system on which they are executed. A fully virtualized application is not installed in the traditional sense; it is just executed as if it is. The application is fooled into believing that it is directly interfacing with the original operating system and all the resources managed by it, when in reality it is not. Application virtualization is just an extension of operating system virtualization where the same basic concepts fool the whole operating system into thinking it is running on a particular type of hardware when it is not.

The concept of virtualization is not a recent development. The use of a virtual machine was a common practice during the mainframe era where extremely large machines were partitioned into smaller, separate virtual machines or domains to allow multiple users to run unique sets of applications and processes simultaneously. Each user constituency used a portion of the total available machine resources, and the virtualization approach made it appear that each domain was an entirely separate machine from all the rest. If you have ever set up a new PC and created a partition on the hard drive, you have taken advantage of virtualization. You have taken one physical drive and created two virtual drives—one for each partition.

Application virtualization is a logical next step from these early roots. The benefits to the enterprise range from the cost savings associated with not having to have multiple platforms for multiple applications, to the energy savings associated with not having a multitude of servers running at low capacity while eating up electricity and generating heat.

A thorough discussion of virtualization is well beyond the scope of this text, but it is rapidly blurring the boundaries between machines and operating systems and operating systems and applications. Add this to the cloud computing concept, and we have the makings of an anytime, anywhere, any machine, any application world.

Toronto's Hospital for Sick Children: Challenges in Making Virtualization Work

Toronto's Hospital for Sick Children has learned the hard way that virtualization efforts won't be successful if vendors aren't ready to support you, according to its director of technology, Ana Andreasian. The hospital (usually referred to as "Sick Kids") has already consolidated a considerable amount of its server infrastructure, which now includes 300 physical and 60 virtual machines. Sick Kids employs about 110 IT staff members who serve more than 5,000 employees.

Andreasian said the biggest issue she's experienced so far has come from vendors who do not properly test their applications before offering them to virtualization customers. "They'll say, 'Give me one CPU, one gig of memory, and I'm good,'" she says. "Then you'll find they need four CPUs and four gigs of RAM. You wind up having a never-ending discussion on how to solve the performance problems."

Another challenge has been vendors who say they're willing to support virtual environments, but not fully. "Some vendors have a condition: if you have a problem, you have to move (the application) out of a virtual environment," she says. "That's just not practical."

Sick Kids Hospital is somewhat unusual in that it started its virtualization journey by focusing on storage systems rather than servers. Andreasian explained that the organization currently manages some 150 terabytes of data, which is always on the increase. Devices to handle that data, meanwhile, always end up going out of support. "We were facing the question: How do you migrate that data? It's a huge cost," she says, adding that no one wants to experience any downtime associated with such a migration. And all this has to happen in such a way that's transparent to the user.

The hospital has also turned to Citrix for application virtualization in order to allow remote support, which is important in a hospital situation where many clinicians may need to work from home. Sick Kids is now using VMware to deal with the more common issues around managing server fleets, such as lack of real estate, power costs, and the need to provision (that is, set up) machines more quickly.

"In the physical world, if you have good planning and processes in place, that will help you with virtualization," says Dennis Corning, HP's worldwide senior manager of product marketing for virtualization.

Andreasian agrees. "Provisioning (a virtual server) is easy. De-provisioning once the business user no longer needs it is where it's difficult," she says. "They might not tell you it's no longer necessary. You need governance and monitoring and process."

SOURCE: Shane Schick, "Hospital CTO Identifies Virtualization Gotchas," *CIO.com*, January 28, 2010.

OTHER SYSTEM MANAGEMENT PROGRAMS

There are many other types of important system management software besides operating systems. These include *database management systems*, which we will cover in Chapter 5, and *network management programs*, which we will cover in Chapter 6. Figure 4.17 compares several types of system software offered by IBM and its competitors.

Several other types of system management software are marketed as separate programs or included as part of an operating system. Utility programs, or **utilities,** are an important example. Programs like Norton Utilities perform miscellaneous housekeeping and file conversion functions. Examples include data backup, data recovery, virus protection, data compression, and file defragmentation. Most operating systems also provide many utilities that perform a variety of helpful chores for computer users.

Other examples of system support programs include performance monitors and security monitors. Performance monitors are programs that monitor and adjust the performance and usage of one or more computer systems to keep them running efficiently. Security monitors are packages that monitor and control the use of computer systems and provide warning messages and record evidence of unauthorized use of computer resources. A recent trend is to merge both types of programs into operating

FIGURE 4.17

Comparing system software offered by IBM and its main competitors.

Software Category	What It Does	IBM Product	Customers	Main Competitor	Customers
Network management	Monitors networks to keep them up and running.	Tivoli	T. Rowe Price uses it to safeguard customer records.	HP OpenView	Amazon.com uses it to monitor its servers.
Application server	Shuttles data between business apps and the Web.	WebSphere	REI uses it to serve up its Web site and distribute data.	BEA WebLogic	Washingtonpost.com builds news pages with it.
Database manager	Provides digital storehouses for business data.	DB2	Mikasa uses it to help customers find its products online.	Oracle 11g	It runs Southwest Airlines' frequent-flyer program.
Collaboration tools	Powers everything from e-mail to electronic calendars.	Lotus	Retailer Sephora uses it to coordinate store maintenance.	Microsoft Exchange	Time Inc. uses it to provide e-mail to its employees.
Development tools	Allows programmers to craft software code quickly.	Rational	Merrill Lynch used it to build code for online trading.	Microsoft Visual Studio .NET	Used to develop management system.

systems like Microsoft's Windows 2008 Datacenter Server or into system management software like Computer Associates' CA-Unicenter, which can manage both mainframe systems and servers in a data center.

Another important software trend is the use of system software known as application servers, which provide a *middleware* interface between an operating system and the application programs of users. *Middleware* is software that helps diverse software applications and networked computer systems exchange data and work together more efficiently. Examples include application servers, Web servers, and enterprise application integration (EAI) software. Thus, for example, application servers like BEA's WebLogic and IBM's WebSphere help Web-based e-business and e-commerce applications run much faster and more efficiently on computers using Windows, UNIX, and other operating systems.

PROGRAMMING LANGUAGES
LO 4-5

To understand computer software, you need a basic knowledge of the role that programming languages play in the development of computer programs. A *programming language* allows a programmer to develop the sets of instructions that constitute a computer program. Many different programming languages have been developed, each with its own unique vocabulary, grammar, and uses.

Machine Languages

Machine languages (or *first-generation languages*) are the most basic level of programming languages. In the early stages of computer development, all program instructions had to be written using binary codes unique to each computer. This type of programming involves the difficult task of writing instructions in the form of strings of binary digits (ones and zeros) or other number systems. Programmers must have a detailed knowledge of the internal operations of the specific type of CPU they are using. They must write long series of detailed instructions to accomplish even simple processing tasks. Programming in machine language requires specifying the storage locations for every instruction and item of data used. Instructions must be included for every switch and indicator used by the program. These requirements make machine language programming a difficult and error-prone task. A machine language program to add two numbers together in the CPU of a specific computer and store the result might take the form shown in Figure 4.18.

Assembler Languages

Assembler languages (or *second-generation languages*) are the next level of programming languages. They were developed to reduce the difficulties in writing machine language programs. The use of assembler languages requires language translator programs called *assemblers* that allow a computer to convert the instructions of such language into machine instructions. Assembler languages are frequently called symbolic

FIGURE 4.18

Examples of four levels of programming languages. These programming language instructions might be used to compute the sum of two numbers as expressed by the formula X = Y + Z.

Four Levels of Programming Languages	
Machine Languages: Use binary coded instructions 1010 11001 1011 11010 1100 11011	**High-Level Languages:** Use brief statements or arithmetic notations BASIC: X = Y + Z COBOL: COMPUTE X = Y + Z
Assembler Languages: Use symbolic coded instructions LOD Y ADD Z STR X	**Fourth-Generation Languages:** Use natural and nonprocedural statements SUM THE FOLLOWING NUMBERS

languages because symbols are used to represent operation codes and storage locations. Convenient alphabetic abbreviations called *mnemonics* (memory aids) and other symbols represent operation codes, storage locations, and data elements. For example, the computation $X = Y + Z$ in an assembler language might take the form shown in Figure 4.18.

Assembler languages are still used as a method of programming a computer in a machine-oriented language. Most computer manufacturers provide an assembler language that reflects the unique machine language instruction set of a particular line of computers. This feature is particularly desirable to *system programmers*, who program system software (as opposed to application programmers, who program application software), because it provides them with greater control and flexibility in designing a program for a particular computer. They can then produce more efficient software—that is, programs that require a minimum of instructions, storage, and CPU time to perform a specific processing assignment. In most cases, however, unless you become an operating system programmer, you will never encounter assembler language. Just know that you are likely to be using software created with it.

High-Level Languages

High-level languages (or *third-generation languages*) use instructions, which are called *statements*, that include brief statements or arithmetic expressions. Individual high-level language statements are actually *macroinstructions*; that is, each individual statement generates several machine instructions when translated into machine language by high-level language translator programs called *compilers* or *interpreters*. High-level language statements resemble the phrases or mathematical expressions required to express the problem or procedure being programmed. The *syntax* (vocabulary, punctuation, and grammatical rules) and *semantics* (meanings) of such statements do not reflect the internal code of any particular computer. For example, the computation $X = Y + Z$ would be programmed in the high-level languages of BASIC and COBOL as shown in Figure 4.18.

High-level languages like BASIC, COBOL, and FORTRAN are easier to learn and program than an assembler language because they have less rigid rules, forms, and syntaxes. However, high-level language programs are usually less efficient than assembler language programs and require a greater amount of computer time for translation into machine instructions. Because most high-level languages are machine-independent, programs written in a high-level language do not have to be reprogrammed when a new computer is installed, and programmers do not have to learn a different language for each type of computer.

Fourth-Generation Languages

The term *fourth-generation language* describes a variety of programming languages that are more *nonprocedural* and *conversational* than prior languages. These languages are called fourth-generation languages (4GLs) to differentiate them from machine languages (first generation), assembler languages (second generation), and high-level languages (third generation).

Most fourth-generation languages are *nonprocedural languages* that encourage users and programmers to specify the results they want, while the computer determines the sequence of instructions that will accomplish those results. Thus, fourth-generation languages have helped simplify the programming process. **Natural languages** are sometimes considered *fifth-generation* languages (5GLs) and are very close to English or other human languages. Research and development activity in artificial intelligence (AI) is developing programming languages that are as easy to use as ordinary conversation in one's native tongue. For example, INTELLECT, a natural language, would use a statement like, "What are the average exam scores in MIS 200?" to program a simple average exam score task. Try going to www.hakia.com, a natural language search engine, and typing a questions like "What is the population of Chicago, IL?" I think you will be surprised at the volume of accurate results. Try entering the same question at www.google.com and you'll immediately get a long list of hits, but at the top you will see "Best guess for Chicago, IL population is 2,896,016." That's natural language!

In the early days of 4GLs, results suggested that high-volume transaction processing environments were not in the range of a 4GL's capabilities. Although 4GLs were characterized by their ease of use, they were also viewed as less flexible than their predecessors, primarily due to their increased storage and processing speed requirements. In today's large-data-volume environment, 4GLs are widely used and no longer viewed as a trade-off between ease of use and flexibility.

Modern (and Automatic?) Code Generation

Twenty years ago, software engineer Fred Brooks famously observed that there was no silver bullet that could slay "the monster of missed schedules, blown budgets and flawed products." Today, the creation of software might seem as expensive, trouble-prone, and difficult as ever—and yet progress is being made. Although no silver bullet is in sight, an array of new techniques promises to further boost a programmer's productivity, at least in some application domains.

The techniques span a broad spectrum of methods and results, but all are aimed at generating software automatically. Typically, they generate code from high-level, machine-readable designs or from domain-specific languages—assisted by advanced compilers—that sometimes can be used by nonprogrammers.

Gordon Novak, a computer science professor at the University of Texas at Austin and a member of the school's Laboratory for Artificial Intelligence, is working on "automatic programming"—using libraries of generic versions of programs, such as algorithms—to sort or find items in a list. Unlike traditional subroutines, which have simple but rigid interfaces and are invoked by other lines of program code, his technique works at a higher level and is therefore more flexible and easier to use.

Novak's users construct "views" that describe application data and principles and then connect the views by arrows in diagrams that show the relationships among the data. The diagrams are, in essence, very high-level flowcharts of the desired program. They get compiled in a way that customizes the stored generic algorithms for the user's specific problem, and the result is ordinary source code such as C, C++, or Java.

Novak says he was able to generate 250 lines of source code for an indexing program in 90 seconds with his system. That's equivalent to a week of productivity for an average programmer using a traditional language. "You are describing your program at a higher level," he says. "And what my program is saying is, 'I can tailor the algorithm for your application for free.'"

Douglas Smith, principal scientist at Kestrel Institute, a nonprofit computer science research firm in Palo Alto, California, is developing tools to "automate knowledge and get it into the computer." A programmer starts with Kestrel's Specware, which is a general-purpose, fifth-generation language that specifies a program's functions without regard to the ultimate programming language, system architecture, algorithms, data structures, and so on. Specware draws on a library of components, but the components aren't code. They are at a higher level and include design knowledge and principles about algorithms, data structures, and so on. Smith calls them "abstract templates."

In addition, Specware can produce proofs that the working code is "correct"—that is, that it conforms to the requirements put in by the user (which, of course, may contain errors). "Some customers want that for very-high-assurance applications, with no security flaws," Smith says. Kestrel does work for NASA and U.S. military and security agencies.

"It's a language for writing down problem requirements, a high-level statement of what a solution should be, without saying how to solve the problem," Smith says. "We think it's the ultimate frontier in software engineering. It's what systems analysts do."

SOURCE: Gary Anthes, "In the Labs: Automatic Code Generators," *Computerworld*, March 20, 2006.

Object-Oriented Languages

Object-oriented languages like Visual Basic, C++, and Java are also considered fifth-generation languages and have become major tools of software development. Briefly, whereas most programming languages separate data elements from the procedures or actions that will be performed on them, object-oriented languages tie them together into **objects.** Thus, an object consists of data and the actions that can be performed on the data. For example, an object could be a set of data about a bank customer's savings account and the operations (e.g., interest calculations) that might be performed on the data. An object also could be data in graphic form, such as a video display window plus the display actions that might be used on it. See Figure 4.19.

In procedural languages, a program consists of procedures to perform actions on each data element. However, in object-oriented systems, objects tell other objects to perform actions on themselves. For example, to open a window on a computer video display, a beginning menu object could send a window object a message to open, and a window would appear on the screen. That's because the window object contains the program code for opening itself.

Object-oriented languages are easier to use and more efficient for programming the graphics-oriented user interfaces required by many applications. Therefore, they are the most widely used programming languages for software development today. Also, once objects are programmed, they are reusable. Therefore, reusability of objects is a major benefit of object-oriented programming. For example, programmers can construct a user interface for a new program by assembling standard objects such as windows, bars, boxes, buttons, and icons. Therefore, most object-oriented programming packages provide a GUI that supports a point-and-click, drag-and-drop visual

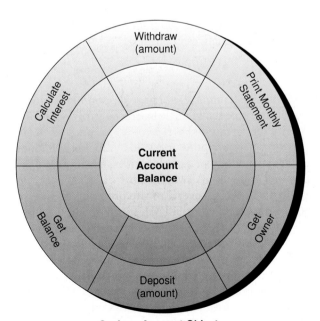

Savings Account Object

FIGURE 4.19

An example of a bank savings account object. This object consists of data about a customer's account balance and the basic operations that can be performed on those data.

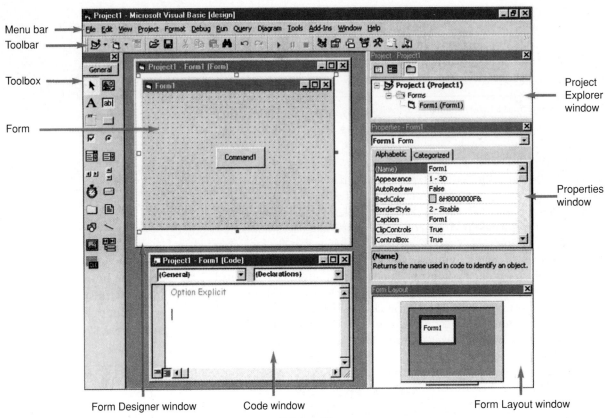

Menu bar
Toolbar
Toolbox
Form

Project Explorer window
Properties window

Form Designer window   Code window   Form Layout window

FIGURE 4.20

The Visual Basic object-oriented programming environment.

SOURCE: Courtesy of Microsoft®.

assembly of objects known as *visual programming*. Figure 4.20 shows a display of the Visual Basic object-oriented programming environment. Object-oriented technology is discussed further in the coverage of object-oriented databases in Chapter 5.

WEB AND INTERNET LANGUAGES AND SERVICES
LO 4-1

HTML, XML, and Java are three programming languages that are important tools for building multimedia Web pages, Web sites, and Web-based applications. In addition, XML and Java have become strategic components of the software technologies that support many Web services initiatives in business.

HTML

HTML (Hypertext Markup Language) is a page description language that creates hypertext or hypermedia documents. HTML inserts control codes within a document at points you can specify that create links (*hyperlinks*) to other parts of the document or to other documents anywhere on the World Wide Web. HTML embeds control codes in the ASCII text of a document that designate titles, headings, graphics, and multimedia components, as well as hyperlinks within the document.

As we mentioned previously, several of the programs in the top software suites automatically convert documents into HTML formats. These include Web browsers, word processing and spreadsheet programs, database managers, and presentation graphics packages. These and other specialized *Web publishing* programs like Microsoft FrontPage, Lotus FastSite, and Macromedia's DreamWeaver provide a range of features to help you design and create multimedia Web pages without formal HTML programming. The important thing to know about HTML is that without it, you would not be enjoying all the great and informative Web sites on the Internet. It is the language of the Web!

XML

XML (eXtensible Markup Language) is not a Web page *format description* language like HTML. Instead, XML describes the *contents of Web pages* (including business documents designed for use on the Web) by applying identifying tags or *contextual labels* to the data in Web documents. For example, a travel agency Web page with airline names and flight times would use hidden XML tags like "airline name" and "flight time" to categorize each of the airline flight times on that page. Or product inventory data available at a Web site could be labeled with tags like "brand," "price," and "size." By classifying data in this way, XML makes Web site information much more searchable, easier to sort, and easier to analyze.

For example, XML-enabled search software could easily find the exact product you specify if the product data on the Web site had been labeled with identifying XML tags. A Web site that uses XML could also more easily determine which Web page features its customers use and which products they investigate. Thus, XML promises to make electronic business and commerce processes a lot easier and more efficient by supporting the automatic electronic exchange of business data between companies and their customers, suppliers, and other business partners.

As mentioned at the beginning of the chapter, this entire textbook was revised and edited for the current edition using an XML-based application called PowerXEditor by Aptara. Let's focus our attention on this unique application of XML intended to create efficiencies in the publishing industry.

Aptara Inc.: Revolutionizing the Publishing Industry through XML

The publishing industry has experienced an upheaval in the past decade or so. The "long tail" of sales of existing books via Web sellers such as Amazon and the improvement in software and hardware technologies that can replicate the experience of reading a book or magazine means publishing houses are printing and selling fewer new books. As a result, many of these companies are venturing into digital publishing.

"All the publishers are shifting from print to digital," said Dev Ganesan, president and CEO of Aptara, which specializes in content transformation. "That's a huge change. What that means for software companies is that they need to develop platforms for content creation that meet the needs of every customer. At the same time, customers are looking at publishing in terms of handling content in terms of authors, editors, and production employees. On top of that, they're trying to automate parts of the production process. And companies must be willing to market products using traditional and new media to reach the widest possible audience. So there are a lot of challenges, but a lot of opportunities, too."

The upshot of all this is that learning professionals can now deliver content more flexibly and at a lower cost. They can make static content dynamic by taking a body of knowledge in print—such as a book—and converting it to a digital format. They can then chunk that content into smaller sizes and organize those nuggets of information according to learners' needs. Moreover, they can get content published and distributed much more quickly via digital, online media. This is critical in an industry such as health care, which faces rapid changes due to technological innovation and regulation, said another Aptara source.

"In addition to the cost savings, they want to turn it around much faster," he said. "Time to market is becoming paramount because there's so much innovation going on. If they don't have their print products out faster, they fall behind."

A breakthrough product from Aptara is called PowerXEditor (PXE). An XML-based application, PXE allows a publisher to upload an existing book layout; edit or revise all elements of the book, including text look and feel, figures, tables, and other elements unique to that book; and output the book to a paging program that sets the book up for final printing. The important issue is that all of this is done in a digital format instead of the previously common method of tear pages and cut-and-paste of figures and tables. Because the PXE content is XML-based, the application can be accessed via the Internet using any conventional Web browser. This means all of the contributors to a textbook can have access to the various chapters and elements no matter where they are. Add in the workflow management aspects of PXE, and all phases of the textbook revising, copyediting, and proofing processes can be handled with ease.

Figure 4.21 shows a typical PXE screen. You might notice that it is in the process of editing the page you are currently reading. Figure 4.22 shows the XML code for the same page.

FIGURE 4.21
The XML-based PowerXEditor allows all of the collaborators on a book project to access the elements of the book via a common Web browser. Here is a screenshot of PXE on the page you are currently reading.

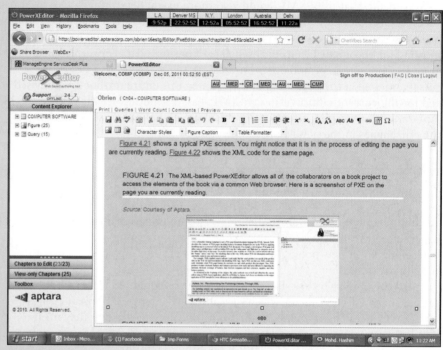

SOURCE: Courtesy of Aptara.

FIGURE 4.22
This is a section of the XML code from the page you are currently reading. While XML looks similar to HTML source code, it is far more powerful and complex.

```
    <internalref type="figure" idref="fig22">Figure 4.22</internalref>
    shows the XML code for the same page.
    </para>
  - <figure id="fig21" numbered="numbered" extra-info="FIGURE 4.21">
      <caption>The XML-based PowerXEditor allows all of. the collaborators on a book
        project to access the elements of the book via a common Web browser. Here is a
        screenshot of PXE on the page you are currently reading.</caption>
      <graphic name="obr76817_0421.jpg" source="source" />
    - <sourcenote>
        <emph type="italics">Source:</emph>
        Courtesy of Aptara.
      </sourcenote>
    </figure>
  - <figure id="fig22" numbered="numbered" extra-info="FIGURE 4.22">
      <caption>This is a section of the XML code from the page you are currently reading.
        While XML looks similar to HTML source code, it is far more powerful and
        complex.</caption>
      <graphic name="obr76817_0422.jpg" source="source" />
    - <sourcenote>
        <emph type="italics">Source:</emph>
        Courtesy of Aptara.
      </sourcenote>
    </figure>
  - <sourcenote>
      Source: Adapted from Brian Summerfield, "Executive Briefings: Balancing Print and
      Digital Media,"
      <emph type="italics">Chief Learning Officer,</emph>
      March 2008.
      <url xlink-type="simple" xlink-
        href="http://www.clomedia.com/includes/printcontent.php?
        aid=2133">http://www.clomedia.com/includes/printcontent.php?aid=2133</url>
    </sourcenote>
```

SOURCE: Courtesy of Aptara.

SOURCE: Brian Summerfield, "Executive Briefings: Balancing Print and Digital Media," *Chief Learning Officer*, March 2008. http://www.clomedia.com/includes/printcontent.php?aid=2133

Java and .NET

Java is an object-oriented programming language created by Sun Microsystems that has revolutionized the programming of applications for the Web, as well as corporate intranets and extranets. Java is related to the C++ and Objective C programming languages but is much simpler and more secure and is computing-platform independent. This means a Java-based program doesn't really care about what kind of computer or what operating system is being used. This makes Java a very powerful programming language. Java is also specifically designed for real-time, interactive, Web-based network applications. Java applications consisting of small application programs, called *applets*, can be executed by any computer and any operating system anywhere in a network.

The ease of creating Java applets and distributing them from network servers to client PCs and network computers is one of the major reasons for Java's popularity. Applets can be small, special-purpose application programs or small modules of larger Java application programs. Java programs are platform-independent, too—they can run on Windows, UNIX, and Macintosh systems without modification.

Microsoft's .NET is a collection of programming support for what are known as *Web services,* the ability to use the Web rather than your own computer for various services (see Figure 4.23). The purpose of .NET is to provide individual and business users with a seamlessly interoperable and Web-enabled interface for applications and computing devices and to make computing activities increasingly Web browser–oriented. The .NET platform includes servers, building-block services such as Web-based data storage, and device software. It also includes Passport, Microsoft's fill-in-the-form-only-once identity verification service.

The .NET platform is expected to enable the entire range of computing devices to work together and have user information automatically updated and synchronized on all of them. In addition, it will provide a premium online subscription service. The service will feature customized access to and delivery of products and services from a central starting point for the management of various applications

FIGURE 4.23

The benefits and limitations of the Java Enterprise Edition 6 (Java EE 6) and Microsoft's .NET software development platforms.

Java EE 5		.NET	
PROS	**CONS**	**PROS**	**CONS**
• Runs on any operating system and application server (may need adjustments). • Handles complex, high-volume, high-transaction applications. • Has more enterprise features for session management, fail-over, load balancing, and application integration. • Is favored by experienced enterprise vendors such as IBM, BEA, SAP, and Oracle. • Offers a wide range of vendor choices for tools and application servers. • Has a proven track record.	• Has a complex application development environment. • Tools can be difficult to use. • Java Swing environment's ability to build graphical user interfaces has limitations. • May cost more to build, deploy, and manage applications. • Lacks built-in support for Web services standards. • Is difficult to use for quick-turnaround, low-cost, and mass-market projects.	• Easy-to-use tools may increase programmer productivity. • Has a strong framework for building rich graphical user interfaces. • Gives developers choice of working in more than 20 programming languages. • Is tightly integrated with Microsoft's operating system and enterprise server software. • May cost less, due in part to built-in application server in Windows, unified management, and less expensive tools. • Has built-in support for Web service standards.	• Framework runs only on Windows, restricting vendor choice. • Users of prior Microsoft tools and technology face a potentially steep learning curve. • New run-time infrastructure lacks maturity. • Questions persist about the scalability and transaction capability of the Windows platform. • Choice of integrated development environments is limited. • Getting older applications to run in new .NET environment may require effort.

SOURCE: Carol Silwa, ".NET vs. Java," *Computerworld,* May 20, 2002, p. 31.

(e.g., e-mail) or software (e.g., Office .NET). For developers, .NET offers the ability to create reusable modules, which should increase productivity and reduce the number of programming errors.

The full release of .NET is expected to take several years to complete, with intermittent releases of products, such as a personal security service and new versions of Windows and Office that implement the .NET strategy coming on the market separately. Visual Studio .NET is a development environment that is now available, and Windows XP supports certain .NET capabilities.

The latest version of Java is Java Enterprise Edition 6 (Java EE 6), which has become the primary alternative to Microsoft's .NET software development platform for many organizations intent on capitalizing on the business potential of Web-based applications and Web services. Figure 4.23 compares the pros and cons of using Java EE 6 and .NET for software development.

Web Services

As discussed above, ***Web services*** are software components that are based on a framework of Web and object-oriented standards and technologies for using the Web that electronically link the applications of different users and different computing platforms. Thus, Web services can link key business functions for the exchange of data in real time within the Web-based applications that a business might share with its customers, suppliers, and other business partners. For example, Web services would enable the purchasing application of a business to use the Web to check the inventory of a supplier before placing a large order, while the sales application of the supplier

FIGURE 4.24

The basic steps in accomplishing a Web services application.

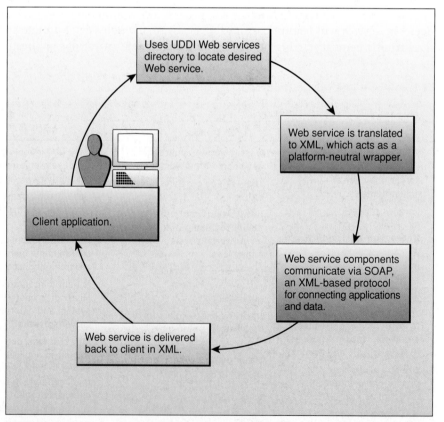

SOURCE: Bala Iyer, Jim Freedman, Mark Gaynor, and George Wyner, "Web Services: Enabling Dynamic Business Networks," *Communications of the Association for Information Systems* 11(2003), p. 543.

could use Web services to automatically check the credit rating of the business with a credit-reporting agency before approving the purchase. Therefore, among both business and IT professionals, the term *Web services* is commonly used to describe the Web-based business and computing functions or services accomplished by Web services software technologies and standards.

Figure 4.24 illustrates how Web services work and identifies some of the key technologies and standards that are involved. The XML language is one of the key technologies that enable Web services to make applications work between different computing platforms. Also important are **UDDI** (Universal Description, Discovery, and Integration), the "yellow pages" directory of all Web services and how to locate and use them, and **SOAP** (Simple Object Access Protocol), an XML-based protocol of specifications for connecting applications to the data that they need.

Web services promise to be the key software technology for automating access to data and application functions between a business and its trading partners. As companies increasingly move to doing business over the Web, Web services will become essential for the development of the easy and efficient e-business and e-commerce applications that will be required. The flexibility and interoperability of Web services will also be essential for coping with the fast-changing relationships between a company and its business partners that are commonplace in today's dynamic global business environment.

Airbus: Flying on SAP and Web Services

European aircraft builder Airbus has implemented a Web services–based travel management application from SAP as a first step in a planned groupwide migration to a service-oriented architecture (SOA). The airplane manufacturer is installing the travel management component of SAP's ERP software, mySAP, which uses SOA technology. "The new system replaces a home-grown system at the company's plant in France, a Lotus-based system in its Spanish operations, and earlier SAP versions at facilities in Germany and the United Kingdom," says James Westgarth, manager of travel technology procurement at Airbus.

"We like the idea of an open architecture, which SOA enables," Westgarth says. "We like the idea of being able to manage everything internally and to cherry-pick for the best solution in every class. Additional components, such as online booking, could also come from SAP—if the software vendor has a superior product for that application," says Westgarth.

The decision to deploy a new Web services–based travel management system was driven in large part by a need to reduce administration costs and improve business processes.

Airbus has a travel budget of 250 million euros, which is used to help pay for more than 180,000 trips annually. The company aims to reduce costs by eliminating the current paper-based reimbursement process, which consumes time and labor, with a system that enables employees to process their own travel expenses online from their desktops or mobile devices.

A key benefit for employees: Reimbursement time will be reduced to 3 days from about 10 days. In addition, the new system allows Airbus to integrate new service providers more easily into its operations, notes Westgarth. The manufacturer has outsourced its valued-added tax reclaim activities to a third party specializing in this service. With the help of application link enablers, Westgarth and his team are able to link their travel management system into the company's other SAP applications, including finance and human resources. Airbus has a strategy to eventually migrate to the mySAP ERP across multiple systems and countries over a number of years.

"The company chose travel management to pilot mySAP ERP," says Westgarth. There have been some issues with the rollout of the travel management application, Westgarth concedes. "Because we're the first big company to implement this technology, we've had difficulty finding enough skilled people on the market," he said. "And some work was required to integrate the Web interface into our portal."

But Airbus employees, Westgarth said, like the Web-based application's new user interface, the single sign-on and the step-by-step guidance. And the company likes the flexibility. "No one was talking about low-cost carriers five years ago," he said. "We need to adapt to the market and to changing needs."

SOURCE: John Blau, "Airbus Flies on Web Services with SAP," *IDG News Service, CIO Magazine,* June 8, 2006.

PROGRAMMING SOFTWARE
LO 4-5

Various software packages are available to help programmers develop computer programs. For example, *programming language translators* are programs that translate other programs into machine language instruction codes that computers can execute. Other software packages, such as programming language editors, are called *programming tools* because they help programmers write programs by providing a variety of program creation and editing capabilities. See Figure 4.25.

Language Translator Programs

Computer programs consist of sets of instructions written in programming languages that must be translated by a ***language translator*** into the computer's own machine language before they can be processed, or executed, by the CPU. Programming language translator programs (or *language processors*) are known by a variety of names. An **assembler** translates the symbolic instruction codes of programs written in an assembler language into machine language instructions, whereas a **compiler** translates high-level language statements.

An **interpreter** is a special type of compiler that translates and executes each statement in a program one at a time, instead of first producing a complete machine

FIGURE 4.25

Using the graphical programming interface of a Java programming tool, Forte for Java, by Sun Microsystems.

SOURCE: Courtesy of Sun Microsystems.

language program, as compilers and assemblers do. Java is an example of an interpreted language. Thus, the program instructions in Java applets are interpreted and executed *on the fly* as the applet is being executed by a client PC.

Programming Tools

Software development and the computer programming process have been enhanced by adding *graphical programming interfaces* and a variety of built-in development capabilities. Language translators have always provided some editing and diagnostic capabilities to identify programming errors or *bugs*. However, most software development programs now include powerful graphics-oriented *programming editors* and *debuggers*. These **programming tools** help programmers identify and minimize errors while they are programming. Such programming tools provide a computer-aided programming environment, which decreases the drudgery of programming while increasing the efficiency and productivity of software developers. Other programming tools include diagramming packages, code generators, libraries of reusable objects and program code, and prototyping tools. All of these programming tools are an essential part of widely used programming languages like Visual Basic, C++, and Java.

CASE TOOLS. Since the early days of programming, software developers have needed automated tools. Initially the concentration was on program support tools such as translators, compilers, assemblers, macroprocessors, and linkers and loaders. However, as computers became more powerful and the software that ran on them grew larger and more complex, the range of support tools began to expand. In particular, the use of interactive timesharing systems for software development encouraged the development of program editors, debuggers, and code analyzers. As the range of support tools expanded, manufacturers began to integrate them into a single application using a common interface. Such tools were referred to as ***CASE tools*** (computer-aided software engineering). CASE tools can take a number of forms and be applied at different stages of the software development process. Those CASE tools that support activities early in the life cycle of a software project (e.g., requirements, design support tools) are sometimes called *front-end* or *upper* CASE tools. Those that are used later in the life cycle (e.g., compilers, test support tools) are called *back-end* or *lower* CASE tools. Exploring the details of CASE tools is beyond the scope of this text, and you will encounter them again when you study systems analysis and design. For now, remember that CASE is an important part of resolving the problems of complex application development and maintenance of software applications.

real world
SOLUTION

Japan Post Network–Savings and Competitive Advantage with Software as a Service

Japan Post Network is a large operator of postal service offices in Japan that resulted from the privatization and breakup of Japan Post, a government-owned private corporation that took over the existing Postal Services Agency. All in all, the company has been providing postal services in one form or another for more than 130 years. In addition to these services, the original Japan Post was a large provider of financial, banking, and insurance services throughout the country. At the time, it was the largest financial services company in the world in terms of assets under custody, as well as Japan's largest individual employer and the largest government creditor, holding one-fifth of the national public debt in government bonds. In addition to Japan Post Network, three other companies (Japan Post Service, Japan Post Bank and Japan Post Insurance) sell their products and services through the offices of Japan Post Network, with the latter acting as an agent of the other companies in the group. This new role for the company, as well as the fact that it is now a separate legal entity from the other companies—which brings new challenges that did not exist before—prompted Japan Post Network to undertake two major application development efforts.

As a result of the competitive bidding process used by the company, salesforce.com was selected to provide the technology underlying the two major business processes required by Japan Post Network, as outlined in the introduction to this chapter. The company chose this approach because it wanted to be able to deploy these applications quickly and gain an early advantage in the now-competitive postal business without having to make large up-front capital outlays in software development staff and infrastructure. Japan Post Network estimates that the combination of cloud computing and provision of services offered by salesforce.com saved it about $10 million in infrastructure hardware and software costs. The company estimates the development costs incurred by going with salesforce.com platform to be about $500,000—an order of magnitude smaller. Because the more than 57,000 who would be end users of the new technologies had varying degrees of IT literacy, differing attitudes toward IT, and new technological developments, Japan Post Network needed to deploy a system that would be as easy to use as possible and that already had an extensive track record among private companies.

The first new application needed to support the cross-selling of products and services from the other companies in the Japan Post group, with Japan Post Network acting as an agent. This initiative was dubbed "Customer Management Information System" and was to be implemented using Salesforce Software as a Service (Saas) CRM application, with NTT Data taking responsibility for systems integration. The target users of this new application were the marketing staff employed at approximately 24,700 postal offices in Japan, as well as other corporate staff located in headquarters; the total number of users was expected to be close to 21,000. The application enables employees to report any compliance and customer-related issues to both regional branches and company headquarters in Tokyo in real time, laying the foundation for improving service levels in the future, as well as strengthening internal compliance. Some of the functionality delivered with this application included checking and searching cross-selling consent forms, viewing and updating customer information, and standardizing that information to make sharing across operations less complicated. It also included work-flow support to comply with applicable laws and regulations, as well as sales proposals that were uniquely matched to specific customer needs.

The second application was geared toward supporting the gathering and analysis of data about various forms of face-to-face interactions with customers at the approximately 24,000 postal offices that Japan Post Network operated throughout the country. Labeled "Accident/Scandal/Complaint Reporting System," it would be implemented using the Force.com application platform (in a rather new innovation at the time, providing Application Platform as a Service, or APaaS, to customers), and Hitachi Software Engineering would take over systems integration work for this application. The new system was targeted to the business departments of all postal offices, with an expected number of end users to be approximately 36,000 overall.

The company was ultimately able to deploy both systems in time for its privatization. In fact, the Accident/Scandal/Complaint Reporting System was fully developed in only three months—probably six months to a year faster than if they had used traditional development methods. This was an important consideration for the company and figured prominently in the specifications that were originally released for competitive bidding—and a major reason the use of a service model was chosen to implement them. The Accident/Scandal/Complaint Reporting System is currently handling 25,000 concurrent users and more than 100,000 new items of information each month with no noticeable performance issues, which are sometimes a concern when cloud computing and Software as a Service are deployed.

"It took about one-fourth the time and cost it would normally require to develop an app and deploy it on conventional infrastructure," says Yoshihiko Ohta, a senior general manager with Japan Post. One downside to working on the Force.com platform is that developers cannot customize as much as would be possible if the applications were developed in-house. At the same time, that may be one of the major benefits of taking this approach. Because the core application logic and most interface functions have already been prebuilt, many applications can be developed and deployed in a fraction of the time. In the future, this should allow for more responsiveness to changes that the business needs to implement.

A number of things went right, which may help other companies that face similar endeavors in the future. First, because of both the confidential nature of the customer data that would be captured and processed by these new applications and the fact that Japan Post Network operations are distributed across literally thousands of sites, application security and service-level considerations were of prime importance. All these were included, in detail, in the specifications the company provided to NTT Data and Hitachi Software. Second, the company took advantage—as much as possible—of the predefined components provided by the Force.com platform, instead of choosing to develop its own. Existing work flows for commonly executed operations were also adopted, and customization—with all of the extensive testing associated with it—were limited to the bare minimum; it was used only for those scenarios where the company had some unique, critical requirements that it needed to meet. In all other cases, standard components were used in the development of the new applications. Finally, one of the system integration partners, Hitachi

Software Engineering, was already using salesforce.com for its own internal applications and had extensive experience with the development platform before taking over parts of the project for Japan Post Network, which made the requirement definition, development, and deployment stages go much more smoothly.

More than eight custom applications have currently been developed, with more than 115 database tables, 340 integration points, and more than 13 million records—all handled outside Japan Post Network. Building new applications on the cloud platform is both easier and more cost-efficient than would be possible if traditional development practices were followed. The company estimates that, moving forward, the cost of ongoing application management and support on the Force.com platform would amount to only 5 to 10 percent of the original development. If the company had done the coding in-house, ongoing maintenance and support would be approximately 30 percent of development costs that were already much higher, also including support for additional data center and infrastructure equipment that would be needed.

"We decided to build the applications on Force.com as we felt it was the only platform that could accomplish the task in our short timescale. Our IT resources are limited, but change is constant. Therefore the key measure of success has been the development productivity, the flexibility, and the ability to change things easily," says Akira Iwasaki, CIO. "We plan on rolling out SaaS for all other areas of IT apart from our core systems and detailed analytics," he adds. In the three years since the applications were rolled out, the company has realized a return on investment of more than 500 percent.

SOURCE: Pete Swabey, "Japan Post," *InformationAge*, March 12, 2009, Charles Babcock, "How Cloud Computing Changes IT Organizations," *InformationWeek*, November 28, 2009, Koji Motoyoshi and Yefim Natis, "Case Study: Japan Post Improves Customer Service Effectiveness with Saas and APaaS," *Gartner Research*, July 15, 2008, "Japan Post Expands Salesforce Platform Deployment to 45,000 Users," *Salesforce.com Press Release*, September 5, 2008, IDC ExpertROI Spotlight, December 2009, and www.japanpost.com, accessed May 16, 2011.

▼ QUESTIONS TO CONSIDER

1. What are the disadvantages, if any, of relying on cloud computing and Software as a Service for the provision of mission-critical applications such as the one enabling the cross-selling of products and services from other companies in the group? What are the most important factors that management should assess as they select these providers?

2. The majority of the development for the two systems discussed here was achieved by putting together components that already existed in the Force.com platform. Is this the best approach—or even a possible one—for all kinds of systems (e.g., strategic, functional, and so forth)?

- **Software.** Computer software consists of two major types of programs: (1) application software that directs the performance of a particular use, or application, of computers to meet the information processing needs of users and (2) system software that controls and supports the operations of a computer system as it performs various information processing tasks. Refer to Figure 4.2 for an overview of the major types of software.

- **Application Software.** Application software includes a variety of programs that can be segregated into general-purpose and application-specific categories. General-purpose application programs perform common information processing jobs for end users. Examples are word processing, electronic spreadsheet, and presentation graphics programs. Application-specific programs accomplish information processing tasks that support specific business functions or processes, scientific or engineering applications, and other computer applications in society.

- **System Software.** System software can be subdivided into system management programs and system development programs. System management programs manage the hardware, software, network, and data resources of a computer system during its execution of information processing jobs. Examples of system management programs are operating systems, network management programs, database management systems, system utilities, application servers, and performance and security monitors. Network management programs support and manage telecommunications activities and network performance telecommunications networks. Database management systems control the development,

integration, and maintenance of databases. Utilities are programs that perform routine computing functions, such as backing up data or copying files, as part of an operating system or as a separate package. System development programs like language translators and programming editors help IS specialists develop computer programs to support business processes.

- **Operating Systems.** An operating system is an integrated system of programs that supervises the operation of the CPU, controls the input/output storage functions of the computer system, and provides various support services. An operating system performs five basic functions: (1) a user interface for system and network communications with users, (2) resource management for managing the hardware resources of a computer system, (3) file management for managing files of data and programs, (4) task management for managing the tasks a computer must accomplish, and (5) utilities and other functions that provide miscellaneous support services.

- **Programming Languages.** Programming languages are a major category of system software. They require the use of a variety of programming packages to help programmers develop computer programs and language translator programs to convert programming language instructions into machine language instruction codes. The five major levels of programming languages are machine languages, assembler languages, high-level languages, fourth-generation languages, and object-oriented languages. Object-oriented languages like Java and special-purpose languages like HTML and XML are being widely used for Web-based business applications and services.

These are the key terms and concepts of this chapter. The page number of their first reference appears in parentheses.

1. Application service provider (ASP) (149)
2. Application software (135)
3. Assembler language (162)
4. CASE tools (173)
5. Cloud computing (150)
6. COTS software (138)
7. Custom software (135)
8. Desktop publishing (DTP) (144)
9. E-mail (142)
10. Fourth-generation language (163)
11. Function-specific application software (139)
12. General-purpose application programs (135)
13. Groupware (147)
14. High-level language (163)
15. HTML (166)
16. Instant messaging (IM) (143)
17. Integrated package (141)
18. Java (169)
19. Language translator (172)
20. Machine language (162)
21. Middleware (162)
22. Multitasking (155)
23. Natural language (163)
24. Object-oriented language (165)
25. Operating system (153)
26. Personal information manager (PIM) (147)
27. Presentation graphics software (146)
28. Programming language (162)
29. Software suites (140)
30. Spreadsheet packages (145)
31. System software (153)
32. User interface (154)
33. Utilities (161)
34. Virtual memory (154)
35. Web browser (141)
36. Web services (170)
37. Word processing software (144)
38. XML (167)

Match one of the previous key terms and concepts with one of the brief examples or definitions that follow. Try to find the best fit for answers that seem to fit more than one term or concept. Defend your choices.

_____ 1. An approach to computing where tasks are assigned to a combination of connections, software, and services accessed over a network.

_____ 2. Programs that direct the performance of a specific use of computers.

_____ 3. A system of programs that manages the operations of a computer system.

_____ 4. Companies that own, operate, and maintain application software for a fee as a service over the Internet.

_____ 5. Integrated software tool that supports the development of software applications.

_____ 6. Software designed in-house for use by a specific organization or set of users.

_____ 7. The function that provides a means of communication between end users and an operating system.

_____ 8. Acronym meaning commercial off-the-shelf.

_____ 9. Provides a greater memory capability than a computer's actual memory capacity.

_____ 10. The ability to do several computing tasks concurrently.

_____ 11. Converts numeric data into graphic displays.

_____ 12. Translates high-level instructions into machine language instructions.

_____ 13. Performs housekeeping chores for a computer system.

_____ 14. A category of application software that performs common information processing tasks for end users.

_____ 15. Software available for the specific applications of end users in business, science, and other fields.

_____ 16. Helps you surf the Web.

_____ 17. Uses your networked computer to send and receive messages.

_____ 18. Creates and displays a worksheet for analysis.

_____ 19. Allows you to create and edit documents.

_____ 20. Enables you to produce your own brochures and newsletters.

_____ 21. Helps you keep track of appointments and tasks.

_____ 22. A program that performs several general-purpose applications.

_____ 23. A combination of individual general-purpose application packages that work easily together.

_____ 24. Software to support the collaboration of teams and workgroups.

_____ 25. Uses instructions in the form of coded strings of ones and zeros.

_____ 26. Uses instructions consisting of symbols representing operation codes and storage locations.

_____ 27. Uses instructions in the form of brief statements or the standard notation of mathematics.

_____ 28. Might take the form of query languages and report generators.

_____ 29. Languages that tie together data and the actions that will be performed on the data.

_____ 30. As easy to use as one's native tongue.

_____ 31. Includes programming editors, debuggers, and code generators.

_____ 32. Produces hyperlinked multimedia documents for the Web.

_____ 33. A Web document content description language.

_____ 34. A popular object-oriented language for Web-based applications.

_____ 35. Windows, Linux, and Mac OS are common examples.

_____ 36. Software that helps diverse applications work together.

_____ 37. Enables you to communicate and collaborate in real time with the online associates in your workgroup.

_____ 38. Links business functions within applications for the exchange of data between companies via the Web.

1. What major trends are occurring in software? What capabilities do you expect to see in future software packages?

2. How do the different roles of system software and application software affect you as a business end user? How do you see this changing in the future?

3. Refer to the Real World Challenge in the chapter. Given the timelines imposed by the privatization process, were there really any alternatives from which Japan Post Network could choose? What is the lesson here about nontechnical constraints that are imposed on this type of project?

4. Why is an operating system necessary? That is, why can't an end user just load an application program into a computer and start computing?

5. Should a Web browser be integrated into an operating system? Why or why not?

6. Refer to the Real World Solution in the chapter. Is there a danger that the development expertise of companies may slowly atrophy as they rely more and more on predesigned, external components for assembling their applications? Is this a good thing or a bad thing?

7. Are software suites, Web browsers, and groupware merging together? What are the implications for a business and its end users?

8. How are HTML, XML, and Java affecting business applications on the Web?

9. Do you think Linux will surpass, in adoption and use, other operating systems for network and Web servers? Why or why not?

10. Which application software packages are the most important for a business end user to know how to use? Explain the reasons for your choices.

1. **Desktop Application Recognition**
   Tool Selection
   ABC Department Stores would like to acquire software to do the following tasks. Identify which software packages they need.

   a. Surf the Web and their intranets and extranets.

   b. Send messages to each other's computer workstations.

   c. Help employees work together in teams.

   d. Use a group of productivity packages that work together easily.

   e. Help sales reps keep track of meetings and sales calls.

   f. Type correspondence and reports.

   g. Analyze rows and columns of sales figures.

   h. Develop a variety of graphical presentations.

   i. Develop and give presentations to clients and other interorganizational departments.

   j. Collect, store, and retrieve organizational information, presenting it to users, giving them the ability to query and modify the data as required.

2. **Y2K Revisited**
   The End of Time
   Decades ago, programmers trying to conserve valuable storage space shortened year values to two digits. This created what became known as the "Y2K" problem or "millennium bug" at the turn of the century. Programmers needed to review billions of lines of code to ensure that important programs would continue to operate correctly. The Y2K problem merged with the **Dot.com** boom and created a tremendous demand for information technology employees. Information system users spent billions of dollars fixing or replacing old software. The IT industry is only now beginning to recover from the post-boom slump. Could such hysteria happen again? It can, and it very likely will.

   Today, most programs now use several different schemes to record dates. One scheme, POSIX time, widely employed on Unix-based systems, requires a signed 32-bit integer to store a number representing the number of seconds since January 1, 1970. "0" represents midnight on January 1, "10" represents 10 seconds after midnight, and "-10" represents 10 seconds *before* midnight. A simple program then converts this into any number of international date formats for display. This scheme works well because it allows programmers to subtract one date/time from another date/time and directly determine the interval between them. It also requires only 4 bytes of storage space. But 32 bits still calculates to a finite number, whereas time is infinite. As a business manager, you will need to be aware of this new threat and steer your organization away from repeating history. The following questions will help you evaluate the situation and learn from history.

   a. Since 1 represents 1 second and 2 represents 2 seconds, how many seconds can be represented in a binary number 32 bits long? Use a spreadsheet to show your calculations.

b. Given that POSIX time starts at midnight, January 1, 1970, in what year will time "run out?" Remember that half the available numbers represent dates before 1970. Use a spreadsheet to show your calculations.

c. As a business manager, what can you do to minimize this problem for your organization?

3. Tracking Project Work
Queries and Reports
You are responsible for managing information systems development projects at AAA Systems. To better track progress in completing projects, you have decided to maintain a simple database table to track the time your employees spend on various tasks and the projects with which they are associated. It will also allow you to keep track of employees'

billable hours each week. The table below provides a sample data set.

a. Build a database table to store the data shown, and enter the records as a set of sample data.

b. Create a query that will list the hours worked for all workers who worked more than 40 hours during production week 20.

c. Create a report grouped by project that will show the number of hours devoted to each task on the project, the subtotal number of hours devoted to each project, and a grand total of all hours worked.

d. Create a report grouped by employee that will show their hours worked on each task and the total hours worked. The user should be able to select a production week and have data only for the week presented.

Project_Name	Task_Name	Employee_ID	Production_Week	Hours_Worked
Fin-Goods-Inv	App. Devel.	456	21	42
Fin-Goods-Inv	DB Design	345	20	20
Fin-Goods-Inv	UI Design	234	20	16
HR	Analysis	234	21	24
HR	Analysis	456	20	48
HR	UI Design	123	20	8
HR	UI Design	123	21	40
HR	UI Design	234	21	32
Shipmt-Tracking	DB Design	345	20	24
Shipmt-Tracking	DB Design	345	21	16
Shipmt-Tracking	DB Development	345	21	20
Shipmt-Tracking	UI Design	123	20	32
Shipmt-Tracking	UI Design	234	20	24

4. Matching Training to Software Use
3-D Graphing
You have responsibility for managing software training for Sales, Accounting, and Operations Department workers in your organization. You have surveyed the workers to get a feel for the amount of time spent using various packages, and the results are shown below. The values shown are the total number of workers in each department and the total weekly hours the department's workers spend using each software package. You have been asked to prepare a spreadsheet summarizing

this data and comparing the use of the various packages across departments.

a. Create a spreadsheet illustrating each application's average use per department. To do this, you will first enter the data shown above. Then compute the average weekly spreadsheet use by dividing spreadsheet hours by the number of sales workers. Do this for each department. Repeat these three calculations for both database and presentation use. Round results to the nearest 1/100th.

Department	Employees	Spreadsheet	Database	Presentations
Sales	225	410	1100	650
Operations	75	710	520	405
Accounting	30	310	405	50

b. Create a three-dimensional bar graph illustrating the averages by department and software package.

c. A committee has been formed to plan software training classes at your company. Prepare a slide presentation with four slides illustrating your findings. The first slide should serve as an introduction to the data. The second slide should contain a copy of the original data table (without the averages). The third slide should contain a copy of the three-dimensional bar graph from the previous answer. The fourth slide should contain your conclusions regarding key applications per department. Use professional labels, formatting, and backgrounds.

5. Office Automation Suites

Not Always Microsoft

WordStar, VisiCalc, dBase, Harvard Graphics: Does any of this software sound familiar? These were word processing, spreadsheet, database, and presentation software applications that represented the state of the art on personal computers long before most of today's university students were born.

When, in 1990, Microsoft introduced Microsoft Office, it proceeded to dominate the office application market for the next two decades.

Lately, however, the computing world has seen a renaissance of office automation offerings, ranging from open source to online. Read PC-World.com's article, *Microsoft Office Alternatives: Productivity Software Showdown* (http://bit.ly/fi0KGN) and answer the following questions.

a. Have you used any of the products mentioned in the article? If so, briefly describe your experience.

b. Use a spreadsheet to create a table to make side-by-side comparisons of each product listed in the article. Organize the products in columns and the features in rows. Sort the features logically. Use an "X" to indicate which products have which features.

c. Select one of the five products mentioned in the article, explore it in detail, and report your results. Do your results match up with the matrix you created in the previous question?

CASE 1

GE, H.B. Fuller Co., and Others: Successful Implementations of Software as a Service

General Electric's supply chain is not just enormous. It's a byzantine web of sourcing partners, touching all corners of the globe: 500,000 suppliers in more than 100 countries that cut across 14 different languages. Each year, GE spends some $55 billion among its vast supplier base.

Long-time GE CIO Gary Reiner knows this problem all too well: Among his other duties, he is responsible for how the $ 173-billion conglomerate spends that $55 billion, utilizing GE's Six Sigma practices and taking advantage of its hefty purchasing power. GE, for instance, buys $150 million in desktops and laptops each year from a single supplier, Dell, "at a very low price," says Reiner.

For years, GE's Global Procurement Group faced a challenging reality: trying to accurately track and make sense of all of the supply chain interactions with half a million suppliers—contracts, compliance initiatives, certifications and other critical data, which needed to be centrally stored, managed, and made accessible to thousands across the globe. GE was using what it called a Global Supplier Library, a homegrown system that, Reiner says, had a "rudimentary capability." Reiner and his staff knew that GE needed something better, but they didn't want to build it. They wanted a supplier information system that was easy to use and install, could unite GE's sourcing empire into one central repository, had multilanguage capabilities, and also offered "self-service" functionality so that each of its suppliers could manage its own data.

The destination was obvious: To achieve one common view of its supplier base, and one version of the truth in all that data, a goal that torments nearly every company today. But to get there, Reiner and his IT and procurement teams took a different route. In 2008, GE bought the application of a little-known Software as a Service (Saas) vendor that would ultimately become the largest SaaS deployment to date.

"When we judge a solution, we are indifferent to whether it's hosted by a supplier or by us," Reiner says. "We look for the functionality of the solution and at the price." And that, he claims, has been the way they've always operated. Reiner says that his group doesn't see a big difference in cost and in capabilities between on-premise and SaaS products. "And let me emphasize," he adds, "we don't see a big difference in cost, either from the point of view of the ongoing operating costs, or the transition costs." Furthermore, Reiner says that when looking at implementation

costs, "they're largely around interfacing with existing systems, process changes and data cleansing," he says. "Those three costs exist regardless of whether GE hosts that application or whether the supplier hosts that application."

The Aravo technology platform was untested at GE's level of requirements, with just 20 or so customers. Coupled with the sheer scale of GE's needs, this did not really concern Reiner. "We could have been concerned about that," he concedes. "But that would have also been a concern if we had hosted the software on our own servers. We knew Aravo could handle it." Plus, Reiner says that no other supply chain vendor offered the type of functionality that Aravo's SIM product offered, and Reiner and his team reasoned that it was much cheaper to buy than to build. "We'd much rather work with them," he says, "than build it on our own." One GE sourcing manager told Aravo that GE's ROI on the project is not just positive, "it's massively positive."

"They're using SaaS for 100,000 users and 500,000 suppliers in six languages: that's a major technology deployment shift," says Mickey North Rizza, research director at AMR Research. She says that the sheer volume of transactions, combined with the fact that GE supply chain and procurement employees around the world can now access the same sourcing partner information, all from the same central spot, is significant not only for the supply chain management space but also for the SaaS and cloud computing world. "Finally we have a very large company tackling the data transparency issue by using a SaaS product," North Rizza says. "It's a huge deal."

So far, the thorny issue of data quality in GE's supplier data has been improved, because suppliers now use the self-service capabilities in the SaaS system to manage their own data. GE has 327,000 employees worldwide, and its sourcing systems have more than 100,000 users. There is still more work to do to the SIM platform—for example, GE sourcing employees will add more work flows and new queries to the system; more languages might be added as well (six are operational now).

Reiner says that GE is committed to working with Aravo for the long term and that the system has performed well so far. And SaaS, as an application delivery mechanism, appears to have a bright future at GE.

When Steven John took over as CIO at specialty chemical manufacturer H.B. Fuller Co., he inherited a North

American payroll system implementation that was expensive and going nowhere. The business units hadn't participated in the technology decision, and the project was bogged down with customization issues and other concerns. John chose to relinquish control of payroll software and switched to SaaS.

"I wanted to do an implementation that was simple and straightforward—to configure but not customize—and see the benefits of a standard, global platform," John says. "This was a way to teach, save money and outsource a non-core system." Giving up control was an easy trade-off compared with the headaches he would face trying to fix the existing software. "You're getting a lot more innovation," says Ray Wang, an analyst at Forrester Research Inc. "The products are a lot more configurable than what most people have in their own applications. You can change fields, rename things, and move attributes and work flows. So there's a good level of control there."

What's more, the configuration choices are more refined and well thought-out, giving users a few good choices instead of myriad options. John found that configuration rather than customization allows H.B. Fuller to maintain its "lean core." "I believe that more standardization leads to more agility," John says. "SaaS allows us to say, 'This is good enough . . . for what we need.' So you don't end up with these horrible situations where you have these highly customized systems. We go with configuration option A, B, or C. If one of those three doesn't meet our need, we can try to influence the next release. But in most cases, A, B, or C is going to meet the need."

At H.B. Fuller, the move to SaaS for human resources tools allowed the company to empower its people. "I can do a reorganization and have it reflected within minutes, and I don't have to call someone in HR to update everything," John says. "I can also pull up other people's organization charts and see where they are and what they're doing and better understand the organization."

When it comes to managing SaaS, neither the IT department nor the business unit using the software should be eager to relinquish control. "The buying decisions are shifting from IT to the business leaders," who often opt to charge the software as an expense rather than wait for approval through the capital budget committee, Wang says. Still, he adds, "it's very important to engage IT in these SaaS decisions because there are overall IT architectures and blueprints to consider." It becomes very costly when applications don't integrate or interoperate well with one another.

"It's good to at least have some parameters and policies in place so that people understand what type of apps will work better within the environment, what will be cheaper to share information and data with," says Wang. One of the problems with SaaS is that if your vendor were to go bankrupt, everything would shut down. You don't own the software. It's on lease. The question is: What do you own? If the vendor doesn't have a separate on-premises deployment option, "you need the ability to take out transactional data, master file information, any kind of migration programs, just in case, so you can convert it to an on-premises alternative if they were to go down," Wang says.

In the long term, Wang envisions an IT culture where SaaS is commonplace. "We may live in a world where everything is provisioned. All our applications don't stay on premises, and business leaders are out procuring applications," he says. "IT teams are testing them to make sure they work well in the environment and there are no bugs or viruses and things integrate well, and basically the IT staff will spend a lot of time provisioning services and implementing, integrating, doing installs. That's where we envision the market in 2020."

SOURCE: Thomas Wailgum, "GE CIO Gets His Head in the Cloud for New SaaS Supply Chain App," *CIO Magazine*, January 22, 2009; and Stacy Collett, "SaaS Puts Focus on Functionality," *Computerworld*, March 23, 2009.

▼ CASE STUDY QUESTIONS

1. What factors should companies take into consideration when making the decision between developing their own applications, purchasing them from a vendor, or taking the SaaS route, as discussed here? Make a list of factors and discuss their importance to this decision.

2. What risks did GE take when they contracted with a small and less experienced vendor? What contingencies could have been put in place to prevent any problems from arising? Provide several examples.

3. What should companies do if none of the "configuration options" perfectly fits their needs? Should they attempt to customize, or select the least-worst alternative? When would they do each?

▼ REAL WORLD ACTIVITIES

1. The case mentions that GE's implementation of SaaS was, at the time, the largest rollout of the technology in the world. What other companies have started to use SaaS extensively since then? Go online and research recent implementations. How are those different from GE's experience? Prepare a report to share your findings.

2. By implementing systems based on SaaS, companies are relinquishing control over ownership of the technology and are putting access to valuable data in the hands of a third party. What are the perils of taking this approach? How could companies guard against them? Break into small groups to discuss these issues and provide some suggestions and recommendations.

U.S. Department of Defense: Enlisting Open-Source Applications

The U.S. Defense Department is enlisting an open-source approach to software development, which is an about-face for such a historically top-down organization. The Department of Defense (DoD) says open-source software is equal to commercial software in almost all cases and by law should be considered by the agency when making technology purchase decisions.

In terms of guidance, the DoD says open-source software (OSS) meets the definition of "commercial computer software," and thus executive agencies are required to include it when evaluating software that meets their computing needs. OSS is defined as "software for which the human-readable source code is available for use, study, reuse, modification, enhancement, and redistribution by the users of that software."

In addition, the DoD lists many open-source advantages, including broad peer-review that helps eliminate defects, modification rights that help speed changes when needed, a reduction in the reliance on proprietary vendors, a licensing model that facilitates quick provisioning, cost reduction in some cases, reduction in maintenance and ownership costs, and favorable characteristics for rapid prototyping and experimentation. "The continuous and broad peer-review enabled by publicly available source code supports software reliability and security efforts through the identification and elimination of defects that might otherwise go unrecognized by a more limited core development team," states deputy CIO David Wennergren in a memo to top military officials.

"I would consider this a milestone day," says John Scott, director of open-source software and open integration for Mercury Federal Systems, a technology consultancy to the U.S. government. Scott helped draft some of the open-source guidance contained in the memo, which took about 18 months to draft. Scott states, "The 2003 policy study was okay to use, but this one goes a bit further in expanding on what open source is and why you would want to use it. But it is not just about usage, it is also about helping create OSS by submitting changes back out to the public."

Scott says he believes this is the first time guidance has been issued about sharing the government's own open-source changes with the public.

Taken together, two developments show how the Defense Department is trying to take advantage of Web-based communities to speed up software development and reduce its costs. Dave Mihelcic, CTO of the Defense Information Systems Agency, says the military believes in the core Web 2.0 philosophy of the power of collaboration.

The military has launched a collaborative platform called Forge.mil for its developers to share software, systems components, and network services. The agency also signed an agreement with the Open Source Software Institute (OSSI) to allow 50 internally developed workforce management applications to be licensed to other government agencies, universities, and companies.

"The Web is a platform for harvesting collective intelligence," Mihelcic says. He points to "remixable data sources, services in perpetual beta and lightweight programming models" as some of the aspects of open-source software development that are applicable to the Defense Department.

One example of the Defense Department's new community-based approach to software development is Forge.mil, which was made generally available for unclassified use within the department in April 2009. Forge.mil is powered by CollabNet Team Forge, a commercial life cycle management platform for distributed software development teams, and is modeled after the popular SourceForge.net.

The Defense Information Systems Agency (DISA) has issued version two of SoftwareForge (software that runs on the Forge.mil site to enable sharing and collaborative development of open-source software) after a three-month trial that grew to 1,300 users. SoftwareForge provides software version control, bug tracking, requirements management, and release packaging for software developers, along with collaboration tools such as wikis, discussion forums, and document repositories, DISA says. DISA also says it will deploy a cloud computing–based version of the SoftwareForge tools for classified environments.

DISA also plans to add software testing and certification services to Forge.mil. Mihelcic says Forge.mil is similar to the "Web 2.0 paradigm of putting services on the Web and making them accessible to a large number of users to increase the adoption of capabilities. We're using the same collaboration approach to speed the development of DOD systems."

Meanwhile, DISA has licensed its Corporate Management Information System (CMIS) to the OSSI to develop an open-source version of the 50-odd applications that DISA uses to manage its workforce. The CMIS applications support human resources, training, payroll, and other personnel management functions that meet federal regulations. DISA, which provides IT services to the Department of Defense, made the decision to share its applications after other agencies expressed interest in them, says Richard Nelson, chief of personnel systems support at DISA's manpower, personnel, and security directorate. "Federal agencies discovered that the applications we have could be of benefit more widely," he says. Interest is coming from states and counties, as well.

DISA worked with the nonprofit OSSI, which promotes the use of open-source software in government and academia. OSSI copyrighted the software stack and licensed it back to DISA, making it available at no cost to government agencies under the Open Software License 3.0. "It's already paid for because the taxpayer paid for us to build it," Nelson says.

OSSI wanted to create a process that could be repeated with other government-built applications. "The opportunity was more than the product," executive director John Weatherby says. "One of the key things was to set up a system, a process that can be replicated by other government agencies."

CMIS comprises more than 50 Web applications, including workforce management, automated work flow, learning management, balanced scorecard, and telework management. CMIS has 16,000 users, including DISA employees and military contractors. Originally written in 1997, CMIS was revamped in January 2006 using the latest Web-based tools, including an Adobe Cold Fusion front-end and a Microsoft SQL Server 2005 back-end.

Nelson says CMIS is easy to use because it takes advantage of modern Web-based interfaces, including drop-down lists for data input. "We've been able to cut down on help desk support so substantially," Nelson says. "With the old version, we were running anywhere from 75 to 100 help desk calls and e-mails a day. Now our average is less than five e-mails and calls. It's not because people are using it less but because it has fewer problems."

Nelson says a key driver for CMIS is that it needs to be so intuitive that users don't need training. "If the customer requires instruction on the product, we have failed and we will do it over," Nelson says. "The reason that we're able to do that so successfully is that we take a somewhat different approach to the way most software is designed. Most software is designed so that business logic and processes need to follow software logic and process. Therefore it requires substantial training. We do it exactly opposite."

The OSSI will make CMIS available in two different licenses: a regular open-source license for government agencies and companies, and a free license for academia. Nelson says CMIS has a cutting-edge approach to learning management, handling everything from training course sign-up to approvals and payment. Another unusual feature of CMIS is its telework management application.

Nelson says he hopes many organizations will license CMIS and start adding new capabilities so DISA can take advantage of a vibrant CMIS community of developers. Within three years, "I would hope that a number of others inside government and beyond are using it," Nelson says. "I'm hoping we all have ready access to qualified developers. I'm hoping that DISA gets access to a substantial number of additional applications . . . without having to build them ourselves."

Going forward, DISA wants to encourage use of and training in Adobe Cold Fusion, which it used to build OSCMIS, to increase the talent pool of OSCMIS developers. "We would even like to start with kids in high school to get them interested in software development as a career," Nelson says.

SOURCE: Carolyn Duffy Marsan, "Military Enlists Open Source Community," *Network World*, April 27, 2009; John Fontana, "DoD: Open Source as Good as Proprietary Software," *Network World*, October 27, 2009; J. Nicholas Hoover, "Defense CIO Touts Benefits of Open Source," *InformationWeek*, October 28, 2009; and J. Nicholas Hoover, "Defense Info Agency Open-Sources Its Web Apps," *InformationWeek*, August 21, 2009.

▼ CASE STUDY QUESTIONS

1. Given the critical nature of defense activities, security in this environment is a primary concern. How do the agencies discussed in the case address this issue? Can you think of anything else they could be doing? Provide some recommendations.

2. The U.S. Department of Defense is arguably one of the largest organizations in the world. Managing technology for such an organization is certainly a major endeavor. Does the shift toward open-source initiatives help in this regard? Does it hurt? Discuss the advantages and disadvantages of adopting open-source applications in large organizations.

3. After reading the case, do you think the shift to open-source software involved a major cultural change for the Department of Defense? Would you expect the same to be the case for large companies? Justify your answer.

▼ REAL WORLD ACTIVITIES

1. While small open-source applications have been around for quite some time, large-scale open-source systems have begun to emerge. Go online and search the Internet for examples of businesses adopting open-source technologies for major organizational systems. Prepare a presentation to highlight several examples from your research.

2. How does the open-source model of application development and distribution differ from the more common, proprietary approach? Do open-source applications present a legitimate threat to commercial software development, or will they remain niche applications? Break into small groups to discuss various reasons that companies may or may not want to adopt open-source technologies.

chapter 5

DATA RESOURCE MANAGEMENT

INFORMATION SYSTEMS

INFORMATION TECHNOLOGIES

LEARNING OBJECTIVES

5-1 Explain the business value of implementing data resource management processes and technologies in an organization.

5-2 Outline the advantages of a database management approach to managing the data resources of a business, compared with a file processing approach.

5-3 Explain how database management software helps business professionals and supports the operations and management of a business.

5-4 Provide examples to illustrate each of the following concepts:
a. Major types of databases.
b. Data warehouses and data mining.
c. Logical data elements.
d. Fundamental database structures.
e. Database development.

Technical Foundations of Database Management

Just imagine how difficult it would be to get any information from an information system if data were stored in an unorganized way or if there were no systematic way to retrieve them. Therefore, in all information systems, data resources must be organized and structured in some logical manner so that they can be accessed easily, processed efficiently, retrieved quickly, and managed effectively. Data structures and access methods ranging from simple to complex have been devised to organize and access data stored by information systems efficiently. In this chapter, we will explore these concepts, as well as the managerial implications and value of data resource management. See Figure 5.1.

It is important to appreciate the value of understanding databases and database management from the beginning. In today's world, just about every piece of data you would ever want to access is organized and stored in some type of database. The question is not so much "Should I use a database?" but rather "What database should I use?" Although many of you will not choose a career in the design of databases, all of you will spend a large portion of your time, in whatever job you choose, accessing data in a myriad of databases. Most database developers consider accessing the data to be the business end of the database world; understanding how data are structured, stored, and accessed can help business professionals gain greater strategic value from their organization's data resources.

Read the Real World Challenge on U.S. Xpress, a major trucking company. We can learn a lot from this case about the challenges presented by the lack of quality data.

FUNDAMENTAL DATA CONCEPTS
LO 5-4c,d

Before we go any further, let's discuss some fundamental concepts about how data are organized in information systems. A conceptual framework of several levels of data has been devised that differentiates among different groupings, or elements, of data. Thus, data may be logically organized into *characters*, *fields*, *records*, *files*, and *databases*, just as writing can be organized into letters, words, sentences, paragraphs, and documents. Examples of these **logical data elements** are shown in Figure 5.2.

Character

The most basic *logical* data element is the **character,** which consists of a single alphabetic, numeric, or other symbol. You might argue that the bit or byte is a more elementary data element, but remember that those terms refer to the *physical* storage elements provided by the computer hardware, as discussed in Chapter 3. Using that understanding, one way to think of a character is that it is a byte used to represent a particular character. In other words, bits and bytes are the method by which a computer-based system represents data. They are not the data, just the way a computer stores the data. As such, from a user's point of view (i.e., from a *logical* as opposed to a physical or hardware view of data), a *character* is the most basic element of data that can be observed and manipulated.

Field

The next higher level of data is the **field,** or data item. A field consists of a *grouping of related characters*. For example, the grouping of alphabetic characters in a person's name may form a name field (or typically, last name, first name, and middle initial

U.S. Xpress–Lots of Data, Not Enough Quality

Trucking companies are really about much more than trucks and cargo; they are also about fuel and maintenance. In addition, they are about customers, sales, operations and—something they share with more and more companies both within and outside the industry—they are especially about data. In this case, the data are about trucks, fuel, cargo, and maintenance. Although everyone would agree that quality data are a prerequisite to making sound business decisions, they may be harder to get than one would think. Consider that at a recent meeting at major trucking company U.S. Xpress, an executive lamented that if she were only to have data about truck idling times, the company could save a small fortune on fuel costs. Trucks are a trucking company's main assets, and idling times—those times when a truck is running but not moving—are very important. Indeed, when you think about it, a truck that is idling is spending money but not making any money. Unfortunately, the data to help solve the problem were just not there.

"It is one of those things where, if you don't measure something, you don't manage it," says "Dale Langley, chief information officer at the Chattanooga, Tennessee–based company, the third largest privately owned trucker in the United States. Engine idle time costs the company more than $2 per hour. Although literally only a couple of bucks, multiply that by thousands of trucks idling for hours each day, and the costs start to add up rather quickly. Clearly, something has to be done about it. "Poor data quality has an insidious effect on business efficiency," says Ivan Chong, executive vice president at vendor Informatica. "Often an organization doesn't even know where the problem is coming from, but clearly realizes the negative impact of poorly performing systems, high operating costs, and missed business opportunities."

U.S. Xpress, founded in 1985, began operations a year later with a fleet of 48 trucks. The company was known in the industry as an early adopter of new technologies, largely because of cofounder and cochairman Max Fuller. In 1987, U.S. Xpress was one of the first carriers to fully integrate satellite communications aboard its fleet. After decades of aggressive growth—16 percent a year since 1994—and a number of acquisitions, the U.S. Xpress fleet today numbers 8,000 tractors and 22,000 trailers. All that growth, however, resulted in a fragmented conglomerate of companies, where each firm has its own information systems and networks. All together, the companies that make up the U.S. Xpress group have 130 different applications that do not integrate data among themselves. "Delving for answers to business questions took weeks and months," says Langley.

With no centralized master database, the company had the same customers appearing in multiple places, as well as major assets such as trucks, trailers, drivers, and customer orders in several different databases. All of this redundancy and duplicated data entry led to data of questionable quality. How many different ways can you spell Wal-Mart? At U.S. Xpress, the number is 178—merely searching for a customer by name is almost impossible under those conditions. "Until you get that kind of thing cleaned up, your data is not worth anything," says Langley.

Let's go back to the engine-idling problem. In an industry with low margins and lots of competition, saving gas could be the difference between being profitable and going bankrupt, since the driver and gas are the main costs of delivering cargo. Years before, U.S. Xpress had installed a truck system called DriverTech, which provided the company with a wealth of information about truck operations, such as when a truck braked, when it stopped, whether it

FIGURE 5.1

Access to accurate and reliable data in the field is the lifeblood for companies such as U.S. Xpress, which have to manage their assets and resources in mobile settings.
SOURCE: © Monty Rakusen/agefotostock.

had any engine problems, and its current location. It also provided navigation, driver performance monitoring, and even training through training videos for drivers. Thus, although a lot of information was available, it was not coming into the company in a way that could be used to implement the necessary efficiencies.

"The data was coming back from the DriverTech system, but the location data wasn't being cleaned or presented in a standard way when it reached us," explains Tim Leonard, chief technology officer, who came to U.S. Xpress from technology giant Dell, where he was a senior manager responsible for data warehousing architecture. "Without reliable data on details such as trucks' location and idle time at the stopping point, it was impossible to report accurately on vehicle movements and bring the truck idle time down." When you consider that each download of data from a truck includes more than 900 components, and the company operates about 8,000 of those trucks, obtaining clean data is a challenge of formidable proportions. In order to create a useful report about truck idling time, Leonard figured he needed the truck number, the name of the fleet manager and the specific driver, and the region in which the truck was driven. DriverTech reported the truck number, but all other pieces would have to come from somewhere else—from those databases with the 178 different spellings of Wal-Mart.

All of a sudden, this has become much bigger than idling times. The types of business reports that one has come to expect from well-run companies—things like dashboards and business intelligence analyses—would not be terribly useful if the inputs could not be trusted. And whispers could be heard in the hallways that management wants to put a customer relationship management (CRM) system in place as well. It is clear to both Langley and Leonard, however, that none of this can build upon dirty data. Building more complex applications without ensuring that the underlying data are up to standards might not be the wisest move. "I told them, we are not even going to start CRM until we have data quality in place," says Langley. Therefore, although the immediate goal may be to help the company save money by reducing idling time—which is very important in and of itself—a number of long-term challenges also need to be addressed before U.S. Xpress can drive itself to the next level.

SOURCE: Rob Lemos, "Big Data: How a Trucking Firm Drove Out Big Errors," *CIO Magazine*, February 28, 2011; "U.S. Xpress Enterprises 'Drives' Savings of $6 Million Annually with Informatica Data Quality," *Informatica Press Release*, July 12, 2010; "An Xcelllent Way of Saving Millions a Year," *Informatica Case Study*; Tim Leonard, "Informatica Data Quality," *Information Management Magazine*, May 1, 2011; William Cassidy, "Trucking Goes to the Cleaners," *Journal of Commerce*, May 24, 2010; and www.usxpress.com, accessed May 22, 2011.

▼ **QUESTIONS TO CONSIDER**

1. This case chronicles the many issues associated with the IT environment in which U.S. Xpress currently operates. How did U.S. Xpress get into this situation? Was this the result of different business priorities in the past? If so, which ones? What are the lessons for companies that frequently acquire other businesses?

2. Moving forward, what does U.S. Xpress need to do in the future regarding its IT infrastructure in general, and its data issues in particular? What do you think should be the next three steps the company should take?

3. Should companies take a periodic (e.g., clean every so often) approach or a continuous, more expensive, approach to data quality? What are the advantages and disadvantages of each?

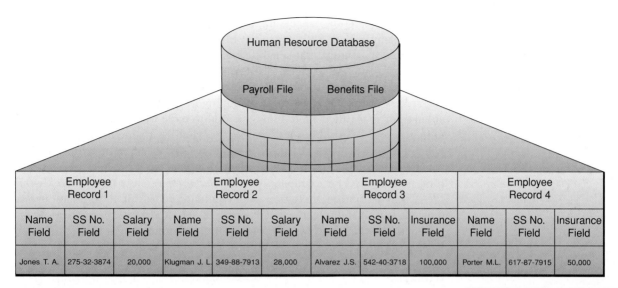

FIGURE 5.2

Examples of the logical data
elements in information systems.
Note especially the examples
of how data fields, records, files,
and databases relate.

fields), and the grouping of numbers in a sales amount forms a sales amount field. Specifically, a data field represents an ***attribute*** (a characteristic or quality) of some ***entity*** (object, person, place, or event). For example, an employee's salary is an attribute that is a typical data field used to describe an entity who is an employee of a business. Generally speaking, fields are organized such that they represent some logical order, for example, last_name, first_name, address, city, state, and zip code. Fields are everywhere you look, especially on the Internet!

Record

All of the fields used to capture, organize, and store the attributes of an entity are grouped to form a ***record.*** Thus, a record represents *a collection of attributes* that describe a single instance of an *entity*. An example is a person's payroll record, which consists of data fields describing attributes such as the person's name, Social Security number, and rate of pay. This record will serve to uniquely describe that person and only that person. Other payroll records may be similar, but none will be exactly the same. *Fixed-length* records contain a fixed number of fixed-length data fields and, therefore, a predetermined maximum number of characters. *Variable-length* records contain a variable number of fields and field lengths and, therefore, can be any length. Another way of looking at a record is that it represents a single *instance* of an entity. Each record in an employee file describes one specific employee.

Normally, the first field in a record is used to store some type of unique identifier for the record. This unique identifier is called the **primary key.** The value of a primary key can be anything that will serve to *uniquely identify one instance of an entity* and distinguish it from another. For example, if we wanted to uniquely identify a single student from a group of related students, we could use a student ID number as a primary key. As long as no one shared the same student ID number, we would always be able to identify the record of that student. If no specific data can be found to serve as a primary key for a record, the database designer can simply assign a record a unique sequential number so that no two records will ever have the same primary key. The important thing about a primary key is that it must be unique, and the manner in which a primary key is created must be consistent for the entire data file.

File

A group of related records is a data ***file*** (sometimes referred to as a *table* or *flat file*). When it is independent of any other files related to it, a single *table* may be referred to as a *flat file*. As a point of accuracy, the term *flat file* may be defined either narrowly or more broadly. Strictly speaking, a flat file database should consist of nothing but data and delimiters (things that separate the fields from each other). More broadly, the term refers to any database that exists in a single file in the form of rows and columns, with no relationships or links between records and fields except the table structure. Regardless of the name used, any grouping of related records in tabular (row-and-column form) is called a *file*. Thus, an employee file would contain the records of the employees of a firm. Files are frequently classified (named) by the application for which they are primarily used, such as a *payroll file* or an *inventory file*, or the type of data they contain, such as a *document file* or a *graphical image file*. Files are also classified by their permanence, for example, a payroll *master file* versus a payroll weekly *transaction file*. A transaction file, therefore, would contain records of all transactions occurring during a period and might be used periodically to update the permanent records contained in a master file. A *history file* is an obsolete transaction or master file retained for backup purposes or for long-term historical storage, called *archival storage*.

Database

A **database** is an *integrated collection of logically related data elements*. A database consolidates records previously stored in separate files into a common pool of data elements that provides data for many applications. The data stored in a database are independent of the application programs using them and of the type of storage devices on which they are stored.

Thus, databases contain data elements describing entities and relationships among entities. For example, Figure 5.3 outlines some of the entities and relationships in a database for an electric utility. Also shown are some of the business applications (billing, payment processing) that depend on access to the data elements in the database.

As stated in the beginning of the chapter, just about all the data we use are stored in some type of database. A database doesn't need to look complex or technical to be a database; it just needs to provide a logical organization method and easy access to the data stored in it. You probably use one or two rapidly growing databases just about every day: How about Facebook, MySpace, Twitter, or YouTube?

All of the pictures, videos, songs, messages, chats, icons, e-mail addresses, and everything else stored on each of these popular social networking Web sites are stored as fields, records, files, or objects in large databases. The data are stored in such a way to ensure that there is easy access to it, it can be shared by its respective owners, and it can be protected from unauthorized access or use. When you stop to think about how

FIGURE 5.3

Some of the entities and relationships in a simplified electric utility database. Note a few of the business applications that access the data in the database.

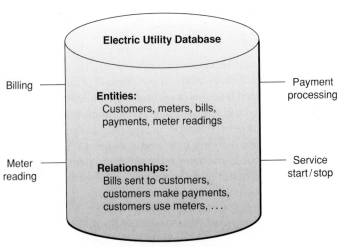

SOURCE: Michael V. Mannino, *Database Application Development and Design* (Burr Ridge, IL: McGraw-Hill/Irwin, 2001), p. 6.

simple it is to use and enjoy these databases, it is easy to forget how large and complex they are.

For example, in August 2006, *The Wall Street Journal* published an article revealing that YouTube was hosting about 6.1 million videos (requiring about 45 terabytes of storage space), and had about 500 accounts. In March 2008, a YouTube search turned up about 77.3 million videos and 2.89 million user channels. In May 2010, YouTube reported that viewers watched more than 2 billion videos every day, describe it as "nearly double the prime-time audience of all three major U.S. television networks combined." Data grows fast, to be sure!

Perhaps an even more compelling example of ease of access versus complexity is found in the popular social networking Web site Facebook. Some of the basic statistics are nothing short of amazing: Facebook reports more than 500 million users logging in at least once each day. The average user has 120 friend relationships established. More than 850 million photos, 8 million videos, 1 billion pieces of content, and 2.5 million events are uploaded or created each month. More than 70 language translations are currently available on the site, with more than 50 other language translations in development. More than 500,000 software applications exist in the Facebook Application Directory, and more than 100 million active users access Facebook through their mobile devices. The size of their databases is best measured in petabytes, which is equal to one quadrillion bytes. All of this from a database and a simple access method launched in 2004 from a dorm room at Harvard University! When it comes to data, little things can become big things in a hurry.

The important point here is that all of this information—in the form of videos, user accounts, and so forth—is easily accessed because the data are stored in some type of structured database system that organizes it so that a particular item can be found on demand.

The relationships among the many individual data elements stored in databases are based on one of several logical data structures, or models. Database management system (DBMS) packages are designed to use a specific data structure to provide end users with quick, easy access to information stored in databases. Five fundamental *database structures* are the *hierarchical*, *network*, *relational*, *object-oriented*, and *multidimensional* models. Simplified illustrations of the first three database structures are shown in Figure 5.4.

DATABASE STRUCTURES LO 5-4d

Hierarchical Structure

Early mainframe DBMS packages used the ***hierarchical structure,*** in which the relationships between records form a hierarchy or treelike structure. In the traditional hierarchical model, all records are dependent and arranged in multilevel structures, consisting of one *root* record and any number of subordinate levels. Thus, all of the relationships among records are *one-to-many* because each data element is related to only one element above it. The data element or record at the highest level of the hierarchy (the department data element in this illustration) is called the root element. Any data element can be accessed by moving progressively downward from a root and along the branches of the tree until the desired record (e.g., the employee data element) is located.

Network Structure

The ***network structure*** can represent more complex logical relationships and is still used by some mainframe DBMS packages. It allows *many-to-many* relationships among records; that is, the network model can access a data element by following one of several paths because any data element or record can be related to any number of other data elements. For example, in Figure 5.4, departmental records can be related to more than one employee record, and employee records can be related to more than

FIGURE 5.4

Example of three fundamental database structures. They represent three basic ways to develop and express the relationships among the data elements in a database.

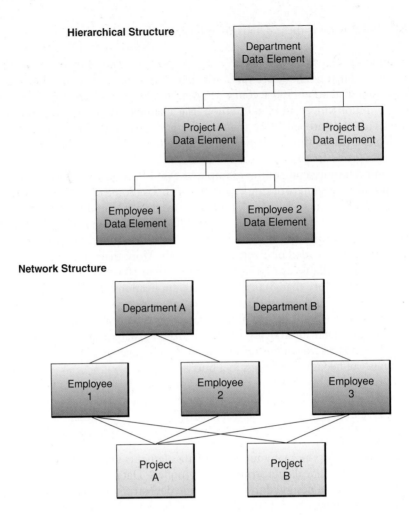

SOURCE: Michael V. Mannino, *Database Application Development and Design* (Burr Ridge, IL: McGraw-Hill/Irwin, 2001), p. 6.

one project record. Thus, you could locate all employee records for a particular department or all project records related to a particular employee.

It should be noted that neither the hierarchical nor the network data structures are commonly found in the modern organization. The next data structure we discuss, the relational data structure, is the most common of all and serves as the foundation for most modern databases in organizations.

Relational Structure

The *relational model* is the most widely used of the three database structures. It is used by most microcomputer DBMS packages, as well as by most midrange and mainframe systems. In the relational model, all data elements within the database are viewed as being stored in the form of simple two-dimensional **tables,** sometimes

Department Table

Deptno	Dname	Dloc	Dmgr
Dept A			
Dept B			
Dept C			

Employee Table

Empno	Ename	Etitle	Esalary	Deptno
Emp 1				Dept A
Emp 2				Dept A
Emp 3				Dept B
Emp 4				Dept B
Emp 5				Dept C
Emp 6				Dept B

FIGURE 5.5

Joining the employee and department tables in a relational database enables you to access data selectively in both tables at the same time.

referred to as *relations*. The tables in a relational database are *flat files* that have rows and columns. Each row represents a single record in the file, and each column represents a field. The major difference between a flat file and a database is that a flat file can only have data attributes specified for one file. In contrast, a database can specify data attributes for multiple files simultaneously and can relate the various data elements in one file to those in one or more other files.

Figure 5.4 illustrates the relational database model with two tables representing some of the relationships among departmental and employee records. Other tables, or relations, for this organization's database might represent the data element relationships among projects, divisions, product lines, and so on. Database management system packages based on the relational model can link data elements from various tables to provide information to users. For example, a manager might want to retrieve and display an employee's name and salary from the employee table in Figure 5.4, as well as the name of the employee's department from the department table, by using their common department number field (Deptno) to link or join the two tables. See Figure 5.5. The relational model can relate data in any one file with data in another file if both files share a common data element or field. Because of this, information can be created by retrieving data from multiple files even if they are not all stored in the same physical location.

Relational Operations

Three basic operations can be performed on a relational database to create useful sets of data. The *select* operation is used to create a subset of records that meet a stated criterion. For example, a select operation might be used on an employee database to create a subset of records containing all employees who make more than $30,000 per year and who have been with the company more than three years. Another way to think of the select operation is that it temporarily creates a table whose rows have records that meet only the selection criteria.

The *join* operation can be used to combine two or more tables temporarily so that a user can see relevant data in a form that looks like it is all in one big table. Using this operation, a user can ask for data to be retrieved from multiple files or databases without having to go to each one separately. This allows multiple data sets from multiple (and often unrelated) locations to be brought together and analyzed. This is one of the most important operations in data mining, which we will talk about in depth in Chapter 10.

Finally, the *project* operation is used to create a subset of the columns contained in the temporary tables created by the select and join operations. Just as the select operation creates a subset of records that meet stated criteria, the project operation creates a subset of the columns, or fields, that the user wants to see. Using a project operation, the user can decide not to view all of the columns in the table, but instead to view only those that have the data necessary to answer a particular question or construct a specific report.

Because of the widespread use of relational models, many commercial products have been created to manage them. Leading mainframe relational database applications include Oracle 11g from Oracle Corp. and DB2 from IBM. A very popular midrange database application is SQL Server from Microsoft. The most commonly used database application for the PC is Microsoft Access.

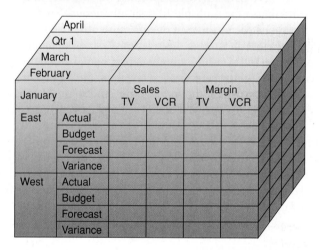

FIGURE 5.6

An example of the different dimensions of a multidimensional database.

Multidimensional Structure

The ***multidimensional model*** is a variation of the relational model that uses multidimensional structures to organize data and express the relationships between data. You can visualize multidimensional structures as cubes of data and cubes within cubes of data. Each side of the cube is considered a dimension of the data. Figure 5.6 is an example that shows that each dimension can represent a different category, such as product type, region, sales channel, and time.

Each cell within a multidimensional structure contains aggregated data related to elements along each of its dimensions. For example, a single cell may contain the total sales for a product in a region for a specific sales channel in a single month. A major benefit of multidimensional databases is that they provide a compact and easy-to-understand way to visualize and manipulate data elements that have many interrelationships. So multidimensional databases have become the most popular database structure for the analytical databases that support *online analytical processing* (OLAP) applications, in which fast answers to complex business queries are expected. We discuss OLAP applications in Chapter 10.

Object-Oriented Structure

The ***object-oriented model*** is considered one of the key technologies of a new generation of multimedia Web-based applications. As Figure 5.7 illustrates, an **object** consists of data values describing the attributes of an entity, plus the operations that can be performed upon the data. This *encapsulation* capability allows the object-oriented model to

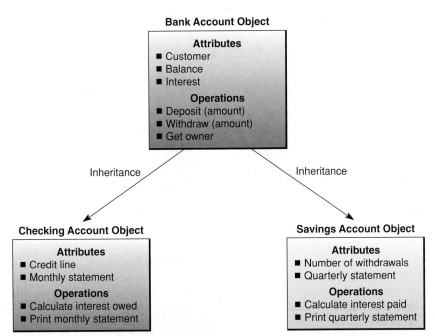

FIGURE 5.7

The checking and savings account objects can inherit common attributes and operations from the bank account object.

SOURCE: Ivar Jacobson, Maria Ericsson, and Agneta Jacobson, *The Object Advantage: Business Process Reengineering with Object Technology* (New York: ACM Press, 1995), p. 65. Copyright © 1995, Association for Computing Machinery. Used by permission.

handle complex types of data (graphics, pictures, voice, and text) more easily than other database structures.

The object-oriented model also supports *inheritance*. Inheritance allows new objects to be automatically created by replicating some or all of the characteristics of one or more *parent* objects. Thus, in Figure 5.7, the checking and savings account objects can inherit both the common attributes and operations of the parent bank account object. Such capabilities have made *object-oriented database management systems* (OODBMS) popular in computer-aided design (CAD) and a growing number of applications. For example, object technology allows designers to develop product designs, store them as objects in an object-oriented database, and replicate and modify them to create new product designs. In addition, multimedia Web-based applications for the Internet and corporate intranets and extranets have become a major application area for object technology.

Object technology proponents argue that an object-oriented DBMS can work with *complex data types* such as document and graphic images, video clips, audio segments, and other subsets of Web pages much more efficiently than relational database management systems. However, major relational DBMS vendors have countered by adding object-oriented modules to their relational software. Examples include multimedia object extensions to IBM's DB2 and Oracle's object-based "cartridges" for Oracle 10g. See Figure 5.8.

Evaluation of Database Structures

The hierarchical data structure was a natural model for the databases used for the structured, routine types of transaction processing characteristic of many business operations in the early years of data processing and computing. Data for these operations can easily be represented by groups of records in a hierarchical relationship. However, as time progressed, there were many cases in which information was needed about records that did not have hierarchical relationships. For example, in some organizations, employees from more than one department can work on more than one project (refer to Figure 5.4). A network data structure could easily handle this many-to-many relationship, whereas a hierarchical model could not. As such, the more flexible

FIGURE 5.8

Databases can supply data to a wide variety of analysis packages, allowing for data to be displayed in graphical form.

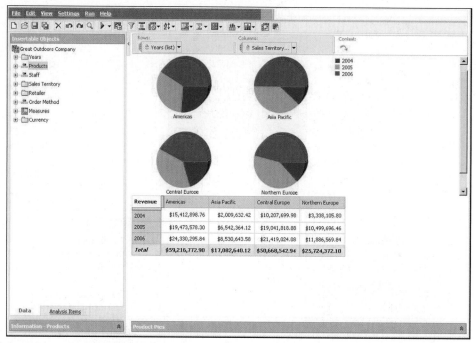

SOURCE: Courtesy of Microsoft®.

network structure became popular for these types of business operations. Like the hierarchical structure, the network model was unable to handle ad hoc requests for information easily because its relationships must be specified in advance, which pointed to the need for the relational model.

Relational databases enable an end user to receive information easily in response to ad hoc requests. That's because not all of the relationships among the data elements in a relationally organized database need to be specified when the database is created. Database management software (such as Oracle 11g, DB2, Access, and Approach) creates new tables of data relationships by using parts of the data from several tables. Thus, relational databases are easier for programmers to work with and easier to maintain than the hierarchical and network models.

The major limitation of the relational model is that relational database management systems cannot process large amounts of business transactions as quickly and efficiently as those based on the hierarchical and network models; they also cannot process complex, high-volume applications as well as the object-oriented model. This performance gap has narrowed with the development of advanced relational database software with object-oriented extensions. The use of database management software based on the object-oriented and multidimensional models is growing steadily, as these technologies are playing a greater role for OLAP and Web-based applications.

Database Pioneer Rethinks the Best Way to Organize Data

Is there a better way to build a data warehouse? For years, relational databases, which organize data in tables composed of vertical columns and horizontal rows, have served as the foundation of data warehouses. Now database pioneer Michael Stonebraker is promoting a different way to organize them, promising much faster response times. As a scientist at the University of California at Berkeley in the 1970s, Stonebraker was one of the original architects of the Ingres relational database, which spawned several commercial variants. A row-based system like Ingres is great for executing transactions, but a column-oriented system is a more natural fit for data warehouses, Stonebraker now says.

SQL Server, Sybase, and Teradata all have rows as their central design point. Yet in data warehousing, faster performance may be gained through a column layout. Stonebraker says all types of queries on "most data warehouses" will run up to 50 times faster in a column database. The bigger the data warehouse, the greater the performance gain.

Why? Data warehouses frequently store transactional data, and each transaction has many parts. Columns cut across transactions and store an element of information that is standard to each transaction, such as customer name, address, or purchase amount. A row, by comparison, may hold 20–200 different elements of a transaction. A standard relational database would retrieve all the rows that reflect, say, sales for a month, load the data into system memory, and then find all sales records and generate an average from them. The ability to focus on just the "sales" column leads to improved query performance.

There is a second performance benefit in the column approach. Because columns contain similar information from each transaction, it's possible to derive a compression scheme for the data type and then apply it throughout the column. Rows cannot be compressed as easily because the nature of the data (e.g., name, zip code, and account balance) varies from record to record. Each row would require a different compression scheme.

Compressing data in columns makes for faster storage and retrieval and reduces the amount of disk required. "In every data warehouse I see, compression is a good thing," Stonebraker says. "I expect the data warehouse market to become completely column-store based."

SOURCE: Charles Babcock, "Database Pioneer Rethinks the Best Way to Organize Data," *InformationWeek*, February 23, 2008.

DATABASE DEVELOPMENT
LO 5-4e

Database management packages like Microsoft Access or Lotus Approach allow end users to develop the databases they need easily. See Figure 5.9. However, large organizations usually place control of enterprisewide database development in the hands of **database administrators (DBAs)** and other database specialists. This delegation improves the integrity and security of organizational databases. Database developers use the *data definition language* (DDL) in database management systems like Oracle 11g or IBM's DB2 to develop and specify the data contents, relationships, and structure of each database, as well as to modify these database specifications when necessary. Such information is cataloged and stored in a database of data definitions and specifications called a *data dictionary*, or *metadata repository*, which is managed by the database management software and maintained by the DBA.

A **data dictionary** is a database management catalog or directory containing **metadata** (i.e., data about data). A data dictionary relies on a specialized database software component to manage a database of data definitions, which is metadata about the structure, data elements, and other characteristics of an organization's databases. For example, it contains the names and descriptions of all types of data records and their interrelationships; information outlining requirements for end users' access and use of application programs; and database maintenance and security.

The database administrator can query data dictionaries to report the status of any aspect of a firm's metadata. The administrator can then make changes to the definitions of selected data elements. Some *active* (versus *passive*) data dictionaries automatically enforce standard data element definitions whenever end users and application programs access an organization's databases. For example, an active data dictionary would not allow a data entry program to use a nonstandard definition of a customer record, nor would it allow an employee to enter a name of a customer that exceeded the defined size of that data element.

FIGURE 5.9

Creating a database table using the Table Wizard of Microsoft Access.

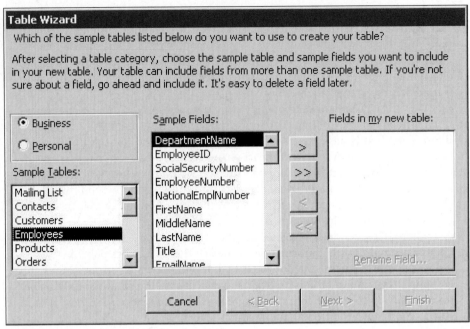

SOURCE: Courtesy of Microsoft®.

Developing a large database of complex data types can be a complicated task. Database administrators and database design analysts work with end users and systems analysts to model business processes and the data they require. Then they determine (1) what data definitions should be included in the database and (2) what structures or relationships should exist among the data elements.

AAA Missouri: Data Quality Is an Important First Step

Although it may sound deceptively simple, keeping data that are both correct and clean is a major challenge for businesses of all makes and sizes. AAA Missouri, which serves Arkansas, Louisiana, Mississippi, and parts of other states (Kansas, Illinois, and Indiana) and processes about 600,000 records a year, came head-to-head against this challenge in the form of customer contact information—in particular, customer address validation.

In recent years, the AAA organization has greatly expanded its offerings of products and services, going from the traditional maps and roadside assistance—although those are still there—into financial services and insurance, especially homeowners and automobile insurance. Although you might think that mailing problems brought about the need for accurate customer address information, for AAA Missouri it was necessary as a result of its expansion into the provision of homeowners insurance. AAA Missouri uses specialized software that retrieves critical property information based on the address provided; the problem is that those addresses must be formatted to U.S. Postal Service standards for the tool to work. And hence the need to work with customer addresses that are perfectly accurate and valid.

After researching a number of offerings, a committee chose to adopt Melissa Data's DQWS (Data Quality Web Service). The solution is hosted off-site by the vendor and is available 24/7 to AAA for real-time address verification. The remote hosting aspect was a major selling point, with its lack of up-front hardware, infrastructure costs, and the long-term maintenance expenses typically associated with systems developed in-house. It was "probably the top reason we went with Melissa," says Dan Perry, a project leader within the AAA Missouri IT Department. "All of the other products required us to host the solution," he explains.

The process itself is quite straightforward. "When a user enters an address and clicks to continue," Perry says, "we call Melissa Data to scrub the address. If there are no errors returned, we save the address to the database." Otherwise, the customer receives an error prompt to recheck the address or, if it belongs to a new subdivision that may still not be in the database, to follow a special process to add it. All of this happens in real time with no evident performance effects due to the transmission of the address to the Web service and back to AAA's Web site. Indeed, the entire process is completely transparent to users.

Ultimately, the goal is to have every single address in the AAA database verified. In the meantime, the Web service is used in a variety of processes, including insurance underwriting, customer care, help desk, and management and reporting. DQWS is also being implemented in new services that AAA Missouri offers. For instance, as the organization added rental dwelling insurance to its offerings, the Web service ran addresses of the prospective customers. That will also be the case when it offers excess liability insurance in the future. "We decided from the beginning that we would use DQWS to validate and format all addresses entered into the system," Perry explains.

SOURCE: Linda L. Briggs, "AAA Drives Up Data Quality with Address Validation," *Business Intelligence Journal* 13, no. 2, 2008, pp. 49–51.

Data Planning and Database Design

As Figure 5.10 illustrates, database development may start with a top-down data planning process. Database administrators and designers work with corporate and end-user management to develop an *enterprise model* that defines the basic business process of the enterprise. They then define the information needs of end users in a business process, such as the purchasing/receiving process that all businesses have.

Next, end users must identify the key data elements that are needed to perform their specific business activities. This step frequently involves developing *entity relationship diagrams* (ERDs) that model the relationships among the many entities involved in business processes. For example, Figure 5.11 illustrates some of the relationships in a purchasing/receiving process. The ERDs are simply graphical models of the various files and their relationships, contained within a database system. End users and database designers could use database management or business modeling software to help them develop ERD models for the purchasing/receiving process. This would help identify the supplier and product data that are required to automate their purchasing/receiving and other business processes using enterprise resource management (ERM) or supply chain management (SCM) software. You will learn about ERDs and other data modeling tools in much greater detail if you ever take a course in systems analysis and design.

Such user views are a major part of a ***data modeling*** process, during which the relationships among data elements are identified. Each data model defines the logical relationships among the data elements needed to support a basic business process. For example, can a supplier provide more than one type of product to us? Can a customer have more than one type of account with us? Can an employee have several pay rates or be assigned to several project workgroups?

Answering such questions will identify data relationships that must be represented in a data model that supports the business processes of an organization. These data models then serve as *logical design* frameworks (called *schema* and *subschema*). These frameworks determine the *physical design* of databases and the development of application programs to support the business processes of the organization. A schema is an overall

FIGURE 5.10

Database development involves data planning and database design activities. Data models that support business processes are used to develop databases that meet the information needs of users.

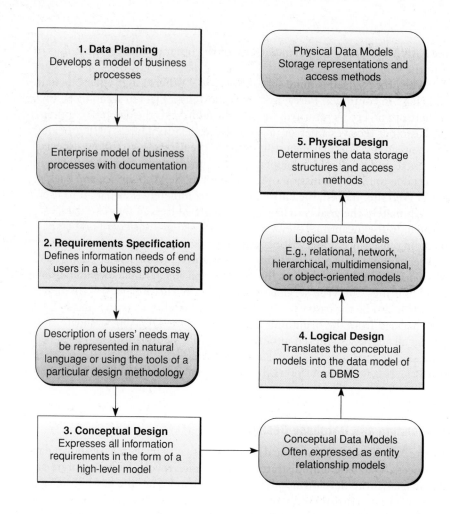

logical view of the relationships among the data elements in a database, whereas the subschema is a logical view of the data relationships needed to support specific end-user application programs that will access that database.

Remember that data models represent logical views of the data and relationships of the database. Physical database design takes a physical view of the data (also called the *internal view*) that describes how data are to be physically stored and accessed on the storage devices of a computer system. For example, Figure 5.12 illustrates these different database views and the software interface of a bank database processing system. This figure focuses on the business processes of checking, savings, and installment lending, which are part of a banking services data model that serves as a logical data framework for all bank services.

FIGURE 5.11

This entity relationship diagram illustrates some of the relationships among the entities (e.g., product, supplier, warehouse) in a purchasing/receiving business process.

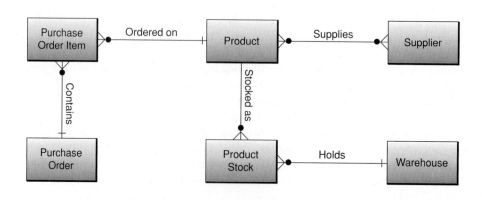

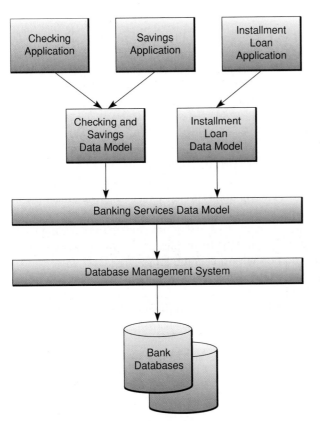

Logical User Views
Data elements and relationships (the subschemas) needed
for checking, savings, or installment loan processing

Data elements and relationships (the schema)
needed for the support of all bank services

Software Interface
The DBMS provides access to the bank's databases

Physical Data Views
Organization and location of data on the storage media

FIGURE 5.12

Example of the logical and
physical database views and the
software interface of a banking
services information system.

Hadoop: Ready for the Large-Scale Data Sets of the Future

Traditional business intelligence solutions can't scale to the degree necessary
in today's data environment. One solution getting a lot of attention recently:
Hadoop, an open-source product inspired by Google's search architecture.
Twenty years ago, most of the data from companies came from fundamental
transaction systems: Payroll, ERP, and so on. The amounts of data seemed
large, but they usually were bounded by well-understood limitations: the
overall growth of the company and the growth of the general economy.

For those companies that wanted to gain more insight, the related data
warehousing systems reflected the structure of the underlying systems: regular
data schema, smooth growth, and well-understood analysis needs. The typical
business intelligence constraint was the amount of processing power that could
be applied. Consequently, a great deal of effort went into the data design to
restrict the amount of processing required to the available processing power.
This led to the now time-honored business intelligence data warehouses: fact
tables, dimension tables, and star schemas.

Today, the nature of business intelligence is totally changed. Computing
is far more widespread throughout the enterprise, so many more systems are
generating data. Companies are on the Internet, generating huge torrents of
unstructured data: searches, click-streams, interactions, and the like. And it's
much harder—if not impossible—to forecast what kinds of analytics a company
might want to pursue.

Today it might be click-stream patterns through the company Web site.
Tomorrow it might be cross-correlating external blog postings with order
patterns. The day after it might be something completely different.

And the system bottleneck has shifted. In the past, the problem was how
much processing power was available, but today the problem is how much data

need to be analyzed. At Internet-scale, a company might be dealing with dozens or hundreds of terabytes. At that size, the number of drives required to hold the data guarantees frequent drive failures, but attempting to centralize the data imposes too much network traffic to conveniently migrate data to processors.

Hadoop is an open-source product inspired by Google's search architecture. Interestingly, unlike previous open-source products that were usually implementations of previously existing proprietary products, Hadoop has no proprietary predecessor. The innovation in this aspect of big data resides in the open-source community, not in a private company.

Hadoop creates a pool of computers, each with a special Hadoop file system. A central master Hadoop node spreads data across each machine in a file structure designed for large block data reads and writes. It uses a clever hash algorithm to cluster data elements that are similar, making processing data sets extremely efficient. For robustness, three copies of all data are kept to ensure that hardware failures do not halt processing.

The advantage of this approach is that very large sets of data can be managed and processed in parallel across the machine pool managed by Hadoop. The power of Hadoop is clear from the way *The New York Times* used it to convert a 4-terabyte collection of its pages from one format to another.

SOURCE: Bernard Golden, "Large Data Set Analysis in the Cloud: Amazon, Cloudera Improve Hadoop," *CIO.com*, April 9, 2009.

Managing Data Resources

Data are a vital organizational resource that need to be managed like other important business assets. Today's business enterprises cannot survive or succeed without quality data about their internal operations and external environment.

> With each online mouse click, either a fresh bit of data is created or already-stored data are retrieved from all those business Web sites. All that's on top of the heavy demand for industrial-strength data storage already in use by scores of big corporations. What's driving the growth is a crushing imperative for corporations to analyze every bit of information they can extract from their huge data warehouses for competitive advantage. That has turned the data storage and management function into a key strategic role of the information age.

That's why organizations and their managers need to practice **data resource management**, a managerial activity that applies information systems technologies like *database management*, *data warehousing*, and other data management tools to the task of managing an organization's data resources to meet the information needs of their business stakeholders. This section will show you the managerial implications of using data resource management technologies and methods to manage an organization's data assets to meet business information requirements. See Figure 5.13.

Continuing developments in information technology and its business applications have resulted in the evolution of several major **types of databases.** Figure 5.14 illustrates several major conceptual categories of databases that may be found in many organizations. Let's take a brief look at some of them now.

Operational Databases

Operational databases store detailed data needed to support the business processes and operations of a company. They are also called *subject area databases* (SADB), *transaction databases*, and *production databases*. Examples are a customer database, human resource database, inventory database, and other databases containing data generated by business operations. For example, a human resource database like that shown in Figure 5.2 would include data identifying each employee and the number of hours worked, compensation, benefits, performance appraisals, training and development

FIGURE 5.13

IT is starting to have major impacts on both medical research and patient treatment.

SOURCE: © Jose Luis Pelaez Inc/Blend Images/Getty Images.

FIGURE 5.14

Examples of some of the major types of databases used by organizations and end users.

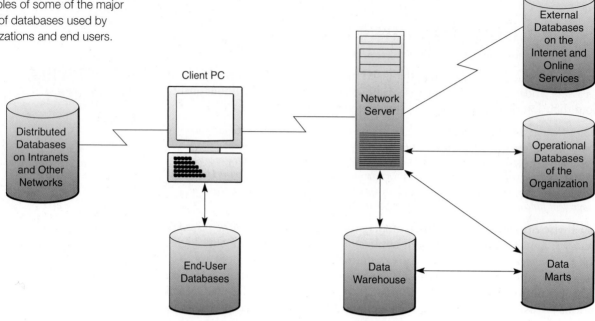

status, and other related human resource data. Figure 5.15 illustrates some of the common operational databases that can be created and managed for a small business using Microsoft Access database management software.

Distributed Databases

Many organizations replicate and distribute copies or parts of databases to network servers at a variety of sites. These *distributed databases* can reside on network servers on the World Wide Web, on corporate intranets or extranets, or on other company networks. Distributed databases may be copies of operational or analytical databases, hypermedia or discussion databases, or any other type of database. Replication and distribution of databases improve database performance at end-user work sites. Ensuring

FIGURE 5.15

Examples of operational databases that can be created and managed for a small business by microcomputer database management software like Microsoft Access.

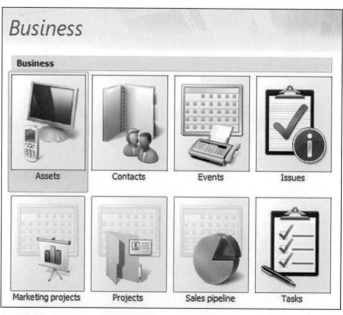

SOURCE: Courtesy of Microsoft®.

that the data in an organization's distributed databases are consistently and concurrently updated is a major challenge of distributed database management.

Distributed databases have both advantages and disadvantages. One primary advantage of a distributed database lies with the protection of valuable data. If all of an organization's data reside in a single physical location, any catastrophic event like a fire or damage to the media holding the data would result in an equally catastrophic loss of use of that data. By having databases distributed in multiple locations, the negative impact of such an event can be minimized.

Another advantage of distributed databases is found in their storage requirements. Often, a large database system may be distributed into smaller databases based on some logical relationship between the data and the location. For example, a company with several branch operations may distribute its data so that each branch operation location is also the location of its branch database. Because multiple databases in a distributed system can be joined together, each location has control of its local data while all other locations can access any database in the company if so desired.

Distributed databases are not without some challenges, however. The primary challenge is the maintenance of data accuracy. If a company distributes its database to multiple locations, any change to the data in one location must somehow be updated in all other locations. This updating can be accomplished in one of two ways: *replication* or *duplication*.

Updating a distributed database using **replication** involves using a specialized software application that looks at each distributed database and then finds the changes made to it. Once these changes have been identified, the replication process makes all of the distributed databases look the same by making the appropriate changes to each one. The replication process is very complex and, depending on the number and size of the distributed databases, can consume a lot of time and computer resources.

The **duplication** process, in contrast, is much less complicated. It basically identifies one database as a master and then duplicates that database at a prescribed time after hours so that each distributed location has the same data. One drawback to the duplication process is that no changes can ever be made to any database other than the master to avoid having local changes overwritten during the duplication process. Nonetheless, properly used, duplication and replication can keep all distributed locations current with the latest data.

One additional challenge associated with distributed databases is the extra computing power and bandwidth necessary to access multiple databases in multiple locations. We will look more closely at the issue of bandwidth in Chapter 6 when we focus on telecommunications and networks.

External Databases

Access to a wealth of information from **external databases** is available for a fee from commercial online services and with or without charge from many sources on the World Wide Web. Web sites provide an endless variety of hyperlinked pages of multimedia documents in *hypermedia databases* for you to access. Data are available in the form of statistics on economic and demographic activity from *statistical* databanks, or you can view or download abstracts or complete copies of hundreds of newspapers, magazines, newsletters, research papers, and other published material and periodicals from *bibliographic* and *full-text* databases. Whenever you use a search engine like Google or Yahoo to look up something on the Internet, you are using an external database—a very, very large one! Also, if you are using Google, you are using one that averages 112 million searches per day.

Hypermedia Databases

The rapid growth of Web sites on the Internet and corporate intranets and extranets has dramatically increased the use of databases of hypertext and hypermedia documents. A Web site stores such information in a **hypermedia database** consisting of

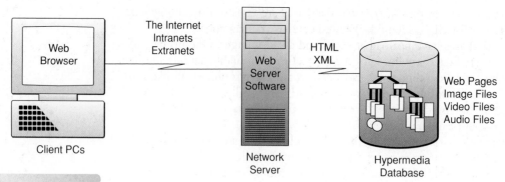

FIGURE 5.16

The components of a Web-based information system include Web browsers, servers, and hypermedia databases.

hyperlinked pages of multimedia (text, graphic and photographic images, video clips, audio segments, and so on). That is, from a database management point of view, the set of interconnected multimedia pages on a Web site is a database of interrelated hypermedia page elements, rather than interrelated data records.

Figure 5.16 shows how you might use a Web browser on your client PC to connect with a Web network server. This server runs Web server software to access and transfer the Web pages you request. The Web site illustrated in Figure 5.16 uses a hypermedia database consisting of Web page content described by HTML (Hypertext Markup Language) code or XML (Extensible Markup Language) labels, image files, video files, and audio. The Web server software acts as a database management system to manage the transfer of hypermedia files for downloading by the multimedia plug-ins of your Web browser.

Coty: Using Real-Time Analytics to Track Demand

In the perfume business, new products like the recent launch of Kate, a fragrance Coty branded for supermodel Kate Moss, can make or break a company's year. But big hits can also lead to big problems. When a product takes off, Coty must respond quickly to keep shelves full, but its ability to ramp up is dependent on glass, packaging, and other suppliers. "If we can't meet demand . . . it annoys the retailers, the consumers lose interest, and we lose sales," says Dave Berry, chief information officer at Coty, whose other brands include Jennifer Lopez, Kenneth Cole, and Vera Wang.

Empty shelves are the scourge of manufacturing and retail. Just look at the annual shortages of the Christmas season's hottest toys or at the rain checks stores must write regularly on sale items. At any given time, 7 percent of all U.S. retail products are out of stock; goods on promotion are out of stock more than 15 percent of the time. That's why manufacturers and retailers are pushing for the next breakthroughs in demand forecasting, what has emerged as the discipline of "demand-signal management." Instead of just relying on internal data such as order and shipment records, manufacturers are analyzing weekly and even daily point-of-sale data from retailers so that they can better see what's selling where. This sort of timely, detailed data lets manufacturers spot trends much sooner by region, product, retailer, and even by individual store.

Handling demand-signal data presents the same problems that real-time data causes in any industry: how to access and integrate high volumes of data, and then combine and analyze it alongside historical information. With the advent of highly scalable data warehouses, low-latency integration techniques, and faster, deeper query and analysis capabilities, the technology is finally here, at a price most can afford. And with easier-to-use business intelligence tools, manufacturers and retailers are pushing analytic tools into the hands of front-line decision makers, most often field sales and marketing people involved in planning, merchandising, and supply chain management.

Over the last two years, Coty has pushed the responsibility for developing accurate forecasts down to its salespeople. Field-level forecasting makes for more accurate and responsive planning, says CIO Berry, who credits an analytics application from vendor CAS with making it easier for salespeople who are new to business intelligence to analyze point-of-sale data and develop forecasts.

An important obstacle to broad adoption of demand-signal analysis has been the lack of standardization in the data supplied by retailers. Coty gets point-of-sale data from the likes of CVS, Target, and Walgreens, but each uses a different format. "The timeliness, accuracy, and depth of the data also varies from retailer to retailer, so it's tough to bring it into a data warehouse," says Berry.

That being said, the payoff from early efforts by Coty has been more accurate forecasting, higher on-shelf availability, and more effective promotions. With faster and more detailed insight into demand, manufacturers can ratchet up revenue by 2 percent to 7 percent, which more than justifies any data-related headaches.

SOURCE: Doug Henschen, "In a Down Economy, Companies Turn to Real-Time Analytics to Track Demand," *InformationWeek*, February 28, 2009.

DATA WAREHOUSES AND DATA MINING
LO 5-4b

A *data warehouse* stores data that have been extracted from the various operational, external, and other databases of an organization. It is a central source of the data that have been cleaned, transformed, and cataloged so that they can be used by managers and other business professionals for data mining, online analytical processing, and other forms of business analysis, market research, and decision support. (We'll talk in-depth about all of these activities in Chapter 10.) Data warehouses may be subdivided into **data marts,** which hold subsets of data from the warehouse that focus on specific aspects of a company, such as a department or a business process.

Figure 5.17 illustrates the components of a complete data warehouse system. Notice how data from various operational and external databases are captured, cleaned, and transformed into data that can be better used for analysis. This acquisition process might include activities like consolidating data from several sources, filtering out unwanted data, correcting incorrect data, converting data to new data elements, or aggregating data into new data subsets.

FIGURE 5.17

The components of a complete data warehouse system.

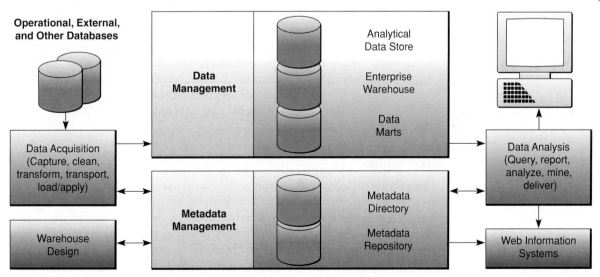

SOURCE: Courtesy of Hewlett-Packard.

FIGURE 5.18

A data warehouse and its data mart subsets hold data that have been extracted from various operational databases for business analysis, market research, decision support, and data mining applications.

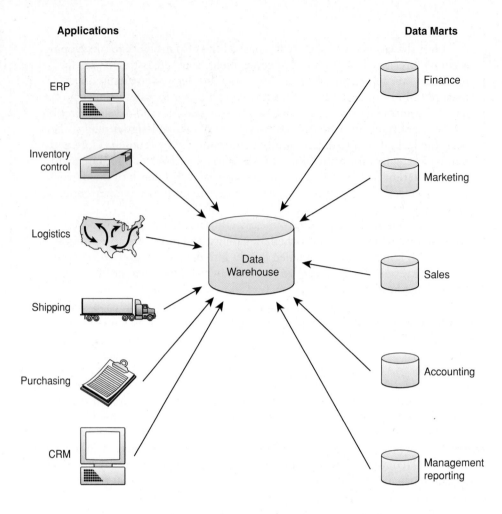

These data are then stored in the enterprise data warehouse, from which they can be moved into data marts or to an *analytical data store* that holds data in a more useful form for certain types of analysis. *Metadata* (data that define the data in the data warehouse) are stored in a metadata repository and cataloged by a metadata directory. Finally, a variety of analytical software tools can be provided to query, report, mine, and analyze the data for delivery via Internet and intranet Web systems to business end users. See Figure 5.18.

One important characteristic about the data in a data warehouse is that, unlike a typical database in which changes can occur constantly, data in a data warehouse are *static*, which means that once the data are gathered up, formatted for storage, and stored in the data warehouse, they will never change. This restriction is so that queries can be made on the data to look for complex patterns or historical trends that might otherwise go unnoticed with dynamic data that change constantly as a result of new transactions and updates.

Data Mining

Data mining is a major use of data warehouse databases and the static data they contain. In data mining, the data in a data warehouse are analyzed to reveal hidden patterns and trends in historical business activity. This analysis can be used to help managers make decisions about strategic changes in business operations to gain competitive advantages in the marketplace. See Figure 5.19.

Data mining can discover new correlations, patterns, and trends in vast amounts of business data (frequently several terabytes of data) stored in data warehouses. Data

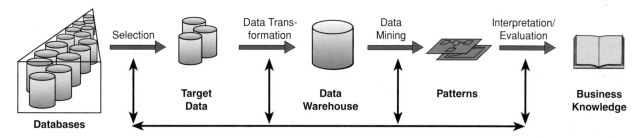

FIGURE 5.19

How data mining extracts business knowledge from a data warehouse.

mining software uses advanced pattern recognition algorithms, as well as a variety of mathematical and statistical techniques, to sift through mountains of data to extract previously unknown strategic business information. For example, many companies use data mining to:

- Perform market-basket analysis to identify new product bundles.
- Find root causes of quality or manufacturing problems.
- Prevent customer attrition and acquire new customers.
- Cross-sell to existing customers.
- Profile customers with more accuracy.

We will discuss data mining further, as well as online analytical processing (OLAP) and other technologies that analyze the data in databases and data warehouses to provide vital support for business decisions, in Chapter 10.

Better Analytics Means Better Care

Southeast Texas Medical Associates (SETMA) is a midsize practice in Beaumont, Texas. In 2010, SETMA reduced its hospital admission rate by 22 percent, and the number of visits by diabetic patients around the holidays—a difficult time—by about 15 percent. How? By keeping their patients healthier. How? By using business analytics to improve the quality of their health care.

Two years ago, SETMA—already an early adopter of NextGen EMR, a system that is used to automate medical practice workflows—implemented software by Cognos, part of IBM, to better analyze data gathered from records of past patient visits and incidents. As a result of these data gathering and consolidating efforts, SETMA now operates a data warehouse that includes records for all of their 65,000 patients. The Cognos implementation included modules used to analyze trends in the data, which are directly used by the doctors and not by middlemen IT specialists. Using the software, SETMA management can better understand the quality of care provided to patients and ensure that doctors adhere to best practices, as outlined by a number of professional organizations, such as the National Committee for Quality Assurance.

"Health care is behind the times in the use of BI," says SETMA CEO James Holly. "But everything that BI can do in other industries, it's doing for us at Southeast Texas Medical Associates, leveraging data to improve care."

SETMA has been able to improve and streamline its operations in many areas as a result of the new tools. Some of this is simply the result of better data about patients. For example, support staff can now run reports about patients before they come in for an appointment. This allows them to identify any missing or overdue tests and arrange for these tests to be taken care of before the patient sees the doctor; then the doctor and patient can go over the test results together. Other analyses are more sophisticated. Using the analytics functionality provided by Cognos, SETMA compared patients who are read-mitted to a hospital after being discharged with those who are not, and used the results to identify how those two groups of patients are different in terms of ethnicity, age, gender, income, and follow-up care. This analysis revealed that patients who live alone are less likely to keep their prescribed medication regimen, and it allowed SETMA to develop improved treatment plans to make sure that did not happen.

Although some of these analyses and reports were theoretically possible before SETMA implemented Cognos, their legacy systems would take 36 hours to provide this kind of information, and with less sophisticated analysis of the results. The practice, then, would always be one day and a half behind the most current information about its patients—and a lot of things can happen to a patient's health in that period of time. With Cognos and the new data ware-house, those reports take a few seconds to run.

"SETMA spent about $500,000 on the Cognos project," says Holly. "It was expensive, but the payoffs are enormous, and we're just scratching the surface," he says.

SOURCE: Marianne Kolbasuk McGee, "Better Clinical Analytics Means Better Clinical Care," *InformationWeek*, May 21, 2011.

TRADITIONAL FILE PROCESSING
LO 5-2

How would you feel if you were an executive of a company and were told that some information you wanted about your employees was too difficult and too costly to obtain? Suppose the vice president of information services gave you the following reasons:

- The information you want is in several different files, each organized in a different way.
- Each file has been organized to be used by a different application program, none of which produces the information you want in the form you need.
- No application program is available to help get the information you want from these files.

That's how end users can be frustrated when an organization relies on *file processing* systems in which data are organized, stored, and processed in independent files of data records. In the traditional file processing approach that was used in business data processing for many years, each business application was designed to use one or more specialized data files containing only specific types of data records. For example, a bank's checking account processing application was designed to access and update a data file containing specialized data records for the bank's checking account customers. Similarly, the bank's installment loan processing application needed to access and update a specialized data file containing data records about the bank's installment loan customers. See Figure 5.20.

Problems of File Processing

The file processing approach finally became too cumbersome, costly, and inflexible to supply the information needed to manage modern business; as we shall soon see, the *database management approach* replaced it. Despite their apparent logic and simplicity, file processing systems had the following major problems:

DATA REDUNDANCY. Independent data files included a lot of duplicated data; the same data (such as a customer's name and address) were recorded and stored in several files. This *data redundancy* caused problems when data had to be updated. Separate *file*

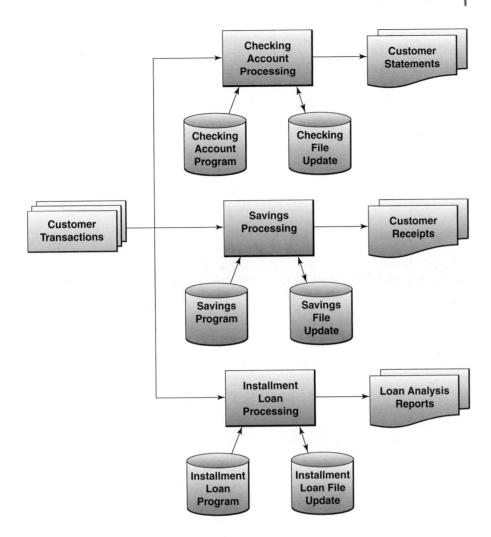

FIGURE 5.20

Examples of file processing systems in banking. Note the use of separate computer programs and independent data files in a file processing approach to the savings, installment loan, and checking account applications.

maintenance programs had to be developed and coordinated to ensure that each file was properly updated. Of course, this coordination proved difficult in practice, so a lot of inconsistency occurred among data stored in separate files.

LACK OF *DATA INTEGRATION.* Having data in independent files made it difficult to provide end users with information for ad hoc requests that required accessing data stored in several different files. Special computer programs had to be written to retrieve data from each independent file. This retrieval was so difficult, time-consuming, and costly for some organizations that it was impossible to provide end users or management with such information. End users had to extract the required information manually from the various reports produced by each separate application and then prepare customized reports for management.

DATA DEPENDENCE. In file processing systems, major components of a system—the organization of files, their physical locations on storage hardware, and the application software used to access those files—depended on one another in significant ways. For example, application programs typically contained references to the specific *format* of the data stored in the files they used. Thus, changes in the format and structure of data and records in a file required that changes be made to all of the programs that used that file. This *program maintenance* effort was a major burden of file processing systems. It proved difficult to do properly, and it resulted in a lot of inconsistency in the data files.

LACK OF *DATA INTEGRITY* OR STANDARDIZATION. In file processing systems, it was easy for data elements such as stock numbers and customer addresses to be defined differently by different end users and applications. This divergence caused serious inconsistency problems in the development of programs to access such data. In addition, the *integrity* (i.e., the accuracy and completeness) of the data was suspect because there was no control over their use and maintenance by authorized end users. Thus, a lack of standards caused major problems in application program development and maintenance, as well as in the security and integrity of the data files needed by the organization.

Online Dating: The Technology behind Finding Love

When Joe wanted to find love, he turned to science.

Rather than hang out in bars or hope that random dates worked out, the 34-year-old aerospace engineer signed up for eHarmony.com, an online dating service that uses detailed profiles, proprietary matching algorithms, and a tightly controlled communications process to help people find their perfect soul mate. Over a three-month period, Joe found 500 people who appeared to fit his criteria. He initiated contact with 100 of them, corresponded with 50, and dated 3 before finding the right match.

The "scientific" matching services, such as eHarmony, PerfectMatch, and Chemistry.com, attempt to identify the most compatible matches for the user by asking anywhere from a few dozen to several hundred questions. The services then assemble a personality profile and use that against an algorithm that ranks users within a set of predefined categories; from there, the system produces a list of appropriate matches.

The technology that powers these dating sites ranges from incredibly simple to incredibly complicated. Unsurprisingly, eHarmony has one of the most sophisticated data centers. "The company stores 4 terabytes of data on some 20 million registered users, each of whom has filled out a 400-question psychological profile," says Joseph Essas, vice president of technology at eHarmony. The company uses proprietary algorithms to score that data against 29 "dimensions of compatibility"—such as values, personality style, attitudes, and interests—and match up customers with the best possible prospects for a long-term relationship.

A giant Oracle 10g database spits out a few preliminary candidates immediately after a user signs up, to prime the pump, but the real matching work happens later, after eHarmony's system scores and matches up answers to hundreds of questions from thousands of users. The process requires just under 1 billion calculations that are processed in a giant batch operation each day. These operations execute in parallel on hundreds of computers and are orchestrated using software written to the open-source Hadoop software platform.

Once matches are sent to users, the users' actions and outcomes are fed back into the model for the next day's calculations. For example, if a customer clicked on many matches that were at the outset of his or her geographical range—say, 25 miles away—the system would assume distance wasn't a deal-breaker and next offer more matches that were just a bit farther away.

"Our biggest challenge is the amount of data that we have to constantly score, move, apply, and serve to people, and that is fluid," Essas says. To that end, the architecture is designed to scale quickly to meet growth and demand peaks around major holidays. The highest demand comes just before Valentine's Day. "Our demand doubles, if not quadruples."

SOURCE: Robert L. Mitchell, "Online Dating: The Technology Behind the Attraction," *Computerworld*, February 13, 2009.

To solve the problems encountered with the file processing approach, the *database management approach* was conceived as the foundation of modern methods for managing organizational data. The database management approach consolidates data records, formerly held in separate files, into databases that can be accessed by many different application programs. In addition, a *database management system* (DBMS) serves as a software interface between users and databases, which helps users easily access the data in a database. Thus, database management involves the use of database management software to control how databases are created, interrogated, and maintained to provide information that end users need.

For example, customer records and other common types of data are needed for several different applications in banking, such as check processing, automated teller systems, bank credit cards, savings accounts, and installment loan accounting. These data can be consolidated into a common *customer database*, rather than being kept in separate files for each of those applications. See Figure 5.21.

THE DATABASE MANAGEMENT APPROACH
LO 5-2
LO 5-3

Database Management System

A *database management system (DBMS)* is the main software tool of the database management approach because it controls the creation, maintenance, and use of the databases of an organization and its end users. As we saw in Figure 5.15, microcomputer database management packages such as Microsoft Access, Lotus Approach, or Corel Paradox allow you to set up and manage databases on your PC, network server, or the World Wide Web. In mainframe and server computer systems, the database management system is an important system software package that controls the development, use, and maintenance of the databases of computer-using organizations. Examples of popular mainframe and server versions of DBMS software are IBM's DB2 Universal Database, Oracle 11g by Oracle Corp., and MySQL, a popular open-source DBMS. See Figure 5.22. Common DBMS components and functions are summarized in Figure 5.23.

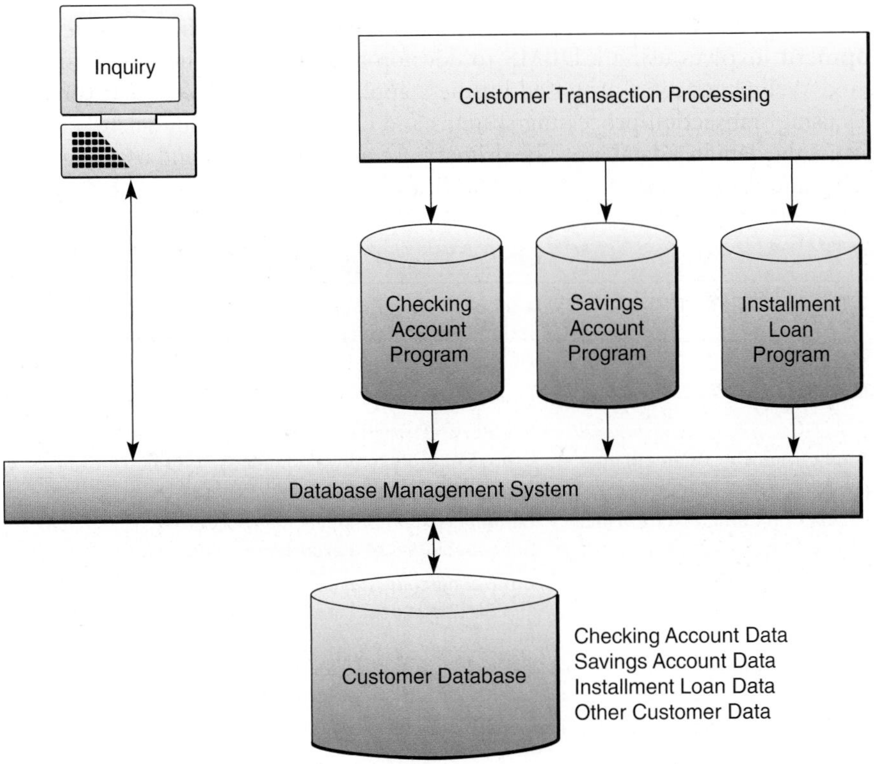

FIGURE 5.21

An example of a database management approach in a banking information system. Note how the savings, checking, and installment loan programs use a database management system to share a customer database. Note also that the DBMS allows a user to make direct, ad hoc interrogations of the database without using application programs.

FIGURE 5.22

Database management software like MySQL, a popular open-source DBMS, supports the development, maintenance, and use of the databases of an organization.

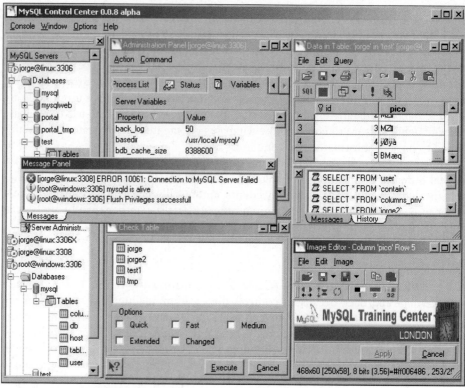

SOURCE: Courtesy of Oracle Corporation.

The three major functions of a database management system are (1) to *create* new databases and database applications, (2) to *maintain* the quality of the data in an organization's databases, and (3) to *use* the databases of an organization to provide the information that its end users need. See Figure 5.24.

Database development involves defining and organizing the content, relationships, and structure of the data needed to build a database. **Database application development** involves using a DBMS to develop prototypes of queries, forms, reports, and Web pages for a proposed business application. **Database maintenance** involves using transaction processing systems and other tools to add, delete, update, and correct the data in a database. The primary use of a database by end users involves employing the *database interrogation* capabilities of a DBMS to access the data in a

FIGURE 5.23

Common software components and functions of a database management system.

Common DBMS Software Components	
• **Database Definition**	Language and graphical tools to define entities, relationships, integrity constraints, and authorization rights.
• **Nonprocedural Access**	Language and graphical tools to access data without complicated coding.
• **Application Development**	Graphical tools to develop menus, data entry forms, and reports.
• **Procedural Language Interface**	Language that combines nonprocedural access with full capabilities of a programming language.
• **Transaction Processing**	Control mechanisms to prevent interference from simultaneous users and recover lost data after a failure.
• **Database Tuning**	Tools to monitor and improve database performance.

SOURCE: Michael V. Mannino, *Database Application Development and Design* (Burr Ridge, IL: McGraw-Hill/Irwin, 2001), p. 7.

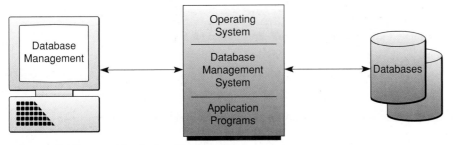

- Create: Database and Application Development
- Maintain: Database Maintenance
- Use: Database Interrogation

FIGURE 5.24
The three major uses of DBMS software are to create, maintain, and use the databases of an organization.

database to selectively retrieve and display information and produce reports, forms, and other documents.

Database Interrogation

A *database interrogation* capability is a major benefit of the database management approach. End users can use a DBMS by asking for information from a database using a *query* feature or a *report generator*. They can receive an immediate response in the form of video displays or printed reports. No difficult programming is required. The **query language** feature lets you easily obtain immediate responses to ad hoc data requests: You merely key in a few short inquiries—in some cases, using common sentence structures just like you would use to ask a question. The **report generator** feature allows you to specify a report format for information you want presented as a report. Figure 5.25 illustrates the use of a DBMS report generator.

SQL QUERIES. SQL (pronounced "see quill"), or ***Structured Query Language,*** is an international standard query language found in many DBMS packages. In most cases, SQL is the language structure used to "ask a question" that the DBMS will retrieve the data to answer. The basic form of a SQL query is:

SELECT . . . FROM . . . WHERE . . .

After SELECT, you list the data fields you want retrieved. After FROM, you list the files or tables from which the data must be retrieved. After WHERE, you specify conditions that limit the search to only those data records in which you are interested. Figure 5.26 compares a SQL query to a natural language query for information on customer orders.

FIGURE 5.25
Using the report generator of Microsoft Access to create an employee report.

Department	Last Name	First Name	Title	Street	City	State	Zip

◀ Department Header

Department

◀ Detail

| | LastName | FirstName | Title | Street | City | State | Zip |

◀ Department Footer

Count =Count([Departmen]

◀ Page Footer

=Now() ="Page " &[Page]& " of " &[Pages]

◀ Report Footer

Grand Count =Count([Departmen]

SOURCE: Courtesy of Microsoft®.

FIGURE 5.26

Comparing a natural language query with a SQL query.

Operations Support Systems

A Sample Natural Language-to-SQL Translation for Microsoft Access

Natural Language

What customers had no orders last month?

SQL

SELECT [Customers].[Company Name],[Customers].[Contact Name]
FROM [Customers]
WHERE not Exists {SELECT [Ship Name] FROM [Orders]
   WHERE Month {[Order Date]}=I and Year {[Order Date]}=2004 and [Customers].
   [Customer ID]=[Orders].[Customer ID]}

BOOLEAN LOGIC. To fully access the power of SQL, a database user needs to have a basic understanding of the concepts behind **Boolean logic.** Developed by George Boole in the mid-1800s, Boolean logic allows us to refine our searches for specific information such that only the desired information is obtained.

Boolean logic consists of three logical operators: (1) AND, (2) OR, and (3) NOT. Using these operators in conjunction with the syntax of a SQL query, a database user can refine a search to ensure that only the desired data are retrieved. This same set of logical operators can be used to refine searches for information from the Internet (which is really nothing more than the world's largest database). Let's look at an example of how the three logical operators work.

Suppose we are interested in obtaining information about cats from the Internet. We could just search on the word *cats*, and a large number of potentially useful Web sites would be retrieved. The problem is that in addition to the Web sites about cats, we would also retrieve Web sites about cats and dogs, pets in general (if the site includes the word *cats*), and probably even sites about the Broadway musical titled *Cats*. To avoid having to sift through all the sites to find what we want, we could use Boolean logic to form a more refined query:

Cats OR Felines AND NOT Dogs OR Broadway.

By using this search query, we would retrieve any Web site with the word *cats* or *felines* but exclude any site that also has the words *dogs* or *Broadway*. Using this approach, we would eliminate any reference to cats and dogs or to the Broadway musical titled *Cats*. This query therefore would result in a more refined search and eliminate the need to look at Web sites that do not pertain to our specific interest. You can try this on Google. Just type the following: cats felines -dogs -broadway. See Figure 5.27.

GRAPHICAL AND NATURAL QUERIES. Many end users (and IS professionals) have difficulty correctly phrasing SQL and other database language search queries. So, most end-user database management packages offer GUI (graphical user interface) point-and-click methods, which are easier to use and are translated by the software into SQL commands. Other packages are available that use *natural language* query statements similar to conversational English (or other languages), as illustrated in Figure 5.26. To see this concept in action, go to Google and click on "Advanced search," which is right below the Search button. You will then see a form that can be filled out to assist in creating your query to Google. Just put the words "cats" and "felines" in the field marked "all these words" and put the words "dogs" and "Broadway" in the field marked "any of these unwanted words." Clicking on

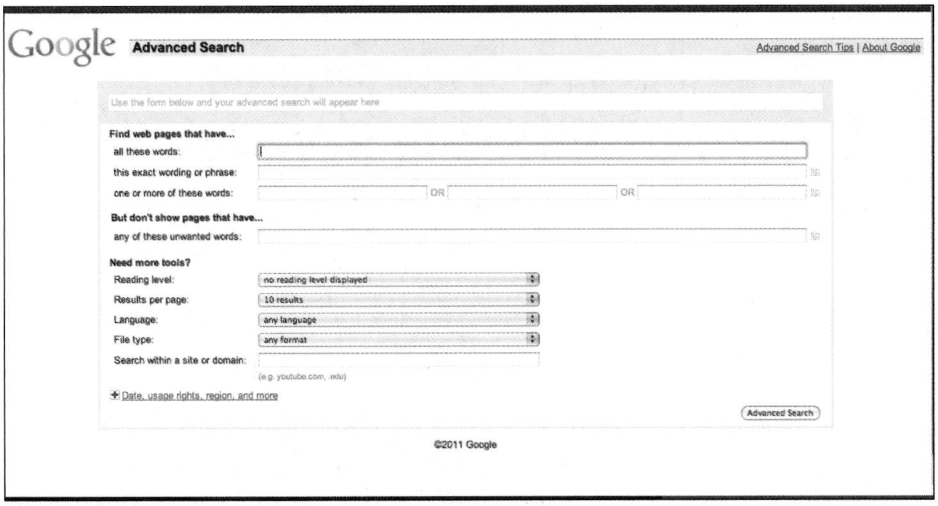

FIGURE 5.27
Using the Advanced Search option in Google to develop a query about cats.

SOURCE: Courtesy of Google®.

Advanced search will produce the same query as above, but with this application, you are asking Google to help you write it correctly.

Database Maintenance

The **database maintenance** process is accomplished by *transaction processing systems* and other end-user applications, with the support of the DBMS. End users and information specialists can also use various utilities provided by a DBMS for database maintenance. The databases of an organization need to be updated continually to reflect new business transactions (e.g., sales made, products produced, inventory shipped) and other events. Other miscellaneous changes also must be made to update and correct data (e.g., customer or employee name and address changes) to ensure the accuracy of the data in the databases. We introduced transaction processing systems in Chapter 1 and will discuss them in more detail in Chapter 7.

Application Development

In addition, DBMS packages play a major role in **application development.** End users, systems analysts, and other application developers can use the internal 4GL programming language and built-in software development tools provided by many DBMS packages to develop custom application programs. For example, you can use a DBMS to develop the data entry screens, forms, reports, or Web pages of a business application that accesses a company database to find and update the data it needs. A DBMS also makes the job of application software developers easier, because they do not have to develop detailed data-handling procedures using conventional programming languages every time they write a program. Instead, they can include features such as *data manipulation language* (DML) statements in their software that call on the DBMS to perform necessary data-handling activities.

real world SOLUTION

U.S. Xpress–Data Quality Drives Millions in Savings

U.S. Xpress is the third largest privately owned trucking company in the United States. Given the recent economic downturn, which has been very problematic for the trucking industry, and the increased competition it is facing, the company started to look for ways in which it could control costs and keep its growth plans on track. Although known in the industry as an early adopter of technology—U.S. Xpress was one of the first companies to fully integrate satellite communications aboard its fleet—management soon realized that the lack of accurate data about its operations would be a major block in the road to better decision making. For example, executives did not have any accurate and reliable information on truck idling times, which consumed gas but did not have any associated benefits. Although seemingly a minor issue, with a large fleet of trucks those costs added up quite rapidly. But there was not much that could be done about them, since the data needed to take action were just not there

The frustration that management voiced was painful for those in IT. After all, one of the main reasons companies invest in IT is to have good data that can be the basis for making good decisions, isn't it? Although the issue surrounding the need to be able to assess and contain gas costs and truck idling times became the focal point of contention, it was a symptom of a larger issue related to the heavily balkanized IT environment in which the company was operating, largely a result of so many mergers and acquisitions over the years. When Tim Leonard, chief technology officer, came to the company from Dell, he found data stored all over the place. Some would be on an AS400 (an IBM hardware product, part of its iSeries server line), and some in other environments. With more than 130 different applications and no integrated, master database, putting together any data for any business purpose was quite complicated, and without a high degree of assurance that the data would be correct. To add insult to injury, much of the data stored in those files was "dirty," that is, incorrect, inconsistent, or incomplete. As a result, IT embarked on the dual task of both cleaning up old data and making sure new data would be already clean before entering its systems. Dale Langley, chief information officer for U.S. Xpress, launched a comprehensive revamping of its IT infrastructure and strategy, with the idling problem becoming the pilot to show the value of this important effort.

"The goal is not to get clean data, because clean data does not get you money," says Rob Karel, principal analyst with Forrester Research. "The goal is to fuel your business processes and decisions in the best way possible."

As part of this initiative, Leonard launched a data quality program using tools from vendor Informatica. Leonard had already used them at his previous job with Dell and had seen firsthand how powerful those tools were. In particular, U.S. Xpress implemented two different products, called Informatica Data Quality, which standardizes common information elements coming from multiple sources, and Informatica Data Explorer, which profiles, discovers, and maps any data records from any source. Using the latter, for example, allowed the company to create a profile of a legacy database that had been created more than 10 years ago, and for the first time really understand how it worked. Using both tools, Leonard embarked on an aggressive program to normalize and aggregate its disparate data sources into a central master database where they could be both cleaned and strictly controlled.

Fast forward four months, and results are starting to show after a lot of hard work. The company used the tools by Informatica to identify duplicate customer and location information across different trucks and locations using prebuilt data-matching rules and integrated geo-coding capabilities. Searching and matching data moving forward is improved by the use of statistical matching algorithms that ensure accurate results. All common components, such as abbreviations, formats, and so forth are standardized across data sources and validated along the way. The new, clean data are stored in a separate database, so the company can always go back to the original data in case it needs to extract new elements or add something that was not needed before. But the two don't mix.

The availability of high-quality data soon started making its mark. Almost immediately, U.S. Xpress was able to create accurate reports on truck idling times, which allowed it to drastically reduce vehicle idle time by issuing new directives regarding best driving practices. This one aspect alone now saves the company $6 million annually across its fleet of trucks. "Almost immediately, we cut the percentage of time our trucks stand idle from the high 80s, to just over 50 percent. That is saving the company millions every year—equivalent to a return on investment in only three months. To say the U.S. Xpress board is ecstatic would underestimate how well the project has been received," says Leonard.

Building on this success, the company created a Web-based dashboard tool that includes a scorecard that measures, among other things, truck idle time. This new system is accessed by about 800 staff who are responsible for managing the logistics operations across the country. This helped pinpoint those areas where deviations were occurring and concentrate efforts where the most savings could be made. IT created an alert process that notifies managers when a truck is idle for more than 24 hours straight, which helps prevent these issues from ever happening in the first place, as the responsible managers are notified in real time that something is about to go wrong. "We contacted one fleet manager and told him he had a parked truck that had been idling for three days," says Leonard. "He said, 'If I had a truck idling for three days, I'd know about it.' Then he walked out and there it was. Somebody parked it and left it running." The system identified an instance in the past where a truck had been running idle for seven days. This is something that, thanks to improved reporting and visibility, will never happen again.

The new master database also allowed operations personnel to enhance truck maintenance routines. Now, with access to current and clean data, they could better predict when trucks should come in for maintenance based on manufacturer standards and historical occurrences, instead of relying on a driver "feeling" that the truck might need to be looked at, or waiting for it to break down. Leonard estimates that this resulted in additional savings of $1.2 million a year, on top of those realized from the reduction of idling times. This also allowed numerous staffers to focus on other tasks. The greatest benefit, however, is in changing the way the business will operate in the future. Lack of data is no longer the limitation that once prevented the company from designing, or even thinking of, new products and services.

"Our Chief Operating Office [COO] recently said to me, 'In my 20 years at U.S. Xpress, it's the first time I've seen data being used the way it should be. IT has done a great job'. And that's coming from someone who's not the greatest fan of IT!" says Leonard. Armed with this string of successes, Leonard is now pushing for a real-time, next-generation data warehouse also based on Informatica technology. Leonard anticipates that the introduction of an enterprise data warehouse may increase savings to between $9 million and $20 million over the next two years. Most important, IT has gone from problem child to helpful business partner in less than a year. Clean and integrated data are giving managers more and more ideas about what they can get out of the same truck. Thus, gaining a better understanding of how a truck is really used gives managers new thoughts about how to manage that asset. Sometimes, managers will point to a piece of data and say that it is wrong—not the data itself, but whatever is going on that results in those reports. And now they have the tools to go out and fix it.

SOURCE: Rob Lemos, "Big Data: How a Trucking Firm Drove Out Big Errors," *CIO Magazine*, February 28, 2011; "U.S. Xpress Enterprises 'Drives' Savings of $6 Million Annually with Informatica Data Quality," *Informatica Press Release*, July 12, 2010; "An Xcelllent Way of Saving Millions a Year," *Informatica Case Study*; Tim Leonard, "Informatica Data Quality," *Information Management Magazine*, May 1, 2011; William Cassidy, "Trucking Goes to the Cleaners," *Journal of Commerce*, May 24, 2010; and www.usxpress.com, accessed May 22, 2011.

▼ QUESTIONS TO CONSIDER

1. Once the technical aspects of data quality are put in place, who should be in charge of making decisions about these issues? Is this a technical responsibility or a business one? What are the advantages and disadvantages of either approach?

2. Are the benefits outlined in the case the result of better technology or improved decision making? Today, is it possible to clearly separate the two anymore? What are the implications for U.S. Xpress as it decides where to go next and how to invest in future projects?

- **Data Resource Management.** Data resource management is a managerial activity that applies information technology and software tools to the task of managing an organization's data resources. Early attempts to manage data resources used a file processing approach in which data were organized and accessible only in specialized files of data records that were designed for processing by specific business application programs. This approach proved too cumbersome, costly, and inflexible to supply the information needed to manage modern business processes and organizations. Thus, the database management approach was developed to solve the problems of file processing systems.

- **Database Management.** The database management approach affects the storage and processing of data. The data needed by different applications are consolidated and integrated into several common databases instead of being stored in many independent data files. Also, the database management approach emphasizes updating and maintaining common databases, having users' application programs share the data in the database, and providing a reporting and an inquiry/response capability so that end users can easily receive reports and quick responses to requests for information.

- **Database Software.** Database management systems are software packages that simplify the creation, use, and maintenance of databases. They provide software tools so that end users, programmers, and database administrators can create and modify databases; interrogate a database; generate reports; do application development; and perform database maintenance.

- **Types of Databases.** Several types of databases are used by business organizations, including opera-

tional, distributed, and external databases. Data warehouses are a central source of data from other databases that have been cleaned, transformed, and cataloged for business analysis and decision support applications. That includes data mining, which attempts to find hidden patterns and trends in the warehouse data. Hypermedia databases on the World Wide Web and on corporate intranets and extranets store hyperlinked multimedia pages on a Web site. Web server software can manage such databases for quick access and maintenance of the Web database.

- **Data Access.** Data must be organized in some logical manner on physical storage devices so that they can be efficiently processed. For this reason, data are commonly organized into logical data elements such as characters, fields, records, files, and databases. Database structures, such as the hierarchical, network, relational, and object-oriented models, are used to organize the relationships among the data records stored in databases. Databases and files can be organized in either a sequential or direct manner and can be accessed and maintained by either sequential access or direct access processing methods.

- **Database Development.** The development of databases can be easily accomplished using microcomputer database management packages for small end-user applications. However, the development of large corporate databases requires a top-down data planning effort that may involve developing enterprise and entity relationship models, subject area databases, and data models that reflect the logical data elements and relationships needed to support the operation and management of the basic business processes of the organization.

These are the key terms and concepts of this chapter. The page number of their first reference appears in parentheses.

1. Data dependence (211)
2. Data dictionary (197)
3. Data integration (211)
4. Data integrity (212)
5. Data mining (208)
6. Data modeling (199)
7. Data redundancy (210)
8. Data resource management (203)
9. Database administrator (DBA) (197)
10. Database interrogation (215)
11. Database management approach (213)
12. Database management system (DBMS) (213)
13. Database structures (191)
    a. Hierarchical structure (191)
    b. Multidimensional model (194)
    c. Network structure (191)
    d. Object-oriented model (194)
    e. Relational model (192)
14. Duplication (205)
15. File processing (210)
16. Logical data elements (186)
    a. Attribute (189)
    b. Character (186)
c. Database (190)
d. Entity (189)
e. Field (186)
f. File (189)
g. Record (189)
17. Metadata (197)
18. Replication (205)
19. Structured Query Language (SQL) (215)
20. Types of databases (203)
    a. Data warehouse (207)
    b. Distributed (204)
    c. External (205)
    d. Hypermedia (205)
    e. Operational (203)

Match one of the key terms and concepts listed previously with one of the brief examples or definitions that follow. Try to find the best fit for answers that seem to fit more than one term or concept. Defend your choices.

_____ 1. The use of integrated collections of data records and files for data storage and processing.

_____ 2. Data in independent files made it difficult to provide answers to ad hoc requests and required special computer programs to be written to perform this task.

_____ 3. A specialist in charge of the databases of an organization.

_____ 4. A nonprocedural computer language used to interrogate a database.

_____ 5. Defines and catalogs the data elements and data relationships in an organization's database.

_____ 6. A feature of database systems that uses queries or report generators to extract information.

_____ 7. The main software package that supports a database management approach.

_____ 8. Databases that are dispersed over the Internet and corporate intranets and extranets.

_____ 9. Databases that organize and store data as objects.

_____ 10. Databases of hyperlinked multimedia documents on the Web.

_____ 11. The management of all the data resources of an organization.

_____ 12. Processing data in a data warehouse to discover key business factors and trends.

_____ 13. Developing conceptual views of the relationships among data in a database.

_____ 14. A customer's name.

_____ 15. A customer's name, address, and account balance.

_____ 16. The names, addresses, and account balances of all of your customers.

_____ 17. An integrated collection of all of the data about your customers.

_____ 18. Business application programs that use specialized data files.

_____ 19. A treelike structure of records in a database.

_____ 20. A tabular structure of records in a database.

_____ 21. Records organized as cubes within cubes in a database.

_____ 22. Databases that support the major business processes of an organization.

_____ 23. A centralized and integrated database of current and historical data about an organization.

_____ 24. Databases available on the Internet or provided by commercial information services.

_____ 25. A problem in the file processing approach where major components of a system are dependent on each other to a large degree.

_____ 26. Different approaches to the logical organization of individual data elements stored in a database.

_____ 27. The most basic logical data element corresponding to a single letter or number.

_____ 28. A feature of distributed databases that identifies changes in one database and then makes appropriate changes in the others.

_____ 29. A characteristic of data that refers to their accuracy and completeness.

_____ 30. Data that describe the structure and characteristics of databases.

_____ 31. A characteristic or quality of some entity used to describe that entity.

_____ 32. Includes, among others, operational, distributed, and hypermedia databases.

_____ 33. The existence of duplicate data among different files in an organization.

_____ 34. An approach to distributed databases that copies the complete content of a master database to others at a prescribed time of the day.

_____ 35. An object, person, place, event, and so on that is of interest to an organization and thus included in a database.

_____ 36. An approach to database structure that improves on the hierarchical model by allowing many-to-many relationships.

_____ 37. Different levels of data groupings that exist in a database.

1. How should a business store, access, and distribute data and information about its internal operations and external environment?

2. What role does database management play in managing data as a business resource?

3. What are the advantages of a database management approach to the file processing approach? Give examples to illustrate your answer.

4. Refer to the Real World Challenge in the chapter. In the case, it is quite evident that data were either unavailable or inaccurate to the point that business decisions could not rely on them too much. Who was responsible for the company being in that state of affairs?

5. What is the role of a database management system in a business information system?

6. In the past, databases of information about a firm's internal operations were the only databases that were considered important to a business. What other kinds of databases are important for a business today?

7. Refer to the Real World Solution in the chapter. Although trucking companies would not generally be considered part of the "new economy," they are nonetheless heavily reliant on data. Are all companies, both old and new, going the way of becoming data-driven when it comes to running them? Was this always the case?

8. What are the benefits and limitations of the relational database model for business applications today?

9. Why is the object-oriented database model gaining acceptance for developing applications and managing the hypermedia databases on business Web sites?

10. How have the Internet, intranets, and extranets affected the types and uses of data resources available to business professionals? What other database trends are also affecting data resource management in business?

1. Training Cost Management Part 1
Joining Tables

You have the responsibility for managing technical training classes within your organization. These classes fall under two general types: highly technical training, and end-user training. Software engineers sign up for the former and administrative staff sign up for the latter. Your supervisor measures your effectiveness in part based upon the average cost per training hour and type of training. In short, your supervisor expects the best training for the least cost.

To meet this need, you have negotiated an exclusive on-site training contract with Hands On Technology Transfer Inc. (HOTT) (www.traininghott.com), a high-quality technical training provider. Your negotiated rates are reproduced below in the pricing table. A separate table contains a sample list of courses you routinely make available for your organization.

a. Using the data below, design and populate a table that includes basic training rate information. Designate the "Technical" field type as "Yes/No" (Boolean).

b. Using the data below, design and populate a course table. Designate the CourseID field as a "Primary Key" and allow your database to automatically generate a value for this field. Designate the "Technical" field type as "Yes/No" (Boolean).

c. Prepare a query that lists each course name and its cost per day of training.

d. Prepare a query that lists the cost per student for each class. Assume maximum capacity and that you will schedule two half-day classes on the same day to take full advantage of HOTT's per day pricing schedule.

PRICING TABLE

Technical	Price Per Day	Capacity
Yes	2680	15
No	2144	30

COURSE TABLE

Course ID	Course Name	Duration	Technical
1	ASP Programming	5	Yes
2	XML Programming	5	Yes
3	PHP Programming	4	Yes
4	Microsoft Word—Advanced	.5	No
5	Microsoft Excel—Advanced	.5	No

...

2. Training Cost Management Part 2
Data Structure

Having determined the cost per student for each of the classes in the previous problem, you now must carefully manage class registration. Since you pay the same flat rates no matter how many students attend (up to capacity), you want to do all you can to ensure maximum attendance. Your training provider, Hands On Technology Transfer Inc., requires two weeks notice in the event that you need to reschedule a class. You want to make sure your classes are at least two-thirds full before this deadline. You also want to make sure you send timely reminders to all attendees so they do not forget to show up. Use the database you created in problem #1 above to perform the following activities:

a. Using the information provided in the sample below, add a course schedule table to your training database. Designate the ScheduleID field as a "Primary Key" and allow your database program to automatically generate a value for this field. Make the CourseID field a number field and the StartDate field a date field.

b. Using the information provided in the sample below, add a class roster table to your training database. Make the ScheduleID field a number field. Make the Reminder and Confirmed fields both "yes/no" (Boolean) fields.

c. Since the Class Schedule table relates to the Course Table and the Course Table relates to the Pricing Table, why is it appropriate to record the Price Per Day information in the Class Schedule table, too?

d. What are the advantages and disadvantages of using the participant's name and e-mail address in the Class Roster table? What other database design might you use to record this information?

e. Write a query that shows how many people have registered for each scheduled class. Include the class name, capacity, date, and count of attendees.

3. Selling the Sawdust
Selling Information By-Products
Sawmill operators are in the business of turning trees into lumber. Products include boards, plywood, and veneer. For as long as there have been sawmills, there have been sawmill operators who have tried to solve the problem of what to do with their principle by-product: sawdust. Numerous creative examples abound.

Likewise, businesses often generate tremendous amounts of data. The challenge then becomes what to do with this by-product. Can a little additional effort turn this into a valuable product? Research the following:

a. What are your college's or university's policies regarding student directory data?

b. Does your college or university sell any of its student data? If your institution sells student data, what data do they sell, to whom, and for how much?

c. If your institution sells data, calculate the revenue earned per student. Would you be willing to pay this amount per year in exchange for maintaining your privacy?

4. Data Formats and Manipulation
Excel: Importing and Formatting
Ms. Sapper, a marketing manager in a global accounting firm, was this year's coordinator for her firm's annual partner meeting. With 400 partners from around the world, Ms. Sapper faced daunting communications tasks that she needed to automate as much as possible. Ms. Sapper received a file containing the names of all partners, as well as additional, personal information from her IT

CLASS SCHEDULE

Schedule ID	Course ID	Location	Start Date	Price Per Day
1	1	101-A	7/12/2004	2680
2	1	101-A	7/19/2004	2680
3	1	101-B	7/19/2004	2680
4	4	101-A8B	7/26/2004	2144
5	5	101-A8B	8/2/2004	2144
. . .				

CLASS ROSTER

Schedule ID	Participant	e-mail	Reminder	Confirmed
1	Linda Adams	adams.l@ . . .	Yes	Yes
1	Fatima Ahmad	ahmad.f@ . . .	Yes	No
1	Adam Alba	alba.a@ . . .	Yes	Yes
4	Denys Alyea	alyea.d@ . . .	No	No
4	Kathy Bara	bara.k@ . . .	Yes	No
. . .				

department. The file ended with the extension "CSV." *Now what?* She wondered to herself.

The CSV, or "comma separated values" format, is a very basic data format that most database applications use to import or export data. As a minimum, the CSV format groups all fields in record into a single line of text. It then separates each field within a line with a comma or other delimiter. When the text information contains commas, the format requires that this text information be placed within quotes. Ms. Sapper needed to get this data into Excel. Given how busy the IT guys appeared, she decided to do this herself.

a. Download and save "partners.csv" from the MIS 11e OLC. Open the file using Microsoft Word. Remember to look for the "csv" file type when searching for the file to open. Describe the data's appearance.

b. Import the "partner.csv" file into Excel. Remember to look for the "csv" file type when searching for the file to open. Does Excel automatically format the data correctly? Save your file as "partner.xls."

c. Describe in your own words why you think database manufacturers use common formats to import and export data from their systems.

5. Cloud Data Transience

AVOS Buys Yahoo's Delicious (http://www.delicious.com**) . . .**

Delicious, Yahoo's poorly named online bookmarking application, has a stagnant but loyal customer base. Delicious allows users to create an account, store their favorite URLs, mark them as private or shared, assign tags to them for easy retrieval, and access them from any computer or mobile device. This utility makes the standard browser-based, hierarchically organized bookmarking approach virtually obsolete.

Yahoo, however, found Delicious to be an unprofitable distraction from its core business and decided to sell it off to AVOS, an Internet start-up by Chad Hurley and Steve Chen, YouTube's founders.

After the big announcement, Delicious sent its users an e-mail explaining that to keep their accounts, they must agree to the transition and accept both AVOS's new privacy policies and its terms of service. Those who fail to agree will lose their accounts and data. Fortunately, Delicious also allows users to download a copy of all of their bookmarks, although without the tag functionality they're pretty useless.

a. What types of data do people maintain online for their personal use? Make a list.

b. Can you transfer your personal notes from MySpace to a new Facebook? What difficulties would you encounter?

c. What are the advantages to keeping data online?

d. What are the disadvantages to keeping data online?

Beyond Street Smarts: Data-Driven Crime Fighting

On a Saturday afternoon last summer, Mark Rasch took his son to his baseball game at a park in Georgetown, Maryland. The ballpark is located in an area that has zone parking with a two-hour limit. Rasch was forced to park in a spot that was a bit of a hike from the ball field. He later eyed an opening closer to the park and moved his car there.

The game ended, Rasch packed up, and was ready to pull away when he noticed a parking enforcement officer writing tickets. "I'm OK, right?" he asked, assuming that because he had moved his car she wouldn't know he'd been parked in the zone longer than two hours.

Wrong. The officer not only knew that he had moved his car, but also when and how long he'd been parked within the zone. Fortunately, she didn't write him a ticket, as he was about to pull out. But the encounter left Rasch, who is a lawyer and a cyber-security consultant, a little spooked at the realization of just how much information law enforcement is generating.

If there was a time when law-enforcement agencies suffered from an information deficit, it's passed. Of the more than 18,000 law-enforcement agencies across the United States, the vast majority has some form of technology for collecting crime-related data in digital form. The biggest city agencies have sophisticated data warehouses, and even the most provincial are database savvy.

So it's not surprising that law-enforcement and criminal justice agencies are running into the same data-related problems that CIOs have been experiencing for years: ensuring data quality and accessibility, developing and enforcing standards for interoperability, and exploiting those digital resources in the most effective manner.

The era of data-driven law enforcement began in the early 1990s in New York City. It was there that police chief William Bratton sought to impress newly elected mayor Rudolph Giuliani with a radical approach to policing that came to be known as CompStat. CompStat put an emphasis on leveraging data—accurate, detailed, and timely—to optimize police work.

"Police departments are powerful collectors of data," says Michael Berkow, president of Altegrity Security Consulting, a newly launched division of security firm Altegrity. Before joining ASC last month, Berkow was chief of the Savannah-Chatham police department, and before that he was second-in-command to Bratton in Los Angeles after Bratton left New York to be chief of the LAPD.

Police departments were motivated to implement or upgrade IT systems by the Y2K frenzy, Berkow says. "By 2000–2001, everybody had some level of digital information," he says. That and CompStat led to a movement known by the initials ILP, which stand for "information-led policing" or, according to some, "intelligence-led policing."

The concept is simple: Leverage data to help position limited police resources where they can do the most good. It's an effort to be more proactive, to "change the environment," Berkow says, from the reactive, response-oriented methods of the past.

To a great extent, data are about the context of criminal behavior. "We know that the same small group of criminals is responsible for a disproportionate amount of crime," says Berkow. Police refer to that group as PPOs: persistent prolific offenders. Past criminal behavior, such as domestic violence, can be a strong indicator of potential future problems. When Berkow was chief in Savannah, his department went through data on recent homicide cases and noticed an interesting data point: Of 20-some arrests for homicide, 18 of those people had prior arrests for possession of firearms. "We started this very detailed review of every aspect of our gun arrests," he says.

Law-enforcement officials often refer to the need for "actionable information." One of the first ways police agencies used incident-report data in digital form was in conjunction with geographical information systems, in support of what's known as electronic crime mapping, or hot-spot analysis.

Police in the city of Edmonton, Alberta, brought in data analysis technology from business intelligence vendor Cognos (now part of IBM) a few years ago. The first project police officials concentrated on was using the reporting tool in conjunction with a new geographic-based resource deployment model being implemented by the agency. "Our business analytics reports became a key component of how we deployed policemen around the city," says John Warden, staff sergeant in the business performance section of the Edmonton Police Service.

Now the agency is using the data to plot criminal activity according to both geographic area and comparative history. "We're really delving into those analytics in terms of place and time," says Warden. The holy grail of information-led policing is what's referred to as predictive policing: being able to predict where and when crimes may occur.

That's where Chicago wants to go. The Chicago PD operates what Jonathan Lewin, commander of information services, refers to as "the largest police transaction database in the United States." Costing $35 million, Chicago's Citizen and Law Enforcement Analysis and Reporting (CLEAR) system processes "all the arrests for all the departments in Cook county—about 120—in real time," Lewin says, and 450 local, state, and federal law enforcement agencies have query access to it. Lewin's IT shop has about 100 staffers and employs between 10 and 20 contract workers from Oracle, whose database technology the system is based on.

Chicago PD is working with the Illinois Institute of Technology (IIT), by way of a $200,000 grant from the National Institute of Justice, on an "initial exploration" of a predictive policing model. The grant was awarded partly on the basis of work done by Dr. Miles Wernick of IIT in the area of medical imaging and pattern recognition, and the project involves exploring "nontraditional disciplines" and how they might apply to crime projection. "We're going to be using all the data in the CLEAR system," Lewin says, including arrests, incidents, calls for service, street-gang activity, as well as weather data and community concerns such as reports of nonworking streetlights. "This model will seek to use all these variables in attempting to model future patterns of criminal activity," he says.

SPSS is a name often associated with predictive policing. The statistical analysis software developer, recently acquired by IBM, has customer histories that tout the success of its tools in the criminal justice environment, such as the Memphis, Tennessee, police force, which SPSS says reduced robberies by 80 percent by identifying a particular "hot spot" and proactively deploying resources there.

But can software really predict crime? "It's not a binary yes or no; it's more of an assessment of risk—how probable something is," says Bill Haffey, technical director for the public sector at SPSS.

The private sector is also doing its part. CargoNet, the first-ever national database of truck theft information, is a joint project from insurance data provider ISO and the National Insurance Crime Bureau (NICB). CargoNet will collect up to 257 fields of data, detailing such things as the destination, plate number, and carrier; the time, date, and location of the theft; as well as serial numbers and other identifying details on the stolen goods. Refreshed several times per day, CargoNet is expected to track more than 10,000 events per year, driving both a national alerting system and a corresponding truck-stop watch program.

Truck theft happens mostly on weekends, and it's rife around the Los Angeles basin, Atlanta, Miami, Dallas/Ft. Worth, and Memphis, Tennessee. Trucks and trailers typically slip away in the dark of night from truck stops, rest areas, distribution centers, and transfer points. The goods most often hit are consumer electronics, food, wine and spirits, clothing, and other items easily sold on the street.

These historical patterns are well known, but cops on the beat need up-to-the-minute information on the latest truck stops and distribution centers hit, the time of day perpetrators strike, and the type of goods stolen. Carriers and manufacturers want fresh, nationwide information so they can change the timing of deliveries and avoid specific truck stops and routes. Insurers want a single source of data so they can get a better gauge risk and bring the problem under control nationwide.

All this collecting, warehousing, and mining crime-related data begs the question: How much is too much? The Georgetown incident still bothers Rasch. "What it meant was that D.C. was keeping a database of people who are legally parked," says Rasch, which, from a privacy standpoint, is "more intrusive than chalking the tires."

Pertinent questions include: How long do they hold on to that data? And with whom do they share it? It's an important discussion to have, both in terms of privacy and effective police methods. After all, as Rasch points out, it was a parking ticket that led to the arrest of serial killer Son of Sam.

SOURCE: John Soat, "Beyond Street Smarts," *InformationWeek*, November 16, 2009, and Doug Henschen, "National Database Tracks Truck Thefts," *InformationWeek*, January 26, 2010.

▼ CASE STUDY QUESTIONS

1. What are some of the most important benefits derived by the law-enforcement agencies mentioned in the case? How do these technologies allow them to better fight crime? Provide several examples.

2. How are the data-related issues faced by law enforcement similar to those that could be found in companies? How are they different? Where do these problems come from? Explain.

3. Imagine that you had access to the same crime-related information as that managed by police departments. How would you analyze this information, and what actions would you take as a result?

▼ REAL WORLD ACTIVITIES

1. The case discusses many issues related to data quality, sharing, and accessibility that are faced by both government bodies and for-profit organizations. Go online and research how these issues manifest themselves in companies, as well as some of approaches used to manage them. Would those issues apply to police departments? Prepare a report to share your findings.

2. The case discusses the large volume of very detailed information collected daily by law-enforcement agencies. Knowing this, how comfortable do you feel about the storing and sharing of that data? What policies would you put in place to assuage some of those concerns? Break into small groups with your classmates to discuss these issues and arrive at some recommendations.

CASE 2

Duke University Health System, Beth Israel Deaconess Medical Center, and Others: Medical IT Is Getting Personal

Personalized medicine brings to mind researchers doing complicated analysis of a single patient's genetic makeup, and fine-tuning medicine and other treatments to those results. But Duke University Health System is using everyday data from the electronic medical records of patients, combined with an analytics tool to personalize its approach to treating patients.

County health officials recently asked Duke how many of its patients would need priority access to the H1N1 flu vaccine. Duke used IBM's Cognos to sift through information on the more than 20 million patients in its Oracle-based clinical data repository and in an hour was able to identify about 120,000 of them with risk factors such as age, pregnancy, respiratory, and other conditions that made them vulnerable to complications from swine flu. And now that the H1N1 vaccine is available, Duke is letting those patients know that they're first in line to get it.

"We put an analytics engine on top of our clinical repository and were able to stratify by age and key illnesses millions of records, and streamline who was most at risk," says Asif Ahmed, chief information officer of diagnostics services for the Duke system, which runs three hospitals and about 100 clinics in the Raleigh/Durham, North Carolina, area and treats more than 1 million patients a year.

This is a practical example of how health care IT is being used to personalize medical care in ways that help doctors make smarter decisions and tailor treatment to an individual's needs. This evolving field covers a broad range of efforts. Beyond analytics systems like Duke's, it includes decision support tools that help doctors pick the best tests and treatments for patients, remote monitoring tools that provide close to real-time care, as well as software that helps researchers identify the best candidates to participate in trials or experimental treatments.

At Beth Israel Deaconess Medical Center in Boston, helping doctors make better treatment choices and arrive at more accurate diagnoses is a big and growing area of personalized medicine. One example is clinical support software to help its 1,600 staff and affiliated physicians choose the best radiology tests for patients.

When ordering CT scans, MRIs, X-rays, ultrasounds, and other radiology tests, doctors enter a patient's electronic

medical record number into the Anvita Health decision support system. Data from Beth Israel's records system, such as recent lab tests and allergies, are automatically loaded into the software. The doctor then adds information on the current complaint, such as symptoms, which area of the body is a concern, and the suspected diagnosis, as well as whether the person has any implants that might interfere with radiology treatment.

The software analyzes the data and rates the best tests for the patient, giving five stars for the top choices and one for the worst ones based on the risks and benefits of each. It can also recommend that the patient forgo radiological testing.

The system can catch details that might otherwise elude a doctor, such as a previous blood test indicating decreased kidney function that could mean the patient can't metabolize the dyes used in certain radiological tests. It also checks how much radiation the patient has already been exposed to.

"Excessive radiation can cause second malignancies," says Dr. Richard Parker, medical director of Beth Israel's physician organization. "The system takes that into account when ordering a scan." For instance, the software might point out that a patient suspected of having pneumonia has enough symptoms and clinical indicators to make that the most likely diagnosis, and that treating the patient for it would be better than exposing him or her to a chest X-ray.

During the three years that the hospital system has used the Anvita software, it has cut out about 5 percent of tests as unnecessary or inappropriate, Parker says.

Beth Israel launched a related pilot project six months ago to analyze a doctor's thought processes when ordering radiology tests. When a doctor orders a test, the system asks what diagnosis the physician is leaning toward, with what percentage of certainty. After the test, the system follows up with an e-mail asking the doctor whether the test confirmed the original diagnosis. The study aims at gaining insight into how doctors decide which tests to use, and learning in which situations doctors are most likely to prescribe the wrong test for a given set of symptoms.

Information technology isn't just helping doctors choose the right test for a patient; it's also making more personalized medical tests possible. For example, diagnostic testing services provider Quest Diagnostics and Vermillion, a molecular diagnostic test developer, have developed a test to assess the likelihood that women diagnosed with pelvic masses have ovarian cancer as opposed to benign tumors. The test is helping those women who are most at risk for cancer be referred to specialists faster.

Many of the newest personalized medicine efforts are focused on giving analytics and decision support tools to doctors and other clinicians. But medical researchers are also still focused on the more complex efforts to analyze genomic data and use the results to create individualized treatments that doctors will use in the future.

One such initiative is Cancer Biomedical Informatics Grid, or caBig, a biomedical informatics network that the National Cancer Institute launched in 2004 with the mission of developing more personalized cancer treatments and getting them into the hands of doctors faster.

Researchers at the about 100 academic and community-based cancer centers that make up caBig use the network to share data and research results. They can make use of the data in analytics, data mining, decision support, and other software tools. Members are using the network's data and software today to identify the best patients to participate in clinical trials of experimental cancer treatments.

Multiple myeloma, a cancer that strikes white blood cells and eventually bone marrow, can be difficult to treat. Now the Dana-Farber Cancer Institute in Boston is harnessing the dual power of business intelligence and Web 2.0-based scientific search tools to gather complex, scattered data to better treat patients and work toward a cure for this formidable disease.

Dana-Farber is a treatment, research, and teaching facility affiliated with Harvard Medical School. Its physicians and researchers regularly slog through complex calculations to find connections between data gleaned from tumor biopsies and other clinical samples and the vast genetic research housed within the organization or spread among three massive public-domain databases.

Dana-Farber officials are working to leverage grant money and other resources to blend data warehousing capabilities with Web-based data collection tools, since vital connections between patient samples and analytical data will almost certainly prove the crux of both effective patient treatment and any potential breakthroughs tied to the disease, according to researchers.

To make the hunt for precious genetic information easier, Dana-Farber officials have stitched together a system that wraps in Oracle's Healthcare Transaction Base, a service-oriented architecture that supports the medical industry's HL7 standard for the electronic exchange of clinical data.

Increased use of e-medical records should make more patient data available for research, says Ken Buetow, director of the center of bioinformatics and IT at the National Cancer Institute. Ultimately, Buetow expects the caBig network, combined with doctors' growing use of electronic data, will shorten the time it takes for research findings to show up as clinical treatments. "We think this could be one of those moments for a big shift," he says.

John Glaser, chief information officer at Partners Healthcare, which operates several Boston-area hospitals, including Massachusetts General and Brigham and Women's, sees that shift coming. As the use of EMRs become more pervasive and the amount of digitized clinical data increases, it will be easier to provide patients with more personalized care, says Glaser, who also is an adviser on the Health IT Policy Committee at the U.S. Department of Health and Human Services. EMRs make data on patients easier to search and analyze. Doctors using them are also more likely to use decision support tools, Glaser says.

"Science is moving rapidly," he says, and health IT helps capture and disseminate to doctors perspectives and research findings that are impossible for even the most diligent physicians to keep up with.

Once the use of EMRs is standard practice, the federal government is likely to put greater emphasis on personalized medicine initiatives, Glaser predicts. In the future, health care providers could be rewarded in terms of patient outcomes, and personalized medical treatments are one of the most likely ways to improve outcomes and improve health care across the board.

SOURCE: Marianne Kolbasuk McGee, "Medical IT Gets Personal," *InformationWeek*, November 16, 2009, and Jennifer McAdams, "Better BI: Dana-Farber Cancer Institute," *Computerworld*, September 1, 2008.

▼ CASE STUDY QUESTIONS

1. What are the benefits that result from implementing the technologies described in the case? How are those different for hospitals, doctors, insurance companies, and patients? Provide examples of each from the case.
2. Many of the technologies described in the case require access to large volumes of data in order to be effective. At the same time, there are privacy considerations involved in the compiling and sharing of such data. How do you balance those?
3. What other industries that manage large volumes of data could benefit from an approach to technology similar to the one described in the case? Develop at least one example with sample applications.

▼ REAL WORLD ACTIVITIES

1. The legal and regulatory environment of the health care industry has changed significantly in recent times. How does this affect technology development and implementation in these organizations? Go online and research new uses of information technology in health care motivated by these developments. Prepare a presentation to share your findings.

2. Some of the technologies described in the case verify the diagnostics made by doctors and can sometimes make their own recommendations. Does this improve the quality of care, or are these organizations putting too much faith in a computer algorithm that did not attend medical school? Break into small groups to discuss this, and provide some recommendations about what organizations should do before deploying these technologies in the field, if anything.

chapter 6

TELECOMMUNICATIONS AND NETWORKS

INFORMATION SYSTEMS

INFORMATION TECHNOLOGIES

CHAPTER HIGHLIGHTS

The Networked Enterprise

Networking the Organization
The Concept of a Network

REAL WORLD CHALLENGE: Adena Health System and Cherokee Health Systems—The Challenges of Medicine in the Rural United States

Trends in Telecommunications
The Business Value of Telecommunications Networks
The Internet Revolution
The Role of Intranets
The Role of Extranets

Telecommunications Network Alternatives

Telecommunications Alternatives
A Telecommunications Network Model
Types of Telecommunications Networks
Digital and Analog Signals
Telecommunications Media
Wired Technologies
Wireless Technologies
Telecommunications Processors
Telecommunications Software
Network Topologies
Network Architectures and Protocols
Bandwidth Alternatives
Switching Alternatives
Network Interoperability

REAL WORLD SOLUTION: Adena Health System and Cherokee Health Systems—Reaching Far Away with the Help of Technology

REAL WORLD CASE: DLA Piper, MetLife, PepsiCo, and Others: Telepresence Is Finally Coming of Age

REAL WORLD CASE: Brain Saving Technologies Inc. and the T-Health Institute: Medicine through Videoconferencing

LEARNING OBJECTIVES

6-1 Understand the concept of a network.

6-2 Apply Metcalfe's law in understanding the value of a network.

6-3 Identify several major developments and trends in the industries, technologies, and business applications of telecommunications and Internet technologies.

6-4 Provide examples of the business value of Internet, intranet, and extranet applications.

6-5 Identify the basic components, functions, and types of telecommunications networks used in business.

6-6 Explain the functions of major components of telecommunications network hardware, software, media, and services.

6-7 Explain the concept of client/server networking.

6-8 Understand the two forms of peer-to-peer networking.

6-9 Explain the difference between digital and analog signals.

6-10 Identify the various transmission media and topologies used in telecommunications networks.

6-11 Understand the fundamentals of wireless network technologies.

6-12 Explain the concepts behind TCP/IP.

6-13 Understand the seven layers of the OSI network model.

The Networked Enterprise

When computers are networked, two industries—computing and communications—converge, and the result is vastly more than the sum of the parts. Suddenly, computing applications become available for business-to-business coordination and commerce, and for small as well as large organizations. The global Internet creates a public place without geographic boundaries—cyberspace—where ordinary citizens can interact, publish their ideas, and engage in the purchase of goods and services. In short, the impact of both computing and communications on our society and organizational structures is greatly magnified.

NETWORKING THE ORGANIZATION

Telecommunications and network technologies are revolutionizing business and society. Businesses have become networked enterprises. The Internet, the Web, and intranets and extranets are networking business processes and employees together and connecting them to their customers, suppliers, and other business stakeholders. Companies and workgroups can thus collaborate more creatively, manage their business operations and resources more effectively, and compete successfully in today's fast-changing global economy. This chapter presents the telecommunications and network foundations for these developments. In real estate, the mantra is "location, location, location." In business, the mantra is "connect, connect, connect!"

Read the Real World Challenge about the problems that health systems face when providing care in rural areas of the United States. See Figure 6.1.

THE CONCEPT OF A NETWORK

LO 6-1
LO 6-2

Because of our focus on information systems and technologies, it is easy for us to think of networks in terms of connected computers. For a full understanding of the value of connecting computers, however, it is important to understand the concept of a network in its broader sense.

By definition, the term **network** means *an interconnected or interrelated chain, group, or system.* Using this definition, we can begin to identify all kinds of networks: a chain of hotels; the road system; the names in a person's address book or PDA; the railroad system; the members of a church, club, or organization; your Facebook page. The examples of networks in our world are virtually endless, and computer networks, though both valuable and powerful, are just one example of the concept.

The concept of networks can be expressed as a mathematical formula that calculates the number of possible connections or interactions in a one-way communication environment: $N(N - 1)$, or $N^2 - N$. In the formula, N refers to the number of *nodes* (points of connection) on the network. If only a few nodes exist on a network, the number of possible connections is quite small. Using the formula, we see that three nodes result in only 6 possible connections: $(3 \times 3 - 3 = 6)$. A network of 10 nodes results in a somewhat larger number—90 connections $(10 \times 10 - 10 = 90)$. It's when a large number of nodes is connected that the possible number of connections grows to significant proportions. A network with 100 nodes has 9,900 possible connections, and a network with 1,000 nodes has 999,000 possible connections. This type of mathematical growth is called *exponential.* This term just means that the growth in number of connections is many times greater than the number of nodes. Adding only one more node to a network makes the number of connections grow many times greater. Think of the effect of adding a new entry and exit ramp on a highway system that connects 30,000 cities and towns. How many more connections does that one new ramp create? Maybe more relevant is the effect of adding one additional person as a friend to your Facebook, MySpace, or Plaxo account. If you have 100 unique friends who each have 100 unique friends and the new friend has 100 unique friends—well, you get the picture. That's what the next section is all about.

real world CHALLENGE

Adena Health System and Cherokee Health Systems— The Challenges of Medicine in the Rural United States

Across countries and cultures, there is at least one thing that all parents worry about: the health and well-being of their children. It is at those very special—and stressful—moments, such as the birth of a baby, or when a small child is sick, when all parents want or need access to the best possible health care for their children. Depending on where they live, however, that care may be dozens or even hundreds of miles away. This is the reality today for a lot of people living in the rural United States.

Consider the case of Adena Health System, an independent, nonprofit health group employing more than 2,000 people in southern Ohio. The group includes the Adena Regional Medical Center in Chillicothe, Ohio, and several smaller clinics in the surrounding areas. Adena has been providing health services since 1895—for 116 years, to be exact. Its story begins with the derailment and subsequent crash of a passenger train a few miles west of Adena's current location; injured passengers had to be taken into private homes because the town had no medical facilities of any kind. The Emergency Hospital was opened, and continued growth during the 20th century led to the opening and expansion of new facilities. Today, Adena provides services to 650,000 people in 13 different counties in southern Ohio, with the Adena Regional Medical Center serving as

the primary hospital facility for 10 of them. In fact, the majority of the residents of those counties have been born in the Adena Regional Medical Center in one or another of the facilities the center has occupied throughout its existence.

Although the medical center has long provided quality care for mothers and newborns since its founding, the hospital has generally had limited access to physicians specialized in neonatal critical care because of its location and the higher wages typically attached to those services. As a result, when complications arise during childbirth—and they always do every now and then, even with the best prenatal care—doctors at Adena Regional Medical Center have little choice but to refer and transfer those newborns requiring specialized care to Nationwide Children's Hospital in Columbus, about 70 miles north of Chillicothe. That means separating babies from their mothers and placing significant strain, both emotional and financial, on parents and patients alike. Adena serves some of the poorest areas in Ohio, and the cost of traveling and staying in Columbus for several days at a time can represent a significant expenditure for many of those families.

"The last thing you want to do after birth is separate the family," says Rachel Brown, MD, attending neonatologist with Nationwide Children's Hospital. "We also want to avoid bringing in patients who are going to be here for a quick, three- to four-day stay," says Brown. "We want to make sure we have beds available for the patients who are going to be here for a longer period, who really need to come."

Cherokee Health Systems, headquartered in Knoxville, Tennessee, faces a similar challenge. Begun in 1960 as a mental health office in Morristown, the organization now operates out of 22 different offices in the eastern part of the state, employs more than 500 professionals, and provides health services to more than 60,000 residents every year. This part of the state is a challenging location for the provision of medical services, and around there Cherokee is known as the place that will care for anyone, regardless of ability to pay. East Tennessee is a mountainous region where a large proportion of residents have low incomes and lack health insurance. The presence of several tourist attractions in the area has the detrimental effect of fostering a large population of predominantly hourly employees with limited flexibility, both in scheduling and finances, to provide adequate health care for their children.

FIGURE 6.1

The provision of quality health care everywhere presents a major challenge for many patients and providers and provides opportunities to leverage technology.

SOURCE: Getty Images/Image Source.

In the Sevier County School System, where the Great Smoky Mountains National Park is located, about 50 percent of the children qualify for free or reduced cost lunches, with some schools reaching more than 80 percent of their student population. For their parents, taking a sick child to the doctor, who may be located more than an hour away, means lost income and concerns about job stability if too many days are missed. And even if they can take their children to the doctor, pediatric services, particularly specialized ones, are expensive. As a result of all of these issues, many children in the area do not have regular access to quality health care, which is clearly an undesirable situation for everyone involved. The Sevier County School System explored the possibility of providing low-cost school clinics staffed with a nurse practitioner, with the dual goal of keeping parents at their jobs—a must for hourly employees for whom missed time means lost wages—and children at school. However, even though the school district includes 17 elementary and middle schools with a population of more than 10,000 students, it did not have the financial resources to staff clinics at all of its locations, and it thus turned to Cherokee Health Systems for help.

Though slightly different, these two health organizations face a similar challenge: finding the best way to provide health services to underserved populations in rural areas of the country. Because of the nature of the populations served, funding for any new health care model is likely to be a major constraint. The unique billing and claim processes of the health care industry, involving multiple actors—parents, medical facilities, providers, insurance companies, and state governments—will also need to be accommodated. In these two cases, however, the services provided by Adena and Cherokee Health Systems are not one of many alternatives that those who live in large cities can choose; rather, they are the only option for the residents of those areas. The central challenge, then, is how to bring large-hospital resources and specialized expertise to those areas where they are most sorely needed. However, the issue of affordable, accessible, high-quality health care for children is not limited to Sevier County, Tennessee, or to southern Ohio. Solutions are needed in rural regions throughout the world.

SOURCE: "Adena Health System," *Computerworld Honors Case Study*, www.adena.org, accessed May 23, 2011; "Cherokee Health Systems," *Computerworld Honors Case Study*; and cherokeehealthsystems.com, accessed May 23, 2011.

▼ QUESTIONS TO CONSIDER

1. What are some of the different ways in which the needed services could be provided? What are the advantages and disadvantages of each? Which resources will be required in each case?
2. What will be the key issues that will define the success of any solution that is implemented? Are those technological or organizational in nature?
3. What are the shared characteristics of the problems that both organizations face? That is, how are the challenges that they face structurally similar?

Metcalfe's Law

Robert Metcalfe founded 3Com Corp. and designed the Ethernet protocol for computer networks. He used his understanding of the concept of networks to express their exponential growth in terms of potential business value. *Metcalfe's law* states that *the usefulness, or utility, of a network equals the square of the number of users*. In other words, every time you add a new user to a network, the value of that network, in terms of potential connections among its members, exactly doubles!

Metcalfe's law becomes easy to understand if you think of a common piece of technology we all use every day: the telephone. The telephone is of very limited use if only you and your best friend have one. If a whole town is on the system, it becomes much more useful. If the whole world is wired, the utility of the system is phenomenal. Add the number of wireless telephone connections, and you have a massive potential for value. To reach this value, however, many people had to have access to a telephone—and they had to have used it. In other words, telephone use had to reach a *critical mass* of users. So it is with any technology.

Until a critical mass of users is reached, a change in technology affects only the technology. Once critical mass is attained, however, social, political, and economic systems change. The same is true of digital network technologies. Consider the Internet. It reached critical mass in 1993, when there were roughly 2.5 million host computers on the network; by November 1997, the vast network contained an estimated 25 million host computers. According to Internet World Stats, the number of users on the Internet in April 2011 topped 1.96 billion! More important, that represents only slightly more than 28 percent of the estimated world population. With computing costs continuing to drop rapidly (remember Moore's law from Chapter 3) and the Internet growing exponentially (Metcalfe's law), we can expect to see more and more value—conceivably for less cost—virtually every time we log on. The Internet is kind of a big deal, and it's getting bigger, even as you read this.

TRENDS IN TELECOMMUNICATIONS
LO 6-3

Telecommunications is the exchange of information in any form (voice, data, text, images, audio, video) over networks. The Internet is the most widely visible form of telecommunications in your daily life. Early telecommunications networks did not use computers to route traffic and, as such, were much slower than today's computer-based networks. Major trends occurring in the field of telecommunications have a significant impact on management decisions in this area. You should make yourself aware of major trends in telecommunications industries, technologies, and applications that significantly increase the decision alternatives confronting business managers and professionals. See Figure 6.2.

Industry Trends

The competitive arena for telecommunications service has changed dramatically in recent years. The telecommunications industry has changed from government-regulated monopolies to a deregulated market with fiercely competitive suppliers of telecommunications services. Numerous companies now offer businesses and consumers a choice of everything from local and global telephone services to communications satellite channels, mobile radio, cable television, cellular phone services, and Internet access. See Figure 6.3.

The explosive growth of the Internet and the World Wide Web has spawned a host of new telecommunications products, services, and providers. Driving and responding to this growth, business firms have dramatically increased their use of the Internet and the Web for electronic commerce and collaboration. Thus, the service and vendor options available to meet a company's telecommunications needs have increased significantly, as have a business manager's decision-making alternatives.

Technology Trends

Open systems with unrestricted connectivity, using ***Internet networking technologies*** as their technology platform, are today's primary telecommunications technology

FIGURE 6.2
Major trends in business telecommunications.

Industry trends — Toward more competitive vendors, carriers, alliances, and network services, accelerated by deregulation and the growth of the Internet and the World Wide Web.

Technology trends — Toward extensive use of Internet, digital fiber-optic, and wireless technologies to create high-speed local and global internetworks for voice, data, images, audio, and videocommunications.

Application trends — Toward the pervasive use of the Internet, enterprise intranets, and interorganizational extranets to support electronic business and commerce, enterprise collaboration, and strategic advantage in local and global markets.

drivers. Web browser suites, HTML Web page editors, Internet and intranet servers and network management software, TCP/IP Internet networking products, and network security firewalls are just a few examples. These technologies are being applied in Internet, intranet, and extranet applications, especially those for electronic commerce and collaboration. This trend has reinforced previous industry and technical moves toward building client/server networks based on an open-systems architecture.

Open systems are information systems that use common standards for hardware, software, applications, and networking. Open systems, like the Internet and corporate intranets and extranets, create a computing environment that is open to easy access by end users and their networked computer systems. Open systems provide greater connectivity, that is, the ability of networked computers and other devices to access and communicate with one another easily and share information. Any open-systems architecture also provides a high degree of network interoperability. Open systems enable

FIGURE 6.3
The spectrum of telecommunications-based services available today.

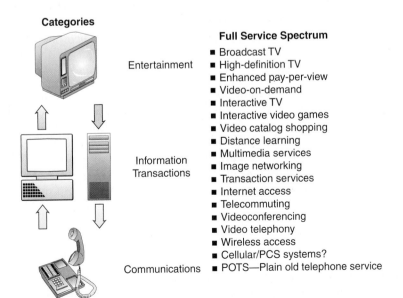

Categories

Entertainment

Information Transactions

Communications

Full Service Spectrum

- Broadcast TV
- High-definition TV
- Enhanced pay-per-view
- Video-on-demand
- Interactive TV
- Interactive video games
- Video catalog shopping
- Distance learning
- Multimedia services
- Image networking
- Transaction services
- Internet access
- Telecommuting
- Videoconferencing
- Video telephony
- Wireless access
- Cellular/PCS systems?
- POTS—Plain old telephone service

the many different activities of end users, using the different varieties of computer systems, software packages, and databases provided by a variety of interconnected networks. Frequently, software known as *middleware* may be used to help diverse systems work together.

Middleware is a general term for any programming that serves to glue together or mediate between two separate, and usually already existing, programs. A common application of middleware is to allow programs written for access to a particular database (e.g., DB2) to access other databases (e.g., Oracle) without the need for custom coding.

Middleware is commonly known as the plumbing of an information system because it routes data and information transparently between different back-end data sources and end-user applications. It's not very interesting to look at—it usually doesn't have much, if any, visible "front end" of its own—but it is an essential component of any IT infrastructure because it allows disparate systems to be joined together in a common framework. More recently, open-systems standards have become so prevalent that the need for middleware is diminishing. Still, many of the networks in place have been there for a long, long time, and scrapping them to update to the latest and greatest can be a significant cost. As such, many organizations can still make a business case for middleware rather than for a brand new system.

Telecommunications is also being revolutionized by the rapid change from analog to digital network technologies. Telecommunications systems have always depended on voice-oriented analog transmission systems designed to transmit the variable electrical frequencies generated by the sound waves of the human voice. However, local and global telecommunications networks are rapidly converting to digital transmission technologies that transmit information in the form of discrete pulses, as computers do. This conversion provides (1) significantly higher transmission speeds, (2) the movement of larger amounts of information, (3) greater economy, and (4) much lower error rates than with analog systems. In addition, digital technologies allow telecommunications networks to carry multiple types of communications (data, voice, video) on the same circuits.

Another major trend in telecommunications technology is a change from reliance on copper wire–based media and land-based microwave relay systems to fiber-optic lines and cellular, communications satellite, and other *wireless technologies. Fiber-optic transmission,* which uses pulses of laser-generated light, offers significant advantages in terms of reduced size and installation effort, vastly greater communication capacity, much faster transmission speeds, and freedom from electrical interference. Satellite transmission offers significant advantages for organizations that need to transmit massive quantities of data, audio, and video over global networks, especially to isolated areas. Cellular, mobile radio, and other wireless systems are connecting cellular phones, PDAs, and other wireless appliances to the Internet and corporate networks.

Business Application Trends

The changes in telecommunications industries and technologies just mentioned are causing a significant change in the business use of telecommunications. The trend toward more vendors, services, Internet technologies, and open systems, and the rapid growth of the Internet, the World Wide Web, and corporate intranets and extranets, dramatically increases the number of feasible telecommunications applications. Thus, telecommunications networks are now playing vital and pervasive roles in Web-enabled e-business processes, e-commerce, enterprise collaboration, and other business applications that support the operations, management, and strategic objectives of both large and small business enterprises.

Internet2

We cannot leave our overview of trends in telecommunications without reiterating that the Internet sits firmly in the center of the action. Despite its importance and seemingly unexplored boundaries, we are already embarking on the next generation of the "network of networks." *Internet2* is a high-performance network that uses an entirely different infrastructure than the public Internet we know today. More than 300 universities and scientific founding institutions and 60,000 member institutions throughout the United States and the rest of the world are already part of the Internet2 network. One big misconception about Internet2 is that it's a sequel to the original Internet and will replace it someday. It never will, because it was never intended to replace the Internet. Rather, its purpose is to build a road map that can be followed during the next stage of innovation for the current Internet. The ideas being honed, such as new addressing protocols and satellite-quality streaming video, will likely be deployed to the Internet, but it might take close to 10 years before we see them.

Furthermore, the Internet2 network may never become totally open; it might remain solely in the domain of universities, research centers, and governments. To be sure, the lightning-fast technologies in use by Internet2 right now must eventually be turned over to the public Internet. For now, the Internet2 project lives for the purpose of sharing, collaborating, and trying new high-speed communication ideas—interestingly, many of the same goals that shaped the early history of today's Internet.

Most of the institutions and commercial partners on the Internet2 network are connected via *Abilene*, a network backbone that will soon support throughput of 10 gigabits per second (Gbps). Several international networks are also plugged into Abilene's infrastructure, and as the project grows, more and more networks will be able to connect to the current framework. The one common denominator among all of the Internet2 partners is their active participation in the development and testing of new applications and Internet protocols with an emphasis on research and collaboration, focusing on things such as videoconferencing, multicasting, remote applications, and new protocols that take advantage of the many opportunities megabandwidth provides. In short, Internet2 is all about high-speed telecommunications and infinite bandwidth.

To give you an idea of exactly how fast this network of the future is, an international team of researchers has already used it to set a new landspeed record. At the end of 2005, the team attained a speed of 131 gigabytes per second. That's roughly five full-length DVD-quality movies on the Internet in one second! The same team is already hard at work, attempting to break its own record.

As we are exploring new ways to gain business advantage through the Internet, a significant effort is being made to make the Internet bigger and faster. In 2011, Internet2 celebrated its 15th anniversary and has significantly expanded in breadth, speed, and storage capacity since its inception in 1996. We'll look at Internet2 again later in this chapter when we discuss Internet-addressing protocols.

What *business value* is created when a company capitalizes on the trends in telecommunications we have just identified? Use of the Internet, intranets, extranets, and other telecommunications networks can dramatically *cut costs, shorten business lead times and response times, support e-commerce, improve the collaboration of workgroups, develop online operational processes, share resources, lock in customers and suppliers,* and *develop new products and services.* These benefits make applications of telecommunications more strategic and vital for businesses that must increasingly find new ways to compete in both domestic and global markets.

THE BUSINESS VALUE OF TELECOMMUNICATIONS NETWORKS

LO 6-4

Figure 6.4 illustrates how telecommunications-based business applications can help a company overcome geographic, time, cost, and structural barriers to business success. Note the examples of the business value of these four strategic capabilities of telecommunications networks. This figure emphasizes how several online business applications can help a firm capture and provide information quickly to end users at remote geographic locations at reduced costs, as well as support its strategic organizational objectives.

For example, traveling salespeople and those at regional sales offices can use the Internet, extranets, and other networks to transmit customer orders from their laptops

Strategic Capabilities	Online Business Examples	Business Value
Overcome geographic barriers: Capture information about business transactions from remote locations.	Use the Internet and extranets to transmit customer orders from traveling salespeople to a corporate data center for order processing and inventory control.	Provide better customer service by reducing delay in filling orders and improve cash flow by speeding up the billing of customers.
Overcome time barriers: Provide information to remote locations immediately after it is requested.	Credit authorization at the point of sale using online POS networks.	Credit inquiries can be made and answered in seconds.
Overcome cost barriers: Reduce the cost of more traditional means of communication.	Desktop videoconferencing between a company and its business partners using the Internet, intranets, and extranets.	Reduce expensive business trips; allow customers, suppliers, and employees to collaborate, thus improving the quality of decisions reached.
Overcome structural barriers: Support linkages for competitive advantage.	Business-to-business electronic commerce Web sites for transactions with suppliers and customers using the Internet and extranets.	Fast, convenient services lock in customers and suppliers.

FIGURE 6.4

Examples of the business value of business applications of telecommunications networks.

or desktop PCs, thus breaking geographic barriers. Point-of-sale terminals and an online sales transaction processing network can break time barriers by supporting immediate credit authorization and sales processing. Teleconferencing can be used to cut costs by reducing the need for expensive business trips, allowing customers, suppliers, and employees to participate in meetings and collaborate on joint projects without traveling.

Finally, business-to-business (B2B) Web sites are used by businesses to establish strategic relationships with their customers and suppliers by making business transactions fast, convenient, and tailored to the needs of the business partners involved.

THE INTERNET REVOLUTION

The explosive growth of the Internet is a revolutionary phenomenon in computing and telecommunications. The Internet has become the largest and most important network of networks today and has evolved into a global *information superhighway*. We can think of the Internet as a network made up of millions of smaller private networks, each with the ability to operate independent of, or in harmony with, all the other millions of networks connected to the Internet. When this network of networks began to grow in December 1991, it had about 10 servers. In January 2004, the Internet was estimated to have more than 46 million connected servers with a sustained growth rate in excess of 1 million servers per month. In January 2007, the Internet was estimated to have more than 1 billion users with Web sites in 34 languages from English to Icelandic. Now that is some growth! Today, the Internet handles 294 billion e-mails per day, has 255 million Web sites (with 10 percent of that occurring in 2010), and is estimated to have more than 75 million servers in its network. I could write more about it, but it would just get bigger.

The Internet is constantly expanding as more and more businesses and other organizations and their users, computers, and networks join its global Web. Thousands of business, educational, and research networks now connect millions of computer systems and users in more than 200 countries. Internet users projected for 2011 topped the 2 billion user mark, which still only represents approximately one-third of the worldwide population. Apply these numbers to Metcalfe's law, and you can see that the number of possible connections is extraordinary.

The Net doesn't have a central computer system or telecommunications center. There are, however, 13 servers called *root servers* that are used to handle the bulk of the routing of traffic from one computer to another. Each message sent has a unique address code, so any Internet server in the network can forward it to its destination. In addition, the Internet does not have a headquarters or governing body. International advisory and standards groups of individual and corporate members, such as the Internet

Society (www.isoc.org) and the World Wide Web Consortium (www.w3.org), promote use of the Internet and the development of new communications standards. These common standards are the key to the free flow of messages among the widely different computers and networks of the many organizations and *Internet service providers* (ISPs) in the system.

Internet Service Providers

One of the unique aspects of the Internet is that nobody really owns it. Anyone who can access the Internet can use it and the services it offers. Because the Internet cannot be accessed directly by individuals, we need to use the services of a company that specializes in providing easy access. An ISP, or **Internet service provider**, is a company that provides access to the Internet to individuals and organizations. For a monthly fee, the service provider gives you a software package, user name, password, and access phone number or access protocol. With this information (and some specialized hardware), you can then log onto the Internet, browse the World Wide Web, and send and receive e-mail.

In addition to serving individuals, ISPs serve large companies, providing a direct connection from the company's networks to the Internet. These ISPs themselves are connected to one another through *network access points*. Through these connections, one ISP can easily connect to another ISP to obtain information about the address of a Web site or user node.

Internet Applications

The most popular Internet applications are e-mail, instant messaging, browsing the sites on the World Wide Web, and participating in *newsgroups* and *chat rooms*. Internet e-mail messages usually arrive in seconds or within a few minutes anywhere in the world and can take the form of data, text, fax, and video files. Internet browser software like Internet Explorer, Mozilla Firefox, or Google Chrome enables millions of users to surf the Web by clicking their way to the multimedia information resources stored on the hyperlinked pages of businesses, government, and other Web sites. Web sites offer information and entertainment and are the launch sites for online transactions between businesses and their suppliers and customers. As we will discuss in Chapter 9, e-commerce Web sites offer all manner of products and services via online retailers, wholesalers, service providers, and online auctions. See Figure 6.5.

FIGURE 6.5

Popular uses of the Internet.

- **Surf.** Point-and-click your way to thousands of hyperlinked Web sites and resources for multimedia information, entertainment, or electronic commerce.

- **e-Mail.** Use e-mail and instant messaging to exchange messages with colleagues, friends, and other Internet users.

- **Discuss.** Participate in discussion forums of special-interest newsgroups, or hold real-time text conversations in Web site chat rooms.

- **Publish.** Post your opinion, subject matter, or creative work to a Web site or Weblog for others to read.

- **Buy and Sell.** Buy and sell practically anything via e-commerce retailers, wholesalers, service providers, and online auctions.

- **Download.** Transfer data files, software, reports, articles, pictures, music, videos, and other types of files to your computer system.

- **Compute.** Log onto and use thousands of Internet computer systems around the world.

- **Connect.** Find out what friends, acquaintances, and business associates are up to.

- **Other Uses.** Make long-distance phone calls, hold desktop videoconferences, listen to radio programs, watch television, play video games, explore virtual worlds, and so forth.

The Internet provides electronic discussion forums and bulletin board systems formed and managed by thousands of special-interest newsgroups. You can participate in discussions or post messages on a myriad of topics for other users with the same interests. Other popular applications include downloading software and information files and accessing databases provided by a variety of business, government, and other organizations. You can conduct online searches for information on Web sites in a variety of ways by using search sites and search engines such as Yahoo!, Google, and Fast Search. Logging on to other computers on the Internet and holding real-time conversations with other Internet users in *chat rooms* are also popular uses of the Internet.

Telepresence: GE Does Training and Meetings Face-to-Face, but Virtually

GE's former CEO and Chairman Jack Welch famously said "The desire, and the ability, of an organization to continuously learn from any source, anywhere, and to rapidly convert this learning into action, is its ultimate competitive advantage." Although he is now retired, the emphasis on education and training that Welch instilled into General Electric—one of the largest and most valuable companies in the world—still exists today, as strong as ever. GE invests about $1.2 billion every year in training, centered on its Crotonville, New York, facility, aptly dedicated to Jack Welch in commemoration of his retirement. Although some types of training can be done individually with prepared materials delivered through computers (i.e., computer-based training), there is an important aspect of training and shared organizational culture that requires people to meet other people in the process. In 2005, however, as part of the effort to reduce its carbon footprint, GE embarked on a project to reduce corporate travel.

The big challenge, then, was how to keep facilitating meetings and training while at the same time limiting the need for people to travel to Crotonville. In addition, flying executives around for meetings and training was quite expensive. GE estimates that an executive flying on a round trip to Asia for a two-hour meeting would cost $30,000, two days lost in transit, and almost 7,000 pounds of carbon dioxide emissions. With the dual goals of replicating face-to-face meetings while at the same time saving money and limiting the environmental impacts of training, GE choose to pilot telepresence technology from Cisco. This technology uses high-definition video to create lifelike meetings. Although it is not strictly part of the technology, meeting rooms are often identically set up across the different locations—same wall color, same furniture, and so forth—to create the impression that all participants are sitting in the same room, when they might be two continents away.

Although the typical telepresence room seats about 10 or 15 people in each location, GE chose to implement the technology in a large conference room with stadium-style seating and capacity for 60. "This Telepresence room is the first of its kind," says Tim Hennen, senior vice president of AV integration with IVCi, the company that implements the technology. "Never before has an integrated Telepresence room been created that can deliver an optimal experience to over 18 participants, and this room's capacity far exceeds that number." GE has already started to use the room for training and meetings, and the experience has far exceeded their expectations. In fact, the ability to conduct any business meeting face-to-face has created a more intimate sense of belonging and connection, which has resulted in improved productivity. To underscore the flexibility provided by the facility, GE held its corporate executive council meeting—where all executives responsible for international operations report on their results—using telepresence instead of flying all of them to a common location, with many obvious benefits in time and money.

"There was no negative impact to the participants who joined the meeting remotely," says Timothy Peterson, GE's lead desk-side support. "The executives were able to do anything they would have done if everyone had been present in the same room."

SOURCE: Nina Parker, "IVCi Case Study: GE Installs Groundbreaking Cisco Telepresence Room," *Cisco Case Study*, June 2009.

Business Use of the Internet

As Figure 6.6 illustrates, business use of the Internet has expanded from an electronic information exchange to a broad platform for strategic business applications. Notice how applications such as collaboration among business partners, providing customer and vendor support, and e-commerce have become major business uses of the Internet. Companies are also using Internet technologies for marketing, sales, and customer relationship management applications, as well as for cross-functional business applications, and applications in engineering, manufacturing, human resources, and accounting.

The Business Value of the Internet

The Internet provides a synthesis of computing and communication capabilities that adds value to every part of the business cycle.

What business value do companies derive from their presence and applications on the Internet? Figure 6.7 summarizes how many companies perceive the business value

FIGURE 6.6

Examples of how a company can use the Internet for business.

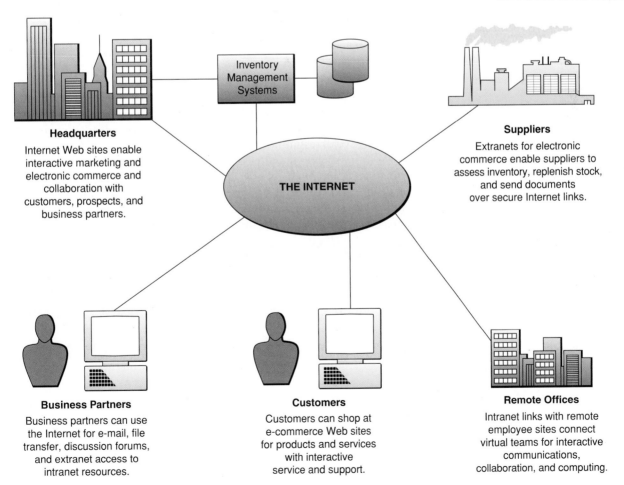

Headquarters
Internet Web sites enable interactive marketing and electronic commerce and collaboration with customers, prospects, and business partners.

Suppliers
Extranets for electronic commerce enable suppliers to assess inventory, replenish stock, and send documents over secure Internet links.

Inventory Management Systems

THE INTERNET

Business Partners
Business partners can use the Internet for e-mail, file transfer, discussion forums, and extranet access to intranet resources.

Customers
Customers can shop at e-commerce Web sites for products and services with interactive service and support.

Remote Offices
Intranet links with remote employee sites connect virtual teams for interactive communications, collaboration, and computing.

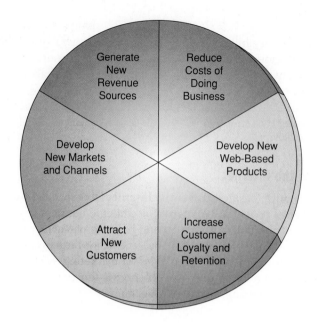

of the Internet for online commerce. Substantial cost savings can arise because applications that use the Internet and Internet-based technologies (like intranets and extranets) are typically less expensive to develop, operate, and maintain than traditional systems. For example, an airline saves money every time customers use its Web site instead of its customer support telephone system.

Generally speaking, with the exception of a very few types of transactions, the transaction cost savings are significant for online versus more traditional channels. For example, booking a reservation over the Internet costs about 90 percent less for the airline than booking the same reservation over the telephone. The banking industry has also found significant cost savings via the Internet. A typical online banking transaction (payments, balance inquiry, check payment) is estimated to cost anywhere from 50 percent to 95 percent less than its bricks-and-mortar counterpart. For the most part, anytime you convert a business process from a manual one to a software-based version, the transaction costs associated with that process can be expected to go down by the order of several magnitudes.

Other primary sources of business value include attracting new customers with innovative marketing and products, as well as retaining present customers with improved customer service and support. Of course, generating revenue through Web-based applications is a major source of business value, which we will discuss in Chapter 9. To summarize, most companies are building Web sites to achieve six major business values:

- Generate new revenue from online sales.
- Reduce transaction costs through online sales and customer support.
- Attract new customers via Web marketing and advertising and online sales.
- Increase the loyalty of existing customers via improved Web customer service and support.
- Develop new Web-based markets and distribution channels for existing products.
- Develop new information-based products accessible on the Web.

**THE ROLE OF
INTRANETS**
LO 6-4

Many companies have sophisticated and widespread intranets, offering detailed data retrieval, collaboration tools, personalized customer profiles, and links to the Internet. Investing in the intranet, they feel, is as fundamental as supplying employees with a telephone.

Before we go any further, let's redefine the concept of an *intranet*, to emphasize specifically how intranets are related to the Internet and *extranets*. As the name implies, an ***intranet*** is a *network inside an organization* that uses Internet technologies (such as Web browsers and servers, TCP/IP network protocols, HTML hypermedia document publishing and databases, and so on) to provide an Internet-like environment within the enterprise for information sharing, communications, collaboration, and the support of business processes. An intranet is protected by security measures such as passwords, encryption, and firewalls, and thus can be accessed by authorized users through the Internet. A company's intranet can also be accessed through the intranets of customers, suppliers, and other business partners via *extranet* links. Just think of an intranet as a private version of the Internet.

The Business Value of Intranets

Organizations of all kinds are implementing a broad range of intranet uses. One way that companies organize intranet applications is to group them conceptually into a few categories of user services that reflect the basic services that intranets offer to their users. These services are provided by the intranet's portal, browser, and server software, as well as by other system and application software and groupware that are part of a company's intranet software environment. Figure 6.8 illustrates how intranets provide an *enterprise information portal* that supports communication and collaboration, Web publishing, business operations and management, and intranet portal management. Notice also how these applications can be integrated with existing IS resources and applications and extended to customers, suppliers, and business partners via the Internet and extranets.

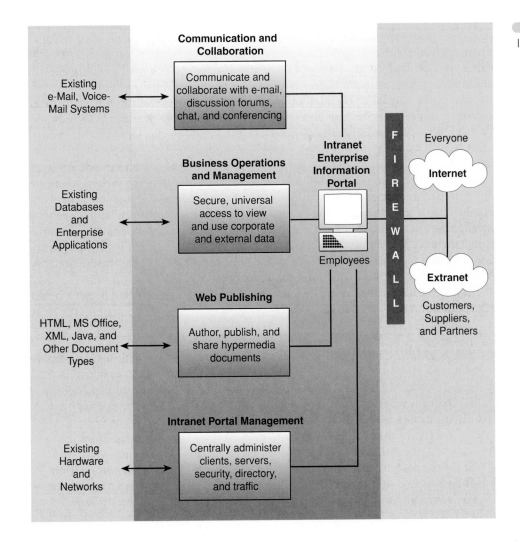

FIGURE 6.8

Intranets can provide an enterprise information portal for applications in communication and collaboration, business operations and management, Web publishing, and intranet portal management.

COMMUNICATIONS AND COLLABORATION. Intranets can significantly improve communications and collaboration within an enterprise. For example, you can use your intranet browser and your PC or mobile device to send and receive e-mail, voice mail, pages, and even faxes to communicate with others within your organization, as well as externally through the Internet and extranets. You can also use intranet groupware features to improve team and project collaboration with services such as discussion groups, chat rooms, and audio and videoconferencing.

WEB PUBLISHING. The advantage of developing and publishing hyperlinked multimedia documents to hypermedia databases accessible on World Wide Web servers has moved to corporate intranets. The comparative ease, attractiveness, and lower cost of publishing and accessing multimedia business information internally via intranet Web sites have been the primary reasons for the explosive growth in the use of intranets in business. For example, information products as varied as company newsletters, technical drawings, and product catalogs can be published in a variety of ways, including hypermedia Web pages, e-mail, and net broadcasting, and as part of in-house business applications. Intranet software browsers, servers, and search engines can help you easily navigate and locate the business information you need.

BUSINESS OPERATIONS AND MANAGEMENT. Intranets have moved beyond merely making hypermedia information available on Web servers or pushing it to users via net broadcasting. Intranets are also being used as the platform for developing and deploying critical business applications to support business operations and managerial decision making across the inter-networked enterprise. For example, many companies are developing custom applications like order processing, inventory control, sales management, and enterprise information portals that can be implemented on intranets, extranets, and the Internet. Many of these applications are designed to interface with and access existing company databases and legacy systems. The software for such business uses is then installed on intranet Web servers. Employees within the company or external business partners can access and run such applications using Web browsers from anywhere on the network whenever needed.

INTRANET PORTAL MANAGEMENT. Organizations must employ IT and IS professionals to manage the functions of the intranet, along with maintaining the various hardware and software components necessary for successful operations. For example, a network administrator must manage the access of users via passwords and other security mechanisms to ensure that each user is able to use the intranet productively while simultaneously protecting the integrity of the data resources. Included in this job are issues related to protection against unauthorized access, computer viruses, directory management, and other highly important functions.

Now let's look at one company's use of an intranet in more detail to get a better idea of how intranets are used in business.

Intranet Dashboard Revs Up Audi Australia

Audi is a brand synonymous with sporty, progressive, and sophisticated cars that embody technological perfection. On the back of the company's year-on-year record growth since 2004—including 30 percent growth in Australia in 2008—the company needed to position itself, and its national dealer network, to manage its future growth.

Audi Australia has a network of 30 dealerships across Australia. It needed to communicate with a range of people within its dealer network and ensure that different roles within the dealership were given access to the right information. There was a complex network of stakeholders who required access: the solution needed to cater to 500 users who were broken into 90 different user groups.

Audi has an existing portal solution that has been built on an open-source solution. Audi's business had outgrown this solution, which had become unreliable and required a lot of technical management. Audi only has one in-house IT staff member, and it needed a solution that could be administered and maintained by nontechnical staff, without intervention from a third-party supplier.

"The old portal wasn't letting us provide all the information we wanted to the dealers. We just couldn't update it frequently enough," says Wolf-Christian Vaross, IT Specialist for Audi Australia. "Administration of the old site wasn't easy—to make changes we had to get a programmer to do it. The software might have been free initially but we didn't have the expertise to support it in house, and we didn't want to keep paying someone outside the company to maintain it."

Audi chose the iD solution because it was able to deliver all the features they required out of the box. Another important component of the project was that the dealer portal had to meet Audi's scrupulous design standards to match Audi's distinctive branding.

As part of the implementation, Audi involved the general managers from across five key departments including sales, corporate communications, and finance to find out what information they needed to share with dealers. This ensured that the broader business would be involved in creating and maintaining the dealer portal and had buy-in to the project. "The preparation process that iD took us through made it easy—they gave us an understanding of how to structure it," says Vaross.

"Now when someone from a dealership logs in, they'll see the latest news relevant to them, and it will only take one mouse click for them to find what they're looking for. It was important to give them the easiest possible route to the information they need," adds Vaross.

Audi's dealer portal was launched on February 1, 2009, and enjoyed rapid uptake by its dealer users. The number of users increased by 450 percent in the second month of use. "As users have discovered that the new portal is easy to use and offers relevant information, they are already beginning to access more information via the portal," says Vaross. "We have seen the number of pages they visit increase by 300 percent in the second month of operation."

SOURCE: *Intranet Dashboard Case Study,* "Intranet Dashboard Revs Up Audi Australia," *Intranet Journal,* October 22, 2009.

THE ROLE OF EXTRANETS
LO 6-4

As businesses continue to use open Internet technologies [extranets] to improve communication with customers and partners, they can gain many competitive advantages along the way—in product development, cost savings, marketing, distribution, and leveraging their partnerships.

As we explained previously, **extranets** are network links that use Internet technologies to *interconnect the intranet of a business with the intranets of its customers, suppliers, or other business partners.* Companies can establish direct private network links among themselves or create private, secure Internet links called *virtual private networks* (VPNs). (We'll look more closely at VPNs later in this chapter.) Or a company can use the unsecured Internet as the extranet link between its intranet and consumers and others but rely on the encryption of sensitive data and its own firewall systems to provide adequate security. Thus, extranets enable customers, suppliers, consultants, subcontractors, business prospects, and others to access selected intranet Web sites and other company databases. See Figure 6.9.

As shown in the figure, an organization's extranet can simultaneously link the organization to a wide variety of external partners. Consultants and contractors can use the extranet to facilitate the design of new systems or provide outsourcing services.

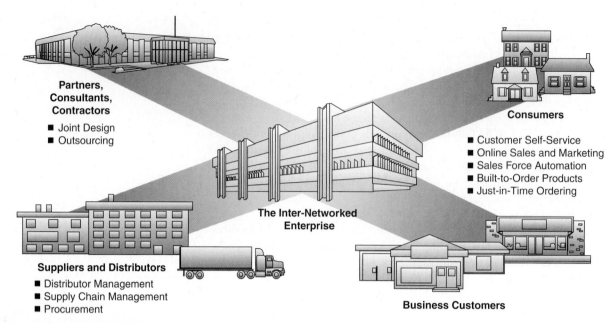

Partners,
Consultants,
Contractors

■ Joint Design
■ Outsourcing

Consumers

■ Customer Self-Service
■ Online Sales and Marketing
■ Sales Force Automation
■ Built-to-Order Products
■ Just-in-Time Ordering

**The Inter-Networked
Enterprise**

Suppliers and Distributors

■ Distributor Management
■ Supply Chain Management
■ Procurement

Business Customers

FIGURE 6.9

Extranets connect the inter-networked enterprise to consumers, business customers, suppliers, and other business partners.

The suppliers of the organization can use the extranet to ensure that the raw materials necessary for the organization to function are in stock or delivered in a timely fashion. The customers of an organization can use the extranet to access self-service functions such as ordering, order status checking, and payment. The extranet links the organization to the outside world in a manner that improves the way it does business.

The business value of extranets is derived from several factors. First, the Web browser technology of extranets makes customer and supplier access of intranet resources a lot easier and faster than previous business methods. Second, as you will see in two upcoming examples, extranets enable a company to offer new kinds of interactive Web-enabled services to their business partners. Thus, extranets are another way that a business can build and strengthen strategic relationships with its customers and suppliers. Also, extranets can enable and improve collaboration by a business with its customers and other business partners. Extranets facilitate an online, interactive product development, marketing, and customer-focused process that can bring better-designed products to market faster. Remember Metcalfe's Law? This is an example of how businesses derive value from applying its principles.

The NFL Scores with New Extranet

The National Football League (NFL) is the most popular sports league in the United States, with the highest per-game attendance numbers of any domestic sport league worldwide. Composed of 32 teams that compete to win the Super Bowl, the league is also well-known for its excellent management and organizational skills; indeed, it has been called "one of America's best-run businesses" by *BusinessWeek* magazine.

Although each team is a separate entity, the league provides central services geared to the production and promotion of the sport, as well as supporting individual teams and other organizations involved in the process, such as television broadcasters, game officials, fans, and the media. In 1997 the NFL was the first major sports league to implement a media-only Web site that could be used to distribute information—team and player statistics, player careers, attendance numbers, schedules, and so forth—to the various journalists and publications that cover the sport, both in the United States and worldwide. "We have a very good relationship with our media and are proud of the services we provide for them. The media portal is an extension of that, which is why we want to keep moving forward and making it the best resource we can," says Leslie Hammond, Director of Media Services for the National Football League.

By 2008, however, the site had become dated and new capabilities were required. The NFL decided to rebuild its media site as a custom portal, which could be used to provide all necessary information in a secure manner and in a way that best meets the needs of the media organizations. With that in mind, the league conducted extensive interviews and surveys with the media to identify which features were deemed most necessary to be included in the new site. As a result of this process, the new portal was organized around specific "pages" that contained information the media needed about specific aspects of the sport. For example, there is a separate Team Page for each team, which consolidates all team-related information, and is most useful for those who exclusively cover one specific team. Then there are Release Pages which contain leaguewide information and press releases, and Game Day Pages which include all information necessary for the coverage of a specific game.

Behind the scenes, the consolidation, editing, production, and publication of content is managed by work-flow tools by IBM Workplace Web Content Management, which is tightly integrated with WebSphere Portal, the underlying technology hosting the portal. "We decided in favor of IBM WebSphere Portal to take advantage of the years of experience behind it and the number of companies that can support it," says Joe Manto, vice president of Business Services and User Support for the National Football League. Since it was first launched, the portal has proved to be a success with both NFL personnel, as well as the media. A number of NFL public relations staff travel constantly, and this allows them to upload and edit content remotely. On the media side, the portal provides customized content that puts all necessary information about a team or game at their fingertips and in a single place, which eliminates the need to navigate to multiple places to get all necessary content. In addition, they can subscribe to receive any news or new content related to teams or games they are covering.

SOURCE: "The NFL Scores a Win with Extranet Media Portal," *IBM Case Study*, February 15, 2008.

Telecommunications Network Alternatives

TELECOMMUNICATIONS ALTERNATIVES

Telecommunications is a highly technical, rapidly changing field of information systems technology. Most business professionals do not need detailed knowledge of its technical characteristics. However, it is necessary that you understand some of the important characteristics of the basic components of telecommunications networks. This understanding will help you participate effectively in decision making regarding telecommunications alternatives. See Figure 6.10.

A TELECOMMUNICATIONS NETWORK MODEL
LO 6-5
LO 6-6

Figure 6.11 outlines key telecommunications component categories and examples. Remember, a basic understanding and appreciation, not a detailed knowledge, is sufficient for most business professionals.

Before we begin our discussion of telecommunications network alternatives, we should understand the basic components of a *telecommunications network.* Generally, a *communications network* is any arrangement in which a *sender* transmits a message

FIGURE 6.10

Information technology is changing the way medicine works by bringing remote patients and doctors together.

SOURCE: Kevin Maloney/The New York Times/Redux.

FIGURE 6.11

Key telecommunications network component categories and examples.

Network Alternative	Examples of Alternatives
Networks	Internet, intranet, extranet, wide area, local area, client/server, network computing, peer-to-peer
Media	Twisted-pair wire, coaxial cable, fiber optics, microwave radio, communications satellites, cellular and PCS systems, wireless mobile and LAN systems
Processors	Modems, multiplexers, switches, routers, hubs, gateways, front-end processors, private branch exchanges
Software	Network operating systems, telecommunications monitors, Web browsers, middleware
Channels	Analog/digital, switched/nonswitched, circuit/message/packet/cell switching, bandwidth alternatives
Topology/Architecture	Star, ring, and bus topologies, OSI and TCP/IP architectures and protocols

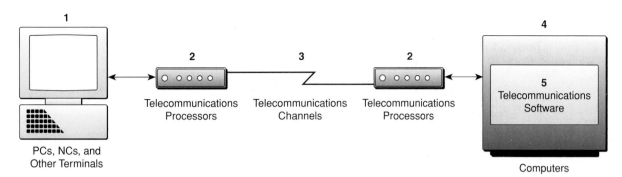

1 — PCs, NCs, and Other Terminals

2 — Telecommunications Processors

3 — Telecommunications Channels

2 — Telecommunications Processors

4 — Computers

5 — Telecommunications Software

FIGURE 6.12

The five basic components in a telecommunications network: (1) terminals, (2) telecommunications processors, (3) telecommunications channels, (4) computers, and (5) telecommunications software.

to a receiver over a *channel* consisting of some type of *medium*. Figure 6.12 illustrates a simple conceptual model of a telecommunications network, which shows that it consists of five basic categories of components:

- **Terminals,** such as networked personal computers, network computers, net boxes, or information appliances. Any input/output device that uses telecommunications networks to transmit or receive data is a terminal, including telephones and the various computer terminals that were discussed in Chapter 3.

- **Telecommunications processors,** which support data transmission and reception between terminals and computers. These devices, such as modems, switches, and routers, perform a variety of control and support functions in a telecommunications network. For example, they convert data from digital to analog and back, code and decode data, and control the speed, accuracy, and efficiency of the communications flow between computers and terminals in a network.

- **Telecommunications channels** over which data are transmitted and received. Telecommunications channels may use combinations of *media,* such as copper wires, coaxial cables, or fiber-optic cables, or use wireless systems like microwave, communications satellite, radio, and cellular systems to interconnect the other components of a telecommunications network.

- **Computers** of all sizes and types are interconnected by telecommunications networks so that they can carry out their information processing assignments. For example, a mainframe computer may serve as a *host computer* for a large network, assisted by a midrange computer serving as a *front-end processor,* while a microcomputer may act as a *network server* in a small network.

- **Telecommunications control software** consists of programs that control telecommunications activities and manage the functions of telecommunications networks. Examples include network management programs of all kinds, such as *telecommunications monitors* for mainframe host computers, *network operating systems* for network servers, and *Web browsers* for microcomputers.

No matter how large and complex real-world telecommunications networks may appear to be, these five basic categories of network components must be at work to support an organization's telecommunications activities. This is the conceptual framework you can use to help you understand the various types of telecommunications networks in use today.

Many different types of networks serve as the telecommunications infrastructure for the Internet and the intranets and extranets of inter-networked enterprises. However, from an end user's point of view, there are only a few basic types, such as wide area and local area networks and client/server, network computing, and peer-to-peer networks.

TYPES OF TELECOMMUNICATIONS NETWORKS
LO 6-7
LO 6-8

Wide Area Networks

Telecommunications networks covering a large geographic area are called *wide area networks (WANs).* Networks that cover a large city or metropolitan area (*metropolitan*

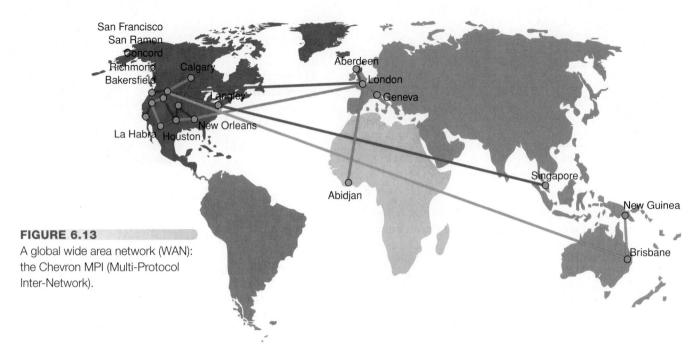

FIGURE 6.13

A global wide area network (WAN): the Chevron MPI (Multi-Protocol Inter-Network).

SOURCE: Courtesy of Cisco Systems Inc.

area networks) can also be included in this category. Such large networks have become a necessity for carrying out the day-to-day activities of many business and government organizations and their end users. For example, WANs are used by many multinational companies to transmit and receive information among their employees, customers, suppliers, and other organizations across cities, regions, countries, and the world. Figure 6.13 illustrates an example of a global wide area network for a major multinational corporation.

Metropolitan Area Network

When a wide area network optimized a specific geographical area, it is referred to as a **metropolitan area network** (MAN). Such networks can range from several blocks of buildings to entire cities. MANs can also depend on communications channels of moderate-to-high data rates. A MAN might be owned and operated by a single organization, but it usually will be used by many individuals and organizations. MANs might also be owned and operated as public utilities. Your local cable provider or a local telephone company is probably operating on a MAN. MANs will often provide means for inter-networking of local area networks.

Local Area Networks

Local area networks (LANs) connect computers and other information processing devices within a limited physical area, such as an office, classroom, building, manufacturing plant, or other work site. LANs are commonplace organizations for providing telecommunications network capabilities that link end users in offices, departments, and other workgroups.

LANs use a variety of telecommunications media, ranging from ordinary telephone wiring, coaxial cable, or even wireless radio and infrared systems, to interconnect microcomputer workstations and computer peripherals. To communicate over the network, each PC usually has a circuit board called a *network interface card.* Most LANs use a more powerful computer with a large hard disk capacity, called a *file server* or *network server,* that contains a network operating system program that controls telecommunications and the use and sharing of network resources. For example, it distributes copies of common data files and software packages to the other computers in the network and controls access to shared laser printers and other network peripherals. See Figure 6.14.

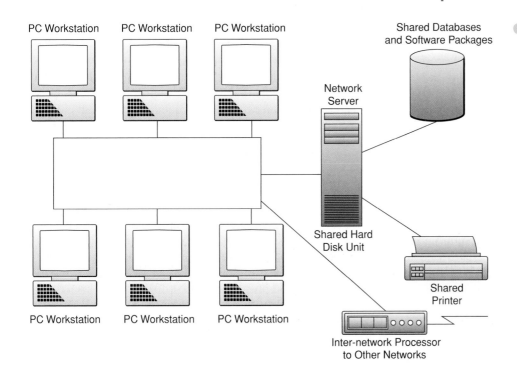

FIGURE 6.14
A local area network (LAN). Note how the LAN allows users to share hardware, software, and data resources.

Virtual Private Networks

Many organizations use ***virtual private networks (VPNs)*** to establish secure intranets and extranets. A virtual private network is a secure network that uses the Internet as its main *backbone network* but relies on network firewalls, encryption, and other security features of its Internet and intranet connections and those of participating organizations. Thus, for example, VPNs would enable a company to use the Internet to establish secure intranets between its distant branch offices and manufacturing plants and secure extranets between itself and its business customers and suppliers. Figure 6.15

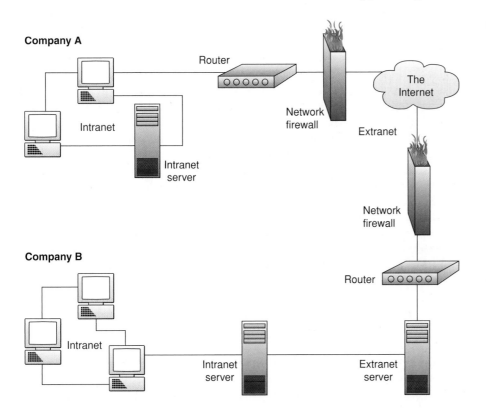

FIGURE 6.15
An example of a virtual private network protected by network firewalls.

illustrates a VPN in which network routers serve as firewalls to screen Internet traffic between two companies. We will discuss firewalls, encryption, and other network security features in Chapter 13. For the time being, we can think of a VPN as a pipe traveling through the Internet. Through this pipe, we can send and receive our data without anyone outside the pipe being able to see or access our transmissions. Using this approach, we can "create" a private network without incurring the high cost of a separate proprietary connection scheme. Let's look at a real-world example about the use of VPN to secure remote and wireless access to sensitive data.

Wireless VPNs: Alternatives for Secure Remote Access

Road warriors wirelessly connect to the corporate network from hot spots at airports or coffee outlets. Just a few years ago, common nightmare stories were told of even casual bystanders being able to eavesdrop on corporate communications made in such circumstances. As a result, there's a widespread acceptance that VPNs are pretty much de rigueur for wireless use on the road.

Fast-growing, New York–based Castle Brands uses a PPTP-based VPN—having first weighed open-source and proprietary VPNs. "We tried to keep the cost down, without compromising security," says Director of IT Andre Preoteasa. "Throw in the up-front cost of some VPNs, the additional hardware, license fees, and yearly support costs, and costs soon climb. With PPTP, if you've got Windows XP, you pretty much have it."

Initial access to the network is password-based, explains Preoteasa, with subsequent access control following role-based rules maintained on the server in the form of Microsoft Active Directory. "People can't just go anywhere and open up anything; the accounting guys get accounting access while the sales guys don't," he says.

At London-based law firm Lawrence Graham, a combination of tokenless, two-factor authentication techniques help ensure secure remote VPN wireless access, says the firm's IT director Jason Petrucci.

"When lawyers log on to the system remotely from a laptop, they are presented with three authentication boxes: one for their username, one for their log-on password, and the last for their combined personal PIN code and passcode," he says. "SecurEnvoy is used to manage and deliver this passcode by preloading three one-time passcodes within a text message, which is delivered to the user's BlackBerry."

As passcodes are used, replacements are automatically sent to each lawyer's BlackBerry. "Our lawyers carry BlackBerrys with them wherever they go. A physical token inevitably runs the risk of being left behind or lost altogether."

Meanwhile, at Fortune 50 insurance company MetLife, protecting against data leakage—especially with respect to client information—is of paramount importance when enabling remote wireless access, says Jesus Montano, assistant vice president of enterprise security.

"The challenge is balancing people's access requirements with our overall security requirements, and then working with them to find ways of creating an effective solution without compromising security," he says.

For wireless access from airports and coffee outlets, he explains, these days that means access via VPN vendor Check Point, solely from MetLife-owned laptops, with log-ons protected by RSA "hard token"–based, two-factor authentication. In addition to the encryption built into the VPN, all the data on the laptop are protected, he adds.

"All wireless traffic is encrypted; the devices are encrypted and wrapped around with a firewall," stresses Montano. "We think we've addressed the most obvious pitfalls in remote access, and think we've got a robust, highly engineered solution."

SOURCE: Malcolm Wheatley, "Wireless VPNs Protecting the Wireless Wanderer," *CSO Magazine*, December 15, 2008.

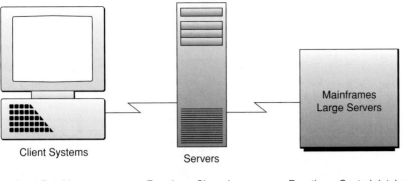

FIGURE 6.16
The functions of the computer
systems in client/server networks.

Client Systems

Servers

Mainframes
Large Servers

- Functions: Provide user interface, perform some/most processing on an application.

- Functions: Shared computation, application control, distributed databases.

- Functions: Central database control, security, directory management, heavy-duty processing.

Client/Server Networks

Client/server networks are the predominant information architecture of enterprise-wide computing, and they are how most, if not all, LANs are designed. In a client/server network, end-user computing workstations are the *clients*. They are interconnected by local area networks and share application processing with network *servers*, which also manage the networks. (This arrangement of clients and servers is sometimes called a *two-tier* client/server architecture.) Local area networks (LANs) are also interconnected to other LANs and wide area networks (WANs). Figure 6.16 illustrates the functions of the computer systems that may be in client/server networks, including optional host systems and superservers.

A continuing trend is the *downsizing* of larger computer systems by replacing them with client/server networks. For example, a client/server network of several interconnected local area networks may replace a large mainframe-based network with many end-user terminals. This shift typically involves a complex and costly effort to install new application software that replaces the software of older, traditional mainframe-based business information systems, now called **legacy systems.** Client/server networks are seen as more economical and flexible than legacy systems in meeting end-user, workgroup, and business unit needs, and more adaptable in adjusting to a diverse range of computing workloads.

Basically, a client/server approach can take one of two forms: *thick client* or *thin client.* A thick approach uses the server to store data and the client to do all of the processing and computing. A thick client approach requires the user to have a computer powerful enough to handle whatever software applications and processing they require. The server is just a big storage mechanism. The important part of a thick client approach is that it requires enough bandwidth to move the data back and forth because all of the software resides on the client side of things. This means a big bandwidth is needed.

In contrast, the *thin client* approach makes the server do all the work. The server becomes the powerful processor and generally houses not only the data but the software applications needed to process the data. In this approach, the client really only needs enough power to *look* at the information being sent to it by the processor. Because of this, the bandwidth necessary is much smaller than with a thick client design. Both approaches have their advantages and disadvantages and, generally speaking, the user doesn't have to know which design they are using as long as it is appropriate for the work needed to be done.

Network Computing

The growing reliance on the computer hardware, software, and data resources of the Internet, intranets, extranets, and other networks has emphasized that, for many users,

FIGURE 6.17

The functions of the computer
systems in network computing.

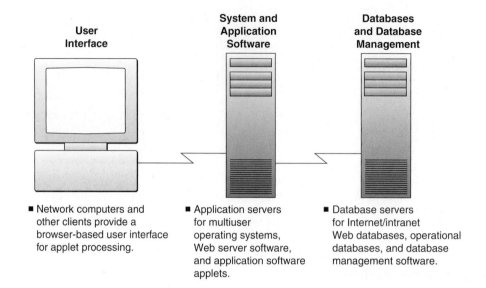

**User
Interface**

**System and
Application
Software**

**Databases
and Database
Management**

■ Network computers and
other clients provide a
browser-based user interface
for applet processing.

■ Application servers
for multiuser
operating systems,
Web server software,
and application software
applets.

■ Database servers
for Internet/intranet
Web databases, operational
databases, and database
management software.

"the network is the computer." This **network computing** or *network-centric* concept
views networks as the central computing resource of any computing environment.

Figure 6.17 illustrates that in network computing, *network computers* and other *thin
clients* provide a browser-based user interface for processing small application programs called *applets*. Thin clients include network computers, netboxes, and other low-
cost network devices or information appliances. Application and database servers
provide the operating system, application software, applets, databases, and database
management software needed by the end users in the network. Network computing is
sometimes called a *three-tier* client/server model because it consists of thin clients,
application servers, and database servers.

Peer-to-Peer Networks

The emergence of peer-to-peer (P2P) networking technologies and applications for the
Internet is being hailed as a development that will have a major impact on e-business
and e-commerce and the Internet itself. Whatever the merits of such claims, it is clear
that peer-to-peer networks are a powerful telecommunications networking tool for
many business applications.

Figure 6.18 illustrates two major models of **peer-to-peer network** technology.
In the central server architecture, P2P file-sharing software connects your PC to a
central server that contains a directory of all of the other users (*peers*) in the network.
When you request a file, the software searches the directory for any other users who
have that file and are online at that moment. It then sends you a list of user names that
are active links to all such users. Clicking on one of these user names prompts the
software to connect your PC to that user's PC (making a *peer-to-peer* connection) and
automatically transfers the file you want from his or her hard drive to yours.

The *pure* peer-to-peer network architecture has no central directory or server.
First, the file-sharing software in the P2P network connects your PC with one of the
online users in the network. Then an active link to your user name is transmitted from
peer to peer to all the online users in the network that the first user (and the other
online users) encountered in previous sessions. In this way, active links to more and
more peers spread throughout the network the more it is used. When you request a
file, the software searches every online user and sends you a list of active file names
related to your request. Clicking on one of these automatically transfers the file from
that user's hard drive to yours.

One of the major advantages and limitations of the central server architecture is
its reliance on a central directory and server. The directory server can be slowed or

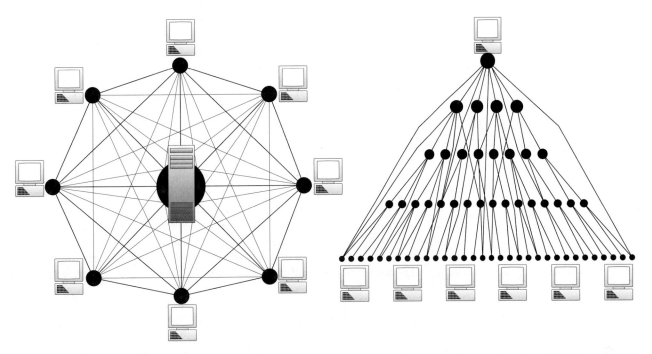

■ A peer-to-peer network architecture with a
directory of all peers on a central server

■ A pure peer-to-peer network architecture
with no central directory server

FIGURE 6.18

The two major forms of
peer-to-peer networks.

overwhelmed by too many users or technical problems. However, it also provides the
network with a platform that can better protect the integrity and security of the content and users of the network. Some applications of pure P2P networks, in contrast,
have been plagued by slow response times and bogus and corrupted files.

The Internet, as originally conceived in the late 1960s, was a peer-to-peer system. The
goal of the original ARPANET (the name of the early version of today's Internet) was
to share computing resources around the United States. The challenge for this effort was to
integrate different kinds of existing networks, as well as future technologies, with one
common network architecture that would allow every host to be an equal player. The first
few hosts on the ARPANET (e.g., UCLA and the University of Utah) were already independent computing sites with equal status. The ARPANET connected them together not
in a master/slave or client/server relationship, but rather as equal computing peers.

One common use for peer-to-peer networks today is the downloading and trading
of files. When the term *peer-to-peer* was used to describe the *Napster* network, it implied that the peer protocol nature was important, but in reality the unique achievement of Napster was the empowerment of the peers (i.e., the fringes of the network)
in association with a central index that made it fast and efficient to locate available
content. The peer protocol was just a common way to achieve this.

Although much media attention has focused on copyright-infringing uses of filetrading networks, there are vast numbers of entirely noninfringing uses. *BitTorrent* was
originally designed to keep sites from getting overwhelmed by "flash crowds" and
heavy traffic. That makes it very suitable for many situations in which there are massive peaks of demand. Most Linux distributions are released via BitTorrent to help
with their bandwidth needs. Another example is *Blizzard Entertainment* (http://www.
blizzard.com), which uses a modified version of BitTorrent to distribute patches to its
game World of Warcraft (http://www.worldofwarcraft.com). Users have often complained about BitTorrent due to a bandwidth cap that almost defeats its purpose.

Other peer-to-peer networks are emerging as well, such as *PeerCast*, which allows
someone to broadcast an Internet radio or television station with very little upstream
bandwidth due to its distributed nature. Other peer-to-peer broadcast tools, sometimes

called *peer-casting,* include the *IceShare* project and *FreeCast.* Since around 2004, peer-to-peer networks represent the largest single contributor to network traffic on the Internet.

DIGITAL AND ANALOG SIGNALS
LO 6-9

We regularly hear the words *analog* and *digital* associated with computers, telephones, and other hardware devices. To be sure that you understand exactly what these terms mean, a short discussion is in order.

Basically, **analog** or **digital** refers to the method used to convert information into an electrical signal. Telephones, microphones, measuring instruments, vinyl record players, CD players, tape decks, computers, fax machines, and so on must convert information into an electrical signal in some manner so that it can be transmitted or processed. For example, a microphone must convert the air pressure waves that we call *sound* into a corresponding electrical voltage or current, which can be sent down a telephone line, amplified in a sound system, broadcast on the radio, and/or recorded on some medium.

In an analog system, an electrical voltage or current is generated that is directly proportional to the quantity being observed. In a digital system, the quantity being observed is expressed as a number. This is really all there is to it, but a few details must still be discussed.

For example, in an electronic analog thermometer, if the temperature being measured is 83 degrees, then the analog system would put out, for example, 83 volts. This level could just as well be 8.3 volts or any other voltage proportional to the temperature. Thus, if the temperature doubled to 166 degrees, the output voltage would double to 166 volts (or perhaps 16.6 volts if the instrument were so scaled). The output voltage is, therefore, "analogous" to the temperature—thus the use of the term *analog*.

In the case of an electronic digital thermometer, however, the output would be the *number* 83 if the temperature were 83 degrees, but the way that number is created is different than analog. Appropriately enough, a digital system is based on "digits." The only thing wrong with this example is that 83 is a decimal number constructed from the 10 symbols 0, 1, 2, . . ., 8, 9. We commonly use 10 symbols in our numbers for historical reasons; it is probably because we have 10 fingers. It is inconvenient, however, to use 10 symbols to express the output as an electrical voltage. It is much more convenient to have only two symbols, *0* and *1*. In this case, for example, 0 could be represented by 0 volts, and 1 by 1 volt. Recall from Chapter 3 that this system is known as a binary (only two symbols) number system, but the principle is still the same: The output of the digital thermometer is a number, that is, "digits."

For the thermometer example above, 83 is the binary number 1010011. The electronic thermometer would send the sequence 1 volt, 0 volts, 1 volt, 0 volts, 0 volts, 1 volt, and 1 volt to express the number 83 in binary. When the digital thermometer receives this binary number, it displays the temperature as 83 degrees. Because a digital system doesn't need to generate a proportionate voltage for every temperature, it requires far less power to operate than an analog thermometer.

A digital system may seem more complicated than an analog system, but it has a number of advantages. The principal advantage is that once the measurement is expressed in digital form, it can be entered into a computer or a microprocessor and manipulated as desired. If we worked with only analog devices, we would eventually have to convert the output of the analog device into digital form if we wanted to input it into a computer. Because computer networks work primarily with digital signals, most of the hardware used by a computer network is digital.

TELECOMMUNICATIONS MEDIA

Telecommunications channels make use of a variety of **telecommunications media.** These include *twisted-pair wire, coaxial cables,* and *fiber-optic cables,* all of which physically link the devices in a network. Also included are *terrestrial microwave, communications satellites, cellular phone systems,* and *packet and LAN radio,* all of which use microwave and other radio waves. In addition, there are *infrared* systems, which use infrared light to transmit and receive data. See Figure 6.19.

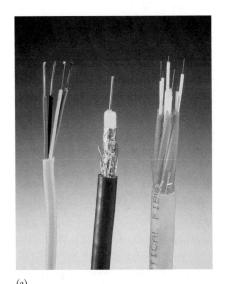

(a)
SOURCE: Phil Degginger/Getty Images.

(b)
SOURCE: © Photodisc/Getty Images.

(c)
SOURCE: © Photodisc/PunchStock.

FIGURE 6.19

Common telecommunications guided media: (a) twisted-pair wire, (b) coaxial cable, and (c) fiber-optic cable.

WIRED TECHNOLOGIES
LO 6-10

Twisted-Pair Wire

Ordinary telephone wire, consisting of copper wire twisted into pairs (twisted-pair wire), is the most widely used medium for telecommunications. These lines are used in established communications networks throughout the world for both voice and data transmission. Twisted-pair wiring is wrapped or shielded in a variety of forms and used extensively in home and office telephone systems and many local area networks and wide area networks. Transmission speeds can range from 2 million bits per second (unshielded) to 100 million bits per second (shielded).

Coaxial Cable

Coaxial cable consists of a sturdy copper or aluminum wire wrapped with spacers to insulate and protect it. The cable's cover and insulation minimize interference and distortion of the signals the cable carries. Groups of coaxial cables may be bundled together in a big cable for ease of installation. These high-quality lines can be placed underground and laid on the floors of lakes and oceans. They allow high-speed data transmission (from 200 million to more than 500 million bits per second—200–500 Mbps) and are used instead of twisted-pair wire lines in high-service metropolitan areas, for cable television systems, and for short-distance connections of computers and peripheral devices. Coaxial cables are also used in many office buildings and other work sites for local area networks. This is the "cable" referred to when we think of "the cable company."

Fiber Optics

Fiber optics uses cables consisting of one or more hair-thin filaments of glass fiber wrapped in a protective jacket. They can conduct pulses of visible light elements (*photons*) generated by lasers at transmission rates as high as trillions of bits per second (terabits per second, or Tbps). This speed is hundreds of times faster than coaxial cable and thousands of times better than twisted-pair wire lines. Fiber-optic cables provide substantial size and weight reductions, as well as increased speed and greater carrying capacity. A half-inch-diameter fiber-optic cable can carry more than 500,000 channels, compared with about 5,500 channels for a standard coaxial cable.

Fiber-optic cables are not affected by and do not generate electromagnetic radiation; therefore, multiple fibers can be placed in the same cable. Fiber-optic cables have less need for repeaters for signal retransmissions than copper wire media. Fiber optics also has a much lower data error rate than other media and is harder to tap than electrical wire and cable. Fiber-optic cables have already been installed in many parts of the world, and they are expected to replace other communications media in many applications.

New optical technologies such as *dense wave division multiplexing* (DWDM) can split a strand of glass fiber into 40 channels, which enables each strand to carry 5 million calls. In the future, DWDM technology is expected to split each fiber into 1,000 channels, enabling each strand to carry up to 122 million calls. In addition, newly developed *optical routers* will be able to send optical signals up to 2,500 miles without needing regeneration, thus eliminating the current need for repeaters every 370 miles to regenerate signals.

The Problem of "The Last Mile"

While on the subject of telecommunication media, we need to understand a pervasive problem in the telecommunications industry: *the problem of the last mile*. The last-mile problem, although simple to understand, is still one of the greatest challenges faced by telecommunications providers.

The basic problem goes something like this: The telecommunications provider adopts a new, faster, better technology that can provide higher bandwidths and faster telecommunication speeds to consumers. A good example of this type of situation is the invention of fiber-optic cable and its related optical technologies. Fiber can move data at lightning speed and handle a much larger volume of data than the more typical twisted-pair wiring commonly found in households. So the telecommunications provider completely reengineers the network and begins laying fiber instead of copper wire in trenches. The fiber, costing $500,000 to $1 million per mile, begins bringing all of its faster, better, and cheaper benefits to the front door of the consumer. This is where the last-mile problem begins. Right out in front of the house lies enough bandwidth to handle more than 100 million telephone calls or download entire movies in a few seconds. The problem is that the house it is connecting to is wired with twisted-pair wiring that just cannot handle the bandwidth provided by fiber. This situation is analogous to hooking up a garden hose directly to the water company. At the end of the day, the amount of water you get is whatever will come out of the garden hose and nothing more. Therefore, the problem is more than just the cost. In many cases, the wiring in a structure simply cannot be upgraded and therefore, the bandwidth right outside the door just cannot be accessed. It's the *last mile* in the connection that causes all the problems and that ultimately dictates the speed and bandwidth of the connection.

Many methods have been offered to solve the last-mile problem. Cable companies are providing a single-wire solution to many modern households. By using sophisticated technologies, they can bring cable television, Internet access, and telephone services into a home using only the coaxial wire originally put there for cable television. Other solutions include bypassing the old wired network completely and providing high-speed services via a satellite or other wireless approach. Regardless of the solution, the problem of the last mile is still very much an issue to consider when designing a telecommunications network.

Although still in the developmental stages, one solution to the last-mile problem may be WiMax. Defined as *Worldwide Interoperability for Microwave Access*, WiMax is intended to provide high-speed, mobile telecommunications services to diverse Internet connections and locations. There are still many issues to work out regarding WiMax, but it looks like we may be able to solve the problem of last-mile connectivity somewhere in the near future.

WIRELESS TECHNOLOGIES
LO 6-11

Wireless telecommunications technologies rely on radio wave, microwave, infrared, and visible light pulses to transport digital communications without wires between communications devices. Wireless technologies include terrestrial microwave, communications satellites, cellular and PCS telephone and pager systems, mobile data radio, wireless LANs, and various wireless Internet technologies. Each technology utilizes specific ranges within the electromagnetic spectrum (in megahertz) of electromagnetic frequencies that are specified by national regulatory agencies to minimize interference and encourage efficient telecommunications. Let's briefly review some of these major wireless communications technologies.

Terrestrial Microwave

Terrestrial microwave involves earthbound microwave systems that transmit high-speed radio signals in a line-of-sight path between relay stations spaced approximately 30 miles apart. Microwave antennas are usually placed on top of buildings, towers, hills, and mountain peaks, and they are a familiar sight in many sections of the country. They are still a popular medium for both long-distance and metropolitan area networks.

Communications Satellites

Communications satellites also use microwave radio as their telecommunications medium. Typically, high-earth orbit (HEO) communications satellites are placed in stationary geosynchronous orbits approximately 22,000 miles above the equator. Satellites are powered by solar panels and can transmit microwave signals at a rate of several hundred million bits per second. They serve as relay stations for communications signals transmitted from earth stations. Earth stations use dish antennas to beam microwave signals to the satellites that amplify and retransmit the signals to other earth stations thousands of miles away.

Whereas communications satellites were used initially for voice and video transmission, they are now also used for high-speed transmission of large volumes of data. Because of time delays caused by the great distances involved, they are not suitable for interactive, real-time processing. Communications satellite systems are operated by several firms, including Comsat, American Mobile Satellite, and Intelsat.

Various other satellite technologies are being implemented to improve global business communications. For example, many companies use networks of small satellite dish antennas known as VSAT (very small aperture terminal) to connect their stores and distant work sites via satellite. Other satellite networks use many low-earth orbit (LEO) satellites orbiting at an altitude of only 500 miles above the earth. Companies like Globalstar offer wireless phone, paging, and messaging services to users anywhere on the globe. Let's look at a real-world example.

View from Space: Satellite Farming for Greener Pastures

Making the most of natural resources of farms is critical in today's environment, where rainfalls are becoming ever so scarce.

Although in Queensland the use of animal recognition technology is being used to conserve water, on the other side of the country, in Western Australia, satellite technology is providing farmers with a suite of tools to accurately estimate the amount of feed in their pastures, how quickly their pastures are growing, and the pasture quality.

For maximum efficiency on a farm, farmers need to use the pasture when it is at its best. According to Gonzalo Mata, who is in charge of farming systems and Web development for the project, the general rule of thumb is that about only 20 to 30 percent of pasture grown is utilized in many beef and sheep production systems.

"Farmers need this information in order to match the animals' nutrient demands for growth and reproduction with the supply of feed, which can be very seasonal. If this is not achieved, production is lower or costs increase through the use of supplements to achieve the balance," Mata adds. According to Mata, you can't manage what you can't measure, hence the need to allow farmers to measure how much pasture there is on their farms.

The tool uses images from a NASA satellite to create a composite greenness index. The climate data are sourced from the Bureau of Meteorology on a weekly basis, and the two data sources are combined in a pasture growth model. Pastures from Space boasts a 97 percent accuracy, and it is possible for farmers with a subscription to have sustainable pasture utilization of more than 50 percent.

"Building data over time allows the farmer to do comparisons for specific areas between seasons or between years, which can be a powerful tool to benchmark production and manage risk," says Mata.

By going online, the farmer can also look at maps of pasture growth grate (PGR) for their farm, giving them a better understanding of why some parts of the farm are performing better than others.

SOURCE: Kathryn Edwards, "View from Space: Satellite Farming for Greener Pastures," *Computerworld Australia*, April 29, 2009.

Cellular and PCS Systems

Cellular and PCS telephone and pager systems use several radio communications technologies. However, all of them divide a geographic area into small areas, or *cells*, typically from one to several square miles in area. Each cell has its own low-power transmitter or radio relay antenna device to relay calls from one cell to another. Computers and other communications processors coordinate and control the transmissions to and from mobile users as they move from one area to another.

Cellular phone systems have long used analog communications technologies operating at frequencies in the 800–900 MHz cellular band. Newer cellular systems use digital technologies, which provide greater capacity and security, and additional services such as voice mail, paging, messaging, and caller ID. These capabilities are also available with PCS (personal communications services) phone systems. PCS operates at 1,900 MHz frequencies using digital technologies that are related to digital cellular. However, PCS phone systems cost substantially less to operate and use than cellular systems and have lower power consumption requirements.

Wireless LANs

Wiring an office or a building for a local area network is often a difficult and costly task. Older buildings frequently do not have conduits for coaxial cables or additional twisted-pair wire, and the conduits in newer buildings may not have enough room to pull additional wiring through. Repairing mistakes in and damage to wiring is often difficult and costly, as are major relocations of LAN workstations and other components. One solution to such problems is installing a *wireless LAN* using one of several wireless technologies. Examples include a high-frequency radio technology similar to digital cellular and a low-frequency radio technology called *spread spectrum*.

The use of wireless LANs is growing rapidly as new high-speed technologies are implemented. A prime example is a new open-standard wireless radio-wave technology technically known as IEEE 802.11b, or more popularly as Wi-Fi (for wireless fidelity). Wi-Fi is faster (11 Mbps) and less expensive than standard Ethernet and other common wire-based LAN technologies. Thus, Wi-Fi wireless LANs enable laptop PCs, PDAs, and other devices with Wi-Fi modems to connect easily to the Internet and other networks in a rapidly increasing number of business, public, and home environments. A faster version (802.11g) with speeds of 54 Mbps promises to make this technology even more widely used. As of December 2009, the newest version, 802.11n, was finalized. This new standard offers speeds of up to 108 Mbps.

Bluetooth

The short-range wireless technology called ***Bluetooth*** is becoming commonplace in computers and other devices. Bluetooth serves as a *cable-free wireless connection* to peripheral devices such as computer printers and scanners. Operating at approximately 1 Mbps with an effective range from 10 to 100 meters, Bluetooth promises to change significantly the way we use computers and other telecommunication devices.

To fully appreciate the potential value of Bluetooth, look around the space where you have your computer. You have your keyboard connected to the computer, as well as a printer, pointing device, monitor, and so on. What joins these together are their associated cables. Cables have become the bane of many offices and homes. Many of us have experienced trying to figure out what cable goes where and getting tangled up in the details. Bluetooth essentially aims to fix this; it is a cable-replacement technology.

Conceived initially by Ericsson and later adopted by a myriad of other companies, Bluetooth is a standard for a small, cheap radio chip to be plugged into computers, printers, mobile phones, and so forth. A Bluetooth chip is designed to replace cables by taking the information normally carried by the cable and transmitting it at a special frequency to a receiver Bluetooth chip, which will then give the information received to the computer, telephone, printer, or other Bluetooth device. Given its fairly low cost to implement, Bluetooth is set to revolutionize telecommunications. The hands-free system in your car for mobile phone communications uses Bluetooth to connect to your phone and allows you to keep your hands on the wheel.

The Wireless Web

Wireless access to the Internet, intranets, and extranets is growing as more Web-enabled information appliances proliferate. Smart telephones, pagers, PDAs, and other portable communications devices have become *very thin clients* in wireless networks. Agreement on a standard *wireless application protocol* (WAP) has encouraged the development of many wireless Web applications and services. The telecommunications industry continues to work on *fourth-generation* (4G) wireless technologies whose goal is to raise wireless transmission speeds to enable streaming video and multimedia applications on mobile devices.

For example, the Smartphone, a PCS phone, can send and receive e-mail and provide Web access via a "Web clipping" technology that generates custom-designed Web pages from many popular financial, securities, travel, sport, entertainment, and e-commerce Web sites. Another example is the Sprint PCS Wireless Web phone, which delivers similar Web content and e-mail services via a Web-enabled PCS phone.

Figure 6.20 illustrates the wireless application protocol that is the foundation of wireless mobile Internet and Web applications. The WAP standard specifies how Web

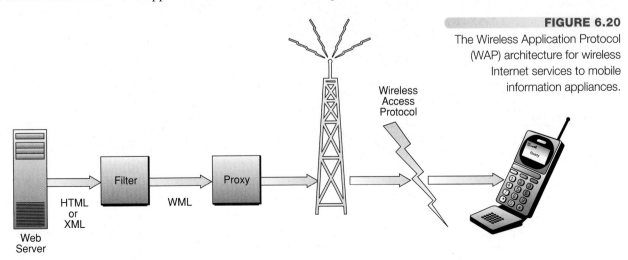

FIGURE 6.20

The Wireless Application Protocol (WAP) architecture for wireless Internet services to mobile information appliances.

pages in HTML or XML are translated into a *wireless markup language* (WML) by *filter* software and preprocessed by *proxy* software to prepare the Web pages for wireless transmission from a Web server to a Web-enabled wireless device.

Around the World: Mobile Buying and Banking

In 2009, many U.S. consumers whipped out their Smartphones in brick-and-mortar stores to find better deals online, tripling mobile shopping revenue in just one year. The relationship between money and mobile devices, however, varies widely from one part of the world to another. Mobile banking grew significantly in India, while Africa, Latin America, and some other parts of the world appeared ready to bypass banking altogether in favor of payments handled by mobile operators.

"Mobile commerce grew far faster in the U.S. than worldwide, vaulting from US$396 million in 2008 to an estimated $1.2 billion in 2009," says analyst Mark Beccue of ABI Research. Drawing on information from multiple sources, ABI concluded that many Smartphone users went shopping in physical stores, looked at products, checked out deals on the same items online and made a purchase without even going home to log onto a computer.

Shopping on the mobile Web has become especially popular in North America, though in Japan, it already accounts for about 20 percent of online purchases, says Beccue. Worldwide, excluding Japan, mobile commerce grew from about $3 billion in 2008 to $4.4 billion in 2009.

Meanwhile, the number of U.S. consumers using mobile banking more than doubled in 2009, from 4 million to 10 million. "That was partly driven by the slumping economy, because many consumers adopt mobile banking to check their balances frequently," says Beccue. In addition, U.S. banks are starting to treat mobile as more than an extension of Web-based banking, with tools such as SMS (Short Message Service).

But mobile banking is most popular in Asia and has made particular gains in India, where much of the country has limited banking infrastructure. Looking to remedy this problem, the Indian government in 2008 started encouraging banks to launch mobile platforms, he says. "They see mobile banking as a way to accelerate the acceptance of personal financial services," Beccue says. More than half of Asia's mobile banking customers in 2009 were in India.

Worldwide, the number of mobile banking users grew from 24.4 million in 2008 to 52.1 million in 2009.

Half of those users were in the Asia-Pacific region. ABI expects to see 407 million people worldwide use mobile banking by 2015. But by that time, nearly as many people will be handling their money through their phones without ever opening a bank account. By then, approximately 405 million people will be using point-to-point payment systems in which the mobile operator takes in and pays out the cash, Beccue says.

Point-to-point payment systems are becoming an important financial platform in countries where most people have never had access to banks. "In many parts of the developing world, mobile is the most common piece of infrastructure that exists," says Beccue. "In many places, there are more mobile phones than there is running water or electricity."

SOURCE: Stephen Lawson, "Mobile Buying Booms in U.S., Banking in India," *CIO.com,* February 17, 2010.

TELECOMMUNICATIONS PROCESSORS
LO 6-6

Telecommunications processors such as modems, multiplexers, switches, and routers perform a variety of support functions between the computers and other devices in a telecommunications network. Let's take a look at some of these processors and their functions. See Figure 6.21.

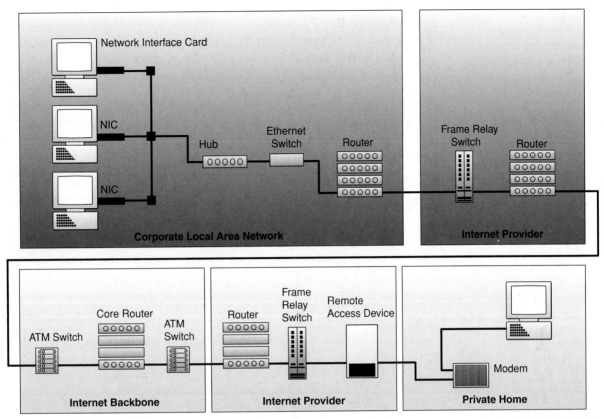

Network Interface Card

NIC

NIC

Hub

Ethernet Switch

Router

Corporate Local Area Network

Frame Relay Switch

Router

Internet Provider

ATM Switch

Core Router

ATM Switch

Internet Backbone

Router

Frame Relay Switch

Remote Access Device

Internet Provider

Modem

Private Home

FIGURE 6.21

Examples of some of the communications processors involved in an Internet connection.

Modems

Modems are the most common type of communications processor. They convert the digital signals from a computer or transmission terminal at one end of a communications link into analog frequencies that can be transmitted over ordinary telephone lines. A modem at the other end of the communications line converts the transmitted data back into digital form at a receiving terminal. This process is known as *modulation* and *demodulation*, and the word *modem* is a combined abbreviation of those two words. Modems come in several forms, including small stand-alone units, plug-in circuit boards, and removable modem cards for laptop PCs. Most modems also support a variety of telecommunications functions, such as transmission error control, automatic dialing and answering, and a faxing capability. As shown in Figure 6.21, a modem is used in the private-home setting to accept the data from the Internet provider and convert it to input for a PC.

Modems are used because ordinary telephone networks were first designed to handle continuous analog signals (electromagnetic frequencies), such as those generated by the human voice over the telephone. Because data from computers are in digital form (voltage pulses), devices are necessary to convert digital signals into appropriate analog transmission frequencies and vice versa. However, digital communications networks that use only digital signals and do not need analog/digital conversion are becoming commonplace. Because most modems also perform a variety of telecommunications support functions, devices called digital modems are still used in digital networks.

Figure 6.22 compares several modem and telecommunications technologies for access to the Internet and other networks by home and business users.

Inter-Network Processors

Telecommunications networks are interconnected by special-purpose communications processors called *inter-network processors,* such as switches, routers, hubs, and gateways. A *switch* is a communications processor that makes connections between

FIGURE 6.22

Comparing modem and telecommunications technologies for Internet and other network access.

Modem (56 Kbps)	DSL (Digital Subscriber Line) Modem
• Receives at 56 Kbps	• Receives at 1.5 Mbps to 5.0 Mbps
• Sends at 33.6 Kbps	• Sends at 128 Kbps to 640 Kbps
• Slowest technology	• Users must be near switching centers
ISDN (Integrated Services Digital Network)	**Cable Modem**
• Sends and receives at 128 Kbps	• Receives at 1.5 Mbps to 20 Mbps
• Users need extra lines	• Sends at 128 Kbps to 2.5 Mbps
• Becoming obsolete	• Speed degrades with many local users
Home Satellite	**Local Microwave**
• Receives at 400 Kbps	• Sends and receives at 512 Kbps to 1.4 Mbps
• Sends via phone modem	• Higher cost
• Slow sending, higher cost	• May require line of sight to base antenna

telecommunications circuits in a network. Switches are now available in managed versions with network management capabilities. A bridge is a device that connects two or more local area networks that use the same communications rules or *protocol*. In contrast, a *router* is an intelligent communications processor that interconnects networks based on different rules or *protocols*, so a telecommunications message can be routed to its destination. A *hub* is a port-switching communications processor. Advanced versions of both hubs and switches provide automatic switching among connections called *ports* for shared access to a network's resources. Workstations, servers, printers, and other network resources are typically connected to ports. Networks that use different communications architectures are interconnected by using a communications processor called a *gateway*. All these devices are essential to providing connectivity and easy access between the multiple LANs and wide area networks that are part of the intranets and client/server networks in many organizations.

Again referring to Figure 6.21, we can see examples of all of these elements. The corporate local area network in the upper left of the figure uses a hub to connect its multiple workstations to the network switch. The switch sends the signals to a series of switches and routers to get the data to their intended destination.

Multiplexers

A *multiplexer* is a communications processor that allows a single communications channel to carry simultaneous data transmissions from many terminals. This process is accomplished in two basic ways. In *frequency division multiplexing* (FDM), a multiplexer effectively divides a high-speed channel into multiple slow-speed channels. In *time division multiplexing* (TDM), the multiplexer divides the time each terminal can use the high-speed line into very short time slots, or time frames.

For example, if we need to have eight telephone numbers for a small business, we could have eight individual lines come into the building—one for each telephone number. Using a digital multiplexer, however, we can have one line handle all eight telephone numbers (assuming we have an eight-channel multiplexer). Multiplexers work to increase the number of transmissions possible without increasing the number of physical data channels.

TELECOMMUNICATIONS SOFTWARE
LO 6-3
LO 6-6

Telecommunications software is a vital component of all telecommunications networks. Telecommunications and network management software may reside in PCs, servers, mainframes, and communications processors like multiplexers and routers. Network servers and other computers in a network use these programs to manage network performance. Network management programs perform functions such as automatically checking client PCs for input/output activity, assigning priorities to data communications requests from clients and terminals, and detecting and correcting transmission errors and other network problems.

For example, mainframe-based wide area networks frequently use *telecommunications monitors* or *teleprocessing* (TP) monitors. The CICS (Customer Identification Control System) for IBM mainframes is a typical example. Servers in local area and other networks frequently rely on *network operating systems* like Novell NetWare or operating systems like UNIX, Linux, or Microsoft Windows 2008 Servers for network management. Many software vendors also offer telecommunications software as *middleware*, which can help diverse networks communicate with one another.

Telecommunications functions built into Microsoft Windows and other operating systems provide a variety of communications support services. For example, they work with a communications processor (such as a modem) to connect and disconnect communications links and to establish communications parameters such as transmission speed, mode, and direction.

Network Management

Network management packages such as network operating systems and telecommunications monitors determine transmission priorities, route (switch) messages, poll terminals in the network, and form waiting lines (queues) of transmission requests. They also detect and correct transmission errors, log statistics of network activity, and protect network resources from unauthorized access. See Figure 6.23.

Examples of major **network management** functions include the following:

- **Traffic Management.** Manage network resources and traffic to avoid congestion and optimize telecommunications service levels to users.

- **Security.** Providing security is one of the top concerns of network management today. Telecommunications software must provide authentication, encryption, firewall, and auditing functions, and enforce security policies. Encryption, firewalls, and other network security defenses are covered in Chapter 13.

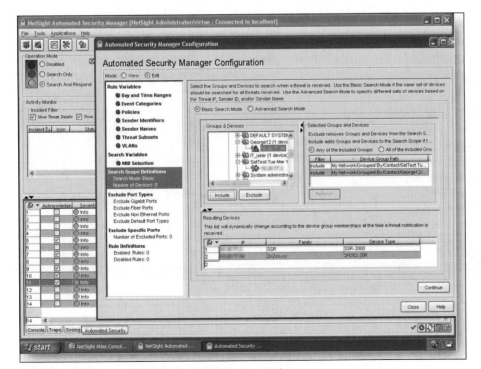

FIGURE 6.23

Network management software monitors and manages network performance.

- **Network Monitoring.** Troubleshoot and watch over the network, informing network administrators of potential problems before they occur.
- **Capacity Planning.** Survey network resources and traffic patterns and users' needs to determine how best to accommodate the needs of the network as it grows and changes.

NETWORK TOPOLOGIES
LO 6-6

There are several basic types of ***network topologies,*** or structures, in telecommunications networks. Figure 6.24 illustrates three basic topologies used in wide area and local area telecommunications networks. A *star* network ties end-user computers to a central computer. A *ring* network ties local computer processors together in a ring on a more equal basis. A *bus* network is a network in which local processors share the same bus, or communications channel. A variation of the ring network is the *mesh* network. It uses direct communications lines to connect some or all of the computers in the ring to one another.

Wired networks may use a combination of star, ring, and bus approaches. Obviously, the star network is more centralized, whereas ring and bus networks have a more decentralized approach. However, this is not always the case. For example, the central computer in a star configuration may be acting only as a *switch*, or message-switching computer that handles the data communications between autonomous local computers. Star, ring, and bus networks differ in their performance, reliability, and cost. A pure star network is considered less reliable than a ring network, because the other computers in the star are heavily dependent on the central host computer. If it fails, there is no backup processing and communications capability, and the local computers are cut off from one another. Therefore, it is essential that the host computer be highly reliable. Having some type of multiprocessor architecture to provide a fault-tolerant capability is a common solution.

FIGURE 6.24

The ring, star, and bus network topologies.

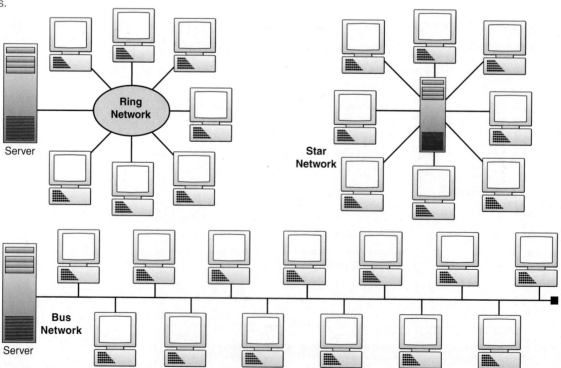

SOURCE: Courtesy of NetSight.

Until quite recently, sufficient standards were lacking for the interfaces among the hardware, software, and communications channels of telecommunications networks. This situation hampered the use of telecommunications, increased its costs, and reduced its efficiency and effectiveness. In response, telecommunications manufacturers and national and international organizations have developed standards called *protocols* and master plans called *network architectures* to support the development of advanced data communications networks.

**NETWORK
ARCHITECTURES
AND PROTOCOLS
LO 6-12
LO 6-13**

Protocols

A *protocol* is a standard set of rules and procedures for the control of communications in a network. However, these standards may be limited to just one manufacturer's equipment or just one type of data communications. Part of the goal of communications network architectures is to create more standardization and compatibility among communications protocols. One example of a protocol is a standard for the physical characteristics of the cables and connectors between terminals, computers, modems, and communications lines. Other examples are the protocols that establish the communications control information needed for *handshaking*, which is the process of exchanging predetermined signals and characters to establish a telecommunications session between terminals and computers. Other protocols deal with control of data transmission reception in a network, switching techniques, inter-network connections, and so on.

Network Architectures

The goal of *network architectures* is to promote an open, simple, flexible, and efficient telecommunications environment, accomplished by the use of standard protocols, standard communications hardware and software interfaces, and the design of a standard multilevel interface between end users and computer systems.

The OSI Model

The *Open Systems Interconnection (OSI)* model is a standard description or "reference model" for how messages should be transmitted between any two points in a telecommunications network. Its purpose is to guide product implementers so that their products will consistently work with other products. The reference model defines seven layers of functions that take place at each end of a communication. Although OSI is not always strictly adhered to in terms of keeping related functions together in a well-defined layer, many, if not most, products involved in telecommunications make an attempt to describe themselves in relation to the OSI model. It is also valuable as a view of communication that furnishes a common ground for education and discussion.

Developed by representatives of major computer and telecommunication companies beginning in 1983, OSI was originally intended to be a detailed specification of interfaces. Instead, the committee decided to establish a common reference model for which others could develop detailed interfaces that in turn could become standards. OSI was officially adopted as an international standard by the International Organization of Standardization (ISO).

The main idea in OSI is that the process of communication between two endpoints in a telecommunication network can be divided into layers, with each layer adding its own set of special, related functions. Each communicating user or program is at a computer equipped with these seven layers of functions. So in a given message between users, there will be a flow of data through each layer at one end down through the layers in that computer; at the other end, when the message arrives, there will be another flow of data up through the layers in the receiving computer and ultimately to the end user or program. The actual programming and hardware that furnishes these seven layers of functions is usually a combination of the computer operating system,

TCP/IP   **The OSI Model**

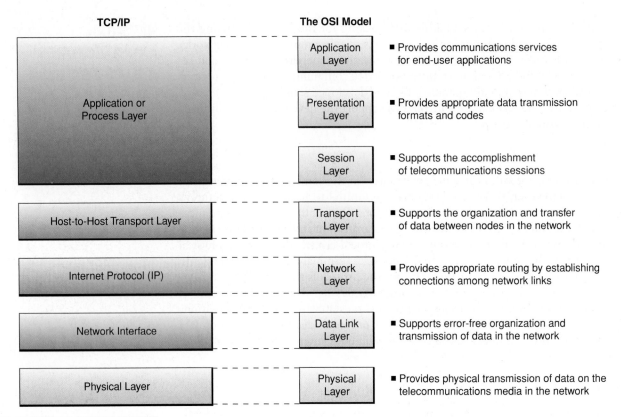

FIGURE 6.25

The seven layers of the OSI communications network architecture, and the five layers of the Internet's TCP/IP protocol suite.

applications (e.g., your Web browser), TCP/IP or alternative transport and network protocols, and the software and hardware that enable you to put a signal on one of the lines attached to your computer.

OSI divides telecommunication into seven layers. Figure 6.25 illustrates the functions of the seven layers of the OSI model architecture.

The layers consist of two groups. The upper four layers are used whenever a message passes to or from a user. The lower three layers (up to the network layer) are used when any message passes through the host computer. Messages intended for this computer pass to the upper layers. Messages destined for some other host are not passed to the upper layers but are forwarded to another host. The seven layers are:

- **Layer 1: The physical layer.** This layer conveys the bit stream through the network at the electrical and mechanical level. It provides the hardware means of sending and receiving data on a carrier.

- **Layer 2: The data link layer.** This layer provides synchronization for the physical level and does bit-stuffing for strings of 1's in excess of 5. It furnishes transmission protocol knowledge and management.

- **Layer 3: The network layer.** This layer handles the routing of the data (sending it in the right direction to the right destination on outgoing transmissions and receiving incoming transmissions at the packet level). The network layer does routing and forwarding.

- **Layer 4: The transport layer.** This layer manages the end-to-end control (e.g., determining whether all packets have arrived) and error checking. It ensures complete data transfer.

- **Layer 5: The session layer.** This layer sets up, coordinates, and terminates conversations, exchanges, and dialogues between the applications at each end. It deals with session and connection coordination.

- **Layer 6: The presentation layer.** This layer, usually part of an operating system, converts incoming and outgoing data from one presentation format to another (e.g., from a text stream into a pop-up window with the newly arrived text). It's sometimes called the syntax layer.

- **Layer 7: The application layer.** At this layer, communication partners are identified, quality of service is identified, user authentication and privacy are considered, and any constraints on data syntax are identified. (This layer is *not* the application itself, although some applications may perform application layer functions.)

The Internet's TCP/IP

The Internet uses a system of telecommunications protocols that has become so widely used that it is now accepted as a network architecture. The Internet's protocol suite is called *Transmission Control Protocol/Internet Protocol* and is known as ***TCP/IP.*** As Figure 6.25 shows, TCP/IP consists of five layers of protocols that can be related to the seven layers of the OSI architecture. TCP/IP is used by the Internet and by all intranets and extranets. Many companies and other organizations are thus converting their client/server and wide area networks to TCP/IP technology, which are now commonly called IP networks.

Although many of the technical aspects of the Internet can appear quite complex, the addressing, routing, and transport protocols, which make sure you get to the right Web site or your e-mail is delivered to the right place, are actually elegantly simple. TCP/IP can be thought of as analogous to how the postal system finds your house and delivers your mail. In this analogy, TCP represents the postal system and the various processes and protocols used to move the mail, while IP represents the zip code and address.

The current IP addressing protocol is called IPv4. When IP was first standardized in September 1981, the specification required that each system attached to the Internet be assigned a unique, 32-bit Internet address value. Systems that have interfaces to more than one network require a unique IP address for each network interface. The first part of an Internet address identifies the network on which the host resides, while the second part identifies the particular host on the given network. Keeping with our postal system analogy, the network address can be thought of as the zip code, and the host address represents the street address. By convention, an IP address is expressed as four decimal numbers separated by periods, such as "127.154.95.6." Valid addresses can range from 0.0.0.0 to 255.255.255.255, creating a total of about 4.3 billion addresses (4,294,967,296 to be exact). Using this two-level addressing hierarchy, any computer connected to the Internet can be located.

IP addressing can identify a specific network connected to the Internet. To provide the flexibility required to support networks of varying sizes, the Internet designers decided that the IP address space should be divided into three address classes—Classes A, B, and C. Each class fixes the boundary between the network prefix and the host number at a different point within the 32-bit address.

Class A networks are defined by the first number in an IP address. The value can range from 000 to 127, creating theoretically 128 unique networks. In reality, however, there are only 126 Class A addresses because both 0.0.0.0 and 127.0.0.0 are reserved for special use. Each Class A network address can support a total of 16,777,214 hosts per network, and they represent 50 percent of the total IPv4 address space. The Class A addresses are normally owned by large Internet service providers or well-established major corporations. For example, General Electric owns 3.0.0.0, IBM owns 9.0.0.0, Ford Motor Co. owns 19.0.0.0, and the U.S. Postal Service owns 56.0.0.0.

Class B network addresses range from 128.0 to 255.254. Using a Class B address, 16,384 networks can be identified with up to 65,534 hosts per network. Because the Class B address allocation contains slightly more than 1 million addresses, it represents 25 percent of the IPv4 address space. Class B addresses are also normally owned by very large service providers and global organizations—AOL uses 205.188.0.0.

Class C addresses range from 192.0.0 to 233.255.255 and represent 12.5 percent of the available IPv4 address space. Slightly less than 2.1 million networks can be identified with a Class C address allowing approximately 537 million hosts. The remaining 12.5 percent of the IPv4 address space is reserved for special use.

You would think that 4.3 billion addresses would be sufficient for quite a while, but the Internet is running out of space. During the early days of the Internet, the seemingly unlimited address space allowed IP addresses to be allocated to an organization based on a simple request rather than on actual need. As a result, addresses were freely assigned to those who asked for them without concerns about the eventual depletion of the IP address space. Now many of the Class A and Class B host addresses are not even in use. To make matters worse, new technologies are extending IP addresses beyond computers to televisions, toasters, and coffeemakers.

This is where IPv6 comes to the rescue. Developed to work with Internet2, IPv6 increases the IP address size from 32 bits to 128 bits to support more levels of the address hierarchy and a much greater number of nodes. IPv6 supports more than 340 trillion trillion trillion addresses, enough for each person in the world to be allocated 1 billion personal IP addresses! That should last for a while.

Voice over IP

One of the newest uses for Internet protocol (IP) is *Internet telephony*—the practice of using an Internet connection to pass voice data using IP instead of using the standard public-switched telephone network. Often referred to as *voice over IP* or **VoIP**, this approach makes use of a packet-based (or switched) network to carry voice calls, instead of the traditional circuit-switched network. In simpler terms, VoIP allows a person to function as if he or she were directly connected to a regular telephone network even when at home or in a remote office. It also skips standard long-distance charges because the only connection is through an ISP. VoIP is being used more and more to keep corporate telephone costs down, as you can just run two network cables to a desk instead of separate network and data cables. VoIP runs right over a standard network infrastructure, but it also demands a very well-configured network to run smoothly.

For those of us who love to talk (and not to pay for it), there is *Skype* (www.skype.com). Skype was founded in 2002 to develop the first peer-to-peer (P2P) telephony network. Today, Skype software allows telephone conversation through a PC and over the Internet instead of a separate phone connection. This proprietary freeware uses a messenger-like client and offers inbound and outbound PSTN (public-switched telephone network) facilities.

Skype users can call to any noncomputer-based landline or mobile telephone in the world and call other Skype users for free. The calls made to or received from traditional telephones are charged a fee, as are the voice-mail messages.

Skype software also provides features like voice mail, instant messaging, call forwarding, and conference calling. Skype users are not billed according to the distance between the two countries. Instead, the users are charged according to the prosperity of the country, the volume of calls made to and from the country, and the access charges. The latest statistical figures show that Skype is one of the fastest-growing companies on the Internet:

- Skype has 54 million members in 225 countries and territories, and the number is swelling—just through word-of-mouth marketing by satisfied users!
- Skype is adding approximately 150,000 users a day, and there are 3 million simultaneous users on the network at any given time.
- Skype has been downloaded 163 million times in 225 countries and territories.
- Skype is available in 27 languages.
- Skype has more users and serves more voice minutes than any other Internet voice communications provider.

Skype continues to grow in the consumer sector and is now offering business-specific services designed to reduce business telecommunication costs while offering more flexible alternatives to current landline or mobile approaches. Skype also demonstrates how VoIP is fast becoming part of the telecommunications infrastructure as shown in the following example.

For those of us to love to talk (and want to pay less than the telephone company wants us to pay), there is *Vonage* (www.vonage.com). The name is a play on their motto: Voice-Over-Net-Age—Vonage. Using VoIP technologies, Vonage offers local and long-distance telephone service to homes and businesses for a single low monthly price. VoIP has come a long way since Vonage, however. Today, you can find dozens of VoIP providers ranging from basic Internet phone services to complex business PBX services that allow for voice mail, auto-attendant features, call queuing and routing and many, many more features and resources. Most important, businesses adopting VoIP phone services are saving on the order of 50 percent or more over their previous landline services.

Ottawa Regional Hospital: Lowering Costs while Converting to VoIP

What started out as an upgrade to the phone system at Ottawa Regional Hospital and Healthcare Center became a badly needed network overhaul that lowered costs and included a conversion to VoIP.

The Ottawa, Illinois–based center was running an analog phone system that wouldn't support an IP phone system, let alone the battery of high-bandwidth medical applications that are becoming more and more necessary, says Curt Sesto, director of facilities, construction management, and electronics for the center.

When he arrived in 2008, his marching order from the CEO was to get a new phone system right away. "It had been on his radar for a couple of years," he says. One goal was to get rid of the estimated $28,000-per-year maintenance cost of the PBXs, for which it was getting increasingly harder to find parts as they grew older. "They could go toes-up at any time," he says.

Sesto checked out Siemens, Cisco, and Avaya VoIP systems. The Siemens system was being pushed by PosTrack, which also supplies Siemens medical gear to Ottawa Health. It was the only bidder that urged a data network evaluation as the first step in the process of moving to VoIP, he says. He liked that and also the fact that the Siemens offer was a hosted service. It would take on the task of network monitoring and maintenance, which frees up two to three full-timers who can focus instead on implementing electronic medical records systems, another priority for the center.

Voice traffic will run over the same network. The voice system is based on Siemens OpenScape servers located at two separate sites in Chicago for redundancy in case one goes down. It consists of a 30-mile connection over the local Medicacom cable TV network to the state-run Illinois Century Network, which is available to hospitals to connect to their local facilities.

The new phone system can be extended to 15 medical office buildings that are off the Ottawa campus, Sesto says. The old PBXs couldn't handle them, so each had its own small Avaya PBX that is being decommissioned as the central VoIP service rollout reaches each building.

The VoIP system has given the center a new voicemail system that integrates with Outlook so users get e-mail notification of voice messages. They system can also ring more than one phone when an extension is called. So an individual could configure the system to ring the office phone, but also the home phone and mobile. Unified communications (UC) features in the system include faxing to e-mails.

The network overhaul was more extensive than the CEO had in mind when he asked for a new phone system, but it's more appropriate to the high-bandwidth medical applications the network needs to support, Sesto says. "The old network was like having bicycle tires on an Indy car," he says.

SOURCE: Tim Greene, "VoIP, Network Overhaul brings Hospital Savings, Unified Communications," *Network World*, November 30, 2009.

FIGURE 6.26

Examples of the telecommunications transmission speeds of various network technologies.

Network Technologies	Typical-Maximum bps
Wi-Fi: wireless fidelity	11-54M
Standard Ethernet or token ring	10-16M
High-speed Ethernet	100M-1G
FDDI: fiber distributed data interface	100M
DDN: digital data network	2.4K-2M
PSN: packet-switching network-X.25	64K-1.5M
Frame relay network	1.5M-45M
ISDN: integrated services digital network	64K/128K-2M
ATM: asynchronous transfer mode	25/155M-2.4G
SONET: synchronous optical network	45M-40G

Kbps = thousand bps or kilobits per second   Gbps = billion bps or gigabits per second
Mbps = million bps or megabits per second

BANDWIDTH ALTERNATIVES
LO 6-10

The communications speed and capacity of telecommunications networks can be classified by **bandwidth**. The frequency range of a telecommunications channel, it determines the channel's maximum transmission rate. The speed and capacity of data transmission rates are typically measured in bits per second (bps). This level is sometimes referred to as the *baud* rate, though baud is more correctly a measure of signal changes in a transmission line.

Bandwidth represents the capacity of the connection. The greater the capacity, the more likely that greater performance will follow. Thus, greater bandwidth allows greater amounts of data to move from one point to another with greater speed. Although the relationship among bandwidth, data volume, and speed is theoretically sound, in practice, this is not always the case. A common analogy is to think of bandwidth as a pipe with water in it. The larger the pipe, the more water that can flow through it. If, however, the big pipe is connected to a small pipe, the effective amount of water that can be moved in a given time becomes severely restricted by the small pipe. The same problem occurs with network bandwidth. If a large bandwidth connection tries to move a large amount of data to a network with less bandwidth, the speed of the transmission will be determined by the speed of the smaller bandwidth.

Narrow-band channels typically provide low-speed transmission rates up to 64 Kbps but can now handle up to 2 Mbps. They are usually unshielded twisted-pair lines commonly used for telephone voice communications and for data communications by the modems of PCs and other devices. Medium-speed channels (*medium-band*) use shielded twisted-pair lines for transmission speeds up to 100 Mbps.

Broadband channels provide high-speed transmission rates at intervals from 256 Kbps to several billion bps. Typically, they use microwave, fiber optics, or satellite transmission. Examples are 1.54 Mbps for T1 and 45 Mbps for T3 communications channels, up to 100 Mbps for communications satellite channels, and between 52 Mbps and 10 Gbps for fiber-optic lines. See Figure 6.26.

SWITCHING ALTERNATIVES

Regular telephone service relies on *circuit switching*, in which a switch opens a circuit to establish a link between a sender and a receiver; it remains open until the communication session is completed. In message switching, a message is transmitted a block at a time from one switching device to another.

Packet switching involves subdividing communications messages into fixed or variable-length groups called packets. For example, in the X.25 protocol, packets are 128 characters long, while in the *frame relay* technology, they are of variable length.

Company	Technology	Why
Sears	Frame relay	Reliable, inexpensive, and accommodates mainframe and Internet protocols
Rack Room	VSAT (very small aperture terminal)	Very inexpensive way to reach small markets and shared satellite dishes at malls
Hannaford	ATM (asynchronous transfer mode)	Very high bandwidth; combines voice, video, and data
7-Eleven	ISDN (integrated services digital network)	Can use multiple channels to partition traffic among different uses

FIGURE 6.27

Why four large retail chains chose different network technologies to connect their stores.

Packet-switching networks are frequently operated by *value-added carriers* who use computers and other communications processors to control the packet-switching process and transmit the packets of various users over their networks.

Early packet-switching networks were X.25 networks. The X.25 protocol is an international set of standards governing the operations of widely used, but relatively slow, packet-switching networks. *Frame relay* is another popular packet-switching protocol and is used by many large companies for their wide area networks. Frame relay is considerably faster than X.25 and is better able to handle the heavy telecommunications traffic of interconnected local area networks within a company's wide area client/server network. ATM (*asynchronous transfer mode*) is an emerging high-capacity cell-switching technology. An ATM switch breaks voice, video, and other data into fixed cells of 53 bytes (48 bytes of data and 5 bytes of control information) and routes them to their next destination in the network. ATM networks are being developed by many companies needing their fast, high-capacity multimedia capabilities for voice, video, and data communications. See Figure 6.27.

Section 256 of the Communications Act, enacted in February 1996, states two key purposes: (1) "to promote nondiscriminatory accessibility by the broadest number of users and vendors of communications products and services to public telecommunications networks used to provide telecommunications service" and (2) "to ensure the ability of users and information providers to seamlessly and transparently transmit and receive information between and across telecommunications networks." To accomplish these purposes, the Federal Communications Commission (FCC) is required to establish procedures to oversee coordinated network planning by providers of telecommunications services. It is also authorized to participate in the development, by appropriate industry standards-setting organizations of public telecommunications, of network interconnectivity standards that promote access.

As you can see, the FCC is a key regulatory agency with regard to telecommunications. Although we tend to think of the FCC as the oversight body for radio and television, it is equally involved in all aspects of data and voice communications. If you reread the first paragraph of this section, it becomes clear that there is an important underlying reason for the FCC to be so involved with telecommunications. The answer lies in the importance of a concept called *network interoperability*.

This interoperability ensures that anyone anywhere on one network can communicate with anyone anywhere on another network without having to worry about speaking a common language from a telecommunications perspective. All that we have discussed in this chapter with regard to business value would not be possible without complete accessibility, transparency, and seamless interoperability across all networks. Without these things, the Internet would not be possible, nor would e-mail, instant messaging, or even common file sharing.

Fortunately for us, everyone in the telecommunications field understands the importance of network interoperability, and as such, they work together to ensure that all networks remain interoperable.

NETWORK INTEROPERABILITY
LO 6-5

real world SOLUTION

Adena Health System and Cherokee Health Systems— Reaching Far Away with the Help of Technology

Adena Health System and Cherokee Health Systems operate in low-income and underserved areas in southern Ohio and east Tennessee, respectively. Although the specific details of the challenges they are facing are slightly different—provision of specialized neonatal care for the former, basic pediatric and care for school-age children in the latter case—the general issue is the same: How to provide quality health care services to rural areas so that access to care, information, and expertise is on par with residents of large cities, where most of these services are commonly available. In the past, some state governments have attempted to address the issue by providing incentives for the establishment of medical facilities in rural areas, but those never caught on. In addition, there are benefits to scale that can be obtained by centralizing expertise in specific locations; the issue is how to make that expertise available regardless of geographical distance. Both organizations turned to telecommunication technology to help them make it happen.

In a joint effort between Adena Health Systems, Nationwide Children's Hospital (the specialized care partner to which Adena often referred newborns) and the Ohio Supercomputer Center, a telemedicine initiative was launched to connect the Adena Regional Medical Center with Nationwide Children's Hospital in Columbus, Ohio. Through a cutting-edge videoconferencing system, doctors in Chillicothe can collaborate with their colleagues in Columbus as if they were down the hall. "In the past, if a newborn was struggling, our doctors would have to work with the critical care specialists in Columbus by phone," says Marcus Bost, chief information officer, Adena Health System. "Physicians would have to try to describe the patient's skin tone, breathing, and other observations as accurately as possible, and fax reports back and forth. Although the process worked, it was always limited. With the technology we have in place now, doctors at Children's Hospital can observe the child themselves. This allows our physicians to make more informed decisions about whether a child needs to be transported to Children's Hospital or can remain here with the family."

Given the very specialized nature of critical neonatal care, not just any approach to videoconferencing would do. In particular, high-definition video was necessary, which in turn requires an incredible amount of bandwidth as well as strong internal networks to support and distribute the traffic. In the months prior to the deployment, the Adena Regional Medical Center had revamped its internal network using Cisco technology, which made it one of the few rural facilities with the capability to pull off this kind of project. In fact, the amount of bandwidth required is so large that the network connecting the two facilities actually runs on Internet2, the high-speed network designed to foster collaboration between universities and research institutions across the country. As a result of the high quality of the video being used, specialists in Columbus would be able to see a newborn as well as if she were in front of them. "With the telemedicine system, we can look at newborns' color, their tone, how much they're able to move," says Stephen E. Welty, MD, chief of neonatology at Nationwide Children's Hospital. "We can look at their profusion, and the resolution is so good that we can actually see how well their skin is being profused, which is a significant marker for the severity of illness."

In addition to the need to navigate the complex billing and reimbursement practices of insurance companies so that "consultations" over the telemedicine system would be treated as any other visit to the doctor, Adena had to make sure it could integrate the technology into the everyday work routines of doctors and nurses on both sides of the arrangement. The key to this issue was that the project was physician-driven from the very beginning, with strong support from executives in both sites as well as state officials interested in seeing how the project could drastically change the quality of care for a medically underserved region. After a year of running the new system, the number of newborns transferred to Columbus dropped by half, thanks largely to more specialized diagnoses that were made remotely by physicians and allowed newborns to be treated locally by Adena staff. For those more complicated cases that needed to be transferred to Columbus, by the time they got there the doctors already had the chance to examine them remotely, and thus knew what to expect and were prepared accordingly. All in all, the project has been a tremendous success, so much so that the state government is working on the implementation of a high-capacity fiber-optic network that will link more rural facilities to specialized health care throughout the state.

At the request of the Sevier County School District, Cherokee Health Systems started examining different models for the provision of on-site health clinics in each of the 17 elementary and middle schools in the county.

Although several alternatives were examined, enrollments at each school were not, by themselves, enough to financially justify the volume necessary to support a full-time nurse practitioner. At the same time, the large overall enrollment for the entire county—about 10,000 students—was more than adequate for the provision of those services; a different operating model, however, was required. The key to this was to be able to leverage that volume by providing services from a centralized location that could simultaneously serve a demand that was very distributed geographically. This is where technology came in, in the form of videoconferencing.

The technology itself was not an obstacle, but funding was. The technology has been there for some time now, and the telecommunications aspect of the project was straightforward: A single metro-ethernet circuit connected Cherokee to Education Networks of Americas, which served as the data services provider for all schools, and no upgrades were necessary. Although high-definition capabilities were considered, limitations in the amount of bandwidth available pushed project sponsors to use regular LCD screens. The setup for each individual school, however, was rather expensive, and this is where things got complicated. Each site was outfitted with a Polycom—a leading provider of conferencing systems—unit, as well as peripheral devices from AMD Telemedicine, which include a camera and illumination unit; an ear, nose, and throat scope; and a stethoscope, all of which integrate directly to the Polycom unit. Add the LCD screens, and the total bill runs to about $17,000 per school in the program.

Fortunately, the Sevier County School District foresaw the many benefits that would arise from the project, and decided to make the majority of the up-front investment itself. Once that issue was addressed, the entire project took only about four months to be implemented, partly the result of strong leadership from the school health director and district superintendent, who drove the process. "Within the first four months of Telemed being implemented, the attendance has increased each 20-day period. All school administrators believe it could be the biggest difference maker in academic improvement in years. Student basic health needs are being addressed with positive results," says Don Best, Coordinator of School Health, Sevier County School System.

The benefits are so clear that both parents and schools have rushed to embrace the new approach. "Parents have often expressed their appreciation of the program and medical help that their child received without leaving school with Telemed," says Nancye Williams, Principal, Pigeon Forge Primary School. At current staffing levels, Cherokee has the capacity to see 27 school patients every school day, an order-of-magnitude improvement from parents missing work to drive their children to remote offices, which are also considerably more expensive. One major challenge that is still being worked upon lies with billing and insurance companies, many of which still consider telemedicine an "experimental" treatment and refuse to cover it. However, since many of the children are covered under TennCare, a state-run program for low-income families that does reimburse for telemedicine "visits," this has not yet been a major hindrance to the program.

Each in its own way, both cases show how communications technology can help break some long-standing barriers to providing quality health care to underserved, rural areas of the country. "As you look forward in medicine, I think this technology is almost limitless," says John Radford, attending pediatrician, Adena Regional Medical Center. "What we're seeing here is the beginning of some pretty amazing innovations in medicine, as far as the ability of tertiary care facilities to reach out to smaller rural hospitals and give them specialty care in a much more sophisticated fashion."

SOURCE: "Adena Health System," *Computerworld Honors Case Study*, www.adena.org, accessed May 23, 2011; "Cherokee Health Systems," *Computerworld Honors Case Study*; and cherokeehealthsystems.com, accessed May 23, 2011.

▼ QUESTIONS TO CONSIDER

1. Although the technologies used in both cases were quite sophisticated, these technologies do not seem to have been a major issue in the implementation. What were the main roadblocks to the rollout of the projects? What are the lessons that can be applied to videoconferencing efforts in other organizations or industries?

2. Which other problems or scenarios would benefit from the technologies discussed in this case? What are the characteristics of situations that could benefit from videoconferencing technologies?

- **Telecommunications Trends.** Organizations are becoming networked enterprises that use the Internet, intranets, and other telecommunications networks to support business operations and collaboration within the enterprise and with their customers, suppliers, and other business partners. Telecommunications has entered a deregulated and fiercely competitive environment with many vendors, carriers, and services. Telecommunications technology is moving toward open, internetworked digital networks for voice, data, video, and multimedia. A major trend is the pervasive use of the Internet and its technologies to build interconnected enterprise and global networks, like intranets and extranets, to support enterprise collaboration, e-commerce, and other e-business applications.

- **The Internet Revolution.** The explosive growth of the Internet and the use of its enabling technologies have revolutionized computing and telecommunications. The Internet has become the key platform for a rapidly expanding list of information and entertainment services and business applications, including enterprise collaboration, electronic commerce, and other e-business systems. Open systems with unrestricted connectivity using Internet technologies are the primary telecommunications technology drivers in e-business systems. Their primary goal is to promote easy and secure access by business professionals and consumers to the resources of the Internet, enterprise intranets, and interorganizational extranets.

- **The Business Value of the Internet.** Companies are deriving strategic business value from the Internet, which enables them to disseminate information globally, communicate and trade interactively with customized information and services for individual customers, and foster collaboration of people and integration of business processes within the enterprise and with business partners. These capabilities allow them to generate cost savings from using Internet technologies, revenue increases from electronic commerce, and better customer service and relationships through better supply chain management and customer relationship management.

- **The Role of Intranets.** Businesses are installing and extending intranets throughout their organizations to (1) improve communications and collaboration among individuals and teams within the enterprise; (2) publish and share valuable business information easily, inexpensively, and effectively via enterprise information portals and intranet Web sites and other intranet

services; and (3) develop and deploy critical applications to support business operations and decision making.

- **The Role of Extranets.** The primary role of extranets is to link the intranet resources of a company to the intranets of its customers, suppliers, and other business partners. Extranets can also provide access to operational company databases and legacy systems to business partners. Thus, extranets provide significant business value by facilitating and strengthening the business relationships of a company with customers and suppliers, improving collaboration with its business partners, and enabling the development of new kinds of Web-based services for its customers, suppliers, and others.

- **Telecommunications Networks.** The major generic components of any telecommunications network are (1) terminals, (2) telecommunications processors, (3) communications channels, (4) computers, and (5) telecommunications software. There are several basic types of telecommunications networks, including wide area networks (WANs) and local area networks (LANs). Most WANs and LANs are interconnected using client/server, network computing, peer-to-peer, and Internet networking technologies.

- **Network Alternatives.** Key telecommunications network alternatives and components are summarized in Figure 6.11 for telecommunications media, processors, software, channels, and network architectures. A basic understanding of these major alternatives will help business end users participate effectively in decisions involving telecommunications issues. Telecommunications processors include modems, multiplexers, internetwork processors, and various devices to help interconnect and enhance the capacity and efficiency of telecommunications channels. Telecommunications networks use such media as twisted-pair wire, coaxial cables, fiber-optic cables, terrestrial microwave, communications satellites, cellular and PCS systems, wireless LANs, and other wireless technologies.

- Telecommunications software, such as network operating systems and telecommunications monitors, controls and manages the communications activity in a telecommunications network.

These are the key terms and concepts of this chapter. The page number of their first reference appears in parentheses.

1. Analog (256)
2. Bandwidth (272)
3. Bluetooth (261)
4. Client/server networks (253)
5. Coaxial cable (257)
6. Communications satellites (259)
7. Digital (256)
8. Extranets (245)
9. Fiber optics (257)
10. Internet networking technologies (234)
11. Internet service provider (ISP) (239)
12. Inter-network processors (263)
13. Intranets (243)
14. Legacy systems (253)
15. Local area networks (LAN) (250)
16. Metcalfe's law (234)
17. Middleware (236)
18. Modems (263)
19. Multiplexer (264)
20. Network (231)
21. Network architectures (267)
    a. Open Systems Interconnection (OSI) (267)
    b. TCP/IP (269)
22. Network computing (254)
23. Network interoperability (273)
24. Network topologies (266)
25. Open systems (235)
26. Peer-to-peer networks (254)
27. Protocol (267)
28. Telecommunications (234)
29. Telecommunications media (256)
30. Telecommunications network (248)
31. Telecommunications processors (262)
32. Telecommunications software (264)
33. Virtual private networks (VPN) (251)
34. VoIP (270)
35. Wide area networks (WAN) (249)
36. Wireless LAN (260)
37. Wireless technologies (236)

Match one of the key terms and concepts listed previously with one of the brief examples or definitions that follow. Try to find the best fit for answers that seem to fit more than one term or concept. Defend your choices.

_____ 1. Technique for making telephone calls over the Internet.

_____ 2. The ability for all networks to connect to one another.

_____ 3. An interconnected or interrelated chain, group, or system.

_____ 4. Software that serves to "glue together" separate programs.

_____ 5. The usefulness, or utility, of a network equals the square of the number of users.

_____ 6. Internet-like networks that improve communications and collaboration, publish and share information, and develop applications to support business operations and decision making within an organization.

_____ 7. Provide Internet-like access to a company's operational databases and legacy systems by its customers and suppliers.

_____ 8. Company that provides individuals and organizations access to the Internet.

_____ 9. A communications network covering a large geographic area.

_____ 10. A communications network in an office, a building, or other work site.

_____ 11. Representation of an electrical signal using binary numbers.

_____ 12. Coaxial cable, microwave, and fiber optics are examples.

_____ 13. A communications medium that uses pulses of laser light in glass fibers.

_____ 14. A short range cable replacement technology for digital devices.

_____ 15. Includes modems, multiplexers, and inter-network processors.

_____ 16. Includes programs such as network operating systems and Web browsers.

_____ 17. A common communications processor for microcomputers.

_____ 18. Helps a communications channel carry simultaneous data transmissions from many terminals.

_____ 19. Star, ring, and bus networks are examples.

_____ 20. Representation of an electrical signal that is analogous to the signal itself.

_____ 21. The communications speed and capacity of telecommunications networks.

_____ 22. Intranets and extranets can use their network firewalls and other security features to establish secure Internet links within an enterprise or with its trading partners.

_____ 23. Sturdy cable that provides high bandwidth on a single conductor.

_____ 24. Standard rules or procedures for control of communications in a network.

_____ 25. An international standard, multilevel set of protocols to promote compatibility among telecommunications networks.

_____ 26. The standard suite of protocols used by the Internet, intranets, extranets, and some other networks.

_____ 27. Information systems with common hardware, software, and network standards that provide easy access for end users and their networked computer systems.

_____ 28. Interconnected networks need communications processors such as switches, routers, hubs, and gateways.

_____ 29. Web sites, Web browsers, HTML documents, hypermedia databases, and TCP/IP networks are examples.

_____ 30. Networks in which end-user PCs are tied to network servers to share resources and application processing.

_____ 31. Network computers provide a browser-based interface for software and databases provided by servers.

_____ 32. End-user computers connect directly with each other to exchange files.

_____ 33. Orbiting devices that provide multiple communication channels over a large geographical area.

_____ 34. Older, traditional mainframe-based business information systems.

_____ 35. Any arrangement in which a sender transmits a message to a receiver over a channel consisting of some type of medium.

_____ 36. Provides wireless network access for laptop PCs in business settings.

_____ 37. Their goal is to improve the telecommunications environment by fostering standardized protocols, communications hardware and software, and the design of standard interfaces, among other things.

_____ 38. A type of communications network consisting of terminals, processors, channels, computers, and control software.

_____ 39. Telecommunications technologies that do not rely on physical media such as cables or fiber optics.

discussion questions

1. The Internet is the driving force behind developments in telecommunications, networks, and other information technologies. Do you agree or disagree? Why?

2. How is the trend toward open systems, connectivity, and interoperability related to business use of the Internet, intranets, and extranets?

3. Refer to the Real World Challenge in the chapter. The problems in the case are framed from the perspective of the health care providers. From that of a patient, what would be your concerns about "visiting" a doctor who is maybe hundreds of miles away? What could be done to alleviate those concerns?

4. How will wireless information appliances and services affect the business use of the Internet and the Web? Explain.

5. What are some of the business benefits and management challenges of client/server networks? Network computing? Peer-to-peer networks?

6. What is the business value driving so many companies to install and extend intranets rapidly throughout their organizations?

7. What strategic competitive benefits do you see in a company's use of extranets?

8. Refer to the Real World Solution in the chapter. Why do some insurance companies refuse to cover telemedicine services, or classify them as "experimental"? What are their concerns? How could those concerns be addressed so that these approaches can be expanded to other geographical areas with similar problems?

9. Do you think that business use of the Internet, intranets, and extranets has changed what businesspeople expect from information technology in their jobs? Explain.

10. The insatiable demand for everything wireless, video, and Web-enabled everywhere will be the driving force behind developments in telecommunications, networking, and computing technologies for the foreseeable future. Do you agree or disagree? Why?

1. IPv4 / IPv6

How many addresses are enough?

The Internet Protocol version 4 assigns each connected computer a four-byte address known as an IP Address. Messages, or packets, each include this address so that routers know where to forward them. They are the Internet's version of a mailing address.

Each region of the world has been given a range of IP addresses to administer locally, with America taking the largest share. Asia, with a significantly larger population, received a disproportionately small range of numbers and fears running out.

Anticipating this problem, the Internet Engineering Task Force adopted IPv6, which uses addresses 16 bytes long. Although slow to be adopted, all Internet Root servers now support IPv6, and Internet Service Providers are rolling it out as needed while maintaining backwards compatibility for IPv4. The U.S. federal government has mandated the change to IPv6 for all federal agencies by 2008.

a. Express as a power of 2 the number of nodes that can exist using IPv4.

b. Express as a power of 2 the number of nodes that can exist using IPv6.

2. MNO Incorporated Communications Network

Calculating Bandwidth

MNO Incorporated is considering acquiring its own leased lines to handle voice and data communications between its 14 distribution sites in three regions around the country. The peak load of communications for each site is expected to be a function of the number of phone links and the number of computers at that site. Communications data are available below. You have been asked to analyze this information.

a. Create a database table with an appropriate structure to store the data below. Enter records shown below and get a printed listing of your table.

Site Location	Region	Phone Lines	Computers
Boston	East	228	95
New York	East	468	205
Richmond	East	189	84
Atlanta	East	192	88
Detroit	East	243	97
Cincinnati	East	156	62
New Orleans	Central	217	58
Chicago	Central	383	160
Saint Louis	Central	212	91
Houston	Central	238	88
Denver	West	202	77
Los Angeles	West	364	132
San Francisco	West	222	101
Seattle	West	144	54

b. Survey results suggest that the peak traffic to and from a site will be approximately 2 kilobits per second for each phone line plus 10 kilobits per second for each computer. Create a report showing the estimated peak demand for the telecommunications system at each site in kilobits. Create a second report grouped by region and showing regional subtotals and a total for the system as a whole.

3. Wireless Radiation

Frying Your Brains?

Radio waves, microwaves, and infrared all belong to the electromagnetic radiation spectrum. These terms reference ranges of radiation frequencies that we use every day in our wireless networking environments. However, the very word "radiation" strikes fear in many people. Cell towers have sprouted from fields all along highways. Tall rooftops harbor many more cell stations in cities. Millions of cell phone users place microwave transmitters/receivers next to their heads each time they make a call. Wireless access points for computer networks have become ubiquitous. Even McDonalds's customers can use their machines to browse the Internet as they eat burgers. With all this radiation zapping about, should we be concerned?

The electromagnetic spectrum ranges from ultra-low frequencies, radio waves, microwaves, infrared, visible light, ultraviolet, X-ray, up to gamma-ray radiation. Is radiation dangerous? The threat appears to come from two different directions, the frequency and the intensity. A preponderance of research has demonstrated the dangers of radiation at frequencies just higher than those of visible light. This even includes the ultraviolet light used in tanning beds, X-rays, and gamma rays. These frequencies are high enough (the wavelengths are small enough) to penetrate and disrupt molecules and even atoms. The results range from burns to damaged DNA that might lead to cancer or birth defects.

However, radiation's lower frequencies ranging from visible light (the rainbow colors you can see), infrared, microwave, and radio waves have long waves unable to penetrate molecules. Indeed, microwave wavelengths are so long that microwave ovens use a simple viewing screen that can block these long waves and yet allow visible light through. As a result, we can watch our popcorn pop without feeling any heat. Keep in mind that visible light consists of radiation frequencies closer to the "danger end" of the spectrum than microwave light.

Lower radiation frequencies can cause damage only if the *intensity* is strong enough, and that damage is limited to common burns. Microwave ovens cook food by drawing 800 or more watts and converting them into a very intense (bright) microwave light. Cellular telephones, by comparison, draw a very tiny amount of current from the phone's battery and uses the resulting microwaves to transmit a signal. In fact, the heat you feel from the cell phone is not from the microwaves but rather from its discharging battery.

a. Use an Internet search engine and report on what the World Health Organization (WHO) has had to say about microwave radiation or non-ionizing radiation.

b. Use an Internet search engine to identify the various complaints posed by stakeholders regarding cell phone towers. Write a one-page paper describing an alternative to cell phone towers that would enable cell phone use and yet mitigate all or most of these complaints.

4. Maximizing Communications
Human Networking

Ms. Sapper, this year's annual partner meeting coordinator for a global accounting firm, faced an interesting challenge. With 400 high-powered partners gathering from all around the world, she wanted to arrange meal seating in a way that maximized diversity at each table. She hoped that this would encourage partners to open up new lines of communication and discourage old cliques from re-forming. The banquet facility included 50 tables, each seating eight guests. Ms. Sapper had all the necessary partner data, but she found herself stumped about how to maximize diversity at each table. Let's walk her through the process.

Download and save "partners.xls" from the IIS 16e OLC. Open the file and note that in addition to partner's names, it also contains industry, region, and gender information. The *Table No.* column has been left blank.

a. In Excel's menu, select "Data" and then "Sort" and then press the "F1" key for help. Read through each of the topics. How would an *ascending* sort arrange the list "Smith; Jones; Zimmerman"?

b. What feature allows users to sort month lists so *January* appears before *April*?

c. Sort the partner data first on Gender, then by Industry, and then by Region, and save the file.

d. Examine the sorted results from the previous step. Notice that assigning the first eight partners to the *same* table would *minimize* diversity. This should also provide a clue about how to *maximize* diversity. Using this insight, assign a table number in the range from 1 to 50 to each partner in your sorted list so as to maximize diversity. Save the file as "partners_sorted.xls", and explain your logic.

5. Dark Shadows
Fixing the Dead Zones

Imagine you've made the leap from commuting to working out of your own home office. You've found an ideal place in the basement: it's cool, it's quiet, and you and your Star Wars action figure collection won't be disturbed. All is well until you make your first call and discover that you don't get cellular phone coverage in your basement. Your phone is a zombie: cold and dead.

Cell phones operate on radio/microwave frequencies, frequencies lower on the spectrum than visible light. Like visible light, they don't pass well through dirt, steel, or concrete, although they can reflect off these surfaces to some extent. In the end, however, your service provider isn't going to build a cell tower in your backyard to fill in the coverage shadow in your basement, but *you* can . . . if you use your brains.

a. Have you experienced dead zones? If so, describe where or under what circumstances?

b. Search for "cell phone signal boosters." Briefly describe what you found.

c. What are the pros and cons to these products?

real world
CASE 1

DLA Piper, MetLife, PepsiCo, and Others: Telepresence Is Finally Coming of Age

Sprawling international law firm DLA Piper has upgraded from videoconferencing to telepresence, which will save the firm nearly $1 million dollars per year in reduced travel costs and lost productivity. The conferencing gear that simulates across-the-table meetings has "a provable and achievable return on investment over five years, and may actually pay for itself before then," says Don Jaycox, chief information officer of DLA Piper U.S.

This involves an "immersive video experience," or technology that provides high-end, high-definition visual and audio communications in a completely integrated environment. The goal is to make anyone involved in these meetings feel as if they're actually in the room with the other meeting participants, regardless of where everyone is physically based.

"Rescheduling half the firm's in-person board meetings as telepresence conferences and relying on at least two attorneys per week to use telepresence rather than travel accounts for significant savings when lost productivity for travel time is factored in," says Jaycox.

"If I look at my total telepresence project cost, which includes equipment, room construction, implementation services, maintenance contract, financing costs, etc., then amortize that over the expected five-year life of the system, it works out to be just a hair under $500,000 per year for our six U.S. sites," he says. "Our early experience suggests that a more accurate number of avoided trips is closer to four or five per week, so the $970,000 projection almost certainly underestimates our actual savings," he notes.

Beyond the financial benefits, telepresence meetings works to bind together the 65 DLA Piper offices in 28 countries and its 3,800 attorneys, he says, by encouraging more meetings. Telepresence sessions are simpler to set up than traditional videoconferencing, and that encourages greater use. "It enables the meetings you otherwise wouldn't have had but probably should have," Jaycox says.

The sites were selected so they put 80 percent of the attorneys within an hour's drive of a telepresence room. Jaycox says he has observed attorneys working together via telepresence conferences, and was struck to see two workgroups formed at either end of the telepresence table, just as they might be if they were all working around the same physical table. "You had the sense all these people were in the same strategy room," he says.

With the economy in a downturn, it's no surprise that companies have been slashing travel budgets. But at MetLife, officials say the focus is also on quality of life for employees, keeping them home as much as possible. As a result, the insurance giant has recently made a big push into telepresence technology.

MetLife is using Cisco Telepresence in three dedicated conference rooms in Chicago, New York, and New Jersey, and plans to expand to other offices nationally and internationally soon. "Instead of having to take people away from their families, you walk down to the room and turn on the lights and have your three-hour meeting and it's extremely effective," says Anthony Nugent, executive vice president of employee benefits sales. He regularly uses telepresence to communicate with his direct reports in Chicago and Somerset, N.J., and the clarity is so good that, he says with a laugh, "Everyone jokes around that they can reach a Coke across the table" from one location to another.

MetLife has seen direct cost savings, as well as better employee time efficiency, and a way to help the company meet its "green initiative" goal of reducing its carbon emissions by 20 percent this year, says Nugent. The company finished its initial telepresence rollout a year ago and hasn't yet determined exact savings, but Nugent estimates the use of the systems will provide double-digit ROI in travel savings alone.

At MetLife, the three Cisco telepresence systems cost just under $1 million to install, according to Paul Galvin, vice president of enterprise services in the information technology group. Nugent says he uses both videoconferencing and telepresence, depending on what his needs are. Videoconferencing is a better choice for one-on-one situations, such as "if someone is going to do a quick presentation to me," he says, but telepresence is ideal for meetings where participants are located in multiple offices.

Telepresence allows him to have face-to-face contact with a broader group "so it allows me to get to know people better," Nugent says. He runs an organization with people based all around the country and used to require that his direct reports come to New York for quarterly reviews. Now they can stay in their offices and he can discuss business with a wider range of employees.

"Using telepresence allows me to see and virtually interact with more people on my team instead of just my direct reports," says Nugent. "When we use telepresence for meetings, people who wouldn't normally be asked to travel to New York have the opportunity to make presentations and get valuable exposure to executive management. It really facilitates face-to-face interaction with a broader cross-section of employees on an economically efficient basis."

MetLife is considering putting a telepresence system at a business processing plant in India to avoid having employees fly over to see it. The company is also looking at ways to utilize telepresence with salespeople across the country. The idea is to have as many people using the system as possible, Nugent says.

"Flying out of Boston for a meeting when I was 20 sounded great, but the sales pitch I always give is we're respecting the time of the employee," he says. "So if we can give a person the effectiveness of being there and then be home with his family, it's two wins."

PepsiCo is deploying Cisco Telepresence systems in its major offices worldwide. PepsiCo CIO Robert Dixon says that using telepresence "will reinvent the way we work" while cutting down on travel, which, in turn, improves productivity and reduces the company's environmental footprint. "In this day and age, it's simply a smarter way of going about our business," he adds. PepsiCo sells products from 18 different product lines in 200 countries and employs nearly 200,000 workers.

The law firm of Lathrop & Gage, LLP, is using both high-definition videoconferencing and telepresence. Employees conduct more than 300 meetings every month at the firm's Kansas City, Missouri headquarters. "It's a more meaningful way to conduct meetings than over the phone," says CEO Joel Voran, who uses the system about three times a week. While he still tries to make it to all of the firm's offices twice a year, Voran says use of the Polycom systems has significantly reduced the need for lawyers to fly to Kansas City.

"The clarity has been impressive," Voran says. "At one of our very first meetings at one of our offices I could see the brand of the beverage someone was drinking and that made the partner sit up and take notice."

"This is a billable-hour profession," notes Ben Weinberger, chief information officer at Lathrop & Gage, who adds that one attorney alone can save over $1,500 in travel expenses and productivity loss by not having to fly somewhere to attend a meeting. Because many lawyers travel monthly, the Polycom system could represent a savings of more than $30,000 in annual travel expenses and productivity loss for a single attorney, he estimates.

Weinberger differentiates between high-end videoconferencing and telepresence by the size of the screens. The rooms that have 50-plus-inch screens and run high-quality, high-definition cameras are utilizing telepresence, he says.

Making it possible for far-flung attorneys to work closely together via telepresence helps drive home that the firm has offices around the world and should have an international focus: a benefit of the system that can't be quantified in dollars and cents. "When you work in one location, you tend to draw inward. We want people to think globally," says Jaycox.

SOURCE: Esther Shein, "Telepresence Catching On, but Hold onto Your Wallet," *Computerworld*, January 22, 2010; Matt Hamblen, "PepsiCo to Deploy Telepresence from Cisco and BT Globally," *Computerworld*, February 2, 2010; and Tim Greene, "Telepresence Cuts Near $1M in Travel Costs for Law Firm," *Network World*, October 7, 2009.

▼ CASE STUDY QUESTIONS

1. Implementing telepresence seems to have other, less tangible, advantages beyond travel cost savings. What are some of those advantages? How do you quantify them to make the case for investing in the technology? Provide at least two fully developed examples.

2. DLA Piper, MetLife, and the other companies featured in the case are very optimistic about the technology. However, other than its cost, what are some potential disadvantages of implementing telepresence in organizations?

3. Do you think meetings conducted through telepresence technology will be similar to face-to-face ones as the technology becomes more pervasive? How would the rules of etiquette change for telepresence meetings? Which would you like best?

▼ REAL WORLD ACTIVITIES

1. Telepresence is described in the case as a green technology because it replaces air travel with a more environmentally friendly alternative. Recently, many organizations are looking to IT to help them cut their carbon footprint. What other technologies can be helpful in this regard? Go online and research different ways in which the "green IT" movement is catching on. Prepare a report to share your findings.

2. The organizations featured in the case are not optimistic about the future of business travel. Taking into account the high quality of current and future telepresence systems, do you believe these companies are missing something by not having people meet face-to-face? Why or why not? Break into small groups with your classmates to discuss this issue.

real world CASE 2

Brain Saving Technologies Inc. and the T-Health Institute: Medicine through Videoconferencing

On average, every 45 seconds, someone in the United States suffers a stroke, the third-leading cause of death, as well as the leading cause of permanent disability in the nation, according to the American Heart Association.

The first three hours after a stroke are critical to a patient's survival and recovery. For instance, depending on the type of stroke a patient suffers, certain drugs can vastly improve the patient's survival and chances for full rehabilitation. Those same drugs, however, can be deadly if given to a patient suffering from another type of stroke. Due in part to a shortage of specialty physicians trained to accurately diagnose and treat stroke victims, not all U.S. hospitals have the expertise and equipment to give stroke patients optimal care, particularly in the critical early hours.

The new Neuro Critical Care Center, operated by Brain Saving Technologies Inc. in Wellesley Hills, Massachusetts, will begin to connect emergency-room doctors at a number of suburban hospitals in the state with a remote university hospital that will act as a "hub" with on-call critical-care neurologists who can assist in making remote diagnoses and treatment recommendations for suspected stroke patients, says Stuart Bernstein, CEO and chief operating officer at Brain Saving Technologies. The connection occurs through a visual communication workstation that can connect via Internet protocol (IP), high-bandwidth communications, or private leased line. The workstation allows the remote specialists to examine and talk to patients, and collaborate with on-site doctors to improve timely diagnosis of strokes and optimize treatment options, Bernstein says.

"Our purpose is to provide member hospitals with a major hospital stroke center, 24/7," Bernstein says. CT scans—digital images of patient's brains—can also be transmitted from the member hospitals to the Neuro Critical Care Center specialists to improve diagnosis of the patients, he says. The images are seen simultaneously by doctors at both locations so they can collaborate. The technology can also help train emergency-room doctors about what characteristics to look for on the CT scans of stroke patients.

A key component of the Neuro Critical Care Center's offering is the Intern Tele-HealthCare Solution from Tandberg, which provides simultaneous audio and video transmission and bidirectional videoconferencing and image-display capabilities to hub and member hospital

doctors. Emergency-room doctors can wheel the mobile Tandberg system to a patient's bedside, Bernstein says.

Tandberg's medical video communication products are also used in other telehealth applications, including situations where doctors need an expert in sign language or a foreign language to communicate with patients or their family members, says Joe D'Iorio, Tandberg's manager of telehealth. "The technology provides real-time visibility and collaboration to help assess patients' well-being and facilitate real-time interaction," he notes.

Doctors have long had a tradition of holding "grand rounds" to discuss patient cases and educate aspiring physicians. The centuries-old practice certainly has its merits, but medical leaders in Arizona want to improve, update, and broaden it to include a larger list of health care practitioners, such as nurses and social workers, regardless of their locations. So the Arizona Telemedicine Program (ATP) drew on its extensive use of videoconferencing equipment to develop the Institute for Advanced Telemedicine and Telehealth, or the T-Health Institute, to facilitate a 21st-century way of teaching and collaborating across disciplines and professions.

"Its specific mission is to use technology to permit interdisciplinary team training," explains Dr. Ronald Weinstein, cofounder and director of the ATP. "Now we're opening it up to a far broader range of participants and patients." The T-Health Institute is a division of the ATP, which Arizona lawmakers established in 1996 as a semi-autonomous entity. The ATP operates the Arizona Telemedicine Network, a statewide broadband health care telecommunications network that links 55 independent health care organizations in 71 communities.

Through this network, telemedicine services are provided in 60 subspecialties, including internal medicine, surgery, psychiatry, radiology, and pathology, by dozens of service providers. More than 600,000 patients have received services over the network.

Project leaders say the goal is to create much-needed discussion and collaboration among professionals in multiple health care disciplines so that they can deliver the best care to patients. "It's the effort to be inclusive," Weinstein says. "Medicine is quite closed and quite limited, but we're counting on telecommunications to bridge some of those communication gaps." The institute is essentially a teleconferencing hub that enables students, professors, and working professionals to participate in live meetings. Its technology also allows them to switch nearly instantly between different discussion groups as easily as they could if they were meeting in person and merely switching chairs.

Gail Barker has noticed that participants who don't speak up during in-person meetings often become much more active in discussions held via videoconferencing. Perhaps it's because they feel less intimidated when they're not physically surrounded by others or because the videoconferencing screen provides a buffer against criticism, says Barker, who is director of the T-Health Institute and a teacher at the University of Arizona's College of Public Health.

When used poorly, videoconferencing can be stiff and dull, just a talking head beaming out across cyberspace without any chance to engage the audience. But Barker and others are finding that when the technology is used in a thoughtful and deliberate manner, it has some advantages over real-life sessions because of its ability to draw more participants into the fray.

"It's literally a new method of teaching medical students. It's a novel approach," says Jim Mauger, director of engineering at Audio Video Resources Inc., a Phoenix-based company hired to design and install the videoconferencing equipment for the T-Health Institute.

The T-Health Institute uses a Tandberg 1500 videoconferencing system, and its video wall has 12 50-inch Toshiba P503DL DLP Datawall RPU Video Cubes. The video wall itself is controlled by a Jupiter Fusion 960 Display Wall Processor utilizing dual Intel Xeon processors. The Fusion 960 allows the wall to display fully movable and scalable images from multiple PC, video, and network sources.

Although Weinstein was able to articulate this vision of interprofessional interaction—that is, he could clearly lay out the user requirements—implementing the technology to support it brought challenges, IT workers say.

Mauger says creating a videoconferencing system that linked multiple sites in one video wall wasn't the challenging part. The real challenge was developing the technology that allows facilitators to move participants into separate virtual groups and then seamlessly switch them around. "The biggest challenges to making this work were the audio isolation among the separate conference participants as well as fast dynamics of switching video and moving participants to meetings," he explains.

He says his team also encountered other challenges—ones that affect more typical IT projects, such as budget constraints, the need to get staffers in different cities to collaborate, and the task of translating user requirements into actionable items. "It's necessary to have someone there on-site who understands all the complex parts of the project," he says. "Someone who is not just meeting with people every now and then, but someone who works with them on a daily basis."

Barker, who teaches in the College of Public Health at the University of Arizona and is a user of the system, led a trial-run training session at the T-Health amphitheater. She met with 13 people, including a clinical pharmacist, two family nurse practitioners, a senior business developer, two program coordinators, a diabetes program case manager, and an A/V telemedicine specialist.

For that event, Barker says the biggest benefit was the time saved by having the facility in place; without the T-Health Institute, some participants would have had to make a four-hour round trip to attend in person. Now the system is opening up to others in Arizona's health care and medical education communities. T-Health Institute officials say they see this as the first step toward a health care system that truly teaches its practitioners to work together across professional disciplines so that they can deliver the best, most efficient, care possible.

"We think," Weinstein says, "that this is the only way you're going to create coordinated health care."

SOURCE: Marianne Kolbasuk McGee, "Telemedicine Improving Stroke Patients' Survival and Recovery Rates," *InformationWeek*, May 11, 2005, and Mary K. Pratt, "Audiovisual Technology Enhances Physician Education," *Computerworld*, February 16, 2009.

▼ CASE STUDY QUESTIONS

1. From the perspective of a patient, how would you feel about being diagnosed by a doctor who could be hundreds or thousands of miles away from you? What kind of expectations or concerns would you have about that kind of experience?

2. What other professions, aside from health care and education, could benefit from the application of some of the technologies discussed in the case? How would they derive business value from these projects? Develop two proposals.

3. The deployment of IT in the health professions is still very much in its infancy. What other uses of technology could potentially improve the quality of health care? Brainstorm several alternatives.

▼ REAL WORLD ACTIVITIES

1. Technology enhances the ability of educational institutes to reach students across geographic boundaries. One recent development in this area is YouTube EDU. Go online to check out the site and prepare a report summarizing its objectives, the kind of content available there, and how it could be used to support traditional modes of education delivery, such as lectures.

2. If widely adopted, these technologies could conceivably lead to a concentration of specialists in a small number of "hub" institutions, essentially creating a two-tier health care system. Do you believe this would lead to an increase or decrease in the availability of these professionals for patients? What could be the positive and negative consequences of this development? Break into small groups with your classmates to discuss these issues.

e-BUSINESS APPLICATIONS

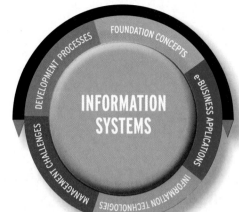

Information Systems
(FOUNDATION CONCEPTS, e-BUSINESS APPLICATIONS, INFORMATION TECHNOLOGIES, MANAGEMENT CHALLENGES, DEVELOPMENT PROCESSES)

How do Internet technologies and other forms of information technology enable better support of business processes, e-commerce, and business decision making? The four chapters of this module show you how such business applications of information systems are accomplished in today's networked enterprises.

- **Chapter 7: e-Business Systems** describes how information systems integrate and support enterprisewide business processes, as well as the business functions of marketing, manufacturing, human resource management, accounting, and finance.

- **Chapter 8: Business Across the Enterprise** outlines the goals and components of systems that span the organization. This chapter focuses on customer relationship management (CRM), enterprise resource planning (ERP), and supply chain management (SCM), with discussion of the benefits and challenges of these major enterprise-spanning applications.

- **Chapter 9: e-Commerce Systems** introduces the basic process components of e-commerce systems and discusses important trends, applications, and issues in e-commerce.

- **Chapter 10: Supporting Decision Making** shows how management information systems, decision support systems, executive information systems, expert systems, and artificial intelligence technologies can be applied to decision-making situations that business managers and professionals face in today's dynamic business environment.

e-BUSINESS SYSTEMS

INFORMATION SYSTEMS

e-BUSINESS APPLICATIONS

LEARNING OBJECTIVES

After reading and studying this chapter, you should be able to:

7-1 Identify the following cross-functional enterprise systems, and give examples of how they can provide significant business value to a company:

    a. Enterprise application integration

    b. Transaction processing systems

    c. Enterprise collaboration systems

7-2 Give examples of how Internet and other information technologies support business processes within the business functions of accounting, finance, human resource management, marketing, and production and operations management.

e-Business Systems

Contrary to popular opinion, e-business is not synonymous with e-commerce. E-business is much broader in scope, going beyond transactions to signify use of the Internet, in combination with other technologies and forms of electronic communication, to enable any type of business activity.

This chapter introduces the fast-changing world of information technology's business applications, which increasingly consists of *e-business systems*, a term originally coined in 1997 by Lou Gerstner, CEO of IBM. Remember that **e-business** is the use of the Internet, as well as other networks and information technologies, to support e-commerce, enterprise communications and collaboration, and Web-enabled business processes—both within a networked enterprise and with its customers and business partners. E-business includes *e-commerce*, which is the buying/selling, marketing, and servicing of products, services, and information over the Internet and other networks. We will discuss e-commerce in Chapter 9.

In this chapter, we will explore some of the major concepts and applications of e-business. Many argue that the term *e-business* is rapidly becoming extinct; today, e-business is just *business*. It is hard to imagine a critical business process that does not either make use of or need information technologies. In this text, however, we will continue to use the term to concentrate our focus on the part of the business that uses a significant amount of IT and IS for operation. We will begin by examining examples of cross-functional enterprise systems, which serve as a foundation for more in-depth coverage of enterprisewide business systems, such as customer relationship management, enterprise resource planning, and supply chain management in Chapter 8. Later in the chapter, we will explore examples of information systems that support essential processes in the functional areas of business.

Read the Real World Challenge on the next page. We can learn a lot from this case about the application integration challenges that large companies face. See Figure 7.1.

Many companies today are using information technology to develop integrated *cross-functional enterprise systems* that cross the boundaries of traditional business functions in order to reengineer and improve vital business processes all across the enterprise. These organizations view cross-functional enterprise systems as a strategic way to use IT to *share information resources and improve the efficiency and effectiveness of business processes*, and *develop strategic relationships with customers, suppliers, and business partners*. See Figure 7.2, which illustrates a cross-functional business process.

Companies first moved from functional mainframe-based *legacy systems* to integrated cross-functional *client/server* applications. This typically involved installing *enterprise resource planning, supply chain management*, or *customer relationship management* software from SAP America, PeopleSoft, Oracle, and others. Instead of focusing on the information processing requirements of business functions (i.e., accounting, finance, or marketing), such enterprise software focuses on supporting integrated *clusters of business processes* involved in the operations of a business by providing a single software-based system that spans the traditional functional boundaries.

Now, as we see continually in the Real World Challenges and Cases in this text, business firms are using Internet technologies to help them reengineer and integrate the flow of information among their internal business processes and their customers and suppliers. Companies all across the world are using the Web and their intranets and extranets as a technology platform for their cross-functional and interenterprise information systems.

Qualcomm—Silos, Silos, Everywhere

Qualcomm Inc., now a Fortune 500 company with a market capitalization of over $90 billion and more than $12 billion in annual revenue, started in 1985 when a group of industry veterans met to share ideas; they decided to form a company with the goal of providing "Quality Communications," which they shortened to Qualcomm. The group started out by providing research and development services to established telecommunications companies, and then launched its first commercial product, OmniTracs, introduced in 1988. Today, it is the largest satellite-based commercial mobile system for the transportation industry. After many other product introductions with major impact in the wireless telecommunications industry—such as CDMA (Code Division Multiple Access), which in one form or another underlies much of 3G technology—Qualcomm now employs more than 17,000 as a world-leading provider of wireless technology and services.

Qualcomm's IT architecture is a composite of multiple application silos, that is, applications that are not well suited to communicating with other applications. In this, Qualcomm is no different from many large enterprises. As a result, its architecture is not very responsive, and a very complex set of technologies is necessary to keep things running more or less smoothly. In short, Qualcomm suffers from an application integration problem. Application integration (sometimes called enterprise application integration or EAI) is the process of incorporating data or a function from one application program with that of another application program. At Qualcomm, the problem is rather severe, and likely to become even worse as the company keeps growing and adding new systems and technologies to its infrastructure. "Connecting these systems requires lots of point-to-point integration and a lot of technologies," says Norm Fjeldheim, chief information officer at Qualcomm. "And the communication was inefficiently done," he adds.

Point-to-point integration, also known as app-to-app (short for application-to-application) integration, involves a fair amount of custom coding that is specifically created only for the purpose of moving data from application A to application B. While this is a tried-and-true method to integrate applications, it does not scale very well. Every new application requires coding for each new integration point that has other applications with which it would need to share data. For example, to integrate 10 applications, you would need 45 point-to-point connections. In addition, the coding is largely application-specific, so code developed to integrate applications by two specific vendors will not necessarily work—at least not without a fair amount of testing and some customization—to integrate applications by other vendors. Currently, Qualcomm uses a homegrown integration tool to connect the various databases and applications that it operates. Although this approach is somewhat successful, it is costly to create, maintain, and support the infrastructure necessary to satisfy the needs of the company. In addition, this method lacks a monitoring tool, which in turn requires that each integration point be supervised manually on its own, making this approach even less scalable, as monitoring resources are needed with every new integration point.

Business applications today rarely live in isolation. Users expect instant access to all business functions an enterprise can offer, regardless of which system the functionality may reside in. The various information technologies that an organization has deployed over time form the lifeblood of the company, and they can either constrain or enable its capacity to create and deliver new products and services to its customers, as well as collaborate with others in order to do so. Although this is true for any large company today, it is particularly important for companies that rely or depend heavily

Current point-to-point integration has become too costly and is starting to constrain the ability of IT to support the business.
SOURCE: © Echo/Cultura/Getty Images.

on digital networks, such as Qualcomm. "We have ERP [Enterprise Resource Planning] systems that have the same data being extracted three times and being sent to three different systems: to a PLM [Product Lifecycle Management], to a CRM [Customer Relationship Management] system, and also to trade export compliance applications," sayas Steve Polaski, director of Enterprise Architecture for Qualcomm. "A lot of our IT budget is consumed in handling integration; some of our core systems have dozens, even hundreds, of integration points. It is a challenge to keep track of them all and is a big expenditure that is starting to slow us down," says Polaski.

One particularly thorny issue is the time taken to be able to provision customers. In telecom parlance, "provisioning" is the process of preparing and equipping a network to allow it to provide (new) services to its users. When a customer wants to add new features or change existing ones, it can be done remotely over the network to which the particular device is connected. It should be rather straightforward; however, it now takes much too long for Qualcomm to execute those changes, which in turn annoys its customers.

A major challenge for Qualcomm's chief information officer—or for any other executive in a similar position—is how to justify the need for a major application integration. On the one hand, chief information officers can focus on IT-specific benefits, such as how improved integration can help reduce software development times and maintenance costs, increase the reliability of the current applications, and help the applications be developed or implemented in the future. On the other hand, business benefits can be realized through better integration, such as supporting the business strategy, improving customer service, cutting down inventory costs, or standardizing idiosyncratic business processes.

Qualcomm management knows that it will eventually have to replace all or part of its legacy systems, and because of the size, variety, and complexity, the cost is going to be significant. There is also the cost, hassle, and sheer complexity of having to rewrite the multitudinous point-to-point application program interfaces. Over the years, generation after generation of interfaces have been constructed to integrate these applications, and layers and layers of rewrites, patches, upgrades, and changes have been made over and over. As its ultimate goal, the IT department would like to be able to share data in real time across multiple applications. For instance, when a new device is provisioned, the billing and CRM applications should know about it instantly, so when a customer calls about the device half an hour after receiving it, whoever picks up the call knows what is going on. Right now, the systems do communicate with each other, but it takes time for a new equipment sale to make its way to the other applications where that information would be necessary—and they know they could do better than that. After all, Qualcomm is in the communications business.

SOURCE: Daniel Dern, "How One Company Broke Down Silos and Improved Application Integration," *CIO.com*, September 15, 2008; Scot Petersen, "Qualcomm Dials in SOAs," *eWeek*, November 22, 2004; "TIBCO Supports Product Engineering and Business Integration at Qualcomm," *TIBCO Success Story*, 2006; www.qualcomm.com, accessed May 28, 2011.

▼ QUESTIONS TO CONSIDER

1. Looking at the situation that Qualcomm faces, how does a large, technology-oriented company get to this point? What would be some of the underlying reasons that would make the development of separate applications a priority over careful orchestrated integration?

2. What does it mean to say that technology can " either constrain or enable its capacity to create and deliver new products and services"? In which ways?

3. Moving forward, what are some of the alternatives open to Qualcomm? Should it replace its integration approach with a different one, or rewrite all of its legacy applications from scratch? Or should it do something in between? What are the advantages and disadvantages of each alternative?

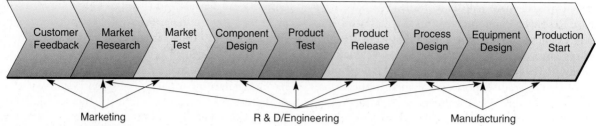

FIGURE 7.2

The new product development process in a manufacturing company. This is an example of a business process that must be supported by cross-functional systems that cross the boundaries of several business functions.

SOURCE: Mohan Sawhney and Jeff Zabin, *Seven Steps to Nirvana: Strategic Insights into e-Business Transformation* (New York: McGraw-Hill, 2001), p. 175.

Enterprise Application Architecture

Figure 7.3 presents an ***enterprise application architecture,*** which illustrates the interrelationships of the major cross-functional enterprise applications that many companies use or are installing today. This architecture does not provide a detailed or exhaustive application blueprint, but it provides a conceptual framework to help you visualize the basic components, processes, and interfaces of these major e-business applications, and their interrelationships to each other. This application architecture also spotlights the roles these business systems play in supporting the customers, suppliers, partners, and employees of a business.

Notice that instead of concentrating on traditional business functions or supporting only the internal business processes of a company, enterprise applications focus on accomplishing fundamental business processes in concert with a company's customer, supplier, partner, and employee stakeholders. Thus, *enterprise resource planning* (ERP) concentrates on the *efficiency* and *effectiveness* of a firm's internal production, distribution, and financial processes. *Customer relationship management* (CRM) focuses on acquiring and retaining profitable customers via marketing, sales, and service processes. *Partner relationship management* (PRM) aims to acquire and retain partners who can enhance the sale and distribution of a firm's products and services. *Supply chain management* (SCM) focuses on developing the most efficient and effective sourcing and procurement processes with suppliers for the products and services that a business needs. *Knowledge management* (KM) applications provide a firm's employees with tools that support group collaboration and decision support.

FIGURE 7.3

This enterprise application architecture presents an overview of the major cross-functional enterprise applications and their interrelationships.

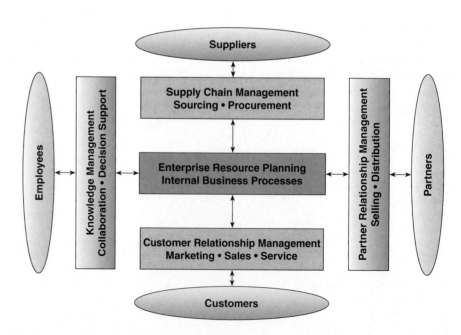

We will discuss CRM, ERP, and SCM applications in detail in Chapter 8 and cover KM applications in Chapter 10. Now let's look at a real-world example of some of the challenges involved in integrating disparate systems to arrive at a unified view of all customer interactions.

Marriott Hotels: Toward a Single View of the Customer

Marriott Hotels operates with a very simple philosophy: *Make Every Interaction Meaningful.* This means that at any point of contact with a customer, the company wants to ensure that something important and valuable will happen, something that will make the customers satisfied and will keep them coming back. However, when a hotel chain operates multiple properties—literally thousands of them—grouped under several different brands and using multiple ways of contacting the customers, it can be a major challenge to keep all this in harmony. Today, Marriott Hotels operates more than 3,200 properties under 19 different brands in more than 67 countries. To make sense of all the customer experiences that happen every moment at every one of those properties, Marriot Hotels went looking for an integrated campaign-management platform.

The company started by forming a cross-functional group of marketing leaders, brand managers, and IT specialists to clearly define the common experience Marriott wanted to provide its customers across all properties and countries in which the company operates. One of the key challenges they identified was a lack of an accessible record of all the interactions each customer had with every property in each brand in the past. To solve this, the company built a data warehouse that supported the use of statistical models that created offers tailored to the preferences and past behavior of each customer, as well as collating the results of past marketing campaigns and how those affected customer experiences. These are also used to better tailor future advertising and promotion efforts.

For the first time, Marriott had the information available to see each customer as a single person who happened to visit different brands on each occasion, as opposed to seeing that person as multiple different customers. Using this information, Marriott could tailor promotions to the way each guest uses the different services the company has to offer. The first e-mail campaign that was created using the new platform consisted of 3 million messages that sent tailored offers to more than 2.9 million recipients. The campaign largely exceeded its revenue goals: After six months, the results were 35 percent higher than planned. The new platform also includes a Web-based self-service system that is used by regional marketers, which has helped reduce the time it takes to develop a regional marketing campaign from about six weeks to two single days.

The new platform allows Marriott Hotels to create an end-to-end business process that provides marketing leaders with the information necessary to develop more relevant, effective, and tailored campaigns and offers to customers. More relevant offers and better tailored services will keep customers happy and coming back. In the end, technology is all about people.

SOURCE: Rick Swanborg, "CRM: How Marriott Broke Down Customer Data Siloes," *CIO.com,* November 11, 2009.

ENTERPRISE APPLICATION INTEGRATION
LO 7-1

How does a business interconnect some of the cross-functional enterprise systems? *Enterprise application integration* (EAI) software is being used by many companies to connect their major e-business applications. See Figure 7.4. EAI software enables users to model the business processes involved in the interactions that should occur between business applications. EAI also provides *middleware* that performs data conversion and

FIGURE 7.4

Enterprise application integration software interconnects front-office and back-office applications.

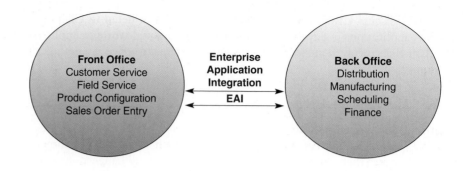

Front Office
Customer Service
Field Service
Product Configuration
Sales Order Entry

Enterprise
Application
Integration
EAI

Back Office
Distribution
Manufacturing
Scheduling
Finance

coordination, application communication and messaging services, and access to the application interfaces involved. Recall from Chapter 6 that middleware is any software that serves to glue together or mediate between two separate pieces of software. Thus, EAI software can integrate a variety of enterprise application clusters by letting them exchange data according to rules derived from the business process models developed by users. For example, a typical rule might be:

When an order is complete, have the order system tell the accounting system to send a bill to the customer and alert shipping to send out the product.

Thus, as Figure 7.4 illustrates, EAI software can integrate the front-office and back-office applications of a business so they work together in a seamless, integrated way. This is a vital capability that provides real business value to a business enterprise that must respond quickly and effectively to business events and customer demands. For example, the integration of enterprise application clusters has been shown to dramatically improve customer call center responsiveness and effectiveness. That's because EAI integrates access to all of the customer and product data that customer representatives need to serve customers quickly. EAI also streamlines sales order processing so products and services can be delivered faster. Thus, EAI improves customer and supplier experience with the business because of its responsiveness. See Figure 7.5.

FIGURE 7.5

An example of a new customer order process showing how EAI middleware connects several business information systems within a company.

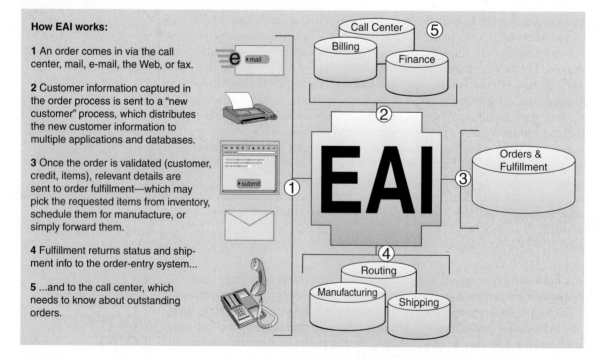

How EAI works:

1 An order comes in via the call center, mail, e-mail, the Web, or fax.

2 Customer information captured in the order process is sent to a "new customer" process, which distributes the new customer information to multiple applications and databases.

3 Once the order is validated (customer, credit, items), relevant details are sent to order fulfillment—which may pick the requested items from inventory, schedule them for manufacture, or simply forward them.

4 Fulfillment returns status and shipment info to the order-entry system...

5 ...and to the call center, which needs to know about outstanding orders.

As a company that manufactures diagnostic imaging, monitoring, and other medical equipment, to Philips Medical Systems, customer satisfaction means saving lives. A division of Royal Philips Electronics, the company distributes its products to more than 100 countries around the world. In order to support more agile and responsive business processes, the company decided it needed to revamp its existing legacy infrastructure. At the time, its highly distributed business—with local operations in more than 30 countries—required more than 50 different systems to function.

The company approached its integration problem by using internally developed point-to-point integration routines that transferred data between systems every night. When immediate data was required, employees needed to know to which systems they should log on to access the data and then how to put it together, often manually. Managers quickly realized that their original approach to integration would require more than 3,000 separate interfaces to create what would look like a fully integrated business model, but would be costly and difficult to maintain. And a migration to a new ERP solution was on the horizon. Clearly, they needed a different approach.

"We operated a traditional corporate computing environment. We had many legacy systems, each responsible for different aspects of manufacturing, sales, and distribution," says Reinier Lodewijks, manager of Global Application Integration at Philips Medical Systems. "But we were looking for a more flexible technology to meet our current and future needs."

Once managers realized that the migration to a new ERP would affect almost every part of the existing systems, they started looking for an integration solution that was robust, but at the same time flexible enough to support a dynamic business environment, and they settled for a service-oriented messaging bus provided by TIBCO Software. In the new approach, all applications simply link to the TIBCO backbone through a software adapter, and then this backbone distributes data to where they are needed. The company started by first installing the messaging backbone and only then implementing the new ERP package, which helped minimize the many disruptions commonly associated with large-scale application changes.

Philips Medical Systems is producing the new adapters needed to connect existing applications to the messaging bus in only two to four weeks, by building upon standard components provided by the TIBCO solution. In addition, managers estimate that integrating each of those applications with the new architecture costs about 25 percent less than they would have spent with the old point-to-point approach. What is even more important, the new infrastructure allows the company to roll out new integration projects in only days; this has resulted in reduced development costs, while at the same time maximizing the flexibility needed to keep the company on the competitive edge of its industry.

Philips Medical Systems: Reaping the Benefits of Enterprise Integration

SOURCE: "Philips Medical Systems and Its Customers Reap the Benefits of Enterprise Integration," *TIBCO Success Story*, 2007.

TRANSACTION PROCESSING SYSTEMS

Transaction processing systems (TPS) are cross-functional information systems that process data resulting from the occurrence of business transactions. We introduced transaction processing systems in Chapter 1 as one of the major application categories of information systems in business.

Transactions are events that occur as part of doing business, such as *sales, purchases, deposits, withdrawals, refunds,* and *payments.* Think, for example, of the data generated whenever a business sells something to a customer on credit, whether in a retail store or at an e-commerce site on the Web. Data about the customer, product, salesperson, store, and so on, must be captured and processed. This in turn prompts additional transactions, such as credit checks, customer billing, inventory changes, and increases in accounts receivable balances, which generate even more data. Transaction processing activities are needed to capture and process such data, or the operations of a business would grind to a halt. Therefore, transaction processing systems play a vital role in supporting the operations of most companies today.

Online transaction processing systems play a strategic role in Web-enabled businesses. Many firms are using the Internet and other networks that tie them electronically to their customers or suppliers for online transaction processing (OLTP). Such *real-time* systems, which capture and process transactions immediately, can help firms provide superior service to customers and other trading partners. This capability also adds value to their products and services, and thus gives them an important way to differentiate themselves from their competitors.

Syntellect's Online Transaction Processing

FIGURE 7.6

The Syntellect pay-per-view online transaction processing system.

For example, Figure 7.6 illustrates an online transaction processing system for cable pay-per-view systems developed by Syntellect Interactive Services. Cable TV viewers can select pay-per-view events offered by their cable companies using the phone or the World Wide Web. The pay-per-view order is captured by Syntellect's interactive voice response system or Web server, then transported to Syntellect database application servers. There the order is processed, customer and sales databases are updated, and the approved order is relayed back to the cable company's video server, which transmits the video of the pay-per-view event to the customer. Thus, Syntellect teams with more than 700 cable companies to offer a very popular and very profitable service.

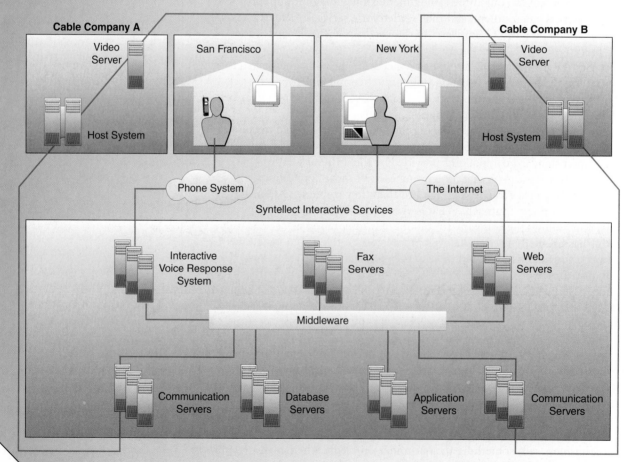

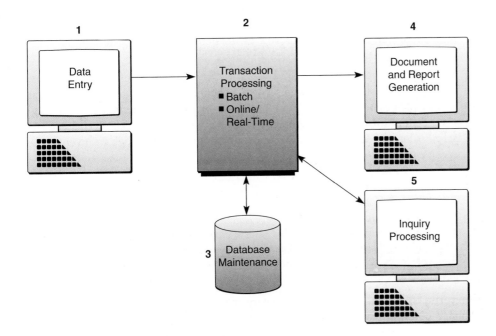

FIGURE 7.7

The transaction processing cycle. Note that transaction processing systems use a five-stage cycle of data entry, transaction processing, database maintenance, document and report generation, and inquiry processing activities

The Transaction Processing Cycle

Transaction processing systems, such as Syntellect's, capture and process data describing business transactions, update organizational databases, and produce a variety of information products. You should understand this as a *transaction processing cycle* of several basic activities, as illustrated in Figure 7.7.

- **Data Entry.** The first step of the transaction processing cycle is the capture of business data. For example, transaction data may be collected by point-of-sale terminals using optical scanning of bar codes and credit card readers at a retail store or other business. Transaction data can also be captured at an e-commerce Web site on the Internet. The proper recording and editing of data so they are quickly and correctly captured for processing is one of the major design challenges of information systems discussed in Chapter 12.

- **Transaction Processing.** Transaction processing systems process data in two basic ways: (1) *batch processing,* where transaction data are accumulated over a period of time and processed periodically, and (2) *real-time processing* (also called online processing), where data are processed immediately after a transaction occurs. All online transaction processing systems incorporate real-time processing capabilities. Many online systems also depend on the capabilities of fault-tolerant computer systems that can continue to operate even if parts of the system fail. We will discuss this fault-tolerant concept in Chapter 13.

- **Database Maintenance.** An organization's databases must be updated by its transaction processing systems so that they are always correct and up-to-date. Therefore, transaction processing systems serve to assist in maintaining the corporate databases of an organization to reflect changes resulting from day-to-day business transactions. For example, credit sales made to customers will cause customer account balances to be increased and the amount of inventory on hand to be decreased. Database maintenance ensures that these and other changes are reflected in the data records stored in the company's databases.

- **Document and Report Generation.** Transaction processing systems produce a variety of documents and reports. Examples of transaction documents include purchase orders, paychecks, sales receipts, invoices, and customer statements.

Transaction reports might take the form of a transaction listing such as a payroll register, or edit reports that describe errors detected during processing.

- **Inquiry Processing.** Many transaction processing systems allow you to use the Internet, intranets, extranets, and Web browsers or database management query languages to make inquiries and receive responses concerning the results of transaction processing activity. Typically, responses are displayed in a variety of prespecified formats or screens. For example, you might check on the status of a sales order, the balance in an account, or the amount of stock in inventory and receive immediate responses at your PC.

ENTERPRISE COLLABORATION SYSTEMS

Really difficult business problems always have many aspects. Often a major decision depends on an impromptu search for one or two key pieces of auxiliary information and a quick ad hoc analysis of several possible scenarios. You need software tools that easily combine and recombine data from many sources. You need Internet access for all kinds of research. Widely scattered people need to be able to collaborate and work the data in different ways.

Enterprise collaboration systems (ECS) are cross-functional information systems that enhance communication, coordination, and collaboration among the members of business teams and workgroups. Information technology, especially Internet technologies, provides tools to help us collaborate—to communicate ideas, share resources, and coordinate our cooperative work efforts as members of the many formal and informal process and project teams and workgroups that make up many of today's organizations. Thus, the goal of *enterprise collaboration systems* is to enable us to work together more easily and effectively by helping us to:

- **Communicate:** Share information with each other.
- **Coordinate:** Organize our individual work efforts and use of resources.
- **Collaborate:** Work together cooperatively on joint projects and assignments.

For example, engineers, business specialists, and external consultants may form a virtual team for a project. The team may rely on intranets and extranets to collaborate via e-mail, videoconferencing, discussion forums, and a multimedia database of work-in-progress information at a project Web site. The enterprise collaboration system may use PC workstations networked to a variety of servers on which project, corporate, and other databases are stored. In addition, network servers may provide a variety of software resources, such as Web browsers, groupware, and application packages, to assist the team's collaboration until the project is completed.

Tools for Enterprise Collaboration

The capabilities and potential of the Internet, as well as intranets and extranets, are driving the demand for better enterprise collaboration tools in business. However, Internet technologies like Web browsers and servers, hypermedia documents and databases, and intranets and extranets provide the hardware, software, data, and network platforms for many of the *groupware tools* for enterprise collaboration that business users want. Figure 7.8 provides an overview of some of the software tools for electronic communication, electronic conferencing, and collaborative work management.

Electronic communication tools include e-mail, voice mail, faxing, Web publishing, bulletin board systems, paging, and Internet phone systems. These tools enable you to send messages, documents, and files in data, text, voice, or multimedia electronically over computer networks. This helps you share everything from voice and text messages to copies of project documents and data files with your team members, wherever they may be. The ease and efficiency of such communications are major contributors to the collaboration process.

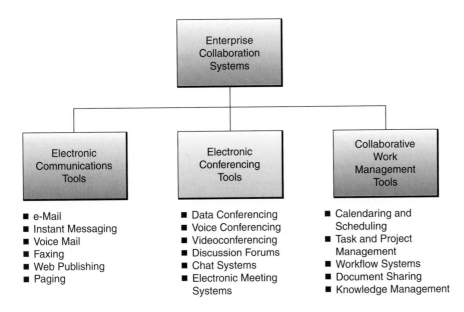

FIGURE 7.8

Electronic communications, conferencing, and collaborative work software tools enhance enterprise collaboration.

Electronic conferencing tools help people communicate and collaborate as they work together. A variety of conferencing methods enable the members of teams and workgroups at different locations to exchange ideas interactively at the same time, or at different times at their convenience. These include data and voice conferencing, videoconferencing, chat systems, and discussion forums. Electronic conferencing options also include *electronic meeting systems* and other *group support systems* where team members can meet at the same time and place in a *decision room* setting, or use the Internet to work collaboratively anywhere in the world. See Figure 7.9.

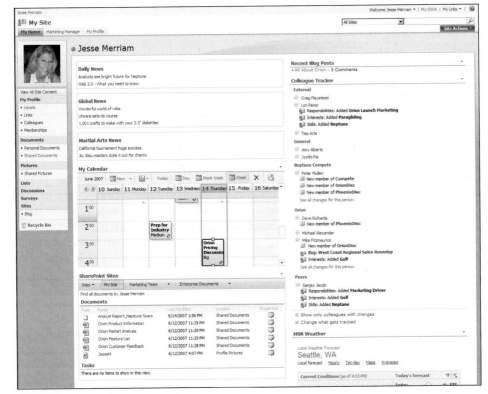

FIGURE 7.9

SharePoint by Microsoft Corporation helps virtual workgroups set up Web-based work spaces for collaborative work assignments.

SOURCE: Courtesy of Microsoft Corporation.

Collaborative work management tools help people accomplish or manage group work activities. This category of software includes calendaring and scheduling tools, task and project management, workflow systems, and knowledge management tools. Other tools for joint work, such as joint document creation, editing, and revision, are found in the software suites discussed in Chapter 4.

Exploring Virtual Worlds as Collaboration Tools

For emergency responders working along Interstate 95, accidents aren't a game; they're a way of life (and death). So it seemed odd to a group of firefighters, cops, and medics when researchers from the University of Maryland suggested that they use a virtual world to collaborate on training for rollovers, multicar pileups, and life-threatening injuries.

The phrase *virtual world* is often associated with Second Life, the much-hyped 3-D environment hosted by Linden Lab that allows users to talk to friends, sell T-shirts, fly around on carpets, and even build amusement parks—in other words, to play. "It wasn't until we started to do elaborate demos that the first responders started to realize the true potential," says Michael Pack, director of research with the University of Maryland's Center for Advanced Transportation Technology, who has since begun rolling out a virtual world pilot project that could accommodate training for hundreds of emergency workers.

Industry analysts and developers of virtual worlds believe that by immersing users in an interactive environment that allows for social interactions, virtual worlds have the potential to succeed where other collaborative technologies, like teleconferencing, have failed. Phone-based meetings begin and end abruptly, at the mercy of the person or service administering it. In a virtual world, conversations between employees can continue within the virtual space—just as they do in company hallways after a meeting ends.

However, businesses must overcome many technical and cultural obstacles before they adopt virtual worlds on a major scale. Perhaps even more important than the technical challenges, companies must tackle the issue of workers' online identities. People's 3-D representations, known as avatars, must be constructed in such a way that allows users of virtual worlds to have faith that they're talking to the right colleague. Security challenges abound; most companies using virtual worlds today do so on a public or externally hosted platform with limited options to protect corporate data.

Pack says training in a virtual world presents a desirable alternative to real-life exercises, which can be pricey and inefficient. "You'd go out in a field and flip a car over and have people act as victims," he says. Trainers couldn't introduce many variables (such as mounting traffic). "It's supposed to be as human as possible, so anything goes," he says. "We've put together lots of scenarios, from fender benders to 20-car pileups. We put [the participants] in dangerous situations to see how they will respond." In virtual worlds, Pack and his team can program multiple scenarios into the software. For example, if a first responder gets out of his car and fails to put on a reflective jacket, the system might respond with a car hitting that person's avatar.

"You want people to be so comfortable in the virtual world that they're not concentrating on how to use them," Pack says. "They can't be worried about how to turn left or talk to someone. They need to be worried about how to do their jobs, just like they would in the real world."

SOURCE: C. G. Lynch, "Companies Explore Virtual Worlds as Collaboration Tools," *CIO Magazine,* February 6, 2008.

Functional Business Systems

INTRODUCTION
LO 7-2

Business managers are moving from a tradition where they could avoid, delegate, or ignore decisions about IT to one where they cannot create a marketing, product, international, organization, or financial plan that does not involve such decisions.

There are as many ways to use information technology in business as there are business activities to be performed, business problems to be solved, and business opportunities to be pursued. As a business professional, you should have a basic understanding and appreciation of the major ways information systems are used to support each of the functions of business that must be accomplished in any company that wants to succeed. Thus, for the rest of the chapter, we will discuss ***functional business systems,*** that is, a variety of types of information systems (transaction processing, management information, decision support, and so on) that support the business functions of *accounting, finance, marketing, operations management,* and *human resource management*. See Figure 7.10.

IT in Business

As a business professional, it is also important that you have a specific understanding of how information systems affect a particular business function (e.g., marketing) or a particular industry (e.g., banking) that is directly related to your career objectives. For example, someone whose career objective is a marketing position in banking should have a basic understanding of how information systems are used in banking and how they support the marketing activities of banks and other firms.

SOURCE: © Ryan McVay/Getty Images.

FIGURE 7.10

Companies are deploying technology and reengineering processes in search of "one source of the truth" across the enterprise.

FIGURE 7.11

Examples of functional business information systems. Note how they support the major functional areas of business.

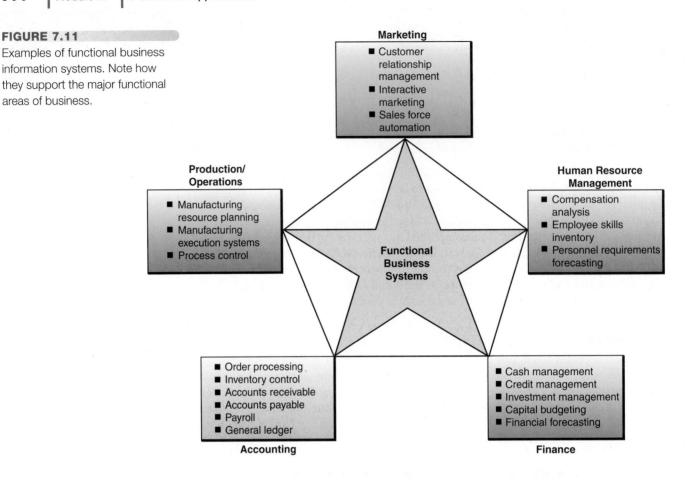

Marketing
- Customer relationship management
- Interactive marketing
- Sales force automation

Production/Operations
- Manufacturing resource planning
- Manufacturing execution systems
- Process control

Human Resource Management
- Compensation analysis
- Employee skills inventory
- Personnel requirements forecasting

Functional Business Systems

- Order processing
- Inventory control
- Accounts receivable
- Accounts payable
- Payroll
- General ledger

Accounting

- Cash management
- Credit management
- Investment management
- Capital budgeting
- Financial forecasting

Finance

Figure 7.11 illustrates how information systems can be grouped into business function categories. Thus, information systems in this part of the chapter will be analyzed according to the business function they support by looking at a few key examples in each functional area. This should give you an appreciation of the variety of functional business systems that both small and large business firms may use.

MARKETING SYSTEMS

The business function of *marketing* is concerned with the planning, promotion, and sale of existing products in existing markets, and the development of new products and new markets to better attract and serve present and potential customers. Thus, marketing performs an essential function in the operation of a business enterprise. Business firms have increasingly turned to information technology to help them perform vital marketing functions in the face of the rapid changes of today's environment.

Figure 7.12 illustrates how *marketing information systems* provide information technologies that support major components of the marketing function. For example, Internet/intranet Web sites and services make an *interactive marketing* process possible where customers can become partners in creating, marketing, purchasing, and improving products and services. *Sales force automation* systems use mobile computing and Internet technologies to automate many information processing activities for sales support and management. Other marketing information systems assist marketing managers in product planning, pricing, and other product management decisions; advertising, sales promotion, and targeted marketing strategies; and market research and forecasting. Finally, enterprisewide systems like customer relationship management (discussed in Chapter 8) link to the portfolio of marketing information systems to provide and obtain data essential to the marketing function. Let's take a closer look at three of these marketing applications.

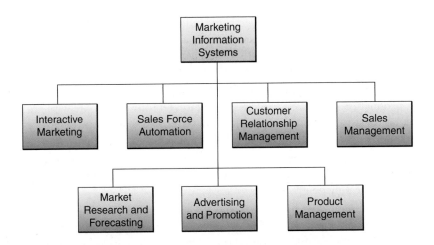

FIGURE 7.12
Marketing information systems provide information technologies to support major components of the marketing function.

Interactive Marketing

The term *interactive marketing* has been coined to describe a customer-focused marketing process that is based on using the Internet, intranets, and extranets to establish two-way transactions between a business and its customers or potential customers. The goal of interactive marketing is to enable a company to use those networks profitably to attract and keep customers who will become partners with the business in creating, purchasing, and improving products and services.

In interactive marketing, customers are not just passive participants who receive media advertising prior to purchase; they are actively engaged in network-enabled proactive and interactive processes. Interactive marketing encourages customers to become involved in product development, delivery, and service issues. This is enabled by various Internet technologies, including chat and discussion groups, Web forms and questionnaires, instant messaging, and e-mail correspondence. Finally, the expected outcomes of interactive marketing are a rich mixture of vital marketing data, new product ideas, volume sales, and strong customer relationships.

Targeted Marketing

Targeted marketing has become an important tool in developing advertising and promotion strategies to strengthen a company's e-commerce initiatives, as well as its traditional business venues. As illustrated in Figure 7.13, targeted marketing is an advertising and promotion management concept that includes five targeting components:

- **Community.** Companies can customize their Web advertising messages and promotion methods to appeal to people in specific communities. They can be *communities of interest,* such as *virtual communities* of online sporting enthusiasts, or arts and crafts hobbyists, or geographic communities formed by the Web sites of a city or other local organization.

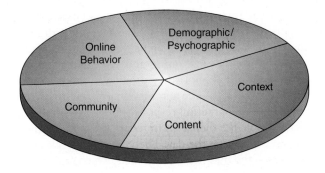

FIGURE 7.13
The five major components of targeted marketing for electronic commerce.

- **Content.** Advertising, such as electronic billboards or banners, can be placed on a variety of selected Web sites, in addition to a company's Web site. The content of these messages is aimed at the targeted audience. An ad for a product campaign on the opening page of an Internet search engine is a typical example.

- **Context.** Advertising appears only in Web pages that are relevant to the content of a product or service. So, advertising is targeted only at people who are already looking for information about subject matter (e.g., vacation travel) that is related to a company's products (e.g., car rental services).

- **Demographic/Psychographic.** Web marketing efforts can be aimed only at specific types or classes of people: for example, unmarried, twenty-something, middle income, male college graduates.

- **Online Behavior.** Advertising and promotion efforts can be tailored to each visit to a site by an individual. This strategy is based on a variety of tracking techniques, such as Web "cookie" files recorded on the visitor's disk drive from previous visits. This enables a company to track a person's online behavior at its Web site so marketing efforts (such as coupons redeemable at retail stores or e-commerce Web sites) can be targeted to that individual at each visit to its Web site.

An interesting and effective marriage between e-business and target marketing is the emergence of the digital billboard. It is estimated that about 450,000 billboard faces exist in the United States. Currently, only about 2,000 of them are digital. While only a tiny fraction of digital billboards exist, the innovative technologies are making a huge impact on markets, and marketing, all over the country.

The concept behind the digital billboard is elegantly simple. A billboard is constructed using hundreds of thousands of small LEDs, which are controlled via a computer interface that can be accessed via the Web. Advertisers can change their messages quickly, including multiple times in one day. For example, a restaurant can feature breakfast specials in the morning and dinner specials in the evening. A realtor can feature individual houses for sale and change the creative content when the house sells. Print and broadcast news media alike use digital billboards to deliver headlines, weather updates, and programming information. WCPO-TV in Cincinnati, Ohio, credits its meteoric rise in the ratings to the use of digital billboards to deliver breaking news and updates to the nightly newscast. The television station went from the bottom of the ratings in 2002 to the third largest ABC affiliate in the nation. When the I-35 bridge collapsed in Minneapolis in 2007, a dangerous situation for unsuspecting drivers existed. Within minutes, a digital billboard network in the area switched from showing advertising copy to informing drivers about the collapse. Later that evening, the digital billboards advised motorists to take alternate routes. Target marketing is in the digital arena, with a new way of doing something old.

Sales Force Automation

Increasingly, computers and the Internet are providing the basis for *sales force automation.* In many companies, the sales force is being outfitted with notebook computers, Web browsers, and sales contact management software that connect them to marketing Web sites on the Internet, extranets, and their company intranets. This not only increases the personal productivity of salespeople, but it dramatically speeds up the capture and analysis of sales data from the field to marketing managers at company headquarters. In return, it allows marketing and sales management to improve the delivery of information and the support they provide to their salespeople. Therefore, many companies are viewing sales force automation as a way to gain a strategic advantage in sales productivity and marketing responsiveness. See Figure 7.14.

For example, salespeople use their PCs to record sales data as they make their calls on customers and prospects during the day. Then each night, sales reps in the field can connect their computers to the Internet and extranets, which can access intranet or other

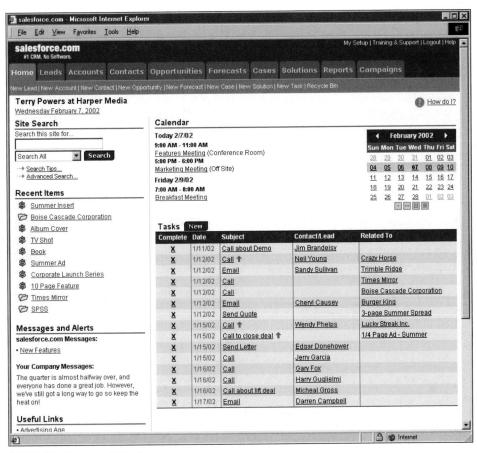

SOURCE: Courtesy of Salesforce.com.

FIGURE 7.14
This Web-based sales force automation package supports sales lead management of qualified prospects, and management of current customer accounts.

network servers at their company. Then, they can upload information on sales orders, sales calls, and other sales statistics, as well as send e-mail messages and access Web site sales support information. In return, the network servers may download product availability data, prospect lists of information on good sales prospects, and e-mail messages.

Wireless Sales Force Automation Drives Sales for adidas America

Located in Portland, Oregon, with more than 1,000 employees, adidas America produces athletic footwear, apparel, accessories and equipment products. With roots reaching back to 1949, adidas America is part of a larger organization that strives to be the global leader in the sporting goods industry. Adidas products are available in virtually every country.

A leader in its industry, adidas America recognized that it could increase its sales potential by automating many components of the sales process. Its team of 200 sales representatives had been using BlackBerry handheld devices for e-mail. Before implementing its wireless sales force automation solution, the company's sales representatives were required to borrow a customer's phone or use their personal mobile phones to check warehouse inventory. The company realized that this slowed sales momentum.

"We wanted to strike while the iron is hot, while the enthusiasm is there for the product," says Tim Oligmueller, sales force automation manager for adidas America. "Real-time wireless access is important because we want the customer to see that we have immediate access to data to meet their needs." Lacking wireless capability, some sales representatives would prepare for a meeting with a customer by checking inventory before they left the office.

However, if an item wasn't available when the sales representative returned to the office, the rep would have to contact the customer to change the order.

At the foundation of adidas America's wireless solution is Atlas2Go, an internally developed sales force automation application. The custom wireless application runs on the sales representatives's BlackBerry devices and performs real-time inventory queries into the company's SAP application data over AT&T's wireless network. Sales reps can view up-to-date inventory information and can choose to receive an e-mail with inventory status, which they can then forward to their customer.

The wireless sales force automation solution has provided adidas America with valuable benefits. Sales representatives can more quickly and easily check inventory from the field while providing improved customer service.

Back-office staff work more efficiently with fewer interruptions from sales representatives. Oligmueller notes that the adidas inventory system receives nearly 120 wireless queries each day, saving time otherwise spent in phone calls between sales and back-office staff.

The application was pushed out over the air to the sales representatives's BlackBerry devices during a regularly scheduled sales meeting. Training was done on the spot at the same meeting. Oligmueller estimates that the company spent less than $10,000 to develop the software application. "It was so inexpensive to do that just one order paid for it," said Oligmueller. "Our return on investment is going to grow and grow."

SOURCE: "Sales Force Automation Case Study—Wireless Sales Force Automation Drives Sales for adidas America," *AT&T Wireless Case Study*, June 30, 2008.

MANUFACTURING SYSTEMS

Manufacturing information systems support the *production/operations* function that includes all activities concerned with the planning and control of the processes producing goods or services. Thus, the production/operations function is concerned with the management of the operational processes and systems of all business firms. Information systems used for operations management and transaction processing support all firms that must plan, monitor, and control inventories, purchases, and the flow of goods and services. Therefore, firms such as transportation companies, wholesalers, retailers, financial institutions, and service companies must use production/operations information systems to plan and control their operations. In this section, we will concentrate on computer-based manufacturing applications to illustrate information systems that support the production/operations function.

Computer-Integrated Manufacturing

Once upon a time, manufacturers operated on a simple build-to-stock model. They built 100 or 100,000 of an item and sold them via distribution networks. They kept track of the stock of inventory and made more of the item once inventory levels dipped below a threshold. Rush jobs were both rare and expensive, and configuration options limited. Things have changed. Concepts like just-in-time inventory, build-to-order (BTO) manufacturing, end-to-end supply chain visibility, the explosion in contract manufacturing, and the development of Web-based e-business tools for collaborative manufacturing have revolutionized plant management.

A variety of manufacturing information systems, many of them Web-enabled, are used to support **computer-integrated manufacturing** (CIM). See Figure 7.15. CIM is an overall concept that emphasizes that the objectives of computer-based systems in manufacturing must be to:

- **Simplify** (reengineer) production processes, product designs, and factory organization as a vital foundation to automation and integration.

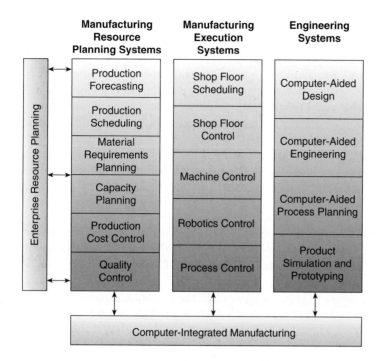

Manufacturing Resource Planning Systems
- Production Forecasting
- Production Scheduling
- Material Requirements Planning
- Capacity Planning
- Production Cost Control
- Quality Control

Manufacturing Execution Systems
- Shop Floor Scheduling
- Shop Floor Control
- Machine Control
- Robotics Control
- Process Control

Engineering Systems
- Computer-Aided Design
- Computer-Aided Engineering
- Computer-Aided Process Planning
- Product Simulation and Prototyping

Enterprise Resource Planning

Computer-Integrated Manufacturing

FIGURE 7.15

Manufacturing information systems support computer-integrated manufacturing. Note that manufacturing resource planning systems are one of the application clusters in an ERP system.

- **Automate** production processes and the business functions that support them with computers, machines, and robots.

- **Integrate** all production and support processes using computer networks, cross-functional business software, and other information technologies.

The overall goal of CIM and other such manufacturing information systems is to create flexible, agile, manufacturing processes that efficiently produce products of the highest quality. Thus, CIM supports the concepts of *flexible manufacturing systems*, *agile manufacturing*, and *total quality management*. Implementing such manufacturing concepts enables a company to respond to and fulfill customer requirements quickly with high-quality products and services.

Manufacturing information systems help companies simplify, automate, and integrate many of the activities needed to produce products of all kinds. For example, computers are used to help engineers design better products using both *computer-aided engineering* (CAE) and *computer-aided design* (CAD) systems, and better production processes with *computer-aided process planning*. They are also used to help plan the types of material needed in the production process, which is called *material requirements planning* (MRP), and to integrate MRP with production scheduling and shop floor operations, which is known as *manufacturing resource planning*. Many of the processes within manufacturing resource planning systems are included in the manufacturing module of enterprise resource planning (ERP) software, which will be discussed in Chapter 8.

Computer-aided manufacturing (CAM) systems are those that automate the production process. For example, this could be accomplished by monitoring and controlling the production process in a factory (manufacturing execution systems) or by directly controlling a physical process (process control), a machine tool (machine control), or machines with some humanlike work capabilities (robots).

Manufacturing execution systems (MES) are performance-monitoring information systems for factory floor operations. They monitor, track, and control the five essential components involved in a production process: materials, equipment, personnel, instructions and specifications, and production facilities. MES includes shop floor scheduling and control, machine control, robotics control, and process control systems. These manufacturing systems monitor, report, and adjust the status and performance of production components to help a company achieve a flexible, high-quality manufacturing process.

Process control is the use of computers to control an ongoing physical process. Process control computers control physical processes in petroleum refineries, cement plants, steel mills, chemical plants, food product manufacturing plants, pulp and paper mills, electric power plants, and so on. A process control computer system requires the use of special sensing devices that measure physical phenomena such as temperature or pressure changes. These continuous physical measurements are converted to digital form by analog-to-digital converters and relayed to computers for processing.

Machine control is the use of computers to control the actions of machines. This is also popularly called *numerical control*. The computer-based control of machine tools to manufacture products of all kinds is a typical numerical control application used by many factories throughout the world.

HUMAN RESOURCE SYSTEMS

The human resource management (HRM) function involves the recruitment, placement, evaluation, compensation, and development of the employees of an organization. The goal of human resource management is the effective and efficient use of the human resources of a company. Thus, *human resource information systems* (HRIS) are designed to support (1) planning to meet the personnel needs of the business, (2) development of employees to their full potential, and (3) control of all personnel policies and programs. Originally, businesses used computer-based information systems to (1) produce paychecks and payroll reports, (2) maintain personnel records, and (3) analyze the use of personnel in business operations. Many firms have gone beyond these traditional *personnel management* functions and have developed human resource information systems that also support (1) recruitment, selection, and hiring; (2) job placement; (3) performance appraisals; (4) employee benefits analysis; (5) training and development; and (6) health, safety, and security. See Figure 7.16.

HRM and the Internet

The Internet has become a major force for change in human resource management. For example, *online HRM systems* may involve recruiting for employees through recruitment sections of corporate Web sites. Companies are also using commercial recruiting services and databases on the World Wide Web, posting messages in selected Internet newsgroups, and communicating with job applicants via e-mail.

FIGURE 7.16

Human resource information systems support the strategic, tactical, and operational use of the human resources of an organization.

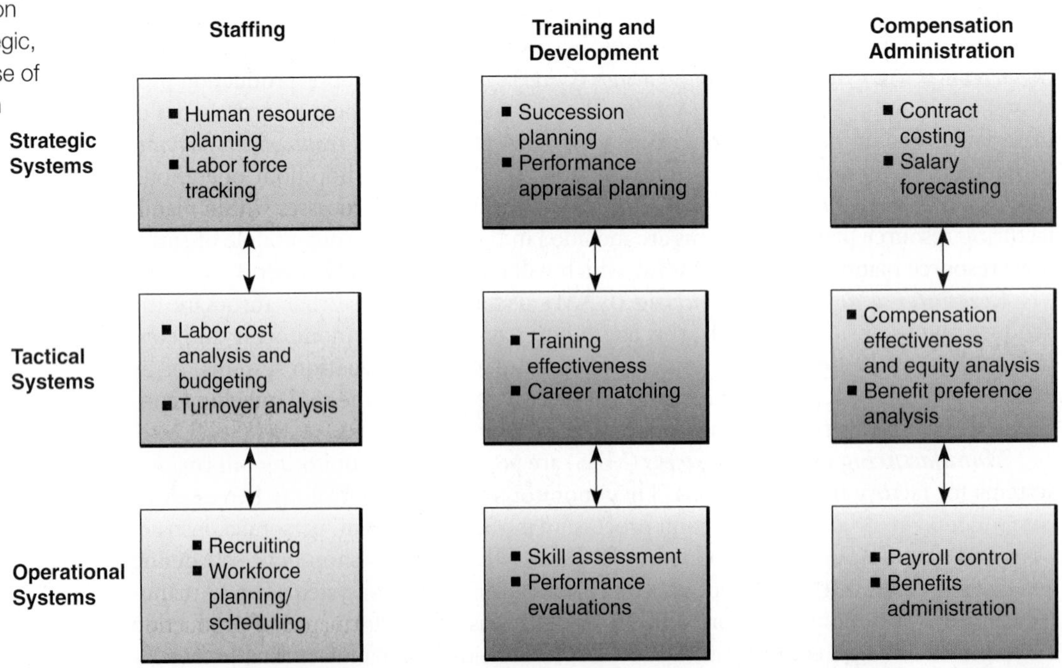

	Staffing	Training and Development	Compensation Administration
Strategic Systems	▪ Human resource planning ▪ Labor force tracking	▪ Succession planning ▪ Performance appraisal planning	▪ Contract costing ▪ Salary forecasting
Tactical Systems	▪ Labor cost analysis and budgeting ▪ Turnover analysis	▪ Training effectiveness ▪ Career matching	▪ Compensation effectiveness and equity analysis ▪ Benefit preference analysis
Operational Systems	▪ Recruiting ▪ Workforce planning/scheduling	▪ Skill assessment ▪ Performance evaluations	▪ Payroll control ▪ Benefits administration

The Internet has a wealth of information and contacts for both employers and job hunters. Top Web sites for job hunters and employers on the World Wide Web include Monster.com, HotJobs.com, and CareerBuilder.com. These Web sites are full of reports, statistics, and other useful HRM information, such as job reports by industry, or listings of the top recruiting markets by industry and profession.

HRM and Corporate Intranets

Intranet technologies allow companies to process most common HRM applications over their corporate intranets. Intranets allow the HRM department to provide around-the-clock services to their customers: the employees. They can also disseminate valuable information faster than through previous company channels. Intranets can collect information online from employees for input to their HRM files, and they can enable managers and other employees to perform HRM tasks with little intervention by the HRM department. See Figure 7.17.

For example, *employee self-service* (ESS) intranet applications allow employees to view benefits, enter travel and expense reports, verify employment and salary information, access and update their personal information, and enter time-sensitive data. Through this completely electronic process, employees can use their Web browsers to look up individual payroll and benefits information online, right from their desktop PCs, mobile computers, or intranet kiosks located around a work site.

Another benefit of the intranet is that it can serve as a superior training tool. Employees can easily download instructions and processes to get the information or education they need. In addition, employees using new technology can view training videos over the intranet on demand. Thus, the intranet eliminates the need to loan out and track training videos. Employees can also use their corporate intranets to produce automated paysheets, the online alternative to time cards. These electronic forms have made viewing, entering, and adjusting payroll information easy for both employees and HRM professionals.

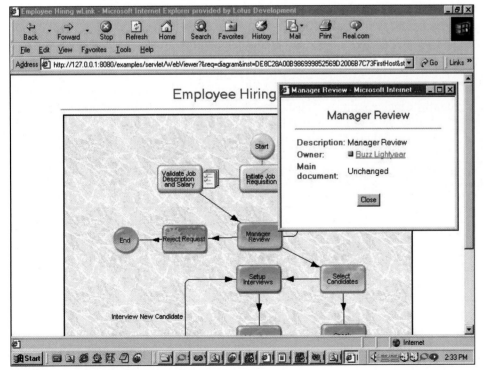

FIGURE 7.17

An example of an employee hiring review system.

SOURCE: Courtesy of IBM.

Chiquita Brands: Finding Out How Many Employees They Have

It seems like a straightforward and simple question that your typical HR application and corporate ERP system should be able to answer: How many employees are working for our company today?

At Chiquita Brands, the Fortune 500 company best known for its blue-stickered bananas, "We couldn't answer that question," recalls Manjit Singh, Chiquita's chief information officer since September 2006.

"It would take us a couple of weeks to get the answer pulled together and by that time, of course, it was all incorrect."

Chiquita boasts a global workforce of 23,000 employees in 70 countries on six continents, although most of the workers are predominantly in Central America. Until 2008, the Cincinnati-based food manufacturer had employed a hodgepodge of legacy HR systems that were inadequate at managing the complex demands of its decentralized workforce. Manual, inefficient work-arounds (Excel spreadsheets and paper-based processes) were frequently used.

When Chiquita hired a new employee, for instance, the HR paper-trail process could contain 20 to 30 steps, Singh notes.

"At any point, if that paper gets lost, things are going to fall through the cracks," he says. "Many times new employees have shown up and haven't had an office, a PC, or a phone. Obviously that causes pain to the employee, it doesn't make the employer look good, and you've lost productivity from the moment the employee walks through the door."

In October 2008, Chiquita went live on Workday HCM with 5,000 U.S.-based employees and 500 managers across 42 countries. Singh took advantage of customization options Workday offered when necessary. But he and his team tried to minimize customization as much as possible, so that they could shorten implementation time lines as they continue phased rollouts to 18,000 Latin America–based employees and nearly 3,000 employees throughout Europe.

Today, Chiquita's North American operations enjoy the fruits of the new system, including core HR functions such as employee hiring, job changes, compensation tracking, and more. "We can see exactly where in the process the employee is, or how the hiring is going, who is holding it up and why it's being held up, so that we can guarantee when an employee walks through the door, they have an office, a phone, a PC, and they've been given access to all of the systems they need to have access to," says Singh.

"That's big, when you talk about the number of employees we hire in a given month," Singh continues. "That drops dollars back down to the bottom line."

Lastly, the new HR system has freed up many of Chiquita's 200 IT staffers to focus on higher-value projects. "I want my folks sitting arm and arm with business folks, talking about process transformation and trying to figure out how to bring products to market even quicker," Singh says, "not keeping the lights on running a system."

SOURCE: Thomas Wailgum, "Why Chiquita Said 'No' to Tier 1 ERP Providers and 'Yes' to SaaS Apps from Upstart Workday," *CIO Magazine*, April 7, 2009.

ACCOUNTING SYSTEMS

Accounting information systems are the oldest and most widely used information systems in business. They record and report business transactions and other economic events. Computer-based accounting systems record and report the flow of funds through an organization on a historical basis and produce important financial statements such as balance sheets and income statements. Such systems also produce forecasts of future conditions such as projected financial statements and financial budgets. A firm's financial performance is measured against such forecasts by other analytical accounting reports.

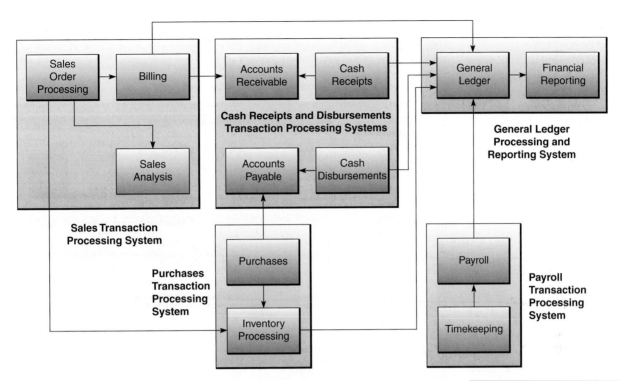

FIGURE 7.18

Important accounting information systems for transaction processing and financial reporting. Note how they are related to each other in terms of input and output flows.

Operational accounting systems emphasize legal and historical record-keeping and the production of accurate financial statements. Typically, these systems include transaction processing systems such as ***order processing, inventory control, accounts receivable, accounts payable, payroll,*** and ***general ledger*** systems. Management accounting systems focus on the planning and control of business operations. They emphasize cost accounting reports, the development of financial budgets and projected financial statements, and analytical reports comparing actual to forecasted performance.

Figure 7.18 illustrates the interrelationships of several important accounting information systems commonly computerized by both large and small businesses. Many accounting software packages are available for these applications. Figure 7.19

FIGURE 7.19

A summary of six essential accounting information systems used in business.

Common Business Accounting Systems
• **Order Processing** Captures and processes customer orders and produces data for inventory control and accounts receivable.
• **Inventory Control** Processes data reflecting changes in inventory and provides shipping and reorder information.
• **Accounts Receivable** Records amounts owed by customers and produces customer invoices, monthly customer statements, and credit management reports.
• **Accounts Payable** Records purchases from, amounts owed to, and payments to suppliers, and produces cash management reports.
• **Payroll** Records employee work and compensation data and produces paychecks and other payroll documents and reports.
• **General Ledger** Consolidates data from other accounting systems and produces the periodic financial statements and reports of the business.

FIGURE 7.20

An example of an online accounting report.

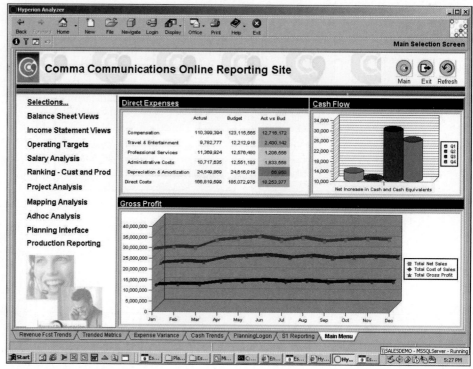

SOURCE: Courtesy of Hyperion.

provides a good summary of the essential purposes of six common, but important, accounting information systems used by both large and small business firms.

Online Accounting Systems

It should come as no surprise that the accounting information systems illustrated in Figures 7.18 and 7.19 are being transformed by Internet technologies. Using the Internet and other networks changes how accounting information systems monitor and track business activity. The interactive nature of *online accounting systems* calls for new forms of transaction documents, procedures, and controls. This particularly applies to systems like order processing, inventory control, accounts receivable, and accounts payable. As outlined in Figure 7.18, these systems are directly involved in the processing of transactions between a business and its customers and suppliers. So naturally, many companies are using Internet and other network links to these trading partners for such online transaction processing systems, as discussed in the beginning of the chapter. Figure 7.20 is an example of an online accounting report.

FINANCIAL MANAGEMENT SYSTEMS

Computer-based *financial management systems* support business managers and professionals in decisions concerning (1) the financing of a business and (2) the allocation and control of financial resources within a business. Major financial management system categories include cash and investment management, capital budgeting, financial forecasting, and financial planning. See Figure 7.21.

For example, the **capital budgeting** process involves evaluating the profitability and financial impact of proposed capital expenditures. Long-term expenditure proposals for facilities and equipment can be analyzed using a variety of return on investment (ROI) evaluation techniques. This application makes heavy use of spreadsheet models

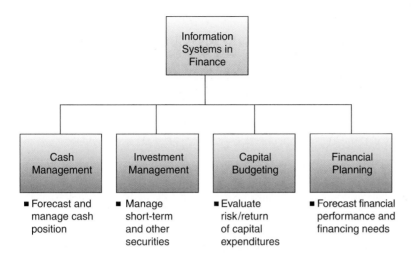

FIGURE 7.21
Examples of important financial management systems.

that incorporate present value analysis of expected cash flows and probability analysis of risk to determine the optimum mix of capital projects for a business.

Financial analysts also typically use electronic spreadsheets and other **financial planning** software to evaluate the present and projected financial performance of a business. They also help determine the financing needs of a business and analyze alternative methods of financing. Financial analysts use financial forecasts concerning the economic situation, business operations, types of financing available, interest rates, and stock and bond prices to develop an optimal financing plan for the business. Electronic spreadsheet packages, DSS software, and Web-based groupware can be used to build and manipulate financial models. Answers to what-if and goal-seeking questions can be explored as financial analysts and managers evaluate their financing and investment alternatives. We will discuss such applications further in Chapter 10. See Figure 7.22.

FIGURE 7.22
An example of strategic financial planning using a multiple scenario approach. Note the effect on earnings per share.

Comshare Planning - C:\DOCUME~1\ADMINI~1\LOCALS~1\TEMP\AQUISITIONS.MD1 - [EPS]

File   Edit   View   Specify   Format   Tools   Transfers   External   Window   Help

Comshare Strategic Planning

Comshare Strategic Planning

Earnings Per Share (EPS) Analysis

	2001	2002	2003	2004	2005	2006
Scenario 1						
Total Revenue	1,350,000	1,350,000	1,440,000	1,440,000	1,440,000	1,440,000
Cost of Goods Sold	405,000	405,000	432,000	432,000	432,000	432,000
Gross Profit	945,000	945,000	1,008,000	1,008,000	1,008,000	1,008,000
Total Direct Costs	882,813	897,646	894,885	895,069	893,304	889,791
Tax Provision	21,144	16,100	38,459	38,397	38,997	40,191
Net Income	41,043	31,253	74,656	74,534	75,699	78,018
Earnings per Share	0.41	0.31	0.75	0.75	0.76	0.78
Scenario 2						
Total Revenue	1,350,000	1,350,000	1,440,000	1,440,000	1,440,000	1,440,000
Cost of Goods Sold	405,000	405,000	432,000	432,000	432,000	432,000
Gross Profit	945,000	945,000	1,008,000	1,008,000	1,008,000	1,008,000
Total Direct Costs	882,813	897,646	894,885	895,069	893,304	889,791
Tax Provision	21,144	16,100	38,459	38,397	38,997	40,191
Net Income	41,043	31,253	74,656	74,534	75,699	78,018
Earnings per Share	0.41	0.31	0.75	0.75	0.76	0.78
Scenario 3						
Total Revenue	1,350,000	1,350,000	1,440,000	1,440,000	1,440,000	1,440,000
Cost of Goods Sold	405,000	405,000	432,000	432,000	432,000	432,000

SOURCE: Courtesy of Comshare.

Qualcomm—Breaking Down Silos and Integrating Applications

Qualcomm Inc. is a large company that engages in the development, design, manufacture, and marketing of digital wireless telecommunications products and services. The company operates in four segments: Qualcomm CDMA Technologies, Qualcomm Technology Licensing, Qualcomm Wireless and Internet, and Qualcomm Strategic Initiatives, as well as having direct—and in many cases full—ownership of a number of other subsidiaries, such as Qualcomm Atheros, Firethorn Mobile Inc., and Qualcomm Labs.

As in many other large companies whose business models rely heavily on, and are enabled by, information technology, Qualcomm's IT infrastructure results from years of special-purpose applications that were developed independently and that now have a hard time communicating with the other systems in the company—in short, multiple application silos. Although the company had developed a homegrown approach over the years to handling those challenges through hand-coding point-to-point integration between the various systems and databases, the limitations of that approach were starting to show and constrain what the company could and could not do, or how well it could serve the needs of its customers.

At some point, Steve Polaski, director of Enterprise Architecture for Qualcomm, realized that they could significantly reduce all three major costs of integration—development, maintenance, and support—by acquiring a product with the necessary capabilities rather than continuing to develop and maintain the in-house tool they had been working on for years. In addition, they were interested in what services could offer for the company, both as an approach to software development as well as an underlying philosophy for their IT infrastructure and environment. A service orientation requires loose coupling of services with operating systems, and other technologies that underlie applications. This approach to application integration and communication is commonly referred to as Service-Oriented Architecture (SOA). SOA separates functions into distinct units, or services, which developers make accessible over a network in order to allow users to combine and reuse them in the production of applications. These services and their corresponding consumers communicate with each other by passing data in a well-defined, shared format, or by coordinating an activity between two or more services. As a result, specific implementations are hidden behind the communication standards, making it much easier to change one application without needing to change another.

"SOA is a concept and a process and a way of thinking about how to move data and how to allow business functions to interoperate with each other," says Polaski. When Qualcomm started looking at Enterprise Application Integration (EAI) approaches, services were only emerging as a viable alternative for making systems and databases talk to each other effortlessly—at least as effortlessly as possible. However, managers quickly became convinced that services were the way to go, and they started looking for products that would let them expose the different functionality of the applications as services that other applications could access without knowing anything about the other side of the transaction. In the end, Qualcomm management selected products from TIBCO software to create their new application environment.

"We have other pieces in our SOA fabric today," says Polaski. "TIBCO products are a major part of this, and we use a number of tools from Oracle, including Oracle BPEL Process Manager. Plus, we use a number of opensource products. But TIBCO was the first set of SOA products we used."

Qualcomm's transition into the new practice of SOA was very structured and carefully planned. First, the company took the necessary time to implement a robust architecture that defined how the various applications and databases would be integrated by exposing them as a service. As a result, before they did any actual integration, managers already had a clear picture of how they wanted things to look when they were done, and as they say, the rest is just implementation. Between the time Tibco was selected as the main software vendor for this effort and the first few services were up and running, more than four months went by in developing and documenting the architecture. The other key piece of the approach was to take a forward-looking view of how to roll out integration through services. Qualcomm started by first setting up the infrastructure and connecting new applications and functionality to it under the new approach; only then were the existing applications and databases considered.

"We started by not attacking our existing integration, anything already in place," says Norm Fjeldheim, chief information officer at Qualcomm. "We built the SOA infrastructure around Tibco. And then as new things came up, instead of using what we had been using, we started using Tibco; and that is how we got things established. So it became our new engine around growth."

As Qualcomm engineers gained more experience with both the software tools and the service-oriented approach in general, new components were added from other applications and vendors, as well as slowly going after the legacy point-to-point integration as the opportunity arose. "It was a good approach for us," says Fjeldheim. "We had a lot we needed to get done, and this let us do it a lot quicker and it was less painful. We were pretty religious about not doing things the old way and adding to the problem. We used Tibco and our SOA infrastructure as much as possible for everything new we created." Each time changes or maintenance was needed in the legacy applications or integration points, managers considered whether they could migrate to the new approach. The logic was that, since changes would have to be made and tested to ensure that they would function appropriately, developers might as well eliminate the old approach and convert the exposed functionality of the application to a service that would then communicate with others in the network, as necessary. In some cases it was the right time, and in others it was not. But the question was asked anew each time.

After all was said and done, the service-oriented architecture has been deployed globally throughout the many business divisions and fully owned subsidiaries that make up Qualcomm Inc. More than 150 different messages are sent between a number of different applications, 58 Web services, and other databases using technology from Tibco, Oracle, and some open-source packages. In addition, more than 180 other integration points have been exposed as services, and they are not nearly done with the project.

Exposing applications as services allows IT to make existing systems available as service calls and then build new applications that combine existing functionality, with little or no new coding necessary. The new skill set and capabilities that developers learned from the move to SOA has

helped them tackle new challenges more effectively. Where a new IT-based solution to a business problem would have taken a week to implement under the old approach, in some cases it has been up and running in as little as three hours using SOA. Moneywise, IT has benefited as well. The new deployment has eliminated about half a million dollars of annual integration costs: A single point-to-point integration piece that used to cost between $30,000 to $150,000 has been cut by a factor of 5 to 10 as a result of the new approach taken, which frees up money to spend on other things. And IT departments never have a shortage of those.

And what about those business benefits discussed in the opening to this chapter? One major benefit was inching Qualcomm close to the real-time sharing of data they had envisioned. For example, one of the first integration projects under SOA was undertaken so the sales representatives could access the existing CRM application through Smartphones, which would allow them to work remotely while at the same time always stay connected and up-to-date. Other projects include the integration of the product data management application with its ERP package and a legacy manufacturing system. And all those issues with the provisioning of new features have been addressed as well. "By changing the architecture and our integration strategy, the time to add features and functions to wireless devices went down to from three hours or so to five seconds," says Polaski. "Customer satisfaction went way up as a result," notes Fjeldheim. "Our internal and external customers were both happy." Also, says Polaski, "We have agility and flexibility to support our changing business models that we didn't before, because the services are being orchestrated, rather than hardwired to each other."

SOURCE: Daniel Dern, "How One Company Broke Down Silos and Improved Application Integration," *CIO.com*, September 15, 2008; Scot Petersen, "Qualcomm Dials in SOAs," *eWeek*, November 22, 2004, "TIBCO Supports Product Engineering and Business Integration at Qualcomm," *TIBCO Success Story*, 2006; and www.qualcomm.com, accessed May 28, 2011.

▼ QUESTIONS TO CONSIDER

1. How are services different than the existing point-to-point integration approach? Where does their value come from?

2. Consider the approach taken by Qualcomm to roll out services into its IT infrastructure. What were its strong points? Were there any weaknesses? What could they have done differently?

- **Cross-Functional Enterprise Systems.** Major e-business applications and their interrelationships are summarized in the enterprise application architecture of Figure 7.2. These applications are integrated cross-functional enterprise systems, such as enterprise resource planning (ERP), customer relationship management (CRM), and supply chain management (SCM). The applications may be interconnected by enterprise application integration (EAI) systems so that business professionals can more easily access the information resources they need to support the needs of customers, suppliers, and business partners. Enterprise collaboration systems (ECS) are cross-functional systems that support and enhance communication and collaboration among the teams and workgroups in an organization. Refer to Figures 7.4 and 7.8 for summary views of the e-business applications in EAI systems and enterprise collaboration systems.

- **Transaction Processing Systems.** Online transaction processing systems play a vital role in business. Transaction processing involves the basic activities of (1) data entry, (2) transaction processing, (3) database maintenance, (4) document and report generation, and (5) inquiry processing. Many firms are using the Internet, intranets, extranets, and other networks for online transaction processing to provide superior service to their customers and suppliers. Figure 7.6 illustrates the basic activities of transaction processing systems.

- **Functional Business Systems.** Functional business information systems support the business functions of marketing, production/operations, accounting, finance, and human resource management through a variety of e-business operational and management information systems summarized in Figure 7.11.

- **Marketing.** Marketing information systems support traditional and e-commerce processes and management of the marketing function. Major types of marketing information systems include interactive marketing at e-commerce Web sites, sales force automation, customer relationship management, sales management, product management, targeted marketing, advertising and promotion, and market research. Thus, marketing information systems assist marketing managers in e-commerce product development and customer relationship decisions, as well as in planning advertising and sales promotion strategies and developing the e-commerce potential of new and present products and new channels of distribution.

- **Manufacturing.** Computer-based manufacturing information systems help a company achieve computer-integrated manufacturing (CIM), and thus simplify, automate, and integrate many of the activities needed to quickly produce high-quality products to meet changing customer demands. For example, computer-aided design using collaborative manufacturing networks helps engineers collaborate on the design of new products and processes. Then manufacturing resource planning systems help plan the types of resources needed in the production process. Finally, manufacturing execution systems monitor and control the manufacture of products on the factory floor through shop floor scheduling and control systems, controlling a physical process (process control), a machine tool (numerical control), or machines with some humanlike work capabilities (robotics).

- **Human Resource Management.** Human resource information systems support human resource management in organizations. They include information systems for staffing the organization, training and development, and compensation administration. HRM Web sites on the Internet or corporate intranets have become important tools for providing HR services to present and prospective employees.

- **Accounting and Finance.** Accounting information systems record, report, and analyze business transactions and events for the management of the business enterprise. Figure 7.19 summarizes six essential accounting systems including order processing, inventory control, accounts receivable, accounts payable, payroll, and general ledger. Information systems in finance support managers in decisions regarding the financing of a business and the allocation of financial resources within a business. Financial information systems include cash management, online investment management, capital budgeting, and financial forecasting and planning.

These are the key terms and concepts of this chapter. The page number of their first reference appears in parentheses.

1. Accounting information systems (308)
2. Accounts payable (309)
3. Accounts receivable (309)
4. Batch processing (295)
5. Computer-aided manufacturing (305)
6. Computer-integrated manufacturing (304)
7. Cross-functional enterprise systems (287)
8. E-business (287)
9. Enterprise application architecture (290)
10. Enterprise application integration (291)
11. Enterprise collaboration systems (296)
12. Financial management systems (310)
13. Functional business systems (299)
14. General ledger (309)
15. Human resource information systems (306)
16. Interactive marketing (301)
17. Inventory control (309)
18. Machine control (306)
19. Manufacturing execution systems (305)
20. Manufacturing information systems (304)
21. Marketing information systems (300)
22. Online accounting systems (310)
23. Online HRM systems (306)
24. Online transaction processing systems (294)
25. Order processing (309)
26. Payroll (309)
27. Process control (306)
28. Real-time processing (295)
29. Sales force automation (302)
30. Targeted marketing (301)
31. Transaction processing cycle (295)

Match one of the key terms and concepts listed previously with one of the brief examples or definitions that follow. Try to find the best fit for the answers that seem to fit more than one term or concept. Defend your choices.

_____ 1. Using the Internet and other networks for e-commerce, enterprise collaboration, and Web-enabled business processes.

_____ 2. Information systems that cross the boundaries of the functional areas of a business in order to integrate and automate business processes.

_____ 3. Information systems that support marketing, production, accounting, finance, and human resource management.

_____ 4. E-business applications fit into a framework of interrelated cross-functional enterprise applications.

_____ 5. Software that interconnects enterprise application systems.

_____ 6. Information systems for customer relationship management, sales management, and promotion management.

_____ 7. Collaborating interactively with customers in creating, purchasing, servicing, and improving products and services.

_____ 8. Using mobile computing networks to support salespeople in the field.

_____ 9. Information systems that support manufacturing operations and management.

_____ 10. A conceptual framework for simplifying and integrating all aspects of manufacturing automation.

_____ 11. Using computers in a variety of ways to help manufacture products.

_____ 12. Use electronic communications, conferencing, and collaborative work tools to support and enhance collaboration among teams and workgroups.

_____ 13. Using computers to operate a petroleum refinery.

_____ 14. Using computers to help operate machine tools.

_____ 15. Information systems to support staffing, training and development, and compensation administration.

_____ 16. Using the Internet for recruitment and job hunting is an example.

_____ 17. Accomplishes legal and historical record-keeping and gathers information for the planning and control of business operations.

_____ 18. An example is using the Internet and extranets to do accounts receivable and accounts payable activities.

_____ 19. Handles sales orders from customers.

_____ 20. Keeps track of items in stock.

_____ 21. Keeps track of amounts owed by customers.

_____ 22. Keeps track of purchases from suppliers.

_____ 23. Produces employee paychecks.

_____ 24. Produces the financial statements of a firm.

_____ 25. Information systems for cash management, investment management, capital budgeting, and financial forecasting.

_____ 26. Performance monitoring and control systems for factory floor operations.

_____ 27. Customizing advertising and promotion methods to fit their intended audience.

_____ 28. Data entry, transaction processing, database maintenance, document and report generation, and inquiry processing.

_____ 29. Collecting and periodically processing transaction data.

_____ 30. Processing transaction data immediately after they are captured.

_____ 31. Systems that immediately capture and process transaction data and update corporate databases.

discussion questions

1. Refer to the Real World Challenge in the chapter, where the difficulty of making a business case for integration projects is discussed. What could managers do to make the benefits of those projects more clear? Should these be evaluated like any other IT project?

2. Why is there a trend toward cross-functional integrated enterprise systems in business?

3. Which of the 17 tools for enterprise collaboration systems summarized in Figure 7.8 do you feel are essential for any business today? Which ones do you feel are optional, depending on the type of business or other factors? Explain.

4. Other than EAI systems, what are some possible solutions to the problem of incompatibility of information systems in business?

5. What are the most important HR applications a company should offer to its employees via a Web-based system? Why?

6. How could sales force automation affect salesperson productivity, marketing management, and competitive advantage?

7. How can Internet technologies help improve a process in one of the functions of business? Choose one example and evaluate its business value.

8. Refer to the Real World Solution in the chapter. What are some of the prerequisites for a successful implementation of the service-oriented approach, as in Qualcomm's case? Would it work in any organizational environment?

9. What are several e-business applications that you might recommend to a small company to help it survive and succeed in challenging economic times? Why?

10. Refer to the example on virtual worlds in the chapter. How do enterprise collaboration systems contribute to bottom-line profits for a business?

analysis exercises

1. **Hybrid Application Service Providers**
ASP Integrated Applications
Revenue from desktop application sales ends with the sale. Or does it? Companies like Microsoft provide updates, fixes, and security patches to its software while developing the next revenue-generating edition. However, they don't make another dime until they release the next edition. But that isn't the only model.

McAfee charges an annual maintenance fee that includes daily application and virus definition updates. McAfee provides it for one year as part of its license. After the first year, license holders may continue to use the software, but they must pay a subscription fee if they want updates. Customers tend to pay for this subscription service in order to protect themselves from new virus threats. Thus, McAfee generates revenue long after the initial sale. In this way, McAfee behaves like an application service provider.

The following questions will help you explore the many ASP-related services that relocate applications, maintenance, and data from your systems and allow you to focus on your mission.

a. Skype offers audio, video, and instant messaging tools (see the Features link at www.skype.com). Compare the Skype tools to the equivalent Google offerings. Prepare a table in Word or write a one-page paper (at your instructor's request) to compare these competing tools. Place Feature, Skype, and Google as column headers. List individual features under "Feature" in the left-most column. Place the symbol "•" in the cell if it's a current feature for each competitor. Leave the cell blank if it isn't available at all. Give the table a professional appearance.

b. Yahoo and Google are in a heated competition for the same user base. Look up the latest developments for Yahoo at next.yahoo.com and for Google at labs.google.com. Prepare a table in Word to compare current and beta features for Yahoo and Google. Place Feature, Google, and Yahoo as column headers. List individual features under "Feature" in the left-most column. Place the symbol "•" in the cell if it's a current feature for each competitor and the symbol "o" in the cell if it's a beta feature.

Leave the cell blank if it isn't available at all. Give the table a professional appearance.

2. In Search of Talent
Online Job Matching and Auctions
Many opportunities await those who troll the big job boards, the free-agent sites, the reverse auction services, and the niche sites for specialized jobs and skills. Presented below are a diverse sample of employment-related Web sites.

- eLance.com (www.elance.com)
- Guru.com (www.guru.com)
- Monster.com (www.monster.com)
- Virtual Worker (www.vworker.com)

a. Prepare a review for each job site listed above. Include target employers, target employees, and notable Web site features.

b. Which site did you find most useful? Why?

3. Integrating Data Capture
Keys to Better Information
Business systems have long served to automate tasks, facilitate data capture, and enable new opportunities. These processes have crept into virtually all businesses and business processes. RE/MAX real estate agent Rosemary Chiaverini well remembers business 20 years ago and the rather cumbersome process of coordinating key exchanges with fellow agents. "It really limited the number of houses we could show in a day."

A key safe increased productivity by allowing real estate agents to open a key safe at each property. The key locked inside the key safe then provides access to the residence. Showing agents would then leave a business card behind to indicate they had shown a property, but the listing agent would have to retrieve these cards personally. "I just didn't know for certain who was seeing my homes or what they thought of them."

GE Security's Supra iBox has changed that. Rosemary now uses an electronic, infrared key to open GE's new key safe, and the key records the transaction. When she synchronizes her key online to update her key's codes, this information goes up to GE's database and is shared with the listing agent. With most agents in her area subscribing to this system, Rosemary has Internet access information about who visited one of her listed homes and when. She uses this information to follow up on each visit and gain valuable insights. "Before, I would waste a lot of time calling busy agents who had arranged to show a home but hadn't."

a. Use a search engine to look up the Supra iBox. Describe the product's capabilities.

b. Describe the next-generation product you might sell Rosemary once keyless locks become commonplace.

4. Word's Mail Merge
Partner Name Tags
Ms. Sapper, this year's annual partner meeting coordinator for a global accounting firm, faced an interesting challenge. She wanted to provide the 400 partners attending the meeting with the opportunity to mix, mingle, and network. Most partners only knew a handful of their peers, and Ms. Sapper wanted to make everyone feel as comfortable as possible. With a list of partners in hand, she decided to prepare name tags for each participant. Each tag would include the partner's first name, last name, practice area, and region. Arranging them alphabetically by last name at the event's welcome desk would allow each partner to quickly find and use the correct name tag.

Complete the following steps to prepare partner name badges.

a. Download and save "partners.xls" from the MIS 16e OLC.

b. Use Microsoft Word's mail merge feature to generate name tags sorted by last name and then first name. Use a suitable name tag template, and format the name tag as illustrated below. Be sure to include first name, last name, industry, and region. Turn in either the first two pages of the merged names or the merged file as per your professor's preference.

Example:

Christoph Aarns
Audit
Asia Pacific

5. Federated Search
Deep into e-Business
Deep Web Technologies (deepwebtech.com) provides "federated search" capabilities for a client base ranging from government agencies to research institutions. Federated searches aren't like standard Internet searches where users search an index of Web pages. Instead, DWT's tools simultaneously search dozens or even hundreds of online databases in real time. Since online databases tend to have their own customized search tools, DWT's de-duplicated and prioritized results can save users hours of time searching across many online databases.

So how does DWT produce this state-of-the-art software? In short, they rely heavily on e-business tools. For example, to recruit qualified jRuby developers, DWT uses human networking via social media such as LinkedIn and Facebook. Programmer training consists primarily of e-books, Web-based resources and developer tools, and hands-on mentoring. Developers provide status updates, collaborate, and banter all hands-free with Skype. Skype enables an open-office feel but with all the conveniences of home. They manage software version control through Subversion, another online tool.

On the business end, DWT uses Google Apps for Business for their productivity software (calendaring, scheduling, e-mail, word processing, spreadsheets). Google's online business applications simplify administration and access control, they operate across multiple platforms, and they allow real-time updating and collaboration. These tools are flexible enough that DWTs developers have used them to create work-flow tools to standardize requests for new database connectors. DWT also uses Redmine, an online tool, to manage help desk tickets, host system documentation, and provide the organization with a wiki-style knowledge base. Lastly, employees with a fast and reliable Internet connection have the option to telecommute.

a. Read up on "federated search." List the obvious strengths and weaknesses.

b. Visit DWT's demo page (http://bit.ly/ k31KKb) and run a couple of searches. Run the same searches through a standard search engine. How does the experience differ? How do the results differ?

c. What advantages do you think DWT gains by using Web-enabled, cloud-based applications to manage its business?

Toyota Europe, Campbell Soup Company, Sony Pictures, and W.W. Grainger: Making the Case for Enterprise Architects

When technology infrastructure lines up with business projects like musicians in a marching band, you know you have a good enterprise architect on staff.

Enterprise architecture focuses on four crucial C's: connection, collaboration, communication, and customers. Imagine needing to manually log onto five different systems to create and track an order, or putting in 20 hours researching a project because you didn't know the information already existed in another department. These situations result from fragmentation and siloed thinking; the goal of enterprise architecture, on the other hand, is to create unity.

Enterprise architecture's goal is IT that enables business strategy today and tomorrow, says Peter Heinckiens, chief enterprise architect at Toyota Europe. "The 'tomorrow' part is especially important," he says. The enterprise architect must map, define, and standardize technology, data, and business processes to make that possible. This means that the architect must have both a macro and micro view: She must understand the business strategy and translate this into an architectural approach (macro view), but she must also be able to work with individual projects and deliver very concrete guidance to these projects that focuses on the successful delivery of the individual project within that macro view. "The enterprise architect transforms tech-speak into the language of business solutions, and he knows what technology is needed to enable business strategy," says Heinckiens.

In other words, an architect knows how to bridge silos. An oft-used metaphor for the enterprise architect's role is that of the city planner, one who also provides the road maps, zoning, common requirements, regulations and strategy—albeit for a company rather than for a city. And this role is increasingly important as enterprise architecture itself becomes more important.

"Enterprise architecture's roots are in the desire to serve what is best for the enterprise versus the individual department or project," says Campbell Soup Company Vice President of IT-Shared Services Andy Croft, who has the enterprise architect role at Campbell's. He speaks of the days when employees within the same company were unable to share information via e-mail, because of incompatible e-mail systems. Each department thought it needed its own brand of PC, even its own network or security system. Finally, Croft says, "People lifted their heads and thought, maybe it's more important to be able to work together rather than me

having the 'best.'" Enterprise architecture gained traction from the bottom up.

That siloed view on projects may come in the form of "I want to use this package" or "I want to build this application," according to Heinckiens. As an architect, he advises, it's important to take a step back: Try to understand what problem the proposed project will solve. Is there already a solution that covers the proposed area being researched? Does the proposed project fit into the wider picture? "Structurally, business units are silos—and therefore often have a limited view—but the enterprise architect ensures that the pieces of the wider-picture puzzle fit together," says Heinckiens.

As an illustration, some projects use data that nobody else in the company will be interested in, while other projects use data that are useful and relevant to everyone in the company. It is the enterprise architect's job to figure out how to make the latter type available to the rest of the company, and one part of that task is creating compliance standards. "It is important that this discussion takes place," says Heinckiens. "Then you see other discussions start to happen." For example, who owns this data? Who should receive permission to access this data? What is a customer? For the marketing department, after-sale department, finance department, the definition of customer is totally different, even though they refer to the same person. In many companies this process is ultimately formalized. At Campbell's, it's called a "blueprint." Before a new project can be started, each technology area must review a proposed project to ensure that it fits into the overall strategy.

Achieving that impressive lockstep between business and IT takes time and practice, of course. Not only that, but an enterprise architect must be a voice that many kinds of people can understand, says Tim Ferrarell, chief information officer and senior vice president of enterprise systems at W.W. Grainger, a $6.4 billion distributor of heavy equipment.

Ideally, Ferrarell says, this person "can think at a strategic level and all the way down to the operating level and understand how to move up and down that chain of abstraction," he says. "And know how to deal with conflicts and trade-offs."

Is that all? Actually, no. That person also has to gain the confidence of the senior leadership team, he says. Execs must believe that the enterprise architect comprehends how the company works, where it wants to go and how technology helps or hinders, he says. Then effective working relationships can bloom.

In 2006, Grainger went live with a companywide SAP project—20 SAP modules and 30 additional applications that would touch 425 locations. To help guard against what could go wrong in a big-bang cutover, Ferrarell took his team of about 20 enterprise architects off their regular jobs and assigned them to design and integration roles on the SAP project. The SAP implementation was such an all-encompassing program that it made sense to re-purpose the enterprise architects into key roles in the project. Their broad business and technical knowledge made them very valuable team members, says Ferrarell.

Grainger's senior business-side managers knew these architects and their business savvy firsthand, he explains. The trust was there, which helped get IT the intense cooperation needed during and after the complicated launch. Their architects played a significant role, not only in shaping the need for completion of the ERP project, but in ensuring that its design would enable their business requirements. The SAP project succeeded, Ferrarell says, in part due to the institutional knowledge and business-IT translation skills the EAs brought to it.

Other companies, though, have to be convinced of the enterprise architect's criticality. Sony Pictures Entertainment launched an enterprise architect role modestly in 2002, focused at first only on technology issues, says David Buckholtz, vice president of planning, enterprise architecture, and quality at the media company.

He had to start small: Sony Pictures Entertainment didn't even have a corporatewide IT department until the late 1990s, Buckholtz says. The company grew from acquisitions and other deals that parent company Sony Corp. of America made in the 1980s and 1990s, such as the acquisition of Columbia TriStar movie studio (*The Karate Kid* and *Ghostbusters*) and the acquisition of Merv Griffin Enterprises (*Wheel of Fortune* and *Jeopardy*).

"We're in a creative industry and people made a lot of decisions on their own," he says. Hence, no central IT until relatively recently and no strong belief in the importance of central IT, he says.

Buckholtz was hired from General Electric to start an enterprise architecture team because Sony Pictures wanted more efficiency and savings from IT, he says. At first, he concentrated on classifying existing and future technology investments. Categories include technologies in development where Sony is doing proofs of concept; technologies in pilot; current and supported; supported but older versions; those headed to retirement; and those that are obsolete and no longer supported except "under extreme duress," Buckholtz says, laughing.

He began this way to demonstrate that IT could be businesslike: investing well, conscious of risk, planning for the future. "This is how you plan enterprise architecture when you don't have business support yet. We had to build up to that."

Once the architecture group has the enterprise IT house under control, it can look for ways to work with different business technology groups to build credibility beyond bits and bytes, he says. One technique Buckholtz used was to install architects in different business groups to work on projects on business turf but using IT's budget. A free trial, in a sense.

By 2005, Buckholtz's group had started a high-profile project with the digital media team to map out how Sony Pictures would digitize content for downloading to mobile phones and other devices. He counts it as a success that the digital media group continues to use that road map today. "We identified high-value work and we were all committed to it," he says. "It was not a group off somewhere, passing down standards."

As the economy tightens, Sony Pictures must make its distribution chain as efficient as possible, he adds. Movies, after all, are a discretionary expense for consumers and if they pull back on luxuries, Sony Pictures will feel it. EAs continuously reinforce to business-side counterparts the expected returns on IT projects as the temptation to cut spending grows. "We make sure we close the loop and quantify hard-dollar costs and benefits for the CFO," Buckholtz says.

SOURCE: Diann Daniel, "The Rising Importance of the Enterprise Architect," *CIO.com*, March 31, 2007, and Kim S. Nash, "The Case for Enterprise Architects," *CIO.com*, December 23, 2008.

▼ CASE STUDY QUESTIONS

1. What does the position of enterprise architect entail? What qualifications or experiences do you think a good enterprise architect should have? Support your answer with examples from the case.
2. Consider the different companies mentioned in the case and their experiences with enterprise architecture. Does this approach seem to work better in certain types of companies or industries than in others? Why or why not?
3. What is the value derived from companies with mature enterprise architectures? Are there any downsides that you can see? Discuss.

▼ REAL WORLD ACTIVITIES

1. Service-oriented architecture (SOA) is a recent approach to systems development and implementation that has much in common with enterprise architecture, as well as some differences. Go online and research these similarities and differences. Prepare a report to summarize your work.
2. Have you considered a career as an enterprise architect? What bundle of courses would you put together to design a major or a track in enterprise architecture? Break into small groups with your classmates to outline the major areas that should be covered.

Nationwide Insurance: Unified Financial Reporting and "One Version of the Truth"

In a span of three short years, between 2000 and 2002, Nationwide Insurance got a new CEO, CIO, and CFO.

Jerry Jurgensen, elected by Nationwide's board in 2000 to replace the retiring CEO, was hired for his financial acumen and his ability to transform a business's culture. Michael Keller was named the company's first enterprisewide chief information officer the following year. He had 25 years of IT experience managing big infrastructure and systems integration projects. In 2002, Robert Rosholt replaced the retiring chief financial officer and joined the others in Nationwide's Columbus headquarters, bringing along deep experience in all things financial.

The three were old buddies who had worked together at financial giant Bank One. Now they held the reins at Nationwide and their goal was to take its dozens of business units, selling a diverse set of insurance and financial products, to a higher level. In 2001, Nationwide was profitable to the tune of $138 million and board members had billion-dollar aspirations for that line item.

But to get there, Jurgensen needed financial snapshots of how Nationwide was doing at any given moment. And getting them wasn't so easy.

In fact, it was almost impossible.

"When you're dealing with 14 general ledger platforms and over 50 applications," Rosholt says, "it was enormous work to get the financials out."

The problem lay knotted in a tangle of systems and applications, and some 240 sources of financial data flowing in and around Nationwide's business units. The units had always run independently, and that's how financial reporting was handled. "There was a variety of [financial reporting] languages," Rosholt says, which affected Nationwide's ability to forecast, budget, and report. "It was difficult," says Rosholt, to ask, "How are we doing?" Keller's situation was no better.

"One of the first questions I was asked when I joined was, How much money do we spend, total, on IT?" Keller recalls. "The answer was, we didn't know. It took weeks to put that answer together."

Jurgensen wanted to be able to run Nationwide as if it were one unified enterprise. He wanted, in Rosholt's words, "to do things that are common, and respect the things that are different. And that was a big change." Indeed, the transformation the company embarked upon in early 2004 was daunting—a master data management makeover that would alter how every Nationwide business reported its financials, how accounting personnel did their jobs, how data was governed and by whom, and how the company's information systems would pull all that together. The goal was simple: one platform; one version of the financial truth. Simple goal. But a difficult challenge.

Says James Kobielus, principal analyst of data management at market researcher Current Analysis, "In the hyper-siloed real world of enterprise networking, master data is scattered all over creation and subjected to a fragmented, inconsistent, rickety set of manual and automated processes." Good master data governance can happen only when the various constituencies that own the data sources agree on a common set of definitions, rules, and synchronized procedures, all of which requires a degree of political maneuvering that's not for the faint of heart.

Nationwide began its finance transformation program, called Focus, with its eyes wide open. The executive troika of Jurgensen, Rosholt, and Keller had pulled off a similar project at Bank One and thought it knew how to avoid the big mistakes. That, in part, is why Rosholt, who had ultimate say on the project, would not budge on its 24-month time line. "The most important aspect was sticking to discipline and not wavering," he recalls. And that's why the technology piece was, from the outset, the last question to be addressed.

"It wasn't a technology project," insists Lynda Butler, whose vice president of performance management position was created to oversee Focus (which stands for Faster, Online, Customer-driven, User-friendly, Streamlined). She says that Nationwide approached Focus first and foremost as a business and financial project.

Nationwide considers the project, which made its deadline, a success, although everyone interviewed for this article stresses that there's more work to be done. Says Keller: "There's a foundation to build on where there wasn't one before."

"Fourteen general ledgers, 12 reporting tools, 17 financial data repositories and 300,000 spreadsheets were used in finance," says Butler. "That's not real conducive to 'one version of the truth.'"

Early in his tenure as chief executive officer, Jurgensen's concerns about the company's financials weren't limited to the timeliness of the data; he was also worried about its integrity and accuracy. He and other execs knew that faster access to more comprehensive data sets would allow for better trend analysis and forecasting decisions, and strengthen budgeting, reporting and accounting processes. For example, because Nationwide had such a variety of businesses, the company carried a lot of risk—some easily visible, some not. "So, if equity markets went down, we were exposed," notes Butler. "But we didn't realize that until the markets actually went down. We needed some enterprise view of the world."

Executives also knew that common data definitions among all the business units would provide comparable financial data for analysis—which was difficult, if not impossible, without those definitions. "We needed consistent data across the organization," Rosholt says. "We were looking for one book of record." CFO Rosholt went back to his Bank One roots and recruited Vikas Gopal, who had proven his mettle on similar projects, to lead the IT team.

With no wiggle room on the time line, the team, with Rosholt's encouragement, followed what it refers to as the "80/20" rule. It knew that it wasn't going to get 100 percent of the desired functionality of the new system, so the team decided that if it could get roughly 80 percent of the project up and running in 24 months, it could fix the remaining 20 percent later. "If we went after perfection," says Rosholt, "we'd still be at it."

Keeping in mind that no one would get everything he wanted, the Focus team interviewed key stakeholders in Nationwide's business units to understand where their pain points were. "We went back to basics," says Gopal. "We said, 'Let's talk about your financial systems, how they help your decision making.'" The team then determined where senior management wanted to focus and presented it with a choice of 10 different financial competencies. "Do we want to be the best company that does transaction recording? Or enterprise risk? Or analytics?" Gopal says.

In other words, people were introduced to the concept of making trade-offs, which allowed the Focus team to target the system's core functionalities and keep control over the project's scope.

It was only after the requirements, definitions, and parameters were mapped out that Gopal's group began looking at technologies. Gopal had two rules to guide them: First, all financial-related systems had to be subscribers to the central book of record. Second, none of the master data in any of the financial applications could ever be out of sync. So the Focus team's final step was to evaluate technologies that would follow and enforce those rules.

The team reasoned that it had neither the time nor the inclination to invent technology at Nationwide. "We wanted to start off on the right footing from a TCO (total cost of ownership) perspective; with only 24 months you don't have a ton of time to build a lot of stuff," Gopal says. His team sought out best-of-breed tool sets from vendors such as Kalido and Teradata that would be able to tie into their existing systems. Gopal wasn't overly "worried about [technology] execution" because he had assembled this type of system before and knew that the technology solutions on the market, even in the most vanilla forms, were robust enough for Nationwide's needs.

What did worry him was Nationwide's legion of financial employees who didn't relish the idea of changing the way they went about their work. At the beginning of the program, Nationwide formed a "One Finance Family" program that tried to unify all the finance folks around Focus. Executives were also able to identify those employees who were most affected through weekly "change meetings" and provide support. In addition, executives placed dedicated communications personnel who were responsible for communicating and managing change through the meetings and media channels.

The Focus team had to remain resolute. The overarching theme, that there would be no compromise in data quality and integrity, was repeated early and often, and execs made sure that the gravity of the change was communicated before anyone saw any new software.

Finally, in March 2005, with three waves of planned deployments ahead of it, the team started rolling out the new Focus system. By fall 2005, there was light at the end of the tunnel. The team could see the new business processes and financial data governance mechanisms actually being used by Nationwide employees. And it all was working. "They saw the value they were creating," recalls Butler. "The 'aha' moment came when we finally got a chance to look in the rear-view mirror."

Nationwide execs concede that the system is still evolving but say substantial gains are everywhere. The first benefit of the transformation that Rosholt mentions is something that didn't happen. "You go through a project such as this, in a period of extreme regulatory and accounting oversight, and these things can cough up more issues, such as earnings restatements. We've avoided that," he says. "That doesn't mean we're perfect, but that's one thing everyone's amazed at. We went through all this change and nothing coughed up. Our balance sheet was right."

Nationwide has one less thing to worry about, one more thing to be confident about.

SOURCE: Thomas Wailgum, "How Master Data Management Unified Financial Reporting at Nationwide Insurance," *CIO.com*, December 21, 2007.

▼ **CASE STUDY QUESTIONS**

1. The project that Nationwide undertook was quite clearly a success. What made this possible? Discuss three different practices that helped Nationwide pull this off. Use examples from the case where necessary.

2. The case notes that Nationwide had in mind a simple goal, but faced a difficult challenge. Why was this so difficult? What was the scenario the three executives faced when they joined Nationwide? How had the company gotten there?

3. What is the business value derived from the successful completion of this project? What can executives at Nationwide do now that they could not do before? Provide some examples.

▼ REAL WORLD ACTIVITIES

1. Technologies and systems involved in financial reporting have received a great deal of attention in the last few years due to renewed regulatory focus on the integrity and reliability of financial information. Go online and research how companies are deploying technology to deal with these issues. Prepare a report to summarize your findings.

2. A number of political and cultural issues were involved in the implementation of the "one version of the truth" approach at Nationwide. Can these obstacles be overcome simply by mandating compliance from top management? What else should companies do to help ease these transitions? Break into small groups with your classmates and brainstorm some possible actions.

chapter 8

BUSINESS ACROSS THE ENTERPRISE

INFORMATION SYSTEMS

e-BUSINESS APPLICATIONS

CHAPTER HIGHLIGHTS

LEARNING OBJECTIVES

After reading and studying this chapter, you should be able to:

8-1 Identify and give examples to illustrate the following aspects of customer relationship management, enterprise resource management, and supply chain management systems:

a. Business processes supported

b. Customer and business value provided

c. Potential challenges and trends

8-2 Understand the importance of managing at the enterprise level to achieve maximum efficiencies and benefits.

Getting All the Geese Lined Up:
Managing at the Enterprise Business Level

Here's a question you probably never expected to find in your information systems text: Have you ever noticed how geese fly? They start out as a seemingly chaotic flock of birds, but very quickly end up flying in a V-shape or echelon pattern like that shown in Figure 8.1. As you might imagine, this consistency in flying formation is not an accident. By flying in this manner, each bird receives a slight, but measurable, benefit in reduced drag from the bird in front. This makes it easier for all of the birds to fly long distances than if they just took up whatever portion of the sky they happened to find. Of course, the lead bird has the toughest job, but geese have figured out a way to help there, as well. Systematically, one of the birds from the formation will fly up to relieve the current lead bird. In this way, the entire flock shares the load as they all head in the same direction.

INTRODUCTION
LO 8-1

Okay, so what does this have to do with information systems? This chapter will focus on systems that span the enterprise and that are intended to support three enterprisewide operations: *customer relationships*, *resource planning*, and *supply chain*. Each operation requires a unique focus and, thus, a unique system to support it, but they all share one common goal: to get the entire organization to line up and head in the same direction, just as the geese do. Without this guidance and control, these three essential activities would very likely go in a variety of directions, with no clear target. So, just like the geese, businesses want to be organized, structured, and focused.

We could cover these important enterprisewide systems in any order, and if we asked three people how to do it, we would most likely get three different approaches. For our purposes, we will start with the focus of every business: the customer. From there, we will expand our view to the back-office operations and, finally, to systems that manage the movement of raw materials and finished goods. The end result, of course, is that we get all the "geese" in the business to fly in the same direction in as efficient a manner as possible.

FIGURE 8.1

Geese fly in a highly organized and efficient V-shaped formation—much like a well-run business.

SOURCE: © Royalty-Free/Corbis.

Customer Relationship Management: The Business Focus

INTRODUCTION
LO 8-1

Today, customers are in charge. It is easier than ever for customers to comparison shop and, with a click of the mouse, to switch companies. As a result, customer relationships have become a company's most valued asset. These relationships are worth more than the company's products, stores, factories, Web addresses, and even employees. Every company's strategy should address how to find and retain the most profitable customers possible.

The primary business value of customer relationships today is indisputable. That's why we emphasized in Chapter 2 that becoming a *customer-focused business* was one of the top business strategies that can be supported by information technology. Thus, many companies are implementing *customer relationship management* (CRM) business initiatives and information systems as part of a customer-focused or *customer-centric* strategy to improve their chances for success in today's competitive business environment. In this section, we will explore basic CRM concepts and technologies, as well as examples of the benefits and challenges faced by companies that have implemented CRM systems as part of their customer-focused business strategy.

Let's start by looking at a Real World Challenge. We can learn a lot about the challenges that result from lack of accesible information about sales and customers. See Figure 8.2.

WHAT IS CRM?

Managing the full range of the customer relationship involves two related objectives: one, to provide the organization and all of its customer-facing employees with a single, complete view of every customer at every touchpoint and across all channels; and, two, to provide the customer with a single, complete view of the company and its extended channels.

Companies are turning to **customer relationship management** to improve their customer focus. CRM uses information technology to create an enterprisewide system that integrates and automates many of the *customer-serving* processes in sales, marketing, and other customer-related services that interact with a company's customers. CRM systems also create an IT framework of Web-enabled software and databases that integrates these processes with the rest of a company's business operations. CRM systems include a family of software modules that provides the tools that enable a business and its employees to deliver fast, convenient, dependable, and consistent service to its customers. Siebel Systems, Oracle, PeopleSoft, SAP AG, Epiphany, and Microsoft are some of the leading vendors of CRM software. Figure 8.3 illustrates some of the major application components of a CRM system. Let's take a look at each of them.

Contact and Account Management

CRM software helps sales, marketing, and service professionals capture and track relevant data about every past and planned contact with prospects and customers, as well as other business and life-cycle events of customers. Information is captured from all customer touchpoints, such as telephone, fax, e-mail, the company's Web site, retail stores, kiosks, and personal contact. CRM systems store the data in a common customer database that integrates all customer account information and makes it available throughout the company via Internet, intranet, or other network links for sales, marketing, service, and other CRM applications.

Sales

A CRM system provides sales representatives with the software tools and company data sources they need to support and manage their sales activities and optimize cross-selling

CHALLENGE

Jelly Belly Candy Company–Getting Your Arms around Sales

Widely known in the United States for its famous jelly beans, the Jelly Belly Candy Company has been in business since 1869. Its founders, German immigrants Gustav and Albert Goelitz, purchased an ice cream and candy store in Belleville, Illinois, where they distributed their sweets to the surrounding communities in a horse-drawn wagon, in addition to selling to the locals. In 1900, the second generation of the family introduced Candy Corn Jelly Belly—still made today with the same original recipe—which helped carry the business through the Great Depression and two world wars. The great-grandsons of the founders are still involved in the business. This business, however, could not be more different today than when everything got started.

Today the company has more than 700 employees and is headquartered in Fairfield, California, with manufacturing facilities there, as well as in Chicago and Thailand. As has always been the case, Jelly Belly is privately owned. The company manufactures more than 1,400 different products and variations, and currently has more than 30,000 active customer accounts. Its signature product, the jelly bean, is responsible for 80 percent of the approximately $200 million in annual revenue. Although today it is best known for jelly beans, the company was essentially a manufacturer of

a buttercream-type candy called Candy Corn for many years. When a shortage of chocolate—which was sent to troops fighting in World War II—forced Americans to start eating other types of candy, nonchocolate sweets became popular. In 1960 the company started to make the jelly beans that still sell so well today. They were a favorite of Ronald Reagan, then governor of California, who once famously stated that "we can hardly start a meeting or make a decision without passing around the jar of jelly beans." Indeed, the beans spent three presidential terms as the preferred candy of Presidents Ronald Reagan and George H.W. Bush. The beans even traveled to space, aboard the space shuttle Challenger.

Over the last decade, the company has experienced rapid growth, in part due to its expansion into international markets and new products. Now, with more than a dozen international representatives, it does business in places as disparate as Sweden, Thailand, Israel, the United Kingdom, New Zealand, and Qatar. As the company started to grow and operations became more complex, management realized the need to improve the IT side of the business. To that end, Jelly Belly installed an enterprise resource planning (ERP) system in 2007, which helped improve the operational side of the company. Sales and marketing, however, still remained very much labor intensive, with little process standardization and measurement. Although a variety of tools are used to track and report sales activities—which are the core of the business—the rigor is just not there. "Our manufacturing operations operate with very little waste and produce extremely consistent results. We wanted that same type of efficiency and consistency in our sales, but we need a tool that will help us achieve that goal," says Dan Rosman, vice president of Information Technology at Jelly Belly.

Because Jelly Belly sells mostly to corporate clients, both big and small, the sales process is somewhat unique to this particular industry. For example, sales teams from Jelly Belly may attend two or three trade shows or industry events every week, where they gather contacts and expressions of interest from attendees, which may later transform into sales leads. Depending on the size of the event, there may be several hundred contacts to follow. After company representatives come back from the shows, however, management has no standardized process to make sure those potential leads are contacted in a timely manner, nor does it have a

FIGURE 8.2

Sales managers who do not know much about their customers have limited options when it comes to serving their needs.
SOURCE: © Reuters.

reporting approach to detail how many of the leads are eventually converted into actual sales—an important number. "Although we've diversified our sales channels, the bedrock of our business remains the same 'mom and pop' candy stores that Herman Goelitz sold candy to when he founded the company in 1869. This customer segment typically requires a significant amount of interaction and follow-up, which means we need to make our sales force as efficient as possible," explains Ryan Schader, vice president of Business Development at Jelly Belly.

Most notably, management lacks visibility into the sales process, which in turn makes it difficult to understand who are the best and worst performers, which tactics are leading to more or less sales, or how outright sales are being achieved. Although management can see what is going on right now through a number of ad hoc processes and tools, it is difficult to identify other useful opportunities that the company should be pursuing, such as those customers that have not placed an order in the last few months. Did they order too much the last time, and are they still working down that inventory? Did their sales go down over the same period? Did they switch to a competitor? Did they go bankrupt? Are they still in business at all? These are all very important questions, with little data to help answer them.

In addition to going after new customers and sales, the company also wanted to take better care of their existing customers, which make up the bulk of the revenues on a year-to-year basis. In an industry and with a signature product that is relatively mature, getting customers to switch from another supplier is both very difficult and quite costly. "It takes a lot more time and energy to acquire new customers than to retain current ones," says Schader. Although a new customer may not be worth twice as much as an existing one (as in the saying "a bird in the hand is worth two in the bush"), it is nonetheless true that reducing customer churn (also known as customer attrition, customer turnover, or customer defection, *churn* describes the loss of customers in a certain time period) can have a major impact on the bottom line for any business. As many other companies know all too well, selling more products to existing customers typically requires less effort—and is thus more profitable—than selling some products to new customers. Caring for existing customers, however, does not just happen. It requires a concerted effort to respond to their emerging needs, to understand the challenges they are facing, and to make those challenges your own. And it also requires data—lots of data—about them.

The Jelly Belly Candy Company took the first step to the modernization of its technology infrastructure with the implementation of an ERP package in 2007, which helped bring operational efficiency to the operations, manufacturing, and logistics side of the business. Sales and marketing, especially sales and customer care, are next. There is no denying that the company has been a success until now, with a flagship product that continues to sell very well after almost four decades since it was first introduced, and extensive expansion into international ventures and new product lines. That being said, if the company wants to continue being a success in the face of increasing competition and market saturation, it will need all the help it can get—big or small. It is clear to management that high-quality information lies at the center of the next step they need to take, whatever it may be.

SOURCE: "Jelly Belly Candy Company," *Microsoft Dynamics Customer Solution Case Study*, 2009; Lauren McKay, "The CRM Elite: Sweetening the Deal," *CRM Magazine*, August 24, 2010; and Jelly Belly Candy Company, www.jellybelly.com, accessed June 4, 2011.

▼ QUESTIONS TO CONSIDER

1. What are the problem, or problems, that management at the Jelly Belly Candy Company is trying to solve? What would be the consequences if they are left unaddressed? Are these problems important to the future of the company?

2. What are the information needs of sales managers at the Jelly Belly Candy Company that are not being satisfied? What is preventing the company from doing so? Why was this not a problem before?

3. Assume that you work for the Jelly Belly Candy Company as a sales manager and you have access to all of the data you could want. What would you ask for? How would you use that data?

FIGURE 8.3

The major application clusters in customer relationship management.

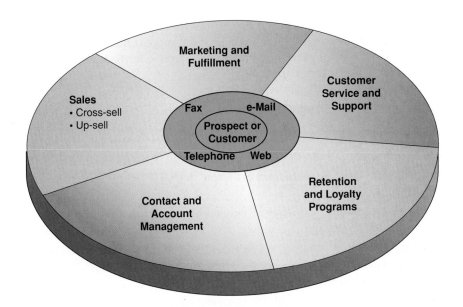

and up-selling. Cross-selling is an approach in which a customer of one product or service, say, auto insurance, might also be interested in purchasing a related product or service, say, homeowners insurance. By using a cross-selling technique, sales representatives can better serve their customers while simultaneously improving their sales. Up-selling refers to the process of finding ways to sell a new or existing customer a better product than they are currently seeking. Additional examples include sales prospect and product information, product configuration, and sales quote generation capabilities. CRM also provides real-time access to a single common view of the customer, enabling sales representatives to check on all aspects of a customer's account status and history before scheduling their sales calls. For example, a CRM system would alert a bank sales representative to call customers who make large deposits to sell them premier credit or investment services. A CRM system would also alert a salesperson to unresolved service, delivery, or payment problems that could be resolved through a personal contact with a customer.

Marketing and Fulfillment

CRM systems help marketing professionals accomplish direct marketing campaigns by automating such tasks as qualifying leads for targeted marketing, and scheduling and tracking direct marketing mailings. Then the CRM software helps marketing professionals capture and manage prospect and customer response data in the CRM database, and analyze the customer and business value of a company's direct marketing campaigns. CRM also assists in the fulfillment of prospect and customer responses and requests by quickly scheduling sales contacts and providing appropriate information on products and services to them, while capturing relevant information for the CRM database.

Customer Service and Support

A CRM system provides service reps with software tools and real-time access to the common customer database shared by sales and marketing professionals. CRM helps customer service managers create, assign, and manage requests for service by customers. *Call center* software routes calls to customer support agents based on their skills and authority to handle specific kinds of service requests. *Help desk* software helps customer service reps assist customers who are having problems with a product or service by providing relevant service data and suggestions for resolving problems. Web-based self-service enables customers to access personalized support information easily at the company Web site, while it gives them an option to receive further assistance online or by phone from customer service personnel.

Retention and Loyalty Programs

Consider the following:

- It costs six times more to sell to a new customer than to sell to an existing one.
- A typical dissatisfied customer will tell 8 to 10 people about his or her experience.
- A company can boost its profits 85 percent by increasing its annual customer retention by only 5 percent.
- The odds of selling a product to a new customer are 15 percent, whereas the odds of selling a product to an existing customer are 50 percent.
- If a company takes care of a service problem quickly, 70 percent of complaining customers will do business with the company again.

That's why enhancing and optimizing customer retention and loyalty is a major business strategy and primary objective of customer relationship management. CRM systems try to help a company identify, reward, and market to their most loyal and profitable customers. CRM analytical software includes data mining tools and other analytical marketing software, while CRM databases may consist of a customer data warehouse and CRM data marts. These tools are used to identify profitable and loyal customers and to direct and evaluate a company's targeted marketing and relationship marketing programs toward them. Figure 8.4 is an example of part of a proposed Web-based report format for evaluating Charles Schwab & Co.'s customer retention performance.

FIGURE 8.4

A proposed report format for evaluating the customer retention performance of Charles Schwab & Co.

	Navigation	Performance	Operations	Environment
Customer Retention	Customer retention rate Household retention rate Average customer tenure	Retention rate by customer cohort Retention rate by customer segment Customer loyalty rating	Percentage of customers who are active Web users Percentage of customers who interact via e-mail Decline in customer activity Propensity to defect	Offers by competitors Share of portfolio Comparative retention Comparative customer tenure
Customer Experience	Satisfaction by customer segment Satisfaction by cohort Satisfaction by customer scenario	Customer satisfaction by: • Task • Touchpoint • Channel partner End-to-end performance by scenario Customer satisfaction with quality of information provided	Elapsed time for commonly performed tasks Accuracy of Web search results Percentage of trades executed with price improvement Percentage of e-mails answered accurately in one hour	Comparative satisfaction: Competitors: • Other online brokers • Other financial service firms • All products and services
Customer Spending	Average revenue per customer Average profitability per customer Growth in customer assets Customer lifetime value	Revenues per customer segment Profits per customer segment Growth in customer assets per segment	Daily log-ins at market opening Revenue trades per day Percentage increase in customer assets Cost to serve by touchpoint	Total brokerage assets Growth in brokerage assets

Back in 2005, Joe Trifoglio, chief information officer of Zip Realty, needed a new e-mail system for his 2,500 real estate agents spread out across 14 major metropolitan areas. His homegrown, open-source e-mail client worked well, but he needed something that would work on top of his custom-built CRM system, known internally as ZAP, the Zip Agent Platform. Prior to shopping for a new messaging system, Trifoglio's real estate agents toggled between their e-mail and CRM app, and they had to manually input a lot of information (such as appointments) between the two.

There was a variety of Web-based e-mail clients for Trifoglio to choose from, including Google and its Google Apps. But because Zip Realty built its CRM system completely from scratch and on Java and open-source components, Trifoglio needed a messaging system built on similar principles. He picked the open-source, Yahoo-owned Zimbra, an e-mail, calendar, and chat (instant messaging) client.

Trifoglio noted that other vendors offered the same features, such as e-mail and instant messaging, "but they had little ability to integrate with our internal systems [mainly ZAP]." After what he describes as moderate development work, Trifoglio says the e-mail system is now embedded on top of his customized CRM, allowing his real estate agents to book showings with better efficiency than ever before.

For example, at the front end of Zip's Web site, people can book appointments with realtors to look at residential properties. That information is fed from the front end of the Web site into Zip's CRM system. Typically, agents had to do a lot of the data input between the CRM app and their calendar app. Now, with Zimbra on top of ZAP, it happens more easily.

When agents come in, they now have a single sign-on that logs them onto both CRM and e-mail at once. With Zimbra, they can also add Zimlets—which are essentially plug-ins, such as one for easy calendaring—that get embedded on top of the application.

"The agents are much happier because it's more feature rich," Trifoglio says. "The system allows end users to use Web 2.0 features, like tagging emails and searching mail."

He says Zimbra also works well on Windows mobile phones, which will be critical for the agents on the move. Currently, agents are testing the Zimbra app on their mobile, and they have given Trifoglio only positive feedback.

Another upside to a Zimbra implementation?

"As far as the cost of purchasing the software, it's a fraction of what it would cost to do Exchange or Lotus Notes or something like that," Trifoglio says.

Zip Realty: E-Mail and CRM Integration with Open-Source Zimbra

SOURCE: C.G. Lynch, "CRM Collaboration: Real Estate Firm Implements Zimbra for All Its Agents," *CIO.com*, June 27, 2008.

THE THREE PHASES OF CRM

Figure 8.5 illustrates another way to think about the customer and business value and components of customer relationship management. We can view CRM as an integrated system of Web-enabled software tools and databases accomplishing a variety of customer-focused business processes that support the three phases of the relationship between a business and its customers.

- **Acquire.** A business relies on CRM software tools and databases to help it acquire new customers by doing a superior job of contact management, sales prospecting, selling, direct marketing, and fulfillment. The goal of these CRM functions is to help customers perceive the value of a superior product offered by an outstanding company.

FIGURE 8.5

How CRM supports the three phases of the relationship between a business and its customers.

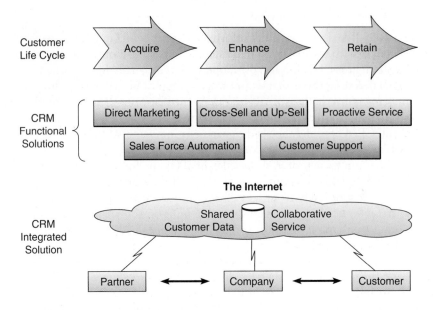

- **Enhance.** Web-enabled CRM account management and customer service and support tools help keep customers happy by supporting superior service from a responsive networked team of sales and service specialists and business partners. In addition, CRM sales force automation and direct marketing and fulfillment tools help companies cross-sell and up-sell to their customers, thus increasing their profitability to the business. The value the customers perceive is the convenience of one-stop shopping at attractive prices.

- **Retain.** CRM analytical software and databases help a company proactively identify and reward its most loyal and profitable customers to retain and expand their business via targeted marketing and relationship marketing programs. The value the customers perceive is of a rewarding personalized business relationship with "their company."

BENEFITS AND CHALLENGES OF CRM

The potential business benefits of customer relationship management are many. For example, CRM allows a business to identify and target its best customers—those who are the most profitable to the business—so they can be retained as lifelong customers for greater and more profitable services. It makes possible real-time customization and personalization of products and services based on customer wants, needs, buying habits, and life cycles. CRM can also keep track of when a customer contacts the company, regardless of the contact point. In addition, CRM systems can enable a company to provide a consistent customer experience and superior service and support across all the contact points a customer chooses. All of these benefits would provide strategic business value to a company and major customer value to its customers.

Hard Rock Hotel and Casino: Drinks—and CRM—Go Mobile

In Las Vegas or in any other major destination, getting service at a bar on weekends can be exhausting. There is pushing and shoving to get to the counter itself, then shouting your order, hoping the bartender got it right, and then more pushing and shoving to get your order and bring it back to your table. The Hard Rock Hotel and Casino in Las Vegas is experimenting with a different take on this full contact sport. It has deployed a system that allows customers who have smartphones to place their orders without leaving their tables, and have their orders brought to where they are sitting (or standing).

The technology is called Kickback, and it is the flagship product of start-up Kickback Mobile. Customers interested in this must download an app that allows them to register their credit card information. Using GPS technology, the system determines which of the seven Hard Rock locations the customer is currently in and shows the appropriate menu. Further, it can also be used for room service. "As long as customers have a smartphone, they are part of the community," says Todd Moreau, vice president of Food and Beverage with Hard Rock.

As interesting as it sounds, it gets even more exciting when you consider the benefits it accrues to the company. Hard Rock integrates all of these orders with its CRM technology and point-of-sale systems, allowing them to track spenders in real time with detailed data on when, where, and what they are spending money on. It could also be used for delivering advertising or marketing campaigns in real time based on customer preferences, location, and past purchases. In the end, CRM is all about the information that it provides about what customers are doing, what they are not doing, what they like, and what they do not like.

Scott Voeller, vice president of Brand Strategy and Advertising at competitor MGM Resorts, says there's no disputing the importance of mobile apps in CRM. "Customers may not always be in front of a computer, but they always have their phones with them," he says. "Assuming they've opted in to your application, it allows them to stay connected with the brand."

SOURCE: Matt Villano, "CRM on a Smartphone," *CIO.com*, April 27, 2011.

CRM Failures

The business benefits of customer relationship management are not guaranteed and, in some cases, have proven elusive at many companies. Surveys by industry research groups include a report that more than 50 percent of CRM projects did not produce the results that were promised. In another research report, 20 percent of businesses surveyed reported that CRM implementations had actually damaged long-standing customer relationships. Furthermore, in a survey of senior management satisfaction with 25 management tools, CRM ranked near the bottom in user satisfaction, even though 72 percent expected to have CRM systems implemented shortly.

The common wisdom of why CRM systems fail includes:

- Lack of senior management sponsorship.
- Improper change management.
- Elongated projects that take on too much, too fast.
- Lack of or poor integration between CRM and core business systems.
- Lack of end-user incentives leading to poor user adoption rates.

Despite the above, research shows that the major reason for CRM failure is a familiar one: *lack of understanding and preparation*. Too often, business managers rely on a major new application of information technology (like CRM) to solve a business problem without first developing the business process changes and change management programs that are required. For example, in many cases, failed CRM projects were implemented without the participation of the business stakeholders involved. Therefore, employees and customers were not prepared for the new processes or challenges that were part of the new CRM implementation. We will discuss the topic of failures in information technology management, system implementation, and change management further in later chapters. For now, remember that information technology and information systems do nothing! It takes people, processes, and internal structuring of the project for IT/IS make a difference. Without the rest, the IT is just a machine, and the IS is just a tool with no skilled user.

Unum Group: The Long Road to CRM

The multiple mergers that formed insurer Unum Group in the late 1990s aggregated billions in revenue, assembled thousands of employees, and created a quagmire of customer data systems that couldn't talk to each other. In all, with Provident, Colonial, Paul Revere, and Unum, there were 34 disconnected policy and claims back-office systems, all loaded with critical customer data. As a result, "it was very difficult to get your hands around the information," understates Bob Dolmovich, Unum Group's vice president of business integration and data architecture. One Unum Group customer's account, for instance, might exist in multiple places within the newly combined company, leading, of course, to a great deal of waste.

For the first couple of years after the mergers, Unum Group used a homegrown data-store solution as a quick fix. But by 2004, the $10 billion disability insurer felt compelled to embark on a new master data management strategy aimed at uniting the company's disparate pockets of customer data, including account activity, premiums, and payments.

Integral to Unum Group's strategy would be a customer data integration (CDI) hub, built on service-oriented architecture, using a standard set of protocols for connecting applications via the Web (in effect, Web services). The project, begun in early 2005, has already improved data quality, soothed the multiple customer records headaches, and created the possibility for a companywide, in-depth customer analysis. But as Dolmovich acknowledges, there's still a long way to go. Of those original 34 systems, he has been able to get rid of only four to date. But he's still optimistic.

Despite the long, slow slog, Dolmovich is hoping that the new CDI approach will ultimately give his company the 360-degree view of the customer that vendors have promised since the dawn of CRM. In the late 1990s, enterprise software vendors like Oracle, PeopleSoft, and Siebel sold the single-customer view as CRM's holy grail.

But implementation flameouts and legacy integration nightmares soured many CIOs on these expensive enterprisewide rollouts. A CDI hub differs from a traditional CRM solution in that a CDI hub allows a company to automatically integrate all of its customer data into one database, while ensuring the quality and accuracy of the data before they are sent to the hub's central store for safekeeping.

A stand-alone CRM system can't do that because it can't be integrated with the billing, marketing, ERP, and supply chain systems that house customer data, and it has no way to address inconsistent data across platforms.

Dolmovich says the first data loaded into the CDI hub in late 2005 came from business customers and brokers. With the new system, Dolmovich says, "We are now able to assimilate and display a broker's entire block of business and create some statistics and a profile of our relationship with that broker." Unum Group is now working to create individual profiles of employer customers so that every time a new customer account is created or accessed—perhaps to change an address or add new customer information—all employees of the insurance company will see that change at the same time, regardless of which system they are using. "The desired end state is a CDI hub that has information about all customers across all products," he says.

SOURCE: Thomas Wailgum, "The Quest for Customer Data Integration," *CIO Magazine*, August 1, 2006.

. . . .
TRENDS IN CRM

Increasingly, enterprises must create tighter collaborative linkages with partners, suppliers, and customers, squeezing out time and costs while enhancing the customer experience and the total value proposition.

Types of CRM	Business Value
Operational CRM	• Supports customer interaction with greater convenience through a variety of channels, including phone, fax, e-mail, chat, and mobile devices. • Synchronizes customer interactions consistently across all channels. • Makes your company easier to do business with.
Analytical CRM	• Extracts in-depth customer history, preferences, and profitability information from your data warehouse and other databases. • Allows you to analyze, predict, and derive customer value and behavior and forecast demand. • Lets you approach your customers with relevant information and offers that are tailored to their needs.
Collaborative CRM	• Enables easy collaboration with customers, suppliers, and partners. • Improves efficiency and integration throughout the supply chain. • Allows greater responsiveness to customer needs through sourcing of products and services outside of your enterprise.
Portal-Based CRM	• Provides all users with the tools and information that fit their individual roles and preferences. • Empowers all employees to respond to customer demands more quickly and become truly customer-focused. • Provides the capability to instantly access, link, and use all internal and external customer information.

FIGURE 8.6

Many companies are implementing CRM systems with some or all of these capabilities.

SOURCE: mySAP Customer Relationship Management, mySAP.com, 2001, p. 7; and Brian Caulfield, "Toward a More Perfect (and Realistic) e-Business," *Business 2.0*, January 2002, p. 80.

Figure 8.6 outlines four types or categories of CRM that are being implemented by many companies today, and it summarizes their benefits to a business. These categories may also be viewed as stages or trends in how many companies implement CRM applications, and the figure also outlines some of the capabilities of CRM software products. Most businesses start out with operational CRM systems such as sales force automation and customer service centers. Then analytical CRM applications are implemented using several analytical marketing tools, such as data mining, to extract vital data about customers and prospects for targeted marketing campaigns.

Increasingly, businesses are moving to *collaborative* CRM systems, to involve business partners and customers in collaborative customer services. This includes systems for customer self-service and feedback, as well as **partner relationship management** (PRM) systems. PRM applications apply many of the same tools used in CRM systems to enhance collaboration between a company and its business partners, such as distributors and dealers, to coordinate and optimize sales and service to customers across all marketing channels. Finally, many businesses are building Internet, intranet, and extranet Web-based CRM portals as a common gateway for various levels of access to all customer information, as well as operational, analytical, and collaborative CRM tools for customers, employees, and business partners. Let's look at a real-world example.

Consider this: A businessman is traveling to Chicago tomorrow. He logs on to Hilton's Web site and decides to stay at Homewood Suites, one of nine Hilton Hotel chains. Next, he goes to the hotel's digital floor plan, takes a look at the rooms available, picks one on the top floor that is far from the pool but close to the elevator, and checks in online. When he gets to the hotel the next day, his key is at the front desk, and the desk clerk welcomes him by name. When he gets to his room, he finds feather pillows and the local newspaper, just as he prefers.	**Integrated CRM: Hilton's Welcome Mat Starts on the Web**

IT-facilitated customer service is what Hilton is all about. From a do-it-all customer information system to self-service kiosks in hotel lobbies to richly interactive Web sites, its singular goal is to keep customers coming back.

CIO Tim Harvey says Hilton's strong tech portfolio is part of the formula that lets the hotel chain charge more than competitors and still fill up rooms. Revenue per room across Hilton brands is more than 7 percent above the industry average, and as much as 28 percent more at Hampton Inn. "Customers are willing to pay more to stay in our hotels for some reason, and the technology enables that," Harvey says.

Hilton doesn't view technology as a cost center, but rather as an enabler of nearly all business processes. The tech team asks, "What value can I add above and beyond the traditional role of IT?" says Chuck Scoggins, vice president of distribution CRM and pricing technology. Hilton's signature IT project is OnQ, a (mostly) internally developed platform for property management, reservations, e-commerce, and CRM.

OnQ includes 3.5 terabytes of data on 22.5 million guests, and the company is spending $20 million to expand it worldwide.

Harvey credits OnQ with letting Hilton build a reservation system to book large blocks of rooms and conference areas for $10 million and roll it out ahead of schedule. It was Hilton's drive to make sites more interactive that led to the feature to choose a room at Homewood Suites by floor plan, the way we can choose airline seats. Homewood, where guests typically stay longer, lagged in online and phone bookings. "People were doing research online, but they just weren't finding what they were looking for," says Scoggins.

Suite Selection lets guests select rooms from floor diagrams, view photos of rooms, and reserve a specific room up to 36 hours before arrival. More than half of those polled by Hilton said Suite Selection improved their travel experience. Homewood now ranks among the top two Hilton properties for online check-ins, with 22 percent of guests doing so.

Whatever the future holds, Hilton can count on one thing: IT will be expected to play a central role in keeping customers happy and coming back.

SOURCE: J. Nicholas Hoover, "Hilton's Welcome Mat Starts on the Web," *InformationWeek*, September 15, 2008.

Enterprise Resource Planning:
The Business Backbone

What do Microsoft, Coca-Cola, Cisco, Eli Lilly, Alcoa, and Nokia have in common? Unlike most businesses, which operate on 25-year-old back-office systems, these market leaders reengineered their businesses to run at breakneck speed by implementing a transactional backbone called enterprise resource planning (ERP). These companies credit their ERP systems with having helped them reduce inventories, shorten cycle times, lower costs, and improve overall operations.

Businesses of all kinds have now implemented *enterprise resource planning* (ERP) systems. ERP serves as a multifunctional enterprisewide backbone that integrates and automates many internal business processes and information systems within the manufacturing, logistics, distribution, accounting, finance, and human resource functions of a company. Large companies throughout the world began to install ERP systems in the 1990s as a conceptual framework and catalyst for reengineering their business processes. ERP also served as the vital software engine needed to integrate and accomplish the cross-functional processes that resulted. Now, ERP is recognized as a necessary ingredient for many companies to gain the efficiency, agility, and responsiveness required to succeed in today's dynamic business environment. See Figure 8.7.

FIGURE 8.7

Companies are realizing the value of ERP.

SOURCE: Patrice Latron/Corbis.

ERP is the technological backbone of e-business, an enterprisewide transaction framework with links into sales order processing, inventory management and control, production and distribution planning, and finance.

Enterprise resource planning is a cross-functional enterprise system driven by an integrated suite of software modules that supports the basic internal business processes of a company. For example, ERP software for a manufacturing company will typically process the data from and track the status of sales, inventory, shipping, and invoicing, as well as forecast raw material and human resource requirements. Figure 8.8 presents the major application components of an ERP system. Figure 8.9 illustrates some of the

• • • • • • • • • •
WHAT IS ERP?
LO 8-1

FIGURE 8.8

The major application components of enterprise resource planning demonstrate the cross-functional approach of ERP systems.

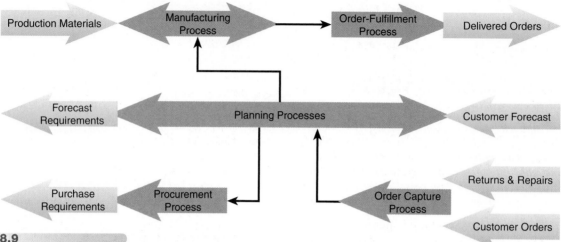

Some of the business process flows and customer and supplier information flows supported by ERP systems.

key cross-functional business processes and supplier and customer information flows supported by ERP systems.

ERP gives a company an integrated real-time view of its core business processes, such as production, order processing, and inventory management, tied together by the ERP application software and a common database maintained by a database management system. ERP systems track business resources (such as cash, raw materials, and production capacity), and the status of commitments made by the business (such as customer orders, purchase orders, and employee payroll), no matter which department (manufacturing, purchasing, sales, accounting, and so on) has entered the data into the system.

ERP software suites typically consist of integrated modules of manufacturing, distribution, sales, accounting, and human resource applications. Examples of manufacturing processes supported are material requirements planning, production planning, and capacity planning. Some of the sales and marketing processes supported by ERP are sales analysis, sales planning, and pricing analysis, while typical distribution applications include order management, purchasing, and logistics planning. ERP systems support many vital human resource processes, from personnel requirements planning to salary and benefits administration, and accomplish most required financial record-keeping and managerial accounting applications. Figure 8.10 illustrates the processes supported by the ERP system that the Colgate-Palmolive Company installed.

The business processes and functions supported by the ERP system implemented by the Colgate-Palmolive Company.

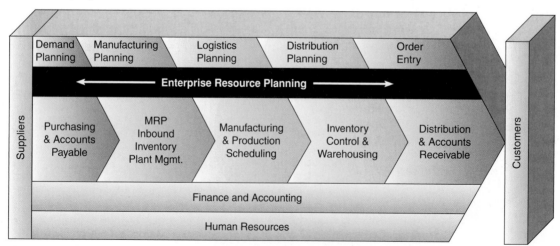

Colgate-Palmolive is a global consumer products company that implemented the SAP R/3 enterprise resource planning system. Colgate embarked on an implementation of SAP R/3 to allow the company to access more timely and accurate data, get the most out of working capital, and reduce manufacturing costs. An important factor for Colgate was whether it could use the software across the entire spectrum of the business. Colgate needed the ability to coordinate globally and act locally. The implementation of SAP across the Colgate supply chain contributed to increased profitability. Now installed in operations that produce most of Colgate's worldwide sales, SAP was expanded to all Colgate divisions worldwide. Global efficiencies in purchasing—combined with product and packaging standardization—also produced large savings.

- Before ERP, it took Colgate U.S. anywhere from one to five days to acquire an order, and another one to two days to process the order. Now, order acquisition and processing combined take four hours, not up to seven days. Distribution planning and picking used to take up to four days; today, they take 14 hours. In total, the order-to-delivery time has been cut in half.

- Before ERP, on-time deliveries used to occur only 91.5 percent of the time, and cases ordered were delivered correctly 97.5 percent of the time. After R/3, the figures are 97.5 percent and 99.0 percent, respectively.

- After ERP, domestic inventories have dropped by one-third, and receivables outstanding have dropped to 22.4 days from 31.4. Working capital as a percentage of sales has plummeted to 6.3 percent from 11.3 percent. Total delivered cost per case has been reduced by nearly 10 percent.

BENEFITS AND CHALLENGES OF ERP

As the example of Colgate-Palmolive has just shown, ERP systems can generate significant business benefits for a company. Many other companies have found major business value in their use of ERP in several basic ways:

- **Quality and efficiency.** ERP creates a framework for integrating and improving a company's internal business processes that results in significant improvements in the quality and efficiency of customer service, production, and distribution.

- **Decreased costs.** Many companies report significant reductions in transaction processing costs and hardware, software, and IT support staff compared to the nonintegrated legacy systems that were replaced by their new ERP systems.

- **Decision support.** ERP provides vital cross-functional information on business performance to managers quickly to significantly improve their ability to make better decisions in a timely manner across the entire business enterprise.

- **Enterprise agility.** Implementing ERP systems breaks down many former departmental and functional walls or "silos" of business processes, information systems, and information resources. This results in more flexible organizational structures, managerial responsibilities, and work roles, and therefore a more agile and adaptive organization and workforce that can more easily capitalize on new business opportunities.

The Costs of ERP

An ERP implementation is like the corporate equivalent of a brain transplant. We pulled the plug on every company application and moved to PeopleSoft software. The risk was certainly disruption of business because if you do not do ERP properly, you can kill your company, guaranteed.

So says Jim Prevo, chief information officer of Green Mountain Coffee of Vermont, commenting on their successful implementation of an ERP system. Although the

FIGURE 8.11

Typical costs of implementing a new ERP system.

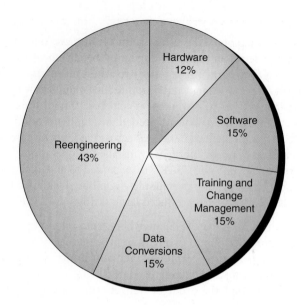

benefits of ERP are many, the costs and risks are also considerable, as we will continue to see in some of the real-world cases and examples in the text. Figure 8.11 illustrates the relative size and types of costs of implementing an ERP system in a company. Notice that hardware and software costs are a small part of total costs, and that the costs of developing new business processes (reengineering) and preparing employees for the new system (training and change management) make up the bulk of implementing a new ERP system. Converting data from previous legacy systems to the new cross-functional ERP system is another major category of ERP implementation costs.

The costs and risks of failure in implementing a new ERP system are substantial. Most companies have had successful ERP implementations, but a sizable minority of firms experienced spectacular and costly failures that heavily damaged their overall business. Big losses in revenue, profits, and market share resulted when core business processes and information systems failed or did not work properly. In many cases, orders and shipments were lost, inventory changes were not recorded correctly, and unreliable inventory levels caused major stock-outs to occur for weeks or months. Companies like Hershey Foods, Nike, A-DEC, and Connecticut General sustained losses running into hundreds of millions of dollars in some instances. In the case of FoxMeyer Drugs, a $5 billion pharmaceutical wholesaler, the company had to file for bankruptcy protection and then was bought out by its arch competitor, McKesson Drugs.

The most recent example of ERP failure is Shane Co., the family owned jewelry retailer and one of the 10 largest jewelry retailers in the world. In January 2009, Shane Co. sought bankruptcy protection, attributing the company's decline to delays and cost overruns in their $36 million SAP AG inventory-management system. Shane Co. claimed SAP took almost three years to install and implement the system instead of one year, while costs "ballooned" to $36 million from a projected maximum of $10 million. Shane, based in Centennial, Colorado, became "substantially overstocked with inventory, and with the wrong mix of inventory" when Walldorf, Germany–based SAP finished the system in September 2007, according to the bankruptcy filing. The software "adversely affected sales" through the first nine months of 2008, it said.

ERP Implementations: When They Fail, They Fail Big

How do you define a "big" ERP implementation failure? Easy—it is one that burns through tons of cash, does not deliver results that are even remotely close to what was expected, takes much longer to complete than originally planned (if ever at all), and destroys careers in the process. Unfortunately, since ERP packages were first introduced, hardly a year goes by without having a catalog of such failures. In fact, you can conceive of these large-scale implementations as being a partnership among three groups: customers, vendors, and system integrators. When any one of these goes down, the whole project goes with it.

In 2010, however, none was larger than the New York City ERP project. Since the original effort started as a modernization of the payroll systems used by the city in 1998, it could easily be classified as the failure of the decade. Amid allegations of corruption and massive waste, the original budget of $60 million pales in comparison to actual expenditures of more than $700 million (and still counting). Mayor Michael Bloomberg has candidly called the project a "disaster," but he argued that the city desperately needs the system anyway. In his opinion, officials just did not know how complex the project really was, and they did not manage scope creep very well. "Once they started, part of it was they just kept adding things that it made sense to do," he said.

But there were other failures. In August, officials in Marin County, California, decided to throw away everything in its botched ERP implementation and start from scratch. In addition, the county sued its integration partner, a major consulting company, alleging that the consultants used the project as a training ground for inexperienced employees, which resulted in a "costly computer system far worse than the legacy systems it was intended to replace." Officials estimate that just keeping the system running "as is" would cost in excess of $34 million over the next 10 years, whereas fixing some of the issues by bringing in more workers would run the tab well into the $50 million over the same period. On the other hand, starting anew would "merely" cost $26 million, and that was the road they took. In November, Lumber Liquidators—the largest retailer of flooring supplies in the United States—attributed weak third-quarter earnings to issues related to its recent SAP implementation. In all fairness, the company indicated that the problems were not with the software itself, but rather with difficulties that employees had in figuring out how it worked. "One feature of our previous system is that it was very flexible and easy to manipulate," says Jeffrey Griffiths, CEO. "SAP is much more structured, you follow steps, but it's much more stable. Because of that it was a change for us."

There are too many other failures to discuss in any detail, and these are only the ones we know about—for some reason or other, they are the ones that made the news. Not all is lost, however. Although these problems continue to arise, the failures seem to be more contained in most cases. In the past, companies would immediately go bankrupt as a result of problematic ERP implementations. (Does anyone remember FoxMeyer, the second largest wholesale drug distributor in the United States at the time? There is a reason the name does not sound familiar. . . . On the other hand, we still have a long way to go before "ERP" and "failure" often go hand in hand in the same sentence.

SOURCE: Chris Kanaracus, "Biggest ERP Failures of 2010," *Computerworld*, December 17, 2010.

Causes of ERP Failures

What have been the major causes of failure in ERP projects? It's sad to say, but in almost every case, the business managers and IT professionals of these companies underestimated the complexity of the planning, development, and training that were needed to prepare for a new ERP system that would radically change their business processes and information systems. Failure to involve affected employees in the planning and development phases and to change management programs, or trying to do too much too fast in the conversion process were typical causes of failed ERP projects. Insufficient training in the new work tasks required by the ERP system and failure to do enough data conversion and testing were other causes of failure. In many cases, ERP failures were also due to overreliance by company or IT management on the claims of ERP software vendors or on the assistance of prestigious consulting firms hired to lead the implementation. The following experience of a company that did it right gives us a helpful look at what is needed for a successful ERP implementation.

Capital One Financial: Success with ERP Systems	Just a few years ago at Capital One Financial Corp., it took 10 human-resources (HR) specialists to sign off on one change-of-address form. With thousands of employees worldwide, that's a lot of paper-pushing. Today, address changes are done via a self-service application that has freed HR to devote time to strategic staffing, program planning, and change management. This example illustrates a big change that has taken place at the $2.6 billion-a-year financial services company since it began to roll out People-Soft applications. "It's a cultural change that has freed people to not deal with minutiae but to deal with business value," says Gregor Bailar, executive vice president and chief information officer. "It really has been transformative." Bailar envisions more automation ahead, with financials following in the footsteps of HR's "lean-process" design to deal with the mountain of data requests the financials team receives and processes within the group. The PeopleSoft ERP system, which serves as Capital One's backbone for financials, HR, asset management, and supply chain processes, supports about 18,000 users, including Capital One's 15,000 associates and some business partners. The applications are accessible via a Web portal based on BEA Systems Inc.'s technology. Capital One is exploring the possibility of partnering with ERP application service providers, now that the hard work of correcting data and linking processes is done. Running the applications may be more of a commodity job at this point, but the applications themselves serve as a pillar for the company's future-of-work initiative. Bailar describes this as "a very mobile, interactive, collaborative environment" designed to support the requirements of the company's biggest asset, its knowledge workers. It's characterized not only by extensive Wi-Fi access, VoIP-enabled laptops, instant messaging, and BlackBerrys, but also by workflows that, for the most part, come to users electronically. Says Bailar, "Everyone's daily life is kind of drawn back to this suite of apps."

SOURCE: Jennifer Zaino, "Modern Workforce: Capital One Puts ERP at Core of Work," *InformationWeek*, July 11, 2005.

TRENDS IN ERP

Today, ERP is still evolving—adapting to developments in technology and the demands of the market. Four important trends are shaping ERP's continuing evolution: improvements in integration and flexibility, extensions to business applications, a broader reach to new users, and the adoption of Internet technologies.

Figure 8.12 illustrates four major developments and trends that are evolving in ERP applications. First, the ERP software packages that were the mainstay of ERP implementations in the 1990s, and were often criticized for their inflexibility, have gradually been modified into more flexible products. Companies that installed ERP systems pressured software vendors to adopt more open, flexible, standards-based software architectures. This makes the software easier to integrate with other application programs of business users, as well as making it easier to make minor modifications to suit a company's business processes. An example is SAP 6.0 Enterprise, released in 2010 by SAP AG as a successor to earlier versions of SAP R/3. Other leading ERP vendors, including Oracle, PeopleSoft, and J.D. Edwards, have also developed more flexible ERP products.

Web-enabling ERP software is a second development in the evolution of ERP. The growth of the Internet and corporate intranets and extranets prompted software companies to use Internet technologies to build Web interfaces and networking

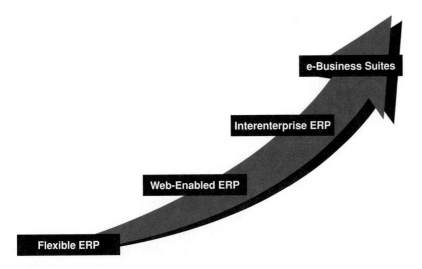

FIGURE 8.12
Trends in the evolution of
ERP applications.

capabilities into ERP systems. These features make ERP systems easier to use and connect to other internal applications, as well as to the systems of a company's business partners. This Internet connectivity has led to the development of interenterprise ERP systems that provide Web-enabled links between key business systems (such as inventory and production) of a company and its customers, suppliers, distributors, and others. These external links signaled a move toward the integration of internal-facing ERP applications with the external-focused applications of supply chain management (SCM) and a company's supply chain partners. We will discuss supply chain management later in the chapter.

All of these developments have provided the business and technological momentum for the integration of ERP functions into *e-business suites.* The major ERP software companies have developed modular, Web-enabled software suites that integrate ERP, customer relationship management, supply chain management, procurement, decision support, enterprise portals, health care functionality, and other business applications and functions. Examples include Oracle's e-Business Suite and SAP's mySAP. Some e-business suites disassemble ERP components and integrate them into other modules, while other products keep ERP as a distinct module in the software suite. Of course, the goal of these software suites is to enable companies to run most of their business processes using one Web-enabled system of integrated software and databases, instead of a variety of separate e-business applications. See Figure 8.13. Let's look at a real-world example.

FIGURE 8.13
The application components in
Oracle's e-Business Suite
software product.

ORACLE E-BUSINESS SUITE

Advanced Planning	Business Intelligence	Contracts
e-Commerce	Enterprise Asset Management	Exchanges
Financials	Human Resources	Interaction Center
Manufacturing	Marketing	Order Fulfillment
Procurement	Product Development	Professional Services Automation
Projects	Sales	Service
Training	Treasury	

SOURCE: Oracle Corporation, "E-Business Suite: Manage by Fact with Complete Automation and Complete Information," Oracle.com, 2002.

Visa International: Implementing the e-Business Suite

Despite the innovations brought to global commerce by Visa's sophisticated consumer payments processing system, Visa International used surprisingly outdated systems to manage some of its most critical internal business processes. "KPMG did an analysis of our business and found that our internal systems were becoming a risk to our organization," said Gretchen McCoy, senior vice president of Visa International. "We were in the red zone."

McCoy found that Visa's internal systems were unnecessarily complex and utilized few of the advantages that technology can bring to an enterprise. The financial management infrastructure was fragmented, complex, and costly to maintain. Data were not standardized, resulting in many different databases making disparate interpretations of business data. Corporate purchasing, accounts payable, and asset management were managed manually, resulting in time-consuming delays and discrepancies. Fragmented internal systems are not unusual in a company that experiences rapid growth. Visa experienced double-digit growth for 11 consecutive years. Visa chose Oracle e-Business Suite to remedy the problems that come with a complex and inefficient back office.

The resulting implementation turned Visa's cumbersome, outdated desktop procedures into Web-based e-business solutions that met Visa's demands for all roles and processes. For example, Oracle Financials automated Visa's old organization and created a more agile system capable of accounting for the impact of financial activities on a global scale. Accounts payable was transformed from a cumbersome manual process into a streamlined system that automatically checks invoices against outgoing payments and requests review of any discrepancies via e-mail. And Oracle iProcurement helped automate Visa's requisitioning and purchasing system by streamlining the entire purchasing process and implementing a self-service model to increase processing efficiency, said McCoy.

Supply Chain Management: The Business Network

INTRODUCTION

Starting a business takes ideas, capital, and technical savvy. Operating one, however, takes supply chain management (SCM) skills. A successful SCM strategy is based on accurate order processing, just-in-time inventory management, and timely order fulfillment. SCM's increasing importance illustrates how a tool that was a theoretical process 10 years ago is now a hot competitive weapon.

That's why many companies today are making *supply chain management* (SCM) a top strategic objective and major business application development initiative. Fundamentally, supply chain management helps a company get the right products to the right place at the right time, in the proper quantity and at an acceptable cost. The goal of SCM is to manage this process efficiently by forecasting demand; controlling inventory; enhancing the network of business relationships a company has with customers, suppliers, distributors, and others; and receiving feedback on the status of every link in the supply chain. To achieve this goal, many companies today are turning to Internet technologies to Web-enable their supply chain processes, decision making, and information flows. See Figure 8.14.

WHAT IS SCM?

Legacy supply chains are clogged with unnecessary steps and redundant stockpiles. For instance, a typical box of breakfast cereal spends an incredible 104 days getting from factory to supermarket, struggling its way through an unbelievable maze of wholesalers, distributors, brokers, and consolidators, each of which has a warehouse. The e-commerce opportunity lies in the fusing of each company's internal systems to those of its suppliers, partners, and customers. This fusion forces companies to better integrate interenterprise supply chain processes to improve manufacturing efficiency and distribution effectiveness.

So *supply chain management* is a cross-functional interenterprise system that uses information technology to help support and manage the links between some of a company's key business processes and those of its suppliers, customers, and business partners. The goal of SCM is to create a fast, efficient, and low-cost network of business relationships, or *supply chain*, to get a company's products from concept to market.

SOURCE: Getty Images.

FIGURE 8.14
Companies are freeing up cash by tightening their supply chain and reducing inventory.

What exactly is a company's supply chain? Let's suppose a company wants to build and sell a product to other businesses. Then it must buy raw materials and a variety of contracted services from other companies. The interrelationships with suppliers, customers, distributors, and other businesses that are needed to design, build, and sell a product make up the network of business entities, relationships, and processes that is called a supply chain. Because each supply chain process should add value to the products or services a company produces, a supply chain is frequently called a *value chain*, a different but related concept that we discussed in Chapter 2. In any event, many companies today are using Internet technologies to create interenterprise business systems for supply chain management that help a company streamline its traditional supply chain processes.

According to the Council of Supply Chain Management Professionals (CSCMP), supply chain management encompasses the planning and management of all activities involved in *sourcing, procurement, conversion,* and *logistics management.* It also includes the crucial components of *coordination and collaboration with channel partners,* which can be suppliers, intermediaries, third-party service providers, and customers. In essence, supply chain management integrates supply and demand management within and across companies. More recently, the loosely coupled, self-organizing network of businesses that cooperate to provide product and service offerings has been called the *Extended Enterprise.*

Figure 8.15 illustrates the basic business processes in the supply chain life cycle and the functional SCM processes that support them. It also emphasizes how many companies today are reengineering their supply chain processes, aided by Internet technologies and supply chain management software. For example, the demands of today's competitive business environment are pushing manufacturers to use their intranets, extranets, and e-commerce Web portals to help them reengineer their relationships with their suppliers, distributors, and retailers. The objective is to significantly reduce costs, increase efficiency, and improve their supply chain cycle times. SCM software can also help to improve interenterprise coordination among supply chain process players. The result is much more effective distribution and channel networks among business partners. The Web initiatives of PC Connection illustrate these developments.

FIGURE 8.15

Supply chain management software and Internet technologies can help companies reengineer and integrate the functional SCM processes that support the supply chain life cycle.

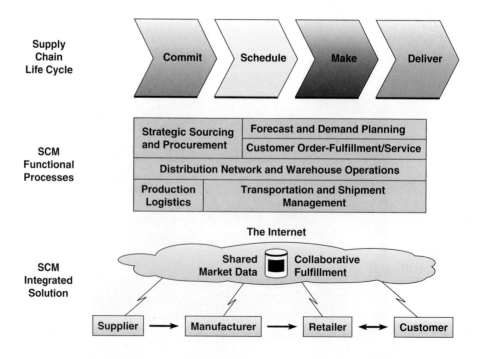

PC Connection has razor-thin margins. To stay healthy, the $1.8 billion-a-year tech reseller has slashed inefficiencies wherever possible in recent years. Yet despite tight financial circumstances, PC Connection invested substantially to overhaul its supply chain, building Web services modules in front of its ERP system for more efficient integration with partners and suppliers. The upgrades will help the company take on new business opportunities, such as selling software licenses, that promise higher margins than hardware.

Although the company has grown significantly over the years, the growth hasn't been without pain. While PC Connection now offers goods and services from more than 1,400 manufacturers, its core ERP system hadn't changed much from the days when the company sold directly to customers. "It was built for the days of pick, pack, and ship," Jack Ferguson, PC Connection's treasurer and chief financial officer, says of the company's Oracle JD Edwards ERP system. That became a growing problem over the last several years as the company expanded its catalog and extended its fulfillment network to include more than a dozen external partners to handle increasingly complex drop-ship orders. "We were faced with a growing number of products, and we also had a desire to cut inventory," Ferguson says.

It soon became apparent that the system wasn't built to handle such a multitiered fulfillment network. "Once you move to drop-ship it gets more complicated," says Ferguson, who notes that even basic requirements, like the calculation of sales tax on an order, were affected by the new drop-ship arrangements. Before long, managers from various departments within PC Connection were requesting ad hoc changes to the company's ERP system to meet new requirements as they evolved. But the process was becoming unmanageable.

As a result, PC Connection decided to embark on a thorough overhaul of its fulfillment system last year.

IT staffers looked at numerous off-the-shelf e-commerce packages, but all were found lacking. Instead, the company launched a labor-intensive campaign to develop new front-end modules internally for the existing JD Edwards system. These modules were built using both Web services and traditional EDI to deal with the company's growing web of fulfillment partners.

The first set of enhancements to the JD Edwards system went online recently, and Ferguson says they're already paying off in terms of time and cost savings. "In the past, much of what our buyers did was very manual and time consuming, with lots of order entry across multiple systems," he says. "This takes 90 percent of the manual part out of their day."

Among other things, there are now modules that can automatically determine the quickest, most economical, way to fulfill an order, whether directly from one of the company's warehouses or through a partner in a particular geographic location. Still, Ferguson says, PC Connection is investing for future growth, and he adds that the new system means customer orders will continue to be filled with greater speed and accuracy, even as business picks up.

"It's a customer satisfaction issue," he says. "To stay in the game, you have to upgrade your system to handle increased requests."

PC Connection: Learning to Stop, Drop, and Ship

SOURCE: Paul McDougall, "PC Connection Learns to Stop, Drop, and Ship," *InformationWeek*, September 15, 2008.

Electronic Data Interchange

Electronic data interchange (EDI) was one of the earliest uses of information technology for supply chain management. EDI involves the electronic exchange of business transaction documents over the Internet and other networks between supply chain trading partners (organizations and their customers and suppliers). Data representing

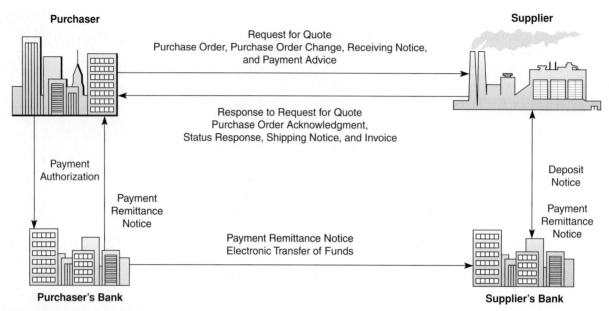

Purchaser

Supplier

Request for Quote
Purchase Order, Purchase Order Change, Receiving Notice,
and Payment Advice

Response to Request for Quote
Purchase Order Acknowledgment,
Status Response, Shipping Notice, and Invoice

Payment
Authorization

Payment
Remittance
Notice

Deposit
Notice

Payment
Remittance
Notice

Payment Remittance Notice
Electronic Transfer of Funds

Purchaser's Bank

Supplier's Bank

FIGURE 8.16

A typical example of electronic data interchange activities, an important form of business-to-business electronic commerce. EDI over the Internet is a major B2B e-commerce application.

a variety of business transaction documents (such as purchase orders, invoices, requests for quotations, and shipping notices) are automatically exchanged between computers using standard document message formats. Typically, EDI software is used to convert a company's own document formats into standardized EDI formats as specified by various industry and international protocols. Thus, EDI is an example of the almost complete automation of an e-commerce supply chain process. EDI over the Internet, using secure *virtual private networks*, is a growing business-to-business (B2B) e-commerce application.

Formatted transaction data are transmitted over network links directly between computers without paper documents or human intervention. Besides direct network links between the computers of trading partners, third-party services are widely used. Value-added network companies like GE Global Exchange Services and CA Technologies (formerly Computer Associates) offer a variety of EDI services for relatively high fees, but many EDI service providers now offer secure, lower-cost EDI services over the Internet. Figure 8.16 illustrates a typical EDI system.

EDI is still a popular data-transmission format among major trading partners, primarily to automate repetitive transactions, although it is slowly being replaced by XML-based Web services. EDI automatically tracks inventory changes; triggers orders, invoices, and other documents related to transactions; and schedules and confirms delivery and payment. By digitally integrating the supply chain, EDI streamlines processes, saves time, and increases accuracy. In addition, by using Internet technologies, lower-cost Internet-based EDI services are now available to smaller businesses.

Telefonica TSAI: Internet EDI	Telefonica is Spain's largest supplier of telecommunications services, serving the Spanish-speaking and Portuguese-speaking world with affiliates in Latin America and the United States. Telefonica Servicios Avanzados de Informacion (TSAI) is a subsidiary of Telefonica that handles 60 percent of Spain's electronic data interchange (EDI) traffic. TSAI's customers are supply chain trading partners—merchants, suppliers, and others involved in business supply chains from design to delivery.
	To tap into the sizable market of smaller businesses that can't afford standard EDI services, TSAI offers an Internet EDI service, InfoEDI, based on ECXpert electronic commerce software. InfoEDI allows transactions to be entered and processed on the Internet, so smaller trading partners no longer

have to buy and install special connections, dedicated workstations, and proprietary software. Instead, they can access the EDI network through the Internet via TSAI's Web portal.

InfoEDI's forms-based interface lets businesses connect with the InfoEDI simply by using modems and Web browsers. They can then interact with the largest suppliers and retailers to send orders, issue invoices based on orders, send invoice summaries, track status of documents, and receive messages. InfoEDI also provides a product database that lists all details of trading partners' products. Once a trading relationship has been established, each partner has encrypted access to details of its own products. Because those details remain accessible on TSAI's Web server, users need enter only minimal information to create links to those data, which are then plugged in as needed.

THE ROLE OF SCM

Figure 8.17 helps us understand the role and activities of supply chain management in business more clearly. The top three levels of Figure 8.17 show the strategic, tactical, and operational objectives and outcomes of SCM planning, which are then accomplished by the business partners in a supply chain at the execution level of SCM. The role of information technology in SCM is to support these objectives with interenterprise information systems that produce many of the outcomes a business needs to manage its supply chain effectively. That's why many companies today are installing SCM software and developing Web-based SCM information systems.

Until recently, SCM software products have typically been developed for either supply chain planning or execution applications. SCM planning software from vendors such as SAP and Oracle support a variety of applications for supply and demand forecasting. SCM execution software from vendors such as RedPrairie and Manhattan Associates support applications like order management, logistics management, and warehouse management. In addition, big ERP vendors like Oracle and SAP are now offering Web-enabled software suites of business applications that include SCM modules. Examples include Oracle's e-Business Suite and SAP AG's mySAP.

Figure 8.18 gives you a good idea of the major planning and execution functions and outcomes that can be provided by SCM software as promised by mySAP's supply chain management module. Now let's look at a real-world example of an SCM system.

FIGURE 8.17

The objectives and outcomes of supply chain management are accomplished for a business with the help of interenterprise SCM information systems.

SCM Objectives		SCM Outcomes
What? Establish objectives, policies, and operating footprint	**Strategic**	• Objectives • Supply policies (service levels) • Network design
How much? Deploy resources to match supply to demand	**Tactical**	• Demand forecast • Production, procurement, logistics plan • Inventory targets
When? Where? Schedule, monitor, control, and adjust production	**Operational**	• Work center scheduling • Order/inventory tracking
Do Build and transport	**Execution**	• Order cycle • Material movement

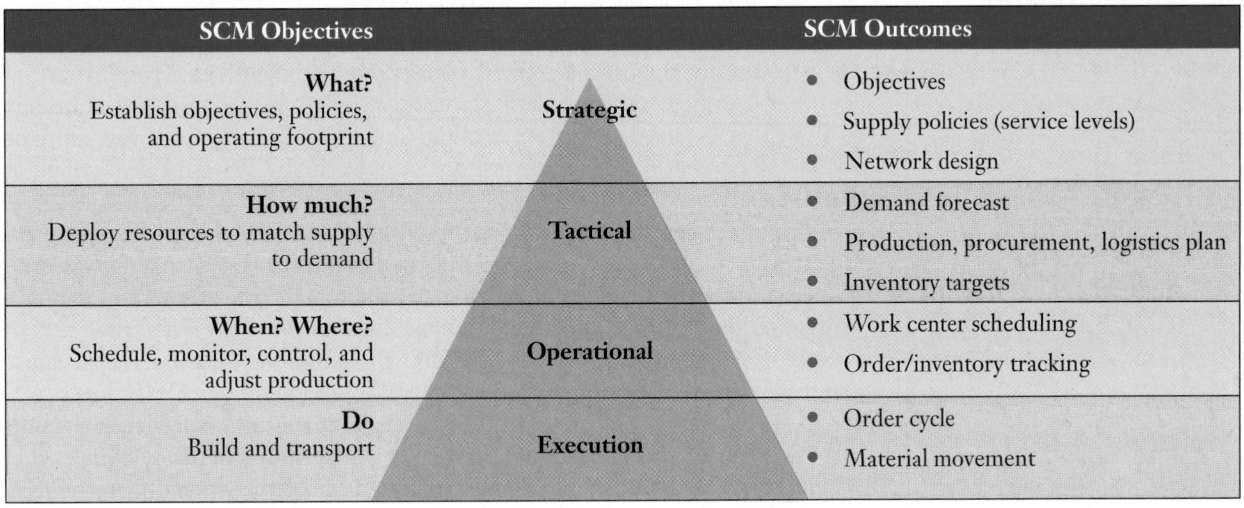

SOURCE: Keith Oliver, Anne Chung, and Nick Samanach, "Beyond Utopia: The Realist's Guide to Internet-Enabled Supply Chain Management," *Strategy and Business*, Second Quarter, 2001, p. 99.

SCM Functions	SCM Outcomes
Planning	
Supply chain design	• Optimize network of suppliers, plants, and distribution centers.
Collaborative demand and supply planning	• Develop an accurate forecast of customer demand by sharing demand and supply forecasts instantaneously across multiple tiers.
	• Internet-enable collaborative scenarios, such as collaborative planning, forecasting, and replenishment (CPFR), and vendor-managed inventory.
Execution	
Materials management	• Share accurate inventory and procurement order information.
	• Ensure materials required for production are available in the right place at the right time.
	• Reduce raw material spending, procurement costs, safety stocks, and raw material and finished goods inventory.
Collaborative manufacturing	• Optimize plans and schedules while considering resource, material, and dependency constraints.
Collaborative fulfillment	• Commit to delivery dates in real time.
	• Fulfill orders from all channels on time with order management, transportation planning, and vehicle scheduling.
	• Support the entire logistics process, including picking, packing, shipping, and delivery in foreign countries.
Supply chain event management	• Monitor every stage of the supply chain process, from price quotation to the moment the customer receives the product, and receive alerts when problems arise.
Supply chain performance management	• Report key measurements in the supply chain, such as filling rates, order cycle times, and capacity utilization.

Imperial Sugar: Supply Chain Management to the Rescue

It was an otherwise ordinary Thursday night in February 2008 when Imperial Sugar CIO George Muller got the call. "There had been an accident. People were hurt," Muller remembers. Some died. "As more and more of the details started to come out, it was horrific."

In the days following the explosion at the company's refinery in Port Wentworth, Georgia, CEO John Sheptor implored his executives to lead with their hearts, not their heads; efforts focused on helping affected employees and their families. But the $522 million sugar refiner—the third largest in the United States—also had customer obligations. The disaster destroyed approximately 60 percent of its production capacity overnight. It wasn't clear when, or if, the plant would operate again.

Imperial Sugar had already weathered some major challenges: bankruptcy, divestiture, and new management. But the Port Wentworth tragedy was the hardest Muller had faced. "Not too many manufacturing companies can withstand that kind of impact to their business and survive," he says.

The Georgia refinery remained offline for 20 months. "We didn't have any safety stockpiles," says Muller. "We were scurrying to fulfill as many orders as we could." Some sugar was imported through its joint venture with Mexican refiner Ingenios Santos, but it wasn't enough. "We disappointed many customers," Muller says. He credits supply chain systems—particularly demand-management software—with helping to make the most of available resources.

In 1998, Imperial Sugar implemented an all-in-one PeopleSoft ERP system, in lieu of best-of-breed software, to manage 20-odd business processes. After several upgrades, it was clear that the demand-management module couldn't handle the complexities of the business. When large beverage and food manufacturers sign an annual contract, Imperial Sugar has to predict how that demand will play out based on seasonal and consumer cycles. "Supply chain is at the heart of our business," says Muller. "For us, it's a differentiator. It's why customers come back."

In 2006, the company added a bolt-on solution from Demand Foresight: software that essentially learns how demand ebbs and flows over time. The tool allows Imperial Sugar to see the impact of a wide range of factors on demand, react to changes quickly, and track performance.

After the refinery catastrophe, Imperial Sugar needed immediate insight into how many customers it could serve with its available inventory. The software gave them that overview by product line, and its "available to promise" functionality allowed everyone—from production to sales—to see what could be delivered in real time.

Muller won't reveal how much he spent on Demand Foresight, saying only that it was a "drop in the bucket" compared to the $5.7 million spent on the last PeopleSoft upgrade and implementation. "It was our saving grace," he says. "It took our demand, our inventory and capacity, and the number of new orders coming in and tied it all together. We couldn't fulfill every order, but we were able to fill more orders than we ever would have had we not had that tool."

SOURCE: Stephanie Overby, "Supply Chain Management to the Rescue," *CIO.com*, March 16, 2010.

BENEFITS AND CHALLENGES OF SCM
LO 8-2

Creating a real-time SCM infrastructure is a daunting and ongoing issue and quite often a point of failure for several reasons. The chief reason is that the planning, selection, and implementation of SCM solutions are becoming more complex as the pace of technological change accelerates and the number of a company's partners increases.

The real-world experiences of companies like Imperial Sugar and the promised outcomes that are outlined in Figure 8.18 emphasize the major business benefits that are possible with effective supply chain management systems. Companies know that SCM systems can provide them with key business benefits such as faster, more accurate, order processing; reductions in inventory levels; quicker times to market; lower transaction and materials costs; and strategic relationships with their suppliers. All of these benefits of SCM are aimed at helping a company achieve agility and responsiveness in meeting the demands of its customers and the needs of its business partners. Let's look at a recent example.

Emerson Transaction Hub: A Bright Idea That's Paying Off

A couple of years ago, some executives at Emerson asked themselves a question: Why pay to send inventory from one supplier on one ship and goods from a second supplier on another ship, when both deliveries are coming from the same place and could be loaded into a single container?

It was an *aha!* moment that ended up saving millions for the St. Louis manufacturer that regularly ships supplies from Asia to North America and Europe. In late 2005, the company started a pilot program in which a logistics provider that specializes in transportation management for freight carriers worked with two Emerson divisions to consolidate multiple orders into the same shipping container. Not only did the pilot program save money, the business units were able to tighten their global supply chains by better tracking shipments and managing inventory.

Naturally, Emerson wanted to expand the program, but here's where things got complicated: Emerson has 70 separate business units that purchase goods from 35,000 suppliers. Each unit communicates with its own suppliers via a combination of e-mail, spreadsheets, faxes, and phone calls. Asking a logistics provider to step into the middle of this tangled transaction web just wasn't feasible. "It's a brittle system," says Steve Hassell, vice president and chief information officer at Emerson. "If a provider or a business unit makes changes, you have to go and touch tens or hundreds of connections."

Instead, Hassell's team envisioned a single hub that everyone would link to using common communications mechanisms and data formats. It would serve as a unified gateway that Emerson's business units, logistics providers, and suppliers could use to exchange information. Of course, for a single communications hub to work, everyone has to speak the same language. Emerson decided to conduct transactions via two data formats: EDI, using the ANSI ASC X12 format, and OAGIS XML.

Here's how the system works: A business unit initiates a transaction, such as a purchase order, through its ERP system. The order is sent to the transaction hub, which translates the message into OAGIS XML. Providers and suppliers then coordinate shipping, and the providers communicate shipment status to the Emerson division through the hub. The hub is processing about 10,000 transactions per day. Once all business units are on board, Emerson expects to see that number jump to 100,000 transactions.

Hassell estimates that Emerson invested about $500,000 in the hub and has recovered those costs more than several times. Putting 10 suppliers in the same shipping container cuts costs by 35 percent. The company has saved millions in transport costs alone by consolidating shipping. Also, with information such as purchase orders and shipping notices in a common format, Emerson has more visibility into its supply chain, increasing inventory control efficiency by ensuring that materials aren't overstocked or understocked.

Finally, whereas Emerson used to look like 70 smaller businesses to its suppliers, it now looks like one big customer. Suppliers can streamline their business processes through the transaction hub while Emerson gains better leverage to negotiate prices and contracts.

SOURCE: Andrew Conry-Murray, "InformationWeek 500: Emerson Transaction Hub: A Bright Idea That's Paying Off in Efficiency, Savings," *InformationWeek*, September 18, 2007.

However, developing effective SCM systems has proved to be a complex and difficult application of information technology to business operations. So achieving the business value and customer value goals and objectives of supply chain management, as illustrated in Figure 8.19, has been a major challenge for most companies.

FIGURE 8.19

The challenge of achieving the goals and objectives of supply chain management.

Objectives of Supply Chain Management

What are the causes of problems in supply chain management? Several reasons stand out. A lack of proper knowledge about demand planning, tools, and guidelines is a major source of SCM failure. Inaccurate or overly optimistic demand forecasts will cause major production, inventory, and other business problems, no matter how efficiently the rest of the supply chain management process is constructed. Inaccurate production, inventory, and other business data provided by a company's other information systems are a frequent cause of SCM problems. In addition, lack of adequate collaboration among marketing, production, and inventory management departments within a company, and with suppliers, distributors, and others, will sabotage any SCM system. Many companies that are installing SCM systems consider even the SCM software tools themselves to be immature, incomplete, and hard to implement. These problems are spotlighted in the real-world example of Nike Inc.

Nike Inc.: Failure (and Bouncing Back) with Supply Chain Management

Roland Wolfram, Nike's vice president of global operations and technology, calls the i2 problem a "speed bump." Some speed bump! The i2 problem is a software glitch that cost Nike more than $100 million in lost sales, depressed its stock price by 20 percent, triggered a flurry of class-action lawsuits, and caused Phil Knight, its chairman, president, and chief executive officer, to lament famously, "This is what you get for $400 million, huh?" In the athletic footwear business, only Nike, with a 32 percent worldwide market share (almost double Adidas, its nearest rival) and a market cap that's more than the rest of the manufacturers and retailers in the industry combined, could afford to talk about $100 million like that.

"For the people who follow this sort of thing, we became a poster child for failed implementations," Wolfram says. Yet there was a lesson too for people who do, in fact, follow "this sort of thing," specifically chief information officers. The lesson of Nike's failure and subsequent rebound lies in the fact that it had a business plan that was widely understood and accepted at every level of the company. Given that, and the resiliency it afforded the company, the i2 failure ultimately turned out to be, indeed, just a speed bump.

Nike's June 2000 problems with its i2 system reflect the double whammy typical of high-profile enterprise computing failures. First, there's a software problem closely tied to a core business process—in this case, factory orders. Then the glitch sends a ripple through product delivery that grows into a wave crashing on the balance sheet. The wave is big enough that the company must reveal the losses at a quarterly conference call with analysts, or risk the wrath of the Securities and Exchange Commission, shareholders, or both.

Wolfram says Nike's demand-planning strategy was and continues to be a mixture of art and technology. Nike sells too many products (120,000) in too many cycles (four per year) to do things by intuition alone. "We've tuned our system so we do our runs against historical models, and then people look at it to make sure it makes sense," he says. The computer models are trusted more when the product is a reliable seller (i.e., just about anything with Michael Jordan's name on it) and the planners' intuition plays a bigger role in new or more volatile products. In this case, says Wolfram, talking with retailers does more good than consulting the system.

So how has Nike's business fared, six years and $500 million later? Wolfram claims that better collaboration with Far East factories has reduced the amount of "prebuilding" of shoes from 30 percent of Nike's total manufacturing units to around 3 percent. The lead time for shoes, he asserts, has gone from nine months to six (in some periods of high demand, seven months). Inventory levels have been reduced by cutting Nike's factory order interval time from one month to a week in some cases. So far, the most direct benefits of the system have been typical for ERP: improved financial visibility, cash flow management, revenue forecasting, and an ability to juggle Nike's cash stockpile in different currencies to take advantage of shifting exchange rates—benefits that are enhanced by the single database that holds all the data.

Yet because Nike developed a plan in 1998 and stuck with it, the company claims it can make a coordinated global effort to cut that lead time. The system to make that happen is in place. Given all that has transpired in the past several years, that is rather remarkable.

SOURCE: Christopher Koch, "Nike Rebounds: How (and Why) Nike Recovered from Its Supply Chain Disaster," *CIO Magazine*, June 15, 2004.

TRENDS IN SCM
LO 8-2

The supplier-facing applications arena will see the continued growth of public as well as private networks that transform linear and inflexible supply chains into nonlinear and dynamic fulfillment networks. Supplier-facing applications will also evolve along another dimension: from automation and integration of supply chains to collaborative sourcing, planning, and design across their supplier networks.

Figure 8.20 illustrates the trends in the use of supply chain management today as three possible stages in a company's implementation of SCM systems. In the first stage, a company concentrates on making improvements to its internal supply chain processes and its external processes and relationships with suppliers and customers. Its e-commerce Web site and those of some of its trading partners provide access to online catalogs and useful supply chain information as they support limited online transactions.

In stage two, a company accomplishes substantial supply chain management applications by using selected SCM software programs internally, as well as externally via intranet and extranet links among suppliers, distributors, customers, and other trading partners. Companies in this stage also concentrate on expanding the business network of Web-enabled SCM-capable trading partners in their supply chain to increase its operational efficiency and effectiveness in meeting their strategic business objectives.

FIGURE 8.20

Stages in the use of supply chain management.

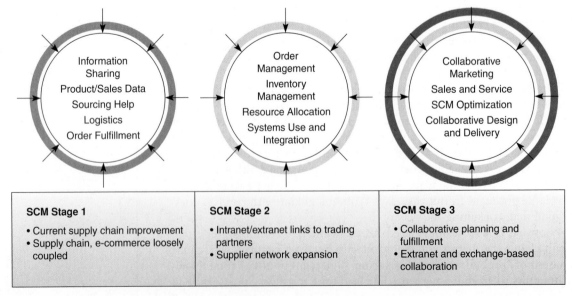

In the third stage, a company begins to develop and implement cutting-edge collaborative supply chain management applications using advanced SCM software, full-service extranet links, and private and public e-commerce exchanges. Examples include collaborative supply chain planning and fulfillment applications like collaborative product design and delivery, and collaborative planning, forecasting, and replenishment (CPFR). In addition, collaborative marketing sales and service applications with trading partners, including customer and partner relationship management systems, may be developed. Companies in this third stage strive to optimize the development and management of their supply chains in order to meet their strategic customer value and business value goals. Let's look at some real-world examples.

CVS, McKesson, and MPT: Web-Based SCM Integration

CVS is a leading drug retail chain, while McKesson is the largest U.S. distributor of pharmaceuticals, health care products, and medical/surgical supplies, with annual sales in excess of $20 billion. Better integration with McKesson is a key strategic move for CVS, as management sees significant potential for improving sales and margins through its enhanced pricing and promotional forecasting systems. Supply chain integration helps the retailer move from pull to push promotions by allowing marketing managers to plan promotions more effectively, using item history taken from historical point-of-sale data on a store-by-store basis. The integration with McKesson substantially reduces the amount of time needed to plan and to stock inventory for individual promotions.

A major objective in the CVS–McKesson chain is to improve business performance through better supply chain integration. This requires much closer cooperation between McKesson and CVS, with McKesson even taking responsibility for CVS stock levels. McKesson monitors CVS's store-level consumption via Web extranet links and replenishes the inventory to meet the agreed-on service levels—true supply chain integration. This cooperative process between supplier and customer is achieved through seamless interenterprise process integration and advanced SCM applications that link CVS directly to McKesson's production department.

Not every supply chain application, however, requires a hefty up-front investment. Modern Plastics Technology (MPT), an injection mold manufacturer in Port Huron, Michigan, spends just several hundred dollars per month to access the i-Supply Service Web-based supply chain application from SupplySolution Inc. The company had been using electronic data interchange transmissions to fill its orders and was having a tough time keeping up with unscheduled changes in orders, says Doug Archer, vice president of Modern Plastics.

Then a large sealant manufacturer that was one of the company's customers persuaded Modern Plastics to connect with its i-Supply Service application. This Web-based SCM system has enabled Modern Plastics to see what its customers need on a real-time basis. Modern Plastics runs 30 to 40 different products through its presses, and i-Supply now allows management to better plan long production runs or prioritize specific product runs. Additionally, i-Supply helps MPT accomplish more accurate demand forecasting and production scheduling.

Jelly Belly Candy Company– Competing with CRM

The Jelly Belly Candy Company (Jelly Belly for short) is a manufacturer of sweets, candies, and confections; it is best known for its flagship products, jelly beans and candy corn. Located in Fairfield, California, and with two other manufacturing locations in Chicago and Thailand, the company produces more than 34 million pounds of candy every year. The first Jelly Belly jelly beans were sold in 1976 in an ice cream parlor in Alhambra, California. Expensive at the time, they were sold in a variety of flavors for $2 a pound. Total sales for the first week were $44, and customers never looked back. Varieties today include Sport Beans, which contain electrolytes and vitamins; Sugar-Free Jelly Belly Jelly Beans; Jelly Belly Cocktail Classics (same flavor but without the alcohol); and a number of other products, including the well-known Candy Corn and Gummi Bears.

Although the company had been growing well for the last decade, including new product launches and international ventures, management realized that the lack of high-quality information about its processes was hindering further improvements. In 2007, the company successfully implemented an ERP package, which resulted in significant operational gains on their manufacturing and logistics functions. Sales and marketing, however, were still managed with a number of ad hoc tools and processes, and managers lacked adequate visibility into the sales process, which made it difficult to improve it. After careful consideration, the company decided that on top of its already successful ERP implementation, a CRM system was necessary, one that could integrate with the ERP data, provide a single view of each customer throughout the company, and better manage and track all ongoing sales, marketing, and customer service efforts. "Without a customer relationship management system integrated with our ERP system, there was little we could do from an organizational standpoint to remedy this problem. Our customer relationship management project was critical," says Ryan Schader, vice president of Business Development at Jelly Belly.

And thus armed with business requirements, the company started the implementation of a CRM package that was compatible with its existing ERP system. After a few months had gone by, however, it was clear to everyone involved that things were not going well. The desired functionality could not all be implemented, and the IT department was fighting a problem, followed by a glitch, followed

by a bug on a daily basis. In addition, the processes that were included in the package were much more convoluted than strictly necessary; even a relatively easy task, such as interfacing with the ERP system, was very complicated. After a year and a half, management decided that if the system was not working already it never would, and it pulled the plug on the project. "Looking forward, I anticipated more work for the IT staff and frustrated business users. We didn't want to sour the organization on customer relationship management," explains Dan Rosman, vice president of Information Technology at Jelly Belly. It was back to square one for Jelly Belly.

After picking up the pieces, the company still needed a CRM solution, so management started looking at alternatives that were compatible with their existing infrastructure—the ERP system in particular—before they got involved again with a problematic solution. Since the majority of that infrastructure, as well as the database underlying their ERP system (Microsoft SQL Server), had been purchased from Microsoft, they decided to give the software giant a try. To prevent getting burned again, they decided to engage Microsoft Gold Certified Partner Webfortis to create a proof-of-concept that would meet all the core requirements before proceeding with any large-scale efforts. In one month, the prototype was up and running, and management was duly impressed. Fast forward two and one-half months later, and Microsoft Dynamics CRM had been fully deployed within Jelly Belly, on time and under budget.

The new system shares information with the database underlying the existing ERP, so all employees now have a comprehensive, holistic view of all customers and their interactions with the company. Whether those interactions are initiated by a salesperson, an order entry clerk, or a customer service representative, the new CRM application keeps track of everything. As a result, there is no longer a disconnect between the many different functions and areas involved in servicing the needs of customers, and everybody has access to the same underlying information; this eliminates the need to reconcile the disparate, and sometimes conflicting, reports coming out of the all of the different applications that existed before. On addition to this common data, the company implemented a set of standardized processes geared to tracking and reporting sales activity, with a host of benefits. For example, the company now has standing arrangements with a few large customers to house company-owned candy bins on their premises. Before this, no mechanism existed for tracking chargebacks when the customers sold candy but did not pay for it; now the profitability of each separate unit can be determined with total accuracy. The application also allows Jelly Belly to see why a store might choose to return the equipment, or whether theft is a significant problem at certain retail locations. It also monitors how long candy has been on the display, and it notifies the stores when they should be replacing it with a fresh batch.

Jelly Belly is also taking advantage of the functionality in the new package to improve its retention of specialty retail clients. In the past, the company would gain as many customers as it would lose in any given year, making the creation of long-standing relationships with this customer segment particularly difficult. Using the new outbound calling features of the application, customer sales representatives place calls to those customers who have not placed an order in the last twelve months, in many cases bypassing the distributors and going directly to the actual customer. "Our Director of Customer Service has been with the company over 30 years and was skeptical that customers would respond positively," says Schader. "But since we've started the calls, we've found that most specialty retailers are happy to hear about new products and what is selling well at other stores. In most cases, they've simply forgotten about us because they're busy." Since implementing the new solution, annual customer churn has decreased by 34 percent. After running the new system for 24 months, the company has gained 4,400 new customers and lost only 2,900. And the company expects this number to get better as they gain more experience with the system and are able to better identify problematic customers well before the customers take their business elsewhere.

This same outbound calling program has also resulted in increased sales activity, in addition to drastically lowering customer churn. Now that these activities can be better tracked, the company is seeing an increase in revenue of more than $60,000 each month that can be directly attributed to sales activity following a sales call using the information now provided by the CRM package. Considering that the implementation of Microsoft Dynamics CRM was not expensive to begin with, these two single improvements paid for the entire project in just three months. Moreover, once installed, most employees do not seem to have too much trouble finding their way around the technology, nor have they encountered any of the bugs, problems, or glitches that were prevalent in the previous project. The support desk gets fewer than a dozen e-mails a week, and most are questions about how to perform some particular activity in the software from those employees who are in the early stages of using it.

The project has also effected a number of changes in the way management runs the company. For example, with the available tools, regional sales managers can now make sure that all sales leads resulting from those trade shows and events are followed up on a timely basis, and see how many of those leads are converted to actual sales. Perhaps more important, it has prompted everyone to look at what else can be done to improve sales now that the problem of reliable sales and customer service information has been solved. "The mantra for our company right now is 'Work smarter, not harder,'" says Schader. "Tools like Microsoft Dynamics CRM are helping us grow even as the economy goes through a rough period."

SOURCE: "Jelly Belly Candy Company," *Microsoft Dynamics Customer Solution Case Study*, 2009; Lauren McKay, "The CRM Elite: Sweetening the Deal," *CRM Magazine*, August 24, 2010; and www.jellybelly.com, accessed June 4, 2011.

▼ QUESTIONS TO CONSIDER

1. What can managers at the Jelly Belly Candy Company do now that they could not do before? What has changed to make that possible? Do they have more data, better processes, both?
2. Managers at the Jelly Belly Candy Company have started to look at what else can they do to improve sales now that the lack of access to necessary information is no longer an issue. What could they be doing with their new setup? What three new initiatives would you consider implementing?

- **Customer Relationship Management: The Business Focus.** Customer relationship management is a cross-functional enterprise system that integrates and automates many of the customer-serving processes in sales, marketing, and customer services that interact with a company's customers. CRM systems use information technology to support the many companies that are reorienting themselves into customer-focused businesses as a top business strategy. The major application components of CRM include contact and account management; sales, marketing, and fulfillment; customer service and support; and retention and loyalty programs, all aimed at helping a company acquire, enhance, and retain profitable relationships with its customers as a primary business goal. However, many companies have found CRM systems difficult to implement properly due to lack of adequate understanding and preparation by management and affected employees. Finally, many companies are moving toward collaborative CRM systems that support the collaboration of employees, business partners, and the customers themselves in enhancing profitable customer relationships.

- **Enterprise Resource Planning: The Business Backbone.** Enterprise resource planning is a cross-functional enterprise system that integrates and automates many of the internal business processes of a company, particularly those within the manufacturing, logistics, distribution, accounting, finance, and human resource functions of the business. Thus, ERP serves as the vital backbone information system of the enterprise, helping a company achieve the efficiency, agility, and responsiveness required to succeed in a dynamic business environment. ERP software typically consists of integrated modules that give a company a real-time cross-functional view of its core business processes, such as production, order processing, and sales, and its resources, such as cash, raw materials, production capacity, and people. However, properly implementing ERP systems is a difficult and costly process that has caused serious business losses for some companies, which underestimated the planning, development, and training that were necessary to reengineer their business processes to accommodate their new ERP systems. However, continuing developments in ERP software, including Web-enabled modules and business software suites, have made ERP more flexible and user friendly, as well as extending it outward to a company's business partners.

- **Supply Chain Management: The Business Network.** Supply chain management is a cross-functional interenterprise system that integrates and automates the network of business processes and relationships between a company and its suppliers, customers, distributors, and other business partners. The goal of SCM is to help a company achieve agility and responsiveness in meeting the demands of its customers and needs of its suppliers, by enabling it to design, build, and sell its products using its supply chain, a fast, efficient, and low-cost network of business partners, processes, and relationships. SCM is frequently subdivided into supply chain planning applications, such as demand and supply forecasting, and supply chain execution applications, such as inventory management, logistics management, and warehouse management. Developing effective supply chain systems and achieving the business goals of SCM have proved to be complex and difficult challenges for many firms. But SCM continues to be a major concern and top business initiative as companies increase their use of Internet technologies to enhance integration and collaboration with their business partners, and improve the operational efficiency and business effectiveness of their supply chains.

These are the key terms and concepts of this chapter. The page number of their first reference appears in parentheses.

1. Customer relationship management (326)
   a. Application components (326)
   b. Business benefits (332)
   c. Challenges (332)
   d. Trends (334)
2. E-business suites (343)
3. Electronic data interchange (347)
4. Enterprise resource planning (337)
   a. Application components (337)
   b. Business benefits (339)
   c. Challenges (339)
   d. Trends (343)
5. Supply chain (345)
6. Supply chain management (345)
   a. Application components (346)
   b. Business benefits (351)
   c. Challenges (351)
   d. Trends (354)

Match one of the key terms and concepts listed previously with each of the brief examples or definitions that follow. Try to find the best fit for answers that seem to fit more than one term or concept. Defend your choices.

_____ 1. A cross-functional enterprise system that helps a business develop and manage its customer-facing business processes.

_____ 2. A cross-functional enterprise system that helps a business integrate and automate many of its internal business processes and information systems.

_____ 3. A cross-functional interenterprise system that helps a business manage its network of relationships and processes with its business partners.

_____ 4. Includes contact and account management; sales, marketing, and fulfillment; and customer service and support systems.

_____ 5. Includes order management, production planning, accounting, finance, and human resource systems.

_____ 6. Includes demand forecasting, inventory management, logistics management, and warehouse management systems.

_____ 7. Acquiring, enhancing, and retaining profitable relationships with customers.

_____ 8. Improvements in the quality, efficiency, cost, and management of internal business processes.

_____ 9. Development of a fast, efficient, and low-cost network of business partners to get products from concept to market.

_____ 10. Resistance from sales and customer service professionals who are not adequately involved in the development of the system.

_____ 11. Failure of order processing and inventory accounting systems that are reengineered to accommodate a new cross-functional system.

_____ 12. A lack of adequate demand-planning knowledge, tools, and guidelines may cause major overproduction and excess inventory problems.

_____ 13. Toward Web portals and collaborative systems involving business partners, as well as customers to coordinate sales and service across all marketing channels.

_____ 14. Toward more flexible, user-friendly, Web-enabled software, integrated into e-business software suites.

_____ 15. Toward the use of Internet technologies to integrate and enhance collaboration with a company's network of business partners.

_____ 16. An integrated system of software modules for customer relationship management, enterprise resource planning, supply chain management, and other business applications.

_____ 17. The automatic exchange of electronic business documents between the networked computers of business partners.

_____ 18. A network of business partners, processes, and relationships that supports the design, manufacture, distribution, and sale of a company's products.

1. Should every company become a customer-focused business? Why or why not?

2. Why would systems that enhance a company's relationships with customers have such a high rate of failure?

3. Refer to the Real World Challenge introduced at the beginning of this chapter. Is the main problem that the Jelly Belly Candy Company faces a lack of reliable information, or is it something else? How important is it to obtain an accurate diagnosis of the situation before throwing technology at it?

4. How could some of the spectacular failures of ERP systems have been avoided?

5. Should companies continue to use EDI systems? Why or why not?

6. Refer to the Real World Solution in the chapter. The company's first attempt at implementing a

CRM package was not successful. What was done differently the second time that resulted in a better experience? What lessons can be drawn from these two projects?

7. How can you avoid the problem of overly enthusiastic demand forecasts in supply chain planning?

8. What challenges do you see for a company that wants to implement collaborative SCM systems? How would you meet such challenges?

9. Refer to the Real World Case on Kennametal, Haworth, Dana Holding, and Others in the chapter. Do the examples discussed in the case show that customization and ERPs should never go together? Discuss.

10. Should companies install e-business software suites or "best of breed" e-business software components? Why or why not?

1. Netsuite's Netsuite
   Enterprise Systems to Go
   NetSuite by NetSuite Inc. (www.netsuite.com) enables small businesses to quickly develop and deploy ERP, CRM, and e-commerce applications. Their Web site presents detailed information about this software suite. Visit NetSuite's Web site and click on their NetSuite product link to see more information about the product's components. Click on the "Customers" link for a list of success stories. Notice the tremendous variety of business types.

   a. Identify and explore NetSuite's components that relate to your business major.

   b. Click on the "customers" link on NetSuite's home page and select a customer in an industry that interests you (or one assigned by your instructor). Read the customer's success story. What benefits were emphasized?

   c. Would you recommend this suite to a small business owner? Why or why not?

2. Collaborative CRM
   Distributed Teams
   A large telecommunications company's real estate holdings include more than 6 million square feet of property. To aid in its 400+ real estate–related transactions each year, the company contracted the services of a corporate real estate company and a law firm that specialized in corporate real estate. Real estate transactions significantly differ based on type and circumstances unique to each property and property owner. Legal specialists help ensure that each transaction meets its client's risk preferences.

   The telecommunications company wanted an information system using the Lotus Notes/Domino messaging platform to link it with the real estate firm and the law firm in order to:

   1. Capture common transaction information such as property location, transaction type, business unit, "opposing party," and lead contacts.

   2. Record and report which tasks have been completed, when they were completed, and who completed them.

   3. Allow ad hoc posting of additional, transaction-specific information into a common electronic file.

   Team members quickly found that by taking time to update the system they would reduce miscommunications and interruptions and therefore save time overall. Management liked the system

because they could track the performance of team members, identify processes open to improvement, and identify project delays before they became costly problems.

   a. How do these property transactions differ from commodity supply chain transactions?

   b. What advantage does the real estate company and the law firm gain by adopting their client's technology platform (Lotus Notes/Domino)?

   c. Find a Lotus Notes/Domino product review on the Web, read it, and report your findings to the class. Your presentation should answer the following questions: Who provided the review? What is the reviewer's relationship to the product? What did the reviewer like? What did the reviewer dislike? Which competitors were mentioned in the review? How did Lotus Notes/Domino compare?

3. Enterprise Sales Support
   Making Up for Missing Features
   Christina Lovan works as an independent agent for Farmers Insurance (www.farmers.com) in O'Fallon, Illinois. As an independent agent, she manages her own office and earns her income entirely from policy sales. Farmers Insurance supports Christina's efforts with training and access to a Web-based suite of applications that helps her manage her business. This *extranet* includes contact, customer, and policy management systems, as well as corporate communications. The system also includes a "feedback" feature agents may use to report software problems or make suggestions regarding future software enhancements.

   Christina enjoys working with people to help them solve their problems. However, to meet these people, Christina needs leads. She purchases leads from Farmers Insurance, Net Quote (www.netquote.com), and InsureMe (www.insureme.com), and she asks each client for three referrals at each meeting. She is a member of Business Networking International (www.bni.com), and she is an active member of the local chambers of commerce.

   Although the software tools provided by Farmers Insurance allow Christina to track prospective customers, they do not measure information quality. It is expensive to purchase or solicit lead information. Christina needs to know the best way to spend her time and money. She hopes Farmers will provide system updates to accommodate this need, but Christina has also developed her own data-quality evaluation tools using Microsoft Excel.

   With a few basic Excel skills, we can duplicate Christina's efforts. Download and save the

Insurance.xls from the MIS 10e OLC and use it to complete the following exercises. Note that the data providers used in this exercise are real, but the data in this spreadsheet are randomly generated.

a. Pending sales need Christina's immediate attention. Help her spot these opportunities by automatically highlighting them. Select the "Sales Leads" spreadsheet and use Excel's *Conditional Formatting* feature to set the cell shading color of each *Status* cell (Life, Auto, Home, Health) to green if the status is "Sale" (S), and red if the status is "Pending" (P).

b. Select the Cover Sheet spreadsheet. In cell C2, use the COUNTA function to count the total number of sales leads in the Sales Leads sheet. In cells C5 through C8, use the COUNTIF function to count the number of sales made for each type of insurance. In cells D5 through D8, divide the sales made by the number of leads to calculate the percentage of sales. Write these formulas so they calculate the correct answers even when Christina later adds more records to the list. Which product has the highest sales rate?

c. When rating the quality of her information, Christina counts whether or not a lead resulted in at least one sale. Using the "IF" and the "OR" functions, write a formula that will display "1" when at least one sale was made to a lead and "0" if the lead generated no sales.

d. Ultimately, Christina needs to know which lead source results in the most sales. Create a pivot table to average the data in the "Sales" for each "Source." Format this result as a percentage. Because a "1" indicates at least one sale and a "0" indicates no sales, the average per source indicates each source's closing rate. Which source had the highest closing rate? Which source had the lowest closing rate?

4. The Future of Enterprise Systems
Plug-in ERP

As enterprise systems grow in size to perform more and more operations for an organization, the software system itself becomes increasingly complex and hard to maintain. Add the fact that organizations typically customize these applications, and it becomes clear why organizations end up with ever-increasing annual software maintenance budgets.

Is there an alternative model to enterprisewide systems that try to do it all? What if third-party developers produced mutually compatible components or modules for enterprise systems? Such components would plug in to a central system much like a printer, mouse, monitor, and modem plugs into a personal computer.

If third parties wrote individual components, they might make them more closely fit the needs of specific types of business. With a better fit, these components would require less customization. Organizations could upgrade or replace components individually and only when needed.

So what is the current state of the art? Visit 20/20 Software Inc.'s Web site (www.2020software.com) and use its "Compare Software" feature to research applications.

a. Identify a system that runs on more than one server operating system.

b. Identify a system that runs on more than one database platform.

c. Describe 2020software's revenue model.

5. Customer Relations Gone Awry
Megabank

Mai Wing's career was off to a brilliant start. Following graduation and two years of hard work for a big-name international accounting and consulting firm, she'd earned her CPA, gained valuable experience, and accepted an offer from a mid-sized firm for 50 percent more pay and a lot less travel. She looked forward to taking a well-deserved vacation, buying her first new car, paying off her student loans, and saving for a home.

Two months after starting her new job, she received a letter from Megabank, where she maintained her direct-deposit checking account. It advised her that since she'd left the big-name accounting firm, she was no longer entitled to free checking, and she should expect a monthly charge for the service.

Annoyed, Mai Wing found another bank with free checking, switched over her direct-deposit and automated bill-paying services, and waited to ensure that the changes took effect. When Mai appeared at Megabank to close her accounts, her account manager appeared surprised.

a. What could Mai Wing have done differently?

b. Was Mai Wing the sort of customer Megabank would want to keep?

c. Were Megabank's policies sound? Why or why not?

d. Who was to blame for losing Mai Wing as a customer: Megabank's information systems department or its marketing managers?

real world

CASE 1

Kennametal, Haworth, Dana Holding, and Others: ERPs Get a Second Lease on Life

Kennametal, a $2 billion maker of construction tools, has spent $10 million on ERP maintenance contracts during the past 13 years and not once could the company take advantage of upgrades, says CIO Steve Hanna. The company's implementation was too customized: The time and effort needed to tweak and test the upgrade outweighed any benefits, he says. But Hanna kept trying. Recently, he priced the cost of consultants to help with an ERP re-implementation, and he was shocked by estimates ranging from $15 million up to $54 million.

The major ERP suites are "old and not as flexible as some newer stuff, and they can't build flexibility in," Hanna says. "Modifying it takes our time and money and training." His ears practically steam from frustration. "You tell me: What am I missing here?"

Kennametal is like many companies when it comes to ERP. The software is essential, but unlike when it was new, it now offers scant opportunity for a business to set itself apart from its competition. It certainly doesn't help bring in new revenue, and running it eats up an increasing share of the IT budget. Yet longtime ERP users aren't pitching the technology. Companies still need it for managing supply chain, financial, and employee data.

As Hanna and other chief information officers are finding, however, behemoth ERP systems are inflexible. Meanwhile, high-priced maintenance plans, as well as the slowness of vendors to support new technologies like mobile and cloud computing, mean that the ERP technology woven through your company can become a liability without careful management.

Your ERP system probably won't collapse if you do nothing; it's not like legacy mainframe applications were a decade ago. But just as you had to adapt your approach to managing mainframes in order to maintain their value in an age of faster, cheaper Web-based apps, you now need to do the same with ERP. And so it's time to rethink business processes, drive a harder bargain on maintenance fees, and find ways to marry ERP to emerging technologies. Achieving an ERP system that delivers future value means managing it differently here and now.

New ERP license revenue dropped by about 24 percent, according to Forrester Research—one effect of the general decline in software spending during 2009. This means vendors are hungry for new business. They'll offer software deals to tempt chief information officers who had put off upgrades or who want to install completely new systems to get the latest capabilities.

Yet chief information officers need to tread carefully: What used to be a good deal may not be one anymore. Steve Stanec is vice president of information systems at Piggly Wiggly Carolina, a privately held supermarket chain with 105 stores, most in the southeast United States. Stanec says he and other chief information officers must depart from the traditional ERP script, where, after lengthy negotiations, vendors hand over software and charge hefty on-going fees. Chief information officers must avoid falling into the same ERP traps they once did, he says.

Buying and installing ERP was never an easy task. Today, though, ERP is the Jack Nicholson of software: Its repertoire hackneyed, the old and expensive dog finds it hard to learn new tricks. It has become a legacy technology, and chief information officers are now finding new ways to manage ERP projects and the ongoing upkeep. Their best advice: Draw a clear project map and modify the software only as a last resort.

Haworth, a $1.7 billion office furniture manufacturer, will use tools from iRise to visually plan its rollouts of SAP systems in its major offices on four continents. The iRise tools simulate how the finished SAP system will look to employees to help them get accustomed to changes before rollout. The company also uses a sales compensation application from Vertex because SAP doesn't support the complicated, multi-tiered compensation model Haworth uses to pay its salespeople, says CIO Ann Harten. These choices stem from Harten's decision to make no custom changes to the core SAP code. The idea is to streamline the implementation project, which started in 2006, and to make future upgrades easier.

Modifying the core is expensive both when you do it and as you live with it, she says. "Next time the vendor does a version upgrade or a patch, your testing requirements are increased several fold," she says. "You want to avoid this at all costs."

ERP of the future is as plain-Jane as possible, agrees Hanna, the chief information officer of Kennametal. The fact that it can take an army of developers to build new features into ERP suites slows the vendors down. But it's also an obstacle for customers. The 6,446 customizations—Hanna counted them—that Kennametal made to its ERP software over the years prevented the company from taking advantage of the new technology its vendor did build in. "We couldn't implement one single enhancement pack ever," he says.

So even if he could pay up to $54 million for integrators and consultants to help Kennametal move to the latest version of the ERP suite, he doesn't want to. Instead, he plans to turn Kennametal's old ERP management strategy on its head by putting in as vanilla a version of SAP as possible. He and CEO Carlos Cardoso are willing to change Kennametal's internal business processes to match the way SAP works, Hanna says, rather than the other way around.

Kennametal will also take on the implementation itself. He hired IBM to consult about requirements definitions and to identify business processes that must be revamped to conform to SAP's procedures. Meanwhile, Kennametal staff will do the legwork. Hanna and Cardoso have committed to the board of directors to have the job done in eight months, he says, implementing at least 90 percent of the SAP software unmodified. The project is so important to Kennametal that it must succeed in order for the company's leaders, including Hanna and Cardoso, to achieve their performance goals for the year. "I'm going to make it work," says Hanna.

Because Kennametal's ERP system has been unable to keep up with changing technologies, Hanna says the company never benefited from the millions in maintenance fees it paid to cover upgrades. "We paid maintenance for nothing."

Doug Tracy, chief information officer at Dana Holding, researched analyst firm estimates about where maintenance money actually goes and found that 90 percent of those fees are pure profit for the vendor. For Tracy, there is no more time or tolerance for vendor games.

The $8.1 billion auto parts supplier has in recent years fought a hostile takeover attempt as well as been in, then emerged from, Chapter 11 bankruptcy protection. Then the auto market tanked, and Dana's sales reflected the 30–70 percent decline. The company had to scale back some ERP projects, and Dana wanted its vendors to work with them to reduce fees. He declines to name Dana's main ERP vendor, but he says he wasn't getting the deal he was looking for.

Dana's vendor didn't lie down. To try to persuade Tracy that maintenance fees are valuable, the vendor analyzed Dana's use of its support, he says. The findings: Dana made 21,000 requests to the vendor between January and September 2009. About 98 percent of them didn't involve human intervention; they were automated lookups on the vendor's knowledge base. "We're not getting much," Tracy concluded.

So he stopped making maintenance payments to his main ERP vendor as of December 31, 2009. "That's a risky strategy, though not as risky as vendors would have you believe," he says. One result of the move away from provider support is that Dana's internal IT people have to be more savvy about the ERP systems the company relies on, and able to fix what may go wrong. But, he says, there have been no technological showstoppers in years because ERP, like other legacy systems, is mature and reliable. Plus, there's plenty of ERP talent.

Eliminating maintenance saves money, because Dana is no longer paying for a service of questionable value, and it sets a precedent with the company's other ERP vendors. "You have to show value every step of the way," Tracy tells his suppliers. "If you try to hold us hostage, I will call what I see as a bluff and just stop payment."

Chief information officers have to take charge of what the future of ERP is going to be. Treating ERP as legacy IT may be hard for some who have invested so much time and energy to plan, implement, and tweak these systems. But adopting this mind-set will help chief information officers move ERP, and their companies, ahead. Modifying the base applications judiciously, if at all, will minimize expense and time devoted to software that now provides the most basic functionality. Everyone does accounts payable, notes Stanec at Piggly Wiggly, so don't waste time customizing it.

Stanec, for one, dreams of one day seeing ERP vendors develop packages that help companies generate revenue. "Then," he says, "we'd have something interesting to negotiate."

SOURCE: Kim S. Nash, "Reviving ERP," *CIO Magazine*, February 1, 2010.

▼ CASE STUDY QUESTIONS

1. Why does ERP customization lead to so many headaches when it is time to upgrade? Why were the systems customized in the first place?
2. Outright cutting payments to ERP vendors may not be possible for smaller companies without the in-house resources that larger organizations have. Are they at the mercy of the software providers? What other alternatives do small companies have? Provide some recommendations.
3. Kennametal's chief information officer complains that they "paid maintenance for nothing." Who do you think is responsible for that state of affairs? Kennametal, the ERP vendor, or both? Justify your answer.

▼ REAL WORLD ACTIVITIES

1. What offerings are available in the ERP marketplace today that were not available when the companies mentioned in the case first started investing in the technology? What new functionality do these offerings have? Research current ERP alternatives and prepare a report comparing their major features.
2. Should companies scrape their existing ERP implementations and start from scratch again, or should they keep trying to make their existing investments pay off? What are the advantages and disadvantages of each approach? Break into small groups to discuss these issues.

Cisco Systems, Black & Decker, and O'Reilly Auto Parts: Adapting Supply Chains to Tough Times

Whether it's a truck, a tsunami, or an economic downturn, the same general rule applies: You're better off if you can see it coming from a safe distance.

There aren't many companies that understand this notion better than Cisco Systems Inc. White-hot during the 90s, the company was pummeled after its vaunted inventory-forecasting system could not, or did not, predict the dot-com bubble's collapse.

The result of this miscalculation was that sales were halved, the company lost 25 percent of its customers in a matter of weeks, and it ultimately wrote off more than $2 billion in inventory. After that experience, Cisco's supply chain team vowed that it would never get blindsided again.

"There is a huge difference cutting head count between now and 2001," says Karl Braitberg, Cisco's vice president of customer value chain management. Back then, Cisco's supply chain model was built on a "push" system, where products were made and inventory was built up in anticipation of market demand based on best-guess forecasts. "Then, when demand dropped, the supply chain froze. Nothing happened," Braitberg says. "We knew we had to build a new system that reacts better than just 'push.'"

Every company must match its supply to consumer demand. In a normal business cycle, how well that job is accomplished determines whether the company is profitable. But this current economic downturn is anything but normal, and businesses are struggling just to stay liquid. There are various strategies to help preserve working capital, including cutting head count, outlets, and manufacturing lines. But for most companies, the key to capital preservation will be how well they can reduce their inventory levels.

Largely, companies are in survival mode, and they're looking to their supply chain management team to free up precious capital to help them do that. While it may not fall directly on IT executives to make that happen, their role in the equation is very strategic.

With globalization, outsourcing, and increased compliance and security concerns, managing supply chain operations becomes increasingly complex. Shorter, more frequent product cycles that target more sophisticated markets create a need to manage more products and parts from remote locations. Add the pressure of shorter cash-to-cash

cycles—the time a business extends credit to build inventory until the time it gets paid—to the equation, and the need for an intelligent, nimble, and timely flow of information becomes critical.

To have visibility as well as command and control, supply chain operations must be tightly integrated with the IT infrastructure. That isn't the case at many companies, and yet it may be the factor that determines success or failure as they endure and emerge from this downturn.

Like bloodletting, reducing inventory is a delicate matter that most people would prefer to avoid. Inventory can range from materials, to parts, to fully assembled products. Nobody wants to run out. If there's too little, customers won't get orders in a timely manner and market opportunities will be missed. Yet if a company carries too much and demand drops, then the inventory must be "bled down," or reduced in price, until it has a buyer.

During a strong economy and when cash flow is loosened, many companies can get by without rigorous inventory-management practices, says Larry Lapide, director of demand management at the MIT Center for Transportation & Logistics in Cambridge, Massachusetts. But during a recession, he adds, "companies had better bleed down inventory to reflect the downturn in sales. If they don't, it just sits there."

Inventory optimization is so critical now because of its impact on available cash, Lapide says. In accounting terms, inventory is an asset. So inventory that is on the books through manufacturing, assembly, and distribution represents credit-funded inventory. With credit at a premium, it's in a company's best interest not only to keep inventory levels tight, but also to sell goods as soon as possible.

Reducing costs and squeezing maximum utility out of fixed assets is nothing new to Black & Decker Corp.'s Hardware and Home Improvement Group in Lake Forest, California. The unit supplies hardware to big-box retailers that have responded to the economic downturn with new low-price strategies. It now falls on Scott Strickland, vice president of IS, to help the group squeeze down its own costs and maintain profit margins.

"We had been loath to drive inventory down to this level," Strickland says. However, the company had gained invaluable experience by deploying an integrated inventory-management system prior to the downturn. The result was that the key decision makers throughout its supply chain were operating with the same information, planners focused only on exceptions, and supplier and material issues were quickly resolved. The system, Strickland says, does the heavy lifting, and as a result, the unit has cut planning cycles from weeks to days and improved forecast accuracy by 10.4 percent.

"If someone had told us nine months ago that we could lower inventory as fast as we could to address a sales decline, we would not have believed it was possible," Strickland says. However, "because of the impetus on freeing up working capital, we have been focused on lowering our inventory and levels. We figured we could do this, and it turned out to not be the bad experience we had imagined."

The effort to lower inventory levels to free up working capital has proved so effective that the Black & Decker unit and its partners are jointly considering making it standard practice even after the economy recovers, Strickland says.

O'Reilly Auto Parts Inc., in Springfield, Missouri, uses inventory as a competitive differentiator, says Greg Beck, vice president of purchasing. One of the largest specialty retailers of automotive aftermarket parts, tools, supplies, and accessories in the United States, O'Reilly is responding to the recession differently than many other companies.

"Business is increasing because of the downturn," Beck says. "People aren't buying new cars but instead are putting more money into fixing old cars."

This isn't to say that O'Reilly lacks supply chain challenges or that it can let down its guard. As the result of an acquisition last year, the company increased its total store count to more than 3,300 and now operates in 38 states. To bolster its competitive advantage, O'Reilly's strategy is to increase customer service levels and replenish inventory on a nightly basis, while at the same time managing an increasing number of products.

The partnership between the supply chain operation and IT was critical to O'Reilly's strategy. The company is using Manhattan Associates Inc.'s replenishment software to collect product data information on the half hour, while updates from the distribution centers are transmitted nightly. The replenishment system uses these data to determine the forecast for these products. As a result, O'Reilly has increased inventory turns by 44 percent, and it still manages to fulfill 97 percent of customer requests immediately, with 3 percent handled through separate channels. At the same time, the company reduced its inventory levels, freeing up $60 million.

Companies say that driving costs out of the supply chain is an important goal, but the big question is whether they can afford to invest in their supply chain IT infrastructures to help make that happen, especially during a recession.

Dwight Klappich, an analyst at Gartner Group, calls that a short-sighted and, in the long term, costly approach. "If this trend continues," Klappich stated in a report, "this myopic focus on short-term tactical issues, while necessary for many businesses, could widen the gap between the best-performing organizations and lower-performing organizations."

Cisco understands this. After the 2001 downturn, it made major system investments to transform its "push-driven," siloed supply chain model into an integrated "pull system" that can extract timely data from suppliers and downstream partners. These reorder data are sent to Cisco after being triggered by specified parameters and algorithms, to shape "demand signals."

The system doesn't operate in a vacuum. Cisco has optimized its forecasting algorithms by bringing together representatives from its marketing, finance, sales, supply chain, and IT departments, and from key customers, as part of its sales and operations planning process. This group collaborates to create a common view of demand signals. This input drives an agreed-upon plan of action to align manufacturing capacity and inventory deployment and meet customer service levels. In short, they work together with the same data to optimally match supply and demand.

"Now, if there are no pull signals, nothing gets brought into the system," says Cisco's Braitberg. Manufacturers don't continue to source and build inventory that may sit in some warehouse waiting for customers who may never buy it. Cash is freed up for other purposes.

While Braitberg acknowledges that even past history can't be used as a template for this downturn, Cisco is confident that it has better visibility into market demand when it goes down, and that it will be ready when the green shoots emerge.

"We now have the techniques in place to be hypersensitive to demand changes," Braitberg says, "and we can manage our way through a downturn."

SOURCE: William Brandel, "Inventory Optimization Saves Working Capital in Tough Times," *Computerworld*, August 24, 2009.

▼ **CASE STUDY QUESTIONS**

1. Cisco Systems went from a "push" to a "pull" approach to its supply chain after the dot-com debacle. How are these two approaches different? Does the state of the economy determine which one should be used? Why?

2. What different elements must come together to bring supply chains to the optimal levels that these companies need? What role does IT play?

3. How is O'Reilly Auto Parts's approach to inventory management different from the approach that Cisco Systems and Black & Decker have taken?

 ## REAL WORLD ACTIVITIES

1. The ability to forecast demand accurately is one of the major issues discussed in the case. Go online and research the technologies that companies are using today to improve this aspect of their supply chains. Prepare a presentation to share your findings with the rest of your class.

2. The case compares short-term tactical needs with long-term strategic investments. How do you make the case, in an economic downturn, for the continued need to invest in technology? Break into small groups and brainstorm some alternatives.

e-COMMERCE SYSTEMS

INFORMATION SYSTEMS

e-BUSINESS APPLICATIONS

LEARNING OBJECTIVES

9-1 Identify the major categories and trends of e-commerce applications.

9-2 Identify the essential processes of an e-commerce system, and give examples of how it is implemented in e-commerce applications.

9-3 Identify and give examples of several key factors and Web store requirements needed to succeed in e-commerce.

9-4 Identify and explain the business value of several types of e-commerce marketplaces.

9-5 Discuss the benefits and trade-offs of several e-commerce clicks-and-bricks alternatives.

e-Commerce Fundamentals

E-commerce is changing the shape of competition, the speed of action, and the streamlining of interactions, products, and payments from customers to companies and from companies to suppliers.

For most companies today, **electronic commerce** is more than just buying and selling products online. Rather, it encompasses the entire online process of developing, marketing, selling, delivering, servicing, and paying for products and services transacted on internetworked, global marketplaces of customers, with the support of a worldwide network of business partners. In fact, much like the term e-business, many consider the term *e-commerce* to be somewhat antiquated. Given that the incoming generation of businesspeople have grown up in a world in which online commerce has always been available, it may soon be time to eliminate the distinction between e-commerce and e-business and accept that it is all just "business as usual." Until then, as before, we will retain the term *e-commerce* because it allows for a clearer picture of the differences between online and more traditional business transactions.

Because e-commerce involves more than just buying or selling something on the Internet, we must have a definition that is broad enough to allow for the vast array of activities defined by it. For our purposes, we will define e-commerce as *the online exchange of value*. Using this definition, all of the activities identified above, and more, can be defined as e-commerce.

As we will see in this chapter, e-commerce systems rely on the resources of the Internet and many other information technologies to support every step of this process. We will also see that most companies, large and small, are engaged in some form of e-commerce activities. Therefore, developing an e-commerce capability has become a competitive necessity for most businesses in today's marketplace.

Read the Real World Challenge on the next page. We can learn a lot about the many issues that companies face as a result of changing customer preferences. See Figure 9.1.

Figure 9.2 illustrates the range of business processes involved in the marketing, buying, selling, and servicing of products and services in companies that engage in e-commerce. Companies involved in e-commerce as either buyers or sellers rely on Internet-based technologies and e-commerce applications and services to accomplish *marketing, discovery, transaction processing*, and *product and customer service processes*. For example, e-commerce can include *interactive marketing, ordering, payment*, and *customer support processes* at e-commerce catalog and auction sites on the World Wide Web. However, e-commerce also includes e-business processes such as extranet access of inventory databases by customers and suppliers (transaction processing), intranet access of customer relationship management systems by sales and customer service reps (service and support), and customer collaboration in product development via e-mail exchanges and Internet newsgroups (marketing/discovery).

The advantages of e-commerce allow a business of virtually any size that is located anywhere on the planet to conduct business with just about anyone, anywhere. Imagine a small olive oil manufacturer in a remote village in Italy selling its wares to major department stores and specialty food shops in New York, London, Tokyo, and other large metropolitan markets. The power of e-commerce allows geophysical barriers to disappear, making all consumers and businesses on earth potential customers and suppliers.

e-Commerce Technologies

Which technologies are necessary for e-commerce? The short answer is that most information technologies and Internet technologies that we discuss in this text are, in some form, involved in e-commerce systems. A more specific answer is illustrated in Figure 9.3,

real world CHALLENGE

Ticketmaster–New Clients, New Outlets, New Needs

It may seem hard to believe, but world leading entertainment ticketing company Ticketmaster started less than 40 years ago, in 1976, in a garage in Phoenix, Arizona, founded by two college students and a businessman. One year later, in 1977, it had signed its first ticketed concert, the Electric Light Orchestra appearing at the University of New Mexico. In 1978 the company signed its first international client in Oslo, Norway; its first major venue (the Louisiana Superdome); and its first major league team, the NBA New Orleans Jazz (now the Utah Jazz). Today, Ticketmaster has become one of the largest e-commerce sites in the world, operating more than 7,000 retail outlets in 20 markets internationally. In 2009, more than one million paperless tickets were sold.

Although most of us may think of Ticketmaster as the place—real or virtual—where we go to buy tickets to a concert, show, or game for our own use, a major portion of Ticketmaster's business relates to the provision of technology and services to more than 10,000 corporate clients such as arenas, stadiums, professional and college sports teams and leagues, museums, theaters, and other entertainment venues. Indeed, in 2008 alone Ticketmaster sold more than 140 million tickets worth more than $9 billion on behalf of these clients. For example, Ticketmaster was

the official ticket provider for the 2008 Summer Olympic Games in Beijing and will do the same for the 2012 Summer Olympic Games in London. These arrangements, however, go beyond "merely" selling the tickets.

When that much money is at stake, it is important for Ticketmaster to provide its corporate clients with the tools necessary to run their businesses more efficiently; this in turn generates even more revenue for the company and more strongly ties its clients to the platform. The ultimate goal—which at the end of the day drives the entire industry—is that we, the final users of those tickets, have the best possible experience when purchasing them and later when attending our favorite events. For that to happen, however, many different things must go right, all behind the scenes.

Consider, for example, the Washington Capitals, an NFL franchise team in Washington, D.C., that makes the Verizon Center its home arena. The season ticket base for the team has about 4,500 ticket holders, with more than 50 percent of them renewing or upgrading their tickets online every year. On the one hand, online renewing and ticketing tremendously reduces the amount of manual labor involved in the production and delivery of those tickets, with obvious benefits for the team. On the other hand, that means that the software that supports the process must be very reliable with little, if any, downtime. In the current economic environment, going out for a game, concert, or the like is a major effort for most end customers—it may be the one big thing they do for the month. As a result, both Ticketmaster and its clients, like the Washington Capitals, want to do all they can to make the process as simple as possible. At the same time, consumers have become more demanding—the economic downturn has helped their attitude as well—and they are not content anymore with just buying a ticket. They want to do much more.

Think about how "buying a ticket" has changed in the last 15 or 20 years. Before, one would stand in line at a stadium or arena, sometimes for hours, to buy tickets to a game or concert. After purchasing the tickets, the next step was to show up at the specified date, time, and place, and enjoy the event. If the ticket holder got sick or had a job commitment, it was too bad, but tickets could not easily be sold or transferred. Unless the ticket holder knew somebody who wanted to go, it was difficult to resell the tickets. Although some places would buy them, the discounts were

The rise of the Internet and new customer practices are putting pressure on the ticketing business to adapt.

SOURCE: © AP Wide World Photos.

FIGURE 9.1

significant. If a game was sold out, and you were not one of the lucky ones to get a ticket, then it was also difficult to buy them in the secondary market. Scalpers charged major premiums, and buying these tickets is illegal in many states; a ticket holder would be uncertain whether the tickets were valid and whether he or she would be able to get into the game. We—the customers—do not want to do any of that today. This means that new tools and services must be made available for both Ticketmaster and its corporate clients so the end customers can be better served.

To meet the increasingly more complex needs of its corporate clients, Ticketmaster sought to develop a ticketing platform that provides granular-level control over seat inventory, customer relationship management, and full ownership of all customer data by the team, franchise, or facility. In addition, the solution would need to handle many different types of transactions quickly, easily, and securely. The goal is not only to provide these clients with a better way to market their events and thus sell more tickets—although that is certainly an important goal—but also to provide better service and support to their fans in a variety of ways. For example, beyond keeping accurate count of the number of available seats in the different pricing sections of the stadium, organizations also want to be able to have the option to offer clients an upgrade to a season or multi-ticket package (say, for the next five home games), or to keep waiting lists to be filled as new tickets become available. And these are just two examples. By providing more options to

ticket holders, any solution implemented would improve the ticket use rate: how much revenue is generated by each individual seat sold. More advanced features, such as gaining insight into patterns of consumption, behavior, and preferences of individual fans is not out of the question either.

Created less than 40 years ago in Arizona, Ticketmaster is a major player in the entertainment industry today, serving thousands of corporate clients, venues, and teams throughout the world. For most large events, Ticketmaster provides the underlying processes related to managing the sales of all tickets and admission, and those are largely based online today. A number of different steps and processes make up a great e-commerce experience, and Ticketmaster, as the leading provider of ticketing services in the world, is determined to enhance each and every one of those steps. At the same time, it is important for Ticketmaster—or any other company contemplating such a major development—to manage the project carefully, lest it fail to deliver superior value on every step because it is trying to achieve too much at once. As in any other major project that involves technology, there are major risks and there are major benefits.

SOURCE: "ARCHTICS," *Computerworld Honors Case Study*, 2010; "Ticketmaster," *Sybase Customer Case Study*, 2010; "The Phoenix Suns Launch Ticketmaster's Team Exchange, Online Ticket Forwarding Technology," *Ticketmaster Press Release*, September 5, 2010; "Ticketmaster and the Golden State Warriors Sign Multi-Year Ticketing Agreement," *Ticketmaster Press Release*, September 26, 2010; and www.ticketmaster.com, accessed May 29, 2011.

▼ QUESTIONS TO CONSIDER

1. List all of the steps that purchasing a ticket entails. How can technology change the way in which each step is carried out? What alternatives could be implemented for each step?
2. What kind of information would be valuable for corporate clients, such as sport franchises, arenas, or the like? What could those corporate clients do with that information?
3. Beyond those features discussed here, what other features should Ticketmaster consider incorporating into its future solution?

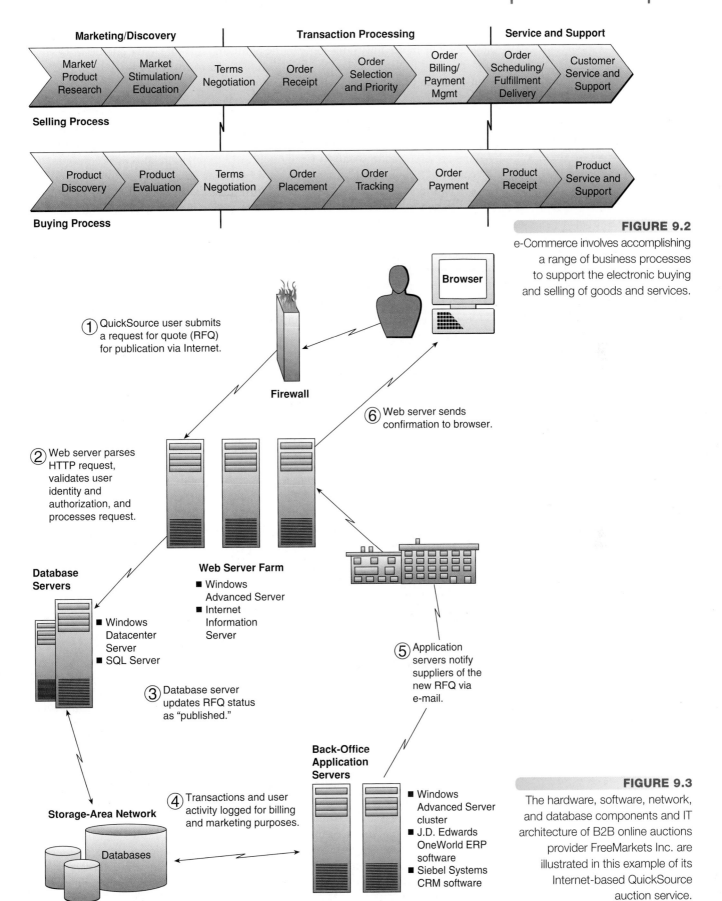

Marketing/Discovery

| Market/ Product Research | Market Stimulation/ Education | Terms Negotiation | Order Receipt | Order Selection and Priority | Order Billing/ Payment Mgmt | Order Scheduling/ Fulfillment Delivery | Customer Service and Support |

Transaction Processing

Service and Support

Selling Process

| Product Discovery | Product Evaluation | Terms Negotiation | Order Placement | Order Tracking | Order Payment | Product Receipt | Product Service and Support |

Buying Process

FIGURE 9.2

e-Commerce involves accomplishing a range of business processes to support the electronic buying and selling of goods and services.

① QuickSource user submits a request for quote (RFQ) for publication via Internet.

Browser

Firewall

⑥ Web server sends confirmation to browser.

② Web server parses HTTP request, validates user identity and authorization, and processes request.

Database Servers

■ Windows Datacenter Server
■ SQL Server

Web Server Farm

■ Windows Advanced Server
■ Internet Information Server

③ Database server updates RFQ status as "published."

⑤ Application servers notify suppliers of the new RFQ via e-mail.

④ Transactions and user activity logged for billing and marketing purposes.

Storage-Area Network

Databases

Back-Office Application Servers

■ Windows Advanced Server cluster
■ J.D. Edwards OneWorld ERP software
■ Siebel Systems CRM software

FIGURE 9.3

The hardware, software, network, and database components and IT architecture of B2B online auctions provider FreeMarkets Inc. are illustrated in this example of its Internet-based QuickSource auction service.

which gives an example of the technology resources required by many e-commerce systems. The figure illustrates some of the hardware, software, data, and network components used by FreeMarkets Inc. to provide business-to-business (B2B) online auction e-commerce services.

Forrester: Web 2.0 Has a Bright Future	As a standard enterprise tool, Web 2.0 has a bright future, one for which companies are expected to spend $4.6 billion by 2013 to integrate into their corporate computing environments, according to a Forrester Research report. Although still considered an upstart technology, Forrester believes that conventional Web 2.0 elements—social networking, RSS, blogs, wikis, mashups, podcasting, and widgets—are fast becoming the norm for communicating with employees and customers. The report highlights megacompanies such as General Motors, McDonald's, Northwestern Mutual Life Insurance, and Wells Fargo among those who have already jumped into the Web 2.0 pool with both feet. In addition, some 56 percent of North American and European enterprises consider Web 2.0 to be a priority.

"If I wanted to be anywhere in the Web 2.0 economy, I'd want to be on the enterprise side," says report author and Forrester Research analyst Oliver Young. "We're seeing enterprise-class software coming from startups, but we're seeing them through very low price points . . . so it [Web 2.0] will never be a mega market," says Young. "It will eventually disappear into the fabric of the enterprise, despite the major effects the technology will have on how businesses market their products and optimize their workforces."

The consumer-facing ad-funded Web 2.0 sites like Facebook, MySpace, and Delicious will also have difficulty as similar technologies are incorporated into the enterprise. "Even Google is having a hard time selling the advertising," Young said. Still, start-ups have much to gain in pursuing the Web 2.0 world, such as understanding how companies are adopting their technology. Small groups within a company are more likely to adopt blogs, wikis, mashups, and widgets. The key to adoption, he adds, is to show how there is a business value in using the Web 2.0 tools. "Web 2.0 is not a critical 'must have' for any company at this point, but it's more than likely that your competition is using it and is showing faster results because of it." |

SOURCE: Michael Singer, "Web 2.0: Companies Will Spend $4.6 Billion by 2013, Forrester Predicts," *InformationWeek*, April 21, 2008.

Categories of e-Commerce

Many companies today are participating in or sponsoring four basic categories of e-commerce applications: ***business-to-consumer, business-to-business, consumer-to-consumer*** and business-to-government e-commerce. Note: We do not explicitly cover business-to-government (B2G) and *e-government* applications because they are beyond the scope of this text, but many e-commerce concepts apply to such applications.

BUSINESS-TO-CONSUMER (B2C) e-COMMERCE. In this form of e-commerce, businesses must develop attractive electronic marketplaces to sell products and services to consumers. For example, many companies offer e-commerce Web sites that provide virtual storefronts and multimedia catalogs, interactive order processing, secure electronic payment systems, and online customer support. The B2C marketplace is growing like a wildfire but still remains the tip of the iceberg when compared with all online commerce.

CONSUMER-TO-CONSUMER (C2C) e-COMMERCE. The huge success of online auctions like eBay, where consumers (as well as businesses) can buy from and sell to one another in an auction process at an auction Web site, makes this e-commerce model an important e-commerce business strategy. Thus, participating in or sponsoring consumer or business auctions is an important e-commerce alternative for B2C, C2B (consumer-to-business), or B2B e-commerce. Electronic personal advertising of products or services to buy or sell by consumers at electronic newspaper sites, consumer e-commerce portals, or personal Web sites is also an important form of C2C e-commerce.

BUSINESS-TO-BUSINESS (B2B) e-COMMERCE. If B2C activities are the tip of the iceberg, B2B represents the part of the iceberg that is under the water—the biggest part. This category of e-commerce involves both e-business marketplaces and direct market links between businesses. For example, many companies offer secure Internet or extranet e-commerce catalog Web sites for their business customers and suppliers. Also very important are B2B e-commerce portals that provide auction and exchange marketplaces for businesses. Others may rely on electronic data interchange (EDI) via the Internet or extranets for computer-to-computer exchange of e-commerce documents with their larger business customers and suppliers.

The essential *e-commerce processes* required for the successful operation and management of e-commerce activities are illustrated in Figure 9.4. This figure outlines the nine key components of an *e-commerce process architecture* that is the foundation of the e-commerce initiatives of many companies today. We concentrate on the role these processes play in e-commerce systems, but you should recognize that many of these components may also be used in internal, noncommerce e-business applications. An example would be an intranet-based human resource system used by a company's employees, which might use all but the catalog management and product payment processes shown in Figure 9.4. Let's take a brief look at each essential process category.

FIGURE 9.4

This e-commerce process architecture highlights nine essential categories of e-commerce processes.

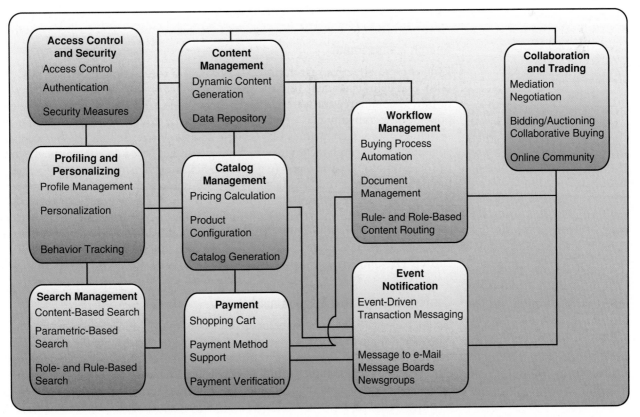

Access Control and Security

E-commerce processes must establish mutual trust and secure access between the parties in an e-commerce transaction by authenticating users, authorizing access, and enforcing security features. For example, these processes establish that a customer and e-commerce site are who they say they are through user names and passwords, encryption keys, or digital certificates and signatures. The e-commerce site must then authorize access to only those parts of the site that an individual user needs to accomplish his or her particular transactions. Thus, you usually will be given access to all resources of an e-commerce site except for other people's accounts, restricted company data, and Web master administration areas. Companies engaged in B2B e-commerce may rely on secure industry exchanges for procuring goods and services or Web trading portals that allow only registered customers to access trading information and applications. Other security processes protect the resources of e-commerce sites from threats such as hacker attacks, theft of passwords or credit card numbers, and system failures. We discuss many of these security threats and features in Chapter 13.

Profiling and Personalizing

Once you have gained access to an e-commerce site, profiling processes can occur that gather data on you and your Web site behavior and choices, as well as build electronic profiles of your characteristics and preferences. User profiles are developed using profiling tools such as user registration, cookie files, Web site behavior tracking software, and user feedback. These profiles are then used to recognize you as an individual user and provide you with a personalized view of the contents of the site, as well as product recommendations and personalized Web advertising as part of a *one-to-one marketing* strategy. Profiling processes are also used to help authenticate your identity for account management and payment purposes and gather data for customer relationship management, marketing planning, and Web site management. Some of the ethical issues in user profiling are discussed in Chapter 13.

Search Management

Efficient and effective search processes provide a top e-commerce Web site capability that helps customers find the specific product or service they want to evaluate or buy. E-commerce software packages can include a Web site search engine component, or a company may acquire a customized e-commerce search engine from search technology companies like Google and Requisite. Search engines may use a combination of search techniques, including searches based on content (e.g., a product description) or parameters (e.g., above, below, or between a range of values for multiple properties of a product). While we tend to think of Google, Yahoo, or Bing when we think of search engines, currently there are more than 30 search engines on the Internet that perform functions that are unique to a particular search need. Try checking out *ChaCha, Faroo, Blekko, Dogpile* or *DuckDuckGo*. You can even search at *Gigablast*, which has more than 200 billion pages and is powered entirely via wind energy!

Content and Catalog Management

Content management software helps e-commerce companies develop, generate, deliver, update, and archive text data and multimedia information at e-commerce Web sites. For example, German media giant Bertelsmann, part owner of BarnesandNoble.com, uses StoryServer content manager software to generate Web page templates that enable online editors from six international offices to easily publish and update book reviews and other product information, which are sold (syndicated) to other e-commerce sites.

E-commerce content frequently takes the form of multimedia catalogs of product information. As such, generating and managing catalog content is a major subset of content management, or catalog management. For example, W.W. Grainger & Co., a multibillion-dollar industrial parts distributor, uses the CenterStage catalog management software suite to retrieve data from more than 2,000 supplier databases, standardize the data, translate it into HTML or XML for Web use, and organize and enhance the data for speedy delivery as multimedia Web pages at its www.grainger.com Web site. At K and G Cycles, a large online motorcycle parts and accessories retailer, more than 250,000 products organized into more than 5,000 categories are managed via X-Cart software such that customers can find whatever they are looking for in four clicks or less (www.kandgcycles.com)!

Content and catalog management software works with the profiling tools we mentioned previously to personalize the content of Web pages seen by individual users. For example, Travelocity.com uses OnDisplay content manager software to push personalized promotional information about other travel opportunities to users while they are involved in an online travel-related transaction.

Finally, content and catalog management may be expanded to include *product configuration* processes that support Web-based customer self-service and the *mass customization* of a company's products. Configuration software helps online customers select the optimum feasible set of product features that can be included in a finished product. For example, both Dell Computer and Cisco Systems use configuration software to sell built-to-order computers and network processors to their online customers.

e-Commerce Tools to Close the Deal

Nothing is as heart-wrenching to an e-tailer as watching a customer abandon a full cart just seconds before consummating the deal. To be so close yet so cashless is more than frustrating; it's harmful to an e-tailer's health. A virtual armory of tools are in use to woo, cajole, prompt, and push consumers to make the buy—but are they working, or are they turning even more customers away?

"Most fall woefully short," says Matthew Brown, senior director of e-commerce and interactive marketing at MarketNet. "Instead of focusing on using tools and technologies to help the customer, much more thought and time needs to go into Web site architecture in the first place."

Many theories are being tossed about as to why consumers turn fickle a hair short of the finish line. For each theory, there are a multitude of technological solutions. "Retailers continue to launch and test technologies and features aimed at reducing abandonment or increasing online conversion," says Jessica Ried, a director of retail strategy at Resource Interactive. "In our experience, it is difficult to know for sure if any particular one is going to be effective for a given retailer without testing it with that retailer's customer base, or at least having a solid understanding of existing customer behaviors on the site through site analytics and surveys."

Once an e-tailer understands the true obstacles to closing the deal, there are a range of tools available to clear the way to bigger profits. The most commonly deployed are live chat, pop-up discounts, and follow-up e-mail programs; some are achieved through the standard use of cookies, others via pixel-based triggers. Third-person endorsements are also frequently used. "Hosting consumer-generated content such as ratings and reviews has typically allowed retailers to improve conversions," explains Ried, "as customers are more confident with their selections. That's because they have access to an 'unbiased' opinion, building trust rather than having to rely solely on the marketing copy on the retailer's site."

"We use Liveperson chat extensively. It has been an incredible tool for answering any last-minute doubts during the last few states of the transaction," notes Adrian Salamunovic, cofounder of DNA 11, a multimillion-dollar e-commerce art retailer. "Our average transaction is over US$500, so this is very important to us."

"It pays for itself many times over each month," he adds. "For us, interrupting the client with pop-ups or invitations to chat really doesn't work—in fact, it does the opposite. We've watched customers bounce (exit) quite quickly after being interrupted with pop-ups."

Therein lies the conundrum. No two customers are identical. At least some personalized customization is essential. There is a point, however, at which actions considered helpful by the retailer are perceived as intrusive by the consumer. "Some customers welcome the help; others are unnerved by the Big Brother effect it can suggest," says Resource Interactive's Ried. "Start by considering what is known about consumer behavior in evaluating which technologies, features, and functionalities to explore first."

SOURCE: Pam Baker, "Rescuing the e-Commerce Deal When the Customer's Walking Way," *E-Commerce Times*, April 24, 2009.

Workflow Management

Many of the business processes in e-commerce applications can be managed and partially automated with the help of *workflow management* software. E-business workflow systems for enterprise collaboration help employees electronically collaborate to accomplish structured work tasks within knowledge-based business processes. Workflow management in both e-business and e-commerce depends on a *workflow software engine* containing software models of the business processes to be accomplished. The workflow models express the predefined sets of business rules, roles of stakeholders, authorization requirements, routing alternatives, databases used, and sequence of tasks required for each e-commerce process. Thus, workflow systems ensure that the proper transactions, decisions, and work activities are performed, and the correct data and documents are routed to the right employees, customers, suppliers, and other business stakeholders.

As many of you begin your business careers, you will be charged with the responsibility of driving cost out of existing business processes while maintaining or improving

FIGURE 9.5

The PleoWorld site serves as the only interface with which customers work, whereas, behind the scenes, the company and its two partners orchestrate the order-fulfillment process.

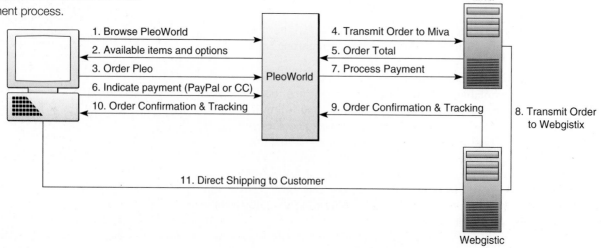

the effectiveness of those processes. As you continue to acquire a greater appreciation for, and understanding of, how technology can benefit business, you will explore work-flow management as the key to this optimization of cost and effectiveness throughout the business.

For example, Figure 9.5 illustrates the e-commerce processes of the PleoWorld site by Innvo Labs. Customers use this site to browse, choose, and order the anima-tronic dinosaur toy Pleo, while partners Miva and Webgistix take care of order valida-tion, billing, and payments—including those in foreign currency—and direct shipping to the customer, all happening behind the interface of the PleoWorld site. Making all these processes transparent to the customer was a major design consideration.

Pleo is an animatronic dinosaur toy designed to emulate the appearance and imagined behavior of a week-old baby Camarasaurus. Created and designed by the inventor of the Furby, this particular species was chosen because its relatively large cranium provided the ideal place to hide the various sensors and motors necessary for its operation. Each individual unit would learn from its unique experiences and would, over time, develop its own personality. It was manufactured and distributed by a company called Ugobe, which went bankrupt in 2008. In 2009, Innvo Labs Corporation was formed and acquired the rights to the toy.

Under Ugobe, orders were placed through a Web site, with order fulfill-ment performed manually at a central location on an order-by-order basis, which significantly slowed down deliveries. Rather, the new owner wanted a process that would be as much "hands-off" as possible, from order to delivery. In addition, the new Web site would need to support international deliveries, order customization, and membership in the site, which allowed registered users to receive news, software updates, and other information. To address fraud concerns associated with international orders, buyer authentication and foreign currency processing were also implemented behind the scenes.

"The most successful e-commerce stores follow a conservative approach to design. The PleoWorld site does that, and allows for shoppers to have a seamless, simple and secure shopping process that promotes a high conversion rate," says Rick Wilson, executive vice president at Miva Merchant, the plat-form vendor selected to run the new site. Another company involved in the project was Webgistix, which provided automated order fulfillment. One key aspect of the site is that as the transaction is processed, customers always stay within the PleoWorld environment; they are not bounced from interface to interface to complete all the steps, which don't require user input. Figure 9.5 shows the complete sequence of steps in more detail.

Since the site went live in 2009, more than 20,000 member registrations have been received, including 7,500 existing Pleo owners who reregistered their existing units. In 2010, Innvo Labs launched a second-generation version, the Pleo rb, which, among other things, snores while it sleeps.

Innvo Labs: Automated e-Commerce Processes

SOURCE: "Innvo Labs—How PleoWorld's Ecommerce Runs Itself," Planetmagpie Case Study, October 2010.

Event Notification

Most e-commerce applications are *event-driven* systems that respond to a multitude of events—from a new customer's first Web site access, to payment and delivery pro-cesses, to innumerable customer relationship and supply chain management activities. That is why event notification processes play an important role in e-commerce systems;

customers, suppliers, employees, and other stakeholders must be notified of all events that might affect their status in a transaction. ***Event notification*** software works with workflow management software to monitor all e-commerce processes and record all relevant events, including unexpected changes or problem situations. Then it works with user-profiling software to notify all involved stakeholders automatically of important transaction events using appropriate user-preferred methods of electronic messaging, such as e-mail, newsgroup, pager, and fax communications. This notification includes a company's management, who then can monitor their employees' responsiveness to e-commerce events and customer and supplier feedback.

For example, when you purchase a product at a retail e-commerce Web site like Amazon.com, you automatically receive an e-mail record of your order. Then you may receive e-mail notifications of any change in product availability or shipment status and, finally, an e-mail message notifying you that your order has been shipped and is complete. This type of event notification uses a software application referred to as an *autoresponder*. As events occur, the autoresponder application is triggered to send a particular email or notice to the customer. Autoresponder events can be timed such that a single event can trigger a series of messages set to be sent a specific intervals in the future.

Collaboration and Trading

This major category of e-commerce processes consists of those that support the vital collaboration arrangements and trading services needed by customers, suppliers, and other stakeholders to accomplish e-commerce transactions. Thus, in Chapter 2, we discussed how a customer-focused e-business uses tools such as e-mail, chat systems, and discussion groups to nurture online *communities of interest* among employees and customers to enhance customer service and build customer loyalty in e-commerce. The essential collaboration among business trading partners in e-commerce may also be provided by Internet-based trading services. For example, B2B e-commerce Web portals provided by companies like Ariba and Commerce One support matchmaking, negotiation, and mediation processes among business buyers and sellers. In addition, B2B e-commerce is heavily dependent on Internet-based trading platforms and portals that provide online exchange and auctions for e-business enterprises. Therefore, the online auctions and exchanges developed by companies like FreeMarkets are revolutionizing the procurement processes of many major corporations. We will discuss these and other e-commerce applications later in the chapter.

ELECTRONIC PAYMENT PROCESSES
LO 9-2

Payment for the products and services purchased is an obvious and vital set of processes in e-commerce transactions. Payment processes, however, are not simple because of the nearly anonymous electronic nature of transactions taking place between the networked computer systems of buyers and sellers and the many security issues involved. E-commerce payment processes are also complex because of the wide variety of debit and credit alternatives, as well as the financial institutions and intermediaries that may be part of the process. Therefore, a variety of ***electronic payment systems*** have evolved over time. In addition, new payment systems are being developed and tested to meet the security and technical challenges of e-commerce over the Internet.

Web Payment Processes

Most e-commerce systems on the Web involving businesses and consumers (B2C) depend on credit card payment processes, but many B2B e-commerce systems rely on more complex payment processes based on the use of purchase orders, as was illustrated in Figure 9.5. However, both types of e-commerce typically use an electronic

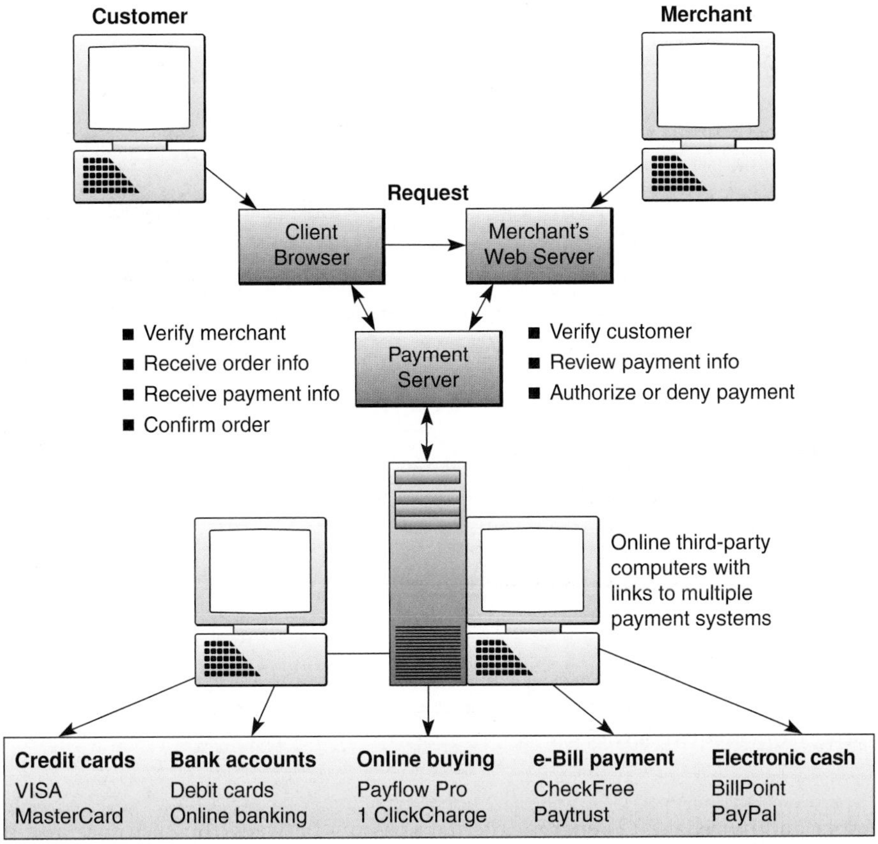

FIGURE 9.6
An example of a secure
electronic payment system with
many payment alternatives.

shopping cart process, which enables customers to select products from Web site catalog displays and temporarily put them in a virtual shopping basket for later checkout and processing. Figure 9.6 illustrates and summarizes a B2C electronic payment system with several payment alternatives.

Electronic Funds Transfer

Electronic funds transfer (EFT) systems are a major form of electronic payment systems in banking and retailing industries. EFT systems use a variety of information technologies to capture and process money and credit transfers between banks and businesses and their customers. For example, banking networks support teller terminals at all bank offices and automated teller machines (ATMs) at locations throughout the world. Banks, credit card companies, and other businesses may support pay-by-phone services. Very popular also are Web-based payment services, such as PayPal and BillPoint for cash transfers, and CheckFree and Paytrust for automatic bill payment, that enable the customers of banks and other bill payment services to use the Internet to pay bills electronically. In addition, most point-of-sale terminals in retail stores are networked to bank EFT systems, which makes it possible for you to use a credit card or debit card to pay instantly for gas, groceries, or other purchases at participating retail outlets.

Secure Electronic Payments

When you make an online purchase on the Internet, your credit card information is vulnerable to interception by *network sniffers*, software that easily recognizes credit card number formats. Several basic security measures are being used to solve this security problem: (1) encrypt (code and scramble) the data passing between the

SOURCE: Courtesy of VeriSign Inc.

customer and merchant, (2) encrypt the data passing between the customer and the company authorizing the credit card transaction, or (3) take sensitive information off-line. Note: Because encryption and other security issues are discussed in Chapter 13, we will not explain how they work in this section.

For example, many companies use the Secure Socket Layer (SSL) security method originally developed by Netscape Communications that automatically encrypts data passing between your Web browser and a merchant's server. However, sensitive information is still vulnerable to misuse once it's decrypted (decoded and unscrambled) and stored on a merchant's server, so a digital wallet payment system was developed. In this method, you add security software add-on modules to your Web browser. That enables your browser to encrypt your credit card data in such a way that only the bank that authorizes credit card transactions for the merchant gets to see it. All the merchant is told is whether your credit card transaction is approved or not.

The Secure Electronic Transaction (SET) standard for electronic payment security extends this digital wallet approach. In this method, software encrypts a digital envelope of digital certificates specifying the payment details for each transaction. VISA, MasterCard, IBM, Microsoft, Netscape, and most other industry players have agreed to SET. Therefore, a system like SET may become the standard for secure electronic payments on the Internet. See Figure 9.7.

e-Commerce Applications and Issues

E-commerce is here to stay. The Web and e-commerce are key industry drivers. It's changed how many companies do business. It's created new channels for our customers. Companies are at the e-commerce crossroads, and there are many ways to go.

Thus, e-commerce is now defining how companies do business both internally and externally with their customers, suppliers, and other business partners. As managers confront a variety of e-commerce alternatives, the way companies apply e-commerce to their businesses is also subject to change. The applications of e-commerce by many companies have gone through several major stages as e-commerce matures in the world of business. For example, e-commerce between businesses and consumers (B2C) moved from merely offering multimedia company information at corporate Web sites (*brochureware*) to offering products and services at Web storefront sites via electronic catalogs and online sales transactions. B2B e-commerce, in contrast, started with Web site support to help business customers serve themselves, and then moved toward automating intranet and extranet procurement systems. One of the most important things to understand about e-commerce is that by converting a business model from bricks and mortar to an e-commerce approach, the transaction costs (i.e., the costs of doing business with a customer or supplier) drop dramatically. Thus, anything that can be digital will be digital. See Figure 9.8.

e-Commerce Trends

Figure 9.9 illustrates some of the trends taking place in the e-commerce applications that we introduced earlier in the chapter. Notice how B2C e-commerce moves from simple Web storefronts to interactive marketing capabilities that provide a personalized shopping experience for customers, and then toward a totally integrated Web store that supports a variety of customer shopping experiences. B2C e-commerce is also moving toward a self-service model in which customers configure and customize the products and services they wish to buy, aided by configuration software and online customer support as needed.

B2B e-commerce participants moved quickly from self-service on the Web to configuration and customization capabilities and extranets connecting trading partners. As B2C e-commerce moves toward full-service and wide-selection retail Web portals, the trend for B2B is toward the use of e-commerce portals that provide catalog, exchange,

SOURCE: © Digital Vision/PunchStock.

FIGURE 9.8
Online opinion leaders may be tapping into underlying trends that are critical to marketers.

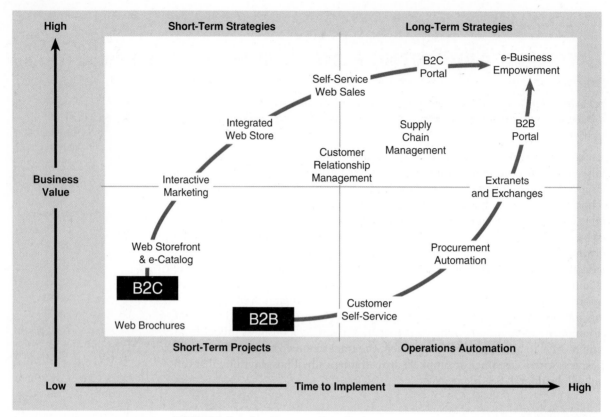

FIGURE 9.9

Trends in B2C and B2B e-commerce, and the business strategies and value driving these trends.

SOURCE: Jonathan Rosenoer, Douglas Armstrong, and J. Russell Gates, *The Clickable Corporation: Successful Strategies for Capturing the Internet Advantage* (New York: The Free Press, 1999), p. 24.

and auction markets for business customers within or across industries. Of course, both of these trends are enabled by e-business capabilities like customer relationship management and supply chain management, which are the hallmarks of the customer-focused and inter-networked supply chains of a fully e-business–enabled company.

BUSINESS-TO-CONSUMER e-COMMERCE

LO 9-3
LO 9-4

E-commerce applications that focus on the consumer share an important goal: to attract potential buyers, transact goods and services, and build customer loyalty through individual courteous treatment and engaging community features.

What does it take to create a successful B2C e-commerce business venture? That's the question that many are asking in the wake of the failures of many pure B2C *dot-com* companies. One obvious answer would be to create a Web business initiative that offers attractive products or services of great customer value, with a business plan based on realistic forecasts of profitability within the first year or two of operation—a condition that was lacking in many failed dot-coms. Such failures, however, have not stemmed the tide of millions of businesses, both large and small, that are moving at least part of their business to the Web. So let's take a look at some essential success factors and Web site capabilities for companies engaged in either B2C or B2B e-commerce. Figure 9.10 provides examples of a few top-rated retail Web companies.

e-Commerce Success Factors

On the Internet, the barriers of time, distance, and form are broken down, and businesses are able to transact the sale of goods and services 24 hours a day, 7 days a week, 365 days a year with consumers all over the world. In certain cases, it is even possible to convert a physical good (CDs, packaged software, a newspaper) to a virtual good (MP3 audio, downloadable software, information in HTML format).

FIGURE 9.10

Examples of a few top-rated
retail Web sites.

Top Retail Web Sites

- **Amazon.com** $34.20B 2010 Web sales volume   **www.amazon.com**
  Amazon.com is the exception to the rule that consumers prefer to shop "real world"
  retailers online. The mother of all shopping sites, Amazon features a vast selection of
  books, videos, DVDs, CDs, toys, kitchen items, electronics, and even home and garden
  goods sold to millions of loyal customers.

- **Staples, Inc.** $9.8B 2010 Web sales volume   **www.staples.com**
  Staples tops the "Big 3" office supply giants in terms of Internet sales, although Office
  Depot and OfficeMax are also members of the top 10 retail Web sites list. Consumers
  can access the entire catalog online and can have their purchases delivered to their
  home or office within 24 hours and often within the same business day.

- **Dell, Inc.** $4.5B 2010 Web sales volume   **www.dell.com**
  Dell has created an online shopping experience for their customers that makes buying
  and configuring a computer system to meet a specific need almost effortless.

- **Apple, Inc.** $4.25B 2010 Web sales volume   **www.apple.com**
  Apple has captured the world with the iPod, iPhone, and iPad. 2011 is expected to be a
  great year for Apple with an estimated 50 million iPhones being sold.

A basic fact of Internet retailing is that all retail Web sites are created equal as far
as the "location, location, location" imperative of success in retailing is concerned. No
site is any closer to its Web customers, and competitors offering similar goods and
services may be only a mouse click away. This scenario makes it vital that businesses
find ways to build customer satisfaction, loyalty, and relationships so that customers
keep coming back to their Web stores. Thus, the key to e-tail (retail business conducted online) success is to optimize several key factors, such as *selection and value,
performance and service efficiency, the look and feel of the site, advertising and incentives to
purchase, personal attention, community relationships,* and *security and reliability.* Let's
briefly examine each of these factors that are essential to the success of a B2C Web
business. See Figure 9.11.

SELECTION AND VALUE. Obviously, a business must offer Web shoppers a good selection of attractive products and services at competitive prices, or the shoppers will
quickly click away from a Web store. However, a company's prices don't have to be

FIGURE 9.11

Some of the key factors for
success in e-commerce.

e-Commerce Success Factors

- **Selection and Value.** Attractive product selections, competitive prices, satisfaction
  guarantees, and customer support after the sale.

- **Performance and Service.** Fast and easy navigation, shopping, and purchasing, and
  prompt shipping and delivery.

- **Look and Feel.** Attractive Web storefront, Web site shopping areas, multimedia product
  catalog pages, and shopping features.

- **Advertising and Incentives.** Targeted Web page advertising and e-mail promotions,
  discounts, and special offers, including advertising at affiliate sites.

- **Personal Attention.** Personal Web pages, personalized product recommendations,
  Web advertising and e-mail notices, and interactive support (online chat, Skype, and so
  forth) for all customers.

- **Community Relationships.** Virtual communities of customers, suppliers, company
  representatives, and others via newsgroups, chat rooms, and links to related sites.

- **Security and Reliability.** Security of customer information and Web site transactions,
  trustworthy product information, and reliable order fulfillment.

- **Great Customer Communication.** Easy-to-find contact information, online order status,
  product support specialists.

the lowest on the Web if it builds a reputation for high-quality, guaranteed satisfaction and top customer support while shopping and after the sale. For example, top-rated e-tailer REI.com helps you select quality outdoor gear for hiking and other activities with a "How to Choose" section and gives a money-back guarantee on your purchases.

PERFORMANCE AND SERVICE. People don't want to be kept waiting when browsing, selecting, or paying in a Web store. A site must be efficiently designed for ease of access, shopping, and buying, with sufficient server power and network capacity to support Web site traffic. Web shopping and customer service must also be friendly and helpful, as well as quick and easy. In addition, products offered should be available in inventory for prompt shipment to the customer.

LOOK AND FEEL. B2C sites can offer customers an attractive Web storefront, shopping areas, and multimedia product catalogs. These could range from an exciting shopping experience with audio, video, and moving graphics to a more simple and comfortable look and feel. Thus, most retail e-commerce sites let customers browse product sections, select products, drop them into a virtual shopping cart, and go to a virtual checkout station when they are ready to pay for their order.

ADVERTISING AND INCENTIVES. Some Web stores may advertise in traditional media, but most advertise on the Web with targeted and personalized banner ads and other Web page and e-mail promotions. Most B2C sites also offer shoppers incentives to buy and return. Typically, these incentives mean coupons, discounts, special offers, and vouchers for other Web services, sometimes with other e-tailers at cross-linked Web sites. Many Web stores also increase their market reach by being part of Web banner advertising exchange programs with thousands of other Web retailers. Figure 9.12 compares major marketing communications choices in traditional and e-commerce marketing to support each step of the buying process.

PERSONAL ATTENTION. Personalizing your shopping experience encourages you to buy and make return visits. Thus, e-commerce software can automatically record details of your visits and build user profiles for you and other Web shoppers. Many sites also encourage you to register with them and fill out a personal interest profile. Then, whenever you return, you are welcomed by name or with a personal Web page, greeted with special offers, and guided to those parts of the site in which you are most interested. This *one-to-one marketing* and relationship-building power is one of the major advantages of personalized Web retailing.

FIGURE 9.12

How traditional and Web marketing communications differ in supporting each step of the buying process.

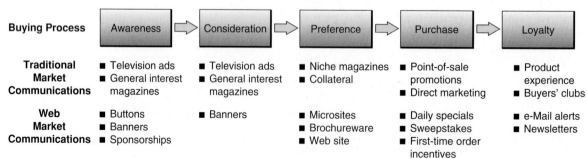

Buying Process	Awareness	Consideration	Preference	Purchase	Loyalty
Traditional Market Communications	■ Television ads ■ General interest magazines	■ Television ads ■ General interest magazines	■ Niche magazines ■ Collateral	■ Point-of-sale promotions ■ Direct marketing	■ Product experience ■ Buyers' clubs
Web Market Communications	■ Buttons ■ Banners ■ Sponsorships	■ Banners	■ Microsites ■ Brochureware ■ Web site	■ Daily specials ■ Sweepstakes ■ First-time order incentives	■ e-Mail alerts ■ Newsletters

COMMUNITY RELATIONSHIPS. Giving online customers with special interests a feeling of belonging to a unique group of like-minded individuals helps build customer loyalty and value. Thus, Web site relationship and affinity marketing programs build and promote virtual communities of customers, suppliers, company representatives, and others via a variety of Web-based collaboration tools. Examples include discussion forums or newsgroups, chat rooms, message board systems, and cross-links to related Web site communities.

SECURITY AND RELIABILITY. As a customer of a successful Web store, you must feel confident that your credit card, personal information, and details of your transactions are secure from unauthorized use. You must also feel that you are dealing with a trustworthy business whose products and other Web site information you can trust to be as advertised. Having your orders filled and shipped as you requested, in the time frame promised, and with good customer support are other measures of an e-tailer's reliability.

GREAT CUSTOMER COMMUNICATIONS. As more consumers shift their habits from the traditional brick-and-mortar approach to an online shopping experience, one thing becomes even more important than ever: the need for constant and informative communication channels with the customer. Despite the conveniences associated with online shopping, consumers still have questions that need to be answered by a human being. Issues ranging from product information to order status or modification are often still handled the "old fashioned way." K and G Cycles, the large online motorcycle parts and accessories retailer, provides telephone, live chat space, and Skype access to customer representatives who will even help you pick out your purchases in real time.

Amazon.com: Partnering and Leveraging Infrastructure

Amazon.com has just launched an application on Facebook that enables members of the social network to buy gifts for each other based on wish lists registered with the online retailer. *Amazon Giver* also provides Facebook members with the option of viewing suggested items for friends based on interests listed on their profile pages. A second Facebook application, *Amazon Grapevine*, provides a news feed of friends' activity on Amazon, such as when they update their wish lists, write reviews, or tag products. Both applications share information only with Facebook members who have opted in to the service.

"By combining Amazon's vast selection of products with Facebook's millions of users, we are able to make activities like gift-giving more efficient and rewarding for Facebook users," says Eva Manolis, vice president of Amazon.

By adding the *Amazon Giver* application to their profile, Facebook members get the option of clicking directly to a secure Amazon checkout page. If the recipient has a wish list, then Amazon can ship the item without the buyer entering a shipping address, which would already be on file. In order for people to view a wish list, it would have to be set as "public." With *Amazon Grapevine*, people have the option to choose what type of activity they would be willing to share with friends through the news feed. Activity updates are entirely opt-in.

Amazon.com has also introduced a new way for online merchants to leverage Amazon's infrastructure to ship physical products. "The *Amazon Fulfillment Web Service* (Amazon FWS) allows merchants to tap in to Amazon's network of fulfillment centers and our expertise in logistics," says Amazon Web

Services evangelist Jeff Barr. "Merchants can store their own products to our fulfillment centers and then, using a simple Web service interface, fulfill orders for the products."

Amazon FWS is designed to complement *Fulfillment By Amazon* (FBA), the fulfillment service Amazon has offered since 2006, by making the fulfillment process accessible programmatically. Amazon also maintains a separate fulfillment program called *Amazon Advantage*, which allows content publishers to send Amazon music, books, and videos for sale on consignment, with a 55 percent fee.

The idea, Barr explains, is to be able to ship a product with a simple Web service call. By making it possible for merchants to further automate their e-commerce and fulfillment efforts, Amazon is demonstrating its commitment to selling "muck," as CEO Jeff Bezos has referred to his company's e-commerce infrastructure.

SOURCE: Antone Gonsalves, "Amazon.com Launches Shopping Apps on Facebook," *InformationWeek*, March 13, 2008; and Thomas Claburn, "Amazon Introduces Fulfillment Web Service," *InformationWeek*, March 20, 2008.

WEB STORE REQUIREMENTS
LO 9-3

FIGURE 9.13

To develop a successful e-commerce business, these Web store requirements must be implemented by a company or its Web site hosting service.

Most business-to-consumer e-commerce ventures take the form of retail business sites on the World Wide Web. Whether a huge retail Web portal like Amazon.com or a small specialty Web retailer, the primary focus of such e-tailers is to develop, operate, and manage their Web sites so they become high-priority destinations for consumers who will repeatedly choose to go there to buy products and services. Thus, these Web sites must be able to demonstrate the key factors for e-commerce success that we have just covered. In this section, let's discuss the essential Web store requirements that you would have to implement to support a successful retail business on the Web, as summarized and illustrated in Figure 9.13.

Developing a Web Store	
Build	**Market**
Web site design tools	Web page advertising
Site design templates	E-mail promotions
Custom design services	Web advertising exchanges with affiliate sites
Web site hosting	Search engine registrations and optimization

Serving Your Customers		
Serve	**Transact**	**Support**
Personalized Web pages	Flexible order process	Web site online help
Dynamic multimedia catalog	Credit card processing	Customer service e-mail
Catalog search engine	Shipping and tax calculations	Discussion groups and chat rooms
Integrated shopping cart	E-mail order notifications	Links to related sites

Managing a Web Store		
Manage	**Operate**	**Protect**
Web site usage statistics	24×7 Web site hosting	User password protection
Sales and inventory reports	Online tech support	Encrypted order processing
Customer account management	Scalable network capacity	Encrypted Web site administration
Links to accounting system	Redundant servers and power	Network firewalls and security monitors

Stork Craft Manufacturing Inc. ("Stork Craft") is an industry leader in the design, manufacture, and distribution of juvenile products. Stork Craft is one of the world's leading juvenile furniture manufacturers. Founded more than 60 years ago in Vancouver, Canada, the company started with its founder selling hand-crafted furniture out of his basement. Over the years it has racked up a number of awards, including the Ernst & Young Entrepreneur of the Year award in 2006, the Sears Supplier of the Year in 2007, and a finalist to Canada's Best Managed Companies in 2008.

Stork Craft has had a retail and distribution partnership with Wal-Mart for the United States and Canada since 2005, with both companies jointly developing a Web site to purchase Stork Craft products in the United States in 2006. The initiative proved very profitable to the company, which was able to acquire its three main competitors in a span of 18 months. In 2008, the goal was to develop a similar partnership with Wal-Mart Canada, with similar results, Stork Craft hoped.

The driving force behind the project was Irene Jeremic, then corporate executive advisor and chief information officer for Stork Craft. "It is not often that you have a business-to-business partner trying to cater to the general public," says Jeremic. "The fact that Wal-Mart was open to this was perhaps the biggest factor in getting the site to work."

Up to then, interested customers could only browse, but not purchase, Stork Craft products through the Web site of Wal-Mart Canada. After assembling a cross-functional team with executives from both companies, Stork Craft's IT group built the entire technology platform, which included a Web site in which Wal-Mart Canada customers could shop, as well as management and administrative functionality. In addition, instead of shipping to Wal-Mart Canada, which in turn would ship to the end customers, Stork Craft agreed to ship its products directly to the final consumers, as well as provide direct-sale support such as handling returns and warranty and service inquiries. As an alternative to in-store sales of Stork Craft products at Wal-Mart stores, the online sale plus direct shipping alternative allowed Stork Craft to cut delivery times by up to 85 percent, as well as keep better control over the delivery process.

The co-branded site, where Wal-Mart Canada gets a portion of every sale made, went live in 2008 when shoppers could purchase more than 200 different cribs, tables, and toddler beds. Since then, more than 350,000 customers have visited the site, which is not an insignificant fraction of the total adult population of the country. Jeremic says the Web site has provided "great value" to both partners.

SOURCE: Matt Villano, "Ringing Up Baby," *CIO Magazine*, August 1, 2009, and www.storkcraftdirect.com, accessed May 30, 2011.

Getting Customers to Find You

Just because your Web store has been launched does not mean customers will come flocking to your cyber front door. Your Web store needs to be discovered by your customers, and this means getting listed in the popular search engines.

You can submit your Web site to search engines such as Yahoo, Google, Live, and others, and each will begin looking at your Web pages and listing you when appropriate search terms are entered. Waiting for your site to show up competitively ranked with all the other similar sites could take weeks and even months. There is a science to search engine ranking and it is an essential element in Web store success.

Search engine optimization (SEO) is considered a subset of search engine marketing, and it focuses on improving the number and/or quality of visitors to a Web site over "natural" (also called "organic" or "algorithmic" search engine) listings. The term SEO can also refer to search engine optimizers, an industry of consultants who carry out optimization projects on behalf of clients.

Search engines display different kinds of listings on a results page, including paid advertising in the form of pay-per-click (PPC) advertisements and paid inclusion listings, as well as unpaid organic search results and keyword-specific listings, such as news stories, definitions, map locations, and images. As an Internet marketing strategy, SEO considers how search engines work and what people search for.

Optimizing a Web site primarily involves editing its content and HTML coding, both to increase its relevance to specific keywords and to remove barriers to the indexing activities of search engines. Because SEO requires making changes to the source code of a site, it is often most effective when incorporated into the initial development and design of a site, leading to the use of the term *search engine friendly* to describe designs, menus, content management systems, and shopping carts that can be optimized easily and effectively.

A range of strategies and techniques are employed in SEO, including changes to a site's code (referred to as *inside SEO*) and getting links from other sites (referred to as *outside SEO*). These techniques include two broad categories: techniques that search engines recommend as part of good design, and those techniques that search engines do not approve of and attempt to minimize the effect of, referred to as spamdexing. Methods such as *link farms*, where a group of Web sites is set up so that all hyperlink to every other Web site in the group, and *keyword stuffing*, where a Web page is loaded with keywords in the meta tags or in content, are examples of techniques considered "black hat" SEO. Such techniques serve only to degrade both the relevance of search results and the user experience of search engines.

SEO, as a marketing strategy, can often generate a good return. However, as the search engines are not paid for the traffic they send from *organic search*, the algorithms used can and do change, and there are many factors that can cause search engine problems when crawling or ranking a site's pages. In contrast to black hat SEO techniques, *white hat SEO* requires a series of tools that constantly look at keywords and variants of search terms for specific items and then assist in the optimization of various pages on a website such that it shows up closer to the front of the pack when a specific set of search terms are entered. This activity can be very demanding when it comes to time and often small businesses must pay large sums of money to outside vendors specializing in SEO services. There are no guarantees of success, either in the short or long term. Because of the lack of guarantees and certainty, SEO is often compared to traditional public relations (PR), with PPC advertising closer to traditional advertising.

Serving Your Customers

Once your retail store is on the Web and receiving visitors, the Web site must help you welcome and serve them personally and efficiently so that they become loyal customers. So most e-tailers use several Web site tools to create user profiles, customer files, and personal Web pages and promotions that help them develop a one-to-one relationship with their customers. This effort includes creating incentives to encourage visitors to register, developing *Web cookie files* to identify returning visitors automatically, or contracting with Web site tracking companies like DoubleClick and others for software to record and analyze the details of the Web site behavior and preferences of Web shoppers automatically.

Of course, your Web site should have the look and feel of an attractive, friendly, and efficient Web store. That means having e-commerce features like a dynamically changing and updated multimedia catalog, a fast catalog search engine, and a convenient shopping cart system that is integrated with Web shopping, promotions, payment, shipping, and customer account information. Your e-commerce order processing software should be fast and able to adjust to personalized promotions and customer options like gift handling, special discounts, credit card or other payments, and shipping and tax alternatives.

Also, automatically sending your customers e-mail notices to document when orders are processed and shipped is a top customer service feature of e-tail transaction processing.

Providing customer support for your Web store is an essential Web site capability. Thus, many e-tail sites offer help menus, tutorials, and lists of FAQs (frequently asked questions) to provide self-help features for Web shoppers. Of course, e-mail correspondence with customer service representatives of your Web store offers more personal assistance to customers. Establishing Web site discussion groups and chat rooms where your customers and store personnel can interact helps create a more personal community that can provide invaluable support to customers, as well as build customer loyalty. Providing links to related Web sites from your Web store can help customers find additional information and resources, as well as earning commission income from the affiliate marketing programs of other Web retailers. For example, the Amazon.com affiliate program pays commissions of up to 15 percent for purchases made by Web shoppers clicking to its Web store from your site.

Managing a Web Store

A Web retail store must be managed as both a business and a Web site, and most e-commerce hosting companies offer software and services to help you do just that. For example, companies like FreeMerchant, Prodigy Biz, and Verio provide their hosting clients with a variety of management reports that record and analyze Web store traffic, inventory, and sales results. Other services build customer lists for e-mail and Web page promotions or provide customer relationship management features to help retain Web customers. Also, some e-commerce software includes links to download inventory and sales data into accounting packages like QuickBooks for bookkeeping and preparation of financial statements and reports.

Of course, Web-hosting companies must enable their Web store clients to be available online 24 hours a day and seven days a week all year. This availability requires them to build or contract for sufficient network capacity to handle peak Web traffic loads and redundant network servers and power sources to respond to system or power failures. Most hosting companies provide e-commerce software that uses passwords and encryption to protect Web store transactions and customer records, as well as to employ network firewalls and security monitors to repel hacker attacks and other security threats. Many hosting services also offer their clients 24-hour tech support to help them with any technical problems that arise. We will discuss these and other e-commerce security management issues in Chapter 13.

Luxury Goes Digital: Fashion House Embraces Online Shopping

Historically, luxury brands have been slow to embrace e-commerce. But in recent years, high-end retail sites like Net-a-Porter and Yoox, as well as discount luxury flash sales like those on Gilt Groupe and Rue La La, are forcing executives to rethink the benefits of online sales. Bain & Co. estimates that the $4.9 billion online luxury market grew by 20 percent in 2009.

Richemont, which owns luxury names like Cartier, Van Cleef & Arpels, Montblanc, and Jaeger-LeCoultre, has a 33 percent stake in Net-a-Porter and will buy the remaining 66 percent of the company, with founder Natalie Massenet remaining as the executive chairman. Richemont made the offer, valuing Net-a-Porter at $534 million.

Net-a-Porter, founded in 2000 by former fashion journalist Natalie Massenet, has been a forerunner in selling expensive designer women's clothes and accessories online. That is a space that was long overlooked by big luxury-goods houses like Richemont, Burberry PLC, and LVMH Moët Hennessy Louis Vuitton SA, which jumped on the online sales bandwagon far later than their lower-priced counterparts did.

With the acquisition of a successful luxury e-tailer—Net-a-Porter saw sales of $183 million in 2009—Richemont is clearly making a commitment to boosting its presence in the online luxury space. Just one month earlier, Cartier had launched its U.S. transactional site.

At the time, Cartier North America CEO Emmanuel Perrin acknowledged the importance of selling on the Web. "The Internet has been a medium taking an increasing part in our client's lifestyle and means of interaction," he says.

Being available online is no longer a stigma to luxury brands, and things like holograms allow them to help consumers identify authorized resellers online. High-end designers like Narciso Rodriguez and Norma Kamali have even created exclusive collections for eBay.

The big luxury brands have made digital retailing a higher priority, having recognized that shoppers are increasingly willing to buy very expensive products on the Web. But selling $1,000 dresses online is different from hawking groceries or secondhand books: Customers want an editorial element, a guiding hand to replace the in-store salesperson and signal what's in style, which is where Net-a-Porter has carved out its niche.

"It's just as much a magazine as it is a store," says Massenet. "That really has served us well, because when you're online you lose the offline experience of walking into a store."

Says Massenet, "Richemont has completely embraced our vision and strategy since they came on board as a shareholder and together we are going to continue to build the 21st-century model for luxury fashion retailing."

That model would be online shopping.

SOURCE: Anne C. Lee, "Luxury Goes Digital: Fashion House Richemont Embraces E-Commerce," *Fast Company*, April 1, 2010; and Paul Sonne, "Richemont to Buy Net-a-Porter," *The Wall Street Journal*, April 2, 2010.

BUSINESS-TO-BUSINESS e-COMMERCE
LO 9-4

Business-to-business e-commerce is the wholesale and supply side of the commercial process, where businesses buy, sell, or trade with other businesses. B2B e-commerce relies on many different information technologies, most of which are implemented at e-commerce Web sites on the World Wide Web and corporate intranets and extranets. B2B applications include electronic catalog systems, electronic trading systems such as exchange and auction portals, electronic data interchange, electronic funds transfers, and so on. All of the factors for building a successful retail Web site that we discussed previously also apply to wholesale Web sites for business-to-business e-commerce.

In addition, many businesses are integrating their Web-based e-commerce systems with their e-business systems for supply chain management, customer relationship management, and online transaction processing, as well as with their traditional, or legacy, computer-based accounting and business information systems. This integration ensures that all e-commerce activities are integrated with e-business processes and supported by up-to-date corporate inventory and other databases, which in turn are automatically updated by Web sales activities.

Avnet Tears Up the B2B e-Commerce Playbook

When does a global distributor of electronic components need to start operating more like Amazon.com and other consumer-focused companies? When the market demands that it move in that direction.

At Avnet Inc., they came to just that realization a few years ago as they saw a shift taking place within their electronic components market. While large manufacturers continued to buy large quantities of components for their designs, a growing segment of engineers and smaller companies wanted to buy low volumes (including product samples) online, instead of by phone or face to face. Many of their customers had to either be really patient or just stubborn to make a successful purchase on the e-commerce site they offered at the time.

Avnet realized the need to shift their B2B e-commerce approach to incorporate a B2C perspective. While they were dealing with business customers, their online purchasing expectations were shaped by their experiences on consumer-friendly Web sites such as Amazon.com and HomeDepot.com. The problem was that the experience and functionality that those kinds of sites provide users isn't easily replicated in a B2B environment, especially within the components industry. For example, Avnet deals with millions of parts, and each part has dozens of technical attributes that must be precisely specified for engineers to determine whether it's the part they need. Additionally, legal and country-specific regulations determine which companies and individuals Avnet can ship certain parts to around the world.

So Avnet went ahead and made a few changes. First, they eliminated the need to register. Previously, all customers had to register to get on the commerce site. To make matters even more complicated, all customers had to qualify for credit before they could search for parts, even if they were purchasing with a credit card. Now anyone can search for part information without having to register and share personal details. Only when customers reach a purchase point does the site then ask them for their information. And if the customer is paying with a credit card, credit checks are out the window.

Previously, customers could search for parts only by entering precise supplier part numbers, which may be up to 50 characters—the equivalent of making a reader search for a book by the unique ISBN number. Furthermore, the search result displayed information on only the part corresponding to the number entered, not on alternative parts that may also meet the customer's requirements. Customers can now search by part number, product name, description, and technical attributes. Returned search results now include similar products that match the engineer's requirements, so the engineer can make informed decisions about alternative parts based on factors such as availability, cost, and manufacturer.

The new e-commerce site, featuring more than 3.5 million electronic components, took two years to develop and deploy, and Avnet keeps on adding functionality based on customer feedback. So far, however, results tell them that customers already like what they see: There has been a 75 percent annual increase in e-commerce revenue and a 50 percent annual increase in site visitors.

SOURCE: Steve Phillips and Beth Ely, "Global CIO: Avnet Tears Up the B2B E-Commerce Playbook," *InformationWeek*, June 15, 2009.

e-COMMERCE MARKETPLACES
LO 9-4

The latest e-commerce transaction systems are scaled and customized to allow buyers and sellers to meet in a variety of high-speed trading platforms: auctions, catalogs, and exchanges.

Businesses of any size can now buy everything from chemicals to electronic components, excess electrical energy, construction materials, or paper products at business-to-business **e-commerce marketplaces**. Figure 9.14 outlines five major types of e-commerce marketplaces used by businesses today. However, many B2B **portals** provide several types of marketplaces. Thus, they may offer an electronic **catalog** shopping and ordering site for products from many suppliers in an industry. Or they may serve as an **exchange** for buying and selling via a bid-ask process or at negotiated prices. Very popular are electronic **auction** Web sites for B2B auctions

FIGURE 9.14

Types of e-commerce marketplaces.

e-Commerce Marketplaces
• **One to Many.** Sell-side marketplaces. Host one major supplier, who dictates product catalog offerings and prices. Examples: Cisco.com and Dell.com.
• **Many to One.** Buy-side marketplaces. Attract many suppliers that flock to these exchanges to bid on the business of a major buyer like GE or AT&T.
• **Some to Many.** Distribution marketplaces. Unite major suppliers who combine their product catalogs to attract a larger audience of buyers. Examples: VerticalNet and Works.com.
• **Many to Some.** Procurement marketplaces. Unite major buyers who combine their purchasing catalogs to attract more suppliers and thus more competition and lower prices. Examples: the auto industry.
• **Many to Many.** Auction marketplaces used by many buyers and sellers that can create a variety of buyers. Examples: eBay and FreeMarkets.

of products and services. Figure 9.15 illustrates a B2B trading system that offers exchange, auction, and reverse auction (where sellers bid for the business of a buyer) electronic markets.

Many of these B2B e-commerce portals are developed and hosted by third-party *market-maker* companies who serve as ***infomediaries*** that bring buyers and sellers together in catalog, exchange, and auction markets. Infomediaries are companies that serve as intermediaries in e-business and e-commerce transactions. Examples are Ariba, Commerce One, and VerticalNet, to name a few successful companies. All provide e-commerce marketplace software products and services to power business Web portals for e-commerce transactions.

These B2B e-commerce sites make business purchasing decisions faster, simpler, and more cost effective because companies can use Web systems to research and transact with many vendors. Business buyers get one-stop shopping and accurate purchasing information. They also get impartial advice from infomediaries that they can't get from the sites hosted by suppliers and distributors. Thus, companies can negotiate or bid for better prices from a larger pool of vendors. Of course, suppliers benefit from easy access to customers from all over the globe. Now, let's look at a real-world example.

FIGURE 9.15

An example of a B2B e-commerce Web portal that offers exchange, auction, and reverse auction electronic markets.

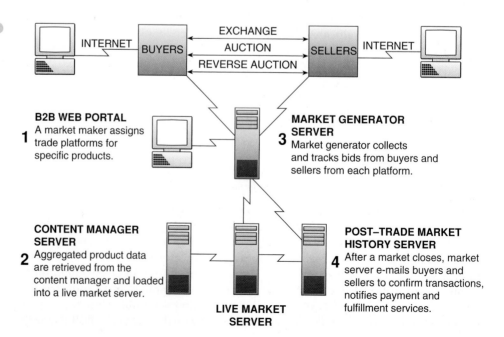

B2B WEB PORTAL

1 A market maker assigns trade platforms for specific products.

MARKET GENERATOR SERVER

3 Market generator collects and tracks bids from buyers and sellers from each platform.

CONTENT MANAGER SERVER

2 Aggregated product data are retrieved from the content manager and loaded into a live market server.

POST–TRADE MARKET HISTORY SERVER

4 After a market closes, market server e-mails buyers and sellers to confirm transactions, notifies payment and fulfillment services.

LIVE MARKET SERVER

Online marketplaces like Craigslist and Freecycle allow consumers to make low-cost sales—or even exchange goods for free—through sophisticated technological systems that make such transactions efficient.

Some companies are attempting to apply a similar model to online business-to-business marketplaces.

The FCC holds auctions to grant licenses for radio spectrums, and most of these are used by cell phone carriers, or for first responders and their communication gear. But some of these spectrums aren't being used for a variety of reasons.

Spectrum Bridge's Web site, SpecEx.com, aims to create a secondary market for these unused spectrums. The company says the site can provide an easy and effective way to connect buyers and sellers. The market could potentially be large, as public safety agencies and major wireless carriers like Verizon Wireless and AT&T routinely purchase spectrums on the secondary market. The cable companies could also become potential buyers, especially as some are eyeing the wireless voice space. Spectrum Bridge makes money by taking a percentage of the transaction.

All transfers of spectrum would have to be approved by the FCC, but the agency has been supportive of spectrum trading in the past.

The idea of organizing the secondary spectrum market isn't a new one, but previous attempts have not been successful because they couldn't get enough buyers and sellers. "The spectrum world is almost tribal," says Peter Stanforth, chief technology officer for Spectrum Bridge. "It consists of small groups of people who know each other—and do everything manually." That is not an efficient system for smaller parcels—SpecEx's sweet spot. "By automating a lot of functions and bringing in a wider audience of buyers and sellers, we are making these smaller pieces more liquid and valuable," explains Stanforth.

Rick Rotondo, chief marketing officer of Spectrum Bridge, compares the SpecEx service to Craigslist, a favorite site for consumer bargains. With its launch several years ago, Craigslist made the sale of small consumer items efficient, which is what SpecEx aims to do with respect to the sale of wireless spectrum parcels. "Let's say you had used sunglasses you wanted to sell, for maybe $25. Before online classifieds were introduced, it would not have been cost-efficient to try to sell them to a huge audience in a paper, because the ad probably would have cost you $20." Same thing with wireless spectrum, he says. "Transaction costs are eating up most of the value for small buyers and sellers."

E-commerce technology can standardize much of the process, notes Stanforth. "What we are trying to do is be the eBay of the wireless spectrum world—a one-stop shop where companies can go to monetize excess or idle spectrum, and spectrum seekers can go to find reasonably priced unused spectrums."

SpecEx.com: B2B Trading of Wireless Spectrum

SOURCE: Erika Morphy, "The Corporate Bargain Hunters' Quest for a Business Model," *E-Commerce Times*, January 20, 2009; and Marin Perez, "Spectrum Bridge Launches Online Secondary Market," *InformationWeek*, September 5, 2008.

Companies are recognizing that success will go to those who can execute clicks-and-mortar strategies that bridge the physical and virtual worlds. Different companies will need to follow very different paths when deciding how closely—or loosely—to integrate their Internet initiatives with their traditional operations.

CLICKS AND BRICKS IN e-COMMERCE
LO 9-5

Figure 9.16 illustrates the spectrum of alternatives and benefit trade-offs that e-business enterprises face when choosing an e-commerce ***clicks-and-bricks strategy.*** E-business managers must answer this question: Should we integrate our e-commerce virtual business operations with our traditional physical business operations or keep them separate? In today's networked world, a bricks-and-mortar business that does not

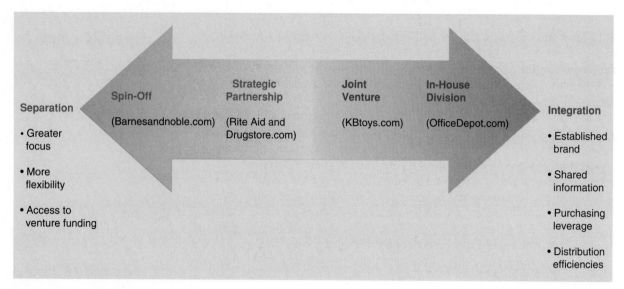

FIGURE 9.16

Companies have a spectrum of alternatives and benefit trade-offs when deciding on an integrated or separate e-commerce business.

adopt a clicks-and-bricks strategy is sometimes referred to as a brink-and-mortar business, suggesting it is on the brink of extinction. While that may be somewhat of an exaggeration, businesses of any size that have not yet adopted an Internet presence, at minimum, are very likely feeling the effects in terms of lost sales and market share.

In February 2011, bricks-and-mortar mainstay Borders Inc. filed for Chapter 11 bankruptcy protection. As competition for consumers intensified amid the growth of the book superstore in the 1990s, Borders made a number of crucial gaffes, including transferring its Internet operations to Amazon in 2001 and embarking on an overseas expansion that swelled its debt. In recent years, Borders had started to shift the focus away from its physical presence by halting expansion plans and identifying unproductive stores for closure, but their recognition of the need for a strategic clicks-and-bricks approach came too late to prevent the bankruptcy. Borders claimed to be focusing on a restructuring plan that would more closely target the Internet sales channel than was done previously. Later in 2011, Borders closed its doors for good. As Figure 9.16 shows, successful companies have implemented a range of integration/separation strategies and made key benefit trade-offs in answering the integration question. Let's take a look at several alternatives.

e-Commerce Integration

The Internet is just another channel that gets plugged into the business architecture.

So says Bill Seltzer, former chief information officer of the office supply retailer Office Depot, which fully integrates its OfficeDepot.com e-commerce sales channel into its traditional business operations. Thus, Office Depot is a prime example of why many companies have chosen integrated clicks-and-bricks strategies, where their e-commerce business is integrated in some major ways into the traditional business operations of a company. The business case for such strategies rests on:

- Capitalizing on any unique strategic capabilities that may exist in a company's traditional business operations that could be used to support an e-commerce business.

- Gaining several strategic benefits of integrating e-commerce into a company's traditional business, such as sharing established brands and key business information, joint buying power, and distribution efficiencies.

For example, Office Depot already had a successful catalog sales business with a professional call center and a fleet of more than 2,000 delivery trucks. Its 1,825 stores and 30 warehouses were networked by a sophisticated information system that provided complete customer, vendor, order, and product inventory data in real time. These business resources made an invaluable foundation for coordinating Office Depot's e-commerce activities and customer services with its catalog business and physical stores. In 2010, Office Depot boasted 9 public Web sites in North America, more than 40 public Web sites outside North America, and more than 15 corporate contract customized Web sites. Thus, customers can shop at OfficeDepot.com at their home, business, or in-store kiosks. Then they can choose to pick up their purchases at the store or have them delivered. In addition, the integration of Web-enabled e-commerce applications within Office Depot's traditional store and catalog operations has helped increase the traffic at their physical stores and improved the catalog operation's productivity and average order size.

IT Lessons from the Demise of Borders

Borders Group Inc. is an international book and music retailer based in Ann Arbor, Michigan. Before filing for bankruptcy protection in 2011 and later going out of business, the company operated close to 1,000 stores in the United States under the Borders and Waldenbooks brands. Computerworld columnist Frank Hayes believes there are a number of IT lessons to be learned from this debacle:

First, you cannot run a company without IT-savvy management. When founded by brothers Tom and Louis Borders, the company had what was then a state-of-the-art punch card system that allowed them to track and adjust inventory in a near real-time basis. It was reportedly one of the main reasons Kmart bought Borders in 1992: to use the system to run its Waldenbooks chain. The brothers, however, cashed out and all managers who came after them never had a strong grasp of IT. Sometimes even the best technology does not scale well; the system worked fine for a few stores, but not for hundreds.

Companies need to keep getting better all of the time. In 2000, according to Forrester, Borders overtook Amazon.com as the best online bookseller. Amazon kept improving, while Borders turned its attention elsewhere. Borders also missed the chance to emulate, borrow, or steal the best ideas that were introduced in the Web site of its main competitor, Amazon. At some point, Borders fell too far behind.

Right now most analysts decry the deal that, in 2001, gave Amazon.com control of the Borders online operations. Then, however, Gartner called it "a step in the right direction for both companies," which would allow Borders a stronger presence online and Amazon a foothold in the brick-and-mortar retail market. It turns out that all media—including books and music—was heading online. After the original deal, Borders tried to revive its inventory management system, but it failed twice (badly the second time).

Finally, Borders never created its own competitor to the Kindle and Nook e-book offerings. Although it sold e-readers from Sony and Kobo in its stores, it never developed the tight integration between reader and bookstore that makes Amazon the preferred place for buying Kindle books, whereas those that have Nooks go to Barnes & Noble.

"Sure, you can save a little money by using exactly the same technology that anyone can buy. But you only get a real business advantage from IT when you are different," says Hayes. "And if you think a little money is better than a real business advantage, consider this: Right now, 'a little money' is all Borders has left."

SOURCE: Frank Hayes, "Seven IT Lessons from the Failure of Borders," *Computerworld*, March 7, 2011.

Other Clicks-and-Bricks Strategies

As Figure 9.16 illustrates, other clicks-and-bricks strategies range from partial e-commerce integration using joint ventures and strategic partnerships to complete separation via the spin-off of an independent e-commerce company.

The strategic partnership of the Rite Aid retail drugstore chain and Drugstore .com is a good example of a less integrated e-commerce venture. Rite Aid only owns about 25 percent of Drugstore.com, which has an independent management team and a separate business brand. However, both companies share the decreased costs and increased revenue benefits of joint buying power, an integrated distribution center, co-branded pharmacy products, and joint prescription fulfillment at Rite Aid stores.

Finally, let's look at an example of the benefits and challenges of a completely separate clicks-and-bricks strategy. Barnesandnoble.com was created as an independent e-commerce company that was spun off by the Barnes & Noble book retail chain. This status enabled it to gain several hundred million dollars in venture capital funding, create an entrepreneurial culture, attract quality management, maintain a high degree of business flexibility, and accelerate decision making. However, the book e-retailer has done poorly since its founding and failed to gain market share from Amazon.com, its leading competitor. Many business analysts say that the failure of Barnes & Noble to integrate some of the marketing and operations of Barnesandnoble.com within their thousands of bookstores meant it forfeited a key strategic business opportunity.

e-Commerce Channel Choices

Some of the key questions that the management of companies must answer in making a clicks-and-bricks decision and developing the resulting e-commerce channel are outlined in Figure 9.17. An *e-commerce channel* is the marketing or sales channel created by a company to conduct and manage its chosen e-commerce activities. How this e-commerce channel is integrated with a company's traditional sales channels (e.g., retail/wholesale outlets, catalog sales, and direct sales) is a major consideration in developing its e-commerce strategy.

Thus, the examples in this section emphasize that there is no universal clicks-and-bricks e-commerce strategy or e-commerce channel choice for every company, industry, or type of business. Both e-commerce integration and separation have major business benefits and shortcomings. Deciding on a clicks-and-bricks strategy and e-commerce channel depends heavily on whether a company's unique business operations provide strategic capabilities and resources to support a profitable business model successfully for its e-commerce channel. As these examples show, most companies are implementing some measure of clicks-and-bricks integration because "the benefits of integration are almost always too great to abandon entirely."

FIGURE 9.17

Key questions for developing an e-commerce channel strategy.

A Checklist for Channel Development
1. What audiences are we attempting to reach?
2. What action do we want those audiences to take? To learn about us, to give us information about themselves, to make an inquiry, to buy something from our site, to buy something through another channel?
3. Who owns the e-commerce channel within the organization?
4. Is the e-commerce channel planned alongside other channels?
5. Do we have a process for generating, approving, releasing, and withdrawing content?
6. Will our brands translate to the new channel or will they require modification?
7. How will we market the channel itself?

When outdoor equipment retailer REI wanted to boost in-store sales, the company looked to its Web site. In June 2003, REI.com launched free in-store pickup for customers who ordered online. The logic behind that thinking: People who visit stores to collect their online purchases might be swayed to spend more money upon seeing the colorful displays of clothing, climbing gear, bikes, and camping equipment.

REI's hunch paid off. "One out of every three people who buy something online will spend an additional $90 in the store when they come to pick something up," says Joan Broughton, REI's vice president of multichannel programs. That tendency translates into a healthy 1 percent increase in store sales.

As Broughton sees it, the mantra for any multichannel retailer should be "a sale is a sale is a sale, whether online, in stores or through catalogs." The Web is not simply an isolated channel with its own operational metrics or exclusive group of customers.

As the Web has matured as a retail channel, consumers have turned to online shopping as an additional place to interact with a retailer, rather than as a replacement for existing channels such as stores or catalogs.

And to make that strategy as cost-efficient as possible, the company uses the same trucks that restock its stores to fulfill online orders slated for in-store pickup. To make this work, REI had to integrate order information from the Web site and replenishment orders from stores at its distribution warehouse in Washington state.

In and of itself, integrating the two types of order information wasn't complex, says Brad Brown, REI's vice president of information services. What was difficult, however, was coordinating fulfillment of both online and replenishment orders because "orders placed on the Web by customers are nothing like replenishment orders that stores place," he says. Online orders are picked from the warehouse at the time of the order and then put in a queue until the appropriate truck is loaded, whereas store orders are picked by an automated replenishment system that typically picks orders at one time based on either a weekly or biweekly replenishment schedule.

To make in-store pickup a reality, Brown's group wrote a "promise algorithm" that informs customers of a delivery date when they place an online order. Timing can get tricky when orders are placed the day before a truck is scheduled to depart the warehouse with a store-replenishment delivery. For example, if an online order is placed on a Monday night and a truck is scheduled to depart Tuesday morning, the system promises the customer a pickup date of a week later, as if the order would be placed on the following week's truck. However, REI will shoot for fulfilling the order that night; if it can do it, REI (and, ultimately, the customer) is happy because the order arrives sooner than was promised.

Creating effective business-to-consumer retail Web sites entails more than just calculating sales figures. It's about delivering the functionality that users expect and using the site to drive sales through other channels. And only IT integration can make this happen.

REI: Scaling e-Commerce Mountain

SOURCE: Megan Santosus, "Channel Integration—How REI Scaled e-Commerce Mountain," *CIO Magazine*, May 15, 2004.

real world SOLUTION

Ticketmaster–Changing the Way Tickets Are Sold

Ticketmaster is the undisputed global leader in the provision of ticketing and related products and services to the live entertainment industry. Since it was founded in 1976, the way in which tickets to events are issued, distributed, purchased, exchanged, and used has changed dramatically, in no small part thanks to the rise of the Internet. Because these operations are so different from when the company started its business, Ticketmaster requires a new approach to its operations.

In order to answer these challenges, Ticketmaster deployed its Advanced Product Suite, at the center of which is a package called ARCHTICS, which handles ticketing. Although it may sound straightforward—you pay for a ticket and a ticket is issued—the package encompasses all steps: creating ticket offers and packages, selling tickets to the fans or customers, managing inventory control, collecting personal and demographic information, and only then taking credit card payments. The package runs on top of a Sybase SQL Anywhere database engine, which features self-tuning and self-managing capabilities that make it ideal for deployment in environments where the clients operating the application (sport teams, stadiums, arenas, theaters, and so forth) may have very limited information technology capabilities. As a result, the application must be as easy to deploy, run, and support as possible.

"Sybase SQL Anywhere does all the complex, heavy lifting of the ARCHTICS platform," says Steve Davidson, vice president of Product Development at Ticketmaster. "Inventory control is absolutely essential to the system—there are only a certain number of seats and each must be accurately assigned. All that control is done through the Sybase database engine."

"The ARCHTICS solution is a phenomenal asset for the Washington Capitals. The reliability and stability of the solution is second to none. The reporting features and the amount of data we can house and pull at any given time is tremendous," says Christopher Sheap, director of Ticket Operations with the Washington Capitals.

The first instantiation of the ARCHTICS platforms was not originally a Ticketmaster development. It was developed by a small company that sold it to a number of clients. Ticketmaster recognized the value of the solution, acquired it, and expanded its capabilities beyond managing season ticket holders, which was the original focus. Par-

ticularly for sport franchises, however, season ticket holders form the core of their annual revenue, and they continue to be the central focus of attention. "Our ARCHTICS installation provides the technology to help us really get to know our fans. We track season ticket holder information in the CRM (customer relationship management) console in ARCHTICS so that we know who our VIP fans are and continuously develop programs to improve their event experience. Our fans are critical to the success of the Boston Celtics and it is imperative that we take good care of them. You need an organized solution to help you do that, and ARCHTICS does that for us," says Paul Cacciatore, senior director of ticketing at the Boston Celtics NBA franchise.

While ARCHTICS is at the center of the Advanced Product Suite solution, Ticketmaster offers more to its customers than ticketing. For example, it also includes MailManager, a module used to manage e-mail campaigns and promotions to fans. The application sends out the e-mails, tracks whether each was opened and, if so, which links in each e-mail were clicked on. It also tracks the activities that users conducted while visiting the sites to which they were sent after clicking on those links—most importantly, whether the promotional e-mail generated a sale after all. All this allows marketing managers at the various sport franchises or venues to accurately pinpoint response rates to their campaigns, as well as to provide insights into what may work better in some scenarios, to fine-tune future efforts.

Selling a ticket, however, is only half—or maybe a third—of the story. From the moment a fan purchases the ticket until the date of the game, a number of different things may prevent the ticket holder from attending the game. What then? In the world before ARCHTICS, the ticket holder would almost certainly lose money and be frustrated by the complicated process. To help simplify the process for the ticket holder, Ticketmaster introduced Ticket Exchange, which also runs on ARCHTICS. The Ticket Exchange platform allows fans to post their tickets for sale, and those who are looking for tickets can search for them in a number of ways: by team, game, price, seating, and so forth. By purchasing tickets through Ticket Exchange, fans know they are getting real tickets posted directly by season ticket holders and other fans. A ticket holder who sells through

Ticket Exchange typically gets a better price than one who sells to a discount ticket broker.

"Ultimately, ARCHTICS helps us run our entire business better and give our valued fans a better purchasing experience, says Sheap. "One feature I particularly like is the online ticket management. It allows our season ticket holders to transfer tickets they are not going to use to someone else or sell them in a safe and secure manner on the open market. Additionally, fans who purchase tickets through Ticket Exchange know that they are getting valid tickets. This goes a long way in helping sell season tickets, and build fan loyalty and retention in the long run."

After a ticket has been originally issued, and maybe changed hands along the way, the last third of the experience is actually coming into the arena to enjoy the game or event. This is where AccessManager, also part of the Advanced Product Suite centered around ARCHTICS, comes into play. At that time, security and fraud are major concerns, as team owners and arena operators want to ensure that only customers with valid tickets are granted access to the venue. In order to achieve this, each ticket features a bar code that is scanned by a handheld device as patrons enter the building. The device connects wirelessly to the local ARCHTICS instance, which validates the ticket on the spot. If it does not check out, you cannot come in. The system also allows managers to deactivate bar codes for tickets that are reported lost or stolen, and then reissue them to the original owners. As a result, the actual patrons can still come into the game, and those who stole their tickets cannot, which is a desirable state of affairs. Although this is certainly useful, a lot of data are collected in the process of security and access control that can be used for something else. Good data are too valuable to let go to waste.

The AccessManager module also identifies when a ticketed patron came into the venue (i.e., date and time information), through which door or gate the patron entered, and how many of the purchased tickets were used that night. All this information feeds back into ARCHTICS to provide team owners with a complete picture of attendance for each game, which in turn provides their marketing managers with the necessary information to boost attendance. After all, a fan who does not come to the game, even one who has paid for a ticket, is a fan who does not purchase something to eat or take a gift or souvenir home; revenues go beyond the price of the ticket alone. Managers can then alert season ticket holders who show a pattern of not regularly coming to the games that they can give their tickets to a friend or family member on a game-by-game basis, with no ongoing commitment; post them for resale for specific games; or use other means to help them come to the games—anything that makes a ticket sold mean that an actual customer comes through the door.

These modules, part of ARCHTICS and the Advanced Product Suite, started out as turnkey systems that Ticketmaster sold to its clients, who were responsible for operating them. The company is now looking to expand into offering remote hosting of the suite for smaller clients, who may not have the necessary in-house IT resources but still want to be able to access all of these features. Today, more than 400 corporate clients—teams, arenas, theaters, and so forth—are using ARCHTICS.

SOURCE: "ARCHTICS," *Computerworld Honors Case Study*, 2010; "Ticketmaster," *Sybase Customer Case Study*, 2010; "The Phoenix Suns Launch Ticketmaster's Team Exchange, Online Ticket Forwarding Technology," *Ticketmaster Press Release*, September 5, 2010; "Ticketmaster and the Golden State Warriors Sign Multi-Year Ticketing Agreement," *Ticketmaster Press Release*, September 26, 2010; and www.ticketmaster.com, accessed May 29, 2011.

▼ QUESTIONS TO CONSIDER

1. Since ARCHTICS and the Advanced Product Suite manage so much of the operational aspects of ticketing today, where does the value added by the independent clients—teams, franchises, and so forth—come from?

2. How would the relationship between Ticketmaster and its corporate clients change if Ticketmaster were to host and operate the applications for them outright? How would its corporate clients benefit? Should the corporate clients have any concerns?

- **e-Commerce.** E-commerce encompasses the entire online process of developing, marketing, selling, delivering, servicing, and paying for products and services. The Internet and related technologies, e-commerce Web sites on the World Wide Web, and corporate intranets and extranets serve as the business and technology platforms for e-commerce marketplaces for consumers and businesses in the basic categories of business-to-consumer (B2C), business-to-business (B2B), and consumer-to-consumer (C2C) e-commerce. The essential processes that should be implemented in all e-commerce applications—access control and security, personalizing and profiling, search management, content management, catalog management, payment systems, workflow management, event notification, and collaboration and trading—are summarized in Figure 9.4.

- **e-Commerce Issues.** Many e-business enterprises are moving toward offering full-service B2C and B2B e-commerce portals supported by integrated customer-focused processes and inter-networked supply chains, as illustrated in Figure 9.9. In addition, companies must evaluate a variety of e-commerce integration or separation alternatives and benefit trade-offs when choosing a clicks-and-bricks strategy and e-commerce channel, as summarized in Figures 9.16 and 9.17.

- **B2C e-Commerce.** Businesses typically sell products and services to consumers at e-commerce Web sites that provide attractive Web pages, multimedia catalogs, interactive order processing, secure electronic payment systems, and online customer support. However, successful e-tailers build customer satisfaction and loyalty by optimizing factors outlined in Figure 9.11, such as selection and value, performance and service efficiency, the look and feel of the site, advertising and incentives to purchase, personal attention, community relationships, and security and reliability. In addition, a Web store has several key business requirements, including building and marketing a Web business, serving and supporting customers, and managing a Web store, as summarized in Figure 9.13.

- **B2B e-Commerce.** Business-to-business applications of e-commerce involve electronic catalog, exchange, and auction marketplaces that use Internet, intranet, and extranet Web sites and portals to unite buyers and sellers, as summarized in Figure 9.14 and illustrated in Figure 9.15. Many B2B e-commerce portals are developed and operated for a variety of industries by third-party market-maker companies called infomediaries, which may represent consortiums of major corporations.

These are the key terms and concepts of this chapter. The page number of their first reference appears in parentheses.

1. Clicks-and-bricks strategy (393)
2. E-commerce channel (396)
3. E-commerce marketplaces (391)
   a. Auction (391)
   b. Catalog (391)
   c. Exchange (391)
   d. Portal (391)
4. E-commerce processes (373)
   a. Access control and security (374)

b. Collaboration and trading (378)
c. Content and catalog management (375)
d. Electronic payment systems (378)
e. Event notification (378)
f. Profiling and personalizing (374)
g. Search management (374)
h. Workflow management (376)

5. Electronic commerce (368)
   a. Business-to-business (B2B) (372)
   b. Business-to-consumer (B2C) (372)
   c. Consumer-to-consumer (C2C) (372)
6. Electronic funds transfer (EFT) (379)
7. Infomediaries (392)
8. Search engine optimization (387)

Match one of the key terms and concepts listed previously with each of the brief examples or definitions that follow. Try to find the best fit for the answers that seem to fit more than one term or concept. Defend your choices.

_____ 1. The online process of developing, marketing, selling, delivering, servicing, and paying for products and services.

_____ 2. Business selling to consumers at retail Web stores is an example.

_____ 3. Using an e-commerce portal for auctions by business customers and their suppliers is an example.

_____ 4. Using an e-commerce Web site for auctions among consumers is an example.

_____ 5. E-commerce applications must implement several major categories of interrelated processes, such as search and catalog management, in order to be effective.

_____ 6. Helps to establish mutual trust between you and an e-tailer at an e-commerce site.

_____ 7. Tracks your Web site behavior to provide you with an individualized Web store experience.

_____ 8. Develops, generates, delivers, and updates information to you at a Web site.

_____ 9. Ensures that proper e-commerce transactions, decisions, and activities are performed to serve you more efficiently.

_____ 10. Sends you an e-mail when your e-commerce order has been shipped.

_____ 11. Includes matchmaking, negotiation, and mediation processes among buyers and sellers.

_____ 12. Companies that serve as intermediaries in e-commerce transactions.

_____ 13. A process aimed at improving the volume and/or quality of traffic to a Web site.

_____ 14. An e-commerce marketplace that may provide catalog, exchange, or auction service for businesses or consumers.

_____ 15. Buyers bidding for the business of a seller.

_____ 16. Marketplace for bid (buy) and ask (sell) transactions.

_____ 17. The most widely used type of marketplace in B2C e-commerce.

_____ 18. The marketing or sales channel created by a company to conduct and manage its e-commerce activities.

_____ 19. The processing of money and credit transfers between businesses and financial institutions.

_____ 20. Ways to provide efficient, convenient, and secure payments in e-commerce.

_____ 21. Companies can evaluate and choose from several e-commerce integration alternatives.

_____ 22. Web sites and portals hosted by individual companies, consortiums, or intermediaries that bring together buyers and sellers to accomplish e-commerce transactions.

_____ 23. A component of e-commerce sites that helps customers find what they are looking for.

1. Most businesses should engage in e-commerce on the Internet. Do you agree or disagree with this statement? Explain your position.

2. Are you interested in investing in, owning, managing, or working for a business that is primarily engaged in e-commerce on the Internet? Explain your position.

3. Consider the Real World Challenge at the beginning of the chapter. The e-commerce practices of today would not be possible without the Internet. Did customers place new demands for products and services on companies like Ticketmaster before the Internet appeared, and the technology allowed the companies to satisfy them? Or are the demands a result of the technology being there in the first place? Which one comes first?

4. What are the critical success factors for retail e-business start-ups?

5. Do the e-commerce success factors listed in Figure 9.11 guarantee success for an e-commerce business venture? Give a few examples of what else could go wrong and how you would confront such challenges.

6. If personalizing a customer's Web site experience is a key success factor, then electronic profiling processes to track visitor Web site behavior are necessary. Do you agree or disagree with this statement? Explain your position.

7. All corporate procurement should be accomplished in e-commerce auction marketplaces, instead of using B2B Web sites that feature fixed-price catalogs or negotiated prices. Explain your position on this proposal.

8. Refer to the Real World Solution in the chapter. Given that corporate clients largely cannot operate without relying on Ticketmaster

today, do you think sport teams and franchises should be concerned about being edged out of the ticketing business by Ticketmaster in the future? What can they do to prevent this from happening?

9. If you were starting an e-commerce Web store, which of the business requirements summarized in Figure 9.13 would you primarily do yourself, and which would you outsource to a Web development or hosting company? Why?

10. Refer to the Real World Case on social networks, mobile commerce, and online shopping in the chapter. Do you think that mobile devices (not just phones anymore) are becoming the major platform for shopping, communication, everything? What are the implications for companies?

analysis exercises

1. **Small Business e-Commerce Portals**
e-Commerce Portals
On the Internet, small businesses have become big business, and a really big business, Microsoft, wants a piece of the action. The company's Small Business Center (www.microsoft.com/smallbusiness) is one of many sites offering advice and services for small businesses moving online. Most features, whether free or paid, are what you'd expect: lots of links and information along the lines established by Google Small Business Network (http://www.google.com/smallbusinessnetwork) or Entrabase.com. Small Business Center, however, stands out for its affordable advertising and marketing services. Go check it out and see what you think.

One program helps businesses create banner ads and places them on a collection of Web sites that it claims are visited by 60 percent of the Web surfing community. With its "Banner Network Ads" program, buyers don't pay a huge fee up front, and they don't run the risk that a huge number of visitors will unexpectedly drive up click-through commissions. Instead, this program allows small business to pay a small, fixed fee for a guaranteed number of click-throughs (people who click on your banner ad to visit your Web site). Small Business Center rotates these banner ads around a network of participating Web sites and removes the ad as soon as it has received the guaranteed number of click-through visitors. This action eliminates the guesswork regarding both traffic and fees. The three packages—100, 250, and 1,000 visitors—break down to 50 cents per visitor.

a. Check out Small Business Center and the other e-commerce portals mentioned. Identify several benefits and limitations for a business using these Web sites.

b. Which Web site is your favorite? Why?

c. Which site would you recommend or use to help a small business wanting to get into e-commerce? Why?

2. **Car Buying**
e-Commerce Web Sites for Car Buying
Nowadays new car buyers can configure the car of their dreams on Microsoft's MSN Autos Web site, as well as those of Ford, GM, and other auto giants. Many independent online car purchase and research companies offer similar services. See Figure 9.18. Car-buying information provided by manufacturers, brokerage sites, car dealers, financial institutions, and consumer advocate Web sites has exploded in the past few years. Yet in the age of the Internet, the auto industry remains a steadfast holdout to innovations that might threaten the well-established and well-connected supply chain, the car dealership. American new car buyers simply cannot skip the middleperson and purchase an automobile directly from the manufacturer. That's not just a business decision by the manufacturers; that's the law. Even so, many car buyers use the Internet as a place to research their purchases. Instead of selling new cars directly, Web sites such as Autobytel.com of Irvine, California, just put consumers in touch with a local dealer where they test-drive a vehicle and negotiate a price. Autobytel.com has been referring buyers to new and used car dealers since 1995. It also offers online financing and insurance. Online car-buying sites on the Web make consumers less dependent on what cars a dealer has on the lot. At online sites, buyers can customize a car—or van, truck, or sport utility vehicle—by selecting trim, paint, color, and other options before purchase. They can also use Web sites such as CarBuyingTips.com to help prepare for the final negotiating process.

a. Check out several of the Web sites shown in Figure 9.18. Evaluate them based on ease of use, relevance of information provided, and other criteria you feel are important. Don't forget the classic: "Did they make you want to buy?"

b. Which sites would you use or recommend if you or a friend actually wanted to buy a car? Why?

Manufacturer's Sites	
Ford Motor Company	(www.ford.com)
Product specifications, pricing, build-your-own feature, finance calculators, and dealer finder.	
General Motors Corporation	(www.gm.com)
With access to nearly 6,000 GM dealerships, car shoppers can get a price quote, schedule a test drive, and buy.	

Pro-Consumer Sites	
Cars.com	(www.cars.com)
Research tools include automotive reviews, model reports, dealer locators, and financial information.	
Auto Web	(www.autoweb.com)
Buy new and used automobiles online, or sell your old one. Go to the new car research center to investigate autos. Find out what rebates and incentives are currently available, link to Kelly Blue Book, or chat with others in the forums.	
Edmunds	(www.edumnds.com)
For an objective opinion, Edmunds.com provides reviews, safety updates, and rebate news for car buyers.	
Kelly Blue Book	(www.kbb.com)
New and used car information and valuation.	
CarSmart	(www.carsmart.com)
Find new car price quotes, dealer locators, and used auto sales at the site "where America shops for cars." Report library allows visitors to download vehicle information and car-buying tips.	
Cars.com	(www.cars.com)
Research tools include automotive reviews, model reports, dealer locators, and financial information.	
CarMax	(www.carmax.com)
More than 20,000 new and used vehicles available to purchase online. Check out their online research tools. If the exact model you want isn't at a nearby store, it can be transferred to your local CarMax for a fee.	
J.D. Power	(www.jdpower.com/auto)
These folks award the coveted J.D. Powers quality awards. Hundreds of vehicles rated by thousands of people. Consistently accurate reviews on cars, boats, insurance, and finance. Automotive Ratings highly respected. Also see powerful buyers guides.	
Cars Direct	(www.carsdirect.com)
"America's #1 way to buy cars online" is now partnered with Amazon.com. Get prices on new cars. Search more than 50,000 used car listings. Anti-theft products, auto accessories, and vehicle history reports too.	
Microsoft MSN Autos	(www.autos.msn.com)
Auto reviews, detailed vehicle specifications, safety ratings, and buying services for new and used cards, including customizing your very own Ford.	

FIGURE 9.18

Top car-buying Web sites.

c. Check out the Consumer Federation of America's study on anticompetitive new car-buying state laws or similar studies online. How much does it estimate consumers would save if they could purchase cars directly from manufacturers online?

3. **Which e-Commerce Site Is Best?**

Comparing e-Commerce Sites

In this exercise, you will experiment with electronic shopping and compare alternative e-commerce sites. First, select a category of product widely available on the Web, such as books, CDs, or toys. Second, select five specific products to price on the Internet, for example, five specific CDs you might be interested in buying. Third, search three prominent e-commerce sites selling this type of product and record the price charged for each product by each site.

a. Using a spreadsheet, record a set of information similar to that shown for each product. (Categories describing the product will vary depending on the type of product you select—CDs might require the title of the CD and the performer[s], whereas toys or similar products would require the name of the product and its description.) See Figure 9.19.

FIGURE 9.19

Table for Problem 3.

Title of Book	Author	Price			Rating		
		Site A	Site B	Site C	A	B	C
The Return of Little Big Man	Berger, T.	15.00	16.95	14.50	2	3	1
Learning Perl/Tk	Walsh, N. & Mui, L.	26.36	25.95	25.95	3	1.5	1.5
Business at the Speed of Thought	Gates, W.	21.00	22.95	21.00	1.5	3	1.5
Murders for the Holidays	Smith, G.		8.25	7.95	4	2	1
Designs for Dullards	Jones	17.95	18.50	18.50	1	2.5	2.5
Sum of ratings (low score represents most favorable rating)					11.5	12	7.5

b. For each product, rank each company on the basis of the price charged. Give a rating of 1 for the lowest price and 3 for the highest, and split the ratings for ties—two sites tying for the lowest price would each receive a 1.5. If a site does not have one of the products available for sale, give that site a rating of 4 for that product. Add the ratings across your products to produce an overall price/availability rating for each site.

c. Based on your experience with these sites, rate them on their ease of use, completeness of information, and order-filling and shipping options. As in Part (b), give a rating of 1 to the site you feel is best in each category, a 2 to the second best, and a 3 to the poorest site.

d. Prepare a set of PowerPoint slides or similar presentation materials summarizing the key results and including an overall assessment of the sites you compared.

4. e-Commerce: The Dark Side
Don't Get Scammed

Anonymous transactions on the Internet may have a dark side. Scams abound. Research each of the terms below on the Web. Prepare a one-page report for each term researched. Your paper should describe the problem and provide real-world examples where possible. Conclude each paper with recommendations on how to guard against each type of fraud.

a. Search using the terms "Ponzi scheme" or "Pyramid scheme." You may find current examples by searching for "cash matrix," or "gifting party."

b. Search using the terms "phishing." Report your results. If possible, include a printout of a real-world example that you or an acquaintance may have received via e-mail.

c. Search using the term "Nigerian scam." Report your results. If possible, include a printout of a real-world example that you or an acquaintance may have received via e-mail.

d. Search using the term "third-party escrow." What legitimate function does this serve? Provide an example of a legitimate third-party escrow service for Internet transactions. How has the third-party escrow system been used to commit fraud on the Internet?

5. Ecosystems and e-Commerce
Does Google Have a Leg Up on Groupon?

If you use Facebook, you've heard of Groupon. Groupon advertises heavily on Facebook where the social networking medium serves not only as a targeted advertising platform but also as a highly effective viral marketing platform.

Groupon uses self-reported demographics, purchase history, and location to match users with money-saving deals. Users get great deals, and vendors attract more customers during slow periods. Groupon also has a mobile app with GPS- enabled searching and paperless coupons that enables on-the-spot savings.

Before buying stock in Groupon just yet, please note that the Google gorilla has entered the room. Google, with its own mobile operating system, Web browser, massive amounts of geographic and user data, and a well-established highly successful, online advertising system may pose a massive threat.

Google's beta application "Google Offers" competes directly with Groupon. Google is now rolling out "Google Wallet": a mobile application that allows users to make secure retail purchases in person directly via any Android-enabled mobile device.

Read Practical Ecommerce's article, "*Google Wallet to Impact Ecommerce Merchants?*" (http://bit.ly/iJZuEf), view the embedded video, and answer the following questions.

a. What are the pros and cons of PCI certification for brick-and-mortar stores?

b. According to the video, what is "fun" about using Google Wallet?

c. Google has had numerous successes and failures. Should Groupon be worried?

Sony, 1-800-Flowers, Starbucks, and Others: Social Networks, Mobile Phones, and the Future of Shopping

A number of major retailers have been driven into bankruptcy protection during this recession, including RedEnvelope and Eddie Bauer, or gone out of business altogether, like Circuit City. Blockbuster, Virgin Megastores and many more have closed stores. Survivors, suffering deflated profits and slow sales, warn of a bleak future.

But smart retailers are going where it's warm: the hot little hands of cellphone- and laptop-toting consumers who want to shop right now, wherever they happen to be sipping their lattes or watching their kids playing soccer. Technology-backed projects to increase revenue include mobile e-commerce, coupons by text message, even storefronts on social networks. As enablers of these projects, chief information officers are moving ever closer to the customer.

"Out of recession develops one picture—finally—of what true business–IT alignment looks like," says Drew Martin, chief information officer of Sony Electronics, "IT is becoming part of the product offerings." Whether that's hotel kiosks, mobile banking, hospital patient portals or retail, chief information officers are getting their IT groups to the front line in the competition for consumer dollars. When a customer logs on to his new Sony e-book reader, for example, the device automatically connects him to his existing customer profile, from which he can start buying e-books. This feature is thanks to Martin's efforts to connect product development with Sony's internal customer relationship management system.

As exciting as it is to live on the progressive edge of the CIO profession, though, it's a new world to navigate at a time when wrong moves can severely hurt a company. "The challenge is that now you're entering into the revenue space," Martin says. "You need to commit to delivering your part of what needs to be delivered."

"Websites and e-mail—that's just too many steps now," says Brett Michalak, chief information officer with Tickets. com, which sells tickets to games, concerts, and other events, as well as its own ticketing technology.

Social media such as Twitter, Facebook, and YouTube take e-mail out of the equation, putting offers in front of customers on sites they already visit. Dell, JetBlue, Whole Foods and other big brands have pounced on Twitter as a marketing and promotion tool, tweeting special deals to followers. Dell, for example, attributes more than $2 mil-

lion in sales to its 14 Twitter accounts that promote offers to 1.4 million followers. ("15% off any Dell Outlet Inspiron laptop. Enter code at checkout . . .")

Sony is using Twitter, among other social networking sites, to hype the SonyReader. A recent tweet included a link to a page at Sony's site comparing the product favorably to Amazon's Kindle. "You can't build a site and expect people to come. We are on YouTube, Facebook, and Twitter to go out and get them," Martin says.

1-800-Flowers intends to find out whether social networkers are also social shoppers. In July 2009, the $714 million flower delivery company launched the first Facebook storefront. Collectively, Facebook's 300 million active members spend 8 billion minutes per day on the site, according to the company. An Experian survey found that dwell time for an adult visiting a social network is 19 minutes and 32 seconds. Meanwhile, 35 percent of adults who had been on a social network in the past month had also bought something online in that time period, the survey found—a ripe demographic.

"Still, there's a lot to do on Facebook, so any shopping has to be fast," says Vibhav Prasad, vice president of Web marketing and merchandising at 1-800-Flowers. The company's Facebook store, therefore, offers only 10 percent to 15 percent of the several hundred bouquets available from the main 1-800-Flowers Web site, and the checkout process has been pared down. No suggestions to buy related products pop up, for example, and four special occasions tabs span the top of the page, instead of the eight on the main site.

"It's a fairly impulsive purchase in this channel," Prasad says. "As simple and as quick as we can make it, the more effective we'll be." Impulsiveness is key. Every time Facebook members log in, they see updates about who among their friends is having a birthday. Prasad wants those regular reminders to spark flower buys. Going social was "a logical extension" for 1-800-Flowers, which was one of the first retailers to put up an e-commerce site, in the early 1990s, notes Kevin Ranford, director of Web marketing. "It comes from listening to customers and responding to the channels in which they're interacting," Ranford says.

Facebook users spend most of their time looking at their own home pages. They read their news feed—a display of their friends' status updates, quizzes taken, notes posted, and games played. So, 1-800-Flowers is planning a way into the news feed. When a fan fills out a wish list to indicate which flowers she'd like to receive, notification would go into the feeds of her friends. Carol logs on to Facebook, sees Alice has a birthday on Thursday and wishes for the "Pleasantly Pink" bouquet. Ding! Carol clicks over to the 1-800-Flowers store and $29.99-plus-shipping later, takes care of that gift without ever leaving Facebook. "We think people will do it because social networking is all about you expressing your interests and your friends responding," says Wade Gerten, chief executive officer of Alvenda, the Minneapolis software developer that built the Facebook store for 1-800-Flowers. "Shopping online can be social again, as it was in person."

People lose their credit cards and forget their wallets. But cell phones? There is perhaps no combination of vices so bursting with commercial promise than that of cell phone-plus-caffeine. Starbucks is there. In September 2009, the $9.8 billion coffee chain began testing a system to let customers pay using their iPhones or iTouch devices. They download the Starbucks Card Mobile App and type in the number of their Starbucks loyalty card, preloaded with spending money. A two-dimensional bar code appears that cashiers can scan.

Royal Oak Music Theatre, a Michigan music and comedy venue where acts such as Train and Bob Saget have played, started mobile ticketing three years ago and has adjusted its marketing to cover for finicky technology.

Anyone who's done self-check out at the supermarket knows that scanning takes a special, knowing touch. Still, scanning bar codes on the screens of mobile devices often requires extra wiggling of the phone and slanting it at different angles. It's slower than scanning paper tickets. To avoid ticking off patrons lined up to run in and grab general admission floor spots, Royal Oak created a separate VIP entrance for the mobile customers. There, staff use the newer model scanners required for reading mobile bar codes, and it's not so apparent that the scanning takes longer, says Diana Williams, box office manager.

Mobile customers are also allowed to get into the theater a few minutes before traditional customers, which encourages more people to buy their tickets by cell phone, she says. That's cheaper for the theater than handling paper tickets—saving money and hassle time is Williams's goal. But it also positions the theater well for collecting future revenue.

"Mobile ticketing skews young," Williams observes. The theater does shows for all ages, and for a typical adult event, 16 percent of tickets sold are through the mobile channel. But for a recent show by the boy-band Hansen, popular with tween girls, mobile accounted for nearly 40 percent of tickets. "There's an age—around 22 or younger—where it would never occur to patrons that you couldn't buy a ticket from your phone," Williams says.

Mobile and social commerce projects will change the business of any company that invests in it, says Russ Stanley, managing vice president of ticket services and client relations for the San Francisco Giants. For example, instead of being a long-planned activity, a Major League Baseball game can become an impulse buy, Stanley says, bringing in more sales for the organization.

Every game day, the Giants have 40,000 seats to sell. If they've sold only 30,000, 10,000 spoil every bit as badly as old pears. Last year, the team changed prices daily on about 2,000 seats. Stanley imagines the day when he'll have a database of fans who, say, live within a mile of the ballpark to whom he can text last-minute offers. "Hey, the Giants have $5 tickets left for tonight. For $5, I'll walk down there," he says. "As they're walking up to the entrance, they're buying on the mobile."

The Giants started to offer mobile tickets midway through the 2008 season, when they sold about 100 tickets that way per game. In 2009, it was about 200 and Stanley expects to do about 400 per game in the coming years. "Fans who use it love it. It's getting the people to use it," he says.

Like hot dogs and cold beer, holding a ticket is part of the rite of baseball, he says. Plus, there's the souvenir value. When pitcher Jonathan Sanchez threw a no-hitter against the San Diego Padres in July 2009, about 50 mobile fans, as well as people who had bought tickets online and printed them on plain paper at home, later requested the team print "real" tickets for them to commemorate the event. "We did that for them. It's good relations," says Stanley. And, he adds, it could turn into a money-making service in the future.

SOURCE: Kim S. Nash, "Facebook, Mobile Phones, and the Future of Shopping," *CIO.com*, November 24, 2009.

▼ CASE STUDY QUESTIONS

1. How do the companies involved benefit from the innovations discussed in the case? Is it about more efficient transaction processing, better reaching out to customers, or both? Use examples from the case to illustrate your answer.

2. "Shopping online can be social again, as it was in person," says Wade Gerten, chief executive officer of Alvenda. Do you think this is a stretch, or are we in the midst of a turning point in online shopping? Explain your answer.

3. Many of the applications discussed in the case are mostly used by the younger demographic, who grew up around technology. How do online behavior patterns change as people become older, with more responsibilities, and more challenging jobs? Do applications like those discussed in the case become less important? More important?

▼ REAL WORLD ACTIVITIES

1. Consider the examples discussed in the case. Go online and research what other companies or industries are doing in terms of the use of social networking sites and mobile commerce. What other examples can you find? Prepare a report that compares those in your research with the ones described here, highlighting similarities and differences. Can you spot any new trends?

2. How often, if ever, do you shop with your mobile phone? What do you think are some of the roadblocks that prevent the widespread adoption of mobile shopping? What would you suggest companies do to overcome those? Break into small groups with your classmates to develop a few recommendations.

LinkedIn, Umbria, Mattel, and Others: Driving the "Buzz" on the Web

David Hahn has spotted a trend. As director of advertising for the popular online business networking site LinkedIn, he's being asked pointed questions by large advertisers about his ability to help them find "influentials": those people within the LinkedIn community who are the most likely to go out and spread the word about a particular product or experience. "Some of them are requesting it specifically, while others are more implying it, but it comes down to the same thing," Hahn says. "Marketers are very interested in the value of online social networks, and how leaders in those networks can be used to drive proactive behaviors in the population."

Hahn isn't alone in his observations. "The notion of the online influencer is quite the thing today in the marketing world," says Janet Edan-Harris, chief executive officer of Umbria, which monitors chatter in cyberspace communities for corporations wanting to know what's being discussed online about their brands and products. "Companies are incredibly eager to get to those people. Do that—or so the conventional wisdom says—and you'll be in marketing heaven."

But new research, as well as growing business experience, suggests that such thinking may be overly simplistic. The effectiveness of using online word-of-mouth campaigns—or using individuals rather than traditional media advertising to spread the word about products or services—is increasingly viewed as an effective way to reach consumers. But the popular notion that frequently accompanies this, that there are special individuals who hold the key to the hearts of entire online communities, is coming under fire.

Dave Balter certainly thinks so. As chief executive officer of BzzAgent, a word-of-mouth marketing firm, Balter had a revelation three years ago: The so-called influentials, or opinion leaders, in online communities can't be influenced in a way that accelerates the success of a word-of-mouth campaign. "We actually believed in the idea that influentials drove market trends at that point," says Balter. "But upon closer look, we found out it didn't add up. The sales data of our campaigns didn't match the profiles of the opinion leaders we had targeted, and it really caused us to re-evaluate some of our core assumptions." Today, when a client comes in with the goal of influencing the influentials, "we tell them that's fools' gold," says Balter. "It

sounds really great, it sounds really sexy, but the results simply don't fly."

This indeed is what Edan-Harris has concluded from her experiences working with online communities. "We said, 'Wait a minute, is this really a correct assumption, that there are individuals on the Internet that have that much influence?'" she says. Her conclusion: "Not nearly as much as everyone seems to think."

Despite this, companies are putting significant dollars into efforts to find these online opinion leaders, whether they're bloggers, contributors to discussion boards, or members of online social networks. Indeed, a whole cottage industry has sprung up based upon the notion that all marketers need to kick off a successful marketing strategy with a list of Internet opinion leaders. And with the expanding universe of blogs, online communities, and social networks such as MySpace, FaceBook, and LinkedIn, the appeal of this idea has become even more entrenched. There's a growing perception that the increasingly ubiquitous availability of broadband, coupled with the rise in popularity of blogs and online communities, make "influentials" even more influential.

It's critical to understand, however, that all these proponents of opinion leaders as drivers of social and commercial trends aren't talking about media stars or personalities, but about otherwise seemingly ordinary members of a community who, through accumulation of knowledge or number of connections with others, act as catalysts for change. Not surprisingly, marketers of all stripes began trying to take advantage of this almost at once—at first offline, and now increasingly within the online social networks rising in popularity.

"The largest companies had already established influence-based programs and are now extending that model into the online social networking space," says Matthew Hurst, a scientist at Microsoft LiveLabs who follows online marketing trends. "It's not the notion of influence that's new, it's the technology that is now enabling it to a greater degree." Not surprisingly, a rapidly increasing number of companies have leaped into the fray to help firms identify the influentials in cyberspace. Buzzlogic is one of them. Launched in 2007, Buzzlogic is dedicated to this idea that opinion leaders in online social networks can be identified, and their influence measured.

An early Buzzlogic beta customer is Protuo.com, a Web-based career management portfolio service that provides matchmaking between employers and potential employees. Not having the funds to buy expensive marketing spots in television, radio, or mainstream print media, Jennifer Gerlach, vice president of marketing, hired Buzzlogic to find the people who are the most influential in the human resource/employee professional space, contact them, and get them to buzz about the product. "We noticed that once one blogger wrote about our service, then suddenly a bunch of other people were writing about it. All at once, there were reviewers everywhere," says Gerlach, who just snagged a major feature in Inc. that she attributes to the online "influentials" campaign. She says she can map increases in site traffic precisely to blog mentions, and she views the campaign as a huge success.

But despite this apparent triumph, a steadily growing number of online marketing experts would argue that, rather than being responsible for the deluge of publicity that Protuo.com is experiencing, the bloggers targeted by Buzzlogic were simply tapping into a sort of zeitgeist waiting to happen—in this case, intense interest in how the Internet could be used to bring employers and candidates together more efficiently than traditional job boards are capable of doing.

Indeed, a growing school of thought is that "influentials" aren't so much leading trends as acting as mouthpieces for underlying social movements that are either already in progress or lying fallow waiting to be triggered. Thus, successful marketing doesn't depend so much on finding influential people and seeding them with ideas so much as doing the kind of research that exposes embryo trends, and then helping "influentials" discover them.

This in fact is what Umbria does by focusing on tracking online conversations taking place in discussion boards and social networks, as well as blogs. "It's much more important to identify those themes that are gaining momentum than try to find opinion leaders," says Edan-Harris. "You want to ride the wave rather than trying to start one on your own." By listening first to the conversations and being nimble enough to use the Internet to craft campaigns that jump on an existing trend, "you get much better results than attempting to generate your own little epicenter," she says.

Protuo.com's Gerlach agreed with some aspects of that. "There has to be a story around your product, and that story has to resonate in the world for the opinion leader strategy to work," she says.

Herein lies the problem with swallowing the "influentials" theory whole cloth. Much of the so-called evidence of how the process works is a matter of reverse engineering. Once something happens—if there's a best-selling book coming out of nowhere, or a surprise political upset—you can always go back to the beginning and find the event or person that seems to have triggered it. You can always tell a causal story in retrospect.

Michael Shore, vice president of worldwide consumer insights for Mattel, directs an organization that increasingly monitors blogs, social networks, discussion boards, and forums to figure out what the market might want from toys in general and Mattel products in particular. But unlike many other global consumer-brands companies, Mattel isn't interested in simply smoking out those individuals who are inordinately influential in their online communities and pushing top-down marketing messages onto them. Despite the fact that this has become the strategy du jour in the online world, Shore's philosophy is a more holistic one.

"We're not just interested in opinion leaders. We'd consider that too narrow a focus," says Shore, who hired MarketTools.com to help him develop and get involved with online communities. Instead, he uses the online universe to do what he calls "cultural assessments" that involve analyzing language, behavioral patterns, and values. Armed with that information, Shore says, Mattel gets valuable information from the Internet that it uses to shape future product development, as well as marketing campaigns.

If there's one thing that everyone agrees on, it's that marketers need to invest a great deal more effort into how online social networks and Internet communities actually work with respect to selling products and services at the grass-roots level.

"It's an emerging medium, and the rules haven't yet been established," says Umbria's Edan-Harris. "We're still learning what does and doesn't work."

SOURCE: Alice LaPlante, "Online Influencers: How the New Opinion Leaders Drive Buzz on the Web," *InformationWeek*, May 5, 2007.

▼ CASE STUDY QUESTIONS

1. How can companies benefit from the "cultural assessments "regularly performed by Mattel? How could the information obtained be used to create business value for those organizations? Provide multiple examples.

2. The case notes that, in spite of disconfirming evidence as to the effectiveness of targeting online opinion leaders, companies are nonetheless increasing their efforts to identify and contact them. Why do you think this is the case?

3. One of the participants in the case states that "you want to ride the wave rather than trying to start one of your own." What does she mean by that? If companies are not starting these "waves," where are they coming from?

REAL WORLD ACTIVITIES

1. A number of technological and cultural developments in recent years has resulted in the emergence of extensive social networks and a large number of avidly followed blogs. Go online to research how companies are tapping into these trends and what new marketing practices have arisen as a result. Prepare a report to summarize your findings.

2. Reflect on your own purchasing behavior. How much do you rely on blogs, feedback, and recommendations from past customers to make your own purchasing decisions? Why do you (or do you not) rely on these sources of information? Do you believe they are largely unbiased? Break into small groups to discuss these issues with your classmates and compare perspectives on them.

chapter 10

SUPPORTING DECISION MAKING

INFORMATION SYSTEMS

e-BUSINESS APPLICATIONS

LEARNING OBJECTIVES

10-1 Identify the changes taking place in the form and use of decision support in business.

10-2 Identify the role and reporting alternatives of management information systems.

10-3 Describe how online analytical processing can meet key information needs of managers.

10-4 Explain the decision support system concept and how it differs from traditional management information systems.

10-5 Explain how the following information systems can support the information needs of executives, managers, and business professionals:

  a. Executive information systems

  b. Enterprise information portals

  c. Knowledge management systems

10-6 Identify how neural networks, fuzzy logic, genetic algorithms, virtual reality, and intelligent agents can be used in business.

10-7 Give examples of several ways expert systems can be used in business decision-making situations.

Supporting Decision Making

INTRODUCTION

LO 10-1

As companies migrate toward responsive e-business models, they are investing in new data-driven decision support application frameworks that help them respond rapidly to changing market conditions and customer needs.

One way to look at an organization is to view it as a intertwining nexus of decisions. The length and breadth of an organization is held together by the relationship between a decision made in one area and a decision made in another. To succeed in business today, companies need information systems that can support the diverse information and decision-making needs of their managers and business professionals. In this chapter, we will explore how this is accomplished by several types of management information, decision support, and other information systems. We concentrate our attention on how the Internet, intranets, and other Web-enabled information technologies have significantly strengthened the role that information systems play in supporting the decision-making activities of every manager and knowledge worker in business.

Read the Real World Challenge on the next page. We can learn a lot about the efforts underlying the global integration of large multinational companies. See Figure 10.1.

Information, Decisions, and Management

Figure 10.2 emphasizes that the type of information required by decision makers in a company is directly related to the *level of management decision making* and the *amount of structure* in the decision situations they face. It is important to understand that the framework of the classic managerial pyramid shown in Figure 10.2 applies even in today's downsized organizations and flattened or nonhierarchical organizational structures. Levels of management decision making still exist, but their size, shape, and participants continue to change as today's fluid organizational structures evolve. Thus, the levels of managerial decision making that must be supported by information technology in a successful organization are:

- **Strategic Management.** Typically, a board of directors and an executive committee of the CEO and top executives develop overall organizational goals, strategies, policies, and objectives as part of a strategic planning process. They also monitor the strategic performance of the organization and its overall direction in the political, economic, and competitive business environment.

- **Tactical Management.** Increasingly, business professionals in self-directed teams, as well as business unit managers, develop short- and medium-range plans, schedules, and budgets and specify the policies, procedures, and business objectives for their subunits of the company. They also allocate resources and monitor the performance of their organizational subunits, including departments, divisions, process teams, project teams, and other workgroups.

- **Operational Management.** The members of self-directed teams, operating managers, or line personnel develop short-range plans such as weekly production schedules. They direct the use of resources and the performance of tasks according to procedures and within budgets and schedules they establish for the teams and other workgroups of the organization.

Information Quality

What characteristics of information products make them valuable and useful to you? To answer this important question, we must first examine the characteristics or

CHALLENGE

Deutsche Post DHL–The Challenges of Creating and Managing a Global Brand

Deutsche Post DHL is the largest logistics service provider in the world today. The corporate group, which includes Deutsche Post, DHL Express, DHL Global Forwarding, DHL Freight, and DHL Supply Chain as its major operating divisions, employs more than 420,000 in more than 220 different countries. In 2008, more than 5 percent of the global trade volume traveled through some arm of the group. Revenues for 2010 were 51,481 million euro, or about $75.5 billion. As an integrated logistics provider, operations lie at the core of the enterprise, with more than 3 million packages and more than 70 million letters delivered every day. The global fleet of vehicles numbers in excess of 150,000, and the company recognizes more than 120,000 different postal codes worldwide. To put these numbers in context, consider that FedEx operates a fleet of almost 44,000 trucks and delivered 3.5 million shipments in 2009.

The Deutsche Post DHL group is the result of the acquisition of DHL by Deutsche Post, which began to accumulate shares in 1998, reached a majority stake in 2001, and finalized the purchase in 2002. Deutsche Post itself is the heir to the German government-run Deutsche Bundespost, which was privatized in 1995, following an overarching movement in the European Union to deregulate monopolistic services. Running a publicly listed company is very different from operating a government-sanctioned monopoly, and as their first order of business senior management tackled the dual issues of declining growth in its existing markets and the many opportunities present due to a lack of international presence and a tendency toward increased globalization of trade. In addition, the exclusivity rights of Deutsche Post to deliver letters within Germany—in essence, the operation of the postal system—was due to expire in 2008 as set forth by the privatization process and European legislation. At the same time, the company was granted a license to deliver mail in the United Kingdom in 2002, effectively terminating the historic monopoly enjoyed by the Royal Mail. In all areas of the business, from local mail to worldwide package distribution and large-scale logistics, competition was increasing. As a result, management decided to build a global logistics business to augment and complement its traditional domestic postal operations.

The acquisition of DHL in 2001–2002 was the first major step in this process, followed by the acquisitions of Airborne Express in the United States in 2003 and British logistics company Exel in 2005. DHL itself was originally founded in 1969 in California. Law student Larry Hillblom (the H in DHL) started running a courier service between San Francisco and Los Angeles to supplement his income, picking up packages for the last flight of the day and returning on the first flight the next morning, five days a week. After graduation, he was joined by friends Adrian Dalsey and Robert Lynn (the D and L, respectively) and launched a niche company that would fly bills of lading for maritime freight between San Francisco and Honolulu, Hawaii. Since the documentation flew in advance of the actual cargo, documents could be processed beforehand with significant time savings. In the following years, the company started expanding aggressively to countries such as the Philippines, Japan, Hong Kong, and Australia. In the beginning, DHL hired couriers in exchange for free airplane tickets to their destinations. DHL was the first international delivery company to offer overnight service. As it is now German-owned, DHL is not affected by U.S. embargoes and thus delivers to countries such as Cuba, Iran, and Burma.

As a result of these various mergers and acquisitions occurring in the relatively short time span of ten years, the company now known as Deutsche Post DHL (DHL

FIGURE 10.1

As Deutsche Post DHL seeks to build a global integrated logistics business, investing with a global brand in mind introduces some significant challenges.

SOURCE: © Carol Kohen/photolibrary.

for short) became a collection of smaller brands with various degrees of recognition across the world. International logistics, however, almost by definition is a global business, and customers who operate on a global scale would very much prefer to do business with a single provider instead of navigating the internal operations of DHL by themselves. As a result, management embarked on a campaign to create a truly unique and global brand that would unify all those operations under the banner of DHL, and that would serve as the umbrella denomination for the regional and specialist companies that conformed the Deutsche Post DHL group. Building a global brand is a challenge for any firm of any size. If the company in question were just founded, then it would not have to deal with the challenges of transitioning existing brands into a global name, as well as deciding which brands, if any, to do away with. For an existing company as large as DHL, those challenges are there.

There are clearly a number of advantages in establishing a global brand, particularly for a business whose customers are global as well. A unified brand aligns company objectives and marketing efforts, providing staff across divisions and countries with clear guidance on how to conduct their marketing activities. From a communications point of view, a global brand simplifies reaching out to customers and creates an image of consistency and integrated operations. This is just what the customers of DHL are looking for, as the majority of them would like to do business with a single unified provider that can take care of their needs from beginning to end. Strong brands also help with customer acquisition and retention; to establish this unique, global brand, it must be present at every point of contact in every office in every country. That means that thousands of employees must be trained to understand,

live, and execute on the brand promise. It is essential for management to decide how to determine which of many possible brand investments would be effective in developing that global brand at the individual country level.

As much as the local employees in each office deliver on the global brand, it is the local marketing managers in each division and country who decide on how marketing dollars (or euros) should be allocated. As part of this process, management focused on answering a specific set of questions:

1. What is the potential growth of the DHL brand in each country, compared to its competitors?

2. In which stages of the purchase process would brand investments offer the most potential return?

3. What are the key attributes on which the brand is evaluated by their customers, and how does DHL perform on those attributes compared to competitors?

4. *How can DHL best allocate marketing resources to best differentiate the brand in ways that are most relevant to its customers?*

The answers to these questions are very likely to differ for each country, depending on the specific customers and competitive structure in each market. Nevertheless, answering the questions would help brand managers determine the best course of action to make local investments that will develop the brand most consistently with the global concept, while remaining flexible to adapt those investments to the needs of their local environment.

SOURCE: Fischer, M., Giehl, W. and Freundt, T. "Managing Global Brand Investments at DHL," *Interfaces*, 2008, and www.dp-dhl.com, accessed June 7, 2011.

▼ QUESTIONS TO CONSIDER

1. What are some of the ways in which local marketing managers can choose to invest their marketing budgets? What are the pros and cons of each? How would you make that allocation decision?

2. Consider the four questions that the company is attempting to answer. How can technology help with

those kind of situations? How would you apply technology to this problem?

3. Is it possible for information technology to supplement (or even replace) the expertise, experience, and judgment of a local marketing manager who knows his industry and/or country? Why?

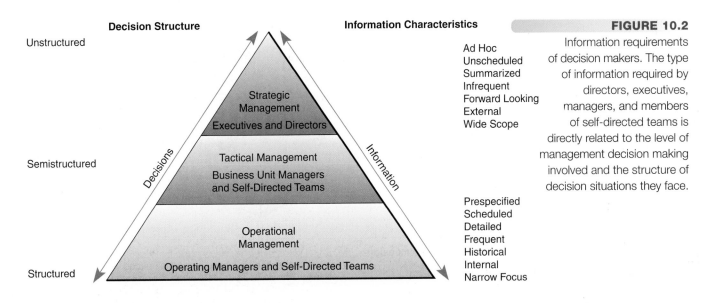

Decision Structure   **Information Characteristics**

Unstructured

Ad Hoc
Unscheduled
Summarized
Infrequent
Forward Looking
External
Wide Scope

Strategic
Management

Executives and Directors

Decisions

Information

Semistructured

Tactical Management

Business Unit Managers
and Self-Directed Teams

Prespecified
Scheduled
Detailed
Frequent
Historical
Internal
Narrow Focus

Operational
Management

Operating Managers and Self-Directed Teams

Structured

FIGURE 10.2

Information requirements of decision makers. The type of information required by directors, executives, managers, and members of self-directed teams is directly related to the level of management decision making involved and the structure of decision situations they face.

attributes of *information quality.* Information that is outdated (or late), inaccurate, or hard to understand is not very meaningful, useful, or valuable to a decision maker. People need information of high quality—that is, information products whose characteristics, attributes, or qualities make the information more valuable to them. While information quality has many attributes, it is useful to think of information quality as having the three dimensions of time, content, and form. Figure 10.3 summarizes the important attributes of information quality and groups them into those three dimensions.

Decision Structure

One way to understand decision making is to look at **decision structure.** Decision structure can be thought of as a continuum anchored on one end with *highly structured* decisions and on the other end with *highly unstructured* decisions. Decisions made at the operational management level tend to be more *structured,* those at the tactical level are more *semistructured,* and those at the strategic management level are more *unstructured.* Structured decisions involve situations in which the procedures to follow, when a decision is needed, can be specified in advance. One of the simplest examples of a highly structured decision is adding 2 + 2. There is a specified procedure for doing it and, if correctly followed, the answer will always be the same. The inventory reorder decisions that most businesses face are another example. There is a formula that, when correctly applied, will provide the best answer as to when to reorder or how much to stock.

In contrast, unstructured decisions involve decision situations in which it is not possible to specify in advance most of the decision procedures to follow. Most decisions related to long-term strategy can be thought of as unstructured (e.g., "What product lines should we develop over the next five years?"). Most business decision situations are semistructured; that is, some decision procedures can be prespecified but not enough to lead to a definite recommended decision. For example, decisions involved in starting new online services or making major changes to employee benefits would probably range from unstructured to semistructured. Finally, decisions that are unstructured are those for which no procedures or rules exist to guide the decision makers toward the correct decision. In these types of decisions, many sources of information must be accessed, and the decision often rests on experience and "gut feeling." One example of an unstructured decision might be the answer to the question, "What business should we be in 10 years

FIGURE 10.3

A summary of the attributes of information quality. This figure outlines the attributes that should be present in high-quality information products.

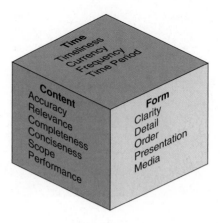

Time Dimension

Timeliness	Information should be provided when it is needed.
Currency	Information should be up-to-date when it is provided.
Frequency	Information should be provided as often as needed.
Time Period	Information can be provided about past, present, and future time periods.

Content Dimension

Accuracy	Information should be free from errors.
Relevance	Information should be related to the information needs of a specific recipient for a specific situation.
Completeness	All the information that is needed should be provided.
Conciseness	Only the information that is needed should be provided.
Scope	Information can have a broad or narrow scope, or an internal or external focus.
Performance	Information can reveal performance by measuring activities accomplished, progress made, or resources accumulated.

Form Dimension

Clarity	Information should be provided in a form that is easy to understand.
Detail	Information can be provided in detail or summary form.
Order	Information can be arranged in a predetermined sequence.
Presentation	Information can be presented in narrative, numeric, graphic, or other forms.
Media	Information can be provided in the form of printed paper documents, video displays, or other media.

from now?" Figure 10.4 provides a variety of examples of business decisions by type of decision structure and level of management.

Therefore, information systems must be designed to produce a variety of information products to meet the changing needs of decision makers throughout an organization. For example, decision makers at the strategic management level may look to *decision support systems* and *business analytical systems* to provide them with more summarized, ad hoc, unscheduled reports, forecasts, and external intelligence to support their more unstructured planning and policymaking responsibilities. Decision makers

FIGURE 10.4

Examples of decisions by the type of decision structure and level of management.

Decision Structure	Operational Management	Tactical Management	Strategic Management
Unstructured	Cash management	Business process reengineering	New e-business initiatives
		Workgroup performance analysis	Company reorganization
Semistructured	Credit management	Employee performance appraisal	Product planning
	Production scheduling	Capital budgeting	Mergers and acquisitions
	Daily work assignment	Program budgeting	Site location
Structured	Inventory control	Program control	

	Management Information Systems	Decision Support Systems
• Decision support provided	Provide information about the performance of the organization	Provide information and decision support techniques to analyze specific problems or opportunities
• Information form and frequency	Periodic, exception, demand, and push reports and responses	Interactive inquiries and responses
• Information format	Prespecified, fixed format	Ad hoc, flexible, and adaptable format
• Information processing methodology	Information produced by extraction and manipulation of business data	Information produced by analytical modeling of business data

FIGURE 10.5

Comparing the major differences in the information and decision support capabilities of management information systems and decision support systems.

at the operational management level, in contrast, may depend on *management information systems* to supply more prespecified internal reports emphasizing detailed current and historical data comparisons that support their more structured responsibilities in day-to-day operations. Figure 10.5 compares the information and decision support capabilities of management information systems and decision support systems, which we will explore in this chapter.

The emerging class of applications focuses on personalized decision support, modeling, information retrieval, data warehousing, what-if scenarios, and reporting.

DECISION SUPPORT TRENDS
LO 10-2

As we discussed in Chapter 1, using information systems to support business decision making has been one of the primary thrusts of the business use of information technology. During the 1990s, however, both academic researchers and business practitioners began to report that the traditional managerial focus originating in classic management information systems (1960s), decision support systems (1970s), and executive information systems (1980s) was expanding. The fast pace of new information technologies like PC hardware and software suites, client/server networks, and networked PC versions of business analytic software made decision support available to lower levels of management, as well as to individual line personnel and self-directed teams of business professionals.

This trend has accelerated with the dramatic growth of the Internet, as well as of intranets and extranets that inter-network with companies and their stakeholders. The e-business and e-commerce initiatives that are being implemented by many companies are also expanding the information and decision support uses and the expectations of a company's employees, managers, customers, suppliers, and other business partners. Figure 10.6 illustrates that all business stakeholders expect easy and instant access to information and Web-enabled self-service data analysis. Today's businesses are responding with a variety of personalized and proactive Web-based analytical techniques to support the decision-making requirements of all of their constituents.

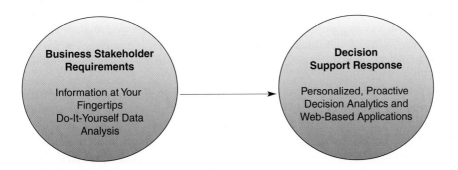

FIGURE 10.6

A business must meet the information and data analysis requirements of its stakeholders with more personalized and proactive Web-based decision support.

Thus, the growth of corporate intranets and extranets, as well as the Web, has accelerated the development and use of "executive-class" information delivery and decision support software tools by lower levels of management and by individuals and teams of business professionals. In addition, this dramatic expansion has opened the door to the use of such ***business intelligence (BI)*** tools by the suppliers, customers, and other business stakeholders of a company for customer relationship management, supply chain management, and other e-business applications.

In 1989, Howard Dresner (later a Gartner Group analyst) proposed BI as an umbrella term to describe "*concepts and methods to improve business decision making by using fact-based support systems.*" It was not until the late 1990s that this usage became widespread. Today, BI is considered a necessary and mission-critical element in crafting and executing a firm's strategy. Consider the following findings from a recent Gartner Group study:

- Because of lack of information, processes, and tools, through 2012, more than 35 percent of the top 5,000 global companies will regularly fail to make insightful decisions about significant changes in their business and markets.

- In 2012, business units will control at least 40 percent of the total budget for business intelligence.

- In 2010, 20 percent of organizations were using an industry-specific analytic application, delivered via software as a service, as a standard component of their business intelligence portfolio.

- In 2009, collaborative decision making emerged as a new product category that combines social software with business intelligence platform capabilities.

When you consider some of these findings, it becomes easy to see that BI is rapidly becoming the mainstay for business decision making in the modern organization. In fact, it is very likely a competitive necessity for many industries.

As with all concepts in business-related technologies, business intelligence has evolved from Dresner's original definition focusing on concepts and methods to a more action-oriented approach referred to as *business analytics*. Business analytics (BA) refers to the *skills, technologies, applications, and practices applied to a continuous iterative exploration and investigation of a business's historical performance to gain insight and drive the strategic business planning process*. Business analytics focuses on developing new insights and understanding of business performance based on data and statistical methods. In contrast, business intelligence traditionally focuses on using a consistent set of metrics to both measure past performance and guide business planning, which is also based on data and statistical methods.

Business analytics makes much more extensive use of data, statistical and quantitative analysis, explanatory and predictive modeling, and fact-based management to drive decision making. Analytics may be used as input for human decisions or may drive fully automated decisions. Business intelligence is more associated with querying, reporting, online analytical processing (OLAP), and "alerts." In other words, querying, reporting, OLAP, and alert tools can answer the questions: *what happened; how many; how often; where; where exactly is the problem;* and *what actions are needed*. Business analytics, in contrast, can answer the questions: *why is this happening; what if these trends continue; what will happen next (that is, predict);* and *what is the best that can happen (that is, optimize)*. One of the most common techniques and approaches associated with business analytics is data mining, a concept introduced in Chapter 5 and discussed in detail later in this chapter.

Figure 10.7 highlights several major information technologies that are being customized, personalized, and Web-enabled to provide key business information and analytical tools for managers, business professionals, and business stakeholders. We highlight the trends toward such business intelligence applications in the various types of information and decision support systems that are discussed in this chapter.

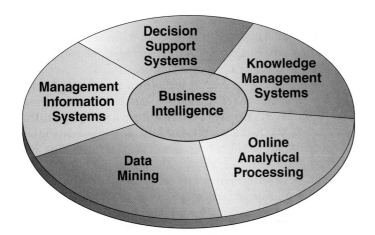

FIGURE 10.7
Business intelligence applications are based on personalized and Web-enabled information analysis, knowledge management, and decision support technologies.

Hyatt Hotels: Dashboards Integrate Financial and Operational Information

A few years ago, executives at Chicago-based Hyatt Hotels decided the company needed a way to consolidate its disparate financial data so that it could more easily forecast future sales and plan its business accordingly. In other words, the company wanted to install a typical financial performance management layer, with dashboards and scorecards for top-level managers. But after some discussion on the matter, the installation grew to be not so typical.

Gebhard Rainer, Hyatt's vice president of hotel finance and systems, wanted to combine these financial elements—budgeting, planning, modeling, and reporting—with operational data from the hotels themselves. The idea was that a complete picture of the company's business, available on a daily basis to executives as well as to hotel managers, was not possible without having the two together in the same dashboard.

The concept was motivated by a changing world, with terrorist risks and natural disasters causing an ever-shifting array of business variables. Rainer, in a Middle Eastern country in the aftermath of a terrorist attack several years ago, confronted these issues firsthand—as did the company, which owns hotels in New Orleans and along the hurricane-ravaged Gulf Coast. The first line of business is the safety of hotel guests. But in terms of the big picture, hotel companies must re-forecast their business goals from the ground up, based on a set of entirely new metrics that deals with issues from resource allocation to skittish tourists who may want to rethink their travel plans. It wasn't a job for spreadsheets.

Hyatt was among the first of Hyperion Inc.'s customers to adopt System 9. (Hyperion Inc. is now part of Oracle.) The company selected Hyperion based on its "integrateability" with its source systems, as well as its user-friendliness. At first, Hyatt wanted a small-scale installation, delivering the System 9 dashboards to about 40 executive users. "This phase was a 'show-me-what-you-can-do' thing," says Sufel Barkat, Hyatt's assistant vice president for financial systems. "We simply wanted to understand the capability of the tools. The next stage will have a much bigger impact." The ultimate plan is to spread the system throughout the Hyatt organization to its many subsidiaries, in the United States and abroad, and to its individual properties—full-blown operational BI. Eventually, hotel managers will have access to dashboards so that everyone is on the same page, and so that local employees can make local decisions based on the same information viewed at headquarters.

Hyatt ended up using a data warehouse from Teradata to cleanse operational information coming from the decentralized ERP systems of Hyatt's individual hotels around the world. The company also uses the warehouse to store and cleanse external marketing data, such as what the competition is up to, or market share in each region.

On the financial side, other sources include the company's proprietary general ledger system and an Oracle database—systems already consolidated and unified through Hyatt's original performance management outlay.

The next step will be to deliver the dashboards to between 500 and 600 users at Hyatt—all the way down to the regional manager level. The full-blown operational BI rollout will target around 3,000 users. So far, in these early stages, Barkat hasn't been able to quantify the results of System 9 with any real figures. But, he says, users have been providing feedback on metrics, which, to him, indicates a strong "cultural and business adaptation" among Hyatt's executive class.

SOURCE: Scott Eden, "Hyatt Merges Financial, Ops Data," *InformationWeek*, January 17, 2006.

DECISION SUPPORT SYSTEMS
LO 10-4

Decision support systems are computer-based information systems that provide interactive information support to managers and business professionals during the decision-making process. Decision support systems use (1) analytical models, (2) specialized databases, (3) a decision maker's own insights and judgments, and (4) an interactive, computer-based modeling process to support semistructured business decisions.

Example

An example might help at this point. Sales managers typically rely on management information systems to produce sales analysis reports. These reports contain sales performance figures by product line, salesperson, sales region, and so on. A decision support system (DSS), however, would also interactively show a sales manager the effects on sales performance of changes in a variety of factors (e.g., promotion expense and salesperson compensation). The DSS could then use several criteria (e.g., expected gross margin and market share) to evaluate and rank alternative combinations of sales performance factors.

Therefore, DSSs are designed to be ad hoc, quick-response systems that are initiated and controlled by business decision makers. Decision support systems are thus able to support directly the specific types of decisions and the personal decision-making styles and needs of individual executives, managers, and business professionals.

DSS Components

Unlike management information systems, decision support systems rely on *model bases,* as well as databases, as vital system resources. A DSS model base is a software component that consists of models used in computational and analytical routines that mathematically express relationships among variables. For example, a spreadsheet program might contain models that express simple accounting relationships among variables, such as Revenue − Expenses = Profit. A DSS model base could also include models and analytical techniques used to express much more complex relationships. For example, it might contain linear programming models, multiple regression forecasting models, and capital budgeting present value models. Such models may be stored in the form of spreadsheet models or templates, or statistical and mathematical programs and program modules. See Figure 10.8.

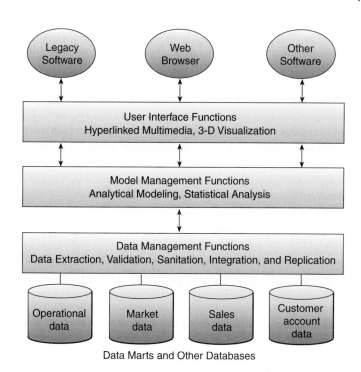

FIGURE 10.8
Components of a Web-enabled marketing decision support system. Note the hardware, software, model, data, and network resources involved.

In addition, DSS software packages can combine model components to create integrated models that support specific types of decisions. DSS software typically contains built-in analytical modeling routines and also enables you to build your own models. Many DSS packages are now available in microcomputer and Web-enabled versions. Of course, electronic spreadsheet packages also provide some of the model building (spreadsheet models) and analytical modeling (what-if and goal-seeking analysis) offered by more powerful DSS software. As businesses become more aware of the power of decision support systems, they are using them in ever-increasing areas of the business. See Figure 10.9.

FIGURE 10.9

Many businesses are turning to decision support systems and their underlying models to improve a wide variety of business functions.

Analytics competitors make expert use of statistics and modeling to improve a wide variety of functions. Here are some common applications:		
Function	**Description**	**Exemplars**
Supply chain	Simulate and optimize supply chain flows; reduce inventory and stockouts.	Dell, Walmart, Amazon
Customer selection, loyalty, and service	Identify customers with the greatest profit potential; increase likelihood that they will want the product or service offering; retain their loyalty.	Harrah's, Capital One, Barclays
Pricing	Identify the price that will maximize yield or profit.	Progressive, Marriott
Human capital	Select the best employees for particular tasks or jobs at particular compensation levels.	New England Patriots, Oakland A's, Boston Red Sox
Product and service quality	Detect quality problems early and minimize them.	Honda, Intel
Financial performance	Better understand the drivers of financial performance and the effects of nonfinancial factors.	MCI, Verizon
Research and development	Improve quality, efficacy, and, where applicable, safety of products and services.	Novartis, Amazon, Yahoo

SOURCE: Thomas H. Davenport, "Competing on Analytics," *Harvard Business Review*, January 2006.

United Agri Products: Making Better Decisions Using Models and Data

You give employees electronic reports, maybe even a dashboard. But are you helping them make better day-to-day decisions?

Companies can't report their way to great results—although you wouldn't know it from their accumulation of underused reports and dashboards. Companies that get this critical point are moving away from IT-centric business intelligence (BI) programs and toward results-focused performance management. True: BI does more than just generate reports. But add in query and analysis tools, as well as sophisticated predictive and statistical analytics, and those tools and technologies are overwhelmingly under IT's control.

In contrast, performance management, or PM, is defined by business needs, providing decision makers with the data they need to make the right moves, ones that fit with company strategy.

Most often, companies incorporate performance management (PM) into their budgeting and financial processes, in what's called corporate or financial PM. The next step is operational PM, where they apply BI to practical, day-to-day decisions in the supply chain, sales, customer service, and other areas.

That's what's happening at United Agri Products (UAP), a unit of $5 billion-a-year chemical and fertilizer supplier Agrium, which started doing operational PM projects using IBM's Cognos BI platform. "After years of IT preaching the value of BI to business, we reached a point of maturity where the roles started to reverse, and the business started coming to us with ideas," says David Wheat, UAP's director of decision support systems.

UAP's director of operations brought one such project to IT. The chief executive officer had asked him to cut end-of-year inventory by $25 million, a difficult task for an agricultural company given ever-changing weather conditions, crop disease, and insect infestations, all happening across a variety of regions.

"The operations director sketched out exactly what he wanted on a whiteboard," Wheat says. Then he said, "If I can know at any point in time what I have in inventory and can forecast what the consumption will be through the end of the season, I'll know what dollar amount I'll have left and I can go after the high-dollar overages."

With that context, Wheat laid out a model for a PM system that included what data he needed and when he had to have them in order to make decisions. And his model came complete with a financial target.

UAP lacked a sales forecasting application, so Wheat's team developed one by integrating relevant information—current inventory levels, open purchase orders, prior-year purchase histories, and predicted overages or shortages—into a single report. The application includes a daily alert that notifies managers in four regions whenever a purchase order has the potential to create excess season-ending inventory.

"All that data presented in one place, with exceptions highlighted in color, made problems jump right to the top for the director and his regional managers," Wheat says. That information led managers to investigate open, unconfirmed purchase orders to see if they're justified. The result: "Within two weeks, UAP had canceled $2 million worth of POs for products that weren't needed."

SOURCE: Dough Henschen, "Decision Time," *InformationWeek*, November 24, 2008.

MANAGEMENT INFORMATION SYSTEMS
LO 10-5

Recall from Chapter 1 that *management information systems* were the original type of information system developed to support managerial decision making. An MIS produces information products that support many of the day-to-day decision-making needs of managers and business professionals. Reports, displays, and responses produced by management information systems provide information that these decision makers have specified in advance as adequately meeting their information needs. Such predefined information products satisfy the information needs of decision makers at the operational and tactical levels of the organization who are faced with more structured types of decision situations. For example, sales managers rely heavily on sales analysis reports to evaluate differences in performance among salespeople who sell the same types of products to the same types of customers. They have a pretty good idea of the kinds of information about sales results (by product line, sales territory, customer, salesperson, and so on) that they need to manage sales performance effectively.

Managers and other decision makers use an MIS to request information at their networked workstations that supports their decision-making activities. This information takes the form of periodic, exception, and demand reports and immediate responses to inquiries. Web browsers, application programs, and database management software provide access to information in the intranet and other operational databases of the organization. Remember, operational databases are maintained by transaction processing systems. Data about the business environment are obtained from Internet or extranet databases when necessary.

Management Reporting Alternatives

Management information systems provide a variety of information products to managers. Four major reporting alternatives are provided by such systems.

- **Periodic Scheduled Reports.** This traditional form of providing information to managers uses a prespecified format designed to provide managers with information on a regular basis. Typical examples of such periodic scheduled reports are daily or weekly sales analysis reports and monthly financial statements.

- **Exception Reports.** In some cases, reports are produced only when exceptional conditions occur. In other cases, reports are produced periodically but contain information only about these exceptional conditions. For example, a credit manager can be provided with a report that contains only information on customers who have exceeded their credit limits. Exception reporting reduces *information overload* instead of overwhelming decision makers with periodic detailed reports of business activity.

- **Demand Reports and Responses.** Information is available whenever a manager demands it. For example, Web browsers, DBMS query languages, and report generators enable managers at PC workstations to get immediate responses or to find and obtain customized reports as a result of their requests for the information they need. Thus, managers do not have to wait for periodic reports to arrive as scheduled.

- **Push Reporting.** Information is *pushed* to a manager's networked workstation. Thus, many companies are using Webcasting software to broadcast reports and other information selectively to the networked PCs of managers and specialists over their corporate intranets. See Figure 10.10.

At a stockholder meeting, the former CEO of PepsiCo, D. Wayne Calloway, said: "Ten years ago I could have told you how Doritos were selling west of the Mississippi. Today, not only can I tell you how well Doritos sell west of the Mississippi, I can also tell you how well they are selling in California, in Orange County, in the town of Irvine, in the local Vons supermarket, in the special promotion, at the end of Aisle 4, on Thursdays."

ONLINE ANALYTICAL PROCESSING
LO 10-3

The competitive and dynamic nature of today's global business environment is driving demands by business managers and analysts for information systems that can provide fast answers to complex business queries. The IS industry has responded to these demands with developments like analytical databases, data marts, data warehouses, data mining techniques, and multidimensional database structures (discussed

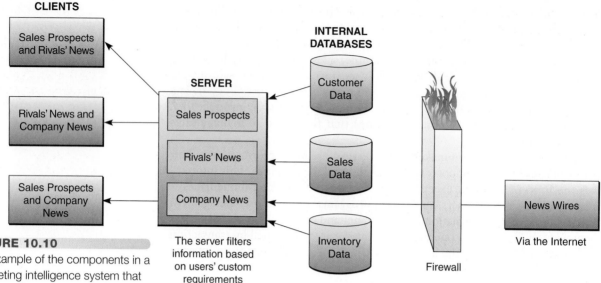

FIGURE 10.10

An example of the components in a marketing intelligence system that uses the Internet and a corporate intranet system to "push" information to employees.

in Chapter 5), and with specialized servers and Web-enabled software products that support *online analytical processing (OLAP)*.

Online analytical processing enables managers and analysts to interactively examine and manipulate large amounts of detailed and consolidated data from many perspectives. OLAP involves analyzing complex relationships among thousands or even millions of data items stored in data marts, data warehouses, and other multidimensional databases to discover patterns, trends, and exception conditions. An OLAP session takes place online in real time, with rapid responses to a manager's or analyst's queries, so that the analytical or decision-making process is undisturbed. See Figure 10.11.

Online analytical processing involves several basic analytical operations, including consolidation, "drill-down," and "slicing and dicing." See Figure 10.12.

- **Consolidation.** Consolidation involves the aggregation of data, which can involve simple roll-ups or complex groupings involving interrelated data. For example, data about sales offices can be rolled up to the district level, and the district-level data can be rolled up to provide a regional-level perspective.

- **Drill-Down.** OLAP can also go in the reverse direction and automatically display detailed data that comprise consolidated data. This process is called drill-down. For example, the sales by individual products or sales reps that make up a region's sales totals could be easily accessed.

FIGURE 10.11

Online analytical processing may involve the use of specialized servers and multidimensional databases. OLAP provides fast answers to complex queries posed by managers and analysts using traditional and Web-enabled OLAP software.

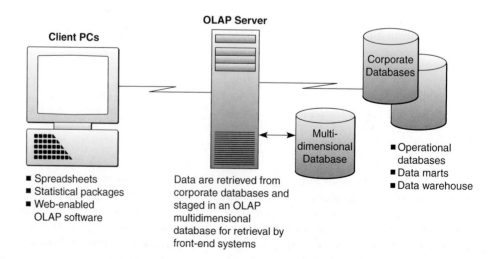

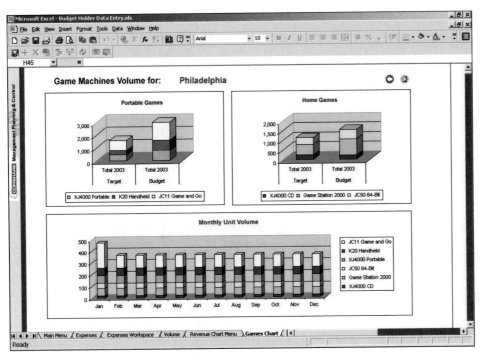

FIGURE 10.12
Comshare's Management Planning and Control software enables business professionals to use Microsoft Excel as their user interface for Web-enabled online analytical processing.

SOURCE: Used with permission from Microsoft®.

- **Slicing and Dicing.** Slicing and dicing refers to the ability to look at the database from different viewpoints. One slice of the sales database might show all sales of a product type within regions. Another slice might show all sales by sales channel within each product type. Slicing and dicing is often performed along a time axis to analyze trends and find time-based patterns in the data.

OLAP Examples

Probably the best way to understand the power of OLAP fully is to look at common business applications of the technique. The real power of OLAP comes from the marriage of data and models on a large scale. Through this marriage, managers can solve a variety of problems that previously would be considered too complex to tackle effectively. Common business areas where OLAP can solve complex problems include:

- Marketing and sales analysis
- Clickstream data
- Database marketing
- Budgeting
- Financial reporting and consolidation
- Profitability analysis
- Quality analysis

Let's look at one or two examples of how OLAP can be used in the modern business setting.

It is near the end of a business quarter, and senior management is worried about the market acceptance of several new products. A marketing analyst is asked to provide an update to senior management. The problem is that the update must be delivered in less than an hour due to a last-minute request from the chief executive officer. The analyst really only has a few minutes to analyze the market acceptance of several new products, so she decides to group 20 products that were introduced between six and nine months ago and compare their sales with a comparable group of 50 products introduced between two and three years ago. The analyst just defines two new, on-the-fly, product groupings and creates a ratio of the new group to the older group. She can then track this ratio of sales revenue or volume by any level of location, over time, by customer sector or by sales group. Defining the new groupings and the ratio takes a couple of minutes, and any of the analyses take a matter of a few seconds to generate, even though the database has tens of thousands of products and hundreds of locations. It takes no more than a total of 15 minutes to spot that some regions have not accepted the new products as fast as others.

Then, the analyst investigates whether this was because of inadequate promotion, unsuitability of the new products, lack of briefings of the sales force in the slow areas, or whether some areas always accept new products more slowly than others. Looking at other new product introductions by creating new groupings of products of different ages, she finds that the same areas are always conservative when introducing expensive new products. She then uses this information to see if the growth in the slow areas is in line with history and finds that some areas have taken off even more slowly than previously. Given the results of this analysis, senior management decides it is premature in its concern and tables further discussion until the next quarterly sales data can be assessed.

In another example, let's consider a general merchandise retailer who has joined the e-tailing ranks, wants the company Web site to be as "sticky" as possible, and has begun to analyze clickstream data to surmise why customers might leave the site prematurely. The company sharpened its analysis to determine the value of abandoned shopping carts. When a customer leaves the site in the middle of a shopping trip, for whatever reason, the company looks to see what products were in the abandoned cart. The data are then compared with similar data from other carts to examine:

- How much revenue the abandoned carts represented (in other words, the amount of revenue that was lost because of the customer's early departure).
- Whether the products in the cart were high-profit items or loss leaders.
- Whether the same products were found in other abandoned carts.
- The volume of products and the number of different product categories in the cart.
- Whether the total bill for the abandoned carts consistently fell within a certain dollar range.
- How the average and total bills for abandoned carts compared with unabandoned carts (those that made it through the checkout process).

The results of using OLAP to conduct this analysis trigger some interesting theories. For instance, it is possible that none of the products in the cart was appealing enough to a particular customer to keep that customer shopping. The customer might have been annoyed by frequent inquiries, such as "Are you ready to check out?" At a particular dollar total, the customer might have changed his or her mind about the entire shopping trip and left. It's also possible that a number or mix of products in a cart reminded the customer of another site that might offer a steeper discount for similar purchases.

Admittedly, some of these theories are mere guesses. After all, maybe the customer's Internet connection was on the fritz, or the site had a bug that abruptly booted the user. When examined regularly and with consistent metrics, however, clickstreams can reveal interesting patterns. After several analyses, the e-tailer decides to make some changes to the Web site.

First, the e-tailer tweaks the site to show a rolling total as items are added to the cart, thereby allowing the customer to see the total charge during the shopping time and to check out once the magic budget limit is reached. In addition, rather than requiring the customer to go to another page for specific product information, the site now invites the customer to see pop-up product information with a click of the right mouse button, keeping the buy mode alive. Finally, the vendor decides to integrate the click-stream data with more specific customer behavior information, including information from the CRM system.

Rather than just examining a customer's navigation patterns and guessing about which actions to take, the e-tailer can combine those patterns with more specific customer data (such as previous purchases in that product category, key demographic and psychographic data, or lifetime value score) to provide a complete view of that customer's value and interests. That kind of analysis will show you whether the lost customer was a one-time-only shopper or a high-value customer. A tailored e-mail message or electronic coupon—perhaps targeting one of the products left behind on a prior trip—could make all the difference the next time that high-value customer logs on.

Here's a real-world example of how OLAP can help solve complex business problems.

Direct Energy: Mining BI to Keep Its Customers

Even before bad debt shook the mortgage industry, Direct Energy was feeling its effects, including eroding revenue streams due to customer churn. Until then, the company effectively mined its way out in the best fashion: business intelligence. "Various groups were pulling data from various systems and not having integrated information," explains John Katsinos, vice president of information systems for Direct Energy's mass markets operations. "There was no way to tie together a customer's end-to-end lifecycle."

Without that holistic view of customer records, it was difficult for Direct Energy analysts to understand, let alone prevent, customer churn. So began BI Jumpstart, the company's initiative to give its analysts insight into customer actions that precipitate into the dropping of Direct Energy services, as well as tools for forecasting bad debt. The result has been savings of tens of millions of dollars and a more proactive approach to customer retention via more accurate pricing, forecasting, and targeted marketing.

"We wanted to mitigate the risk to our business and customer base, and to grow our customer base and revenue," Katsinos adds.

"That meant being able to understand customer data at a level where we can forecast and predict behavior." Katsinos kicked off BI Jumpstart by assembling a crack analytics team consisting of an IS project manager, a data modeler, a pair of ETL developers, an analytic developer, a BI architect, and a BI administrator. That group then implemented a "multilayered business intelligence" strategy that, Katsinos explains, comprises data warehousing, data marts, OLAP repositories, and ETL.

The result is a data miner's dream: Direct Energy analysts can use the integrated BI program to predict which customers in which areas are likely to turn over, and then adjust the company's services, pricing, and marketing campaigns accordingly.

For example, with BI Jumpstart in place, Direct Energy can now determine why one of its offerings experiences a 2 percent churn while another sees 20 percent of its customers dropping the service.

More than an initiative geared toward new revenue streams, BI Jumpstart helps Direct Energy make the most of what it already has. "Now, we can slice and dice any way we want," Katsinos says.

SOURCE: Tom Sullivan, "Direct Energy Mines BI to Conserve Revenue Streams," *InfoWorld*, November 17, 2008.

Geographic Information and Data Visualization Systems

Geographic information systems (GIS) and *data visualization systems (DVS)* are special categories of DSS that integrate computer graphics with other DSS features. A geographic information system is a DSS that uses *geographic databases* to construct and display maps, as well as other graphics displays that support decisions affecting the geographic distribution of people and other resources. Many companies are using GIS technology along with *global positioning system* (GPS) devices to help them choose new retail store locations, optimize distribution routes, or analyze the demographics of their target audiences. For example, companies like Levi Strauss, Arby's, Consolidated Rail, and Federal Express use GIS packages to integrate maps, graphics, and other geographic data with business data from spreadsheets and statistical packages. GIS software such as MapInfo and Atlas GIS is used for most business GIS applications. See Figure 10.13.

Data visualization systems represent complex data using interactive, three-dimensional, graphical forms such as charts, graphs, and maps. DVS tools help users interactively sort, subdivide, combine, and organize data while the data are in their graphical form. This assistance helps users discover patterns, links, and anomalies in business or scientific data in an interactive knowledge discovery and decision support process. Business applications like data mining typically use interactive graphs that let users drill down in real time and manipulate the underlying data of a business model to help clarify their meaning for business decision making. Figure 10.14 is an example of airline flight analysis by a data visualization system.

The concept of the geographic information system and data visualization is not a new one. One of the first recorded uses of the concept occurred in September 1854. During a 10-day period, 500 people, all from the same section of London, England, died of cholera. Dr. John Snow, a local physician, had been studying this cholera epidemic for some time. In trying to determine the source of the cholera, Dr. Snow located every cholera death in the Soho district of London by marking the location of

FIGURE 10.13

Geographic information systems facilitate the mining and visualization of data associated with a geophysical location.

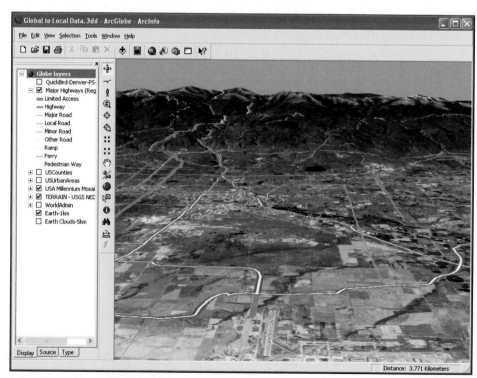

SOURCE: Courtesy of Rockware Inc.

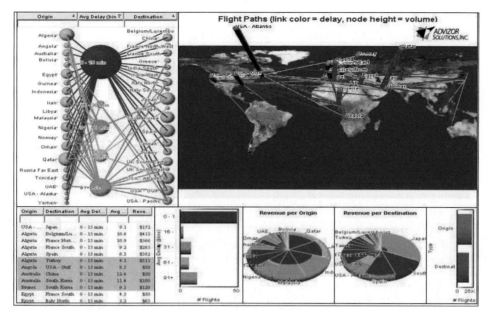

SOURCE: Courtesy of ADVIZOR Solutions, Inc. www.advizorsolutions.com.

FIGURE 10.14

Using a data visualization system to analyze airplane flights by segment and average delay, with drill-down to details.

the home of each victim with a dot on a map he had drawn. Figure 10.15 contains a replica of his original map.

As can be seen on the map, Dr. Snow marked the deaths with dots, and the 11 *X*s represent water pumps. By examining the scattering and clustering of the dots, Dr. Snow observed that the victims of the cholera shared one common attribute: They all lived near—and drank from—the Broad Street water pump. To test his hypothesis, Dr. Snow requested that the handle of the pump be removed, thus rendering it inoperable. Within a very short time, the cholera epidemic, which claimed more than 500 lives, was over.

You have probably used a GIS without knowing it. One of the most commonly used GIS websites is Google Maps. You can "drop pins" on desired locations to see a proposed route or just to mark places on a map.

SOURCE: E.R. Tufte, *The Visual Display of Quantitative Information*, 2nd ed. (Cheshire, Connecticut; Graphics Press, 2001), p. 24.

FIGURE 10.15

Replica of Dr. John Snow's cholera epidemic map.

JPMorgan and Panopticon: Data Visualization Helps Fixed Income Traders

Visualizing and understanding vast quantities of credit market data can be overwhelming using traditional techniques such as charts and tables. Navigating through this data to find specific reports and analytical information can also prove daunting, and traditional information delivery mechanisms have tended to provide unruly volumes of data.

The Internet is today the obvious delivery mechanism for such market data and proprietary analyses, yet the providers of such services must deliver more intuitive visualization and navigation to provide better value to their customers.

Fixed income research and analytics providers are looking at new means of visualizing data to provide more valuable and intuitive services to their users by going beyond simple online tables, charts, and document repositories.

JPMorgan created their CreditMap application using Panopticon Developer in order to provide their customers with a graphical representation of real-time activity in the corporate bond market. JPMorgan blurred the lines between providing informative research and valuable analytics, which has enabled them to win the Euromoney award for "Best Online Fixed Income Research."

JPMorgan was able to provide their users with quicker access to their existing online information using new visualization and navigation tools. To do this, they implemented Panopticon's interactive treemap visualization as a presentation layer and navigation system that provides a bird's-eye view of the data, at the same time allowing the user to drill down to specific reports and analytics.

JPMorgan's CreditMap allows users to visualize information through the use of color, size, and proximity in any way they desire with an easily customizable interface. This interface acts as a catalyst, enabling users to recognize patterns, analyze information, and make decisions more quickly and more accurately than ever before. Before CreditMap, the brokerage firm's customers could read text reports on the corporate bond market and view various tables of statistical information. But the market is so extensive that it could be difficult to keep things in perspective or to be aware of many of the investment opportunities.

CreditMap presents the corporate bond universe as a quilt of rectangles on a computer screen. The quilt is divided into industry sectors, and the rectangles within each sector represent bond issues. The size of the rectangle indicates the size of the issue, and the color indicates the issue's performance. So at a glance, investors can see which sectors and which individual issues are hot, and whether an issue's size fits their investment needs. Clicking on a rectangle opens a window that gives basic information on the issue—including its ratings and the name and phone number of the analyst who covers the issue—along with a drop-down menu offering detailed research.

"Panopticon treemaps have greatly enhanced our users' ability to visualize the credit markets and utilize analytics—it was an important contributing factor to us winning the Euromoney award," says Lee McGinty, head of European Portfolio & Index Strategy at JPMorgan.

SOURCE: *Case Study: JPMorgan CreditMap*, www.panopticon.com, March 2008.

USING DECISION SUPPORT SYSTEMS
LO 10-3

A decision support system involves an interactive ***analytical modeling*** process. For example, using a DSS software package for decision support may result in a series of displays in response to alternative what-if changes entered by a manager. This differs from the demand responses of management information systems because decision makers are not demanding prespecified information; rather, they are exploring possible alternatives. Thus, they do not have to specify their information needs in advance. Instead, they use the DSS, and its underlying models, to find the information

Type of Analytical Modeling	Activities and Examples
What-if analysis	Observing how changes to selected variables affect other variables. *Example:* What if we cut advertising by 10 percent? What would happen to sales?
Sensitivity analysis	Observing how repeated changes to a single variable affect other variables. *Example:* Let's cut advertising by $100 repeatedly so we can see its relationship to sales.
Goal-seeking analysis	Making repeated changes to selected variables until a chosen variable reaches a target value. *Example:* Let's try increases in advertising until sales reach $1 million.
Optimization analysis	Finding an optimum value for selected variables, given certain constraints. *Example:* What's the best amount of advertising to have, given our budget and choice of media?

FIGURE 10.16

Activities and examples of the major types of analytical modeling.

they need to help them make a decision. This is the essence of the decision support system concept.

Four basic types of analytical modeling activities are involved in using a decision support system: (1) *what-if analysis*, (2) *sensitivity analysis*, (3) *goal-seeking analysis*, and (4) *optimization analysis*. Let's briefly look at each type of analytical modeling that can be used for decision support. See Figure 10.16.

What-If Analysis

In *what-if analysis,* a user makes changes to variables, or relationships among variables, and observes the resulting changes in the values of other variables. For example, if you were using a spreadsheet, you might change a revenue amount (a variable) or a tax rate formula (a relationship among variables) in a simple financial spreadsheet model. Then you could command the spreadsheet program to recalculate all affected variables in the spreadsheet instantly. A managerial user would be able to observe and evaluate any changes that occurred to the values in the spreadsheet, especially to a variable such as net profit after taxes. To many managers, net profit after taxes is an example of the *bottom line*, that is, a key factor in making many types of decisions. This type of analysis would be repeated until the manager was satisfied with what the results revealed about the effects of various possible decisions. Figure 10.17 is an example of what-if analysis.

Sensitivity Analysis

Sensitivity analysis is a special case of what-if analysis. Typically, the value of only one variable is changed repeatedly, and the resulting changes on other variables are observed. As such, sensitivity analysis is really a case of what-if analysis that involves repeated changes to only one variable at a time. Some DSS packages automatically make repeated small changes to a variable when asked to perform sensitivity analysis. Typically, decision makers use sensitivity analysis when they are uncertain about the assumptions made in estimating the value of certain key variables. In our previous spreadsheet example, the value of revenue could be changed repeatedly in small increments, and the effects on other spreadsheet variables observed and evaluated. This process would help a manager understand the impact of various revenue levels on other factors involved in decisions being considered. A typical example might be determining at what point the interest rate on a loan makes a project no longer feasible. By varying the interest rate used in a net present value calcuation, for example, a

FIGURE 10.17

This what-if analysis, performed by @RISK for Excel, involves the evaluation of probability distributions of net income and net present value (NPV) generated by changes to values for sales, competitors, product development, and capital expenses.

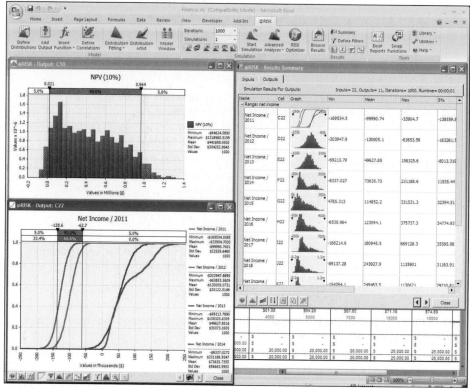

SOURCE: @RISK software. Image courtesy of Palisade Corporation.

manager can determine the range of acceptable interest rates under which a project can move forward. Approaching the problem this way allows the manager to make decisions about a forthcoming project without knowing the actual cost of the money being borrowed.

Goal-Seeking Analysis

Goal-seeking analysis reverses the direction of the analysis done in what-if and sensitivity analyses. Instead of observing how changes in a variable affect other variables, goal-seeking analysis (also called *how-can* analysis) sets a target value (goal) for a variable and then repeatedly changes other variables until the target value is achieved. For example, you could specify a target value (goal) of $2 million in net profit after taxes for a business venture. Then you could repeatedly change the value of revenue or expenses in a spreadsheet model until you achieve a result of $2 million. Thus, you would discover the amount of revenue or level of expenses the business venture needs to reach the goal of $2 million in after-tax profits. Therefore, this form of analytical modeling would help answer the question, "How can we achieve $2 million in net profit after taxes?" instead of the question, "What happens if we change revenue or expenses?" So, goal-seeking analysis is another important method of decision support.

Optimization Analysis

Optimization analysis is a more complex extension of goal-seeking analysis. Instead of setting a specific target value for a variable, the goal is to find the optimum value for one or more target variables, given certain constraints. Then one or more other variables are changed repeatedly, subject to the specified constraints, until you discover the best values for the target variables. For example, you could try to determine the highest possible level of profits that could be achieved by varying the values for selected revenue sources and expense categories. Changes to such variables could be subject to constraints, such as the limited capacity of a production process or limits to available financing. Optimization typically is accomplished using software like the Solver tool in Microsoft Excel and other software packages for optimization techniques, such as linear programming.

	Casual Male Retail Group: On-Demand Business Intelligence
Ask Dennis Hernreich, chief operating officer and chief financial officer of Casual Male Retail Group, what his life was like before he switched to an on-demand business intelligence reporting application, and he remembers the frustration all too easily.	

Ask Dennis Hernreich, chief operating officer and chief financial officer of Casual Male Retail Group, what his life was like before he switched to an on-demand business intelligence reporting application, and he remembers the frustration all too easily.

Casual Male Retail Group, a specialty retailer of big and tall men's apparel with $464 million in annual sales, was using a legacy on-premise reporting application for its catalog operations. (The company also has 520 retail outlets and e-commerce operations.) Yet the reporting features built into the system were "extremely poor," as Hernreich describes them: "Visibility to the business? Terrible. Real-time information? Doesn't exist. How are we doing with certain styles by size? Don't know."

"It was unacceptable," Hernreich says. In addition, you could only view those "canned" reports (which lacked features such as exception reporting) by making a trip to the printer for a stack of printouts. "It was hundreds of pages," he recalls. "That's just not how you operate today."

It's not as though Casual Male didn't have all this information; it just didn't have an intuitive and easy way to see the sales and inventory trends for its catalog business in real time. That changed in 2004, when Casual Male began to use a on-demand BI tool from vendor Oco (www.oco-inc.com), which takes all of Casual Male's data, builds and maintains a data warehouse for it off-site, and creates "responsive, real-time reporting dashboards that give us and our business users information at their fingertips," Hernreich says.

Today, Hernreich and Casual Male's merchandise planners and buyers have access to easy-to-consume dashboards full of catalog data: "What styles are selling today? How much inventory are we selling today? Where are we short? Where do we need to order? How are we selling by size? What are we out of stock in?" he says. "All of these basic questions, in terms of running the business—that's what we're learning every day from these reports."

Best of all, those annoying trips to the printer have ended.

SOURCE: Thomas Wailgum, "Business Intelligence and On-Demand: The Perfect Marriage?" *CIO Magazine*, March 27, 2008.

Data Mining for Decision Support

We discussed *data mining* and data warehouses in Chapter 5 as vital tools for organizing and exploiting the data resources of a company. Thus, data mining's main purpose is to provide decision support to managers and business professionals through a process referred to as *knowledge discovery*. Data mining software analyzes the vast stores of historical business data that have been prepared for analysis in corporate data warehouses and tries to discover patterns, trends, and correlations hidden in the data that can help a company improve its business performance.

Data mining software may perform regression, decision tree, neural network, cluster detection, or market basket analysis for a business. See Figure 10.18. The data mining process can highlight buying patterns, reveal customer tendencies, cut redundant costs, or uncover unseen profitable relationships and opportunities. For example, many companies use data mining to find more profitable ways to perform successful direct mailings, including e-mailings, or discover better ways to display products in a store, design a better e-commerce Web site, reach untapped profitable customers, or recognize customers or products that are unprofitable or marginal.

FIGURE 10.18

Data mining software helps discover patterns in business data, like this analysis of customer demographic information.

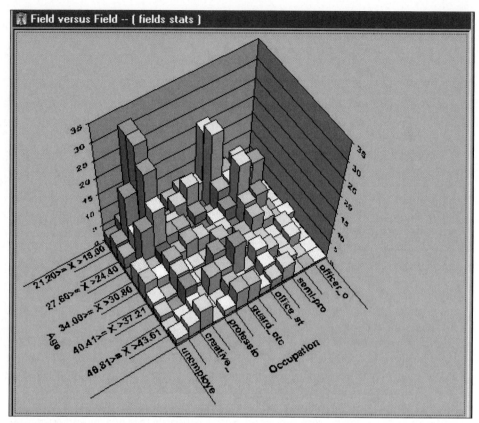

SOURCE: Courtesy of XpertRule Software.

Market basket analysis (MBA) is one of the most common and useful types of data mining for marketing and is a key technique in business analytics. The purpose of market basket analysis is to determine which products customers purchase together with other products. MBA takes its name from the concept of customers throwing all of their purchases into a shopping cart (a market basket) during grocery shopping. It can be very helpful for a retailer or any other company to know which products people purchase as a group. A store could use this information to place products frequently sold together into the same area, and a catalog or World Wide Web merchant could use it to determine the layouts of a catalog and order form. Direct marketers could use the basket analysis results to determine which new products to offer their prior customers.

In some cases, the fact that items are sold together is obvious; every fast-food restaurant asks its customers "Would you like fries with that?" whenever a customer orders a sandwich. Sometimes, however, the fact that certain items would be sold together is far from obvious. A well-known example is the relationship between beer and diapers. A supermarket performing a basket analysis discovered that diapers and beer sell well together on Thursdays. Although the result makes some sense—couples stock up on supplies for themselves and for their children before the weekend starts—it's far from intuitive. The strength of market basket analysis is as follows: By using computer data mining tools, it's not necessary for a person to think of which products consumers would logically buy together; instead, the customers' sales data speak for themselves. This is a good example of data-driven marketing.

Consider some of the typical applications of MBA:

- **Cross-Selling.** Offer the associated items when customer buys any items from your store.

- **Product Placement.** Items that are associated (such as bread and butter, tissues and cold medicine, potato chips and beer) can be put near each other. If the customers see them, it has higher probability that they will purchase them together.

- **Affinity Promotion.** Design the promotional events based on associated products.

- **Survey Analysis.** The fact that both independent and dependent variables of market basket analysis are nominal (categorical) data type makes MBA very useful to analyze questionnaire data.

- **Fraud Detection.** Based on credit card usage data, we may be able to detect certain purchase behaviors that can be associated with fraud.

- **Customer Behavior.** Associating purchase with demographic, and socioeconomic data (such as age, gender, and preference) may produce very useful results for marketing.

Once it is known that customers who buy one product are likely to buy another, it is possible for a company to market the products together or make the purchasers of one product target prospects for another. If customers who purchase diapers are already likely to purchase beer, they'll be even more likely to buy beer if there happens to be a beer display just outside the diaper aisle. Likewise, if it's known that customers who buy a sweater from a certain mail-order catalog have a propensity toward buying a jacket from the same catalog, sales of jackets can be increased by having the telephone representatives describe and offer the jacket to anyone who calls in to order the sweater. By targeting customers who are already known to be likely buyers, the effectiveness of a given marketing effort is significantly increased—regardless of whether the marketing takes the form of in-store displays, catalog layout design, or direct offers to customers.

Warner Home Video: Predicting Harry Potter DVD Sales

Being accurate when forecasting demand for a tangible product is very important. If you overestimate demand, then you are stuck with boxes of something you cannot sell, or that you will have to discount to move off the shelf. Underestimate and you could lose significant revenue, as well as irritate customers who must line up at stores to get one of the "limited number" of items you have available for sale. And when the item in question is Harry Potter's latest DVD release, we are talking about a lot of money riding on accurate demand forecasting.

Since its debut in the big screen in 2001, the Harry Potter franchise has generated more than $1.7 billion in U.S. box office revenue for its distributor, Warner Bros. Entertainment. Most people are not aware of this, but movie companies make about half of their overall sales in the first week a DVD comes out. As a result, even choosing the right week to release a movie is an important decision. To help with sales forecasting, Warner Home Video has implemented business intelligence applications that allows them to fine-tune forecasts to make sure retail stores have the right number of discs on hand when customers show up to buy them in those first few days—not too many, not too few. Before this implementation, forecasting was accurate within 40 percent of the actual number, which is not really that good. The first key steps involved standardizing data definitions across business groups, so everybody is now working from the same set of statistics, and moving shared data to a common location instead of having them stored in each computer, which also helps with keeping everybody on the same page. Analytical tools are from SAS.

Better data and analysis has allowed the company to improve its manufacturing and distribution operations by only making and shipping the right number of discs to each retailer. Custom-developed scripts in SAS analyze each individual release in terms of genre, cast, plot, and so forth to develop a specific forecast for each title. The company can also add data, both from its own similar movies and from those sold by competitors, to improve the accuracy of the model. As the company readies the home release of the new Harry Potter, Thomas Tileston, vice president of Business Decision Support at Warner Home Video expects its forecast to be within 10 percent of actual sales—an order of magnitude improvement. "You would love to be dead-on from the start," he says, "but it is the history that helps you refine and refine."

SOURCE: Kim Nash, "Using Business Intelligence to Predict Harry Potter DVD Sales," *CIO.com*, November 2, 2010.

EXECUTIVE INFORMATION SYSTEMS
LO 10-5a

Executive information systems (EIS) are information systems that combine many of the features of management information systems and decision support systems. When they were first developed, their focus was on meeting the strategic information needs of top management. Thus, the first goal of executive information systems was to provide top executives with immediate and easy access to information about a firm's *critical success factors* (CSFs), that is, key factors that are critical to accomplishing an organization's strategic objectives. For example, the executives of a retail store chain would probably consider factors such as its e-commerce versus traditional sales results or its product line mix to be critical to its survival and success.

Yet managers, analysts, and other knowledge workers use executive information systems so widely that they are sometimes humorously called "everyone's information systems." More popular alternative names are enterprise information systems (EIS) and executive support systems (ESS). These names also reflect the fact that more features, such as Web browsing, e-mail, groupware tools, and DSS and expert system capabilities, are being added to many systems to make them more useful to managers and business professionals.

In recent years, the term EIS has lost some of its popularity in favor of terms such as *business intelligence* and *business analytics*. Regardless, the concept remains in place as an important part of the organization's decision support processes.

Features of an EIS

In an EIS, information is presented in forms tailored to the preferences of the executives using the system. For example, most executive information systems emphasize the use of a graphical user interface, as well as graphics displays that can be customized to the information preferences of executives using the EIS. Other information presentation methods used by an EIS include exception reporting and trend analysis. The ability to *drill down*, which allows executives to retrieve displays of related information quickly at lower levels of detail, is another important capability.

Figure 10.19 shows one of the displays provided by the Web-enabled Hyperion executive information system. Notice that this display is simple and brief, and note how it provides users of the system with the ability to drill down quickly to lower levels of detail in areas of particular interest to them. In addition to the drill-down capability, the Hyperion EIS emphasizes trend analysis and exception reporting. Thus, a business user can quickly discover the direction in which key factors are heading and the extent to which critical factors are deviating from expected results.

Executive information systems have spread into the ranks of middle management and business professionals as their feasibility and benefits have been recognized and as less expensive systems for client/server networks and corporate intranets became available. For example, one popular EIS software package reports that only 3 percent of its users are top executives.

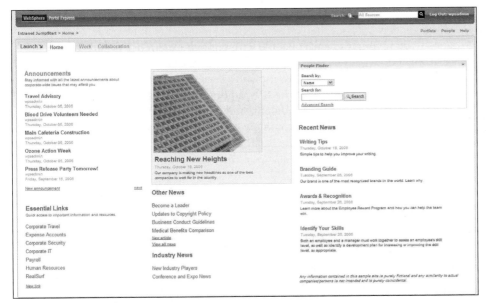

FIGURE 10.19
This Web-based executive information system provides managers and business professionals with a variety of personalized information and analytical tools for decision support.

SOURCE: Courtesy of International Business Machines Corporation.

PureSense and Farming: Watering Plans Based on Minute-by-Minute Data

Derk VanKonynenburg used to think the information he got from measuring the soil moisture every 15 minutes on his 1,500-acre fruit and almond orchard was as precise as he could possibly need. He gets the data from probes that measure moisture in the soil and send readings over a wireless link to a collection station. From there, it's relayed to a data center, and VanKonynenburg accesses the data online from a PC, helping him decide when and how much to water the trees.

Once VanKonynenburg and his partners got accustomed to the feed, however, they wanted even more data, and they wanted better data. "We decided we needed a measurement every minute," he says.

That's right. On this one midsize farm around Modesto, California, a farmer is measuring the soil moisture every single minute of the day to make irrigation decisions.

Understand that VanKonynenburg isn't looking at that moisture count minute-by-minute like a stock ticker, waiting to hit the water switch. He looks about once a day to create an irrigation plan. But because the farm irrigates in bursts—say, seven minutes on and 14 minutes off—collecting readings every 15 minutes wasn't accurate enough. With better understanding of moisture needs, "We think it may allow us to lower our water use another 10 percent," says VanKonynenburg, "and 10 percent is a huge number."

PureSense was founded by a team of technologists and farmers determined to give farmers a better sense of what's going on in the ground on their farms, beyond just giving them weather data and related calculations. Farmers have been "running blind for years," says John Williamson, cofounder and chief operating officer of PureSense, which says it has about 200 customers, mostly in California.

VanKonynenburg is also looking for more uses for the data he's collecting on soil moisture, temperature, and sunshine. He'd like to use the dashboard he gets from PureSense, which is focused on irrigation decisions, to determine risks for certain pests, fungus, and bacteria to determine the best time to spray for them. Like any busy executive, he wants one decision-making dashboard.

Irrigation, like most elements of farming, won't become automated. Soil moisture provides insight into what's happening in the fields and allows more informed decisions, but there are still critical judgments to be made. "You need data and then you need smart people with enough experience to interpret that," VanKonynenburg says. "A lot of those decisions are subjective."

Although he could access his moisture sensor data on an iPhone, he laughs off the idea. "I'm 69 years old," he says, adding that checking data once a day on the computer is fine. Then, a moment later, VanKonynenburg can't help but confess: "I suspect that a year from now, I will be carrying one."

SOURCE: Chris Murphy, "Make Every Drop Count," *InformationWeek*, November 16, 2009.

ENTERPRISE PORTALS AND DECISION SUPPORT
LO 10-5b

Don't confuse portals with the executive information systems that have been used in some industries for many years. Portals are for everyone in the company, and not just for executives. You want people on the front lines making decisions using browsers and portals rather than just executives using specialized executive information system software.

We mentioned previously in this chapter that major changes and expansions are taking place in traditional MIS, DSS, and EIS tools for providing the information and modeling managers need to support their decision making. Decision support in business is changing, driven by rapid developments in end-user computing and networking; Internet and Web technologies; and Web-enabled business applications. One of the key changes taking place in management information and decision support systems in business is the rapid growth of enterprise information portals.

Enterprise Information Portals

A user checks his e-mail, looks up the current company stock price, checks his available vacation days, and receives an order from a customer—all from the browser on his desktop. That is the next-generation intranet, also known as a corporate or enterprise information portal. With it, the browser becomes the dashboard to daily business tasks.

An ***enterprise information portal (EIP)*** is a Web-based interface and integration of MIS, DSS, EIS, and other technologies that give all intranet users and selected extranet users access to a variety of internal and external business applications and services. For example, internal applications might include access to e-mail, project Web sites, and discussion groups; human resources Web self-services; customer, inventory, and other corporate databases; decision support systems; and knowledge management systems. External applications might include industry, financial, and other Internet news services; links to industry discussion groups; and links to customer and supplier Internet and extranet Web sites. Enterprise information portals are typically tailored or personalized to the needs of individual business users or groups of users, giving them a personalized *digital dashboard* of information sources and applications. See Figure 10.20.

The business benefits of enterprise information portals include providing more specific and selective information to business users, providing easy access to key corporate intranet Web site resources, delivering industry and business news, and providing better access to company data for selected customers, suppliers, or business partners. Enterprise information portals can also help avoid excessive surfing by employees across company and Internet Web sites by making it easier for them to receive or find the information and services they need, thus improving the productivity of a company's workforce.

Figure 10.21 illustrates how companies are developing enterprise information portals as a way to provide Web-enabled information, knowledge, and decision support to their executives, managers, employees, suppliers, customers, and other business partners. The enterprise information portal is a customized and personalized

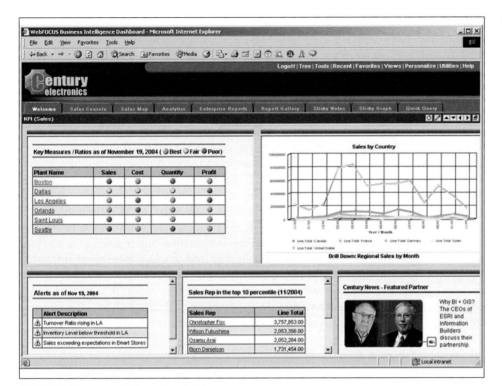

SOURCE: Courtesy of Information Builders.

FIGURE 10.20

An enterprise information portal can provide a business professional with a personalized workplace of information sources, administrative and analytical tools, and relevant business applications.

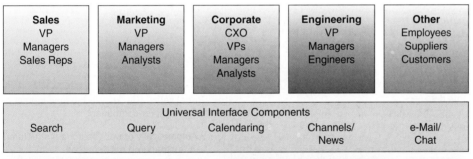

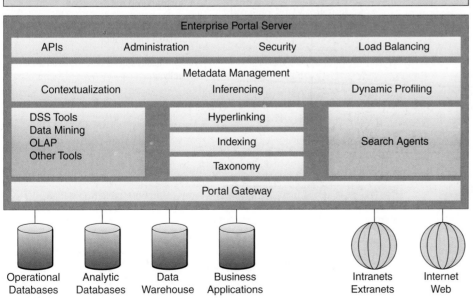

FIGURE 10.21

The components of this enterprise information portal identify it as a Web-enabled decision support system that can be personalized for executives, managers, employees, suppliers, customers, and other business partners.

Web-based interface for corporate intranets, which gives users easy access to a variety of internal and external business applications, databases, and services. For example, the EIP in Figure 10.20 might give a qualified user secure access to DSS, data mining, and OLAP tools; the Internet and the Web; the corporate intranet; supplier or customer extranets; operational and analytical databases; a data warehouse; and a variety of business applications.

KNOWLEDGE MANAGEMENT SYSTEMS
LO 10-5c

We introduced **knowledge management systems** (KMS) in Chapter 2 as the use of information technology to help gather, organize, and share business knowledge within an organization. Recall that the idea of a KMS is to enable employees to have ready access to the organization's documented base of facts, sources of information, and solutions. For example, a typical claim justifying the creation of a KM system might run something like this: an engineer could know the metallurgical composition of an alloy that reduces sound in gear systems. Sharing this information organizationwide can lead to more effective engine design and it could also lead to ideas for new or improved equipment. In many organizations, hypermedia databases at corporate intranet Web sites have become the *knowledge bases* for storage and dissemination of business knowledge. This knowledge frequently takes the form of best practices, policies, and business solutions at the project, team, business unit, and enterprise levels of the company.

For many companies, enterprise information portals are the entry to corporate intranets that serve as their knowledge management systems. That's why such portals are called **enterprise knowledge portals** by their vendors. Thus, enterprise knowledge portals play an essential role in helping companies use their intranets as knowledge management systems to share and disseminate knowledge in support of business decision making by managers and business professionals. See Figure 10.22. Now let's look at an example of a knowledge management system in business.

FIGURE 10.22

This example of the capabilities and components of an enterprise knowledge portal emphasizes its use as a Web-based knowledge management system.

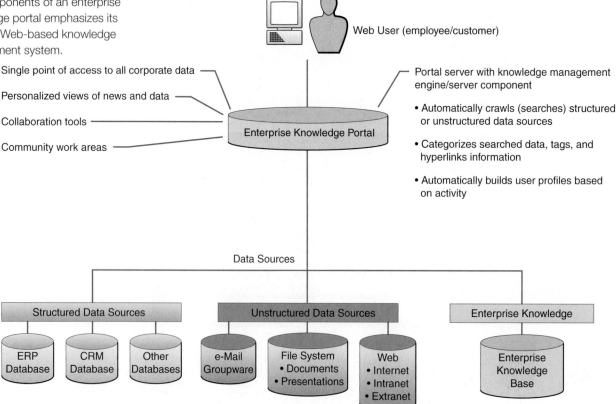

Web User (employee/customer)

Single point of access to all corporate data

Personalized views of news and data

Collaboration tools

Community work areas

Enterprise Knowledge Portal

Portal server with knowledge management engine/server component

- Automatically crawls (searches) structured or unstructured data sources
- Categorizes searched data, tags, and hyperlinks information
- Automatically builds user profiles based on activity

Data Sources

Structured Data Sources	Unstructured Data Sources	Enterprise Knowledge
ERP Database CRM Database Other Databases	e-Mail Groupware File System • Documents • Presentations Web • Internet • Intranet • Extranet	Enterprise Knowledge Base

The Mitre Corporation is a nonprofit organization that administers a number of federally funded research centers supporting various government agencies, such as the Department of Defense, the Federal Aviation Administration, amd the Internal Revenue Service, among others. For more than 13 years it has been implementing and refining a knowledge management environment that fosters a culture of sharing in support of customer needs. Mitre employs more than 6,000 scientists and engineers, the vast majority of whom are experts in their respective fields. The challenge that the organization faces involved making all that expertise available to each other while keeping a low overhead and while those same scientists and engineers kept working at their regular jobs.

Working from project management records, human resource systems, and time sheets, Mitre put together the Mitre Information Infrastructure, which reflected the historical groupings of people as they moved from project to project; information about project characteristics populated the skills or expertise fields that indicated what each engineer or scientist was involved with. Instead of requiring employees to volunteer this information, which for a number of companies has been ineffective and not overly reliable, the system was built from actual data. "This capability connected people to projects to organizations and to their open document spaces, allowing staff to navigate across all these dimensions," says Jean Tatalias, director of Knowledge Management. Other improvements include an Expertise Finder, a collection of engineering and project management best practices, and technology exchange meetings. The key is not to be afraid to experiment to see what works better for your unique organization.

Legendary innovator 3M took a different approach to getting people connected. Recognizing that it needed to include more employees into its ideation process—the very first stage of an innovation—the company implemented an internal social networking platform open to all employees. In its first two weeks of operation, more than 1,200 people had signed up and contributed more than 700 new ideas, which eventually resulted in nine new markets for the company. "Although not an easy task, leaders recognized that this was the ideal time to inject new fuel into the process of defining future markets," says Barry Dayton, Knowledge Management Strategist at 3M.

3M employs more than 75,000 globally; that is a lot of people to connect. The goal was to get employees to focus on the future of the company while the economy fixes itself. The Corporate Knowledge Management group partnered with Corporate Strategy and Corporate IT to deploy the technology necessary to expand the innovation process to anybody who had something to contribute. Most notable is the fact that they went from idea to live project in only eight weeks. In addition to the plethora of new ideas—nine new markets is no small feat—the initiative also greatly enhanced employee engagement with the company, which is likely to provide benefits of its own in the future.

SOURCE: Rick Swanborg, "Mitre's Knowledge Management Journey," *CIO.com*, February 27, 2009, and Rick Swanborg, "Social Networks in the Enterprise: 3M's Innovation Process," *CIO.com*, April 29, 2010.

Advanced Technologies
for Decision Support

Artificial intelligence (AI) technologies, such as the virtual reality system shown in Figure 10.23, are being used in a variety of ways to improve the decision support provided to managers and business professionals in many companies. For example:

> *AI-enabled applications are at work in information distribution and retrieval, database mining, product design, manufacturing, inspection, training, user support, surgical planning, resource scheduling, and complex resource management.*
>
> *Indeed, for anyone who schedules, plans, allocates resources, designs new products, uses the Internet, develops software, is responsible for product quality, is an investment professional, heads up IT, uses IT, or operates in any of a score of other capacities and arenas, AI technologies already may be in place and providing competitive advantage.*

AN OVERVIEW OF ARTIFICIAL INTELLIGENCE
LO 10-6

What is *artificial intelligence*? **Artificial intelligence (AI)** is a field of science and technology based on disciplines such as computer science, biology, psychology, linguistics, mathematics, and engineering. The goal of AI is to develop computers that can simulate the ability to think, as well as see, hear, walk, talk, and feel. A major thrust of artificial intelligence is the computer simulation of functions normally associated with human intelligence, such as reasoning, learning, and problem solving, as summarized in Figure 10.24.

Debate has raged about artificial intelligence since serious work in the field began in the 1950s. Technological, moral, and philosophical questions about the possibility of intelligent, thinking machines are numerous. AI research is highly technical and specialized, and deeply divided into subfields that often fail to communicate with each other. These subfields have grown up around particular institutions (often universities), the work of individual researchers, the solution of specific problems, long-standing differences of opinion about how AI should be done and the application of widely differing tools. The central problems of AI include such traits as reasoning, knowledge, planning, learning, communication, perception, and the ability to move and manipulate objects. General intelligence (or "strong AI") is still among the field's long-term goals.

For example, British AI pioneer Alan Turing in 1950 proposed a test to determine whether machines could think. According to the Turing test, a computer could demonstrate intelligence if a human interviewer, conversing with an unseen human

FIGURE 10.23

Virtual reality technologies enable companies to develop and test new products without actually making them.

SOURCE: © Toru Hanai/Reuters/Landov.

Attributes of Intelligent Behavior
• Think and reason.
• Use reason to solve problems.
• Learn or understand from experience.
• Acquire and apply knowledge.
• Exhibit creativity and imagination.
• Deal with complex or perplexing situations.
• Respond quickly and successfully to new situations.
• Recognize the relative importance of elements in a situation.
• Handle ambiguous, incomplete, or erroneous information.

FIGURE 10.24
Some of the attributes of intelligent behavior. AI is attempting to duplicate these capabilities in computer-based systems.

and an unseen computer, could not tell which was which. Although much work has been done in many of the subgroups that fall under the AI umbrella, critics believe that no computer can truly pass the Turing test. They claim that it is just not possible to develop intelligence to impart true humanlike capabilities to computers, but progress continues. Only time will tell whether we will achieve the ambitious goals of artificial intelligence and equal the popular images found in science fiction.

One derivative of the Turing test that is providing real value to the online community is a CAPTCHA. A CAPTCHA (Completely Automated Public Turing test to tell Computers and Humans Apart) is a type of challenge-response test used in a wide variety of computing applications to determine that the user is really a human and not a computer posing as one. A CAPTCHA is sometimes described as a reverse Turing test because it is administered by a machine and targeted to a human, in contrast to the standard Turing test that is typically administered by a human and targeted to a machine. The process involves one computer (such as a server for a retail Web site) asking a user to complete a simple test that the computer is able to generate and grade. Because other computers are unable to solve the CAPTCHA, any user entering a correct solution is presumed to be human. A common type of CAPTCHA requires that the user type the letters of a distorted image, sometimes with the addition of an obscured sequence of letters or digits that appears on the screen. Figure 10.25 shows several common examples of CAPTCHA patterns.

FIGURE 10.25
Examples of typical CAPTCHA patterns that can be easily solved by humans but prove difficult to detect by a computer.

One of the newest examples of AI reasoning is Watson. Watson is an artificial intelligence computer system capable of answering questions posed in natural language, developed in IBM's DeepQA project by a research team led by principal investigator David Ferrucci. Watson was named for IBM's first president, Thomas J. Watson. In 2011, as a test of its abilities, Watson competed on the quiz show *Jeopardy!* in the show's only human-versus-machine matchup. In a two-game, combined-point match, broadcast in three *Jeopardy!* episodes, Watson outperformed Brad Rutter, the biggest all-time money winner on *Jeopardy!* and Ken Jennings, the record holder for the longest-running streak as *Jeopardy!* champion. For its performance, Watson received the first prize of $1 million. All three contestants pledged their winnings to various charities. Watson consistently outperformed its human opponents on the game's signaling device, but it had trouble responding to a few categories, notably those having short clues containing only a few words. For each clue, Watson's three most probable responses were displayed by the television screen. Watson had access to 200 million pages of structured and unstructured content consuming four terabytes of disk storage, including the full text of Wikipedia. Watson was at no point connected to the Internet during the game.

The Domains of Artificial Intelligence

Figure 10.26 illustrates the major **domains** of AI research and development. Note that AI applications can be grouped under three major areas—*cognitive science, robotics,* and *natural interfaces*—although these classifications do overlap, and other classifications can be used. Also note that expert systems are just one of many important AI applications. Let's briefly review each of these major areas of AI and some of their current technologies. Figure 10.27 outlines some of the latest developments in commercial applications of artificial intelligence.

COGNITIVE SCIENCE. This area of artificial intelligence is based on research in biology, neurology, psychology, mathematics, and many allied disciplines. It focuses on researching how the human brain works and how humans think and learn. The results of such research in *human information processing* are the basis for the development of a variety of computer-based applications in artificial intelligence.

Applications in the cognitive science area of AI include the development of *expert systems* and other *knowledge-based systems* that add a knowledge base and some reasoning capability to information systems. Also included are *adaptive learning systems* that can modify their behaviors on the basis of information they acquire as they operate. Chess-playing systems are primitive examples of such applications, although many more applications are being implemented. *Fuzzy logic* systems can process data that are

FIGURE 10.26

The major application areas of artificial intelligence. Note that the many applications of AI can be grouped into the three major areas of cognitive science, robotics, and natural interfaces.

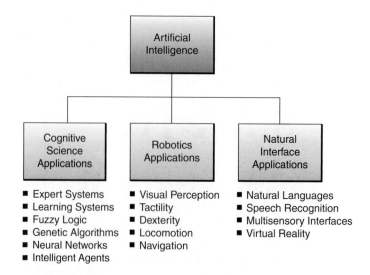

Commercial Applications of AI
Decision Support
• Intelligent work environment that will help you capture the *why* as well as the *what* of engineered design and decision making.
• Intelligent human-computer interface (HCI) systems that can understand spoken language and gestures, and facilitate problem-solving by supporting organizationwide collaborations to solve particular problems.
• Situation assessment and resource allocation software for uses that range from airlines and airports to logistics centers.
Information Retrieval
• AI-based intranet and Internet systems that distill tidal waves of information into simple presentations.
• Natural language technology to retrieve any sort of online information, from text to pictures, videos, maps, and audio clips, in response to English questions.
• Database mining for marketing trend analysis, financial forecasting, maintenance-cost reduction, and more.
Virtual Reality
• X-ray-like vision enabled by enhanced-reality visualization that allows brain surgeons to "see through" intervening tissue to operate, monitor, and evaluate disease progression.
• Automated animation interfaces that allow users to interact with virtual objects via touch (e.g., medical students can "feel" what it's like to suture severed aortas).
Robotics
• Machine-vision inspections systems for gauging, guiding, identifying, and inspecting products and providing competitive advantage in manufacturing.
• Cutting-edge robotics systems, from microrobots and hands and legs to cognitive robotic and trainable modular vision systems.

FIGURE 10.27

Examples of some of the latest commercial applications of AI.

incomplete or ambiguous, that is, *fuzzy data*. Thus, they can solve semistructured problems with incomplete knowledge by developing approximate inferences and answers, as humans do. *Neural network* software can learn by processing sample problems and their solutions. As neural nets start to recognize patterns, they can begin to program themselves to solve such problems on their own. *Genetic algorithm* software uses Darwinian (survival of the fittest), randomizing, and other mathematics functions to simulate evolutionary processes that can generate increasingly better solutions to problems. In addition, *intelligent agents* use expert system and other AI technologies to serve as software surrogates for a variety of end-user applications.

ROBOTICS. AI, engineering, and physiology are the basic disciplines of **robotics.** This technology produces robot machines with computer intelligence and computer-controlled, humanlike physical capabilities. This area thus includes applications designed to give robots the powers of sight, or visual perception; touch, or tactile capabilities; dexterity, or skill in handling and manipulation; locomotion, or the physical ability to move over any terrain; and navigation, or the intelligence to find one's way to a destination.

NATURAL INTERFACES. The development of natural interfaces is considered a major area of AI applications and is essential to the natural use of computers by humans. For example, the development of *natural languages* and speech recognition are major thrusts of this area of AI. Being able to talk to computers and robots in conversational human languages and have them "understand" us as easily as we understand each other is a goal of AI research. This goal involves research and development in linguistics, psychology, computer science, and other disciplines. Other natural interface research applications include the development of multisensory devices that use a variety of body movements to operate computers, which is related to the emerging application area of *virtual reality*. Virtual reality involves using multisensory human–computer interfaces that enable human users to experience computer-simulated objects, spaces, activities, and "worlds" as if they actually exist. Now, let's look at some examples of how AI is becoming increasingly more relevant in the business world.

Artificial Intelligence Gets Down to Business

Today, AI systems can perform useful work in "a very large and complex world," says Eric Horvitz, an AI researcher at Microsoft Research (MSR). "Because these small software agents don't have a complete representation of the world, they are uncertain about their actions. So they learn to understand the probabilities of various things happening, they learn the preferences of users and costs of outcomes and, perhaps most important, they are becoming self-aware."

These abilities derive from something called machine learning, which is at the heart of many modern AI applications. In essence, a programmer starts with a crude model of the problem he's trying to solve but builds in the ability for the software to adapt and improve with experience.

Speech recognition software gets better as it learns the nuances of your voice, for example, and over time Amazon.com more accurately predicts your preferences as you shop online. Machine learning is enabled by clever algorithms, of course, but what has driven it to prominence in recent years is the availability of huge amounts of data, both from the Internet and, more recently, from a proliferation of physical sensors.

For instance, Microsoft Research has combined sensors, machine learning, and analysis of human behavior in a road traffic prediction model. Predicting traffic bottlenecks would seem to be an obvious and not very difficult application of sensors and computer forecasting. But MSR realized that most drivers hardly need to be warned that the interstate heading out of town will be jammed at 5 p.m. on Monday. What they really need to know is where and when anomalies, or "surprises," are occurring and, perhaps more important, where they will occur. So MSR built a "surprise forecasting" model that learns from traffic history to predict surprises 30 minutes in advance based on actual traffic flows captured by sensors. In tests, it has been able to predict about 50 percent of the surprises on roads in the Seattle area, and it is in use now by several thousand drivers who receive alerts on their Windows Mobile devices.

Few organizations need to make sense of as much data as do search engine companies. For example, if a user searches Google for "toy car" and then clicks on a Walmart ad that appears at the top of the results, what's that worth to Walmart, and how much should Google charge for that click? The answers lie in an AI specialty that employs "digital trading agents," which companies like Walmart and Google use in automated online auctions.

Michael Wellman, a University of Michigan professor and an expert in these markets, explains: "There are millions of keywords, and one advertiser may be interested in hundreds or thousands of them. They have to monitor the prices of the keywords and decide how to allocate their budget, and it's too hard for Google or Yahoo to figure out what a certain keyword is worth. They let the market decide that through an auction process."

When the "toy car" query is submitted, Google looks up in a fraction of a second which advertisers are interested in those keywords, then looks at their bids and decides whose ads to display, and where to put them on the page. "The problem I'm especially interested in," Wellman says, "is how should an advertiser decide which keywords to bid on, how much to bid and how to learn over time—based on how effective their ads are—how much competition there is for each keyword."

SOURCE: Gary Anthes, "Future Watch: A.I. Comes of Age," *Computerworld*, January 26, 2009.

One of the most practical and widely implemented applications of artificial intelligence in business is the development of expert systems and other knowledge-based information systems. A *knowledge-based information system* (KBIS) adds a knowledge base to the major components found in other types of computer-based information systems. An ***expert system (ES)*** is a knowledge-based information system that uses its knowledge about a specific, complex application area to act as an expert consultant to end users. Expert systems provide answers to questions in a very specific problem area by making humanlike inferences about knowledge contained in a specialized knowledge base. They must also be able to explain their reasoning process and conclusions to a user, so expert systems can provide decision support to end users in the form of advice from an expert consultant in a specific problem area.

Components of an Expert System

The components of an expert system include a knowledge base and software modules that perform inferences on the knowledge in the knowledge base and communicate answers to a user's questions. Figure 10.28 illustrates the interrelated components of an expert system. Note the following components:

- ***Knowledge Base.*** The knowledge base of an expert system contains (1) facts about a specific subject area (e.g., *John is an analyst*) and (2) heuristics (rules of thumb) that express the reasoning procedures of an expert on the subject (e.g., *IF John is an analyst, THEN he needs a workstation*). There are many ways that such knowledge is represented in expert systems. Examples are *rule-based, frame-based, object-based*, and *case-based* methods of knowledge representation. See Figure 10.29.

- **Software Resources.** An expert system software package contains an inference engine and other programs for refining knowledge and communicating with users. The ***inference engine*** program processes the knowledge (such as rules and facts) related to a specific problem. It then makes associations and inferences resulting in

EXPERT SYSTEMS
LO 10-7

FIGURE 10.28
Components of an expert system. The software modules perform inferences on a knowledge base built by an expert and/or knowledge engineer. This provides expert answers to an end user's questions in an interactive process.

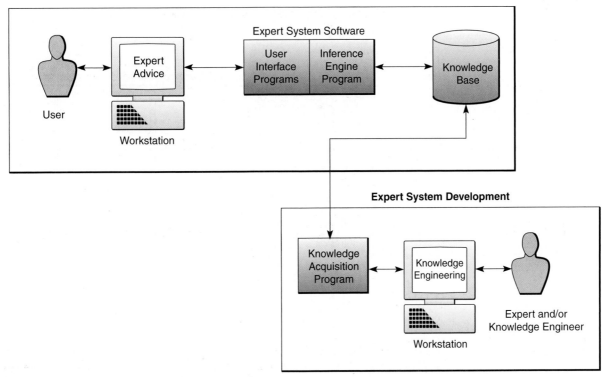

FIGURE 10.29

A summary of four ways that knowledge can be represented in an expert system's knowledge base.

Methods of Knowledge Representation
• **Case-Based Reasoning.** Representing knowledge in an expert system's knowledge base in the form of cases, that is, examples of past performance, occurrences, and experiences.
• **Frame-Based Knowledge.** Knowledge represented in the form of a hierarchy or network of *frames*. A frame is a collection of knowledge about an entity consisting of a complex package of data values describing its attributes.
• **Object-Based Knowledge.** Knowledge represented as a network of objects. An object is a data element that includes both data and the methods or processes that act on those data.
• **Rule-Based Knowledge.** Knowledge represented in the form of rules and statements of fact. Rules are statements that typically take the form of a premise and a conclusion, such as If (condition), Then (conclusion).

recommended courses of action for a user. User interface programs for communicating with end users are also needed, including an explanation program to explain the reasoning process to a user if requested. Knowledge acquisition programs are not part of an expert system but are software tools for knowledge base development, as are *expert system shells*, which are used for developing expert systems.

Expert System Applications

Using an expert system involves an interactive computer-based session in which the solution to a problem is explored, with the expert system acting as a consultant to an end user. The expert system asks questions of the user, searches its knowledge base for facts and rules or other knowledge, explains its reasoning process when asked, and gives expert advice to the user in the subject area being explored. For example, Figure 10.30 illustrates an expert system application.

Expert systems are being used for many different types of applications, and the variety of applications is expected to continue to increase. You should realize, however, that expert systems are typically put to one or more generic uses. Figure 10.31

FIGURE 10.30

Tivoli Business Systems Manager by IBM automatically monitors and manages the computers in a network with proactive expert system software components based on IBM's extensive mainframe systems management expertise.

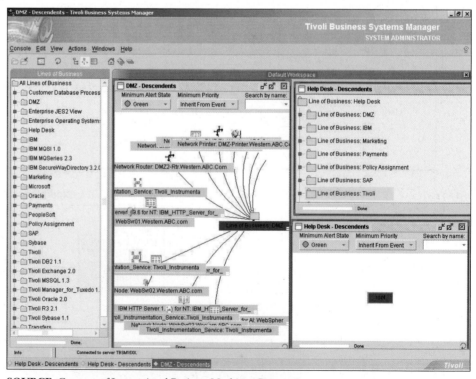

SOURCE: Courtesy of International Business Machines Corporation.

Application Categories of Expert Systems

- **Decision Management.** Systems that appraise situations or consider alternatives and make recommendations based on criteria supplied during the discovery process:

  Loan portfolio analysis
  Employee performance evaluation
  Insurance underwriting
  Demographic forecasts

- **Diagnostic/Troubleshooting.** Systems that infer underlying causes from reported symptoms and history:

  Equipment calibration
  Help desk operations
  Software debugging
  Medical diagnosis

- **Design/Configuration.** Systems that help configure equipment components, given existing constraints:

  Computer option installation
  Manufacturability studies
  Communications networks
  Optimum assembly plan

- **Selection/Classification.** Systems that help users choose products or processes, often from among large or complex sets of alternatives:

  Material selection
  Delinquent account identification
  Information classification
  Suspect identification

- **Process Monitoring/Control.** Systems that monitor and control procedures or processes:

  Machine control (including robotics)
  Inventory control
  Production monitoring
  Chemical testing

FIGURE 10.31

Major application categories and examples of typical expert systems. Note the variety of applications that can be supported by such systems.

outlines five generic categories of expert system activities, with specific examples of actual expert system applications. As you can see, expert systems are being used in many different fields, including medicine, engineering, the physical sciences, and business. Expert systems now help diagnose illnesses, search for minerals, analyze compounds, recommend repairs, and do financial planning. So from a strategic business standpoint, expert systems can be and are being used to improve every step of the product cycle of a business, from finding customers to shipping products to providing customer service.

Benefits of Expert Systems

An expert system captures the expertise of an expert or group of experts in a computer-based information system. Thus, it can outperform a single human expert in many problem situations. That's because an expert system is faster and more consistent, can have the knowledge of several experts, and does not get tired or distracted by overwork or stress. Expert systems also help preserve and reproduce the knowledge of experts. They allow a company to preserve the expertise of an expert before she leaves the organization. This expertise can then be shared by reproducing the software and knowledge base of the expert system. Sounds like Watson, doesn't it?

Limitations of Expert Systems

The major limitations of expert systems arise from their limited focus, inability to learn, maintenance problems, and developmental cost. Expert systems excel only in solving specific types of problems in a limited domain of knowledge. They fail miserably in solving problems requiring a broad knowledge base and subjective problem solving. They do well with specific types of operational or analytical tasks but falter at subjective managerial decision making.

Expert systems may also be difficult and costly to develop and maintain. The costs of knowledge engineers, lost expert time, and hardware and software resources may be too high to offset the benefits expected from some applications. Also, expert systems can't maintain themselves; that is, they can't learn from experience but instead must be taught new knowledge and modified as new expertise is needed to match developments in their subject areas.

Although there are practical applications for expert systems, applications have been limited and specific because, as discussed, expert systems are narrow in their domain of knowledge. An amusing example of this is the user who used an expert system designed to diagnose skin diseases to conclude that his rusty old car had likely developed measles. In addition, once some of the novelty had worn off, most programmers and developers realized that common expert systems were just more elaborate versions of the same decision logic used in most computer programs. Today, many of the techniques used to develop expert systems can now be found in most complex programs without any fuss about them.

Healthways: Applying Expert Systems to Health Care

Healthways, the U.S. leader in health and care support for well and chronically ill populations, relies on SAS to identify high-risk patients and implement preventative actions. The company knows that a key to successful disease management is the correct identification of those members in greatest need of care. Using SAS, Healthways reduces costs and helps to improve member health outcomes by predicting who is at most risk for developing specific health problems. In doing so, it is able to coordinate intervention plans that address care designed to avoid complications down the road.

Healthways provides disease and care management to more than two million health-plan members in all 50 states, the District of Columbia, Guam, and Puerto Rico. The company provides its services on behalf of the nation's leading health plans. It employs thousands of nurses at call centers throughout the country who collect data and provide clinical support to health-plan members and their physicians.

At Healthways, the goal is to empower health-plan members to manage their health effectively. The company achieves its objective using SAS for data mining and a group of robust artificial intelligence neural networks. To support predictive analytics, Healthways accesses hundreds of data points involving care for millions of health-plan members.

"We want to develop predictive models that not only identify and classify patients who are at risk, but also anticipate who is at the highest risk for specific diseases and complications and then determine which of those are most likely to comply with recommended standards of care," says Adam Hobgood, Director of Statistics at Healthways' Center for Health Research. "Most of all we want to predict their likelihood of success with our support programs. By identifying high-risk patients and implementing preventative actions against future conditions, we hope to head off the increased costs of care before they occur."

With SAS, Healthways builds predictive models that assess patient risk for certain outcomes and establishes starting points for providing services. Once Healthways loads patient risk-stratification levels into its own "clinical expert system," the system evaluates clinical information from hospitals, data that nurses collect by phone, and information that employer groups and health-plan members report.

Finally, the clinical expert system adjusts the initial risk-stratification levels based on the new inputs and expert clinical judgment. The resulting approach to member stratification is a hybrid solution that incorporates sophisticated artificial intelligence neural network predictive models, clinically relevant rule-based models, and expert clinician judgment.

"It's a very powerful hybrid solution, and we have worked closely with clinical experts in the company to integrate the neural network predictive model with our world-class clinical expert system," says Matthew McGinnis, Senior Director of Healthways's Center for Health Research. "The ability of our highly experienced clinicians to use their expert clinical judgment further complements the model and rounds out our hybrid approach to stratification. We believe that sophisticated statistical models are necessary to help risk-stratify our significant member populations, and by coupling this with the expertly trained clinical mind, we have created a hybrid solution that is unrivaled in the industry."

SOURCE: "Healthways Heads Off Increased Costs with SAS," www.sas.com, accessed April 25, 2009.

What types of problems are most suitable to expert system solutions? One way to answer this question is to look at examples of the applications of current expert systems, including the generic tasks they can accomplish, as were summarized in Figure 10.31. Another way is to identify criteria that make a problem situation suitable for an expert system. Figure 10.32 outlines some important criteria.

DEVELOPING EXPERT SYSTEMS
LO 10-7

Figure 10.32 emphasizes that many real-world situations do not fit the suitability criteria for expert system solutions. Hundreds of rules may be required to capture the assumptions, facts, and reasoning that are involved in even simple problem situations. For example, a task that might take an expert a few minutes to accomplish might require an expert system with hundreds of rules and take several months to develop.

The easiest way to develop an expert system is to use an ***expert system shell*** as a developmental tool. An expert system shell is a software package consisting of an expert system without its kernel, that is, its knowledge base. This leaves a *shell* of software (the inference engine and user interface programs) with generic inferencing and user interface capabilities. Other development tools (e.g., rule editors, user interface generators) are added in making the shell a powerful expert system development tool.

Expert system shells are now available as relatively low-cost software packages that help users develop their own expert systems on microcomputers. They allow trained users to develop the knowledge base for a specific expert system application. For example, one shell uses a spreadsheet format to help end users develop IF–THEN

Suitability Criteria for Expert Systems
• **Domain.** The domain, or subject area, of the problem is relatively small and limited to a well-defined problem area.
• **Expertise.** Solutions to the problem require the efforts of an expert. That is, a body of knowledge, techniques, and intuition is needed that only a few people possess.
• **Complexity.** Solution of the problem is a complex task that requires logical inference processing, which would not be handled as well by conventional information processing.
• **Structure.** The solution process must be able to cope with ill-structured, uncertain, missing, and conflicting data, and a problem situation that changes with the passage of time.
• **Availability.** An expert exists who is articulate and cooperative, and who has the support of the management and end users involved in the development of the proposed system.

FIGURE 10.32

Criteria for applications that are suitable for expert systems development.

FIGURE 10.33

Using the Visual Rule Studio and Visual Basic to develop rules for a credit management expert system.

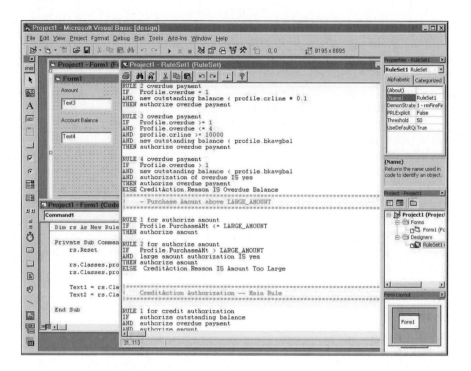

rules, automatically generating rules based on examples furnished by a user. Once a knowledge base is constructed, it is used with the shell's inference engine and user interface modules as a complete expert system on a specific subject area. Other software tools may require an IT specialist to develop expert systems. See Figure 10.33.

Knowledge Engineering

A *knowledge engineer* is a professional who works with experts to capture the knowledge (facts and rules of thumb) they possess. The knowledge engineer then builds the knowledge base (and the rest of the expert system if necessary), using an iterative, prototyping process until the expert system is acceptable. Thus, knowledge engineers perform a role similar to that of systems analysts in conventional information systems development.

Once the decision is made to develop an expert system, a team of one or more domain experts and a knowledge engineer may be formed. Experts skilled in the use of expert system shells could also develop their own expert systems. If a shell is used, facts and rules of thumb about a specific domain can be defined and entered into a knowledge base with the help of a rule editor or other knowledge acquisition tool. A limited working prototype of the knowledge base is then constructed, tested, and evaluated using the inference engine and user interface programs of the shell. The knowledge engineer and domain experts can modify the knowledge base, and then retest the system and evaluate the results. This process is repeated until the knowledge base and the shell result in an acceptable expert system.

NEURAL NETWORKS
LO 10-6

Neural networks are computing systems modeled after the brain's meshlike network of interconnected processing elements, called *neurons*. Of course, neural networks are a lot simpler in architecture (the human brain is estimated to have more than 100 billion neuron brain cells!). Like the brain, however, the interconnected processors in a neural network operate in parallel and interact dynamically. This interaction enables the network to "learn" from data it processes. That is, it learns to recognize patterns and relationships in these data. The more data examples it receives as input, the better it can learn to duplicate the results of the examples it processes. Thus, the neural network will change the strengths of the interconnections between the processing elements in response to changing patterns in the data it receives and the results that occur. See Figure 10.34.

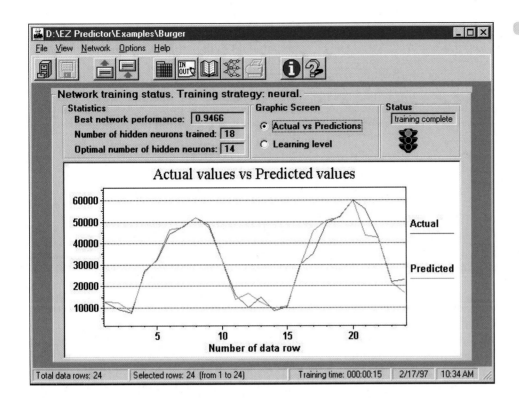

BioPassword: Neural Networks Applied to Authentication

Computer security is a never-ending challenge involving a number of important trade-offs. On the one hand, we want information that is accessible at all times over a variety of devices, applications, and networks for a constantly changing population of employees, users, and customers. On the other hand, we want to keep control over who accesses what, authenticate users, grant them the right privileges, protect the privacy of data, comply with all applicable laws and regulations, and protect corporations from internal and external fraud. And all this must be accomplished without crippling the business or inconveniencing customers—in other words, we want to have our cake and eat it too.

BioPassword is pioneering a new approach to user authentication. In addition to something you know (such as a user name and password combination), something you have (such as a smart card), and who you are (i.e., biometrics such as fingerprints), the company is implementing the use of behavioral biometrics to better identify users: in particular, using a user's behavioral keystroke dynamics, our own "typing rhythm." Keystroke dynamics measures the series of key down and key up event timings while a user types a phrase on a keyboard, separated into "dwell time," the time between pressing and releasing each key, and "flight time," the time between releasing one key and pressing the next. Once keystroke data timing is captured for a user, a neural algorithm generates a unique pattern that can be employed for future comparison, that is, authentication.

The underlying idea is that, even if someone steals your password, the typing rhythm of the thief will be different from yours and then, even if the same password is typed, the system will not let that person through, or will require additional authentication procedures. Over time, however, as we become more familiar with our user names and passwords, our timing signature evolves. Using neural networks again, BioPassword incorporates adaptive learning into the solution, letting the pattern templates used for verification evolve over time—the longer a user stays with the same template, the better the system becomes at recognizing her. Key to this is the adaptive aspect of the solution.

This approach has a number of advantages over commonly used ones. It does not require any external change in user behavior, employs a device that is already widely prevalent in any computer environment (i.e., a keyboard), and is relatively inexpensive to deploy. A user's typing rhythm, unlike a password, cannot be shared, lost, or stolen. Although the templates can be easily reset, a stolen fingerprint is forever. On this last count, behavioral approaches like this one may go a long way to address the privacy concerns employees have toward biometric security. Furthermore, the development of Web-based remote authentication services by the company even does away with the need to deploy and operate a local implementation—"behavioral security as a service" is in the works.

SOURCE: "Authentication Solutions through Keystroke Dynamics," *BioPassword Whitepaper*, 2006.

For example, a neural network can be trained to learn which credit characteristics result in good or bad loans. Developers of a credit evaluation neural network could provide it with data from many examples of credit applications and loan results to process, with opportunities to adjust the signal strengths between its neurons. The neural network would continue to be trained until it demonstrated a high degree of accuracy in correctly duplicating the results of recent cases. At that point, it would be trained enough to begin making credit evaluations on its own.

FUZZY LOGIC SYSTEMS
LO 10-6

In spite of their funny name, *fuzzy logic* systems represent a small, but serious, application of AI in business. Fuzzy logic is a method of reasoning that resembles human reasoning, in that it allows for approximate values and inferences (fuzzy logic) and incomplete or ambiguous data (fuzzy data) instead of relying only on *crisp data*, such as binary (yes/no) choices. For example, Figure 10.35 illustrates a partial set of rules (fuzzy rules) and a fuzzy SQL query for analyzing and extracting credit risk information on businesses that are being evaluated for selection as investments.

Notice how fuzzy logic uses terminology that is deliberately imprecise, such as *very high, increasing, somewhat decreased, reasonable,* and *very low*. This language enables fuzzy systems to process incomplete data and quickly provide approximate, but acceptable, solutions to problems that are difficult for other methods to solve. Thus, fuzzy logic queries of a database, such as the SQL query shown in Figure 10.35, promise to improve the extraction of data from business databases. It is important to note that fuzzy logic isn't fuzzy or imprecise thinking. Fuzzy logic actually brings precision to decision scenarios where it previously didn't exist.

FIGURE 10.35

An example of fuzzy logic rules and a fuzzy logic SQL query in a credit risk analysis application.

Fuzzy Logic Rules

Risk should be acceptable
If debt-equity is very high
   then risk is positively increased
If income is increasing
   then risk is somewhat decreased
If cash reserves are low to very low
   then risk is very increased
If PE ratio is good
   then risk is generally decreased

Fuzzy Logic SQL Query

Select companies
  from financials
     where revenues are very large
      and pe_ratio is acceptable
      and profits are high to very high
      and (income/employee_tot) is reasonable

Fuzzy Logic in Business

Examples of applications of fuzzy logic are numerous in Japan but rare in the United States. The United States has preferred to use AI solutions like expert systems or neural networks, but Japan has implemented many fuzzy logic applications, especially the use of special-purpose fuzzy logic microprocessor chips, called fuzzy process controllers. Thus, the Japanese ride on subway trains, use elevators, and drive cars that are guided or supported by fuzzy process controllers made by Hitachi and Toshiba. Many models of Japanese-made products also feature fuzzy logic microprocessors. The list is growing and includes autofocus cameras, autostabilizing camcorders, energy-efficient air conditioners, self-adjusting washing machines, and automatic transmissions.

The use of ***genetic algorithms*** is a growing application of artificial intelligence. Genetic algorithm software uses Darwinian (survival of the fittest), randomizing, and other mathematical functions to simulate an evolutionary process that can yield increasingly better solutions to a problem. Genetic algorithms were first used to simulate millions of years in biological, geological, and ecosystem evolution in just a few minutes on a computer. Genetic algorithm software is being used to model a variety of scientific, technical, and business processes.

    Genetic algorithms are especially useful for situations in which thousands of solutions are possible and must be evaluated to produce an optimal solution. Genetic algorithm software uses sets of mathematical process rules (*algorithms*) that specify how combinations of process components or steps are to be formed. This process may involve trying random process combinations (*mutation*), combining parts of several good processes (*crossover*), and selecting good sets of processes and discarding poor ones (*selection*) to generate increasingly better solutions. Figure 10.36 illustrates a business use of genetic algorithm software.

GENETIC ALGORITHMS
LO 10-6

FIGURE 10.36

Risk Optimizer software combines genetic algorithms with a risk simulation function in this airline yield optimization application.

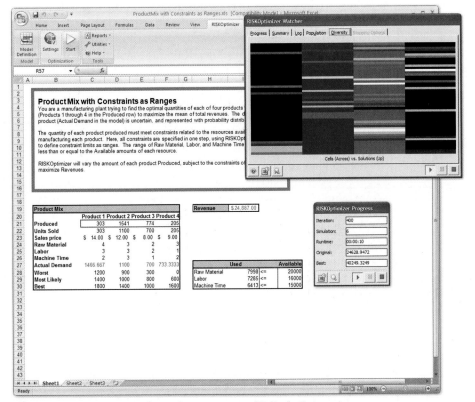

SOURCE: RISKOptimizer software. Image courtesy of Palisade Corporation.

United Distillers: Moving Casks Around with Genetic Algorithms

United Distillers (now part of Diageo PLC) is the largest and most profitable spirits company in the world. United Distillers' two grain distilleries account for more than one-third of total grain whiskey production, and the company's Johnnie Walker brand is the world's top whiskey, achieving sales of up to 120 million bottles a year.

Nevertheless, Christine Wright, Inventory and Supply Manager at United Distillers, points out that some parts of the business attract less attention than others: "Each week, 20,000 casks are moved in and out of our 49 warehouses throughout Scotland to provide the whiskey needed for the blending program. Warehousing is a physical and laborious process and has tended to be the forgotten side of the business." The introduction of genetic algorithm computer technology, however, during the past year has given a fillip to the blend selection process at United Distillers.

"We want to maximize our operational efficiency without compromising the quality," states Wright. United Distillers' Blackgrange warehouse site alone houses approximately 3 million casks, indicating the scale of the challenge. Of the 20,000 casks that are moved each week, 10,000 are not used but are moved only to allow access to those identified by the selection process. "Although we had 100 percent accurate positional information about all the stock, casks had to be selected numerically. Given the practical challenges involved in warehouse management, casks are seldom stored numerically."

Information held on the system about recipes, site constraints, and the blending program is given to the XpertRule package, which works out the best combinations of stocks to produce the blends. This information is supplemented with positional information about the casks. The system then optimizes the selection of required casks, keeping to a minimum the number of "doors" (warehouse sections) from which the casks must be taken and the number of casks that need to be moved to clear the way. Other constraints must be satisfied, such as the current working capacity of each warehouse and the maintenance and restocking work that may be in progress. Lancashire-based expert systems specialist XpertRule Software Limited has worked closely with United Distillers to develop the software application using XpertRule. The system is based on the use of genetic algorithms and adopts the Darwinian principle of natural selection to optimize the selection process.

"The incidence of non-productive cask movements has plummeted from a high of around 50 percent to a negligible level of around 4 percent and our cask handling rates have almost doubled." Wright adds: "The new technology enables staff to concentrate on what they want to achieve, rather than the mechanism of how to go about it. They can concentrate on the constraints that they wish to impose and get the system to do the legwork of finding the best scenario within those constraints. It means that the business can be driven by primary objectives." "Not only does the lack of wasted effort allow warehouse staff to get on with their work, but it enables them to plan ahead and organize long-term maintenance programs. It encourages a mind-set that is strategic, rather than reactive, and empowers managers to manage their own sites."

SOURCE: XpertRule Case Study, "A Break from Tradition in Blend Selection at United Distillers & Vintners," http://www.xpertrule.com/pages/case_ud.htm, accessed April 23, 2008.

VIRTUAL REALITY
LO 10-6

Virtual reality (VR) is computer-simulated reality. Virtual reality is a fast-growing area of artificial intelligence that had its origins in efforts to build more natural, realistic, multisensory human–computer interfaces. So virtual reality relies on multisensory input/output devices such as a tracking headset with video goggles and stereo earphones,

SOURCE: © George Steinmetz/Corbis.

FIGURE 10.37

This landscape architect uses a virtual reality system to view and move through the design of the Seattle Commons, an urban design proposal for downtown Seattle.

a *data glove* or jumpsuit with fiber-optic sensors that track your body movements, and a *walker* that monitors the movement of your feet. Then you can experience computer-simulated "virtual worlds" three-dimensionally through sight, sound, and touch. For example, you can enter a computer-generated virtual world, look around and observe its contents, pick up and move objects, and move around in it at will. Thus, virtual reality allows you to interact with computer-simulated objects, entities, and environments as if they actually exist. See Figure 10.37.

One specific form of VR is *telepresence*. This concept refers to a set of technologies that allow a person to feel present, and give the appearance of being present, in a meeting environment other than the person's true location. Telepresence requires that the senses of the user, or users, are provided with the appropriate stimuli as to give the feeling of being in the remote location. Life-sized images, eye contact, and spatial sound are all examples of the stimulus cues a telepresence system delivers. In terms of actual technology, there are very few differences between a telepresence system and traditional video conferencing. Both systems use the same technologies. The primary difference between a telepresence system and a traditional video conferencing system is in how the systems are installed and configured. Providing telepresence stimuli that is rich enough requires a permanent, dedicated installation: a room configured and used specifically for the telepresence system. A typical telepresence installation is actually more of a studio than it is a conference room. Cameras must be positioned in specific ways so as to present life-size images of people while constantly establishing full eye contact between the remote participants.

In addition to the cameras, the position of each meeting participant must be precise. Telepresence also limits the number of participants physically located in a room. For example, the Cisco Telepresence 3000 supports three 65-inch screens, two people per screen, for a total of six people per location. Other key factors in effecting telepresence include lighting and furniture, which are actually provided as components of the Cisco Telepresence system. One of the most important components of a telepresence system is the availability of bandwidth. Telepresence requires a large bandwidth, with a minimum of 2 to 3 mbps of up and downlink bandwidth per screen for the full immersive effect. Telepresence studios must use dedicated Internet access to ensure against any drop below the minimum required levels, which will result in audio jitter and noticable delays, thus destroying the immersive experience. Many organizations are intrigued by the capabilities of telepresence systems but the initial cost of the conferencing studio and the recurring network fees put these systems out of the reach of all but the largest and wealthiest companies. There are also organizations that do not have the space to dedicate an entire room to telepresence. Or, if they have the space, the rooms may lack the required dimensions. For now, the conventional video conference (VC) and the desktop VC are the standards.

VR Applications

Current applications of virtual reality are wide-ranging and include computer-aided design (CAD), medical diagnostics and treatment, scientific experimentation in many physical and biological sciences, flight simulation for training pilots and astronauts, product demonstrations, employee training, and entertainment—especially 3-D video arcade games. CAD is the most widely used industrial VR application. It enables architects and other designers to design and test electronic 3-D models of products and structures by entering the models themselves and examining, touching, and manipulating sections and parts from all angles. This scientific visualization capability is also used by pharmaceutical and biotechnology firms to develop and observe the behavior of computerized models of new drugs and materials, as well as by medical researchers to develop ways for physicians to enter and examine a virtual reality of a patient's body.

A recent support technology to virtual reality is the advent of the three dimensional (3-D) printer. This is a form of additive manufacturing technology where a three-dimensional object is created by putting down successive layers of a material such as plastic or resin. Such printers offer product developers the ability to "print" 3-D prototypes of parts and assemblies made of several materials with different mechanical and physical properties in a single build process. Advanced 3-D printing technologies yield models that closely emulate the look, feel, and functionality of product prototypes. A 3-D printer works by taking a 3-D computer file, such as a CAD file, and using it to make a series of cross-sectional slices. Each slice is then printed one on top of the other to create the 3-D object. Since 2003, there has been large growth in the sale of 3-D printers, and the cost of 3-D printers has declined in recent years. The technology also finds use in the jewelry, footwear, industrial design, architecture, engineering and construction (AEC), automotive, aerospace, dental, and medical industries.

The hottest VR application today is Linden Lab's *Second Life*. Here, users can create avatars to represent themselves, teleport to any of the thousands of locations in *Second Life*, build personal domains, "buy" land, and live out their wildest fantasies. *Second Life* has grown to enormous proportions, although actual statistics regarding size and number of users are constantly in dispute. Today, *Second Life* is home to individuals, commercial organizations, universities, governments (the Maldives was the first country to open an embassy in *Second Life*), churches, sports entertainment, art exhibits, live music, and theater. Just about anything goes in *Second Life* and, as technologies advance, the lines between your first life and your second one may begin to blur—stay tuned.

There has been increasing interest in the potential social impact of new virtual reality technologies. It is believed by many that virtual reality will lead to a number of important changes in human life and activity. For example:

- Virtual reality will be integrated into daily life and activity and will be used in various human ways.
- Techniques will be developed to influence human behavior, interpersonal communication, and cognition (i.e., virtual genetics).
- As we spend more and more time in virtual space, there will be a gradual "migration to virtual space," resulting in important changes in economics, worldview, and culture.

- The design of virtual environments may be used to extend basic human rights into virtual space, to promote human freedom and well-being or to promote social stability as we move from one stage in sociopolitical development to the next.

- Virtual reality will soon engage all of the senses including smell, taste, and touch.

Real Students Practice on Virtual Surgeries

A new technology developed by the University of Melbourne, the Australian Commonwealth Scientific and Research Organization (CSIRO), and medical technology company Medic Vision will allow medical students to perform complex ear "surgeries" in a simulator under the guidance of faculty, who may even be remotely located. The technology is called temporal bone simulator, and potentially represents a major advance in medical education in the area of ear, nose, and throat specialization, which has so far always relied on cadavers to provide the necessary practice to students. The system will enable surgeons to undertake initial training for major ear surgery in a virtual reality environment rather than using temporal bone samples from cadavers.

The training environment incorporates a realistic sense of touch, enabled via force feedback devices, and 3-D visualization in order to match the surgical situation as closely as possible. "By clearly showing the intricate anatomy of the ear and allowing students to drill away the bone over and over again, under direct supervision, the system provides an amazing teaching and learning experience," says Dr. Mathew Hutchins of the CSIRO ICT Centre.

The educational experience is integrated with additional materials provided via textbooks and more traditional curricular activities. While carrying out simulated surgical procedures, trainees will also have access to further educational materials, as well as guidance from experienced practitioners. Using this tool, medical students could train for complex procedures like repeated cochlear implants, facing slightly different variations implemented by experienced surgeons in order to introduce the variability that is seen in the field. By the time students are faced with a real, live patient, they would have performed the procedure a number of times and be much better prepared than has been possible before.

"This provides an enhanced level of sophistication and access for surgical training. Feeling is believing—the realism the technology conveys is remarkable," says Professor Vijoleta Braach-Maksvytis, deputy vice-chancellor at the University of Melbourne.

SOURCE: Darren Pauli, "Australian University Students Practice Virtual Surgery," *Computerworld Today (Australia)*, July 10, 2006, and "CSIRO, Medic Vision and University of Melbourne Commercialise VR Ear Surgery Training System," *CSIRO Media Release*, 2006.

INTELLIGENT AGENTS
LO 10-6

Intelligent agents are growing in popularity as a way to use artificial intelligence routines in software to help users accomplish many kinds of tasks in e-business and e-commerce. An intelligent agent is a *software surrogate* for an end user or a process that fulfills a stated need or activity. An intelligent agent uses its built-in and learned knowledge base about a person or process to make decisions and accomplish tasks in a way that fulfills the intentions of a user. Sometimes an intelligent agent is given a graphic representation or persona, such as Einstein for a science advisor, Sherlock Holmes for an information search agent, and so on. Thus, intelligent agents (also called *software robots* or "bots") are special-purpose, knowledge-based information systems that accomplish specific tasks for users. Figure 10.38 summarizes major types of intelligent agents.

FIGURE 10.38

Examples of different types of
intelligent agents.

Types of Intelligent Agents
User Interface Agents
• **Interface Tutors.** Observe user computer operations, correct user mistakes, and provide hints and advice on efficient software use.
• **Presentation Agents.** Show information in a variety of reporting and presentation forms and media based on user preferences.
• **Network Navigation Agents.** Discover paths to information and provide ways to view information that are preferred by a user.
• **Role-Playing Agents.** Play what-if games and other roles to help users understand information and make better decisions.
Information Management Agents
• **Information Brokers.** Provide commercial services to discover and develop information resources that fit the business or personal needs of a user.
• **Information Filters.** Receive, find, filter, discard, save, forward, and notify users about products received or desired, including e-mail, voice mail, and all other information media.

The wizards found in Microsoft Office and other software suites are among the most well-known examples of intelligent agents. These wizards are built-in capabilities that can analyze how an end user is using a software package and offer suggestions on how to complete various tasks. Thus, wizards might help you change document margins, format spreadsheet cells, query a database, or construct a graph. Wizards and other software agents are also designed to adjust to your way of using a software package so that they can anticipate when you will need their assistance. See Figure 10.39.

The use of intelligent agents is growing rapidly as a way to simplify software use, search Web sites on the Internet and corporate intranets, and help customers do comparison shopping among the many e-commerce sites on the Web. Intelligent agents are becoming necessary as software packages become more sophisticated and powerful, as the Internet and the World Wide Web become more vast and complex, and as information sources and e-commerce alternatives proliferate exponentially. In fact, some commentators forecast that much of the future of computing will consist of intelligent agents performing their work for users.

FIGURE 10.39

Intelligent agent software such
as Copernic can help you access
information from a variety of
categories and from a variety
of sources.

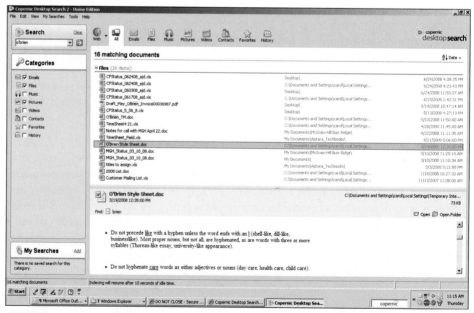

SOURCE: Courtesy of Copernic.

In 2002, the Army began to use intelligent software agents instead of people to route the background files of soldiers who required security clearance to the proper authorities for review. The result: A process that once took days now takes 24 hours. The Army reduced its year-long backlog, and the Army Central Clearance Facility in Fort Meade, Maryland, can now handle 30 percent more requests a year. The intelligent agent retrieves the necessary background information from existing records and builds an electronic folder for each case. It then examines the file to determine whether it's a clean case or there are warning signs, such as financial problems, arrests, or anything to indicate that a person might be susceptible to improper influence. Human investigators take closer looks at the tough cases.

Intelligent agents are semiautonomous, proactive, and adaptive software systems that can act on a user's behalf. Give an intelligent agent a goal, such as to help a U.S. ambassador pick a safe evacuation route following a terrorist attack in a foreign country, and it creates the best plan after gathering weather information, news reports, airplane schedules, road information, and police reports.

Such agents can also help investigators identify unusual patterns of activity, says Henry Lieberman, research scientist and leader of the Software Agents Group at the MIT Media Lab in Cambridge, Massachusetts. "Law enforcement can say to an intelligent agent, 'Let me know when any person arrived from a sensitive Middle Eastern country that was recently involved in a large bank transfer.' Or government agencies like the Securities and Exchange Commission can use them to monitor financial statements for fraud. Maybe they could have caught the whole Enron thing earlier."

Nevertheless, the issue of trust may deter their widespread adoption in business. "People just aren't used to using these kinds of things yet," says Lieberman. "When you first start using one of these agents, you have to watch it closely to make sure it's doing what you want. But performance improves over time. And the agent just makes a proposal. Then it's up to you."

Security Uses of Intelligent Software Agents

SOURCE: Stephanie Overby, "Security Strategy Includes Intelligent Software Agents," *CIO Magazine,* January 1, 2003.

Deutsche Post DHL–Decision Support for Local Brand Investments

Deutsche Post DHL is the result of the acquisition of DHL, a courier company that originated in California and expanded into extensive international operations, by Deutsche Post, the heir of the government-run postal operator in Germany. As a result of this and a series of major acquisitions between 2000 and 2005, the Deutsche Post DHL group found itself as the umbrella organization owning a complex portfolio of several regional and specialist brands. As the company focused more and more on the international logistics business, creating a strong and unique global brand became an important aspect of that transition. As many of its customers also operate on a global scale, the development of a strong DHL brand was key. In 2002, DHL began an ambitious brand-building effort that would ultimately transform the entire organization.

Many marketers consider brand management to be more art than science. Indeed, creativity figures prominently in brand management courses and articles. Although it is certainly important, there is also room for more fact-based approaches that can shed some light on the kind of questions faced by DHL. Convinced of this, Dr. Klaus Zumwinkel, then chief executive officer of Deutsche Post DHL, initiated a project under the auspices of the department of corporate brand management that brought together market research, academic experts, and consultants to answer those questions and develop a tool to help implement the answers across DHL's worldwide operations.

The brand-building effort took place in stages spanning years of work and research. Underlying the entire project is the notion that customers progress through a series of steps in the purchasing process that represent different stages of consumer development. For the particular case of DHL, those stages were identified as brand awareness, brand consideration, brand usage, choice of main provider, and choice of sole provider. This theoretical model is based on a hierarchical approach to decision making; for example, a customer must first be aware of a brand or product in order to judge it. To evaluate the strengths and weaknesses of the DHL brand across these different stages, large random samples of customers in each country were interviewed, answering questions about DHL as it compares to the other major providers (e.g., FedEx, UPS, TNT, or any major local brand). These data were collected worldwide in two waves

in 2004 and 2006, with a new wave planned every five years or so for updating purposes.

The analysis of these data, which ultimately led to building a tool to support local managers in allocating their marketing resources, proceeded in five stages. First, the sequential choice model outlined above was overimposed on the data to better understand in which of the five purchasing stages the DHL brand was particularly strong and in which it was not. The overall objective of the entire project, of course, is to move as many customers as possible to the last stage: DHL as their "choice of sole provider." This first analysis also compared DHL to a benchmark competitor with the most market share in the particular market under examination. The results were very revealing. In the U.K. market, for example, DHL had an advantage over TNT in the percentage of customers who both knew the brand and considered it part of the relevant set of alternative service providers—a 10 percent advantage. By the time customers reached the "main provider" stage, the tables had turned and the 10 percent advantage become a 7 percent disadvantage compared to TNT.

These results were fed into the second stage of the process to understand how much of that gap could be closed by improving the brand. In this step, specific brand attributes of both DHL and TNT were compared across stages of the customer choice process to understand in which attributes and stages the differences in branding efforts could be responsible for the problems observed in the customer conversion process. This analysis identifies which specific attributes may need to be targeted, and what could be the increases in revenue derived from those efforts—on the assumption that if the most relevant attributes at each stage were improved beyond those of TNT (or any other competitor), increased sales would follow. The key in this step of the process is that not all brand attributes appear to be equally valuable. Stages three and four further refined these results by employing mathematical models and optimization algorithms to derive optimal weights for each specific combination of brand attribute and stage. Using a simple visualization tool based on the relevance for purchase of each attribute and how well DHL fared against its competitors, a matrix mapping all these for both DHL and TNT along these two axes highlighted where DHL should focus in the future.

All the previously discussed results were used as input into the final step of the process, the development of a tool that would support the optimal allocation of local marketing resources across media and activities. When you think about it, there are a number of choices as to what marketers may do with their budget. They may launch an advertising campaign in television and print media, or focus on targeted direct mailing, use online media, or sponsor sport events, just to name a few. It can also be used to revamp the stores, and train employees in ways that enhance the interaction of the face of DHL with its customers. The choice of medium and activity should be largely determined by the brand attributes that are being targeted. For example, changing perceptions about how "environmentally conscious" DHL is as a company will most likely require a very different approach from communicating that it offers "great service at low prices."

However, because financial resources are always limited, these choices must be made under a budget constraint. Using previous results, the researchers derived an elasticity for each brand attribute, which represents the expected increase in revenue which comes from an increase in perceptions of a particular brand attribute. Then, brand attributes should be targeted based on their effectiveness, which will vary for each particular country or market. Underlying all this is the optimization of a constrained-profit-maximization problem, but the support tool itself can be easily implemented in a spreadsheet. The results were quite dramatic: In the U.K. market, for example, all attributes were given relatively similar weights when allocating marketing dollars (pounds actually) to them. The new tool, on the other hand, recommended allocating 54 percent of resources to two specific attributes, 38 percent to three other attributes, and spreading out the resulting 8 percent. This new allocation scheme is expected to result in a net increase of 4.8 percent in sales over the existing approach.

The global brand-building effort resulted in an improved perception of DHL as a global partner for several customers. Bernie Ecclestone, president and chief executive officer of Formula One Management, attested to the success of DHL's brand strategy: "We are obviously very proud and very happy to be partners with a very successful brand." Pascal Eymery, vice president of Supply Chain and Logistics at Airbus, highlighted trust as a core perception of the brand, resulting in joint advertising campaigns: "DHL has earned our trust because they are committed to very good performance standards in terms of quality, service, and costs." The collection of data and their subsequent analysis for each individual country helped highlight that each market is somewhat unique in what needs to be done in order to strengthen the global brand. It also helped communicate that both brand strategy and fact-based decision making were here to stay—indeed, brand strategy discussions are now a permanent item in global board meetings.

On the financial side, the impacts of the project and the resulting tool have also greatly exceeded all expectations. While the "value" of a brand is notoriously difficult to quantify, conservative estimates indicate that the value of the DHL global brand increased from $4.19 billion in 2003 to $5.51 billion in 2008, or 5.6 percent per annum. Using the cost of capital of DHL, obtaining such an improvement should have cost $265 million in brand expenditures, whereas actual brand expenditures over the same period were lower at $200 million—a return on investment of 38 percent for the project. Not controlling for the effects of brand acquisition, at the end of 2008, the global DHL brand was internally valued at $8.22 billion. This compares well with an independent valuation of $9.72 billion by an external report, which noted that "Sometimes it looks like an overnight success. But it rarely is. The brand achieved its position due to hard work over many years, developing and communicating clear and sustainable benefits." It is indisputable that its brand is now a key DHL asset.

SOURCE: Fischer, M., Giehl, W. and Freundt, T. "Managing Global Brand Investments at DHL," *Interfaces*, 2008, and www.dp-dhl.com, accessed June 7, 2011.

▼ QUESTIONS TO CONSIDER

1. What are some of the assumptions on which the new allocation tool was built? How likely are those assumptions to stay the same in the future? In other words, how enduring would this tool be?

2. What are some of the challenges Deutsche Post DHL may face as it seeks to implement the new tool worldwide? How do these challenges change the job of the local marketing managers?

- **Information, Decisions, and Management.** Information systems can support a variety of management decision-making levels and decisions. These include the three levels of management activity (strategic, tactical, and operational decision making) and three types of decision structures (structured, semistructured, and unstructured). Information systems provide a wide range of information products to support these types of decisions at all levels of the organization.

- **Decision Support Trends.** Major changes are taking place in traditional MIS, DSS, and EIS tools for providing the information, and modeling managers need to support their decision making. Decision support in business is changing, driven by rapid developments in end-user computing and networking; Internet and Web technologies; and Web-enabled business applications. The growth of corporate intranets and extranets, as well as the Web, has accelerated the development of "executive-class" interfaces like enterprise information portals and Web-enabled business intelligence software tools, as well as their use by lower levels of management and individuals, and teams of business professionals. In addition, the growth of e-commerce and e-business applications has expanded the use of enterprise portals and DSS tools by the suppliers, customers, and other business stakeholders of a company.

- **Management Information Systems.** Management information systems provide prespecified reports and responses to managers on a periodic, exception, demand, or push reporting basis to meet their need for information to support decision making.

- **OLAP and Data Mining.** Online analytical processing interactively analyzes complex relationships among large amounts of data stored in multidimensional databases. Data mining analyzes the vast amounts of historical data that have been prepared for analysis in data warehouses. Both technologies discover patterns, trends, and exception conditions in a company's data that support business analysis and decision making.

- **Decision Support Systems.** Decision support systems are interactive, computer-based information systems that use DSS software and a model base and database to provide information tailored to support semistructured and unstructured decisions faced by individual managers. They are designed to use a decision maker's own insights and judgments in an ad hoc, interactive, analytical modeling process leading to a specific decision.

- **Executive Information Systems.** Executive information systems are information systems originally designed to support the strategic information needs of top management; however, their use is spreading to lower levels of management and business professionals. EISs are easy to use and enable executives to retrieve information tailored to their needs and preferences. Thus, an EIS can provide information about a company's critical success factors to executives to support their planning and control responsibilities.

- **Enterprise Information and Knowledge Portals.** Enterprise information portals provide a customized and personalized Web-based interface for corporate intranets to give their users easy access to a variety of internal and external business applications, databases, and information services that are tailored to their individual preferences and information needs. Thus, an EIP can supply personalized Web-enabled information, knowledge, and decision support to executives, managers, and business professionals, as well as to customers, suppliers, and other business partners. An enterprise knowledge portal is a corporate intranet portal that extends the use of an EIP to include knowledge management functions and knowledge base resources so that it becomes a major form of knowledge management system for a company.

- **Artificial Intelligence.** The major application domains of artificial intelligence (AI) include a variety of applications in cognitive science, robotics, and natural interfaces. The goal of AI is the development of computer functions normally associated with human physical and mental capabilities, such as robots that see, hear, talk, feel, and move, and software capable of reasoning, learning, and problem solving. Thus, AI is being applied to many applications in business operations and managerial decision making, as well as in many other fields.

- **AI Technologies.** The many application areas of AI are summarized in Figure 10.26, including neural networks, fuzzy logic, genetic algorithms, virtual reality, and intelligent agents. Neural nets are hardware or software systems based on simple models of the brain's neuron structure that can learn to recognize patterns in data. Fuzzy logic systems use rules of approximate reasoning to solve problems when data are incomplete or ambiguous. Genetic algorithms use selection, randomizing, and other mathematic functions to simulate an evolutionary process that can yield increasingly better solutions to problems. Virtual reality systems are multisensory systems that enable human users to experience computer-simulated environments as if they actually existed. Intelligent agents are knowledge-based software surrogates for a user or process in the accomplishment of selected tasks.

- **Expert Systems.** Expert systems are knowledge-based information systems that use software and a knowledge base about a specific, complex application area to act as expert consultants to users in many business and technical applications. Software includes an inference engine program that makes inferences based on the facts and rules stored in the knowledge base. A knowledge base consists of facts about a specific subject area and heuristics (rules of thumb) that express the reasoning procedures of an expert. The benefits of expert systems (such as preservation and replication of expertise) must be balanced with their limited applicability in many problem situations.

---

key terms and concepts

These are the key terms and concepts of this chapter. The page number of their first reference appears in parentheses.

1. Analytical modeling (430)
   a. Goal-seeking analysis (432)
   b. Optimization analysis (432)
   c. Sensitivity analysis (431)
   d. What-if analysis (431)
2. Artificial intelligence (AI) (442)
3. Business intelligence (BI) (418)
4. Data mining (433)
5. Data visualization system (DVS) (428)
6. Decision structure (415)
7. Decision support system (420)
8. Enterprise information portal (EIP) (438)
9. Enterprise knowledge portal (440)
10. Executive information system (EIS) (436)
11. Expert system (ES) (447)
12. Expert system shell (451)
13. Fuzzy logic (454)
14. Genetic algorithms (455)
15. Geographic information system (GIS) (428)
16. Inference engine (447)
17. Intelligent agent (459)
18. Knowledge base (447)
19. Knowledge engineer (452)
20. Knowledge management system (440)
21. Management information system (422)
22. Model base (420)
23. Neural network (452)
24. Online analytical processing (OLAP) (424)
25. Robotics (445)
26. Virtual reality (VR) (456)

---

review quiz

Match one of the key terms and concepts listed previously with one of the brief examples or definitions that follow. Try to find the best fit for answers that seem to fit more than one term or concept. Defend your choices.

_____ 1. Decision-making procedures cannot be specified in advance for some complex decision situations.

_____ 2. Information systems for the strategic information needs of top and middle managers.

_____ 3. Systems that produce predefined reports for management.

_____ 4. Provide an interactive modeling capability tailored to the specific information needs of managers.

_____ 5. Provides business information and analytical tools for managers, business professionals, and business stakeholders.

_____ 6. A collection of mathematical models and analytical techniques.

_____ 7. Analyzing the effect of changing variables and relationships and manipulating a mathematical model.

_____ 8. Changing revenues and tax rates to see the effect on net profit after taxes.

_____ 9. Changing revenues in many small increments to see revenue's effect on net profit after taxes.

_____ 10. Changing revenues and expenses to find how you could achieve a specific amount of net profit after taxes.

_____ 11. Changing revenues and expenses subject to certain constraints to achieve the highest profit after taxes.

_____ 12. Real-time analysis of complex business data.

_____ 13. Attempts to find patterns hidden in business data in a data warehouse.

_____ 14. Represents complex data using three-dimensional graphical forms.

_____ 15. A customized and personalized Web interface to internal and external information resources available through a corporate intranet.

_____ 16. Using intranets to gather, store, and share a company's best practices among employees.

_____ 17. An enterprise information portal that can access knowledge management functions and company knowledge bases.

_____ 18. Information technology that focuses on the development of computer functions normally associated with human physical and mental capabilities.

_____ 19. Development of computer-based machines that possess capabilities such as sight, hearing, dexterity, and movement.

_____ 20. Computers that can provide you with computer-simulated experiences.

_____ 21. An information system that integrates computer graphics, geographic databases, and DSS capabilities.

_____ 22. A knowledge-based information system that acts as an expert consultant to users in a specific application area.

_____ 23. A collection of facts and reasoning procedures in a specific subject area.

_____ 24. A software package that manipulates a knowledge base and makes associations and inferences leading to a recommended course of action.

_____ 25. A software package consisting of an inference engine and user interface programs used as an expert system development tool.

_____ 26. An analyst who interviews experts to develop a knowledge base about a specific application area.

_____ 27. AI systems that use neuron structures to recognize patterns in data.

_____ 28. AI systems that use approximate reasoning to process ambiguous data.

_____ 29. Knowledge-based software surrogates that do things for you.

_____ 30. Software that uses mathematical functions to simulate an evolutionary process.

discussion questions

1. Are the form and use of information and decision support systems for managers and business professionals changing and expanding? Why or why not?

2. Has the growth of self-directed teams to manage work in organizations changed the need for strategic, tactical, and operational decision making in business?

3. What is the difference between the ability of a manager to retrieve information instantly on demand using an MIS versus the capabilities provided by a DSS?

4. Refer to the Real World Challenge at the beginning of the chapter. Does DHL stand to lose anything by integrating its operations under a single, global brand? If so, what? Is there a way to keep the best of both alternatives?

5. In what ways does using an electronic spreadsheet package provide you with the capabilities of a decision support system?

6. Are enterprise information portals making executive information systems unnecessary? Explain your reasoning.

7. Refer to the Real World Solution in the chapter. How would a local marketing manager decide that the tool is no longer applicable, or maybe not to a particular situation? If the use of the tool eventually does away with the need for local marketing managers, then what?

8. Can computers think? Will they ever be able to? Explain why or why not.

9. Which applications of AI have the most potential value for use in the operations and management of a business? Defend your choices.

10. What are some of the limitations or dangers you see in the use of AI technologies such as expert systems, virtual reality, and intelligent agents? What could be done to minimize such effects?

analysis exercises

1. **e-Commerce Web Site Reviews**
BizRate.com
BizRate (www.bizrate.com) instantly provides information about hundreds of online stores. Supported product lines include books, music, electronics, clothes, hardware, gifts, and more. Customer reviews help shoppers select products and retailers with confidence. BizRate also features a "Smart Choice" tag that balances retailer reviews, price, and other variables to recommend a "best buy."

a. Use BizRate.com to check out a product of interest. How thorough, valid, and valuable were the product and retailer reviews to you? Explain.

b. How could nonretail businesses use a similar web-enabled review system? Give an example.

c. How is BizRate's Web site functionality similar to a decision support system (DSS)?

2. **Enterprise Application Integration**
Digital Desktops
Information coming from a variety of business systems can appear on the executive desktop as a consolidated whole. Often referred to as a "digital dashboard," the information contained in such a view might include the executive's schedule, current e-mail, a brief list of production delays, major accounts past due, current sales summaries, and a financial market summary. Although it isn't possible

to fit all of an organization's information on a single screen, it is possible to summarize data in ways specified by the executive and then act as a launching point or portal for further point-and-click inquiries.

How might such a system look? Portals such as my.Excite.com, my.MSN.com, "I, Google" (www.google.com/ig), and my.Yahoo.com make good general-purpose information portals. These Web sites contain characteristics in common with their business-oriented brethren. They provide information from many different sources such as e-mail, instant messages, calendars, task lists, stock quotes, weather, and news. They allow users to determine what information sources they see. For example, a user may choose to list only business-related news and omit sports, lottery results, and horoscopes. They allow users to filter the information they see. For example, a user may choose to view only local weather, news containing specific keywords, or market results only for stocks they own. They allow users to arrange their own information space so that information a user finds most important appears in the right place. Lastly, they allow a user to drill down into the information they find important to receive more detail.

Once a user has set up an account and identified his or her preferences, these public portals remember the user's preferences and deliver only what the user has requested. Users may change their preferences as often as they wish, and the controls to make these changes require only point-and-click programming skills.

a. Visit one of the portal sites listed above. Configure the site to meet your own information needs. Provide a printout of the result.

b. Look up "Digital Dashboard" on the 20/20 Software Web site (www.2020software.com), read about products with this feature, and describe these features in your own words.

3. Case-Based Marketing
Selling on Amazon.com
A case-based reasoning system is a type of "expert system." It attempts to match the facts on hand to a database of prior "cases." When a case-based reasoning system finds one or more cases in its database that closely matches the facts at hand, it then evaluates and reports the most common outcomes. Given enough cases, such a system can prove very useful. Even better, if a case-based system automatically captures cases as they occur, then it will become a powerful tool that continually fine-tunes its results as it gains experience.

Amazon.com relies on just such a system to refer books to its customers. Like many e-commerce sites, Amazon allows visitors to search for, buy, and review books. Amazon.com takes its database interactivity a step further. Given a particular book title, its case-based reasoning engine examines all past sales of that book to see if the customers who bought that book shared other book purchases in common. It then produces a short list and presents that list to the user. The overall effect approaches that of a sales clerk who says "Oh! If you like this book, then you'll really like reading these as well." However, Amazon's system has the experience of hundreds of millions more transactions than the most wizened and well-read sales clerk.

Equipped with this information, a customer may consider purchasing additional books; better information increases the customer's confidence in the purchase and encourages sales.

a. What is the source of expertise behind Amazon's online book recommendations?

b. How do you feel about online merchants tracking your purchases and using this information to recommend additional purchases?

c. What measures protect consumers from their government obtaining their personal shopping histories maintained by Amazon?

d. Although Amazon doesn't share personal information, it still capitalizes on the shopping data of its customers. Is this ethical? Should Amazon offer its customers the right to opt out of this information gathering?

e. What obligations do organizations have to secure your private data from unauthorized access?

4. Palm City Police Department
Goal Seeking
The Palm City Police Department has eight defined precincts. The police station in each precinct has primary responsibility for all activities in its precinct area. The table below lists the current population of each precinct, the number of violent crimes committed in each precinct, and the number of officers assigned to each precinct. The department has established a goal of equalizing access to police services. Ratios of population per police officer and violent crimes per police officer should be calculated for each precinct. These ratios for the city as a whole are shown below.

a. Build a spreadsheet to perform the analysis described above and print it out.

b. Currently, no funds are available to hire additional officers. Based on the citywide ratios,

Precinct	Population	Violent Crimes	Police Officers
Shea Blvd.	96,552	318	85
Lakeland Heights	99,223	582	108
Sunnydale	68,432	206	77
Old Town	47,732	496	55
Mountainview	101,233	359	82
Financial District	58,102	511	70
Riverdale	78,903	537	70
Cole Memorial	75,801	306	82
Total	**625,978**	**3,315**	**629**
Per Officer	**995.196**	**5.270**	

the department has decided to develop a plan to shift resources as needed in order to ensure that no precinct has more than 1,100 residents per police officer and no precinct has more than seven violent crimes per police officer. The department will transfer officers from precincts that easily meet these goals to precincts that violate one or both of these ratios. Use "goal seeking" on your spreadsheet to move police officers between precincts until the goals are met. You can use the goal seek tool to see how many officers would be required to bring each precinct into compliance and then judgmentally reduce officers in precincts that are substantially within the criteria. Print out a set of results that allow the departments to comply with these ratios and a memorandum to your instructor summarizing your results and the process you used to develop them.

5. **Are You Getting All the Information You Need?**

Filter Bubbles

Internet search engines and many consumer Web sites use a variety of parameters to tailor search results, product recommendations, and advertising to individual preferences. In short, these types of Web sites try to show you what they think you want to see. Never mind the privacy issues, they're having great success.

But it's not all puppies and kittens. If we're all getting information tailored to our preferences, are we still getting all the information we *need*? Watch Eli Pariser's video *"What the Internet knows about you"* (http://bit.ly/l9s1Kb) produced by TED.com (see also CNN's article by the same author [http://bit.ly/jDreSY]) and do the following.

a. Recruit a classmate who routinely uses the same search engine you use. Conduct identical searches. What search engine did you use? Did you indeed get different results?

b. Analyze the first page of results from the experiment in question "a." How are your results different? What assumptions did the search engine make about your preferences?

c. Assume you have been tasked with finding a suitable location in the United States for a new manufacturing site. How might a search engine's assumptions affect your research regarding public acceptance?

Valero Energy, Elkay Manufacturing, J&J, and Overstock.com: The Move toward Fact-Based Decision Making

It's 7 a.m. in San Antonio, Texas, and Rich Marcogliese, chief operating officer of Valero Energy, is holding his usual morning meeting with the plant managers of 16 major refineries throughout the United States and Canada. On the walls of the headquarters's operations center are a series of monitors centered by a giant screen with a live display of the company's Refining Dashboard. Whether the executives are in the room or connected remotely, all eyes are trained on the Web-accessible gauges and charts, which are refreshed with the latest data every five minutes.

"They review how each plant and unit is performing compared to the plan," says Valero CIO Hal Zesch, "and if there is any deviation, the manager explains what's going on at their plant."

For Valero, surprisingly little-known for a Fortune 10 (that's right, one-zero) company with more than $118 billion (with a "b") in revenue, just one dashboard needle moving from green to red might signal millions of dollars at stake. The point of the dashboard isn't to call managers out; it's to give executives timely information so they can take corrective action.

Valero's Refining Dashboard is just the sort of cutting-edge decision support tool that thousands, if not tens of thousands, of companies are now attempting to create. Those companies have embraced the idea that decisions based on fact will consistently beat those based on gut. Business bestsellers including "Competing on Analytics," "Super Crunchers," and "The Numerati" have documented that it's an approach that works. Financial analysts, board members, and even the news media increasingly expect sound, data-backed analyses from top management. And when things go wrong, regulators and, in some cases, even district attorneys follow the numbers to trace bad decisions.

Plenty of obstacles stand in the way of better decision support, from backward-looking metrics and ill-advised goals to antiquated budgeting approaches and technophobic executives. For management teams that can make use of the data—and these days there's always plenty of data—there are huge opportunities to improve efficiency, develop innovative products, get closer to customers, and outsell competitors.

Valero rolled out its dashboard in early 2008 at the behest of COO Marcogliese. He had launched a Commitment to Excellence program aimed at improving performance, and he wanted to see real-time data related to plant and equipment reliability, inventory management, safety, and energy consumption. Real-time performance data are compared against daily and monthly targets, and there are executive-level, refinery-level, and even individual system-operator-level dashboard views. It's rare among business intelligence deployments to get fresh data every five minutes, but Valero has tapped directly into "process historian" systems at each plant in a six-month deployment of SAP's Manufacturing Integration and Intelligence application.

A major focus of Valero's Commitment to Excellence program is reducing energy consumption, so the company is rolling out separate dashboards that show detailed statistics on power consumption by unit and plant. "Based on the data, managers can share best practices and make changes in operations to reduce energy consumption while maintaining production levels," CIO Zesch explains. Estimated savings to date: $140 million per year for the seven plants where the dashboards are in use, with expected total savings of $230 million per year once the dashboards are rolled out at all 16 refineries.

The terms *scorecard* and *dashboard* are often used interchangeably, but there's an important distinction. Scorecards are all about tracking against defined metrics, and most scorecards are attached to a methodology, such as the Balanced Scorecard or TQM, says Mychelle Mollot, vice president of worldwide marketing, analytics, and performance management at IBM. "Top executives have actually laid out a map for where they want to drive the business, and they've created metrics that will drive the behavior that will get them there," Mollot says.

Whether they call their decision support tools scorecards or dashboards, only a small percentage of leading companies have actually mapped out enterprisewide goals with a formal methodology. Some companies come up with their own methodologies, but the key question is whether it's a comparative decision support interface: Does it track performance trends relative to predefined goals? A much larger chunk of companies use dashboard-style interfaces that simply monitor the health of the business. "These types of decision-support tools aren't often attached to a grand methodology or linked down to the bottom of the organization," Mollot says.

At Elkay Manufacturing, a $1 billion plumbing fixture and cabinetry maker, the chief financial officer has led the company to embrace new approaches toward evaluation and reporting. The conventional budgeting process, by contrast, often takes too long, it's a fixed contract, and "compensation schemes tied to it tend to encourage all sorts of bad behavior, like people sandbagging or just budgeting amounts based on last year's budget," says Adam Bauer, corporate planning manager at Elkay.

Elkay's stated strategy is to grow profitably, so its sales-related scorecards and dashboards include profit metrics so that salespeople don't just drive revenue at the expense of the bottom line. Controller John Hrudicka says the company's decision support tools have identified initiatives that produced more than $13 million in hard-dollar profit improvements while "helping us transform our culture to a profit mind-set."

Elkay put most of its decision-support technologies in place over the last two years. It tapped Host Analytics' Software as a Service financial performance management system, which it uses for budgeting, planning, reporting, and end-of-quarter financial consolidation. The system also supported the move, completed in September, to 18-month budgeting and planning cycles. Elkay chose Acorn Performance Analyzer software for activity-based costing—analyses that reveal the true cost of delivering products (including manufacturing, distribution, sales and marketing, and warranty claims)—as well as the true cost of sustaining customers (including products purchased, discounts applied, and ongoing service and support costs).

For decision support, Oracle Business Intelligence Enterprise Edition pulls information from multiple enterprise systems to deliver multilevel scorecards and dashboards. "It starts with the corporate scorecard and it rolls down from there to the divisions and all the way down to individual-employee goals that affect bonuses at the end of the year," Bauer says. Bottom-up feedback, he says, is gathered during quarterly strategy reviews.

Few companies have worked as hard or as long at data-driven decision making as Johnson & Johnson. There is an iterative process of assessing opportunities, developing goals, implementing improvements, and then monitoring their success with the aid of decision support tools. Indeed, fact-based decision making is now "part of the culture at J&J," says Karl Schmidt, vice president of business improvement, who leads a 9-person internal management consulting group.

Johnson & Johnson is decentralized, so there's no single, overarching corporate dashboard. There are separate dashboards—or in some cases, balanced scorecards—within the pharmaceutical, consumer, and medical device and diagnostics product divisions, and the dozens of companies in each of those groups. The key performance indicators include a mix of financial metrics (revenue, net income, cash flow); customer metrics (satisfaction, loyalty, market share); internal process metrics (product development, manufacturing efficiency, fulfillment); and employee metrics (engagement, satisfaction).

"It comes down to fact-based decision making," he says. "In tough economic times, you want the best available data and analysis to make better decisions."

Some of the most decision-support-savvy executives can be found in e-commerce. For example, Patrick Byrne, chief executive officer of Overstock.com, is said to use dashboards to help set his daily schedule. If the problem of the day is gross profit margins, that will drive who he calls in for a discussion. "If you get invited into a meeting with that kind of metrics-oriented CEO, you better have your hands on the data, including the detail at the next level down," says David Schrader, director of strategy and marketing at Teradata, the vendor behind Overstock's data warehousing environment.

Overstock can roll up its profit and loss statement every two hours, "which is absolutely world class," Schrader says. That capability gives executives accurate, up-to-date insight into the financial results they can expect, and it also drives operational decisions such as spot buys of TV advertising.

Whether a company is an e-commerce powerhouse or not, digital marketing channels like e-mail, social media, and online advertising networks are increasingly important. Thus, top executives should be watching forward-looking, upstream measures such as Web site performance, Web-driven lead generation, and sales pipeline information. Here, again, you must be careful to select the right metrics.

"A lot of people are measuring the wrong thing, like how many people came in the door," Schrader says. "What you really want to measure is how many people came in the door and became qualified leads."

And once prospects become customers, you'll want to know if they are good or bad customers. That's where analyses such as activity-based costing and customer segmentation come in. Lessons learned should come full circle and be reapplied to lead-generation campaigns and marketing offers.

Considering all the IT systems now in place, the growing dominance of Internet-based marketing, and the intensely digital nature of services-based industries, there's no doubt that data-driven decision making is the way forward. But the key questions are: How prepared are these organizations to synthesize and share key performance indicators? and How prepared are executives to draw insight from information?

SOURCE: Doug Henschen, "Execs Want Focus on Goals, Not Just Metrics," *InformationWeek*, November 13, 2009.

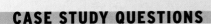

CASE STUDY QUESTIONS

1. What is the difference between a "dashboard" and a "scorecard"? Why is it important that managers know the difference between the two? What can they learn from each of them?

2. In what ways have the companies mentioned in the case benefited from their adoption of "fact-based" decision making? Provide several examples from the case to illustrate your answer.

3. Information quality is central to the approach that these organizations have taken toward decision making. What other elements must be present for this approach to be successful (technology, people, culture, and so on)?

REAL WORLD ACTIVITIES

1. A number of major companies have launched projects geared toward improving their business analytics and decision-making capabilities in the last few years. Go online and research other examples in this trend. What are the similarities with the ones chronicled in the case? What are the differences? Prepare a report that includes a section contrasting your new examples with the ones in the case.

2. If you had to apply the ideas discussed in the case to your academic career, what would your "dashboard" and/or "scorecard" look like? What would be the sources of information? How you would measure whether you are making progress toward attaining your goals? Break into small groups to discuss these issues.

Kimberly-Clark Corp.: Shopping for Virtual Products in Virtual Stores

Using a new tool developed by Kimberly-Clark Corp., a woman stood surrounded by three screens showing a store aisle, a retina-tracking device recording her every glance. At Kimberly-Clark, innovation doesn't stop with developing more absorbent diapers or stronger paper towels. The consumer-goods maker is also using IT to help retailers market and sell products—and not just the ones made by Kimberly-Clark.

Virtual reality technology has found its footing in many industries and applications, including health care, automotive, and aerospace. Now, consumer-goods manufacturer Kimberly-Clark has incorporated proprietary virtual reality technology into its new Innovation Design Studio, and it expects big payback from its technological leap.

Asked by a Kimberly-Clark researcher to find a "big box" of Huggies Natural Fit diapers in size three, she pushed forward on a handle like that of a shopping cart, and the video simulated her progress down the aisle. Spotting Huggies's red packages, she turned the handle to the right to face a dizzying array of diapers. After pushing a button to get a kneeling view of the shelves, she reached forward and tapped the screen to put the box she wanted in her virtual cart.

Kimberly-Clark hopes these virtual shopping aisles will help it better understand consumer behavior and make testing new products faster, more convenient, and more precise. The mobile testing unit is usually based in a new high-tech studio that Kimberly-Clark completed in the basement of a nondescript office building in Appleton, Wisconsin. The cavernous room also features a U-shaped floor-to-ceiling screen that recreates in vivid detail interiors of the big retailers that sell the company's products: a tool that the company will use in presentations to executives in bids to win shelf space. A separate area is reserved for real replicas of store interiors, which can be customized to match the flooring, light fixtures, and shelves of retailers such as Target Corp. and Wal-Mart Stores Inc.

As the fragmented television market raises doubts about the effectiveness of traditional ads and competition for shelf space increases, manufacturers and retailers are intensifying their focus on ways to get consumers' attention while they are in the store.

The efforts go well beyond the usual cardboard displays and sample handouts. A group including manufacturers Procter & Gamble Co., Coca-Cola Co. and General Mills Inc., and retailers Kroger Co. and Wal-Mart announced the results of a test that tracked the movement of shoppers in stores using a combination of infrared beams and human observation. Nielsen Co. plans to syndicate such data and sell it to clients, much as it does with television ratings.

"By engaging ourselves and our customers in this virtual world, we can spark better ideas to improve the shopping experience and collaborate on new product concepts and innovations," says Ramin Elvaz, Kimberly-Clark vice president of North Atlantic Insight, Strategy and Growth.

Kimberly-Clark says its studio allows researchers and designers to get a fast read on new product designs and displays without having to stage real-life tests in the early stages of development. Doing the research in a windowless basement, rather than an actual test market, also avoids tipping off competitors early in the development process.

"We're trying to test ideas faster, cheaper and better," says Ramin Eivaz, a vice president at Kimberly-Clark focusing on strategy. Before, new product testing typically took eight months to two years. Now, that time is cut in half, he says. Projects that test well with the virtual reality tools will be fast-tracked to real-store trials, Mr. Eivaz says.

Once product design options have been determined, Kimberly-Clark brings retail executives into the studio so they can see how the new product would actually look on the shelf and fit in with the existing assortment—an important factor in decisions the retailers make on space.

The company declined to reveal how much it spent to build the Appleton studio. "We made a significant investment in the studio and expect it will yield a positive return for our customers in the future," a spokesman says.

The battle for shelf space is accelerating as consumer-products companies have introduced more and more new products. Meanwhile, retailers are churning out more of their own private-label products. The rate of new product launches has grown steadily since 2000, introducing more than 40,000 new packaged goods in 2007, says Tom Vierhile, director of Productscan Online, market research firm Datamonitor's database of new products.

However, Kimberly-Clark is particularly enthusiastic about how the design center can help its retail partners improve their in-store designs and merchandising. For example, using the virtual reality technology and K-C SmartStation, the manufacturer can create store models, allowing retailers to envision hypothetical store designs and merchandising concepts. Likewise, eye-tracking technology in the high-tech kiosk allows them to study the reactions of consumers in simulated shopping settings to determine how different environments or packaging affect buying decisions.

Inside the center's virtual reality theater, visitors are surrounded by screens on which rear-projection equipment displays virtual images powered by applications running on eight Hewlett-Packard high-end rack-mount PCs. The system's 3-D capabilities were developed with RedDotSquare. Sensors embedded in the walls, ceilings, and floor detect movements of the visitors, track their locations, and can even tell exactly what the visitors are looking at, says Kurt Schweitzer, director, IT business partner for marketing, strategy, and innovation. This allows the system to further immerse visitors by making things happen around them. such as opening a door near where they're standing or changing their perspective on what's going on, he says.

The center lets store managers use "multiple senses and not just visualization" to assess product display effectiveness, Schweitzer says. The front screen of the immersion center is more than 20 feet wide and is flanked by two side screens that rest at 45-degree angles, creating a wraparound effect. The wings can move inward to 90-degree angles, forming a three-sided box. "When you step into that 8-foot-high physical space, the word immersive takes on a whole new meaning," Schweitzer says.

To sell retailers on new products, manufacturers are revealing more about their product pipelines to drum up interest early on. Over the past several months, Kimberly-Clark says it has brought in executives from major chains, including Target, Wal-Mart and Kroger, to see the Appleton facility. Kimberly-Clark uses the data from its virtual reality tests with consumers to tout the performance of products in development.

"It no longer works to show up on a retailer's doorstep with your new product and say, 'Isn't this pretty?'" Mr. Eivaz says. "We need to be an indispensable partner to our retailers and show we can do more for them."

When grocery chain Safeway Inc. asked its major manufacturers for display suggestions to lift traffic through its center aisles in late 2005, Kimberly-Clark used an early version of the virtual reality modeling technology it was developing for the new studio to pitch for more room for its Huggies diapers and other baby products. The company created three-dimensional models of a store display that resembled a nursery, complete with a giant, colorful bathtub. The company had consumers navigate the store virtually, testing how easily they could find certain items in the area.

"We hadn't seen that type of technology applied to that type of traditional merchandising and store decor before," says Michael Minasi, Safeway's president of marketing. When it tested the display inside its stores, sales of items in that section increased. Nevertheless, in the end, reality set limits. "Some of the decor and decoration components were easier to do virtually than they were to do in the real world, mostly from a cost and implementation standpoint," Minasi says. However, a version of Kimberly-Clark's concept was put in place at a handful of Safeway stores.

In the store-model section of its new studio, Kimberly-Clark goes to elaborate lengths with its re-creations aimed to impress retail executives. Once, the company readied the studio for visitors from Target. The store's branded shopping carts were lined up at the doorway, next to a stand holding recent Target sales fliers and a faux ATM. Standing behind a pharmacy counter was a Kimberly-Clark employee outfitted in a lab coat with a Target logo. Target's standard white tiles covered the floor, its beige light fixtures hung above, and Target store shelves were fully stocked with diapers and other baby products made by Kimberly-Clark and its competitors.

"What if you just spent a lot of money on a package's shade of red but it doesn't look good in their store?" says Don Quigley, president of Kimberly-Clark's consumer sales and customer development, North America. "This is where you can spot that, before you ship a single case of product."

SOURCE: Ellen Byron, "A Virtual View of the Store Aisle," *Wall Street Journal*, October 3, 2007; Jill Jusko, "Kimberly-Clark Embraces Virtual Reality," *IndustryWeek*, December 1, 2007; and Marianne Kolbasuk McGee, "InformationWeek 500: Kimberly-Clark's Virtual Product Demo Center Yields Real Ideas on How to Sell More Products," *InformationWeek*, September 17, 2007.

▼ CASE STUDY QUESTIONS

1. What are the business benefits derived from the technology implementation described in the case? Also discuss benefits other than those explicitly mentioned in the case.

2. Are virtual stores like this one just an incremental innovation in the way marketing tests new product designs? Or do they have the potential to radically reinvent the way these companies work? Explain your reasons.

3. What other industries could benefit from deployments of virtual reality like the one discussed in the case? If cost were not an issue, what new products or services could you envision within those industries? Provide several examples.

▼ REAL WORLD ACTIVITIES

1. What is the current cutting-edge technology in virtual reality, and what is it being used for by companies? Go online to research this topic and prepare a presentation to share your work.

2. With technologies like these, will consumers do away with retailers entirely in the future and shop only through virtual representations of a retail store? Will consumers even want it to look like a retail store? Break into small groups to propose arguments for and against these questions.

DEVELOPMENT PROCESSES

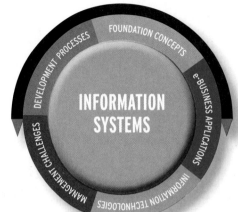

INFORMATION SYSTEMS

How can business professionals plan, develop, and implement strategies and solutions that use information technologies to help meet the challenges and opportunities faced in today's business environment? The chapters of this module will answer that question by concentrating on the processes and challenges in planning, developing, and implementing IT-based business strategies and applications.

- **Chapter 11: Business/IT Strategies for Development** emphasizes the importance of the strategic planning process in developing IT/business solutions and the implementation strategies necessary to consider when introducing new IT-based business strategies and applications into an organization.

- **Chapter 12: Implementing Business/IT Solutions** introduces the traditional, prototyping, and end-user approaches to the development of information systems and discusses the processes and managerial issues in the implementation of new business applications of information technology.

INFORMATION SYSTEMS

DEVELOPMENT PROCESSES

chapter 11

BUSINESS/IT STRATEGIES FOR DEVELOPMENT

CHAPTER HIGHLIGHTS

IT Planning Fundamentals

Introduction
Organizational Planning
The Scenario Approach

REAL WORLD CHALLENGE: Sloan Valve Company—
ERP, Business Processes, and the Need to Change

Planning for Competitive Advantage
Business Models and Planning
Business/IT Architecture Planning
Identifying Business/IT Strategies
Business Application Planning

Implementation Challenges

Implementation
Implementing Information Technology
End-User Resistance and Involvement
Change Management

REAL WORLD SOLUTION: Sloan Valve Company—
**IT and the Redesign of the New Product
Development Process**

REAL WORLD CASE: IT Leaders: IT/Business
Alignment Takes on a Whole New Meaning

REAL WORLD CASE: Centene, Flowserve, and Shaw
Industries: Relationships, Collaboration, and Project
Success

LEARNING OBJECTIVES

After reading and studying this chapter, you should be able to:

11-1 Discuss the role of planning in the business use of information technology, using the scenario approach and planning for competitive advantage as examples.

11-2 Discuss the role of planning and business models in the development of business/IT strategies, architectures, and applications.

11-3 Identify several change management solutions for end-user resistance to the implementation of new IT-based business strategies and applications.

476

IT Planning Fundamentals

Imagine taking a caravan of thousands of people on a journey with no map, no plan, no one in charge, no logistical support, no way to keep everyone informed, no scouting reports to assess and update progress, and no navigational instruments. It would be sheer madness, yet that's how most companies are handling the transition to e-business.

Information technology has created a seismic shift in the way companies do business. Just knowing the importance and structure of e-business is not enough. You need to create and implement an action plan that allows you to make the transition from an old business design to a new e-business design.

That is why you need to learn some fundamental planning concepts, which is the goal of this part of the chapter. We will first discuss several strategic planning concepts and then talk more specifically about developing IT-based business strategies and other planning issues. Later we will discuss the process of implementing IT-based business plans and the challenges that arise when introducing new IT strategies and applications within a company.

Read the Real World Challenge on the next page. We can learn a lot about the problems companies face as they seek to change their business processes. See Figure 11.1.

Introducing new IT/IS–based solutions into an organization is a huge undertaking. Companies often make the mistake of relying solely on the IT department to plan, design, develop, and implement such solutions. This is the biggest, and unfortunately the most common, mistake that could be made. Enterprisewide solutions require an enterprisewide planning, development, and implementation process to be successful. Figure 11.2 illustrates the components of an ***organizational planning*** process. This fundamental planning process consists of (1) team building, modeling, and consensus; (2) evaluating what an organization has accomplished and the resources they have acquired; (3) analyzing their business, economic, political, and societal environments; (4) anticipating and evaluating the impact of future developments; (5) building a shared vision and deciding what goals they want to achieve; and (6) deciding which actions to take to achieve their goals.

The result of this process is what we call a *plan*, which formally articulates the actions we feel are necessary to achieve our goals. Thus, a plan is an action statement. Plans lead to actions, actions produce results, and part of planning is learning from results. In this context, the planning process is followed by implementation, which is monitored by control measures, which provide feedback for planning.

Strategic planning deals with the development of an organization's mission, goals, strategies, and policies. Corporations may begin the process by developing a shared vision using a variety of techniques, including team building, scenario modeling, and consensus-creating exercises. Team planning sessions frequently include answering *strategic visioning* questions such as those shown in Figure 11.3. *Tactical planning* involves the setting of objectives and the development of procedures, rules, schedules, and budgets. *Operational planning* is done on a short-term basis to implement and control day-to-day operations. Typical examples are project planning and production scheduling.

Many organizational planning methodologies are used in business today. Let's concentrate on two of the most popular methodologies: the *scenario approach* and *planning for competitive advantage*.

Planning and budgeting processes are notorious for their rigidity and irrelevance to management action. Strict adherence to a process of rapid or efficient completion may only make the process less relevant to the true management agenda.

Managers and planners continually try different approaches to make planning easier, more accurate, and more relevant to the dynamic, real world of business.

CHALLENGE

Sloan Valve Company–ERP, Business Processes, and the Need to Change

Sloan Valve Company was founded in 1906 in downtown Chicago by prolific inventor William E. Sloan. Drawing on earlier experiences as a pipe fitter in his native Missouri, and later as a foreman, superintendent, and independent contractor in Chicago, Sloan developed a lifelong interest in inventions and new products. In fact, Sloan was credited with 64 different inventions during his life. His most notable invention—which is how the company got started—would eventually be known as the Royal Flushometer, a revolutionary device that discharged water using pressure from the water supply system rather than the law of gravity. Although the new product offered a number of benefits, customers were slow to embrace it. In the first year of business as an independent company, Sloan Valve sold a total of one valve. In the second year, sales doubled to two valves. By the third year, however, they sold 150 valves and sales started to ramp up.

Today, the company has more than 1,000 employees and remains privately held, with revenues of more than $1 billion. Headquartered at a 400,000-square-foot facility in Franklin Park, Illinois, the best-selling product is that very same valve, using a design that is amazingly similar to the original. The company is led today, as it has always been, by a descendant of the founder: CEO Charles S. Allen, grandson of William E. Sloan. "Over the years, Sloan Valve has

continued to focus on its core business—flush valves," says Allen, who has also been president of the company for the past 29 years. "In the late 1970s, Sloan Valve made a very important strategic move into electronic plumbing. For years, the company had evaluated different technologies, but finally identified infrared sensing as a reliable, cost-effective solution. Sloan Valve has now become a market leader in electronic plumbing." Growing domestic operations in Michigan, Massachusetts, and Arkansas as well as a new plant in Suzhou, China, and operations in Mexico, have helped the company solidify its position as an industry leader.

Ever since its founding, the company has fostered a strong culture of innovation. "Sloan Valve has always been able to change with the times," noted water conservation manager Jim Allen, great-grandson of W. E. Sloan. "Meeting and exceeding industry expectations has been what sets us apart. Many times, Sloan has been the driving force between an industry change." To maintain its leading position in the marketplace, the company has been focused on continuously introducing new products and technologies that help advance the value proposition it offers to its customers. "All new products must provide an element of value for the owner who invests in properties, for the contractor who installs it, to the maintenance person who ultimately interfaces with the product on a daily basis," says Pete Jahrling, Director of Design Engineering. "We are constantly introducing new technologies into our products in small advancements and complete customer solutions." As a result, new product development is a core strategic competency of the Sloan Valve Company, and it must continue to be such in the future, if the company is to keep growing and competing.

Although its new development processes had functioned well until the late 1990s, it became evident to management that they needed a new approach. Sixteen different functional units were involved the process, which introduced a fairly significant amount of complex coordination among them to make anything happen. As a result, the time-to-market of new ideas, an important measure of how well a company manages its innovation processes, was slow, taking between one year and a half to two years from idea to product. The company's ad hoc and very informal process led to roughly half of the ideas being dropped, sometimes

FIGURE 11.1

Companies are increasingly turning to IT for expertise in improving or changing business processes.

SOURCE: © Jon Feingersh/Iconica/Getty Images.

after significant, and costly, prototyping and design work had been already conducted, thus increasing the overall costs of entire process. As there was not a single person, group, or function in charge of the new product development process, accountability for results was also a major challenge.

Management believed that replacing the company's internal network to transfer information with a modern ERP would eventually contribute to solving many of the communication and coordination issues plaguing the organization; it would do so by providing a single, common database where a "single version of the truth" could be established, as well as replacing a myriad of legacy applications then in use. Sloan Valve chose SAP as its ERP vendor and spent about 11 months implementing the new system, with no significant returns. Management encountered several problems in the implementation process and, as one was solved, others raised their ugly heads. Understandably concerned about this issue, management hired a new chief information officer in 2000. "The ERP system very vaguely supported the business as it existed. It was not crafted to support any new business process that we wanted, especially in new product development," says CEO Charles Allen. In addition to fixing the ERP, Tom Coleman, the newly appointed chief information officer, needed to set a new direction for the entire IT function—one that would integrate responsibility for IT with the management of business processes.

Soon after getting settled into his new job, Coleman, who came to Sloan Valve from Motorola with extensive IT experience, realized that the ERP was actually working as it should be. Rather, the problems were with the processes themselves. When Sloan Valve installed the ERP package, it extensively customized the package to fit its existing processes, rather than the other way around—changing the way the company worked to match the process structures embedded in the new software. As Coleman saw this, the problems were broader than the ERP itself, and had to do with the way the company was structured and got work done. "At the time, the company had many folks reporting directly to the CEO from multiple silos. I immediately started talking about how we had to look at cross-functional business processes as a way to get value from the ERP system," says Coleman.

But changing deeply ingrained ways of doing things is not easy. Following the advice of a heavyweight senior executive, management decided to embark on a project of incremental improvement, using the logistics process as a pilot experiment. After seven months of work, results were nowhere to be seen. Looking deeply into the problem, it became evident that making changes to one specific process would affect the ways in which interacted with others—no business process lives in isolation from others. As a result, focusing on just one single process was not going to do it. This much was clear from this failed effort. Where to go from here, on the other hand, was not as evident.

SOURCE: Balaji, S., Ranganathan, C. and Coleman, T. "IT-Led Process Reengineering: How Sloan Valve Redesigned Its New Product Development Process," *MIS Quarterly Executive*, 2011; Martin, M., "Celebrating 100 Years . . . Sloan Valve Continues to Build on Strong Foundation," *The Wholesaler*, May 2011; and www.sloanvalve.com, accessed June 10, 2011.

▼ QUESTIONS TO CONSIDER

1. What is a company seeking to achieve when it extensively customizes an ERP system? Are you surprised at what the Sloan Valve Company obtained as a result of its efforts?

2. Given the structure of the company and its processes at the time, what would be the major bottlenecks or issues that make it difficult to develop new products successfully? How can IT help alleviate those issues?

3. The case states that innovation processes worked well until the late 1990s, when it became evident that they were not cutting it anymore. What would be some reasons for this change? Why would ad hoc and informal work before but not anymore?

FIGURE 11.2

The components of an organizational planning process.

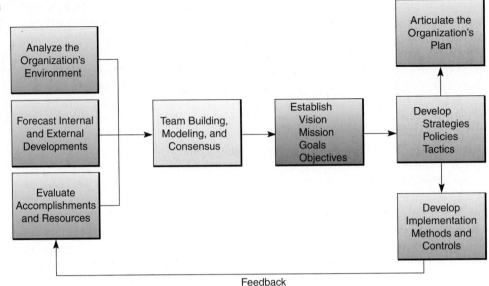

The **_scenario approach to planning_** has gained in popularity as a less formal, but more realistic, strategic planning methodology for business professionals to use.

In the scenario approach, teams of managers and other planners participate in what management author Peter Senge calls _microworld_, or _virtual world_, exercises. A microworld is a simulation exercise that is a microcosm of the real world. In a microworld exercise, managers can safely create, experience, and evaluate a variety of scenarios of what might be happening, or what might happen in the real world.

> _When a work team goes white-water rafting or engages in some other outdoor team-building exercise, the team members are creating a microworld to reflect on and improve the way they work together. When personnel staff create a role-playing exercise to be used in a supervisory training, they are creating a microworld. Many team retreats serve as microworlds._

Scenario planning is, in large part, an adaptation and generalization of classic methods used by military intelligence. In the original method, a group of analysts

FIGURE 11.3

Examples of strategic visioning questions in planning for e-business initiatives.

Strategic Business Visioning	
• **Understanding the Customer**	Who are our customers?
	How are our customers' priorities shifting? Who should be our target customers?
	How will an e-business help reach our target customer segments?
• **Customer Value**	How can we add value for the customer with e-business services?
	How can we become the customer's first choice?
• **Competition**	Who are our real competitors? What is our toughest competitor's business model?
	What are they doing in e-business and e-commerce? Are our competitors potential partners, suppliers, or customers in an e-business venture?
• **Value Chain**	How would we design a value chain if we were just starting an e-business?
	Who would be our supply chain partners? What roles should we play: e-commerce Web site, B2C portal, B2B marketplace, or partner in an e-commerce alliance?

would generate various simulation games for policy makers. The games would combine known facts about the future, such as *demographics, geography, military, political, industrial information,* and *mineral reserves,* with plausible alternative *social, technical, economic, environmental, educational, political* and *aesthetic* (STEEEPA) trends, which are key driving forces. In business applications, the emphasis on gaming the behavior of opponents is shifting more toward a game against nature, although specific competitor gaming situations can be crafted. Scenario planning may involve aspects of Systems thinking (discussed in greater detail in Chapter 12), specifically the recognition that many factors may combine in complex ways to create sometimes surprising future events or outcomes. Scenario planning also allows the inclusion of factors that are difficult to formalize, such as novel insights about the future, deep shifts in values, unprecedented regulations, or inventions. Systems thinking used in conjunction with scenario planning leads to plausible scenario story lines because the causal relationship between factors can be demonstrated. In cases when scenario planning is integrated with a systems thinking approach to scenario development, it is sometimes referred to as *structural dynamics.*

In the past, strategic plans have often considered only the "official future," which was usually a linear graph of current trends extended into the future—say, five years. Often the accounting department generated the trend lines, and they lacked discussions of demographics, or qualitative differences in social conditions. Although these simplistic guesses are surprisingly good most of the time, they often fail to consider qualitative social changes that can dramatically affect a business organization. Well-crafted scenarios focus on the joint effect of many factors. Scenario planning helps an organization understand how the various strands of a complex tapestry move if one or more threads are pulled. When you only list possible causes, you may tend to discount any one factor in isolation. But when you explore the factors together, you realize that certain combinations could magnify each other's impact or likelihood. For instance, an increased trade deficit may trigger an economic recession, which in turn creates unemployment and reduces domestic production.

Scenario planning starts by dividing knowledge into two broad domains: (1) *things we believe we know something about* and (2) *elements we consider uncertain or unknowable.* The first component—*trends*—casts the past forward, recognizing that our world possesses considerable momentum and continuity. For example, we can safely make assumptions about demographic shifts and, perhaps, substitution effects for certain new technologies. The second component—*uncertainties*—involves indeterminables, such as future interest rates, outcomes of political elections, rates of innovation, fads and fashions in markets, and so on. The art of scenario planning lies in blending the known and the unknown into a limited number of internally consistent views of the future that span a very wide range of possibilities.

Numerous organizations have applied scenario planning to a broad range of issues, from relatively simple, tactical decisions to the complex process of strategic planning and vision building. The power of scenario planning for business was originally established by Royal Dutch/Shell, which has used scenarios since the early 1970s as part of a process for generating and evaluating its strategic options. Shell has been consistently better in its oil forecasts than other major oil companies, and saw the overcapacity in the tanker business and Europe's petrochemicals earlier than its competitors. Scenario planning is as much art as science, and prone to a variety of traps (both in process and content). Nonetheless, it is a common and useful practice used by organizations to "see" into the future and craft suitable strategic responses to the possible outcomes.

Thus, in the scenario approach to strategic IS planning, teams of business and IS managers create and evaluate a variety of business scenarios. For example, they make assumptions about what a business will be like three to five years or more into the future, and the role that information technology can or will play in those future scenarios. Alternative scenarios are created by the teams or by business simulation

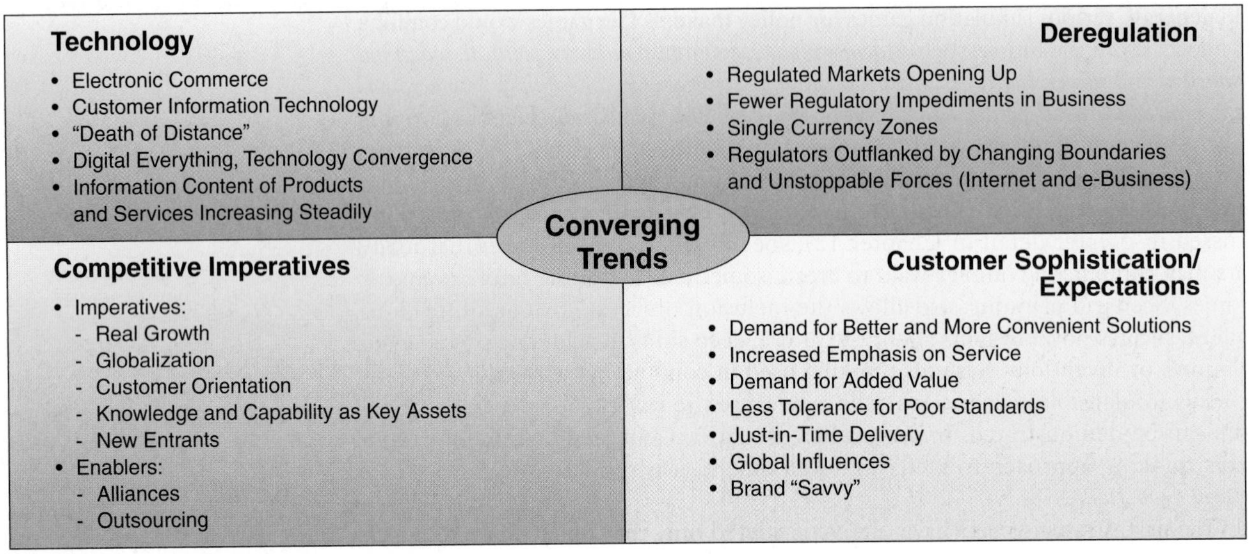

Technology	Deregulation
• Electronic Commerce • Customer Information Technology • "Death of Distance" • Digital Everything, Technology Convergence • Information Content of Products and Services Increasing Steadily	• Regulated Markets Opening Up • Fewer Regulatory Impediments in Business • Single Currency Zones • Regulators Outflanked by Changing Boundaries and Unstoppable Forces (Internet and e-Business)
Competitive Imperatives	**Customer Sophistication/ Expectations**

• Imperatives:
  - Real Growth
  - Globalization
  - Customer Orientation
  - Knowledge and Capability as Key Assets
  - New Entrants
• Enablers:
  - Alliances
  - Outsourcing
	• Demand for Better and More Convenient Solutions
	• Increased Emphasis on Service
	• Demand for Added Value
	• Less Tolerance for Poor Standards
	• Just-in-Time Delivery
	• Global Influences
	• Brand "Savvy"

Converging Trends

FIGURE 11.4

Converging business, political, and technological trends that are shaping strategic business/IT planning.

software, based on combining a variety of developments, trends, and environmental factors, including political, social, business, and technological changes that might occur. For example, Figure 11.4 outlines key business, political, and technological trends that could help guide business/IT planning.

Risk Assessment and Mitigation

Chief information officers are frequently asked, "What are our IT risks?" Unfortunately, this question is too generic because there are multiple kinds of risk. Before starting any risk assessment, IT needs to understand both the concern prompting the request and which risks need to be assessed. Moreover, everyone needs to understand that nearly all risks that affect an IT organization affect the entire business. Risks fall into four categories that require different mitigation tools:

Business operations risk. An assessment determines the risks involved in addressing or ignoring a particular competitive threat. Analyzing competitive threats helps the company decide whether to invest the resources necessary to combat the threat. Determining appropriate responses to competitive threats from nontraditional sources can be particularly difficult. The appropriate mitigation tool is a good business case that evaluates all associated risks. For new business opportunities, a thorough risk assessment may be as important to success as accurate financial projections.

Program risk. For approved or existing programs, management concerns focus on whether the program or project will be delivered on time, within budget, and with high quality. Effective project management and regular monitoring mitigate risk.

Business interruption risk. This type of risk affects the company's ability to continue operating under difficult circumstances. Scenarios run the gamut from a failed server to a destroyed building. In most cases, a failed server causes minor problems for certain people. In contrast, a destroyed building can bring all company operations to a halt. A continuity-of-operations plan that describes how the business will function in the event of various difficulties can mitigate risk.

Market risk. This category is divided into geopolitical and industry-specific risks. Geopolitical risks include war, terrorism, and epidemics, as well as nationalization and import restrictions. These risks vary depending on the country, the complexity of the corporate supply chain, and the importance of the industry to political leadership. Industry-specific risks also vary. Scenario planning mitigates risk by developing responses to various unlikely events. Most important, it attempts to discover previously unknown risks because the most dangerous risk is often the one you don't identify.

Before embarking on any risk assessment, clarify which types of risk are of concern to your executive management; then select the appropriate mitigation tools to address potential difficulties. Depending on the financial consequences, risk insurance may be warranted. Thorough risk assessments leverage creative thinking into constructive preparations for addressing potential threats, and they're essential to success. As the old adage goes, "Forewarned is forearmed."

SOURCE: Bart Perkins, "Know Which Risks Matter," *Computerworld*, December 17, 2007.

Betting on new IT innovations can mean betting the future of the company. Leading-edge firms are sometimes said to be on the "bleeding edge." Almost any business executive is aware of disastrous projects that had to be written off, often after large cost overruns, because the promised new system just did not work.

In contrast to the scenario planning approach, is another highly visible and commonly used strategic planning method: *planning for competitive advantage.*

Planning for competitive advantage is especially important in today's competitive business arena and complex information technology environment. So, strategic business/IT planning involves an evaluation of the potential benefits and risks a company faces when using IT-based strategies and technologies for competitive advantage. In Chapter 2, we introduced a model of *competitive forces* (competitors, customers, suppliers, new entrants, and substitutes) and *competitive strategies* (cost leadership, differentiation, growth, innovation, and alliances), as well as a value chain model of basic business activities. These models can be used in a strategic planning process to help generate ideas for the strategic use of information technologies to support new e-business initiatives.

Popular in strategic business/IT planning approach is the use of a *strategic opportunities matrix* to evaluate the strategic potential of proposed business/IT opportunities, as measured by their risk/payoff probabilities. See Figure 11.5.

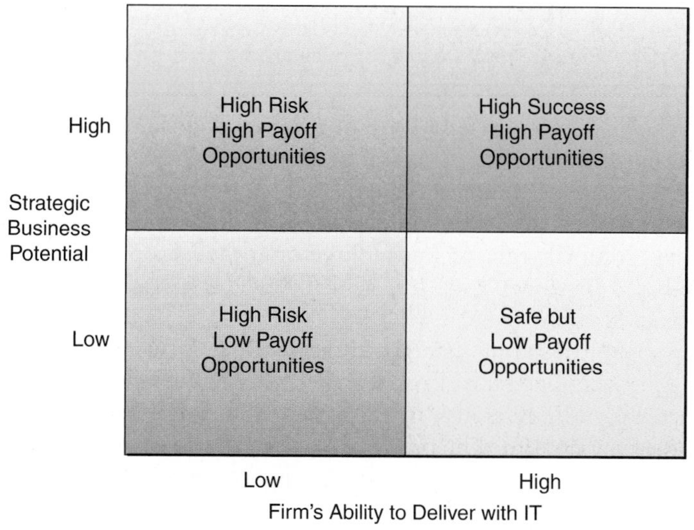

PLANNING FOR COMPETITIVE ADVANTAGE
LO 11-1

	Low	High
High	High Risk High Payoff Opportunities	High Success High Payoff Opportunities
Low	High Risk Low Payoff Opportunities	Safe but Low Payoff Opportunities

Strategic Business Potential

Firm's Ability to Deliver with IT

FIGURE 11.5

A strategic opportunities matrix helps to evaluate the strategic risk/payoff potential of proposed business/IT opportunities.

Strengths	Weaknesses	Opportunities	Threats
Market reputation	Shortage of trained consultants at the operating level	Well-established market niche	Large consultancies operating at a minor market level
Partner-level expertise in HRM	Lack of ability to manage multidisciplinary assignments	New market opportunities for consulting in areas other than HRM	Many small consultancies looking to invade the marketplace

TABLE 11.1

Example of a SWOT Analysis by a Human-Resources Consulting Firm

SWOT Analysis

SWOT analysis (*strengths, weaknesses, opportunities,* and *threats*) is used to evaluate the impact that each possible strategic opportunity can have on a company and its use of information technology. A company's *strengths* are its core competencies and resources in which it is one of the market or industry leaders. *Weaknesses* are areas of substandard business performance compared to others in the industry or market segments. *Opportunities* are the potential for new business markets or innovative breakthroughs that might greatly expand present markets. *Threats* are the potential for business and market losses posed by the actions of competitors and other competitive forces, changes in government policies, disruptive new technologies, and so on.

An example of SWOT analysis might come from a marketing problem. In competitor analysis, marketers build detailed profiles of each competitor in the market, focusing especially on their relative competitive strengths and weaknesses. Marketing managers may examine each competitor's cost structure; sources of profits, resources, and competencies; competitive positioning and product differentiation; degree of vertical integration; historical responses to industry developments; and other factors.

Marketing management often finds it necessary to invest in research to collect the data required to perform accurate marketing analysis. As such, they often conduct market research to obtain this information; although marketers use a variety of techniques, some of the more common methods include:

- Qualitative marketing research, such as focus groups.
- Quantitative marketing research, such as statistical surveys.
- Experimental techniques, such as test markets.
- Observational techniques, such as ethnographic (on-site) observation.
- Marketing managers may also design and oversee various environmental scanning and competitive intelligence processes to help identify trends and inform the company's marketing analysis.

Table 11.1 shows the content of a typical SWOT analysis. Now let's look at a real-world example of how a company used technology to support SWOT analyses, and much more.

Bristow Helicopters: Technology-Supported SWOT, and Much More

When Bristow Helicopters Ltd. started losing market share in the 1990s, executives moved to improve business processes across the Redhill, England–based company. "We needed to change facilities and maintenance processes, improve the efficiencies of the staff, improve the interface between sales and clients," says John Cloggie, technical director at the European business unit of Houston-based Bristow Group Inc., which provides helicopter services to the oil and gas industry.

A key goal of this reengineering effort was to cut several million dollars from the operating budget of Bristow Helicopters. The company managed the project using MindGenius, "mind-mapping" software from East Kilbride, Scotland–based Gael Ltd. The product enabled it to conduct a SWOT analysis (an assessment of its strengths, weaknesses, opportunities, and threats), carve out various process reengineering tasks, and delegate them to appropriate groups. Each team then took the high-level version of the map and created its own subcategories, tasks, and deadlines for its designated work segment. Since beginning the project in 2004, says Cloggie, the company has managed to cut $6 million from its operating budget.

"Mind mapping, of course, didn't directly create our $6 million savings, but it did allow us to control the project while it was being delivered," he says. "The speed with which you can map processes and capture knowledge is a huge return."

Mind mapping has been around for centuries, but it didn't garner much attention until psychologist Tony Buzan began to promote information visualization techniques in the 1970s. A mind map is a diagram that radially arranges words and images around a central theme. It's based on the cognitive theory that many people learn and recall information more easily through graphical representations. Mind mapping—increasingly called business mapping as it makes inroads into corporate settings—is used for a range of problem-solving and brainstorming activities, including managing projects, mapping business processes, creating workflows, planning events, and programming software.

At Bristow Helicopters, mind mapping is used for "virtually all business strategy projects," says Cloggie. Bristow has also used MindGenius for managing employee-retention efforts, and the company always uses it when introducing new aircraft types. "We have a [mind map] template that's 90 percent usable for any aircraft type. It's not just a checklist; it's a tool to help the engineer understand the processes by which he'll bring the aircraft in," says Cloggie. "Through it, he understands the interface with manufacturing, among different departments within the company, and with the Civil Aviation Authority."

As key business strategies are developed around mind maps, the technology will need to move beyond its status as a desktop product to better facilitate collaboration, say users. In fact, Cloggie was recently invited, along with other mind-map software users from various industries, to speak on this need before the Scottish Parliament.

"We talked about the need to take mind maps from being a personal tool to a cross-departmental business tool; you can't extract their true, cross business abilities if you can't work on maps simultaneously," says Cloggie. "With real-time collaboration, you can have experts develop templates and facilitators work with different teams to create maps, with the business as a whole sharing them."

SOURCE: Kym Gilhooly, "Business on the Map," *Computerworld*, July 3, 2006.

BUSINESS MODELS AND PLANNING
LO 11-2

"Business model" was one of the great buzzwords of the Internet boom, routinely invoked, as the writer Michael Lewis put it, "to invoke all manner of half-baked plans." A good business model, however, remains essential to every successful organization, whether it's a new venture or an established player.

A **business model** is a conceptual framework that expresses the underlying economic logic and system that prove how a business can deliver value to customers at an appropriate cost and make money. A business model answers vital questions about the fundamental components of a business, such as: *Who are our customers? What do our customers value? How much will it cost to deliver that value to our customers? How do we make money in this business?*

A business model specifies what value to offer customers, which customers should receive this value, which products and services will be supplied, and what the price will be. It also specifies how the business will organize and operate to have the capability to provide this value and sustain any advantage from providing this value to its customers.

FIGURE 11.6

Questions that illustrate the components of all business models. A good business model effectively answers these questions.

Component of Business Model	Questions for All Business Models
Customer value	Is the firm offering its customers something distinctive or at a lower cost than its competitors?
Scope	To which customers (demographic and geographic) is the firm offering this value? What is the range of products/services offered that embody this value?
Pricing	How does the firm price the value?
Revenue source	Where do the dollars come from? Who pays for what value and when? What are the margins in each market and what drives them? What drives value in each source?
Connected activities	What set of activities does the firm have to perform to offer this value and when? How connected (in cross section and time) are these activities?
Implementation	What organizational structure, systems, people, and environment does the firm need to carry out these activities? What is the fit between them?
Capabilities	What are the firm's capabilities and capabilities gaps that need to be filled? How does a firm fill these capabilities gaps? Is there something distinctive about these capabilities that allows the firm to offer the value better than other firms and that makes them difficult to imitate? What are the sources of these capabilities?
Sustainability	What is it about the firm that makes it difficult for other firms to imitate it? How does the firm keep making money? How does the firm sustain its competitive advantage?

Figure 11.6 outlines more specific questions about the components of a business that all business models must answer. Figure 11.7 lists questions that illustrate the essential components of e-business models.

A business model is a valuable planning tool because it focuses attention on how all the essential components of a business fit into a complete system. Done properly,

FIGURE 11.7

Questions that illustrate the components of e-business models that can be developed as part of the strategic business/IT planning process.

Component of Business Model	Questions Specific to e-Business Models
Customer value	What is it about Internet technologies that allows your firm to offer its customers something distinctive? Can Internet technologies allow you to solve a new set of problems for customers?
Scope	What is the scope of customers that Internet technologies enable your firm to reach? Does the Internet alter the product or service mix that embodies the firm's products?
Pricing	How does the Internet make pricing different?
Revenue source	Are revenue sources different with the Internet? What is new?
Connected activities	How many new activities must be performed as a result of the Internet? How much better can Internet technologies help you to perform existing activities?
Implementation	How do Internet technologies affect the strategy, structure, systems, people, and environment of your firm?
Capabilities	What new capabilities do you need? What is the impact of Internet technologies on existing capabilities?
Sustainability	Do Internet technologies make sustainability easier or more difficult? How can your firm take advantage of it?

it forces entrepreneurs and managers to think rigorously and systemically about the value and viability of the business initiatives they are planning. Then the strategic planning process can be used to develop unique business strategies that capitalize on a firm's business model to help it gain competitive advantages in its industry and the markets it wants to dominate.

Iridium Satellite: Finding the Right Business Model

Left for dead by many observers in the IT and telecommunications worlds just a few years ago, the reborn Iridium Satellite LLC, which provides satellite-based communications services, is showing new signs of life. Nowhere near the revenue and customer numbers posted by huge wireless telecommunications companies such as Verizon Wireless and AT&T, it's definite progress for a company that was brought out of bankruptcy in 2000 and remodeled with a new focus and direction.

The first Iridium marketed itself as a consumer satellite telephone service, but its original phone was too bulky and its service too expensive for general adoption. There were also some service quirks consumers wouldn't accept, such as the need for line-of-sight connection to a satellite, which precluded using the phones indoors. After the buyout, the company recreated itself as a telecommunications provider that could offer reliable service in remote areas where cellular phones and landlines won't work, such as barren deserts, the Earth's poles, deep wilderness, disaster areas, and other isolated and harsh environments.

"Originally Iridium was focused on the wrong business, on the mass-market consumer business selling directly to customers," says Matt Desch, the company's CEO and chairman. Since its rebirth in 2001, the company has worked with more than 150 partner companies to find new business uses and niches for Iridium service in industries from mining to manufacturing to oil and gas exploration to forestry to emergency response needs. "We've developed an ecosystem around ourselves," Desch said. "That's a big difference."

Not all of Iridium's service is provided using handsets. An increasing part of its business is in machine-to-machine communications, using a sensor device about the size of a deck of playing cards that is attached to a ship, truck, container, or similar item. The device can send and receive short bursts of communications data to a satellite wherever it is on Earth. Some of these sensors are even located on buoys in the ocean, where weather agencies can monitor wave heights, winds, and other storm data in real time to provide warnings for onrushing storms. "That's the real fast part of our growth," Desch said of the short-burst data communications segment.

Max Engel, an analyst with Frost & Sullivan in Palo Alto, California, said that although Iridium's original idea to be a satellite phone service for the masses "was an obvious example of stupid failure," the change in business plan raises the service's prospects. "What the new management did when they bought it was it took the assets that originally cost billions, but were now freed of those expectations," Engel said. "They then asked, 'what can we do with this' and enlisted many partners" to create a more workable business model. "Yes, they're very nichy, but as long as you've got bunches of niches, who cares?" says Engel. "They've redesigned their business to suit their assets instead of creating an asset to do business."

"We're obviously hitting our stride," says Desch. "We're a lifeline where no other device can be used."

SOURCE: Todd Weiss, "Defying Naysayers, Iridium Satellite Finds a Business Model," *Computerworld,* July 27, 2007.

BUSINESS/IT ARCHITECTURE PLANNING
LO 11-2

Figure 11.8 illustrates the ***business/IT planning*** process, which focuses on discovering innovative approaches to satisfying a company's customer value and business value goals. This planning process leads to development of strategies and business models for new e-business and e-commerce platforms, processes, products, and services. Then a company can develop IT strategies and an IT architecture that supports building and implementing its newly planned business applications.

Both the CEO and the chief information officer (CIO) of a company must manage the development of complementary business and IT strategies to meet its customer value and business value vision. This *coadaptation* process is necessary because, as we have seen so often in this text, information technologies are a fast-changing but vital component in many strategic business initiatives. The business/IT planning process has three major components:

- **Strategic Development.** Developing business strategies that support a company's business vision, for example, using information technology to create innovative e-business systems that focus on customer and business value. We will discuss this process in more detail shortly.

- **Resource Management.** Developing strategic plans for managing or outsourcing a company's IT resources, including IS personnel, hardware, software, data, and network resources.

- **Technology Architecture.** Making strategic IT choices that reflect an information technology architecture designed to support a company's e-business and other business/IT initiatives.

Information Technology Architecture

The ***information technology architecture*** that is created by the strategic business/IT planning process is a conceptual design, or blueprint, that includes the following major components:

- **Technology Platform.** The Internet, intranets, extranets, and other networks, computer systems, system software, and integrated enterprise application software provide a computing and communications infrastructure, or platform, that supports the strategic use of information technology for e-business, e-commerce, and other business/IT applications.

- **Data Resources.** Many types of operational and specialized databases, including data warehouses and Internet/intranet databases (as reviewed in Chapter 5) store and provide data and information for business processes and decision support.

FIGURE 11.8

The business/IT planning process emphasizes a customer and business value focus for developing business strategies and models, and an IT architecture for business applications.

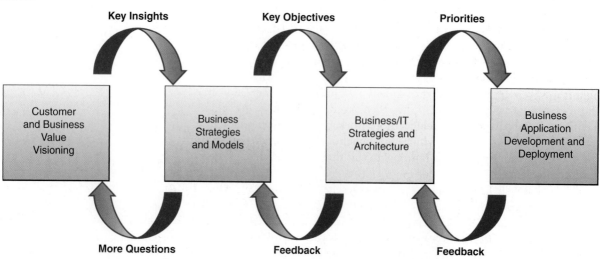

- **Applications Architecture.** Business applications of information technology are designed as an integrated architecture of enterprise systems that support strategic business initiatives, as well as cross-functional business processes. For example, an applications architecture should include support for developing and maintaining interenterprise supply chain applications, as well as integrated enterprise resource planning and customer relationship management applications as we discussed in Chapter 8.

- **IT Organization.** The organizational structure of the IS function within a company and the distribution of IS specialists are designed to meet the changing strategies of a business. The form of the IT organization depends on the managerial philosophy and business/IT strategies formulated during the strategic planning process. We will discuss the IT organization in Chapter 14.

Balanced Scorecard

In 1992, Robert S. Kaplan and David Norton introduced the **balanced scorecard** (BSC), a method for measuring a company's activities in terms of its vision and strategies. It gives managers a comprehensive view of the performance of a business and has become a popular business and IT planning tool.

BSC is a strategic management system that forces managers to focus on the important performance metrics that drive success. It balances a financial perspective with customer, internal process, and learning and growth perspectives. The system consists of four processes: (1) translating the vision into operational goals; (2) communicating the vision and linking it to individual performance; (3) business planning; (4) feedback and learning, and then adjusting the strategy accordingly.

The **scorecard** seeks to measure a business from the following perspectives:

- **Financial Perspective.** This measures reflecting financial performance; for example, number of debtors, cash flow, or return on investment. The financial performance of an organization is fundamental to its success. Even **nonprofit organizations** must make the books balance. Financial figures suffer from two major drawbacks:
  - They tell us what has happened to the organization historically, but they may not tell us what is currently happening or be a good indicator of future performance.
  - It is common for the current market value of an organization to exceed the market value of its assets. Tobin's q measures the ratio of the value of a company's assets to its market value. The excess value can be thought of as intangible assets. These figures are not measured by normal financial reporting.

- **Customer Perspective.** This measures having a direct impact on customers; for example, time taken to process a phone call, results of customer surveys, number of complaints, or competitive rankings.

- **Business Process Perspective.** This measures reflecting the performance of key business processes; for example, time spent prospecting, number of units that required rework, or process cost.

- **Learning and Growth Perspective.** This measures describing the company's learning curve; for example, number of employee suggestions or total hours spent on staff training.

The balanced scorecard approach is not without its detractors, however. A major criticism of the balanced scorecard is that the scores are not based on any proven economic or financial theory and have no basis in the decision sciences. The process is entirely subjective and makes no provision to assess quantities like risk and economic value in a way that is actuarially or economically well-founded. The

FIGURE 11.9

An example of a balanced scorecard analysis.

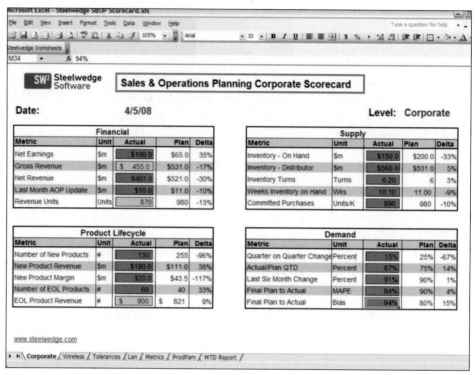

SOURCE: Courtesy of Steelwedge Software, Inc.

BSC does not provide a bottom-line score or a unified view with clear recommendations; rather, it is only a list of metrics. Positive responses from users of BSC may merely be a type of placebo effect, as there are no empirical studies linking the use of balanced scorecard to better decision making or improved financial performance of companies.

Despite these criticisms, BSC can be found in many organizations and is a common strategic planning tool. Figure 11.9 shows an example of a balanced scorecard analysis.

IDENTIFYING BUSINESS/ IT STRATEGIES
LO 11-2

Companies need a strategic framework that can bridge the gap between simply connecting to the Internet and harnessing its power for competitive advantage. The most valuable Internet applications allow companies to transcend communication barriers and establish connections that will enhance productivity, stimulate innovative development, and improve customer relations.

Internet technologies and e-business and e-commerce applications can be used strategically for competitive advantage, as this text repeatedly demonstrates. However, in order to optimize this strategic impact, a company must continually assess the strategic value of such applications. Figure 11.10 is a strategic positioning matrix that can help a company identify where to concentrate its strategic use of Internet technologies to gain a competitive advantage. Let's take a look at the strategies that each quadrant of this matrix represents.

- **Cost and Efficiency Improvements.** This quadrant represents a low amount of internal company, customer, and competitor connectivity and use of IT via the Internet and other networks. One recommended strategy would be to focus on improving efficiency and lowering costs by using the Internet and the World Wide Web as a fast, low-cost way to communicate and interact with customers, suppliers, and business partners. The use of e-mail, chat systems, discussion groups, and a company Web site are typical examples.

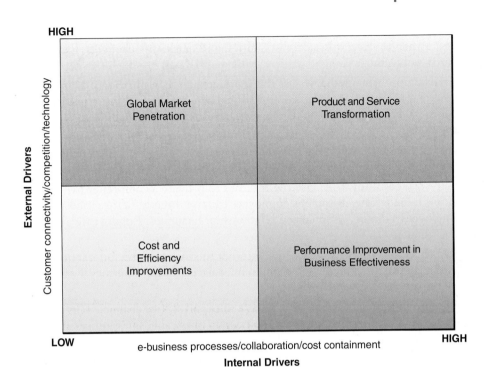

FIGURE 11.10

A strategic positioning matrix helps a company optimize the strategic impact of Internet technologies for e-business and e-commerce applications.

- **Performance Improvement in Business Effectiveness.** Here a company has a high degree of internal connectivity and pressures to improve its business processes substantially, but external connectivity by customers and competitors is still low. A strategy of making major improvements in business effectiveness is recommended. For example, widespread internal use of Internet-based technologies like intranets and extranets can substantially improve information sharing and collaboration within the business and with its trading partners.

- **Global Market Penetration.** A company that enters this quadrant of the matrix must capitalize on a high degree of customer and competitor connectivity and use of IT. Developing e-business and e-commerce applications to optimize interaction with customers and build market share is recommended. For example, e-commerce Web sites with value-added information services and extensive online customer support would be one way to implement such a strategy.

- **Product and Service Transformation.** Here a company and its customers, suppliers, and competitors are extensively networked. Internet-based technologies, including e-commerce Web sites and e-business intranets and extranets, must now be implemented throughout the company's operations and business relationships. This enables a company to develop and deploy new Internet-based products and services that strategically reposition it in the marketplace. Using the Internet for e-commerce transaction processing with customers at company Web sites and e-commerce auctions and exchanges for suppliers are typical examples of such strategic e-business applications. Let's look at more specific examples.

Market creator. Use the Internet to define a new market by identifying a unique customer need. This model requires you to be among the first to market and to remain ahead of competition by continuously innovating. Examples: Amazon.com and E*TRADE.

Channel reconfiguration. Use the Internet as a new channel to access customers, make sales, and fulfill orders directly. This model supplements,

e-Business Strategy Examples

rather than replaces, physical distribution and marketing channels. Example: Cisco and Dell.

Transaction intermediary. Use the Internet to process purchases. This transactional model includes the end-to-end process of searching, comparing, selecting, and paying online. Examples: Microsoft, Expedia, and eBay.

Infomediary. Use the Internet to reduce the search cost. Offer the customer a unified process for collecting information necessary to make a large purchase. Examples: HomeAdvisor and Auto-By-Tel.

Self-service innovator. Use the Internet to provide a comprehensive suite of services that the customer's employees can use directly. Self-service affords employees a direct, personalized relationship. Examples: Employease and Healtheon.

Supply chain innovator. Use the Internet to streamline the interactions among all parties in the supply chain to improve operating efficiency. Examples: McKesson and Ingram Micro.

Channel mastery. Use the Internet as a sales and service channel. This model supplements, rather than replaces, the existing physical business offices and call centers. Example: Charles Schwab.

SOURCE: Joan Magretta, "Why Business Models Matter," *Harvard Business Review*, May 2002.

BUSINESS APPLICATION PLANNING
LO 11-2

The ***business application planning*** process begins after the strategic phase of business/IT planning has occurred. Figure 11.11 shows that the application planning process includes the evaluation of proposals made by the IT management of a company for using information technology to accomplish the strategic business priorities developed earlier in the planning process, as was illustrated in Figure 11.8. Then, company executives and business unit managers evaluate the business case for investing in proposed e-business development projects based on the strategic business priorities that they decide are most desirable or necessary at that time. Finally, business application planning involves developing and implementing business applications of IT, as well as managing their development projects. We will cover the application development and implementation process in Chapter 12. Now, let's examine a real-world example.

FIGURE 11.11

A business application planning process includes consideration of IT proposals for addressing the strategic business priorities of a company and planning for application development and implementation.

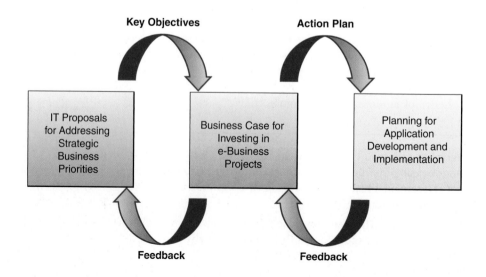

It must be great to be the chief information officer of FedEx, General Electric, or Credit Suisse—or any other one of those places where IT and the business are so tightly aligned that they cannot be torn apart without creating some serious damage. In such a place, chief information officers would spend their time looking at big picture problems, and chief executive officers would seek their counsel. That being said, most places are not that kind of IT Wonderland. The majority of chief information officers work in companies where not even the business has a clear strategic direction, much less IT. In these companies, IT may not be as valued, or be invited to sit at the big table of strategy. For most chief information officers, then, putting together a strategic IT plan is very difficult, but it must be done nonetheless.

Vicki Petit is the vice president of Information Services for KI, an office furniture manufacturer and provider of movable wall solutions for the education, health care, government, and corporate markets, headquartered in Green Bay, Wisconsin. When she first came on board as the IT leader, the business itself had no business strategy per se, so it was understandable that no one had ever thought of creating one for IT. When the business finally created a corporate strategy, it was not really a plan, but rather a 200-page-long tome containing mostly operational objectives, and nothing about IT. So Petit went ahead and created a strategic IT plan herself, with long term goals and everything. Every six months she goes back to it and revises according to progress. Now, the chief financial officer—her boss—requires a similar plan for all departments. "They love me," she jokes. But the plan has proved to be very useful. "We can use what is in there to help us justify IT's direction or say no to a project instead of just reacting to what the users want." In essence, to make long term strategic decisions about IT.

When Petit created her first plan in 2003 it was a nice big step, but she knew it was neither perfect nor ideal. "The first pass was really just internal to IS in order to create some principles for how we wanted to operate, and specific objectives," says Petit. "A better model would be to work with functional leaders and get their take on what we should be doing." This translates to "IT strategic planning cannot be done in a vacuum." Instead, the strategic plan communicates to the rest of the company the value that IT has to offer, and that should not be something that happens in a remote island out there. Although Petit herself is not involved in crafting corporate strategy, she has identified a set of stakeholders and started meeting with them to better understand what their objectives are and how they are rewarded and measured. Petit is essentially figuring out what IT can do that will make it easier for the business leaders to earn their bonus, which shows that you do not necessarily need to have a seat at the table to involve the business in IT planning; rather, doing so could be the way to earn that place in the future.

SOURCE: Stephanie Overby, "How to Get Real About Strategic Planning," *CIO.com*, January 18, 2008.

Business/IT Architecture Planning

Another way to look at the business/IT planning process, which is growing in acceptance and use in industry, is shown in Figure 11.12. ***E-business architecture planning*** combines contemporary strategic planning methods (for example, SWOT analysis and alternative planning scenarios) with more recent business modeling and application development methodologies (for example, component-based development). As illustrated in Figure 11.13, strategic e-business initiatives, including strategic goals,

FIGURE 11.12

Fostering relationships between IT and business partners through a formal business/IT planning process has a major impact on project success.

SOURCE: © Manchan/Getty Images.

constraints, and requirements, are developed based on SWOT analysis and other planning methods. Application developers then use business process engineering methods to define how strategic business requirements are to be implemented; they use organizational, process, and data models to create new internal and interenterprise e-business processes among a company's customers, suppliers, and other business partners.

Component-based e-business and e-commerce applications are then developed to implement the new business processes using application software and data components stored in a *repository* of reusable business models and application components. Of course, the business process engineering and component-based application development activities are supported by a company's technology infrastructure; this includes all the resources of its IT architecture, as well as the necessary component development technologies. So, e-business architecture planning links strategy development to business modeling and component development methodologies in order to produce the strategic e-business applications that a company needs.

FIGURE 11.13

E-business architecture planning integrates business strategy development and business process engineering to produce e-business and e-commerce applications using the resources of the IT architecture, component development technologies, and a repository of business models and application components.

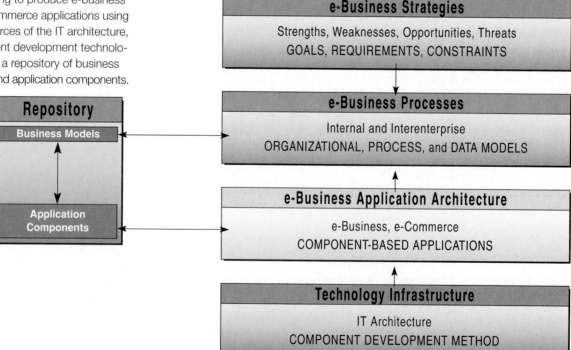

SOURCE: Peter Fingar, Harsha Kumar, and Tarun Sharma, *Enterprise E-Commerce: The Software Component Breakthrough for Business to Business Commerce* (Tampa, FL: Meghan-Kiffer Press, 2000), p. 68.

The Role of IT in Business Process Redesign

For a long time the idea that IT would be in charge of business processes would not fit well with anybody. After a number of years and disappointing results from enterprise IT projects, it dawned on many senior managers that IT people—who often have a more comprehensive view of the organization than many functional or divisional heads, and who are largely concerned with their specific areas—may be in a unique position to effect changes in business processes. The more so since, today, all those processes are IT-enabled. "Having a focus on the whole process is paramount and helps to build the leadership foundation to promote and sustain change," says Heather M. Hartman, director of IS Technical Services for Care New England Health System.

Hartman's earlier experience in IT consulting helped her land the job of overseeing infrastructure at Care New England Health System. Quickly, she was applying her experience not only to "IT problems" but to outright business issues. For example, one of the organizations in the group needed desperately to cut the time and cost of dictation and transcription services, and another was looking for new dictation and transcription software. The focus on both cases had been purely on IT, however, and as a result the project were stalling. Hartman was asked to look into it.

After analyzing the two cases, it became evident to Hartman that the issues lay with the end-to-end processes, and not solely with the technology used to support them. She created process maps that identified the main issues and bottlenecks and what could be done to improve them. More importantly, she reached out to those involved knee-deep in the problem itself—the transcriptionists at both of the two organizations and other hospitals—since the only way to really understand a process is to talk to the people who are part of it. Within a month, the improvements put in place had exceeded the cost-cutting goals by 120 percent, and this was even before any new IT systems were installed, just out of better processes. Eventually, transcriptionists were able to work full-time from home, which raised employee satisfaction as well. The key step in the process was to have the stakeholders claim ownership of the process and make it their own—that is when real change happens.

"My work within the business helped me as an IS leader by bringing me out of the data center onto the floor with them," says Hartman. "It gave me a great opportunity to learn a critical part of our operations and how the IT systems they use support that part of the business." Hopefully, says Hartman, the learning was a two-way street. "I think it helped them understand that IT is more than just the systems and technology. It is a part of everyone's world."

SOURCE: Stephanie Overby, "Experience Base: Executing an Operational or Process Improvement," *CIO.com*, June 9, 2010.

Implementation Challenges

IMPLEMENTATION

Many companies plan really well, yet few translate strategy into action, even though senior management consistently identifies e-business as an area of great opportunity and one in which the company needs stronger capabilities.

Implementation is an important managerial responsibility. An interesting characteristic of the word *implementation* is that it can be applied as either a noun or a verb. In one sense, implementation is an event that happens: the system has been implemented. In yet another sense, implementation can be thought of as a process that is being applied to effect an outcome. Regardless, implementation is just doing what you planned to do. You can view ***implementation*** as a process that carries out the plans for changes in business/IT strategies and applications that were developed in the planning process we covered in the beginning of the chapter. See Figure 11.14.

IMPLEMENTING INFORMATION TECHNOLOGY
LO 11-3

Moving to an e-business environment involves a major organizational change. For many large, global, companies, becoming an e-business is the fourth or fifth major organizational change they have undergone since the early 1980s. Many companies have gone through one or more rounds of business process reengineering (BPR); installation and major upgrades of an ERP system; upgrading legacy systems to be Y2K compliant; creating shared service centers; implementing just-in-time (JIT) manufacturing; automating the sales force; contract manufacturing; and the major challenges related to the introduction of euro currency.

Implementation of new e-business strategies and applications is only the latest catalyst for major organizational changes enabled by information technology. Figure 11.14 illustrates the impact and the levels and scope of business changes that applications of information technology introduce into an organization. For example, implementing an application such as online transaction processing brings efficiency to single-function or core business processes. Yet, implementing e-business applications such as enterprise resource management or customer relationship management requires a reengineering of core business processes internally and with supply chain partners, thus forcing a company to model and implement business practices by leading firms in their industry. Of course, any major new business initiatives can enable a company to redefine its core lines of business and precipitate dramatic changes within the entire interenterprise value chain of a business.

FIGURE 11.14

The impact and the levels and scope of business change introduced by implementations of information technology.

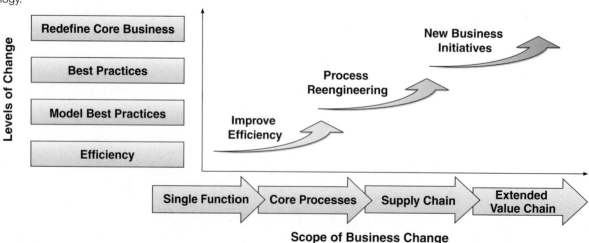

SOURCE: Craig Fellenstein and Ron Wood, *Exploring E-Commerce, Global E-Business and E-Societies* (Upper Saddle River, NJ: Prentice Hall, 2000), p. 97.

Intranet Enterprise Portal Challenges	Enterprise Resource Planning Challenges
• Security, security, security	• Getting end-user buy-in
• Defining the scope and purpose of the portal	• Scheduling/planning
• Finding the time and the money	• Integrating legacy systems/data
• Ensuring consistent data quality	• Getting management buy-in
• Getting employees to use it	• Dealing with multiple/international sites and partners
• Organizing the data	• Changing culture/mind-sets
• Finding technical expertise	• IT training
• Integrating the pieces	• Getting, keeping IT staff
• Making it easy to use	• Moving to a new platform
• Providing all users with access	• Performance/system upgrades

FIGURE 11.15

The 10 greatest challenges of developing and implementing intranet enterprise portals and enterprise resource planning systems reported by 100 companies.

As we will see in the remainder of this chapter, implementing new business/IT strategies requires managing the effects of major changes in key organizational dimensions such as business processes, organizational structures, managerial roles, employee work assignments, and stakeholder relationships that arise from the deployment of new business information systems. For example, Figure 11.15 emphasizes the variety and extent of the challenges reported by 100 companies that developed and implemented new enterprise information portals and ERP systems. In this sense, planning for implementation of a new system is as important as actually performing the implementation successfully. There is much more to implementation than just getting the new system installed.

END-USER RESISTANCE AND INVOLVEMENT
LO 11-3

Any new way of doing things generates some resistance from the people affected. For example, the implementation of new work support technologies can generate employees' fear and resistance to change. Customer relationship management (CRM) is a prime example of a key e-business application for many companies today. It is designed to implement a business strategy of using IT to support a total customer care focus for all areas of a company. Yet CRM projects have a history of a high rate of failure in meeting their objectives. For example, according to a report from Meta Group, a staggering 55 percent to 75 percent of CRM projects fail to meet their objectives, often as a result of sales-force automation problems and "unaddressed cultural issues"—sales staffs that are often resistant to, or even fearful of, using CRM systems.

Société de Transport de Montréal: Smooth Ride after a Bumpy Start

Suburban sprawl might make a great business case for a transit agency, but when it came to servers, Canada's Société de Transport de Montréal (STM) drew the line. Mike Stefanakis, senior systems engineer at STM, says that the main reason he started looking at virtualization technology was to prevent server sprawl. He wanted consolidation, particularly for development servers at the agency, which provides more than 360 million bus and metro rides each year.

"We crunched the numbers and realized that our growth was going to cause a few problems in the near future," he says. If things kept going as they had, the agency would need an additional 20 to 30 servers each year, on top of its existing base of 180 primarily Wintel machines. "Too many servers were going to be needed to feed the needs of our users and clients," Stefanakis says.

But even though staffers were convinced of virtualization's benefits pretty early on, the agency's end users didn't necessarily feel the same way. Several factors contributed to the initial resistance. For starters, there was a fear of the unknown. There were questions like "How stable is this new technology?" and "What do you mean I will be sharing my resources with other servers?" Potential users thought the new technology might slow them down.

To help users get over their fears, Stefanakis focused on giving people the information they needed, while explaining the advantages of the new technology. Among them: great response time for business applications and baked-in disaster recovery. If anything does fail, restoration is just a quickly restored image away.

Stefanakis and his staff kept "talking up" the technology and its benefits. "Virtualization came up in every budget, strategy, and development meeting we had," he recalls. "We made sure the information was conveyed to the proper people so that everyone in our department knew that virtualization was coming."

STM has been staging production servers in its virtual environment since December 2005. The first virtual machine was staged in STM's testing center as a means of quickly recovering a downed production server. Once the first few applications were implemented, user resistance quickly became history. "After people see the advantages, stability and performance available to them on a virtual platform, they tend to lose any inhibitions they previously may have had. The psychological barrier for virtualization has been broken," Stefanakis says, "and now users will ask for a new server as if they are ordering a coffee and danish."

SOURCE: Mary Ryan Garcia, "After Bumpy Start, Transit Agency Finds Virtualization a Smooth Ride," *Computerworld*, March 8, 2007.

One of the keys to solving problems of ***end-user resistance*** to new information technologies is proper education and training. Even more important is ***end-user involvement*** in organizational changes and in the development of new information systems. Organizations have a variety of strategies to help manage business change, and one basic requirement is the involvement and commitment of top management and all business stakeholders affected by the planning processes that we described earlier in the chapter.

Direct end-user participation in business planning, as well as application development projects before a new system is implemented, is especially important in reducing the potential for end-user resistance. That's why end users frequently are members of systems development teams or do their own development work. Such involvement helps ensure that end users assume ownership of a system and that its design meets their needs. Systems that tend to inconvenience or frustrate users cannot be effective systems, no matter how technically elegant they are and how efficiently they process data. For example, Figure 11.16 illustrates some of the major obstacles to knowledge management systems in business. Notice that end-user resistance to sharing knowledge is the biggest obstacle to the implementation of knowledge management applications. Let's look at a real-world example that spotlights resistance to change and what one company did about it.

FIGURE 11.16

Obstacles to knowledge management systems. Note that end-user resistance to knowledge sharing is the biggest obstacle.

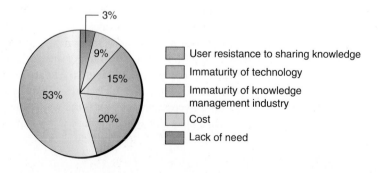

Understanding the Science Behind Change

Kevin Sparks, at the time the chief information officer at Blue Cross and Blue Shield of Kansas City (and now its chief operating officer, which shows that IT executives can make the jump to running a business), could not convince his staffers to change the way they monitored and supported the data center. After trying to convince them for a year, he was starting to get frustrated. Not that anyone disagreed that the changes were necessary, and the monitoring software under consideration would be a major improvement in the way things were done. He had even taken layoffs off the table—assuming the staff thought the monitoring software would result in a loss of jobs through automation—and things still did not happen, and with no seemingly rational explanation.

In the last few years, advances in brain analysis technology have allowed researchers to gain a better understanding of how the brain reacts to exposure to different stimuli, as well as more fully understand our most deeply ingrained responses. When it comes to change, those responses are both consistent and predictable, at least from a neurological perspective. We all react to change in the same way; that is, we avoid it as much as possible. It turns out that change hurts. Exposure to change lights up an area of the brain—the prefrontal cortex—that is both expensive to operate and has limited working capacity. Extensive exposure to change causes fatigue, and even anger, as a result of the many ties of the prefrontal cortex to the emotional centers of the brain.

This also helps explain why, even though everyone in the IT group at Blue Cross and Blue Shield of Kansas City agreed that the new approach was better, nobody seemed willing to implement it. The current approach, while somewhat more troublesome, is familiar and more predictable. Familiar actions run off from the basal ganglia in our brain, which controls habit-based behavior and is not expensive, from a physiological perspective, to operate. In a nutshell: Problematic but familiar beats new and better. The way to solve this problem is to help people come to their own resolution with the new concepts—have an epiphany, if you will—since our brain seems to reward insight, although the specific mechanisms are not yet well understood. Once that insight has happened, repetition is now necessary to reinforce the new behaviors until they too become familiar. Feeling uncomfortable, however, is a natural part of change, and leaders should emphasize that it is perfectly natural.

And so Kevin Sparks changed gears and brought in an outside consultant to talk about how the monitoring project fit with the overall strategic direction of the IT department. "We had an outstanding instructor, and she was able to address many of the questions people had," recalls Sparks. "I could begin to see the lights come on in some of the skeptics. After a long meeting, one of my people stood up and said, 'You know, we should have started working on this automated monitoring six months ago.'"

SOURCE: Christopher Koch, "Change Management—Understanding the Science of Change," *CIO Magazine*, September 15, 2006.

CHANGE MANAGEMENT
LO 11-3

Figure 11.17 illustrates some of the key dimensions of *change management,* as well as the level of difficulty and business impact involved. Notice some of the people, process, and technology factors involved in the implementation of business/IT strategies and applications, or other changes caused by introducing new information technologies into a company. Some of the technical factors listed, such as systems integrators and outsourcing, will be discussed in more detail in the next few chapters. For example, systems integrators are consulting firms or other outside contractors who may be paid to assume the responsibility for developing and implementing a new e-business application, including designing and leading its change management activities. In addition, notice that people factors have the highest level of difficulty and longest time to resolve of any dimension of change management.

	Technology	Process	People
Strategic	• Enterprise Architecture • Supplier Partnership • Systems Integrators • Outsourcing	• Ownership • Design • Enterprisewide Processes • Interenterprise Processes	• Change Leaders • Loose/Tight Controls • Executive Sponsorship and Support • Aligning on Conditions of Satisfaction
Operational	• Technology Selection • Technology Support • Installation Requirements	• Change Control • Implementation Management • Support Processes	• Recruitment • Retention • Training • Knowledge Transfer

Impact on Business (High / Low — vertical axis)

Level of Difficulty/Time to Resolve (Low → High — horizontal axis)

FIGURE 11.17

Some of the key dimensions of change management. Examples of the people, process, and technology factors involved in managing the implementation of IT-based changes to an organization.

SOURCE: Grant Norris, James Hurley, Kenneth Hartley, John Dunleavy, and John Balls, *E-Business and ERP: Transforming the Enterprise*, p. 120. Copyright © 2000 by John Wiley & Sons, Inc. Reprinted by permission.

Thus, people are a major focus of organizational change management. This includes activities such as developing innovative ways to measure, motivate, and reward performance. It is important to design programs to recruit and train employees in the core competencies required in a changing workplace. Change management also involves analyzing and defining all changes facing the organization, as well as developing programs to reduce the risks and costs and to maximize the benefits of change. For example, implementing a new e-business application such as customer relationship management might involve developing a *change action plan*, assigning selected managers as *change sponsors*, developing employee *change teams*, and encouraging open communications and feedback about organizational changes. Some key tactics that change experts recommend include:

- Involve as many people as possible in e-business planning and application development.
- Make constant change an expected part of the culture.
- Tell everyone as much as possible about everything as often as possible, preferably in person.
- Make liberal use of financial incentives and recognition.
- Work within the company culture, not around it.

DHL Express: The Challenges of Global Change

Depending on the business pressure *du jour*, large IT shops tend to swing back and forth from one organizational model to another. Need to save money and promote technology standards across the organization? Centralize. Need to respond more quickly to local market demands and better align with the business? Decentralize. "It's a constant tension between the two extremes of the pendulum," says Ron Kifer, senior vice president and chief information officer for the United States and Canada at DHL Express.

The global transportation and logistics services giant began to centralize and consolidate IT infrastructure and services six years ago, building a massive computing supercenter in Kuala Lumpur to manage IT for most of its operations in the Asia-Pacific and emerging markets, Kifer says. Two years ago, DHL opened a supercenter in Scottsdale, Arizona, to consolidate IT for the United States, Canada, and parts of Central and South America; and this year, the company set up a supercenter in Prague to condense IT for most of Europe and the Mediterranean.

Although centralization drove down costs, it did make it harder for business units to ensure that IT spending was in sync with business strategy. "It was difficult to get the right people from the business together with the right people from IT to define project requirements in a manner that was suitable for design and specification," Kifer says. Multiple iterations of project requirement specs were continually shifting between the business and IT (because of their remoteness to each other), adding cost and time to project life cycles, he says.

DHL has now embarked on an IT transformation that aims to give it the best of both worlds. The arrangement separates the supply side of DHL's IT organization from the demand side, and it puts IT demand management under the business's control. "Demand CIOs" report to regional CEOs and manage the region's IT budget, Kifer says, to align IT spending more closely with business strategy. The demand management function—Express Business IT (EbIT)—is staffed by IT employees who were previously focused on demand management aspects of IT. Under the new model, Kifer says, DHL will be able to reap the cost savings of its centralized computing supercenters, as well as the alignment benefits of having IT closely tied to regional operations. All regions of DHL are adopting this organizational model. Regional teams are in charge of implementing the EbIT functions within their regions, Kifer says, but a "thin global group" under a single CIO is coordinating to ensure a consistent approach, standards, processes, and tools from region to region. DHL also has a global corporate transformation office supporting this initiative.

For many employees, the reorganization means a dramatic change in roles, reporting relationships, and processes, Kifer says. DHL's change management plan emphasizes education and training to help employees understand the benefits of these changes to the company as a whole—and to them personally.

SOURCE: "Case Study: DHL's Global Change Management Plan," *CIO Magazine*, November 1, 2005.

A Change Management Process

An eight-level process of change management for organizations is illustrated in Figure 11.18. This change management model is only one of many that could be applied to manage organizational changes caused by new business/IT strategies and applications and other changes in business processes. For example, this model suggests that the business vision created in the strategic planning phase should be communicated in a compelling *change story* to the people in the organization. Evaluating the readiness for changes within an organization, then developing change strategies and choosing and training change leaders and champions based on that assessment, could be the next steps in the process.

These change leaders are the change agents who would then be able to lead change teams of employees and other business stakeholders in building a business case for changes in technology, business processes, job content, and organizational structures. They could also communicate the benefits of these changes and lead training

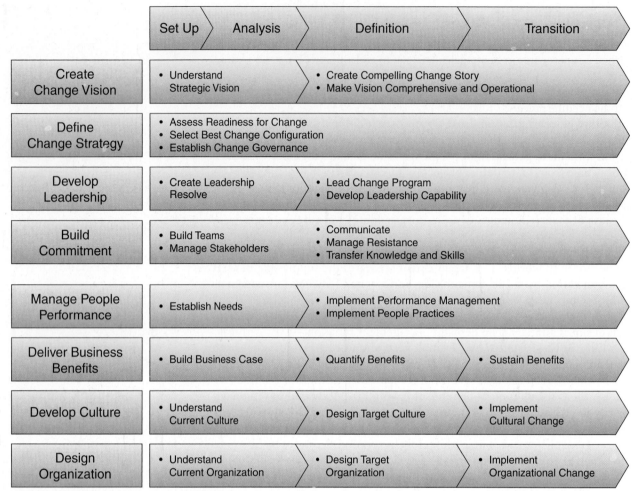

FIGURE 11.18

A process of change management. Examples of the activities involved in successfully managing organizational change caused by the implementation of new business processes.

SOURCE: Martin Diese, Conrad Nowikow, Patric King, and Amy Wright, *Executive's Guide to E-Business: From Tactics to Strategy*, p. 190. Copyright © 2000 by John Wiley & Sons, Inc. Reprinted by permission.

programs on the details of new business applications. Of course, many change management models include methods for performance measurement and rewards to provide financial incentives for employees and stakeholders to cooperate with changes that may be required. In addition, fostering a new e-business culture within an organization by establishing communities of interest for employees and other business stakeholders via Internet, intranet, and extranet discussion groups could also be a valuable change management strategy. Such groups would encourage stakeholder involvement and buy-in for the changes brought about by implementing new e-business applications of information technology.

Reuters: Implementing Global Shared Services

The late 1990s and the Internet revolution did not bode well for Reuters (now part of Thomson Reuters). Much of its core content became commoditized, and the widespread availability of financial information significantly eroded its competitive advantage. Even worse, the premium rates the company had been able to charge were rapidly disappearing. Indeed, the company went from a profit of £297 million in 2000 to a loss of £94 million in 2001, and a further loss of £493 million in 2002. Internally, things were not faring much better. Rapid growth had resulted in duplicate back offices and financial processes, which made integration very difficult. In particular, senior management noticed that its finance operating model exceeded 2.3 percent of revenue, where comparable costs across the best-run companies indicated they should be about 1.5 percent. This is a major difference when you consider that revenue for 2002 was £3,575 million.

In 2001, the corporate chief financial officer decided to do something about it, and launched a global initiative to reduce finance costs by standardizing operations across the board and moving away from decentralized business units to six new regional, shared service centers. According to Accenture, shared services can be defined as the consolidation of support functions into a stand-alone entity whose goal is to provide them as efficiently and effectively as possible. For Reuters, the transition involved four different change programs, implemented in two separate phases: business process redesign (what business processes the organization will perform), organizational redesign (where business processes will be performed), sourcing redesign (who performs the business processes), and technology enablement (how those processes will be implemented). Phase 1 ran from 2001 to 2004, while Phase 2 went from 2005 to 2006. Figure 11.19 shows the ordering of the phases, its major challenges and activities, and the results obtained from each.

After all the dust settled, Reuters was able to realize its vision for efficiently and effectively delivering financial services through shared global

FIGURE 11.19

Reuters moved through several stages of organizational transformation as it sought to implement global shared service centers for its financial services function.

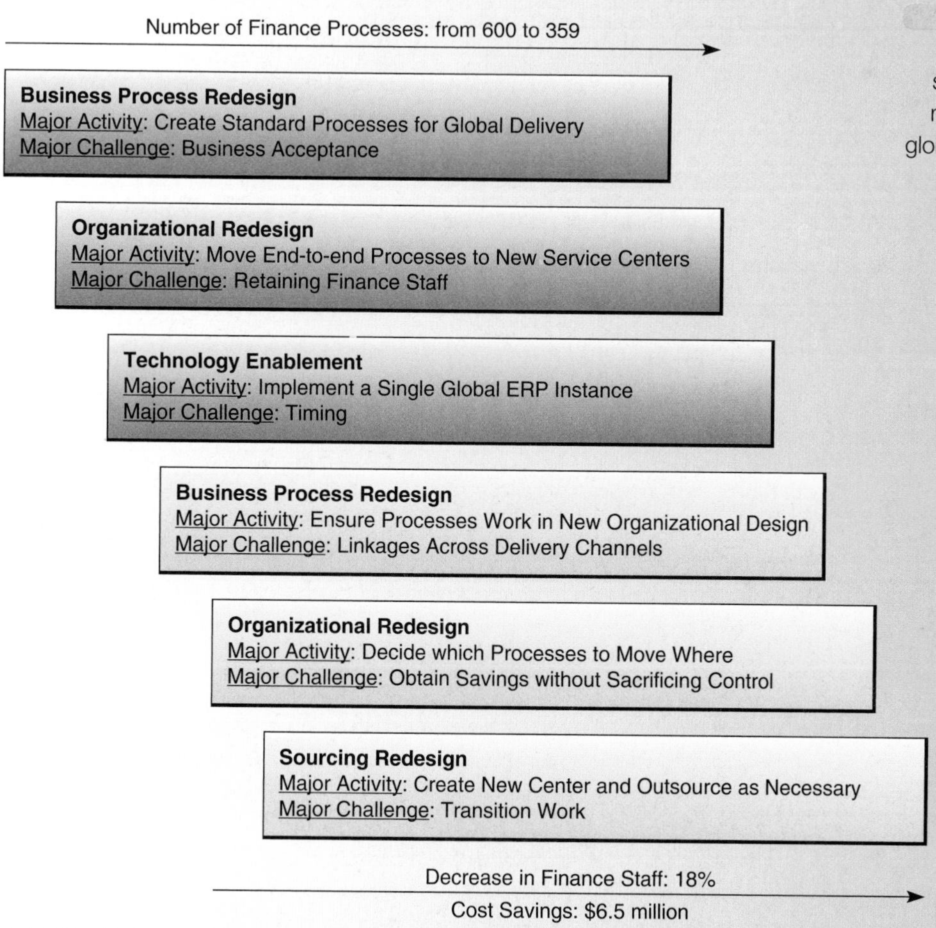

Number of Finance Processes: from 600 to 359

Business Process Redesign
Major Activity: Create Standard Processes for Global Delivery
Major Challenge: Business Acceptance

Organizational Redesign
Major Activity: Move End-to-end Processes to New Service Centers
Major Challenge: Retaining Finance Staff

Technology Enablement
Major Activity: Implement a Single Global ERP Instance
Major Challenge: Timing

Business Process Redesign
Major Activity: Ensure Processes Work in New Organizational Design
Major Challenge: Linkages Across Delivery Channels

Organizational Redesign
Major Activity: Decide which Processes to Move Where
Major Challenge: Obtain Savings without Sacrificing Control

Sourcing Redesign
Major Activity: Create New Center and Outsource as Necessary
Major Challenge: Transition Work

Decrease in Finance Staff: 18%
Cost Savings: $6.5 million

SOURCE: M. Lacey and J. Fox, "Creating Global Shared Services: Lessons from Reuters," *MIS Quarterly Executive*, 2008, and ke.thomsonreuters.com, accessed June 11, 2011.

services. Finance employees who remained in the business units now focus only on strategic activities, while those who moved to the regional shared services deliver them in highly standardized processes, and to those that require close proximity to customers. Reuters reduced financial service staff by 35 percent and reduced finance costs from 2.3 percent of revenue to 1.8 percent—much closer to the benchmark for world-class companies. In addition to financial outcomes, the work became much more simplified. Prior to the beginning of the project, Reuters had 600 distinct finance processes, which were reduced to 359 after Phase 1. Of those, processes, 279 were globally standardized, while the remaining 80 represented specialized processes due to localized needs. And all this was achieved without reduction in service levels or control standards, which are key for finance operations. By the end of 2006, Reuters had regained both revenue and profit.

SOURCE: Lacity, M. and Fox, J. "Creating Global Shared Services: Lessons from Reuters," *MIS Quarterly Executive*, 2008, and ke.thomsonreuters.com, accessed June 11, 2011.

Sloan Valve Company—IT and the Redesign of the New Product Development Process

The Sloan Valve Company, founded in 1906 and headquartered in Franklin Park, Illinois, is a family-owned manufacturer of faucets, flushometers, showerheads, and sinks with growing domestic and international operations. The company has always taken pride in its ability to develop and introduce new products and innovations as a leader in its industry. Indeed, its mission explicitly notes "the ability to develop, manufacture, market and distribute breakthrough products and services" as a major goal of the organization. As a result of an increasing awareness that its approach to the development of new products was no longer delivering on that goal, management sought to introduce changes into the process. A new ERP package, while arguably well-implemented, did little to help. A project to incrementally improve the logistic process was also abandoned after months of work resulted in little to show for it.

After the less-than-successful attempt to drive incremental improvements into the logistic process—a result of the complex interdependency of this process with many others in the company—management at Sloan Valve started looking for an alternative approach. Part of the problem was the need to change the way IT was perceived inside the company. Traditionally, employees viewed IT at Sloan Valve as a support function for individual departments, which resulted in well-defined boundaries between IT and those other functions. IT-enabled business processes, on the other hand, tend to cut across those same functions, so a new approach was needed. Recognizing these issues, senior management appointed the existing chief information officer (CIO) to the additional role of chief process officer (CPO). In fact, senior management went so far as to announce, in 2004, than these were not two different responsibilities held by the same person, but rather a single role. "It was a clear signal from top management. The CIO is typically seen as a person in charge of technology. By combining the CIO and CPO roles, management sent a clear message that the CIO would from now on lead as a business executive and take on the role of a business leader as well," says a manager at Sloan Valve.

Given its critical importance to the company, the New Product Development process was the first one targeted through a series of initiatives undertaken by Tom Coleman, now CIO/CPO. The first step was to procure exposure and training on business process reengineering for the entire senior management team. Eventually, all senior and middle managers, business analysts, and program managers underwent formal training. Senior management worked with reluctant executives to win them over to the new approach and gain their full commitment to the project. A few who had strongly opposed the plan left the company, and others were assigned to new functions. In order to obtain commitment and support from all involved, the CIO/CPO created a two-level governance structure. The strategic level would be composed of key members from each functional department, led by the CEO, and would enable cross-function coordination and communication. The process level would oversee efforts in particular processes. Tom Coleman took the role of architect and visionary, raising awareness of the new process orientation across the organization, and a strong IT manager with extensive business knowledge was made responsible for the day-to-day progress of the project.

For the New Product Development process, the Director of Design Engineering became the process owner. The BPM manager appointed by the CIO/CPO led the redesign team, which included members from manufacturing, design, engineering, IT, finance, marketing, and operations—in short, from all areas of the company, as the process is integral to the organization and cuts across every single function. The team spent nine months studying the current process, identifying subprocesses, associated activities, and interfaces with other processes, as well as any other interdependencies that needed to be considered. Visualization tools from iGrafx aided analysis of a such a complex undertaking, which allowed the team to create a visual representation of the process and how information flowed from one to another of the sixteen functions included in it. This process map also served as a communication tool and to educate the company as to the many problems and deficiencies that existed in the current process. Indeed, for most people it was the first time they saw the entire process in action. "This technique typically shocks senior management in terms of how the company actually runs," says Coleman. The graphical representation was also effective in a different way. When making a presentation about what the new process would look like, the manager in charge of the effort would bring down the 'as-is' diagram with all the steps across the sixteen functions from the wall and tear it up in front of everybody in the room—that typically had the effect of conveying to everybody how serious the company was about changing the way it worked.

A series of metrics were identified to help measure the extent to which the new project would be deemed successful. Chief among these were the metrics that reflected the main objectives the company wanted to achieve with the process redesign: namely, time-to-market, innovation rate, and total new products. These metrics were incorporated into strategy maps and balanced scorecards that further helped align the new process with the strategy of the organization. The CIO/CPO also decided to upgrade the ERP package into the MySAP business suite, which added customer relationship management, supply chain management, and product lifecycle management capabilities. The basic components of the latter were put in place in 2006, with all the upgrades being completed by 2007. However, upgrading the ERP package at the same time the New Product Development process was being redesigned and continually improved was a major challenge for the company, as the software modules needed to be customized repeatedly for each new iteration of the process. The major issues, however, were not technical, but rather organizational. Says Coleman, "The major issues we faced with NPD [New Product Development] and other process efforts were leadership, change management, and slow organizational changes needed to make process work 'sing.' The technology issues are challenging but not nearly as difficult as the human side of change."

The new process introduced at Sloan Valve consisted of six subprocesses, each grouping a logical set of activities. Employees from each of the individual functions that interacted with the old process were transferred to one of the subprocesses, with commensurate changes in their objectives and reward structures. A new program management office was created to coordinate the new product initiatives as they moved along the process, and to make sure the necessary resources—human or technological—were made available at the appropriate times, as well as overseeing project prioritization. In 2008, management created a new role for a senior vice president of New Product Development to lead the new process and take executive ownership of it.

Given the earlier issues with the original implementation of the ERP, the CIO/CPO wanted to develop strong IT capabilities to support the newly designed process effectively. These took the form of an "Ideation Portal," an intranet platform that was deployed to provide structure to the management of new product ideas, which was done in a very ad hoc manner before, and effective use of the Product Lifecycle Module that was implemented when the company migrated to MySAP. The module allowed the process owner to get a complete picture of every project at every stage of the process, and track and allocate resources as necessary to different ideas, as well as see which were lagging behind schedule. The software also solved the communication and coordination challenges faced by the company with the implementation of a centralized repository of all documents, reports, design templates, and other project files, which were available from any location due to the Web-enabled nature of the product.

The implementation of the new process has resulted in a number of benefits for the Sloan Valve Company. Most notably, the time-to-market of new ideas went from 18–24 months to less than 12 months, which significantly improves the agility and responsiveness of the company to bring new products to market and swiftly react to new demands or preferences from its customers. The governance structure of the process is much simplified, from 16 different units having to collaborate and coordinate among themselves to a two-tier governance structure led by top-level executives. The ability to see the entire process from end-to-end enabled managers to identify bottlenecks and quickly move to improve the flow of new ideas and products, an aspect that is enhanced by the increased accountability integrated into the new process. Increased emphasis in the idea-generation stage—further supported by technologies such as the Ideation Portal—allowed the company to sift through the many new ideas earlier than before, resulting in less design and prototyping work conducted for ideas that were eventually discarded, with significant savings. As a result, those ideas that did proceed to the later stages and eventually made it to market yielded a better return on investment, as only the solid ideas made it that far. This is, at the end of the day, what new product development is all about.

SOURCE: Balaji, S., Ranganathan, C. and Coleman, T. "IT-Led Process Reengineering: How Sloan Valve Redesigned Its New Product Development Process," *MIS Quarterly Executive*, 2011; Martin, M., "Celebrating 100 Years . . . Sloan Valve Continues to Build on Strong Foundation," *The Wholesaler*, May 2011; and www.sloanvalve.com, accessed June 10, 2011.

▼ **QUESTIONS TO CONSIDER**

1. The endeavor chronicled here would arguably be considered a success. What were the key success factors—changes, practices, techniques, and so on—that made this possible? How did each contribute to the positive outcomes of the project?

2. The company adopted a two-level governance structure with a strategic and a process level. How would this approach work? What kind of issues should be discussed in each level? What are the advantages of taking such an approach?

- **Organizational Planning.** Managing information technology requires planning for changes in business goals, processes, structures, and technologies. Planning is a vital organizational process that uses methods like the scenario approach and planning for competitive advantage to evaluate an organization's internal and external environments; forecast new developments; establish an organization's vision, mission, goals, and objectives; develop strategies, tactics, and policies to implement its goals; and articulate plans for the organization to act upon. A good planning process helps organizations learn about themselves and promotes organizational change and renewal.
- **Business/IT Planning.** Strategic business/IT planning involves aligning investment in information technology with a company's business vision and strategic goals such as reengineering business processes or gaining competitive advantages. It results in a strategic plan that outlines a company's business/IT strategies and technology architecture. The technology architecture is a conceptual blueprint that specifies a company's technology platform, data resources, applications architecture, and IT organization.
- **Implementing Business Change.** Implementation activities include managing the introduction and implementation of changes in business processes, organizational structures, job assignments, and work relationships resulting from business/IT strategies and applications such as e-business initiatives, reengineering projects, supply chain alliances, and the introduction of new technologies. Companies use change management tactics such as user involvement in business/IT planning and development to reduce end-user resistance and maximize acceptance of business changes by all stakeholders.

These are the key terms and concepts of this chapter. The page number of their first reference appears in parentheses.

1. Business model (485)
2. Business/IT planning (488)
   a. Business application planning (492)
   b. E-business architecture planning (493)
   c. Strategic planning (477)
3. Change management (499)
4. End-user involvement (498)
5. End-user resistance (498)
6. Implementation (496)
7. Information technology architecture (488)
8. Organizational planning (477)
9. Planning for competitive advantage (483)
10. Scenario approach to planning (480)
11. SWOT analysis (484)

Match one of the key terms and concepts listed previously with each of the brief examples or definitions that follow. Try to find the best fit for answers that seem to fit more than one term or concept. Defend your choices.

_____ 1. An organization should create a shared business vision and mission, and plan how it will achieve its strategic goals and objectives.

_____ 2. Outlines a business vision, business/IT strategies, and technical architecture for a company.

_____ 3. A blueprint for information technology in a company that specifies a technology platform, applications architecture, data resources, and IT organization structure.

_____ 4. Evaluating strategic business/IT opportunities based on their risk/payoff potential for a company.

_____ 5. Planning teams simulate the role of information technology in various hypothetical business situations.

_____ 6. Evaluating IT proposals for new business application development projects.

_____ 7. Evaluating strategic business opportunities based on a company's capabilities and the competitive environment.

_____ 8. Accomplishing the strategies and applications developed during organizational planning.

_____ 9. Managing the introduction of new technologies and IT-based strategies in organizations.

_____ 10. End users frequently resist the introduction of new technology.

_____ 11. End users should be part of planning for organizational change and business/IT project teams.

_____ 12. Expresses how a business can deliver value to customers and make money.

_____ 13. Identifying and developing e-business strategies for a company would be an example.

_____ 14. A combination of traditional planning methods with business modeling and application development.

discussion questions

1. "Planning is a useless endeavor because developments in e-business and e-commerce and in the political, economic, and societal environments are moving too quickly nowadays." Do you agree or disagree with this statement? Why?

2. "Planning and budgeting processes are notorious for their rigidity and irrelevance to management action." How can planning be made relevant to the challenges facing a business?

3. Refer to the Real World Challenge introduced at the beginning of this chapter. If the ERP package implemented by the Sloan Valve Company "vaguely supported the business as it existed" and "it was not crafted to support any new business process that we wanted," according to the CEO, then why do you think it was implemented in the first place? Were these issues—that it was not going to have a great impact on the business—evident at the outset?

4. What planning methods would you use to develop business/IT strategies and applications for your own business? Explain your choices.

5. What are several e-business and e-commerce strategies and applications that should be developed and implemented by many companies today? Explain your reasoning.

6. Refer to the Real World Solution in the chapter. The CIO/CPO of the Sloan Valve Company mentioned that although technology issues were challenging, it was really the people issues that were the most difficult. Why is this the case?

7. How can a company use change management to minimize the resistance to, and maximize the acceptance of, changes in business and technology? Give several examples.

8. "Many companies plan really well, yet few translate strategy into action." Do you think this statement is true? Why or why not?

9. Review the real-world examples on user resistance and involvement in the chapter. What else would you recommend to encourage user acceptance in both cases? Explain your recommendations.

10. What major business changes beyond e-business and e-commerce do you think most companies should be planning for in the next 10 years? Explain your choices.

analysis exercises

1. **Business on the Fly**
   Remote Point of Sales in Mexico
   Melissa and "Rook" Nelson, co-owners of Skydive Chicago, shut down their northern operations in mid-December each year. With heavy cloud cover and frigid temperatures, they just cannot find enough skydivers willing to jump over the frozen Chicago landscape. Without customers, valued staff members would migrate to southern drop zones, and more than a million dollars in aircraft assets would sit in a hanger. Some northern drop-zone owners turn to hauling freight. Others lease their aircraft to southern dropzones. Melissa and Rook, world-champion skydivers themselves, developed other plans.

   Each winter, Skydive Chicago moves their operations to sunny Ixtapa, Mexico. By moving south, Skydive Chicago keeps its aircraft in operation, provides year-round employment for valued staff members, gives its northern customers a sunny winter holiday destination, and introduces skydiving to crowds of tourists seeking to enjoy the beach from a new angle.

   When Skydive Chicago relocates to Ixtapa, they take their computers with them. "We use them for everything," said Rook. "Everything" includes Web site updates, newsletters, video editing, photo printing, jump manifesting, e-mail, customer account management, and credit card processing. With three computers, a credit card reader, a router, an Internet connection through Telmex, and credit card clearing through Authorize.Net, business continues in a *much* more hospitable climate.

a. Research credit card readers. What are the popular brands? What features do they offer? How much do they cost?

b. Research mobile point-of-sales devices. What are the popular brands? What features do they offer? How much do they cost?

c. Look up "Authorize.Net" and explore the Web site as a prospective retail merchant. Read and summarize a retail merchant case study.

2. **Online University Degrees**

Distance Learning

"Distance learning" is a growth business with an increasing number of accredited universities adding new online degrees to their offerings every year. However, prospective employers often value these degrees little more than the mail-order degree variety. University administrators would like to bring in additional revenue but without compromising their degree's integrity or cannibalizing their traditional student base.

a. Use news.google.com to find and read three articles about successful online degree programs. What are the key elements for success mentioned in the articles?

b. Prepare a SWOT analysis describing this business opportunity for your university's administration.

c. What sorts of concerns might the faculty have about an online degree program? What steps would you recommend the administration take in order to make an online degree initiative attractive to the faculty whose help is required to make the endeavor a success?

3. **Strategic Opportunities Matrix**

Planning Tool

The Strategic Opportunities Matrix described in this chapter provides a simple analysis tool for strategic planning groups. It places all plans in direct competition with each other and allows participants to rapidly identify the most promising plans to evaluate in greater detail.

Use the Internet and your own experience to evaluate each of the following opportunities and place them appropriately on a "Strategic Opportunities Matrix." Explain how you assessed each decision.

a. Online sale and distribution of digital college textbooks.

b. Customized news alerts by topic, industry, region, business function, or other key word.

c. Online college degrees from accredited universities.

d. Brainstorm opportunities that might fit both the "High Ability to Deliver with IT" and the "High Strategic Business Potential" categories. Present your best idea to the class and explain how it fits both classifications.

4. **Practical Change Management**

Work Culture

"Culture" evolves from and sets boundaries for interactions between people in an environment defined by rules, rule enforcement, and the example set by leadership. Conversely, culture can play a significant impact on what rule changes leadership can impose, as well as on the cost of these changes.

New software systems invariably mean change. At a minimum, new software will require new procedures. In many cases, new systems herald significant organizational change. Managers responsible for implementing these systems must take an organization's culture into consideration when planning implementation.

To see these challenges for yourself, find an example of a proposed rule change within your student government organization. Read about or monitor the debate, and interview representatives from each side of the issue.

a. Briefly describe the proposed change.

b. What group or groups oppose the change? What motivates them?

c. What group or groups benefit from the change? What motivates them?

d. Apply the change management principles outlined in this chapter to describe the steps you think leadership could take to ensure success at the lowest reasonable cost.

5. **Planning and Culture**

Facial Recognition Backlash

Facebook has recently rolled out a facial-recognition feature that has caused significant consternation among privacy advocates. The feature scans through photos users upload to Facebook to see if they contain the faces of any of their friends. For every match Facebook finds, it makes the appropriate tag suggestion.

Tags in Facebook serve to link notes or photos to other user accounts. If the software works correctly, it will not make tag suggestions for faces of people who are not in the user's friends list. Users may opt out, thereby causing Facebook not to make tag recommendations for photos friends might upload of them. And, of course, Facebook users are free to remove tags linking them to other people's photos and notes.

As part of the planning process, we can assume Facebook's legal advisors found no problems with this feature. Facebook also took care to roll this feature out gradually so management could evaluate user participation and monitor feedback. Initial participation and feedback was overwhelmingly positive. This feature simply helped automate an otherwise tedious tagging process and made using Facebook more enjoyable.

Yet four advocacy groups have filed a complaint with the Federal Trade Commission, and the attorney general for Connecticut has demanded a meeting with Facebook's leadership.

Read CNN Money's article, *Facebook Facial Recognition Draws Ire of Connecticut Attorney General*, for a more detailed overview (http://bit.ly/jbowWg).

Read Chris Pirillo's article (or view his video), *Will Smartphones and Face Recognition Destroy Anonymity?* for examples of how this technology might be abused (http://bit.ly/mTgLnD).

a. Could Facebook's leadership have anticipated this backlash?

b. Why do you think Facebook's leadership chose to make this an opt-out rather than an opt-in feature?

c. Should Facebook change the feature so users must opt in? Should they remove the feature entirely? Why or why not?

d. After viewing Pirillo's video, do you believe that privacy is (or will soon be) an illusion?

IT Leaders: IT/Business Alignment Takes on a Whole New Meaning

Chief information officers thought they knew what business/IT alignment was. But fighting the dark forces of recession has really taught the lesson. To some of them, anyway.

At a truly aligned company with all cylinders firing, every executive, every manager, and every employee works on one goal: to win customers. In the past, chief information officers saw their role as, say, to install business intelligence tools so that the marketing group could analyze customer data. Or perhaps it was to upgrade enterprise resource planning software for the supply chain guys to improve order fulfillment. Vital work, of course, but inwardly focused and a few steps removed from living, breathing, money-spending customers. But now, as shown in the 2010 State of the CIO survey by CIO Magazine, top technology executives increasingly see bringing home the bacon as their job, too.

Nearly one-third—30 percent—of the IT leaders polled say meeting or beating business goals is a personal leadership competency critically needed by their organizations, up significantly from the 18 percent who said so one year ago. Eighteen percent also named "external customer focus" as a critical skill, double the 9 percent in 2009. Double!

Meanwhile, 22 percent cited "identifying and seizing on commercial opportunities"—up more than triple from the year before. Yes, triple.

It's clear that the recession has deepened the chief information officer's understanding of and commitment to business beyond IT. Chief information officers are interacting with customers directly and working side by side with product engineers to build IT into new goods and services.

"In so many of the products offered now, the differentiating component is the IT capability," says Drew Martin, chief information officer of Sony Electronics. Certain Sony televisions, for example, can stream movies wirelessly, one of several products and features that Sony's IT group itself helped make possible. Chief information officers should get their IT departments involved in product development—if IT can truly step up. "You have to have an awareness of where your business is trying to go," he says. "Then you have to make sure you have the capability to support that."

"At Konica Minolta USA, the IT group also influences what the company sells," says Nelson Lin, chief information officer of the U.S. unit that is part of the $9.7 billion Konica Minolta Holdings in Japan. For example, Konica Minolta printers, measurement devices, and medical tools contain enough computer technology that when they break or get replaced, customers must dispose of them carefully to avoid environmental hazards.

Lin saw end-of-life equipment disposal as a service that customers would pay for. Lin and other senior executives view Konica Minolta as an advanced technology company and through that prism, he says, the chief information officer's input becomes even more valuable. He stepped up to lead discussion of equipment disposal as a moneymaker. "I'm doing it for our own e-waste already. It's now a matter of doing this large scale," he says. "It's the right thing to do, everyone knows. But it could be revenue for us, too."

Denise Coyne, chief information officer of Chevron's corporate departments and services companies, was previously chief information officer of the oil and gas giant's marketing group, as well as manager of 200 Chevron gas stations. She would go to conventions to talk up the company's point-of-sale system with gas station operators. "I found out what they wanted," she says. Her MBA and nine years in marketing have shaped how she approaches IT, she says, assessing projects from finance and business perspectives, for example.

Patti Reilly White has been with Darden Restaurants for 20 years, 10 of them as chief information officer. IT has "always" been customer-focused at Darden, she insists, but the past two years have been particularly intense. Projects in development include a system to text customers when their tables are ready, doing away with the flashing-light buzzers that restaurant greeters now hand out to waiting diners. "What our guests want is for us to value their time and personalize the experience for them. We in IT try to find ways to do that," Reilly White says.

Some chief information officers even run businesses themselves. In addition to overseeing internal IT for the $3.6 billion Nasdaq OMX Group, executive vice president and chief information officer Anna Ewing runs Market Technology, a division that sells Nasdaq's technology to financial exchanges around the world. The unit brought in $359 million in contracts in 2008, for everything from advisory services (helping customers set up various kinds of exchanges) to trading, clearing, and post-trade systems.

Before coming to Nasdaq in 2000, Ewing didn't have profit-and-loss responsibility in her previous positions at CIBC World Markets or at Merrill Lynch. But at those companies, she chose a commercial direction as much as she could: at CIBC, she was a founding member of the financial services company's e-commerce site. Among several positions at Merrill, she led client technology. She was named Nasdaq's chief information officer in 2005.

At Nasdaq, Ewing and her team recently launched a free iPhone application for checking stock quotes as a way to experiment with hot new consumer technology and seed the ground for some revenue-generating app in the future. The app debuted on a Friday. By Tuesday, without advertising, the stock-checker app was the fifth most downloaded free financial app at Apple's site. "We wanted to see if the appetite was there," Ewing says. "It is." A chief information officer's ability to spot new business opportunities comes from thinking like a chief executive officer, she says. "Product development and technology go hand-in-hand."

Still, most chief information officers have no profit-and-loss duties. That's a mistake, says Bill Deam, chief information officer of Quintiles Transnational, a $2.7 billion medical research company. Starting in 2007, most of Quintiles' top executives, including the chief operating officer, the head of corporate development, and Deam himself, were assigned one key customer account. Deam says he tries to cultivate good relations with senior managers at his assignment, a $15 billion biotech and pharmaceuticals firm. Quintiles helps the biotech firm conduct clinical trials for medicines in development. Deam reviews the account with an executive at the customer company every Friday and visits every six months. He hopes his efforts not only produce closer ties but also more business between the two companies. But that takes time.

"They want to make sure that all the work we do for them is performed excellently, without issues," Deam says. "Then we can go to the next phase of the relationship; this is very much about the business side," he says. For example, Quintiles would like to sell customers on the idea of outsourcing their technology infrastructures, Deam says, and he sees a pivotal role for himself in that strategic sales process. "My job is to make sure senior executives feel comfortable enough to talk to each other."

Doing sales calls is a relatively simple way for a chief information officer to learn about customers. The chief information officer's presence also adds weight to what the salesmen claim. Having a chief information officer on a sales call isn't uncommon, but it's especially important now when so many products and services rely on IT, says Hilton Sturisky, senior vice president for information and communication technology with the $14 billion BCD Travel.

BCD manages travel for big companies whose employees use BCD's Web technologies to book flights and hotels, for instance. Special services, such as tools for analyzing your company's travel data for ways to cut costs, are also available. When Sturisky went out with BCD's sales team recently, it wasn't so much to contribute but to listen, he says. BCD hasn't yet won the contract; sales cycles are 9 to 12 months in the travel services industry, he says. But he thinks his presence made a difference. "There was appreciation that we take a collective approach to serving customers and that added credibility to what the sales professionals were saying," he says. As a result of those conversations, Sturisky is considering how to provide such new services as sending notifications of canceled flights to travelers' smartphones, along with alternative itineraries.

Chief information officers who want to focus on external customers may have to deal with internal resistance. The way to overcome that, says Coyne of Chevron, is to be visible. When she is trying to change how people work, for example, she meets in person as much as possible with colleagues above and below her. At "Dining with Denise" lunches, she talks with lower-level employees about corporate change. At meetings once or twice a year with Chevron's senior-most executives, she explains the value of IT. In between there are monthly meetings with departments and governance boards. All the while, it's her voice, her face out there. "Blogs, e-mail, town halls, dining. The objective for me is to continuously remind everyone of the bigger picture."

Reilly White, too, is aware of her visibility at Darden and tries to use it as a tool. When restaurant operations crews see IT managers and staff in kitchens and dining rooms, they know Reilly White takes their partnership seriously. If you're not "out there" she says, you risk not understanding what your business needs.

SOURCE: Kim S. Nash, "2010 State of the CIO: Today's Focus for IT Departments—Business Opportunities," *CIO.com*, December 17, 2009.

▼ CASE STUDY QUESTIONS

1. How does the job of the chief information officer change with the assumption of customer responsibilities? Do you agree with this new development? Why or why not?

2. Why would there be internal resistance to chief information officers becoming more externally, customer-focused than they were before? Does this present a threat to executives in other areas of a company?

3. How do companies benefit from having their chief information officer meet customers and generally become more involved with product development? What can companies do now that was not possible before? Provide a few examples.

▼ REAL WORLD ACTIVITIES

1. The IT function is notorious for being dynamic, and its leaders are no exception. Go online to research recent trends affecting the traditional roles of senior IT executives and how those are changing. Prepare a presentation to share your findings with the rest of the class.

2. "In the future, the prevalence of IT in product offerings will blur the distinction between IT and other areas of the company, to the extent that the IT function will cease to exist as a separate entity." Do you agree with this statement? Why or why not? Break into small groups with your classmates to see if you can reach a consensus on the issue.

Centene, Flowserve, and Shaw Industries: Relationships, Collaboration, and Project Success

Managed care provider Centene has just finished deploying a new financial system. CIO Don Imholz says the project, which involved multiple PeopleSoft modules as well as financial planning and reporting software from Hyperion, was completed "very quickly"—in 12 months—and on budget.

Imholz believes the project was successful for a number of reasons, including that the company implemented proven technology and hired a systems integrator experienced with PeopleSoft to help. Most importantly, Imholz says the project was successful because of "good teaming between the IT organization, the finance organization and the systems integration resources."

In other words, much of the project's success came down to people skills.

The constructive relationship between IT and finance—and in particular, between Imholz and Centene's chief financial officer, William Scheffel—ultimately kept the project on track when the going got tough. And it did get tough.

For example, at one point, the project team was having trouble setting up the technical environment needed to deploy a Hyperion module that a third-party was going to host. The difficulties that IT encountered put the project's schedule at risk, says Imholz. Had the relationship between IT and finance been acrimonious, the organizations would have pointed fingers at each other—a counterproductive move that would have further delayed the project. Instead, says Imholz, they worked together to recover the lost time and keep the implementation on schedule.

"We could have blamed each other and told each other we can't help," says the chief information officer. "But there's no value in doing that. It delays getting to the solution. If IT or finance tried to recover the schedule alone it wouldn't have happened. We had to do it together."

Good relationships—between IT and business partners, project managers and IT staff, and project managers and stakeholders—keep IT projects on track, say IT leaders and project management experts. Bad relationships, however, are a leading cause of project failure.

Faced with mounting operational and regulatory pressures, Linda Jojo, Flowserve's chief information officer, knew it was time to simplify the company's entire IT infrastructure—an endeavor that would bring about sweeping changes across an enterprise spanning more than 56 countries.

At Flowserve, a world leader in the supplying of pumps, valves, seals, automation, and services to the power, oil, gas, chemical, and other industries, Jojo's assignment was heavy on IT change as the company sought to update processes and systems: establishing a common IT infrastructure, introducing global help desk capabilities and cutting dozens of disparate ERP systems. But that didn't stop her from taking a decidedly business approach to simplifying Flowserve's IT footprint.

"The first step was making sure that this wasn't viewed as an IT project," says Jojo. "From our CEO, our leadership team and our board of directors on down, we've made sure that this project is something we talk about in terms of its business impact."

It's a tactic that helped set the scope for a project that could have otherwise become unwieldy. For starters, Jojo helped assemble 35 divisional representatives from across the globe at the company's world headquarters. Here, holed up in a conference room for 17 weeks, these divisional representatives pored over disparate systems and processes, deciding what was—and wasn't—worthy of improvement. Throughout this period, Flowserve also called on internal subject-matter experts, from engineers to sales representatives, to offer their in-the-trenches take on the company's shortcomings.

The result: a blueprint for business standards, the design of a common financial chart of accounts, and the creation of a set of data standards for customers and suppliers. In addition to creating project perimeters, Jojo says that by involving business leaders in the critical design phase, she was able to garner widespread support for a company-wide strategic business initiative costing more than $60 million over four years.

"I've seen projects that should have been successful fail purely because of relationship issues," says Greg Livingston, director of IS planning and system development at Shaw Industries, a flooring manufacturer.

On the other hand, when mutual trust exists between IT project managers and stakeholders, "IT project managers are more likely to discuss problems that could threaten the project as they arise," says Imholz. If bad blood exists between the two groups, project managers may not be inclined to point out those issues, or they may try to cover them up.

"If you look at projects that fail, invariably someone on those projects knew things were going bad," says Imholz. "If you don't have relationships and trust, those things don't surface. And when you don't do something about problems in a timely manner, those problems invariably get bigger. In many cases, minor problems become more serious because they're not addressed in a timely manner. A culture of openness is absolutely essential to good project performance."

Furthermore, when something does go wrong with a project, business partners are less likely to place the sole blame for them on IT if they respect IT, says Livington, of Shaw Industries. In fact, they're more likely to give IT some leeway with the project schedule, he says.

"It doesn't matter what technology you're using, how talented your technology staff is, and how knowledgeable the business partners are on process and business improvement: Every system initiative will have issues," says Livingston. "If you don't have a relationship, you resort to pointing fingers as opposed to being transparent and admitting 'we messed up' or 'we didn't test that as well.' If you have a good relationship, you'll sit down and find a way to make it work."

Decisions affecting the project also get made more promptly when everyone involved gets along. "Fast and good decisions are crucial to keeping projects on track," says Imholz. "The failure of senior people to make decisions means decisions are made at lower levels of the organization. If you have a software developer who's waiting for a decision on a business requirement, there's three things that can happen: He can guess what to do and guess right. He can wait for a decision and while he's waiting he's not as productive. Third, he can guess and guess wrong. If those are equal possibilities, two-thirds of the time it will be detrimental to the project. And if you stack enough of those decisions on top of each other, it will negatively impact the project."

Despite the positive impact good relationships have on project management, IT project managers rely more heavily on software and methodologies than on building relations when they need to improve their delivery. It's no wonder: Compared to the time it takes to build relationships, software seems like a quick fix. IT project managers are also most comfortable with tools.

Livingston of Shaw Industries is using Scrum, an agile software development practice, to improve relationships between IT and business partners and to ensure project success. With Scrum, says Livingston, business partners meet with IT during a four- to eight-hour planning meeting to look at all the projects in the backlog and to jointly determine which one will bring the greatest value to Shaw Industries. IT then divides the project into sprints—30-day increments of work. When IT completes a sprint, business partners assess IT's progress and suggest any necessary changes.

"The agile development methodology, just by design, promotes better relationships," says Livingston. "Scrum and Agile force interaction on a more frequent basis. By doing so, IT delivers solutions on an incremental basis to the business, as opposed to the waterfall method, where it's a year and a half before the business sees the fruits of an initiative."

Livingston says it's not necessary for IT and other business functions to get along swimmingly for Agile to work effectively. Agile can work even if there's initial tension between the groups, he says. "We've had groups with troubled relationships, and certainly initial meetings are not always effective out of the gate," he says. "But at least we can agree that we're going to focus on 15 key items in the next 30 days, and at the end of the 30 days, we'll get back to you."

The process forces IT and business partners to prioritize projects together and agree on the 15 items IT will complete in 30 days. Scrum also then drives IT's behavior. At the end of that 30 days, IT has to show something for its work. Scrum makes IT accountable to the business.

When business partners see IT making tangible progress every thirty days, their confidence in IT grows. Says Livingston, "If the business partner sees results more frequently than they used to, relationships can get better. Agile promotes better relationships just by forcing a process, forcing interaction."

Between the structure that Scrum imposes and the relationships that grow out of it, project delivery improves. Livingston says Shaw Industries is seeing this happen: "Better collaboration results in better value for the business," he says.

SOURCE: Meridith Levinson, "Project Management: How IT and Business Relationships Shape Success," *CIO.com*, September 16, 2009, and Cindy Waxer, "Using IT to Transform the Business: Three Keys to Success," *CIO.com*, August 6, 2007.

CASE STUDY QUESTIONS

1. Why do you think the practices described in the case would lead to success for these companies? How do they change the structure of projects such that the likelihood of a positive outcome goes up?

2. In the case of Shaw Industries, how did Scrum help? Provide three specific examples from the case and explain where and how those activities helped the company move their projects along.

3. Using examples from the case and your own understanding of how those worked, can you distill a set of recommendations that companies should follow when managing technology-based projects? Would these be universal, or would you add any limitations to their applicability?

▼ REAL WORLD ACTIVITIES

1. The Scrum approach to project management has become quite popular in recent years. Go online and research other companies that are using it to organize their projects. Have those experiences been positive as well? What can you tell about how the approach works from your research? Prepare a report to summarize your findings.

2. Would the issues discussed in the case be solved by making a business executive the head of any projects involving IT? Why or why not? Break into small groups with your classmates and develop a justification for both alternatives.

chapter 12

IMPLEMENTING BUSINESS/IT SOLUTIONS

INFORMATION SYSTEMS

DEVELOPMENT PROCESSES

CHAPTER HIGHLIGHTS

Developing Business Systems

IS Development
The Systems Approach

REAL WORLD CHALLENGE: Starwood Hotels and Resorts—Success and Growth Bring on IT Challenges

Systems Analysis and Design
The Systems Development Life Cycle
Starting the Systems Development Process
Systems Analysis
Systems Design
End-User Development
Technical Note: Overview of Object-Oriented Analysis and Design

Implementing Strategic Business Systems

The World of Systems Implementation
Implementing New Systems
Project Management
Evaluating Hardware, Software, and Services
Other Implementation Activities

REAL WORLD SOLUTION: Starwood Hotels and Resorts—Toward a Completely New Infrastructure

REAL WORLD CASE: Microsoft, SiCortex, and Others: How Virtualization Helps Software Developers

REAL WORLD CASE: JetBlue Airways, WestJet Airlines, and Others: The Difficult Path to Software Upgrades

LEARNING OBJECTIVES

After reading and studying this chapter, you should be able to:

12-1 Use the systems development process outlined in this chapter and the model of IS components from Chapter 1 as problem-solving frameworks to help you propose information systems solutions to simple business problems.

12-2 Describe and give examples to illustrate how you might use each of the steps of the information systems development life cycle to develop and implement a business information system.

12-3 Explain how prototyping can be used as an effective technique to improve the process of systems development for end users and IS specialists.

12-4 Understand the basics of project management and its importance to a successful systems development effort.

12-5 Identify the activities involved in the implementation of new information systems.

12-6 Compare and contrast the four basic system conversion strategies.

12-7 Describe several evaluation factors that should be considered in evaluating the acquisition of hardware, software, and IS services.

Developing Business Systems

Suppose the chief executive of the company where you work asks you to find a Web-enabled way to get information to and from the salespeople in your company. How would you start? What would you do? Would you just plunge ahead and hope you could come up with a reasonable solution? How would you know whether your solution was a good one for your company? Do you think there might be a systematic way to help you develop a good solution to the CEO's request? There is a way, and it's a problem-solving process called *the systems approach*.

IS DEVELOPMENT

When the systems approach to problem-solving is applied to the development of information systems solutions to business problems, it is called *information systems development* or *application development*. We will show you how the systems approach can be used to develop business systems and applications that meet the business needs of a company, as well as its employees and stakeholders.

Refer to the Real World Challenge on the next page. We can learn a lot about why companies undertake major systems development projects. See Figure 12.1.

THE SYSTEMS APPROACH

LO 12-1

The **systems approach** to problem-solving uses a systems orientation to define problems and opportunities and then develop appropriate, feasible solutions in response. Analyzing a problem and formulating a solution involve the following interrelated activities:

1. Recognize and define a problem or opportunity using *systems thinking*.
2. Develop and evaluate alternative system solutions.
3. Select the system solution that best meets your requirements.
4. Design the selected system solution.
5. Implement and evaluate the success of the designed system.

Systems Thinking

Using **systems thinking** to understand a problem or opportunity is one of the most important aspects of the systems approach. Management consultant and author Peter Senge calls systems thinking *the fifth discipline*. Senge argues that mastering systems thinking (along with the disciplines of *personal mastery, mental models, shared vision*, and *team learning*) is vital to personal fulfillment and business success in a world of constant change. The essence of the discipline of systems thinking is "seeing the forest *and* the trees" in any situation by:

- Seeing *interrelationships* among *systems* rather than linear cause-and-effect chains whenever events occur.
- Seeing *processes* of change among *systems* rather than discrete "snapshots" of change, whenever changes occur.

One way of practicing systems thinking is to try to find systems, subsystems, and components of systems in any situation you are studying. This is also known as using a *systems context*, or having a *systemic view* of a situation. For example, the business organization or business process in which a problem or opportunity arises could be viewed as a system of input, processing, output, feedback, and control components. Then to understand a problem and solve it, you would determine whether these basic systems functions are being properly performed. See Figure 12.2.

real world CHALLENGE

Starwood Hotels and Resorts— Success and Growth Bring on IT Challenges

Starwood Hotels and Resorts is one of the largest hotel and leisure companies in the world, operating under a number of different brand names, operating more than 300,000 rooms in more than 1,000 properties around the world. The group has close to 145,000 staff members, of which 26 percent are located in the United States, and does business under the St. Regis, Luxury Collection, W, Westin, Le Méridien, Sheraton, Four Points, Aloft, and Element brands. In 2010 the company had revenue over $5 billion, net income over $300 million, and almost $10 billion in assets. The company derives most of its revenue from hotel operations, generally emphasizing the luxury and upscale segments of the hospitality industry. It also derives income from the development, ownership, and operation of vacation ownership resorts; marketing and selling vacation ownership interests in the resorts; and providing financing to customers who purchase timeshare interests in the properties.

By any measure, Starwood Hotels and Resorts is a very successful company. The hotel and timeshare industry, however, is highly competitive, with both location and availability being the key factors in fostering occupancy. Over the years, the company has been able to continue

FIGURE 12.1

From the perspective of the customer, the hotel reservation system *is* the hotel.
SOURCE: © Digital Vision/Getty Images.

growing and staying competitive with both locally-owned properties in its prime markets, as well as against other national and global hospitality chains. All this growth and success, however, comes with a price. As more and more customers chose one of Starwood's properties as their business or vacation destination, the reservation system that underlies the core processes of the company started to show some strain. Without question, a reservation system is the core operational technology of a hotel, as it manages not only the process of searching for availability and making a reservation, from a customer perspective, but also provides multiple functions that managers and staff use to operate the properties on a daily basis.

Even more important, reservation systems are the key point of contact with customers. From their perspective, the reservation system *is* the hotel. "Our websites are key points of interaction with our guests. If online services are unavailable or poorly performing, customer loyalty and profitability is quickly affected," says Keith Kelly, vice president, Information Technology at Starwood Hotels and Resorts. Up to eight million requests for rooms are received and processed by the company every day, the vast majority of them—not surprisingly, in this day and age—through its Web sites. Given the competitive nature of the industry, the company was facing increased demands from guests, rapidly evolving business requirements and strategies, and a rapidly growing business that was becoming increasingly global. Early on, management recognized that the fastest growing segments for luxury and upscale properties do not lie in the traditional markets of North America and Western Europe, but rather in the growing emergent economies. As a result, the company has been involved in a major plan of international expansion over time.

Central reservation systems for a hotel group as large as Starwood Hotels and Resorts represent major investments, which often lead to them having very long life spans. In this particular case, the current system has been in use for more than 20 years and is based on mainframe technology (from IBM, with systems developed in Cobol), which is typically the case in most large hospitality companies that have been in business for more than a couple of decades. This introduced another major risk to the project: As Starwood would be the first large company in the industry to migrate away from a mainframe environment, it had no proven template or experiences to draw from. The company would be breaking new ground, with all the risks and rewards that doing so entails. If done well, the new system would have a dramatic impact on how the company could compete in the marketplace, with new functionality and capabilities that its competitors could only dream about; at the same time, it could push them behind the pack if things did not go quite as planned.

Something, however, has to be done, as the current mainframe system is too limiting in what it will allow the company to do. "It is too difficult to add capabilities to our systems, do proper search to find properties—basically many of the things a modern IT environment needs," says Israel del Rio, with Technology Solutions at Starwood Hotels and Resorts. The current system is also having trouble handling all that increased traffic—those eight million daily requests. Hospitality professionals look at something they call the "look-to-book" ratio, which represents how many searches or requests eventually lead to an actual reservation. When online reservations got started, the ratio was 50:1. Now it is 300:1 and growing; thus, the company needs an IT environment that can handle those requests. Although they could embark on a multimillion-dollar project to upgrade the current mainframe environment, senior managers have reached a consensus that the future lies elsewhere.

Any major changes will involve replacing the backbone system that underlies the business itself, which carries significant risks to the continuing operation of the company and the servicing of current and future guests. As a result, not only would any new solutions need to provide an improved customer experience and superior system functionality, but should also strive to minimize—or outright prevent—disruptions; due to the mission-critical nature of the system, no interruptions should occur during develop-

ment, implementation, or the subsequent rollout to all properties. Failure of any kind would not only tarnish the reputation of IT, which could lead to a loss of confidence from the business, but would also most likely result in a loss of revenue and negatively affect the customer experience. To make things worse, in the hospitality industry there are no downtime periods that could be used to roll out new customer-facing applications; hotels are open and running every hour of every day of the year.

In essence, Starwood Hotels and Resorts is looking to achieve the holy grail of systems development and implementation; that is, a new technology that can be seamlessly rolled out without any disruptions, replaces a major mission-critical system, and enables them to provide an improved experience to customers while better enabling the company to run the business. While they are at it, coming in on time and on budget would be nice, too. Preliminary estimates indicate that a project of this magnitude will take over five years to complete and will cost more than $140 million over that period. As a strategic business project that involves major IT changes and developments touching the very heart of its operations, it is essential that IT and the business work hand-in-hand to deliver a solution that will offer great value to the business, improved service to guest, and can be deployed without any disruptions—a tall order for any company in any industry anywhere in the world.

SOURCE: "Starwood Hotels and Resorts," *Computerworld Honors Case Study*, 2010; "Case Study, Starwood Hotels Uses SOA to Improve Guest Services and Cut Costs," *CIO Insight*, April 27, 2006; Cowley, S., "Starwood Nears End of SOA Revamp," *InfoWorld*, July 20, 2005; "Starwood Hotels and Resorts," *Computer Associates Customer Success Story*, 2009; Babcock, C. "Starwood Hotels Continues Its Migration from Mainframe to Services-Oriented Architecture," *InformationWeek*, July 21, 2005; and www.starwoodhotels.com, accessed June 13, 2011.

▼ QUESTIONS TO CONSIDER

1. What are some of the alternative ways or approaches in which Starwood Hotels and Resorts could carry out this project? What are the advantages and disadvantages of each?

2. How do you plan for the necessary capacity and performance that will be needed years from now? How would you know that you are, or will be, hitting those targets as the development of the new system unfolds?

3. If no one else in its industry has so far moved away from the legacy mainframe environment, should Starwood Hotels and Resorts wait, as well? When is it a good idea to be the first company in an industry to break new ground? When is it not?

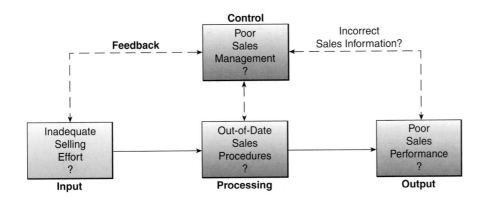

FIGURE 12.2

An example of systems thinking. You can better understand a sales problem or opportunity by identifying and evaluating the components of a sales system.

EXAMPLE. The sales process of a business can be viewed as a system. You could then ask: Is poor sales performance (output) caused by inadequate selling effort (input), out-of-date sales procedures (processing), incorrect sales information (feedback), or inadequate sales management (control)? Figure 12.2 illustrates this concept.

SYSTEMS ANALYSIS AND DESIGN

The overall process by which information systems are designed and implemented within organizations is referred to as *systems analysis and design* (SAD). Within this process are contained activities that include the identification of business problems; the proposed solution, in the form of an information system (IS), to one or more of the problems identified; and the design and implementation of that proposed solution to achieve the desired and stated goals of the organization.

Today, there are many approaches to SAD. The two most common approaches are *object-oriented analysis and design* and the *life cycle approach*. Although each has its advantages and disadvantages, and the two approaches differ in many respects, both are concerned with the analysis and design of a successful information system. In most cases, the choice will depend upon the type of system under study and the degree to which users are able to specify their needs and requirements clearly. A thorough discussion of both approaches is beyond the scope of this text, so we will focus on the most common method: the life cycle approach.

THE SYSTEMS DEVELOPMENT LIFE CYCLE
LO 12-2

One method of using the systems approach to develop information system solutions, and the most prevalent one in organization systems analysis and design, can be viewed as a multistep, iterative process called the *systems development life cycle* (SDLC). Figure 12.3 illustrates what goes on in each stage of this process: (1) investigation, (2) analysis, (3) design, (4) implementation, and (5) maintenance.

It is important to realize, however, that all of the activities involved in the SDLC are highly related and interdependent. In actual practice, therefore, several developmental activities may be occurring at the same time, while certain activities within a given step may be repeated. This means both users and systems analysts may repeat previous activities at any time to modify and improve a system under development. We will discuss the activities and products of each step of the systems development cycle in this chapter.

STARTING THE SYSTEMS DEVELOPMENT PROCESS

Do we have strategic opportunities? What are our business priorities? How can information technologies provide information system solutions that address our business priorities? These are the questions that have to be answered in the *preliminary feasibility analysis* stage (sometimes referred to as *systems investigation*), which is the first step in the systems development process. This stage may involve consideration of proposals generated by a formal business case or strategic planning process, which we will discuss in detail in Chapter 14. The investigation stage also includes the preliminary feasibility study of proposed information system solutions to meet a company's business priorities and opportunities as identified in a planning process.

The traditional information systems development life cycle. Note how the five steps of the cycle are based on the stages of the systems approach. Also note the products that result from each step in the cycle, and that you can recycle back to any previous step if more work is needed.

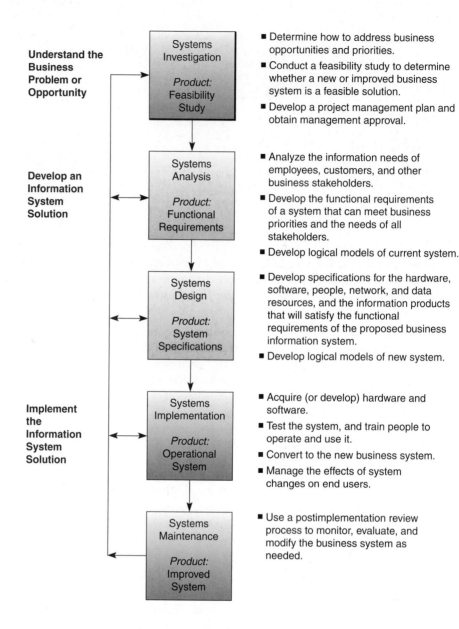

Understand the Business Problem or Opportunity

Systems Investigation

Product: Feasibility Study

- Determine how to address business opportunities and priorities.
- Conduct a feasibility study to determine whether a new or improved business system is a feasible solution.
- Develop a project management plan and obtain management approval.

Develop an Information System Solution

Systems Analysis

Product: Functional Requirements

- Analyze the information needs of employees, customers, and other business stakeholders.
- Develop the functional requirements of a system that can meet business priorities and the needs of all stakeholders.
- Develop logical models of current system.

Systems Design

Product: System Specifications

- Develop specifications for the hardware, software, people, network, and data resources, and the information products that will satisfy the functional requirements of the proposed business information system.
- Develop logical models of new system.

Implement the Information System Solution

Systems Implementation

Product: Operational System

- Acquire (or develop) hardware and software.
- Test the system, and train people to operate and use it.
- Convert to the new business system.
- Manage the effects of system changes on end users.

Systems Maintenance

Product: Improved System

- Use a postimplementation review process to monitor, evaluate, and modify the business system as needed.

Feasibility Studies

Because the process of development can be costly, the systems investigation stage typically requires the development of a *feasibility study.* At this stage, this is a preliminary study where the information needs of prospective users and the resource requirements, costs, benefits, and feasibility of a proposed project are determined. A team of business professionals and IS specialists might then formalize the findings of this study in a written report that includes preliminary specifications and a developmental plan for a proposed business application. If the management of the company approves the recommendations of the feasibility study, the development process can continue.

By design, the preliminary feasibility study of a project is a very rough analysis of its viability that must be continually refined over time. It is, nonetheless, a necessary first step in making the final commitment of organizational resources to the development of the proposed system. In some cases, however, the preliminary feasibility assessment is unnecessary. For extremely small or obvious projects, it may actually represent a waste of valuable time. Also, certain changes in the business environment may dictate the need for change, regardless of the assessed feasibility of such change. If the government changes the tax structure for employee income, an organization has no choice but to make the necessary changes to their payroll system. If a critical program has a major bug in it, the organization has no choice but to address and resolve it. In other words, there is little point in assessing the feasibility of a problem that must be solved. In these cases, the feasibility assessment may be better directed to the analysis of alternative approaches to the solution rather than the problem itself. Nevertheless, a thorough preliminary feasibility study should be the default standard in the organization, and a decision to eliminate this first step in the process should always be carefully scrutinized and justified.

Thus, the goal of the preliminary feasibility study is to evaluate alternative system solutions and to propose the most feasible and desirable business application for development. The feasibility of a proposed business system can be evaluated in terms of five major categories, as illustrated in Figure 12.4.

Operational Feasibility

The *operational feasibility* assessment focuses on the degree to which the proposed development project fits in with the existing business environment and objectives with regard to development schedule, delivery date, corporate culture, and existing business processes. Further, this assessment also determines the degree to which the project meets the specific business objectives set forth during the proposal phase. In the early stages of operational feasibility assessment, we are primarily interested in determining whether the identified problem is worth solving or the proposed solution actually solves the problem at hand. Additionally, we must concern ourselves with an initial assessment of schedule feasibility: Can we identify and solve the problem at hand within a reasonable time period? In the latter stages of operational feasibility assessment, such as during the physical design phase of the SDLC, we shift our focus to one of strategic fit and organizational impact, such as determining to what degree the proposed physical system will require changes in our organizational structure, or what changes in the current spans of authority need to be made to accommodate the new system.

Economic Feasibility

The purpose of the *economic feasibility* assessment is to determine the extent to which the proposed system will provide positive economic benefits to the organization. This

Operational Feasibility	Economic Feasibility
• How well the proposed system supports the business priorities of the organization.	• Cost savings.
	• Increased revenue.
• How well the proposed system will solve the identified problem.	• Decreased investment requirements.
	• Increased profits.
• How well the proposed system will fit with the existing organizational structure.	• Cost/benefit analysis.
Technical Feasibility	**Human Factors Feasibility**
• Hardware, software, and network capability, reliability, and availability.	• Employee, customer, supplier acceptance.
	• Management support.
	• Determining the right people for the various new or revised roles.
Legal/Political Feasibility	
• Patent, copyright, and licensing.	
• Governmental restrictions.	
• Affected stakeholders and reporting authority.	

FIGURE 12.4

Operational, economic, technical, human, and legal/political factors. Note that there is more to feasibility than cost savings or the availability of hardware and software.

determination involves the identification, and quantification, of all benefits expected from the system, as well as the explicit identification of all expected costs of the project. In the early stages of the project, defining and assessing all of the benefits and costs associated with the new system is impossible. Thus, the economic feasibility assessment is an ongoing process in which the definable short-term costs are constantly being weighed against the definable long-term benefits. If a project cannot be accurately judged as economically feasible using hard costs, then the project should not proceed, regardless of the other assessment category outcomes.

The assessment of economic feasibility typically involves the preparation of a *cost/benefit analysis.* If costs and benefits can be quantified with a high degree of certainty, they are referred to as *tangible;* if not, they are called *intangible.* Examples of *tangible costs* are the costs of hardware and software, employee salaries, and other quantifiable costs needed to develop and implement an IS solution. *Intangible costs* are difficult to quantify; they include the loss of customer goodwill or employee morale caused by errors and disruptions arising from the installation of a new system.

Tangible benefits are favorable results, such as the decrease in payroll costs caused by a reduction in personnel or a decrease in inventory carrying costs caused by reduction in inventory. *Intangible benefits* are harder to estimate. Such benefits as better customer service or faster and more accurate information for management fall into this category. Figure 12.5 lists typical tangible and intangible benefits with examples. Possible tangible and intangible costs would be the opposite of each benefit shown.

Technical Feasibility

The assessment of *technical feasibility* is focused on gaining an understanding of the present technical resources of the organization and their applicability to the expected needs of the proposed system. The analyst must assess the degree to which the current technical resources, including hardware, software, and operating environments, can be upgraded or added to such that the needs of the proposed system can be met. If the current technology is deemed sufficient, then the technical feasibility of the project is clear. If this is not the case, however, the analyst must determine whether the technology necessary to meet the stated specifications exists. The danger is that the project may

FIGURE 12.5

Possible benefits of new information systems, with examples. Note that an opposite result for each of these benefits would be a cost or disadvantage of new systems.

Tangible Benefits	Example
• Increase in sales or profits.	• Development of IT-based products.
• Decrease in information processing costs.	• Elimination of unnecessary documents.
• Decrease in operating costs.	• Reduction in inventory carrying costs.
• Decrease in required investment.	• Decrease in inventory investment required.
• Increased operational efficiency.	• Less spoilage, waste, and idle time.
Intangible Benefits	**Example**
• Improved information availability.	• More timely and accurate information.
• Improved abilities in analysis.	• OLAP and data mining.
• Improved customer service.	• More timely service response.
• Improved employee morale.	• Elimination of burdensome job tasks.
• Improved management decision making.	• Better information and decision analysis.
• Improved competitive position.	• Systems that lock in customers.
• Improved business image.	• Progressive image as perceived by customers, suppliers, and investors.

Operational Feasibility	Economic Feasibility
• How well a proposed e-commerce system fits the company's plans for developing Web-based sales, marketing, and financial systems.	• Savings in labor costs. • Increased sales revenue. • Decreased investment in inventory. • Increased profits. • Acceptable return on investment.

Technical Feasibility	Human Factors Feasibility
• Capability, reliability, and availability of Web store hardware, software, and management services.	• Acceptance of employees. • Management support. • Customer and supplier acceptance. • Staff developers have necessary skills.

Legal/Political Feasibility
• No patent or copyright violations. • Software licensing for developer side only. • No governmental restrictions. • No changes to existing reporting authority.

FIGURE 12.6

Examples of how a feasibility study might measure the feasibility of a proposed e-commerce system for a business.

require technology that does not yet exist in a stable form. Despite the claims of vendors that they can supply whatever is required, the analyst must be able to assess accurately the degree to which the needed technology exists in a form suitable for the proposed project. See Figure 12.6.

Human Factors Feasibility

It is one thing to assess the degree to which a proposed system can work and quite another to evaluate whether the system will work. The *human factors feasibility* assessment focuses on the most important components of a successful system implementation: the managers and end users. No matter how elegant the technology, the system will not work if the end users and managers do not perceive it to be relevant and, therefore, do not support it. In this category, we assess the degree of resistance to the proposed system, the perceived role of the end users in the development process, the degree of change to the end users' working environment as a result of the new system, and the current state of human resources available to conduct the project and to manage and use the system on completion.

Legal/Political Feasibility

This category of assessment is often overlooked during the early stages of project initiation and analysis. The *legal and political feasibility* of a proposed project includes a thorough analysis of any potential legal ramifications resulting from the construction and implementation of the new system. Such legal issues include copyright or patent infringements, violation of existing antitrust laws (such as in the antitrust suit brought against Microsoft Corporation over Windows and Internet Explorer by the U.S. Justice Department in 1998), foreign trade restrictions, or any existing contractual obligations of the organization.

The political side of the assessment focuses on understanding who the key stakeholders are within the organization and the degree to which the proposed system may positively or negatively affect the distribution of power. Such distribution can have major political repercussions and may cause disruption or failure of an otherwise relevant development effort.

SYSTEMS ANALYSIS
LO 12-2

What is systems analysis? Whether you want to develop a new application quickly or are involved in a long-term project, you will need to perform several basic activities of systems analysis. Many of these activities are an extension of those used in conducting a feasibility study. Systems analysis is not a preliminary study; however, it is an in-depth study of end-user information needs that produces *functional requirements* that are used as the basis for the design of a new information system. Systems analysis traditionally involves a detailed study of:

- The information needs of a company and end users like yourself.
- The activities, resources, and products of one or more of the present information systems being used.
- The information system capabilities required to meet your information needs, and those of other business stakeholders that may use the system.

Organizational Analysis

An *organizational analysis* is an important first step in systems analysis. How can people improve an information system if they know very little about the organizational environment in which that system is located? They can't. That's why the members of a development team have to know something about the organization, its management structure, its people, its business activities, the environmental systems it must deal with, and its current information systems. Someone on the team must know this information in more detail for the specific business units or end-user workgroups that will be affected by the new or improved information system being proposed. For example, a new inventory control system for a chain of department stores cannot be designed unless someone on a development team understands a great deal about the company and the types of business activities that affect its inventory. That's why business end users are frequently added to systems development teams.

Analysis of the Present System

Before you design a new system, it is important to study the system that will be improved or replaced (assuming there is one). You need to analyze how this system uses hardware, software, network, and people resources to convert data resources, such as transactions data, into information products, such as reports and displays. Then you should document how the information system activities of input, processing, output, storage, and control are accomplished.

For example, you might evaluate the format, timing, volume, and quality of input and output activities. Such *user interface* activities are vital to effective interaction between end users and a computer-based system. Then, in the systems design stage, you can specify what the resources, products, and activities should be to support the user interface in the system you are designing.

Prometric: Understanding Application Performance

Prometric is the global leader in technology-enabled testing and assessment services. With a network of more than 10,000 locations in 160 different countries, the company delivered more than nine million exams worldwide in 2008 alone. Headquartered in Baltimore, Maryland, the company employs more than 2,500 and has international corporate sites in Dublin, Singapore, Johannesburg, Tokyo, and Seoul, to name just a few. More than 450 organizations rely on the services of Prometric to guarantee the integrity of the testing and licensing process. These include such disparate certifications or exams as the GRE (Graduate Record Examination, a commonly required test to gain acceptance to graduate programs in the United States), licensing to sell securities in Japan, and a driver's license in Ireland. The company also administers information technology testing for companies such as Microsoft, Oracle, Apple, Hewlett-Packard, and IBM.

The key application that makes all of this possible is the Web-based scheduling and registration system used by thousands every day to make appointments to take examinations and upload results from remote testing sites. Given the mission-critical nature of this application, Prometric is always eager to make any adjustments or changes that may improve its functionality and responsiveness to increasing customer demand. At the same time, there is little room for performance problems or outright downtime; if the application is not working, then people cannot register, which directly affects the satisfaction of test takers, test providers, and ultimately, revenue. As a result, before any changes are made, the company wants to be able to understand really well what is going on with the application. With this goal in mind, Prometric adopted an Application Performance Management (APM) package from vendor Panorama. This type of package focuses on monitoring and managing the performance and availability of software applications. It uses extensive data collection and analysis tools to detect, diagnose, and report on application performance issues as they occur in real time. The most commonly monitored metrics are application response time or application throughput, which highlight how fast transactions are completed. But others are possible, based on the particular business model of the company implementing this approach to software management.

In the case of Prometric, managers wanted to improve customer satisfaction with the registration and results processes by gaining a better understanding of the performance of this central application. The new package provided them with performance sampling on a second-by-second basis, as well as extensive analytical reporting features. This trove of information allowed them to pinpoint where performance bottlenecks were occurring—for example, to distinguish among issues related to the application code, the underlying database, or the delivery of functionality through the Web-based interface. Within eight weeks of deploying the APM package, managers at Panorama had already made 10 minor configuration changes that significantly improved the application performance, all without touching the code or architecture. Customer satisfaction scores, which were what the company was after, improved measurably after these changes took place.

SOURCE: "Prometric Deploys OPNET Panorama to Improve Application Performance," *Opnet Technologies, Inc. Case Study*, 2009, and www.prometric.com, accessed June 14, 2011.

Logical Analysis

One of the primary activities that occur during the analysis phase is the construction of a *logical model* of the current system. The logical model can be thought of as a blueprint of the current system that displays only *what* the current system does without regard for *how* it does it. By constructing and analyzing a logical model of the current system, a systems analyst can more easily understand the various processes, functions, and data associated with the system without getting bogged down with all the issues surrounding the hardware or the software. Also, by creating a logical model, the various noncomputer components of a system can be incorporated, analyzed, and understood. For example, in the physical version of a system, a person's inbox may be the location where new orders are stored until they have been entered into the computer. In the logical model, that inbox is treated just like a computer hard drive or other electronic storage media. In a logical sense, it is just another place to store data.

Logical and physical models are not limited to use in the design of an information system. They are commonly used in a variety of situations with which you are familiar. Take, for example, the remodeling of your house.

Let's say you want to knock out a wall to expand two small bedrooms into one big one. You also want to add a second bathroom for your guests. One way to approach this

FIGURE 12.7

Examples of functional requirements for a proposed e-commerce system for a business.

Examples of Functional Requirements
• **User Interface Requirements** Automatic entry of product data and easy-to-use data entry screens for Web customers.
• **Processing Requirements** Fast, automatic calculation of sales totals and shipping costs.
• **Storage Requirements** Fast retrieval and update of data from product, pricing, and customer databases.
• **Control Requirements** Signals for data entry errors and quick e-mail confirmation for customers.

would be to call in the contractor and have him start tearing out the wall and adding the plumbing. The problem with this approach is that you have no blueprint for what you are trying to accomplish. You may find that the wall you want removed also holds up part of the second floor. Tearing it out would make for a bad day. Using this approach, you are proceeding with the redesign of the physical model without analyzing the logical model.

A better approach would be to have an architect look at the blueprints to see the feasibility of accomplishing your goals. If it is discovered that the wall cannot be removed, no harm is done. Then, alternative designs—say, putting in an archway between the two rooms—can be easily tested without any costly mistakes. Once the logical model of the remodeling project has been determined to be sound, the physical model can be redone with the expected, and desired, positive consequences. The same approach is used when designing or redesigning information systems.

So, think of the logical model as a blueprint of *what* needs to be done. Once we have that blueprint, we can focus on the various options available to us with regard to *how* we plan to do what we have set out to do.

Functional Requirements Analysis and Determination

This step of systems analysis is one of the most difficult. You may need to work as a team with IS analysts and other end users to determine your specific business information needs. For example, first you need to determine what type of information each business activity requires; what its format, volume, and frequency should be; and what response times are necessary. Second, you must try to determine the information processing capabilities required for each system activity (input, processing, output, storage, control) to meet these information needs. As with the construction of the logical model, your main goal is to identify *what should be done*, not *how to do it*.

When this step of the life cycle is complete, a set of *functional requirements* for the proposed new system will exist. Functional requirements are end-user information requirements that are not tied to the hardware, software, network, data, and people resources that end users presently use or might use in the new system. That is left to the design stage to determine. For example, Figure 12.7 shows examples of functional requirements for a proposed e-commerce application for a business.

SYSTEMS DESIGN
LO 12-3

Once the analysis portion of the life cycle is complete, the process of systems design can begin. Here is where the logical model of the current system is modified until it represents the blueprint for the new system we want to build. This version of the logical model represents what the new system will do. During the physical design portion of this step, users and analysts will focus on determining *how* the system will accomplish its objectives. This is where issues related to hardware, software, networking, data storage, security, and many others will be discussed and determined. As such, systems design consists of design activities that ultimately produce physical system specifications satisfying the functional requirements that were developed in the systems analysis process.

A useful way to look at systems design is illustrated in Figure 12.8. This concept focuses on three major products, or *deliverables*, that should result from the design

Systems Design

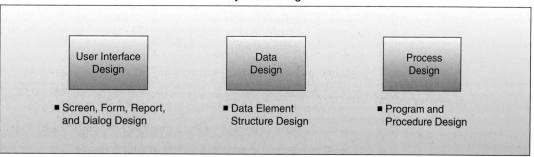

FIGURE 12.8

Systems design can be viewed as the design of user interfaces, data, and processes.

stage. In this framework, systems design consists of three activities: user interface, data, and process design. This results in specifications for user interface methods and products, database structures, and processing and control procedures.

Prototyping

During the design phase, the development process frequently takes the form of, or includes, a *prototyping* approach. **Prototyping** is the rapid development and testing of working models, or *prototypes*, of new applications in an interactive, iterative process that can be used by both IS specialists and business professionals. Prototyping, as a development tool, makes the development process faster and easier, especially for projects where end-user requirements are hard to define. Prototyping has also opened up the application development process to end users because it simplifies and accelerates systems design. Thus, prototyping has enlarged the role of the business stakeholders affected by a proposed system and helps make possible a quicker and more responsive development process called *agile systems development* (ASD). See Figure 12.9.

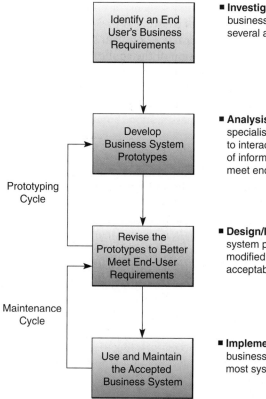

- **Investigation/Analysis.** End users identify their business needs and assess the feasibility of several alternative information system solutions.

- **Analysis/Design.** End users and/or IS specialists use application development tools to interactively design and test prototypes of information system components that meet end-user business needs.

- **Design/Implementation.** The business system prototypes are tested, evaluated, and modified repeatedly until end users find them acceptable.

- **Implementation/Maintenance.** The accepted business system can be modified easily since most system documentation is stored on disk.

FIGURE 12.9

Application development using prototyping. Note how prototyping combines the steps of the systems development life cycle and changes the traditional roles of IS specialists and end users.

Example of Prototyping Development
• **Team.** A few end users and IS developers form a team to develop a business application.
• **Schematic.** The initial prototype schematic design is developed.
• **Prototype.** The schematic is converted into a simple point-and-click prototype using prototyping tools.
• **Presentation.** A few screens and routine linkages are presented to users.
• **Feedback.** After the team gets feedback from users, the prototype is reiterated.
• **Reiteration.** Further presentations and reiterations are made.
• **Consultation.** Consultations are held with IT consultants to identify potential improvements and conformance to existing standards.
• **Completion.** The prototype is used as a model to create a finished application.
• **Acceptance.** Users review and sign off on their acceptance of the new business system.
• **Installation.** The new business software is installed on network servers.

The Prototyping Process

Prototyping can be used for both large and small applications. Typically, large business systems still require using a traditional systems development approach, but parts of such systems can frequently be prototyped. A prototype of a business application needed by an end user is developed quickly using a variety of application development software tools. The prototype system is then repeatedly refined until it is acceptable.

As Figure 12.9 illustrates, prototyping is an iterative, interactive process. End users with sufficient experience with application development tools can do prototyping themselves. Alternatively, you could work with an IS specialist to develop a prototype system in a series of interactive sessions. For example, you could develop, test, and refine prototypes of management reports, data entry screens, or output displays.

Usually, a prototype is modified several times before end users find it acceptable. Program modules are then generated by application development software using conventional programming languages. The final version of the application system is then turned over to its end users for operational use. While prototyping is a useful method of allowing an end user to develop small software applications, its real power is as a development tool, within a life cycle project, to help analysts and users finalize the various interfaces and functions of a large business system. Figure 12.10 outlines a typical prototyping-based systems development process for a business application.

The Determinants of Project Success

What makes a project successful? What should I be doing to make sure—or at least make it likely—that my project will be a success? These are the kinds of questions that project managers have been asking themselves for decades now. In no arena are these questions as important and evident as in the development and implementation of technology-based solutions—in other words, software. Projects succeed or fail for a variety of reasons, but it would be important to know which reasons have the most impact. Is it having a great team of skilled coders? Is it heavy user involvement and stakeholder commitment? Both of these things are surely important. Recent research by training company Insights Learning and Development, in conjunction with chapters of the Project Management Institute, suggests that the single most important factor affecting project success is its link to the organization's business strategy and the project manager's understanding of how the project supports the business strategy (ok, maybe the single two most important factors).

The research was conducted between May and September 2009, and surveyed 609 project managers in North America, the United Kingdom, India, and Spain. Respondents were asked to rank the different challenges they encountered in their projects, as well as indicate whether they believed their project had direct strategic value to their organization. In the group that cited fewer problems, 68 percent believed their projects were progressing according to plan. For those reporting the most problems, only 47 percent were moving along satisfactorily. More than three-fourths of the respondents indicated that their projects had direct strategic value to the organization. Looking deeper into that number, of the 77 percent of project managers who stated that their projects had direct strategic value, only 24 percent knew that because they had been involved in direct communication with others in the company or had seen how their projects fit with the plans laid out by the organization. When you combine all of these factors, a clear picture emerges: The projects with fewer challenges—those that encounter the least number of problems along the way and are more likely to succeed—are the ones where the project itself is strategic to the organization, and the project managers know (rather than think) that this is the case. The latter gives managers "the context required to flag when the project is veering from its original intent and course-correct towards the intended strategic outcome," notes the report.

One possible reason that project managers do not know—or are not entirely sure—whether their projects are indeed strategic to the organization is the generally ad hoc approach to project selection that exists in many companies today. Half of the respondents indicated that their projects were selected out of stakeholder insistence or through some other informal process, or that they did not know how their project had been given the green light. The top challenge cited by project managers was that changing priorities among projects has an impact on the resources available to the project team. When there is no structured, formal approach to select the projects, it is quite likely that resource availability will grow and wane as new projects are added to the mix. Although retaining some degree of flexibility is certainly important, some predictability is also valuable.

SOURCE: Meridith Levinson, "Business Strategy: The 'Best Determinant' of Project Success," *CIO.com*, November 17, 2009.

User Interface Design

Let's take a closer look at ***user interface design***, since it is the system component closest to business end users and the one they will most likely help design. The user interface design activity focuses on supporting the interactions between end users and their computer-based applications. Designers concentrate on the design of attractive and efficient forms of user input and output, such as easy-to-use Internet or intranet Web pages.

As we mentioned earlier, user interface design is frequently a *prototyping* process, where working models or prototypes of user interface methods are designed and modified several times with feedback from end users. The user interface design process produces detailed design specifications for information products such as display screens, interactive user/computer dialogues (including the sequence or flow of dialogue), audio responses, forms, documents, and reports. Figure 12.11 gives examples of user interface design elements and other guidelines suggested for the multimedia Web pages of e-commerce Web sites. Figure 12.12 presents actual before-and-after screen displays of the user interface design process for a work scheduling application of State Farm Insurance Company.

FIGURE 12.11

Useful guidelines for the design of business Web sites.

Checklist for Corporate Web Sites

- **Remember the Customer.** Successful Web sites are built solely for the customer, not to make company vice presidents happy.

- **Aesthetics.** Successful designs combine fast-loading graphics and simple color palettes for pages that are easy to read.

- **Broadband Content.** The Web's coolest stuff can't be accessed by most Web surfers. Including a little streaming video isn't bad, but don't make it the focus of your site.

- **Easy to Navigate.** Make sure it's easy to get from one part of your site to another. Providing a site map, accessible from every page, helps.

- **Searchability.** Many sites have their own search engines; very few are actually useful. Make sure yours is.

- **Incompatibilities.** A site that looks great on a PC using Internet Explorer can often look miserable on an iBook running Netscape.

- **Registration Forms.** Registration forms are a useful way to gather customer data. But make your customers fill out a three-page form, and watch them flee.

- **Dead Links.** Dead links are the bane of all Web surfers—be sure to keep your links updated. Many Web-design software tools can now do this for you.

FIGURE 12.12

An example of the user interface design process. State Farm developers changed this work scheduling and assignment application's interface after usability testing showed that end users working with the old interface (at top) didn't realize that they had to follow a six-step process. If users jumped to a new page out of order, they would lose their work. The new interface (at bottom) made it clearer that a process had to be followed.

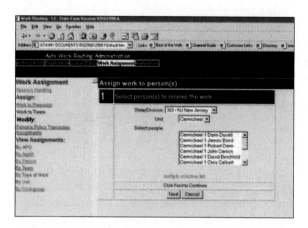

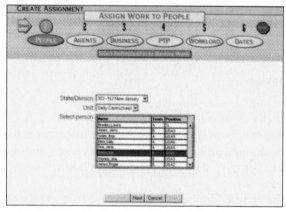

SOURCE: Courtesy of the Usability Lab of State Farm.

Google's Interface: Balancing Freedom and Consistency

For most people, including its own executives, Google still means search. On both the query page and the results pages, design flourishes have been legendarily kept to a minimum, with layout decisions based on what will provide the user with the fastest, most efficient service. Nonetheless, engineers and analysts pore over streams of data to assess the impact of experiments with colors, shading, and the position of every element on the page. Even changes at the pixel level can affect revenue.

But as Google products proliferate beyond search, design decisions become more critical if the company wants a coherent brand image. "More than anything, Google prefers to make design decisions based on what performs well. And as a company, Google cares about being fast, so we want our user experience to be fast," says Irene Au, Google's Director of User Experience. That's not just in terms of front-end latency—how long it takes the page to download—it's also about making people use their computers more efficiently. "A lot of our design decisions are really driven by cognitive psychology research that shows that, say, people online read black text against a white background much faster than white against black, or that sans serif fonts are more easily read than serif fonts online," says Au.

Google has a big culture of being bottom-up and that can make it difficult to get a coherent design experience. There's a federation of people doing whatever they think is best for their product and not looking out for the bigger picture. "We don't want everything to be dictated and top-down, but we do want to find a balance," says Au. "For example, Google apps all look different from each other. As you move from one app to another, the keyboard shortcuts are different, the save model is different. The interaction consistency is not there. For good reason: These were all different startups using different backends. But we're trying to pull all that together. More and more, these experiences are going to get integrated with each other, or there'll be reusable components that might be built for applications but also appear in a search experience. It's becoming increasingly critical for us to have common UIs [user interfaces] and common infrastructure," she notes.

At Google, there's top-down support for consistency, but not a mandate. But middle layers of management are hearing loud and clear from Larry Page and Sergey Brin and the executives that there should be one way to do things. "Inconsistency drives Larry and Sergey crazy. So there's growing appreciation and awareness and with that comes motivation. As a group, we're trying to be very opportunistic and pragmatic. The design team has to be a few steps out—we're designing the target for all the different products to converge towards," says Au.

SOURCE: Helen Walters, "Google's Irene Au: On Design Challenges," *BusinessWeek Online*, March 18, 2009.

System Specifications

System specifications formalize the design of an application's user interface methods and products, database structures, and processing and control procedures. Therefore, systems designers will frequently develop hardware, software, network, data, and personnel specifications for a proposed system. Figure 12.13 shows examples of system specifications that could be developed for an e-commerce system of a company.

In a traditional systems development cycle, your role as a business end user is similar to that of a customer or a client. Typically, you make a request for a new or improved system, answer questions about your specific information needs and information processing problems, and provide background information on your existing business systems. IS professionals work with you to analyze your problem and suggest alternative solutions. When you approve the best alternative, it is designed and implemented. Here again, you may be involved in a prototyping design process or be on an implementation team with IS specialists.

In **end-user development,** however, IS professionals play a consulting role while you do your own application development. Sometimes, user consultants may be available to help you and other end users with your application development efforts. This may include training in the use of application packages; selection of hardware and software; assistance in gaining access to organization databases; and, of course, assistance in analysis, design, and implementation of the business application of IT that you need.

END-USER DEVELOPMENT
LO 12-4

FIGURE 12.13

Examples of system specifications for a new e-commerce system for a business.

Examples of System Specifications
• **User Interface Specifications** Use personalized screens that welcome repeat Web customers and that make product recommendations.
• **Database Specifications** Develop databases that use object/relational database management software to organize access to all customer and inventory data and to multimedia product information.
• **Software Specifications** Acquire an e-commerce software engine to process all e-commerce transactions with fast responses, i.e., retrieve necessary product data and compute all sales amounts in less than one second.
• **Hardware and Network Specifications** Install redundant networked Web servers and sufficient high-bandwidth telecommunications lines to host the company e-commerce Web site.
• **Personnel Specifications** Hire an e-commerce manager and specialists and a Webmaster and Web designer to plan, develop, and manage e-commerce operations.

Focus on IS Activities

It is important to remember that end-user development should focus on the fundamental activities of any information system: input, processing, output, storage, and control, as we described in Chapter 1. Figure 12.14 illustrates these system components and the questions they address.

When analyzing a potential application, you should first focus on the *output* to be produced by the application. What information is needed and in what form should it be presented? Next, look at the *input* data to be supplied to the application. What data are available? From what sources? In what form? Then you should examine the *processing* requirements. What operations or transformation processes will be required to convert the available inputs into the desired output? Among

FIGURE 12.14

End-user development should focus on the basic information processing activity components of an information system.

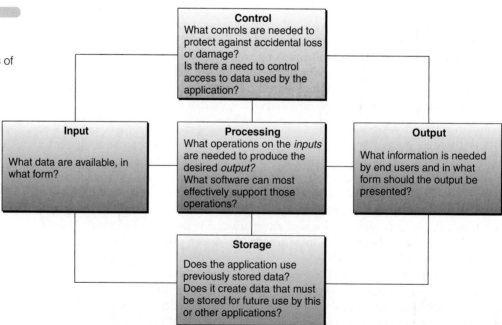

SOURCE: James N. Morgan, *Application Cases in MIS*, 4th ed. (New York: Irwin/McGraw-Hill, 2002), p. 31.

software packages the developer is able to use, which package can best perform the operations required?

You may find that the desired output cannot be produced from the inputs that are available. If this is the case, you must either make adjustments to the output expected, or find additional sources of input data, including data stored in files and databases from external sources. The *storage* component will vary in importance in end-user applications. For example, some applications require extensive use of stored data or the creation of data that must be stored for future use. These are better suited for database management development projects than for spreadsheet applications.

Necessary *control* measures for end-user applications vary greatly depending upon the scope and duration of the application, the number and nature of the users of the application, and the nature of the data involved. For example, control measures are needed to protect against accidental loss or damage to end-user files. The most basic protection against this type of loss is to make backup copies of application files on a frequent and systematic basis. Another example is the cell protection feature of spreadsheets that protects key cells from accidental erasure by users.

Doing End-User Development

In end-user development, you and other business professionals can develop new or improved ways to perform your jobs without the direct involvement of IS specialists. The application development capabilities built into a variety of end-user software packages have made it easier for many users to develop their own computer-based solutions. For example, Figure 12.15 illustrates a Web site development tool you could use to help you develop, update, and manage an intranet Web site for your business unit. You might choose instead to use an electronic spreadsheet package as a tool to develop an easy way to analyze weekly sales results for the sales managers in a company. You could also use a Web site development package to design Web pages for a small business Web store or a departmental intranet Web site. See Figure 12.16.

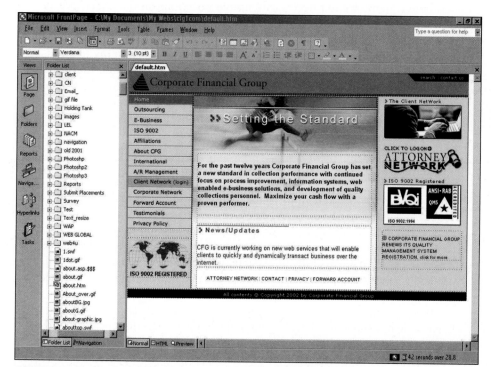

FIGURE 12.15
Microsoft FrontPage is an example of an easy-to-use end-user Web site development tool.

SOURCE: Courtesy of Microsoft® and the Corporate Financial Group.

FIGURE 12.16

How companies are encouraging and managing intranet Web site development by business end users.

Encouraging End-User Web Development
• **Look for Tools That Make Sense.** Some Web development tools may be more powerful and more costly than what your business end users really need.
• **Spur Creativity.** Consider a competition among business departments for the best Web site, to help spur users to more creative uses of their intranet sites.
• **Set Some Limits.** Yes, you have to keep some control. Consider putting limits on exactly which parts of a Web page users can change and who can change which pages. You still want some consistency across the organization.
• **Give Managers Responsibility.** Make business unit managers sign off on who will be Web publishing from their groups, and make the managers personally responsible for the content that goes on their Web sites. That will help prevent the publishing of inappropriate content by some users.
• **Make Users Comfortable.** Training users well on the tools will help users become confident in their ability to properly manage and update their sites—and save IT the trouble of fixing problems later on or providing continuous support for minor problems.

Blue Prism: "Shadow" IT Is Becoming More Pervasive

Businesses increasingly accept the existence of a "shadow" IT culture, in which end users install uncontrolled rogue technology to make good the shortcomings of overstretched IT departments. Rogue IT includes users who install software or tamper with existing software or macros without the IT department's consent, according to a survey by integration specialist Blue Prism. Budget and resource constraints often lead to elements of rogue behavior, reported by 67 percent of respondents to the survey. Twenty-four percent believed that rogue IT isn't used in their organizations, and 10 percent admitted that they didn't know.

These systems are not necessarily simple variations on the Excel spreadsheet. On the contrary, they can be very sophisticated—rivaling and even exceeding any technological solution produced by IT departments. Such systems range from consumer solutions like Google Apps to highly tailored ones. It seems that end users are increasingly aware nowadays that their IT department cannot always deliver a practical solution for their needs, which can lead to the creation of a shadow IT culture within an organization, whereby users actively install their own applications or find their own workaround solutions in order to do their day-to-day jobs.

This is often because IT departments have to manage business-critical projects, sometimes at the expense of helping business users with tactical change requests. Indeed, more than 52 percent reported that working on strategic projects was the main focus for their department, with 40 percent saying that delivering day-to-day business change requests was their priority.

The Blue Prism survey, however, also challenges the traditional perception that IT departments frown upon rogue behavior by users. The survey concludes that many IT departments fully understand why pockets of rogue behavior exist, and it reveals that these departments were equally pragmatic when asked for the best way of dealing with it.

With this change in the relationship between end users and technology, the IT department's singular claim to technology knowledge is disappearing, and with it, its position of power. The more technologists try to counter this effect by enforcing the old ways, the more defunct and isolated they will become;

their decisions will be ignored and their solutions will be unused. One of the primary reasons shadow systems succeed is that people at the front lines of organizations need them.

They know that when they have a problem and when they find a solution that works well for them, their needs are met. IT departments, on the other hand, focus too strongly on the technology to solve a problem rather than on the problem itself—to the extent that when end users do not use officially sanctioned solutions, IT may proceed on radical search-and-destroy missions of user-created systems. In doing so, it ignores why the user did not use its solutions in the first place and, in effect, it destroys one of the few sources of IT strategic and competitive advantage an organization has.

SOURCE: Tom Jowitt, "Shadow IT Culture on the Rise for Businesses," *CIO Magazine*, July 5, 2007, and Sandy Behrens, "Time to Rethink Your Relationship with End Users," *CIO Magazine*, July 24, 2007.

TECHNICAL NOTE: OVERVIEW OF OBJECT-ORIENTED ANALYSIS AND DESIGN
LO 12-1

As stated at the beginning of the chapter, there are two common approaches to analysis and design: SDLC and object-oriented. Whereas the SDLC remains the predominant approach to software development, the object-oriented approach is gaining favor, particularly among programmers focusing on complex systems that require handling a wide variety of complex data structures, such as audio, video, images, documents, Web pages, and other types of data.

We introduced the concepts of objects and object oriented databases in Chapter 5. Thorough coverage of the object-oriented approach to analysis and design is beyond the scope of this text, but a brief overview is presented here. Let's begin with a simple definition of anything object-oriented.

An *object-oriented system* is composed of *objects*. An object can be anything a programmer wants to manage or manipulate—cars, people, animals, savings accounts, food products, business units, organizations, customers—literally anything. Once an object is defined by a programmer, its characteristics can be used to allow one object to interact with another object or pass information to another object. The behavior of an object-oriented system entails collaboration between these objects, and the state of the system is the combined state of all the objects in it.

Collaboration between objects requires them to send messages or information to one another. The exact semantics of message sending between objects varies, depending on the kind of system being modeled. In some systems, "sending a message" is the same as "invoking a method." In others, "sending a message" might involve sending data using a pre-prescribed medium. The three areas of interest to us in an object-oriented system are object-oriented programming, object-oriented analysis, and object-oriented design.

Object-oriented programming (OOP) is the programming paradigm that uses "objects" to design applications and computer programs. It employs several techniques from previously established paradigms, including:

- **Inheritance.** The ability of one object to inherit the characteristics of a higher-order object. For example, all cars have wheels; therefore, an object defined as a *sports car* and as a special type of the object *cars* must also have wheels.

- **Modularity.** The extent to which a program is designed as a series of interlinked yet stand-alone modules.

- **Polymorphism.** The ability of an object to behave differently depending on the conditions in which its behavior is invoked. For example, two objects that inherit the behavior *speak* from an object class *animal* might be a dog object and a cat object. Both have a behavior defined as *speak*. When the dog object is commanded to speak, it will *bark*, whereas when the cat object is commanded to speak, it will *meow*.

- **Encapsulation.** Concealing all of the characteristics associated with a particular object inside the object itself. This paradigm allows objects to inherit characteristics simply by defining a subobject. For example, the object *airplane* contains all of the characteristics of an airplane: wings, tail, rudder, pilot, speed, altitude, and so forth.

Even though it originated in the 1960s, OOP was not commonly used in mainstream software application development until the 1990s. Today, many popular programming languages (e.g., ActionScript, Ada95/2005, C+, C++, Delphi, Java, JavaScript, Lisp, Objective-C, Perl, PHP, Python, RealBasic, Ruby, Squeak, VB.Net, Visual FoxPro, and Visual Prolog) support OOP.

Object-oriented analysis (OOA) aims to model the *problem domain*, that is, the problem we want to solve, by developing an object-oriented (OO) system. The source of the analysis is a set of written requirements statements and/or diagrams that illustrate the statements.

Similar to the SDLC-developed model, an object-oriented analysis model does not take into account implementation constraints, such as concurrency, distribution, persistence, or inheritance, nor how the system will be built. Because object-oriented systems are modular, the model of the system can be divided into multiple domains, each of which are separately analyzed and represent separate business, technological, or conceptual areas of interest. The result of object-oriented analysis is a description of what is to be built, using concepts and relationships between concepts, often expressed as a conceptual model. Any other documentation needed to describe what is to be built is also included in the results of the analysis.

Object-oriented design (OOD) describes the activity when designers look for logical solutions to solve a problem using objects. Object-oriented design takes the conceptual model that results from the object-oriented analysis and adds implementation constraints imposed by the environment, the programming language, and the chosen tools, as well as architectural assumptions chosen as the basis of the design.

The concepts in the conceptual model are mapped to concrete classes, abstract interfaces, and roles that the objects take in various situations. The interfaces and their implementations for stable concepts can be made available as reusable services. Concepts identified as unstable in OOA will form the basis for policy classes that make decisions and implement environment or situation-specific logics or algorithms. The result of OOD is a detailed description of how the system can be built, using objects.

Thus, the object-oriented world bears many similarities to the more conventional SDLC approach. This approach just takes a different view of the programming domain and thus approaches the problem-solving activities inherent in system development from a different direction.

Later in the chapter, we will continue to look at systems development, changing our focus from design to implementation.

Implementing Strategic Business Systems

Once a new information system has been designed, it must be implemented as a working system and maintained to keep it operating properly. The implementation process that we cover here follows the investigation, analysis, and design stages of the systems development life cycle we discussed earlier in this chapter. Implementation is a vital step in the deployment of information technology to support the employees, customers, and other business stakeholders of a company. See Figure 12.17.

Figure 12.18 illustrates that the *systems implementation* stage involves hardware and software acquisition, software development, testing of programs and procedures, conversion of data resources, and a variety of conversion alternatives. It also involves the education and training of end users and specialists who will operate a new system.

Implementation can be a difficult and time-consuming process; however, it is vital in ensuring the success of any newly developed system. Even a well-designed system will fail if it is not properly implemented, which is why the *implementation process* typically requires a project management effort on the part of IT and business unit managers. They must enforce a project plan, which includes job responsibilities, timetables for major stages of development, and budgets. This is necessary if a project is to be completed on time and within its established budget, while still meeting its design objectives. Figure 12.19 illustrates the activities and timetables that might be required to implement an intranet for a new employee benefits system in the human-resources department of a company.

FIGURE 12.17
Airlines run on more than airplanes and jet fuel. The software systems behind the scenes are what make the processes smooth and transparent.

SOURCE: © Ryan McVay/Getty Images.

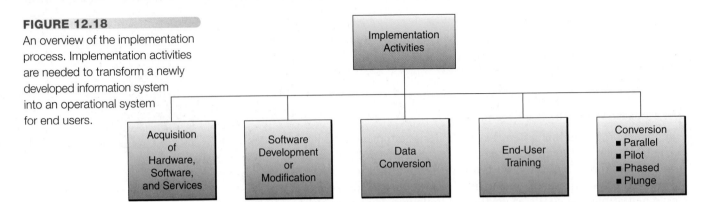

FIGURE 12.18

An overview of the implementation process. Implementation activities are needed to transform a newly developed information system into an operational system for end users.

FIGURE 12.19

An example of the implementation process activities and timetables for a company installing an intranet-based employee benefits system in its human-resources management department.

Intranet Implementation Activities	Month 1	Month 2	Month 3	Month 4
Acquire and install server hardware and software				
Train administrators				
Acquire and install browser software				
Acquire and install publishing software				
Train benefits employees on publishing software				
Convert benefits manuals and add revisions				
Create Web-based tutorials for the intranet				
Hold rollout meetings				

Project Portfolio Management: Shoot the Bad Projects, Keep the Good Ones

IT departments are either the darlings or the despised of corporate America, and some practitioners would debate which extreme causes the most pain. Let's face it: Nowadays, the reward for doing a great job is more work. Once an IT group earns the trust of business units, it must then survive the onslaught of new projects. Good organizations, like good bosses, don't want you to take on more than you can handle and collapse in the process.

Smart organizations have a grip on project portfolio management (PPM) and are willing to prioritize and, when needed, end projects when they turn bad. Like risk management, PPM is nothing new for mature disciplines. "We've picked up where construction and engineers have been for years," says John Nahm, an IT project manager for the state of Virginia.

The highest performers in the IT world, as defined in a recent study by the IT Process Institute, are those most likely to cancel projects—at a rate double that of their lower-performing counterparts, in fact. "It's counterintuitive until you think about it," says Kurt Milne, managing director of the institute. The business world is accustomed to trying new initiatives but is willing to move on if they don't work. But, as Milne points out, in IT there's value in stability, so we're hesitant to pull the trigger. "I don't know that that's a skill that IT folks think they need to have, but logically, it makes sense to shoot your bad projects and move on."

Line-of-business executives understand capacity planning and prioritization, Milne says, but they expect these choices to be presented in business language. What they don't understand is when IT overpromises and then underdelivers, failing to meet deadlines or not completing a project. Unless IT becomes skilled at PPM, we'll never close this credibility gap.

Once you put a process in place, the other P-word—politics—will inevitably appear. The magic behind PPM is that, when you do it right, it becomes clear why a given project shouldn't get done in the context of your overall IT governance strategy. Consider the following situation: Your portfolio management process comes up with a "not now" or a "no" for a business unit's project, but the business unit (which has its own budget and a degree of autonomy) moves ahead without IT's approval; this rogue project then creates urgent unplanned work for IT as the improperly planned technology spirals out of control or fails to integrate with enterprise systems. What do you do in this case?

ITPI's Milne answers this question with a question: "How do you handle it when your corporate strategy says, 'We're not going into the Latin America market,' and a line business does it anyway?" If your PPM process is sufficiently integrated into executive corporate strategy, units that are totally out of line will not need to be nailed by IT; the organization will rein them in, with or without IT's participation.

SOURCE: Jonathan Feldman, "Project Management Keeps IT from Being a Victim of Success," *InformationWeek*, April 5, 2008.

PROJECT MANAGEMENT
LO 12-4

Any discussion of information systems design and development would be incomplete without including a discussion of basic ***project management*** concepts, techniques, and tools. Before we progress any further in our discussion of implementation, we need to understand how our project, which we hope is on time and within budget, got to this point. Although a thorough discussion of project management is far beyond the scope of this text, we can, nonetheless, look at the big picture and acquaint ourselves with the necessary steps in the process. It is important to note that the skills and knowledge necessary to be a good project manager will translate into virtually any project environment, and most organizations regularly seek people who have acquired these skills.

What Is a Project?

A project is a special set of activities with a clear beginning and end. Every project has a set of *goals*, *objectives*, and *tasks*. Every project must also deal with a set of *limitations* or *constraints*. Finally, although the content can vary from one project to the next, there are many important similarities in the process. The first, and probably the greatest, contribution of the modern project management approach is to identify the project as a series of steps or phases. The SDLC is a project management approach tailored toward the design and development of information systems. Before we return our focus to a specific project management approach such as the SDLC, let's look at a more generic picture of project management and see how it compares. No matter what the project, three elements will be necessary to manage it effectively and efficiently: *process*, *tools*, and *techniques*.

The Process of Project Management

The modern project management approach has identified five phases in the process. Figure 12.20 illustrates the five phases.

INITIATING AND DEFINING. The first phase of the project management process serves as a foundation for all that follows. The most important objective to achieve during this phase is the clear and succinct statement of the problem that the project is to solve or

FIGURE 12.20

The five phases of project management.

Project Management Phase	Example Activities
Initiating/Defining	• State the problem(s)/goal(s). • Identify the objectives. • Secure resources. • Explore costs/benefits in feasibility study.
Planning	• Identify and sequence activities. • Identify the "critical path." • Estimate time and resources needed for completion. • Write a detailed project plan.
Executing	• Commit resources to specific tasks. • Add additional resources/personnel if necessary. • Initiate project work.
Controlling	• Establish reporting obligations. • Create reporting tools. • Compare actual progress with baseline. • Initiate control interventions if necessary.
Closing	• Install all deliverables. • Finalize all obligations/commitments. • Meet with stakeholders. • Release project resources. • Document the project. • Issue final report.

the goals that the project is to achieve. Any ambiguity at this point often spells doom for even the best-executed projects. Also during this phase, it is necessary to identify and secure the resources needed to execute the project, explore the costs and benefits, and identify any risks. As you have probably recognized, this is exactly what happens during the systems investigation phase of the SDLC.

PLANNING. The next phase in the project management process involves planning the project. Here every project objective and every activity associated with that objective must be identified and sequenced. Several tools have been created to assist in the sequencing of these activities, including simple *dependence diagrams*, *program evaluation and review* (PERT), *critical path method* (CPM), and a commonly used time-line diagram known as a *Gantt chart*. Although all of these tools have a particular use in project management, their common use is to help plan and sequence activities associated with the objectives of the project so that nothing is left out, performed out of logical sequence, or done twice. These same tools also help the project manager determine how long each activity will take and, thus, how long the project will take. Later in the project process, the tools will help determine whether the project is on schedule and, if not, where the delays occurred and what can be done to remedy the delay.

EXECUTING. Once all of the activities in the planning phase are complete and all detailed plans have been created and approved, the execution phase of the project can begin. It is here that all of the plans are put into motion. Resources, tasks, and schedules are brought together, and the necessary work teams are created and set forth on their assigned paths. In many respects, this is the most exciting part of the project management process. The phases of systems analysis and system design are the primary phases associated with project execution in the SDLC.

CONTROLLING. Some project management experts suggest that controlling is just an integral part of the execution phase of project management; others suggest it must be viewed as a separate set of activities that, admittedly, occur simultaneous to the execution phase. In either case, it is important to give sufficient attention to the controlling activities to ensure that the project objectives and deadlines are met.

Probably the single most important tool for project control is the report. Three common types of reports are generated to assist with project control. The *variance report* contains information related to the difference between actual and planned project progress. It helps identify when a project is off track but provides little evidence as to what is causing the delay.

The second and third types of reports are more helpful in determining the cause of delays and the appropriate corrections. The *status report* is an open-ended report that details the process that led to the current project state. By analyzing this report, a project manager can pinpoint where the delay began and can create a plan to get past it and possibly make up for lost time. This is where the *resource allocation* report becomes useful. This report identifies the various resources (people, equipment, and so on) that are being applied to specific project activities, as well as where currently unused, or *slack*, resources may be available.

CLOSING. This last phase of the project management process focuses on bringing a project to a successful end. The beginning of the end of a project is the implementation and installation of all of the project deliverables. The next step is the formal release of the project resources so they can be redeployed into other projects or job roles. The final step in this phase is to review the final documentation and publish the final project report. This is where the good and bad news concerning the project are documented, and the elements necessary for a postproject review are identified.

Many airline pilots (and passengers, for that matter) identify the final approach and landing as one of the most critical elements of any flight. It is during those remaining moments that even the smoothest of flights can come to an undesirable conclusion. Projects are quite similar in this regard. The most beautifully planned, executed, and controlled project can be deemed a failure if it is poorly implemented. As such, we must turn our attention back to the issues of systems implementation; we hope that this time it will be with a clearer understanding of how we arrived at this point and the process we will follow to do it again in another project.

EVALUATING HARDWARE, SOFTWARE, AND SERVICES
LO 12-7

A major activity during the implementation phase of the SDLC is the acquisition of the hardware and software necessary to implement the new system. How do companies evaluate and select hardware, software, and IT services, such as those shown in Figure 12.21? Large companies may require suppliers to present bids and proposals based on system specifications developed during the design stage of systems development. Minimum acceptable physical and performance characteristics for all hardware and software requirements are established. Most large business firms and all government agencies formalize these requirements by listing them in a document called an RFP (request for proposal) or RFQ (request for quotation). Then they send the RFP or RFQ to appropriate vendors, who use it as the basis for preparing a proposed purchase agreement.

Companies may use a *scoring* system of evaluation when there are several competing proposals for a hardware or software acquisition. They give each evaluation factor a certain number of maximum possible points. Then they assign each competing proposal points for each factor, depending on how well it meets the user's specifications. Scoring evaluation factors for several proposals helps organize and document the evaluation process. It also spotlights the strengths and weaknesses of each proposal.

Hardware
Full range of offerings, including xSeries servers, iSeries midrange servers for small and midsize businesses, RS/6000 servers for UNIX customers, and z900 mainframes for large enterprises. Also has full range of storage options.

Software
Web server: Lotus DominoGo Web server.
Storefront: WebSphere Commerce Suite (formerly known as Net.Commerce) for storefront and catalog creation, relationship marketing, and order management. Can add Commerce Integrator to integrate with back-end systems and Catalog Architect for content management.
Middleware/transaction services: WebSphere application server manages transactions. MQ Series queues messages and manages connections. CICS processes transactions.
Database: DB2 Universal Database.
Tools: WebSphere Studio includes set of predefined templates and common business logic.
Other applications include: IBM Payment Suite for handling credit cards and managing digital certificates.

Services
IBM Global Services, which includes groups organized by each major industry, including retail and financial. Can design, build, and host e-commerce applications.

Whatever the claims of hardware manufacturers and software suppliers, the performance of hardware and software must be demonstrated and evaluated. Independent hardware and software information services (such as Datapro and Auerbach) may be used to gain detailed specification information and evaluations. Other users are frequently the best source of information needed to evaluate the claims of manufacturers and suppliers. That's why Internet newsgroups and Weblogs established to exchange information about specific software or hardware vendors and their products have become one of the best sources for obtaining up-to-date information about the experiences of users of the products.

Large companies frequently evaluate proposed hardware and software by requiring the processing of special *benchmark* test programs and test data. Benchmarking simulates the processing of typical jobs on several computers and evaluates their performances. Users can then evaluate test results to determine which hardware device or software package displayed the best performance characteristics.

Hardware Evaluation Factors

When you evaluate the hardware needed by a new business application, you should investigate specific physical and performance characteristics for each computer system or peripheral component to be acquired. Specific questions must be answered concerning many important factors. Ten of these *hardware evaluation factors* and questions are summarized in Figure 12.22.

Notice that there is much more to evaluating hardware than determining the fastest and cheapest computing device. For example, the question of obsolescence must be addressed by making a technology evaluation. The factor of ergonomics is also very important. Ergonomic factors ensure that computer hardware and software are user-friendly, that is, safe, comfortable, and easy to use. Connectivity is another important evaluation factor because so many network technologies and bandwidth alternatives are available to connect computer systems to the Internet, intranet, and extranet networks.

Hardware Evaluation Factors	Rating
Performance What is its speed, capacity, and throughput?	
Cost What is its lease or purchase price? What will be its cost of operation and maintenance?	
Reliability What is the risk of malfunction and what are its maintenance requirements? What are its error control and diagnostic features?	
Compatibility Is it compatible with existing hardware and software? Is it compatible with hardware and software provided by competing suppliers?	
Technology In what year of its product life cycle is it? Does it use a new untested technology, or does it run the risk of obsolescence?	
Ergonomics Has it been "human factors engineered" with the user in mind? Is it user-friendly, designed to be safe, comfortable, and easy to use?	
Connectivity Can it be easily connected to wide area and local area networks that use different types of network technologies and bandwidth alternatives?	
Scalability Can it handle the processing demands of a wide range of end users, transactions, queries, and other information processing requirements?	
Software Are system and application software available that can best use this hardware?	
Support Are the services required to support and maintain it available?	
Overall Rating	

FIGURE 12.22

A summary of 10 major hardware evaluation factors. Notice how you can use this to evaluate a computer system or a peripheral device.

SAS: Services Key in Mainframe Migration Project

Scandinavian Airlines International (SAS) has embarked on a long-term project to migrate away from more than a dozen homegrown mainframe applications and integrate all that functionality into three commercial packages. These applications have been in place for more than 10 or 15 years in some cases; although they were certainly useful when first implemented, the business looks much different now, and those applications are due for replacement. With more than 1,000 flights a day on more than 300 airplanes, the company needs a degree of responsiveness and flexibility that the legacy applications just cannot provide any longer. One of the problems of the current set of mainframe applications is that they are very closely integrated—"tightly coupled" in IT parlance—with each other and the databases on which they operate. As a result, changes in one function in one place trigger the need for changes in the many other modules that rely on that function to operate in a very specific manner. This also leads to extensive testing of the entire system when changes are made, as the company must ensure that nothing has been "broken" as a result.

To avoid these problems, the new set of applications will be loosely coupled; instead of communicating directly among them, they will communicate through the use of messaging services provided by a package from TIBCO, a leading provider of the technology. "The messaging backbone will let the company map the data from disparate systems, route messages, ensure that services are delivered in the correct order, and enforce security rules," says Jonas Berggren, vice president of Production Systems at SAS Group, the parent company to the airline. For example, every time a plane takes off or lands, a message is sent through the central messaging bus to all of the systems that need to know about such an event. Some of these systems are internal to the company, others are operated by suppliers, while yet others belong to business partners. These messages will flow through the central messaging channel—which ensures that those messages are delivered, and only to the intended recipients—and automatically update all necessary applications. The current system, on the other hand, performs periodic batch updates.

The company expects that the move away from proprietary mainframe applications and into a service-oriented architecture with commercial packages will enable them to react more quickly to unexpected events such as weather delays and equipment repairs. By using the message package from TIBCO, SAS estimates it will shave three to six months off the project, compared to developing a messaging solution in-house. Once the mainframes are gone, IT maintenance costs should decrease by about $250,000 a month.

SOURCE: Heather Havenstein, "ESB, SOA Keys in Airline Migration Project," *Computerworld*, May 7, 2007.

Software Evaluation Factors

You should evaluate software according to many factors that are similar to those used for hardware evaluation. Thus, the factors of performance, cost, reliability, availability, compatibility, modularity, technology, ergonomics, and support should be used to evaluate proposed software acquisitions. In addition, however, the software evaluation factors summarized in Figure 12.23 must also be considered. You should answer the questions they generate in order to evaluate software purchases properly. For example,

FIGURE 12.23

A summary of selected software evaluation factors. Note that most of the hardware evaluation factors in Figure 12.22 can also be used to evaluate software packages.

Software Evaluation Factors	Rating
Quality Is it bug-free, or does it have many errors in its program code?	
Efficiency Is the software a well-developed system of program code that does not use much CPU time, memory capacity, or disk space?	
Flexibility Can it handle our business processes easily, without major modification?	
Security Does it provide control procedures for errors, malfunctions, and improper use?	
Connectivity Is it *Web-enabled* so it can easily access the Internet, intranets, and extranets, on its own, or by working with Web browsers or other network software?	
Maintenance Will new features and bug fixes be easily implemented by our own software developers?	
Documentation Is the software well documented? Does it include help screens and helpful software agents?	
Hardware Does existing hardware have the features required to best use this software?	
Other Factors What are its performance, cost, reliability, availability, compatibility, modularity, technology, ergonomics, scalability, and support characteristics? (Use the hardware evaluation factor questions in Figure 12.22.)	
Overall Rating	

Evaluation Factors for IS Services	Rating
Performance What has been their past performance in view of their past promises?	
Systems Development Are Web site and other e-business developers available? What are their quality and cost?	
Maintenance Is equipment maintenance provided? What are its quality and cost?	
Conversion What systems development and installation services will they provide during the conversion period?	
Training Is the necessary training of personnel provided? What are its quality and cost?	
Backup Are similar computer facilities available nearby for emergency backup purposes?	
Accessibility Does the vendor provide local or regional sites that offer sales, systems development, and hardware maintenance services? Is a customer support center at the vendor's Web site available? Is a customer hotline provided?	
Business Position Is the vendor financially strong, with good industry market prospects?	
Hardware Do they provide a wide selection of compatible hardware devices and accessories?	
Software Do they offer a variety of useful e-business software and application packages?	
Overall Rating	

FIGURE 12.24

Evaluation factors for IS services. These factors focus on the quality of support services business users may need.

some software packages are notoriously slow, hard to use, bug-filled, or poorly documented. They are not a good choice, even if offered at attractive prices.

Evaluating IS Services

Most suppliers of hardware and software products and many other firms offer a variety of IS services to end users and organizations. Examples include assistance in developing a company Web site; installation or conversion of new hardware and software; employee training; and hardware maintenance. Some of these services are provided without cost by hardware manufacturers and software suppliers.

Other types of IS services needed by a business can be outsourced to an outside company for a negotiated price. For example, *systems integrators* take over complete responsibility for an organization's computer facilities when an organization outsources its computer operations. They may also assume responsibility for developing and implementing large systems development projects that involve many vendors and subcontractors. Value-added resellers (VARs) specialize in providing industry-specific hardware, software, and services from selected manufacturers. Many other services are available to end users, including systems design, contract programming, and consulting services. Evaluation factors and questions for IS services are summarized in Figure 12.24.

Testing, data conversion, documentation, and training are keys to successful implementation of a new business system.

Testing

System testing may involve testing and debugging software, testing Web site performance, and testing new hardware. An important part of testing is the review of prototypes of displays, reports, and other output. Prototypes should be reviewed by end users of the proposed systems for possible errors. Of course, testing should not occur only during

OTHER IMPLEMENTATION ACTIVITIES

LO 12-5

LO 12-6

the system's implementation stage, but throughout the system's development process. For example, you might examine and critique prototypes of input documents, screen displays, and processing procedures during the systems design stage. Immediate end-user testing is one of the benefits of a prototyping process.

Data Conversion

Implementing new information systems for many organizations today frequently involves replacing a previous system and its software and databases. One of the most important implementation activities required when installing new software in such cases is called *data conversion.* For example, installing new software packages may require converting the data elements in databases that are affected by a new application into new data formats. Other data conversion activities that are typically required include correcting incorrect data, filtering out unwanted data, consolidating data from several databases, and organizing data into new data subsets, such as databases, data marts, and data warehouses. A good data conversion process is essential because improperly organized and formatted data are frequently reported to be one of the major causes of failures in implementing new systems.

During the design phase, the analysts create a data dictionary that not only describes the various data elements contained in the new system but also specifies any necessary conversions from the old system. In some cases, only the name of the data element is changed, as in the old system field CUST_ID becoming CLIENT_ID in the new system. In other cases, the actual format of the data is changed, thus requiring some conversion application to be written to filter the old data and put them into the new format. An example of this might be the creation of a new CUSTOMER_ID format to allow for expansion or to make two merged systems compatible with one another. This type of data element conversion requires additional time to occur because each element must be passed through the conversion filter before being written into the new data files.

Yet another issue is the time necessary to transfer the data from the old data files into the files for the new system. Although it is possible that the new system may have been designed to use the existing data files, this is not normally the case, especially in situations where a new system is replacing a legacy system that is fairly old. The time necessary to transfer the old data can have a material impact on the conversion process and on the strategy that is ultimately selected. Consider the following situation.

Suppose the conversion to the new system requires the transfer of data from 10 different data files. The average record length across the 10 files is 1,780 bytes, and the total number of records contained in the 10 files is 120 million. With this information and an estimate of the transfer time in bytes per minute, the total transfer time can be easily calculated as follows: Assume a transfer rate of 10.5 megabytes per second (Mbps) (Fast Ethernet) with no conversion algorithm.

1,780 bytes × 120 million records = 213,600,000,000 bytes.

213,600,000,000 bytes/10.5 Mbps × 20,343 seconds.

20,343 seconds = 5.65 hours.

Although the preceding calculations appear to be such that the conversion process does not take an inordinate amount of time, we must also be aware that they assume an error-free transfer, no format conversion, and 100 percent use of available network bandwidth. If the transfer is done using a slower communication medium, say 1.25 Mbps, the time jumps to 47.47 hours (just under two days).

The important consideration here is not just the time necessary to effect the transfer but the preservation of the integrity of the current system data files during the process. If the transfer turns out to be about 4.5 hours, then it could theoretically occur after business hours and be easily accomplished by the opening of the next day's business. If, however, the process takes two full days, then it would need to begin at the close of business on Friday and would not be complete until late Sunday afternoon. Should any glitches show up in the process, either the transfer would have to wait a week to be rerun, or the possibility of disrupting daily operations or losing new data would be very real. As you can see, careful thought to the logistics associated with data transfer must be given when recommending the most appropriate conversion strategy for the new system.

Documentation

Developing good user *documentation* is an important part of the implementation process. Sample data entry display screens, forms, and reports are good examples of documentation. When *computer-aided systems engineering* methods are used, documentation can be created and changed easily because it is stored and accessible on disk in a *system repository*. Documentation serves as a method of communication among the people responsible for developing, implementing, and maintaining a computer-based system. Installing and operating a newly designed system or modifying an established application requires a detailed record of that system's design. Documentation is extremely important in diagnosing errors and making changes, especially if the end users or systems analysts who developed a system are no longer with the organization.

Training

Training is a vital implementation activity. IS personnel, such as user consultants, must be sure that end users are trained to operate a new business system or its implementation will fail. Training may involve only activities like data entry, or it may also involve all aspects of the proper use of a new system. In addition, managers and end users must be educated in how the new technology affects the company's business operations and management. This knowledge should be supplemented by training programs for any new hardware devices, software packages, and their use for specific work activities. Figure 12.25 illustrates how one business coordinated its end-user training program with each stage of its implementation process for developing intranet and Internet access within the company.

FIGURE 12.25

How one company developed training programs for the implementation of an e-commerce Web site and intranet access for its employees.

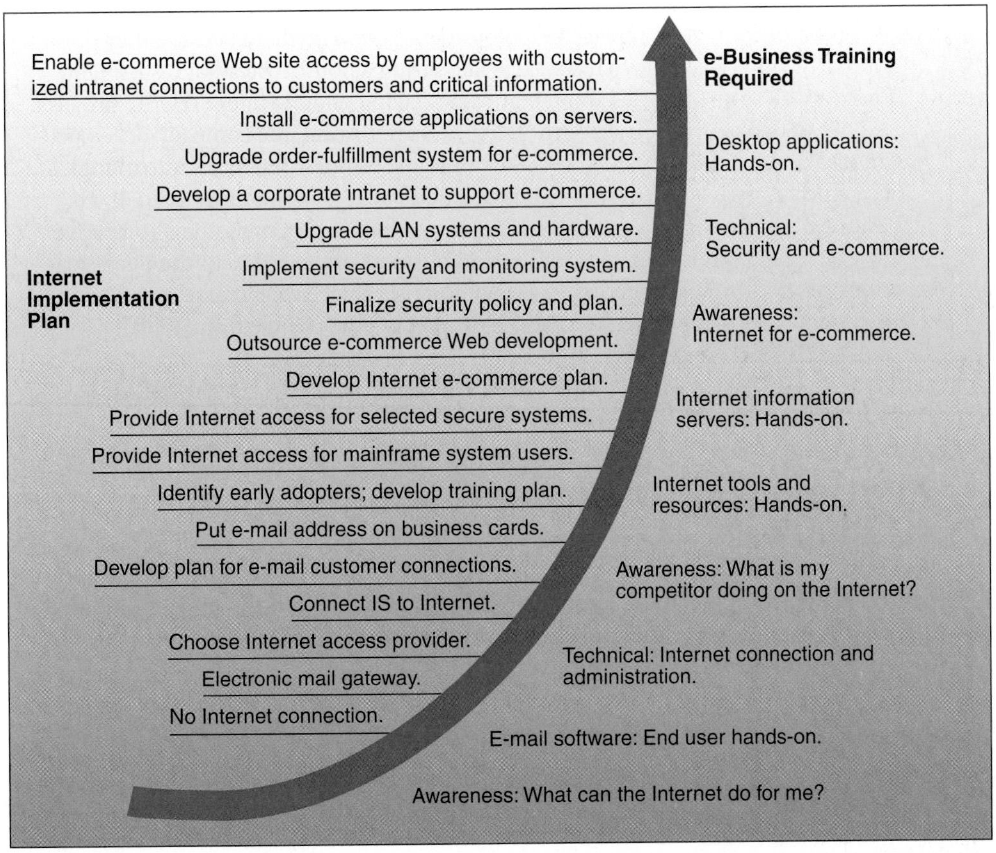

Owens & Minor: The Mainframe Goes, but Cobol Stays

The year is 1980. The *Voyager 1* probe confirms the existence of Janus, a moon of Saturn. The United States severs relationships with Iran, following the taking of hostages the year before. *The Empire Strikes Back* and *Superman II* are the top-grossing films in the United States, and Queen and AC/DC top the billboard charts. And Owens & Minor, a medical supplies company, implements their ERP system.

A lot has changed since 1980, and so has the ERP system. Originally a packaged application, over time the company adapted it to better suit its needs, creating a highly customized application with more than 10 million lines of code. Today, more than 30 years later, the ERP system is still there, running the core applications of the company, including order and inventory management, purchasing, pricing, accounts receivable, and accounts payable. The company itself is more than 130 years old, with more than $8 billion in reported revenue in 2009. As the ERP grew and became more and more complex, managers realized that bigger does not necessarily mean better. For example, each "green screen" application had a different and separate user interface, requiring the purchase of larger and larger monitors over time so that different applications could be displayed at the same time. At some point, something has to give; surprisingly, it will not be the ERP software itself.

Managers at Owens & Minor have decided to move the ERP system off the mainframe where it currently resides and into an x86 machine with Windows clients. This is possible because the original ERP itself runs from a Unix emulator. Although many companies replaced this kind of system with a commercial package or sought to rewrite the logic using a more modern language, Rick Mears, chief information officer at Owens & Minor, says that the logic contained in the ERP system was too valuable to lose. He says he is convinced that either replacing or rewriting the system would have cost $100 million to $200 million more than what it will cost them to move it off the mainframe. The cost of operating the new servers is about half of the maintenance cost of the mainframe itself.

"A lot of companies replace Cobol systems or rewrite them because they do not like the interface," says Mears. "It is like razing a house instead of restoring it. There are all sorts of stories about companies taking on nine figure rewrite projects. I do not understand the payback for that," he says. Instead, the company developed a new set of user interfaces that combine multiple business functions into a single access point, with some dramatic changes. For instance, the more than 400 customer service representations had to access four different systems to resolve an issue, each with its separate screen and business logic. Now, all the necessary information is brought together in a graphical user interface, increasing processing speeds and improving order accuracy. Now that is a big change from 1980.

SOURCE: Patrick Thibodeau, "One Firm's Story: The Mainframe Goes, but Cobol Stays Behind," *Computerworld*, April 20, 2010.

System Conversion Strategies

The initial operation of a new business system can be a difficult task. This typically requires a *conversion* process from the use of a present system to the operation of a new or improved application. Conversion methods can soften the impact of introducing new information technologies into an organization. Four major forms of system conversion are illustrated in Figure 12.26. They include:

- Parallel conversion
- Phased conversion
- Pilot conversion
- Direct conversion

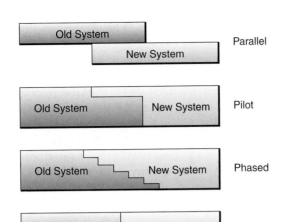

FIGURE 12.26

The four major forms of conversion to a new system.

Direct Conversion

The simplest conversion strategy, and probably the most disruptive to the organization, is the *direct cutover* approach. This method, sometimes referred to as the slam dunk or cold-turkey strategy, is as abrupt as its name implies. Using this approach, the old system is just turned off, and the new system is turned on in its place. Although this method is the least expensive of all available strategies and may be the only viable solution in situations where activating the new system is an emergency or when the two systems cannot coexist under any conditions, it is also the one that poses the greatest risk of failure. Once the new system becomes operational, the end users must cope with any errors or dysfunctions, and depending on the severity of the problem, this approach can have a significant effect on the quality of the work performed. Direct conversion should be considered only in extreme circumstances where no other conversion strategy is viable.

Parallel Conversion

At the opposite end of the risk spectrum is the *parallel conversion* strategy. Here, the old and new systems are run simultaneously until the end users and project coordinators are fully satisfied that the new system is functioning correctly and the old system is no longer necessary. Using this approach, a parallel conversion can be effected with either a *single cutover*, where a predetermined date for stopping the parallel operation is set, or a *phased cutover*, where some predetermined method of phasing in each piece of the new system and turning off a similar piece of the old system is employed.

Although clearly having the advantage of low risk, the parallel approach also brings with it the highest cost. To execute a parallel approach properly, the end users must literally perform all daily functions with both systems, thus creating a massive redundancy in activities and literally double the work. In fact, unless the operational costs of the new system are significantly less than the old system, the cost of parallel operation can be as much as three to four times greater than the old system alone. During a parallel conversion, all outputs from both systems are compared for concurrency and accuracy, until it is determined that the new system is functioning at least as well as the one it is replacing. Parallel conversion may be the best choice in situations where an automated system is replacing a manual one. In certain circumstances where end users cannot cope with the often-confusing redundancy of two systems, the parallel conversion strategy may not be viable. Also, parallel conversion may not be possible if the organization does not have the available computing resources to operate two systems at the same time.

Pilot Conversion

In some situations, the new system may be installed in multiple locations, such as a series of bank branches or retail outlets. In other cases, the conversion may be able to be planned from a geographic perspective. When these types of scenarios exist, the possibility of using a *pilot conversion* strategy exists. This approach allows for the conversion to the new system, using either a direct or parallel method, at a single location. The advantage to this approach is that a location can be selected that best represents the conditions across the organization but also may be less risky in terms of any loss of time or delays in processing. Once the installation is complete at the pilot site, the process can be evaluated and any changes to the system made to prevent problems encountered at the pilot site from reoccurring at the remaining installations. This approach may also be required if the individual sites or locations have certain unique characteristics or idiosyncrasies making either a direct or parallel approach infeasible.

Phased Conversion

A *phased* or gradual conversion strategy attempts to take advantage of the best features of both the direct and parallel approaches, while minimizing the risks involved. This incremental approach to conversion allows for the new system to be brought online as a series of functional components that are logically ordered to minimize disruption to the end users and the flow of business.

Phased conversion is analogous to the release of multiple versions of an application by a software developer. Each version of the software should correct any known bugs and should allow for 100 percent compatibility with data entered into or processed by the previous version. Although it has the advantage of lower risk, the phased approach takes the most time and, thus, creates the most disruption to the organization over time.

Postimplementation Activities

When all is said and done, the single most costly activity occurs after the system implementation is complete: the *postimplementation maintenance phase*. The primary objectives associated with systems maintenance are to correct errors or faults in the system, provide changes to effect performance improvement, or adapt the system to changes in the operating or business environment. In a typical organization, more programmers and analysts are assigned to application maintenance activities than to application development. Further, although a new system can take several months or years to design and build and can cost hundreds of thousands or millions of dollars, the resulting system can operate around the clock and last for 5 to 10 years, or longer. One major activity in postimplementation involves making changes to the system after the users have finally had an opportunity to use it. These are called *change requests*. Such requests can range from fixing a software bug not found during testing to designing an enhancement to an existing process or function.

Systems Maintenance

Managing and implementing change requests is only one aspect of the **systems maintenance** phase activities. In some ways, once the maintenance phase begins, the life cycle starts over again. New requirements are articulated, analyzed, designed, checked for feasibility, tested, and implemented. Although the range and nature of specific maintenance requests vary from system to system, four basic categories of maintenance can be identified: (1) *corrective*, (2) *adaptive*, (3) *perfective*, and (4) *preventive*.

The activities associated with *corrective maintenance* are focused on fixing bugs and logic errors not detected during the implementation testing period. *Adaptive maintenance* refers to those activities associated with modifying existing functions or adding new functionality to accommodate changes in the business or operating environments. *Perfective maintenance* activities involve changes made to an existing system that are intended to improve the performance of a function or interface. The final category of maintenance activities, *preventive maintenance*, involves those activities intended to reduce the chances of a system failure or extend the capacity of a current system's useful life. Although often the lowest-priority maintenance activity, preventive maintenance is, nonetheless, a high-value-adding function and is vital to an organization realizing the full value of its investment in the system.

Postimplementation Review

The maintenance activity also includes a ***postimplementation review*** process to en-sure that newly implemented systems meet the business objectives established for them. Errors in the development or use of a system must be corrected by the mainte-nance process. This includes a periodic review or audit of a system to ensure that it is operating properly and meeting its objectives. This audit is in addition to continually monitoring a new system for potential problems or necessary changes.

Project Success (or Failure): What We Know but Choose to Ignore

There is no mystery as to why most projects succeed or fail; people have been writing about effective project management for millennia. More than 2,000 years ago, Sun Tzu described how to organize a successful, highly complex project (a military campaign) in *The Art of War*. Fred Brooks's classic book, *The Mythical Man-Month*, offers management advice targeted at running large IT projects. The U.K. National Audit Office recently published an excellent guide to deliver-ing successful IT-enabled business change. Over the past 10 years, virtually every major IT publication has printed articles on why large projects succeed or fail.

Despite all the excellent advice available, more than half of the major projects undertaken by IT departments still fail or get canceled. We know what works. We just don't do it.

An ineffective executive sponsor. A weak or, even worse, nonexistent execu-tive sponsor almost guarantees business project failure. Under weak executive leadership, all projects become IT projects rather than business initiatives with IT components.

A poor business case. An incomplete business case allows incorrect expecta-tions to be set—and missed.

The business case is no longer valid. Marketplace changes frequently invalidate original business assumptions, but teams often become so invested in a project that they ignore warning signs and continue as planned.

The project is too big. Bigger projects require more discipline.

A lack of dedicated resources. Large projects require concentration and dedication for the duration. But key people are frequently required to support critical projects while continuing to perform their existing full-time jobs.

Out of sight, out of mind. If your suppliers fail, you fail, and you own it. Don't take your eyes off them.

Unnecessary complexity. Projects that attempt to be all things to all people usually result in systems that are difficult to use, and they eventually fail.

Cultural conflict. Projects that violate cultural norms of the organization seldom have a chance.

No contingency. Stuff happens. Projects need flexibility to address the inevi-table surprises.

Too long without deliverables. Most organizations expect visible progress in six to nine months.

Long projects without intermediate products risk losing executive interest, support, and resources.

Betting on a new, unproven technology. Enough said.

An arbitrary release date. Date-driven projects have little chance of success. Companies should learn to plan the project before picking a release date, not the other way around.

Anything here that doesn't make sense? *That's exactly the point.*

SOURCE: Bart Perkins, "12 Things You Know About Projects but Choose to Ignore," *Computerworld*, March 12, 2007.

Starwood Hotels and Resorts—Toward a Completely New Infrastructure

Starwood Hotels and Resorts is a large, multinational, leading hotel group in the upscale and luxury segments of the industry, operating more than 300,000 rooms in more than 1,000 properties around the world. Like all the other large companies in the industry, the backbone of the company was a reservation system developed in Cobol and run on an IBM mainframe, which had been in place for more than 20 years. And all that was now about to change, a project that would affect every aspect of the company.

A key aspect of the overall effort was that no performance issues or disruptions should occur as a result of the new technology implementation. In order to ensure this, the company implemented an application performance management tool to control the development and implementation process itself. Through the use of this tool, the business defined the quality and performance targets and thresholds that were considered sufficient to judge the outcome of the project a success—or at least adequate enough that the new system would not negatively impact the throughput of reservations coming in—and then used it to measure the new application and all its components as they were developed, tested, and rolled out. As a result, the development team was able to ensure, to themselves and the business, that all application and performance issues were addressed prior to the final cutoff date. They were also able to show that the new technology would be able to handle the load that was necessary, even in peak times of the day. Looking forward, this same approach can be used to monitor the performance of the now-running system and highlight which issues need attention before they turn into actual problems that need to be fixed.

Given the need for a flawless transition, the development group really got to know the existing systems in and out before attempting to develop a replacement. In particular, large amounts of data about the current performance of the systems in place were gathered—transaction volumes throughout each day, type and frequency of different requests, sources of each transaction, and so forth—and used to create a set of transaction profiles for each day of the week. This resulted in an improved understanding of transaction trends throughout each day and each hour of each day, identifying the busiest times and the key sources, types, and volume of transactions that the new reservation system should be able to handle gracefully. These data were also

used to set the targets and thresholds that the application performance management tool monitored. Actual performance data were reviewed at multiple times during the development process, which included testing up to twice the required transaction volume to ensure that the new system could handle peaks in demand—and would remain useful for years to come, as well.

In addition to these technical targets, the company also established business metrics that should be measured and displayed through a series of reports and dashboards, effectively allowing managers to run their business in real time. These included booking volumes, average rates, transaction types, sources of requests and bookings, or daily revenue, to name a few. These could then be aggregated or monitored over time to provide trends that could be useful in future analyses, or eventually loaded into a data warehouse from which reports could be created. In addition, the new system also includes a dashboard that immediately displays the business impact of any problems happening in the underlying technology, which greatly underscores that the technology is an intricate part of the business—no technology, no business—and should thus be treated as any other business asset.

In order to accomplish all this, Starwood Hotels and Resorts opted to move away from a mainframe environment and embrace a full-service-oriented architecture and applications internally developed in Java. "It was the best way to let us map our technology with our various brands," says Israel del Rio, Technology Solutions, at Starwood. Rather than having each brand develop its own set of applications, the new architecture allowed the brands to share the same features and functionality as needed, while permitting customization that would reflect each hotel's unique look and feel. For example, the search function, when initiated from the main Sheraton Web site, may deliver information in a different manner than if it had been called from the W site; while the functionality—that is, search—is the same, the way in which the information is delivered and then displayed can reflect the unique preferences of the customers to frequent each particular hotel chain. "That way we benefit from using all the same tools that can be called up by different applications and interfaces," says del Rio.

The open framework nature of service-oriented environments also means that there is now greater flexibility to create and deploy new applications. For example, there is now a program in place that will keep track of frequent guest preferences as the guests move from one site to the next, something that was not possible—at least not without a fair amount of custom work—when the mainframes were still around. The quality of the information provided by the new system has also led to improvements in the way in which services are provided to guests and partners. For example, the system flags each instance where a customer is told that there is no availability for a specific date at a particular property. Doing so enables operations to go back and check that this reflects either a business decision, such as blocking a number of rooms for a specific event or convention, or that there are indeed no more rooms available fpr those dates. However, it could also be a problem with the system, and flagging those instances allows staff to verify that is not the case—and to do so in real time.

The key technology behind all this is the new, sophisticated reservation system named Valhalla (in Norse mythology, a majestic hall where fallen warriors and heroes go when they die), a massive Java-based application with multiple processing engines that are linked in a complex matrix of interdependencies, which orchestrates the interaction of the many services needed to process any particular transaction request. Although taking this approach leads to many efficiencies, it is not without its share of issues. When there is a problem with one transaction, it is difficult to diagnose exactly where—that is, in which of the many services involved—the problem lies. "With services we are always battling this 'needle in the haystack' issue. Application performance management allows us to isolate performance issues quickly, helping us understand the exact source of any problem," says Keith Kelly, vice president of Information Technology at Starwood Hotels and Resorts.

After five years and $140 million, the new system went live without a glitch—which is rather unheard of, particularly for something as big as this. That is not to say there were no issues. The company faced some stiff initial resistance from its own developers, who were used to building their own tools in-house and were not too sure about the need for a single, standard (and commercial) solution for monitoring the performance of both the development process and the new system itself. The most challenging times came right before deployment, when the business naturally became very nervous about the immensity of the effort, and they took some convincing. However, thanks to the extensive use of application monitoring, targets and metrics, and extensive testing much beyond what was strictly required of the new system, the development group was able to provide the necessary assurances that all would go smoothly—and it did—which, again, is rather unheard of.

On the other hand, given the strategic nature of the project, funding was not an issue and the business was closely involved every step of the way. This was achieved by creating a vision of what the company could do with the new technology that ensured that everyone bought into the need for a new central reservation system. Frequent meetings and reviews were held with all involved stakeholders to keep everyone appraised of the current status and progress of the project. Kelly is quite candid about the importance of the new technology, and the approach IT took toward its development. "We bet the farm on developing Valhalla using services," he says. "It would have been virtually impossible without an application performance management product. However, the overhead is very low, and it is easy to use. To me, the return on investment is almost immeasurable."

SOURCE: "Starwood Hotels and Resorts," *Computerworld Honors Case Study*, 2010, "Case Study, Starwood Hotels Uses SOA to Improve Guest Services and Cut Costs," *CIO Insight*, April 27, 2006; Cowley, S., "Starwood Nears End of SOA Revamp," *InfoWorld*, July 20, 2005; "Starwood Hotels and Resorts," *Computer Associates Customer Success Story*, 2009; Babcock, C. "Starwood Hotels Continues Its Migration from Mainframe to Services-Oriented Architecture," *InformationWeek*, July 21, 2005; and www.starwoodhotels.com, accessed June 13, 2011.

 QUESTIONS TO CONSIDER

1. The case discussed here would most likely be considered a successful deployment. What key aspects of the way in which the company handled this project made that success possible? For each key aspect that you identify, explain how it contributed to the outcome.

2. What are the advantages and disadvantages of examining existing systems—which will be replaced in any case—in a high level of detail? When would that be a sound practice? When would it not be the best approach?

- **The Systems Development Life Cycle.** Business end users and IS specialists may use a systems approach to help them develop information system solutions to meet business opportunities. This frequently involves a systems development life cycle where IS specialists and end users conceive, design, and implement business systems. The stages, activities, and products of the information systems development life cycle are summarized in Figure 12.3.

- **Prototyping.** Prototyping is a major alternative methodology to the traditional information systems development life cycle. It includes the use of prototyping tools and methodologies, which promote an iterative, interactive process that develops prototypes of user interfaces and other information system components. See Figure 12.9.

- **End-User Development.** The application development capabilities built into many end-user software packages have made it easier for end users to develop their own business applications. End users should focus their development efforts on the system components of business processes that can benefit from the use of information technology, as summarized in Figure 12.14.

- **Implementing IS.** The implementation process for information system projects is summarized in Figure 12.27. Implementation involves acquisition, testing, documentation, training, installation, and conversion activities that transform a newly designed business system into an operational system for end users.

- **Evaluating Hardware, Software, and Services.** Business professionals should know how to evaluate the acquisition of information system resources. IT vendors' proposals should be based on specifications developed during the design stage of systems development. A formal evaluation process reduces the possibility of incorrect or unnecessary purchases of hardware or software. Several major evaluation factors, summarized in Figures 12.22, 12.23, and 12.24, can be used to evaluate hardware, software, and IS services.

FIGURE 12.27

An overview of the implementation process. Implementation activities are needed to transform a newly developed information system into an operational system for end users.

Implementing New Systems
Acquisition Evaluate and acquire necessary hardware and software resources and information system services. Screen vendor proposals.
Software Development Develop any software that will not be acquired externally as software packages. Make any necessary modifications to software packages that are acquired.
Data Conversion Convert data in company databases to new data formats and subsets required by newly installed software.
Training Educate and train management, end users, customers, and other business stakeholders. Use consultants or training programs to develop user competencies.
Testing Test and make necessary corrections to the programs, procedures, and hardware used by a new system.
Documentation Record and communicate detailed system specifications, including procedures for end users and IS personnel and examples of input screens and output displays and reports.
Conversion Convert from the use of a present system to the operation of a new or improved system. This may involve operating both new and old systems in *parallel* for a trial period, operation of a *pilot* system on a trial basis at one location, *phasing* in the new system one location at a time, or a *direct cutover* to the new system.

These are the key terms and concepts of this chapter. The page number of their first reference appears in parentheses.

1. Conversion (550)
2. Cost/benefit analysis (524)
3. Data conversion (548)
4. Documentation (549)
5. Economic feasibility (523)
6. End-user development (533)
7. Feasibility study (522)
8. Functional requirements (528)
9. Human factors feasibility (525)
10. Implementation process (539)
11. Intangible (524)
    a. Benefits (524)
    b. Costs (524)
12. Legal/political feasibility (525)
13. Logical model (527)
14. Operational feasibility (523)
15. Organizational analysis (526)
16. Postimplementation review (553)
17. Project management (541)
18. Prototyping (529)
19. Systems analysis and design (521)
20. Systems approach (518)
21. Systems development life cycle (521)
22. Systems implementation (539)
23. Systems maintenance (552)
24. System specifications (533)
25. Systems thinking (518)
26. System testing (547)
27. Tangible (524)
    a. Benefits (524)
    b. Costs (524)
28. Technical feasibility (524)
29. User interface design (531)

Match one of the key terms and concepts listed previously with each of the brief examples or definitions that follow. Try to find the best fit for answers that seem to fit more than one term or concept. Defend your choices.

_____ 1. Using an organized sequence of activities to study a problem or opportunity using systems thinking.

_____ 2. Trying to recognize systems and the new interrelationships and components of systems in any situation.

_____ 3. Evaluating the success of a solution after it has been implemented.

_____ 4. Your evaluation shows that benefits outweigh costs for a proposed system.

_____ 5. The costs of acquiring computer hardware, software, and specialists.

_____ 6. Loss of customer goodwill caused by errors in a new system.

_____ 7. Increases in profits caused by a new system.

_____ 8. Improved employee morale caused by efficiency and effectiveness of a new system.

_____ 9. A multistep process to conceive, design, and implement an information system.

_____ 10. A diagram or blueprint of a system that shows what it does without regard to how it does it.

_____ 11. Determines the organizational, economic, technical, and operational feasibility of a proposed information system.

_____ 12. The goal of this feasibility analysis category is to determine whether the proposed system will provide positive economic benefits.

_____ 13. Reliable hardware and software are available to implement a proposed system.

_____ 14. Determining whether or not any copyright or patent infringements may exist as the result of a new system.

_____ 15. Do we have the right people to operate the new system?

_____ 16. A multistage process for studying in detail the information needs of users and any information systems presently used, and then developing a system to correct a problem or improve operations.

_____ 17. A detailed description of user information needs and the input, processing, output, storage, and control capabilities required to meet those needs.

_____ 18. Systems design should focus on developing user-friendly input and output methods for a system.

_____ 19. A detailed description of the hardware, software, people, network, and data resources and information products required by a proposed system.

_____ 20. Acquiring hardware and software, testing and documenting a proposed system, and training people to use it.

_____ 21. Making improvements to an operational system.

_____ 22. An interactive and iterative process of developing and refining information system prototypes.

_____ 23. Managers and business specialists can develop their own e-business applications.

_____ 24. Correcting, converting, filtering, consolidating, and organizing data when replacing an old system.

_____ 25. Operate in parallel with the old system, use a test site, switch in stages, or cut over immediately to a new system.

_____ 26. Checking whether hardware and software work properly for end users.

_____ 27. A user manual communicates the design and operating procedures of a system.

_____ 28. Keeping an IS project on time and within its budget would be a major goal.

_____ 29. Cost and benefits that can be quantified with a high degree of certainty.

_____ 30. The degree to which a proposed system fits with the business environment and organizational objectives.

_____ 31. Costs and benefits of a new system that are hard to quantify.

_____ 32. A phase within systems analysis focused on understanding the organization and its environment.

_____ 33. The process by which a system goes from designs and blueprints to becoming a working system.

discussion questions

1. Why has prototyping become a popular way to develop business applications? What are prototyping's advantages and disadvantages?

2. Refer to the Real World Challenge faced by Starwood Hotels and Resorts in the chapter. Other companies in the industry had not taken any steps to change their IT infrastructure at the time. What should the company make of this? Why wouldn't other companies take similar steps? Do they know something that management at this company does not?

3. What does SDLC stand for? What are the phases of the SDLC? Explain in one or two sentences of your own words what happens in each phase. If problems occur during the SDLC, is it better to identify and solve those problems near the beginning or the end of the SDLC process?

4. What are the three most important factors you would use in evaluating computer hardware? Computer software? Explain why.

5. Assume that in your first week on a new job you are asked to use a type of business software that you have never used before. What kind of user training should your company provide to you before you start?

6. Refer to the Real World Solution in this chapter. Consider the example of the search functionality discussed there. What are the advantages and disadvantages of a highly modular, that is, loosely coupled, approach to systems development?

7. What is the difference between the parallel, direct (or plunge), phased, and pilot forms of IS conversion? Which conversion strategy is best? Explain why.

8. Review the Google real-world example in the chapter. How might you change the user interface of Google's search pages and those of some of its other products on the Web? Defend your proposals.

9. Review the real-world example discussing the factors involved in project failure in the chapter. If these are well-known, why would companies choose to ignore them over and over again? What could be the reasons behind such behavior?

10. Pick a business task you would like to computerize. How could you use the steps of the information systems development life cycle as illustrated in Figure 12.3 to help you? Use examples to illustrate your answer.

analysis exercises

1. **SDLC in Practice**
Community Action
The Systems Development Life Cycle (SDLC) provides a structured problem-solving software development methodology. However, what works for information system-related problems also works for many business problems. The SDLC provides a framework that requires adherents to follow a logical sequence. This sequence promotes careful analysis and helps ensure that you are _doing the right thing_ as well as _doing the thing right_.

You can apply the SDLC toward addressing many business problems. Think about a problem in your community. Your community may include your campus, your work, or your neighborhood. Your instructor may provide additional guidelines. Select a problem, complete each step in turn, and prepare a report detailing each step. Due to the location-specific nature of this exercise, expect to conduct first-hand research and interviews.

   a. Select a problem and quantify its effects.

   b. Identify the cause or causes of the problem.

c. Describe various solutions to this problem. Include estimated costs and benefits for each solution.

d. Select a solution and prepare a plan for its implementation.

e. Identify the parties responsible for monitoring and maintaining the solution. What metrics should they use to monitor the results?

2. Planning for Success
Project Planning

Projects have many dependencies, any of which could become points of failure. Without the cooperation or input from even one vital resource, a project may fail to meet its objectives. Effective project planning helps project managers think through a project before it starts and prepare communication strategies in advance. Experts say that 10–20 percent of your project time should be spent in the first phase of the SDLC, that is, Investigation (some professionals call this phase Planning). Remember the old adage: Prior Planning Prevents Poor Performance!

a. Read the article "*How to Create a Clear Project Plan*," www.cio.com.au, September 2004 (http://bit.ly/jinIqg), and summarize its main points.

b. Read through the "SDLC in Practice" exercise above, and select a problem as directed by your professor.

c. Prepare a project plan for the problem you selected above.

d. Present your project plan to your class. Solicit your peer's suggestions for improvement.

3. Americans with Disabilities Act
Enabling Technologies

The Americans with Disabilities Act prohibits discrimination on the basis of disability to public accommodations and commercial facilities. This act has been interpreted to include certain information systems as well. All information systems development projects should take ADA issues into consideration during development. Accommodating disabled employees and customers must never become an afterthought.

Even if you do not presently experience physical limitations, you may in the future, or you may have employees under your supervision who require special tools to enable access to information systems. Research information systems access solutions. Be sure to include a detailed description of the hardware or software solution, solution provider, and cost of accommodating each limitation listed below.

a. Partial visual impairment

b. Total visual impairment

c. Manual dexterity impairment

4. Central London Congestion Charging Scheme
Conversion Strategies

The city of London has been well known for its many historic sites, live theatre, and heavy traffic. In spite of a sophisticated underground subway system known locally as the "tube," traffic delays, car exhaust, noise pollution, and vehicle-pedestrian accidents have plagued Londoners for decades. After long deliberation, London's city government adopted the Central London Congestion Charging Scheme. This plan involved establishing a toll perimeter around London's center. Rather than stopping cars to collect tolls, however, London set up video cameras at each toll zone crossing. These cameras link to a billing system that charges each vehicle's registered owner a one-day access toll with same-day reentrance privileges. The steep toll, approximately $8, discourages vehicle traffic into London's city center.

Londoners who live within the toll zone receive a special discount, as do residents living near the toll zone boundary, certain government workers, and businesses operating fleets of vehicles. Tolls remain in effect during working hours on work days. Car owners have until the end of the day to pay their toll through e-mail, SMS messaging, telephone, Web site, or kiosk.

The toll has resulted in a significant decrease in automobile traffic, increased use of mass transit, fewer accidents, and faster driving times. The tolls have had a negligible effect on business operations and most residents. They have also generated significant revenue that London uses to maintain the system and to enhance public transportation.

Consider the massive work involved in educating the public, marking all streets entering the toll zone, setting up cameras, and building the information systems. The information systems alone must process the raw images, match license plates to a payment database, receive payments, send out nonpayment notices, and process appeals. Police also use the system's databases for a variety of law enforcement–related work.

a. Briefly describe the advantages and disadvantages of each conversion strategy—parallel, pilot, phased, and plunge (or direct)—as they apply to the Central London Congestion Charging Scheme project.

b. Which conversion strategy would you recommend for this project?

c. Defend your recommendation in detail.

5. End-User Software Development
Managing Nonprofessionals
Various office productivity suites with word processing and spreadsheet applications such as Google Docs, Open Office, and Microsoft Office allow users to create their own macros, functions, and even programs. These features are open to end users to help them improve their own productivity—especially with spreadsheets.

Although this sounds great in principle, most users aren't professional developers, and their mistakes can be costly.

Assume the role of an IT director for a mid-sized company and answer the following questions:

a. Would you ban end-user development as too risky? Why or why not?

b. Search the Internet for risks associated with end user development and list what you find.

c. What could you do to help support end-user development in your organization?

Microsoft, SiCortex, and Others: How Virtualization Helps Software Developers

Virtualization's big push to fame was arguably kickstarted by VMware's Workstation product, which allowed individual users to run a bunch of operating systems (OS), versions, or instances (similar to multiple application windows) instead of having a one-at-a-time multi-boot environment. In many companies, virtualization arrived with developers first using the technology quietly to do testing and development, then introducing the virtualization tools to IT higher-ups.

Although today computer virtualization fuels many production environments (e.g., servers, desktop infrastructures, and as a provisioning tool), virtualization is also used by a still-growing number of software developers. For starters, they use virtualization tools to provide a range of target environments for development and testing (such as different operating systems, OS versions, and browsers), and also to provision/re-provision configuration instances quickly and easily.

Mark Friedman, a senior software architect, works in Microsoft's Developer Division, where upwards of 3,000 people create Visual Studio and the .NET Framework. Friedman himself works mainly on the performance tools that ship with Microsoft's Visual Studio Team System. "About two-thirds of the people in my division are in development and testing—and most of these developers and testers are using system virtualization (via Microsoft's Hyper-V technology) as one of their key productivity tools," says Friedman, who is also a board director of The Computer Measurement Group.

One key advantage is virtualization's ability to set apart an unstable environment, which is something any developer expects in early phases of application design. As the Microsoft tools are developed, says Friedman, testing early versions may destabilize a developer's entire computing environment.

"That's the nature of the beast," he says. "Almost anything except the simplest desktop application can crash the system. I often tell my developers that if they aren't crashing the system regularly, they are not trying hard enough. We appreciate virtualization technologies, because they save time, and let our developers spend more of their time on the challenging stuff, not the mundane and extremely time-consuming aspects of prepping test environments."

Like other virtualization tools, Microsoft Hyper-V lets users "snapshot" the system at a "last-known good version." "We create a rollback that allows us to restore the system to that previous good state within minutes," Friedman says. "The alternative is having to re-image the computer or re-build the environment, which can take hours," says Friedman. "This is a tremendous timesaver."

Friedman's group also makes extensive use of virtualization and virtual machine images in quality assurance (QA) testing. "Once you get past unit testing by the developers, we like to talk about the test matrix—what versions of the OS does it run on, for example," he says. "Then we need to test against both the 32-bit or 64-bit versions of each. Using Virtual Machine (VM) images is the fastest, cheapest, most flexible way to maintain a variety of testing environments. In our QA labs, we are doing this all the time; we do a lot of automated testing, so we stockpile these images as VMs, and point our test suite at them. It's invaluable. We save so much time you wouldn't believe it."

The ability to snapshot, and restore a working image within minutes, rather than wait hours for a rebuilt system, is particularly important. "You're often looking at bugs where you have to spend a day or two to set up the environment just to reproduce a bug, so the time you spend having to rebuild again and again—that's a time waster," says Friedman. "That is loss of productivity."

For example, when a bug causes a system crash, the developer has to work backward to identify the point where the system crashed. "People often initially set breakpoints too far into the process and the system crashes again. Since a developer can easily be crashing the system several times a day, being able to restore quickly and then re-run the debugging session while the problem is still fresh in their minds is a great benefit," Friedman says. "When you're troubleshooting a complicated bug, it's good to stay in that groove."

Virtualization is a great boon to iterative testing, developers say. "We have lots of test systems for use by our developers—each of which needs its own x86 control system. Rather than get a lot of PCs, even whatever's cheapest, we're using virtualization to create VMs which then 'attach' to the external cluster boards," says Adam Moskowitz, senior software engineer at SiCortex, which builds and sells a range of energy-efficient computers.

A primary benefit of virtualizing the control systems, says Moskowitz, is ease of testing. "Want an experimental system? Clone a standard VM and away you go," he says. The tool set is also valuable because of its ease of configuration; developers can build a VM with the latest software once, then clone it as many times as needed.

Mike Brescia, who works for a company making real-time environmental data recording and retrieval, says, "In addition to offering its system as a virtual appliance, our company's developers use virtualization to put up different test environments, e.g. Windows and Linux, on fewer hardware boxes." Cloning a clean computer system for testing purposes is much easier than copying a disk image and using Clonezilla, Brescia says. "Running VM does not require tearing down and wiping a complete system; we only need to be careful not to overload resources on the host machine," adds Brescia.

The 15 Web developers at design and marketing firm Eli Kirk have to cater to a number of Web browsers and operating systems, says Connor Boyack, Eli Kirk's senior Web developer, who uses Parallels version 4 on Mac OS X Leopard, and runs VMs of Windows XP, OpenSUSE 11 and Windows 7 Beta. "Creating functional and aesthetically identical sites requires a great deal of browser testing, which makes virtualization a must," says Boyack. "Virtualization allows me to use multiple operating systems and multiple browsers all collaboratively and seamlessly."

There's a huge advantage in the ability to test a dozen different scenarios simultaneously to ensure a consistent user experience, agrees Nick Gauthier, a developer at SmartLogic Solutions. "Another advantage is being able to boot up a specific version and browser when a client has a complaint. We no longer have to say 'Well, I don't run that browser, I'm on Linux'; now we can say, 'One moment please; ah, I see the problem and I'm fixing it now.'"

"We use virtualization to test our software on the platforms and applications we support (for QA), and to replicate customer environments when there are customer issues for support," says Eric Floehr, chief technology officer at 3X Systems, a start-up that developed and sells a remote back-up appliance. "Virtualization allows us to quickly bring up and tear down environments, and allows us to do so with a minimum amount of physical hardware." The ability to test against a large number of platforms and environments with a minimum of capital outlay is especially important in a small start-up company. Plus, "It greatly improves the quality and reliability of our product," adds Floehr.

There are, developers acknowledge, parts of the process where virtualization can't help.

"One area where virtualization doesn't help is in stress testing our product, which is a network-based backup appliance," notes 3X's Floehr. "While we could test 10 simultaneous clients virtually, it isn't a true stress test because the 10 clients are only going through, say, four physical CPUs and two NICs, which are constraints that would not exist if they were 10 physical clients in the real world."

"For load testing or scaling, you have to run on the raw hardware, the physical machine," says Microsoft's Mark Friedman. "Performance characteristics, unless you expect to deploy on a VM, are very different. And the same applies to the state of the art for performance measurements; you can't trust the [Physical Machines] you get on a VM currently." Although, Friedman notes, over time he expects this to be fixed.

Also, says Friedman, the para-virtualization approach used by the virtualization industry can and does change some underlying aspects of the OS, notably the OS drivers. "So if you have a dependency on specific drivers or hardware environment, that will be impacted. For example, there's a virtual NIC, and there's a specific driver. The driver is 'virtualization-aware.' You have to understand that if you need testing against a native set of drivers, you won't see that within a VM. So this impacts people doing driver development, but not web developers, etc."

Despite those quibbles, virtualization already gives developers real benefits. "Virtualization makes our developers more productive once they learn to work with the technology," says Microsoft's Friedman. "It allows them to spend more of their time in coding, testing and debugging. It eliminates a lot of time and delay spent in set-up and preparation, which isn't where we want them to be spending the bulk of their time."

SOURCE: Daniel Dern, "How Virtualization Improves Software Development," *CIO.com*, February 11, 2009.

▼ CASE STUDY QUESTIONS

1. How does virtualization work? In your own words, describe what you understand about the virtualization process as depicted in the case.
2. In software development and testing, where does virtualization help, and where it does not? Why?
3. What are the business benefits of implementing virtualization technologies in software development? Classify them into those that enhance the effectiveness and the efficiency of the development and testing process.

▼ REAL WORLD ACTIVITIES

1. Go online and research other uses of virtualization technology (backup and disaster recovery being one of those). How do they differ from the ones described in the case? How are they similar? Prepare a report to summarize your findings.
2. If virtualization technology were eventually to allow end users to run any environment of their choice in the same device, does that mean the choice of computing platform (desktop, notebook, or smartphone; Windows, Linux, or Mac OS) becomes irrelevant? Break into small groups to discuss this issue.

JetBlue Airways, WestJet Airlines, and Others: The Difficult Path to Software Upgrades

Few things in the airline business are more daunting than upgrading to a new reservations system. Do it well, and customers are none the wiser; mess it up, and a carrier risks losing customers and tarnishing its brand. Discount carriers JetBlue Airways Corp. and WestJet Airlines Ltd. both recently switched reservations systems. The differing outcomes are a reminder of how the implementation of new technology can be just as crucial as the technology itself.

Despite months of planning, when WestJet flipped the switch on its new system, its Web site crashed repeatedly and its call center was overwhelmed. It took months to resolve all of the issues. JetBlue, which later upgraded to the same software, smoothed its transition by building a backup Web site and hiring 500 temporary call-center workers.

Reservations are at the heart of a customer's relationship with an airline. So messing with the reservations system "is certainly not for the faint of heart," says Rick Zeni, a vice president of JetBlue who led the Forest Hills, N.Y., carrier through its transition.

Both WestJet and JetBlue previously used a system designed for start-up airlines with simpler needs. As the carriers grew, they needed more processing power to deal with increasing numbers of customers. They also wanted additional functions, such as the ability to link their prices and seat inventories to other airlines with whom they might wish to cooperate.

After studying alternatives, WestJet and JetBlue independently selected a system offered by Sabre Holdings Corp., a provider of such technology to 300 airlines and owner of Travelocity and other online travel agencies. JetBlue says the new system cost about $40 million, including $25 million in capital spending and $15 million in one-time operating expenses. WestJet did not disclose its costs.

The system sells seats and collects passenger payments, but it also controls much of the passenger experience: shopping on the airline's Web site, interacting with reservation agents, using airport kiosks, selecting seats, checking bags, boarding at the gate, rebooking, and getting refunds for cancellations. "It has a very big circle of influence and has to integrate with other systems in the airline," says Steve Clampett, an executive at Sabre Airline Solutions division. "It's as visible a technology upgrade as in almost any industry."

WestJet, which has 88 planes and is Canada's second-largest airline, switched to Sabre in October 2009 after it had shifted to a lighter winter schedule and canceled some flights.

A big challenge was the overnight transition of 840,000 files—transactions of customers who had already purchased flights—from WestJet's old reservations server in Calgary to Sabre's servers in Tulsa, Oklahoma. It didn't go well, says Bob Cummings, WestJet's executive vice president of marketing and sales, because the migration required WestJet agents to go through complex steps to process the data.

Making matters worse, WestJet didn't reduce the number of passengers on the flights operating after the cutover, nor did it tell customers of its upgrade plans until the day of the switch. "We didn't want to telegraph dates so a competitor would put on a big fare sale," Mr. Cummings says. WestJet's customer loyalty scores tumbled as a result of long waits and booking difficulties. The airline sent apology letters, offered flight credits to some customers, and a month later bolstered its call center with temporary staffers in India.

"We were in pretty good shape in mid-January from a service perspective," Mr. Cummings says. "But this is a three- to six-month recovery process." He says WestJet remains enthusiastic about the new system's potential, which will allow the airline to fulfill its plans to begin cooperating with U.S. and international airlines.

JetBlue, which has 151 aircraft, had the benefit of observing WestJet's transition, at WestJet's invitation. JetBlue decided to make its switch on a Friday night because Saturday traffic tends to be low. It trimmed its schedule that January weekend and sold abnormally low numbers of seats on remaining flights. With WestJet's crashing Web site in mind, JetBlue developed a backup site that it used twice for a few hours.

JetBlue also contracted for 500 outside reservations agents. After the switch, in which 900,000 passenger records were moved to Tulsa from Minneapolis, JetBlue routed basic calls to the temporary workers, leaving its own call staff to tackle more complex tasks. The extra agents stayed in place for two months, "one of the wisest investments we made," Zeni says.

There were still glitches. Call wait times increased, and not all of the airport kiosks and ticket printers came online right away. JetBlue still must add some booking functions in the future. But having Sabre, says JetBlue CEO Dave Barger, was an important factor in the airline's recent decision to cooperate on some routes in and out of Boston and New York with AMR Corp.'s American Airlines.

The word *upgrade* has long been a virtual bogeyman for SAP customers, given the historical pain, time, and cost of moving to a new version of the vendor's ERP software. For some time, SAP has been trying to entice users onto the modern ECC 6.0 through its "enhancement pack" program, which promises to let users add new features without the pain of a full technical upgrade. Customers can't take advantage of the packs until they move to 6.0.

For legacy customers who don't yet wish to upgrade, this means an increase in cost for vendor support, a jump to a third-party maintenance provider—which has its own uncertainties, given ongoing high-profile lawsuits—or a decision to go with no paid support at all. The pack strategy is therefore crucial for SAP, which needs to preserve lucrative maintenance revenue while making life easier for customers and stemming defections to other options, particularly SaaS (software as a service) applications, where upgrades are handled by the vendor.

SAP's strategy with the packs "makes a lot of sense," says Tim Ferguson, chief information officer at Northern Kentucky University. "Relatively speaking, compared to previous ways that SAP did this, they're very easy to install." NKU has served as a beta tester for the packs, which helped the school influence SAP to add key features it desired.

Although NKU's core SAP functions for billing, payroll, and other areas are fairly stable, the systems that touch students each day must evolve regularly, Ferguson says. One of the packs provided a new Web service that allows students to register for classes through their iPhones, for example. "The students that are coming out, this generation, they expect different types of services. We have to change to meet those needs," says Ferguson.

SAP's pack strategy is apparently pleasing some customers, but it still involves some work. "I've mostly heard good things," says Jon Reed, an independent analyst who closely tracks SAP. "But they're not quite as painless as SAP's marketing sometimes presented it."

System testing remains a crucial factor, Reed says. "Things break during an on-premise implementation and there's a preferred method of handling that, including sandboxing and testing, so when you pull that lever there are no problems. Customers still need to anticipate how it might break their system."

But SourceGas, a U.S. natural gas utility, had only one issue when installing the enhancement packs, specifically a problem with the "flexible real estate" functionality in SAP, says Michael Catterall, director of enterprise solutions. The company uses that module to manage information regarding the many property easements and right-of-ways it maintains for its infrastructure around the country.

"When we brought up enhancement pack 4, because of how we had it configured, we kind of broke it a little bit," he says. SourceGas plans to "keep watching the enhancement packs as they are coming out," Catterall says. "First, we're looking at where we can improve and get more out of modules we put in."

Meanwhile, there is the substantial task of getting to ECC 6.0 in the first place. Upgrade expenses can amount to 50–85 percent of the original implementation costs, with the price tag varying, depending on factors like the number of integration points and customizations, according to analyst Ray Wang, partner with Altimeter Group.

"Ultimately, upgrading makes sense for R/3 customers who are still committed to SAP and want new functionality provided in the packs," says Wang. But those customers potentially have other options these days, in the form of third-party maintenance from companies such as Rimini Street, as well as SaaS applications. Meanwhile, on-demand products from vendors such as Workday, which makes human-resources software, and CRM (customer relationship management) specialist Salesforce.com are being used by some legacy SAP customers, who are finding that integrating them back to the core ERP system isn't overly difficult, Wang says.

SOURCE: Susan Carey, "Two Paths to Software Upgrade," *Wall Street Journal*, April 13, 2010, and Chris Kanaracus, "SAP Users: Upgrading Has Its Benefits," *CIO.com*, April 9, 2010.

▼ CASE STUDY QUESTIONS

1. In the case, both airlines upgraded to the same application, but approached the upgrade process differently. What were those differences, and how much impact did they have on the outcome of the project?
2. What precautions did the organizations in the case take to prevent software upgrade problems? To what extent do you believe those precautions helped?

3. SAP customers have the choice between upgrading to the most recent version of the application suite or integrating third-party products into their existing infrastructure. What are the advantages and disadvantages of each alternative?

▼ REAL WORLD ACTIVITIES

1. Why are ERP upgrades so complex and expensive? What role does ERP customization, if any, play in this process? Go online and research other examples, discussing ERP upgrades. Can you discern a pattern in what seems to be the major cost drivers of the upgrade process?

2. Place yourself in the position of a WestJet or JetBlue customer while the upgrading was being implemented. What, if anything, would you have done differently if the companies told you a major software upgrade would be happening soon? Should they have told you? Break into small groups with your classmates and discuss these questions.

MANAGEMENT CHALLENGES

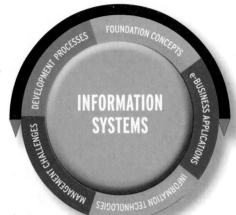

What managerial challenges do information systems pose for today's business enterprises? The two chapters of this module emphasize how managers and business professionals can manage the successful use of information technologies in a global economy.

- **Chapter 13: Security and Ethical Challenges** discusses the threats against and defenses needed for the performance and security of business information systems, as well as societal impact and ethical implications of information technology.

- **Chapter 14: Enterprise and Global Management of Information Technology** discusses the major challenges that information technology presents to business managers, the components of information systems management, and the managerial implications of the use of information technology in global business.

chapter 13

SECURITY AND ETHICAL CHALLENGES

INFORMATION SYSTEMS

MANAGEMENT CHALLENGES

LEARNING OBJECTIVES

13-1 Identify several ethical issues regarding how the use of information technologies in business affects employment, individuality, working conditions, privacy, crime, health, and solutions to societal problems.

13-2 Identify several types of security management strategies and defenses and explain how they can be used to ensure the security of business applications of information technology.

13-3 Propose several ways that business managers and professionals can help lessen the harmful effects and increase the beneficial effects of the use of information technology.

Security, Ethical, and Societal Challenges of IT

INTRODUCTION

There is no question that the use of information technology in business presents major security challenges, poses serious ethical questions, and affects society in significant ways. Therefore, in this chapter, we explore the threats to businesses and individuals as a result of many types of computer crime and unethical behavior. Later in the chapter, we will examine a variety of methods that companies use to manage the security and integrity of their business systems. Now let's look at a real-world example.

Read the Real World Challenge on the next page. We can learn a lot from this problem regarding the security and ethical issues that result from the pervasive use of IT in organizations and society today. See Figure 13.1.

The Nexus of IT, Ethics, Security, and Safety

The convenience we enjoy through the use of information technologies—having information at our fingertips, instant access to money and payment, and digital communications from anywhere on the planet—often comes with a hefty price tag. Technologies are introduced into an organization or society often without regard to the potentially negative impact or unintended consequences that such technologies might have. As we continue to invent new and more innovative technologies, we must consider the impact on society that these technologies have and what ethical issues exist in the areas of crime, privacy, individuality, employment, health, and working conditions. See Figure 13.2.

In other words, it is important to understand that information technology has had beneficial results, as well as detrimental effects, on society and people in each of these areas. For example, computerizing a manufacturing process may have the beneficial result of improving working conditions and producing products of higher quality at lower cost, but it also has the adverse effect of eliminating jobs and contributing to unemployment. Credit cards and digital money have made our lives easier and our transactions more convenient, but they have also created many new risks to our privacy, credit ratings, and even our identities. Wherever and whenever possible, your job as a manager or business professional should involve managing your work activities and those of others to minimize the detrimental effects of business applications of information technology and optimize their beneficial effects. That would represent an ethically responsible use of information technology.

ETHICAL RESPONSIBILITY OF BUSINESS PROFESSIONALS
LO 13-1

In any discussion of business ethics or ethical behavior, the level of debate rises and the number perspectives on what to do or not do rises exponentially. People have their own personal definitions of ethics and use those definitions to guide their actions. At the end of the day, ethics is something that "I can't really define, but I know it when I see it." As a business professional, you have a responsibility to promote ethical uses of information technology in the workplace. Whether or not you have managerial responsibilities, you should accept the ethical responsibilities that come with your work activities. That includes properly performing your role as a vital human resource in the business systems you help develop and use in your organization. As a business professional, it is your responsibility to make decisions about business activities and the use of information technologies that may have an ethical dimension that must be considered.

For example, should you electronically monitor your employees' work activities and e-mail? Should you let employees use their work computers for private business,

Harland Clarke– Reinventing the Company, Reinventing Security

Just a few years ago, Harland Clarke—then Clarke American—was best known as a manufacturer of checks and check-related products for financial institutions, businesses, and consumers. In essence, the company was a relatively simple manufacturing operation without a lot of heavy IT involvement. Very much in line with this identity, security then was more of a tactical concern than a strategic preoccupation, and it was largely focused on physical security for the nine manufacturing plants that the company operated in various locations within the United States. The company is headquartered in San Antonio, Texas, with regional corporate offices in Decatur, Georgia. Harland Clarke employs more than 4,500 in the United States and serves more than 11,000 clients of all kinds, with annual revenue of approximately $1.2 billion.

Today, Harland Clarke offers (1) checks and related products, as well as forms and treasury supplies, to financial

FIGURE 13.1

There are security implications to almost everything we do.
SOURCE: © Punchstock.

services, retail, and software providers; (2) direct marketing services, including direct marketing campaigns, direct mail, database marketing, telemarketing, and e-mail marketing; (3) check-related delivery and fraud prevention services; and (4) stationery, business cards, and other business and home office products to consumers and small businesses. Through its Harland Financial Solutions segment the company provides technology products and services comprising lending and mortgage compliance and origination applications, risk management solutions, business intelligence solutions, Internet and mobile banking applications, branch automation solutions, and core processing systems to financial services clients. Much has changed in a short time.

As the company sought to expand beyond its check manufacturing roots and started adding other products and services, such as customer service centers, direct response marketing and electronic commerce capabilities, its approach to security also began to change. In the midst of a CEO-driven reinvention of the company, John Petrie, now chief information security officer, joined the organization in 2004. "There were issues around protecting electronic data, and our printing processes had changed over to the digital age, so there was a transformation that had occurred," Petrie says. "We knew we had to change our risk management structure." More broadly, the way in which the company culture viewed security—as a technical issue, mostly dealing with physical problems—had to change. As the company moved toward becoming a secure provider of checks and check-related services, and not just a manufacturer, other processes and management practices needed to be put in place. By 2005, most of the financial institutions doing business with Harland Clarke were demanding more security and stricter controls from their suppliers due to new regulations that required them to provide evidence of end-to-end security in their supply chains. To put into context the magnitude of the role that Harland Clarke plays in those supply chains, the company fulfilled more than 110 million checks throughout the country in 2006 alone.

"Harland Clarke has a responsibility to our clients and their customers, shareholders, and employees to keep our organization secure by adhering to high levels of integrated security standards," says Petrie, underscoring that security is not only an internal concern for a company, but can also significantly affect the way in which it conducts business with its customers, suppliers, and partners. In the current organizational structure, security is a decentralized function that is governed jointly by the chief information officer and the various plant managers. The chief information security officer—that is, John Petrie—reports directly to the chief information officer. Physical security, on the other hand, belongs to a chief security officer, who also owns incident management. The current chief security officer, former FBI Special Agent-in-Charge Pat Patterson, reports to the senior vice president of Administrative Services, together with other support areas such as human resources, general counsel, compliance and privacy, and so forth. The senior vice president in turn reports to the chief executive officer of the company. As John Petrie started outlining a transition plan for a new security mind-set throughout the company, he wondered where he wanted to go with this. In his mind, security should not be a collection of isolated efforts here and there, but rather a concerted action by the entire company to achieve the desired results. Going there would require incorporating security into the daily work routines of all employees, a major change because they were not used to having to worry about those issues. "We wanted to make sure security was not a thing that sits out there and functions on its own," says Petrie.

Next, Petrie believes that security, although surely requiring a strong technical foundation, is also very much a business issue. Once you start thinking about it, there are security implications in a lot of different business activities where, at first sight, one would not think that to be the case. For example, it is now commonplace to hear that "this call is being recorded for training and quality assurance purposes." When those calls involve financial services or offer acceptances by customers, regulations also required that they be recorded as a means of assuring that the customer willingly entered into a contract. What happens to those calls afterwards? That is a security issue, as well. Come to think of it,

any time a company captures and stores data of any kind, there will be some security implications.

Finally, we must also decide what kind of security we are talking about. Security is surely about passwords and user names, and maybe about biometrics, transaction logs, and access times. There is also role-based security to ensure that the employee who authorizes payments to vendors cannot at the same time modify the master vendor list, which would open the door to payments to fictitious vendors and fraud. Surely, it is also about virus, worms, malware, and spyware; unauthorized downloading and installing of software on company equipment; storing and sharing illegal copies of songs or movies; and general concerns about unauthorized use by employees. This all falls under the heading of security. However, it is also about access cards, closed-circuit video cameras, and disaster recovery and business continuity; patches to software and operating systems; firewalls and networks; and upgrading to new applications. These are all issues related to security—how and where each issue should be managed is a great question. Maybe Petrie should start looking at convergence: the integration of logical security, information security, physical and personnel security, business continuity, disaster recovery, and safety risk management.

Are all of these issues equally important? Or equally likely to happen? Should Petrie worry more about downloading songs, or weak passwords? Unsecured operating systems or missing access cards? How to best prioritize where to allocate his limited resources?

So many questions, so little time! Where should Petrie—and Harland Clarke—go from here?

SOURCE: Mary Brandel, "Harland Clarke Rechecks Risk Management," *CSO*, October 16, 2007; "Verizon Business Recognizes Harland Clarke's Security Excellence with Prestigious Security Certification," *PRNewsWire*, March 13, 2009; and www.harlandclarke.com, accessed June 14, 2011.

QUESTIONS TO CONSIDER

1. How should John Petrie handle the fact that, realistically, not all security issues are equally important? In any case, how do you define importance in this context?

2. What does the reporting structure of a company say about the importance of a particular function or department? What changes, if any, would you make at Harland Clarke?

3. How do you get people who are not usually security-conscious, or at least never had to be, to be more aware of the potential security implications of their daily routines? What kind of initiatives would you introduce? Provide some examples.

FIGURE 13.2

Important aspects of the security, ethical, and societal dimensions of the use of information technology in business. Remember that information technologies can support both beneficial and detrimental effects on society in each of the areas shown.

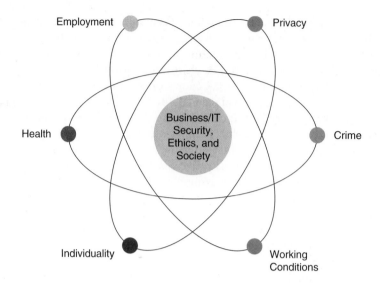

or let them take home copies of software for their personal use? Should you electronically access your employees' personnel records or workstation files? Should you sell customer information extracted from transaction processing systems to other companies? These are a few examples of the types of decisions you will have to make that have an ethical dimension. So let's take a closer look at several *ethical foundations* in business and information technology.

Business Ethics

Business ethics is concerned with the numerous ethical questions that managers must confront as part of their daily business decision making. For example, Figure 13.3 outlines some of the basic categories of ethical issues and specific business practices that have serious ethical consequences. Notice that the issues of intellectual property rights, customer and employee privacy, security of company records, and workplace safety are highlighted because they have been major areas of ethical controversy in information technology.

How can managers make ethical decisions when confronted with business issues such as those listed in Figure 13.3? Several important alternatives based on theories of corporate social responsibility can be used. For example, in business ethics, the *stockholder theory* holds that managers are agents of the stockholders, and their only ethical responsibility is to increase the profits of the business without violating the law or engaging in fraudulent practices.

In contrast, the *social contract theory* states that companies have ethical responsibilities to all members of society, which allows corporations to exist according to a social contract. The first condition of the contract requires companies to enhance the economic

FIGURE 13.3

Basic categories of ethical business issues. Information technology has caused ethical controversy in the areas of intellectual property rights, customer and employee privacy, security of company information, and workplace safety.

Equity	Rights	Honesty	Exercise of Corporate Power
Executive salaries	Corporate due process	Employee conflicts of interest	Product safety
Comparable worth	Employee health screening	**Security of company information**	Environmental issues
Product pricing	**Customer privacy**	Inappropriate gifts	Disinvestment
Intellectual property rights	**Employee privacy**	Advertising content	Corporate contributions
Noncompetitive agreements	Sexual harassment	Government contract issues	Social issues raised by religious organizations
	Affirmative action	Financial and cash management procedures	Plant/facility closures and downsizing
	Equal employment opportunity	Questionable business practices in foreign countries	Political action committees
	Shareholder interests		**Workplace safety**
	Employment at will		
	Whistle-blowing		

satisfaction of consumers and employees. They must do that without polluting the environment or depleting natural resources, misusing political power, or subjecting their employees to dehumanizing working conditions. The second condition requires companies to avoid fraudulent practices, show respect for their employees as human beings, and avoid practices that systematically worsen the position of any group in society.

In yet another perspective, the *stakeholder theory* of business ethics maintains that managers have an ethical responsibility to manage a firm for the benefit of all of its stakeholders, that is, all individuals and groups that have a stake in, or claim on, a company. These stakeholders usually include the corporation's stockholders, employees, customers, suppliers, and the local community. Sometimes the term is broadened to include all groups who can affect or be affected by the corporation, such as competitors, government agencies, and special-interest groups. Balancing the claims of conflicting stakeholders is obviously not an easy task for managers.

Ethical Use of Technology

In addition to the general ethical perspectives outlined above, another important ethical dimension deals specifically with the ethics of the use of any form of technology. For example, Figure 13.4 outlines four principles of technology ethics. These principles can serve as basic ethical requirements that companies should meet to help ensure the ethical implementation of information technologies and information systems in business.

One common example of technology ethics involves some of the health risks of using computer workstations for extended periods in high-volume data entry job positions. Many organizations display ethical behavior by scheduling work breaks and limiting the time that data entry workers stare at a computer monitor to minimize their risk of developing a variety of work-related health disorders, such as hand or eye injuries. The health impact of information technology is discussed later in this chapter.

Ethical Guidelines

We have outlined a few ethical principles that can serve as the basis for ethical conduct by managers, end users, and IS professionals. But what more specific guidelines might help your ethical use of information technology? Many companies and organizations answer that question today with detailed policies for ethical computer and Internet usage by their employees. For example, most policies specify that company computer workstations and networks are company resources that must be used only for work-related uses, whether using internal networks or the Internet.

Another way to answer this question is to examine statements of responsibilities contained in codes of professional conduct for IS professionals. A good example is the code of professional conduct of the Association of Information Technology Professionals (AITP), an organization of professionals in the computing field. Its code of conduct outlines the ethical considerations inherent in the major responsibilities of an IS professional. Figure 13.5 is a portion of the AITP code of conduct.

Principles of Technology Ethics
• **Proportionality.** The good achieved by the technology must outweigh the harm or risk. Moreover, there must be no alternative that achieves the same or comparable benefits with less harm or risk.
• **Informed Consent.** Those affected by the technology should understand and accept the risks.
• **Justice.** The benefits and burdens of the technology should be distributed fairly. Those who benefit should bear their fair share of the risks, and those who do not benefit should not suffer a significant increase in risk.
• **Minimized Risk.** Even if judged acceptable by the other three guidelines, the technology must be implemented so as to avoid all unnecessary risk.

FIGURE 13.4

Ethical principles to help evaluate the potential harms or risks of the use of new technologies.

FIGURE 13.5

Part of the AITP standards of professional conduct. This code can serve as a model for ethical conduct by business end users as well as IS professionals.

AITP Standards of Professional Conduct
In recognition of my obligation to my employer I shall:
• Avoid conflicts of interest and ensure that my employer is aware of any potential conflicts.
• Protect the privacy and confidentiality of all information entrusted to me.
• Not misrepresent or withhold information that is germane to the situation.
• Not attempt to use the resources of my employer for personal gain or for any purpose without proper approval.
• Not exploit the weakness of a computer system for personal gain or personal satisfaction.
In recognition of my obligation to society I shall:
• Use my skill and knowledge to inform the public in all areas of my expertise.
• To the best of my ability, ensure that the products of my work are used in a socially responsible way.
• Support, respect, and abide by the appropriate local, state, provincial, and federal laws.
• Never misrepresent or withhold information that is germane to a problem or a situation of public concern, nor will I allow any such known information to remain unchallenged.
• Not use knowledge of a confidential or personal nature in any unauthorized manner to achieve personal gain.

SOURCE: 2007 PricewaterhouseCoopers Global Security Survey.

Business and IS professionals can live up to their ethical responsibilities by voluntarily following such guidelines. For example, you can be a responsible professional by (1) acting with integrity, (2) increasing your professional competence, (3) setting high standards of personal performance, (4) accepting responsibility for your work, and (5) advancing the health, privacy, and general welfare of the public. Then you would be demonstrating ethical conduct, avoiding computer crime, and increasing the security of any information system you develop or use.

Enron Corporation: Failure in Business Ethics

Much has been said about the driven, cultlike ethos of the organization that styled itself "the world's leading company." Truth be told, for all its razzle-dazzle use of Internet technology, a lot of the things Enron did weren't so very exceptional: paying insanely large bonuses to executives, for example, often in the form of stock options (a practice that not only hid true compensation costs but also encouraged managers to keep the stock price up by any means necessary); promising outlandish growth, year after year, and making absurdly confident predictions about every new market it entered, however untested; scarcely ever admitting a weakness to the outside world; and showing scant interest in the questions or doubts of some in its own ranks about its questionable, unethical, and even illegal business and accounting practices.

Credibility comes hard in business. You earn it slowly by conducting yourself with integrity year in and year out, or by showing exceptional leadership in exceptional circumstances, such as on September 11, 2001. The surest way to lose it, short of being caught in an outright lie, is to promise much and deliver little. Those, at least, are two conclusions suggested by an exclusive survey of executives that Clark, Martire, and Bartolomeo conducted for *Business 2.0*.

Executives rated Enron Chairman and CEO Ken Lay the least credible of the business figures in the survey. Perhaps it had something to do with statements like:

- "Our performance has never been stronger; our business model has never been more robust; our growth has never been more certain. . . . I have never felt better about the prospects for the company." —E-mail to employees, August 14, 2001

- "The company is probably in the strongest and best shape that it has ever been in." —Interview in *BusinessWeek*, August 24, 2001

- "Our 26 percent increase in [profits] shows the very strong results of our core wholesale and retail energy businesses and our natural gas pipelines." —Press release, October 16, 2001

Yet three weeks later, Enron admitted that it had overstated earnings by $586 million since 1997. Within a few more weeks, Enron also disclosed a stunning $638 million third-quarter loss and then filed for Chapter 13 bankruptcy.

Dick Hudson, former chief information officer of Houston-based oil drilling company Global Marine Inc. and now president of Hudson & Associates, an executive IT consulting firm in Katy, Texas, thinks Enron started with a good business strategy and that if it hadn't pushed the envelope, it could well have been a successful Fortune 1000 firm. Instead, it aimed for the Fortune 10, so it got into markets such as broadband, which is a tough nut to crack even for the industry's leaders. "Those good old boys in Houston, they had to walk with the big dogs," accuses Hudson. "They are a textbook case of greed and mismanagement."

On May 25, 2006, Kenneth Lay was convicted on six counts of securities and wire fraud and faced a total of 45 years in prison. Lay died on July 5, 2006, before sentencing could be passed. His protégé, Jeffrey K. Skilling, was convicted of 19 of 28 counts, and was sentenced to 24 years in prison. Andrew S. Fastow, the former chief financial officer, was sentenced to six years in prison for his role in the conspiracy that led to the collapse of Enron. His former lieutenant, Michael Kopper, received a reduced sentence of 37 months for cooperating with the investigation.

SOURCE: Melissa Solomon and Michael Meehan, "Enron Lesson: Tech Is for Support," *Computerworld*, February 18, 2002.

COMPUTER CRIME
LO 13-2

Cyber-crime is becoming one of the Net's growth businesses. Today, criminals are doing everything from stealing intellectual property and committing fraud to unleashing viruses and committing acts of cyberterrorism.

Computer crime, a pervasive threat to society, is caused by the criminal or irresponsible actions of individuals who are taking advantage of the widespread use and vulnerability of computers and the Internet and other networks. It presents a major challenge to the ethical use of information technologies. Computer crime also poses serious threats to the integrity, safety, and survival of most business systems and thus makes the development of effective security methods a top priority. See Figure 13.6.

Computer crime is defined by the Association of Information Technology Professionals (AITP) as including (1) *the unauthorized use, access, modification, and destruction of hardware, software, data, or network resources;* (2) *the unauthorized release of information;* (3) *the unauthorized copying of software;* (4) *denying an end user access to his or her own hardware, software, data, or network resources;* and (5) *using or conspiring to use computer or network resources to obtain information or tangible property illegally.* This definition was promoted by the AITP in a Model Computer Crime Act and is reflected in many computer crime laws.

Equally important is the understanding that computers don't commit crimes; rather, people commit crimes using computers. From such an understanding, we can better see where the source of the criminal threat comes from and how to tailor or manage our technology to create an effective deterrent to computer crime. As with most criminal acts, opportunity and ease of commision are often at the heart of the motivation to commit the crime. The harder it is to commit the crime, the less likely

FIGURE 13.6
How large companies are protecting themselves from cyber-crime.

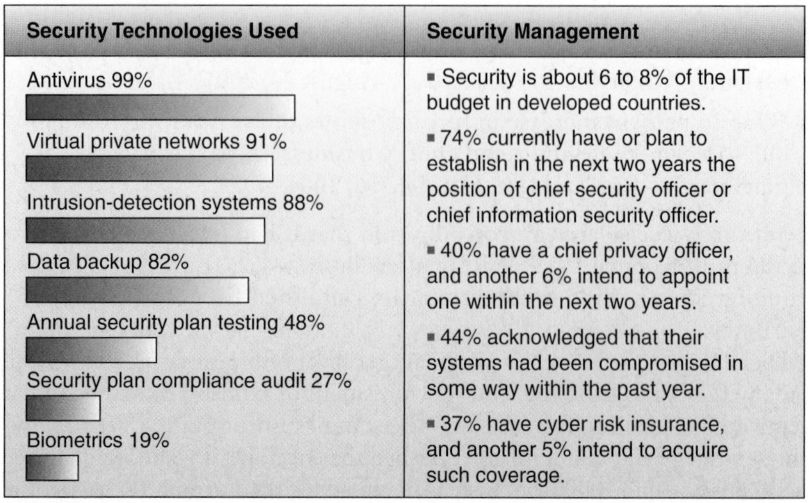

Security Technologies Used	Security Management
Antivirus 99%	■ Security is about 6 to 8% of the IT budget in developed countries.
Virtual private networks 91%	■ 74% currently have or plan to establish in the next two years the position of chief security officer or chief information security officer.
Intrusion-detection systems 88%	
Data backup 82%	■ 40% have a chief privacy officer, and another 6% intend to appoint one within the next two years.
Annual security plan testing 48%	■ 44% acknowledged that their systems had been compromised in some way within the past year.
Security plan compliance audit 27%	
Biometrics 19%	■ 37% have cyber risk insurance, and another 5% intend to acquire such coverage.

SOURCE: 2007 PricewaterhouseCoopers Global Security Survey.

the crime will be committed. The problem with this seemingly simple approach is that as we make the deterrent more effective (i.e., make it harder to commit the crime), we often find that our access to the technology becomes less efficient. Think of it this way: The more locks you have, the harder it is for a crook to break in through the door. That said, the more locks you have, the harder it is for you to unlock and pass through your door. That is the essence of the constant trade-off that business professionals face when managing technology to prevent its use in a criminal or unethical manner.

The Online Crusade against Phishing

Until just a few years ago, Gary Warner did not have the kind of day job you'd expect from an antiphishing crusader. He didn't work for a security vendor or a bank, or any kind of company you'd expect to care about phishing. Warner's career as a cyber-sleuth began on Halloween 2000. That's when his company's Web site was defaced by an entity named Pimpshiz as part of a pro-Napster Internet graffiti campaign.

"My boss came to me and said, 'Find out who did this and put them in jail,'" said Warner, who was at the time an IT staffer with Energen, a Birmingham, Alabama, oil and gas company. It was an eye-opening experience. "I called the police and they were like, 'What do you want us to do?'" he said. Months later, when Pimpshiz struck servers at NASA, Warner reached out, calling staff there and saying "Hey, we know who this guy is. Here's his name and address."

Since then, Warner has quietly become one of the most-respected authorities on phishing in the United States—the kind of guy that federal agents and banking IT staff call when they want to know how to catch the bad guys and shut down their credit-card-stealing Web sites.

With Warner's help, authorities eventually arrested Pimpshiz, whose real name is Robert Lyttle, in connection with the defacements.

Warner said that the Pimpshiz case was formative, underlining how hard it is for law enforcement to catch the bad guys on the Internet. "The experience showed me that it's not that they don't care," Warner said. "Their hands are tied by the legal process."

In July 2007, with recommendations from FBI and Secret Service agents, Warner took a job as Director of Research in Computer Forensics with the University of Alabama at Birmingham (UAB). He also began working with law enforcement, not only educating FBI and Secret Service agents on how crimes were committed, but also helping to track down the criminals and helping with takedowns.

For Warner, the work isn't so much a job, as it's his moral responsibility as a computer scientist. "One of the things that really bothered me from the very beginning was people who were using my field to attack other people," he said. "The way I see it, this is our Internet. I'm going to stand at the end of my driveway and protect what's mine."

Warner is now focusing on fighting cyber-crime full-time and on training a new generation of network forensics investigators.

"You wouldn't believe the looks in their eyes the first time they got an e-mail back from a Webmaster saying, 'Thanks for letting me know. I just shut that down.'" Five days after final exams at the University of Alabama at Birmingham and though it would have no effect on their grades, four students were still coming into the labs to help shut down phishers.

"That idea that as a private citizen, you can help, that's the kind of thing we're trying to inspire," he says.

SOURCE: Robert McMillan, "Crime and Punishment: The White Knight of Phish-Busting," *Computerworld*, December 31, 2007.

Hacking and Cracking

Cyber-thieves have at their fingertips a dozen dangerous tools, from "scans" that ferret out weaknesses in Web site software programs to "sniffers" that snatch passwords.

Hacking, in computerese, is the obsessive use of computers or the unauthorized access and use of networked computer systems. Hackers can be outsiders or company employees who use the Internet and other networks to steal or damage data and programs. One of the issues in hacking is what to do about a hacker who commits only *electronic breaking and entering,* that is, gets access to a computer system and reads some files but neither steals nor damages anything. This situation is common in computer crime cases that are prosecuted. In most cases, courts have found that the typical computer crime statute language prohibiting malicious access to a computer system did apply to anyone gaining unauthorized access to another's computer networks. See Figure 13.7.

Hackers can monitor e-mail, Web server access, or file transfers to extract passwords, steal network files, or plant data that will cause a system to welcome intruders. A hacker may also use remote services that allow one computer on a network to execute programs on another computer to gain privileged access within a network. Telnet, an Internet tool for interactive use of remote computers, can help hackers discover information to plan other attacks. Hackers have used Telnet to access a computer's e-mail port, for example, to monitor e-mail messages for passwords and other information about privileged user accounts and network resources. These are just some of the typical types of computer crimes that hackers commit on the Internet on a regular basis. That's why Internet security measures like encryption and firewalls, as discussed in the next section, are so vital to the success of e-commerce and other e-business applications.

The hacking community is quick to make the distinction between hacking and cracking. A cracker (also called a black hat or darkside hacker) is a malicious or criminal hacker. This term is seldom used outside of the security industry and by some modern programmers. Usually a cracker is a person who maintains knowledge of the vulnerabilities he or she finds and exploits them for private advantage, not revealing them to either the general public or the manufacturer for correction. Many crackers promote individual freedom and accessibility over privacy and security. Crackers may seek to expand holes in systems; any attempts made to patch software are generally to prevent others from also compromising a system over which they have already obtained

FIGURE 13.7

Examples of common hacking tactics to assault companies through the Internet and other networks.

Common Hacking Tactics and Security Exploits
Denial of Service. This is becoming a common networking prank. By hammering a Web site's equipment with too many requests for information, an attacker can effectively clog the system, slowing performance or even crashing the site. This method of overloading computers is sometimes used to cover up an attack.
Vulnerability Scans. Widespread probes of the Internet to determine types of computers, services, and connections. That way the bad guys can take advantage of weaknesses in a particular make of computer or software program.
Packet Sniffer. Programs that covertly search individual packets of data as they pass through the Internet, capturing passwords or the entire contents.
Spoofing (Phishing). Faking an e-mail address or Web page to trick users into passing along critical information like passwords or credit card numbers.
Trojan Horse. A program that, unknown to the user, contains instructions that exploit a known vulnerability in some software.
Back Doors. In case the original entry point has been detected, having a few hidden ways back makes reentry easy—and difficult to detect.
Malicious Applets. Tiny programs, sometimes written in the popular Java computer language, that misuse your computer's resources, modify files on the hard disk, send fake e-mail, or steal passwords.
War Dialing. Programs that automatically dial thousands of telephone numbers in search of a way in through a modem connection.
Logic Bombs. An instruction in a computer program that triggers a malicious act.
Buffer Overflow. A technique for crashing or gaining control of a computer by sending too much data to the buffer in a computer's memory.
Password Crackers. Software that can guess passwords.
Social Engineering. A tactic used to gain access to computer systems by talking unsuspecting company employees out of valuable information such as passwords.
Dumpster Diving. Sifting through a company's garbage to find information to help break into their computers. Sometimes the information is used to make a stab at social engineering more credible.

secure control. In the most extreme cases, a cracker may work to cause damage maliciously or make threats to do so for blackmail purposes.

The term *cracker* was coined by Richard Stallman to provide an alternative to abusing the existing word *hacker* for this meaning. This term's use is limited (as is "black hat") mostly to some areas of the computer and security field and, even there, is considered controversial. One group that refers to themselves as hackers consists of skilled computer enthusiasts. The other, and more common usage, refers to people who attempt to gain unauthorized access to computer systems. Many members of the first group attempt to convince people that intruders should be called crackers rather than hackers, but the common usage remains ingrained.

Cyber-Theft

Many computer crimes involve the theft of money. In the majority of cases, they are inside jobs that involve unauthorized network entry and fraudulent alteration of computer databases to cover the tracks of the employees involved. Of course, many computer crimes involve the use of the Internet. One early example was the theft of $11 million from Citibank in late 1994. Russian hacker Vladimir Levin and his accomplices in St. Petersburg used the Internet for an electronic break-in of Citibank's mainframe systems in New York. They then succeeded in transferring the funds from several Citibank accounts to their own accounts at banks in Finland, Israel, and California.

In most cases, the scope of such financial losses is much larger than the incidents reported. Companies don't usually reveal that they have been targets or victims of computer crime. They fear scaring customers and provoking complaints by shareholders. In fact, several British banks, including the Bank of London, paid hackers more than a half million dollars not to reveal information about electronic break-ins.

Cyberterrorism

Cyberterrorism is the leveraging of an organization's or government's computers and information, particularly via the Internet, to cause physical, real-world harm or severe disruption of infrastructure. There are some that argue cyberterrorism is really a form of hacking or information warfare. They disagree with labeling it terrorism because of the unlikelihood of the creation of fear, significant physical harm, or death in a population using electronic means, considering current attack and protective technologies.

The National Conference of State Legislatures (NCSL) puts a much finer point on the definition of the term:

> *the use of information technology by terrorist groups and individuals to further their agenda. This can include use of information technology to organize and execute attacks against networks, computer systems and telecommunications infrastructures, or for exchanging information or making threats electronically.*

Cyberterrorism can have a serious large-scale influence on significant numbers of people. It can significantly weaken a country's economy, thereby denying it access to vital resources and making it more vulnerable to military attack. Cyberterror can also affect Internet-based businesses. Like bricks and mortar retailers and service providers, most Web sites that produce income (whether by advertising, monetary exchange for goods, or paid services) could stand to lose money in the event of downtime created by cyber-criminals. As Internet businesses have increasing economic importance to countries, what is normally cyber-crime becomes more political and therefore "terror" related.

To date, there have been no reported cyber-attacks on the United States. There have, however, been several large-scale examples of cyberterrorism in other countries. One such example occurred in Romania when cyberterrorists illegally gained access to the computers controlling the life-support systems at an Antarctic research station, endangering the 58 scientists involved. However, the culprits were stopped before damage actually occurred. Mostly nonpolitical acts of sabotage have caused financial and other damage, as in a case where a disgruntled employee caused the release of untreated sewage into water in Maroochy Shire, Australia. Computer viruses have degraded or shut down some nonessential systems in nuclear power plants, but this is not believed to have been a deliberate attack.

More recently, in May 2007, Estonia was subjected to a mass cyber-attack in the wake of the removal of a Russian World War II war memorial from downtown Talinn. The attack was a distributed denial of service attack in which selected sites were bombarded with traffic in order to force them off-line; nearly all Estonian government ministry networks, as well as two major Estonian bank networks, were knocked off-line; in addition, the political party Web site of Estonia's current prime minister, Andrus Ansip, featured a counterfeit letter of apology from Ansip for removing the memorial statue. Despite speculation that the attack had been coordinated by the Russian government, Estonia's defense minister admitted he had no evidence linking cyber attacks to Russian authorities. Russia called accusations of its involvement "unfounded," and neither NATO nor European Commission experts were able to find any proof of official Russian government participation. In January 2008, a man from Estonia was convicted for launching the attacks against the Estonian Reform Party Web site and fined.

Cyber-Warfare

A new term, cyber-warfare, was coined by government security expert Richard A. Clarke, in his book Cyber War, and defined as "*actions by a nation-state to penetrate another nation's computers or networks for the purposes of causing damage or disruption.*" In 2009, U.S. President Barack Obama declared America's digital infrastructure to be a "strategic national asset," and in May 2010 the Pentagon set up its new U.S. Cyber Command (USCYBERCOM), headed by General Keith B. Alexander, director of the National Security Agency (NSA), to defend American military networks and attack other countries' systems. The United Kingdom has also set up a cybersecurity and "operations centre" based in Government Communications Headquarters (GCHQ), the British equivalent of the NSA. In the United States, however, Cyber Command is only set up to protect the military, whereas the government and corporate infrastructures are primarily the responsibility of the Department of Homeland Security and private companies, respectively.

In February 2010, top American lawmakers warned that the threat of a crippling attack on telecommunications and computer networks was sharply on the rise. Many interested government and private agencies have taken the position that numerous key sectors of the U.S. economy, along with that of other nations, are currently at risk, including cyber-threats to public and private facilities, banking and finance, transportation, manufacturing, medical, education, and government, all of which are now dependent on computers for daily operations. Many reports suggest China and Russia, among other countries, are organizing for cyber-war. Iran boasts of having the world's second-largest cyber-army. James Gosler, a government cybersecurity specialist, worries that the United States has a severe shortage of computer security specialists; he estimates that there are only about 1,000 qualified people in the country today, but that we need a force of 20,000 to 30,000 skilled experts. This is a new job opportunity for IS/IT professionals that will only continue to grow.

Leaving Your Job? Don't Take Anything with You

Consider the following scenario: A senior executive has been laid off. As she leaves the company building, she takes her family photographs, various office mementos, and the passwords of several hundred employees. Or this other example: One of your most experienced salespeople hears through the grapevine that there will be layoffs, so she downloads to her free e-mail account the list of A+ customers with their ordering and payment histories. Scenarios like these occur every day, and experts say that even the most trusted employees can be driven to data theft and other crimes when faced with the prospect of job layoffs.

In a 2008 survey by IT security firm Cyber-Ark Software, more than half of those concerned about upcoming layoffs said they had already downloaded competitive corporate data which they planned to use to land a new—or better— job. In fact, 58 percent of Wall Street workers admitted to doing so; 71 percent of all workers said they would definitely take data with them if faced with the prospect of an immediate layoff. "When people are desperate to pay for the roof over their head or put food on the table, they are capable of doing things they would not normally do, which is why crime goes up when the economy suffers," says David Griffeth, vice president of Business Line Integration and Reporting at RBS Citizens Bank. "That does not go away because you have a bachelor's degree or a master's degree. It is a common fear based on need. You have a different level of comfort with the crime you commit."

Things can get even more complicated when those laid off are IT staffers themselves, who often have more access to data, passwords, and so forth than most other people. As an example, consider Roger Duronio, a former IT worker at UBS Paine Webber who was convicted—and sentenced to eight years in prison—for planting a software logic bomb (code that triggers malicious functions under certain conditions; for example, delete all customer accounts on a certain date). He was able to do this because he "had access everywhere," in his own words. System administrators and those with special access privileges pose an even bigger threat.

Also somewhat surprising—and upsetting—is the fact that many companies do not have the processes in place to manage IT security after employees leave the company, whether on their own or as a result of layoffs, which are so-called orphaned accounts. A study of IT and HR executives by Symark International shows that 4 out of 10 companies do not know whether user accounts remain active after employees leave; in fact, 30 percent of those executives reported that they have no process to locate and disable orphaned accounts. What is even more troublesome is that 38 percent of them do not even know if those accounts register any activity after people no longer work there.

SOURCE: Julia King, "Securing All Exits," *Computerworld*, March 2, 2009.

Unauthorized Use at Work

The ***unauthorized use*** of computer systems and networks can be called *time and resource theft*. A common example is unauthorized use of company-owned computer networks by employees. This use may range from doing private consulting or personal finances to playing video games to unauthorized use of the Internet on company networks. Network monitoring software, called *sniffers*, is frequently used to monitor network traffic to evaluate network capacity, as well as to reveal evidence of improper use. See Figure 13.8.

According to one survey, 90 percent of U.S. workers admit to surfing recreational sites during office hours, and 84 percent say they send personal e-mail from work. So this kind of activity alone may not get you fired from your job; however, other Internet activities at work can bring instant dismissal. For example, *The New York Times* fired

FIGURE 13.8

Internet abuses in the workplace.

Internet Abuses	Activity
General E-mail Abuses	Include spamming, harassments, chain letters, solicitations, spoofing, propagations of viruses/worms, and defamatory statements.
Unauthorized Usage and Access	Sharing of passwords and access into networks without permission.
Copyright Infringement/Plagiarism	Using illegal or pirated software that costs organizations millions of dollars because of copyright infringements. Copying of Web sites and copyrighted logos.
Newsgroup Postings	Posting of messages on various non-work-related topics from sex to lawn care advice.
Transmission of Confidential Data	Using the Internet to display or transmit trade secrets.
Pornography	Accessing sexually explicit sites from the workplace as well as the display, distribution, and surfing of these offensive sites.
Hacking	Hacking of Web sites, ranging from denial of service attacks to accessing organizational databases.
Non-Work-Related Download/Upload	Propagation of software that ties up office bandwidth. Use of programs that allow the transmission of movies, music, and graphical materials.
Leisure Use of the Internet	Loafing around the Internet, which includes shopping, sending e-cards and personal e-mail, gambling online, chatting, game playing, auctioning, stock trading, and doing other personal activities.
Usage of External ISPs	Using an external ISP to connect to the Internet to avoid detection.
Moonlighting	Using office resources such as networks and computers to organize and conduct personal business (side jobs).

SOURCE: Keng Siau, Fiona Fui-Hoon Nah, and Limei Teng, "Acceptable Internet Use Policy," *Communications of the ACM*, January 2002, p. 76.

23 workers because they were distributing racist and sexually offensive jokes on the company's e-mail system.

Xerox Corp. fired more than 40 workers for spending up to eight hours a day on pornography sites on the Web. Several employees even downloaded pornographic videos, which took so much network bandwidth that it choked the company network and prevented coworkers from sending or receiving e-mail. Xerox instituted an eight-member SWAT team on computer abuse that uses software to review every Web site its 40,000 computer users view each day. Other companies clamp down even harder by installing software like SurfWatch, which enables them to block and monitor access to off-limit Web sites.

Survey: E-mail and Internet Abuse Can Get You Fired

Think you can get away with using e-mail and the Internet in violation of company policy? *Think again.* A new survey found that more than one-quarter of employers have fired workers for misusing e-mail, and one-third have fired workers for misusing the Internet on the job. The study, conducted by the American Management Association and the ePolicy Institute, surveyed 304 U.S. companies of all sizes.

The vast majority of bosses who fired workers for Internet misuse, 84 percent, said the employee was accessing porn or other inappropriate content. Although it is obviously wrong to look at inappropriate content on company time, a surprising number of people were fired just for surfing the Web. As many as 34 percent of managers in the study said they let workers go for excessive personal use of the Internet, according to the survey.

Among managers who fired workers for e-mail misuse, 64 percent did so because the employee violated company policy and 62 percent said the workers' e-mail contained inappropriate or offensive language. More than a quarter of bosses said they fired workers for excessive personal use of e-mail, and 22 percent said their workers were fired for breaching confidentiality rules in e-mail.

Companies are worried about the inappropriate use of the Internet, and so 66 percent of those in the study said they monitor Internet connections. As many as 65 percent of them use software to block inappropriate Web sites. Eighteen percent of the companies block URLs (uniform resource locators) to prevent workers from visiting external blogs.

Companies use different methods to monitor workers' computers, with 45 percent of those participating in the survey tracking content, keystrokes, and time spent at the keyboard. An additional 43 percent store and review computer files. Twelve percent monitor blogs to track content about the company, and 10 percent monitor social-networking sites.

The researchers found that even though only two states require companies to notify their workers that they're monitoring them, most tell employees of their monitoring activities. Of the companies that monitor workers in the survey, 83 percent said they tell employees that they are monitoring content, keystrokes, and time spent at the keyboard. As many as 84 percent tell employees that they review computer activity, and 71 percent alert workers that they monitor their e-mails.

SOURCE: Nancy Gohring, "Over 50% of Companies Fire Workers for E-Mail, 'Net Abuse," *CIO Magazine*, February 28, 2008.

Software Piracy

Computer programs are valuable property and thus subject to theft from computer systems. However, unauthorized copying of software, or ***software piracy,*** is also a major form of software theft. Software piracy by company employees is widespread, which has resulted in lawsuits by the Software Publishers Association, an industry association of software developers, against major corporations that allowed unauthorized copying of their programs.

Unauthorized copying is illegal because software is intellectual property that is protected by copyright law and user licensing agreements. For example, in the United States, commercial software packages are protected by the Computer Software Piracy and Counterfeiting Amendment to the Federal Copyright Act. In most cases, the purchase of a commercial software package is really a payment to license its fair use by an individual end user. Therefore, many companies sign *site licenses* that legally allow them to make a certain number of copies for use by their employees at a particular location. Other alternatives are *shareware*, which allows you to make copies of software for others, and *public domain software*, which is not copyrighted.

The most recent study by the Business Software Alliance (http://portal.bsa.org/globalpiracy2010), an antipiracy group whose members include Apple Computer, IBM, Intel, and Microsoft, shows that in 2010, pirated software accounts for 42 percent of software in use worldwide. Reported losses from software piracy in 2010 were almost $59 billion—up $8 billion from the year before. "That's over a third of the industry's revenue," says Bob Kruger, the group's vice president for enforcement. According to the findings, only $50 billion of the $100 billion in software purchased in 2010 was legally acquired. In other words, for every dollar spent on software purchased legitimately worldwide, there was 50 cents worth of software that was obtained illegally. Half of the 116 economies studied in 2010 had piracy rates of 62 percent or higher, and two-thirds had at least one software program pirated for every one installed legally.

For example, Carol Bartz, former president and chairman of Autodesk, Inc. (www.autodesk.com) and recently ex-chairman of Yahoo, reported that one of their flagship products, AutoCAD, had 90 percent of the computer-aided design (CAD) market in China, yet sales were virtually negligible due to the widespread acceptance of software piracy. Bartz also stated that many software companies are reluctant to pursue the educational market due to concerns that several copies of purchased software may lead to millions of copies of illegal software, produced "in the name of educating children."

Theft of Intellectual Property

Software is not the only property that is subject to computer-based piracy. Other ***intellectual property theft*** occurs in the form of infringements of copyrighted material, such as music, videos, images, articles, books, and other written works, which most courts have deemed illegal. Digitized versions can easily be captured by computer systems and made available for people to access or download at Internet Web sites or can be readily disseminated by e-mail as file attachments. The development of peer-to-peer (P2P) networking technologies (discussed in Chapter 6) has made digital versions of copyrighted material even more vulnerable to unauthorized use. For example, P2P file-sharing software enables direct MP3 audio file transfers of specified tracks of music between your PC and those of other users on the Internet. Thus, such software creates a *peer-to-peer network* of millions of Internet users who electronically trade digital versions of copyrighted or public domain music stored on their PC's hard drives. More recently, music publishers and manufacturers are offering legal, and relatively inexpensive, methods to access online music in a variety of formats. Because of this proactive posture, the music industry reports that illegal downloading of music and video properties is down and continuing to drop significantly. Let's look at the ongoing debate in this controversial area more closely with a real-world example that emphasizes the threat of developments in IT to intellectual property rights.

Music Piracy: The Long War

"Canadian pirates" is what the music dealers call publishing houses across the line who are flooding this country, they say, with spurious editions of the latest copyrighted popular songs. They use the mails [sic] to reach purchasers, so members of the American Music Publishers' Association assert, and as a result the legitimate music publishing business of the United States has fallen off 50 percent in the past twelve months. Their investigation has revealed that all of the most popular pieces have been counterfeited, despite the fact that they are copyrighted, and by unknown publishers are sold at from 2 cents to 5 cents per copy, though the original compositions sell at from 20 to 40 cents per copy.

Sounds somewhat familiar? You may be a little too young to remember, but it was published in *The New York Times* some time ago—June 13, 1897, to be exact. As you can see, music piracy is hardly a recent phenomenon. It has, however, reached staggering proportions in the last two decades or so, from Napster to torrents, and including the less sophisticated but widely available CD burners.

However, only a few years after Napster's launch, online song-swapping took a big hit from a dogged legal campaign by the Recording Industry Association of America (RIAA) to shut down the top services, Napster and Audiogalaxy. Others—like Kazaa and Morpheus—went on the run, as their users were being sued by the RIAA.

Other networks, like Gnutella, had been built to withstand legal assault. By avoiding centralized servers and spreading the goods around the globe, the free-music hackers hoped their networks would be impossible to shut down. Too bad they also became impossible to use. Shawn Fanning (the creator of Napster) had a hit because Napster provided quick and easy access to a huge trove of music. His deservedly nameless imitators required far more work to find far fewer tunes.

At times, the attention moved to the pirating and copying of physical CDs. Look at the numbers: Industry estimates say that more than 6 billion blank CDs were sold worldwide in 2003—that's one for every person alive today—along with 44 million drives on which to burn them. By 2004, worldwide sales of CD-Audio, CD-ROM, and CD-R all together surpassed 30 billion units. In addition, millions of people now own writable drives—far more than the most optimistic membership claims made by Napster or any of its heirs. "You'll find one on nearly every consumer PC," cites Gartner analyst Mary Craig, one of the more bearish forecasters in the business. "They're not using them for backups."

Today, peer-to-peer (P2P) torrent clients have spread broadly. LimeWire, a grizzled veteran of the peer-to-peer (P2P) file-sharing scene, remains the most popular software for exchanging music, video, and software—much of it pirated—through the Internet, with µTorrent a not-too-close second. LimeWire was used on 17.8 percent of PCs in September of 2007, according to a Digital Media Desktop Report. Since about half of surveyed PCs have at least one peer-to-peer sharing application installed, that gives LimeWire a 36.4 percent share—more than three times the 11.3 percent share of the next-most-popular client, µTorrent.

SOURCE: Paul Boutin, "Burn Baby Burn," *Wired*, December 2002, and Eric Lai, "Study: LimeWire Remains Top P2P Software; µTorrent Fast-Rising No. 2," *Computerworld*, April 17, 2008.

Computer Viruses and Worms

One of the most destructive examples of computer crime involves the creation of a **computer virus** or *worm*. *Virus* is the more popular term, but technically, a virus is a program code that cannot work without being inserted into another program. A worm is a distinct program that can run unaided. In either case, these programs copy annoying or destructive routines into the networked computer systems of anyone who accesses computers infected with the virus or who uses copies of magnetic disks taken from infected computers. Thus, a computer virus or worm can spread destruction among many users. Although they sometimes display only humorous messages, they more often destroy the contents of memory, hard disks, and other storage devices. See Figure 13.9.

Top Five Virus Families of All Time	
1. Storm Worm	**First Discovered: November 2006** The Storm Worm is a Trojan horse program. Its payload is another program, although not always the same one. Some versions of the Storm Worm turn computers into zombies or bots. As computers become infected, they become vulnerable to remote control by the person behind the attack. Some hackers use the Storm Worm to create a botnet and use it to send spam mail across the Internet. Many versions of the Storm Worm fool the victim into downloading the application through fake links to news stories or videos. The people behind the attacks will often change the subject of the e-mail to reflect current events. For example, just before the 2008 Olympics in Beijing, a new version of the worm appeared in e-mails with subjects like "a new deadly catastrophe in China" or "China's most deadly earthquake." The e-mail claimed to link to video and news stories related to the subject, but in reality clicking on the link activated a download of the worm to the victim's computer. Several news agencies and blogs named the Storm Worm one of the worst virus attacks in years. By July 2007, an official with the security company Postini claimed that the firm detected more than 200 million e-mails carrying links to the Storm Worm during an attack that spanned several days. Fortunately, not every e-mail led to someone downloading the worm.
2. Leap-A	**First Discovered: May 2006** The Leap-A virus, also known as Oompa-A, debuted on a Mac. It uses the iChat instant messaging program to propagate across vulnerable Mac computers. After the virus infects a Mac, it searches through the iChat contacts and sends a message to each person on the list. The message contains a corrupted file that appears to be an innocent JPEG image. The Leap-A virus doesn't cause much harm to computers, but it does show that even a Mac computer can fall prey to malicious software. As Mac computers become more popular, we'll probably see more hackers create customized viruses that could damage files on the computer or snarl network traffic.
3. Sasser/Netsky	**First Discovered: March 2004** A 17-year-old German named Sven Jaschan unleashed two of the worst viruses in history onto the Internet. The Sasser worm attacked computers through a Microsoft Windows vulnerability. Unlike other worms, it didn't spread through e-mail. Instead, once the virus infected a computer, it looked for other vulnerable systems. It contacted those systems and instructed them to download the virus. The virus would scan random IP addresses to find potential victims. The virus also altered the victim's operating system in a way that made it difficult to shut down the computer without cutting off power to the system. The Netsky virus moves through e-mails and Windows networks. It spoofs e-mail addresses and propagates through a 22,016-byte file attachment. As it spreads, it can cause a denial of service (DoS) attack as systems collapse while trying to handle all the Internet traffic. At one time, security experts at Sophos believed Netsky and its variants accounted for 25 percent of all computer viruses on the Internet. It also tries to spread via peer-to-peer file-sharing applications by copying itself into the shared folder used by the file-sharing applications (it searches for folders whose name contains the string "share" or "sharing"), renaming itself to pose as one of 26 other common files along the way.
4. MyDoom	**First Discovered: February 2004** MyDoom searched victim computers for e-mail addresses as part of its replication process. But it would also send a search request to a search engine and use e-mail addresses found in the search results. Eventually, search engines like Google began to receive millions of search requests from corrupted computers. These attacks slowed down search engine services and even caused some to crash. MyDoom spread through e-mail and peer-to-peer networks. According to the security firm MessageLabs, one in every 12 e-mail messages carried the virus at one time.
5. Sapphire	**First Discovered: January 2003** Spreads by exploiting a vulnerability in SQL-based servers, spreading from machine to machine with no user intervention required. Only a few minutes after infecting its first Internet server, the Sapphire virus was doubling its number of victims every few seconds. Fifteen minutes after its first attack, the virus infected nearly half of the servers that act as the pillars of the Internet. The Bank of America's ATM service crashed, the city of Seattle suffered outages in 911 service, and Continental Airlines had to cancel several flights due to electronic ticketing and check-in errors.
The Cost of All This . . .	More than 2 million new malware signatures are identified each month. • As many as 11 million computers worldwide—mostly within homes and small organizations—are now believed to be permanently infected and are used by criminal syndicates or malevolents to send out spam; mount distributed denial of service (DDoS) attacks; carry out extortion, identity theft, and phishing scams; or disseminate new viruses. • The total economic damage worldwide from malware proliferation is now estimated to be in excess of $13 billion. • Malware software market exceeded $30 billion by the end of 2007.

SOURCE: CERN https://security.web.cern.ch, 2010 Ponemon Institute Study.

FIGURE 13.9

The top five virus families of all time.

583

Computer viruses typically enter a computer system through e-mail and file attachments via the Internet and online services or through illegal or borrowed copies of software. Copies of *shareware* software downloaded from the Internet can be another source of viruses. A virus usually copies itself into the files of a computer's operating system. Then the virus spreads to the main memory and copies itself onto the computer's hard disk and any inserted floppy disks. The virus spreads to other computers through e-mail, file transfers, other telecommunications activities, or floppy disks from infected computers. Thus, as a good practice, you should avoid using software from questionable sources without checking for viruses. You should also regularly use *antivirus programs* that can help diagnose and remove computer viruses from infected files on your hard disk. We will discuss defense against viruses further later in the chapter.

Oldies but Goodies: Old Threats That Just Won't Go Away

Worried about the virulent Storm worm that has been buffeting the Internet with mass mailings? Symantec Corp. researchers said that the "Storm Trojan," aka "Peacomm," is now spreading via AOL Instant Messenger (AIM), Google Talk, and Yahoo Messenger.

An alert to some Symantec customers pegged the new infection vector as "insidious" because the message—such as the cryptic "LOL;)"—and the included URL can be dynamically updated by the attacker. Even worse, according to Alfred Huger, senior director of Symantec's security response team, "it injects a message and URL only into already open windows. It's not just some random message that pops up, but it appears only to people you are already talking to. That makes the approach very effective."

Well, you should be concerned about the Storm worm, but Gunter Ollmann, director of security strategy at IBM's Internet Security Systems, says the most common malware attack today is coming from the Slammer worm. *No, you didn't misread that last sentence.* The Slammer worm, which hit in January 2003, is still working its way around the Internet and within corporate networks, according to Ollmann. And it's still spreading in a big way. Slammer isn't the only piece of old-time malware that is still wreaking havoc.

"The stuff malware authors wrote a while ago is still out there and still propagating and still infecting machines," he said. "Some have more infections now than they did when they were headline news. All those old vulnerabilities haven't all gone away." Slammer, the worm that brought many networks to their knees by attacking Microsoft's SQL Server, is at the top of Ollmann's list of current malware problems.

"When we hear about the latest worm and zero-day, Slammer still beats them by a long shot," he added. "Slammer is still out there on a large number of infected hosts and it's still sending out malicious network traffic—malicious packets. . . . When people restore data after a crash, it probably is from an old system and it may not have the patches so it can easily be re-infected."

Another problem is that some users just don't do the patching they should, while other users aren't even aware that Microsoft SQL Server is running on their desktop because it's common to several other applications. If they don't know it's there, they don't know to take care of it.

"All these old viruses are never going to go away," said Ollmann.

SOURCE: Sharon Gaudin, "Oldies but Goodies: Slammer Worm Still Attacking," *InformationWeek*, August 24, 2007, and Gregg Keizer, "'Storm Trojan' Ignites Worm War," *Computerworld*, February 12, 2007.

Adware and Spyware

Two more recent entries into the computer vulnerabilities arena are ***adware*** and ***spyware***. By definition, adware is software that, while purporting to serve some useful function and often fulfilling that function, also allows Internet advertisers to display advertisements as banners and pop-up ads without the consent of the computer user. In the extreme, adware can also collect information about the user of its host computer and send it over the Internet to its owner. This special class of adware is called spyware and is defined as any software that employs users' Internet connection in the background without their knowledge or explicit permission. Spyware programs collect specific information about you, ranging from general demographics like name, address, and Internet surfing habits to credit card, Social Security number, user names, passwords, or other personal information. It is important to understand that not all adware programs are spyware. Proper adware represents a viable, albeit sometimes irritating, revenue model for many software companies that allows you to get products for free and, when used correctly, does not pose any significant privacy threat. In contrast, spyware is and should be considered a clear threat to your privacy.

Whereas proper adware generally allows the computer user to opt in to its use in exchange for free use of a piece of software, spyware operates under a rather bizarre ethical model. Consider the following:

- You illegally enter a bank's computer system and place a stealth piece of software in their system. If you are detected or caught, you might be prosecuted and may go to jail.

- You write a worm or virus and spread it around the Internet or other networks. If you are detected or caught, you might be prosecuted and may go to jail.

- You write a program that spreads a spyware agent across computer systems connected to the Internet that steals the private information of the users it infects, manipulates their Internet experience, and uses other people's Web sites and browsers to display your advertising. If you are detected or caught, you may get rich, you don't go to jail, and the computer users are left with possibly rebuilding their computer system to get rid of your spyware.

Spyware has a variety of characteristics, beyond its potential for stealing valuable private information, which make it undesirable to most computer users. At the very least, it plagues the user of the infected machine with unwanted advertising. More often, it watches everything a user does online and sends that information back to the marketing company that created the spyware. Often, spyware applications add advertising links to Web pages owned by other people, for which the Web page owner does not get paid, and may even redirect the payments from legitimate affiliate-fee advertisers to the makers of the spyware. Other undesirable characteristics include setting an infected system's browser home page and search settings to point to the spyware owner's Web sites (generally loaded with advertising), often in a manner that prevents you from changing back the settings (referred to as home-page hijacking). In the extremes, spyware can make a dial-up modem continually call premium-rate phone numbers, thus causing large telephone charges (and usually fees to the spyware owner) or leave security holes in an infected system allowing the makers of the spyware—or, in particularly bad cases, anyone at all—to download and run software on the infected machine (such downloads are called *Trojans*). In almost all cases, spyware severely degrades system performance. As you can see, spyware doesn't have any redeeming features except for the benefits to its owner. Its use is pervasive, and failing to protect against it virtually ensures that your system will eventually become infected.

Protecting against adware and spyware generally requires the purchase and installation of one of a variety of programs designed to prevent the software from being downloaded and installed. Once a computer is infected, however, removal programs are often not completely successful in eliminating the nuisance.

Commtouch: Trends in Internet Threats

Spam: The first quarter of 2011 saw large variations in the amount of spam sent during this period. Partly responsible for this was the takedown of the Rustock botnet, which was reportedly responsible for sending about 50 billion spam messages daily. Even so, the average daily spam in February 2011 was 165 billion e-mails, which compares to 162 billion daily in October 2010. After the Rustock takedown, the level dropped to 119 billion e-mails a day at the end of the quarter. Still, those are staggeringly large numbers. The majority of spam was related to pharmacy and drug-related issues (28 percent), so-called 419 scams, which are most commonly a letter pretending to be from Nigeria asking the recipient to advance some money with the promise of receiving a larger payout later (13 percent), and dating (12 percent).

Zombie Activity: The first quarter saw an average of 258,000 new zombies activated every day for malicious purposes. This number compares favorably with 288,000 in the fourth quarter of 2010 and 339,000 in the third quarter of 2010. India remains the top hotspot for zombie activity, with about 17 percent of the total global zombie population. Other major areas are Brazil (12 percent), Vietnam (9 percent) and the Russian Federation (7 percent).

Malware: Over the last few years, distributors of malware have switched from e-mail attachments to Web-based methods. At the same time, however, in March 2011 about 30 percent of all e-mails sent during the period contained either an attachment or were related to malware in some way. The most common one was a purported message from UPS about tracking information; the DHL name was also used. Other common approaches include purported PDF files and fake Facebook chat windows; attached PowerPoint presentations with funny or interesting topics are still used as well. As part of their analysis of spam trends, Commtouch monitors the domains that are used by spammers in the "from" field of spam e-mails. Although these are, of course, fake addresses, they can sometimes fool antispam filters to give the impression that they may belong to a reputable source. The most commonly used domains were gmail.com, att.net, yahoo.com, yahoogroups.com, and hotmail.com.

Compromised Web Sites: During the first quarter of 2011, Commtouch analyzed which categories of Web sites were most likely to be compromised with malware or phishing. For the first time in over a year, pornographic and sexually explicit sites have been displaced by parked domains and spam sites as being the most compromised categories of sites. The most common Web sites affected by phishing scams were those in the games, health and medicine, portal, and computers and technology categories.

SOURCE: "Internet Threats Trend Report April 2011," *Commtouch Report*, 2011.

PRIVACY ISSUES
LO 13-1

Information technology makes it technically and economically feasible to collect, store, integrate, interchange, and retrieve data and information quickly and easily. This characteristic has an important beneficial effect on the efficiency and effectiveness of computer-based information systems. The power of information technology to store and retrieve information, however, can have a negative effect on the *right to privacy* of every individual. For example, confidential e-mail messages by employees are monitored by many companies. Personal information is being collected about individuals every time someone visits a site on the World Wide Web. Confidential information on individuals contained in centralized computer databases by credit bureaus, government agencies, and private business firms has been stolen or misused, resulting in the invasion of privacy, fraud, and other injustices. The unauthorized use of such information has badly damaged the privacy of individuals. Errors in such databases could seriously hurt the credit standing or reputation of an individual.

Governments around the world, but none more than in the United States, are debating privacy issues and considering various forms of legislation. With regard to the Internet, **opt-in** versus **opt-out** is central to the debate over privacy legislation. Consumer protection groups typically endorse an opt-in standard, making privacy the default. An opt-in system automatically protects consumers who do not specifically allow data to be compiled about them. Most business interests back opt-out, arguing it doesn't disrupt the flow of e-commerce. Interestingly, current laws in this regard differ between the United States and Europe. In the United States, opt-out is the default position, whereas in Europe, consumers must opt-in or their information cannot be used.

Additional privacy issues under debate include:

- Accessing private e-mail conversations and computer records and collecting and sharing information about individuals gained from their visits to Internet Web sites and newsgroups (violation of privacy).

- Always knowing where a person is, especially as mobile and paging services become more closely associated with people rather than places (computer monitoring).

- Using customer information gained from many sources to market additional business services (computer matching).

- Collecting telephone numbers, e-mail addresses, credit card numbers, and other personal information to build individual customer profiles (unauthorized personal files).

There are now cases appearing in courts of all levels challenging a person's right to privacy with regard to digital assets such as e-mail. United States v. Warshak is a criminal case decided by the U.S. Court of Appeals for the Sixth Circuit, holding that government agents violated the defendant's Fourth Amendment rights by compelling his Internet Service Provider (ISP) to turn over his e-mails without first obtaining a search warrant based on probable cause. However, constitutional violation notwithstanding, the evidence obtained with these e-mails was admissible at trial because the government agents relied in good faith on the Stored Communications Act (SCA). Under the SCA, agents of the government can request access to e-mails using an administrative subpoena or by obtaining a court order, depending on certain statutory classifications. Government agents ordered Warshak's ISP to store e-mails citing 18 U.S.C. § 2703(f) as granting them that authority. The government then ordered the ISP to turn over the content of Warshak's e-mails using a subpoena. Warshak was not informed that his ISP was archiving his e-mail, and he did not receive notice of the subpoena and order to his ISP until May 2006, nearly one year after the government served the subpoena.

The court further declared that the SCA is unconstitutional to the extent that it allows the government to obtain e-mails without a warrant. This case is notable because it is the first decision from the U.S. Circuit Court of Appeals to explicitly hold that there is a reasonable expectation of privacy in the content of e-mails stored on third-party servers and that the content of these e-mails is subject to Fourth Amendment protection.

Privacy on the Internet

If you don't take the proper precautions, any time you send an e-mail, access a Web site, post a message to a newsgroup, or use the Internet for banking and shopping . . . whether you're online for business or pleasure, you're vulnerable to anyone bent on collecting data about you without your knowledge. Fortunately, by using tools like encryption and anonymous remailers—and by being selective about the sites you visit and the information you provide—you can minimize, if not completely eliminate, the risk of your privacy being violated.

The Internet is notorious for giving its users a feeling of anonymity when in reality they are highly visible and open to violations of their privacy. Most of the Internet and its World Wide Web, e-mail, chat, and newsgroups are still a wide open, unsecured electronic frontier, with no tough rules on what information is personal and private.

Information about Internet users is captured legitimately and automatically each time you visit a Web site or newsgroup and is recorded as a "cookie file" on your hard disk. Then the Web site owners or online auditing services like DoubleClick may sell the information from cookie files and other records of your Internet use to third parties. To make matters worse, much of the Net and Web is an easy target for the interception or theft by hackers of private information furnished to Web sites by Internet users.

Of course, you can protect your privacy in several ways. For example, sensitive e-mail can be protected by encryption, if both e-mail parties use compatible encryption software built into their e-mail programs. Newsgroup postings can be made privately by sending them through *anonymous remailers* that protect your identity when you add your comments to a discussion. You can ask your Internet service provider not to sell your name and personal information to mailing list providers and other marketers. Finally, you can decline to reveal personal data and interests on online service and Web site user profiles to limit your exposure to electronic snooping.

Identity Theft: As Easy as Stealing a Check

Frank W. Abagnale Jr. was a check forger for five years in the 1960s. Currently he runs Abagnale and Associates, a financial fraud consultancy company. His life story provided the inspiration for the feature film *Catch Me If You Can*, starring Leonardo DiCaprio, as Frank Abagnale Jr., as well as Tom Hanks.

Forty years ago, few people could have predicted that identity theft would become as big an epidemic as it is today. Few could have imagined that protecting your identity would mean taking mail to the post office instead of leaving it in our mailboxes for pickup, shredding documents before throwing them in the trash, or that a $2 pen could help prevent a crime.

"We need to find ways to protect ourselves before identity theft strikes. We can make drastic improvements toward diminishing this crime, but it will never disappear altogether. If you haven't been a victim of identity theft, it is because thieves haven't gotten to you yet. If things fail to change, your turn will come. Prevention is not simply a matter of following a checklist of tips, it is about education—the primary factor in protecting ourselves," says Frank W. Abagnale Jr.—and he should know.

Although more and more people are using online banking, America's 78 million baby boomers, who make up 15 percent of the U.S. population, continue to be a paper-driven majority. This group also accounts for 30 percent of fraud victims, as estimated by Consumer Action, a consumer-advocacy group.

"A check holds all of the information needed to steal your identity: name, address, bank account, routing number. If written with a ball point pen, information can easily be removed by a process called check washing, a common form of identity theft. It is the process of taking a check or document that has already been filled out, removing the ink with a regular household chemical, then re-writing in a new dollar amount and recipient," says Abagnale. If you are careless, your personal check could contribute to the 1.2 million fraudulent checks written every day. That's more than 13 per second.

The American Bankers Association states that check fraud is growing 25 percent per year. To slow this growth, it is important to understand how it works. "I know firsthand how easy it is to perform check fraud. About 40 years ago, I cashed $2.5 million in fraudulent checks in every state and 26 foreign countries over a five-year period. I was involved in a high-stakes game of stolen identities. And to know how easy it can be to perform, I know it is just as easy to prevent," he notes.

Criminals rely on our mistakes to make their job easier. Taking a few precautions will make you less attractive to predators. Don't leave mail in your mailbox overnight or over the weekend. When writing checks and filling out important documents, use a gel pen, so thieves can't remove the ink and change the information. In addition, shred or tear up unwanted documents that contain personal information before discarding them. The cost of a high-quality shredder is far less than the cost of having your identity stolen.

"Let's face it; we can't always control what is happening in our world, so we must take steps to control what we can. Technology is here to stay, but there are still simple and inexpensive ways to prevent identity theft when writing checks. Remember that a crook always looks for the easiest route to riches. Don't hand him a map. Be proactive and start protecting yourself today," says Abagnale.

SOURCE: Frank Abagnale, "Abagnale: Top Tips to Prevent Identity Theft and Fraud," *CIO Magazine*, May 24, 2007.

Computer Matching

Computer profiling and mistakes in the ***computer matching*** of personal data are other controversial threats to privacy. Individuals have been mistakenly arrested and jailed and people have been denied credit because their physical profiles or personal data have been used by profiling software to match them incorrectly or improperly with the wrong individuals. Another threat is the unauthorized matching of computerized information about you extracted from the databases of sales transaction processing systems and sold to information brokers or other companies. A more recent threat is the unauthorized matching and sale of information about you collected from Internet Web sites and newsgroups you visit, as we discussed previously. You are then subjected to a barrage of unsolicited promotional material and sales contacts as well as having your privacy violated.

Privacy Laws

Many countries strictly regulate the collection and use of personal data by business corporations and government agencies. Many government *privacy laws* attempt to enforce the privacy of computer-based files and communications. For example, in the United States, the Electronic Communications Privacy Act and the Computer Fraud and Abuse Act prohibit intercepting data communications messages, stealing or destroying data, or trespassing in federal-related computer systems. Because the Internet includes federal-related computer systems, privacy attorneys argue that the laws also require notifying employees if a company intends to monitor Internet usage. Another example is the U.S. Computer Matching and Privacy Act, which regulates the matching of data held in federal agency files to verify eligibility for federal programs.

More recently, new legislation intended to protect individual privacy has created some new challenges for organizations. Sarbanes-Oxley, the Health Insurance Portability and Accountability Act (HIPAA), Gramm-Leach-Bliley, the USA PATRIOT Act, the California Security Breach Law, and Securities and Exchange Commission Rule 17a-4 are but a few of the compliance challenges facing organizations. In an effort to comply with these new privacy laws, it is estimated that a typical company will spend 3–4 percent of its IT budget on compliance applications and projects.

HIPAA. The Health Insurance Portability and Accountability Act (HIPAA) was enacted by the U.S. Congress in 1996. It is a broad piece of legislation intended to address a wide variety of issues related to individual health insurance. Two important sections of HIPAA include the privacy rules and the security rules. Both of these portions of the law are intended to create safeguards against the unauthorized use, disclosure, or distribution of an individual's health-related information without their specific consent or authorization. While the privacy rules pertain to all Protected Health Information (PHI) including paper and electronic, the security rules deal specifically with Electronic Protected Health Information (EPHI). These rules lay out three types of security safeguards required for compliance: *administrative*, *physical*, and *technical*. For each of these types, the rules identify various security standards, and for each standard, name both required and addressable implementation specifications. Required specifications must be adopted and administered as dictated by the HIPAA regulation. Addressable specifications are more flexible. Individual covered entities can evaluate their own situation and determine the best way to implement addressable specifications.

SARBANES-OXLEY. The Sarbanes-Oxley Act of 2002, also known as the Public Company Accounting Reform and Investor Protection Act of 2002 and commonly called Sarbanes-Oxley, Sarbox, or SOX, is a U.S. federal law enacted on July 30, 2002, as a reaction to a number of major corporate and accounting scandals, including those affecting Enron, Tyco International, Adelphia, Peregrine Systems, and WorldCom. These scandals, which cost investors billions of dollars when the share prices of affected companies collapsed, shook public confidence in the nation's securities markets. Named after sponsors U.S. Senator Paul Sarbanes and U.S. Representative Michael G. Oxley, the act was approved by the House by a vote of 334-90 and by the Senate 99-0. President George W. Bush signed it into law, stating it included "the most far-reaching reforms of American business practices since the time of Franklin D. Roosevelt."

The legislation set new or enhanced standards for all U.S. public company boards, management, and public accounting firms. It does not, however, apply to privately held companies. The act contains 11 sections, ranging from additional corporate board responsibilities to criminal penalties, and requires the Securities and Exchange Commission (SEC) to implement rulings on requirements to comply with the new law.

Debate continues over the perceived benefits and costs of SOX. Supporters contend the legislation was necessary and has played a useful role in restoring public confidence in the nation's capital markets by, among other things, strengthening corporate accounting controls. Opponents of the bill claim it has reduced America's international competitive edge against foreign financial service providers, saying SOX has introduced an overly complex and regulatory environment into U.S. financial markets.

Computer Libel and Censorship

The opposite side of the privacy debate is the right of people to know about matters others may want to keep private (freedom of information), the right of people to express their opinions about such matters (freedom of speech), and the right of people to publish those opinions (freedom of the press). Some of the biggest battlegrounds in the debate are the bulletin boards, e-mail boxes, and online files of the Internet and public information networks such as America Online and the Microsoft Network. The weapons being used in this battle include *spamming, flame mail*, libel laws, and censorship.

Spamming is the indiscriminate sending of unsolicited e-mail messages (*spam*) to many Internet users. Spamming is the favorite tactic of mass mailers of unsolicited advertisements, or *junk e-mail*. Spamming has also been used by cyber-criminals to spread computer viruses or infiltrate many computer systems.

Flaming is the practice of sending extremely critical, derogatory, and often vulgar e-mail messages (*flame mail*) or newsgroup postings to other users on the Internet or online services. Flaming is especially prevalent on some of the Internet's special-interest newsgroups.

There have been many incidents of racist or defamatory messages on the Web that have led to calls for censorship and lawsuits for libel. In addition, the presence of sexually explicit material at many World Wide Web locations has triggered lawsuits and censorship actions by various groups and governments.

THE CURRENT STATE OF CYBER LAW
LO 13-3

Cyber law is the term used to describe laws intended to regulate activities over the Internet or via the use of electronic data communications. Cyber law encompasses a wide variety of legal and political issues related to the Internet and other communications technologies, including intellectual property, privacy, freedom of expression, and jurisdiction. These laws have been described as "paper laws" for a "paperless environment."

The intersection of technology and the law is often controversial. Some feel that the Internet should not (or possibly cannot) be regulated in any form. Furthermore, the development of sophisticated technologies, such as encryption and cryptography, make traditional forms of regulation extremely difficult. Finally, the fundamental end-to-end nature of the Internet means that if one mode of communication is regulated or shut down, another method will be devised and spring up in its place. In the words of John Gilmore, founder of the Electronic Frontier Foundation, "the Internet treats censorship as damage and simply routes around it."

One example of advancements in cyber law is found in the Federal Trade Commission's (FTC) *Consumer Sentinel Project*. Consumer Sentinel is a unique investigative cyber-tool that provides members of the Consumer Sentinel Network with access to data from millions of consumer complaints. Consumer Sentinel includes complaints about identity theft, do-not-call registry violations, computers, the Internet, and on-line auctions, telemarketing scams, advance-fee loans, and credit scams, sweepstakes, lotteries, and prizes, business opportunities and work-at-home schemes, health and weight-loss products, debt collection, credit reports, and other financial matters.

Consumer Sentinel is based on the premise that sharing information can make law enforcement even more effective. To that end, the Consumer Sentinel Network provides law-enforcement members with access to complaints provided directly to the Federal Trade Commission by consumers, as well as providing members with access to complaints shared by data contributors.

According to the FTC Sentinel Report for 2007, more than 800,000 complaints were processed through Sentinel with Internet-related offenses representing 11 percent of the total complaints, and computer-related identity theft representing 23 percent. While many of these complaints are difficult, if not impossible to prosecute, we are beginning to see more resources being committed to addressing cyber-related crime.

Cyber law is a new phenomenon, having emerged after the onset of the Internet. As we know, the Internet grew in a relatively unplanned and unregulated manner. Even the early pioneers of the Internet could not have anticipated the scope and far-reaching consequences of the cyberspace of today and tomorrow. Although major legal disputes related to cyber activities certainly arose in the early 1990s, it was not until 1996 and 1997 that an actual body of law began to emerge. The area, clearly in its infancy, remains largely unsettled. The debate continues regarding the applicability of analogous legal principles derived from prior controversies that had nothing to do with cyberspace. As we progress in our understanding of the complex issues in cyberspace, new and better laws, regulations, and policies will most likely be adopted and enacted.

OTHER CHALLENGES

Let's now explore some other important challenges that arise from the use of information technologies in business, as illustrated in Figure 13.2. These challenges include the potential ethical and societal impact of business applications of IT in the areas of employment, individuality, working conditions, and health.

Employment Challenges

The impact of information technologies on employment is a major ethical concern that is directly related to the use of computers to achieve automation of work activities. There can be no doubt that the use of information technologies has created new jobs and increased productivity while also causing a significant reduction in some types of job opportunities. For example, when computers are used for accounting systems or the automated control of machine tools, they are accomplishing tasks formerly performed by many clerks and machinists. Also, jobs created by information technology may require different types of skills and education than do the jobs that are eliminated. Therefore, people may become unemployed unless they can be retrained for new positions or new responsibilities.

However, there can be no doubt that Internet technologies have created a host of new job opportunities. Many new jobs, including Internet Web masters, e-commerce directors, systems analysts, and user consultants, have been created to support e-business and e-commerce applications. Additional jobs have been created because information technologies make possible the production of complex industrial and technical goods and services that would otherwise be impossible to produce. Thus, jobs have been created by activities that are heavily dependent on information technology, in such areas as space exploration, microelectronic technology, and telecommunications.

Computer Monitoring

One of the most explosive ethical issues concerning workplace privacy and the quality of working conditions in business is *computer monitoring.* That is, computers are being used to monitor the productivity and behavior of millions of employees while they work. Supposedly, computer monitoring occurs so employers can collect productivity data about their employees to increase the efficiency and quality of service. However, computer monitoring has been criticized as unethical because it monitors individuals, not just work, and is done continually, which violates workers' privacy and personal freedom. For example, when you call to make a reservation, an airline reservation agent may be timed on the exact number of seconds taken per caller, the time between calls, and the number and length of breaks taken. In addition, your conversation may be monitored. See Figure 13.10.

Computer monitoring has been criticized as an invasion of the privacy of employees because, in many cases, they do not know that they are being monitored or don't know how the information is being used. Critics also say that an employee's right of due process may be harmed by the improper use of collected data to make personnel decisions. Because computer monitoring increases the stress on employees who must work under constant electronic surveillance, it has also been blamed for causing health problems among monitored workers. Finally, computer monitoring has been blamed for robbing workers of the dignity of their work. In its extremes, computer monitoring can create an "electronic sweatshop," in which workers are forced to work at a hectic pace under poor working conditions.

Political pressure is building to outlaw or regulate computer monitoring in the workplace. For example, public advocacy groups, labor unions, and many legislators are pushing for action at the state and federal level in the United States. The proposed laws would regulate computer monitoring and protect the worker's right to know and right to privacy. In the meantime, lawsuits by monitored workers against employers are increasing. So computer monitoring of workers is one ethical issue in business that won't go away.

FIGURE 13.10

Computer monitoring can be used to record the productivity and behavior of people while they work.

SOURCE: © LWA-JDC/Corbis.

Challenges in Working Conditions

Information technology has eliminated monotonous or obnoxious tasks in the office and the factory that formerly had to be performed by people. For example, word processing and desktop publishing make producing office documents a lot easier to do, and robots have taken over repetitive welding and spray painting jobs in the automotive industry. In many instances, this shift allows people to concentrate on more challenging and interesting assignments, upgrades the skill level of the work to be performed, and creates challenging jobs requiring highly developed skills in the computer industry and computer-using organizations. Thus, information technology can be said to upgrade the quality of work because it can upgrade the quality of working conditions and the content of work activities.

Of course, some jobs in information technology—data entry, for example—are quite repetitive and routine. Also, to the extent that computers are used in some types of automation, IT must take some responsibility for the criticism of assembly-line operations that require the continual repetition of elementary tasks, thus forcing a worker to work like a machine instead of like a skilled craftsperson. Many automated operations are also criticized for relegating people to a "do-nothing" standby role, where workers spend most of their time waiting for infrequent opportunities to push some buttons. Such effects do have a detrimental effect on the quality of work, but they must be compared against the less burdensome and more creative jobs created by information technology.

Challenges of Individuality

A frequent criticism of information systems centers on their negative effect on the individuality of people. Computer-based systems are criticized as impersonal systems that dehumanize and depersonalize activities that have been computerized because they eliminate the human relationships present in noncomputer systems.

Another aspect of the loss of individuality is the regimentation that seems required by some computer-based systems. These systems do not appear to possess any flexibility. They demand strict adherence to detailed procedures if the system is to work. The negative impact of IT on individuality is reinforced by horror stories that describe how inflexible and uncaring some organizations with computer-based processes are when it comes to rectifying their own mistakes. Many of us are familiar with stories of how computerized customer billing and accounting systems continued to demand payment and send warning notices to a customer whose account had already been paid, despite repeated attempts by the customer to have the error corrected.

However, many business applications of IT are designed to minimize depersonalization and regimentation. For example, many e-commerce systems stress personalization and community features to encourage repeated visits to e-commerce Web sites. Thus, the widespread use of personal computers and the Internet has dramatically improved the development of people-oriented and personalized information systems.

The use of information technology in the workplace raises a variety of health issues. Heavy use of computers is reportedly causing health problems like job stress, damaged arm and neck muscles, eyestrain, radiation exposure, and even death by computer-caused accidents. For example, computer monitoring is blamed as a major cause of computer-related job stress. Workers, unions, and government officials criticize computer monitoring as putting so much stress on employees that it leads to health problems.

HEALTH ISSUES
LO 13-1

People who sit at PC workstations or visual display terminals (VDTs) in fast-paced, repetitive keystroke jobs can suffer a variety of health problems known collectively as *cumulative trauma disorders* (CTDs). Their fingers, wrists, arms, necks, and backs may become so weak and painful that they cannot work. Strained muscles, back pain, and nerve damage may result. In particular, some computer workers may suffer from *carpal tunnel syndrome*, a painful, crippling ailment of the hand and wrist that typically requires surgery to cure.

Prolonged viewing of video displays causes eyestrain and other health problems in employees who must do this all day. Radiation caused by the cathode ray

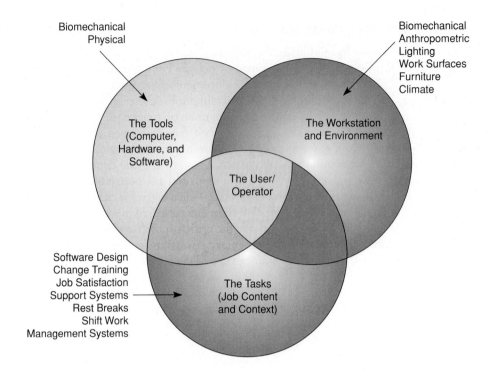

FIGURE 13.11

Ergonomic factors in the workplace. Note that good ergonomic design considers tools, tasks, the workstation, and the environment.

tubes (CRTs) that produce video displays is another health concern. CRTs produce an electromagnetic field that may cause harmful radiation of employees who work too close for too long in front of video monitors. Some pregnant workers have reported miscarriages and fetal deformities due to prolonged exposure to CRTs at work. Studies have failed to find conclusive evidence concerning this problem; still, several organizations recommend that female workers minimize their use of CRTs during pregnancy.

Ergonomics

Solutions to some of these health problems are based on the science of ***ergonomics,*** sometimes called *human factors engineering*. See Figure 13.11. The goal of ergonomics is to design healthy work environments that are safe, comfortable, and pleasant for people to work in, thus increasing employee morale and productivity. Ergonomics emphasizes the healthy design of the workplace, workstations, computers and other machines, and even software packages. Other health issues may require ergonomic solutions emphasizing job design rather than workplace design. For example, this approach may require policies providing for work breaks from heavy video monitor use every few hours, while limiting the CRT exposure of pregnant workers. Ergonomic job design can also provide more variety in job tasks for those workers who spend most of their workday at computer workstations.

SOCIETAL SOLUTIONS
LO 13-3

As we noted at the beginning of the chapter, the Internet and other information technologies can have many beneficial effects on society. We can use information technologies to solve human and social problems through ***societal solutions*** such as medical diagnosis, computer-assisted instruction, governmental program planning, environmental quality control, and law enforcement. For example, computers can help diagnose an illness, prescribe necessary treatment, and monitor the progress of hospital patients. Computer-assisted instruction (CAI) and computer-based training (CBT) enable interactive instruction tailored to the needs of students. Distance learning is supported by telecommunications networks, videoconferencing, e-mail, and other technologies.

Information technologies can be used for crime control through various law-enforcement applications. For example, computerized alarm systems allow police to identify and respond quickly to evidence of criminal activity. Computers have been used to monitor the level of pollution in the air and in bodies of water, detect the sources of pollution, and issue early warnings when dangerous levels are reached. Computers are also used for the program planning of many government agencies in such areas as urban planning, population density and land-use studies, highway planning, and urban transit studies. Computers are being used in job placement systems to help match unemployed persons with available jobs. These and other applications illustrate that information technology can be used to help solve the problems of society.

Obviously, individuals or organizations that do not accept ethical responsibility for their actions cause many of the detrimental effects of information technology. Like other powerful technologies, information technology possesses the potential for great harm or great good for all humankind. If managers, business professionals, and IS specialists accept their ethical responsibilities, then information technology can help improve living and working conditions for all of society.

Security Management of Information Technology

INTRODUCTION

With Internet access proliferating rapidly, one might think that the biggest obstacle to e-commerce would be bandwidth. But it's not; the number one problem is security. And part of the problem is that the Internet was developed for interoperability, not impenetrability.

As we saw in the beginning of the chapter, there are many significant threats to the security of information systems in business. That's why this part of the chapter is dedicated to exploring the methods that companies can use to manage their security. Business managers and professionals alike are responsible for the security, quality, and performance of the business information systems in their business units. Like any other vital business assets, hardware, software, networks, and data resources need to be protected by a variety of security measures to ensure their quality and beneficial use. That's the business value of security management. See Figure 13.12.

TOOLS OF SECURITY MANAGEMENT
LO 13-2

The goal of ***security management*** is the accuracy, integrity, and safety of all information system processes and resources. Thus, effective security management can minimize errors, fraud, and losses in the information systems that interconnect today's companies and their customers, suppliers, and other stakeholders. As Figure 13.13 illustrates, security management is a complex task. As you can see, security managers must acquire and integrate a variety of security tools and methods to protect a company's information system resources. We discuss many of these security measures here.

FIGURE 13.13

Examples of important security measures that are part of the security management of information systems.

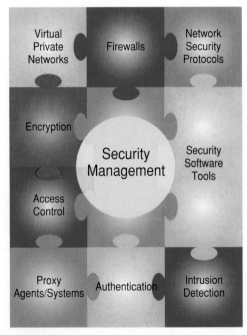

SOURCE: Courtesy of Wang Global.

FIGURE 13.12

The proliferation of end-user devices is making end-point security more important than ever.

SOURCE: © Bloomberg/Getty Images.

What do chief executive officers and other business leaders really think about information security? A recent survey and interviews conducted by *InformationWeek* reveal that they're more aligned with "infosec" (information security) teams than you might think—when comes to information security, non-IT executives just might get it. The results suggest that C-level executives not only recognize the importance of information security, but actively support the efforts of their IT organizations to protect corporate assets and reduce risk.

At times, that comes as a surprise. The rants from IT pros about stingy executives who are ignorant of critical security issues and regard security as an impediment to doing business are quite common. Indeed, conflicts between executives and IT organizations are still common. Moneymaking opportunities that present considerable security risks still go forward over the objections of information security teams. Conversely, security teams don't always appreciate that risk can't be entirely eliminated, or that some security measures go so far as to make information and technology too cumbersome to be useful.

Among the more security-minded executives is William McNabb, chief executive officer of investment firm Vanguard Group. He sums up his company's information security responsibility this way: "We manage more than a trillion dollars of other people's money. That's important trust they've placed with us, and we have to do everything in our power to protect it." Seventy-five percent of survey respondents say information security is among the highest of corporate priorities.

There are four major reasons for this high level of executive support. First is the rise of high-volume theft of credit card information, Social Security numbers, and other personal data. Such attacks began to make headlines in 2005, when DSW Shoe Warehouse and ChoicePoint were hit. In the DSW case, thieves stole 1.4 million credit card numbers from stores in 25 states. Meanwhile, poor controls at ChoicePoint enabled scam artists posing as legitimate businesses to access consumer records and perpetrate identity theft. Since then, a string of larger information thefts from the likes of the Hannaford Bros. grocery chain, job site Monster.com, retailer TJX, and, most recently, Heartland Payment systems has put executives on notice: Such breaches can no longer be dismissed merely as isolated incidents.

Second, the high-profile thefts have triggered a number of state breach-disclosure laws, which compel companies to publicize the theft or loss of personally identifiable information. Companies also face industry data-protection standards, the most prominent of which is the Payment Card Industry Data Security Standard, which requires a variety of security measures for businesses that accept and process credit cards.

The third trend changing executives' attitudes about security is the rising cost of information breaches.

From lawsuit payouts to fines to the expense of setting up credit-monitoring services for victimized customers, executives can see exactly how much a security failure costs. U.S. companies paid an average of $202 per exposed record in 2008, up from $197 in 2007, according to a report by the Ponemon Institute, a privacy management researcher. The report also says the average total cost per breach for each company was $6.6 million in 2008, up from $6.3 million in 2007 and $4.7 million in 2006.

The fourth major trend is the damage to a company's brand and reputation. Although it's hard to put a price on the loss of customer trust or efforts to repair a brand, no CEO wants to have to try to do that math.

Top Executives Agree: Information Security Is a Top Priority

SOURCE: Andrew Conry-Murray, "A Unified Front," *InformationWeek*, February 16, 2009.

INTER-NETWORKED SECURITY DEFENSES LO 13-2

Few professionals today face greater challenges than those IT managers who are developing Internet security policies for rapidly changing network infrastructures. How can they balance the need for Internet security and Internet access? Are the budgets for Internet security adequate? What impact will intranet, extranet, and Web application development have on security architectures? How can they come up with best practices for developing Internet security policy?

The security of today's networked business enterprises is a major management challenge. Many companies are still in the process of getting fully connected to the Web and the Internet for e-commerce and are reengineering their internal business processes with intranets, e-business software, and extranet links to customers, suppliers, and other business partners. Vital network links and business flows need to be protected from external attack by cyber-criminals and from subversion by the criminal or irresponsible acts of insiders. This protection requires a variety of security tools and defensive measures and a coordinated security management program. Let's take a look at some of these important security defenses.

Encryption

Encryption of data has become an important way to protect data and other computer network resources, especially on the Internet, intranets, and extranets. Passwords, messages, files, and other data can be transmitted in scrambled form and unscrambled by computer systems for authorized users only. Encryption involves using special mathematical algorithms, or keys, to transform digital data into a scrambled code before they are transmitted, and then to decode the data when they are received. The most widely used encryption method uses a pair of public and private keys unique to each individual. For example, e-mail could be scrambled and encoded using a unique *public key* for the recipient that is known to the sender. After the e-mail is transmitted, only the recipient's secret *private key* could unscramble the message. See Figure 13.14.

FIGURE 13.14

How public key/private key encryption works.

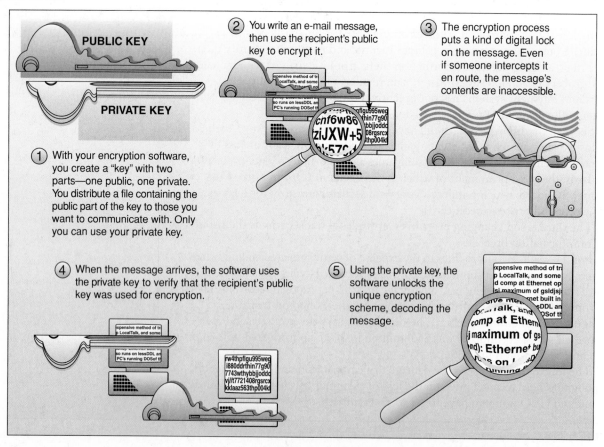

Encryption programs are sold as separate products or built into other software used for the encryption process. There are several competing software encryption standards, but the top two are RSA (by RSA Data Security) and PGP (which stands for "pretty good privacy"), a popular encryption program available on the Internet. Software products including Microsoft Windows XP, Novell NetWare, and Lotus Notes offer encryption features using RSA software.

Firewalls

Another important method for control and security on the Internet and other networks is the use of *firewall* computers and software. A network firewall can be a communications processor, typically a *router*, or a dedicated server, along with firewall software. A firewall serves as a gatekeeper system that protects a company's intranets and other computer networks from intrusion by providing a filter and safe transfer point for access to and from the Internet and other networks. It screens all network traffic for proper passwords or other security codes and only allows authorized transmissions in and out of the network. Firewall software has also become an essential computer system component for individuals connecting to the Internet with DSL or cable modems because of their vulnerable, "always-on" connection status. Figure 13.15 illustrates an Internet/intranet firewall system for a company.

Firewalls can deter, but not completely prevent, unauthorized access (hacking) into computer networks. In some cases, a firewall may allow access only from trusted locations on the Internet to particular computers inside the firewall, or it may allow only "safe" information to pass. For example, a firewall may permit users to read e-mail from remote locations but not run certain programs. In other cases, it is impossible to distinguish the safe use of a particular network service from unsafe use, so all requests must be blocked. The firewall may then provide substitutes for some network services (such as e-mail or file transfers) that perform most of the same functions but are not as vulnerable to penetration.

FIGURE 13.15

An example of the Internet and intranet firewalls in a company's networks.

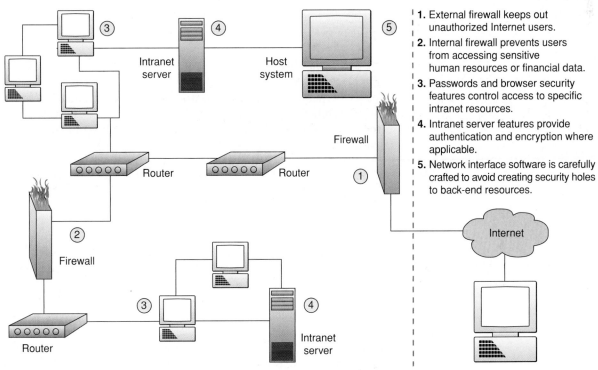

1. External firewall keeps out unauthorized Internet users.
2. Internal firewall prevents users from accessing sensitive human resources or financial data.
3. Passwords and browser security features control access to specific intranet resources.
4. Intranet server features provide authentication and encryption where applicable.
5. Network interface software is carefully crafted to avoid creating security holes to back-end resources.

WhiteHat Security: "Black Box Testing" Mimics Hackers to Discover Vulnerabilities

Jeremiah Grossman wants you to know that firewalls and SSL encryption won't prevent a hacker from breaking into your e-commerce Web site, compromising your customers' data, and possibly stealing your money. That's because most Web site attacks these days exploit bugs in the Web application itself, rather than in the operating system on which the application is running.

Grossman is the founder and chief technology officer of WhiteHat Security, a Silicon Valley firm that offers an outsourced Web site vulnerability management service. Using a combination of proprietary scanning and so-called ethical hacking, WhiteHat assesses the security of its clients' Web sites, looking for exploitable vulnerabilities.

WhiteHat does its scanning without access to the client's source code and from outside the client's firewall using the standard HTTP Web protocol. This approach is sometimes called "black box testing" because the Web site's contents are opaque to the security assessors. The problem with black box testing, of course, is that it is sure to miss many vulnerabilities and back doors that are hidden in the source code. Black box testing can only find vulnerabilities that are visible to someone who is using your Web site, but the advantage of this approach is that it precisely mimics how a hacker would most likely conduct his reconnaissance and break-in.

From his vantage point at WhiteHat, Grossman has seen several organizations migrate Web sites from Microsoft's original ASP to ASP.NET. "ASP classic, the first generation of ASP websites, are generally riddled with vulnerabilities," he says. Yet when these organizations rewrote their applications using ASP.NET, suddenly their applications improved tremendously security-wise. "Same developers, two different frameworks. It wasn't an education problem; it was a technology problem."

At another company—a financial institution—WhiteHat discovered an easily exploited vulnerability that would have let customers steal money. WhiteHat called up the company, and the problem was hot-fixed within 24 hours. A few months later, the vulnerability came back. "The developers were working on the next release, set to come out in two to three months. Some developer did not back-port the hot-fix from the production server to the development server. So when the push occurred three months later, they pushed the vulnerability again." Ugh!

You may not be a big fan of this approach to security, but if you talk to Grossman for a couple of hours, he will convince you that it's a necessary part of today's e-commerce Web sites. Yes, it would be nice to eliminate these well-known bugs with better coding practices, but we live in the real world. It's better to look for the bugs and fix them than to just cross your fingers and hope that they aren't there.

SOURCE: Simson Garfinkel, "An Introduction to the Murky Science of Web Application Security," *CIO Magazine*, May 11, 2007.

Denial of Service Attacks

Major attacks against e-commerce and corporate Web sites in the past few years have demonstrated that the Internet is extremely vulnerable to a variety of assaults by criminal hackers, especially ***distributed denial of service (DDoS)*** attacks. Figure 13.16 outlines the steps organizations can take to protect themselves from DDoS attacks.

Denial of service assaults via the Internet depend on three layers of networked computer systems: (1) the victim's Web site, (2) the victim's Internet service provider (ISP), and (3) the sites of "zombie" or slave computers that the cyber-criminals commandeered. For example, in early 2000, hackers broke into hundreds of servers, mostly

Defending against Denial of Service
• **At the zombie machines:** Set and enforce security policies. Scan regularly for Trojan horse programs and vulnerabilities. Close unused ports. Remind users not to open .exe mail attachments.
• **At the ISP:** Monitor and block traffic spikes. Filter spoofed IP addresses. Coordinate security with network providers.
• **At the victim's Web site:** Create backup servers and network connections. Limit connections to each server. Install multiple intrusion-detection systems and multiple routers for incoming traffic to reduce choke points.

FIGURE 13.16

How to defend against denial
of service attacks.

poorly protected servers at universities, and planted Trojan horse .exe programs, which were then used to launch a barrage of service requests in a concerted attack on e-commerce Web sites like Yahoo! and eBay.

As Figure 13.16 shows, defensive measures and security precautions must be taken at all three levels of the computer networks involved. These are the basic steps companies and other organizations can take to protect their Web sites from denial of service and other hacking attacks. Now let's take a look at a real-world example of a more sophisticated defense technology.

In December 2010, a group calling themselves "Anonymous" launched orchestrated DDoS attacks on organizations such as Mastercard.com, PayPal, Visa.com and PostFinance, as part of the ongoing Operation Payback campaign, which originally targeted antipiracy organizations in support of the whistle-blowing site Wikileaks.ch and its founder, Julian Assange. The attack successfully brought down the Mastercard, PostFinance, and Visa Web sites. PostFinance, the bank that had frozen Julian Assange's account as part of an international criminal investigation, was brought down for more than 16 hours due to the attacks. However, the bank issued a statement that the outage was caused by an overload of inquiries, rather than admit that a bunch of notorious Internet users took down their Web site. DDoS attacks are one of the most common and debilitating attacks on the Internet.

As If Phishing Wasn't Enough: Denial of Service Attacks

Kevin Dougherty has seen his share of spam and phishing scams, as has any IT leader in the financial services industry. But the sender's name on this particular e-mail sent a shudder down his spine: It was from one of his board members at the Central Florida Educators' Federal Credit Union (CFEFCU). The e-mail claimed in convincing detail that there was a problem with the migration to a new Visa credit card that the board member was promoting to the credit union's customers. The fraudulent message urged customers to click on a link—to a phony Web site set up by criminals—and enter their account information to fix the problem.

But what happened later that Friday afternoon—after Dougherty, who is senior vice president of IT and marketing, had wiped the credit card migration information off the Web site and put up an alert warning customers of the scam—really scared him.

Around 2 p.m., the site suddenly went dark, like someone had hit it with a baseball bat. That's when Dougherty realized that he was dealing with something he hadn't seen before. And he couldn't describe it with conventional terms like phishing or spamming. This was an organized criminal conspiracy targeting his bank. "This wasn't random," he says. "They saw what we were doing with the credit card and came at us hard."

Dougherty's Web site lay in a coma from a devastating distributed denial of service (DDOS) attack that, at its peak, shot more than 600,000 packets per second of bogus service requests at his servers from a coordinated firing squad of compromised computers around the globe. That the criminals had the skill and foresight to launch a two-pronged attack against Dougherty and his customers was a clear indication of how far online crime, which is now a $2.8 billion business according to research company Gartner, has come in the past few years.

Obviously, the first thing Dougherty had to do was stop the attack. He had to hurriedly assemble a coalition of vendors and consultants to help him, and then he had to convince his chief executive officer that drastic steps were needed—steps that would temporarily cut off customers from any possibility of getting to their accounts online until the problems were completely eradicated. Dougherty wanted to have the site temporarily blacklisted with his telecom provider, BellSouth, to deflect the attack, thereby reducing pressure on the site and giving him the time and flexibility to make protective changes. But his chief executive officer resisted—as might anyone who has not experienced an attack. "He wanted to keep it up so we could service the members," says Dougherty.

At 11 p.m., after a long night of battling the attackers and plotting strategy, Dougherty finally convinced his chief executive officer to have the site black-listed and to take a break until morning.

Continuing in a tired and emotional state would have played into the attackers' hands. "It's a mind game," says Dougherty.

By Saturday morning, Dougherty had RSA, a security vendor he called in when the attacks began, working to set up a "takedown" service that seeks out and dispatches criminal Web sites (in this case, more than 30) with its own cyber baseball bat. Meanwhile, BellSouth began beefing up security around the credit union site to try to thwart attacks.

The site was back up by Saturday evening. In the end, 22 customers gave up their information to the thieves and the total losses were "less than five figures," says Dougherty. Although the credit union had averted disaster, "it was a rude awakening," he says.

SOURCE: Nancy Weil, "Your Plan to Fight Cyber Crime," *CIO Magazine*, June 15, 2007.

E-mail Monitoring

Spot checks just aren't good enough anymore. The tide is turning toward systematic monitoring of corporate e-mail traffic using content-monitoring software that scans for troublesome words that might compromise corporate security. The reason: Users of monitoring software said they're concerned about protecting their intellectual property and guarding themselves against litigation.

As we mentioned earlier in the chapter, Internet and other online e-mail systems are one of the favorite avenues of attack by hackers for spreading computer viruses or breaking into networked computers. E-mail is also the battleground for attempts by companies to enforce policies against illegal, personal, or damaging messages by employees versus the demands of some employees and others who see such policies as violations of privacy rights.

BNSF Railway: Well-Balanced Web-Use Monitoring

Burlington Northern Santa Fe (BNSF) Railway is headquartered in Fort Worth, Texas, and operates one of the largest railway systems in the world. With more than 32,000 miles of tracks, more than 38,000 employees, and 2009 operating revenue of more than $14 billion, the company relies heavily on the Internet to manage its operations. This extensive use of the Internet, on the other hand, also means that it needs to be careful about the undesirable consequences of wide-spread access by employees, including network security, legal liability issues, and productivity concerns. Most of these arise as a result of employee Web-surfing.

To achieve the best balance between productivity, flexibility, and privacy of employee activities, BNSF has developed a multipronged strategy to address the issue, which combines clear policies and monitoring tools, as well as progressive management practices. On the first count, the BNSF Internet and Intranet Policy clearly defines acceptable and unacceptable use practices. This policy is communicated in writing, as well as covered in orientation sessions for new employees. BNSF does not approach this issue exclusively from a technology standpoint, but rather recognizes that the appropriate use is a business issue. As a result, the policy emphasizes workforce behavior rather than system or network performance issues. The policy is also considered a live document, in that it is frequently revised in light both of new technology developments and of changes in employee behavior over time.

With more than 39,000 widely dispersed computer accounts, monitoring activities and enforcing the policy is no small challenge. BNSF uses a centrally controlled approach based on a monitoring tool called Cyfin Reporter, which is installed at company headquarters in Texas. BNSF management specifies the appropriate use settings, which the administrator uses to set up the application. The tool then produces reports indicating use across a wide variety of standard or company-created categories. For example, two of the most commonly useful results include "indications of excessive personal surfing in seemingly innocent areas, e.g., shopping, sports and news (thus reducing productivity)" and "indications of personal surfing in especially inappropriate and/or potentially dangerous areas, e.g., pornography, hate and crime." It is easy to see from these reports that some innocent personal use is allowed as long as it is not considered excessive; dangerous use, however, is flagged instantly regardless of time spent on it.

The tool can also be used to obtain more finely-grained data about employee Web use. For example, surfing can be categorized based on the kinds of sites visited (sports, shopping, financial, and so forth), or by the group a user belongs to (such as by department or geographical area). Handling large volumes of data are also important; consider that log files of surfing activity alone amount to 2.5 Gb a day. It can also provide automatic abuse detection by setting acceptable limits for specific categories and automatically flagging those occurrences for later review, which allows managers to quickly focus on the really important issues. As far as the Internet goes, things are bound to get more complicated before they get any easier, and companies like BNSF must stay on top of these issues. At the end of the day, employee monitoring is a risk management obligation.

SOURCE: "Employee Web-Use Monitoring at BNSF Railway," *Wavecrest Computing Case Study*, 2007.

VIRAL DEFENSES
LO 13-2
LO 13-3

Is your PC protected from the latest viruses, worms, Trojan horses, and other malicious programs that can wreak havoc on your PC? Chances are it is, if it's periodically linked to the corporate network. These days, corporate antivirus protection is a centralized function of information technology. Someone installs it for you on your PC and notebook or, increasingly, distributes it over the network. The antivirus software runs in the background, popping up every so often to reassure you. The trend right now is to automate the process entirely.

Many companies are building defenses against the spread of viruses by centralizing the distribution and updating of ***antivirus software*** as a responsibility of their IS departments. Other companies are outsourcing the virus protection responsibility to their Internet service providers or telecommunications or security management companies.

FIGURE 13.17

An example of security suite PC software that includes antivirus and firewall protection.

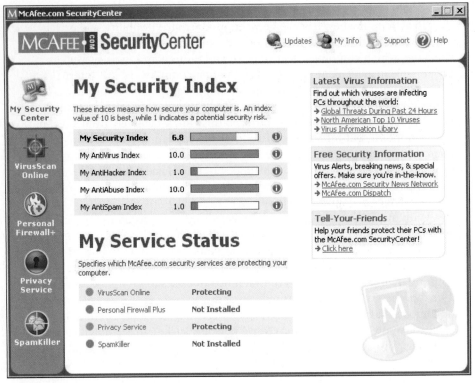

SOURCE: Courtesy of McAfee.

One reason for this trend is that the major antivirus software companies like McAfee (VirusScan) and Symantec (Norton Antivirus) have developed network versions of their programs, which they are marketing to ISPs and others as a service they should offer to all their customers. The antivirus companies are also marketing *security suites* of software that integrate virus protection with firewalls, Web security, and content-blocking features. See Figure 13.17.

The Future of Antivirus

Antivirus software makes Greg Shipley so mad he has to laugh. "The relationship between signature-based antivirus companies and the virus writers is almost comical. One releases something and then the other reacts, and they go back and forth. It's a silly little arms race that has no end."

Shipley, chief technology officer at Neohapsis, a security consulting firm in Chicago, says the worst part is that the arms race isn't helpful either to him or to his clients. "I want to get off of signature-based antivirus as rapidly as possible. I think it's a broken model, and I think it's an incredible CPU hog."

Antivirus as an industry has modeled itself on the human immune system, which slaps a label on things like viruses so it knows to attack them when it sees that same label, or signature, again. Signature-based antivirus has moved well beyond that simple type of signature usage (although, at the beginning, it did look for specific lines of code). The number of malware signatures that security software company F-Secure tracked doubled in 2007, and while you might cynically expect such a company to say there's more malware out there, 2007's total doubled the number of signatures F-Secure had built up over the previous 20 years.

Antivirus firms think that reports of their death are greatly exaggerated, thank you very much—even those that aren't overly reliant on signatures, like BitDefender, which says that signature-based techniques account for only 20 percent of the malware it catches. Corporate CISOs (chief information security officers) certainly don't expect to find one answer to their problems. "If you rely on signatures for security, you're pretty much dead in the water," says Ken Pfeil, head of information security for the Americas region of WestLB, a German bank. Pfeil thinks signatures are useful and his firm uses them, but when new malware appears, he often finds it faster to try to break it down himself to understand its potential effects, rather than wait for his vendor to give him an update. His firm has also adopted tools that use heuristics techniques and anomaly testing, to add oomph to its antivirus approach.

That kind of layered approach to software fits with where Natalie Lambert, an analyst at Forrester Research, thinks the market is going. "Signature-based antivirus plus techniques like heuristic information processing systems, or HIPS, which look for suspicious actions by software, like an application opening itself from the Temp folder." The downside to these technologies is that none is as simple and alluring as the old signature-based antivirus, which she called a "set it and forget it" technology. She notes that HIPS technologies are difficult to manage and will never be as simple as the old model, although she expects they will get easier over time.

Antivirus firms agree that they are becoming something different; however, David Harley, administrator of Avien, the antivirus information exchange network, thinks that there are psychological reasons that antivirus software is unlikely to go away. "The idea of a solution that stops real threats and doesn't hamper nonmalicious objects and processes is very attractive. People (at any rate, those who aren't security specialists) like the idea of threat-specific software, as long it catches all incoming malware and doesn't generate any false positives, because then they can just install it and forget about it. Unfortunately, that's an unattainable ideal."

Note to Greg Shipley: Don't hold your breath on getting rid of your antivirus software.

SOURCE: Michael Fitzgerald, "The Future of Antivirus," *Computerworld*, April 14, 2008.

Let's now briefly examine a variety of security measures that are commonly used to protect business systems and networks. These include both hardware and software tools, like fault-tolerant computers and security monitors, and security policies and procedures, like passwords and backup files. All are part of an integrated security management effort at many companies today.

OTHER SECURITY MEASURES
LO 13-2

Security Codes

Typically, a multilevel *password* system is used for security management. First, an end user logs on to the computer system by entering his or her unique identification code, or user ID. Second, the end user is asked to enter a password to gain access into the system. (Passwords should be changed frequently and consist of unusual combinations of upper- and lowercase letters and numbers.) Third, to access an individual file, a unique file name must be entered. In some systems, the password to read the contents of a file is different from that required to write to a file (change its contents). This feature adds another level of protection to stored data resources. For even stricter security, however, passwords can be scrambled, or *encrypted*, to avoid their theft or improper use, as we will discuss shortly. In addition, *smart cards*, which contain microprocessors that generate random numbers to add to an end user's password, are used in some secure systems.

Backup Files

Backup files, which are duplicate files of data or programs, are another important security measure. Files can also be protected by *file retention* measures that involve storing copies of files from previous periods. If current files are destroyed, the files from previous periods can be used to reconstruct new current files. Sometimes, several generations of files are kept for control purposes. Thus, master files from several recent periods of processing (known as *child*, *parent*, and *grandparent* files) may be kept for backup purposes. Such files may be stored off-premises, that is, in a location away from a company's data center, sometimes in special storage vaults in remote locations.

Security Monitors

Security of a network may be provided by specialized system software packages known as *system security monitors.* See Figure 13.18. System security monitors are programs that monitor the use of computer systems and networks and protect them from unauthorized use, fraud, and destruction. Such programs provide the security measures needed to allow only authorized users to access the networks. For example, identification codes and passwords are frequently used for this purpose. Security monitors also control the use of the hardware, software, and data resources of a computer system. For

FIGURE 13.18

The eTrust security monitor manages a variety of security functions for major corporate networks, including monitoring the status of Web-based applications throughout a network.

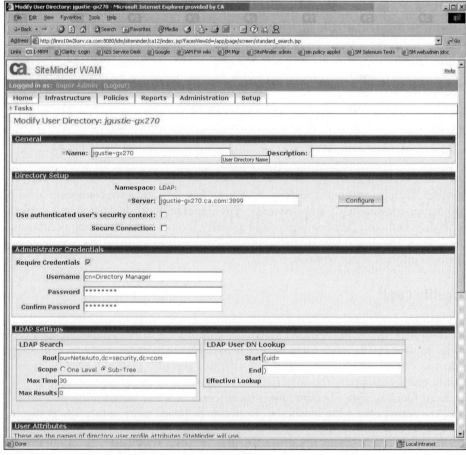

SOURCE: Courtesy of Site Minder.

Evaluation of Biometric Techniques			
User Criteria		**System Criteria**	
Intrusiveness	Effort	Accuracy	Cost
Dynamic signature verification			
Excellent	Fair	Fair	Excellent
Face geometry Good	Good	Fair	Good
Finger scan Fair	Good	Good	Good
Hand geometry Fair	Good	Fair	Fair
Passive iris scan Poor	Excellent	Excellent	Poor
Retina scan Poor	Poor	Very good	Fair
Voice print Very good	Poor	Fair	Very good

FIGURE 13.19

An evaluation of common biometric security techniques based on user requirements, accuracy, and cost.

example, even authorized users may be restricted to the use of certain devices, programs, and data files. In addition, security programs monitor the use of computer networks and collect statistics on any attempts at improper use. They then produce reports to assist in maintaining the security of the network.

Biometric Security

Biometric security is a fast-growing area of computer security. These are security measures provided by computer devices that measure physical traits that make each individual unique, such as voice verification, fingerprints, hand geometry, signature dynamics, keystroke analysis, retina scanning, face recognition, and genetic pattern analysis. Biometric control devices use special-purpose sensors to measure and digitize a biometric profile of a person's fingerprints, voice, or other physical trait. The digitized signal is processed and compared to a previously processed profile of the individual stored on magnetic disk. If the profiles match, the individual is allowed entry into a computer network and given access to secure system resources. See Figure 13.19.

Notice that the examples of biometric security listed in Figure 13.19 are rated according to the degree of intrusiveness (how much the technique interrupts a user) and the relative amount of effort required by the user to authenticate. Also, the relative accuracy and cost of each are assessed. As you can see, trade-offs in these four areas exist in every example. Whereas face geometry is judged easy on the user in terms of intrusiveness and effort, its accuracy is not considered as high as that of other methods. Biometrics is still in its infancy, and many new technologies are being developed to improve on accuracy while minimizing user effort.

Computer Failure Controls

"Sorry, our computer systems are down" is a well-known phrase to many end users. A variety of controls can prevent such computer failure or minimize its effects. Computer systems fail for several reasons—power failures, electronic circuitry malfunctions, telecommunications network problems, hidden programming errors, computer viruses, computer operator errors, and electronic vandalism. For example, computers are available with automatic and remote maintenance capabilities. Programs of preventive maintenance of hardware and management of software updates are commonplace. A backup computer system capability can be arranged with *disaster recovery organizations*. Major hardware or software changes are usually carefully scheduled and implemented to avoid problems. Finally, highly trained data center personnel and the use of performance and security management software help keep a company's computer system and networks working properly.

FIGURE 13.20
Methods of fault tolerance in
computer-based information
systems.

Layer	Threats	Fault-Tolerant Methods
Applications	Environment, hardware, and software faults	Application-specific redundancy and rollback to previous checkpoint
Systems	Outages	System isolation, data security, system integrity
Databases	Data errors	Separation of transactions and safe updates, complete transaction histories, backup files
Networks	Transmission errors	Reliable controllers; safe asynchrony and handshaking; alternative routing; error-detecting and error-correcting codes
Processes	Hardware and software faults	Alternative computations, rollback to checkpoints
Files	Media errors	Replication of critical data on different media and sites; archiving, backup, retrieval
Processors	Hardware faults	Instruction retry; error-correcting codes in memory and processing; replication; multiple processors and memories

Fault-Tolerant Systems

Many firms also use **fault-tolerant** computer systems that have redundant processors, peripherals, and software that provide a *fail-over* capability to back up components in the event of system failure. This system may provide a *fail-safe* capability so that the computer system continues to operate at the same level even if there is a major hardware or software failure. Many fault-tolerant computer systems, however, offer a *fail-soft* capability so that the computer system can continue to operate at a reduced but acceptable level in the event of a major system failure. Figure 13.20 outlines some of the fault-tolerant capabilities used in many computer systems and networks.

What If the Internet Went Down . . . and Didn't Come Back Up?

Yes. We know we all rely on the Internet. But how much?

Imagine, if you will, a world with no Internet. No e-mail. No e-commerce. And no BlackBerrys. E-mail would be supplanted by snail mail; cell phones by land lines.

Now imagine what the future would look like. Futurists say virtual business services of all sorts, accounting, payroll and even sales would come to a halt, as would many companies.

If the Internet were to cease functioning today, the effect would be similar for many people. Increasingly, we are growing up with ubiquitous communication, information at our fingertips, and shopping at the click of a mouse. Many businesses would also come to a crashing halt. Customer lists consisting solely of e-mail addresses are singularly useless without e-mail, and online brochures and catalogs are simply computer wallpaper without the wherewithal to allow potential customers to browse them. And for software developers and others who rely on customer downloads and online credit card payments, the business world would come to an end until they completely rebuilt their business model.

Yes, the corporate landscape would certainly have a very different look, and a lot of businesses would definitely not be able to adjust. Amazon.com? Forget it. E-Bay—gone. E-Trade—bye-bye. In fact, any online shopping would be toast, unless it was conducted through a proprietary service using its dedicated lines (at considerably higher cost). So would payment systems that depend on Internet connections, payroll services, online banking, and Web-based backup services and customer support.

And a lot of media outlets that have moved most of their operations online would scramble madly to resurrect hard copy and its associated advertising revenues.

And don't even think about the blind panic of last-minute Christmas shopping without all those e-tailers promising next-day delivery!

On the plus side, we'd be forever rid of those infernal "male member enhancement" e-mail messages and the kind offers of millions of dollars from strangers on foreign shores that clutter up our inboxes. "One of the things which would disappear with the Internet would be machine-made fame. Modern mass communications have created centripetal attention structures that bottle celebrity, and celebrities, for sale," says futurist Thornton May. "Our adoration of princesses, movie stars, and basketball players would come to an end. This is not necessarily a bad thing."

Could we really go back to the pre-Internet days over time? "We wouldn't do that. We'd recreate the Internet," says May. He adds, "Would Net2 that would be erected to replace Net1 be better? And how long would it take to get Net2 up?"

And then how long would it take us to catch up with our e-mail?

SOURCE: Lynn Greiner, "What If the Internet Went Down . . . and Didn't Come Back Up?" *CIO*, January 15, 2008.

Disaster Recovery

Natural and human-made disasters do happen. Hurricanes, earthquakes, fires, floods, criminal and terrorist acts, and human error can all severely damage an organization's computing resources and thus the health of the organization itself. Many companies, especially online e-commerce retailers and wholesalers, airlines, banks, and Internet service providers, for example, are crippled by losing even a few hours of computing power. Many firms could survive only a few days without computing facilities. That's why organizations develop *disaster recovery* procedures and formalize them in a *disaster recovery plan*. It specifies which employees will participate in disaster recovery and what their duties will be; what hardware, software, and facilities will be used; and the priority of applications that will be processed. Arrangements with other companies for use of alternative facilities as a disaster recovery site and off-site storage of an organization's databases are also part of an effective disaster recovery effort.

Two final security management requirements that need to be mentioned are the development of information system controls and auditing business systems. Let's take a brief look at these two security measures.

SYSTEM CONTROLS AND AUDITS

LO 13-2
LO 13-3

Information System Controls

Information system controls are methods and devices that attempt to ensure the accuracy, validity, and propriety of information system activities. Information system (IS) controls must be developed to ensure proper data entry, processing techniques, storage methods, and information output. Thus, IS controls are designed to monitor

FIGURE 13.21

Examples of information system controls. Note that they are designed to monitor and maintain the quality and security of the input, processing, output, and storage activities of an information system.

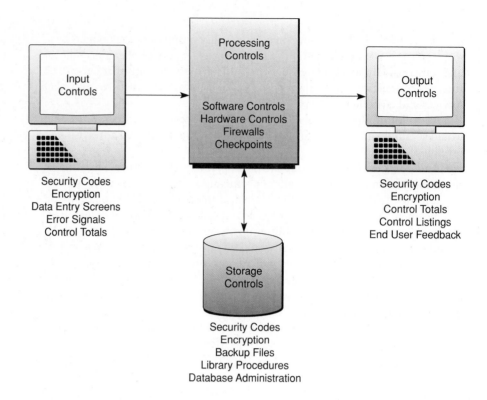

and maintain the quality and security of the input, processing, output, and storage activities of any information system. See Figure 13.21.

For example, IS controls are needed to ensure the proper entry of data into a business system and thus avoid the garbage in, garbage out (GIGO) syndrome. Examples include passwords and other security codes, formatted data entry screens, and audible error signals. Computer software can include instructions to identify incorrect, invalid, or improper input data as it enters the computer system. For example, a data entry program can check for invalid codes, data fields, and transactions, and conduct "reasonableness checks" to determine if input data exceed specified limits or are out of sequence.

Auditing IT Security

IT security management should be periodically examined, or audited, by a company's internal auditing staff or external auditors from professional accounting firms. Such audits review and evaluate whether proper and adequate security measures and management policies have been developed and implemented. This process typically involves verifying the accuracy and integrity of the software used, as well as the input of data and output produced by business applications. Some firms employ special computer security auditors for this assignment. They may use special test data to check processing accuracy and the control procedures built into the software. The auditors may develop special test programs or use audit software packages.

Another important objective of business system audits is testing the integrity of an application's *audit trail*. An **audit trail** can be defined as the presence of documentation that allows a transaction to be traced through all stages of its information processing. This journey may begin with a transaction's appearance on a source document and end with its transformation into information in a final output document or report. The audit trail of manual information systems is quite visible and

Security Management for Internet Users	
1. Use antivirus and firewall software and update it often to keep destructive programs off your computer.	6. Use the most up-to-date version of your Web browser, e-mail software, and other programs.
2. Don't allow online merchants to store your credit card information for future purchases.	7. Send credit card numbers only to secure sites; look for a padlock or key icons at the bottom of the browser.
3. Use a hard-to-guess password that contains a mix of numbers and letters, and change it frequently.	8. Use a security program that gives you control over "cookies" that send information back to Web sites.
4. Use different passwords for different Web sites and applications to keep hackers guessing.	9. Install firewall software to screen traffic if you use DSL or a cable modem to connect to the Net.
5. Install all operating system patches and upgrades.	10. Don't open e-mail attachments unless you know the source of the incoming message.

FIGURE 13.22

How to protect yourself from cyber-crime and other computer security threats.

easy to trace. However, computer-based information systems have changed the form of the audit trail. Now auditors must know how to search electronically through disk and tape files of past activity to follow the audit trail of today's networked computer systems.

Many times, this *electronic audit trail* takes the form of *control logs* that automatically record all computer network activity on magnetic disk or tape devices. This audit feature can be found on many online transaction processing systems, performance and security monitors, operating systems, and network control programs. Software that records all network activity is also widely used on the Internet, especially the World Wide Web, as well as on corporate intranets and extranets. Such an audit trail helps auditors check for errors or fraud, but also helps IS security specialists trace and evaluate the trail of hacker attacks on computer networks.

Figure 13.22 summarizes 10 security management steps you can take to protect your computer system resources from hacking and other forms of cyber-crime.

Georgetown University: All Systems Go

When Bill Badertscher—now senior engineer for facility and safety control systems—first came to Georgetown University in 2008, a number of different departments handled campuswide security with little or no coordination among them. Georgetown had experienced a number of security breaches and project failure occurrences; thus, at a high level it was recognized that a new approach was needed to address systems in the facilities and security spaces. By redefining the enterprise risk management processes to include nontraditional systems, they got the safety and information services departments to work together as they never had before. The new strategy was led by CIO Dave Lambert and led to the formation of several new groups within IT.

The first step in the new program was to establish a budget to replace aging legacy systems, such as access control and video surveillance. It became apparent quite quickly, however, that existing needs were much larger than that. An initial assessment identified more than $60 million required for new spending. That much money, however, was not available, and so Bill and his team had to start focusing on assessing the potential risks arising from all those issues and figuring out which ones to tackle first. The new approach, however, is not only about facilities and security control systems. New groups have appeared, all under the umbrella of the chief information officer, to handle scholarly information systems, research and regulatory administration, data security policies, and so forth. This collection of groups is now working together to address risks across the entire organization—in business terms, enterprise risk management. That still includes facilities and security control systems, of course, but is now much broader than that.

Prioritizing risks is central to this. "A lot of security decisions are made on an emotional basis or in response to incidents," says Badertscher. However, the most significant risks faced by the university have to do with incidents that may lead to lawsuits or otherwise negatively affect its reputation. Media scrutiny is also important in such a high-profile organization. One of the big challenges the new take on enterprise risk has faced has been the existing organizational structure, which was heavily centered around vertical siloes—each with its own administration and responsibilities—which initially led to a fair amount of defensiveness. In particular, people wanted to know why the information systems department was stepping on their turf. There are also various stakeholders involved, each with its own ideas about what "security" means. For some, it means access cards; for others, it means cameras; yet for others, it means monitoring student usage of computer equipment that may open the university to lawsuits in the future. "We base our decisions on a clear understanding of the risks involved," says Badertscher. "This includes identifying our assets and assessing the threat environment and our vulnerabilities—and then communicating our plans."

SOURCE: Joan Goodchild, "Enterprise Risk Management: All Systems Go," *CSO*, May 31, 2010.

Harland Clarke-Toward a Comprehensive Risk Management Program

Originally a manufacturer of checks and check-related products, Harland Clarke essentially underwent a reinvention of the company from the mid-2000s onward—into a provider of technology solutions to financial services institutions, other businesses, and individual customers. As part of this transformation, and recognizing that major changes in its approach to security would be required to carry out the new mission of the organization, the company asked John Petrie to join in 2004 as chief information security officer for the San Antonio, Texas-based organization. Major changes would be required to go from what was originally a tactical function with responsibility distributed among individual plant managers into a world-class risk management shop that could make sure the company would not stumble into any major problems along the way.

As a result, the company decided to implement a new, comprehensive security program that encompassed all operations in all areas of the organization. A winner of the 2001 Malcolm Baldrige National Quality Award—a prestigious recognition—the company decided to implement the same kind of quality processes that led to the distinction of their security practices in order to enjoy cost savings. "We were able to take advantage of the solutions we implemented for quality in the areas of identification, notification and prevention," says Petrie. For example, each plant had some personnel dedicated to monitoring and maintaining quality process. Now, those same employees would also be in charge of identifying events that could have security implications as well as potentially having quality effects. To highlight the new role of security in the company, the reporting structure was modified; now, John Petrie reports directly to the chief security officer, who has integrated responsibility for all security-related aspects of all operations, whereas the chief information officer is no longer directly in charge of these efforts.

The next step was to transform security from a technical function into one that identifies, understands, and manages risks—understanding which risks to accept, and which to mitigate—throughout the company. Doing so required the implementation of new processes to support each of those functions. One of these is an annual business impact analysis, conducted by an external consultant who reviews existing risk management processes and practices and identifies vulnerabilities or threats that the company may have overlooked. Some of those may not appear to be, at first sight, strictly related to security—but they are. Consider, for example, marketing campaigns. "Because we are getting consumer information, we need to look at how to protect that, and once controls are in place, how that would affect the flow of the marketing campaign, which in turn will determine acceptable risk levels," says Petrie. Even marketing has security implications to it.

Relying on external parties who have no stake in the outcome is a tried-and-true method of getting an objective evaluation. On the technology side, Harland Clarke works with Verizon Business—which acquired Cybertrust, their original security consultancy—to conduct monthly reviews of the entire enterprise. Results from those reviews are discussed with management to determine if any issues or vulnerabilities found are within what the company considers acceptable risks. "Risk is not finite, it is not a Yes or No decision," says Petrie. "It depends on what is acceptable to the business to operate."

Results from this kind of analyses are used to develop an annual risk management matrix that is then presented to the executive team for consideration. Part of the transformation of the security function is that now senior executives take ultimate responsibility for which risks they are or are not willing to accept, a major change from the old days of each plant manager on his own. Each identified threat is assessed on a 10-point scale as to its potential damage and its probability of materializing. These form the basis of discussion and subsequent decision making regarding risk. The overall risk profile of a threat is determined by multiplying these factors. For example, a zero-day worm (a previously unknown piece of malicious code for which antivirus signatures are not yet available) may be assigned a potential damage score of 7 or 8, but a likelihood of occurrence of only 2 or 3 because the company has strong controls in place to prevent it from ever getting through the security perimeter. Add to this what it would cost to shut down the network, identify an infected machine, segregate it and apply any necessary fixes, and you have the overall cost of that one risk. Now, is it worth doing anything about it?

"The risk matrix is a tool to help you assign a quantitative number to which you can then decide to assign resources and assets to mitigate the risk," says Petrie.

However, because those resources are limited, managers have to make tough trade-offs when deciding where to focus them, just as you would do when choosing which R&D projects to fund, or which new application development initiatives to green-light. "Now, security is similar to any other line of business," says Petrie. So much so that security has to develop its annual performance indicators in much the same manner as any other area of the company. Right now security is working with a portfolio of 8 Key Performance Indicators, or KPIs for short, which are in turn supported by more than 30 different metrics, which are in turn regularly monitored. "If we do not meet the metrics within information security, that has an impact on our business goals," says Petri.

With all these processes in place, the security group now has the tools required to make security decisions on an ongoing basis. For example, a review by Verizon revealed that operating systems at a production line in one of the manufacturing plants had not been patched adequately. Over seven months before that, the software vendor had told the company that patches for the systems were available, but managers had made the conscious decision not to go ahead, as they did not consider the risk a major issue and were more concerned about the possibility of a disruption or outage of the production equipment. That is the kind of carefully considered rational decision that one can make when all the necessary information is available—that is, taking a calculated risk. The recent review, however, indicated that a newly developed worm that specifically targeted those systems was now active, which led the company to revisit the decision. After running penetration tests over a 30-day period to collect the data necessary to make a sound assessment of the situation, the new findings were presented to the executive team. "The chances were fairly high that even a low-level worm or virus would shut those systems down," says Petrie. "We determined that it was not an acceptable risk to not apply this patch, particularly since it could be done during programmed maintenance downtime for the equipment. The whole process was a complete review of the decision we had already made several months

earlier," he says. "That is why a risk management program is so critical—the threat had changed, so we had to reassess our decision and make a new one based on that. Risk management is not a stagnant process but a continuous one," underscores Petrie.

Another example involves the recording systems that are used to monitor the plants and office facilities of the company. A spot check showed that one of the systems, based on VHS tapes, was malfunctioning, which affected the 20 to 30 cameras that were attached to it. After examining the problem, the group came up with two alternatives for addressing it. First, the company could switch off equipment in other locations to replace the problematic system, as its age made it impossible to find an actual replacement. Alternatively, the entire system could be upgraded to digital equipment. On the one hand, the upgrade represented a one-time cost increase of 20 to 30 percent compared to VHS equipment; on the other hand, reduced physical storage needs and simple maintenance requirements of the digital system represented a 20 percent reduction in ongoing annual costs. From a controls perspective, the digital system was a clear winner, but the costs were in the millions of dollars. Once again, armed with all these data, the question was posed to the executive team, who decided to go ahead with the upgrade. The entire process took only four months.

Fast forward to 2009, and Harland Clarke has been awarded the coveted Verizon Business Security Management Program Cybertrust Certification, which demonstrates continued commitment to high-quality security practices, for the third year in a row. This is a very rigorous program with annual recertification requirements, which only about half of the companies that apply have been able to satisfy. It cannot get any more different from where they were just five years before.

SOURCE: Mary Brandel, "Harland Clarke Rechecks Risk Management," *CSO*, October 16, 2007; "Verizon Business Recognizes Harland Clarke's Security Excellence with Prestigious Security Certification," *PRNewsWire*, March 13, 2009; and www.harlandclarke.com, accessed June 14, 2011.

▼ QUESTIONS TO CONSIDER

1. How has the way in which decisions about security were made changed with the new approach? What are the key differences? What are the most likely effects of the new procedures?

2. Should companies always patch and fix all systems immediately? Why would they take the risk of not doing so? Can you think of any other examples beyond those presented in the case?

summary

- **Ethical and Societal Dimensions.** The vital role of information technologies and systems in society raises serious ethical and societal issues in terms of their impact on employment, individuality, working conditions, privacy, health, and computer crime, as illustrated in Figure 13.2.

  Employment issues include the loss of jobs—a result of computerization and automation of work—versus the jobs created to supply and support new information technologies and the business applications they make possible. The impact on working conditions involves the issues of computer monitoring of employees and the quality of the working conditions of the jobs that use information technologies heavily. The effect of IT on individuality addresses the issues of the depersonalization, regimentation, and inflexibility of some computerized business systems.

  Employees' heavy use of computer workstations for long periods raises issues about and may cause work-related health disorders. The use of IT to access or collect private information without authorization, as well as for computer profiling, computer matching, computer monitoring, and computer libel and censorship, raises serious privacy issues. Computer crime issues surround activities such as hacking, computer viruses and worms, cyber-theft, unauthorized use at work, software piracy, and piracy of intellectual property.

  Managers, business professionals, and IS specialists can help solve the problems of improper use

  of IT by assuming their ethical responsibilities for the ergonomic design, beneficial use, and enlightened management of information technologies in our society.

- **Ethical Responsibility in Business.** Business and IT activities involve many ethical considerations. Basic principles of technology and business ethics can serve as guidelines for business professionals when dealing with ethical business issues that may arise in the widespread use of information technology in business and society. Examples include theories of corporate social responsibility, which outline the ethical responsibility of management and employees to a company's stockholders, stakeholders, and society, and the four principles of technology ethics summarized in Figure 13.4.

- **Security Management.** One of the most important responsibilities of the management of a company is to ensure the security and quality of its IT-enabled business activities. Security management tools and policies can ensure the accuracy, integrity, and safety of the information systems and resources of a company and thus minimize errors, fraud, and security losses in its business activities. Examples mentioned in the chapter include the use of encryption of confidential business data, firewalls, e-mail monitoring, antivirus software, security codes, backup files, security monitors, biometric security measures, computer failure controls, fault-tolerant systems, disaster recovery measures, information system controls, and security audits of business systems.

These are the key terms and concepts of this chapter. The page number of their first reference appears in parentheses.

key terms and concepts

1. Antivirus software (603)
2. Audit trail (610)
3. Backup files (606)
4. Biometric security (607)
5. Business ethics (570)
6. Computer crime (573)
7. Computer matching (589)
8. Computer monitoring (592)
9. Computer virus (582)
10. Cyber law (590)
11. Disaster recovery (609)
12. Distributed denial of service (DDoS) (600)
13. Encryption (598)
14. Ergonomics (594)
15. Ethical foundations (570)
16. Fault-tolerant (608)
17. Firewall (599)
18. Flaming (590)
19. Hacking (575)
20. Information system controls (609)
21. Intellectual property theft (581)
22. Opt-in/Opt-out (587)
23. Password (605)
24. Security management (596)
25. Societal solutions (594)
26. Software piracy (580)
27. Spamming (590)
28. Spyware/Adware (585)
29. System security monitor (606)
30. Unauthorized use (579)

Match one of the key terms and concepts listed previously with one of the brief examples or definitions that follow. Try to find the best fit for the answers that seem to fit more than one term or concept. Defend your choices.

_____ 1. Ensuring the accuracy, integrity, and safety of business/IT activities and resources.

_____ 2. Control totals, error signals, backup files, and security codes are examples.

_____ 3. Software that can control access and use of a computer system.

_____ 4. A computer system can continue to operate even after a major system failure if it has this capability.

_____ 5. A computer system that serves as a filter for access to and from other networks by a company's networked computers.

_____ 6. Laws and regulations focused on issues related to the Internet and other forms of networked communications.

_____ 7. The presence of documentation that allows a transaction to be traced through all stages of information processing.

_____ 8. Using your voice or fingerprints to identify yourself electronically.

_____ 9. A plan to continue IS operations during an emergency.

_____ 10. Scrambling data during its transmission.

_____ 11. Ethical choices may result from decision-making processes, cultural values, or behavioral stages.

_____ 12. Managers must confront numerous ethical questions in their businesses.

_____ 13. Sending unsolicited e-mail indiscriminately.

_____ 14. Software that can infect a machine and transmit private information back to its owner.

_____ 15. Two different perspectives on the use of private information.

_____ 16. Using computers to identify individuals who fit a certain profile.

_____ 17. Using computers to monitor the activities of workers.

_____ 18. Overwhelming a Web site with requests for service from captive computers.

_____ 19. Using computers and networks to steal money, services, software, or data.

_____ 20. Using company computers to access the Internet during work hours for personal business.

_____ 21. Unauthorized copying of software.

_____ 22. Unauthorized copying of copyrighted material.

_____ 23. Electronic breaking and entering into a computer system.

_____ 24. A program that makes copies of itself and destroys data and programs.

_____ 25. Finds and eliminates computer viruses.

_____ 26. Sending extremely critical, derogatory, and vulgar e-mail messages.

_____ 27. Designing computer hardware, software, and workstations that are safe, comfortable, and easy to use.

_____ 28. Applications of information technology that have beneficial effects for society at large.

_____ 29. Duplicate files of programs or data that are periodically copied and stored elsewhere in case the original is damaged and needs to be restored.

_____ 30. A piece of data, known only to an authorized user, that is used to gain access to a system.

1. What can be done to improve the security of business uses of the Internet? Give several examples of security measures and technologies you would use.

2. What potential security problems do you see in the increasing use of intranets and extranets in business? What might be done to solve such problems? Give several examples.

3. Refer to the real-world example about copying CDs and music downloading in the chapter. Is copying music CDs an ethical practice? How about Internet music downloading? Explain.

4. What are your major concerns about computer crime and privacy on the Internet? What can you do about it? Explain.

5. What is disaster recovery? How could it be implemented at your school or workplace?

6. Refer to the Real World Challenge in the introduction to this chapter. Should "IS" security be managed in a different way than physical security? How are the two areas different? How are they similar?

7. Is there an ethical crisis in business today? What role does information technology play in unethical business practices?

8. What are several business decisions that you will have to make as a manager that have both ethical and IT dimensions? Give examples to illustrate your answer.

9. Refer to the Real World Solution in the chapter. Can you apply the "likelihood and magnitude" approach to any kind of risk that a company faces? Can you think of any examples that would not be suitable for that kind of analysis? How should companies evaluate those situations?

10. What would be examples of one positive and one negative effect of the use of information technologies in each of the ethical and societal dimensions illustrated in Figure 13.2? Explain several of your choices.

1. **Problems with Passwords**

   Authentication

   Network and application managers need to know who is accessing their systems in order to determine appropriate access levels. Authentication has three basic forms:

   1. Something you KNOW (a password)
   2. Something you HAVE (such as a key to a locked room or building)
   3. Something you ARE (biometrics)

   Typically, managers require users to create secret passwords. A secret password, known only to the user, allows an administrator to feel confident of that user's identity. A systems administrator even has the authority to determine the characteristics of a password. For example, the administrator may set a minimum length and require that a password include numbers, symbols, or mixed letter case, as well as require the user to change the password every few weeks or months. These approaches have numerous problems.

   - Users often forget complicated or frequently changing passwords. This results in frequent calls to a help desk. The help desk employee then faces the burden of identifying the employee by some other means and resetting the password. This process takes time and is subject to *social engineering*.

   - Users may write down their passwords. However, this leaves passwords subject to discovery and theft. Statistics show that the most popular places to hide passwords are a "sticky note" on the underside of the company phone list in a desk drawer, or taped to the bottom of either the keyboard or the underside of a CRT monitor.

   - Users often pick the same password for many different accounts. Therefore, someone who discovers one of these passwords then has the keys to all of the accounts.

   - Users may pick an easy-to-remember password. However, these passwords are easy to anticipate and therefore easy to guess. Password-cracking programs cycle through entire dictionaries of English language words and common word/number combinations such as "smart1" or "2smart4U."

   - Lastly, users may give away their passwords over the phone (*social engineering*) or via e-mail (*phishing*, a type of social engineering) to someone representing themselves as a system administrator. Perhaps you have already received e-mails purportedly from a financial institution claiming identity or account difficulties and asking you to reconfirm your account information on their authentic-looking Web site.

   As you can see, using passwords to identify a person is fraught with problems. Here are some alternatives to explore. Look up each authentication approach listed below on the Internet, describe the method in your own words (be sure to cite your sources), and briefly list the advantages and disadvantages.

   a. Biometrics (biological measuring)

   b. Smart cards

   c. Bio chips

2. **Your Internet Job Rights**

   Three Ethical Scenarios

   Whether you're an employer or an employee, you should know what your rights are when it comes to Internet use in the workplace. Recently federal and state courts have ruled that e-mail has little or no expectation of privacy in many circumstances. A number of employees have been terminated or warned for misuse, improper use, or inappropriate use of organizational resources by sending/reading personal e-mail on the firm's computers and networks while on their own time (during lunch, or before/after work hours). The type of Internet use also comes into question, particularly when surfing Web sites the firm may consider "questionable" or "adult" (i.e., pornography). Generally, these types of materials fall into three groups: pornographic, obscene, or indecent, and definitions and penalties vary from state to state, and even from town to town. A firm should have written policies for computer and network use, and employees should be schooled in these requirements. Many firms today require employees to sign a statement that they have been advised of these policies.

Mark Grossman, a Florida attorney who specializes in computer and Internet law, gives answers to some basic questions.

Scenario 1

Nobody told you that your Internet use in the office was being monitored. Now you've been warned you'll be fired if you use the Internet for recreational surfing again. What are your rights?

Bottom Line. When you're using your office computer, you have virtually no rights. You'd have a tough time convincing a court that the boss invaded your privacy by monitoring your use of the company PC on company time. You should probably be grateful you got a warning.

Scenario 2

Your employees are abusing their Internet privileges, but you don't have an Internet usage policy. What do you do?

Bottom line. Although the law isn't fully developed in this area, courts are taking a straightforward approach: If it's a company computer, the company can control the way it's used. You don't need an Internet usage policy to prevent inappropriate use of your company computers. To protect yourself in the future, distribute an Internet policy to your employees as soon as possible.

Scenario 3

Employee John Doe downloads adult material to his PC at work, and employee Jane Smith sees it. Smith then proceeds to sue the company for sexual harassment. As the employer, are you liable?

Bottom line. Whether it comes from the Internet or from a magazine, adult material simply has no place in the office. So Smith could certainly sue the company for allowing a sexually hostile environment. The best defense is for the company to have an Internet usage policy that prohibits visits to adult sites. Of course, you have to follow through. If someone is looking at adult material in the office, you must at least send the offending employee a written reprimand. If the company lacks a strict Internet policy, though, Smith could prevail in court.

a. Do you agree with the advice of attorney Mark Grossman in each of the scenarios? Why or why not?

b. What would your advice be? Explain your positions.

c. Identify any ethical principles you may be using in explaining your position in each of the scenarios.

3. **Exploiting Security Weaknesses**
Social Engineering

An employee who needs permission to access an electronic workspace, database, or other information systems resource typically fills in a request form and obtains approval from the responsible manager. The manager then routes the request to one of the system's administrators.

Highly trusted and well-trained systems administrators spend a significant amount of time doing nothing more technical than adding or removing names from access control lists. In large organizations, it's not unusual for systems administrators to have never met any of the people involved in a specific request. The administrators may not even work in the same office.

Hackers have learned to take advantage of this approach to access authorization. They begin by "probing" an organization. The hacker doesn't expect to compromise the system during this initial probe. He or she simply starts by making a few phone calls to learn who is responsible for granting access and how to apply. A little more probing helps the hacker learn who's who within the organization's structure. Some organizations even post this information online in the form of employee directories. With this information in hand, the hacker knows whom to talk to, what to ask for, and what names to use in order to sound convincing. The hacker is now ready to try to impersonate an employee and trick a systems administrator into revealing a password and unwittingly granting unauthorized access.

Organizations determine who needs access to what applications. They also need a system through which they can authenticate the identity of an individual making a request. Finally, they need to manage this process both effectively and inexpensively.

a. Describe the business problems presented by this exercise.

b. Suggest several ways to reduce an organization's exposure to social engineering.

c. Prepare an orientation memo to new hires in your IT department describing "social engineering." Suggest several ways employees can avoid being tricked by hackers.

4. **Privacy Statements**
The Spyware Problem

Web surfers may feel anonymous as they use the Internet, but that feeling isn't always justified. IP addresses, cookies, site log-in procedures, and credit card purchases all help track how often users visit a site and what pages they view. Some companies go further.

Some free screensaver software and peer-to-peer file sharing come with spyware embedded within their applications. Once loaded, these applications run in the background. What they actually track depends on the specific software. To stay on the right side of U.S. law, these companies outline their software's functions in general terms and include this information in the small print within their end-user licensing agreement (EULA) and or privacy policy. In fact, these agreements may even include a stipulation that users not disable any part of their software as a condition for free use.

Since most users don't read these policies, they have no idea what privacy rights they may have given up. They may indeed get their free file-sharing program or screen saver, but they may be getting a lot more. Some spyware programs even remain on hard drives and stay active even after users have uninstalled their free software.

a. Use a search engine to search on "spyware," "spyware removal," "adware," or other related terms. Prepare a one-page summary of your results. Include URLs for online sources.

b. Select three of your favorite Web sites and print out their privacy policies. What do they share in common? How do they differ?

c. Write your own Web site privacy policy, striking a balance between both customer and business needs.

5. Security and Ethics
WikiLeaks Takes on Washington
In 1971 *The* New York Times began publishing excerpts from a leaked document popularly

known as the *Pentagon Papers*. These documents, classified "Top Secret," contained a history of U.S. involvement in Vietnam up through 1968, including details about deceptions perpetrated by four presidential administrations against the American people.

The U.S. Supreme Court ruled against *prior restraint* in this case and allowed newspapers to publish excerpts of this classified document. The subsequent case against the leaker, Daniel Ellsberg, ended in a mistrial. The papers' publication significantly affected popular opinion and most likely hastened America's exit from southeast Asia.

Fast forward nearly 30 years. In 2010 WikiLeaks published a classified video showing an air strike that killed two unarmed Reuters reporters (see http://bit.ly/mkGXmG for video and analysis), a counterintelligence analysis report discussing WikiLeaks and how to stop them, and a selection of U.S. diplomatic cables from among a collection of nearly a quarter million cables classified "Secret." These publications significantly embarrassed the United States and resulted in the arrest of Bradley Manning, the suspected leaker, and criticism of Julian Assange, WikiLeaks publisher.

a. If Assange is prosecuted in the United States, who gets to decide if he broke the law?

b. Should Manning qualify as a whistle-blower?

c. Was Assange's publication of the diplomatic cables ethical?

d. Was Assange's publication of the video moral?

Texas Health Resources and Intel: Ethics, IT, and Compliance

The IT staff at Texas Health Resources Inc. must deliver more than technical functionality. And it needs to deliver more than the business requirements; it also has to meet the organization's ethical standards.

To that end, its systems must help ensure that Texas Health complies with laws and regulations. And they also have to promote the right behaviors and prevent or flag undesirable ones, says Michael Alverson, vice president and deputy chief information officer at the Arlington-based nonprofit health care system. Consider the challenge of handling patients' medical records. Even though the federal Health Insurance Portability and Accountability Act mandates that agencies keep those records private, caregivers still need to access them—when appropriate.

So the organization's electronic health records system "gives doctors and nurses who are caring directly for patients quick access when they use the right authentication," Alverson says. But additional authentication is required to get records for patients who aren't under the provider's immediate care. The system records who gets access to what, allowing officials to audit and review cases to ensure there's no inappropriate access.

"The IT staff holds itself to similar ethical standards, too," Alverson says. The department has policies that prohibit taking gifts and endorsing vendors, to help guarantee that workers make procurement decisions only based on quality and needs. And when there's any question—such as when a vendor proposes a deep discount if Texas Health agrees to be an early adopter of a new technology—IT leaders can turn to the systemwide Business and Ethics Council for guidance.

"If we really want everyone to subscribe to the idea that working at Texas Health is special, then we have to have people actively believe in doing the right thing," Alverson says.

Companies are increasingly looking at their ethics policies and articulating specific values that address a range of issues, from community commitment to environmental sustainability, which employees can use to guide their work. The need to comply with federal laws and regulations drives some of this, while consumer expectations, employee demands, and economic pressures also play a part.

Information technology consultant Dena L. Smith lays out a hypothetical dilemma: Should an IT department hire a more expensive vendor because the vendor shares its own company's ethics standards, or should it go with a lower-cost provider that doesn't?

Companies with established ethical standards that guide how they conduct business frequently confront this kind of question, Smith says, but it's a particularly tough question today, given the recession. With IT departments forced to cut budgets and staff, chief information officers will find it difficult to allocate dollars for applications that promote corporate ethics.

"The decisions were easier in the days when the economics were favorable, but the choices may have to be more limited now," says former CIO John Stevenson, president of consultancy JG Stevenson Associates. "Now it's how much can you afford to do versus how much do you have to do so you don't get burned." Stevenson says companies that had moved toward certain ethical goals before the economic crisis—whether those goals involved green initiatives or corporate responsibility programs—aren't giving up their gains. "But if they haven't done that yet, it gets more difficult to say we'll spend more money than we have to," he says.

"Companies use the term 'corporate ethics' to mean many different things. In many organizations, if not the majority, it means compliance with a set of legal and minimum standards. In other organizations, corporate ethics means defining a set of corporate values that are integral to how they go about business," says Kirk O. Hanson, executive director of the Markkula Center for Applied Ethics at Santa Clara University.

Either way, chief information officers have an opportunity to show how technology can further their companies' ethics objectives.

"Policy decisions at the very senior level need the sensitivity that IT experts can bring to the table," Hanson says. "CIOs will know the capabilities of IT and be able to contribute that to corporate strategy. They will also know the misuses of those capabilities and be able to flag those and prevent the organization from stepping in scandals."

Hanson cites a 15-year-old case in which marketing workers at a large telephone company spent millions of dollars to develop a list of customers with ties to the Washington area that they planned to sell to other marketers. In violation of company policy, they compiled the list using the company's database of customers who frequently placed calls to the District of Columbia.

Executives learned about the list before the marketing department sold it. IT then developed a system to monitor use and block future unauthorized access to such information, Hanson says. However, it came a bit late, since IT should have developed the application in advance, anticipating the need to protect the information as well as detect any efforts to breach it.

Hanson says IT today can build systems that can screen potential subcontractors and vendors to see if they share certain values. It's also possible to create tools that flag contracts whose costs exceed expectations in ways that suggest bribery or other improprieties, or set up systems that analyze customer satisfaction surveys to find evidence of unethical behaviors on the part of workers.

Meanwhile, companies that put green initiatives at the top of their ethical concerns can have IT create applications that track energy consumption to flag anomalies that indicate inefficiencies or calculate the corporate carbon footprint and identify ways to reduce it.

"You have to step back a minute and ask, 'What is the role of technology around ethics?'" says Smith. "Technology can help from a monitoring, protection, and prevention standpoint in a lot of ways." The notion of corporate ethics hasn't always been so broad, says Mike Distelhorst, a law professor at Capital University Law School, a former adjunct professor of business ethics at the Capital School of Management and Leadership and former executive director for the university's Council for Ethical Leadership. "You'd be hard-pressed to find any company that doesn't have a beautiful ethics and compliance program," Distelhorst says. "They're talking about it, and they're working it all out in various strategic documents. But the question is whether they're actually living by it. Some are, and clearly some aren't."

Regardless of where a company stands in the process, IT leaders should be ready to contribute, he says.

"These policies are worked out on the ethics and compliance committees below the board level, and they're having the CIO as a key player," Distelhorst explains.

That's the case at Intel Corp., says the company's chief information officer, Diane Bryant.

Intel's Ethics and Compliance Oversight Committee established the following five principles for the company and its workers: Intel should conduct business with honesty and integrity; the company must follow the letter and spirit of the law; employees are expected to treat one another fairly; employees should act in the best interests of Intel and avoid conflicts of interest; and employees must protect the company's assets and reputation.

"Intel's IT staff builds and maintains the systems that allow the company to meet its legal and regulatory requirements, such as those laid out for accounting and governance by the Sarbanes-Oxley Act," Bryant says. It also developed applications and a team of workers to handle document retention, which is crucial should there be a legal case with electronic discovery requests.

But IT also enables Intel to enforce its own values, and not just meet regulatory requirements, Bryant explains. So there are applications to help perform rigorous checks on suppliers to ensure that they have sufficient business continuity plans and environmental sustainability plans, as well as ethical stances that match Intel's own. IT has also delivered sophisticated systems that monitor the power consumption and carbon dioxide emissions of Intel's data centers. And it developed systems that monitor for potential malicious behavior, such as violations of access management rights or the public release of Intel's intellectual property.

"We put solutions in place that help protect Intel's five principles," Bryant says.

Few companies are that advanced in their use of technology to further an ethical agenda. "Companies recognize that they have to be on record as being committed, but they're not yet as convinced that they have to manage it like other parts of their business," Hanson explains.

But when companies do decide to move in that direction, that's when chief information officers can shine, offering ideas on what metrics to use and what to measure.

"That's where IT can be a real leader," Hanson says, "since they know what can be measured and captured."

SOURCE: Mary K. Pratt, "Business Ethics: Steering Clear of Scandal," *Computerworld*, August 23, 2009, and Mary K. Pratt, "The High Cost of Ethics Compliance," *Computerworld*, August 24, 2009.

▼ CASE STUDY QUESTIONS

1. What are the two meanings of "corporate ethics" in organizations today? What does each definition imply for IT practices? How does the economic environment affect this?

2. How does IT provide more opportunities for difficult ethic issues to arise? How does IT help address those

opportunities? Use examples from the case to justify your answer.

3. Should organizations pursue high ethical standards regardless (or in spite of) their bottom-line impact? Or should they limit themselves to those scenarios where "good ethics make for good business"?

REAL WORLD ACTIVITIES

1. The passage of the Sarbanes-Oxley Act in the United States has greatly increased the compliance obligations of publicly traded companies. Go online to research how this landmark legislation affected the obligations of IT departments, and the way in which they develop and implement new technologies. Prepare a presentation to synthesize your findings.

2. Should an IT department hire a more expensive vendor because the vendor shares its own company's ethics standards, or should it go with a lower-cost provider that doesn't? This is an important question posed in the case above. What do you think? Break into small groups with your classmates to discuss your positions. Can you reach a consensus on this issue?

CASE 2

Wyoming Medical Center, Los Angeles County, and Raymond James: End-Point Security Gets Complicated

Users say protecting network end points is becoming more difficult as the type of end-point devices—desktops, laptops, smartphones—grows, making security a complex moving target. The problem is compounded by the range of what groups within corporations do on these devices, which translates into different levels of protection for classes of users on myriad devices.

"Deciding the appropriate device defense becomes the No. 1 job of endpoint security specialists," says Jennifer Jabbush, chief information security officer of Carolina Advanced Digital consultancy. Depending on the device and the user's role, end points need to be locked down to a greater or lesser degree.

For instance, Wyoming Medical Center in Casper, Wyoming, has four classifications of PCs: "open PCs in hallways for staff use; PCs at nursing stations; PCs in offices; and PCs on wheels that move between patient rooms and handle very specific, limited applications," says Rob Pettigrew, manager of technical systems and help desk for the center.

Pettigrew is deploying Novell ZenWorks to 850 of the center's 900 PCs in order to make sure each class has the right software. With 110 applications and 40 major medical software systems to contend with, that makes a huge matrix of machine types and restrictions to contend with, he says.

In addition, physicians in affiliated clinics can access via SSL VPN (a kind of VPN that is accessible over Web browsers), but they are limited to reaching Web servers in a physician's portal that is protected from the hospital data network. Some Citrix thin-clients are also used to protect data from leaving the network, but overall the strategy for unmanaged machines is a work in progress, Pettigrew says. "We're hoping to get more help desk to deal with the external physicians," he says.

One concern that can be addressed by end-point security is data privacy, which is paramount for the Los Angeles County Department of Health Services in California, says Don Zimmer, information security officer for the department. He supports about 18,000 desktops and laptops and operates under the restrictions of Health Insurance Portability and Accountability Act (HIPAA) regulations. "That means disk encryption," he says.

"If it's not encrypted and there is a breach, then we have to start calling people," he says. To avoid violating patients' privacy and a loss of public trust, the department encrypts the drives of all the PC end points with software from PointSec.

Equally important is keeping sensitive information off movable media that can plug into USB ports. The department uses Safend's USB Port Protector product that either denies access to sensitive documents or requires that they be encrypted and password-protected before being placed on the removable device.

Everyone's talking about the insider threat. But protecting data can't supersede the requirement to give users the access they need to do their jobs—otherwise, soon you'll have neither business data nor employees to worry about.

Striking a balance between access and protection isn't easy, however. In an InformationWeek Analytics/DarkReading.com Endpoint Security Survey of 384 business technology pros, 43 percent classify their organizations as "trusting," allowing data to be copied to USB drives or other devices with no restrictions or protective measures.

Still, IT is aware of the need to move from a stance of securing end points to assuming that laptops and smartphones will be lost, good employees will go bad, and virtual machines will be compromised. Instead of focusing on end points, let fortifications follow the data: Decide what must be protected, find out everywhere it lives, and lock it down against both inside and outside threats, whether via encryption, multitiered security suites, or new technologies like data loss prevention (DLP).

DLP suites combine network scanning and host-based tools to collect, categorize, and protect corporate intellectual property. These products can maintain an archive of data and documents, along with associated permissions by group, individual, and other policies. They then actively scan internal networks and external connections looking for anomalies. This takes data protection beyond perimeter or end-point protection: DLP facilitates internal safety checks, allowing "eyes only" data to remain eyes only and minimizing the risk that sensitive data will be viewed by the wrong folks, even in-house.

Zimmer says he is looking into data loss prevention software as well that can restrict the access that individual devices have to data. Although the technology can be effective, it also requires that businesses locate and classify their data so they can set policies surrounding them—a job that can seem insurmountable, depending on how data have been stored.

For Pettigrew, this means finding the 5 percent of sensitive data stored outside the medical center's electronic medical records system.

Rather than deal with many vendors for specific end-point protection products, some businesses opt for end-point security suites, such as those that evolved from the antivirus roots of vendors, including McAfee and Symantec.

Sam Ghelfi, chief security officer at financial firm Raymond James, opted for Sophos' Endpoint Protection and Data Security Suite, which offers firewall, antivirus, data loss prevention, antispyware, encryption and network access control (NAC). The company wants tight control over what Web content is available to users to minimize the malware coming in via basic Web browsing. The company uses a Sophos Web proxy that filters sites based on reputation but also the content that sites return.

Mobile devices that could contain confidential company information are disk encrypted, again using Sophos agents. If a device is lost or stolen, the encryption key is wiped out, making it impossible to decrypt the contents of the hard drive.

Ghelfi says he believes in personal firewalls on individual machines because they can stop groups of devices from talking to other groups. "Centrally managed, they can reveal network traffic patterns," he says.

He doesn't use all the features of the Sophos suite, though. For instance, he is just getting around to implementing NAC to let unmanaged guest machines get on the network but still minimize risk that they are infected.

That will clear them based on authentication, access method, and type of machine, but for contractors that require access to the main network, he also insists that they install the Sophos suite. Other unmanaged machines such as those of guests are allowed access only through a dedicated wireless network that leads to a limited set of servers in a network segment flanked by firewalls, he says.

"Such endpoint security suites can be attractive financially," Jabbusch says, "because customers can wind up with reduced agent, license and support fees and less management overhead." There may be a certain amount of convenience if customers decide to layer on more applications within a suite.

The newest class of device—smartphones—is presenting ongoing challenges as organizations figure out how to deal with them. Particularly dicey is whether to allow employees to use their personally owned devices for business and to access the business network.

The jury is still out, at least among state government chief information officers. A recent survey by the National Association of State Chief Information Officers says that of 36 states responding to a survey, 39 percent say they allow personal smartphones if they are protected by state security measures. Twenty-seven percent say they don't allow personal smartphones on their networks, 17 percent say they are reviewing state policy, and 17 percent say they don't have statewide control—each agency sets its own policies.

A separate Forrester Research survey says 73 percent of businesses surveyed are at least somewhat concerned about smartphones being authorized for business use. According to DeviceLock, its survey of more than 1,000 IT professionals found that less than 40 percent of respondents said yes to the question: "Have you taken any steps to secure your business against the security threat posed by iPhones?"

Analyzing the responses by region, researchers found that only 25 percent of respondents in North America and Western Europe said yes to the question, suggesting this is a back-burner security issue, says the end-point data leak prevention specialist.

Jabbush says the type of smartphone is a factor. "I can't imagine allowing an iPhone," she says. "A BlackBerry is somewhat better," because BlackBerrys have a management infrastructure and the devices can be locked down to corporate policies.

Mobile device security is one of those areas that should get more attention. However, it is likely that this topic will remain buried—until a lost or stolen iPhone leads to a visible and costly security breach.

SOURCE: Tim Greene, "Endpoint Security Gets Complicated," *Network World*, April 1, 2010, and Joe Hernick, "InformationWeek Analytics: Endpoint Security and DLP," *InformationWeek*, April 27, 2009.

▼ CASE STUDY QUESTIONS

1. What is the underlying issue behind end-point security, and why is it becoming increasingly difficult for companies to address it? Define the problem in your own words using examples from the case.

2. What are the different approaches taken by the organizations in the case to address this issue? What are the advantages and disadvantages of each? Provide at least two examples for each alternative.

3. A majority of respondents to a survey discussed in the case described their company as " trusting." What does this mean? What is the upside of a company being "trusting"? What is the downside? Provide some examples to illustrate your answers.

▼ REAL WORLD ACTIVITIES

1. Data Loss Prevention (DLP) was a technology mentioned in the case, and one that is garnering more and more attention from corporate security departments. Go online and research what DLP involves, and look for examples of its application to actual problems, and their outcomes. Prepare a report to summarize your work.

2. Whether to allow employees to use their own smartphone (or other devices yet to be invented) on corporate networks is quickly becoming a contested issue. What do companies stand to gain, or lose, in either case? What about employees? Break into small groups with your classmates to discuss these questions.

chapter 14

ENTERPRISE AND GLOBAL MANAGEMENT OF INFORMATION TECHNOLOGY

INFORMATION SYSTEMS

MANAGEMENT CHALLENGES

CHAPTER HIGHLIGHTS

Managing IT for the Enterprise

Business and IT

Managing Information Technology

REAL WORLD CHALLENGE: State Street Corporation—The Need to Reshape IT Infrastructure

Business/IT Planning

Managing the IT Function

Organizing IT

Outsourcing and Offshoring IT and IS

Failures in IT Management

Managing Global IT

The International Dimension

Global IT Management

Cultural, Political, and Geoeconomic Challenges

Global Business/IT Strategies

Global Business/IT Applications

Global IT Platforms

Global Data Access Issues

Global Systems Development

REAL WORLD SOLUTION: State Street Corporation—Changing the "Where, When, and How" of IT

REAL WORLD CASE: Reinventing IT at BP

REAL WORLD CASE: Cadbury, Forrester Research, A.T. Kearney, and Others: IT Leaders Face New Challenges in a Globalized World

LEARNING OBJECTIVES

14-1 Identify each of the three components of IT management and use examples to illustrate how they might be implemented in a business.

14-2 Explain how failures in IT management can be reduced by the involvement of business managers in IT planning and management.

14-3 Identify several cultural, political, and geoeconomic challenges that confront managers in the management of global information technologies.

14-4 Explain the effect on global business/IT strategy of the trend toward a transnational business strategy by international business organizations.

14-5 Identify several considerations that affect the choice of IT applications, IT platforms, data access policies, and systems development methods by a global business enterprise.

14-6 Understand the fundamental concepts of outsourcing and offshoring, as well as the primary reasons for selecting such an approach to IS/IT management.

Managing IT for the Enterprise

The strategic and operational importance of information technology in business is no longer in question at any level of business. As the 21st century unfolds, many companies throughout the world are intent on transforming themselves into global business powerhouses through major investments in global e-business, e-commerce, and other IT initiatives. Thus, there is a real need for business managers and professionals to understand how to manage this vital organizational function. In this chapter, we explore how the IS function can be organized and managed, and we emphasize the importance of a customer and business value focus for the management of information technologies. Whether you plan to be an entrepreneur and run your own business, a manager in a corporation, or a business professional, managing information systems and technologies will be one of your major responsibilities.

Read the Real World Challenge on the next page. We can learn a lot from this case about the IT infrastructure needs of global businesses. See Figure 14.1.

As we have seen throughout this text, information technology is an essential component of business success for companies today; however, information technology is also a vital business resource that must be properly managed. Thus, we have also seen many real-world examples in which the management of information technologies plays a pivotal role in ensuring the success or contributing to the failure of a company's strategic business initiatives. Therefore, managing the information systems and technologies that support the modern business processes of companies today is a major challenge for both business and IT managers and professionals.

How should information technology be managed? Figure 14.2 illustrates one popular approach to *managing information technology* in a large company. This managerial approach has three major components:

- **Managing the Joint Development and Implementation of Business/IT Strategies.** Led by the CEO (chief executive officer) and CIO (chief information officer), proposals are developed by business and IT managers and professionals regarding the use of IT to support the strategic business priorities of the company. This business/IT planning process *aligns* IT with strategic business goals. The process also includes evaluating the business case for investing in the development and implementation of each proposed business/IT project.

- **Managing the Development and Implementation of New Business/IT Applications and Technologies.** This step is the primary responsibility of the CIO and CTO (chief technology officer). This area of IT management involves managing the processes for information systems development and implementation we discussed in Chapter 12, as well as the responsibility for research into the strategic business uses of new information technologies.

- **Managing the IT Organization and the IT Infrastructure.** The CIO and IT managers share responsibility for managing the work of IT professionals, who are typically organized into a variety of project teams and other organizational subunits. In addition, they are responsible for managing the IT infrastructure of hardware, software, databases, telecommunications networks, and other IT resources, which must be acquired, operated, monitored, and maintained.

Let's look at a real-world example.

State Street Corporation— The Need to Reshape IT Infrastructure

In 1792 the New York Stock Exchange opened its doors, and then Massachusetts Governor John Hancock—yes, that John Hancock—signed the charter for the newly established Union Bank. Until its merger with the State Street Corporation in 1925, the Union Bank was the state's oldest bank in continuous existence, and America's second oldest. State Street Corporation as it exists today is the result of a series of mergers and acquisitions dating back more than 200 years. Local legend maintains that during the Great Boston Fire, James Beal, then-president of State Street's ancestor, Second National Bank, gathered the bank's securities, money, and other valuables in a cart and took them to his Back Bay home for safekeeping. In 1924 State Street was named custodian of the first U.S. mutual fund. Today, the company remains the largest provider of mutual fund custody and accounting services in the United States, servicing 56 percent of the funds in the U.S. mutual fund market and calculating 40 percent of the U.S. mutual fund prices provided to NASDAQ daily.

State Street Corporation employs more than 29,000 in more than 26 countries worldwide. With more than $22.6 trillion in assets under custody and administration and $2.1 trillion under management, State Street is a financial heavyweight. In its Europe and Asia-Pacific markets, State Street is actually growing faster than the markets themselves. As one of the world's leading investment service providers, the company delivers customized solutions to asset managers, pension funds, insurance companies, collective funds, mutual funds, and nonprofit institutions. State Street focuses exclusively on serving institutional investors.

Historically, the company's approach to information technology has been heavily influenced by a focus on meeting the needs of its customers, large institutional investors. Taking advantage of the sheer magnitude of its operations to drive scale and efficiency savings—which translate into added value for the customers—has always been a major goal of the IT group. To that end, the IT strategy has been closely aligned with the business model, with IT leaders embedded with the business units helping prioritize project development, ensuring business goals are met, and leveraging synergies wherever possible. At State Street, IT is not yet another function or department, but a very much integrated part of the business itself. The IT group alone comprises more than 6,900 employees and contractors around the world, with an internal culture very reliant on cooperation and teamwork. "State Street's clients are among the world's most sophisticated investors, and our deep, long-term relationships with them are a strategic advantage for us. They trust us with large volumes of assets and rely on us as the collaborative partner they need to reach their goals. Technology is a fundamental part of everything we do at State Street," says Christopher Perretta, executive vice president and chief information officer.

Nowhere is this clearer than in the amount of resources that the company has historically allocated to technology and technology development: A full 20–25 percent of the operating expense budget under the control of the chief information officer goes to new projects and initiatives every year. Over the years, the company has also become well known for its "green" IT efforts; it has been awarded numerous distinctions for these efforts, as well as making the rankings at places such as Computerworld, InfoWorld, and Newsweek. Starting in early 2001, a new corporate data center was designed to minimize environmental impacts, and the company started to transition out of cathode ray tube monitors and into flat screens, which reduced energy use and environmental impact as well.

FIGURE 14.1

A global company serving global customers requires a global IT infrastructure.

SOURCE: © Getty Images.

As State Street started to heavily expand internationally and its customers became as global as the company (or the other way around), it became evident that the existing approach to management of technology needed to adapt to the times. Doing so, however, required much more than just opening new offices in remote locations, although that was certainly part of it. It required changing the way everything worked. For instance, existing data centers and processes were designed with the idea that in the quiet hours of the night maintenance and batch processes could be run without affecting operational performance; in a globalized world where operations run 24/7, that is no longer the case. Applications that were designed for local use now may be accessed remotely from across the world; this requires changing both current, existing applications and the way in which new applications are developed, as well as retraining developers in new methods and practices. Network administrators now must be concerned with setting up interorganizational security models, and lawyers must learn—and worry—about privacy and compliance issues in a number of new jurisdictions. Most notably, people both requiring and providing IT support had never been separated by language, distance, and time zones before.

This is not to say that State Street did not already have an extensive international presence, which was certainly not the case. However, international offices were supported by local or regional IT groups. As such, IT was international, but not global; this means that a collection of independent local offices, rather than a set of integrated operations, served the corporation globally. However, as the business model was starting to move in that direction—one global customer, one global company—IT would need to follow suit, and quickly. There are not many other industries like financial services where things move close to the speed of light. Things started to get really complicated when the company was in the process of opening its new office in Krakow, Poland. After the location for the office had been selected, arrangements were made for a provider to host the local IT infrastructure. Two weeks before opening, however, it was determined that those arrangements would not work. Staff had been hired, the premises were prepared, the business was ready, but something was missing: the IT infrastructure. Now what?

Without the option of local infrastructure, the team had to find an alternative way to make things work, lest it be responsible for delaying the opening of the new office. Instead, they designed a solution that allowed the company to support the soon-to-be-opened Krakow office remotely, delivering business, operational and desktop functionality from a regional data center without any performance hitches or issues. Moreover, the new process was more cost-effective than the original option—a local provider hosting the infrastructure—had been. A new way of doing business had been born. The challenge ahead would be to see if this could be scaled to the rest of the world, and to get State Street IT on the road to becoming a global provider of technology services. At the end of the day, this would keep the group aligned with the business strategy, which was so heavily emphasized throughout the company: one global customer, one global provider, one global IT.

SOURCE: "State Street Corporation: Zero Footprint, Maximum Impact," *Computerworld Honors Case Study*, 2008; Penny Crosman, "Q&A: Madge Meyer, State Street's EVP, IT Global Infrastructure Services," *Wall Street Technology*, September 16, 2009; "State Street Corporation: IT Infrastructure Transformation 360," *Computerworld Honors Case Study*, 2009; and www.statestreet.com, accessed June 15, 2011.

▼ QUESTIONS TO CONSIDER

1. What are the advantages and disadvantages of local versus global management of information technology infrastructure? What should be the criteria for making a choice between those two alternatives (or any hybrid approach)?

2. From a practical perspective, what does moving from local to global management of IT entail? What are the many things that managers at State Street should worry about as they undergo that transition?

3. The case discusses a number of issues associated with the ways in which development and provisioning of IT differ when done locally compared with when operations become integrated. Does State Streeet's approach to global IT infrastructure solve any of these issues? How? Which ones remain unaddressed?

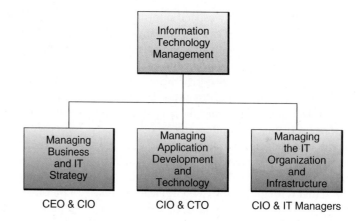

FIGURE 14.2
The major components of information technology management. Note the executives with primary responsibilities in each area.

Managing IT: There Is More Than One Way to Skin the Cat

FIGURE 14.3
Comparing conventional and e-business-driven IT management approaches.

Figure 14.3 contrasts two approaches to IT management for the enterprise. Notice that the strategic approach uses the model of IT management illustrated in Figure 14.2. For example, in technology management, a strategic IT organization can use a best-of-breed approach that supports business needs, instead of enforcing a standardized and homogeneous choice of hardware, software, database, and networking technologies. In managing the IT organization using this approach, IS professionals must be hired who are skilled in the integration of technology with business. These IS professionals are organized in workgroups around business/IT initiatives that focus on building IT-enabled business services for customers.

IT Management	Conventional Practices	Strategic Business/IT Practices
Technology Management	• Approach to IT infrastructure may sacrifice match with business needs for vendor homogeneity and technology platform choices.	• Best-of-breed approach to IT infrastructure in which effective match with business needs takes precedence over commitment to technology platform choices and vendor homogeneity.
Managing the IT Organization	• Hire "best by position" who can bring specific IT expertise. • Departments organized around IT expertise with business liaisons and explicit delegation of tasks. • IT projects have separable cost/value considerations. Funding typically allocated within constraints of yearly budget for IT function.	• Hire "best athletes" IS professionals who can flexibly integrate new IT and business competencies. • Evolving workgroups organized around emerging IT-intensive business initiatives with little explicit delegation of tasks. • IT funding typically based on value proposition around business opportunity related to building services for customers. IT project inseparable part of business initiative.

BUSINESS/IT PLANNING
LO 14-2

Figure 14.4 illustrates the ***business/IT planning process,*** which focuses on discovering innovative approaches to satisfying a company's customer value and business value goals. This planning process leads to the development of strategies and business models for new business applications, processes, products, and services. Then a company can develop IT strategies and an IT architecture that supports building and implementing its newly planned business applications.

Both the CEO and the CIO of a company must manage the development of complementary business and IT strategies to meet its customer value and business value vision. This co-adaptation process is necessary because, as we have seen so often in

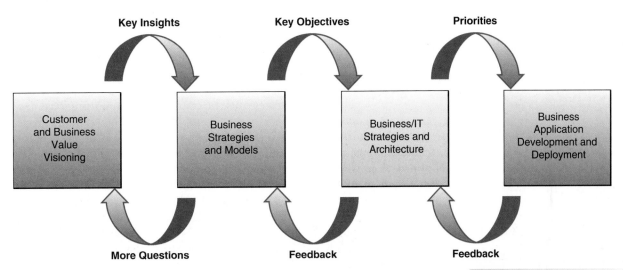

FIGURE 14.4

The business/IT planning process emphasizes a customer and business value focus for developing business strategies and models and an IT architecture for business applications.

this text, information technologies are a fast-changing but vital component in many strategic business initiatives. The business/IT planning process has three major components:

- **Strategy Development.** Developing business strategies that support a company's business vision. For example, using information technology to create innovative e-business systems that focus on customer and business value. We will discuss this process in more detail shortly.

- **Resource Management.** Developing strategic plans for managing or outsourcing a company's IT resources, including IS personnel, hardware, software, data, and network resources.

- **Technology Architecture.** Making strategic IT choices that reflect an information technology architecture designed to support a company's business/IT initiatives.

Information Technology Architecture

The *IT architecture* created by the strategic business/IT planning process is a conceptual design, or blueprint, that includes the following major components:

- **Technology Platform.** The Internet, intranets, extranets, and other networks, computer systems, system software, and integrated enterprise application software provide a computing and communications infrastructure, or platform, that supports the strategic use of information technology for e-business, e-commerce, and other business/IT applications.

- **Data Resources.** Many types of operational and specialized databases, including data warehouses and Internet/intranet databases (as reviewed in Chapter 5), store and provide data and information for business processes and decision support.

- **Applications Architecture.** Business applications of information technology are designed as an integrated architecture *or portfolio* of enterprise systems that support strategic business initiatives, as well as cross-functional business processes. For example, an applications architecture should include support for developing and maintaining the interenterprise supply chain applications and integrated enterprise resource planning and customer relationship management applications discussed in Chapters 7 and 9.

- **IT Organization.** The organizational structure of the IS function within a company and the distribution of IS specialists are designed to meet the changing strategies of a business. The form of the IT organization depends on the managerial philosophy and business/IT strategies formulated during the strategic planning process.

Business/IT Planning: Being Proactive

Figure 14.5 outlines the strategic planning process for business/IT initiatives and compares it with conventional IT planning approaches. A strategic approach weaves both business and IT strategic planning together co-adaptively under the guidance of the chief executive officer and the chief information officer, instead of developing IT strategy just by tracking and supporting business strategies. This approach also locates IT application development projects within the business units that are involved in an e-business initiative to form centers of business/IT expertise throughout the company. Finally, a strategic approach uses a prototyping application development process with rapid deployment of new business applications instead of a traditional systems development approach. This application development strategy trades the risk of implementing incomplete applications with the benefits of gaining competitive advantages from early deployment of new e-business services to employees, customers, and other stakeholders and of involving them in the fine-tuning phase of application development.

FIGURE 14.5

Comparing conventional IT planning and strategic business/IT planning approaches.

Conventional IT Planning	Strategic Business/IT Planning
• Strategic alignment: IT strategy tracks specified enterprise strategy.	• Strategic improvisation: IT strategy and enterprise business strategy co-adaptively unfold based on the clear guidance of a focus on customer value.
• CEO endorses IT vision shaped through CIO.	• CEO proactively shapes IT vision jointly with CIO as part of e-business strategy.
• IT application development projects functionally organized as technological solutions to business issues.	• IT application development projects co-located with e-business initiatives to form centers of IT-intensive business expertise.
• Phased application development based on learning from pilot projects.	• Perpetual application development based on continuous learning from rapid deployment and prototyping with end-user involvement.

MANAGING THE IT FUNCTION
LO 14-5

A radical shift is occurring in corporate computing—think of it as the recentralization of management. It's a step back toward the 1970s, when a data processing manager could sit at a console and track all the technology assets of the corporation. Then came the 1980s and early 1990s. Departments got their own PCs and software; client/server networks sprang up all across companies.

Three things have happened in the past few years: The Internet boom inspired businesses to connect all those networks; companies put on their intranets essential applications without which their businesses could not function; and it became apparent that maintaining PCs on a network is very, very expensive. Such changes create an urgent need for centralization.

ORGANIZING IT

In the early years of computing, the development of large mainframe computers and telecommunications networks and terminals caused a *centralization* of computer hardware and software, databases, and information specialists at the corporate level of organizations. Next, the development of minicomputers and microcomputers accelerated a *downsizing* trend, which prompted a move back toward *decentralization* by many business firms. Distributed client/server networks at the corporate, department, workgroup, and team levels came into being, which promoted a shift of databases and information specialists to some departments and the creation of *information centers* to support end-user and workgroup computing.

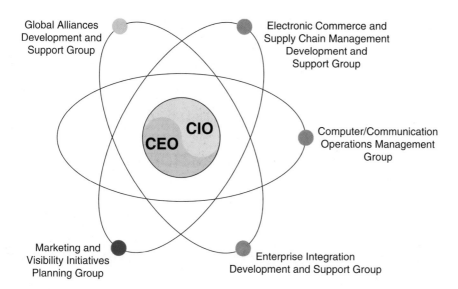

FIGURE 14.6
The components of the IT function in a modern organization.

Lately, the trend is to establish more centralized control over the management of the IT resources of a company while still serving the strategic needs of its business units, especially their e-business and e-commerce initiatives. This trend has resulted in the development of hybrid structures with both centralized and decentralized components. See Figure 14.6.

Some companies spin off their information systems function into IS *subsidiaries* that offer IS services to external organizations, as well as to their parent company. Other companies create or spin off their e-commerce and Internet-related business units or IT groups into separate companies or business units. Corporations also *outsource*, that is, turn over all or parts of their IS operations to outside contractors known as *systems integrators*. In addition, some companies are outsourcing software procurement and support to *application service providers* (ASPs), which provide and support business application and other software via the Internet and intranets to all of a company's employee workstations. We will discuss outsourcing in greater detail shortly. In the meantime, let's take a few minutes to review, and expand on, what we know about managing the various functions and activities in IS.

Managing Application Development

Application development management involves managing activities such as systems analysis and design, prototyping, applications programming, project management, quality assurance, and system maintenance for all major business/IT development projects. Managing application development requires managing the activities of teams of systems analysts, software developers, and other IS professionals working on a variety of information systems development projects. Thus, project management is a key IT management responsibility if business/IT projects are to be completed on time, within their budgets, and meet their design objectives. In addition, some systems development groups have established *development centers* staffed with IS professionals. Their role is to evaluate new application development tools and help information systems specialists use them to improve their application development efforts.

Managing IS Operations

IS operations management is concerned with the use of hardware, software, network, and personnel resources in the corporate or business unit **data centers** (computer centers) of an organization. Operational activities that must be managed include computer system operations, network management, production control, and production support.

FIGURE 14.7

The CA-Unicenter TNG system performance monitor includes an Enterprise Management Portal module that helps ITspecialists monitor and manage a variety of networked computer systems and operating systems.

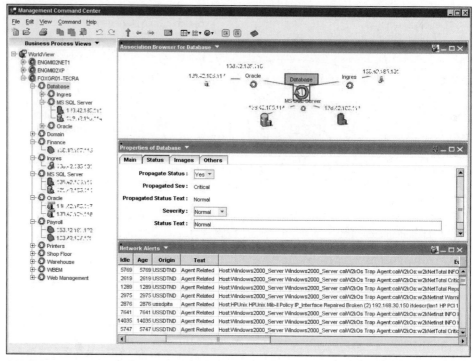

SOURCE: Courtesy of Computer Associates.

Most operations management activities are being automated by the use of software packages for computer system performance management. These *system performance monitors* look after the processing of computer jobs, help develop a planned schedule of computer operations that can optimize computer system performance, and produce detailed statistics that are invaluable for effective planning and control of computing capacity. Such information evaluates computer system utilization, costs, and performance. This evaluation provides information for capacity planning, production planning and control, and hardware/software acquisition planning. It is also used in quality assurance programs, which emphasize the quality of services to business end users. See Figure 14.7.

System performance monitors also supply information needed by *chargeback systems* that allocate costs to users on the basis of the information services rendered. All costs incurred are recorded, reported, allocated, and charged back to specific end-user business units, depending on their use of system resources. When companies use this arrangement, the information services department becomes a service center whose costs are charged directly to business units rather than being lumped with other administrative service costs and treated as overhead costs.

Many performance monitors also feature *process control* capabilities. Such packages not only monitor but also automatically control computer operations at large data centers. Some use built-in expert system modules that are based on knowledge gleaned from experts in the operations of specific computer systems and operating systems. These performance monitors provide more efficient computer operations than human-operated systems. They also enable "lights out" data centers at some companies, where computer systems are operated unattended, especially after normal business hours.

IT Staff Planning

The success or failure of an information services organization rests primarily on the quality of its people. Many firms consider *IT staff planning,* or recruiting, training, and retaining qualified IS personnel, as one of their greatest challenges. Managing information services functions involves the management of managerial, technical, and clerical personnel. One of the most important jobs of information services managers is to recruit qualified personnel and develop, organize, and direct the capabilities of existing personnel. Employees must be continually trained to keep up with the latest developments in a fast-moving and highly technical field. Employee job performances must be continually evaluated, and outstanding performances must be rewarded with salary increases or promotions. Salary and wage levels must be set, and career paths must be designed so that individuals can move to new jobs through promotion and transfer as they gain seniority and expertise.

The CIO and Other IT Executives

The *chief information officer (CIO)* oversees all use of information technology in many companies and brings it into alignment with strategic business goals. Thus, all traditional computer services, Internet technology, telecommunications network services, and other IS technology support services are the responsibility of this executive. The CIO does not direct day-to-day information services activities; instead, CIOs concentrate on business/IT planning and strategy. They also work with the CEO and other top executives to develop strategic uses of information technology in e-business and e-commerce that help make the firm more competitive in the marketplace. Many companies have also filled the CIO position with executives from the business functions or units outside the IS field. Such CIOs emphasize that the chief role of information technology is to help a company meet its strategic business objectives.

Top IT Jobs: Requirements and Compensation

- **Chief information officer**
  Base salary range: $194,000–$303,000+; varies by location
  Bonus range: Up to 40 percent of salary
  The top position in IT isn't all about technology. To land this job, you need to be a Business Technologist with a big "B" and a big "T." If you understand the business, the organization's strategy, and the broad spectrum of technologies, systems, applications, and people necessary to execute it, you will be in great demand by organizations.

- **Chief technology officer**
  Base salary range: $162,000–$245,000+; varies by location
  Bonus range: Up to 40 percent of salary
  If you're second in command to the CIO or chief technology officer and you have years of applications development experience, your next move should be into the chief technology officer's spot. To land this job, you'll need to be a passionate problem solver with a demonstrated record of reducing development time.

- **Chief security officer**
  Base salary range: $142,000–$205,000+; varies by location
  Bonus range: Up to 40 percent of salary
  If you understand the issues related to securing the data resources and information assets of the organization, then this is the job for you. Strong candidates with a deep understanding of both the technical and managerial sides of the field are in great demand.

- **E-commerce architect**
  Base salary range: $115,000–$170,000+; varies by location
  Bonus range: Up to 15 percent of salary
  If you know Java, Perl, C++, and Web services; have experience in systems architecture; and can design an Internet solution from concept through implementation, many companies want you to plan and develop their e-commerce sites.

- **Technical team leader**
  Base salary range: $75,000–$100,000+; varies by location
  Bonus range: Up to 20 percent of salary
  Senior technical team leaders with good communication, project management, and leadership skills, as well as knowledge of Web languages and databases, are still in great demand.

- **Practice manager**
  Base salary range: $70,000–$100,000+; varies by location
  Bonus range: Up to 20 percent of salary
  If you've got a background in IT assessment and a pedigree in business development (MBA preferred), you can land a job as a point person for big projects. You'll need skills in IT operations and software assessment, as well as in marketing, staffing, budgeting, and building customer relationships.

- **Systems analyst**
  Base salary range: $56,000–$100,000+; varies by location
  Bonus range: Up to 25 percent of salary
  If you have problem-solving skills and a degree in information systems (BS or MBA), you can be assured of finding a good job as a systems analyst. You'll need to have excellent interpersonal skills, good technical skills, and an ability to apply your problem-solving and critical-thinking skills to the design of new systems.

SOURCE: www.salary.com.

Technology Management

The management of rapidly changing technology is important to any organization. Changes in information technology, like the rise of the PC, client/server networks, and the Internet and intranets, have come swiftly and dramatically and are expected to continue into the future. Developments in information systems technology have had, and will continue to have, a major impact on the operations, costs, management work environment, and competitive position of many organizations.

Thus, all information technologies must be managed as a technology platform for integrating internally focused or externally facing business applications. Such technologies include the Internet, intranets, and a variety of e-commerce and collaboration technologies, as well as integrated enterprise software for customer relationship management, enterprise resource planning, and supply chain management. In many companies, ***technology management*** is the primary responsibility of a ***chief technology officer (CTO)***, who is in charge of all information technology planning and deployment.

Managing User Services

Teams and workgroups of business professionals commonly use PC workstations, software packages, and the Internet, intranets, and other networks to develop and apply information technology to their work activities. Thus, many companies have responded by creating ***user services,*** or *client services*, functions to support and manage end-user and workgroup computing.

End-user services provide both opportunities and problems for business unit managers. For example, some firms create an *information center* group staffed with user liaison specialists or Web-enabled intranet help desks. IS specialists with titles such as user consultant, account executive, or business analyst may also be assigned to end-user workgroups. These specialists perform a vital role by troubleshooting problems, gathering and communicating information, coordinating educational efforts, and helping business professionals with application development.

In addition to these measures, most organizations still establish and enforce policies for the acquisition of hardware and software by end users and business units. This process ensures their compatibility with company standards for hardware, software, and network connectivity. Also important is the development of applications with proper security and quality controls to promote correct performance and safeguard the integrity of corporate and departmental networks and databases.

An increasingly popular approach to managing the IS and IT functions of the organization is to adopt an outsourcing strategy. *Outsourcing,* in broad terms, is the purchase of goods or services that were previously provided internally from third-party partners. Outsourcing is a generic term used for a broad range of information technology functions that are selectively contracted to an external service provider.

OUTSOURCING AND OFFSHORING IT AND IS LO 14-6

Outsourcing

A commonly outsourced IS function is software application development. This process includes contracting (or subcontracting) with an external organization for the development of complete or partial software products/projects, the purchase of packaged or customized package software products, or activities and/or resources that aid in the software development life cycle. Figure 14.8 lists the functions typically outsourced, the reasons behind the decision to outsource, and several aspects associated with successful vendor selection and a successful outsourcing effort.

Although companies can, theoretically, choose to outsource any organization function for any reason, there are five main reasons behind a decision to outsource:

Save Money—Achieve Greater Return on Investment (ROI)

- Outsourcing IS/IT functions to skilled service providers is often a strategic approach to stretching strained budgets. Companies that take a well-managed approach to outsourcing can gain cost savings of upwards of 40–80 percent.

FIGURE 14.8

Outsourcing's Top 10. Notice that, despite all of the media coverage, application development is No. 3.

Top 10 Reasons Companies Outsource	Top 10 Factors in Vendor Selection
1. Reduce and control operating costs	1. Commitment to quality
2. Improve company focus	2. Price
3. Gain access to world-class capabilities	3. References/reputation
4. Free internal resources for other purposes	4. Flexible contract terms
5. Necessary resources are not available internally	5. Scope of resources
6. Accelerate reengineering benefits	6. Additional value-added capability
7. Function is difficult to manage internally or is out of control	7. Cultural match
8. Make capital funds available	8. Existing relationship
9. Share risks	9. Location
10. Cash infusion	10. Other
Top 10 Factors for Successful Outsourcing	**Top 10 IT Areas Being Outsourced**
1. Understand company goals and objectives	1. Maintenance and repair
2. A strategic vision and plan	2. Training
3. Select the right vendor	3. Applications development
4. Ongoing management of the relationships	4. Consulting and reengineering
5. A properly structured contract	5. Mainframe data centers
6. Open communication with affected individuals/groups	6. Client/server services and administration
7. Senior executive support and involvement	7. Network administration
8. Careful attention to personnel issues	8. Desktop services
9. Near-term financial justification	9. End-user support
10. Use of outside expertise	10. Total IT outsourcing

SOURCE: The Outsourcing Institute.

Focus on Core Competencies

- Outsourced professionals allow an organization and its employees to focus on the business they are in rather than a business in which they are not. By using an outsourcing strategy for application development, an organization can focus its IS professionals on identifying and solving business problems rather than on programming and prototyping new applications.

Achieve Flexible Staffing Levels

- Strategic use of an outsourcing approach to IS/IT functions can result in business growth without increasing overhead. Outsourcing provides a pool of qualified professionals available for unique, niche, or overflow projects. If the unique skill set required by an organization is difficult to find or expensive to maintain in-house, outsourcing can allow for the acquisition of the needed expertise.

Gain Access to Global Resources

- The Outsourcing Institute asserts that the rules for successfully growing a business have changed: "It's no longer about what you own or build. . . . [Instead] success is hinged to resources and talent you can access." Using global expertise allows an organization to gain the advantage of skilled labor, regardless of location, and significantly increase the quality of its deliverables. As such, outsourcing can create opportunities for smaller businesses that might not otherwise be possible due to costs or geophysical constraints.

Decrease Time to Market

- Outsourcing extends the traditional small business benefits of flexibility and responsiveness, allowing smaller organizations to compete effectively against bigger firms. Supplementing an existing workforce with offshore support could allow for productivity 24 hours a day. Having access to resources able to work on key projects even while local employees are asleep can serve to accelerate time to market and provide a key competitive advantage.

Offshoring

Although often confused with outsourcing, offshoring is also increasingly becoming part of a strategic approach to IS/IT management. *Offshoring* can be defined as a relocation of an organization's business processes (including production/manufacturing) to a lower-cost location, usually overseas. Offshoring can be considered in the context of either *production* offshoring or *services* offshoring. After its accession to the World Trade Organization (WTO), China emerged as a prominent destination for production offshoring. After technical progress in telecommunications improved the possibilities of trade in services, India became a country that chose to focus on this domain.

The growth of services offshoring in information systems is linked to the availability of large amounts of reliable and affordable communication infrastructure following the telecom bust of the late 1990s. Coupled with the digitization of many services, it became possible to shift the actual delivery location of services to low-cost locations in a manner theoretically transparent to end users.

India, the Philippines, Ireland, and Eastern European countries benefited greatly from this trend due to their large pool of English-speaking and technically qualified workers. India's offshoring industry took root in IT functions in the 1990s and has since moved to back-office processes, such as call centers and transaction processing, as well as high-end jobs such as application development.

Offshoring is often enabled by the transfer of valuable information to the offshore site. Such information and training allows the remote workers to produce results of comparable value previously produced by internal employees. When such transfer includes proprietary materials, such as confidential documents and trade secrets, protected by nondisclosure agreements, then intellectual property has been transferred or exported. The documentation and valuation of such exports is quite difficult but should be considered because it comprises items that may be regulated or taxable.

Offshoring has been a controversial issue with heated debates. On one hand, it is seen as benefiting both the origin and destination country through free trade. On the other hand, job losses in developed countries have sparked opposition to offshoring. Some critics agree that both sides will benefit in terms of overall production and numbers of jobs created but that the subjective quality of the new jobs will be lower than the quality of the old ones. While this debate continues, companies continue to use offshoring as a viable IS/IT management approach. Let's look at a real-world example of global outsourcing.

<table>
<tr>
<td>

Royal Dutch Shell has signed a five-year, $4 billion outsourcing deal with three global IT and telecommunications suppliers. The value of the contracts for the three suppliers is $1.6 billion with AT&T, $1 billion for EDS, and $1.6 billion with T-Systems.

Shell announced that it has contracted T-Systems, AT&T, and EDS under a master service agreement (MSA), for "significant improvements" to its efficiency and productivity that will see an axing of some tech jobs and a transfer of 3,000 IT staff to the service providers. Under the MSA, Shell will outsource its IT infrastructure in three service bundles: "AT&T for network and telecommunications, T-Systems for hosting and storage, and EDS for end user computing services and for integration of the infrastructure services."

The suppliers will provide integrated services to more than 1,500 sites worldwide. "Shell's approach combines all the advantages of decentralised service provision with the benefits and efficiency of a centralised governance structure," says Elesh Khakhar, a partner at consultant firm TPI, which is an advisor to Shell. Khakar added that the multisupplier deal has been designed to "encourage collaborative behavior" between suppliers, while it allows Shell to "retain full control of strategy and service integration. In addition to all of the usual business benefits, Shell will be able to exploit emerging commoditized services designed for the consumer market, such as email or internet phone services, and integrate them within their services when they become robust enough for commercial use."

Shell CIO Alan Matula said: "This deal is a major strategic choice for Shell. Partnering with EDS, T-Systems and AT&T gives us greater ability to respond to the growing demands of our businesses. It allows Shell IT to focus on Information Technology that drives competitive position in the oil and gas market, whilst suppliers focus on improving essential IT capability."

</td>
<td>

Royal Dutch Shell: Multisupplier Global Outsourcing Deal

</td>
</tr>
</table>

SOURCE: Siobhan Chapman, "Shell Signs $4 Billion, Multi-Supplier Outsourcing Deal," *CIO Magazine,* April 3, 2008.

Trends in Outsourcing and Offshoring

While in the past much of the motivation to outsource and offshore various portions of the IT/IS operation of a firm were driven primarily by cost, a more recent and troubling trend is the increasing motivation to find highly qualified IT/IS talent. Jobs are plentiful in the United States for today's IS graduate, but enrollments in the United States' IS programs remain down. This results in a decreasing supply of qualified labor for the best-paying jobs in the field. To combat this, firms are looking at the science and engineering graduates of other countries to fill their needs. As we discussed in Chapter 2, the jobs that were outsourced and offshored in the late 1990s and early 2000s were not the ones typically benchmarked by university-level IS programs. As such, no real job opportunities were lost to qualified graduates. Today, however, the lack of qualified IS graduates means companies have to turn elsewhere to fill these jobs. The jobs are staying here, but the labor is being imported. The single most effective method to counter this trend is for more young people to seek a career in the information systems field. IS/IT is one of the hottest fields on the planet for job opportunities, and the word needs to get out. Many organizations are focusing on outreach programs that extend down to the pre-high school levels to begin educating, or reeducating, the public with regard to these vast opportunities.

FAILURES IN IT MANAGEMENT
LO 14-2

Managing information technology is not an easy task. The information systems function often has performance problems in many organizations. The promised benefits of information technology have not occurred in many documented cases. Studies by management consulting firms and university researchers have shown that many businesses have not been successful in managing their use of information technology. Thus, it is evident that in many organizations, information technology is not being used effectively and efficiently, and there have been failures in IT management. For example:

- Information technology is not being used *effectively* by companies that use IT primarily to computerize traditional business processes instead of developing innovative e-business processes involving customers, suppliers, and other business partners, e-commerce, and Web-enabled decision support.

- Information technology is not being used *efficiently* by information systems that provide poor response times and frequent downtimes, or by IS professionals and consultants who do not properly manage application development projects.

Let's look more closely, using a real-world example.

Risk without Reward: Weak IT Controls at Société Générale

It's a lethal combination of process oversights and system failures that is the stuff of CIO nightmares: An investigation into rogue trader Jerome Kerviel's fraudulent actions at Société Générale bank uncovered an apparent breakdown in financial and internal IT controls, subverted by an employee with IT know-how and authorized systems access. IT experts say the case should serve as a warning that businesses can do better to manage IT-related risk.

"Much time is spent on protecting the external threat," says J.R. Reagan, managing director and global solution leader for risk, compliance and security at BearingPoint. "But the internal threat can be even larger in terms of risk to the company." In the case of Société Générale, not only were IT security controls insufficient, but the bank's staff did not fully investigate red flags that did arise. Recent research by the Ponemon Institute concludes that "insider threats represent one of the most significant information security risks." In a survey of 700 IT practitioners, 78 percent said they believe individuals have too much access to information that isn't pertinent to their jobs, whereas 59 percent said such access presents business risks. What's more, IT professionals see a disconnect with business leaders: 74 percent said senior management does not view governance of access to information as a strategic issue.

One of Société Générale's primary business lines is derivatives—financial instruments that allow traders to make contracts on a wide range of assets (such as equities, bonds, or commodities) and attempts to reduce (or hedge) the financial risk for one party in the deal. Trading derivatives, however, necessitates some aggressiveness and can be fraught with risk.

Reagan observes that in the case of Société Générale, "their activities deal with high volume, high velocity and quick tempo trading of stock," and it's likely business leaders "wouldn't put up with" security measures that would slow them down. For example, Société Générale employed single-factor authentication (using one method, such as passwords, to grant access to its systems) rather than stronger dual-factor authentication (requiring that individuals employ two methods of identifying themselves to gain access). "The security team needs to explain the risk exposure and the possibility of losing billions in fraudulent trades if security is not adequately addressed," Reagan says. "But most security guys aren't well enough in tune with the business to be able to articulate a business case like that."

That disconnect can be enormously destructive, as the Société Générale incident shows. "The Société Générale case brings to the fore the fact that business risk can be directly exposed through IT," says Scott Crawford, a security expert and research director at Enterprise Management Associates. "Kerviel allegedly manipulated the IT controls on the business systems based on his midoffice experience and back-office knowledge and expertise."

"Businesses are just now beginning to awaken to the controls within the IT environment," Crawford says. "If you're betting the farm and strategy on the IT controls, it behooves the organization to ensure that those controls are reasonably resistant to subversion."

SOURCE: Nancy Weil, "Risk without Reward," *CIO Magazine*, May 1, 2008.

Management Involvement

What is the solution to failures in the information systems function? There are no quick and easy answers. However, the experiences of successful organizations reveal that extensive and meaningful *managerial and end-user involvement* is the key ingredient of high-quality information systems performance. Involving business managers in the governance of the IS function and business professionals in the development of IS applications should thus shape the response of management to the challenge of improving the business value of information technology. See Figure 14.9.

Involving managers in the management of IT (from the CEO to the managers of business units) requires the development of *governance structures* (e.g., executive councils, steering committees) that encourage their active participation in planning and controlling the business uses of IT. Thus, many organizations have policies that require managers to

FIGURE 14.9

Senior management needs to be involved in critical business/ IT decisions to optimize the business value and performance of the IT function.

IT Decision	Senior Management's Role	Consequences of Abdicating the Decision
• **How much should we spend on IT?**	Define the strategic role that IT will play in the company, and then determine the level of funding needed to achieve that objective.	The company fails to develop an IT platform that furthers its strategy, despite high IT spending.
• **Which business processes should receive our IT dollars?**	Make clear decisions about which IT initiatives will and will not be funded.	A lack of focus overwhelms the IT unit, which tries to deliver many projects that may have little companywide value or can't be implemented well simultaneously.
• **Which IT capabilities need to be companywide?**	Decide which IT capabilities should be provided centrally and which should be developed by individual businesses.	Excessive technical and process standardization limit the flexibility of business units, or frequent exceptions to the standards increase costs and limit business synergies.
• **How good do our IT services really need to be?**	Decide which features—for example, enhanced reliability or response time—are needed on the basis of their costs and benefits.	The company may pay for service options that, given its priorities, aren't worth their costs.
• **What security and privacy risks will we accept?**	Lead the decision making on the trade-offs between security and privacy on one hand and convenience on the other.	An overemphasis on security and privacy may inconvenience customers, employees, and suppliers; an underemphasis may make data vulnerable.
• **Whom do we blame if an IT initiative fails?**	Assign a business executive to be accountable for every IT project; monitor business metrics.	The business value of systems is never realized.

SOURCE: Jeanne W. Ross and Peter Weill, "Six IT Decisions Your IT People Shouldn't Make," *Harvard Business Review*, November 2002, p. 87.

be involved in IT decisions that affect their business units. This requirement helps managers avoid IS performance problems in their business units and development projects. With this high degree of involvement, managers can improve the strategic business value of information technology. Also, as we noted in Chapter 12, only direct end-user participation in system development projects can solve the problems of employee resistance and poor user interface design. Overseeing such involvement is another vital management task.

IT Governance

Information technology governance (ITG) is a subset discipline of corporate governance focused on the information technologies (IT), information systems (IS), their performance, use, and associated risks. The rising interest in IT governance is due, in part, to governmental compliance initiatives such as Sarbanes-Oxley in the United States and its counterpart in Europe, Basel II. Additional motivation comes from the acknowledgment that IT projects can easily get out of control and profoundly affect the performance of an organization.

A characteristic theme of IT governance discussions is that the IT capability can no longer be thought of as a mystical black box, the contents of which are known only to the IT personnel. This traditional handling of IT management by board-level executives is due to limited technical experience and the perceived complexity of IT. Historically, key decisions were often deferred to IT professionals. IT governance implies a system in which all stakeholders, including the board, internal customers, and related areas such as finance, have the necessary input into the decision-making process. This prevents a single stakeholder, typically IT, from being blamed for poor decisions. It also prevents users from later complaining that the system does not behave or perform as expected.

The focus of ITG is specifying decision inputs and rights along with an accountability framework such that desirable behaviors toward and in the use of IT are developed. It highlights the importance of IT-related matters in contemporary organizations and ensures that strategic IT decisions are owned by the corporate board, rather than by the CIO or other IT managers. The primary goals for information technology governance are to (1) assure that the significant organizational investments in IT and IS generate their maximum business value and (2) mitigate the risks that are associated with IT. This is accomplished by implementing an organizational structure with well-defined roles for the responsibility of the decisions related to the management and use of IT such as infrastructure, architecture, investment, and use.

One very popular approach to IT governance is COBIT (Control Objectives for Information and related Technology). COBIT is a framework of best practices for IT management created by the Information Systems Audit and Control Association (ISACA) and the IT Governance Institute (ITGI). COBIT provides all members of the organization with a set of generally accepted measures, indicators, processes, and best practices to help them maximize the benefits derived through the use of information technology and in developing appropriate IT governance and control structures in a company.

COBIT has 34 high-level processes covering 210 control objectives categorized in four domains: (1) Planning and Organization, (2) Acquisition and Implementation, (3) Delivery and Support, and (4) Monitoring. Managers benefit from COBIT because it provides them with a foundation upon which IT-related decisions and investments can be based. Decision making is more effective because COBIT helps management define a strategic IT plan, define the information architecture, acquire the necessary IT hardware and software to execute an IT strategy, ensure continuous service, and monitor the performance of the IT system. IT users benefit from COBIT because of the assurance provided to them by COBIT's defined controls, security, and process governance. COBIT also benefits auditors because it helps them identify IT control issues within a company's IT infrastructure, and it helps them corroborate their audit findings. Figure 14.10 illustrates the relationships between the four domains in COBIT and categorizes both the high-level processes and control objectives associated with them.

Let's look at a real-world example of COBIT in action.

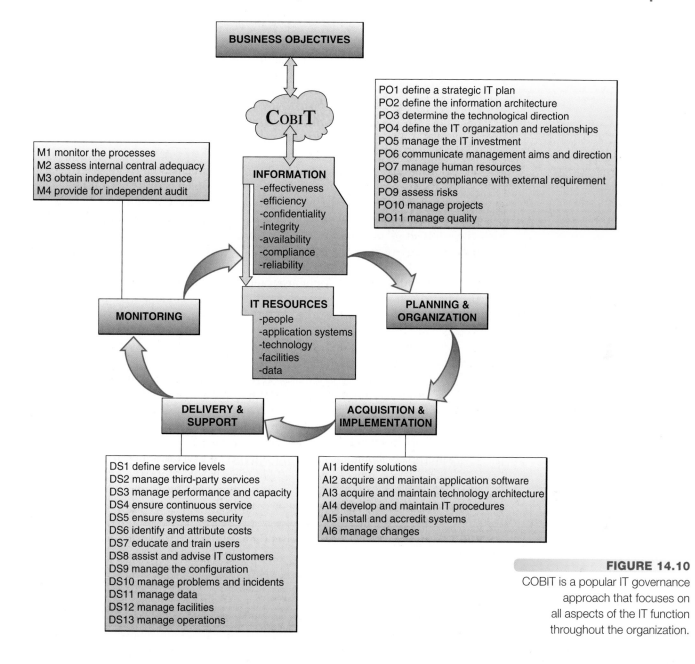

BUSINESS OBJECTIVES

COBIT

M1 monitor the processes
M2 assess internal central adequacy
M3 obtain independent assurance
M4 provide for independent audit

INFORMATION
-effectiveness
-efficiency
-confidentiality
-integrity
-availability
-compliance
-reliability

PO1 define a strategic IT plan
PO2 define the information architecture
PO3 determine the technological direction
PO4 define the IT organization and relationships
PO5 manage the IT investment
PO6 communicate management aims and direction
PO7 manage human resources
PO8 ensure compliance with external requirement
PO9 assess risks
PO10 manage projects
PO11 manage quality

MONITORING

IT RESOURCES
-people
-application systems
-technology
-facilities
-data

PLANNING &
ORGANIZATION

DELIVERY &
SUPPORT

ACQUISITION &
IMPLEMENTATION

DS1 define service levels
DS2 manage third-party services
DS3 manage performance and capacity
DS4 ensure continuous service
DS5 ensure systems security
DS6 identify and attribute costs
DS7 educate and train users
DS8 assist and advise IT customers
DS9 manage the configuration
DS10 manage problems and incidents
DS11 manage data
DS12 manage facilities
DS13 manage operations

AI1 identify solutions
AI2 acquire and maintain application software
AI3 acquire and maintain technology architecture
AI4 develop and maintain IT procedures
AI5 install and accredit systems
AI6 manage changes

FIGURE 14.10

COBIT is a popular IT governance
approach that focuses on
all aspects of the IT function
throughout the organization.

Blue Cross and Blue Shield of North Carolina is a leading health services company that delivers quality products, information, and services to help its customers improve their health and well-being.

In 2004, external audit firms raised the bar on the level of IT controls because of the U.S. Sarbanes-Oxley Act of 2002. In response, Blue Cross and Blue Shield of North Carolina, USA (BCBSNC), created a remediation program that addressed each Sarbanes-Oxley–related issue individually.

In 2006, BCBSNC began preparing for the National Association of Insurance Commissioners's (NAIC) Sarbanes-Oxley–like compliance requirements, called the Model Audit Rule.

Because of the team's research into and selection of the COBIT IT governance framework, BCBSNC was aware that COBIT could also be leveraged to meet Sarbanes-Oxley compliance requirements.

Blue Cross and Blue Shield of North Carolina: Reaping Benefits from a Successful COBIT Implementation

BCBSNC used a couple of unique requirements to help provide focus and set priorities. First, the financially significant applications had to be addressed. The second requirement was called "COBIT Lite." The team used the financially significant applications to narrow the scope of what they looked at and self-tested. For example, when the team looked at backup and recovery, they only looked at the platforms that housed the financially significant applications.

"COBIT Lite" referred to the pragmatic approach the team adopted. The work was performed by employees in addition to their day jobs so they focused on reasonable and prudent controls for the environment.

BCBSNC received numerous benefits from implementing the COBIT framework. Notable benefits include formalizing and documenting control policies and procedures. For the most part, the required controls were in place when they set off on this odyssey; however, little was documented, and procedures were informal.

Many areas achieved benefits from the self-testing program, including noticing minor exceptions right away and being able to correct them before they became any larger. The team also found that it could use COBIT as a common language, which worked internally among various process areas, as well as with internal auditors.

Any undertaking of this size has some great lessons. It is best to build the controls into the process. It makes the controls easier to sustain and it makes self-testing more efficient and effective. If the controls are not built into the process, the area performing the self test may have to pull and review a quarter's worth of documentation. This can take numerous hours. If the control point is built into the process as a quality assurance step, self-testing is always done; they just have to submit the documentation/evidence.

Enterprises should also limit the number of processes they attempt to implement at one time. BCBSNC took on 14 partial processes, and it took them *two and one-half years* to get everything in place and operating. And that was without encountering any major roadblocks.

SOURCE: Marty King, "COBIT Case Study: Blue Cross and Blue Shield of North Carolina," *ISACA CaseStudies.*

Managing Global IT

THE INTERNATIONAL DIMENSION

Whether they are in Berlin or Bombay, Kuala Lumpur or Kansas, San Francisco or Seoul, companies around the globe are developing new models to operate competitively in a digital economy. These models are structured, yet agile; global, yet local; and they concentrate on maximizing the risk-adjusted return from both knowledge and technology assets.

International dimensions have become a vital part of managing a business enterprise in the inter-networked global economies and markets of today. Whether you become a manager in a large corporation or the owner of a small business, you will be affected by international business developments and deal in some way with people, products, or services whose origin is not your home country.

GLOBAL IT MANAGEMENT LO 14-4

Figure 14.11 illustrates the major dimensions of the job of managing global information technology that we cover here. Notice that all global IT activities must be adjusted to take into account the cultural, political, and geoeconomic challenges that exist in the international business community. Developing appropriate business and IT strategies for the global marketplace should be the first step in **global information technology management.** Once that is done, end users and IS managers can move on to developing the portfolio of business applications needed to support business/IT strategies; the hardware, software, and Internet-based technology platforms to support those applications; the data resource management methods to provide necessary databases; and finally the systems development projects that will produce the global information systems required.

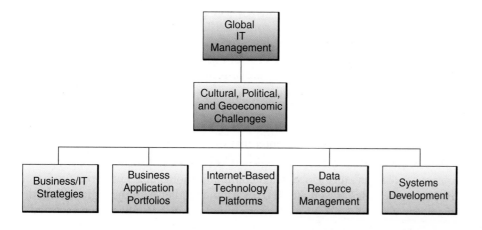

FIGURE 14.11
The major dimensions of global e-business technology management.

We seem to have reached a point where virtually every chief information officer is a global chief information officer—a leader whose sphere of influence (and headaches) spans continents. The global chief information officer's most common challenge, according to CIO Executive Council members, is managing global virtual teams. In an ideal world, human-resources policies across the global IT team should be consistent, fair, and responsive. Titles and reporting structures (if not compensation) should be equalized.

The council's European members, representing Royal Dutch Shell, Galderma, Olympus, and others, commissioned a globalization playbook that collects and codifies best practices in this and other globalization challenges.

Global Teams: It's Still a Small World

Obtain local human-resources expertise. Companies must have a local human-resources person in each country to deal with local laws. "Hiring, firing, and training obligations must be managed very differently in each location, and you need someone with local expertise on the laws and processes," says Michael Pilkington, former chief information officer of Euroclear, the Brussels-based provider of domestic and cross-border settlement for bond, equity, and fund transactions.

Create job grade consistency across regions. Euroclear is moving toward a job evaluation methodology that organizes job types into vertical categories, such as managing people/process, product development, business support, and project management. This provides a basis for comparing and managing roles and people across locations. Grade level is not the same thing as a title; people's titles are much more subject to local conventions.

Manage dispersed staff as portfolio teams. ON Semiconductor has IT staff that support sales in Slovakia, where ON has a factory; in Hong Kong, where ON has a major sales office; in Shenzhen, China, where a customer service center is located; and in Kuala Lumpur, Malaysia, at its regional development center. ON overcomes potential disconnects by having a single sales IT portfolio owner, based at headquarters in Phoenix, Arizona, who sets objectives and distributes work to the members of that team no matter where they reside.

Make the work meaningful. To keep morale high and turnover low, be sure that each remote location contributes to important projects. Don't send remote workers a steady diet of maintenance. Pilkington suggests building a center of excellence in each remote location.

Clearly defining the roles of remote groups can also help knit them together. For example, global company leaders can hold meetings at all levels to discuss the distinct purposes of corporate headquarters, the regions, and the local units. Knowing what their roles are in the larger picture and what they can expect from others "creates a sense of identity and purpose," says Nariman Karimi, senior vice president and chief information officer of DHL Asia Pacific.

Bring remote staff to headquarters. ON Semiconductor brings its foreign-based employees to the United States to work on key initiatives and interact with other business units at corporate headquarters. This may not be a monetary reward, but in many cultures it represents an endorsement and a source of pride.

Foster communication across regional boundaries. Videoconferencing is an obvious tool to enhance global team communication, but it's important to have in-person meetings as well. At DHL, Karimi, together with the regional board members, visits one of the top 10 sites around the Asia Pacific region each month; each gets at least one personal visit a year. The visits include time for the local unit to showcase itself, and there is also unstructured time for informal and personal interaction.

SOURCE: Richard Pastore, "Global Team Management: It's a Small World After All," *CIO Magazine*, January 23, 2008.

CULTURAL, POLITICAL, AND GEOECONOMIC CHALLENGES

LO 14-3

"Business as usual" is not good enough in global business operations. The same holds true for global e-business technology management. There are too many cultural, political, and geoeconomic (geographic and economic) realities that must be confronted for a business to succeed in global markets. As we have just mentioned, global information technology management must focus on developing global business IT strategies and managing global e-business application portfolios, Internet technologies, platforms, databases, and systems development projects. Managers, however, must also accomplish this task from a perspective and through methods that take into account the cultural, political, and geoeconomic differences that exist when doing business internationally.

For example, a major political challenge is that many countries have rules regulating or prohibiting transfer of data across their national boundaries (*transborder data flows*), especially personal information such as personnel records. Others severely restrict, tax, or prohibit imports of hardware and software. Still others have local content laws that specify the portion of the value of a product that must be added in that country if it is to be sold there. Some countries have reciprocal trade agreements that require a business to spend part of the revenue it earns in a country in that nation's economy.

Geoeconomic challenges in global business and IT refer to the effects of geography on the economic realities of international business activities. The sheer physical distances involved are still a major problem, even in this day of Internet telecommunications and jet travel. For example, it may still take too long to fly in specialists when IT problems occur in a remote site. It is still difficult to communicate in real time across the world's 24 time zones. It is still difficult to get good-quality telephone and telecommunications service in many countries. There are still problems finding the job skills required in some countries or enticing specialists from other countries to live and work there. Finally, there are still problems (and opportunities) in the great differences in the cost of living and labor costs in various countries. All of these geoeconomic challenges must be addressed when developing a company's global business and IT strategies.

Cultural challenges facing global business and IT managers include differences in languages, cultural interests, religions, customs, social attitudes, and political philosophies. Obviously, global IT managers must be trained and sensitized to such cultural differences before they are sent abroad or brought into a corporation's home country. Other cultural challenges include differences in work styles and business relationships. For example, should you take your time to avoid mistakes or hurry to get something done early? Should you go it alone or work cooperatively? Should the most experienced person lead, or should leadership be shared? The answers to such questions depend on the culture you are in and highlight the cultural differences that might exist in the global workplace. Let's take a look at a real-world example about what it takes to be global.

CIO Careers: The Importance of Global Experience

When you think about it, chief information officers have not been around for long; the profession is only about 25 years old. They come from all walks of life, and so it is difficult to identify a typical career path. One thing is clear, though: International experience can be a major career boost.

This is not as easy as it seems. For many, it involves uprooting a family, learning a new language (or two), and changing cultures. It is much more complicated than simply booking a flight and looking for a new place. Thus, it is important to know what you can and cannot do. "My first step was to talk with my family about location," says Curt Petrucelli, who in 1997 moved from Pfizer's U.S. IT organization to run the company's IT group in Brussels, Belgium, after realizing that as the company was becoming increasingly globalized he would have to leave New York if he wanted a top senior role one day. "This way, when opportunities arose, I could be clear about my availability," he says. Brussels turned out to be a great fit, and when he returned stateside he had a whole new, different perspective on things. Moreover, he credits his international experience as a major consideration in getting his new job at biopharmaceutical giant AstraZeneca, where he is the current U.S. chief information officer.

"The culture of your company will be grounded in the culture of the country," says Pieter Schoelhuijs, who in 1999 left his job with IBM in the Netherlands to take over as IT Director for Flowserve in Texas, and then moved to Engelhard, BASF, and Church & Dwight. "Arrive a few weeks early and get to know the culture before you start work," advises Schoelhuijs. There are a lot of small nuances that change from place to place, from the right tone to use in a performance evaluation meeting to the way in which people are let go. You need to get those right, on the first try, or problems will loom ahead.

Mike Capone, chief information officer of ADP, says networks and contacts are extremely valuable, as well. When he was selected to become part of an integration team for a large, overseas acquisition, he realized the value of having rotated through multiple departments during his years with ADP. "You will face situations you have never faced before," says Capone. "How do you set up call centers in central Europe? How do you attract local talent? I relied on my networks to compare notes," he says. Finally, be willing to question everything. You may find that people may assume a certain product or service will not fly under a country's regulations, but nobody has really checked—you may find a different answer if you do.

SOURCE: Martha Heller, "Global Work Experience as a Career Boost," *CIO.com*, June 25, 2009.

GLOBAL BUSINESS/ IT STRATEGIES
LO 14-4

FIGURE 14.12

Companies operating internationally are moving toward transnational business and IT strategies. Note some of the chief differences among international, global, and transnational business and IT strategies.

Businesses are moving away from *international* strategies in which foreign subsidiaries are autonomous but depend on headquarters for new processes, products, and ideas; or from *global* strategies, in which a company's worldwide operations are closely managed by corporate headquarters. Instead, companies are moving toward a ***transnational strategy,*** where the company's business depends heavily on its information systems and Internet technologies to help it integrate its global business activities. Instead of having independent IS units at its subsidiaries, or even a centralized IS operation directed from its headquarters, a transnational business tries to develop an integrated and cooperative worldwide hardware, software, and Internet-based architecture for its IT platform. Figure 14.12 compares the three approaches

Comparing Global Business/IT Strategies		
International	**Global**	**Transnational**
• Autonomous operations	• Global sourcing	• Virtual business operations via global alliances
• Region specific	• Multiregional	
• Vertical integration	• Horizontal integration	• World markets and mass customization
• Specific customers	• Some transparency of customers and production	• Global e-commerce and customer service
• Captive manufacturing		• Transparent manufacturing
• Customer segmentation and dedication by region and plant	• Some cross-regionalization	• Global supply chain and logistics
		• Dynamic resource management
Information Technology Characteristics		
• Stand-alone systems	• Regional decentralization	• Logically consolidated, physically distributed, Internet connected
• Decentralized/no standards	• Interface dependent	
• Heavy reliance on interfaces	• Some consolidation of applications and use of common systems	• Common global data resources
• Multiple systems, high redundancy, and duplication of services and operations		• Integrated global enterprise systems
	• Reduced duplication of operations	• Internet, intranet, extranet, and Web-based applications
• Lack of common systems and data	• Some worldwide IT standards	• Transnational IT policies and standards

Tactic	Global Alliances	Global Sourcing and Logistics	Global Customer Service
Examples	British Airways/ American Delta/ Air France	Benetton	American Express
IT Environment	Global network (online reservation system).	Global network, EPOS terminals in 4,000 stores, CAD/CAM in central manufacturing, robots and laser scanner in automated warehouse.	Global network linked from local branches and local merchants to the customer database and medical or legal referrals database.
Results	• Coordination of schedules • Code sharing • Coordination of flights • Co-ownership	• Produce 2,000 sweaters per hour using CAD/CAM • Quick response (in stores in 10 days) • Reduced inventories (just-in-time)	• Worldwide access to funds • "Global Assist" hotline • Emergency credit card replacement • 24-hour customer service

FIGURE 14.13

Examples of how transnational business and IT strategies were implemented by global companies.

to global business/IT strategy. Figure 14.13 illustrates how transnational business and IT strategies have been implemented by global companies.

GLOBAL BUSINESS/IT APPLICATIONS
LO 14-5

The applications of information technology developed by global companies depend on their global business/IT strategies and their expertise and experience in IT. Their IT applications, however, also depend on a variety of *global business drivers,* that is, business requirements caused by the nature of the industry and its competitive or environmental forces. One example would be companies like airlines or hotel chains that have global customers who travel widely or have global operations. Such companies need global IT capabilities for online transaction processing so that they can provide fast, convenient service to their customers—or face losing them to their competitors. The economies of scale provided by global business operations are other business drivers that require the support of global IT applications. Figure 14.14 summarizes some of the business requirements that make global IT a competitive necessity.

Of course, many global IT applications, particularly finance, accounting, and office applications, have been in operation for many years. For example, most multinational companies have global financial budgeting, cash management systems, and office automation applications such as fax and e-mail systems. As global operations expand and global competition heats up, however, there is increasing pressure for companies to install

Business Drivers of Global IT
• **Global Customers.** Customers are people who may travel anywhere or companies with global operations. Global IT can help provide fast, convenient service.
• **Global Products.** Products are the same throughout the world or are assembled by subsidiaries throughout the world. Global IT can help manage worldwide marketing and quality control.
• **Global Operations.** Parts of a production or assembly process are assigned to subsidiaries based on changing economic or other conditions. Only global IT can support such geographic flexibility.
• **Global Resources.** The use and cost of common equipment, facilities, and people are shared by subsidiaries of a global company. Global IT can keep track of such shared resources.
• **Global Collaboration.** The knowledge and expertise of colleagues in a global company can be quickly accessed, shared, and organized to support individual or group efforts. Only global IT can support such enterprise collaboration.

FIGURE 14.14

Some of the business reasons driving global business applications.

global e-commerce and e-business applications for their customers and suppliers. Examples include global e-commerce Web sites and customer service systems for customers, and global supply chain management systems for suppliers. In the past, such systems relied almost exclusively on privately constructed or government-owned telecommunications networks; now the explosive business use of the Internet, intranets, and extranets for e-commerce has made such applications much more feasible for global companies.

Omnicom Group Drives Global ERP Deployment

Omnicom Group Inc. is a strategic holding company that manages a portfolio of leading advertising and marketing services agencies. Omnicom has more than 60,000 employees worldwide and reported annual revenue of $13 billion in 2008.

Many of Omnicom's agencies needed more capable and efficient enterprise resource planning (ERP) and accounting systems to meet the increasing client demands for more detailed information and the financial reporting deadlines that the parent company sets.

Zimmerman Advertising, an Omnicom subsidiary that AdWeek ranks as the 14th-largest advertising firm in the United States, was saddled with a cumbersome financial management application. "Our system had not been updated or enhanced in many years—it was in maintenance mode," says Joe Weiner, vice president and corporate controller at Zimmerman. "We were left with few options in terms of improving the existing system. As a result, our financial reporting capabilities were limited and we had minimal ability to reengineer processes and to import and export data."

To improve financial management at its agencies and corporate reporting, Omnicom made the strategic decision to standardize on Microsoft Dynamics AX. "We needed to implement best-in-class financial management software that would allow our agencies to report in faster time frames and meet the varying client demands for information," says Wayne Wilson, global program manager for Omnicom. "Additionally, Microsoft Dynamics AX had the scalability and localization capabilities—both language and statutory—that we required as a global organization."

Omnicom created a template for Microsoft Dynamics AX that would streamline deployments across locations, set standards needed for reporting, and make it easier to customize the solution at the local level to meet the unique needs of individual agencies. For quick and easy access to information, Omnicom implemented Enterprise Portal for Microsoft Dynamics AX, which provides Web-based access to key information.

At Zimmerman, the efficiencies gained with the new system have been dramatic. "Microsoft Dynamics AX offers a multidimensional chart of accounts that vastly improves our revenue and expense reporting," says Chuck Miller, financial systems manager at Zimmerman. "We're also seeing many other efficiencies in our processes.

We save 80 hours each month with our new process for importing transactions, and our ability to capture more detailed information is better as well. We're also using the online document-handling function to save and retrieve documents electronically, and we have established automatic workflows."

"As a global company, we had to ensure we had alignment between our strategic goals at the corporate level and the individual implementations that were occurring throughout the agencies," explains Wilson. "We aligned the Microsoft product, our corporate goals, and the agencies' local requirements. The coordinated efforts of the consulting and development teams made it so that knowledge gained in one area of the program was incorporated into other areas of the program."

SOURCE: *Microsoft Case Study*, "Omnicom Group Drives Global ERP Deployment with Strategy and Development Support," January 29, 2010.

The management of technology platforms (also called the technology infrastructure) is another major dimension of global IT management—that is, managing the hardware, software, data resources, telecommunications networks, and computing facilities that support global business operations. The management of a global IT platform not only is technically complex but also has major political and cultural implications.

For example, hardware choices are difficult in some countries because of high prices, high tariffs, import restrictions, long lead times for government approvals, lack of local service or spare parts, and lack of documentation tailored to local conditions. Software choices can also present unique problems. Software packages developed in Europe may be incompatible with American or Asian versions, even when purchased from the same hardware vendor. Well-known U.S. software packages may be unavailable because there is no local distributor or because the software publisher refuses to supply markets that disregard software licensing and copyright agreements.

Managing international data communications networks, including Internet, intranet, extranet, and other networks, is a key global IT challenge. Figure 14.15 outlines the top international data communications issues as reported by IS executives in Fortune 500 multinational companies. Notice how political issues dominate the top-10 listing over technology issues, clearly emphasizing their importance in the management of global telecommunications.

Establishing computing facilities internationally is another global challenge. Companies with global business operations usually establish or contract with systems integrators for additional data centers in their subsidiaries in other countries. These data centers meet local and regional computing needs and even help balance global computing workloads through communications satellite links. Offshore data centers, however, can pose major problems in headquarters' support, hardware and software acquisition, maintenance, and security. That's why many global companies turn to application service providers or systems integrators like EDS or IBM to manage their overseas operations.

International Data Communications Issues
Network Management Issues
• Improving the operational efficiency of networks
• Dealing with different networks
• Controlling data communication security
• Burgeoning growth of data
Regulatory Issues
• Dealing with transborder data flow restrictions
• Managing international telecommunication regulations
• Handling international politics
• User auditability
Technology Issues
• Managing network infrastructure across countries
• Managing international integration of technologies
• Limits on scalability of data management platforms
• The need for 24/7 data and application recovery services
Country-Oriented Issues
• Reconciling national differences
• Dealing with international tariff structures
• Lack of qualified people
• Data security and transborder data regulations

FIGURE 14.15

The top issues in managing international data communications.

Orbitz.com: Toward an Integrated Global Platform

Originally established through a partnership of major airlines, and subsequently owned by various entities, Orbitz.com—the flagship brand of Orbitz Worldwide—has been in operation since 2001. Now it's undertaking a major upgrade to improve its online platform and enhance its ability to do business worldwide. All of this has to happen without disrupting Orbitz's ongoing operations.

Orbitz must interface with an array of systems to conduct business: It still has ties into the reservation systems of its original airline owners and those of other airlines it has partnered with along the way. It also must tap into the global distribution systems that still account for a great deal of the airline reservation business. And Orbitz isn't only about airline tickets. The real action and the real profits in the travel industry these days are in hotel rooms, car rentals, train trips, luxury cruises, bus tours, event tickets, and all of that rolled up into vacation packages.

Orbitz was left without a chief information officer after the departure of Bahman Koohestani. "I certainly understand enough about IT to run this organization," says Mike Nelson, chief operations officer, who has a background in financial planning and operations, not technology.

Jack Staehler, group vice president of technology, isn't worried about the lack of a CIO title. "The global platform, that's my charter," he says.

Code-named Austin, Orbitz's new online platform is a component-based system that uses a great deal of the Java code underpinning Orbitz's current platform.

What's different is that it can support multiple Web sites, both internal and external to Orbitz. It features standards-based user-interface technology able to incorporate dynamic updates and accessible from a range of devices. The idea is to be able to plug in data feeds from Orbitz's systems, like CheapTickets.com, and those of its partners and potential partners. It's multilingual and multicurrency, yet location specific.

For example, it understands what a domestic flight is wherever it's being accessed; previously, "domestic" was hardwired into the Orbitz system as referring to the United States.

Orbitz began rolling out Austin in 2008, starting with the Ebookers site in England. "The new Web site aims to make booking decisions easier through simpler navigation and more product choice," the company said in a release. Hooking into the Orbitz system, for instance, tripled hotel inventory available to Ebookers customers.

One reason Orbitz is in such a hurry is that the online travel industry isn't standing still. Travel search engines like Kayak.com, which can operate across platforms, threaten online travel sites with some of the same disintermediation that travel sites brought to travel agencies years ago. And some observers wonder when, not if, the 800-pound Internet gorilla, Google, will enter the online travel market.

"We're trying to accelerate this as much as possible, but it's a huge task," Nelson says. "You can only throw bodies at it so much, and that doesn't mean it's going to happen any faster."

SOURCE: John Soat, "Orbitz's Long, Strange Trip to a New Online Platform," *InformationWeek*, February 9, 2008.

The Internet as a Global IT Platform

What makes the Internet and the World Wide Web so important for international business? This interconnected matrix of computers, information, and networks that reaches tens of millions of users in more than 100 countries is a business environment free of traditional boundaries and limits. Linking to an online global infrastructure offers companies unprecedented potential for expanding markets, reducing costs, and improving profit margins at a price that is typically a

Key Questions
• Will you have to develop a new navigational logic to accommodate cultural preferences?
• What content will you translate, and what content will you create from scratch to address regional competitors or products that differ from those in the United States?
• Should your multilingual effort be an adjunct to your main site, or will you make it a separate site, perhaps with a country-specific domain name?
• What kinds of traditional and new media advertising will you have to do in each country to draw traffic to your site?
• Will your site get so many hits that you'll need to set up a server in a local country?
• What are the legal ramifications of having your Web site targeted at a particular country, such as laws on competitive behavior, treatment of children, or privacy?

FIGURE 14.16

Key questions for companies establishing global Internet Web sites.

small percentage of the corporate communications budget. The Internet provides an interactive channel for direct communication and data exchange with customers, suppliers, distributors, manufacturers, product developers, financial backers, information providers—in fact, with all parties involved in a given business venture.

So the Internet and the World Wide Web have now become vital components in international business and commerce. Within a few years, the Internet, with its interconnected network of thousands of networks of computers and databases, has established itself as a technology platform free of many traditional international boundaries and limits. By connecting their businesses to this online global infrastructure, companies can expand their markets, reduce communications and distribution costs, and improve their profit margins without massive cost outlays for new telecommunications facilities. Figure 14.16 outlines key considerations for global e-commerce Web sites.

The Internet, along with its related intranet and extranet technologies, provides a low-cost interactive channel for communications and data exchange with employees, customers, suppliers, distributors, manufacturers, product developers, financial backers, information providers, and so on. In fact, all parties involved can use the Internet and other related networks to communicate and collaborate to bring a business venture to its successful completion. As Figure 14.17 illustrates, amazing growth has occurred worldwide with regard to the Internet; however, much work needs to be done to bring secure Internet access and e-commerce to more people in more countries. Nonetheless, the trend is clearly toward continued expansion of the Internet as it becomes a pervasive IT platform for global business.

FIGURE 14.17

Current numbers of Internet users by world region. Note: Internet usage and population statistics, updated on December 31, 2010.

World Internet Usage and Population Statistics						
World Regions	**Population (2009 Est.)**	**Population (% of World)**	**Internet Usage, Latest Data**	**Usage Growth 2000–2010 (%)**	**Penetration (% Population)**	**World Users (%)**
Africa	1,013,779,050	14.81	110,931,700	2,357.3%	10.9%	5.6%
Asia	3,834,792,852	56.02	825,094,396	621.8%	21.5%	42.0%
Europe	813,319,511	11.88	475,069,448	352.0%	58.4%	24.2%
Middle East	212,336,924	3.10	63,240,946	1,825.3%	29.8%	3.2%
North America	344,124,450	5.03	266,224,500	146.3%	77.4%	13.5%
Latin America/Caribbean	592,556,972	8.66	204,689,836	1,032.8%	34.5%	10.4%
Oceania/Australia	34,700,201	0.51	21,263,990	179.0%	61.3%	1.1%
WORLD TOTAL	6,845,609,960	100.0	1,966,514,816	444.8%	28.7%	100.0

SOURCE: www.internetworldstats.com.

FIGURE 14.18

Key data privacy provisions of the agreement to protect the privacy of consumers in e-commerce trans-actions between the United States and the European Union.

U.S.–E.U. Data Privacy Requirements
• Notice of purpose and use of data collected
• Ability to opt out of third-party distribution of data
• Access for consumers to their information
• Adequate security, data integrity, and enforcement provisions

GLOBAL DATA ACCESS ISSUES
LO 14-3

Global **data access issues** have been a subject of political controversy and technology barriers in global business operations for many years but have become more visible with the growth of the Internet and the pressures of e-commerce. A major example is the issue of **transborder data flows (TDF),** in which business data flow across international borders over the telecommunications networks of global information systems. Many countries view TDF as a violation of their national sovereignty because these data flows avoid customs duties and regulations for the import or export of goods and services. Others view TDF as a violation of their laws to protect the local IT industry from competition or their labor regulations for protecting local jobs. In many cases, the data flow business issues that seem especially politically sensitive are those that affect the movement out of a country of personal data in e-commerce and human-resource applications.

Many countries, especially those in the European Union (E.U.), may view transborder data flows as a violation of their privacy legislation because, in many cases, data about individuals are being moved out of the country without stringent privacy safeguards. For example, Figure 14.18 outlines the key provisions of a data privacy agreement between the United States and the European Union. The agreement exempts U.S. companies engaging in international e-commerce from E.U. data privacy sanctions if they join a self-regulatory program that provides E.U. consumers with basic information about, and control over, how their personal data are used. Thus, the agreement is said to provide a "safe harbor" for such companies from the requirements of the E.U.'s Data Privacy Directive, which bans the transfer of personal information on E.U. citizens to countries that do not have adequate data privacy protection.

Europe: Tighter Laws Worry Security Professionals

Moves by several European countries to tighten laws against computer hacking worry security professionals who often use the same tools as hackers but for legitimate purposes. The United Kingdom and Germany are among the countries that are considering revisions to their computer crime laws in line with the 2001 Convention on Cybercrime, a Europe-wide treaty, and with a similar E.U. measure passed in early 2005.

But security professionals are scrutinizing those revisions out of concern for how prosecutors and judges could apply the laws. Security professionals are especially concerned about cases where the revisions apply to programs that could be used for bad or good. Companies often use hacking programs to test the mettle of their own systems.

"One useful utility in the wrong hands is a potentially malicious hacking tool," says Graham Cluley, senior technology consultant at Sophos in Abingdon, England. The proposed revisions would make it illegal to create or supply a tool to someone who intends to use it for unauthorized computer access or modification. Likewise, the proposed changes to German law would also criminalize making and distributing hacking tools. The German government said the changes will bring it into compliance with the 2001 Convention on Cybercrime. Several German security companies are planning to lobby against the law, as they fear it could hamper those who test security systems, says Alexander Kornbrust, founder and chief executive officer of Red-Database-Security in Neuenkirchen, Germany. For example, tools to check the strength of passwords, often freely distributed, could also be used by malicious hackers, he says.

"The security community is very unhappy with this approach," Kornbrust says. "The concern is that the usage and possession of so-called hacker tools will become illegal."

The United Kingdom and Germany are trying to align their laws with Article 6 of the convention, which bans the creation of computer programs for the purpose of committing cyber-crime. So far, 43 countries have signed the convention, which indicates their willingness to revise their laws to comply. Fifteen have ratified the convention. After a country changes its laws, it can ratify the convention and put it into force.

Fast forward to June 9, 2011, and the issue is still not fully resolved. In a meeting of ministers from all 27 member countries, they extended the regulation draft to include "the production and making of tools for committing offenses" as a criminal offense. Although the draft mentions "malicious software designed to create botnets or unrightfully obtained computer passwords," it does not indicate how two different tools such as a password cracker and a password recovery tool would be considered if the new law came to pass. Illegal access, illegal system interference, and illegal data interference, as well as instigating, aiding, abetting, and attempting to commit offences are already crimes under current E.U. law.

SOURCE: Dave Gradijan, "Euro Computer Crime Laws Have Security Pros Worried," *CSO Magazine*, September 29, 2006, and Jennifer Baker, "EU Ministers Seek to Ban Creation of 'Hacking Tools'," *Network World*, June 15, 2011.

Internet Access Issues

The Paris-based organization Reporters Without Borders (RSF) reports that there are 45 countries that "restrict their citizens' access to the Internet." At its most fundamental, the struggle between Internet censorship and openness at the national level revolves around three main means: controlling the conduits, filtering the flows, and punishing the purveyors. In countries such as Burma, Libya, North Korea, Syria, and the countries of Central Asia and the Caucasus, Internet access is either banned or subject to tight limitations through government-controlled ISPs, says the RSF.

Figure 14.19 outlines the restrictions to public Internet access by the governments of the countries deemed most restrictive by the Paris-based Reporters Without Borders (RSF). See their Web site at www.rsf.fr.

As an example, Internet censorship in the People's Republic of China is conducted under a wide variety of laws and administrative regulations. In accordance

Global Government Restrictions on Internet Access
• **High Government Access Fees** Kazakhstan, Kyrgyzstan
• **Government-Monitored Access** China, Iran, Saudi Arabia, Azerbaijan, Uzbekistan
• **Government-Filtered Access** Belarus, Cuba, Iraq, Tunisia, Sierra Leone, Tajikistan, Turkmenistan, Vietnam
• **No Public Access Allowed** Burma, Libya, North Korea

FIGURE 14.19

Countries that restrict or forbid Internet access by their citizens.

with these laws, more than 60 Internet regulations have been made by the People's Republic of China (PRC) government, and censorship systems are vigorously implemented by provincial branches of state-owned ISPs, business companies, and organizations. Most national laws of the People's Republic of China do not apply to the Special Administrative Regions of Hong Kong or Macau. There are no known cases of the PRC authorities censoring critical political or religious content in those areas.

The escalation of the government's effort to neutralize critical online opinion comes after a series of large anti-Japanese, anti-pollution, and anti-corruption protests, many of which were organized or publicized using instant messaging services, chat rooms, and text messages. The size of the Internet police is estimated at more than 30,000. Critical comments appearing on Internet forums, blogs, and major portals such as Sohu and Sina usually are erased within minutes.

The apparatus of the PRC's Internet repression is considered more extensive and more advanced than in any other country in the world. The regime not only blocks Web site content but also monitors the internet access of individuals. Amnesty International notes that China "has the largest recorded number of imprisoned journalists and cyber-dissidents in the world." The offenses of which they are accused include communicating with groups abroad, opposing the persecution of the Falun Gong, signing online petitions, and calling for reform and an end to corruption.

So the Internet has become a global battleground over public access to data and information at business and private sites on the World Wide Web. Of course, this becomes a business issue because restrictive access policies severely inhibit the growth of e-commerce with such countries. Most of the rest of the world has decided that restricting Internet access is not a viable policy but in fact would hurt their countries' opportunities for economic growth and prosperity. Instead, national and international efforts are being made to rate and filter Internet content deemed inappropriate or criminal, such as Web sites for child pornography or terrorism. In any event, countries that significantly restrict Internet access are also choosing to restrict their participation in the growth of e-commerce.

To RSF and others, these countries' rulers face a losing battle against the Information Age. By denying or limiting Internet access, they stymie a major engine of economic growth. By easing access, however, they expose their citizenry to ideas that potentially might destabilize the status quo. Either way, many people will get access to the electronic information they want. "In Syria, for example, people go to Lebanon for the weekend to retrieve their e-mail," says Virginie Locussol, RSF's desk officer for the Middle East and North Africa.

GLOBAL SYSTEMS DEVELOPMENT
LO 14-5

Just imagine the challenges of developing efficient, effective, and responsive applications for business end users domestically. Then, multiply that by the number of countries and cultures that may use a global e-business system. That's the challenge of managing global systems development. Naturally, there are conflicts over local versus global system requirements, as well as difficulties agreeing on common system features, such as multilingual user interfaces and flexible design standards. All of this effort must take place in an environment that promotes involvement and "ownership" of a system by local end users.

Other *systems development issues* arise from disturbances caused by systems implementation and maintenance activities. For example, "An interruption during a third shift in New York City will present midday service interruptions in Tokyo." Another major development issue relates to the trade-offs between developing one system that can run on multiple computer and operating system platforms or letting each local site customize the software for its own platform.

Other important global systems development issues are concerned with global standardization of data definitions. Common data definitions are necessary for sharing data among the parts of an international business. Differences in language, culture, and technology platforms can make global data standardization quite difficult. For example, a sale may be called an "order booked" in the United Kingdom, an "order scheduled" in Germany, and an "order produced" in France. Yet, businesses are moving ahead to standardize data definitions and structures. By moving their subsidiaries into data modeling and database design, they hope to develop a global data architecture that supports their global business objectives.

Systems Development Strategies

Several strategies can be used to solve some of the systems development problems that arise in global IT. The first strategy is to transform an application used in the home office into a global application. Often, the system that has the best version of an application will be chosen for global use. Another approach is to set up a *multinational development team* with key people from several subsidiaries to ensure that the system design meets the needs of local sites, as well as corporate headquarters.

A third approach is called *parallel development*. That's because parts of the system are assigned to different subsidiaries and the home office to develop at the same time, based on the expertise and experience at each site. Another approach is the concept of *centers of excellence*. In this approach, an entire system may be assigned for development to a particular subsidiary based on its expertise in the business or technical dimensions needed for successful development. A final approach that has rapidly become a major development option is to outsource the development work to global or *offshore* development companies that have the skills and experience required to develop global business/IT applications. Obviously, all of these approaches require development team collaboration and managerial oversight to meet the global needs of a business. So, global systems development teams are making heavy use of the Internet, intranets, groupware, and other electronic collaboration technologies. See Figure 14.20.

FIGURE 14.20

An example of Internet-enabled collaboration in global IT systems development. Note the roles played by the client company, offshore outsource developer, global open-source community, and just-in-time development team.

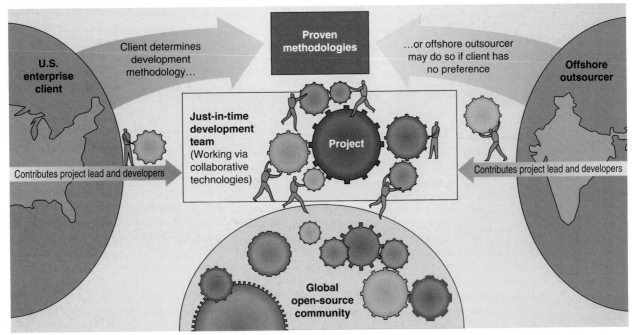

SOURCE: Jon Udell, "Leveraging a Global Advantage," *Infoworld*, April 21, 2003, p. 35.

Genus: The Need for Follow-the-Sun Capability

Genus plc is a British-based business primarily involved in the application of genetics and biotechnology to the development of products for the animal breeding industry. Operating in more than 30 countries, it serves a global supply chain of farmers, breeders, processors, distributors, and consumers. The company is headquartered in Basingstoke, England, and is a member of the FTSE 250 stock index. Annual revenue for 2010 was about £285 million (roughly $460 million).

During the last 40 years, the company expanded from a single office location with 125 staff members to international operations employing more than 1,800. Throughout this expansion, their IT group used a tracking system, designed to be locally hosted and run, to manage the change and release procedures associated with the deployment of internally developed applications, as well as commercially available software packages and infrastructure equipment. As the company expanded, however, support technicians in the new offices found out they could not track incidents over the system, which was directly connected to the local LAN in the headquarters building. In order to manage support processes over different time zones, "follow-the-sun" capability was needed (follow-the-sun is a type of global workflow in which tasks are passed around daily between work sites that are many time zones apart).

As a result, the company implemented a Web-based system by LiveTime Software, which followed ITIL best practices and was able to interconnect with Genus's disparate IT environment, a mixture of open-source and Oracle applications, databases, and middleware. In addition to connectivity and ease of use, the application has allowed support staff at Genus to quickly update tickets involving multiple projects at the same time, as well as raise problems and communicate with other personnel with specific expertise in real time through the application. Most importantly, the Genus IT support team can now provide global, high-quality, around-the-clock service in a cohesive and integrated manner.

SOURCE: "Genus Improve Efficiency by Adopting ITIL Best Practices with LiveTime," *LiveTime Software Case Study*, August 14, 2009.

State Street Corporation— Changing the "Where, When, and How" of IT

State Street Corporation, through its subsidiaries, provides various financial services and products to institutional investors worldwide. With a market capitalization of more than $20 billion, more than $22.6 trillion in assets under custody and administration and $2.1 trillion under management, and more than 29,000 employees worldwide, the company is a leading participant in the increasingly globalized financial services industry. From a technological standpoint, management has historically recognized that IT is a major part of its ability to successfully deliver innovative products and services to its customers, and has devoted a large pool of resources to new projects and developments over time. In line with an ongoing trend of increasing globalization, the IT group at State Street started to explore new ways in which it could provide more flexible, efficient, and cost-effective services to the many locations in which the company operates around the globe.

After the close call during the opening of the new offices in Krakow, Poland, and the realization that a better way existed, management at State Street Corporation launched an initiative to drastically change the way in which IT services were provisioned and provided for at all State Street locations around the world. The approach, which came to be known as "Zero Footprint, Maximum Impact," was geared toward providing the capabilities necessary to deploy information technology to support business demands in a more timely and cost-effective manner than before. The core of the approach is to use a mix of new—and not so new—technologies in order to minimize or entirely eliminate the need for local hosting or deployment of applications and systems. Rather, those applications and systems can be provided by regional data centers; it is far more efficient to operate a few locations to capacity rather than a number of distributed ones, each requiring its own version of the same equipment, infrastructure, and physical facilities. In addition, the local office would not likely use the distributed offices to the full extent of its possibilities.

By reducing the need for local infrastructure deployments, both the time and cost involved in rolling out new applications—or new offices—is greatly reduced. Environmental impacts of IT infrastructure, which are dear to State Street management, are also limited. The other major aspect of the new strategy is transforming the service and support staff involved into a global team that can be tightly coupled with local and regional staff in order to provide "around the clock and around the world" support to the business. Through the establishment of standardized and repeatable processes to help quickly incorporate new staff and reduce language and time zone barriers, support staff based in the United States have quickly realized that middle-of-the-night phone calls, which they had long believed to be just part of their job, can be greatly reduced or eliminated when there is someone else awake who is equipped to solve those problems.

Three technologies are at the center of the transformation. First, there is Wide Area Application Service (WAAS), which uses proprietary algorithms to improve the performance of applications delivered over a network. Because applications are now remotely hosted in regional data centers that are geographically distant from where end users are located, ensuring that distance would not impact performance was a major consideration. One key benchmark used by the company is the time it takes for a file of a known size to be transferred between two geographically distant locations. For example, sending a file from India to Boston used to take about 10 minutes; with the new technology, that time has been reduced to 8 seconds. This ability to share information seamlessly with other employees who may be next door or thousands of miles away has enabled the operation of real-time business processes around the world.

A second key technology is desktop virtualization. One major aspect of servicing an IT infrastructure—even if it does not come quickly to mind—is the development of standards about the kind of equipment, operating systems, and applications that will be used throughout a company. In addition to hardware, the software—and in particular, the desktop environment—is commonly standardized; that is, every employee of the company has access to the same set of basic desktop functionality, applications, and so on, while taking into consideration security and access privileges, of course. Having a standardized desktop environment means that IT only has to worry about supporting one common configuration, and that every time an application needs to be upgraded there is only one environment in which the upgrade or patch will have to be tested before it can be deployed. This much is commonplace among large corporations.

State Street, however, took the practice one step further. In addition to standardizing the desktop environment, they centrally deliver it to all users from a single location. Now, instead of the same common set of applications deployed across thousands of individual computers each in its own location—which was certainly better than different sets of applications deployed across thousands of individual computers each in its own location—State Street is working from a common desktop environment in one single location. The best thing is that this is all transparent to the end users, who do not need to know, worry, or care about where this is happening. For a workforce that is becoming increasingly mobile, being able to log in to the same environment from anywhere in the world—including at home—has greatly contributed to increasing productivity. Moreover, employees who may not have ever met each other face to face can now work from the exact same set of tools, which contributes to the user experience of employees working together, but separately.

The final major technology deployed in the new approach is server and storage virtualization. Through the use of a variety of techniques, State Street is now able to provide capacity on-demand. For example, the provisioning of a new office can be accomplished with minimal lead time, also allowing immediate recovery and business continuity. Downtime for scheduled maintenance, relatively easy to schedule when local operations shut down at night and local data centers are not heavily used, becomes much more difficult to manage once you are working with global capabilities and around-the-clock application service. The virtualization of servers and storage capabilities also helps with this. Moreover, the consolidation of those within regional data centers, in addition to obvious benefits derived from scale and cost efficiencies, allows a more effective management of those resources, as well as increased security, data retention, and controls, even in the face of rapid growth. Before, those were managed by the local facilities, who were not as well equipped to handle them. Reduced equipment and skill redundancies have also proved to be important benefits of doing things this way.

There have been some challenges to make this happen, to be sure. The most important dealt with the transition from a geographically distributed infrastructure to a globally integrated one. The least problematic issues were those related to the technologies themselves. Although technically complex, the technologies were well-defined and understood, and the use of clear success criteria and metrics allowed managers to closely monitor the development, integration, and performance of all three major technology components to ensure satisfactory quality of service. In terms of technology processes, the company relied on ITIL (Information Technology Infrastructure Library, a set of detailed descriptions of a number of important IT practices and comprehensive checklists, tasks, and procedures that any IT organization can tailor to its needs) to adopt industry best practices. The most complex challenges were those related to the nature of globalization itself. By moving away from locally deployed, hosted and managed infrastructure, the company entered the world of diverse time zones, languages, and cultures. Project management practices that had performed well under local conditions needed to be adapted or entirely replaced with newly developed ones to address the kind of issues that arise as a result of integrated global operations. Time and effort estimates that worked well in the past did not take into account the need to coordinate work across time zones; and language, knowledge, and cultural differences made establishing common technology requirements an important challenge. Over time, however, the necessary degree of trust and relationships between people were established that made it possible to move forward with the new initiative.

The "Zero Footprint, Maximum Impact" approach has now been in use for some time. Over a span of 18 months, seven new office buildings were provisioned, serving more than 5,000 new staff members. The benefits have started to spill over to other areas that were not part of the original business case for the new approach. For example, State Street can now deploy technology configurations that, under the old regime, were too expensive to make the cut in cost–benefit analyses—now the new business ideas supported by those configurations are a reality. All these make it possible for the Global Infrastructure Services group at State Street to quickly set up and configure an IT solution for any new acquisition or expansion in any existing or new market around the globe. The most significant advantage provided by these capabilities is being able to accomplish what every IT infrastructure group dreams of: becoming an enabler to the business, rather than an impediment to success.

SOURCE: "State Street Corporation: Zero Footprint, Maximum Impact," *Computerworld Honors Case Study*, 2008; Penny Crosman, "Q&A: Madge Meyer, State Street's EVP, IT Global Infrastructure Services," *Wall Street Technology*, September 16, 2009; "State Street Corporation: IT Infrastructure Transformation 360," *Computerworld Honors Case Study*, 2009; www.statestreeet.com, accessed June 15, 2011.

▼ QUESTIONS TO CONSIDER

1. What are some of the different project management practices that should be implemented when working on IT projects spanning different languages, time zones, cultures, and so forth? How would those practices be different from the ones you would use for local projects?

2. What would be the next step or steps for State Street Corporation, now that their global approach to IT infrastructure has been put into place and is working as expected? Where should they go next?

- **Managing Information Technology.** This can be viewed as managing three major components: (1) the joint development and implementation of e-business and IT strategies, (2) the development of e-business applications and the research and implementation of new information technologies, and (3) IT processes, professionals, and subunits within a company's IT organization and IS function.

- **Failures in IT Management.** Information systems are not being used effectively or efficiently by many organizations. The experiences of successful organizations reveal that the basic ingredient of high-quality information system performance is extensive and meaningful management, as well as user involvement in the governance and development of IT applications. Thus, managers may serve on executive IT groups and create IS management functions within their business units.

- **Managing Global IT.** The international dimensions of managing global information technologies include dealing with cultural, political, and geoeconomic challenges posed by various countries; developing appropriate business and IT strategies for the global marketplace; and developing a portfolio of global e-business and e-commerce applications and an Internet-based technology platform to support them. In addition, data access methods have to be developed and systems development projects managed to produce the global e-business applications that are required to compete successfully in the global marketplace.

- **Global Business and IT Strategies and Issues.** Many businesses are becoming global companies and moving toward transnational business strategies in which they integrate the global business activities of their subsidiaries and headquarters. This transition requires that they develop a global IT platform— that is, an integrated worldwide hardware, software, and Internet-based network architecture. Global companies are increasingly using the Internet and related technologies as a major component of this IT platform to develop and deliver global IT applications that meet their unique global business requirements. Global IT and end-user managers must deal with limitations to the availability of hardware and software; restrictions on transborder data flows, Internet access, and movement of personal data; and difficulties with developing common data definitions and system requirements.

These are the key terms and concepts of this chapter. The page number of their first reference appears in parentheses.

1. Application development management (633)
2. Business/IT planning process (630)
3. Centralization or decentralization of IT (632)
4. Chargeback systems (634)
5. Chief information officer (CIO) (635)
6. Chief technology officer (CTO) (636)
7. Data center (633)
8. Downsizing (632)
9. Global business drivers (649)
10. Global information technology management (645)
    a. Data access issues (654)
    b. Systems development issues (656)
11. IS operations management (633)
12. IT architecture (631)
13. IT staff planning (634)
14. Managerial and end-user involvement (641)
15. Managing information technology (627)
16. Offshoring (638)
17. Outsourcing (637)
18. System performance monitor (634)
19. Technology management (636)
20. Transborder data flows (TDF) (654)
21. Transnational strategy (648)
22. User services (636)

Match one of the key terms and concepts listed previously with one of the brief examples or definitions that follow. Try to find the best answer, even though some seem to fit more than one term or concept. Defend your choices.

_____ 1. Focuses on discovering innovative approaches to satisfying a company's customer value and business value goals with the support of IT.

_____ 2. Concerned with the use of hardware, software, network, and IS personnel resources within the corporate or business unit.

_____ 3. Managing business/IT planning and the IS function within a company.

_____ 4. A conceptual design, or blueprint, of an organization's IS/IT functions, hardware, and software created by a strategic business/IT planning process.

_____ 5. Many organizations have both centralized and decentralized IT units.

_____ 6. Managing the creation and implementation of new business applications.

_____ 7. End users need liaison, consulting, and training services.

_____ 8. Involves recruiting, training, and retaining qualified IS personnel.

_____ 9. Corporate locations for computer system operations.

_____ 10. Rapidly changing technological developments must be anticipated, identified, and implemented.

_____ 11. A relocation of an organization's business processes (including production/manufacturing) to a lower-cost location, usually overseas.

_____ 12. The executive responsible for strategic business/IT planning and IT management.

_____ 13. The executive in charge of researching and implementing new information technologies.

_____ 14. Software that helps monitor and control computer systems in a data center.

_____ 15. The cost of IS services may be allocated back to end users.

_____ 16. Many business firms are replacing their main-frame systems with networked PCs and servers.

_____ 17. The purchase of goods or services from third-party partners that were previously provided internally.

_____ 18. Managing IT to support a company's international business operations.

_____ 19. A business depends heavily on its information systems and Internet technologies to help it integrate its global business activities.

_____ 20. Global customers, products, operations, resources, and collaboration.

_____ 21. Global telecommunications networks like the Internet move data across national boundaries.

_____ 22. Agreement is needed on common user interfaces and Web site design features in global IT.

_____ 23. Security requirements for personal information in corporate databases within a host country are a top concern.

_____ 24. Business managers should oversee IT decision making and projects that are critical to their business units' success.

discussion questions

1. What has been the impact of information technologies on the work relationships, activities, and resources of managers?

2. What can business unit managers do about performance problems in the use of information technology and the development and operation of information systems in their business units?

3. Refer to the Real World Challenge in the introduction to this chapter. Does the fact that State Street Corporation is in the financial services industry have anything to do with their decision to take IT infrastructure global? Is this the way all large companies will be going in the future, and State Street is just going there sooner than most?

4. How are Internet technologies affecting the structure and work roles of modern organizations? For example, will middle management wither away? Will companies consist primarily of virtual (location independent) project teams of knowledge workers? Explain your answers.

5. Should an organization centralize or decentralize its strategic IS decision-making function? Use the Internet to find recent developments to support your answer.

6. Refer to the Real World Solution in the chapter. Does the new approach taken by State Street Corporation to their IT infrastructure leave them more vulnerable to disasters (natural or otherwise) or equipment failure? What should they be doing about it?

7. How might cultural, political, or geoeconomic challenges affect a global company's use of the Internet? Give several examples.

8. What effect does the Internet have on the transnational business strategy of a global business? Explain.

9. How might the Internet, intranets, and extranets affect the business drivers or requirements responsible for a company's use of global IT, as shown in Figure 14.13? Give several examples to illustrate your answer.

10. Should Google continue to do business in China—or in any country—that requires them to filter/censor their search results? Explain.

1. **Top-Rated Web Sites for Executives**
   CEO Express
   Check out CEO Express (www.ceoexpress.com), a top-rated Web portal for busy executives. See Figure 14.21. The site provides links to top U.S. and international newspapers, business and technology magazines, and news services. Hundreds of links to business and technology research sources and references are provided, as well as travel services, online shopping, and recreational Web sites. Premium services include e-mail, contact management, calendaring and scheduling, community networking, and powerful information organizing and sharing tools.

   a. Evaluate the CEO Express Web site as a source of useful links to business and technology news, analysis, and research sources for business executives and professionals.

   b. Compare CEO Express with Google News (news.google.com) and Google IG (www.google.com/ig). What advantages does CEO Express provide?

   c. Select the featured article from the "Editor's Corner." What was the source? Summarize the article. Was it useful to you?

2. **Information and Communications for Development**
   Assessing Global Capabilities
   Over a billion people take their electrical and telecommunications systems for granted. However, for billions more, the service-on-demand mentality remains a distant dream and Internet access only a rumor. Recognizing the need to promote global information and communications technologies (GICT), the World Bank has undertaken numerous technology infrastructure assessment and development projects.

   a. What is the World Bank (www.worldbank.org) doing to address third-world computer literacy needs?

   b. What is MIT (www.mit.edu) doing to help increase global computer literacy?

3. **Overseas Assignments**
   Incompatible Electricity?
   Traveling outside one's country poses special challenges for business travelers who need to remain connected, especially those working out of their hotel rooms. Electricity varies by voltage, cycles, and electrical plug shape. Likewise, telephone jacks may vary from country to country, and American cell phones work pretty much only in America.

   If you find yourself on an overseas assignment, how will you keep your laptop computer charged? How will you access the Internet? Can you free yourself from expensive hotel telephone surcharges?

   Pick a country to "visit" (your professor may assign one instead), and report on specific solutions to each question. *Be sure to include the manufacturer*

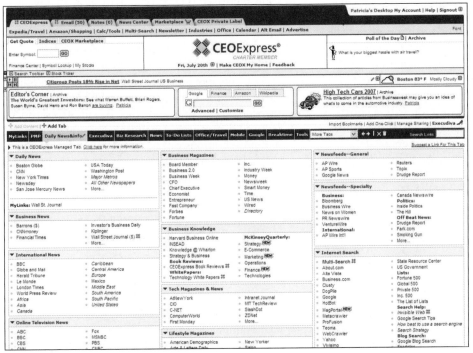

FIGURE 14.21
The CEO Express Web site.

SOURCE: Courtesy of CEO Express.

and model number of any hardware you may require. Cite all your sources.

   a. What do you need to bring with you to keep your laptop computer charged?

   b. What do you need to bring with you to connect your laptop's modem to the local telephone network?

   c. What will you use in place of your handy cell phone?

   d. Use a collaboration-enabled system such as Blackboard, Dreamweaver, or MS Expression Web to merge, organize, and publish your results with the rest of your class to create an online resource.

4. **Knowledge Work on the Move**
   Business Process Outsourcing
   Having discovered knowledge work's location independence, many organizations seek to lower their labor costs by moving their digital operations overseas. When evaluating such opportunities, managers must consider the following regional attributes:

   - Political and regulatory environment
   - Infrastructure (electrical, telecommunications)
   - Professionally skilled labor force
   - Information systems skilled labor force

   All prospective locations must have a supportive political and regulatory environment. However, variations within the other three attributes will pose special limitations. For example, India has millions of well-educated workers but notoriously unreliable telecommunications and electrical grids. Organizations setting up outsourcing operations in India build their own islands of stability with backup power and satellite telecommunications systems. A region with a shortage of professionally skilled labor may offer labor intensive activities such as call centers or data entry instead, yet even these jobs require basic computer literacy.

   The value of services provided depends primarily on the expertise or creativity involved in its performance. List suitable job titles for each work characteristic below. Rank each item in order of value provided.

   a. Digitize: convert data or information into a digital form.

   b. Distribute: process information in one direction or another based on strict rules and nondigital inputs (if the inputs were digital, a computer could probably do the job).

   c. Analyze: process information based on human expertise.

   d. Create: create new information or products based on human expertise.

5. **Global Training**
   Accommodating Global Diversity
   ICF, an international consulting firm, has more than 300 offices located in nearly every country in the world. Its partners number just over 2,000, and it employs nearly 50,000 additional consultants and support staff of all nationalities. When ICF's IT leadership committee decided to roll out new collaborative tools, they faced an international headache: how to get so many people representing so many cultures on board.

   Undaunted, the IT committee agreed early on that if they could win over all the partners while making the applications and training available to everyone, they'd succeed. This still left them with a significant challenge: Partners have management responsibilities, performance requirements, and pressures from clients. Furthermore, the tools that earned them the coveted partnership position didn't involve online collaboration, so the partners may view these tools as an unnecessary distraction.

   The partners on the IT leadership committee, on the other hand, had adopted these tools themselves and integrated them into their committee work. The committee members found the new tools increased their productivity and effectiveness. Processes that used to take weeks to complete could often be handled in days, and automated tracking provided them with useful performance data.

   The committee considered a variety of options to "sell" the new software to the partners and train them to use it. For each approach listed below, provide several pros and cons. Be sure to consider cultural differences. Assume all training, materials, and presentations can be translated into the appropriate languages.

   a. Demonstration video illustrating the software's usefulness

   b. Online, interactive training

   c. Training classes conducted at ICF's main training facility

   d. Training classes conducted locally

   e. Software demonstration kiosks set up in the vicinity of regional partner meetings

   f. Training personal coaches or mentors in each office who are available to the office's partners in addition to their regular duties

Reinventing IT at BP

A few years ago, the CEO of one of the world's largest corporations laid some very tough love on his 500 top managers. Despite having annual revenue of about $300 billion, BP had become, said CEO Tony Hayward, "a serial underperformer" that had "promised a lot but not delivered very much."

At that March 2008 meeting, those same 500 top BP managers also heard a Morgan Stanley oil and gas analyst tell them that while the rest of the energy industry was undertaking rapid change, BP was building a legacy of consistent failure both in finding and extracting new energy, and in refining and marketing finished products. And unless BP transformed its entire global business dramatically and rapidly, the analyst predicted, "BP will not exist in four to five years' time in its current form."

One of the people in that meeting was BP chief information officer and group vice president Dana Deasy, who'd joined the company four months earlier as its first global CIO.

As Deasy listened to the sobering comments from his chief executive officer and from a highly influential analyst, he thought about the transformation he had already launched within IT, an organization he thought had become, like the company overall, bloated, passive, unfocused, and unconcerned with performance and accountability.

Deasy wanted to strip out $800 million in expenses from BP's overall IT budget of $3 billion; cut in half the more than 2,000 IT vendors it had; overhaul BP's ranks of 4,200 IT employees; rationalize and reduce the 8,500 applications in use at BP worldwide; and turn IT from a tactical services unit to a business-driven and intimately embedded strategic weapon.

No stranger to challenging CIO roles, Deasy took the post with full knowledge of the tumultuous times ahead. "We were several billion dollars behind our competitors in oil and gas, and there was a real and very pressing concern in the company due to that," Deasy says. "Another part of the gap that Tony wanted to see closed was around organizational simplification: fewer layers of management, smaller corporate staffs, and deeper talent across key functions."

While noting that BP at the time had some great people in IT and some cutting-edge systems for exploration, Deasy also understood that he was going to have to drive enormous change in personnel, processes, and objectives across the entire IT organization in order to support and enhance the larger overhaul taking place across all of BP.

He saw a fundamental problem with the 4,200 IT employees BP had. "What was most startling to me about that number, only 55% of those IT professionals were actually BP-badged. The rest were contractors," he says. "So I was really struck by the very deep dependency we had on outside contractors."

Then there was the complexity that lay behind that $3 billion IT budget: "That encompassed everything, from the back office to the coalface," says Deasy, including everything from PCs and networks to the IT that supports refineries.

And so in the face of that sprawl in people, budget, priorities, requirements, business objectives, suppliers, and priorities, and inspired by Hayward's stark assessment of BP managers promising more than they delivered, Deasy committed in late 2007 to a three-year overhaul of every facet of BP's IT operations—an overhaul he and his team ultimately completed in two years.

Now, you might say, "Well, what's the big deal? Anybody starting with a $3 billion budget and a lackluster organization could come in and do a few things and look like a genius." That's naive at best and foolish at worst. "I viewed this as one of the top 5 CIO jobs in the world, and I fully understood it was a truly daunting challenge. But that's one of the reasons it appealed to me," Deasy says. "Could we make this work?"

"The team will say to this day that it's hard to imagine if we went back two years and looked at what lay before us that this is where we'd be today. And so we chuckle about that and say that if we knew then what we know now about what we'd have to do, we would've said, 'No, that is just not possible.'" The ability to dig into those kinds of massive challenges, knowing there's no "magic answer," is a big part of the IT culture Deasy sees: "So when we got the first $400 million in costs out, our people started to have a completely different strut around themselves and a new confidence, so that when we said, 'Hey, do you think we can find another $400 million?' they grimaced, but they also said, 'Yeah, we can do this. Bring it on.'"

While he had many urgent challenges, Deasy made BP's talent pool his top priority. "We desperately needed a baseline," he explains. "If we were going to impose the types of staggering changes we needed to meet the objectives

CEO Tony Hayward was laying out, then we had to know if we had the wherewithal to do it."

There was major turnover within those positions, and Deasy says the biggest and most significant change involves the capabilities of the new BP IT organization. "In just 11 months from the time I arrived here at BP, we replaced 80% of the top IT leadership within the organization, with those being the people reporting to me," Deasy says. "In the next level down, we replaced 25% of global management in the first year with new people we went out and selectively targeted and brought into BP. And it was very inspiring to be told that, yes, you can go out and hire the best people in the world to help you make this transformation possible. And that's exactly what we did."

In year one, BP's IT was highly decentralized. "The company didn't know it spent $3 billion in total on IT, or that it had 4,200 people in IT," Deasy says. "So we decided the right approach was to go a little draconian, and I just exerted control over all the people and all the spend. I knew that wasn't the right long-term model or cultural model for the company, but in the short term I wanted to be able to get enough control to be able to move to an 'embedded IT' model, which we have today."

Each business unit chief information officer now works for the business leader and also reports to Deasy. "Accountability No. 1 for those CIOs is that they're there to help deliver enablement through IT to drive new revenue, and also for helping to ensure they're driving standardized shared services to keep our costs down," Deasy says.

"With suppliers, I knew we had way too many from all of our decentralized legacy, and when we tried to round them up we stopped counting at around 2,200," he says. It wasn't only the sheer number; the 20 largest suppliers accounted for only 30% of IT spending, so "we ended up with a huge tail," Deasy says.

So in 2009, BP took 65 percent of its annual global IT spending, about $1.5 billion, and put it up for rebid in one year. It let BP cut 1,200 IT suppliers, and Deasy estimates it will end up saving the company $900 million over the next five years.

Deasy contends that the buyer-seller tension he has created is good for both parties, as long as each side is honest with the other about expectations and objectives. "You've got to be realistic: What's a vendor's job over the next five years? Well, when you strip away all the fancy talk, it's to claw back all that money they gave up in our rebids. So in 2010, how do we ensure that we don't lose the value of the efficiency play we worked so hard to establish? How can we take our five application development and application maintenance vendors and ensure they keep improving their service and delivering more value to us?"

"We just spent two very hard years rebuilding this organization, and one thing you learn in transforming an organization is that it's not a linear process," he says. "No sooner do you have contracts done, and they're effective, and they're delivering value, than you have to start the control process again.

"It is not linear—not at all—and that means that once you get to the enablement phase, you have to resist the temptation that makes you think you can just live there forever. And believe me, that temptation is very strong. But you've got to resist it and go back and once again begin to exert control, because by that time the organization is not the same as the one over which you first exerted control. It's a process that has to repeat itself because, as much as it might appear to be linear, I can assure you that it's not."

SOURCE: Bob Evans, "BP's IT Transformation," InformationWeek, March 8, 2010.

▼ **CASE STUDY QUESTIONS**

1. The case mentions the dependence of BP's IT organization on external contractors. Why would this be an issue? When is it a good idea for IT departments to hire contractors, and when is it not? Discuss some scenarios.

2. The culture of the IT organization is mentioned as an important issue. How do you think it changed throughout the period covered here? What did it look like when Deasy came on board? What does it look like now?

3. How did BP get to the situation mentioned at the beginning of the transformation process? Does it appear to be the result of a conscious decision? Use examples from the case to illustrate your answer.

▼ **REAL WORLD ACTIVITIES**

1. Go online and research the performance of BP since the time chronicled in the case. Did the transformation process pay out in the end? What was the role of IT in the outcome, if any? Prepare a report and compare BP's performance with that of their competitors.

2. Go back and reread the last two paragraphs in the case. What do you think Deasy means when he discusses the nonlinear and iterative nature of the process? What does he mean by 'temptation'? Break into small groups with your classmates to discuss these questions.

Cadbury, Forrester Research, A.T. Kearney, and Others: IT Leaders Face New Challenges in a Globalized World

Wayne Shurts had no experience overseeing IT operations in emerging markets when Cadbury CEO Todd Stitzer appointed him global CIO the summer of 2009. The geographic parameters of Shurts's responsibilities at the sweets maker—with a presence everywhere from Pakistan to Palau—multiplied overnight. The former chief information officer for North America now spends most of his time globe-trotting from his home base in Parsippany, New Jersey, to London headquarters, to operations on six continents.

Shurts also had to shift his thinking. The $7.8 billion company has made a concerted effort to expand in the developing world, giving it the biggest and most dispersed emerging markets business in the confectionery industry. In fact, Cadbury's business in rapidly developing markets was a major driver in Kraft's $19.5 billion takeover bid for the British candy maker. Last year, 60 percent of the company's growth came from emerging markets.

"That means that my world as CIO does not solely revolve around big economies of North America, Europe, Australia, and New Zealand," explains Shurts. "Emerging markets are not afterthoughts to me. They demand—and get—a lot of my attention." Shurts isn't alone. In industries ranging from consumer goods and agriculture to banking and electronics, multinationals are investing more in the Middle East, Asia, Eastern Europe, Africa, and South America.

"Companies are going to tap those markets as mature markets stagnate or decline," says Bob Haas, a partner and vice president with A.T. Kearney who leads the consultancy's strategic IT practice for North America. "And CIOs are gaining more and more responsibility for those emerging markets since IT is one of the most globally integrated corporate functions."

The work amounts to much more than just bringing some distant locations into the IT fold. Setting up shop in Bogotá or in Bursa, Turkey, is clearly a different proposition than supporting a new office in Boise, Idaho, or Brussels. Infrastructure limitations, local talent supply, unfamiliar business and cultural norms, limited vendor support and restricted budgets require creative solutions. At the same time, there is pressure to integrate these often one-off extensions of the company into the global infrastructure.

Bobby Cameron, vice president and principal analyst with Forrester Research, got a call recently from the chief information officer of a U.S.-based agribusiness building a new manufacturing plant in a tiny Peruvian fishing village. "It's 250 miles away from Lima. There's no water. There's no electricity. There's nothing there," Cameron says. "What's that about?"

It's about having an ideal port for moving goods throughout South America. All the chief information officer has to do is figure out how to build something from nothing without many of the support structures—vendors, a trained workforce, infrastructure—he'd have in a mature market. "And once you get through all of that," says Cameron," then you have to figure out how to connect it to the global infrastructure."

It's an extreme example, but supporting business in developing regions rarely lends itself to cookie-cutter IT. Moreover, the importance of emerging markets today means IT leaders can't fob off second-hand technology to non-Western locations. "The strategy of many corporations was basically to develop things in major markets then hand down those solutions to the emerging markets," Shurts says. "Hey, this laptop is two years old, maybe we pass that down, too."

That's not the case at Cadbury, explains Shurts. "I have to deliver strategies that address the specific needs of emerging markets. It requires some creativity and new thinking."

Understanding your company's business model for developing markets is critical. "Will there be manufacturing? Will you distribute from this market? How will your salesforce engage customers and what is their role while engaged?" says Ed Holmes, vice president of Global IT for Stiefel, an $812 million skin care company, acquired by GlaxoSmithKline, that operates in 28 countries.

You may end up providing technology and services similar to those you supply in established markets, Holmes adds, "but you must challenge the baseline assumptions in order to ensure that your solution will fit the market both economically and culturally."

Obstacles vary by location. Many developing markets face disadvantages due to decades of having closed economies, including limited exposure to global business practices. But two overriding—and sometimes conflicting—considerations for global chief information officers are cost structure and scalability. "From an IT perspective, these markets need to grow at an investment rate that makes sense for them," Shurts explains. "What they need today may not be what they need tomorrow. And tomorrow might actually mean tomorrow."

In its early days, an operation in an emerging market country may not need, nor could it support, the complexity and cost of a full-fledged ERP system. "Then, suddenly, through organic growth and an acquisition, everything changes and you do need the disciplines and features that an ERP system provides," Shurts says.

For instance, there's little support for emerging market needs among IT vendors, which means global chief information officers and their teams go it, for the most part, alone. Traditional solutions from IT vendors can be "too heavy and expensive for emerging markets," says Shurts. "It is very easy and neat and comfortable to walk around with that developed-market mind-set. There's a whole industry of people who would love for you to do that—hardware, software companies that have built their businesses focused on the developed market," Shurts says. "It's much harder to get out of that comfort zone."

Typical of global chief information officers, Shurts finds that exciting. "Many of them enjoy starting from scratch," says Forrester's Cameron. "They can't turn to IBM or SAP and have them solve all of their problems."

Cadbury does try to take advantage of corporate-level IT investments where possible. "We can leverage some systems from our developed markets and adapt that to emerging markets at a much lower cost," Shurts says. SAP instances, for example, where 80 percent of the investment has been made in a more established market, may be used in a developing market, even if that new market can't support all the same capabilities, has different legal or regulatory needs, or requires unique functionality. The Australia instance has been leveraged in parts of Asia; the Britain/Ireland instance has been reused in South Africa; and the initial instance in Brazil is being recycled for use throughout Latin America.

Other IT priorities just don't apply. In the United States, Canada, and Australia, Cadbury IT is laser-focused on trade promotion management. Sophisticated tools are used to analyze the amount of money Cadbury spends and the types of corporate programs it uses to promote its products. None of that will do a lick of good in South America or India, where the mom-and-pop shop still rules, and there are no big promotions to manage with Wal-Mart. Rather, the focus is on lower-end tools to determine the right delivery routes, make sales calls, and take orders. The good news is that there are similarities across the company's locations. "Route-to-market tools, salesforce automation and supply chain planning are important to all emerging markets," Shurts says.

Every country has its own particular problems. In some, the concept of urgency—embedded in the workplace culture of established markets—is foreign. In others, it is about infrastructure—or lack thereof. For instance, notes Shurts, most countries in Africa still struggle with broadband access. This problem will be alleviated somewhat by submarine cable projects on either side of the continent, scheduled to go live this fall, but "that's the most frustrating thing for us," Shurts says. "We do a lot of satellite in Africa and with our global applications—HR, finance. You'll notice slower response rates and latency."

Importing hardware and software may be the best way to go in Dubai and Abu Dhabi. But chief information officers managing IT in Brazil—including Shurts and Holmes—know that heavy tariffs there mean it's cheaper to buy everything in-country. "Our standard procurement solution doesn't really work there," says Holmes. "The only way you learn about these country-specific challenges is by engaging with other CIOs, talking to your HR leads in those locations and paying attention to previous challenges in other business functions."

"You have the ability to completely rethink the norms. This lets you create new solutions that would not have otherwise been viable," says Holmes. "The best opportunity is learning something that can then be translated back to a larger, more costly country." Less-developed regions of the world can also serve as testing grounds for new technologies or processes, says Haas, because the IT environment is less complex.

It's a big job, but lots of CIOs are going to have to do it, says Haas, who thinks developing markets experience is becoming a rite of passage for tomorrow's multinational CIOs. "Because we're a business with a very big presence in emerging markets, I am faced with the challenges of supporting IT in developing markets more than my peers," says Shurts. "But for others, it's coming. It's absolutely coming."

SOURCE: Stephanie Overby, "Globalization: New Management Challenges Facing IT leaders," CIO.com, November 12, 2009.

▼ CASE STUDY QUESTIONS

1. What are the challenges faced by the chief information officers mentioned in the case? Group them into categories and use examples from the case to define each.
2. The case mentions that the traditional approach toward emerging countries had been to develop technology in the corporate offices and then hand them down to satellite operations. How has that changed, as discussed in the case?
3. "IT is one of the most globally integrated corporate functions." How is IT different from other business areas when it comes to global integration? Why do you think this is the case?

▼ **REAL WORLD ACTIVITIES**

1. Go online and search for other examples of large multinational organizations facing similar challenges. Summarize your findings and compare them to the ones chronicled in the case. Can you find any new ones not mentioned here?

2. Do you think some form of international experience is key to your long-term career success? Have you ever considered taking a position abroad? Why or why not? Break into small groups with your classmates to discuss the advantages and disadvantages of moving abroad to gain these experiences.

review quiz answers

CHAPTER 1

Foundations of Information Systems in Business

1. 19	8. 22*b*	15. 3	22. 24	29. 16*d*	36. 11	43. 22*a*
2. 23	9. 8	16. 14	23. 24*a*	30. 16*e*	37. 7	44. 4
3. 23*a*	10. 9	17. 16	24. 24*b*	31. 26	38. 26*d*	45. 26*f*
4. 23*b*	11. 10	18. 17	25. 22	32. 26*c*	39. 5	46. 20
5. 23*c*	12. 25	19. 13	26. 16*a*	33. 26*b*	40. 6	47. 26*e*
6. 15	13. 12	20. 13*a*	27. 16*b*	34. 26*a*	41. 14*a*	48. 26*g*
7. 1	14. 2	21. 13*b*	28. 16*c*	35. 18	42. 21	

Competing with Information Technology

1. 3	4. 11	7. 6	10. 2	13. 8
2. 4	5. 5	8. 14	11. 1	14. 9
3. 12	6. 13	9. 10	12. 15	15. 7

Computer Hardware

1. 3	9. 20	17. 18	25. 16	33. 36	41. 30	49. 33*d*
2. 2	10. 1	18. 34	26. 32	34. 33*a*	42. 9	50. 33*g*
3. 5	11. 7	19. 10	27. 23	35. 33*f*	43. 11	
4. 8	12. 13	20. 27*c*	28. 27	36. 30*b*	44. 22	
5. 26	13. 14	21. 33*e*	29. 27*a*	37. 30*a*	45. 27*b*	
6. 29	14. 17	22. 25	30. 33*c*	38. 35	46. 27*d*	
7. 24	15. 9*a*	23. 12	31. 4	39. 6	47. 33*b*	
8. 21	16. 19	24. 15	32. 33	40. 31	48. 28	

Computer Software

1. 5	7. 32	13. 33	19. 37	25. 20	31. 28	37. 16
2. 2	8. 6	14. 12	20. 8	26. 3	32. 15	38. 36
3. 31	9. 34	15. 11	21. 26	27. 14	33. 38	
4. 1	10. 22	16. 35	22. 17	28. 10	34. 18	
5. 4	11. 27	17. 9	23. 29	29. 24	35. 25	
6. 7	12. 19	18. 30	24. 13	30. 23	36. 21	

Data Resource Management

1. 11	7. 12	13. 6	19. 13*a*	25. 1	31. 16*a*	37. 16
2. 3	8. 20*b*	14. 16*e*	20. 13*e*	26. 13	32. 20	
3. 9	9. 13*d*	15. 16*g*	21. 13*b*	27. 16*b*	33. 7	
4. 19	10. 20*d*	16. 16*f*	22. 20*e*	28. 18	34. 14	
5. 2	11. 8	17. 16*c*	23. 20*a*	29. 4	35. 16*d*	
6. 10	12. 5	18. 15	24. 20*c*	30. 17	36. 13*c*	

CHAPTER 6
Telecommunications and Networks

1. 34	7. 8	13. 9	19. 24	25. 21*a*	31. 22	37. 21
2. 23	8. 11	14. 3	20. 1	26. 21*b*	32. 26	38. 30
3. 20	9. 35	15. 31	21. 2	27. 25	33. 6	39. 37
4. 17	10. 15	16. 32	22. 33	28. 12	34. 14	
5. 16	11. 7	17. 18	23. 5	29. 10	35. 28	
6. 13	12. 29	18. 19	24. 27	30. 4	36. 36	

CHAPTER 7
e-Business Systems

1. 8	6. 21	11. 5	16. 23	21. 3	26. 19	31. 24
2. 7	7. 16	12. 11	17. 1	22. 2	27. 30	
3. 13	8. 29	13. 27	18. 22	23. 26	28. 31	
4. 9	9. 20	14. 18	19. 25	24. 14	29. 4	
5. 10	10. 6	15. 15	20. 17	25. 12	30. 28	

CHAPTER 8
Business Across the Enterprise

1. 1	5. 4*a*	9. 6*b*	13. 1*d*	17. 3
2. 4	6. 6*a*	10. 1*c*	14. 4*d*	18. 5
3. 6	7. 1*b*	11. 4*c*	15. 6*d*	
4. 1*a*	8. 4*b*	12. 6*c*	16. 2	

CHAPTER 9
e-Commerce Systems

1. 5	7. 4*f*	13. 8	19. 6
2. 5*b*	8. 4*c*	14. 3*d*	20. 4*d*
3. 5*a*	9. 4*b*	15. 3*a*	21. 1
4. 5*c*	10. 4*e*	16. 3*c*	22. 3
5. 4	11. 4*b*	17. 3*b*	23. 4*g*
6. 4*a*	12. 7	18. 2	

CHAPTER 10
Supporting Decision Making

1. 6	8. 1*d*	15. 8	22. 11	29. 17
2. 10	9. 1*c*	16. 20	23. 18	30. 14
3. 21	10. 1*a*	17. 9	24. 16	
4. 7	11. 1*b*	18. 2	25. 12	
5. 3	12. 24	19. 25	26. 19	
6. 22	13. 4	20. 26	27. 23	
7. 1	14. 5	21. 15	28. 13	

CHAPTER 11
Business/IT Strategies for Development

1. 8	5. 10	9. 3	13. 2*c*
2. 2	6. 2*a*	10. 5	14. 2*b*
3. 7	7. 11	11. 4	
4. 9	8. 6	12. 1	

CHAPTER 12
Implementing Business/IT Solutions

1. 20	7. 27*a*	13. 28	19. 24	25. 1	31. 11
2. 25	8. 11*a*	14. 12	20. 22	26. 26	32. 15
3. 16	9. 19	15. 9	21. 23	27. 4	33. 10
4. 2	10. 13	16. 21	22. 18	28. 17	
5. 27*b*	11. 7	17. 8	23. 6	29. 27	
6. 11*b*	12. 5	18. 29	24. 3	30. 14	

CHAPTER 13
Security and Ethical Challenges

1. 24	7. 2	13. 27	19. 6	25. 1
2. 20	8. 4	14. 28	20. 30	26. 18
3. 29	9. 11	15. 22	21. 26	27. 14
4. 16	10. 13	16. 7	22. 21	28. 25
5. 17	11. 15	17. 8	23. 19	29. 3
6. 10	12. 5	18. 12	24. 9	30. 23

CHAPTER 14
Enterprise and Global Management of Information Technology

1. 2	7. 22	13. 6	19. 21
2. 11	8. 13	14. 18	20. 9
3. 15	9. 7	15. 4	21. 20
4. 12	10. 19	16. 8	22. 10*b*
5. 3	11. 16	17. 17	23. 10*a*
6. 1	12. 5	18. 10	24. 14

selected references

preface

Sawhney, Mohan, and Jeff Zabin. *The Seven Steps to Nirvana: Strategic Insights into e-Business Transformation.* New York: McGraw-Hill, 2001.

chapter 1

Barlas, D. "Accessing Suppliers," *LINE56.com*, article ID=3810, 2002.

Central Intelligence Agency. *CIA Factbook.* August 2003.

"Citibank E-Mail Hoax and Webpage Scam," http://www.millersmiles.co.uk/identitytheft/citibank-email-verification-hoax.htm, November 2003.

Institute for Development Policy and Management. http://www.egov4dev.org/home.htm and http://www.e-devexchange.org/eGov/home.htm, March 2004.

Kalakota, Ravi, and Marcia Robinson. *e-Business 2.0: Roadmap for Success.* Reading, MA: Addison-Wesley, 2001.

Lee, Allen. "Inaugural Editor's Comments." *MIS Quarterly*, March 1999.

Leinfuss, Emily. "Making the Cut." *Computerworld*, September 20, 1999.

Norris, Grant; James Hurley; Kenneth Hartley; John Dunleavy; and John Balls. *e-Business and ERP: Transforming the Enterprise.* New York: John Wiley & Sons, 2000.

Radcliff, Deborah. "Aligning Marriott." *Computerworld*, April 20, 2000.

Rosencrance, L. "Citibank Customers Hit with e-Mail Scam." *Computerworld*, October 24, 2003.

Steadman, Craig. "Failed ERP Gamble Haunts Hershey." *Computerworld*, November 1, 1999.

Vijayan, Jaikumar. "E-Procurement Talks Back." *Computerworld*, Premiere 100 Best in Class supplement, March 11, 2002.

Weiss, Todd. "Hershey Upgrades R/3 ERP System without Hitches." *Computerworld*, September 9, 2002.

chapter 2

"Agilent Technologies ERP Information for Customers," http://www.tmintl.agilent.com/model/index.shtml, n.d.

Applegate, Lynda; Robert D. Austin; and F. Warren McFarlan. *Corporate Information Systems Management: Text and Cases.* 6th ed. Burr Ridge, IL: Irwin/McGraw-Hill, 2003.

Bowles, Jerry. "Best Practices for Global Competitiveness." *Fortune*, Special Advertising Section, November 24, 1997.

Caron, J. Raymond; Sirkka Jarvenpaa; and Donna Stoddard. "Business Reengineering at CIGNA Corporation: Experiences and Lessons from the First Five Years." *MIS Quarterly*, September 1994.

Christensen, Clayton. *The Innovator's Dilemma: When New Technologies Cause Great Firms to Fail.* Boston: Harvard Business School Press, 1997.

Cronin, Mary. *The Internet Strategy Handbook.* Boston: Harvard Business School Press, 1996.

Davenport, Thomas H. *Process Innovation: Reengineering Work through Information Technology.* Boston: Harvard Business School Press, 1993.

El Sawy, Omar, and Gene Bowles. "Redesigning the Customer Support Process for the Electronic Economy: Insights from Storage Dimensions." *MIS Quarterly*, December 1997.

El Sawy, Omar; Arvind Malhotra; Sanjay Gosain; and Kerry Young. "IT-Intensive Value Innovation in the Electronic Economy: Insights from Marshall Industries." *MIS Quarterly*, September 1999.

Frye, Colleen. "Imaging Proves Catalyst for Reengineering." *Client/Server Computing*, November 1994.

Garner, Rochelle. "Please Don't Call IT Knowledge Management!" *Computerworld*, August 9, 1999.

Goldman, Steven; Roger Nagel; and Kenneth Preis. *Agile Competitors and Virtual Organizations: Strategies for Enriching the Customer.* New York: Van Nostrand Reinhold, 1995.

Grover, Varunand Pradipkumar Ramanlal. "Six Myths of Information and Markets: Information Technology Networks, Electronic Commerce, and the Battle for Consumer Surplus." *MIS Quarterly*, December 1999.

Hamm, Steve, and Marcia Stepaneck. "From Reengineering to E-Engineering." *BusinessWeek e.biz*, March 22, 1999.

Hoffman, T. "In the Know: Knowledge Management Case Study Pays Off for BAE Systems." *Computerworld*, October 14, 2002.

"Intel Telecom Case Studies, Best Known Call Center Practices," http://www.intel.com/network/csp/resources/case_studies/enterprise/7867web.htm, n.d.

Kalakota, Ravi, and Marcia Robinson. *e-Business 2.0: Roadmap for Success.* Reading, MA: Addison-Wesley, 2001.

Kettinger, William; Varun Grover; and Albert Segars. "DoStrategic Systems Really Pay Off? An Analysis of Classic Strategic IT Cases." *Information Systems Management*, Winter 1995.

Kettinger, William; James Teng; and Subashish Guha. "Business Process Change: A Study of Methodologies, Techniques, and Tools." *MIS Quarterly*, March 1997.

"New Wal-Mart Fulfillment Distribution Center to Provide Service to Wal-Mart.com," Walmartstores.com, August 2, 2000.

Nonaka, Ikujiro. "The Knowledge Creating Company." *Harvard Business Review*, November–December 1991.

Porter, Michael, and Victor Millar. "How Information Gives You Competitive Advantage." *Harvard Business Review*, July–August 1985.

Prokesch, Steven. "Unleashing the Power of Learning: An Interview with British Petroleum's John Browne." *Harvard Business Review*, September–October 1997.

Sambamurthy, V.; Anandhi Bharadwaj; and Varun Grover. "Shaping Agility through Digital Options: Reconceptualizing the Role of Information Technology in Contemporary Firms." *MIS Quarterly*, June 2003.

Seybold, Patricia. *Customers.com: How to Create a Profitable Business Strategy for the Internet and Beyond.* New York: Times Books, 1998.

Shapiro, Carl, and Hal Varian. *Information Rules: A Strategic Guide to the Network Economy.* Boston: Harvard Business School Press, 1999.

Siekman, Philip. "Why Infotech Loves Its Giant Job Shops." *Fortune*, May 12, 1997.

Songini, Marc. "ERP Effort Sinks Agilent Revenue." *Computerworld*, August 26, 2002.

Strategy Works. "Retrieval Is the Key to the New Economy," http://www.thestrategyworks.com/articles/knowledge2.htm, August 31, 2000.

Weill, Peter, and Michael Vitale. *Place to Space: Migrating to e-Business Models.* Boston: Harvard Business School Press, 2001.

chapter 3

Computerworld, *PC Week*, *PC Magazine*, and *PC World* are just a few examples of many good magazines for current information on computer systems hardware and its use in end-user and enterprise applications.

The World Wide Web sites of computer manufacturers such as Apple Computer, Dell Computer, Gateway, IBM, Hewlett-Packard, Compaq, and Sun Microsystems are good sources of information on computer hardware developments.

Alexander, Steve. "Speech Recognition." *Computerworld*, November 8, 1999.

"Computing in the New Millennium." *Fortune*, Technology Buyers Guide, Winter 2000.

Guyon, Janet. "Smart Plastic." *Fortune*, October 13, 1997.

"Hardware." *Fortune*, Technology Buyer's Guide, Winter 1999.

Hecht, Jeff. "Casino Chips to Carry RFID Tags." *New Scientist*, January 2004.

Joch, Alan. "Fewer Servers, Better Service." *Computerworld*, June 4, 2001.

Kennedy, Ken; Charles Bender; John Connolly; et al. "A Nationwide Parallel Computing Environment." *Communications of the ACM*, November 1997.

Messerschmitt, David. *Networked Applications: A Guide to the New Computing Infrastructure.* San Francisco: Morgan Kaufmann, 1999.

Ouellette, Tim. "Goodbye to the Glass House." *Computerworld*, May 26, 1997.

Ouellette, Tim. "Tape Storage Put to New Enterprise Uses." *Computerworld*, November 10, 1997.

Reimers, Barbara. "Blades Spin ROI Potential." *Computerworld*, February 11, 2002.

Simpson, David. "The Datamation 100." *Datamation*, July 1997.

"Top 500 Supercomputer Sites: ASCII White," www.top500.org, May 18, 2003.

chapter 4

Examples of many good magazines for current information and reviews of computer software for business applications can be found at ZD Net, the Web site for ZD Publications (www.zdnet.com), including *PC Magazine, PC Week, PC Computing, Macworld, Inter@ctive Week,* and *Computer Shopper.*

The Web sites of companies like Microsoft, Sun Microsystems, Lotus, IBM, Apple Computer, and Oracle are good sources of information on computer software developments.

Ascent Solutions Inc. http://www.ascentsolutionsus.com/erp.htm.

Citrix i-Business Report. "Achieving Business Transformation through Application Service Providers." *Business Communications Review,* May 3, 2002.

Gonsalves, A. "At Orbitz, Linux Delivers Double the Performance at One-Tenth the Cost." *InternetWeek.com,* July 1, 2003.

Iyer, Bala; Jim Freedman; Mark Gaynor; and George Wyner. "Web Services: Enabling Dynamic Business Networks." *Communications of the Association for Information Systems,* Volume 11, 2003.

Mearian, Lucas. "Fidelity Makes Big XML Conversion." *Computerworld,* October 1, 2001.

Microsoft Corporation. "Introducing the Windows 2003 Family," http://www.microsoft.com, July 1, 2003.

Oracle Corporation. "Visa to Save Millions a Year by Automating Back-Office Processes with Oracle e-Business Suite," Customer Profile, www.oracle.com, September 13, 2002.

Orbitz Corporate. http://www.orbitz.com/App/about/about.jsp?z=63z0&r=42.

Sliwa, Carol. ".Net vs. Java." *Computerworld,* May 20, 2002.

Smith, T. "How Web Services Help Wells Fargo Customers." *InternetWeek,* May 13, 2003.

Transchannel, LLC. "Transchannel Announces ie2 for People-Soft," http://www.prnewswire.com/, 2002.

Vogelstein, Fred. "Servers with a Smile." *Fortune,* September 30, 2002.

Wainewright, Ivan. "An Introduction to Application Service Providers (ASPs)." *TechSoup,* May 1, 2000.

chapter 5

Amato-McCoy, D. "Enterprise Data Solution Finds a Home at BofA." *Financial Technology Network,* http://www.financetech.com/story/BNK/BNK20021210S0030, December 10, 2002.

Fox, Pimm. "Extracting Dollars from Data." *Computerworld,* April 15, 2002.

IBM Case Study Series. "Kingslake Connects Customers in Sri Lanka with DB2 Everywhere," http://www.306.ibm.com/software/success/cssdb.nsf/cs/NAVO4VPV97?OpenDocument&Site=indwireless, n.d.

IBM Corporation. "DB2 Business Intelligence," www.ibm.com, July 27, 2003.

Jacobsen, Ivar; Maria Ericsson; and Ageneta Jacobsen. *The Object Advantage: Business Process Reengineering with Object Technology.* New York: ACM Press, 1995.

Kalakota, Ravi, and Marcia Robinson. *e-Business 2.0: Roadmap for Success.* Reading, MA: Addison-Wesley, 2002.

Kingslake International Press Release. "Kingslake Helps Sri Lankan Manufacturers Profit and Grow." 2003.

Lorents, Alden, and James Morgan. *Database Systems: Concepts, Management and Applications.* Fort Worth, TX; Dryden Press, 1998.

MacSweeney, G. "Aetna Mines Ethnic Health Data." *InsuranceTech,* April 1, 2003.

Mannino, Michael. *Database Application Development and Design.* New York: McGraw-Hill/Irwin, 2001.

Nance, Barry. "Managing Tons of Data." *Computerworld,* April 23, 2001.

Teradata Corporation Case Report. "State of Iowa: Closing the Tax Gap in Iowa," http://www.teradata.com/t/pdf.aspx?a=83673&b=87463, 2002.

Whiting, R. "The Data Warehousing Advantage, Part II." InformationWeek, July 28, 2003.

chapter 6

Armor, Daniel. *The e-Business (R)Evolution: Living and Working in an Interconnected World.* Upper Saddle River, NJ: Prentice Hall, 2000.

Barksdale, Jim. "The Next Step: Extranets." *Netscape Columns: The Main Thing,* December 3, 1996.

"Boeing 777: A Case Study," http://www.eweek.org/2002/nbm/collaborate/collab01.html, n.d.

Bresnick, Alan. "Verizon Turns Up Heat in Online Data Wars." *Cable Datacom News,* June 1, 2003.

"Cable Modem Info Center," www.cabledatacomnews.com, July 26, 2003.

Caputo, L. "JHI Online Directory Up and Running for Student Users." *The Johns Hopkins Newsletter,* January 28, 1999.

Chatterjee, Samir. "Requirements for Success in Gigabit Networking." *Communications of the ACM,* July 1997.

"Countrywide Home Loans Uses Netscape Platform to Develop Extensive Internet and Intranet Solutions." Netscape Corporate Public Relations Press Release, August 15, 1996.

Cronin, Mary. *Doing More Business on the Internet.* New York: Van Nostrand Reinhold, 1995.

CyberAtlas Inc. "The Big Picture: Geographics: Population Explosion!" www.cyberatlas.internet.com, June 23, 2003.

"Holiday Autos," http://www.itcasestudies.com/case/ser30.html, n.d.

Housel, Thomas, and Eric Skopec. *Global Telecommunications Revolution: The Business Perspective.* New York: McGraw-Hill/Irwin, 2001.

"Johns Hopkins International: Bridging the Communication Gap among Remote Office Employees," *Intranets.com Case Study,* http://www.intranets.com/ProductInfo/CaseStudies/Johns_Hopkins.asp, 2004.

Kalakota, Ravi, and Marcia Robinson. *e-Business 2.0: Roadmap for Success.* Reading, MA: Addison-Wesley, 2001.

Lais, Sami. "Satellites Link Bob Evans Farms." *Computerworld,* July 2, 2001.

Messerschmitt, David. *Network Applications: A Guide to the New Computing Infrastructure.* San Francisco: Morgan Kaufmann, 1999.

Murphy, Kate. "Cruising the Net in Hyperdrive." *BusinessWeek,* January 24, 2000.

Norris, G. "Boeing's Seventh Wonder," *IEEE Spectrum,* http://www.spectrum.ieee.org/publicaccess/1095b777.html, 1995.

O'Brien, Atiye. "Friday Intranet Focus." *Upside.com: Hot Private Companies.* Upside, 1996.

Orenstein, David. "Price, Speed, Location All Part of Broadband Choice." *Computerworld,* July 26, 1999.

Papows, Jeff. "Endquotes." *NetReady Adviser,* Winter 1997.

Schultz, B. "User Excellence Award Honorable Mentions." *Network World,* November 13, 2000.

"Snap-On Tools Company Uses Netscape Software for Extranet Solution." Netscape Corporate Public Relations Press Release, March 6, 1997.

Stuart, Anne. "Cutting the Cord." *Inc. Tech,* March 2001.

UPS corporate Web site. "About UPS," http://www.ups.com/content/us/en/about/index.html, n.d.

chapter 7

Afuah, Allan, and Christopher Tucci. *Internet Business Models and Strategies.* New York: McGraw-Hill/Irwin, 2001.

"Baker Tanks Leverages salesforce.com's Wireless Access to Extend Range of Customer Service." Salesforce.com, 2002.

Clark, Charles; Nancy Cavanaugh; Carol Brown; and V. Sambamurthy. "Building Change-Readiness Capabilities in the IS Organization: Insights from the Bell Atlantic Experience." *MIS Quarterly,* December 1997.

Cole-Gomolski, Barbara. "Users Loath to Share Their Know-How." *Computerworld,* November 17, 1997.

Collett, S. "SAP: Whirlpool's Rush to Go Live Leads to Shipping Snafus." *Computerworld,* November 4, 1999.

"Communications Leader Becomes Customer-Focused e-Business," *Siebel.com,* March 12, 2001.

Cronin, Mary. *The Internet Strategy Handbook.* Boston: Harvard Business School Press, 1996.

Cross, John; Michael Earl; and Jeffrey Sampler. "Transformation of the IT Function at British Petroleum." *MIS Quarterly,* December 1997.

Das, Sidhartha; Shaker Zahra; and Merrill Warkentin. "Integrating the Content and Process of Strategic MIS Planning with Competitive Strategy." *Decision Sciences Journal,* November–December 1991.

De Geus, Arie. "Planning as Learning." *Harvard Business Review*, March–April 1988.

Earl, Michael. "Experiences in Strategic Information Systems Planning." *MIS Quarterly*, March 1993.

El Sawy, Omar, and Gene Bowles. "Redesigning the Customer Support Process for the Electronic Economy: Insights from Storage Dimensions." *MIS Quarterly*, December 1997.

Gates, Bill. *Business @ the Speed of Thought.* New York: Warner Books, 1999.

Grover, Varun; James Teng; and Kirk Fiedler. "IS Investment Priorities in Contemporary Organizations." *Communications of the ACM*, February 1998.

Hawson, James, and Jesse Beeler. "Effects of User Participation in Systems Development: A Longitudinal Field Experiment." *MIS Quarterly*, December 1997.

Hoffman, Thomas. "Intranet Helps Workers Navigate Corporate Maze." *Computerworld*, June 4, 2001.

Kalakota, Ravi, and Marcia Robinson. *e-Business 2.0: Roadmap for Success.* Reading, MA: Addison-Wesley, 2001.

Keen, Peter, and Craigg Ballance. *Online Profits: A Manager's Guide to Electronic Commerce.* Boston: Harvard Business School Press, 1997.

Kettinger, William; James Teng; and Subashish Guha. "Business Process Change: A Study of Methodologies, Techniques, and Tools." *MIS Quarterly*, March 1997.

Koudsi, Suzanne. "Actually, It Is Like Brain Surgery." *Fortune*, March 20, 2000.

KPMG Case Study. "Think Different: Apple Americas Transforms Its US Business with SAP/R3 in Just Twelve Months." 1999.

Levinson, M. "Cleared for Takeoff." *CIO*, April 1, 2002.

Martin, Chuck. *The Digital Estate: Strategies for Competing, Surviving, and Thriving in an Internetworked World.* New York: McGraw-Hill, 1997.

Orenstein, David. "Enterprise Application Integration." *Computerworld*, October 4, 1999.

Robb, Drew. "Rediscovering Efficiency." *Computerworld*, July 16, 2001.

Sawhney, Mohan, and Jeff Zabin. *The Seven Steps to Nirvana: Strategic Insights into e-Business Transformation.* New York: McGraw-Hill, 2001.

chapter 8

Afuah, Allan, and Christopher Tucci. *Internet Business Models and Strategies.* New York: McGraw-Hill/Irwin, 2001.

Clark, Charles; Nancy Cavanaugh; Carol Brown; and V. Sambamurthy. "Building Change-Readiness Capabilities in the IS Organization: Insights from the Bell Atlantic Experience." *MIS Quarterly*, December 1997.

Cole-Gomolski, Barbara. "Users Loath to Share Their Know-How." *Computerworld*, November 17, 1997.

Collett, Stacy. "SAP: Whirlpool's Rush to Go Live Leads to Shipping Snafus." *Computerworld*, November 4, 1999.

Collett, Stacy. "SWOT Analysis." *Computerworld*, July 19, 1999.

Cronin, Mary. *The Internet Strategy Handbook.* Boston: Harvard Business School Press, 1996.

Cross, John; Michael Earl; and Jeffrey Sampler. "Transformation of the IT Function at British Petroleum." *MIS Quarterly*, December 1997.

Das, Sidhartha; Shaker Zahra; and Merrill Warkentin. "Integrating the Content and Process of Strategic MIS Planning with Competitive Strategy." *Decision Sciences Journal*, November–December 1991.

De Geus, Arie. "Planning as Learning." *Harvard Business Review*, March–April 1988.

De Geus, Arie. "The Living Company." *Harvard Business Review*, March–April 1997.

Deise, Martin; Conrad Nowikow; Patrick King; and Amy Wright. *Executive's Guide to e-Business: From Tactics to Strategy.* New York: John Wiley & Sons, 2000.

Earl, Michael. "Experiences in Strategic Information Systems Planning." *MIS Quarterly*, March 1993.

El Sawy, Omar, and Gene Bowles. "Redesigning the Customer Support Process for the Electronic Economy: Insights from Storage Dimensions." *MIS Quarterly*, December 1997.

El Sawy, Omar; Arvind Malhotra; Sanjay Gosain; and Kerry Young. "IT-Intensive Value Innovation in the Electronic Economy: Insights from Marshall Industries." *MIS Quarterly*, September 1999.

Fingar, Peter; Harsha Kumar; and Tarun Sharma. *Enterprise E-Commerce: The Software Component Breakthrough for Business to Business Commerce.* Tampa, FL: Meghan-Kiffer Press, 2000.

Grover, Varun; James Teng; and Kirk Fiedler. "IS Investment Priorities in Contemporary Organizations." *Communications of the ACM*, February 1998.

Hawson, James, and Jesse Beeler. "Effects of User Participation in Systems Development: A Longitudinal Field Experiment." *MIS Quarterly*, December 1997.

Hills, Melanie. *Intranet Business Strategies.* New York: John Wiley & Sons, 1997.

Kalakota, Ravi, and Marcia Robinson. *e-Business: Roadmap for Success.* Reading, MA: Addison-Wesley, 1999.

Keen, Peter G.W. *Shaping the Future: Business Design through Information Technology.* Boston: Harvard Business School Press, 1991.

Kettinger, William; James Teng; and Subashish Guha. "Business Process Change: A Study of Methodologies, Techniques, and Tools." *MIS Quarterly*, March 1997.

Koudsi, Suzanne. "Actually, It Is Like Brain Surgery." *Fortune*, March 20, 2000.

Levinson, M. "Cleared for Takeoff." *CIO*, April 1, 2002.

Maglitta, Joseph. "Rocks in the Gears: Reengineering the Workplace." *Computerworld*, October 3, 1994.

Magretta, Joan. "Why Business Models Matter." *Harvard Business Review*, May 2002.

Norris, Grant; James Hurley; Kenneth Hartley; John Dunleavy; and John Balls. *e-Business and ERP: Transforming the Enterprise.* New York: John Wiley & Sons, 2000.

Peppers & Rogers Group. "Honeywell Aerospace Trains a New Breed of Sales Force on CRM." SearchCRM.com, http://searchcrm.techtarget.com/original Content/0%2C289142%2Csid11_gci859703%2C00.html, October 29, 2002.

Prokesch, Steven. "Unleashing the Power of Learning: An Interview with British Petroleum's John Browne." *Harvard Business Review*, September–October 1997.

Senge, Peter. *The Fifth Discipline: The Art and Practice of the Learning Organization.* New York: Currency Doubleday, 1994.

Whirlpool Corporation corporate Web site. http://www.whirlpoolcorp.com/about/default.asp, n.d.

chapter 9

Armor, Daniel. *The e-Business (R)Evolution: Living and Working in an Interconnected World.* Upper Saddle River, NJ: Prentice Hall, 2000.

Cross, Kim. "Need Options? Go Configure." *Business 2.0*, February 2000.

Davis, Jeffrey. "How IT Works." *Business 2.0*, February 2000.

Davis, Jeffrey. "Mall Rats." *Business 2.0*, January 1999.

Enterasys Company Info. http://www.enterasys.com/corporate, n.d.

Essex, David. "Betting on Win 2K." *Computerworld*, February 26, 2001.

Fellenstein, Craig, and Ron Wood. *Exploring E-Commerce, Global e-Business, and E-Societies.* Upper Saddle River, NJ: Prentice Hall, 2000.

Fingar, Peter; Harsha Kumar; and Tarun Sharma. *Enterprise E-Commerce.* Tampa, FL: Meghan-Kiffer Press, 2000.

Georgia, Bonnie. "Give Your E-Store an Edge." *Smart Business*, October 2001.

Gulati, Ranjay, and Jason Garino. "Get the Right Mix of Clicks and Bricks." *Harvard Business Review*, May–June 2000.

Hoque, Faisal. *E-Enterprise: Business Models, Architecture and Components.* Cambridge, UK: Cambridge University Press, 2000.

Kalakota, Ravi, and Marcia Robinson. *e-Business 2.0: Roadmap for Success.* Reading, MA: Addison-Wesley, 2001.

Kalakota, Ravi, and Andrew Whinston. *Electronic Commerce: A Manager's Guide.* Reading, MA: Addison-Wesley, 1997.

Keenan, Faith, and Timothy Mullaney. "Let's Get Back to Basics." *BusinessWeek e.biz*, October 29, 2001.

Leon, Mark. "Trading Spaces." *Business 2.0*, February 2000.

May, Paul. *The Business of E-Commerce: From Corporate Strategy to Technology.* Cambridge, UK: Cambridge University Press, 2001.

Microsoft IT Showcase. "MS Market: Business Case Study," http://download.microsoft.com/download/6/5/9/659955d7-0cb7-42b6-8e78-daf1e9c49a75/MSMarketBCS.doc, 2002.

Morgan, Cynthia. "Dead Set against SET?" *Computerworld*, March 29, 1999.

Nesdore, P. "Customer Relationship Management: Getting Personal," e-commerceIQ.com, http://www.ecommerceiq.com/special_interests/crm/80-eCommerceIQ_crm.html, 2003.

"Pay-Per-Click Marketing," http://www.pay-per-click-adwords.com/pay-per-click-adwords.html, n.d.

Rayport, Jeffrey, and Bernard Jaworski. *Introduction to e-Commerce*. New York: McGraw-Hill/Irwin, 2001.

Riley, M.; S. Laiken; and J. Williams. "Digital Business Designs in Financial Services," Mercer Management Consulting Commentary, http://www.mercermc.com/Perspectives/WhitePapers/Commentaries/Comm00DBDinFinancialServices.pdf, 2002.

Rosenoer, Jonathan; Douglas Armstrong; and J. Russell Gates. *The Clickable Corporation: Successful Strategies for Capturing the Internet Advantage*. New York: The Free Press, 1999.

"Servers with a Smile." *Fortune*, Technology Buyers Guide, Summer 2000.

Seybold, Patricia, with Ronnie Marshak. *Customers.Com: How to Create a Profitable Business Strategy for the Internet and Beyond*. New York: Times Business, 1998.

Sliwa, Carol. "Users Cling to EDI for Critical Transactions." *Computerworld*, March 15, 1999.

"Tech Lifestyles: Shopping." *Fortune*, Technology Buyers Guide, Winter 2001.

"Telefónica Servicios Avanzados De Informació Leads Spain's Retail Industry into Global Electronic Commerce," www.netscape.com/solutions/business/profiles, March 1999.

Young, Eric. "Web Marketplaces That Really Work." *Fortune/CNET Tech Review*, Winter 2002.

chapter 10

"AmeriKing," Customer Profile, Plumtree.com, October 25, 2002.

Ashline, Peter, and Vincent Lai. "Virtual Reality: An Emerging User-Interface Technology." *Information Systems Management*, Winter 1995.

Beacon Analytics Case Study. "Analyzing Key Measures in a Retail Environment," http://www.beaconus.com/downloads/Beacon%20Case%20Study-The%20GAP.pdf, 2003.

Begley, Sharon. "Software au Naturel." *Newsweek*, May 8, 1995.

Belcher, Lloyd, and Hugh Watson. "Assessing the Value of Conoco's EIS." *MIS Quarterly*, September 1993.

Bioluminate Inc. press release. "Bioluminate to Develop 'Smart Probe' for Early Breast Cancer Detection," http://www.bioluminate.com/press_rel1.html, December 5, 2000.

Bose, Ranjit, and Vijayan Sugumaran. "Application of Intelligent Agent Technology for Managerial Data Analysis and Mining." *The Data Base for Advances in Information Systems*, Winter 1999.

Botchner, Ed. "Data Mining: Plumbing the Depths of Corporate Databases." *Computerworld*, Special Advertising Supplement, April 21, 1997.

Brown, Eryn. "Slow Road to Fast Data." *Fortune*, March 18, 2002.

Brown, Stuart. "Making Decisions in a Flood of Data." *Fortune*, August 13, 2001.

Bylinsky, Gene. "The e-Factory Catches On." *Fortune*, August 13, 2001.

Cox, Earl. "Relational Database Queries Using Fuzzy Logic." *AI Expert*, January 1995.

Darling, Charles. "Ease Implementation Woes with Packaged Datamarts." *Datamation*, March 1997.

Deck, Stewart. "Data Visualization." *Computerworld*, October 11, 1999.

Deck, Stewart. "Data Warehouse Project Starts Simply." *Computerworld*, February 15, 1999.

Deck, Stewart. "Early Users Give Nod to Analysis Package." *Computerworld*, February 22, 1999.

Freeman, Eva. "Desktop Reporting Tools." *Datamation*, June 1997.

Gantz, John. "The New World of Enterprise Reporting Is Here." *Computerworld*, February 1, 1999.

"GAP, Inc. at a Glance," http://www.gapinc.com/about/At_A_Glance.pdf, Summer 2004.

Glode, M. "Scans: Most Valuable Player." *Wired Magazine*, July 22, 1997.

Goldberg, David. "Genetic and Evolutionary Algorithms Come of Age." *Communications of the ACM*, March 1994.

Gorry, G. Anthony, and Michael Scott Morton. "A Framework for Management Information Systems." *Sloan Management Review*, Fall 1971; republished Spring 1989.

Hall, Mark. "Get Real." *Computerworld*, April 1, 2002.

Hall, Mark. "Supercomputing: From R&D to P&L." *Computerworld*, December 13, 1999.

Hoffman, Thomas. "In the Know." *Computerworld*, October 14, 2002.

Jablonowski, Mark. "Fuzzy Risk Analysis: Using AI Systems." *AI Expert*, December 1994.

Kalakota, Ravi, and Marcia Robinson. *e-Business 2.0: Roadmap for Success*. Reading, MA: Addison-Wesley, 2001.

Kalakota, Ravi, and Andrew Whinston. *Electronic Commerce: A Manager's Guide*. Reading, MA: Addison-Wesley, 1997.

King, Julia. "Sharing GIS Talent with the World." *Computerworld*, October 6, 1997.

Kurszweil, Raymond. *The Age of Intelligent Machines*. Cambridge, MA: MIT Press, 1992.

Lundquist, Christopher. "Personalization in E-Commerce." *Computerworld*, March 22, 1999.

Machlis, Sharon. "Agent Technology." *Computerworld*, March 22, 1999.

Mailoux, Jacquiline. "New Menu at PepsiCo." *Computerworld*, May 6, 1996.

McNeill, F. Martin, and Ellen Thro. *Fuzzy Logic: A Practical Approach*. Boston: AP Professional, 1994.

Mitchell, Lori. "Enterprise Knowledge Portals Wise Up Your Business." *Infoworld.com*, December 2000.

Murray, Gerry. "Making Connections with Enterprise Knowledge Portals." White Paper. *Computerworld*, September 6, 1999.

"NASA Ames Research Center Report," Smart Surgical Probe, Bioluminate Inc., http://technology.arc.nasa.gov/success/probe.html, 2003.

Norsk Hydro Corporate Background. http://www.hydro.com/en/about/index.html, 2004.

Orenstein, David. "Corporate Portals." *Computerworld*, June 28, 1999.

Ouellette, Tim. "Opening Your Own Portal," *Computerworld*, August 9, 1999.

Pimentel, Ken, and Kevin Teixeira. *Virtual Reality through the New Looking Glass*. 2nd ed. New York: Intel/McGraw-Hill, 1995.

Rosenberg, Marc. *e-Learning: Strategies for Delivering Knowledge in the Digital Age*. New York: McGraw-Hill, 2001.

Schlumberger Information Solutions. "Norsk Hydro Makes a Valuable Drilling Decision," Schlumberger Technical Report GMP-5911, http://www.sis.slb.com/media/software/success/ir_drillingdecision.pdf, 2002.

Shay, S. "Trendlines." *CIO Magazine*, February 1, 1998.

Turban, Efraim, and Jay Aronson. *Decision Support Systems and Intelligent Systems*. Upper Saddle River, NJ: Prentice Hall, 1998.

Vandenbosch, Betty, and Sid Huff. "Searching and Scanning: How Executives Obtain Information from Executive Information Systems." *MIS Quarterly*, March 1997.

Wagner, Mitch. "Reality Check." *Computerworld*, February 26, 1997.

Watson, Hugh, and John Satzinger. "Guidelines for Designing EIS Interfaces." *Information Systems Management*, Fall 1994.

Watterson, Karen. "Parallel Tracks." *Datamation*, May 1997.

Winston, Patrick. "Rethinking Artificial Intelligence." Program Announcement, Massachusetts Institute of Technology, September 1997.

Wreden, Nick. "Enterprise Portals: Integrating Information to Drive Productivity." *Beyond Computing*, March 2000.

chapter 11

Afuah, Allan, and Christopher Tucci. *Internet Business Models and Strategies*. New York: McGraw-Hill/Irwin, 2001.

Clark, Charles; Nancy Cavanaugh; Carol Brown; and V. Sambamurthy. "Building Change-Readiness Capabilities in the IS Organization: Insights from the Bell Atlantic Experience." *MIS Quarterly*, December 1997.

Cole-Gomolski, Barbara. "Users Loath to Share Their Know-How." *Computerworld*, November 17, 1997.

Collett Stacy. "SWOT Analysis." *Computerworld*, July 19, 1999.

Cronin, Mary. *The Internet Strategy Handbook*. Boston: Harvard Business School Press, 1996.

Cross, John; Michael Earl; and Jeffrey Sampler. "Transformation of the IT Function at British Petroleum." *MIS Quarterly*, December 1997.

Das, Sidhartha; Shaker Zahra; and Merrill Warkentin. "Integrating the Content and Process of Strategic MIS Planning with Competitive Strategy." *Decision Sciences Journal*, November–December 1991.

De Geus, Arie. "Planning as Learning." *Harvard Business Review*, March–April 1988.

De Geus, Arie. "The Living Company." *Harvard Business Review*, March–April 1997.

Deise, Martin; Conrad Nowikow; Patrick King; and Amy Wright. *Executive's Guide to e-Business: From Tactics to Strategy*. New York: John Wiley & Sons, 2000.

Earl, Michael. "Experiences in Strategic Information Systems Planning." *MIS Quarterly*, March 1993.

El Sawy, Omar, and Gene Bowles. "Redesigning the Customer Support Process for the Electronic Economy: Insights from Storage Dimensions." *MIS Quarterly*, December 1997.

El Sawy, Omar; Arvind Malhotra; Sanjay Gosain; and Kerry Young. "IT-Intensive Value Innovation in the Electronic Economy: Insights from Marshall Industries." *MIS Quarterly*, September 1999.

Fingar, Peter; Harsha Kumar; and Tarun Sharma. *Enterprise E-Commerce: The Software Component Breakthrough for Business to Business Commerce*. Tampa, FL: Meghan-Kiffer Press, 2000.

Grover, Varun; James Teng; and Kirk Fiedler. "IS Investment Priorities in Contemporary Organizations." *Communications of the ACM*, February 1998.

Hawson, James, and Jesse Beeler. "Effects of User Participation in Systems Development: A Longitudinal Field Experiment." *MIS Quarterly*, December 1997.

Hills, Melanie. *Intranet Business Strategies*. New York: John Wiley & Sons, 1997.

Kalakota, Ravi, and Marcia Robinson. *e-Business: Roadmap for Success*. Reading, MA: Addison-Wesley, 1999.

Keen, Peter G. W. *Shaping the Future: Business Design through Information Technology*. Boston: Harvard Business School Press, 1991.

Kettinger, William; James Teng; and Subashish Guha. "Business Process Change: A Study of Methodologies, Techniques, and Tools." *MIS Quarterly*, March 1997.

Koudsi, Suzanne. "Actually, It Is Like Brain Surgery." *Fortune*, March 20, 2000.

Maglitta, Joseph. "Rocks in the Gears: Reengineering the Workplace." *Computerworld*, October 3, 1994.

Magretta, Joan. "Why Business Models Matter." *Harvard Business Review*, May 2002.

Norris, Grant; James Hurley; Kenneth Hartley; John Dunleavy; and John Balls. *e-Business and ERP: Transforming the Enterprise*. New York: John Wiley & Sons, 2000.

Prokesch, Steven. "Unleashing the Power of Learning: An Interview with British Petroleum's John Browne." *Harvard Business Review*, September–October 1997.

Senge, Peter. *The Fifth Discipline: The Art and Practice of the Learning Organization*. New York: Currency Doubleday, 1994.

chapter 12

Anthes, Gary. "The Quest for IT E-Quality." *Computerworld*, December 13, 1999.

Clark, Charles; Nancy Cavanaugh; Carol Brown; and V. Sambamurthy. "Building Change-Readiness Capabilities in the IS Organization: Insights from the Bell Atlantic Experience." *MIS Quarterly*, December 1997.

Cole-Gomolski, Barbara. "Companies Turn to Web for ERP Training." *Computerworld*, February 8, 1999.

Cole-Gomolski, Barbara. "Users Loath to Share Their Know-How." *Computerworld*, November 17, 1997.

Cronin, Mary. *The Internet Strategy Handbook*. Boston: Harvard Business School Press, 1996.

Deise, Martin; Conrad Nowikow; Patrick King; and Amy Wright. *Executive's Guide to e-Business: From Tactics to Strategy*. New York: John Wiley & Sons, 2000.

"Design Matters." *Fortune*, Technology Buyers Guide, Winter 2001.

E-Government for Development Information Exchange. "Failed Electronic Voter Registration in Uganda," http://www.egov4dev.org/iecuganda. htm#title, 2002.

Hawson, James, and Jesse Beeler. "Effects of User Participation in Systems Development: A Longitudinal Field Experiment." *MIS Quarterly*, December 1997.

Hills, Melanie. *Intranet Business Strategies*. New York: John Wiley & Sons, 1997.

Kalakota, Ravi, and Marcia Robinson. *e-Business 2.0: Roadmap for Success*. Reading, MA: Addison-Wesley, 2001.

King, Julia. "Back to Basics." *Computerworld*, April 22, 2002.

Lazar, Jonathan. *User-Centered Web Development*. Sudbury, MA: Jones and Bartlett, 2001.

McDonnel, Sharon. "Putting CRM to Work." *Computerworld*, March 12, 2001.

Melymuka, Kathleen. "An Expanding Universe." *Computerworld*, September 14, 1998.

Melymuka, Kathleen. "Energizing the Company." *Computerworld*, August 13, 2001.

Melymuka, Kathleen. "Profiting from Mistakes." *Computerworld*, April 20, 2001.

Morgan, James N. *Application Cases in MIS*. 4th ed. New York: Irwin/McGraw-Hill, 2002.

Neilsen, Jakob. "Better Data Brings Better Sales." *Business 2.0*, May 15, 2001.

Nielsen, Jakob. "Design for Process, Not for Products." *Business 2.0*, July 10, 2001.

Orenstein, David. "Software Is Too Hard to Use." *Computerworld*, August 23, 1999.

Ouellette, Tim. "Giving Users the Key to Their Web Content." *Computerworld*, July 26, 1999.

Ouellette, Tim. "Opening Your Own Portal." *Computerworld*, August 9, 1999.

Panko, R. "Application Development: Finding Spreadsheet Errors." *InformationWeek*, May 29, 1995.

Panko, R. "What We Know about Spreadsheet Errors." *Journal of End-User Computing*, 10:2, 1998, pp. 15–21.

Schwartz, Matthew. "Time for a Makeover." *Computerworld*, August 19, 2002.

Senge, Peter. *The Fifth Discipline: The Art and Practice of the Learning Organization*. New York: Currency Doubleday, 1994.

Sliwa, Carol. "E-Commerce Solutions: How Real?" *Computerworld*, February 28, 2000.

Solomon, Melissa. "Filtering Out the Noise." *Computerworld*, February 25, 2002.

Songini, Marc. "GM Locomotive Unit Puts ERP RolloutBack on Track." *Computerworld*, February 11, 2002.

"Uganda," U.S. Library of Congress Country Study, http://lcweb2.loc.gov/cgi-bin/ query/r?frd/cstdy: (DOCID+ug0000), 2000.

Whitten, Jeffrey, and Lonnie Bentley. *Systems Analysis and Design Methods*. 5th ed. New York: McGraw-Hill/Irwin, 2000.

chapter 13

Alexander, Steve, and Matt Hamblen. "Top-Flight Technology." *Computerworld*, September 23, 2002.

Anthes, Gary. "Biometrics." *Computerworld*, October 12, 1998.

Anthes, Gary. "When Five 9s Aren't Enough." *Computerworld*, October 8, 2001.

Berniker, M. "Study: ID Theft Often Goes Unrecognized," *Internetnews.com*, http://www.internetnews.com/ec-news/article.php/3081881, 2003.

Boutin, Paul. "Burn Baby Burn." *Wired*, December 2002.

Deckmyn, Dominique. "More Managers Monitor E-Mail." *Computerworld*, October 18, 1999.

Dejoie, Roy; George Fowler; and David Paradice, eds. *Ethical Issues in Information Systems*. Boston: Boyd & Fraser, 1991.

Donaldson, Thomas. "Values in Tension: Ethics Away from Home." *Harvard Business Review*, September–October 1996.

Dunlop, Charles, and Rob Kling, eds. *Computerization and Controversy: Value Conflicts and Social Choices*. San Diego: Academic Press, 1991.

Elias, Paul. "Paid Informant." *Red Herring*, January 16, 2001.

Harrison, Ann. "Virus Scanning Moving to ISPs." *Computerworld*, September 20, 1999.

"In Depth: Security." *Computerworld*, July 9, 2001.

Johnson, Deborah. "Ethics Online." *Communications of the ACM*, January 1997.

Joy, Bill. "Report from the Cyberfront." *Newsweek*, February 21, 2000.

Lardner, James. "Why Should Anyone Believe You?" *Business 2.0*, March 2002.

Levy, Stephen, and Brad Stone. "Hunting the Hackers." *Newsweek*, February 21, 2000.

Madsen, Peter, and Jay Shafritz. *Essentials of Business Ethics*. New York: Meridian, 1990.

McCarthy, Michael. "Keystroke Cops." *The Wall Street Journal*, March 7, 2000.

Nance, Barry. "Sending Firewalls Home." *Computerworld*, May 28, 2001.

Naughton, Keith. "CyberSlacking." *Newsweek*, November 29, 1999.

Neumann, Peter. *Computer-Related Risks*. New York: ACM Press, 1995.

Phillips, Robert. *Stakeholder Theory and Organizational Ethics*. San Francisco: Berrett-Koehler, 2003.

Radcliff, Deborah. "Cybersleuthing Solves the Case." *Computerworld*, January 14, 2002.

Robinson, Lori. "How It Works: Viruses." *Smart Computing*, March 2000.

Rothfeder, Jeffrey. "Hacked! Are Your Company Files Safe?" *PC World*, November 1996.

Rothfeder, Jeffrey. "No Privacy on the Net." *PC World*, February 1997.

Sager, Ira; Steve Hamm; Neil Gross; John Carey; and Robert Hoff. "Cyber Crime." *BusinessWeek*, February 21, 2000.

Schoepke, P., and G. Milner, "Phishing Scams Increase 180% in April Alone!" *BankersOnline.com*, http://www.bankersonline.com/technology/tech_phishing052404.html, 2004.

Smith, H. Jefferson, and John Hasnas. "Debating the Stakeholder Theory." *Beyond Computing*, March–April 1994.

Smith, H. Jefferson, and John Hasnas. "Establishing an Ethical Framework." *Beyond Computing*, January–February 1994.

Solomon, Melissa, and Michael Meehan. "Enron Lesson: Tech Is for Support." *Computerworld*, February 18, 2002.

Spinello, Richard. *Cyberethics: Morality and Law in Cyberspace.* 2nd ed. Sudbury, MA: Jones and Bartlett, 2003.

Sullivan, B. "ID Theft Victims Face Tough Bank Fights," MSNBC.com, http://msnbc.msn.com/id/4264051/, 2004.

VanScoy, Kayte. "What Your Workers Are Really Up To." *Ziff Davis Smart Business*, September 2001.

Verton, Dan. "Insider Monitoring Seen as Next Wave in IT Security." *Computerworld*, March 19, 2001.

Vijayan, Jaikumar. "Nimda Needs Harsh Disinfectant." *Computerworld*, September 24, 2001.

Vijayan, Jaikumar. "Securing the Center." *Computerworld*, May 13, 2002.

Willard, Nancy. *The Cyberethics Reader.* Burr Ridge, IL: Irwin/McGraw-Hill, 1997.

York, Thomas. "Invasion of Privacy? E-Mail Monitoring Is on the Rise." *InformationWeek Online*, February 21, 2000.

Youl, T. "Phishing Scams: Understanding the Latest Trends." *FraudWatch International*, White Paper, 2004.

chapter 14

Bryan, Lowell; Jane Fraser; Jeremy Oppenheim; and Wilhelm Rall. *Race for the World: Strategies to Build a Great Global Firm.* Boston: Harvard Business School Press, 1999.

Christensen, Clayton. *The Innovator's Dilemma: When New Technologies Cause Great Firms to Fail.* Boston: Harvard Business School Press, 1997.

Cronin, Mary. *Global Advantage on the Internet.* New York: Van Nostrand Reinhold, 1996.

"Delta Signs Offshore Call Center Agreement." *South Florida Business Journal*, October 7, 2002.

El Sawy, Omar; Arvind Malhotra; Sanjay Gosain; and Kerry Young. "IT-Intensive Value Innovation in the Electronic Economy: Insights from Marshall Industries." *MIS Quarterly*, September 1999.

Gilhooly, Kym. "The Staff That Never Sleeps." *Computerworld*, June 25, 2001.

Grover, Varun; James Teng; and Kirk Fiedler. "IS Investment Opportunities in Contemporary Organizations." *Communications of the ACM*, February 1998.

Hall, Mark. "Service Providers Give Users More IT Options." *Computerworld*, February 7, 2000.

Ives, Blake, and Sirkka Jarvenpaa. "Applications of Global Information Technology: Key Issues for Management." *MIS Quarterly*, March 1991.

Kalakota, Ravi, and Marcia Robinson. *e-Business 2.0: Roadmap for Success.* Reading, MA: Addison-Wesley, 2001.

Kalin, Sari. "The Importance of Being Multiculturally Correct." Global Innovators Series, *Computerworld*, October 6, 1997.

Kirkpatrick, David. "Back to the Future with Centralized Computing." *Fortune*, November 10, 1997.

LaPlante, Alice. "Global Boundaries.com." Global Innovators Series, *Computerworld*, October 6, 1997.

Leinfuss, Emily. "Blend It, Mix It, Unify It." *Computerworld*, March 26, 2001.

McDougall, P. "Opportunity on the Line." *InformationWeek*, October 20, 2003.

Mearian, Lucas. "Citibank Overhauls Overseas Systems." *Computerworld*, February 4, 2002.

Mische, Michael. "Transnational Architecture: A Reengineering Approach." *Information Systems Management*, Winter 1995.

Palvia, Prashant; Shailendra Palvia; and Edward Roche, eds. *Global Information Technology and Systems Management.* Marietta, GA: Ivy League, 1996.

Radcliff, Deborah. "Playing by Europe's Rules." *Computerworld*, July 9, 2001.

Ross, Jeanne, and Peter Weill. "Six IT Decisions Your IT People Shouldn't Make." *Harvard Business Review*, November 2002.

Songini, Marc, and Kim Nash. "Try, Try Again." *Computerworld*, February 18, 2002.

Thibodeau, Patrick. "Europe and U.S. Agree on Data Rules." *Computerworld*, March 20, 2000.

Vitalari, Nicholas, and James Wetherbe. "Emerging Best Practices in Global Systems Development." In *Global Information Technology and Systems Management*, ed. Prashant Palvia et al. Marietta, GA: Ivy League, 1996.

West, Lawrence, and Walter Bogumil. "Immigration and the Global IT Workforce." *Communications of the ACM*, July 2001.

glossary for business professionals

Accounting Information Systems   Information systems that record and report business transactions and the flow of funds through an organization, and then produce financial statements. These statements provide information for the planning and control of business operations, as well as for legal and historical recordkeeping.

Accounts Payable   Those accounts that represent what a business owes to others.

Accounts Receivable   Those accounts that represent what others owe to a business.

Ada   A programming language named after Augusta Ada Byron, considered the world's first computer programmer. Developed for the U.S. Department of Defense as a standard high-order language.

Ad Hoc Inquiries   Unique, unscheduled, situation-specific information requests.

Adware   Software that pushes advertising to a particular machine. Adware is usually not considered to be malicious, as it is often incorporated with a useful piece of software desired by a user.

Agile Company   A company that employs agile manufacturing practices. Also, a company that has converted to a primarily software-based business model and is more quickly able to respond to changing market conditions.

Agile Competition   The ability of a company to operate profitably in a competitive environment of continual and unpredictable changes in customer preferences, market conditions, and business opportunities.

Algorithm   A set of well-defined rules or processes for solving a problem in a finite number of steps.

Analog Computer   A computer that operates on data by measuring changes in continuous physical variables such as voltage, resistance, and rotation. Contrast with Digital Computer.

Analytical Database   A database of data extracted from operational and external databases to provide data tailored to online analytical processing, decision support, and executive information systems.

Analytical Modeling   Interactive use of computer-based mathematical models to explore decision alternatives using what-if analysis, sensitivity analysis, goal-seeking analysis, and optimization analysis.

Antivirus Software   Software specifically intended to protect a particular machine or network from the intrusion of software-based viruses.

Applet   A small, limited-purpose application program or small, independent module of a larger application program.

Application Development   See Systems Development.

Application Development Management   The process by which an organization manages the in-house development of software applications.

Application Generator   A software package that supports the development of an application through an interactive terminal dialogue, where the programmer/analyst defines screens, reports, computations, and data structures.

Application Portfolio   A planning tool used to evaluate present and proposed information systems applications in terms of the amount of revenue or assets invested in information systems that support major business functions and processes.

Application Server   System software that provides a middleware interface between an operating system and the application programs of users.

Application Service Provider (ASP)   A company that specializes in providing turnkey services for various software applications such that an organization can avoid the administration associated with licensing and updates of common software platforms used throughout the company.

Application Software   Programs that specify the information processing activities required for the completion of specific tasks of computer users. Examples are electronic spreadsheet and word processing programs or inventory or payroll programs.

Application-Specific Programs   Application software packages that support specific applications of end users in business, science and engineering, and other areas.

Applications Architecture   A conceptual planning framework in which business applications of information technology are designed as an integrated architecture of enterprise systems that support strategic business initiatives and cross-functional business processes.

Arithmetic-Logic Unit (ALU)   The unit of a computing system containing the circuits that perform arithmetic and logical operations.

Artificial Intelligence (AI)   A science and technology whose goal is to develop computers that can think, as well as see, hear, walk, talk, and feel. A major thrust is the development of computer functions normally associated with human intelligence, for example, reasoning, inference, learning, and problem solving.

ASCII: American Standard Code for Information Interchange   A standard code used for information interchange among data processing systems, communication systems, and associated equipment.

Assembler   A computer program that translates an assembly language into machine language.

Assembly Language A programming language that utilizes symbols to represent operation codes and storage locations.

Asynchronous A sequence of operations without a regular or predictable time relationship. Thus, operations do not happen at regular timed intervals, but an operation will begin only after a previous operation is completed. The data transmission involves the use of start and stop bits with each character to indicate the beginning and end of the character being transmitted. Contrast with Synchronous.

Attribute A characteristic or quality of some object, person, place, or event that is of interest to an organization. Represented in a database through the use of a data field.

Audit Trail The presence of media and procedures that allow a transaction to be traced through all stages of information processing, beginning with its appearance on a source document and ending with its transformation into information in a final output document.

Automated Teller Machine (ATM) A special-purpose transaction terminal used to provide remote banking services.

Back-End Processor Typically, a smaller, general-purpose computer dedicated to database processing using a database management system (DBMS). Also called a database machine or server.

Background Processing The automatic execution of lower-priority computer programs when higher-priority programs are not using the resources of the computer system. Contrast with Foreground Processing.

Backup Files Files that have been copied and stored via a backup process to protect against damage or loss of the original files.

Backward-Chaining An inference process that justifies a proposed conclusion by determining if it will result when rules are applied to the facts in a given situation.

Bandwidth The frequency range of a telecommunications channel, which determines its maximum transmission rate. The speed and capacity of transmission rates are typically measured in bits per second (bps). Bandwidth is a function of the telecommunications hardware, software, and media used by the telecommunications channel.

Bar Codes Vertical marks or bars placed on merchandise tags or packaging that can be sensed and read by optical character-reading devices. The width and combination of vertical lines are used to represent data.

Barriers to Entry Technological, financial, or legal requirements that deter firms from entering an industry.

BASIC: Beginner's All-Purpose Symbolic Instruction Code A programming language developed at Dartmouth College and designed for programming by end users.

Batch Processing A category of data processing in which data are accumulated into batches and processed periodically. Contrast with Real-Time Processing.

Baud A unit of measurement used to specify data transmission speeds. It is a unit of signaling speed equal to the number of discrete conditions or signal events per second. In many data communications applications, it represents one bit per second.

Binary Pertaining to a characteristic or property involving a selection, choice, or condition in which there are two possibilities, or pertaining to the number system that utilizes a base of 2.

Biometric Controls Computer-based security methods that measure physical traits and characteristics such as fingerprints, voice prints, and retina scans. Also called Biometric Security.

Bit A contraction of "binary digit." It can have the value of either 0 or 1.

Block A grouping of contiguous data records or other data elements that are handled as a unit.

Bluetooth A method by which two or more devices can wirelessly connect to each other while in close proximity.

Branch A transfer of control from one instruction to another in a computer program that is not part of the normal sequential execution of the instructions of the program.

Browser See Web Browser.

Buffer Temporary storage used when transmitting data from one device to another to compensate for a difference in rate of flow of data or time of occurrence of events.

Bug A mistake or malfunction.

Bulletin Board System (BBS) A service of online computer networks in which electronic messages, data files, or programs can be stored for other subscribers to read or copy.

Bundling The inclusion of software, maintenance, training, and other products or services in the price of a computer system.

Bus A set of conducting paths for movement of data and instructions that interconnects the various components of the CPU.

Business Ethics An area of philosophy concerned with developing ethical principles and promoting ethical behavior and practices in the accomplishment of business tasks and decision making.

Business Application Planning A process that comprises the evaluation of proposals for using information technology in ways that seek to accomplish the strategic objectives of an organization.

Business Intelligence (BI) A term primarily used in industry that incorporates a range of analytical and decision support applications in business including data mining, decision support systems, knowledge management systems, and online analytical processing.

Business/IT Planning The process of developing a company's business vision, strategies, and goals, as well as how they will be supported by the company's information technology architecture and implemented by its business application development process.

Business Model A conceptual representation of how an organization delivers value to its customers in a cost-effective manner.

Business Process Reengineering (BPR) Restructuring and transforming a business process by a fundamental rethinking and redesign to achieve dramatic improvements in cost, quality, speed, and so on.

Business-to-Business (B2B) e-Commerce transactions where both parties involved are companies. The largest portion of e-Commerce.

Business-to-Consumer (B2C) e-Commerce transactions between companies and individual consumers.

Consumer-to-Consumer (C2C) e-Commerce transactions where both parties involved are individual consumers.

Byte A sequence of adjacent binary digits operated on as a unit and usually shorter than a computer word. In many computer systems, a byte is a grouping of eight bits that can represent one alphabetic or special character or that can be packed with two decimal digits.

C A low-level structured programming language that resembles a machine-independent assembler language.

C++ An object-oriented version of C that is widely used for software package development.

Cache Memory A high-speed temporary storage area in the CPU for storing parts of a program or data during processing.

Capacity Management The use of planning and control methods to forecast and control information processing job loads, hardware and software usage, and other computer system resource requirements.

CASE Tools Specialized software applications intended to support the development of software. CASE is an acronym for computer-aided (or -assisted) software engineering.

Case-Based Reasoning Representing knowledge in an expert system's knowledge base in the form of cases, that is, examples of past performance, occurrences, and experiences.

Cathode Ray Tube (CRT) An electronic vacuum tube (television picture tube) that displays the output of a computer system.

CD-ROM An optical disk technology for microcomputers featuring compact disks with a storage capacity of over 500 megabytes.

Cellular Phone Systems A radio communications technology that divides a metropolitan area into a honeycomb of cells to greatly increase the number of frequencies and thus the number of users that can take advantage of mobile phone service.

Central Processing Unit (CPU) The unit of a computer system that includes the circuits that control the interpretation and execution of instructions. In many computer systems, the CPU includes the arithmetic-logic unit, the control unit, and the primary storage unit.

Centralization and Decentralization of IT Two extremes in a continuum of ways of organizing the provision of IT services within a company. When centralized, these services are provided by a distinct group at the corporate level. In the decentralized alternative, smaller IT units are located within each business unit.

Change Management Managing the process of implementing major changes in information technology, business processes, organizational structures, and job assignments to reduce the risks and costs of change and optimize its benefits.

Channel (1) A path along which signals can be sent. (2) A small special-purpose processor that controls the movement of data between the CPU and input/output devices.

Character A single alphabetic, numeric, or other symbol. The most basic logical data element.

Chargeback Systems Methods of allocating costs to end-user departments on the basis of the information services rendered and information system resources utilized.

Chat Systems Software that enables two or more users at networked PCs to carry on online, real-time text conversations.

Check Bit A binary check digit: for example, a parity bit.

Check Digit A digit in a data field that is utilized to check for errors or loss of characters in the data field as a result of data transfer operations.

Checkpoint A place in a program where a check or a recording of data for restart purposes is performed.

Chief Information Officer A senior management position that oversees all information technology for a firm concentrating on long-range information system planning and strategy.

Chief Technology Officer A senior IT management position that oversees all information technology planning and deployment from a technology perspective.

Clicks-and-Bricks Strategy A business model that combines both a bricks-and-mortar approach and an online presence.

Client (1) An end user. (2) The end user's networked microcomputer in client/server networks. (3) The version of a software package designed to run on an end user's networked microcomputer, such as a Web browser client and a groupware client.

Client/Server Network A computer network where end-user workstations (clients) are connected via telecommunications links to network servers and possibly to mainframe superservers.

Clock A device that generates periodic signals utilized to control the timing of a computer. Also, a register whose contents change at regular intervals in such a way as to measure time.

Cloud Computing A method of computing in which an individual or an organization makes use of another organization's excess computing power or data storage capacity.

Coaxial Cable A sturdy copper or aluminum wire wrapped with spacers to insulate and protect it. Groups of coaxial cables may also be bundled together in a bigger cable for ease of installation.

COBOL: Common Business Oriented Language A widely used business data processing programming language.

Code Computer instructions.

Cognitive Science An area of artificial intelligence that focuses on researching how the human brain works, and how humans think and learn, to apply such findings to the design of computer-based systems.

Cognitive Styles Basic patterns in how people handle information and confront problems.

Cognitive Theory Theories about how the human brain works and how humans think and learn.

Collaborative Work Management Tools Software that helps people accomplish or manage joint work activities.

Communications Satellite Earth satellites placed in stationary orbits above the equator that serve as relay stations for communications signals transmitted from earth stations.

Competitive Advantage Developing products, services, processes, or capabilities that give a company a superior business position relative to its competitors and other competitive forces.

Competitive Forces A firm must confront (1) rivalry of competitors within its industry, (2) threats of new entrants, (3) threats of substitutes, (4) the bargaining power of customers, and (5) the bargaining power of suppliers.

Competitive Strategies A firm can develop cost leadership, product differentiation, and business innovation strategies to confront its competitive forces.

Compiler A program that translates a high-level programming language into a machine-language program.

Computer A device that has the ability to accept data; internally store and execute a program of instructions; perform mathematical, logical, and manipulative operations on data; and report the results.

Computer-Aided Design (CAD) The use of computers and advanced graphics hardware and software to provide interactive design assistance for engineering and architectural design.

Computer-Aided Engineering (CAE) The use of computers to simulate, analyze, and evaluate models of product designs and production processes developed using computer-aided design methods.

Computer-Aided Manufacturing (CAM) The use of computers to automate the production process and operations of a manufacturing plant. Also called factory automation.

Computer-Aided Planning (CAP) The use of software packages as tools to support the planning process.

Computer-Aided Software Engineering (CASE) Same as Computer-Aided Systems Engineering, but emphasizing the importance of software development.

Computer-Aided Systems Engineering (CASE) Using software packages to accomplish and automate many of the activities of information systems development, including software development or programming.

Computer Application The use of a computer to solve a specific problem or accomplish a particular job for an end user. For example, common business computer applications include sales order processing, inventory control, and payroll.

Computer-Assisted Instruction (CAI) The use of computers to provide drills, practice exercises, and tutorial sequences to students.

Computer-Based Information System An information system that uses computer hardware and software to perform its information processing activities.

Computer Crime Criminal actions accomplished through the use of computer systems, especially with intent to defraud, destroy, or make unauthorized use of computer system resources.

Computer Ethics A system of principles governing the legal, professional, social, and moral responsibilities of computer specialists and end users.

Computer Generations Major stages in the historical development of computing.

Computer Graphics Using computer-generated images to analyze and interpret data, present information, and create computer-aided design and art.

Computer Industry The industry composed of firms that supply computer hardware, software, and services.

Computer-Integrated Manufacturing (CIM) An overall concept that stresses that the goals of computer use in factory automation should be to simplify, automate, and integrate production processes and other aspects of manufacturing.

Computer Matching Using computers to screen and match data about individual characteristics provided by a variety of computer-based information systems and databases to identify individuals for business, government, or other purposes.

Computer Monitoring Using computers to monitor the behavior and productivity of workers on the job and in the workplace.

Computer Program A series of instructions or statements in a form acceptable to a computer, prepared to achieve a certain result.

Computer System Computer hardware as a system of input, processing, output, storage, and control components. Thus, a computer system consists of input and output devices, primary and secondary storage devices, the central processing unit, the control unit within the CPU, and other peripheral devices.

Computer Terminal Any input/output device connected by telecommunications links to a computer.

Computer Virus or Worm Program code that copies its destructive program routines into the computer systems of anyone who accesses computer systems that have used the program, or anyone who uses copies of data or programs taken from such computers. This spreads the destruction of data and programs among many computer users. Technically, a virus will not run unaided but must be inserted into another program, whereas a worm is a distinct program that can run unaided.

Concurrent Processing The generic term for the capability of computers to work on several tasks at the same time, that is, concurrently. This may involve specific capabilities such as overlapped processing, multiprocessing, multiprogramming, multitasking, and parallel processing.

Connectivity The degree to which hardware, software, and databases can be easily linked together in a telecommunications network.

Control (1) The systems component that evaluates feedback to determine whether the system is moving toward the achievement of its goal and then makes any necessary adjustments to the input and processing components of the system to ensure that proper output is produced. (2) A management function that involves observing and measuring organizational performance and environmental activities and modifying the plans and activities of the organization when necessary.

Control Listing A detailed report that describes each transaction occurring during a period.

Control Totals Accumulating totals of data at multiple points in an information system to ensure correct information processing.

Control Unit A subunit of the central processing unit that controls and directs the operations of the computer system. The control unit retrieves computer instructions in proper sequence, interprets each instruction, and then directs the other parts of the computer system in their implementation.

Conversion The process in which the hardware, software, people, network, and data resources of an old information system must be converted to the requirements of a new information system. This usually involves a parallel, phased, pilot, or plunge conversion process from the old to the new system.

Cooperative Processing Information processing that allows the computers in a distributed processing network to share the processing of parts of an end user's application.

Cost/Benefit Analysis Identifying the advantages or benefits and the disadvantages or costs of a proposed solution.

COTS (Commercial Off-the-Shelf) Sofware Software developed by an application development company external to the organization who is acquiring it. Whether it is sold, leased or licensed, the developer retains all intellectual property rights associated with it. Source code is not distributed with the application.

Critical Success Factors A small number of key factors that executives consider critical to the success of the enterprise. These are key areas in which successful performance will assure the success of the organization and attainment of its goals.

Cross-Functional Information Systems Information systems that are integrated combinations of business information systems, thus sharing information resources across the functional units of an organization.

Cursor A movable point of light displayed on most video display screens to assist the user in the input of data.

Customer Relationship Management (CRM) A cross-functional e-business application that integrates and automates many customer-serving processes in sales, direct marketing, account and order management, and customer service and support.

Custom Software Applications developed internally by an organization for its exclusive use, and based on its unique technology needs.

Customer Value A strategic business focus that highlights quality, rather than merely price, as the main determinant of value from the point of view of customers.

Cyber Law Describes laws and regulations covering activities and transactions conducted over the Internet or other electronic data communicatio networks.

Cycles per Second A measure of computer processing power expressed in Hertz, commonly called the *clock speed* of a microprocessor.

Cybernetic System A system that uses feedback and control components to achieve a self-regulating capability.

Cylinder An imaginary vertical cylinder consisting of the vertical alignment of tracks on each surface of magnetic disks that are accessed simultaneously by the read/write heads of a disk drive.

Data Facts or observations about physical phenomena or business transactions. More specifically, data are objective measurements of the attributes (characteristics) of entities such as people, places, things, and events.

Data Access Issues A term that encompasses all issues associated with the capture, storage, and transfer of data across borders.

Data Administration A data resource management function that involves the establishment and enforcement of policies and procedures for managing data as a strategic corporate resource.

Database An integrated collection of logically related data elements. A database consolidates many records previously stored in separate files so that a common pool of data serves many applications.

Database Administration A data resource management function that includes responsibility for developing and maintaining the organization's data dictionary, designing and monitoring the performance of databases, and enforcing standards for database use and security.

Database Administrator (DBA) A specialist responsible for maintaining standards for the development, maintenance, and security of an organization's databases.

Database Interrogation A database capability that allows users to retrieve information using queries or report generators.

Database Maintenance The activity of keeping a database up to date by adding, changing, or deleting data.

Database Management Approach An approach to the storage and processing of data in which independent files are consolidated into a common pool, or database, of records available to different application programs and end users for processing and data retrieval.

Database Management System (DBMS) A set of computer programs that controls the creation, maintenance, and utilization of the databases of an organization.

Database Processing Utilizing a database for data processing activities such as maintenance, information retrieval, or report generation.

Data Center An organizational unit that uses centralized computing resources to perform information processing activities for an organization. Also known as a computer center.

Data Conferencing Users at networked PCs can view, mark up, revise, and save changes to a shared whiteboard of drawings, documents, and other material.

Data Conversion Converting data into new data formats required by a new business application and its software and databases. Also includes correcting incorrect data, filtering out unwanted data, and consolidating data into new databases and other data subsets.

Data Dependence Occurs when major components of a system—such as file structures, physical storage, and application programs—depend on one another in significant ways, whcih typically leads to inconsistence in data files.

Data Design The design of the logical structure of databases and files to be used by a proposed information system. This design produces detailed descriptions of the entities, relationships, data elements, and integrity rules for system files and databases.

Data Dictionary A software module and database containing descriptions and definitions concerning the structure, data elements, interrelationships, and other characteristics of a database.

Data Entry The process of converting data into a form suitable for entry into a computer system. Also called data capture or input preparation.

Data Flow Diagram A graphic diagramming tool that uses a few simple symbols to illustrate the flow of data among external entities, processing activities, and data storage elements.

Data Integration (Lack of) Occurs when related or duplicated data are stored in independent files, thus requiring ad-hoc programs to be written in order to retrieve and integrate those data.

Data Integrity (Lack of) Occurs when the same data element is defined in different ways across data files and applications. Also referred to as lack of data standardization.

Data Management Control program functions that provide access to data sets, enforce data storage conventions, and regulate the use of input/output devices.

Data Mining Using special-purpose software to analyze data from a data warehouse to find hidden patterns and trends.

Data Model A conceptual framework that defines the logical relationships among the data elements needed to support a basic business or other process.

Data Modeling A process in which the relationships between data elements are identified and defined to develop data models.

Data Planning A corporate planning and analysis function that focuses on data resource management. It includes the responsibility for developing an overall information policy and data architecture for the firm's data resources.

Data Processing The execution of a systematic sequence of operations performed on data to transform them into information.

Data Redundancy The storage of a particular data element or elements in more than one physical location or form.

Data Resources One of the major resources of an Information System, encompassing any and all data captured, processed and stored by an organization, regarledss of their particular form.

Data Resource Management   A managerial activity that applies information systems technology and management tools to the task of managing an organization's data resources. Its three major components are database administration, data administration, and data planning.

Data Visualization System (DVS)   A type of decision support system which represents complex data in innovative ways using interactive and three-dimensional formats, such as charts, graphs and maps.

Data Warehouse   An integrated collection of data extracted from operational, historical, and external databases and cleaned, transformed, and cataloged for retrieval and analysis (*data mining*) to provide business intelligence for business decision making.

Debug   To detect, locate, and remove errors from a program or malfunctions from a computer.

Decision Structure   Characteristics of a problem that dictate the extent to which the procedures to follow in order to make a decision can be specified in advance.

Decision Support System (DSS)   An information system that utilizes decision models, a database, and a decision maker's own insights in an ad hoc, interactive analytical modeling process to reach a specific decision by a specific decision maker.

Demand Reports and Responses   Information provided whenever a manager or end user demands it.

Desktop Publishing   The use of microcomputers, laser printers, and page makeup software to produce a variety of printed materials that were formerly produced only by professional printers.

Desktop Videoconferencing   The use of end-user computer workstations to conduct two-way interactive video conferences.

Development Centers   Systems development consultant groups formed to serve as consultants to the professional programmers and systems analysts of an organization to improve their application development efforts.

Digital Computer   A computer that operates on digital data by performing arithmetic and logical operations on the data. Contrast with Analog Computer.

Digitizer   A device that is used to convert drawings and other graphic images on paper or other materials into digital data that are entered into a computer system.

Direct Access   A method of storage in which each storage position has a unique address and can be individually accessed in approximately the same period without having to search through other storage positions. Same as Random Access. Contrast with Sequential Access.

Direct Access Storage Device (DASD)   A storage device that can directly access data to be stored or retrieved, for example, a magnetic disk unit.

Direct Data Organization   A method of data organization in which logical data elements are distributed randomly on or within the physical data medium. For example, logical data records distributed randomly on the surfaces of a magnetic disk file. Also called direct organization.

Direct Input/Output   Methods such as keyboard entry, voice input/output, and video displays that allow data to be input into or output from a computer system without the use of machine-readable media.

Disaster Recovery   Methods for ensuring that an organization recovers from natural and human-caused disasters that have affected its computer-based operations.

Discussion Forum   An online network discussion platform to encourage and manage online text discussions over a period among members of special-interest groups or project teams.

Distributed Databases   The concept of distributing databases or portions of a database at remote sites where the data are most frequently referenced. Sharing of data is made possible through a network that interconnects the distributed databases.

Distributed Denial of Service   A malicious attack on a computer system by using a wide distribution of computers to simultaneously and continuously send requests to a single computer or Web site thus making legitimate requests almost impossible to accomodate.

Distributed Processing   A form of decentralization of information processing made possible by a network of computers dispersed throughout an organization. Processing of user applications is accomplished by several computers interconnected by a telecommunications network, rather than relying on one large centralized computer facility or on the decentralized operation of several independent computers.

Document   (1) A medium on which data have been recorded for human use, such as a report or invoice. (2) In word processing, a generic term for text material such as letters, memos, and reports.

Documentation   A collection of documents or information that describes a computer program, information system, or required data processing operations.

Downsizing   Moving to smaller computing platforms, such as from mainframe systems to networks of personal computers and servers.

Downtime   The time interval during which a device is malfunctioning or inoperative.

DSS Generator   A software package for a decision support system that contains modules for database, model, and dialogue management.

Duplex   In communications, pertains to a simultaneous two-way independent transmission in both directions.

Duplication A backup process where a master database is duplicated at specified times to distributed locations, such that each location has an updated copy of the master data.

EBCDIC: Extended Binary Coded Decimal Interchange Code An eight-bit code that is widely used by mainframe computers.

e-Business (Electronic Business) The use of Internet technologies to inter-network and empower business processes, electronic commerce, and enterprise communication and collaboration within a company and with its customers, suppliers, and other business stakeholders.

e-Business Architecture Planning A corporate planning approach which combines business strategy development and process engineering to create novel applications that draw on the existing resources of the company.

e-Business Suites Modular and web-enabled software suites that combine and integrate the functionality traditionally associated with disparate software applications, such as ERP, CRM, SCM, procurement, etc.

Echo Check A method of checking the accuracy of data transmission in which the received data are returned to the sending device for comparison with the original data.

e-Commerce (Electronic Commerce) The buying and selling, marketing and servicing, and delivery and payment of products, services, and information over the Internet, intranets, extranets, and other networks, between an inter-networked enterprise and its prospects, customers, suppliers, and other business partners. Includes business-to-consumer (B2C), business-to-business (B2B), and consumer-to-consumer (C2C) e-commerce.

e-Commerce Channel The sales and marketing channel created by a company in order to carry out its e-Commerce activities.

e-Commerce Marketplaces Internet, intranet, and extranet Web sites and portals hosted by individual companies, consortiums of organizations, or third-party intermediaries providing electronic catalog, exchange, and auction markets to unite buyers and sellers to accomplish e-commerce transactions.

Economic Feasibility Whether expected cost savings, increased revenue, increased profits, and reductions in required investment exceed the costs of developing and operating a proposed system.

EDI: Electronic Data Interchange The automatic electronic exchange of business documents between the computers of different organizations.

Edit To modify the form or format of data. For example, to insert or delete characters such as page numbers or decimal points.

Edit Report A report that describes errors detected during processing

Electronic Communications Tools Software that helps communicate and collaborate with others by electronically sending messages, documents, and files in data, text, voice, or multimedia over the Internet, intranets, extranets, and other computer networks.

Electronic Conferencing Tools Software that helps networked computer users share information and collaborate while working together on joint assignments, no matter where they are located.

Electronic Data Interchange (EDI) A business technology that involves the transmission of transaction documents between commercial partners over the Internet or other electronic networks, using standard document formats.

Electronic Data Processing (EDP) The use of electronic computers to process data automatically.

Electronic Document Management An image-processing technology in which an electronic document may consist of digitized voice notes and electronic graphics images, as well as digitized images of traditional documents.

Electronic Funds Transfer (EFT) The development of banking and payment systems that transfer funds electronically instead of using cash or paper documents such as checks.

Electronic Mail (e-mail) Sending and receiving text messages between networked PCs over telecommunications networks. E-mail can also include data files, software, and multimedia messages and documents as attachments.

Electronic Meeting Systems (EMS) Using a meeting room with networked PCs, a large-screen projector, and EMS software to facilitate communication, collaboration, and group decision making in business meetings.

Electronic Payment Systems Alternative cash or credit payment methods using various electronic technologies to pay for products and services in electronic commerce.

Electronic Spreadsheet Package An application program used as a computerized tool for analysis, planning, and modeling that allows users to enter and manipulate data into an electronic worksheet of rows and columns.

Emulation To imitate one system with another so that the imitating system accepts the same data, executes the same programs, and achieves the same results as the imitated system.

Encryption To scramble data or convert them, prior to transmission, to a secret code that masks the meaning of the data to unauthorized recipients. Similar to enciphering.

End User Anyone who uses an information system or the information it produces.

End-User Computing Systems   Computer-based information systems that directly support both the operational and managerial applications of end users.

End-User Development   The process by which the end user of a software application is also the primary developer of the software.

End-User Involvement   The process and activities associated with involving the end user or end-user representative in the various phases of complex software development. User involvement is considered a necessary but not sufficient condition for software success.

End-User Resistance   A common occurence when new technologies are implemented, and can contribute greatly to their failure.

Enterprise Application Architecture   A graphical representation of the many interrelationships that exist between the portfolio of applications in operation at any given point in time.

Enterprise Application Integration (EAI)   A cross-functional e-business application that integrates front-office applications like customer relationship management with back-office applications like enterprise resource management.

Enterprise Collaboration Systems   The use of groupware tools and the Internet, intranets, extranets, and other computer networks to support and enhance communication, coordination, collaboration, and resource sharing among teams and workgroups in an inter-networked enterprise.

Enterprise Information Portal   A customized and personalized Web-based interface for corporate intranets and extranets that gives qualified users access to a variety of internal and external e-business and e-commerce applications, databases, software tools, and information services.

Enterprise Knowledge Portal   An enterprise information portal that serves as a knowledge management system by providing users with access to enterprise knowledge bases.

Enterprise Model   A conceptual framework that defines the structures and relationships of business processes and data elements, as well as other planning structures, such as critical success factors and organizational units.

Enterprise Resource Planning (ERP)   Integrated cross-functional software that reengineers manufacturing, distribution, finance, human resources, and other basic business processes of a company to improve its efficiency, agility, and profitability.

Entity   Some object, place, person or event that is of interest to an organization and about which data are captured and processed. See Entity Relationship Diagram.

Entity Relationship Diagram (ERD)   A data planning and systems development diagramming tool that models the relationships among the entities in a business process.

Entropy   The tendency of a system to lose a relatively stable state of equilibrium.

Ergonomics   The science and technology emphasizing the safety, comfort, and ease of use of human-operated machines such as computers. The goal of ergonomics is to produce systems that are user-friendly: safe, comfortable, and easy to use. Ergonomics is also called human factors engineering.

Ethical Foundations   Various approaches to considering ethical situations in business.

Exception Reports   Reports produced only when exceptional conditions occur, or reports produced periodically that contain information only about exceptional conditions.

Executive Information System (EIS)   An information system that provides strategic information tailored to the needs of executives and other decision makers.

Executive Support System (ESS)   An executive information system with additional capabilities, including data analysis, decision support, electronic mail, and personal productivity tools.

Expert System (ES)   A computer-based information system that uses its knowledge about a specific complex application area to act as an expert consultant to users. The system consists of a knowledge base and software modules that perform inferences on the knowledge and communicate answers to a user's questions.

Expert System Shell   An expert system software package that does not contain a knowledge base, but does include an inference engine and interface functionality.

External Database   Databases hosted by a third-party external to the user company.

Extranet   A network that links selected resources of a company with its customers, suppliers, and other business partners, using the Internet or private networks to link the organizations' intranets.

Facilities Management   The use of an external service organization to operate and manage the information processing facilities of an organization.

Fault-Tolerant Systems   Computers that have multiple central processors, peripherals, and system software and that are able to continue operations even if there is a major hardware or software failure.

Faxing (Facsimile)   Transmitting and receiving images of documents over the telephone or computer networks using PCs or fax machines.

Feasibility Study   A preliminary study that investigates the information needs of end users and the objectives, constraints, basic resource requirements, costs/benefits, and feasibility of proposed projects.

Feedback (1) Data or information concerning the components and operations of a system. (2) The use of part of the output of a system as input to the system.

Fiber Optics The technology that uses cables consisting of very thin filaments of glass fibers that can conduct the light generated by lasers for high-speed telecommunications.

Field A data element that consists of a grouping of characters that describe a particular attribute of an entity. For example, the name field or salary field of an employee.

Fifth Generation The next generation of computers. Major advances in parallel processing, user interfaces, and artificial intelligence may provide computers that will be able to see, hear, talk, and think.

File A collection of related data records treated as a unit. Sometimes called a data set.

File Management Controlling the creation, deletion, access, and use of files of data and programs.

File Processing Organizing data into specialized files of data records designed for processing only by specific application programs. Contrast with Database Management Approach.

Financial Management Systems Information systems that support financial managers in the financing of a business and the allocation and control of financial resources. These include cash and securities management, capital budgeting, financial forecasting, and financial planning.

Firewall Computers, communications processors, and software that protect computer networks from intrusion by screening all network traffic and serving as a safe transfer point for access to and from other networks.

Firmware The use of microprogrammed read-only memory circuits in place of hard-wired logic circuitry. See also Microprogramming.

Flaming The practice of sending excessively critical, derogatory, or vulgar e-mail messages.

Floating Point Pertaining to a number representation system in which each number is represented by two sets of digits. One set represents the significant digits or fixed-point "base" of the number, while the other set of digits represents the "exponent," which indicates the precision of the number.

Floppy Disk A small plastic disk coated with iron oxide that resembles a small phonograph record enclosed in a protective envelope. It is a widely used form of magnetic disk media that provides a direct access storage capability for microcomputer systems.

Flowchart A graphical representation in which symbols are used to represent operations, data, flow, logic, equipment, and so on. A program flowchart illustrates the structure and sequence of operations of a program, whereas a system flowchart illustrates the components and flows of information systems.

Foreground Processing The automatic execution of the computer programs that have been designed to preempt the use of computing facilities. Contrast with Background Processing.

Format The arrangement of data on a medium.

FORTRAN: FORmula TRANslation A high-level programming language widely utilized to develop computer programs that perform mathematical computations for scientific, engineering, and selected business applications.

Forward Chaining An inference strategy that reaches a conclusion by applying rules to facts to determine if any facts satisfy a rule's conditions in a particular situation.

Fourth-Generation Languages (4GL) Programming languages that are easier to use than high-level languages such as BASIC, COBOL, or FORTRAN. They are also known as nonprocedural, natural, or very high-level languages.

Frame A collection of knowledge about an entity or other concept consisting of a complex package of slots, that is, data values describing the characteristics or attributes of an entity.

Frame-Based Knowledge Knowledge represented in the form of a hierarchy or network of frames.

Front-End Processor Typically a smaller, general-purpose computer that is dedicated to handling data communications control functions in a communications network, thus relieving the host computer of these functions.

Functional Business Systems Information systems within a business organization that support one of the traditional functions of business such as marketing, finance, or production. Functional business systems can be either operations or management information systems.

Functional Requirements The information system capabilities required to meet the information needs of end users. Also called system requirements.

Function-Specific Application Software Software packages designed to support specific functions or applications in business and other fields.

Fuzzy Logic Systems Computer-based systems that can process data that are incomplete or only partially correct, that is, fuzzy data. Such systems can solve unstructured problems with incomplete knowledge, as humans do.

General Ledger Accounting software used to keep track of the balances and transactions of an organization.

General-Purpose Application Programs Programs that can perform information processing jobs for users from all application areas. For example, word processing programs, electronic spreadsheet programs, and graphics programs can be used by individuals for home, education, business, scientific, and many other purposes.

General-Purpose Computer A computer that is designed to handle a wide variety of problems. Contrast with Special-Purpose Computer.

Generate To produce a machine-language program for performing a specific data processing task based on parameters supplied by a programmer or user.

Genetic Algorithm An application of artificial intelligence software that uses Darwinian (survival of the fittest) randomizing and other functions to simulate an evolutionary process that can yield increasingly better solutions to a problem.

Geographic Information Systems A Decision Support System that uses geographic information to construct and display maps overlayed with data that are used in decision-making.

Gigabyte One billion bytes. More accurately, 2 to the 30th power, or 1,073,741,824 in decimal notation.

GIGO An acronym of "Garbage In, Garbage Out," which emphasizes that information systems will produce erroneous and invalid output when provided with erroneous and invalid input data or instructions.

Global Business Drivers Business requirements caused by the nature of an industry and its competitive forces.

Global Company A business that is driven by a global strategy so that all of its activities are planned and implemented in the context of a whole-world system.

Global e-Business Technology Management Managing information technologies in a global e-business enterprise, amid the cultural, political, and geoeconomic challenges involved in developing e-business/IT strategies, global e-business and e-commerce applications portfolios, Internet-based technology platforms, and global data resource management policies.

Global Information Technology The use of computer-based information systems and telecommunications networks using a variety of information technologies to support global business operations and management.

Globalization Becoming a global enterprise by expanding into global markets, using global production facilities, forming alliances with global partners, and so on.

Goal-Seeking Analysis Making repeated changes to selected variables until a chosen variable reaches a target value.

Graphical User Interface A software interface that relies on icons, bars, buttons, boxes, and other images to initiate computer-based tasks for users.

Graphics Pertaining to symbolic input or output from a computer system, such as lines, curves, and geometric shapes, using video display units or graphics plotters and printers.

Graphics Pen and Tablet A device that allows an end user to draw or write on a pressure-sensitive tablet and have the handwriting or graphics digitized by the computer and accepted as input.

Graphics Software A program that helps users generate graphics displays.

Group Decision Making Decisions made by groups of people coming to an agreement on a particular issue.

Group Decision Support System (GDSS) A decision support system that provides support for decision making by groups of people.

Group Support Systems (GSS) An information system that enhances communication, coordination, collaboration, decision making, and group work activities of teams and workgroups.

Groupware Software to support and enhance communication, coordination, and collaboration among networked teams and workgroups, including software tools for electronic communications, electronic conferencing, and cooperative work management.

Hacking (1) Obsessive use of a computer. (2) The unauthorized access and use of computer systems.

Handshaking Exchange of predetermined signals when a connection is established between two communications terminals.

Hard Copy A data medium or data record that has a degree of permanence and that can be read by people or machines.

Hardware (1) Machines and media. (2) Physical equipment, as opposed to computer programs or methods of use. (3) Mechanical, magnetic, electrical, electronic, or optical devices. Contrast with Software.

Hash Total The sum of numbers in a data field that are not normally added, such as account numbers or other identification numbers. It is utilized as a control total, especially during input/output operations of batch processing systems.

Header Label A machine-readable record at the beginning of a file containing data for file identification and control.

Heuristic Pertaining to exploratory methods of problem solving in which solutions are discovered by evaluation of the progress made toward the final result. It is an exploratory trial-and-error approach guided by rules of thumb. Opposite of algorithmic.

Hierarchical Data Structure A logical data structure in which the relationships between records form a hierarchy or tree structure. The relationships among records are one to many, because each data element is related to only one element above it.

High-Level Language A programming language that utilizes macro instructions and statements that closely resemble human language or mathematical notation to describe the problem to be solved or the procedure to be used. Also called a compiler language.

Homeostasis   A relatively stable state of equilibrium of a system.

Host Computer   Typically a larger central computer that performs the major data processing tasks in a computer network.

HTML   See Hypertext Markup Language.

Human Factors   Hardware and software capabilities that can affect the comfort, safety, ease of use, and user customization of computer-based information systems.

Human Information Processing   A conceptual framework about the human cognitive process that uses an information processing context to explain how humans capture, process, and use information.

Human Resource Information Systems (HRIS)   Information systems that support human resource management activities such as recruitment, selection and hiring, job placement and performance appraisals, and training and development.

Hybrid AI Systems   Systems that integrate several AI technologies, such as expert systems and neural networks.

Hypermedia   Documents containing multiple forms of media, including text, graphics, video, and sound, that can be interactively searched, like hypertext.

Hypertext   Text in electronic form that has been indexed and linked (hyperlinks) by software in a variety of ways so that it can be randomly and interactively searched by a user.

Hypertext Markup Language (HTML)   A popular page description language for creating hypertext and hypermedia documents for World Wide Web and intranet Web sites.

Icon   A small figure on a video display that looks like a familiar office or other device, such as a file folder (for storing a file) or a wastebasket (for deleting a file).

Image Processing   A computer-based technology that allows end users to electronically capture, store, process, and retrieve images that may include numeric data, text, handwriting, graphics, documents, and photographs. Image processing makes heavy use of optical scanning and optical disk technologies.

Impact Printers   Printers that form images on paper through the pressing of a printing element and an inked ribbon or roller against the face of a sheet of paper.

Implementation Process   The process and activities associated with installing a software application and preparing it for actual use.

Index   An ordered reference list of the contents of a file or document, together with keys or reference notations for identification or location of those contents.

Index Sequential   A method of data organization in which records are organized in sequential order and also referenced by an index. When utilized with direct access file devices, it is known as index sequential access method, or ISAM.

Inference Engine   The software component of an expert system, which processes the rules and facts related to a specific problem and makes associations and inferences resulting in recommended courses of action.

Infomediaries   Third-party market-maker companies that serve as intermediaries to bring buyers and sellers together by developing and hosting electronic catalog, exchange, and auction markets to accomplish e-commerce transactions.

Information   Data placed in a meaningful and useful context for an end user.

Information Appliances   Small Web-enabled microcomputer devices with specialized functions, such as handheld PDAs, TV set-top boxes, game consoles, cellular and PCS phones, wired telephone appliances, and other Web-enabled home appliances.

Information Architecture   A conceptual framework that defines the basic structure, content, and relationships of the organizational databases that provide the data needed to support the basic business processes of an organization.

Information Center   A support facility for the end users of an organization. It allows users to learn to develop their own application programs and accomplish their own information processing tasks. End users are provided with hardware support, software support, and people support (trained user consultants).

Information Float   The time that a document is in transit between the sender and receiver and thus unavailable for any action or response.

Information Processing   A concept that covers both the traditional concept of processing numeric and alphabetic data and the processing of text, images, and voices. It emphasizes that the production of information products for users should be the focus of processing activities.

Information Products   Information produced by information sytems that can be used in both our work and our personal lives. Examples include messages, reports, forms, etc.

Information Quality   The degree to which information has content, form, and time characteristics that give it value for specific end users.

Information Resource Management (IRM)   A management concept that views data, information, and computer resources (computer hardware, software, networks, and personnel) as valuable organizational resources that should be efficiently, economically, and effectively managed for the benefit of the entire organization.

Information Retrieval The methods and procedures for recovering specific information from stored data.

Information Superhighway An advanced high-speed Internet-like network that connects individuals, households, businesses, government agencies, libraries, schools, universities, and other institutions with interactive voice, video, data, and multimedia communications.

Information System (1) A set of people, procedures, and resources that collects, transforms, and disseminates information in an organization. (2) A system that accepts data resources as input and processes them into information products as output.

Information System Controls Methods, devices, practices and procedures put in place to ensure the quality (accuracy, validity and propriety) of information system activities.

Information System Model A conceptual framework that views an information system as a system that uses the resources of hardware (machines and media), software (programs and procedures), people (users and specialists), and networks (communications media and network support) to perform input, processing, output, storage, and control activities that transform data resources (databases and knowledge bases) into information products.

Information Systems Development See Systems Development.

Information Systems Operations Management Management of all operations concerned with the use of hardware, software, network and personnel resources in a corporate or business unit data center.

Information System Specialist A person whose occupation is related to the providing of information system services, for example, a systems analyst, programmer, or computer operator.

Information Technology (IT) Hardware, software, telecommunications, database management, and other information processing technologies used in computer-based information systems.

Information Technology Architecture A conceptual blueprint that specifies the components and interrelationships of a company's technology infrastructure, data resources, applications architecture, and IT organization.

Information Technology Management Managing information technologies by (1) the joint development and implementation of business and IT strategies by business and IT executives, (2) managing the research and implementation of new information technologies and the development of business applications, and (3) managing the IT processes, professionals, subunits, and infrastructure within a company.

Information Theory The branch of learning concerned with the likelihood of accurate transmission or communication of messages subject to transmission failure, distortion, and noise.

Infomediaries Companies that serve as intermediaries in e-business transactions by virtue of bringing buyers and sellers together.

Input Pertaining to a device, process, or channel involved in the insertion of data into a data processing system. Opposite of Output.

Input/Output (I/O) Pertaining to either input or output, or both.

Input/Output Interface Hardware Devices such as I/O ports, I/O buses, buffers, channels, and I/O control units, which assist the CPU in its input/output assignments. These devices make it possible for modern computer systems to perform input, output, and processing functions simultaneously.

Inquiry Processing Computer processing that supports the real-time interrogation of online files and databases by end users.

Instant Messaging Conferencing technology that allows connected users to chat (using text and/or video) in real-time with their contacts.

Instruction A grouping of characters that specifies the computer operation to be performed.

Intangible Benefits and Costs The nonquantifiable benefits and costs of a proposed solution or system.

Integrated Circuit A complex microelectronic circuit consisting of interconnected circuit elements that cannot be disassembled because they are placed on or within a continuous substrate such as a silicon chip.

Integrated Packages Software that combines the ability to do several general-purpose applications (such as word processing, electronic spreadsheet, and graphics) into one program.

Intellectual Property Theft Infringement on copyrighted material.

Intelligent Agent A special-purpose knowledge-based system that serves as a software surrogate to accomplish specific tasks for end users.

Intelligent Terminal A terminal with the capabilities of a microcomputer that can thus perform many data processing and other functions without accessing a larger computer.

Interactive Marketing A dynamic collaborative process of creating, purchasing, and improving products and services that builds close relationships between a business and its customers, using a variety of services on the Internet, intranets, and extranets.

Interactive Processing A type of real-time processing in which users can interact with a computer on a real-time basis.

Interactive Video   Computer-based systems that integrate image processing with text, audio, and video processing technologies, which makes interactive multimedia presentations possible.

Interenterprise Information Systems   Linked extranets that connect partners, customers, suppliers and competitors into an integrated, virtual enterprise.

Interface   A shared boundary, such as the boundary between two systems. For example, the boundary between a computer and its peripheral devices.

Internet   A rapidly growing computer network of millions of business, educational, and governmental networks connecting hundreds of millions of computers and their users in more than 200 countries.

Inter-Network Processor   Communications processors used by local area networks to interconnect them with other local area and wide area networks. Examples include switches, routers, hubs, and gateways.

Inter-Networks   Interconnected local area and wide area networks.

Internet Networking Technologies   Collectively, all open technologies that underlie the connectivity behind the Internet. Examples include Web browsers, network servers, and TCP/IP products, to name a few.

Internet Service Provider   A company that provides access to the Internet.

Interoperability   Being able to accomplish end-user applications using different types of computer systems, operating systems, and application software, interconnected by different types of local and wide area networks.

Interorganizational Information Systems   Information systems that interconnect an organization with other organizations, such as a business and its customers and suppliers.

Interpreter   A computer program that translates and executes each source language statement before translating and executing the next one.

Interrupt   A condition that causes an interruption in a processing operation during which another task is performed. At the conclusion of this new assignment, control may be transferred back to the point at which the original processing operation was interrupted or to other tasks with a higher priority.

Intranet   An Internet-like network within an organization. Web browser software provides easy access to internal Web sites established by business units, teams, and individuals, and other network resources and applications.

Inventory Control   Software used to manage and keep track of stocked inventory items for sale.

Inverted File   A file that references entities by their attributes.

IT Architecture   A conceptual design for the implementation of information technology in an organization, including its hardware, software, and network technology platforms, data resources, application portfolio, and IS organization.

IT Staff Planning   Recruiting, training, and retaining qualified IS personnel.

Iterative   Pertaining to the repeated execution of a series of steps.

Java   An object-oriented programming language designed for programming real-time, interactive, Web-based applications in the form of applets for use on clients and servers on the Internet, intranets, and extranets.

Job   A specified group of tasks prescribed as a unit of work for a computer.

Job Control Language (JCL)   A language for communicating with the operating system of a computer to identify a job and describe its requirements.

Joystick   A small lever set in a box used to move the cursor on the computer's display screen.

K   An abbreviation for the prefix *kilo*, which is 1,000 in decimal notation. When referring to storage capacity, it is equivalent to 2 to the 10th power, or 1,024 in decimal notation.

Key   One or more fields within a data record that are used to identify it or control its use.

Keyboarding   Using the keyboard of a microcomputer or computer terminal.

Kilobyte   A unit of measure of computer storage capacity, equivalent to 1,024 bytes.

Knowledge Base   A computer-accessible collection of knowledge about a subject in a variety of forms, such as facts and rules of inference, frames, and objects.

Knowledge-Based Information System   An information system that adds a knowledge base to the database and other components found in other types of computer-based information systems.

Knowledge Creating Company   Also known as learning organizations, refers to those companies that consistently create and disseminate new knowledge within the company as well as its products and services.

Knowledge Engineer   A specialist who works with experts to capture the knowledge they possess to develop a knowledge base for expert systems and other knowledge-based systems.

Knowledge Management   Organizing and sharing the diverse forms of business information created within an organization. Includes managing project and enterprise document libraries, discussion databases, intranet Web site databases, and other types of knowledge bases.

Knowledge Workers   People whose primary work activities include creating, using, and distributing information.

Language Translator Program   A program that converts the programming language instructions in a computer program into machine language code. Major types include assemblers, compilers, and interpreters.

Large-Scale Integration (LSI)   A method of constructing electronic circuits in which thousands of circuits can be placed on a single semiconductor chip.

Legacy Systems   The older, traditional, mainframe-based business information systems of an organization.

Leverage Investment in IT   Refers to the development of products and services that would not have been possible without a previous investment in a strategic technology platform.

Legal and Political Feasibility   The analysis of any potential legal and political ramifications arising from the construction and implementation of a new system.

Light Pen   A photoelectronic device that allows data to be entered or altered on the face of a video display terminal.

Liquid Crystal Displays (LCDs)   Electronic visual displays that form characters by applying an electrical charge to selected silicon crystals.

List Organization   A method of data organization that uses indexes and pointers to allow for nonsequential retrieval.

List Processing   A method of processing data in the form of lists.

Local Area Network (LAN)   A communications network that typically connects computers, terminals, and other computerized devices within a limited physical area such as an office, building, manufacturing plant, or other work site.

Locking In Customers and Suppliers   Building valuable relationships with customers and suppliers that deter them from abandoning a firm for its competitors or intimidating it into accepting less profitable relationships.

Logical Data Elements   Data elements that are independent of the physical data media on which they are recorded.

Logical Model   A blueprint of an existing system that depicts what is being accomplished by it without regard for how the system is performing those operations.

Logical System Design   Developing general specifications for how basic information systems activities can meet end-user requirements.

Loop   A sequence of instructions in a computer program that is executed repeatedly until a terminal condition prevails.

Machines   Computers and other electronic equipment.

Machine Control   The use of computers to control the actions of manufacturing equipment.

Machine Cycle   The timing of a basic CPU operation as determined by a fixed number of electrical pulses emitted by the CPU's timing circuitry or internal clock.

Machine Language   A programming language in which instructions are expressed in the binary code of the computer.

Macro Instruction   An instruction in a source language that is equivalent to a specified sequence of machine instructions.

Magnetic Disk   A flat, circular plate with a magnetic surface on which data can be stored by selective magnetization of portions of the curved surface.

Magnetic Ink   An ink that contains particles of iron oxide that can be magnetized and detected by magnetic sensors.

Magnetic Ink Character Recognition (MICR)   The machine recognition of characters printed with magnetic ink. Primarily used for check processing by the banking industry.

Magnetic Tape   A plastic tape with a magnetic surface on which data can be stored by selective magnetization of portions of the surface.

Magnetic Stripe Card   A plastic, wallet-size card with a strip of magnetic tape on one surface; widely used for credit/debit cards.

Mainframe   A larger computer system, typically with a separate central processing unit, as distinguished from microcomputer and minicomputer systems.

Management Information System (MIS)   A management support system that produces prespecified reports, displays, and responses on a periodic, exception, demand, or push reporting basis.

Management Support System (MSS)   An information system that provides information to support managerial decision making. More specifically, an information-reporting system, executive information system, or decision support system.

Managerial End User   A manager, entrepreneur, or managerial-level professional who personally uses information systems. Also, the manager of the department or other organizational unit that relies on information systems.

Managerial Roles   Management of the performance of a variety of interpersonal, information, and decision roles.

Managing Information Technology   Overall approach to the management of all IT resources in a company, which includes business/IT strategies, applications and infrastructure.

Manual Data Processing   Data processing that requires continual human operation and intervention and that utilizes simple data processing tools such as paper forms, pencils, and filing cabinets.

Manufacturing Execution Systems   Performance-monitoring information systems designed to help oversee factory floor operations.

Manufacturing Information Systems Information systems that support the planning, control, and accomplishment of manufacturing processes. This includes concepts such as computer-integrated manufacturing (CIM) and technologies such as computer-aided manufacturing (CAM) or computer-aided design (CAD).

Marketing Information Systems Information systems that support the planning, control, and transaction processing required for the accomplishment of marketing activities, such as sales management, advertising, and promotion.

Mass Storage Secondary storage devices with extra-large storage capacities, such as magnetic or optical disks.

Master File A data file containing relatively permanent information that is utilized as an authoritative reference and is usually updated periodically. Contrast with Transaction File.

Mathematical Model A mathematical representation of a process, device, or concept.

Media All tangible objects on which data are recorded.

Megabyte One million bytes. More accurately, 2 to the 20th power, or 1,048,576 in decimal notation.

Memory See Storage.

Menu A displayed list of items (usually the names of alternative applications, files, or activities) from which an end user makes a selection.

Menu Driven A characteristic of interactive computing systems that provides menu displays and operator prompting to assist an end user in performing a particular job.

Metadata Data about data; data describing the structure, data elements, interrelationships, and other characteristics of a database.

Metcalfe's Law A theory advanced by Robert Metcalfe that suggests that the value of a given network will double with the additional of each successive connection or node.

Microcomputer A very small computer, ranging in size from a "computer on a chip" to handheld, laptop, and desktop units, and servers.

Micrographics The use of microfilm, microfiche, and other microforms to record data in greatly reduced form.

Microprocessor A microcomputer central processing unit (CPU) on a chip. Without input/output or primary storage capabilities in most types.

Microprogram A small set of elementary control instructions called microinstructions or microcode.

Microprogramming The use of special software (microprograms) to perform the functions of special hardware (electronic control circuitry). Microprograms stored in a read-only storage module of the control unit interpret the machine language instructions of a computer program and decode them into elementary microinstructions, which are then executed.

Microsecond A millionth of a second.

Middleware Software that helps diverse software programs and networked computer systems work together, thus promoting their interoperability.

Midrange Computer A computer category between microcomputers and mainframes. Examples include minicomputers, network servers, and technical workstations.

Millisecond A thousandth of a second.

Minicomputer A type of midrange computer.

MIPS Million of instructions per second, a measuring of computer processing speed.

Model Base An organized software collection of conceptual, mathematical, and logical models that express business relationships, computational routines, or analytical techniques.

Modem (MOdulator-DEModulator) A device that converts the digital signals from input/output devices into appropriate frequencies at a transmission terminal and converts them back into digital signals at a receiving terminal.

Monitor Software or hardware that observes, supervises, controls, or verifies the operations of a system.

Moore's Law A theory advanced by Gordon Moore that suggests that computing power will double every 18 to 24 months at a given price point.

Mouse A small device that is electronically connected to a computer and is moved by hand on a flat surface to move the cursor on a video screen in the same direction. Buttons on the mouse allow users to issue commands and make responses or selections.

Multidimensional Structure A database model that uses multidimensional structures (such as cubes or cubes within cubes) to store data and relationships between data.

Multimedia Presentations Providing information using a variety of media, including text and graphics displays, voice and other audio, photographs, and video segments.

Multiplex To interleave or simultaneously transmit two or more messages on a single channel.

Multiplexer An electronic device that allows a single communications channel to carry simultaneous data transmissions from many terminals.

Multiprocessing Pertaining to the simultaneous execution of two or more instructions by a computer or computer network.

Multiprocessor Computer Systems Computer systems that use a multiprocessor architecture in the design of their central processing units. This includes the use of support microprocessors and multiple instruction processors, including parallel processor designs.

Multiprogramming Pertaining to the concurrent execution of two or more programs by a computer by interleaving their execution.

Multitasking The concurrent use of the same computer to accomplish several different information processing tasks. Each task may require the use of a different program or the concurrent use of the same copy of a program by several users.

Nanosecond One-billionth of a second.

Natural Language A programming language that is very close to human language. Also called very high-level language.

Network An interconnected system of computers, terminals, and communications channels and devices.

Network Architecture A master plan designed to promote an open, simple, flexible, and efficient telecommunications environment through the use of standard protocols, standard communications hardware and software interfaces, and the design of a standard multilevel telecommunications interface between end users and computer systems.

Network Computer A low-cost networked microcomputer with no or minimal disk storage, which depends on Internet or intranet servers for its operating system and Web browser, Java-enabled application software, and data access and storage.

Network Computing A network-centric view of computing in which "the network is the computer," that is, the view that computer networks are the central computing resource of any computing environment.

Network Data Structure A logical data structure that allows many-to-many relationships among data records. It allows entry into a database at multiple points, because any data element or record can be related to many other data elements.

Network Interoperability The ability of users in one network to communicate with users or resources in another network even when those networks use different protocols or communication standards.

Network Resources One of the key resources present in all information systems. Includes all devices involved in the provision of telecommunication and access services.

Network Server Powerful microcomputers that coordinate communications and resource sharing in small local area networks and Web sites.

Network Terminal Computer terminals with limited local processing capabilities that depend on external servers for their operating systems and software.

Network Topologies The various configurations by which computers can be networked and connected together.

Neural Networks Computer processors or software whose architecture is based on the human brain's mesh-like neuron structure. Neural networks can process many pieces of information simultaneously and learn to recognize patterns and programs to solve related problems on their own.

Node A terminal point in a communications network.

Nonprocedural Languages Programming languages that allow users and professional programmers to specify the results they want without specifying how to solve the problem.

Numerical Control Automatic control of a machine process by a computer that makes use of numerical data, generally introduced as the operation is in process. Also called machine control.

Object A data element that includes both data and the methods or processes that act on those data.

Object-Based Knowledge Knowledge represented as a network of objects.

Object-Oriented Language An object-oriented programming (OOP) language used to develop programs that create and use objects to perform information processing tasks.

Object-Oriented Model An approach to database design that emphasizes the concepts of encapsulation and inheritance.

Object Program A compiled or assembled program composed of executable machine instructions. Contrast with Source Program.

OEM: Original Equipment Manufacturer A firm that manufactures and sells computers by assembling components produced by other hardware manufacturers.

Office Automation (OA) The use of computer-based information systems that collect, process, store, and transmit electronic messages, documents, and other forms of office communications among individuals, workgroups, and organizations.

Off-line Pertaining to equipment or devices not under control of the central processing unit.

Offshoring A relocation of an organization's business processes to a lower-cost location overseas.

Online Pertaining to equipment or devices under control of the central processing unit.

Online Accounting Systems Accounting systems that process and monitor transactions in real-time.

Online Analytical Processing (OLAP) A capability of some management, decision support, and executive information systems that supports interactive examination and manipulation of large amounts of data from many perspectives.

Online HRM Systems Human Resource Management (HRM) systems that operate using the Internet as their major platform for most applications such as recruiting, training, etc.

Online Transaction Processing (OLTP) A real-time transaction processing system.

Open Systems Information systems that use common standards for hardware, software, applications, and networking to create a computing environment that allows easy access by end users and their networked computer systems.

Open Systems Interconnection (OSI) A standard that describes how messages should be transmitted between any two points in a telecommunications network. Its goal is to guide vendors to make their products compatible with those of other providers.

Operand That which is operated upon. That part of a computer instruction that is identified by the address part of the instruction.

Operating Environment Software packages or modules that add a graphics-based interface among end users, the operating system, and their application programs and that may also provide multitasking capability.

Operating System The main control program of a computer system. It is a system of programs that controls the execution of computer programs and may provide scheduling, debugging, input/output control, system accounting, compilation, storage assignment, data management, and related services.

Operational Feasibility The willingness and ability of management, employees, customers, and suppliers to operate, use, and support a proposed system.

Operation Code A code that represents specific operations to be performed upon the operands in a computer instruction.

Operations Support System (OSS) An information system that collects, processes, and stores data generated by the operations systems of an organization and produces data and information for input into a management information system or for the control of an operations system.

Operations System A basic subsystem of the business firm that constitutes its input, processing, and output components. Also called a physical system.

Optical Character Recognition (OCR) The machine identification of printed characters through the use of light-sensitive devices.

Optical Disks A secondary storage medium using CD (compact disk) and DVD (digital versatile disk) technologies to read tiny spots on plastic disks. The disks are currently capable of storing billions of characters of information.

Optical Scanner A device that optically scans characters or images and generates their digital representations.

Opt-In/Opt-Out Two alternatives in what should be the default stance in privacy considerations.

Optimization Analysis Finding an optimum value for selected variables in a mathematical model, given certain constraints.

Order Processing Sequence of steps and operations involved in capturing order information from customers, checking stock availability and verifying customer credit.

Organizational Feasibility How well a proposed information system supports the objectives of an organization's strategic plan for information systems.

Organizational Analysis An analysis of an organization in terms of its management structure, people, business activities, and environment that is used as part of the assessment of feasibility for a new system.

Organizational Planning The process by which organizations articulate the sequence of steps and actions necessary to transform desired goals into results.

Output Pertaining to a device, process, or channel involved with the transfer of data or information out of an information processing system. Opposite of Input.

Outsourcing Turning over all or part of an organization's information systems operation to outside contractors, known as systems integrators or service providers.

Packet A group of data and control information in a specified format that is transmitted as an entity.

Packet Switching A data transmission process that transmits addressed packets such that a channel is occupied only for the duration of transmission of the packet.

Page A segment of a program or data, usually of fixed length.

Paging A process that automatically and continually transfers pages of programs and data between primary storage and direct access storage devices. It provides computers with multiprogramming and virtual memory capabilities.

Parallel Processing Executing many instructions at the same time, that is, in parallel. Performed by advanced computers using many instruction processors organized in clusters or networks.

Parity Bit A check bit appended to an array of binary digits to make the sum of all the binary digits, including the check bit, always odd or always even.

Pascal A high-level, general-purpose, structured programming language named after Blaise Pascal. It was developed by Niklaus Wirth of Zurich in 1968.

Passwords A sequence of characters only known to a specific user that is employed to prevent unauthorized access to a system or other resource.

Pattern Recognition The identification of shapes, forms, or configurations by automatic means.

Payroll Systems used to process hours worked, contractual salary information, and taxes and related information to create paychecks for employees.

PCM: Plug-Compatible Manufacturer A firm that manufactures computer equipment that can be plugged into existing computer systems without requiring additional hardware or software interfaces.

People Resources All individuals involved in the creation, operation, and use of information systems. Includes end users and IS specialist.

Peer-to-Peer Network (P2P) A computing environment in which end users' computers connect, communicate, and collaborate directly with one another via the Internet or other telecommunications network links.

Pen-Based Computers Tablet-style microcomputers that recognize handwriting and hand drawing done by a pen-shaped device on their pressure-sensitive display screens.

Performance Monitor A software package that monitors the processing of computer system jobs, helps develop a planned schedule of computer operations that can optimize computer system performance, and produces detailed statistics that are used for computer system capacity planning and control.

Periodic Reports Providing information to managers using a prespecified format designed to provide information on a regularly scheduled basis.

Peripheral Devices In a computer system, any unit of equipment, distinct from the central processing unit, that provides the system with input, output, or storage capabilities.

Personal Digital Assistant (PDA) Handheld microcomputer devices that enable you to manage information such as appointments, to-do lists, and sales contacts, send and receive e-mail, access the Web, and exchange such information with your desktop PC or network server.

Personal Information Manager (PIM) A software package that helps end users store, organize, and retrieve text and numerical data in the form of notes, lists, memos, and a variety of other forms.

Petabyte A unit of computer storage capacity equivalent to 1,024 terabytes.

Physical System Design Design of the user interface methods and products, database structures, and processing and control procedures for a proposed information system, including hardware, software, and personnel specifications.

Picosecond One-trillionth of a second.

Plasma Display Output devices that generate a visual display with electrically charged particles of gas trapped between glass plates.

Plotter A hard-copy output device that produces drawings and graphical displays on paper or other materials.

Pointer A data element associated with an index, a record, or other set of data that contains the address of a related record.

Pointing Devices Devices that allow end users to issue commands or make choices by moving a cursor on the display screen.

Pointing Stick A small buttonlike device on a keyboard that moves the cursor on the screen in the direction of the pressure placed upon it.

Point-of-Sale (POS) Terminal A computer terminal used in retail stores that serves the function of a cash register as well as collecting sales data and performing other data processing functions.

Port (1) Electronic circuitry that provides a connection point between the CPU and input/output devices. (2) A connection point for a communications line on a CPU or other front-end device.

Postimplementation Review Monitoring and evaluating the results of an implemented solution or system.

Presentation Graphics Using computer-generated graphics to enhance the information presented in reports and other types of presentations.

Prespecified Reports Reports whose format is specified in advance to provide managers with information periodically, on an exception basis, or on demand.

Primary Storage Unit The memory of a computer.

Private Branch Exchange (PBX) A switching device that serves as an interface between the many telephone lines within a work area and the local telephone company's main telephone lines or trunks. Computerized PBXs can handle the switching of both voices and data.

Procedure-Oriented Language A programming language designed for the convenient expression of procedures used in the solution of a wide class of problems.

Procedures Sets of instructions used by people to complete a task.

Process Control The use of a computer to control an ongoing physical process, such as petrochemical production.

Process Design The design of the programs and procedures needed by a proposed information system, including detailed program specifications and procedures.

Processing Speed The processing power of a computer, measured in millions of instructions per second or millions of cycles per second.

Processor A hardware device or software system capable of performing operations on data.

Program A set of instructions that causes a computer to perform a particular task.

Programmed Decision A decision that can be automated by basing it on a decision rule that outlines the steps to take when confronted with the need for a specific decision.

Programmer A person mainly involved in designing, writing, and testing computer programs.

Programming   The designing, writing, and testing of a program.

Programming Language   A language used to develop the instructions in computer programs.

Programming Tools   Software packages or modules that provide editing and diagnostic capabilities and other support facilities to assist the programming process.

Project Management   Managing the accomplishment of an information system development project according to a specific project plan, so a project is completed on time, is within its budget, and meets its design objectives.

Prompt   Messages that assist a user in performing a particular job. This would include error messages, correction suggestions, questions, and other messages that guide an end user.

Protocol   A set of rules and procedures for the control of communications in a communications network.

Prototype   A working model. In particular, a working model of an information system that includes tentative versions of user input and output, databases and files, control methods, and processing routines.

Prototyping   The rapid development and testing of working models, or prototypes, of new information system applications in an interactive, iterative process involving both systems analysts and end users.

Pseudocode   An informal design language of structured programming that expresses the processing logic of a program module in ordinary human language phrases.

Pull Marketing   Marketing methods that rely on the use of Web browsers by end users to access marketing materials and resources at Internet, intranet, and extranet Web sites.

Push Marketing   Marketing methods that rely on Web broadcasting software to push marketing information and other marketing materials to end users' computers.

Quality Assurance   Methods for ensuring that information systems are free from errors and fraud and provide information products of high quality.

Query Language   A high-level, humanlike language provided by a database management system that enables users to easily extract data and information from a database.

Queue   (1) A waiting line formed by items in a system waiting for service. (2) To arrange in or form a queue.

RAID   Redundant array of independent (or inexpensive) disks. Magnetic disk units that house many interconnected microcomputer hard disk drives, thus providing large, fault-tolerant storage capacities.

Random Access   Same as Direct Access. Contrast with Sequential Access.

Random-Access Memory (RAM)   One of the basic types of semiconductor memory used for temporary storage of data or programs during processing. Each memory position can be directly sensed (read) or changed (written) in the same length of time, regardless of its location on the storage medium.

Reach and Range Analysis   A planning framework that contrasts a firm's ability to use its IT platform to reach its stakeholders with the range of information products and services that can be provided or shared through IT.

Read-Only Memory (ROM)   A basic type of semiconductor memory used for permanent storage. Can only be read, not "written," that is, changed. Variations are Programmable Read-Only Memory (PROM) and Erasable Programmable Read-Only Memory (EPROM).

Real Time   Pertaining to the performance of data processing during the actual time a business or physical process transpires so that results of the data processing can be used to support the completion of the process.

Real-Time Processing   Data processing in which data are processed immediately rather than periodically. Also called online processing. Contrast with Batch Processing.

Record   A collection of related data fields treated as a unit.

Reduced Instruction Set Computer (RISC)   A CPU architecture that optimizes processing speed by the use of a smaller number of basic machine instructions than traditional CPU designs.

Redundancy   In information processing, the repetition of part or all of a message to increase the chance that the correct information will be understood by the recipient.

Register   A device capable of storing a specified amount of data, such as one word.

Relational Data Structure   A logical data structure in which all data elements within the database are viewed as being stored in the form of simple tables. DBMS packages based on the relational model can link data elements from various tables as long as the tables share common data elements.

Remote Access   Pertaining to communication with the data processing facility by one or more stations that are distant from that facility.

Remote Job Entry (RJE)   Entering jobs into a batch processing system from a remote facility.

Report Generator   A feature of database management system packages that allows an end user to quickly specify a report format for the display of information retrieved from a database.

Replication   A backup process that looks for changes made in each distributed database and then makes all necessary changes to all other databases to ensure consistency of data across them.

Reprographics   Copying and duplicating technology and methods.

Resource Management   An operating system function that controls the use of computer system resources such as primary storage, secondary storage, CPU processing time, and input/output devices by other system software and application software packages.

RFID   Radio Frequency Identification. A system for tagging and identifying objects by means of wireless signals.

Robotics   The technology of building machines (robots) with computer intelligence and humanlike physical capabilities.

Routine   An ordered set of instructions that may have some general or frequent use.

RPG: Report Program Generator   A problem-oriented language that utilizes a generator to construct programs that produce reports and perform other data processing tasks.

Rule   Statements that typically take the form of a premise and a conclusion, such as if–then rules: If (condition), Then (conclusion).

Rule-Based Knowledge   Knowledge represented in the form of rules and statements of fact.

Sales Force Automation   Providing sales force personnel with technology (computers, software) to help streamline and improve their productivity.

Scalability   The ability of hardware or software to handle the processing demands of a wide range of end users, transactions, queries, and other information processing requirements.

Scenario Approach   A planning approach in which managers, employees, and planners create scenarios of what an organization will be like three to five years or more into the future and identify the role IT can play in those scenarios.

Schema   An overall conceptual or logical view of the relationships between the data in a database.

Scientific Method   An analytical methodology that involves (1) recognizing phenomena, (2) formulating a hypothesis about the causes or effects of the phenomena, (3) testing the hypothesis through experimentation, (4) evaluating the results of such experiments, and (5) drawing conclusions about the hypothesis.

Search Management   Web site capabilities to help customers find the specific product or service they want to purchase.

Search Engine Optimization   A process by which a Web site can advance the likelihood that it will be listed for a particular Web site query.

Secondary Storage   Storage that supplements the primary storage of a computer. Synonymous with auxiliary storage.

Sector   A subdivision of a track on a magnetic disk surface.

Security Codes   Passwords, identification codes, account codes, and other codes that limit the access and use of computer-based system resources to authorized users.

Security Management   Protecting the accuracy, integrity, and safety of the processes and resources of an internetworked e-business enterprise against computer crime, accidental or malicious destruction, and natural disasters, using security measures such as encryption, firewalls, antivirus software, fault-tolerant computers, and security monitors.

Security Monitor   A software package that monitors the use of a computer system and protects its resources from unauthorized use, fraud, and vandalism.

Semiconductor Memory   Microelectronic storage circuitry etched on tiny chips of silicon or other semiconducting material. The primary storage of most modern computers consists of microelectronic semiconductor storage chips for random-access memory (RAM) and read-only memory (ROM).

Semistructured Decisions   Decisions involving procedures that can be partially prespecified but not enough to lead to a definite recommended decision.

Sensitivity Analysis   Observing how repeated changes to a single variable affect other variables in a mathematical model.

Sequential Access   A sequential method of storing and retrieving data from a file. Contrast with Random Access and Direct Access.

Sequential Data Organization   Organizing logical data elements according to a prescribed sequence.

Serial   Pertaining to the sequential or consecutive occurrence of two or more related activities in a single device or channel.

Server   (1) A computer that supports applications and telecommunications in a network, as well as the sharing of peripheral devices, software, and databases among the workstations in the network. (2) Versions of software for installation on network servers designed to control and support applications on client microcomputers in client/server networks. Examples include multiuser network operating systems and specialized software for running Internet, intranet, and extranet Web applications, such as electronic commerce and enterprise collaboration.

Service Bureau   A firm offering computer and data processing services. Also called a computer service center.

Smart Products   Industrial and consumer products, with "intelligence" provided by built-in microcomputers or microprocessors that significantly improve the performance and capabilities of such products.

Societal Solutions   Technologies that help solve large-scale human and social problems, such as those related to medicine and law enforcement issues.

Software   Computer programs and procedures concerned with the operation of an information system. Contrast with Hardware.

Software Package   A computer program supplied by computer manufacturers, independent software companies, or other computer users. Also known as canned programs, proprietary software, or packaged programs.

Software Piracy   Unauthorized copying of software.

Software Resources   All information processing instructions. Includes programs (which direct and control computer hardware) and procedures (which are directed to people).

Software Suites   A combination of individual software packages that share a common graphical user interface and are designed for easy transfer of data between applications.

Solid State   Pertaining to devices such as transistors and diodes whose operation depends on the control of electric or magnetic phenomena in solid materials.

Source Data Automation   The use of automated methods of data entry that attempt to reduce or eliminate many of the activities, people, and data media required by traditional data entry methods.

Source Document   A document that is the original formal record of a transaction, such as a purchase order or sales invoice.

Source Program   A computer program written in a language that is subject to a translation process. Contrast with Object Program.

Spamming   A process in which a single advertiser sends thousands of messages to computer users without their permission. The computer version of junk mail.

Special-Purpose Computer   A computer designed to handle a restricted class of problems. Contrast with General-Purpose Computer.

Speech Recognition   Direct conversion of spoken data into electronic form suitable for entry into a computer system. Also called voice data entry.

Spooling   Simultaneous peripheral operation online. Storing input data from low-speed devices temporarily on high-speed secondary storage units, which can be quickly accessed by the CPU. Also, writing output data at high speeds onto magnetic tape or disk units from which it can be transferred to slow-speed devices such as a printer.

Spreadsheet Packages   A computer application that simulates a paper worksheet by means of a two-dimensional grid containing columns and rows.

Spyware   Also called Adware.

Stage Analysis   A planning process in which the information system's needs of an organization are based on an analysis of its current stage in the growth cycle of the organization and its use of information systems technology.

Standards   Measures of performance developed to evaluate the progress of a system toward its objectives.

Storage   Pertaining to a device into which data can be entered, in which they can be held, and from which they can be retrieved at a later time. Same as Memory.

Strategic Information Systems   Information systems that provide a firm with competitive products and services that give it a strategic advantage over its competitors in the marketplace. Also, information systems that promote business innovation, improve business processes, and build strategic information resources for a firm.

Strategic Planning   The process by which executives in an organization develop its mission, goals, strategies, and policies.

Strategic Opportunities Matrix   A planning framework that uses a matrix to help identify opportunities with strategic business potential, as well as a firm's ability to exploit such opportunities with IT.

Structure Chart   A design and documentation technique to show the purpose and relationships of the various modules in a program.

Structured Decisions   Decisions that are structured by the decision procedures or decision rules developed for them. They involve situations in which the procedures to follow when a decision is needed can be specified in advance.

Structured Programming   A programming methodology that uses a top-down program design and a limited number of control structures in a program to create highly structured modules of program code.

Structured Query Language (SQL)   A query language that is becoming a standard for advanced database management system packages. A query's basic form is SELECT . . . FROM . . . WHERE.

Subroutine   A routine that can be part of another program routine.

Subschema   A subset or transformation of the logical view of the database schema that is required by a particular user application program.

Subsystem   A system that is a component of a larger system.

Supercomputer   A special category of large computer systems that are the most powerful available. They are designed to solve massive computational problems.

Superconductor   Materials that can conduct electricity with almost no resistance. This allows the development of extremely fast and small electronic circuits. Formerly only possible at super-cold temperatures near absolute zero. Recent developments promise superconducting materials near room temperature.

Supply Chain   The network of business processes and interrelationships among businesses that are needed to build, sell, and deliver a product to its final customer.

Supply Chain Management   Integrating management practices and information technology to optimize information and product flows among the processes and business partners within a supply chain.

System Security Monitor   Software that monitors the use of computer systems and networks to protect them from unauthorized use, fraud, and destruction.

Switch   (1) A device or programming technique for making a selection. (2) A computer that controls message switching among the computers and terminals in a telecommunications network.

Switching Costs   The costs in time, money, effort, and inconvenience that it would take a customer or supplier to switch its business to a firm's competitors.

SWOT Analysis   A business planning process in which various aspects of a business situation are analyzed and compared. SWOT is an acronym for Strengths, Weaknesses, Opportunities, and Threats.

Synchronous   A characteristic in which each event, or the performance of any basic operation, is constrained to start on, and usually to keep in step with, signals from a timing clock. Contrast with Asynchronous.

System   (1) A group of interrelated or interacting elements forming a unified whole. (2) A group of interrelated components working together toward a common goal by accepting inputs and producing outputs in an organized transformation process. (3) An assembly of methods, procedures, or techniques unified by regulated interaction to form an organized whole. (4) An organized collection of people, machines, and methods required to accomplish a set of specific functions.

System Flowchart   A graphic diagramming tool used to show the flow of information processing activities as data are processed by people and devices.

System Performance Monitor   Software used to manage the performance of computer systems by overseeing the processing of computer jobs, developing schedules of computer operations, and providing statistical control information.

Systems Analysis   (1) Analyzing in detail the components and requirements of a system. (2) Analyzing in detail the information needs of an organization, the characteristics and components of presently utilized information systems, and the functional requirements of proposed information systems.

Systems Approach   A systematic process of problem solving that defines problems and opportunities in a systems context. Data are gathered describing the problem or opportunity, and alternative solutions are identified and evaluated. Then the best solution is selected and implemented, and its success is evaluated.

Systems Design   Deciding how a proposed information system will meet the information needs of end users. Includes logical and physical design activities and user interface, data, and process design activities that produce system specifications that satisfy the system requirements developed in the systems analysis stage.

Systems Development   (1) Conceiving, designing, and implementing a system. (2) Developing information systems by a process of investigation, analysis, design, implementation, and maintenance. Also called the systems development life cycle (SDLC), information systems development, or application development.

Systems Development Tools   Graphical, textual, and computer-aided tools and techniques used to help analyze, design, and document the development of an information system. Typically used to represent (1) the components and flows of a system, (2) the user interface, (3) data attributes and relationships, and (4) detailed system processes.

Systems Implementation   The stage of systems development in which hardware and software are acquired, developed, and installed; the system is tested and documented; people are trained to operate and use the system; and an organization converts to the use of a newly developed system.

Systems Investigation   The screening, selection, and preliminary study of a proposed information system solution to a business problem.

Systems Maintenance   The monitoring, evaluating, and modifying of a system to make desirable or necessary improvements.

System Software   Programs that control and support operations of a computer system. System software includes a variety of programs, such as operating systems, database management systems, communications control programs, service and utility programs, and programming language translators.

System Specifications   The product of the systems design stage. It consists of specifications for the hardware, software, facilities, personnel, databases, and the user interface of a proposed information system.

Systems Thinking   Recognizing systems, subsystems, components of systems, and system interrelationships in a situation. Also known as a systems context or a systemic view of a situation.

System Testing   Part of the system implementation process where the various components of a new system are reviewed to check their accuracy and correctness.

System Support Programs   Programs that support the operations, management, and users of a computer system by providing a variety of support services. Examples are system utilities and performance monitors.

Tangible Benefits and Costs   The quantifiable benefits and costs of a proposed solution or system.

Targeted Marketing Advertising and promotion that is targeted to specific groups of current or potential customers based on one or more targeting parameters, such as content, context, or demographic characteristics.

Task and Project Management Managing team and workgroup projects by scheduling, tracking, and charting the completion status of tasks within a project.

Task Management A basic operating system function that manages the accomplishment of the computing tasks of users by a computer system.

TCP/IP Transmission control protocol/Internet protocol. A suite of telecommunications network protocols used by the Internet, intranets, and extranets that has become a de facto network architecture standard for many companies.

Technical Feasibility Whether reliable hardware and software capable of meeting the needs of a proposed system can be acquired or developed by an organization in the required time.

Technology Management The organizational responsibility to identify, introduce, and monitor the assimilation of new information system technologies into organizations.

Telecommunications Pertaining to the transmission of signals over long distances, including not only data communications but also the transmission of images and voices using radio, television, and other communications technologies.

Telecommunications Channel The part of a telecommunications network that connects the message source with the message receiver. It includes the hardware, software, and media used to connect one network location to another for the purpose of transmitting and receiving information.

Telecommunications Controller A data communications interface device (frequently a special-purpose mini- or microcomputer) that can control a telecommunications network containing many terminals.

Telecommunications Control Program A computer program that controls and supports the communications between the computers and terminals in a telecommunications network.

Telecommunications Media The physical media over which telecommunication activities are conducted (e.g., twisted-pair wire, coaxial cable, etc.)

Telecommunications Network Any arrangement where a sender transmits a message to a receiver over a channel consisting of some type of medium.

Telecommunications Monitors Computer programs that control and support the communications between the computers and terminals in a telecommunications network.

Telecommunications Processors Inter-network processors such as switches and routers and other devices such as multiplexers and communications controllers that allow a communications channel to carry simultaneous data transmissions from many terminals. They may also perform error monitoring, diagnostics and correction, modulation-demodulation, data compression, data coding and decoding, message switching, port contention, and buffer storage.

Telecommunications Software Software used to manage the various components and activities involved in the operation of a telecommunications network.

Telecommuting The use of telecommunications to replace commuting to work from one's home.

Teleconferencing The use of video communications to allow business conferences to be held with participants who are scattered across a country, continent, or the world.

Telephone Tag The process that occurs when two people who wish to contact each other by telephone repeatedly miss each other's phone calls.

Teleprocessing Using telecommunications for computer-based information processing.

Terabyte One trillion bytes. More accurately, 2 to the 40th power, or 1,009,511,627,776 in decimal notation.

Text Data Words, phrases, sentences, and paragraphs used in documents and other forms of communication.

Throughput The total amount of useful work performed by a data processing system during a given period.

Timesharing Providing computer services to many users simultaneously while providing rapid responses to each.

Total Quality Management Planning and implementing programs of continuous quality improvement, where quality is defined as meeting or exceeding the requirements and expectations of customers for a product or service.

Touch-Sensitive Screen An input device that accepts data input by the placement of a finger on or close to the computer screen.

Track The portion of a moving storage medium, such as a drum, tape, or disk, that is accessible to a given reading head position.

Trackball A rollerball device set in a case used to move the cursor on a computer's display screen.

Transaction An event that occurs as part of doing business, such as a sale, purchase, deposit, withdrawal, refund, transfer, or payment.

Transaction Document A document produced as part of a business transaction, for example, a purchase order, paycheck, sales receipt, or customer invoice.

Transaction File A data file containing relatively transient data to be processed in combination with a master file. Contrast with Master File.

Transaction Processing Cycle A cycle of basic transaction processing activities including data entry, transaction processing, database maintenance, document and report generation, and inquiry processing.

Transaction Processing System (TPS) An information system that processes data arising from the occurrence of business transactions.

Transaction Terminals Terminals used in banks, retail stores, factories, and other work sites to capture transaction data at their point of origin. Examples are point-of-sale (POS) terminals and automated teller machines (ATMs).

Transborder Data Flows (TDF) The flow of business data over telecommunications networks across international borders.

Transform Algorithm Performing an arithmetic computation on a record key and using the result of the calculation as an address for that record. Also known as key transformation or hashing.

Transnational Strategy A management approach in which an organization integrates its global business activities through close cooperation and interdependence among its headquarters, operations, and international subsidiaries and its use of appropriate global information technologies.

Turnaround Document Output of a computer system (such as customer invoices and statements) that is designed to be returned to the organization as machine-readable input.

Turnaround Time The elapsed time between submission of a job to a computing center and the return of the results.

Turnkey Systems Computer systems in which all of the hardware, software, and systems development needed by a user are provided.

Unauthorized Use Usage of company-owned computing resources by employees that lies beyond that what is needed for the conduct of company-related business.

Unbundling The separate pricing of hardware, software, and other related services.

Uniform Resource Locator (URL) An access code (such as http://www.sun.com) for identifying and locating hypermedia document files, databases, and other resources at Web sites and other locations on the Internet, intranets, and extranets.

Universal Product Code (UPC) A standard identification code using bar coding printed on products that can be read by optical scanners such as those found at a supermarket checkout.

Unstructured Decisions Decisions that must be made in situations in which it is not possible to specify in advance most of the decision procedures to follow.

User Friendly A characteristic of human-operated equipment and systems that makes them safe, comfortable, and easy to use.

User Interface That part of an operating system or other program that allows users to communicate with it to load programs, access files, and accomplish other computing tasks.

User Services Functions or departments responsible for providing support to end-user and workgroup computing.

User Interface Design Designing the interactions between end users and computer systems, including input/output methods and the conversion of data between human-readable and machine-readable forms.

Utility Program A standard set of routines that assists in the operation of a computer system by performing some frequently required process such as copying, sorting, or merging.

Value-Added Carriers Third-party vendors who lease telecommunications lines from common carriers and offer a variety of telecommunications services to customers.

Value-Added Resellers (VARs) Companies that provide industry-specific software for use with the computer systems of selected manufacturers.

Value Chain Viewing a firm as a series, chain, or network of basic activities that adds value to its products and services and thus adds a margin of value to the firm.

Videoconferencing Real-time video and audio conferencing (1) among users at networked PCs (desktop videoconferencing) or (2) among participants in conference rooms or auditoriums in different locations (teleconferencing). Videoconferencing can also include whiteboarding and document sharing.

Virtual Communities Groups of people with similar interests who meet and share ideas on the Internet and online services and develop a feeling of belonging to a community.

Virtual Company A form of organization that uses telecommunications networks and other information technologies to link the people, assets, and ideas of a variety of business partners, no matter where they may be, to exploit a business opportunity.

Virtual Machine Pertaining to the simulation of one type of computer system by another computer system.

Virtual Mall An online multimedia simulation of a shopping mall with many different interlinked retail Web sites.

Virtual Memory The use of secondary storage devices as an extension of the primary storage of the computer, thus giving the appearance of a larger main memory than actually exists.

Virtual Private Network A secure network that uses the Internet as its main backbone network to connect the intranets of a company's different locations or to establish extranet links between a company and its customers, suppliers, or other business partners.

Virtual Reality The use of multisensory human/computer interfaces that enable human users to experience computer-simulated objects, entities, spaces, and "worlds" as if they actually existed.

Virtual Storefront   An online multimedia simulation of a retail store shopping experience on the Web.

Virtual Team   A team whose members use the Internet, intranets, extranets, and other networks to communicate, coordinate, and collaborate with one another on tasks and projects, even though they may work in different geographic locations and for different organizations.

VLSI: Very-Large-Scale Integration   Semiconductor chips containing hundreds of thousands of circuits.

Voice Conferencing   Telephone conversations shared among several participants via speaker phones or networked PCs with Internet telephone software.

Voice Mail   Unanswered telephone messages that are digitized, stored, and played back to the recipient by a voice messaging computer.

Voice over IP (VoIP)   A process where the Internet is used as the network carrier for telephone or voice communication.

Volatile Memory   Memory (such as electronic semiconductor memory) that loses its contents when electrical power is interrupted.

Wand   A handheld optical character recognition device used for data entry by many transaction terminals.

Web Browser   A software package that provides the user interface for accessing Internet, intranet, and extranet Web sites. Browsers are becoming multifunction universal clients for sending and receiving e-mail, downloading files, accessing Java applets, participating in discussion groups, developing Web pages, and other Internet, intranet, and extranet applications.

Web Publishing   Creating, converting, and storing hyperlinked documents and other material on Internet or intranet Web servers so that they can be easily shared via Web browsers with teams, workgroups, or the enterprise.

Web Services   A collection of Web and object-oriented technologies for linking Web-based applications running on different hardware, software, database, or network platforms. For example, Web services could link key business functions within the applications a business shares with its customers, suppliers, and business partners.

What-If Analysis   Observing how changes to selected variables affect other variables in a mathematical model.

Whiteboarding   See Data Conferencing.

Wide Area Network (WAN)   A data communications network covering a large geographic area.

Window   One section of a computer's multiple-section display screen, each section of which can have a different display.

Wireless LANs   Using radio or infrared transmissions to link devices in a local area network.

Wireless Technologies   Using radio wave, microwave, infrared, and laser technologies to transport digital communications without wires between communications devices. Examples include terrestrial microwave, communications satellites, cellular and PCS phone and pager systems, mobile data radio, and various wireless Internet technologies.

Word   (1) A string of characters considered as a unit. (2) An ordered set of bits (usually larger than a byte) handled as a unit by the central processing unit.

Word Processing   The automation of the transformation of ideas and information into a readable form of communication. It involves the use of computers to manipulate text data to produce office communications in the form of documents.

Word Processing Software   A software package that supports the creation, editing, revising, and printing of documents.

Workflow Management   Ensuring that proper transactions and activities are conducted in accordance with a prespecified workflow model.

Workgroup Computing   Members of a networked workgroup may use groupware tools to communicate, coordinate, and collaborate and to share hardware, software, and databases to accomplish group assignments.

Workstation   (1) A computer system designed to support the work of one person. (2) A high-powered computer to support the work of professionals in engineering, science, and other areas that require extensive computing power and graphics capabilities.

World Wide Web (WWW)   A global network of multimedia Internet sites for information, education, entertainment, e-business, and e-commerce.

XML (Extensible Markup Language)   A Web document content description language that describes the content of Web pages by applying hidden identifying tags or contextual labels to the data in Web documents. By categorizing and classifying Web data this way, XML makes Web content easier to identify, search, analyze, and selectively exchange between computers.

subject index